Logic Programming

Logic Programming

Ehud Shapiro, editor

Koichi Furukawa, Jean-Louis Lassez, Fernando Pereira, and David H. D. Warren, associate editors

The Art of Prolog: Advanced Programming Techniques, Leon Sterling and Ehud Shapiro, 1986

Logic Programming: Proceedings of the Fourth International Conference (volumes 1 and 2), edited by Jean-Louis Lassez, 1987

Concurrent Prolog: Collected Papers (volumes 1 and 2), edited by Ehud Shapiro, 1987

Logic Programming: Proceedings of the Fifth International Conference and Symposium (volumes 1 and 2), edited by Robert A. Kowalski and Kenneth A. Bowen, 1988

Constraint Satisfaction in Logic Programming, Pascal Van Hentenryck, 1989

Logic-Based Knowledge Representation, edited by Peter Jackson, Han Reichgelt, and Frank van Harmelen, 1989

Logic Programming: Proceedings of the Sixth International Conference, edited by Giorgio Levi and Maurizio Martelli, 1989

Meta-Programming in Logic Programming, edited by Harvey Abramson and M. H. Rogers, 1989

Logic Programming: Proceedings of the North American Conference 1989 (volumes 1 and 2), edited by Ewing L. Lusk and Ross A. Overbeek, 1989

Logic Programming: Proceedings of the 1990 North American Conference, edited by Saumya Debray and Manuel Hermenegildo, 1990

Logic Programming: Proceedings of the Seventh International Conference, edited by David H. D. Warren and Peter Szeredi, 1990

The Craft of Prolog, Richard A. O'Keefe, 1990

The Practice of Prolog, edited by Leon S. Sterling, 1990

Eco-Logic: Logic-Based Approaches to Ecological Modelling, David Robertson, Alan Bundy, Robert Muetzelfeldt, Mandy Haggith, and Michael Uschold, 1991

Warren's Abstract Machine: A Tutorial Reconstruction, Hassan Aït-Kaci, 1991

Parallel Logic Programming, Evan Tick, 1991

Logic Programming: Proceedings of the Eighth International Conference, edited by Koichi Furukawa, 1991

Logic Programming: Proceedings of the 1991 International Symposium, edited by Vijay Saraswat and Kazunori Ueda, 1991

Foundations of Disjunctive Logic Programming, Jorge Lobo, Jack Minker, and Arcot Rajasekar, 1992

Types in Logic Programming, edited by Frank Pfenning, 1992

Logic Programming: Proceedings of the Joint International Conference and Symposium on Logic Programming, edited by Krzysztof Apt, 1992

Logic Programming

Proceedings of the Joint International Conference
and Symposium on Logic Programming

The Boston Computer Society
One Kendall Square
Cambridge, Massachusetts 02139

BCS 12/92

edited by Krzysztof Apt

The MIT Press
Cambridge, Massachusetts
London, England

Contents

The Boston Computer Society
One Kendall Square
Cambridge, Massachusetts 02139

Semantics

Addendum

Conference Chair

Jack Minker   University of Maryland, United States

Program Committee

Krzysztof R. Apt, Chair	CWI, The Netherlands
Hassan Aït-Kaci	Digital Paris Research Laboratory, France
Maurice Bruynooghe	Catholic University of Leuven, Belgium
Keith L. Clark	Imperial College, England
John S. Conery	University of Oregon, United States
Seif Haridi	SICS, Sweden
Manuel V. Hermenegildo	University of Madrid, Spain
Alexander Herold	ECRC, Germany
Joxan Jaffar	IBM T. J. Watson Research Center, United States
Paris Kanellakis	Brown University, United States
Feliks Kluzniak	University of Warsaw, Poland
John Lloyd	University of Bristol, England
Jan Maluszynski	Linköping University, Sweden
Alberto Martelli	University of Torino, Italy
Dale Miller	University of Pennsylvania, United States
Catuscia Palamidessi	University of Pisa, Italy
Frank Pfenning	Carnegie Mellon University, United States
Antonio Porto	University of Lisbon, Portugal
Teodor Przymusinski	University of California, Riverside, United States
Taisuke Sato	Electrotechnical Laboratory, Japan
Ehud Shapiro	Weizmann Institute of Science, Israel
Rodney Topor	Griffith University, Australia
David H. D. Warren	University of Bristol, England
David S. Warren	SUNY Stony Brook, United States
Kazunori Ueda	ICOT, Japan
Carlo Zaniolo	University of California, Los Angeles, United States

The Association for Logic Programming

The Association for Logic Programming (ALP) was founded in 1986 at the International Conference on Logic Programming, held that year in London. In addition to this conference (JICSLP'92), the ALP has sponsored International Conferences and Symposia in Melbourne (1987), Seattle (1988), Lisbon (1989), Cleveland (1989), Jerusalem (1990), Austin (1990), Paris (1991), and San Diego (1991). The proceedings of all these meetings are published by The MIT Press, with the exception of the London conference which was published by Springer-Verlag.

The Association sponsors workshops, contributes support to other meetings related to logic programming, and provides limited support for attendance at its sponsored conferences and workshops by participants in financial need. Members receive the Association's newsletter quarterly and can subscribe to the Journal of Logic Programming at a reduced rate.

The affairs of the Association are overseen by the Executive Council. Current members are Krzysztof Apt, Koichi Furukawa, Jean-Louis Lassez, Giorgio Levi, Dale Miller, David H.D. Warren, David S. Warren, Association President Hervé Gallaire, and Past-President Keith Clark. Past members of the Council are Maurice Bruynooghe, John Lloyd, and Ehud Shapiro. The current officers of the Association are: Robert Kowalski, Secretary; Fariba Sadri, Treasurer; David S. Warren, Conference Coordinator; Keith Clark, Conference Budget Auditor; and Andrew Davidson, Newsletter Editor. Further information about the Association may be obtained from:

Cheryl Anderson
ALP Administrative Secretary
Department of Computing
Imperial College
180 Queen's Gate
London SW7 2BZ, UK
Tel: +44 (071) 589 5111 ext. 5011
Fax: +44 (071) 589 1552
E-mail: alp@doc.ic.ac.uk

Series Foreword

The logic programming approach to computing investigates the use of logic as a programming language and explores computational models based on controlled deduction.

The field of logic programming has seen a tremendous growth in the last several years, both in depth and in scope. This growth is reflected in the number of articles, journals, theses, books, workshops, and conferences devoted to the subject. The MIT Press Series in Logic Programming was created to accomodate this development and to nurture it. It is dedicated to the publication of high-quality textbooks, monographs, collections, and proceedings in logic programming.

Ehud Shapiro
The Weizmann Institute of Science
Rehovot, Israel

Preface

It is a funny thing to be a program committee chairman. In practice it means that for a long time nothing happens, then you are literally drowned by packets with submissions and emails about the "real deadline" (some 40 % papers were submitted on time). Next, you have to distribute these papers in record time (my score: 9 hours work) to other program committee members and referees and, somehow, two and half months later get the referee reports back (the record fax had more than 50 pages).

Here are the bare figures for this conference: 173 submissions from 23 countries and more than 600 referee reports generated.

The program committee met on June 15 and 16 and after lively discussions based on these referee reports selected 50 high quality papers.

Additionally, Professor G. Mints agreed to deliver the Keynote Address, Professors M. Chandy, W. Mitchell and J. Pearl accepted to give invited talks, and Professors S. Abiteboul, M. Fitting, M. Hermenegildo, R. Overbeek, E. Tick and A. Troelstra were willing to present advanced tutorials. The outcome is the volume you are holding in your hands.

Of course I would have been completely lost had I not been helped by a number of people. First of all, I would like to thank here Frans Snijders whose help was instrumental for my survival. Also, my thanks go to Anna Baanders, Mieke Brune, Marjan Koot-de Groot and Ruth Oria for their valuable assistance. Bob Prior from The MIT Press provided me with precise information about the production of the volume.

Finally, last but not least, it was a real pleasure to work with Jack Minker and Johanna Weinstein who were always ready to provide me with instant answers to numerous questions and requests.

Also, I would like to express here my thanks to the authors of all submitted papers, invited speakers, presenters of advanced tutorials, program committe members and the referees. Thanks to all of them this conference could take place.

Krzysztof R. Apt
Program Committee Chair

Referees

A. Aiba
H. Aït-Kaci
K. Ali
M. Alpuente
J. Andreoli
K.R. Apt
P. Atzeni
J. Baptista
M. Baudinet
A.J. Beaumont
R. Ben-Eliyahu
H. Blair
F. de Boer
R.N. Bol
P. Bonatti
S. Bonnier
A. Bossi
D. Boulanger
A. Bowers
J. Boye
A. Brodsky
A. Brogi
M. Bruynooghe
F. Bry
F. Bueno Carrillo
D. Cabeza Gras
L. Caires
A. Callebout
M. Carro Linares
W. Chen
T. Chikayama
D. Chu
K.L. Clark
N. Cocco
M. Codish
L. Colussi
J.S. Conery
L. Console
J.N. Crossley
J. Cunningham

G. David
L. De Raedt
D. De Schreye
L. Degerstedt
B. Demoen
M. Denecker
Y. Deville
A. Di Pierro
A. Dias
K. Doets
W. Drabent
M. Ducasse
B. Dumant
Phan Minh Dung
I.C. Dutra
M. Falaschi
Y. Feldman
A. Felty
J.A. Fernandez
G. File
M. Ford
T. Fruhwirth
H. Fujita
K. Furukawa
M. Gabbrielli
J.P. Gallagher
H, Gao
M. Garcia Clemente
J. Garcia Martin
A. Garcia Serrano
M.J. Garcia de la Banda
R. Giacobazzi
L. Giordano
A. Goto
S. Greco
S. Gregory
A. Guessoum
G. Gupta
C. Gurr
M. Hanus

S. Haridi
J.A. Harland
N. Heintze
M.V. Hermenegildo
A. Herold
P.M. Hill
K. Horiuchi
T. Hortala
J. Jaffar
G. Janssen
S. Jansson
C.S. Jutla
M. Kalsbeek
T. Kanamori
P. Kanellakis
R. Karlsson
R. Katserstein
D. Kemp
Y. Kinosita
S. Kliger
J.W. Klop
F. Kluzniak
V. Kuchenhoff
T. Kwamura
E. Lalovic
B. Le Charlier
A. Lefebvre
Leung Ho-Fung
F. Levi
G. Levi
P. Lim
J. Lipton
L. Yuan
J.W. Lloyd
M.J. Maher
J. Maluszynski
M. Mamede
P. Mancarella
E. Marchiori
A. Marien

J. Marino Carvallo

K.G. Marriott

A. Martelli

M. Martelli

B. Martens

A. Masini

B. Massey

Y. Matsumoto

Y. Matumoto

M. McCord

F. Mccabe

M. Meier

M.C. Meo

S. Michaylov

D. Miller

K. Milsted

J. Minker

A. Montanari

L. Monteiro

D. Montesi

J. Moreno Navarro

Y. Moscowitz

Ch. Moss

A. Mulkers

M. Murakami

G. Nadathur

L. Naish

M. Nilson

U. Nilsson

N. Olivetti

C. Palamidessi

L. Palopoli

R. Pareschi

D. Pedreschi

F. Pereira

L. Pereira

F. Pfenning

L. Pluemer

A. Porto

H. Przymusinska

T. Przymusinski

C. Ribeiro

G. Ringwood

M. Rodriguez Artalejo

P. Rosado

C. Ruiz

K.F. Sagonas

D. Sahlin

T. Sakama

V. Santos Costa

M.L. Sapino

A. V. S. Sastry

T. Sato

A. Sattar

M. Schaerf

J. Schimpf

H. Seki

M. Sergot

E. Shapiro

K. Shen

E. Shibayama

E. Shilcrat

T. Sjoland

G. Smolka

H. Sondergaard

L. Sterling

P.J. Stuckey

H. Sugano

R. Sundararajan

T. Swift

Y. Takayama

D. Theseider Dupre'

E. Tick

R.W. Topor

P. Torasso

R. Torlone

K. Ueda

P. Van Hentenryck

P. Van Roy

H. Vandecasteele

A. Veron

K. Verschaetse

A. Voronkov

M. Wallace

D.H.D. Warren

D.S. Warren

C. Witteveen

B. Wutherich

R. Yang

R. Yap

E. Yardeni

H. Yasukawa

C. Zaniolo

X. Zhong

Invited Talks

The Derivation of Compositional Programs

K. Mani Chandy and Carl Kesselman [1]
California Institute of Technology
Pasadena, California 91125, USA
mani@vlsi.caltech.edu, carl@vlsi.caltech.edu

Abstract

This paper proposes a parallel programming notation and a method of reasoning about programs with the following characteristics:

1. Parallel Composition The notation provides different forms of interfaces between processes; the more restrictive the interface, the simpler the proofs of process composition. A flexible interface is that of cooperating processes with a shared address space; proofs of programs that use this interface are based on non-interference [OG76] and temporal logic [Pnu81, CM88, Lam91]. We also propose more restrictive interfaces and specifications that allow us to use the following *specification-conjunction* rule: the strongest specification of a parallel composition of processes is the conjunction of the strongest specifications of its components. This rule is helpful in deriving parallel programs.

2. Determinism A process that does not use certain primitives of the notation is guaranteed to be deterministic. Programmers who wish to prove that their programs are deterministic are relieved of this proof obligation if they restrict their programs to a certain subset of the primitives.

1   Parallel Composition

VLSI is an example of parallel programming as Chuck Seitz asserts. The success of VLSI is due in part to a hierarchy of interfaces for composing circuits: from composing transistors to form memory units, to composing microprocessors to form multicomputers. A designer putting transistors together has to be concerned with issues such as parasitic capacitance. A designer putting microprocessors together works with a more restrictive interface that does not deal with such details; the interface is such that a microprocessor behaves as a microprocessor regardless of the circuits to which it is connected. Composing transistors and composing microprocessors are both instances of parallel composition; the interfaces between transistors is different from the interfaces between microprocessors, and therefore, the ways of reason-

---

[1]This research is funded by the NSF Center for Research on Parallel Computing under grant CCR-8809615 and DARPA under grant N00014-91-J-4014.

ing about compositions of transistors is different from the ways of reasoning about compositions of microprocessors.

What is the analogy to composing processes? There are situations where we may want to employ flexible interfaces between concurrent processes and other situations in which we want to use more restrictive interfaces between processes. In general, more restrictive interfaces allow for simpler proof techniques and more flexible interfaces can provide more efficiency. We propose a notation and methods of reasoning about programs that allow programmers to design different kinds of interfaces between concurrent processes. Programmers can balance flexibility on the one hand with ease of reasoning on the other, in designing their own interfaces.

A very flexible interface between concurrent processes is where processes share variables, and use atomicity and **await** commands [OG76]; in this case methods of reasoning are based on non-interference [OG76] or temporal logic and its derivatives [Pnu81, CM88, Lam91]. More restrictive interfaces and specifications allow us to use the powerful specification-conjunction rule for reasoning about parallel composition.

Consider a simple example that illustrates the problem of interfaces between concurrent processes.

Example   The process p:

do x = 0 $\rightarrow$ x := x+2   []   x = 1 $\rightarrow$ x := -1 od

satisfies the specification: $(x = 0) \rightsquigarrow (x \geq 2)$, if $x = 0$ at any point in its computation, then at a later point in its computation $x \geq 2$.

The same specification is satisfied by the process q:

do ((x = 0) $\vee$ (x = 1)) $\rightarrow$ x := x + 1 od

The parallel composition of p and q, p$\|$q, does not satisfy the specification, because q can change the value of x from 0 to 1, and then p can change the value of x to -1, after which x remains unchanged.

The parallel composition of processes, all of which have a common specification R, may not satisfy specification R, because the shared-memory interface between processes is flexible and allows one process to "interfere" with the proof of another [OG76]. Later, we define more restrictive interfaces and specifications that permit simpler proofs.

1.1   Processes

We define processes in terms of transition systems [Pnu81, Lam91, CM88]. A system is a set $\mathcal{P}$ of processes and a set $\mathcal{G}$ of global variables. A process is (i) a set L of *local variables*, (ii) a set G of *shared variables* where $G \subseteq \mathcal{G}$, (iii) the *initial values* of its variables $L \cup G$, and (iv) a set of atomic *actions*. The name space of local variables of a process is local to the process; by contrast, the name space of shared variables is global to the system.

A state of a process is defined by the values of the variables of the process. (Program counters or other methods of representing the locus of control are treated as variables, as in [CM88].) The initial state of a process is given by the initial values of its variables.

An action is a binary relation on states of the process. We shall say that an action A takes a process from a state S to a state S' if and only if $(S, S') \in A$. An action A is *executable* in a state S if there exists an S' such that A takes the process from S to S',

1.2 System States and Transitions

The state of a system is a tuple of states of its component processes where the values of shared variables are consistent among all processes, i.e., if v is shared by p and q, and $v = v'$ in the state of process p in the tuple, then $v = v'$ in the state of process q in the tuple as well.

The initial state of a system is a tuple of initial states of its component processes if the values of shared variables are consistent in the tuple. If initial shared-variable values are inconsistent, the initial system state is undefined.

Transitions between system states are labeled with actions of component processes. There exists a transition labeled A from a system state S to a system state S' if and only if there exists a transition A in a component process p such that

1. values of all variables other than those referenced by p are identical in S and S', and

2. action A takes the values of variables referenced by p from their values in S to their values in S'.

1.3 Computations

A *computation* of a process p is an initial state S_0 of the process, and a sequence of pairs (A_i, S_i) where $i > 0$ and action A_i takes the process from process-state S_{i-1} to process-state S_i, and the sequence satisfies the following *fairness rule*:

For all infinite computations, if action B is executable at some point in the computation then there is a later point in the computation at which either B is executed or B is not executable.

B is executable in $S_i \Rightarrow$
$\quad (\exists j : j > i : (A_j = B) \vee (B$ is not executable in $S_j))$

A *terminal* process-state is a state S such that all actions of the process are disabled in S. A *maximal computation* of a process is either an infinite computation or a computation that ends in a terminal state.

System computations, terminal system states, and maximal computations of systems are defined in the same way as for processes (except that system states replace process states in the definitions).

1.4   Process Properties and Open Systems

A conventional definition of process *properties* is as follows:

Closed-System Definition of Properties
A property R of a process p is a predicate on maximal computations of p where all maximal computations of p satisfy R.

With this definition, $p\|q$ does not have a property common to both p and q. How can we define process properties so as to use the following rule:

A property of p is a property of $p\|q$, for all processes q?

An obvious solution is to redefine properties in a somewhat unconventional way:

Open-System Definition of Properties
R is a property of p if and only if for all processes q, R is a predicate on maximal computations of $p\|q$, and R holds for all maximal computations of $p\|q$.

The conventional definition of process properties is sometimes referred to as the *closed-system* definition, and the alternative definition is called an *open-system* definition; this nomenclature is because the conventional definition defines properties of a process executing in isolation, whereas the alternative definition defines properties of a parallel composition of a process with some arbitrary "environment."

Relative Advantages of Open and Closed Systems   The primary disadvantage of the open-system definition is that the properties that we can prove about open-systems are weak. To prove a property of a process p we have to consider computations of p executing concurrently with q, for *all* processes q. So, we are forced to consider processes that the designer of p had no intention of composing with p. For instance, we cannot prove that a multiplier circuit multiplies because it can be connected to a megavolt power supply that fries the multiplier!

The primary disadvantage of the closed-system definition is that we do not enjoy the benefits of specification-conjunction. When we wish to prove properties about the parallel composition of processes we use noninterference [OG76] or prove properties from the *text* of the component programs [CM88] as opposed to the preferred mode of composing specifications without regard to program text.

2   The Proper Interface Approach

An approach that enjoys some of the advantages of both open and closed systems is the *proper interface* approach. We define a *proper* interface (or protocol) by which processes cooperate. We restrict attention to process composition in which the interface between processes is proper; we call composition with proper interfaces *proper composition*. We define process properties as for open systems, but we restrict attention to proper interfaces:

Proper-Interface Definition of Properties

A property of a process p is a predicate on maximal computations of $p\|q$, that holds for all maximal computations of $p\|q$, for all q *such that the interface between p and q is proper.*

Are the properties we can prove, using proper interfaces, too weak to be useful? That depends on the definition of proper interfaces — the more flexible the interface, the weaker the properties.

One of the advantages of hardware modules is that engineers have developed a set of proper interfaces. A hardware module is specified in terms of its inputs and outputs for a proper interface. When hardware modules are composed, the designer proves that the interfaces are proper (and this is usually straightforward) and then the designer can use specification-conjunction. Design is simplified greatly by being able to assert that the output of a multiplier circuit is the product of its inputs, regardless of the circuits with which the multiplier is composed, provided that the interfaces are proper. The designer of a multiplier circuit does not have to be concerned about the circuit being connected to a megavolt power supply because such an interface is not proper. The designer has to be concerned, however, with *all* possible environments with proper interfaces.

A problem with concurrent programming is that we do not usually specify software processes in terms of standard interfaces with clearly defined inputs and outputs; and we define process properties in terms of closed systems; and, therefore, we cannot use specification-conjunction to prove properties of concurrent programs. A proper-interface approach is particularly helpful in designing libraries of processes, all of which use the same interface.

2.1   A Collection of Proper Interfaces

For an open-systems specification, we specify an interface of a process in terms of the outputs of the process and the outputs of the environment of the process. The form of outputs (messages, shared-variables,...) is not important at this stage. There are many ways of designing interfaces, but to simplify design we will design processes and proper interfaces that satisfy the following rules.

Rule 1:   An action is one of the following three types:

1. **Inputs:** The action reads shared variables as input and (possibly) reads or modifies local variables.

2. **Outputs:** The action modifies shared variables as output and (possibly) reads or modifies local variables.

3. **Internal:** The action does not reference shared variables.

The output actions and internal actions of a process are nonblocking because they depend only on the state of the process (and are otherwise independent of the state of the system).

Rule 2: If an input action B is executable at some point in a computation, then it remains executable until it is executed.

$(B \text{ is executable in } S_i) \wedge (B \neq A_{i+1}) \Rightarrow (B \text{ is executable in } S_{i+1})$

This rule disallows probes [Mar85] and other nonmonotonic operators on inputs. A probe checks whether an input is present and takes some action if there is no input; this action can be disabled when an input arrives. But, according to the rule, if an action is executable, it must remain executable until the action is taken.

This rule also prohibits a process from changing an earlier output value; a process can *add* to its earlier output but it cannot change its earlier output. Thus, we have an ordering relation on the "length" of outputs and inputs. For now, assume that outputs and inputs are sequences of values. We can consider other data structures such as trees, provided "length" is defined properly, but this is not central to our discussion.

Rule 3: An input of a process is a prefix of an output of at most one process.

If an input to a process were an output of two or more processes, we would have to deal with interference between processes writing to the same input.

The input to a process may not equal the output from a process because of delays in transmission; hence, we require the input to be an initial subsequence of the output.

An output can feed an arbitrary number of inputs. If x is a process output, and y and z are process inputs, we can have:

$(x \text{ is a prefix of } y) \wedge (x \text{ is a prefix of } z)$

Consider the example, given earlier, of processes p and q sharing a variable x, where though both p and q have a property R, the parallel composition $p\|q$ does not have property R. What are the inputs to p? One definition is that the inputs to p are the sequence of values of x prior to actions by p; these are the sequence of values of the shared variable, projected on p's computation. A definition of the outputs of q are the values of x at the termination of actions of q. But, with this definition, the rules for inputs and outputs are not satisfied! One process can modify x with no impact on the computation of the other process. There seems to be no convenient way to define inputs and outputs so that the input of one process is a prefix of the output of the other.

Next we propose a few proper interfaces that satisfy the rules.

2.2   Examples

Modify Privileges   At most one process has the privilege of modifying a shared variable. The modify-privilege for a shared-variable can be passed between processes; the methods by which privileges are passed is not important at this point in the discussion. An input of a process p, and an output of a process q is the sequence of values of a shared variable at the points in the computation at which the modify-privilege for the shared variable is passed from q to p.

Single-Assignment   Associated with each shared variable x is a boolean x.assigned which is initially false. When a value is assigned to x, the boolean x.assigned becomes true — i.e., a postcondition to every assignment to x is x.assigned.

A value can be assigned to a shared variable at most once in a computation; therefore, if the precondition to an assignment to x is x.assigned holds, then the postcondition is that error holds, where error is a boolean that indicates whether an error has occurred.

The booleans x.assigned cannot appear in the program text. Note that rule 2 prohibits testing whether a variable is unassigned.

The execution of a process reading an unassigned shared variable is suspended until the variable is assigned a value. Each shared variable referenced by a process is either an input or an output variable of the process, and a shared variable is an output variable of at most one process.

An output (input) of a process is the value (if any) assigned to an output (input) variable of the process

Computations of unbounded length are achieved by using data structures, such as lists, of unbounded length.

Message Passing   The shared variables are first-in-first-out channels. The state of a channel is a queue of messages. The length of the queue is unbounded. A channel is empty initially. At most one process can send messages on a channel (append to the queue) and at most one process can receive messages on a channel (delete from the queue). Sending is nonblocking — i.e. the executability of a send action of a process p depends only on the state of p. Receives are blocking — a receive on a channel is executable only if the channel is nonempty. Probes are not permitted: a channel cannot be tested to determine if it is empty.

An output of a process p is the sequence of messages that p sends on a channel. An input of a process p is the sequence of messages received by p

on a channel.

The privilege to send messages, and to receive messages, on a channel can also be sent from one process to another [FC92].

2.3 Reasoning about Programs

A property of a process is a temporal logic formula, and the only rule we have for parallel composition is: if R is a property of p then R is a property of $p\|q$, for any q such that the interface between p and q is proper.

Because, we have an ordering on the lengths of inputs and outputs, an operator that is useful is *establishes* [CT91]. Let R be a predicate on process states. Process p *establishes* R if and only if for all maximal computations of $p\|q$, where q is any process such that the interface between p and q is proper, there exists a suffix of the computation such that R holds for each state of the suffix.

In temporal-logic terms, p establishes R means "eventually always R."

The proof that establishes is conjunctive is straightforward [CT91].

$(p \text{ establishes } R) \wedge (p \text{ establishes } T) \Rightarrow (p \text{ establishes } R \wedge T)$

$(p \text{ establishes } R) \wedge (q \text{ establishes } T) \Rightarrow (p\|q \text{ establishes } R \wedge T)$

The following example illustrates the use of *establishes*.

Consider a single-assignment interface. Process p has inputs x and output y. Process q has inputs x and y and output z. The body of p is: y = x+1 and the body of q is z = x*y

We can prove:

p establishes (x.assigned $\Rightarrow$ y.assigned $\wedge$ y = x+1)
q establishes ((x.assigned $\wedge$ y.assigned) $\Rightarrow$ z.assigned $\wedge$ z = x*y)

Using specification-conjunction and predicate calculus:

$p\|q$ establishes
((x.assigned $\Rightarrow$ y.assigned $\wedge$ z.assigned $\wedge$ y = x+1 $\wedge$ z = x*y)

The use of *establishes* simplifies proofs of parallel composition with proper interfaces. The operator *establishes* was proposed within the context of the PCN theory. Here, we observe that the same constructs can be extended to other proper interfaces.

3 Determinism

We can prove that if each process in a parallel composition is deterministic, and the parallel composition satisfies our 3 rules for proper interfaces, then the parallel composition is deterministic as well: Different executions of the parallel composition produce identical output.

4 Programming Languages and Proper Composition

Next, we consider language support for the design of families of interfaces for parallel composition. We wish to support flexible interfaces with which we use closed-systems specifications and we also wish to support more restrictive interfaces with which we use proper-interface specifications.

We have based our research on the C++ programming language [ES90]. A major objective of C++ is to provide a language framework for constructing program libraries with well defined, compiler enforced interfaces. These features, along with its widespread, use motivated our choice of C++. Our design methodology is supported by C++ augmented by small number of simple extensions. We call the resulting language Compositional C++ or CC++. A detailed discussion of CC++ can be found in [CK92].

Parallel composition in CC++ is provided by parallel blocks (equivalent to parbegin/parend) and a parallel loop construct. Any statement can appear in a parallel block; blocks can be nested. The execution of a parallel block terminates when all statements in the block terminate.

A generalization of the single assignment rule is used to synchronize operations between statements executing in parallel. Primitive data types can be declared to be synchronization or **sync** objects. A process reading an uninitialized **sync** object suspends until the object is initialized by an assignment. Multiple initialization of the same variable is an error. CC++ generalizes single assignment variables in that *user-defined* data types can also be made **sync**. The designer of the data type has complete control over the semantics of user defined **sync** objects and the operations that can be performed on such a data object.

In C++, one can associate a function with a user-defined data type; such a function can only be applied to an object of the appropriate type. These functions control the manner in which a data type can be used. Such functions are commonly invoked through a pointer to an object of that data type. If a pointer to an object is a global variable of a system, invoking a function through such a pointer corresponds to a remote procedure call. If a reference to an object is shared by more than one statement in a **par** block, nondeterministic execution can result. As part of the interface specification for a data type, we can indicate that the operations of a function take place atomically.

5 The Relationship between CC++ and Logic Programming

In our work, we have focused on language mechanisms that facilitate the design of interfaces for parallel composition. The design of CC++ draws ideas from a wide range of parallel programming languages. These include data flow languages with single-assignment variables [TE68, Ack82], remote procedure calls [TA90], message passing [Sei91], actors [Agh86], concurrent logic programming [FT90, Ued86, Sha86] and compositional languages, particularly PCN [CT91]. While a range of comparisons are possible, the following discussion will focus on the relationship between CC++ and concurrent logic programming languages.

A "pure" logic program has a declarative reading. Such a program does not presuppose any ordering on the actions the program performs. The execution of a program produces a consistent set of variable bindings. As long as the bindings are consistent between program components, the order in which the bindings are determined is not specified. Thus, the conjunction and disjunction operators in a logic program can be viewed as specifying a parallel composition. Clearly, in a pure logic program, one that does not utilize predicates with side effects, all compositions are proper. One may write an open-system specification for a program component, however, that specification is restricted to use only logical variables. If predicates with side effects are used (i.e. such as cut, input/output, assert), then the specification must be weakened.

The situation in the committed choice languages such as Strand [FT90], FCP [Sha86], GHC [Ued86] or Parlog [Gre87] is not as clear cut. In these languages, only one solution path is explored, there is no backtracking or or-parallel search. In order to control which solution path is followed, modify access to variables is restricted. A consequence of read only variables is that the programmer has additional proof obligations, or the open-system specification is weakened. For example, a procedure can deadlock if the environment with which it is composed does not follow an appropriate resource acquisition protocol.

Concurrent logic programming languages provide the safety net that all programs written in such a language conform to the protocol of a proper declarative composition. By contrast, CC++ places the burden of designing interfaces and their proofs on the programmer. We observe, however, that in many large scale parallel programs, efficiency and system concerns dictate that some parts of the program be written in an imperative programming language. Indeed multilingual programming using a concurrent logic programming language as the interface had been proposed as a useful parallel programming paradigm [FO90, FO91, FT90, CT91] and most logic programming languages include "foreign language" interfaces. However, once foreign language components are introduced into a system, the tasks of designing interfaces and their proofs falls back onto the user.

It is important to recognize that a sync variable in CC++ is a pure single assignment variable and not a logical variable. In particular, the assignment x = y suspends until y has a value; variable-to-variable assignments are not made. Consequently, structured sync data behaves more like an I-Structure [AT80] from the dataflow language Id [Ack82] than a tuple from a logic programming language. The use of single assignment variables in place of logical variables has the advantages that assignment semantics are completely consistent with C++, and that pointer dereferencing is not required prior to variable use. The disadvantage is that some concurrent logic programming techniques, such as the short circuit technique [Tak89] become sequentialized. This is not a significant drawback, however, because termination of parallel blocks is easily determined.

CC++ has many ideas in common with the parallel programming language PCN [CT91] which in turn draws heavily from committed choice concurrent logic programming languages such as Strand [FT90]. There are, however, fundamental differences between them. These include:

- CC++ provides a general shared memory model. This includes having pointers to data objects.

- PCN permits x = y as an equality. CC++ treats all assignment operators as assignment of value.

- Remote procedure call is a primitive operation in CC++.

- There are no nondeterministic language constructs in CC++ as opposed to PCN. Nondeterminism in CC++ is obtained through interleaving of atomic actions.

- The emphasis in CC++ is on the development of families of interfaces and proofs. PCN provides a single-assignment interface and proof theory.

6   A Programming Example

To demonstrate how CC++ supports parallel program design through proper interfaces, we present a simple example. The parallel program we wish to construct is a producer/consumer system. The producer process produces a sequence of values. The values are processed in order by a consumer process. Both the producer and the consumer execute in parallel. One of the advantages of CC++ is that the parallel code is quite similar to the sequential C++ code that solve the same problem. The primary difference is the use of sync variables and the introduction of parallel blocks.

We will solve this problem using three different interfaces: i) a declarative interface, ii) a modify-privileges interface, and iii) a message passing interface.

Figure 1 shows how a producer/consumer program is constructed using a declarative interface. The sequence of values is passed from the producer to the consumer on a list. The list structure is declared so that both the value being placed on the list, and the pointer to the next cell of the list are sync. The producer iterates, creating new list cells, initializing their values and setting the next field of the previous cell to point to the newly created cell. The consumer is passed a `sync` pointer to a list cell. It cannot proceed until that pointer is assigned a list cell. Furthermore, the value field of the list cell cannot be used until it is initialized. Within the main routine, the producer and consumer execute in parallel.

The modify-privileges interface is essentially the same as the declarative interface. The only difference is that the `value` field of the list cell is *not* `sync`. The modify-privileges interface protocol requires that shared values can only be modified by the procedure with modification privileges. Modify privileges are passed from the producer to the consumer when the `sync next` pointer is initialized. Thus we must ensure that the value component of the list is initialized before the next pointer is set.

Our final example is a message passing interface. In a message passing interface, we must have an entity to send a message to. Therefore, we will define the producer and consumer as user defined types. We associate a set of functions with each user defined type. Thus the `produce` function can be applied to a variable of type `producer`, while the `insert_queue` and `consume` operations can be applied to a variable of type `consumer`. The consumer also has a `get_queue` operation which is only accessible to variables of type `consumer`.

The main program creates a `producer` and `consumer` variable and applies the `produce` and `consume` operations to the `producer` and `consumer` respectively. The `producer` inserts a data value directly into the queue of the `consumer` by calling applying the `insert_queue` operation. The `consumer` then extract the data values and processes them. The operations on the queue must be made atomic to prohibit `insert_queue` and `get_queue` operations from occurring simultaneously.

References

[Ack82]   William B. Ackerman. Data flow languages. *Computer*, 15(2):15–25, feb 1982.

[Agh86]   Gul Agha. *ACTORS: A Model of Concurrent Computation in Distributed Systems*. MIT Press, 1986.

[AT80]   Arvind and R.E. Thomas. I-Structures: An efficient data structure for functional languages. Technical Report TM-178, MIT, 1980.

[CK92]   K. Mani Chandy and Carl Kesselman. Compositional C++: Compositional parallel programming. Technical Report Caltech-CS-TR-92-13, California Institute of Technology, 1992.

[CM88]   K. Mani Chandy and Jayadev Misra. *Parallel Program Design*. Addison-Wesley, 1988.

[CT91]   K. Mani Chandy and Stephen Taylor. *An Introduction to Parallel Programming*. Bartlett and Jones, 1991.

15

[ES90] Margaret A. Ellis and Bjarne Stroustrup. *The Annotated C++ Reference Manual*. Addison-Wesley, 1990.

[FC92] Ian Foster and K. Mani Chandy. Fortran M: Modular Fortran for parallel programming. Technical report, Argonne National Laboratory, 1992.

[FO90] Ian Foster and Ross Overbeek. Experiences with bilingual parallel programming. In *The Proceedings of the Fifth Distributed Memory Computer Conference*, 1990.

[FO91] Ian Foster and Ross Overbeek. Bilingual parallel programming. In *Proceedings of the Third Workshop on Parallel Computing and Compilers*. MIT Press, feb 1991.

[FT90] Ian Foster and Stephen Taylor. *Strand: New Concepts in Parallel Programming*. Prentice Hall, 1990.

[Gre87] Steve Gregory. *Parallel Logic Programming in PARLOG*. International Series in Logic Programming. Addison-Wesley, 1987.

[Lam91] Leslie Lamport. Temporal logic of actions. Technical report, DEC-SRC, 1991.

[Mar85] Alain J. Martin. The Probe: An addition to communication primitives. *Information Processing Letters*, 20:125–130, April 1985.

[OG76] S. Owicki and D. Gries. An axiomatic proof technique for parallel programs I. *Acta Informatica*, 6(1):319–340, 1976.

[Pnu81] Amir Pnueli. The temporal semantics of concurrent programs. *Theoretical Computer Science*, 13:45–60, 1981.

[Sei91] Charles Seitz. *Developments in Concurrency and Communication*, chapter 5, pages 131–200. Addison Wesley, 1991.

[Sha86] Ehud Shapiro. Concurrent Prolog: A program report. *IEEE Computer*, 19(8):44–58, August 1986.

[TA90] B. H. Tay and A. L. Ananda. A survey of remote procedure calls. *ACM Operating Systems Review*, 24(3), July 1990.

[Tak89] Akikazu Takeuchi. How to solve it in Concurrent Prolog. Unpublished note., 1989.

[TE68] L. Tesler and H. Enea. A language for concurrent processes. In *Proceedings of AFIPS SJCC*, number ANL-91/38, 1968.

[Ued86] Kazunori Ueda. Guarded horn clauses. In *Logic Programming '85*, pages 168–179. Springer-Verlag, 1986.

```
// The value of the list element and the pointer to the
// next list cell are both sync variables

struct list {
  sync T value;
  struct list * sync next;
}

producer(list * sync * ptr) {
    // A producer iterates allocating a new list cell, storing the pointer to
    // it into the sync next pointer from the previous iteration and
    // initializing the value field of the list cell.

    list * tmp;        // tmp is a pointer to a list cell
    while (1) {
      tmp = new list;                // Allocate a new list cell
      tmp->value = producer_value();  // Initialize the value being produced
      (*ptr)->next = tmp;            // Pass modify privileges
      ptr = & (tmp->next);    // Get a pointer to the next field
    }
}

consumer(list * sync ptr) {
    // Iterate over the list created by the consumer.  Because they
    // are both sync, we have to wait for both the value and the
    // next pointer to be initialized before continuing.

    while (1) {
      consume_value(ptr-> value);
      ptr = ptr->next;
    }
}

main() {
  list * sync X;
  // Run the producer and consumer in parallel.  The consumer waits for
  // the list pointer X to be assigned a value.  The producer is passed
  // a non-sync pointer to the list so that it doesn't have to wait.

  par { producer(& X); consumer(X); }
}
```

Figure 1: A producer/consumer example using a declarative interface.

```
// Produce a value by sending it directly to the consumer
struct producer {
  produce(consumer * ptr) {
      while (1) { ptr->insert_queue(producer_value()); }
  }
}

// A consumer is a user defined data type with three operations associated with
// it.
struct consumer {
  atomic insert_queue(T); // Insert a value into the consumers queue
  void consume(list sync * ptr) // Consume the values put in the queue
     {
        while (1) { consume_value(get_queue()); }
     }
private:
    atomic T get_queue();    // Extract a value from the queue.
}

main() {
  producer P;                      // Create a producer object
  consumer C; // Create a consumer object

  // Start the producer and consumer
  par { P.produce( &C ); C.consume(); }
}
```

Figure 2: A producer/consumer example using a message passing interface.

Empirical Semantics for Defeasible Databases

Judea Pearl
Cognitive Systems Laboratory
Computer Science Department
University of California, Los Angeles, CA 90024
judea@cs.ucla.edu

Abstract

Sentences in general logic programs are normally interpreted as introspective prescriptions for building coherent sets of epistemic beliefs, given other beliefs or lack of beliefs. As these prescriptions become more complex, they tend to behave more like procedural programs than sentences in logic, forcing programmers to guard carefully against strange, unintended consequences of slight nuances of expression. There are, however, many applications where the interaction between sentences can be made significantly simpler to understand and compute. Such applications require matter-of-fact knowledge about the external world, to which we do not need to attribute complicated modalities such as knowledge, beliefs and desires. Knowledge about the world includes, for example, the typical properties of objects and classes, what an agent should expect given facts observed in the world, and how the world would react to actions taken by the agent.

Defeasible databases express such facts and expectations, respectively, in the form of propositional and conditional sentences (or defaults) that admit exceptions. Some exceptions are represented explicitly in the database (e.g., specific birds that do not fly) and some are implicit in vague expressions or in chains of conflicting expectations.

In this talk, I will survey current attempts to give such databases empirical semantics in terms of infinitesimal probabilities, to be regarded as qualitative abstractions of an agent's experience. This semantics can be described in terms of rankings on models, where higher ranked models stand for more surprising (or less likely) situations. At the heart of this formulation is the concept of *default priorities*, namely, a natural ordering of the conditional sentences that can be derived automatically from the knowledge base and that can be used to answer queries without computing explicit rankings of worlds or formulas. The result is a model-theoretic account of plausible beliefs which, as in classical logic, are qualitative and deductively closed and, as in probability, are subject to retraction and to varying degrees of firmness.

Topics to be discussed include:

1. Criteria for consistency of defeasible databases.

2. Criteria and procedures for deriving plausible conclusions.

3. Analysis of behavior (specificity vs. irrelevance).

4. Analysis of complexity.

5. Background knowledge vs. contingent observations.

6. Representation of causal relations, actions and change.

7. Semantics of counterfactuals and nested conditionals.

8. Belief revision and belief update.

9. Imprecise observations and vague queries.

References

- Ernest Adams. *The Logic of Conditionals.* Dordrecht, Netherlands: D. Reidel, Chapter 2, 1975.

- Craig Boutilier. Conditional logics for default reasoning and belief revision. Ph.D. dissertation, University of Toronto, 1992. Also Technical Report 91-1, Department of Computer Science, University of British Columbia.

- Hector Geffner. *Default Reasoning: Causal and Conditional Theories.* Cambridge, MA: MIT Press, 1992.

- Hector Geffner and Judea Pearl. Conditional entailment: Bridging two approaches to default reasoning. *Artificial Intelligence,* 53, 209-244, 1992.

- Moisés Goldszmidt and Judea Pearl. System-Z^+: A formalism for reasoning with variable-strength defaults. *Proceedings, AAAI-91.* Anaheim, CA, 1: 399-404, July 1991.

- Moisés Goldszmidt and Judea Pearl. On the consistency of defeasible databases. *Artificial Intelligence,* 52, 121-149, 1991.

- Moisés Goldszmidt and Judea Pearl. Default ranking: A practical framework for evidential reasoning, belief revision and update. *Proceedings of the Third International Conference on Knowledge Representation and Reasoning.* Cambridge, MA: MIT Press, October 1992.

- Moisés Goldszmidt and Judea Pearl. Stratified rankings for causal modeling. *Proceedings of the Fourth International Workshop on Nonmonotonic Reasoning.* Plymouth, VT, 99-110, May 1992.

- Moisés Goldszmidt and Judea Pearl. Reasoning with qualitative probabilities can be tractable. *Proceedings of the Eighth Conference on Uncertainty in Artificial Intelligence.* San Mateo, CA: Morgan Kaufmann, 112-120, 1992.

- Moisés Goldszmidt, Paul Morris, and Judea Pearl. A maximum entropy approach to nonmonotonic reasoning. *Proceedings, AAAI-90.* Boston, MA, 646-652, 1990. Forthcoming, *IEEE, Transactions PAMI.*

- Daniel Lehmann and Menachem Magidor. What does a conditional knowledge base entail? *Artificial Intelligence,* 55, 1-60, 1992.

- Judea Pearl. *Probabilistic Reasoning in Intelligent Systems.* San Mateo, CA: Morgan Kaufmann, 1988.

- Judea Pearl. System Z: A natural ordering of defaults with tractable applications to nonmonotonic reasoning. In R. Parikh (Ed.), *Theoretical Aspects – Reasoning about Knowledge.* San Mateo, CA: Morgan Kaufmann, 121-135, 1990.

- Judea Pearl. Probabilistic semantics for nonmonotonic reasoning: A survey. In R. Cummins and J. Pollock (Eds.), *Philosophy and Artificial Intelligence - Essays at the Interface.* Cambridge, MA: Bradford Books/MIT Press, 157-187, 1991.

- Judea Pearl. Epsilon-Semantics. *Encyclopedia of AI, 2nd Edition.* New York: John Wiley, 468-475, 1992.

- Wolfgang Spohn. A general non-probabilistic theory of inductive reasoning. In W.L. Harper and B. Skyrms (Eds.), *Causation in Decision, Belief Change, and Statistics, II.* Dordecht, Netherlands: D. Reidel, 105-134, 1988.

Advanced Tutorials

Many-Valued Semantics for Logic Programming

Melvin Fitting
Lehman College - CUNY
Department of Mathematics and Computer Science
Bedford Park Boulevard West
Bronx, NY 10468, USA
mlflc@cunyvm.cuny.edu

Abstract

Many-valued semantics play two distinct roles in the area of logic programming. One role — which so far is the minor one but which has the most promising long-term potential — is in the investigation of logic programming paradigms that go beyond those that are currently standard. For instance, suggestions have been made to take probabilities, or sets of nodes in a distributed database, as truth values. The other role for many-valued semantics lies in the varied attempts to understand logic programs in the more conventional sense — e.g. the role of negation as failure. Here we discuss both aspects of many-valued semantics; it turns out they are not as separate as they might seem (at first encounter).

Conventional logic programming, allowing negation as failure, is the area where a many-valued approach is most likely to be encountered. Such approaches are three-valued (it is even a little misleading to call them many-valued). Instead one can look at the situation as: logic is classical; our knowledge (expressed in a program) is limited; in some cases truth values can not be determined; consequently *partial* truth assignments must be considered. Seen this way, *partial logic* looks hard to avoid. Now, introducing a third truth value of *unknown* is just a reification of ignorance that turns out to have technical advantages, simplifying arguments and suggesting new paradigms. We discuss the basic ideas of partial logic — these are quite straightforward. Then we discuss how they give rise to a three-valued logic.

The three-valued (or partial) approach to conventional logic programming is not monolithic. So-called Kripke-Kleene semantics is closest to the classical semantics developed for logic programs without negation. Kunen introduced a variation that is better behaved in some respects, but which requires consideration of non-Herbrand models. More importantly, he established some important connections between two- and three-valued semantics that have important consequences. Finally, well-founded and stable model semantics, though originally introduced as two-valued, quickly developed three-valued versions, and these were in many ways better behaved and more natural. Thus, three-valued, or partial, semantics is a family, and we discuss its members and their interrelationships.

The next most interesting number of truth values after three is four. Four-valued logic can still be thought of as essentially classical logic; but now the information embodied in a program can be not only incomplete but also inconsistent. Hence we need truth assignments that are partial, and that sometimes assign both true and false to an atom. If we make inconsistency into a truth-value, we get a natural four-valued logic whose introduction in the scientific literature antedates its application to logic programming. We show that working in a four-valued setting can aid in the understanding of stable model and well-founded semantics. In many ways, technical details and intuitions mesh nicely in this setting.

The four-valued logic mentioned above is the simplest example of a *bilattice*. These are many-valued logics, and many of them have particularly nice algebraic structure. In addition they arise naturally and provide one possible link between conventional logic programming with negation, as we have been discussing it, and logic programming based on other paradigms such as probabilities. We conclude with a sketch of the basic ideas of bilattices and how they do unify ideas from several approaches.

Advanced Tutorial:
Concurrent Logic Programming

E. Tick
Dept. of Computer Science
University of Oregon
Eugene, OR 97403, USA
tick@cs.uoregon.edu

Abstract

This tutorial reviews practical, concurrent logic programming languages exploiting several paradigms of concurrency and parallelism. Abstract models and formal semantics are critical in the development of better (e.g., more expressive, faster) languages, but practical experience with actual implmented languages is also important, and will be stressed here.

Rather than give a "bottom-up" taxonomy of languages from the point of view of exploitable parallelism, a "top-down" view is taken. Standard exposition about parallel logic programming is to decompose languages into those that exploit AND-parallelism and OR-parallelism. Our approach here is to decompose languages into their professed programming paradigms and goals:

- Speedup of sequential Prolog to transparently exploit multiprocessor power (Aurora, Muse, and &-Prolog).

- Removing backtracking of standard logic programs to enable concurrent execution of tasks synchronized on logic variable bindings (FGHC, etc.).

- Ability to write bilingual programs in logic programming and imperative languages, to facilitate writing scientific applications (PCN).

- Further removal of the broadcast facility (multiple writers of a logical variable) of standard logic programs to enable implementation speeds approaching that of imperative languages (Janus).

- Combining backtracking with stream communication to enable a wide range of algorithms while retaining the power of the logical variable (Andorra, AKL, Pandora).

Each group will be reviewed, with key implementation issues summarized and performance analyzed. These languages and systems (and others in their corresponding families) are given as examples because they are accessible in the public domain.

Deductive and Object-Oriented Databases

Serge Abiteboul
I.N.R.I.A.,
78153 Le Chesnay, France.
Serge.Abiteboul@inria.fr

This tutorial is concerned with database management systems (DBMS's). The acronym *dDBMS* is used for a deductive one and *ooDBMS* for an object-oriented one. Finally, *dooDBMS* are obtained by combining deduction and object-orientation. The purpose of the tutorial is to try to clarify these concepts.

A DBMS provides easy access to a *persistent, shared, large volume of data.* Each of the terms is important to understand those systems. For instance, because of the volume of data, secondary storage management including index management, data clustering, query optimization, is critical in terms of performance although it is not directly visible to the user. There have already been a number of DBMS generations, in particular, the "relational revolution". We are concerned here with future generations. To consider the next generations, it is important to understand the major limitations of relational systems. The first one stems from the nature of the data structure, the relation, which is too simplistic for many DB applications. The second one is that the core of the relational model is essentially a query language, i.e. a language for accessing data. To write real database applications, one also needs the full power of a programming language. Thus one has to use an embedding of the query language in a programming language (e.g., C+SQL) which leads to the so-called *impedance mismatch.*

To overcome these problems, two main directions have been followed. One is based on the integration of logic-programming features and the second on the object-oriented paradigm.

Deduction. A deductive DBMS incorporates aspects of logic programming and thereby provides advantages over pure relational systems by bridging the gap towards knowledge bases. Standard logic-programming languages such as Prolog are viewed as too procedural, too complicated for database users and too rich to be efficiently optimized. The deductive approach has centered around the study of Datalog, i.e., pure Horn rules without function symbols. In the database perspective, logic is viewed as essential to integrate knowledge in various forms: passive (integrity constraints), implicit (deduction) or active (triggers).

Most of the effort in deductive databases has been devoted to optimizing Datalog. Other research directions are: providing declarative semantics to negation (e.g., stratification, well-founded), introducing more complex data structures and in particular set-based data structures, or adding updates.

Object-orientation. The integration of object-orientation in database systems is now mastered from an implementation point of view and several ooDBMS's are already commercially exploited. The main purpose of this new technology was to enlarge the range of applications that could benefit from database technology (e.g., engineering or CAD databases). A measure of its success is that standard relational systems are now commonly adopting object-oriented features.

However, ooDBMS's lack the formal basis of relational systems. Furthermore, although some of them offer a query language, this is in the best case a variant of SQL which does not encompass any deductive capability and does not even take advantage in a real sense of object-orientation.

dooD. In the case of relational DBMS's, there was the rare convergence (in the sixties and seventies) of intense experimental activities and theoretical studies. The situation is less clear now since with notable exceptions, the experimental activities over the last five years have been concentrated around ooDBMS's whereas the theoretical ones preferred the deductive paradigm. This resulted in a theory with almost no implementation and systems with fragile theoretical basis. The third part of the tutorial will deal with dooDB which is an attempt to reconcile the two approaches.

On the negative side, one may be tempted to believe that the triangular integration of database, logic-programming and object-oriented technologies would lead to a monster. Indeed, this could be the case. We will argue optimistically that to the contrary, (i) object-orientation provides the basis for incorporating deductive capabilities in *real* database systems, and (ii) the logical framework is the natural candidate for providing a sound theoretical basis to ooDB's.

We will survey the main achievements of (d)(oo)DBMS and consider the open problems. We draw particularly from work described in the following references.

References

[1] S. Abiteboul. Towards a deductive object-oriented language. In W. Kim, J.-M. Nicolas, and S. Nishio, editors, *Deductive and Object-Oriented Databases*, pages 453–472. Elsevier Science Publishers B.V., 1990.

[2] S. Abiteboul and C. Beeri. On the manipulation of complex objects. Technical report, INRIA and Hebrew Univ., 1988. to appear in *ACM Transactions on Database Systems*.

[3] S. Abiteboul and P.C. Kanellakis. Object identity as a query language primitive. In *Proc. ACM SIGMOD Symp. on the Management of Data*, pages 159–173, 1989. to appear in *J. ACM*.

[4] A.M. Alashqur, S.Y.W. Su, and H. Lam. A rule-based language for deductive object-oriented databases. In *International Conf. on Data Engineering*, pages 58–67, 1990.

[5] F. Bancilhon, S. Cluet, and C. Delobel. Query languages for object-oriented database systems: the O_2 proposal. In *proc. Second Intern. Work. on Data Base Programming Languages*, 1989.

[6] C. Beeri and T. Milo. Functional and predicative programming in oodb's. In *pods*, pages 176–190, 1992.

[7] C. Beeri, S. Naqvi, R. Ramakrishnan, O. Shmueli, and S. Tsur. Sets and negation in a logic database language (LDL1). In *Proc. ACM Symp. on Principles of Database Systems*, pages 21–37, 1987.

[8] F. Cacace, S. Ceri, S. Crespi-Reghizzi, L. Tanca, and R. Zicari. The Logres project: integrating object-oriented data modelling with a rule-based programming paradigm. Technical Report 89-039, Politecnico di Milano, 1989.

[9] Y. Caseau. an object-oriented deductive language. *Annals of Mathematics and Artificial Intelligence*, 3:211–258, 1991.

[10] S. Danforth, E. Simon, F. Cacace, S. Ceri, and L. Tanca. the design of the RL language. Technical Report 2443, Esprit, 1990.

[11] A. Heuer and P. Sander. Semantics and evaluation of rules over complex objects. In W. Kim, J.-M. Nicolas, and S. Nishio, editors, *Deductive and Object-Oriented Databases*, pages 473–492. Elsevier Science Publishers B.V., 1990.

[12] M. Jarke and M. Jeusfeld. Rule representation and management in ConceptBase. *Sigmod Record*, 18:3:46–51, 1989.

[13] M. Kifer and G. Lausen. F-logic: A higher-order language for reasoning about objects. In *sigmod*, 1989.

[14] G. Kuper and M.Y. Vardi. A new approach to database logic. In *Proc. ACM Symp. on Principles of Database Systems*, pages 86–96, 1984.

[15] Y. Lou and Z. M. Ozsoyoglu. LLO: an object-oriented deductive language with methods and method inheritance. In *sigmod*, pages 198–207, 1991.

[16] D. Maier. A logic for objects. In *Workshop on foundations of deductive databases and logic programming*, pages 6–26, 1986.

[17] D. Maier, J. Zhu, and H. Ohkawa. Features in the TEDM object model. In W. Kim, J.-M. Nicolas, and S. Nishio, editors, *Deductive and Object-Oriented Databases*, pages 511–530. Elsevier Science Publishers B.V., 1990.

[18] E. Bertino D. Montesi. Toward a logical-object oriented programming language for databases. In *edbt*, pages 168–183, 1992.

[19] L. Wong. Inference rules in object-oriented programming systems. In W. Kim, J.-M. Nicolas, and S. Nishio, editors, *Deductive and Object-Oriented Databases*, pages 493–509. Elsevier Science Publishers B.V., 1990.

[20] C. Zaniolo. Object identity and inheritance in deductive databases – an evolutionary approach. In W. Kim, J.-M. Nicolas, and S. Nishio, editors, *Deductive and Object-Oriented Databases*, pages 7–21. Elsevier Science Publishers B.V., 1990.

Tutorial on Linear Logic

A. S. Troelstra
Faculteit Wiskunde en Informatica
Universiteit van Amsterdam
Plantage Muidergracht 24, 1018TV Amsterdam, Netherlands
anne@fwi.uva.nl

Abstract

Linear logic is a "resource-conscious" logic: if we think of formulas as indicating resources (or the types of resources), it matters whether a formula appears n times, only once, or not at all; an n-fold occurrence refers to n-fold use of the same (type of) resource. The usual logical systems motivated by the concept of truth do not permit us to make these distinctions; n times asserting A still means just means asserting the truth of A.

In a sequent-calculus formulation the resource-consciousness is expressed by the suppression of the so-called structural rules of weakening and contraction (not exchange). Logical systems without (some of) the structural rules have appeared in other contexts too (relevance logic, BCK-logic, Lambek calculus), but in the case of linear logic the possibility of contraction and weakening is reintroduced in a controlled way via the logical operators of storage, denoted by !, and its dual, denoted by ?. It will be obvious that a logic which keeps track of the number of times a formula is used is of potential interest for the theory of logic programming as well.

We first discuss some of the principal aspects of linear logic by means of a "baby example": the calculus of conjunction. In particular we look at the role of the structural rules, the contrast between "additive" and "multiplicative" operators in the absence of such rules, the role of cut-elimination, the formulas-as-types paradigm, and the categorical approach.

Next we consider the full calculus for classical and intuitionistic linear logic, and in particular we discuss the storage operator and its dual. For a formula $!A$ in the antecedent of a sequent contraction and weakening holds, and similarly for a formula $?A$ in the succedent of a sequent. Classical linear logic exhibits the same symmetry between antecedent and succedent of sequents as ordinary classical logic does; intuitionistic linear logic on the other hand permits at most one formula in the succedent, resembling in this respect the sequent formulation of ordinary intuitionistic logic.

Some elementary syntactic properties of the calculus are reviewed, the proof of cut-elimination is sketched. We also describe embeddings of intuitionistic and classical logic into linear logic.

For intuitionistic linear logic, there is an interesting and useful alternative formalism: natural deduction. This is not satisfactory for classical linear logic, in that case we need Girard's theory of proof nets. For the so-called multiplicative fragment without constants a simple presentation of proof-nets is possible.

Linear logic has "logical" and "type-theoretical" models; after discussing this distinction, we present a simple type-theoretical model, the calculus of relations. Then we turn to the (logical) quantale semantics and give a sketch of the completeness proof.

We conclude the tutorial with a brief discussion of the undecidability of linear logic.

Of the many items in the rapidly expanding literature on the subject we mention only two, the paper of Girard which started the topic in its present form, and my lecture notes which are suitable for further orientation.

References

[1] J.-Y Girard. Linear Logic. *Theoretical Computer Science*, 50:1–102, 1987.

[2] A.S. Troelstra *Lectures on Linear Logic*. Center for the Study of Language and Information, Stanford; CSLI Lecture Notes no.29, 1992.

Logic Programming and Genetic Sequence Analysis: a Tutorial

Ross A. Overbeek

Abstract

Approximately 3.5 to 4 billion years ago, a self-replicating "organism" appeared on earth. The mechanism of evolution produced alternatives that adapted to specific environments, and the variety of life gradually emerged.

Now, we live in a period in which the molecular mechanisms that characterize life forms are rapidly being determined. With the ability to actually "sequence the genome" of living organisms, we have gained access to the blueprints that govern the molecular details of life. With such knowledge comes not only the ability to create advances in medicine; it also allows one to seriously consider the task of gradually elucidating the historical development of the fundamental mechanisms, gradually shedding light on the billions of years of evolution since the existence of the universal ancestor (the latest common ancestor of all extant life forms – not the original life form). Many of the key insights will result from the comparison of blueprints. From the similarities and differences, one gains appreciation of what is essential, what is accidental, and what alternative designs have emerged for the mechanisms that drive life. This exploration of the blueprints (i.e., genomes) may well be the most exciting scientific quest for the coming few decades.

To fully understand the role that logic programming might play in this endeavor, one must have a basic grasp of both the essential molecular mechanisms and how the search for clarification will continue. While it is impossible to convey that information in a short tutorial, I will attempt to give an outline, along with suggestions on what references might be most helpful. Finally, I will end my presentation with some specific problems that might be of interest to logic programmers. These problems represent computational tasks that might be considered by those wishing an introduction to computational issues in genetic sequence analysis.

In the remainder of this abstract, I will offer a highly abbreviated outline of what will be presented.

What is known about the molecular mechanisms of life?

Consider a small, single-celled organism like a bacterium. In a reductionist view, it is essentially an enclosed environment in which a relatively small set of chemical reactions determine its self-replicating behavior. These reactions convert energy to usable forms, synthesize critical molecules, breakdown large molecules into reusable subcomponents, and so forth. They frequently require the presence of auxiliary little molecular machines in order to operate efficiently; these machines (called enzymes) are protein molecules.

A central activity of the cell involves synthesizing the needed proteins from instructions encoded in a blueprint. The blueprint for an organism is encoded in large DNA molecules. When the organism needs to manufacture a given protein, a copy of the blueprint is made onto a mRNA molecule, which may be thought of as a "tape" containing the detailed instructions needed to make the protein. The tape is fed into a machine called the ribosome which manufactures the desired protein.

The Role of Logic Programming

In order to clarify the exact functioning of this exquisite automaton, we will need to

1. lay out exactly what reactions characterize its existence and sustain its self-replication,

2. determine which enzymes are needed to facilitate these reactions,

3. locate where each enzymes is described in the blueprint, and

4. determine how the cell regulates when to cause the instructions on how to build an enzyme to be used.

That is, we will need to clarify exactly how such machines function. The problems associated with understanding multicellular organisms (like us) are profoundly more difficult, but will build on knowledge about these simpler organisms.

The challenge of clarifying the molecular basis of life forms will necessarily involve computational support. In particular,

• databases that record what is known about life forms will play a central role,

• phylogenetic analysis will allow us to understand the historical relationships between species,

• comparative analysis of the exact blueprints of the enzymes will gradually reveal the alternative designs of structural units (revealing how mutations break or enhance their function), and

• structural analysis of these enzyme molecules will eventually allow us to understand how the function of each enzyme is actually achieved.

Logic programming can play a useful and growing role in this scientific effort – arguably the most interesting and profound project of this century.

The most comprehensive integration of biological databases now exists within a Prolog implementation which is available to the community. Improving and extending this effort is of major importance.

Phylogenetic analysis requires extremely large amounts of computation, making it an obvious candidate for parallel processing. One implementation of the best available phylogenetic analysis system has been done in PCN, a language based on committed-choice logic programming.

The central tool of comparative analysis is multiple-sequence alignment. Some of the better implementations have been done in Prolog, Strand, and KL1.

Structural analysis of protein molecules is an ongoing activity with teams in Europe, Japan, and America all actively working on creating a knowledge-based approach that might lay the foundation for eventually attacking this extremely difficult problem.

In my tutorial, I will try to amplify and clarify these remarks, including an attempt to provide concrete examples of problems that might profitably be explored using different technologies from the logic programming research world.

Unification

Checking the Soundness
of Resolution Schemes

Bruno Dumant
Digital,Paris Research Laboratory,
85 av. Victor Hugo,
92563 Rueil Malmaison Cedex, France.
dumant@prl.dec.com

Abstract

Any theorem-prover manipulating Horn clauses and working in the domain of finite trees should provide the unification algorithm with occur-check, but this test slows down execution significantly. Recently, P. Deransart et al. ([3]) presented sufficient conditions to check that a program may be soundly executed by any resolution scheme never performing the occur-check.

We extend this work, putting forward conditions to guarantee that a program may be soundly executed by a resolution scheme which only performs the occur-check in some known places. Our conditions take into account the order in which unifications are carried out during the execution of the program. Therefore, the method may be applied to any theorem-prover, for example, an industrial implementation of Prolog with delaying primitives or a bottom-up parser.

If a resolution strategy is given, those conditions can also be used to build algorithms designed to determine at compile time when the occur-check can be safely avoided during execution.

1   Introduction

Logic programming languages can be distinguished through the domain of interpretation of the terms they manipulate. Some of them use rational trees to interpret terms, the others only use finite trees, which means that the occur-check should be performed in order to guarantee the correctness of the answer.

Actually, most Prolog compilers and interpreters of the latter family do not perform occur-check for efficiency reasons: The unification of a variable with a term is a basic operation in any Prolog interpreter or compiler; without occur-check, it can be done in constant time, but with occur-check, this time is linear in the size of the term. And it is generally admitted that industrial Prolog programs "usually" don't need occur-check.

When programs cannot be soundly interpreted over rational trees — it is often the case for instance with programs using difference lists — it would be safer to make sure that the occur-check is performed when it is *necessary*. But this test should not be carried out otherwise, to preserve efficiency. Unfortunately, the problem of determining exactly when the occur-check is necessary is undecidable ([6]).

Many works have been devoted to this problem. Most of them try to determine in a program a number of arguments which should be unified with occur-check in order to guarantee the soundness of the answer ([10], [11], [2]). Some of these works use abstract interpretation techniques to solve this problem, assuming that the resolution scheme is the standard Prolog one, and put forward compile-time tests. J. Beer ([1]) deals with the problem in a different way in that his solution is partially dynamic: He proposes to use a new tag in the Warren Abstract Machine ([12]) to keep information about the context in which a variable is used; this enables him to optimize the WAM code, and also to avoid calls to the occur-check routine, but it is still dependent on the strategy, and there is a little overhead at run-time.

Another possible approach (see [5], [3]), is to determine classes of programs for which the occur-check is never needed, what [3] call NSTO (Not Subject To Occur-check) programs. This approach is based on the study of the relations between logic programs and attribute grammars, and one of its main advantages is its independence with regard to the resolution scheme.

Nevertheless, the places where the occur-check has to be carried out depend on the resolution scheme. Consider for instance the following program:

```
?- test(L,L)
test(L1,L2) :- empty(L1,[a,b,c|L2]).
empty(T,T).
```

If a top-down scheme is used, empty(L1,[a,b,c|L2]) and empty(T,T) should be unified with occur-check, but if a bottom-up scheme is used, the occur-check is only necessary when unifying test(L,L) and test(L1,L2).

In this paper, we extend the framework of [3] to be able to take into account the resolution scheme. We aim at finding conditions to check statically that a given resolution scheme is *sound*. For example, it is well known that, given a top-down strategy, the occur-check may be omitted when the head of clause to unify is linear (i.e. with no repeated variables): Such a resolution scheme is sound.

In Section 3, we focus on systems of term equations. We give conditions to guarantee that a given unification algorithm is *sound*, namely it performs the occur-check each time it is necessary.

The idea on which our analysis relies is quite simple. Let E be a system of equations and S the subsystem of E containing the equations solved by the algorithm without occur-check. We assume that S is fixed at compile time. [3] prove that any resolution of so-called *safe* systems of equations doesn't necessitate occur-checks. As all the equations of S are solved without occur-check, imposing the "safety" of S seems to be a reasonable condition.

Obviously, this is not sufficient. Consider the following example:

$$E : \{X = t(U); g(X) = U\} \text{ and } S : \{X = t(U)\}$$

It is very easy to prove that S is safe, but if $g(X) = U$ is solved first, S loses this property. To check the soundness of the algorithm, we have to prove that S will remain safe even if equations not belonging to S are solved. To do that, we introduce a dependency relation between equations which has the following property:

S will remain safe if, each time an equation e_u not belonging to S is solved, all the equations of S on which e_u depends have already been solved.

Therefore, to guarantee the soundness of an algorithm, we just have to check that the equations are solved in a correct order.

In Section 4, we extend our result to logic programs and resolution schemes. A logic program and a resolution scheme specify a family of systems of equations to be solved, and algorithms to solve them. If all the specified algorithms are sound, then the resolution scheme itself is sound. Like [3], we use attribute grammars to formalize this extension, using attribute dependencies to model equation dependencies. Before that, we present our notations and some previous results.

2   Theoretical background

In all this paper, P is a program, namely a set of Horn clauses. We first define skeletons (introduced in [6]), which can be seen as derivation trees where no unification has been performed.

Definition 2.1 Skeletons
A skeleton Σ is either:

- *a one-node tree $\bot$ or c, where c is a fact of P;*

- *or a tree $c(\Sigma_1, \ldots, \Sigma_m)$ where:*

  - *c is a clause of the form $h :\text{-} b_1 \ldots b_m$;[1]*

  - *$\Sigma_1, \ldots, \Sigma_m$ are skeletons;*

  - *for all i, if $\Sigma_i \neq \bot$, the predicate symbol in b_i is the same as in the head (denoted h_i) of the clause which labels the root of Σ_i.*

All clauses labelling nodes in Σ are renamed apart, i.e. if c and c' label two nodes of Σ, $Var(c) \cap Var(c') = \emptyset$.
With the notations above, we define the associated system of equations $\mathcal{E}(\Sigma)$ of Σ recursively by:

- *$\mathcal{E}(\Sigma) = \emptyset$ if Σ is a one node tree;*

- *$\mathcal{E}(\Sigma) = \bigcup_{i \in I} \{h_i = b_i\} \cup \mathcal{E}(\Sigma_i)$ otherwise, where I is the set of i such that $\Sigma_i \neq \bot$.*

Example 2.1 *Consider the following program:*
c_1 : ?- foo([X|L],L), bar(L,[]).
c_2 : foo([a|L1],L2) :- fuz(L1,L2).
c_3 : fuz([b|T],T).
c_4 : bar(M,M).
$c_1(c_2(c_3), c_4)$ *is a skeleton, and may be represented this way:*

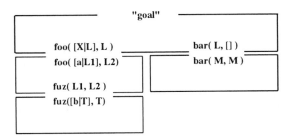

Figure 1

The system of equations associated with this skeleton is:

```
foo([X|L],L)=foo([a|L1],L2)
fuz(L1,L2)=fuz([b|T],T)
bar(L,[])=bar(M,M)
```

---

[1]If c is a goal clause, we assume that h is some special symbol "goal"

During the execution of a program, skeletons are built, and their associated systems of equations are solved. An *equation solving step* is one of the steps of the following unification algorithm (adapted from [9]):

Unification algorithm:
Given a system S of equations, perform any of the following steps; if no step applies, stop with success.

1. *EQUATION INVERSION:*
   Select any equation of the form $t = X$, where X is a variable and t is not a variable, and replace it by $X = t$;

2. *EQUATION ELIMINATION:*
   Select any equation of the form $X = X$, X being a variable, and erase it;

3. *EQUATION SPLITTING:*
   Select any equation of the form $f(\ldots, t_i, \ldots) = f(\ldots, t'_i, \ldots)$, and replace it by the system of equations $\{t_i = t'_i\}$; if f is a constant, simply erase the equation;

4. *FAILURE by DISEQUATION:*
   Select any equation of the form $f(\ldots)=g(\ldots)$ where f and g are distinct functors (a "disequation"), and stop with failure;

5. *PARTIAL EVALUATION:*
   Select any equation of the form $X = t$, where X is a variable which appears at least twice in the system, and $t \neq X$;
   if *X occurs in t*
   then *Stop with Failure (POSITIVE OCCUR CHECK)*
   else *apply the substitution $\{X \leftarrow t\}$ to all the other equations of the system;*

Definition 2.2 Transformed systems
Let E be a system of equations; Let S be a subsystem of E (or E itself); S^n denotes the system obtained from S after n steps of unification have been performed on E. S^n can be defined inductively by:

- *$S^0 = S$;*

- *Let us suppose that a unification step is applied to an equation e of E^p:*

  - *If $e \in S^p$, S^{p+1} is the system obtained after application of the unification step to S^p;*

  - *If $e \equiv (X = t) \notin S^p$, and the unification step is a step 5, S^{p+1} is the system obtained after application of the substitution $\{X \leftarrow t\}$ to S^p;*

  - *otherwise, $S^{p+1} = S^p$.*

If for some p, e is an equation of a subsystem S^p, we'll say that e is stemming from S.

[3] define two NSTO notions, one for the systems of equations, the other for the programs:

Definition 2.3 NSTO property for a system of equations
A system of equations is said to be Not Subject To Occur-check (NSTO) iff the test of step 5 is always negative regardless of the order in which the steps are applied.

Definition 2.4 NSTO property for a program
A program P is said to be NSTO iff the associated system of equation $\mathcal{E}(S)$ of any skeleton S built with clauses of P is NSTO.

[6] prove that the NSTO property is undecidable. Therefore the only solution is to give sufficient conditions. The condition they give is based on a dependency relation between equations.

It is well known that the occur-check is not necessary to solve an equation $t = t'$ where t is a linear term which doesn't share a variable with t', i.e. when all the variables of t occur only once in the equation. Hence, to prove that a system is NSTO, we can try to guarantee that *one* of the members of each equation satisfies this condition, in every step of the solving.

To model this asymmetry, we choose an orientation of the equations and decide that in each equation, the *left-hand side* should satisfy the condition. Hence, an equation e_1 "depends on" an equation e_2 if the left-hand side *lhs* of e_1 may be modified when e_2 is solved, namely if a variable of *lhs* also occurs in e_2.

This way, an equation depends on itself if a variable of its left-hand side occurs twice in the equation: There is a risk of a positive occur-check. More generally, there is a risk of a positive occur-check if the $\xrightarrow{+}$ relation (the transitive closure of $\rightarrow$) is cyclic, for any orientation of the equations (see Proposition 2.1).

Definition 2.5 $\rightarrow$: Dependency relation on equations
Let E be a system of equations. Let e_1 and e_2 be two equations such that e_1 is oriented.
$e_1 \rightarrow e_2$ iff a variable of the left-hand side of e_1 has another occurrence in e_2.

Example 2.2 *Let E be the following system, where all the equations are oriented from left to right.*

e_1: $X = f(U)$
e_2: $t(f(V)) = t(X)$
e_3: $g(Z) = V$
e_4: $r(U, U) = a$

We obtain the following relations:
$e_1 \rightarrow e_2$ *and* $e_2 \rightarrow e_3$;
$e_4 \rightarrow e_4$.

The *sufficiently refined* equations of a system are the equations which can be solved (or proved unsolvable) by the above unification algorithm, without any partial evaluation step.

Definition 2.6 Sufficiently refined equations
Let e be an equation of a system E. e is sufficiently refined *if all the equations obtained from e after having applied as many steps of equation splitting, equation inversion, or equation elimination as possible, are "disequations" or equations of the form $X = t$, where X appears only once in E.*

Those equations may be for instance equations of the form $t = t$ (where t may be any term). They cannot lead to a positive occur-check, nor can equations with a ground member. Therefore, our conditions will only take into account the other equations, called *candidate equations*[2] ("candidate to an occur-check").

---

[2] This terminology is used in [3], but our notion of candidate equation is slightly more refined than that of [3]

Definition 2.7 System of candidate equations
Let E be a system of equations. The system of candidate equations of E is the system obtained from E by removing all the sufficiently refined equations and the equations having a ground member.

The two following definitions allow to express in a simple way the NSTO sufficient condition proposed by [3].

Definition 2.8 Well-oriented system of equations
Let S be an oriented system of equations, and S_c the system of its candidate equations.
S is well-oriented *if the restriction of $\xrightarrow{+}$ to S_c contains no cycle.*

Definition 2.9 Safe system of equations
A system of equations is safe *if there exists an orientation that makes it well-oriented (it is "well-orientable").*

We obtain now (cf. [8]):

Proposition 2.1 NSTO sufficient condition for a system of equations
If a system of equations is safe, then it is NSTO.

Example 2.3 *Consider the system E of the previous example. The system of candidate equations is $\{e_1, e_2, e_3\}$, and the relation $\xrightarrow{+}$ contains no cycle with the given orientation: E is well-oriented, hence safe, hence NSTO.*

This result on the systems of equations may be applied to the logic programs. [3] propose a sufficient and decidable condition to check that the associated system of *any* skeleton is safe, and this is sufficient to show that the program itself is NSTO.

3 Partially NSTO systems of equations

3.1 Intuition and notations

We will use this example throughout this section:

Example 3.1 *Consider the following system:*

e_1: $X = t(Y)$
e_2: $Y = t(Z)$
e_3: $f(Z) = f(X)$

Let us assume that the unification algorithm:
1. unifies e_1 and e_2 without occur-check;
2. then unifies e_3 with occur-check.

The unification algorithm used to solve a system of equations can be seen as the "resolution scheme" of the system. We are interested in unification algorithms which do not carry out the occur-check every time an equation $Var = term$ is solved, and we suppose that the family $\mathcal{F}$ of equations which are unified without occur-check is known at compile time. In the above example, $\mathcal{F}$ is the set of all equations of the form $Var = term$ stemming from e_3. Such an algorithm may be described in the same way as above, except the step 5:

5. PARTIAL EVALUATION:
> *Select any equation e of the form $X = t$, where X is a variable which appears*
> *somewhere else in the system, and $t \neq X$;*
> **if** $e \notin \mathcal{F}$ **then**
>   **if** X *occurs in* t **then**
>   *Stop with Failure (POSITIVE OCCUR CHECK)*
>   **end-if**
> **end-if**
> *Apply the substitution $\{X \leftarrow t\}$ to all the other equations of the system.*

In the following, we always assume the selection rule is fixed. The soundness of such an algorithm may be defined this way:

Definition 3.1 Soundness of the unification algorithm of a system of equations
Let E be a system of equations, and A the unification algorithm used to solve E. We consider now another algorithm A', which is identical to A, except that the family $\mathcal{F}$ it uses is empty. A is sound iff every positive occur-check detected by A' is also detected by A.

How can we prove that a given algorithm A is sound? In a first step, we consider a system E, and a subsystem S of E such that all the equations of $\mathcal{F}$ stem from equations of S, and we try to find sufficient conditions on S to make sure the algorithm is sound.

This is guaranteed if all the equations $X = t$ stemming from S are NSTO: Hence, it is natural to check that S is safe.

Condition 1 *S is safe.*

Example 3.1 (continued) *We have to show that $\{e_1, e_2\}$ is a safe system of equations. If we consider X and Y as the respective left-hand sides of e_1 and e_2, we obtain the following dependencies:*
> $e_2 \rightarrow e_1$ *and* $e_1 \rightarrow e_3$.
> *We see that there is no cycle, hence $\{e_1, e_2\}$ is safe. Note that there is no need to give an orientation to e_3.*

In the following, we assume that this condition is satisfied, and that S is well-oriented. Let $U = E - S$. As in the Introduction, we want to make sure that S will not lose its safety during execution. Let us suppose that p steps of unification have been performed, and that S^p is safe. If the next unification step makes S^{p+1} unsafe, a variable occurring in the left-hand side of an equation e_s^p of S^p must have been substituted, producing a cycle. Thus, the unification step is necessarily the partial evaluation of an equation e_u^p of $U^p{}^3$, and $e_s^p \rightarrow e_u^p$. To preclude this situation, we could impose a condition like the following one:.

> For all $e_s^p \in S^p$, $e_u^p \in U^p$, if $e_s^p \rightarrow e_u^p$, then e_s^p is solved before e_u^p

In fact, we need not impose this condition on S^p, but only on the system of its candidate equations, as the non-candidates have no influence on the safety of S^p. Moreover, to obtain a static test, we need to find conditions independent from p. It is possible, since no new dependency is created during the execution ([8]), namely: If e_s and e_u are respectively equations of S and U, e_s^p and e_u^p equations stemming from e_s and e_u, and if $e_s^p \rightarrow e_u^p$, then $e_s \xrightarrow{+} e_u$. Hence, our condition becomes:

---

[3] and not of S^p, otherwise being safe would not be a sufficient condition for being NSTO.

For all $e_s \in S$, $e_u \in U$, if e_s is candidate, and if $e_s \xrightarrow{+} e_u$, then e_s is solved before e_u.

We have to define more precisely what "e_s *is solved before* e_u" really means. Actually, we just have to give a condition on the order in which the partial evaluation steps are applied on equations stemming from e_s and e_u, as we have seen that the other steps don't matter.

Definition 3.2 $\prec_e$: (partial) order of evaluation
Let E be a system of equations, and e_1 and e_2 two equations of E.
$e_1 \prec_e e_2$ iff a partial evaluation step on an equation stemming from e_2 will only be performed when no equation stemming from e_1 is candidate.

It is important to notice that the $\prec_e$ order depends only on the selection rule used by the unification algorithm. If nothing is known about this selection rule, then $\prec_e$ is empty. The condition above can be seen as a compatiblity condition of $\rightarrow$ with $\prec_e$.

Definition 3.3 Compatibility of $\rightarrow$ with $\prec_e$
$\rightarrow$ is compatible with $\prec_e$ if the following condition is satisfied:
For all the candidate equations e_s of S and all the equations e_u of U, if $e_s \xrightarrow{+} e_u$, then $e_s \prec_e e_u$.

Our second condition can now be expressed:

Condition 2 $\rightarrow$ *is compatible with $\prec_e$.*

Example 3.1 (continued) *With our hypotheses, we have $e_1 \prec_e e_3$ and $e_2 \prec_e e_3$: This second condition is satisfied.*

Actually, as we don't take into account the order in which all the unification steps are applied, but only the order of evaluation, our conditions are sufficient to prove that a system may be soundly solved by a *family* of algorithms, and not only one.

Definition 3.4 Partially NSTO system of equations
Let E be a system of equations; Let $\prec_e$ be a partial order on E, and S a subsystem of E.
E is partially NSTO w.r.t. S and $\prec_e$ iff any unification algorithm respecting $\prec_e$ and not performing the occur-check on equations $X = t$ stemming from S, is sound.

3.2 Results

The proofs of the following results may be found in [8].

Theorem 1 *Let E be a system of equations. Let S be a subsystem of E. If there exists an orientation of S such that:*

- *S is well-oriented;*

- *$\rightarrow$ is compatible with $\prec_e$;*

then E is partially NSTO w.r.t. S and $\prec_e$.

Intuitively, "S is well oriented" means that S can be solved without occur-check, if it is taken independently from its context; the second condition guarantees that the context has no influence on the properties of S. If both conditions are satisfied, the equations stemming from S may be unified without occur-check.

Example 3.1 (continued) *The system is p-NSTO w.r.t. $\{e_1, e_2\}$ and $\prec_e$: The algorithm used to solve it is sound*

This theorem can be refined thanks to the following result:

Proposition 3.1 *Let E be a system of equations. Let E' be the system obtained from E after having performed an arbitrary number of equation elimination, inversion, or splitting steps. Let S' be a subsystem of E'.*

Let A be the unification algorithm, and $\prec_e$ an order on equations of E' compatible with A ; we assume that A does not perform the occur-check on equations $X = t$ stemming from S'.

A is sound if E' is partially NSTO w.r.t. S' and $\prec_e$.

Example 3.2 *Consider the following system:*
$e_1 : X = t(Y)$
$e_2 : h(Y, f(Z)) = h(t(Z), f(X))$
Let us assume that the unification algorithm first solves e_1 without occur-check, then splits e_2, solves $Y = t(Z)$ without occur-check, and finally solves $f(Z) = f(t(t(Z)))$ with occur-check.

If we apply theorem 1, we cannot prove that the algorithm is sound since there is always a cycle $e_2 \rightarrow e_2$, whatever orientation is chosen for e_2.

But if we apply one step of equation splitting on e_2, we obtain exactly the system of example 3.1, and the $\prec_e$ order is unchanged: Hence, the algorithm is sound.

4 Soundness of a resolution scheme

We give in this section sufficient conditions to check the soundness of resolution schemes, using our result on systems of equations.

4.1 From equations to programs

A resolution scheme carries out two different tasks:

- It builds skeletons;

- It solves the equations associated with those skeletons, some of them with occur-check, the others without.

Given a resolution scheme and a skeleton Σ, it is possible to define a partial order of evaluation in the associated system of equations $\mathcal{E}(\Sigma)$.

Example 4.1 *Consider the following program (the same as in example 2.1):*

```
c₁ : ?- foo([X|L],L), bar(L,[]).
c₂ : foo([a|L1],L2) :- fuz(L1,L2).
c₃ : fuz([b|T],T).
c₄ : bar(M,M).
```

If we suppose that this program is solved with the standard Prolog strategy, then the skeleton of Figure 1 is built, and the equations are solved in the following order:

```
foo([X|L],L)=foo([a|L1],L2)
fuz(L1,L2)=fuz([b|T],T)
bar(L,[])=bar(M,M)
```

The resolution scheme specifies for each skeleton a unification algorithm to solve the system of its associated equations. In particular, we assume that the family $\mathcal{F}$ of equations that will be solved without occur-check is known. For instance, if the occur-check is only performed when the head of the clause to unify is not linear, the set $\mathcal{F}$ of equations corresponding to the skeleton of Figure 1 is the set of equations of the form $Var = term$ stemming from the first equation.

Thus, the formalism of the previous section lets us define the soundness of a resolution scheme precisely:

Definition 4.1 Soundness of a resolution scheme
Let P a program, and R the resolution scheme used to execute it. To every possible skeleton built by R, we can associate a system of equations, solved by an algorithm which is determined by R.
R is sound iff all the algorithms determined this way are sound.

4.2 From programs to attribute grammars

It is of course impossible to consider all the skeletons and try to check that each corresponding algorithm is sound. Actually, this problem is very close to problems encountered in the field of attribute grammars, where properties of dependency relations have to be satisfied in *any* derivation tree. We use those similarities to obtain sufficient conditions to guarantee the soundness of a resolution scheme.

The results we obtain are based on a close correspondence between the possible skeletons built during the execution of the program and derivation trees of a given grammar[4].

The non-terminals of the grammar are 3-tuples $< c, i, c' >$ where c and c' are clauses and the ith literal in the body of c has the same predicate as the head of c'. There is also a special non-terminal: $< goal >$.

Example 4.2 *The non-terminals associated with the program of Example 2.1 are:*
$< goal >$, $< c_1, 1, c_2 >$, $< c_1, 2, c_4 >$ *and* $< c_2, 1, c_3 >$

Let c be a clause with n literals in the body ($n \geq 0$). A rule *generated* by c has the form:

$$N_0 \rightarrow N_1, \ldots, N_n.$$

where N_0 is some $< c_0, i, c >$ if such a non-terminal exists, and $< goal >$ otherwise, and N_i ($1 \leq i \leq n$) is some $< c, i, c_i >$. If for some j, the predicate of the jth literal in the body of c has no definition (hence there is no $< c, j, c_j >$), there is no N_j in the rule.

Example 4.3 *With the previous program, we obtain the following rules:*

---

[4]The formal construction of the grammar will not be given here; the reader is referred to [3] for more details. Except the definition of the grammar, the formalism we use here is not strictly identical to that of [3].

$< goal > \rightarrow < c_1, 1, c_2 >, < c_1, 2, c_4 >$.
$< c_1, 1, c_2 > \rightarrow < c_2, 1, c_3 >$.
$< c_2, 1, c_3 > \rightarrow$.
$< c_1, 2, c_4 > \rightarrow$.

We assume now that the resolution scheme is fixed. Let us consider a skeleton Σ, and its associated system of equations $\mathcal{E}(\Sigma)$. To show that the algorithm used to solve $\mathcal{E}(\Sigma)$ is sound, we can use Proposition 3.1, but then we have to refine the equations of $\mathcal{E}(\Sigma)$ and orient some of them. As we cannot do this for *every* skeleton, we fix the way it is done, using the non-terminals.

Let $< c, i, c' >$ be a non-terminal, b_i the ith literal in the body of c, and h_i the head of c'. It is possible to associate the equation $b_i = h_i$ with $< c, i, c' >$, and any equation of the associated system of a given skeleton is an instance of such an equation. This equation may be partially solved, yielding a *system of "subequations"*.

Definition 4.2 System of subequations of a non-terminal
We associate with each non-terminal N a system of subequations $Sub(N)$:

- *$Sub(< goal >)$ is empty;*

- *If $N = < c, i, c' >$: Apply to $b_i = h_i$ the following steps a number of times:*
    - *equation splitting;*
    - *remove an equation with a ground member;*
    - *remove a sufficiently refined equation.*

  $Sub(< c, i, c' >)$ is the obtained system of equations.

Example 4.4 *Let us consider $< c_1, 1, c_2 >$. If we apply no step, we obtain a first system of subequations which has only one element:*
`foo([X|L],L)= foo([a|L1],L2)`
If we apply one step (a splitting), we obtain the following system:
`[X|L]=[a|L1]`
`L=L2`
If the steps are applied as many times as possible, we obtain another system:
`L=L1`
`L=L2`
All these systems are possible choices for $Sub(< c_1, 1, c_2 >)$.

The *attributes* of a non-terminal are the equations which may be unified without occur-check.

Definition 4.3 Attributes of a non-terminal
We associate with each non-terminal N a system $Attr(N)$:

- *$Attr(< goal >)$ is empty;*

- *$Attr(< c, i, c' >)$ is the subsystem of $Sub(< c, i, c' >)$ such that every equation stemming from $Sub(< c, i, c' >)$ and solved without occur-check, stems from an equation of $Attr(< c, i, c' >)$.*

To give an orientation to the equations which are instances of attributes, we use a *d-assignment*.

Definition 4.4 d-assignment
Let Attr the set of all the attributes. A direction assignment (d-assignment) is a mapping from Attr into $\{\downarrow, \uparrow\}$. If an attribute is assigned $\downarrow$, we will say it is inherited, *otherwise we will say it is* synthesized.

Definition 4.5 Orientation
Let $< c, i, c' >$ be a non-terminal, and a: $t_c = t_{c'}$ an attribute of $< c, i, c' >$, where t_c is a subterm of the ith atom in the body of c, and $t_{c'}$ the corresponding subterm of the head of c'.

- *If a is synthesized, we choose t_c as the left-hand side of the equation;*

- *If a is inherited, we choose $t_{c'}$ as the left-hand side of the equation.*

We still need to model the dependencies between subequations:

Definition 4.6 Positions in a rule
A position in a rule $N_0 \rightarrow N_1, \ldots, N_n$ is a pair (j,s) where $0 \leq j \leq n$ and $s \in Sub(N_j)$.
A position (j,s) is input *iff s is an attribute, and:*
 – either j=0 and s is inherited;
 – or $j \geq 1$ and s is synthesized.
It is output *if s is an attribute, and (j,s) is not input.*

The local dependency relation in a rule is a restriction of the $\rightarrow$ relation to the equations associated with the positions of the rule:

Definition 4.7 Local dependencies
Let r be a rule. The local dependency relation d_r is defined on the positions of r as follows: If p_1 and p_2 are two positions of r, e_1 and e_2 are the equations associated to p_1 and p_2, then, p_1 d_r p_2 iff p_1 is input and $e_1 \rightarrow e_2$.

Example 4.5 *We still consider the same program, and we assume that the second argument of* fuz *is unified with* occur-check, *and not the others. We choose the following subequations and d-assignment:*

non-terminals	subequations and d-assignment	
$< c_1, 1, c_2 >$	[X|L]=[a|L1] ($\uparrow$)	L2=L ($\downarrow$)
$< c_1, 2, c_4 >$	M=L ($\downarrow$)	
$< c_2, 1, c_3 >$	L1=[b|T] ($\uparrow$)	L2=T (non oriented)

The second subequation of $< c_2, 1, c_3 >$ is not an attribute.
 Figure 2 shows the local dependencies within the rule: $< c_1, 1, c_2 > \rightarrow < c_2, 1, c_3 >$. Input positions have their direction pointing to the "inside" of the rule, and vice versa for output positions.

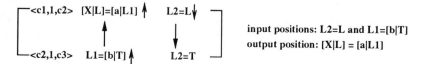

input positions: L2=L and L1=[b\|T]
output position: [X\|L] = [a\|L1]

Figure 2

Definition 4.8 Global dependencies
A position in a derivation tree of the grammar is a pair (n,s), where n is a node of the derivation tree whose label is a non-terminal N, and s ∈ Sub(N).

A derivation tree can be seen as a collection of rules which are pasted together, and the positions in the tree are instances of positions of the rules. The global dependency relation is the relation on the positions in the tree defined by pasting together all the local dependency relations in the rules. This relation is denoted $\mathcal{D}$.

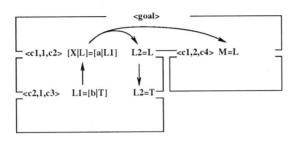

Figure 3

Example 4.6 *Figure 3 shows the global dependencies within the derivation tree corresponding to the skeleton of Figure 1.*

4.3 Results

Our result is based on the correspondence between the derivation trees of the grammar and the skeletons built by the resolution scheme. Figure 1 and 2 give the intuition of this correspondence. In this example, we see that the set of all the subequations corresponds to the associated system of equations of the skeleton, after some steps of equation splitting have been applied, and some non-candidate equations removed. The d-assignment gives an orientation to the equations which may be unified without occur-check, and the global dependency relation corresponds to the dependency relation on the equations of the associated system. Lastly, the resolution scheme defines an evaluation order on the positions.

Thanks to those correspondences, we can give sufficient conditions to check the soundness of a resolution scheme.

Theorem 2 Sufficient conditions for the soundness of a resolution scheme
Let P be a program and R the resolution scheme used to execute P. Let G be the grammar built from P using the construction described above. If there is a d-assignment such that, in any derivation tree:

- *the global dependency relation is non circular;*

- *the global dependency relation is compatible with the order of evaluation of the positions;*

then R is sound.

A formal proof of this theorem is given in [8], and is mainly based on the correspondence between skeletons and syntax trees in the grammar, established by [6].

Example 4.7 *Look at Figure 3, and assume that we only know that the program is solved with the standard Prolog strategy. The conditions of Theorem 2 are not satisfied since:*

$$\text{L1=[b|T]} \xrightarrow{+} \text{L2=T}$$

and we don't know which equation is solved first: We can prove that the scheme is sound if L1=[b|T] *is solved before* L2=T.

4.4 Applications

This framework is more general than that described in [3]. A program is NSTO if any scheme never performing the occur-check is sound. To prove this with Theorem 2, we just have to find for each non-terminal in the grammar, a system of subequations such that the global dependency relation is non-circular. The second condition of the theorem is automatically satisfied since all subequations are attributes. We can prove easily that the condition we obtain is equivalent to the condition proposed by [3].

But our framework can also be useful if the program is not NSTO. We can use it to build algorithms to find where an occur-check should be performed and where it can be avoided.

A compiler based for instance on the Warren Abstract Machine gives useful information about the order of evaluation by distinguishing between the first occurrence of a variable in a clause and the following ones. It also detects constant terms. It is natural not to perform the occur-check when unifying constants, or the variables occurring for the first time in the heads of clauses (i.e. when performing any instruction which is not a *_value one). This (very simple) method already gives interesting results ([7]) but we can still improve it. Being practical imposes some restrictions on the possible choices of subequations and d-assignments.

What is interesting is to tell which unification instructions should be performed with occur-check. Unification is controlled by the compiling instructions of the heads of clauses: Therefore, for every non-terminal $< c, i, c' >$, we have to find a system of subequations which is independent from c; the direction of each attribute should also be independent from c. The number of relevant non-terminals is limited by the indexing of the clauses in the compiler.

A priori, the best possible subequations correspond to the equations between the arguments of the predicates. Finding a non-trivial system of attributes, and the corresponding d-assignment is still not easy in the general case. To achieve this, we can use the existing classification of the attribute grammars ([4]): The conditions of Theorem 2 are much easier to check if the grammar we buid is "one-sweep" for instance. We know in some cases how to generate d-assignments such that the obtained attribute grammar belongs to a proper class.

5 Conclusion

In this paper, we have presented a theoretical framework to check statically the soundness of resolution schemes with respect to occur-check. We first consider the set S of all the unifications carried out without occur-check, and check that they actually don't need it: This is the "safety" condition. Then, we check that the order of unification is such that the safety of S will be preserved during the execution of the program.

The most general conditions we give would lead us to build unrealistic tests[5]. But it is possible to restrict some conditions in order to build algorithms of reasonable complexity, able to find in logic programs where the occur-check has to be carried out in order to ensure the soundness of the execution.

6   Acknowledgements

I thank Pierre Deransart for his help and his comments troughout this work, started under his supervision at INRIA, and Peter Van Roy and Andreas Podelski for their careful reviewing of this paper.

References

[1] Joachim Beer. The Occur-Check Problem Revisited. *Journal of Logic Programming*, 5:243–261, 1988.

[2] Marc Michel Corsini. *Interprétation abstraite en programmation logique, théorie et applications.* PhD thesis, Université de Bordeaux I, 1989.

[3] Pierre Deransart, Gérard Ferrand, and Michel Téguia. NSTO Programs. In *ILPS'91*, pages 533–547, October 1991.

[4] Pierre Deransart, Martin Jourdan, and Bernard Lorho. *Attribute Grammars: Main Results, Existing Systems and Bibliography.* LNCS 323. Springer Verlag, 1988.

[5] Pierre Deransart and Jan Maluszynski. Relating logic programs and attribute grammars. *Journal of Logic Programming*, 2:119–155, 1985.

[6] Pierre Deransart and Jan Maluszynski. *A Grammatical View of Logic Programming.* MIT Press, 1992. *To appear.*

[7] Peter Dreussen, Wolfgang Rosentiel, Klaus Erik Schauser, and Jörg Wedeck. Architecture Design of a RISC Processor for Prolog. In *Euromicro 89*, 1989.

[8] Bruno Dumant. Sound Resolution Schemes. Research report, Digital PRL and INRIA, 1992. *To appear.*

[9] A. Martelli and Ugo Montanari. An efficient unification algorithm. *ACM Trans. on Prog. Lang.*, 4(2):399–425, April 1982.

[10] David Plaisted. The Occur Check Problem in Prolog. *Journal of Logic Programming*, 2:309–322, 1984.

[11] Harald Sondergaard. An Application of Abstract Principles of Logic Programs: Occur-Check Reduction. In *European Symposium on Programming*, pages 327–338, 1986.

[12] David H.D. Warren. An Abstract Prolog Instruction Set. Technical note 309, SRI International, October 1983.

---

[5]It is more complex to check our conditions than the NSTO sufficient conditions given by [3], which are decidable, but several times exponential.

Higher-Order E-Unification for Arbitrary Theories

Zhenyu Qian
Kang Wang
FB Mathematik/Informatik
Universität Bremen
2800 Bremen 33, Germany
qian@informatik.uni-bremen.de/wang@pc-labor.uni-bremen.de

Abstract

We present an algorithm consisting of three transformation rules for pre-unification of simply typed λ-terms w.r.t. α, β and η conversions and an arbitrary first-order equational theory E. The algorithm is parameterized by E-unification algorithms that admit free function symbols. It is proved that the algorithm is complete if the given E-unification algorithm is complete. The result is relevant to implementations of higher-order logic programming languages and higher-order proof systems.

1 Introduction

Typed λ-calculi are suitable frameworks for succinctly representing logical languages with bound variables. This is not only because they can be directly and intuitively used in encoding logical terms and formulae, but also because some of them have been turned into computational realities, e.g. in the logic programming languages λProlog [15] and Elf [20], and in the generic theorem prover Isabelle [19], due to the pioneer work on unification in the simply typed λ-calculus by Huet [10].

In order to enhance the expressiveness, first-order equational theories have been integrated into typed λ-calculi [3, 4]. Snyder was the first to study the unification problem for simply typed λ-terms w.r.t. α, β and η conversions and a first-order equational theory E [22], which is called *higher-order E-unification*. In the spirit of "universal unification" [7], he presented a set of transformation rules that yield an algorithm enumerating a complete set of unifiers, where the presentation of E itself is used in the unification process. The problem with this general algorithm is its nontermination and high nondeterminism. Recently, Dougherty and Johann [6] solved higher-order E-unification problems for the restricted case of convergent E by translating the unification problems into a combinatory logic framework. Although the approach provides a uniform setting for treating higher- and first-order E-unification, the intuitive clarity of λ-notation was lost.

Following the idea of combining unification and matching algorithms for disjoint equational theories [24, 13, 9, 21, 16, 2, 1], Nipkow and Qian [18, 17] adopted a modular approach. Their algorithms are extensions of those by

Snyder and Gallier [23] and parameterized by complete E-unification algorithms. The pre-unification algorithm was proved to be complete for collapse-free regular theories E, and the full unification algorithm for regular theories E and for E-unification algorithms admitting arbitrary free constants.

This paper presents three transformation rules for higher-order equational pre-unification with arbitrary equational theories in the modular approach (Section 3). The idea is to push as much of the unification task as possible into given E-unification algorithms. The price is to require that the given E-unification algorithms admit not only free constants but also arbitrary free function symbols. This is not a strong restriction because the problem of extending arbitrary E-unfications with arbitrary free function symbols has been solved elsewhere [21, 2, 1].

We prove (in Section 4) that under some special control strategies the transformation rules yield complete algorithms of higher-order equational pre-unification.

The new algorithm is not only theoretically significant, but more importantly, of great practical value, since pushing as much as possible into the first-order E-unification algorithm increases the efficiency tremendously: Firstly, we may make use of efficient E-unification algorithms resulting from the intensive research in the recent years (cf. e.g. [11]); Secondly, the number of switches between the pure higher-order and equational unification processes are minimized. Although higher-order unification is in general undecidable, our pre-unification algorithm is terminating enough for practical applications like theorem proving [19] and higher-order logic programming [15, 20]. The idea of pre-unification goes back to Huet [10] and is crucial in making any kind of higher-order unification practical.

To give a rough impression about how a given E-unification algorithm is used in our algorithm, let us consider the simple unification problem

$$\lambda x.F(x) \stackrel{?}{=} \lambda x.F(x) * G(x) * x$$

w.r.t. the equations of Boolean ring with constants $0, 1, +$ and $*$, where F, G are free variables. Our algorithm solves the unification problem by performing the following steps:

1. Construct a underlying E-unification problem by replacing the subterm $F(x)$ by a new variable X and the subterm $G(x)$ by a new variable Y. The result is $\lambda x.X =^? \lambda x.X * Y * x$.

2. Use the given E-unification algorithm to compute an E-unifier of the resulting underlying E-unification problem, where the λ-abstraction λx is regarded as a new unary function symbol and the other occurrence of x as a new constant. Obviously we may compute an E-unifier $\{X \mapsto Y * x * Z\}$ with Z being a new variable.

3. Replace back the newly introduced variable X by $F(x)$ and Y by $G(x)$ in the above E-unifier. Replace each variable newly introduced in the E-unification by a term $H(x)$ with H being a new variable. Finally put the λ-abstraction λx at the outermost place of each side of $\mapsto$. The resulting $\lambda x.F(x) \mapsto \lambda x.G(x) * x * H(x)$ is a higher-order E-unifier of the original problem.

2 Preliminaries

We use $\mathcal{T}_0$ to denote the set of *base types*, $\mathcal{T}$ the set of *types*, and write $\alpha_1 \rightarrow \cdots \rightarrow \alpha_n \rightarrow \beta$ and $\overline{\alpha_n} \rightarrow \beta$ for $(\alpha_1 \rightarrow \cdots (\alpha_n \rightarrow \beta))$. In $\overline{\alpha_n} \rightarrow \beta$, β is assumed in $\mathcal{T}_0$. For each $\alpha \in \mathcal{T}$, $\mathcal{C}_\alpha$ and $\mathcal{V}_\alpha$ denote pairwise disjoint denumerable sets of *function constants* and *variables*, resp. Let $\mathcal{C} = \bigcup_{\alpha \in \mathcal{T}} \mathcal{C}_\alpha$ and $\mathcal{V} = \bigcup_{\alpha \in \mathcal{T}} \mathcal{V}_\alpha$. The sets of *atoms* are $\mathcal{A} = \mathcal{C} \cup \mathcal{V}$ and $\mathcal{A}_\alpha = \mathcal{C}_\alpha \cup \mathcal{V}_\alpha$.

The set $\mathcal{L}_\alpha$ of *terms of type* $\alpha \in \mathcal{T}$ is defined by the usual construction of *application* and *abstraction*. Let $\mathcal{L} = \bigcup_{\alpha \in \mathcal{T}} \mathcal{L}_\alpha$. We also use $\tau(t)$ to denote α for $t \in \mathcal{L}_\alpha$. In an abstraction $\lambda x.t$ the term t is said to be *covered* by or *in the scope* of the λ-*abstraction* λx. The term $(\ldots(a\ t_1)\ldots t_n)$ may be written as $a(t_1, \ldots, t_n)$ or $a(\overline{t_n})$, and $\lambda x_1. \cdots. \lambda x_k.t$ as $\lambda \overline{x_k}.t$, where t is not an abstraction unless otherwise stated

In the higher-order setting, terms are only compared modulo α-conversion. Bound and free variables are defined as usual. For the time being, it is also assumed that in a term no variable is bound more than once and no variable occurs both bound and free. The set of all bound variables in a syntactic object O is denoted by $\mathcal{BV}(O)$ and that of all free variables by $\mathcal{FV}(O)$. We also use $\mathcal{C}(O)$ and $\mathcal{A}(O)$ to denote the sets of all function constants and of all atoms in O.

For $\mathcal{X} \in \{\beta, \eta, \beta\eta\}$, we use $\longrightarrow_{\mathcal{X}}$ to denote one step $\mathcal{X}$-reduction and $=_{\mathcal{X}}$ the equivalence relation induced by $\longrightarrow_{\mathcal{X}}$. Let s be a term. Then $s\!\downarrow_{\mathcal{X}}$ denotes the $\mathcal{X}$-normal form such that $s \longrightarrow^*_{\mathcal{X}} s\!\downarrow_{\mathcal{X}}$. If t is a β-normal form, then t must be of the form $\lambda \overline{x_k}.a(\overline{t_n})$ with $a \in \mathcal{A}$ and each t_i a β-normal form. The atom a is called the *head* and denoted by $\mathcal{H}ead(t)$. The β-normal form t is called *flexible* if $a \in \mathcal{FV}(t)$, *rigid* if not. A β-normal form $\lambda \overline{x_k}.a(\overline{t_n})$ may also be called an η-*long form* if $a(\overline{t_n})$ is of a base type and each t_i is a η-long form. Let $s\!\downarrow_{l\eta}$ denote the η-long form (uniquely) obtained by η-expanding $s\!\downarrow_\beta$. For single variable F, $F\!\downarrow_{l\eta}$ may still be written as F.

A *substitution* σ is a function $\{x_1 \mapsto t_1, \cdots, x_n \mapsto t_n\}$ or $\{\overline{x_n \mapsto t_n}\}$ with $x_i \in \mathcal{V}$, $t_i \in \mathcal{L}$, $\tau(x_i) = \tau(t_i)$, $i = 1, \ldots, n$, the *domain* $\mathcal{D}om(\sigma) = \{x_1, \cdots, x_n\}$, and the *range* $\mathcal{R}an(\sigma) = \bigcup_{i=1,\cdots,n} \mathcal{FV}(t_i)$. Let s be a term. To avoid capture of free variables of $\mathcal{R}an(\sigma)$ in $\sigma(s)$ it is assumed that all bound variables in s have been α-converted such that $\mathcal{BV}(s) \cap \mathcal{R}an(\sigma) = \emptyset$. It is also assumed that $\mathcal{BV}(s) \cap \mathcal{D}om(\sigma) = \emptyset$. Hence, $\sigma(\lambda x.t) = \lambda x.\sigma(t)$ holds automatically for every term t. The *composition* of substitutions is defined by $(\sigma \circ \theta)(x) = \sigma(\theta(x))$ for every $x \in \mathcal{V}$. The *union* $\sigma \cup \theta$ are defined as usual, provided $\mathcal{D}om(\sigma) \cup \mathcal{D}om(\theta) = \emptyset$. Let $\mathcal{W} \subseteq \mathcal{V}$. The *restriction* $\sigma_{|\mathcal{W}}$ is a substitution defined by $\sigma_{|\mathcal{W}}(x) = \sigma(x)$ for $x \in \mathcal{W}$, $\sigma_{|\mathcal{W}}(x) = x$ otherwise.

A substitution σ is said to be *away from* $\mathcal{W}$ if $\mathcal{R}an(\sigma) \cap \mathcal{W} = \emptyset$. It is *normalized* if $\sigma(x)$ is η-long for each $x \in \mathcal{D}om(\sigma)$. Normalized σ satisfies $\sigma(t){\downarrow}_{l\eta} = \sigma(t){\downarrow}_\beta$ for any η-long form t. Only normalized substitutions are considered in this paper.

The set of *algebraic terms* $\alpha\mathcal{L}$ is the smallest set containing $\bigcup_{\beta \in \mathcal{T}_0} \mathcal{A}_\beta$ and satisfying that if $f \in \mathcal{C}_{\overline{\beta_n} \to \beta}$ with $\{\beta_1, \ldots, \beta_n, \beta\} \subseteq \mathcal{T}_0$, and $s_i \in \alpha\mathcal{L} \cap \mathcal{L}_{\beta_i}$ for $1 \leq i \leq n$, then $f(\overline{s_n}) \in \alpha\mathcal{L}$. The set $\bigcup_{\{\beta_1,\ldots,\beta_n,\beta\} \subseteq \mathcal{T}_0} \mathcal{C}_{\overline{\beta_n} \to \beta}$ is called the set of *algebraic function constants* and denoted by $\alpha\mathcal{C}$. *Algebraic atoms* are elements in $\alpha\mathcal{A} = \alpha\mathcal{C} \cup \bigcup_{\beta \in \mathcal{T}_0} \mathcal{V}_\beta$. An *algebraic theory* E is a set of unordered pairs $l \simeq r$ of terms in $\alpha\mathcal{L}$ with $\tau(l) = \tau(r)$, called *algebraic equations*. Function constants not occurring in E are also said to be *free* in E. We use $=_{\beta\eta E}$ to denote the equivalence relation induced by E-equivalence and $\beta\eta$-reduction. For any terms u and v, $u =_{\beta\eta E} v \Longleftrightarrow u{\downarrow}_{l\eta} =_E v{\downarrow}_{l\eta}([3])$.

Let $\mathcal{W} \subseteq \mathcal{V}$. For any substitutions σ and θ, $\sigma =_{\beta\eta E} \theta \ [\mathcal{W}]$ means $\sigma(x) =_{\beta\eta E} \theta(x)$ for each $x \in \mathcal{W}$. Furthermore, $\sigma \leq_{\beta\eta E} \theta \ [\mathcal{W}]$ means that there is a substitution ρ such that $\rho \circ \sigma =_{\beta\eta E} \theta \ [\mathcal{W}]$. $[\mathcal{W}]$ may be omitted if $\mathcal{W} = \mathcal{V}$. For any substitution σ and finite $\mathcal{W} \supseteq \mathcal{D}om(\sigma)$, there always exists a substitution σ' such that $\mathcal{D}om(\sigma') \cap \mathcal{R}an(\sigma') = \emptyset$, $\mathcal{D}om(\sigma) = \mathcal{D}om(\sigma')$ and $\sigma \leq_{\beta\eta E} \sigma' \ [\mathcal{W}]$ and $\sigma' \leq_{\beta\eta E} \sigma \ [\mathcal{W}]$. Since $\mathcal{W}$ is usually known in a context, we may restrict our attention only to the substitutions like σ' without loss of generality. Note that $\mathcal{D}om(\sigma') \cap \mathcal{R}an(\sigma') = \emptyset$ implies $\sigma' \circ \sigma' =_{\beta\eta E} \sigma'$.

In the rest of this paper, we use α, β and γ to denote types, s, t, u and v terms, f and g function constants, a and b atoms, x, y and z bound variables, X, Y, Z, F, G and H free variables, σ, θ and η substitutions.

3 Higher-order equational pre-unification via transformations

In this section a set $\mathcal{HEU}$ of transformation rules is presented for higher-order equational pre-unification. The rules assume a given E-unification algorithm that admits arbitrary free algebraic function constants. Following Huet [10], only *pre-unification* is considered where a solution is a substitution with a set of solvable constraints of flex-flex unification pairs.

A *unification pair* $u =^? v$ is an unordered pair of η-long terms with $\tau(u) = \tau(v)$. It is said to be *rigid-rigid* if both terms are rigid, *flex-rigid* if u is flexible and v rigid, *flex-flex* if both terms are flexible. A *unification problem* S is a finite multiset of unification pairs.

A unification pair $F =^? t \in S$ is said to be *solved in* S, and F is called a *solved variable in* S, if $F \notin \mathcal{FV}(t) \cup \mathcal{FV}(S - \{F =^? t\})$. A unification problem S is said to be *presolved* if every unification pair in S is either solved or flex-flex. For a presolved S, we denote $\sigma_S = \{F \mapsto t \mid F =^? t \text{ is solved in } S\}$.

We fix a unification problem S and an algebraic theory E from now on. A substitution θ is called a λE-*unifier of* S if $\theta(u) =_{\beta\eta E} \theta(v)$ for each $u =^? v \in S$. The set of all λE-unifiers of S is denoted by $\mathcal{U}_{\lambda E}(S)$. A *complete set of* λE-*unifiers of* S, denoted as $\mathcal{CSU}_{\lambda E}(S)$, is defined as usual. Without loss of generality it is assumed that

$$\forall \sigma \in \mathcal{CSU}_{\lambda E}(S).\mathcal{D}om(\sigma) \subseteq \mathcal{FV}(S), \mathcal{R}an(\sigma) \cap (\mathcal{D}om(\sigma) \cup \mathcal{W}) = \emptyset$$

where $\mathcal{W} \subseteq \mathcal{V}$ is a finite variable set containing all free variables used before. For a substitution $\theta = \{\overline{x_n \mapsto t_n}\}$, $[\theta]$ denotes $\{\overline{x_n =^? t_n}\}$.

Our transformation process includes the following steps:

(i) Construct underlying E-unification pairs of unification pairs by abstracting subterms not acceptable to the given E-unification algorithm into new variables;

(ii) Solve E-unification pairs by the given E-unification algorithm;

(iii) Bind free variables occurring as heads of unification pairs by *partial bindings* as in [23].

A λ-abstraction of the form λx or an atom not in $\mathcal{C}(E)$ may be given as an *alien symbol*. Intuitively, it is a symbol not acceptable to a given E-unification algorithm. In order to obtain the maximal top layer of a term acceptable to the given E-unification algorithm, maximal subterms that start with alien symbols, called *maximal alien subterms*, should be first identified. Sometimes, a maximal alien subterm may occur more than once in a term, and its occurrences covered by different λ-abstractions have to be distinguished. Let u be an η-long term. Use $\mathcal{PMAS}(u)$ to denote the set of all pairs of maximal alien subterms in u and the lists of their covering λ-abstractions in a top-down order. Formally, we may have $\mathcal{PMAS}(u) = PMAS(u, \langle \rangle)$ with $PMAS$ being a simple procedure defined as follows:

$$
\begin{aligned}
PMAS(\lambda y.s, \langle \overline{y_m} \rangle) &= PMAS(s, \langle \overline{y_m}, y \rangle) && \text{if } \lambda y \text{ is not alien} \\
PMAS(a(\overline{s_n}), \langle \overline{y_m} \rangle) &= \bigcup_{i=1,\cdots,n} PMAS(s_i, \langle \overline{y_m} \rangle) && \text{if } a \text{ is not alien} \\
PMAS(\lambda y.s, \langle \overline{y_m} \rangle) &= \{(\lambda y.s, \langle \overline{y_m} \rangle)\} && \text{if } \lambda y \text{ is alien} \\
PMAS(a(\overline{s_n}), \langle \overline{y_m} \rangle) &= \{(a(\overline{s_n}), \langle \overline{y_m} \rangle)\} && \text{if } a \text{ is alien}
\end{aligned}
$$

where $\lambda y.s, a(\overline{s_n})$ are η-long terms, $\overline{y_m}$ is a list $y_1, \cdots, y_m$ of bound variables. We use $\mathcal{MAS}(u) = \{s \mid (s, list) \in \mathcal{PMAS}(u)\}$ to denote the set of all maximal alien subterms in u. The above definition is generic, since different sets of alien symbols may lead to different sets of maximal alien subterms. For example, the maximal alien subterms in [3] may be obtained by the above definition with $\mathcal{A} - \alpha\mathcal{A}$ being the set of alien symbols.

Let u be an η-long term with $\mathcal{MAS}(u) = \{s_1, \ldots, s_n\}$. We can define a mapping $\phi = \{\overline{s_n \mapsto t_n}\}$ with each t_i being a term and $\tau(u_i) = \tau(t_i)$, and use $\phi(u)$ to denote the result of replacing each occurrence of s_i by t_i, $i = 1, \cdots, n$.

A lemma in [3] can be formulated in our general case.

Lemma 3.1 *Let u and v be η-long forms. Assume $\mathcal{MAS}(u) \cup \mathcal{MAS}(v) = \{s_1, \ldots, s_n\}$. Let $\phi = \{\overline{s_n \mapsto Y_n}\}$ be a mapping with new variables $Y_1, \ldots, Y_n$ such that $Y_i = Y_j$ iff $s_i =_E s_j$. Then $u =_E v$ if and only if $\phi(u) =_E \phi(v)$.*

Proof Let $u_1 =_E \cdots =_E u_m$ with each step $u_i =_E u_{i+1}$ resulting from the application of an equation of E. We prove by induction on m. For $m = 1$, it is trivial. Let $m = k + 1$. Consider $u_k =_E u_{k+1}$. For any maximal alien subterm s in u_k, since the outermost symbol of s is not in $\mathcal{C}(E)$, the application of the equation in E either happens within s, or independent of s, or s is in the instance of some variable of the equation. Replace all maximal alien subterms in the derivations as required. Then s in u_k and the result of s in u_{k+1} in the first case are replaced by the same variable. By the induction assumption, it is easy to check that the above claim holds. $\square$

Since our idea is to push as much as possible of the top layer of a higher-order E-unification pair into the given E-unification algorithm, we take all free variables as our alien symbols in the sequel, unless otherwise stated. In this case, maximal alien subterms are in fact flexible subterms of the form $F(\overline{s_n})$ with F being a free variable. Occurrences of λ-abstractions and bound variables should be regarded as free function constants in the given E-unification algorithm.

When fixing λ-abstractions as free function constants, no explicit α-conversion is possible. Therefore unification pairs should be α-converted before so that no explicit α-conversion is needed any more. For doing this, assume an infinite list of new bound variables for every type. An η-long term is said to be α-converted if each λ-abstraction in the term always uses the first bound variable in a list that has not been used by other covering λ-abstractions. For example, $\lambda y_1.f(\lambda y_2.\lambda y_3.y_2, \lambda y_2.y_2)$ is an α-converted form, provided that f is of the type $(\alpha \to \alpha \to \alpha) \to (\alpha \to \alpha) \to \beta$ and $y_1, y_2, y_3, \cdots$, a list of bound variables of type α. Note that a variable may be bound more than once in an α-converted form, but they can only happen in independent subterms. The following lemma asserts that explicit α-conversion is not needed in proving E-equivalence of α-converted terms.

Lemma 3.2 *Let* $u =_E v$ *with* α-*converted* u *and* v. *Then* $u =_E v$ *can be derived without using* α-*conversion.*

Proof Assume $u_1 =_1 u_2 =_2 \cdots =_n u_m$, where $=_i$ is either $=_\alpha$ or a step $=_E$ resulted from an application of an equation in E. The lemma can be prove by induction on the number of one-step $=_E$. $\square$

The above lemma also requires that occurrences of the same λ-abstraction should be regarded as the occurrences of the same function constant in regarding λ-abstractions as new function constants. To satisfy this, we just view each λ-abstraction λx as a new function constant and each occurrence of the form $\lambda x.t$ as $\lambda x(t)$.

The function constants of higher-order function types cause no real difficulties in first-order E-unification, provided that the given algorithm admits arbitrary free algebraic function constants. In fact no type information is needed in the E-unification, since atoms of different types are distinct.

From now on terms in unification problems are assumed to be α-converted. Let us define a few more notions. A subterm $H(\overline{x_k})$ of an η-long t is called a *trivial variable subterm* if H is a free variable and $\overline{x_k}$ is the list of the bound variables of all λ-abstractions top-down covering $H(\overline{x_k})$; otherwise a subterm of the form $H(\overline{t_m})$ is called a *proper variable subterm*. For example, $F(x, y)$ and the second $G(x)$ are trivial variable subterms in $\lambda x.f(\lambda y.f(F(x, y), G(x), F(y, x)), F(x, a), G(x))$, whereas $F(y, x)$, $F(x, a)$ and the first $G(x)$ are proper variable subterms. A free variable H is called *trivial in S* if it *only* occurs in trivial variable subterms in S; otherwise, it is called *proper in S*. A unification problem S is called *E-acceptable* if no proper variable subterms occur in S.

Denote $\mathcal{PMAS}(S) = \bigcup_{u=^? v \in S} \mathcal{PMAS}(u) \cup \mathcal{PMAS}(v)$. Let u be an η-long form with $\mathcal{PMAS}(u) = \{(u_1, \langle \overline{x_{k_1}^1} \rangle) \ldots (u_n, \langle \overline{x_{k_n}^n} \rangle)\}$. Then we can define an extended mapping $\phi = \{(u_n, \langle \overline{x_{k_n}^n} \rangle) \mapsto t_n\}$ with each t_i being a term of the same type as u_i. We use $\phi(u)$ to denote the result of replacing occurrences of u_i with covering λ-abstractions $\lambda x_1^i, \cdots, \lambda x_{k_i}^i$, by t_i, $i = 1, \cdots, n$.

To construct a top E-acceptable layer from a term u, maximal alien subterms are replaced by trivial variable subterms. For efficiency, occurrences of a maximal alien subterm with the same covering λ-abstractions are replaced by the same term. The bound variables in trivial variable subterms serve to prevent from losing unifiers. For example, $\lambda x.F(a, x) =^? \lambda x.x$ has a unifier $\{F \mapsto \lambda xy.y\}$, but $\lambda x.H =^? \lambda x.x$ after replacing $F(a, x)$ by H would not be unifiable. As an *abstracting rule* in $\mathcal{HEU}$ we have

$$\frac{\{u =^? v\} \cup S}{\{\phi(u) =^? \phi(v), H_1 =^? \lambda \overline{x_{k_1}^1} u_1, \ldots, H_n =^? \lambda \overline{x_{k_n}^n} u_n\} \cup S} \quad \text{(Abs)}$$

where

1. at least one of u and v is rigid,

2. $\mathcal{PMAS}(u) \cup \mathcal{PMAS}(v) = \{(u_1, \langle \overline{x_{k_1}^1} \rangle) \ldots (u_n, \langle \overline{x_{k_n}^n} \rangle)\}$,

3. ϕ is $\{(u_n, \langle \overline{x_{k_n}^n} \rangle) \mapsto H_n(\overline{x_{k_n}^n})\}$ with distinct new variables $H_1, \cdots, H_n$.

Now the unifiers of $\phi(u) =^? \phi(v)$ can be obtained by the given E-unification algorithm, where the newly introduced $H_1(\overline{x_{k_1}^1}), \ldots, H_n(\overline{x_{k_n}^n})$ are regarded as variables of base types, λ-abstractions and occurrences of bound variables as constants. To do this, an E-unification rule may be formulated in $\mathcal{HEU}$:

$$\frac{S_1 \cup S_2}{[\theta] \cup \theta(S_2)\downarrow_\beta} \quad \text{(E-Uni)}$$

where

1. S_1 is E-acceptable,

2. let $H_1(\overline{x_{k_1}^1}), \ldots, H_n(\overline{x_{k_n}^n})$ be all trivial variable subterms in S_1 and $\rho = \{H_n(\overline{x_{k_n}^n}) \mapsto Y_n\}$ a mapping with distinct new variables $Y_1, \ldots, Y_n$,

3. let σ be a first-order E-unifier of $\rho(S_1) = \{\rho(s) =^? \rho(t) \mid s =^? t \in S_1\}$, where λ-abstractions and bound variables are regarded as constants,

4. let $\phi_i = \{(Z, \overline{y_m}) \mapsto Z'(\overline{x_{k_i}^i}, \overline{y_m}) \mid (Z, \overline{y_m}) \in \mathcal{PMAS}(\sigma Y_i)\}, 1 \leq i \leq n$, be extended mappings with each Z' being a new variable for each $Z, x_1^i, \cdots, x_{k_i}^i, y_1, \cdots, y_m$, and

5. $\theta = \{H_1 \mapsto \lambda \overline{x_{k_1}^1}.\phi_1(\sigma Y_1), \cdots, H_n \mapsto \lambda \overline{x_{k_n}^n}.\phi_n(\sigma Y_n)\}$.

The substitution θ in item 5 is well-defined since the mapping ρ implies an one-to-one correspondence between H_i and Y_i.

The example given in Section 1 is in fact an example of using rule (E-Uni). In that example, $F(x), G(x), X$ and Y are $H_1(\overline{x_{k_1}^1}), H_2(\overline{x_{k_2}^2}), Y_1$ and Y_2 in item 2 with $\overline{x_{k_1}^1} = \overline{x_{k_2}^2} = x$. Instead of choosing the unifier $\sigma = \{X \mapsto Y * Z * x\}$ as there, we choose its equivalent form $\sigma = \{X \mapsto Z_1 * Z_2 * x, Y \mapsto Z_1\}$ with new variables Z_1 and Z_2 here. Furthermore, ϕ_1 in item 4 may be chosen as $\{Z_1 \mapsto Z_1'(x), Z_2 \mapsto Z_2'(x)\}$ with new variables Z_1' and Z_2', ϕ_2 as $\{Z_1 \mapsto Z_1'(x)\}$. The final substitution θ is $\{F \mapsto \lambda x.Z_1'(x) * Z_2'(x) * x, G \mapsto \lambda x.Z_1'(x)\}$. It is a unifier of the original unification problem.

The mappings $\phi_1, \ldots, \phi_n$ in item 4 should have as a whole a net effect in item 5 of lifting variables introduced in the E-unifier σ to trivial variable subterms with new variables at heads, and thus constructing a λE-unifier θ of S_1, which mimics σ. For this purpose, these mappings should lift occurrences of the same variable to occurrences of the same trivial variable subterm as long as possible, as both ϕ_1 and ϕ_2 map Z_1 to $Z_1'(x)$ in the above example. However, this is not always possible. Let Z be a variable in σY_i and σY_j with lists $\overline{y_{m_1}^1}$ and $\overline{y_{m_2}^2}$ of bound variables of covering λ-abstractions such that $\overline{x_{k_i}^i}, \overline{y_{m_1}^1} \neq \overline{x_{k_j}^j}, \overline{y_{m_2}^2}$. Then the two occurrences of Z cannot be lifted to the same trivial variable subterm. To this end a generalization of σ has to be made by ϕ_i and ϕ_j, which map the two occurrences of Z to trivial variable subterms $Z'(\overline{x_{k_i}^i}, \overline{y_{m_1}^1})$ and $Z''(\overline{x_{k_j}^j}, \overline{y_{m_2}^2})$ with distinct Z' and Z''.

Before proving that the resulting θ after the generalization is a λE-unifier of S_1 we first give a simple example. Let

$$S_1 = \{f(\lambda x.H_1(x), \lambda y.H_2(y)) \stackrel{?}{=} f(\lambda x.H_3(x), \lambda y.H_4(y))\}, \quad \text{where } x \neq y.$$

Let $\rho = \{H_1(x) \mapsto Y_1, H_2(y) \mapsto Y_2, H_3(x) \mapsto Y_3, H_4(y) \mapsto Y_4\}$. Then $\sigma = \{Y_i \mapsto Z \mid i = 1, 2, 3, 4\}$ is a unifier of $\{f(\lambda x.Y_1, \lambda y.Y_2) =^? f(\lambda x.Y_3, \lambda y.Y_4)\}$. The mappings required in item 4 are $\phi_1 = \phi_3 = \{Z \mapsto Z'(x)\}$ and $\phi_2 = \phi_4 = \{Z \mapsto Z''(y)\}$. Fortunately, the resulting substitution

$$\theta = \{H_i \mapsto \lambda x.Z'(x) \mid i = 1, 3\} \cup \{H_i \mapsto \lambda y.Z''(y) \mid i = 2, 4\}$$

is still a unifier of S_1. The real first-order underlying E-unifier for θ is not σ but a more general one $\sigma^* = \{Y_i \mapsto X_1 \mid i = 1, 3\} \cup \{Y_i \mapsto X_2 \mid i = 2, 4\}$.

In general we can prove that the substitution θ in rule (E-Uni) is a λE-unifier of S_1.

Assume the notations in rule (E-Uni). Let $\psi_i = \{(Z, \overline{y_m}) \mapsto X \mid (Z, \overline{y_m}) \in \mathcal{PMAS}(\sigma Y_i)\}$, $i = 1, \cdots, n$ be mappings such that X is a new variable for each $Z, x_1^i, \cdots, x_{k_i}^i, y_1, \cdots, y_m$. Construct a substitution $\sigma^* = \{Y_n \mapsto \psi_n(\sigma Y_n)\}$. Obviously, θ is a unifier of S_1 if σ^* is an E-unifier of $\rho(S_1)$. Take as alien symbols all λ-abstractions, all variables and all free function constants except those in $\mathcal{C}(E)$. By repeatedly applying Lemma 3.1, a set of E-equalities containing only function constants in $\mathcal{C}(E)$ and variables of base types may be produced from $\sigma(\rho(S_1))$ such that all of these E-equalities hold if and only if so do all E-equalities in $\sigma(\rho(S_1))$. Note that the difference between $\sigma^*(\rho(S_1))$ and $\sigma(\rho(S_1))$ is only that occurrences of the same variable in $\sigma(\rho(S_1))$ covered by different λ-abstractions are renamed into occurrences of different variables in $\sigma^*(\rho(S_1))$. Thus the same set of E-equalities can also be produced from $\sigma^*(\rho(S_1))$ in a similar way, since subterms under different covering free function constants cannot be generated as E-equivalent anyway. Therefore, σ^* is also an E-unifier of $\rho(S_1)$, which is more general than σ. Hence, θ is a λE-unifier of S_1.

In order to deal with flex-rigid pairs $\lambda\overline{x_k}.F(\overline{u_n}) =^? \lambda\overline{x_k}.a(\overline{v_m})$, a *binding* rule based on the notion of *partial binding* of imitation and projection (analog to rules (4a) and (4b) in [23]) is needed. We take the notion of *partial binding* as in [23] and give the rule as follows:

$$\frac{\{\lambda\overline{x_k}.F(\overline{u_n}) =^? \lambda\overline{x_k}.a(\overline{v_m})\} \cup S}{\{F =^? t\} \cup \{F \mapsto t\}(\{\lambda\overline{x_k}.F(\overline{u_n}) =^? \lambda\overline{x_k}.a(\overline{v_m})\} \cup S)\!\downarrow_\beta} \quad \text{(Bin)}$$

where $\lambda\overline{x_k}.F(\overline{u_n}) =^? \lambda\overline{x_k}.a(\overline{v_m})$ is flex-rigid and t is a partial binding

$$\lambda\overline{y_n}.b(\overline{\lambda\overline{z_{pq}^q}.H_q(\overline{y_n}, \overline{z_{pq}^q})})$$

appropriate to F with b being an arbitrary atom satisfying that

- in the case of imitation if $a \in \mathcal{C} - \mathcal{C}(E)$ then $b \in \{a\} \cup \mathcal{C}(E)$, and

- in the case of projection if $b = y_i$ for some $1 \leq i \leq n$, and $a \in \mathcal{C} - \mathcal{C}(E)$ then $\mathcal{Head}(u_i)$ is either a free variable or a constant in $\{a\} \cup \mathcal{C}(E)$.

The above choice of partial bindings t has to be more nondeterministic than in the corresponding rules of [23] because of the presence of equations E. For example, in the case of imitation, if $a(\overline{X_m}) = X_i \in E$ then the head of v_i may be chosen as b. Optimizations may be done when we know more about the given equations in E.

We use $S \Longrightarrow_r S'$ (short $S \Longrightarrow S'$) to denote that S' can be obtained from S by applying $\mathcal{HEU}$-rule (r). The proof of the soundness of $\mathcal{HEU}$ can be accomplished by showing that each rule of $\mathcal{HEU}$ is sound. We omit the tedious proof here, (except that part of it has already been given in the explanations above,) and state the result directly.

Theorem 3.3 *(Soundness) If $S \Longrightarrow^* S'$ then $U_{\lambda E}(S') \subseteq U_{\lambda E}(S)$.*

4 Completeness and control strategy

Completeness of the higher-order unification in simply typed λ-calculus usually means the *non-deterministic completeness*: if S is unifiable then there exists a finite sequence of transformations which leads to a unifier of S. In order to prove this, a special control strategy is used, which can be refined and used in implementations.

To define the strategy, S is uniquely split into four parts:

$$S = S_{|Sol} \cup S_{|E-Uni} \cup S_{|FF} \cup S_{|Res}$$

where

- $S_{|Sol}$ is the set of solved unification pairs in S,

- $S_{|E-Uni}$ is the set of all unification pairs in $S - S_{|Sol}$ whose free variables are all trivial in S,

- $S_{|FF}$ is the set of flex-flex unification pairs in $S - (S_{|Sol} \cup S_{|E-Uni})$,

- $S_{|Res}$ is the rest of S, i.e. $S - (S_{|Sol} \cup S_{|E-Uni} \cup S_{|FF})$,

Intuitively, $S_{|E-Uni}$ is an E-acceptable set of the unification pairs in $S - S_{|Sol}$ that should be E-unified by rule (E-Uni). The set $S_{|FF}$ consists of flex-flex unification pairs that need not be considered in pre-unification. Note that only flex-rigid and rigid-rigid unification pairs may be included in $S_{|Res}$.

Our strategy is to update the current unification problem S in the following way until S becomes presolved:

1. Repeatedly apply rule (Abs) to some unification pair in the current $S_{|Res}$. If $S_{|Res}$ is empty, go to the next step.

2. Apply once rule (E-Uni) to the whole current $S_{|E-Uni}$ and go to the next step;

3. Apply once rule (Bin) to a unification pair in the current $S_{|Res}$, and go to Step 1.

Note that the above strategy is of course not the unique one that leads to a unifier: the breadth-first traversal of the transformation tree is another (slow) one. Our strategy is efficient in the sense that it delays the "guess" step (Bin) to some extent and pushes unification problems as much as possible in the given E-unification algorithm.

To keep track of the transformation process of $\mathcal{HEU}$ the following set $\mathcal{CHEU}$ of transformations on $\langle \theta, S \rangle$ with $\theta \in \mathcal{U}_{\lambda E}(S)$ is needed. The same rule names as in $\mathcal{HEU}$ are intentionally used to suggest their correspondence. If $\{u =^? v\} \cup S \implies_{Abs} \{s =^? t, \overline{H_n =^? s_n}\} \cup S$, then define

$$\langle \theta, \{u =^? v\} \cup S \rangle \implies_{Abs} \langle \theta \cup \{\overline{H_n \mapsto \theta(s_n)\!\downarrow_\beta}\}, \{s =^? t, \overline{H_n =^? s_n}\} \cup S \rangle$$

If $S_1 \cup S_2 \implies_{E-Uni} [\sigma] \cup \sigma(S_2)\!\downarrow_\beta$ with $\sigma \leq_{\beta\eta E} \theta$, let σ' be such that $\sigma' \circ \sigma =_{\beta\eta E} \theta[Dom(\sigma)]$ and $Dom(\sigma') = Ran(\sigma)$, then define
$$\langle \theta, S_1 \cup S_2 \rangle \implies_{E-Uni} \langle \theta \cup \sigma', [\sigma] \cup \sigma(S_2)\!\downarrow_\beta \rangle$$
Note that all variables in $Ran(\sigma)$ are new. So $Dom(\sigma') \cap Dom(\theta) = \emptyset$ and $\theta \cup \sigma'$ is well-defined. Furthermore, $\theta \cup \sigma'$ is a unifier of $[\sigma] \cup \sigma(S_2)\!\downarrow_\beta$.

If $\{\lambda\overline{x_k}.F(\overline{u_n}) =^? \lambda\overline{x_k}.v\} \cup S \implies_{Bin} [\sigma] \cup \sigma(\{\lambda\overline{x_k}.F(\overline{u_n}) =^? \lambda\overline{x_k}.v\} \cup S)\!\downarrow_\beta$ with $\sigma = \{F \mapsto t\}$, then define
$$\langle \theta, \{\lambda\overline{x_k}.F(\overline{u_n}) =^? \lambda\overline{x_k}.v\} \cup S \rangle \implies_{Bin} \langle \theta', [\sigma] \cup \sigma(\{\lambda\overline{x_k}.F(\overline{u_n}) =^? \lambda\overline{x_k}.v\} \cup S)\!\downarrow_\beta \rangle$$
where two subcases may be distinguished depending on whether $F \in Dom(\theta)$:

- *(Bin-1)* If $F \in Dom(\theta)$ with $\theta(F) = \lambda\overline{y_n}.a(\overline{s_m})$, then set

$$t = \lambda\overline{y_n}.a(\overline{\lambda z_{p_m}^m.H_m(\overline{y_n}, \overline{z_{p_m}^m})}) \quad \text{and} \quad \theta' = \theta \cup \{\overline{H_m \mapsto \lambda\overline{y_n}.s_m}\}$$

- *(Bin-2)* If $F \notin Dom(\theta)$ then F could be regarded as a constant in unification. Let c be a new constant with the type of F. Set

$$t = \lambda\overline{y_n}.c(\lambda\overline{z_{p_1}^1}.H_1(\overline{y_n}, \overline{z_{p_1}^1}), \cdots, \lambda\overline{z_{p_n}^n}.H_n(\overline{y_n}, \overline{z_{p_n}^n}))$$
$$\theta' = \theta \cup \{F \mapsto c, H_1 \mapsto \lambda\overline{y_n}.y_1, \cdots, H_n \mapsto \lambda\overline{y_n}.y_n\}$$

Note that $\theta'(t) =_{\beta\eta} c$.

The $\mathcal{CHEU}$-transformations imitate $\mathcal{HEU}$-transformations under the guidance of a given unifier, thus may be used in proving the completeness of $\mathcal{HEU}$. However, it is worth to point out that our strategy is independent of any initial unifiers: All unifiers of the original unification problem can be enumerated under our strategy.

In the rest of this section we assume to start with an arbitrary pair $\langle \hat{\theta}_0, \hat{S}_0 \rangle$ satisfying $\hat{\theta}_0 \in \mathcal{U}_{\lambda E}(\hat{S}_0)$, and use $\langle \hat{\theta}_1, \hat{S}_1 \rangle$, $\langle \hat{\theta}_2, \hat{S}_2 \rangle$ and $\langle \hat{\theta}_3, \hat{S}_3 \rangle$ to denote the unification problems produced by $\mathcal{CHEU}$-transformations after step 1, 2 and 3 of our control strategy, resp.

The proof is in two steps: The first step is to prove that for any pair $\langle \hat{\theta}_0, \hat{S}_0 \rangle$ with a non-presolved $\hat{S}_0$, $\langle \hat{\theta}_3, \hat{S}_3 \rangle$ with $\hat{\theta}_3 \in \mathcal{U}_{\lambda E}(\hat{S}_3)$ can be produced by $\mathcal{CHEU}$-transformations under our strategy; The second step is to prove that $\mathcal{CHEU}$-transformations starting from $\langle \hat{\theta}_0, \hat{S}_0 \rangle$ under our strategy terminate on a presolved unification problem. Unifiers of the original unification problem can be constructed from the presolved unification problem.

We start with two lemmas showing properties of $\mathcal{HEU}$-rule (E-Uni).

Lemma 4.1 *For any E-acceptable S, if $\theta_1 \in \mathcal{U}_{\lambda E}(S)$, then there exists $\theta_2 \leq_{\beta\eta E} \theta_1$ such that $S \implies_{E-Uni} [\theta_2]$.*
Proof The proof is based on Lemma 3.1. □

Lemma 4.2 *The set $\hat{S}_{2|E-Uni}$ is empty, and $\hat{S}_{2|Res}$ may only contain flex-rigid unification pairs with proper variables at the heads of the flex sides.*
Proof Follows from that rule (E-Uni) only finds bindings for trivial variables. □

Now we finish the first step of the completeness with the following lemma.

Lemma 4.3 *If any of the above pairs $\langle \hat{\theta}_i, \hat{S}_i \rangle, i = 0, 1, 2, 3$, is not in pre-solved form, then it can be further $\mathcal{CHEU}$-transformed according to our control strategy. Furthermore, for any $\mathcal{CHEU}$-transformation $\langle \theta, S \rangle \Longrightarrow_r \langle \theta', S' \rangle$ the following hold:*

(i) $S \Longrightarrow_r S'$

(ii) $\theta =_{\beta \eta E} \theta'[\mathcal{D}om(\theta)]$ and $\mathcal{D}om(\theta) \subseteq \mathcal{D}om(\theta')$

(iii) $\theta' \in \mathcal{U}_{\lambda E}(S')$

Proof For an arbitrary pair $\langle \hat{\theta}_0, \hat{S}_0 \rangle$, step 1 of our strategy can always be performed. Step 2 is always possible due to Lemma 4.1. By Lemma 4.2, $\hat{S}_{2|E-Uni} = \emptyset$ and $\hat{S}_{2|Res}$ may only contain flex-rigid unification pairs with proper variables at the heads of the flex sides. If $\hat{S}_2$ is non-presolved, then $\hat{S}_{2|Res} \neq \emptyset$. Thus, $\mathcal{CHEU}$-transformation (Bin-1) or (Bin-2) can be applied as required in step 3.

The proof of (i) and (ii) is easy by the definition of $\mathcal{CHEU}$. (iii) holds obviously for rules (Abs) and (Bin-1). Assume $\langle \theta, S_1 \cup S_2 \rangle \Longrightarrow_{E-Uni} \langle \theta \cup \sigma', [\sigma] \cup \sigma(S_2) \downarrow_\beta \rangle$. It can be proved that $\theta \cup \sigma' \in \mathcal{U}_{\lambda E}([\sigma] \cup \sigma(S_2) \downarrow_\beta)$. Consider the case (Bin-2), we have $\langle \theta, S \rangle \Longrightarrow_{Bin} \langle \theta', [\sigma] \cup \sigma(S) \downarrow_\beta \rangle$, with $\sigma = \{F \mapsto t\}$, $F \notin \mathcal{D}om(\theta)$, new variables $H_1, \ldots, H_n$ and a new constant c. Obviously $\theta \cup \{F \mapsto c\} = \{F \mapsto c\} \circ \theta \in \mathcal{U}_{\lambda E}(S)$. Let $\theta' = \theta \cup \{F \mapsto c, \overline{H_n \mapsto (\lambda \overline{y_n}.y_n)}\}$. Then $\theta' \in \mathcal{U}_{\lambda E}(S)$. Since θ' unifies $[\sigma]$, we have $\theta' \in \mathcal{U}_{\lambda E}([\sigma] \cup \sigma(S))$. □

We turn to the second step to prove the termination of $\mathcal{CHEU}$-transformations under our control strategy. First it is easy to prove

Lemma 4.4 *$\mathcal{CHEU}$-transformation (Abs) in step 1 of our strategy strictly reduces the number of the unification pairs in current $S_{|Res}$.*

Therefore, successive $\mathcal{CHEU}$-transformations from Step 1 to 3 of our control strategy terminate. Now we need only to prove that the whole process of Step 1 to 3 cannot be repeated infinitely.

Define the *size* $|t|$ *of a term* t as the number of atomic subterms in t. The whole process of Step 1 to 3 can only be repeated finitely many times since it strictly reduces the complexity measure $I(\theta, S) = \langle L(\theta, S), M(\theta, S) \rangle$ for $\theta \in \mathcal{U}_{\lambda E}(S)$, where

- $L(\theta, S)$ is the number of proper variables which are not in $\mathcal{D}om(\theta)$ and

- $M(\theta, S)$ is the sum of the sizes of the θ-bindings of proper variables, i.e. $M(\theta, S) = \sum \{|\theta(x)| \mid x \in \mathcal{D}om(\theta) \text{ is proper in } S\}$.

Lemma 4.5 *For $\theta \in \mathcal{U}_{\lambda E}(S)$, if $\langle \theta, S \rangle \Longrightarrow^* \langle \hat{\theta}_3, \hat{S}_3 \rangle$ and $\hat{S}_3$ is not a presolved form then $I(\hat{\theta}_3, \hat{S}_3) < I(\theta, S)$ where $<$ is the standard lexicographic ordering on pairs of numbers.*

Proof Since rule (Abs) does not introduce new proper variables $I(\hat{\theta}_1, \hat{S}_1) = I(\theta, S)$. Let $\hat{S}_2 = [\sigma] \cup \sigma(S') \downarrow_\beta$ for some S'. Since neither $\hat{S}_{1|E-Uni}$ of $\hat{S}_1$ nor $[\sigma]$ contains proper variables, $\hat{S}_2$ contains the same proper variables as $\hat{S}_1$. Thus $I(\hat{\theta}_2, \hat{S}_2) = I(\hat{\theta}_1, \hat{S}_1)$.

In the case (Bin-1) of Step 3, $M(\hat{\theta}_3, \hat{S}_3) < M(\hat{\theta}_2, \hat{S}_2)$ and $L(\hat{\theta}_3, \hat{S}_3) = L(\hat{\theta}_2, \hat{S}_2)$. In case of (Bin-2), $L(\hat{\theta}_3, \hat{S}_3) < L(\hat{\theta}_2, \hat{S}_2)$. Thus in both cases, $I(\hat{\theta}_3, \hat{S}_3) < I(\hat{\theta}_2, \hat{S}_2)$.

If rule (Bin) is not applicable, the set $\hat{S}_{2|Res}$ of $\hat{S}_2$ is empty. By Lemma 4.2, $\hat{S}_2$ must be in presolved form. □

Now we give the main result of this subsection:

Theorem 4.6 *(Completeness) If $\theta \in U_{\lambda E}(S)$ then there exists some finite sequence of transformations in $\mathcal{CHEU}$ under our strategy $\langle \theta, S \rangle \Longrightarrow^* \langle \theta', S' \rangle$, where S' is presolved, $\theta =_{\beta\eta E} \theta'[\mathcal{D}om(\theta)]$ and $\theta' \in U_{\lambda E}(S')$.*

Note that $\theta =_{\beta\eta E} \theta'[\mathcal{FV}(S)]$ is not true in general because of the case (Bin-2), nor is $\sigma_{S'} \leq \theta[\mathcal{FV}(S)]$. However, an S'' can be constructed from S' by deleting all the unification pairs $F =^? \lambda \overline{x_k}.c(\overline{u_n})$ with c being a constant not in $\mathcal{C}(S) \cup \mathcal{C}(E)$, and it can be shown that $\sigma_{S''} \leq_{\beta\eta E} \theta \, [\mathcal{FV}(S)]$.

5   An example

In this section, an example is given to show the use of $\mathcal{HEU}$-rules. Let

$$S_0 = \{\lambda x.F(x,Y) + x \stackrel{?}{=} \lambda x.0\}$$

be a unification problem in the presence of equations of Boolean Ring with the usual function constants $0, 1, +, *$, where F, Y are free variables. Obviously, $F(x, Y)$ is an alien subterm. Applying rule (Abs) to S_0 will yield

$$S_1 = \{\lambda x.H(x) + x \stackrel{?}{=} \lambda x.0, \ \lambda x.H(x) \stackrel{?}{=} \lambda x.F(x,Y).\}$$

The first unification pair of S_1 is E-acceptable and the second flex-flex. Rule (E-Uni) may be used to solve the first unification pair. Let $\rho = \{H(x) \mapsto Z\}$ be the abstracting mapping, and $\{\lambda x.Z + x =^? \lambda x.0\}$ the underlying E-unification pair where λx and x are treated as free function constants. The E-unification algorithm of Boolean Ring (admitting free function constants) may find a unifier $\sigma = \{Z \mapsto x\}$ of $\{\lambda x.Z + x =^? \lambda x.0\}$, which is most general in this case. Since there are no new variables in $\sigma(Z)$, $\phi = \emptyset$. Therefore $\theta = \{H \mapsto \lambda x.x\}$. The result of the transformation is:

$$S_2 = \{H \stackrel{?}{=} \lambda x.x, \ \lambda x.F(x,Z) \stackrel{?}{=} \lambda x.x\}.$$

Using rule (Bin), S_2 can be further transformed into

$$S_3 = \{H \stackrel{?}{=} \lambda x.x, \ F \stackrel{?}{=} \lambda xy.x, \ \lambda x.x \stackrel{?}{=} \lambda x.x\}$$

with a projection $F \mapsto \lambda xy.x$.

There is a trivial unification pair $\lambda x.x =^? \lambda x.x$ in S_3. If there is a rule deleting such unification pairs, we are done. If not, we may apply rule (E-Uni) again such that $\lambda x.x =^? \lambda x.x$ will be deleted as the E-acceptable part with $\theta = \emptyset$. The final presolved unification problem is

$$\{H \stackrel{?}{=} \lambda x.x, \ F \stackrel{?}{=} \lambda xy.x\}$$

which directly implies a unifier of the initial unification problem S_0.

6 Conclusions and directions for future investigation

This paper is clearly an important step towards a complete solution to the problem of integrating first-order equational and higher-order unification algorithms.

It is planned to study hardware verification problems of [8] and [5] in this context. The possibility of embedding the unification in the theory of Boolean Ring, for instance, into higher-order unification might provide further power and convenience.

Another obvious direction for further research is to study the integration of E-unification into the so-called *simple* higher-order unification [14], where the higher-order unification is unitary. This might lead to a practical higher-order equational logic programming language.

Finally, it is also interesting to consider whether the idea here can be used to solve the unification problem in other typed λ-calculi, e.g. that with dependent types [20] or with higher-order rewrite rules [12].

Acknowledgements

Zhenyu Qian wishes to thank Tobias Nipkow for cooperation on related work. Qian's research is partially supported by ESPRIT Basic Research WG *COMPASS* 3264.

References

[1] A. Boudet. Unification in a combination of equational theories: an efficient algorithm. In M. Stickel, editor, *Proc. 10th Int. Conf. Automated Deduction*, pages 292–307, LNCS 449, 1990.

[2] A. Boudet, J. Jouannaud, M. Schmidt-Schauß. Unification in boolean rings and abelien groups. *J. Symbolic Computation* 8, 1989

[3] V. Breazu-Tannen. Combining algebra and higher-order types. In *Proc. 3rd IEEE Symp. Logic in Computer Science*, pages 82–90, 1988.

[4] V. Breazu-Tannen and J. Gallier. Polymorphic rewriting conserves algebraic strong normalization and confluence. In *Proc. 16th Int. Coll. Automata, Languages and Programming*, LNCS 372, 1988.

[5] W. Büttner and H. Simonis. Embedding boolean expression into logic programming. *J. Symbolic Computation*, 4:191–205, 1987.

[6] D. Dougherty and P. Johann. A combinatory logic approach to higher-order E-unification. In *Proc. 11th Int. Conf. on Automated Deduction*, pages 79–93, LNCS 607, 1992.

[7] J. Gallier and W. Snyder. Complete sets of transformations for general E-unification. *Theoretical Computer Science*, 67:203–260, 1988.

[8] M. Gordon. Why higher-order logic is a good formalism for specifying and verifying hardware. In G. Milne and P. Subrahmanyam, editors, *Formal Aspect of VLSI Design*, page , North Holland, 1986.

[9] A. Herold. Combination of unification algorithms. In *Proc. 8th Int. Conf. Automated Deduction*, LNCS 230, 1986.

[10] G. Huet. A unification algorithm for typed λ-calculus. *Theoretical Computer Science*, 1:27–57, 1975.

[11] J. Jouannaud and C. Kirchner. Solving equations in abstract algebras: a rule-based survey of unification. In J. Lassez and G. Plotkin, editors, *Computational Logic: Essays in Honor of Alan Robinson*, MIT Press.

[12] J. Jouannaud and M. Okada. Embedding first-order and higher-order rewriting into λ-calculus. In *Proc. 6th LICS*, 1991.

[13] C. Kirchner. *Méthodes et outils de conception systématique d'algorithmes d'unification dans les théories équationnelles*. Technical Report, Thèse d'état de l'Université de Nancy I, 1985.

[14] D. Miller. A logic programming language with lambda-abstraction, function variables, and simple unification. In P. Schroeder-Heister, editor, *Extensions of Logic Programming*, pages 253–281, LNCS 475, 1991.

[15] G. Nadathur and D. Miller. An overview of λProlog. In R. A. Kowalski and K. A. Bowen, editors, *Proc. 5th Int. Logic Programming Conference*, pages 810–827, MIT Press, 1988.

[16] T. Nipkow. Combining matching algorithms: the regular case. In N. Dershowitz, editor, *Proc. 3rd Int. Conf. Rewriting Techniques and Applications*, pages 343–358, LNCS 355, 1989.

[17] T. Nipkow and Z. Qian. *Higher-Order E-Unification for Collapse-Free and Regular Theories E*. Technical Report, Universität Bremen, 1991.

[18] T. Nipkow and Z. Qian. Modular higher-order E-unification. In R. Book, editor, *Proc. 4th Int. Conf. Rewriting Techniques and Applications*, pages 200–214, LNCS 488, 1991.

[19] L. Paulson. Isabelle: the next 700 theorem provers. In P. Odifreddi, editor, *Logic and Computer Science*, Academic Press, 1990.

[20] F. Pfenning. Logic programming in the LF logical framework. In G. Huet and G. D. Plotkin, editors, *Logical Frameworks*, pages 66–78, Cambridge University Press, 1991.

[21] M. Schmidt-Schauß. Unification in a combination of arbitrary disjoint equational theories. *J. Symbolic Computation*, 8:51–99, 1989.

[22] W. Snyder. Higher-order E-unification. In *Proc. 10th Int. Conf. Automated Deduction*, pages 573–587, LNCS 449, 1990.

[23] W. Snyder and J. Gallier. Higher-order unification revisited: complete sets of transformations. *J. Symbolic Computation*, 8:101–140, 1989.

[24] K. Yelick. Unification in combinations of collapse-free regular theories. *J. Symbolic Computation*, 3:153–181, 1987.

A Predicate Transformer for Unification

Livio Colussi
Dipartimento di Matematica Pura ed Applicata
Università di Padova
Via Belzoni 7, 35131 Padova, Italy
colussi@pdmat1.unipd.it

Elena Marchiori
Centre for Mathematics and Computer Science
Kruislaan 413, 1098 SJ Amsterdam, The Netherlands
elena@cwi.nl
and
Dipartimento di Matematica Pura ed Applicata
Università di Padova
Via Belzoni 7, 35131 Padova, Italy

Abstract

In this paper we study unification as predicate transformer. Given a unification problem expressed as a set of sets of terms $\mathcal{U}$ and a predicate P, we are interested in the strongest predicate R (w.r.t. the implication) s.t. if P holds before the unification of $\mathcal{U}$ then R holds when the unification is performed. We introduce a Dijkstra-style calculus that given P and $\mathcal{U}$ computes R. We prove the soundness, completeness and termination of the calculus. The predicate language considered contains monotonic predicates together with some non-monotonic predicates like var, $\neg ground$, $share$ and $\neg share$. This allows to use the calculus for the static analysis of run-time properties of Prolog programs.

1 Introduction

The standard view of logic programming is declarative, i.e. a program describes some predicate or function without referring to the way it will be computed. Nevertheless computational aspects become fundamental for the study of run-time properties of Prolog programs, like the actual form of the arguments of a goal before and after its call. In Prolog unification is the main computational mechanism since it produces the value of the variables during the execution of a goal in a program. To study its effect on the values of variables we study unification by means of predicate transformers. The use of predicate transformers for semantic analysis has been studied in the setting of imperative programming: it was advocated by Floyd [5] and by Dijkstra [3] for program verification. The use of predicate transformers in the framework of logic programming is new. Given a unification problem expressed by a set of sets of terms $\mathcal{U}$, we introduce the predicate transformer $sp.\mathcal{U}$ such that $sp.\mathcal{U}.P$ is semantically equivalent to the strongest predicate R (w.r.t. implication) s.t. if P holds before the unification of $\mathcal{U}$, then R holds when the unification is performed. We show that $sp.\mathcal{U}.P$ could be computed in one step if P were a monotonic predicate. Since our aim is to infer run-time properties of Prolog programs, then the predicate language considered contains also non-monotonic predicates like *var* or *share*. For this reason a careful analysis of some intermediate steps of the unification process is necessary. This yelds to a non-trivial system of syntactic rules to compute $sp.\mathcal{U}.P$. The soundness, completeness and termination of the system is proved. The calculus can be used to infer run-time properties of logic programs. In Cousot and Cousot's original paper on abstract interpretation of imperative programs [2] everything was couched in terms of predicate transformers. Predicate transformers were used to define deductive semantics. Deductive semantics was used to design approximate program analysis frameworks. To propose a similar approach for logic programs we need the correspondent of program point for a logic program. In [7] Nilsson introduced a scheme for inferring run-time properties of logic programs based on a semantic description of logic programs that uses the concept of program point. We will show that the predicate transformer sp can be easily cast in such a theory.

The rest of the paper is organized as follows. The next section contains some preliminaries and introduces the predicate transformer $sp.\mathcal{U}$. Section 3 introduces the transformation rules to compute $sp.\mathcal{U}.P$. In section 4 the soundness, completeness and termination of the calculus are proved. In section 5 we illustrate the use of the calculus for defining a forward semantics of Prolog programs.

2 Unification as Predicate Transformer

The computational meaning of unification in Prolog relies on the concept of substitution. A *substitution* is a mapping from variables to terms such that $dom(\vartheta) \stackrel{\text{def}}{=} \{v \mid v\vartheta \neq v\}$ is finite. The notion of unification can be given w.r.t. a set of sets of terms [4] or w.r.t. a set of equations [6]. We choose the first approach. Let $\mathcal{U}$ be a finite set of sets of terms. A *unifier* for $\mathcal{U}$ is a substitution ϑ such that every set in $\mathcal{U}$, under the application of ϑ, becomes a singleton, i.e. $\forall S \in \mathcal{U} \; \forall t, t' \in S \; (t\vartheta = t'\vartheta)$. A *most general unifier* for $\mathcal{U}$ is a unifier ϑ such that for every unifier σ there exists a substitution γ such that $\vartheta\gamma = \sigma$. The *set of idempotent most general unifiers* for $\mathcal{U}$ will be denoted by $mgu(\mathcal{U})$. The operational meaning of $\mathcal{U}$ can be described as the partial function $\lambda\alpha.\alpha\mu$, where α is a substitution and μ is a fixed mgu in $mgu(\mathcal{U}\alpha)$; clearly $\lambda\alpha.\alpha\mu$ is undefined if $mgu(\mathcal{U}\alpha) = \emptyset$. We study unification by means of the predicate transformer $sp.\mathcal{U}$ (where sp stands for strongest postcondition [5]) with the following operational meaning.

Definition 2.1 $sp.\mathcal{U}.P$ is true in precisely those substitutions $\alpha\mu$ such that $P\alpha$ is true and $\mu \in mgu(\mathcal{U}\alpha)$.

The choice to represent the unification process as set of sets of terms is motivated by the following observations:
$mgu(\{\{f(t_1,\ldots,t_n),f(s_1,\ldots,s_n)\}\}) = mgu(\{\{t_1,s_1\},\ldots,\{t_n,s_n\}\})$ and
$mgu(\{S_1,\ldots,S_n\}) = mgu(\{S_1 \cup S_2, S_3,\ldots,S_n\})$ if $S_1 \cap S_2 \neq \emptyset$.
These two equalities will be used in our calculus for $sp.\mathcal{U}$ and they clearly lead to consider sets of sets of terms. For sake of clarity, we use double square brackets to enclose sets of terms $S = [\![t_1,\ldots,t_m]\!]$ and braces to enclose sets of sets of terms $\mathcal{U} = \{S_1,\ldots,S_n\}$.

We call a predicate P *monotonic* if it is (semantically) invariant under instantiation, that is for all substitutions α,β if $P\alpha$ is true then $P\alpha\beta$ is true. Now let $\mathcal{U}$ be $\{[\![t^1_1,\ldots,t^1_{n_1}]\!],\ldots,[\![t^m_1,\ldots,t^m_{n_m}]\!]\}$: we denote by U the predicate $((t^1_1 = \ldots = t^1_{n_1}) \wedge \ldots \wedge (t^m_1 = \ldots = t^m_{n_m}))$. Then the following lemma holds.

Lemma 2.2 *Let P be a monotonic predicate. Then $P \wedge U$ is equivalent to $sp.\mathcal{U}.P$.*

Proof. Let α be s.t. $P\alpha$ is true and let $\mu \in mgu(\mathcal{U}\alpha)$. Then $U\alpha\mu$ is true and from P monotonic it follows that $P\alpha\mu$ is true.
Viceversa let α be s.t. $(P \wedge U)\alpha$ is true. Then $P\alpha$ is true and $\epsilon \in mgu(\mathcal{U}\alpha)$. So by Definition 2.1 $(sp.\mathcal{U}.P)\alpha$ is true. □

Lemma 2.2 allows to compute $sp.\mathcal{U}.P$ when P is a monotonic predicate.

2.1 The Language

However we are interested also in properties that describe the structure of terms, like *var* or *¬ground*, since we want to use the predicate transformer to infer runtime properties of logic programs. Thus we introduce the language $\mathcal{A}$ defined on the alphabet containing the following classes of symbols:

- a countable set VAR of *variables*;
- a set FUN of *functions*;
- a set $PRED = Pred\cup\{free, var, \neg ground, share, \neg share, inst\}$ of *predicate symbols* where $Pred$ is a finite set of monotonic predicate symbols s.t. $=$, $ground$, $\neg var$, $\prec$, $\preceq$, $invar$ are in $Pred$;
- the *connectives* $\wedge$ and $\vee$;
- the *existential quantifier* $\exists$;
- (and) as punctuation symbols.

Variables will be normally denoted by the letters u, v, w, x, y, z (possibly subscripted or superscripted) and functions will be normally denoted by the letters f, g, h (possibly subscripted). Let $TERM$ be the set of *terms* built on FUN and VAR. Terms will be normally denoted by the letters r, s, t (possibly subscripted or superscripted). Given a term t, the set $vars(t) \subseteq VAR$ denotes the set of variables that occur in t. We call *structured term* a term of the form $f(t_1, \ldots, t_m)$, where $m \geq 1$; we call *proper subterm* of t every subterm of t but t. We assume that sequences are contained in $\mathcal{A}$. We denote by $\underline{t}$ a sequence $t_1, \ldots, t_k$ and we write $\underline{t}_{(k)}$ or $\langle t_1, \ldots, t_k \rangle$ if respectively the size or the elements of the sequence are relevant. Moreover we indicate with $\underline{x}\rho$ the sequence of terms obtained applying the substitution ρ to every element of the sequence $\underline{x}$. We call *atom* a predicate of the form $p(t_1, \ldots, t_n)$ where p is a predicate symbol of arity n and $t_1, \ldots, t_n$ are terms. When ambiguity does not arise we write $r(t_1, \ldots, t_m)$ as a shorthand for the predicate $r(t_1) \wedge \ldots \wedge r(t_m)$, where r is a predicate symbol of arity 1.

The *truth value of a predicate* $P \in \mathcal{A}$ w.r.t. a substitution α s.t. $vars(P) \subseteq dom(\alpha)$ is defined inductively on the structure of P, and the meaning of an atom is specified as follows:

- $\neg var(t)\alpha$ is true iff $t\alpha \notin VAR$;
- $ground(t)\alpha$ is true iff $vars(t\alpha) = \emptyset$;
- $(t_1 = t_2)\alpha$ is true iff $t_1\alpha = t_2\alpha$ syntactically;
- $(s \preceq t)\alpha$ is true iff $s\alpha$ is a subterm of $t\alpha$;
- $(s \prec t)\alpha$ is true iff $s\alpha$ is a proper subterm of $t\alpha$;
- $invar(s, t)\alpha$ is true iff $vars(s\alpha) \subseteq vars(t\alpha)$;
- $free(x)\alpha$ is true iff $x\alpha \in VAR$ and $x\alpha \notin vars(y\alpha)$ for all $y \in dom(\alpha)$ s.t. $y \neq x$;
- $var(x)\alpha$ is true iff $x\alpha \in VAR$;
- $\neg ground(t)\alpha$ is true iff $vars(t\alpha) \neq \emptyset$;
- $share(s, t)\alpha$ is true iff $vars(s\alpha) \cap vars(t\alpha) \neq \emptyset$;
- $\neg share(s, t)\alpha$ is true iff $vars(s\alpha) \cap vars(t\alpha) = \emptyset$;
- $inst(x, r_1, r_2, y)\alpha$ is true iff $r_1\alpha$ is the sequence $\langle x_1, \ldots, x_m \rangle$, with $x_i \in vars(x\alpha)$ and $x_i \notin vars(y\alpha)$ for $i \in [1, m]$, $r_2\alpha$ is the sequence $\langle t_1, \ldots, t_m \rangle$ and $\{x_1/t_1, \ldots, x_m/t_m\} \in mgu(\{[\![x\alpha, y\alpha]\!]\})$.

Notice that x and y in $inst(x, r_1, r_2, y)$ represent two terms the second of which is an instance of the first. Thus the predicate $inst$ expresses a special case of the unification.

Given two predicates P and Q, we write $P \equiv Q$ to indicate that P and Q are semantically equivalent. We can assume that the predicates $TRUE$ (the predicate true w.r.t. all substitutions) and $FALSE$ (the predicate false w.r.t. all substitutions) are in $\mathcal{A}$, since $TRUE \equiv (var(x) \vee \neg var(x))$ and $FALSE \equiv (var(x) \wedge \neg var(x))$.

Predicates in $\mathcal{A}$ are not in general monotonic, since all atoms built on predicate symbols not in $Pred$ are non-monotonic by definition. So Lemma 2.2 is not sufficient to characterize $sp.\mathcal{U}$: consider for instance the unification $\{[\![x, a]\!]\}$ and the predicate $var(x)$. Thus a careful analysis of the effect of the unification process on non-monotonic predicates is necessary. The fact that the connective $\neg$ is not in our language guarantees that atoms built on predicate symbols not in $Pred$ are the only non-monotonic atoms of the language; this allows a case analysis of the effect of unification on non-monotonic predicates.

We introduce now some assumptions that will be used to simplify the form of the rules for $sp.\mathcal{U}$ that will be introduced in the next section.
Predicates are of the form $\exists \underline{x} P$ where P doesn't contain any quantifier, it is in disjunctive normal form (i.e. it is a disjunction of conjunctions of atoms) and the equalities that occur in each conjunct are expressed by a set of equations in solved form. Atoms with predicate symbol $free$, var, $\neg var$, $ground$, $\neg ground$, $share$, $\neg share$, $invar$ have variables as arguments. For any formula $sp.\mathcal{U}.P$ the predicate P does not contain (existential) quantifiers.
All assumptions are not restrictive. Here the proof for the last one.

Lemma 2.3 *If the variable x does not occur in $\mathcal{U}$ then $sp.\mathcal{U}.\exists x P$ is equivalent to $\exists x(sp.\mathcal{U}.P)$ w.r.t. Definition 2.1.*

Proof. Since x doesn't occur in $\mathcal{U}$ then the truth value of $\exists x(sp.\mathcal{U}.P)\beta$ and of $(sp.\mathcal{U}.\exists x P)\beta$ does not depend on $x\beta$. Thus we can assume without loss of generality $x \notin dom(\beta)$. Then $(sp.\mathcal{U}.\exists x P)\beta$ is true iff there exist α and μ s.t. $x \notin dom(\alpha)$, $x \notin dom(\mu)$, $\mu \in mgu(\mathcal{U}\alpha)$, $(\exists x P)\alpha$ is true and $\beta = \alpha\mu$ iff there exist α, μ and t s.t. $x \notin dom(\alpha)$, $x \notin dom(\mu)$, $\mu \in mgu(\mathcal{U}\alpha)$, $P(\alpha \cup \{x/t\})$ is true and $\beta = \alpha\mu$ iff there exist α, μ and t s.t. $\mu \in mgu(\mathcal{U}(\alpha \cup \{x/t\}))$, $P(\alpha \cup \{x/t\})$ is true and $(\beta \cup \{x/t\}) = (\alpha \cup \{x/t\})\mu$ iff $(sp.\mathcal{U}.P)(\beta \cup \{x/t\})$ is true iff $(\exists x sp.\mathcal{U}.P)\beta$ is true. $\square$

3   A Calculus for $sp.\mathcal{U}$

The following conditions on P and $\mathcal{U}$ characterize the types of formulas which will specify the scope of applicability of the rules for $sp.\mathcal{U}.P$.

(i) P is a conjunction of atoms.
(ii) For each equation $x = t$ in P, x does not occur in $\mathcal{U}$.
(iii) For every x occurring in $\mathcal{U}$ either $var(x)$ or $\neg var(x)$ occurs in P.
(iv) For all distinct variables x occurring in $\mathcal{U}$ and y occurring in P either $share(x,y)$ or $\neg share(x,y)$ occurs in P.
(v) $\mathcal{U} = \{S_1, \ldots, S_n\}$ contains disjoint sets, i.e. $S_i \cap S_j = \emptyset$ for $i \neq j$.
(vi) Each set in $\mathcal{U}$ contains more than one element.
(vii) Each set in $\mathcal{U}$ contains at most one structured element $f(v_1, \ldots, v_m)$ and in such a case $free(v_1), \ldots, free(v_m)$ occur in P.
(viii) Every element x of a set $S \in \mathcal{U}$ is s.t. $free(x)$ occurs in P if x occurs in the structured element of another set in $\mathcal{U}$ and $\neg var(x)$ occurs in P otherwise. Moreover, each set that contains a structured element also contains an element

y s.t. $free(y)$ occurs in P. (Hence y occurs in the structured element of another set).

We introduce 3 types of formulas $sp.\mathcal{U}.P$ as follows.

> **type 1:** those which satisfy conditions (i)–(iii).
> **type 2:** those which satisfy conditions (i)–(vii).
> **type 3:** those which satisfy conditions (i)–(viii).

Each type of formula characterizes a simpler form of P and $\mathcal{U}$. The final form will be a disjunction of formulas in the so called *reduced form*.

A formula $sp.\mathcal{U}.P$ is in **reduced form** if P is a conjunction of atoms, for each equation $x = t$ in P x does not occur in $\mathcal{U}$, $\mathcal{U}$ contains only disjoint sets of two or more variables, for all x occurring in $\mathcal{U}$ both $\neg var(x)$ and $\neg ground(x)$ occur in P and for all x occurring in $\mathcal{U}$ and y occurring in P either $share(x, y)$ or $\neg share(x, y)$ occurs in P.

We are now ready to present the rules for $sp.\mathcal{U}.P$. The notation E_t^x will be used to indicate the formula obtained by replacing the occurrences of x in E with t.

- If $P = P_1 \vee \ldots \vee P_n$ then

$$sp.\mathcal{U}.P \equiv sp.\mathcal{U}.P_1 \vee \ldots \vee sp.\mathcal{U}.P_n \qquad\qquad \textbf{OR}$$

- If x occurs in $\mathcal{U}$ and neither $var(x)$ nor $\neg var(x)$ occurs in P then

$$sp.\mathcal{U}.P \equiv sp.\mathcal{U}.(P \wedge var(x)) \vee sp.\mathcal{U}.(P \wedge \neg var(x)) \qquad\qquad \textbf{VAR1}$$

- If P is a conjunction of atoms and $x = t$ occurs in P then:

$$sp.\mathcal{U}.P \equiv sp.\mathcal{U}_t^x.P \qquad\qquad \textbf{EQ}$$

- $sp.\mathcal{U}.FALSE \equiv FALSE \qquad\qquad \textbf{F}$

The following eight rules may be applied only to **type 1** formulas.

- If x occurs in $\mathcal{U}$ and y occurs in P and neither $share(x, y)$ nor $\neg share(x, y)$ occurs in P then

$$sp.\mathcal{U}.P \equiv sp.\mathcal{U}.(P \wedge share(x, y)) \vee sp.\mathcal{U}.(P \wedge \neg share(x, y)) \qquad\qquad \textbf{SH1}$$

- If $\mathcal{U} = \{[\![f_1(\underline{s}), f_2(\underline{t}), \ldots]\!], S_2, \ldots, S_n\}$ and $f_1 \neq f_2$, then

$$sp.\mathcal{U}.P \equiv FALSE \qquad\qquad \textbf{MIS1}$$

- If $\mathcal{U} = \{[\![x, s, \underline{t}]\!], S_2, \ldots, S_n\}$ and either $x \in vars(s)$ or the conjunct $x \prec s$ occurs in P then

$$sp.\mathcal{U}.P \equiv FALSE \qquad\qquad \textbf{MIS2}$$

- If $\mathcal{U} = \{[\![f(\underline{s}^1_{(k)}), \ldots, f(\underline{s}^m_{(k)})]\!], S_2, \ldots, S_n\}$ then

$$sp.\mathcal{U}.P \equiv sp.\mathcal{U}'.P \qquad\qquad\qquad \textbf{STR1}$$

where $\mathcal{U}' = \{[\![\underline{s}^{(m)}_j]\!]_{j \in [1,k]}, S_2, \ldots, S_n\}$

- If $\mathcal{U} = \{[\![f(\underline{s}^1_{(k)}), \ldots, f(\underline{s}^i_{(k)}), x_{i+1}, \ldots, x_m]\!], S_2, \ldots, S_n\}$ with $i < m$ and either $i \geq 2$ or at least one s^i_j is not a variable or at least one s^i_j is a variable such that $\neg var(s^i_j)$ occurs in P, then

$$sp.\mathcal{U}.P \equiv \exists \underline{y}_{(k)} \big(sp.\mathcal{U}'.P' \big) \qquad\qquad\qquad \textbf{STR2}$$

where $\mathcal{U}' = \{[\![f(\underline{y}_{(k)}), x_{i+1}, \ldots, x_m]\!], [\![y_j, \underline{s}^{(i)}_j]\!]_{j \in [1,k]}, S_2, \ldots, S_n\}$,
$P' = P \wedge free(\underline{y}_{(k)})$ and $\underline{y}_{(k)}$ are fresh variables.

- If $\mathcal{U} = \{[\![t, \underline{t}_{(m)}]\!], [\![t, \underline{s}_{(m')}]\!], S_3, \ldots, S_n\}$ then

$$sp.\mathcal{U}.P \equiv sp.\mathcal{U}'.P \qquad\qquad\qquad \textbf{SH2}$$

where $\mathcal{U}' = \{[\![t, \underline{t}_{(m)}, \underline{s}_{(m')}]\!], S_3, \ldots, S_n\}$

- If $\mathcal{U} = \{[\![t]\!], S_2, \ldots, S_n\}$ then

$$sp.\mathcal{U}.P \equiv sp.\mathcal{U}'.P \qquad\qquad\qquad \textbf{SI}$$

where $\mathcal{U}' = \{S_2, \ldots, S_n\}$

The following two rules may be applied only to **type 2** formulas.

- If $\mathcal{U} = \{[\![t, \underline{x}_{(m)}]\!], S_2, \ldots, S_n\}$ where x_m does not occur in the structured term of any set of $\mathcal{U}$, $var(x_m)$ and $\neg share(x_m, y)$ occurs in P for all $y \in vars(t)$, then

$$sp.\mathcal{U}.P \equiv \exists \underline{z}' \, sp.\mathcal{U}'.R \qquad\qquad\qquad \textbf{VAR2}$$

where $\mathcal{U}' = \{[\![t, \underline{x}_{(m-1)}]\!], S_2, \ldots, S_n\}$,
$R = (\bigwedge_{z \in \underline{z}} inst(z\rho, \langle x_m \rho\rangle, \langle t\rangle, z) \wedge P' \wedge x_m = t)$,
$\underline{z} = \langle z \in vars(P) \mid P \Rightarrow share(z, x_m) \rangle$, $\underline{z}' = \underline{z}\rho$ is a variant of $\underline{z}$ disjoint from P and $P' = P^{\underline{z}}_{\underline{z}'}$.

- If $\mathcal{U} = \{[\![f(\underline{s}_{(k)}), \underline{x}_{(m)}]\!], S_2, \ldots, S_n\}$ and $\neg var(x_1), \ldots, \neg var(x_m)$ occur in P then

$$sp.\mathcal{U}.P \equiv \exists \underline{y} \, sp.\mathcal{U}'.(P \wedge x_1 = f(\underline{y}^1_{(k)}) \wedge \ldots \wedge x_m = f(\underline{y}^m_{(k)})) \qquad \textbf{VAR3}$$

where $\mathcal{U}' = \{[\![s_i, \underline{y}^{(m)}_i]\!]_{i \in [1,k]}, S_2, \ldots, S_n\}$ and $\underline{y}$ is the sequence $\underline{y}^1_{(k)}, \ldots, \underline{y}^m_{(k)}$ of fresh variables.

The following three rules may be applied only to **type 3** formulas.

- If there is a set $S \in \mathcal{U}$ that contains a structured term then

$$sp.\mathcal{U}.P \equiv FALSE \qquad \qquad \textbf{MIS3}$$

- If x occurs in $\mathcal{U}$ and neither $ground(x)$ nor $\neg ground(x)$ occurs in P then

$$sp.\mathcal{U}.P \equiv sp.\mathcal{U}.(P \wedge ground(x)) \vee sp.\mathcal{U}.(P \wedge \neg ground(x)) \qquad \qquad \textbf{GR1}$$

- If $\mathcal{U} = \{[\![\underline{x}_{(m)}]\!], S_2, \ldots, S_n\}$ and $ground(x_m)$ occurs in P then

$$sp.\mathcal{U}.P \equiv \exists \underline{x}', z_{\underline{x}}, y_{\underline{x}} \ sp.\mathcal{U}'.R \qquad \qquad \textbf{GR2}$$

where $\mathcal{U}' = \{S_2, \ldots, S_n\}$,
$\underline{x} = \langle x \in vars(P) \mid P \Rightarrow share(x, x_i) \text{ for some } i \in [1, m-1]\rangle$, $\underline{x}' = \underline{x}\rho$ is a variant of $\underline{x}$ disjoint from P, $z_{\underline{x}}$ and $y_{\underline{x}}$ are the sequences of fresh variables z_x and y_x with $x \in \underline{x}$, $P' = P^{\underline{x}}_{\underline{x}'}$ and R is the predicate

$$\bigwedge_{x \in \underline{x}} (inst(x\rho, z_x, y_x, x) \bigwedge_{i \mid P \Rightarrow share(x, x_i)} invar(z_x, x_i) \bigwedge_{y \in vars(P)} \neg share(z_x, y))$$
$$\wedge P' \wedge x_1 = \ldots = x_m.$$

To a formula in **reduced form** we can apply the following rule.

- If $sp.\mathcal{U}.P$ is in reduced form, where $\mathcal{U} = \{[\![\underline{x}^1_{(m_1)}]\!], \ldots, [\![\underline{x}^n_{(m_n)}]\!]\}$, then

$$sp.\mathcal{U}.P \equiv \exists \underline{x}', z_{\underline{x}}, y_{\underline{x}} \ (R \wedge U) \qquad \qquad \textbf{RF}$$

where U is the predicate $(x^1_1 = \ldots = x^1_{m_1}) \wedge \ldots \wedge (x^n_1 = \ldots = x^n_{m_n})$,
$\underline{x} = \langle x \in vars(P) \mid P \Rightarrow share(x, x^j_i) \text{ for some } i \in [1, m_j], j \in [1, n]\rangle$, $\underline{x}' = \underline{x}\rho$ is a variant of $\underline{x}$ disjoint from P, $z_{\underline{x}}$ and $y_{\underline{x}}$ are the sequences of fresh variables z_x and y_x with $x \in \underline{x}$, $P' = P^{\underline{x}}_{\underline{x}'}$ and $R = (\bigwedge_{x \in \underline{x}} inst(x\rho, z_x, y_x, x) \wedge P')$.

The previous rules are natural abstractions of the relative unification step except rules **MIS3, VAR2, GR2** and **RF**. Rule **MIS3** relies on the condition that the formula is of type 3 and $\mathcal{U}$ contains at least a set with a structured element. In this case it can be proven that $\mathcal{U}$ has no unifier.

Rules **VAR2, GR2** and **RF** take into account how sharing among variables can propagate the bindings produced by the considered transformation and how the transformations affect the truth of the non-monotonic atoms. To keep track of the way the predicate is modified suitable variables are renamed with fresh variables existentially quantified and suitable predicates are introduced to specify the link among the original variables and the renamed ones.

All the rules are syntactic. Thus the set of rules provides a (nondeterministic) algorithm. We will see in the following section that this algorithm terminates and computes $sp.\mathcal{U}.P$. We conclude this section with some examples.

Let $P = free(x, y)$ and $\mathcal{U} = \{[\![f(x), y]\!], [\![g(y), x]\!]\}$. Since $sp.\mathcal{U}.P$ is of **type 3**, then by rule **MIS3** it is equivalent to $FALSE$. In fact an occur check does occur.

Let $P = (free(x,y) \land \neg share(x,y))$ and $\mathcal{U} = \{[\![f(y),x]\!]\}$. Since $sp.\mathcal{U}.P$ is of **type 2**, then we can apply rule **VAR2**. We obtain
$$\exists x'(sp.\{[\![f(y)]\!]\}.(P_{x'}^x \land inst(x',\langle x'\rangle,\langle f(y)\rangle,x) \land x = f(y))).$$
By rules **SI** and **RF** we obtain
$$\exists x'(P_{x'}^x \land inst(x',\langle x'\rangle,\langle f(y)\rangle,x) \land x = f(y)),$$
which is equivalent to $(free(y) \land x = f(y))$.

Let $P = (ground(y) \land \neg var(x) \land \neg ground(x) \land \neg share(x,y))$ and $\mathcal{U} = \{[\![x,y]\!]\}$. Since $sp.\mathcal{U}.P$ is of **type 3**, then we can apply rule **GR2**. We obtain
$$\exists x', z_x, y_x(sp.\{\ \}.$$
$$(P_{x'}^x \land inst(x', z_x, y_x, x) \land invar(z_x, z_x) \land \neg share(z_x, x) \land \neg share(z_x, y) \land x = y)).$$
By rule **RF** we obtain
$$\exists x', z_x, y_x(P_{x'}^x \land inst(x', z_x, y_x, x) \land invar(z_x, z_x) \land$$
$$\neg share(z_x, x) \land \neg share(z_x, y) \land x = y)$$
which is equivalent to $(ground(y) \land \neg var(y) \land y = x)$.

Let $P = (\neg var(x,y) \land \neg ground(x,y) \land share(x,y))$ and $\mathcal{U} = \{[\![x,y]\!]\}$. Since $sp.\mathcal{U}.P$ is in **reduced form**, then we can apply rule **RF**. We obtain
$$\exists x', y', z_x, y_x, z_y, y_y(P_{x',y'}^{x,y} \land inst(x', z_x, y_x, x) \land$$
$$inst(x', z_x, y_x, y) \land inst(y', z_y, y_y, y) \land x = y)),$$
which is equivalent to $(x = y \land \neg var(x,y))$, if CON contains at least a function of arity greater than one and a constant; otherwise it is equivalent to $(x = y \land \neg var(x,y) \land \neg ground(x,y))$.

4 Soundness and Completeness of the Calculus

We indicate by $\mathcal{H}_{sp}$ the set of rules but **RF**. We first show that all the rules are equivalences. Then we show that a formula $sp.\mathcal{U}.P$ can be reduced in a finite number of steps to a disjunction of formulas in reduced form, by applying rules from $\mathcal{H}_{sp}$. Finally rule **RF** applied to each disjunct will give the desired predicate (of $\mathcal{A}$) relative to $sp.\mathcal{U}.P$.

Theorem 4.1 *All rules are equivalences (with respect to Definition 2.1)*

Proof. The proof is not difficult except for rules **MIS3**, **VAR2**, **GR2** and **RF** which have a quite technical proof.

MIS3 By hypothesis the formula is of type 3 and $\mathcal{U}$ contains at least a set with a structured element. Then by condition (vii) each set that contains a structured element $f(y_1, \ldots, y_k)$ also contains at least a variable x that occurs in the structured element of another set. In such a situation we can eventually extract from $\mathcal{U}$ a subset $\{S_1, \ldots, S_t\}$ of sets such that

$$S_1 = [\![f_1(\ldots, x_t, \ldots), x_1, \ldots]\!]$$
$$S_2 = [\![f_2(\ldots, x_1, \ldots), x_2, \ldots]\!]$$

$$\cdots$$
$$S_t = \llbracket f_t(\ldots, x_{t-1}, \ldots), x_t, \ldots \rrbracket.$$
Clearly $\{S_1, \ldots, S_t\}\alpha$ has no unifier.

In the next proofs we use the following properties of most general unifiers:
1) Let $\mathcal{U} = \{\llbracket t_{(m)} \rrbracket, S_2, \ldots S_n\}$. If $\beta \in mgu(\{\llbracket t_{(i)} \rrbracket\})$ and $\mu \in mgu(\mathcal{U}\beta)$ then $\mu \cup \mu' \in mgu(\mathcal{U})$, where $\mu' = (\beta\mu)_{|dom(\beta)}$.
2) $mgu(\{\llbracket t \rrbracket, S_2, \ldots S_n\}) = mgu(\{S_2, \ldots S_n\})$.

VAR2 Let α be such that $P\alpha$ is true and let $\mu \in mgu(\mathcal{U}\alpha)$. Let α' be such that

$$x\alpha' = \begin{cases} t\alpha & \text{if } x = x_m, \\ z\alpha & \text{if } x = z\rho, \\ (x\alpha)_{t\alpha}^{x_m\alpha} & \text{otherwise.} \end{cases}$$

Let A' be an atom in P'. Then $A' = A_{z'}^{z}$ with A atom in P. If A' is monotonic then $A'\alpha'$ is an instance of $A\alpha$. Otherwise $A'\alpha' = A\alpha$. Thus in both cases $A'\alpha'$ is true. From $t\alpha' = t\alpha$ it follows that $inst(z\rho, \langle x_m\rho \rangle, \langle t \rangle, z)\alpha'$ and $(x_m = t)\alpha'$ are both true. Then $R\alpha'$ is true. Now let μ' be s.t. $\mu = \mu' \cup \{x_m\alpha/t\alpha\mu'\}$. Then from $\mathcal{U}'\alpha' = (\mathcal{U}\alpha)_{t\alpha}^{x_m\alpha}$ it follows by property 1) that $\mu' \in mgu(\mathcal{U}'\alpha')$. Thus $(sp.\mathcal{U}'.R)\alpha'\mu'$ is true and, since $x\alpha\mu = x\alpha'\mu'$ for all x in P, then $(\exists \underline{z}' \ sp.\mathcal{U}'.R)\alpha\mu$ is true.
Viceversa let α' be such that $R\alpha'$ is true and let $\mu' \in mgu(\mathcal{U}'\alpha')$. Let α be such that

$$x\alpha = \begin{cases} x\rho\alpha' & \text{if } x \text{ in } \underline{z}, \\ x\alpha' & \text{otherwise.} \end{cases}$$

Then $P\alpha = P'\alpha'$ is true. Let $\mu = \mu' \cup \{x_m\alpha/t\alpha\mu'\}$. By $inst(z\rho, \langle x_m\rho \rangle, \langle t \rangle, z)\alpha'$ true for all z in $\underline{z}$ it follows that $\mathcal{U}'\alpha' = (\mathcal{U}\alpha)_{t\alpha}^{x_m\alpha}$. Then by property 1) $\mu \in mgu(\mathcal{U}\alpha)$. Thus $(sp.\mathcal{U}.P)\alpha\mu$ is true and, since $x_m\alpha'\mu' = t\alpha'\mu' = t\alpha\mu' = x_m\alpha\mu$, then $(sp.\mathcal{U}.P)\alpha'\mu'$ is true.

GR2 Let α and μ be such that $P\alpha$ is true and $\mu \in mgu(\mathcal{U}\alpha)$, let $\mu_i = \mu_{|vars(x_i\alpha)}$. From $ground(x_m)\alpha$ true it follows that $x_i\alpha\mu = x_m\alpha$ for $i \in [1, m-1]$. Let α' be s.t.

$$w\alpha' = \begin{cases} x\alpha & \text{if } w = x\rho \text{ with } x \text{ in } \underline{x}, \\ x_m\alpha & \text{if } w = x_i \text{ for } i \in [1, m_1], \\ y^1 \ldots y^{m-1} & \text{if } w = z_x \text{ with } x \text{ in } \underline{x}, \\ (y^1 \ldots y^{m-1})\mu & \text{if } w = y_x \text{ with } x \text{ in } \underline{x}, \\ (w\alpha)\mu_1 \ldots \mu_{m-1} & \text{otherwise.} \end{cases}$$

where y^i is the sequence of variables in $vars(x\alpha) \cap vars(x_i\alpha)$ for $i \in [1, m-1]$. Let A' be an atom of P'. Then $A' = A_{\underline{x}'}^{\underline{x}}$ with A atom in P. If A' is monotonic then $A'\alpha'$ is an instance of $A\alpha$. If A' is non-monotonic then $A'\alpha' = A\alpha$. In both cases $A'\alpha'$ is true. Moreover $(x_1 = \ldots = x_m)\alpha'$ is true because $x_m\alpha' = x_m\alpha = x_i\alpha'$ for all $i \in [1, m-1]$, $\neg share(z_x, x)\alpha'$ is true because all variables in $z_x\alpha'$ occur in $x_i\alpha$ for some $i \in [1, m-1]$ and $x\alpha'$ is obtained replacing the variables in all $x_i\alpha$ with ground terms, $inst(x\rho, z_x, y_x, x)\alpha'$ is true because $x\rho\alpha' = x\alpha$, $x\alpha' = (x\alpha)^{z_x\alpha'}_{y_x\alpha'}$ and $\neg share(z_x, x)\alpha'$ true imply $\{z_x\alpha'/y_x\alpha'\} \in mgu(\{[\![x\rho\alpha', x\alpha']\!]\})$; finally $invar(z_x, \langle z_{x_1}, \ldots, z_{x_{m-1}}\rangle)\alpha'$ is true by construction. Thus $R\alpha'$ is true. Now let $\mu' = \mu_{|vars(\mathcal{U}'\alpha')}$. We have that $\mu_1 \ldots \mu_{m-1}$ is in $mgu(\{[\![x_1, \ldots, x_m]\!]\}\alpha)$, $range(\mu_1 \ldots \mu_{m-1}) = \emptyset$ because $x_m\alpha$ is ground, $\mathcal{U}'\alpha' = \mathcal{U}'\alpha\mu_1 \ldots \mu_{m-1}$. Then $\mu = \mu' \cup \mu_1 \ldots \mu_{m-1}$ and by properties 1) and 2) μ' is in $mgu(\mathcal{U}'\alpha')$. Then $(sp.\mathcal{U}'.R)\alpha'\mu'$ is true and, since $x\alpha'\mu' = x\alpha\mu$ for all x occurring in P, then $(\exists \underline{x}, z_{\underline{x}}, y_{\underline{x}}\ sp.\mathcal{U}.R)\alpha\mu$ is true. Viceversa let α' be such that $R\alpha'$ is true and let $\mu' \in mgu(\mathcal{U}'\alpha')$. Let α be s.t.

$$x\alpha = \begin{cases} x\rho\alpha' & \text{if } x \text{ in } \underline{x}, \\ x\alpha' & \text{otherwise.} \end{cases}$$

Then $P\alpha = P'\alpha'$ is true. Let $\mu = \mu' \cup \beta$ with $\beta = \{(z_{x_i}\alpha'/y_{x_i}\alpha')_{i\in[1,m-1]}\}$. From $inst(x\rho, z_x, y_x, x)\alpha'$, $\neg share(z_{x_j}, x)\alpha'$ and $invar(z_x, \langle z_{x_1}, \ldots, z_{x_{m-1}}\rangle)\alpha'$ true it follows that $x\alpha' = x\alpha\beta$ for all $x \in \underline{x}$. If $x \notin \underline{x}$ then from $\neg share(z_y, x)\alpha'$ true for all y it follows that $x\alpha' = (x\alpha')\beta = x\alpha\beta$. Then $x\alpha' = x\alpha\beta$ for all x occurring in P. Then $\mathcal{U}'\alpha' = \mathcal{U}'\alpha\beta$. From $x_1\alpha' = \ldots = x_m\alpha'$ true, $x_m\alpha'$ ground and $inst(x_i\rho, z_{x_i}, y_{x_i}, x_i)\alpha'$ true for all $i \in [1, m-1]$ it follows that $\beta \in mgu(\{[\![x_1, \ldots, x_m]\!]\}\alpha)$. Then by properties 1) and 2) it follows that $\mu \in mgu(\mathcal{U}\alpha)$. Thus $(sp.\mathcal{U}.P)\alpha\mu$ is true and, since $x\alpha'\mu' = (x\alpha)\beta\mu' = x\alpha\mu$ for all x occurring in P, then $(sp.\mathcal{U}.P)\alpha'\mu'$ is true.

RF Let α and μ be such that $P\alpha$ is true, $\mu \in mgu(\mathcal{U}\alpha)$. Let α' be s.t.

$$w\alpha' = \begin{cases} x\alpha & \text{if } w = x\rho \text{ with } x \text{ in } \underline{x}, \\ w\alpha\mu & \text{if } w \text{ occurs in } P, \\ \underline{y} & \text{if } w = z_x \text{ with } x \text{ in } \underline{x}, \\ \underline{y}\mu & \text{if } w = y_x \text{ with } x \text{ in } \underline{x}. \end{cases}$$

where $\underline{y}$ is the sequence of variables occurring in $dom(\mu_{|vars(x\alpha)})$. Now $U\alpha'$ is true because $x_i^j\alpha' = x_i^j\alpha\mu$ for every $i \in [1, m_j]$, $j \in [1, n]$. Let A' be an atom of P'. Then $A' = A^x_{x'}$ with A atom in P. If A' is monotonic then $A'\alpha'$ is an instance of $A\alpha$. If A' is non-monotonic then $A'\alpha' = A\alpha$. In both cases $A'\alpha'$ is true. Moreover $inst(x\rho, z_x, y_x, x)\alpha'$ is true because $x\rho\alpha' = x\alpha$, $x\alpha' = x\alpha\mu$ and the substitution relative to the two sequences $z_x\alpha'$ and $y_x\alpha'$ is equal to $\mu_{|vars(x\alpha)}$. Since μ is idempotent by hypothesis, then $\mu_{|vars(x\alpha)} \in mgu(\{[\![x\alpha, x\alpha\mu]\!]\})$. Then $(R \wedge U)\alpha'$ is true and, since $x\alpha' = x\alpha\mu$ for every x occurring in P, then $(\exists \underline{x}', z_{\underline{x}}, y_{\underline{x}}(R \wedge U))\alpha\mu$ is true. Viceversa let α' be s.t. $(R \wedge U)\alpha'$ is true. Let α be s.t.

$$x\alpha = \begin{cases} x\rho\alpha' & \text{if } x \text{ in } \underline{x}, \\ x\alpha' & \text{otherwise.} \end{cases}$$

Then $P\alpha = P'\alpha'$ is true. Let μ be the substitution relative to the sequences $z_{x_i^j}\alpha'$, $y_{x_i^j}\alpha'$ for all $i \in [1, m_j]$, $j \in [1, n]$. Then $\mu \in mgu(\mathcal{U}\alpha)$. Thus $(sp.\mathcal{U}.P)\alpha\mu$

is true and, since $x\alpha\mu = x\rho\alpha'\mu = x\alpha'$ for every x that occurs in P, then $(sp.\mathcal{U}.P)\alpha'$ is true. □

Theorem 4.2 *The system $\mathcal{H}_{sp}$ is terminating.*

Proof. (Sketch)

We show that no proof tree built using $\mathcal{H}_{sp}$ has an infinite branch. Rules **F**, **MIS1**, **MIS2** and **MIS3** have a predicate as right hand side, so they cannot belong to an infinite branch. To prove that only finitely many applications of the remaining rules are allowed, consider the tuple

$$\tau = (leq, comp, funct, elem, disj, unvar, unshare, unground)$$

of natural numbers with the lexicographic order. A structured term $f(t_1, \ldots, t_n)$ will be called *compound* if either some t_i is not a variable or the variables $t_1, \ldots, t_n$ are not distinct. Then leq denotes the number of variables in $\mathcal{U}$ that occur as left hand side of an equation in P, $comp$ denotes the number of occurences of compound subterms of terms in $\mathcal{U}$, $funct$ denotes the number of occurences of functor symbols in $\mathcal{U}$, $elem$ denotes the total number of elements in the sets of $\mathcal{U}$, $disj$ denotes the number of disjuncts in the disjunctive normal form of P, $unvar$ denotes the number of variables x in P such that neither $P \Rightarrow var(x)$ nor $P \Rightarrow \neg var(x)$ holds, $unshare$ denotes the number of variables x in P such that neither $P \Rightarrow share(x, y)$ nor $P \Rightarrow \neg share(x, y)$ holds for some variable y distinct by x, $unground$ denotes the number of variables x in P such that neither $P \Rightarrow ground(x)$ nor $P \Rightarrow \neg ground(x)$ holds.

It is not difficult to check that the application of every rule of $\mathcal{H}_{sp}$ decreases the value of τ. □

Corollary 4.3 *Rules of $\mathcal{H}_{sp}$ transform $sp.\mathcal{U}.P$ in a (semantically unique) disjunction of formulas in reduced form.*

Proof. (Sketch)

By Theorem 4.1 all transformations are equivalences (w.r.t. Definition 2.1). By Theorem 4.2 there is a final form. Thus the final form is semantically unique. By contraposition it is not difficult to show that if the final form is not a disjunction of formulas in reduced form then one of the rules in $\mathcal{H}_{sp}$ may be applied. □

5 Applications

Predicate transformers are related to the core of abstract interpretation of imperative programs. In [2] predicate transformers are used to define deductive semantics. Deductive semantics is used to design approximate program analysis frameworks. To propose a similar approach in the setting of logic programming we need the correspondent of program point for a logic program. In [7] Nilsson introduced a scheme for inferring run-time properties of logic programs based on a semantic description of logic programs that uses the concept of program point. The predicate transformer sp can be easily cast in such a theory. A clause of a logic program $\mathcal{P}$ is interpreted as a sequence of procedure calls. To each call A there corresponds a *calling point* $_{\bullet}A$ and a *success point* $A_{\bullet}$. The leftmost and rightmost points in the body of a clause C are called respectively *entry-* and *exit points* of the clause and are indicated respectively by $_{\bullet}C$ and $C_{\bullet}$. Goals are represented as elements of the set $Cgoals := (\mathcal{P}oints \times \mathcal{E}nv)^{*}$, where $\mathcal{P}oints$ denotes the set of program points of $\mathcal{P}$ and $\mathcal{E}nv$ is the set of predicates $\mathcal{A}$. A transition system for $\mathcal{P}$ can be defined through two state transition schemes that transform elements of $Cgoals$ as follows.

$$\langle C_{\bullet}; R\rangle :: y \models y,$$

$$\langle _{\bullet}A; R\rangle :: y \models (\langle _{\bullet}C; TRUE\rangle :: \langle A_{\bullet}; R\rangle :: y)(T\sigma^{-1}),$$

where A is a body atom, $C\sigma$ is a variant of a clause C of $\mathcal{P}$ s.t. $vars(\langle _{\bullet}A; R\rangle ::$ $y) \cap vars(C\sigma) = \emptyset$, $T \equiv sp.\{[A, head(C\sigma)]\}.(R \wedge free(vars(C\sigma))) \not\equiv FALSE$. We assume that the program clauses are disjoint and that the definition of $\mathcal{U}$ in sp is generalized in the obvious way to atoms or terms. The application of a predicate R to a C-goal is defined as follows:
$(nil)R = R$,
$(\langle x; T\rangle :: y)R = \langle x; T \bullet R\rangle :: yR$,
where $T \bullet R$ is (equivalent to) $T' \wedge R$, with T' the strongest assertion (w.r.t. implication) s.t. $T \rightarrow T'$ and $(T' \wedge R) \not\equiv FALSE$. Notice that $T \bullet R$ is defined when R is consistent. For instance if $T = (x = y \wedge var(x))$ and $R = ground(y)$ then $T \bullet R \equiv (x = y \wedge ground(y))$.

The previous transitions schemes are obtained from those in [7] by taking as enviroment $\mathcal{E}nv$ predicates instead of substitutions, by using the predicate transformer sp instead of the mgu as operation in the transition and the operation $\bullet$ to model the application of a predicate to a C−goal.

To each program point i is associated a set Θ_i of states which specifies when the program point becomes current. The set of states is defined as $Cgoals \times Cgoals$, where the first component describes the C-goal that invoked the clause containing point i and the second component is the C-goal when the point is current. The semantics of $\mathcal{P}$ is defined as the least fixpoint of the system of equations relative to its program points. Every program point is either the entry point of a clause or the success point of a body atom. Then it is sufficient to define the meaning of entry- and success points:

$$\Theta_{\bullet C} = \bigcup\nolimits_{A\leadsto C}\{\langle G_i; G_{i+1}\rangle \mid \exists G(\langle G; G_i\rangle \in \Theta_{\bullet A} \wedge G_i \models^C G_{i+1})\},$$

$$\Theta_{A_{\bullet}} = \bigcup\nolimits_{A\leadsto C}\{\langle G; tail(G_j)\rangle \mid \exists G_i(\langle G; G_i\rangle \in \Theta_{\bullet A} \wedge \langle G_i; G_j\rangle \in \Theta_{C_{\bullet}})\}.$$

Example Consider the following simple case of concatenation of two lists:

$C_0 : \leftarrow_1 append([a], [], z)_2$.
$C_1 : append([H|L1], L2, [H|L3]) \leftarrow_3 append(L1, L2, L3)_4$.

$C_2 : \; append([\,], L, L) \leftarrow_5$.

Here the program points are explicitly labelled by integers. The meaning of this program, when $append([a], [\,], z)$ is called with z *free* variable, can be given as least fixpoint of the following set of equations, where we use the notation of [7].

$\Theta_1 = \{\langle nil \; ; \; \langle _\bullet C_0; free(z)\rangle :: nil\rangle\},$
$\Theta_2 = \{\langle G; tail(G_j)\rangle \mid \exists G_i(\langle G; G_i\rangle \in \Theta_1 \wedge (\langle G_i; G_j\rangle \in \Theta_4 \vee \langle G_i; G_j\rangle \in \Theta_5))\},$
$\Theta_3 = \{\langle G_i; G_{i+1}\rangle \mid \exists G((\langle G; G_i\rangle \in \Theta_1 \vee \langle G; G_i\rangle \in \Theta_3) \wedge G_i \models^{C_1} G_{i+1})\},$
$\Theta_4 = \{\langle G; tail(G_j)\rangle \mid \exists G_i(\langle G; G_i\rangle \in \Theta_3 \wedge (\langle G_i; G_j\rangle \in \Theta_4 \vee \langle G_i; G_j\rangle \in \Theta_5))\},$
$\Theta_5 = \{\langle G_i; G_{i+1}\rangle \mid \exists G((\langle G; G_i\rangle \in \Theta_1 \vee \langle G; G_i\rangle \in \Theta_3) \wedge G_i \models^{C_2} G_{i+1})\}.$

Notice that in this case the fixpoint can be computed in finite time since the program terminates. We first calculate Θ_3. We need to compute

$$sp.\{[\![append([a], [\,], z), append([H|L1], L2, [H|L3])]\!]\}.(free(z, H, L1, L2, L3)).$$

By rule **STR1**, rule **VAR2** applied to $L2$ and z, rules **SI**, **STR1** and rule **VAR2** applied to H and $L1$ we obtain the predicate

$$T \equiv (H = a \wedge L1 = [\,] \wedge L2 = [\,] \wedge z = [a|L3] \wedge free(L3)).$$

Since $(free(z) \bullet T) = T$ then $\langle _\bullet C_0; free(z)\rangle :: nil \models^{C_1} \langle _\bullet C_1; T\rangle :: \langle C_{0\bullet}; T\rangle :: nil.$

By rules **STR1** and **MIS1**
$$sp.\{[\![append(L1, L2, L3), append([H'|L1'], L2', [H'|L3'])]\!]\}.$$
$$(free(H', L1', L2', L3') \wedge T)$$
is equivalent to $FALSE$. Hence

$\Theta_3 = \{\langle\langle _\bullet C_0; free(z)\rangle :: nil; \langle _\bullet C_1; T\rangle :: \langle C_{0\bullet}; T\rangle :: nil\rangle\}.$

Consider now Θ_5. We need to compute

$$sp.\{[\![append([\,], L, L), append(L1, L2, L3)]\!]\}.(free(L) \wedge T).$$

By rule **STR1**, rule **EQ** applied to $L1$ and $L2$, rule **SI**, rule **SH2** applied to L and rule **VAR2** applied to L and $L3$ we obtain the predicate

$$R \equiv ((H = a \wedge L1 = L2 = L3 = L = [\,] \wedge z = [a]).$$

Since $T \bullet R = R$ then

$$\langle _\bullet C_1; T\rangle :: \langle C_{0\bullet}; T\rangle :: nil \models^{C_2} \langle _\bullet C_2; R\rangle :: \langle C_{1\bullet}; R\rangle :: \langle C_{0\bullet}; R\rangle :: nil.$$

By rules **STR1** and **MIS1**
$$sp.\{[\![append([a], [\,], z), append([\,], L, L)]\!]\}.(free(L) \wedge T)$$
is equivalent to $FALSE$. Hence

$\Theta_5 = \{\langle\langle _\bullet C_1; T\rangle :: \langle C_{0\bullet}; T\rangle :: nil; \langle _\bullet C_2; R\rangle :: \langle C_{1\bullet}; R\rangle :: \langle C_{0\bullet}; R\rangle :: nil\rangle\}.$

Finally Θ_2 and Θ_4 can be easily calculated.

$$\Theta_2 = \{\langle nil; \langle C_{0\bullet}; R \rangle :: nil \rangle\};$$

$$\Theta_4 = \{\langle \langle_\bullet C_0; free(z) \rangle :: nil; \langle C_{1\bullet}; R \rangle :: \langle C_{0\bullet}; R \rangle :: nil \rangle\}.$$

Every set Θ_i describes the states associated to the program point i. Thus for instance Θ_3 specifies that the program point 3 becomes current only when the goal $append([a], [\ ], z)$ invokes C_1 with z free variable and in such a case H becomes equal to a, $L1$ and $L2$ become equal to the empty list $[\ ]$ and $L3$ remains a free variable.

Acknowledgements This research was supported by "Progetto Finalizzato Sistemi Informatici e Calcolo Parallelo" of CNR under the grant n. 89.00026.69.

References

[1] P. Cousot, R. Cousot. Abstract Interpretation : a Unified Lattice Model for Static Analysis of Programs by Construction or Approximation of Fixpoints. *Proceedings of the 4th ACM Symposium on Principles of Programming Languages*, 238–251, 1977.

[2] P. Cousot, R. Cousot. Systematic Design of Program Analysis Frameworks. *Proceedings of the 6th ACM Symposium on Principles of Programming Languages*, 269–282, 1979.

[3] E. W. Dijkstra. A Discipline of Programming. *Prentice-Hall*, 1976.

[4] E. Eder. Properties of Substitutions and Unifications. *Journal of Symbolic Computation*, 1: 31–46, 1985.

[5] R.W. Floyd. Assigning Meanings to Programs. *Proc. Symp. Appl. Math., American Math. Society, Providence, Rhode Island*, 19: 15–32, 1967.

[6] J-L. Lassez, M.J. Maher, K. Marriott. Unification revisited. *Fundations of Logic and Functional Programming, LNCS 306*, 1987.

[7] Ulf Nilsson. Systematic Semantics Approximations of Logic Programs. *Proceedings of PLILP '90, Springer-Verlag*, 1990.

Programming Languages Issues

Integrating Modes and Subtypes into a Prolog Type-checker

Yann Rouzaud, Lan Nguyen-Phuong
Laboratoire de Génie Informatique
Institut d'Informatique et de Mathématiques Appliquées de Grenoble
BP 53X, 38041 Grenoble Cedex, France
email: rouzaud@imag.imag.fr nguyen-lan@imag.imag.fr

Abstract

We present a declaration-based polymorphic type system with subtypes, designed to help debugging Prolog programs. A key feature is that modes are integrated to types, so predicate declarations may specify input and output types of arguments. Mode information is also necessary to ensure type consistency when subtyping is involved. When all input and output types are identical and complete (without any information about instantiation degree of terms), our system is equivalent to Mycroft-O'Keefe's one. Type-checking works locally on each clause of a program, so it is not expensive. Type-checking is sound: a well-typed program never goes "wrong" (every goal encountered during execution have correct arguments).

1   Introduction

It is evident that static type checking in programming languages allows automatic detection of errors, which makes debugging easier. Type information may also be used by a compiler to produce various optimizations. Therefore many researchers tried to introduce type disciplines in Prolog which is primarily untyped, except for primitive domains like *integers* and predicates such as *is/2*.

Those works are generally classified depending upon two approaches ([7]): a descriptive one, where types describe some semantic properties of programs, and a prescriptive one, where types reflect the programmer's intent (following [12], types are part of specification). [6] qualifies those approaches as respectively liberal (a type is a postcondition) and conservative (a type is a precondition), and considers them as two extremes of a spectrum of "bipartisan types". This point of view is clearly connected to [4], where classical results of Floyd and Hoare about assertion method for imperative languages are adapted to Prolog.

Types may be declared by the users or inferred by the system. Generally, type inference restricts the domain of types, to ensure a decidable calculus ([1], [9]). Especially, overloading and subtyping are generally rejected, so the expressive power is less important than in declarative systems, where type-checking is an easy task. The declarative approach also reinforces documentation about programs.

We follow a *declarative bipartisan approach*: declaration of predicates includes input and output types of arguments. An input type is a precondition for arguments of a goal at calling time, and an output type is a postcondition for answers whenever it succeeds. Note that in contrast to others type systems, a variable may have many type assignments, forming a descending chain of types. Output types are always subtypes of input types.

Programs are statically type-checked, and no run-time checks are necessary. Standard semantic of Prolog is assumed, but a semantic in the spirit of [6], mimicking run-time type-checking, could be defined.

Subtyping is a feature which can lead to unsound type consistency by naively processing type inclusions in predicate calls, without dataflow treatment.

Example 1 Consider the following ill-typed program.

$type$
$tau = a,$
$tau1 = f(tau),$
$tau2 = b|f(tau).$
$profile$
$p(tau1),$
$q(tau2),$
$r(tau1).$
$p(X) :- q(X), \ r(X).$
$q(b).$
$q(f(Z)).$

Here the syntax for type declarations is nearly the same as in the Mycroft-O'Keefe's system [11]. In the clause of $p/1$, X has initially type $tau1$, so it cannot be a valid argument for $q/1$, because we do not know if X denotes an instantiated term. For instance, the resolution of goal $:- p(Y)$ leads to instantiate Y to b after the completion of $q(Y)$. The term denoted by Y has no more type $tau1$, therefore it cannot be an argument of $r/1$.

A polymorphic type system with subtypes has been studied in [3], which requires in addition, for type consistency, dataflow information (input-output instantiation degree, or mode) about arguments of a clause. For example, in the program above, with the following declaration of modes

$mode \ p(out), \ q(out), \ r(in)$

which imply that in the clause $p/1$ there is a dataflow from occurrence of X in $q(X)$ to the one in $p(X)$, so the type of X in $q(X)$ must be included in the type of X in $p(X)$, and the clause is ill-typed. But with

$mode \ p(in), \ q(in), \ r(in)$

the clause is well-typed, and the goal $:- p(Y)$ is rejected.

Knowledge of modes is always necessary to ensure soundness of a type system with subtypes. But we have a different approach to this problem.

We remark in this example that if $p/1$ is always called with an instantiated argument of the form $f(t)$ with t not necessarily ground, the clause can be safely accepted: such a term is always instantiated to a term in $tau1$ by any substitution which instantiates it to a term in $tau2$. So we have in mind to define type $tau1$ by:

$type\ tau1 = +f(tau)$

which contains all terms instantiable to $f(a)$, free variables excepted. With this definition, the clause $p/1$ is well-typed, and the goal $:- p(Y)$ is rejected.

To be able to define such types, unlike other type systems for Prolog, we consider a type as a set of terms which are not necessarily ground. Type inclusion in a predicate call is only accepted when a supplementary condition on instantiation degree of terms holds (this is our order relation $\ll$).

The paper is organised as follows. In Section 2 we present our definition of types which integrates the notion of mode. In Section 3 we describe the type language used in our system. Section 4 defines the order relation $\ll$. Section 5 gives computation rules to deduce types for subterms of a term and an important lemma about unification. In Section 6 the notion of well-typing of a program is defined and illustrated by examples. The Theorem of type consistency of well-typed programs is given in section 7, and further work is described in the last section. Detailed proofs can be found in [13].

Throughout that paper, $Term$ denotes the set of terms, Var the set of variables, $vars(t)$ the set of variables occurring in a term t, and Σ the set of substitutions over terms. A term t is said to be more general than a term t' ($t \leq t'$), if $\exists \sigma \in \Sigma$, $\sigma t = t'$.

2   Types

Definition 1 *Let E be a set of terms.*

- $prod(E) = \{t \in E \mid \exists t'\ ground\ \in E, t \leq t'\}$

  $prod(E)$ *is the set of productive terms of E*

- $gen(E) = \{t \in Term \mid \exists t' \in E, t \leq t'\}$

  $gen(E)$ *is the set of more general terms of E*

Definition 2 (Tuple-distributivity) *Let $t[(t'_1, \ldots, t'_n)/(t_1, \ldots, t_n)]$ be the replacement by $(t'_1, \ldots, t'_n)$ of a n-tuple $(t_1, \ldots, t_n)$ occurring in a term t. A set of terms E is* tuple-distributive *if:*

$prod(\cup\{D_{t,t'} \mid t, t' \in E,\ t' = t[(t'_1, \ldots, t'_n)/(t_1, \ldots, t_n)]\}) \subseteq E,$
$where\ D_{t,t'} = \{t[(t''_1, \ldots, t''_n)/(t_1, \ldots, t_n)] \mid t''_i = t_i\ or\ t''_i = t'_i\}.$

Definition 3 (Type definition) *A set of terms E is a* type *if:*

- *E is closed under renaming substitutions:* $\forall t \in E$, $\forall t' \in Term$, *if* $t \leq t'$ *and* $t' \leq t$, *then* $t' \in E$.

- *E is continuous:* $\forall t_1, t_2 \in E$, $\forall t \in Term$, $t_1 \leq t \leq t_2 \Rightarrow t \in E$.

- *E is productive:* $prod(E) = E$

- *E is tuple-distributive.*

If a type τ contains a term $f(t_1, \ldots, t_n)$, f/n is said to be a *main functor* of τ. Types closed under *gen* are called *complete types*, other ones are called *instantiated types*. For instance, $\tau_1 = \{f(X) \mid X \in Var\} \cup \{a, f(b)\}$ is an instantiated type, and $\tau_2 = \tau_1 \cup Var$ is a complete type. Note that an instantiated type contains only terms whose main functor is known.

Closedness under renaming substitutions is evidently a necessary property, because resolution uses variants of clauses.

Continuity is necessary to prove Unification Lemma (section 5), so it ensures type consistency during program execution.

Productivity is related to Herbrand models ([8]): it ensures that every term in a type can represent a ground term. Note that Var is not a type.

Tuple-distributivity is an extension of a classical definition ([10], [15]) to non ground terms, preserving productivity. It is a necessary condition for Decomposition Lemma (this section).

Definition 4 *Let* $\tau_1, \ldots, \tau_n$ *be types, and* f/n *a n-ary functor. The following sets are types:*

- $\tau_1 \& \tau_2 = prod(\tau_1 \cap \tau_2)$, $\&\{\tau_i \mid i \in I\} = prod(\cap_{i \in I}\tau_i\}$

  (greatest type included in intersection of types)

- $+f(\tau_1, \ldots, \tau_n) = prod(\{f(t_1, \ldots, t_n) \mid t_i \in \tau_i\})$

- $f(\tau_1, \ldots, \tau_n) = gen(+f(\tau_1, \ldots, \tau_n))$

The following property is a direct consequence of definitions. It allows us to denote a type as an enumeration of subtypes having distinct main functors.

Property 1 *Let* $\tau_1, \tau_1', \ldots, \tau_n, \tau_n'$ *be types, and* f/n, f'/n' *distinct functors.*

- $f(\tau_1, \ldots, \tau_n) \cup f'(\tau_1', \ldots, \tau_n')$ *is a type.*

- $+f(\tau_1, \ldots, \tau_n) \cup +f'(\tau_1', \ldots, \tau_n')$ *is a type.*

Lemma 1 (Decomposition Lemma) *Let* τ *be a type, and* f/n *a main functor of* τ. *There are exactly one set of terms E and n types* $\tau_1, \ldots, \tau_n$ *such that* $\tau = +f(\tau_1, \ldots, \tau_n) \cup E$, *and no term in E has main functor* f/n.

3 The Type Language

The Type Language is based on regular trees ([10]), with a syntax close to [11]. In this article type names and functor names are assumed to belong to disjoint sets, so we may omit irrelevant details of the implemented language. Type names are not essential because type equivalence is structural.

Example 2
> $type$
> $\quad tau1 = a \mid b,$
> $\quad tau2 = a \mid f(tau1) \mid g(c,d),$
> $\quad tau3 = + a \mid f(tau1) \mid g(+c,d),$
> $\quad list(T) = [\,] \mid [T \mid list(T)],$
> $\quad inlist(T) = + [\,] \mid [T \mid inlist(T)].$
> $profile$
> $\quad p(tau2 \rightarrow tau3),$
> $\quad q(tau1),$
> $\quad append(inlist(T), inlist(T), \rightarrow inlist(T)).$

A type is defined by an enumeration of components ("|" is disjoint union), optionally preceded by a sign "+". An unsigned enumeration denotes a complete type, a signed enumeration denotes an instantiated type ("+" applies to every component). To ensure tuple distributivity, main functors of components must be distinct.

By using definition 4, we obtain:
> $tau1 = Var \cup \{a,b\},$
> $tau2 = Var \cup \{a\} \cup \{f(t) \mid t \in Var \cup \{a,b\}\}$
> $\qquad\quad \cup \{g(t,t') \mid t \in Var \cup \{c\}, t' \in Var \cup \{d\}, t \neq t'\}$
> $tau3 = \{a\} \cup \{f(t) \mid t \in Var \cup \{a,b\}\} \cup \{g(t,t') \mid t \in \{c\}, t' \in Var \cup \{d\}\}$

$list(T)$ and $inlist(T)$ are *polymorphic types*, which as usual are interpreted as functions on types. For example,
> $inlist(a|b) = \{[t_1, \ldots, t_n] \mid n \geq 0, t_i \in Var \cup \{a,b\}\}$

A component of a polymorphic type may be a type variable, which is called an *inclusive parameter*. For instance: $type\ tree(T) = +[\,] \mid [T \mid inlist(T)] \mid T$.

Because components are disjoint sets, an inclusive parameter has a restricted domain: $tree(T)$ is defined for all T containing neither $[\,]$ nor $[\_|\_]$ (T represents types which are not lists).

A profile $p(\tau_1 \rightarrow \tau_1', \ldots, \tau_n \rightarrow \tau_n')$ for a predicate p/n defines input and output types for each argument. A necessary condition is that $\tau_i' \ll \tau_i$ (see next section). Note that a predicate may have several profiles. We allow the following supplementary notations for type arguments:

- τ means $\tau \to \tau$,

- $\to \tau$ means $gen(\tau) \to \tau$

A polymorphic profile defines a set of profiles, for all type variables instantiated into their domains (as if type variables were universally quantified). So the profile $append(inlist(T), inlist(T), \to inlist(T))$ means that arguments of predicate $append/3$ (standard list concatenation) must be lists of some type T. List functors of first two arguments must be known at calling time, and those of third argument will be known when the goal succeeds. Note that list elements need not to be instantiated, so the following goal is well-typed:
$:- append([a, X, b], [Y], [Z|U])$

4 Type relation $\ll$

Definition 5 *Let τ_1 and τ_2 be types. $\tau_1 \ll \tau_2$ (τ_1 is* more instantiated *than τ_2), iff $\tau_1 \subseteq \tau_2$, and $\forall t \in \tau_1$, $\forall \sigma \in \Sigma$, $\sigma t \in \tau_2 \Rightarrow \sigma t \in \tau_1$.*

For instance, let $\tau = f(a|b, a|b)$, $\tau' = +f(a|b, b)$ and $\tau'' = +f(a|b, +b)$. $\tau' \not\ll \tau$, because $\{X/a\}f(a, X) = f(a, a) \notin \tau$. But $\tau'' \ll \tau$.

An interesting consequence of the definition is that if a term t is in type $\tau' \ll \tau$, then a call $p(t)$ of a predicate p, which always instantiates its argument into τ ($p(\tau)$ is well-typed), necessarily instantiates t into τ'.

To characterize relation $\ll$, we need classical notion of occurrences (or positions) of subterms of a term as sequences of natural numbers. For instance, variable X has positions 1.1 and 2.2 in term $f(g(X, Y), h(Z, X))$.

Definition 6 *Let τ be a type, and $t \in gen(\tau)$. The type position u of a subterm t' of t, written $p(\tau, t, u)$, is defined by structural induction on t:*

- $p(\tau, t, \epsilon) = \tau$ *if $t \in Var$*

- $p(+f(\tau_1, \ldots, \tau_n) \cup E, f(t_1, \ldots, t_n), \epsilon) = +f(\tau_1, \ldots, \tau_n)$

- $p(+f(\tau_1, \ldots, \tau_n) \cup E, f(t_1, \ldots, t_n), i.u) = p(\tau_i, t_i, u)$

Lemma 2 *Let τ_1 and τ_2 be types. $\tau_1 \ll \tau_2$ iff $\tau_1 \subseteq \tau_2$ and $\forall t \in \tau_1$, $\forall x \in vars(t)$, $\forall u$ position of V in t, $p(\tau_1, t, u) = p(\tau_2, t, u)$.*

In the example above, let $t = f(a, X) \in \tau'$, then $p(\tau', t, 2) = a$, and $p(\tau, t, 2) = a|b$, so $p(\tau', t, 2) \neq p(\tau, t, 2)$, and $\tau' \not\ll \tau$.

5 Unification Lemma

Definition 7 *Let τ a type and t a term $\in gen(\tau)$.*

- $d(\tau, t)$, type deduction *from τ on t, is a relation between variables and types, defined by:*

  $d(\tau, t) = \{x : p(\tau, t, u) \mid x \in vars(t), u \text{ position of } x \text{ in } t\}.$

- $\forall x \in vars(t), d(\tau, t, x) = \{\tau \mid x : \tau \in d(\tau, t)\}.$

- $d(\tau, t)$ *is* functional *if $\forall x \in vars(t), d(\tau, t, x)$ is a singleton.*

- $d(\tau, t)$ *is* functional with respect to $\ll$, *if $\forall x \in vars(t), \exists \tau_m \in d(\tau, t, x)$ such that $\forall \tau_x \in d(\tau, t, x), \tau_m \ll \tau_x$.*

For instance, let $\tau = +f(+a, \ a|b, \ a|c)$ and $t = f(X, X, X)$:

$d(\tau, t) = \{X : +a, \ X : a|b, \ X : a|c\},$

$d(\tau, t, X) = \{+a, \ a|b, \ a|c\},$

$\tau_m = +a = \&d(\tau, t, X),$

$d(\tau, t)$ is functional with respect to $\ll$, but it is not functional.

$d(\tau, t)$ is functional means that all occurrences of the same variable in t have the same type. Let us call a term $t \in \tau$ with $d(\tau, t)$ functional, a *safe term* of τ.

$d(\tau, t)$ is functional with respect to $\ll$ means that the set of deduced types for any variable has a least element. Note that in this case, $\forall x \in vars(t)$, $\&d(\tau, t, x) = \tau_m$.

In clauses, an effective argument having type τ is generally represented by a more general term $t \in gen(\tau)$. Let us call a term $t \in gen(\tau)$ with $d(\tau, t)$ functional with respect to $\ll$, a *safe representative* of τ.

It follows that, for any types τ, τ_1, τ_2:

- $\forall t \in gen(\tau), \ \forall x \in vars(t), \ \&d(\tau, t, x) \neq \emptyset,$

- $\forall t \in gen(\tau), \ t \in \tau$ iff $\forall x \in vars(t), \ \&d(\tau, t, x)$ is complete.

- If $t \in \tau_1$ and $\tau_1 \ll \tau_2$, then $d(\tau_1, t) = d(\tau_2, t)$.

Note that a type is not necessarily closed under unification. For instance, if $\tau = +f(a, a|b)$, then $t = f(X, X) \in \tau$ and $t' = f(Y, b) \in \tau$, but the unification $t = t'$ gives $f(b, b) \notin \tau$. This problem is due to variable aliasing. The following results give sufficient conditions for preserving the type of a term by substitution and unification.

Lemma 3 *Let τ a type, $t \in gen(\tau)$, $\sigma \in \Sigma$ such that $\forall x \in vars(t)$, $\sigma x \in gen(\&d(\tau, t, x))$, and $D = \bigcup_{x \in vars(t)}\{d(\tau_x, \sigma x) \mid \tau_x \in d(\tau, t, x)\}$.*

- *If $\forall x' \in \sigma t$, $\&\{\tau \mid x' : \tau \in D\} \neq \emptyset$, then $\sigma t \in gen(\tau)$.*

- *If $\forall x \in t$, $\sigma x \in \&d(\tau, t, x)$, and D is functional, then $\sigma t \in \tau$.*

Lemma 4 (Unification Lemma) *Let τ be a type, and t, t' terms such that:*

- $t \in gen(\tau)$, $t' \in \tau$

- $d(\tau, t)$ *is functional with respect to $\ll$, $d(\tau, t')$ is functional*

- $\forall x \in vars(t) \cap vars(t')$, $\&d(\tau, t, x) = \tau_x$, *where* $\{\tau_x\} = d(\tau, t', x)$

- t *and* t' *are unifiable by a most general unifier θ.*

Then $\theta t = \theta t' \in \tau$, and $d(\tau, \theta t)$ is functional.

This lemma has been proved by induction on the Robinson's Unification algorithm (see [8]).

Conditions of lemma mean that t is a safe representative of τ and t' is a safe term of τ. Note the dissymmetry between conditions about t and t' : in next sections, t' will occur in a goal and t in the head of a clause. Unification Lemma ensures that θt is a safe term of τ.

For instance, let $t = f(X, X)$, $t' = f(a, Y)$, $\tau = f(+a, a|b)$: then $d(\tau, t) = \{X : +a, X : a|b\}$ is functional with respect to $\ll$, and $d(\tau, t') = \{Y : a|b\}$, so the lemma conditions hold, and indeed $\theta t = \theta t' = f(a, a) \in \tau$.

6   Well-typing of a program

Let us use the following notations:

- $\bar{t}$ denotes a n-tuple $(t_1, \ldots, t_n)$,

- $p\bar{t}$ denotes a n-ary predicate p apllied to a n-tuple $\bar{t} = (t_1, \ldots, t_n)$,

- $d(\bar{\tau}, \bar{t})$, where $\bar{\tau} = (\tau_1, \ldots, \tau_n)$, $\bar{t} = (t_1, \ldots, t_n)$ denotes type deduction on tuples, defined by: $d(\bar{\tau}, \bar{t}) = \cup_i d(\tau_i, t_i)$.

Definition 8 *Let P be a Prolog program, Pred the set of its predicates. P is called Π-typed if a set Π is given, and $\forall p \in Pred$, $\exists p^{\bar{\tau} \to \bar{\tau}'} \in \Pi$, where $\Pi = \{p^{\bar{\tau} \to \bar{\tau}'} \mid p$ n-ary predicate, $\bar{\tau} = (\tau_1, \ldots, \tau_n)$, $\bar{\tau}' = (\tau_1', \ldots, \tau_n'), \bar{\tau}' \ll \bar{\tau}\}$*

$p^{\bar{\tau} \to \bar{\tau}'}$ is called a profile of predicate p, $\bar{\tau}$ is the input type, $\bar{\tau}'$ is the output type of p arguments, τ_i and τ_i' correspond to ith argument.

Definition 9 *A Π-typed clause of P is in the form:*

$$p_0\bar{t}_0^{\;\bar{\tau}_0\to\bar{\tau}'_0} :- \; p_1\bar{t}_1^{\;\bar{\tau}_1\to\bar{\tau}'_1}, \; \ldots, \; p_n\bar{t}_n^{\;\bar{\tau}_n\to\bar{\tau}'_n}$$

where $p_0\bar{t}_0 :- \; p_1\bar{t}_1, \; \ldots, \; p_n\bar{t}_n$ is a clause of P and $p_i^{\;\bar{\tau}_i\to\bar{\tau}'_i} \in \Pi$, $0 \le i \le n$.

Definition 10 *A clause (C) $p_0\bar{t}_0 :- \; p_1\bar{t}_1, \; \ldots, \; p_n\bar{t}_n$ of a Π-typed program P is Π-well-typed, if $\forall p_0^{\;\bar{\tau}_0\to\bar{\tau}'_0} \in \Pi$, $\exists p_i^{\;\bar{\tau}_i\to\bar{\tau}'_i} \in \Pi$, $1 \le i \le n$, such that in the obtained Π-typed clause $p_0\bar{t}_0^{\;\bar{\tau}_0\to\bar{\tau}'_0} :- \; p_1\bar{t}_1^{\;\bar{\tau}_1\to\bar{\tau}'_1}, \; \ldots, \; p_n\bar{t}_n^{\;\bar{\tau}_n\to\bar{\tau}'_n}$ the following conditions hold:*

- $\bar{t}_i \in gen(\bar{\tau}'_i)$, $0 \le i \le n$,

  $d(\bar{\tau}_0, \bar{t}_0)$ *is functional with respect to* $\ll$,

  $\forall x \in Var$, $m = \min\{j \mid x \in vars(\bar{t}_j)\}$ *and* $m \ne 0 \Rightarrow d(\bar{\tau}_m, \bar{t}_m, x)$ *is functional and its element is a complete type*

- *Let* $A_0 = \{x : \&d(\bar{\tau}_m, \bar{t}_m, x) \mid m = \min\{j \mid V \in vars(\bar{t}_j)\}\}$,

  $A_i = \{x : A_{i-1}(x) \; \& \; (\&d(\bar{\tau}'_i, \bar{t}_i, x))\}$, $1 \le i \le n$

  Then $\forall x \in vars(\bar{t}_i)$, $1 \le i \le n$, $\forall \tau_x \in d(\bar{\tau}_i, \bar{t}_i, x)$, $A_{i-1}(x) \ll \tau_x$

  $\forall x \in vars(\bar{t}_0)$, $\forall \tau_x \in d(\bar{\tau}'_0, \bar{t}_0, x)$, $A_n(x) \ll \tau_x$

In this definition, each A_i denotes the types of clause variables after the completion of subgoal $p_i\bar{t}_i$. In A_0, each variable has a type deduced from input type of its first occurrence . Note that variables occurring only in the clause body have an initial complete type. After each subgoal, new types for variables are defined by intersecting their previous types and their outputs types (based on output type of that subgoal). Note that $\forall x \in vars(C)$, $A_{i-1}(x) \ll A_i(x), 1 \le i \le n$.

Definition 11

- *A goal $p\bar{t}$ is Π-well-typed, if there is a profile $p^{\bar{\tau}\to\bar{\tau}'} \in \Pi$ such that $\bar{t}$ is a safe term of $\bar{\tau}$.*

- *A Π-typed program is well-typed, if its goal is Π-well-typed, and for all profiles $p^{\bar{\tau}\to\bar{\tau}'}$, all clauses of p are Π-well-typed.*

Example 3

> *type $inlist(T) = + \; [\,] \mid [T \mid inlist(T)]$.*
> *profile*
>   *$append(inlist(T), \; inlist(T), \; \to inlist(T))$,*
>   *$reverse(inlist(T), \; \to inlist(T))$.*
> *$append([\,], \; L, \; L)$.*
> *$append([A \mid L], \; M, \; [A \mid N]) :- \; append(L, \; M, \; N)$.*
> *$reverse([\,], \; [\,])$.*
> *$reverse([A \mid L], \; R) :- \; reverse(L, \; R1), \; append(R1, \; [A], \; R)$.*

All these clauses are well-typed. Consider, for instance, second clause of $append/3$. For the two occurrences of A in the clause head, deduced types are T and $gen(T)$. But $T \ll gen(T)$, so the types of head variables are
$$A_0 = \{A : T,\ L : inlist(T),\ M : inlist(T),\ N : gen(inlist(T))\}.$$
These types satisfy the input condition for the body call : $inlist(T) \ll inlist(T')$, $gen(inlist(T)) \ll gen(inlist(T'))$, with $T' = T$. After the body execution, N has type: $gen(inlist(T))\&inlist(T))$, which is $inlist(T)$, so
$$A_1 = \{A : T,\ L : inlist(T),\ M : inlist(T),\ N : inlist(T)\}$$
Second clause of $reverse/2$ gives the following computation of variable types:
$$A_0 = \{A : T,\ L : inlist(T),\ R : gen(inlist(T)),\ R1 : gen(inlist(T))\}$$
$$A_1 = \{A : T,\ L : inlist(T),\ R : gen(inlist(T)),\ R1 : inlist(T)\}$$
$$A_2 = \{A : T,\ L : inlist(T),\ R : inlist(T),\ R1 : gen(inlist(T))\}.$$

Example 4 Consider the following declarations and first clause of a predicate $diff/3$ which specifies the symbolic differentiation of arithmetic expressions ([3]):

> $type$
> $\quad symbol = x \mid y \mid z,$
> $\quad exp = symbol \mid integer \mid add(exp, exp).$
> $profile\ diff(exp,\ +symbol,\ exp).$
> $diff(X,\ X,\ 1).$

This clause, rejected by the system of Mycroft-O'Keefe, is well-typed in our system, because deduced types for X are $+symbol$ and exp, and $+symbol \ll exp$, so $A_0 = \{X : +symbol\}$ and then the output condition of the predicate is satisfied. The query :- $diff(x + y, X, 1)$ will be rejected by the type checker, because the variable X corresponds to the position of the type $+symbol$ which must be instantiated, so the goal is ill-typed.

Example 5 the following program is ill-typed:

> $type$
> $\quad tau1 = a,$
> $\quad tau2 = a \mid b.$
> $profile$
> $\quad p(tau1,\ tau2),$
> $\quad q(tau1,\ tau2),$
> $\quad r(tau2),\ s(tau1).$
> $p(X, Y)\ :-\ q(X, Y),\ r(Y),\ s(X).$
> $q(X,\ X).$
> $q(\_,\ b).$
> $r(b).$

One can see that the resolution of the well-typed goal :- $p(X, Y)$ leads to instantiate X to Y in $q(X, Y)$, and then Y to b after $r(Y)$ completion. In consequence, X is instantiated to b which is not in the expected type of $s/1$. This problem comes from second clause of $q/2$ which is indeed ill-typed: neither $tau1 \ll tau2$, nor $tau2 \ll tau1$

7 Type consistency

We have proved the type consistency of a well-typed program by the Inductive Assertion Method for Logic Programs of Drabent and Maluszynski ([4]). The proof is based on the following lemma.

Lemma 5 *Let $p_0\bar{t}$ be a well-typed goal with profile $p^{\bar{\tau}\rightarrow\bar{\tau}'}$, (C) a well-typed clause $p_0\bar{t_0}^{\bar{\tau_0}\rightarrow\bar{\tau}'_0} :- p_1\bar{t_1}^{\bar{\tau_1}\rightarrow\bar{\tau}'_1}, \ldots, p_n\bar{t_n}^{\bar{\tau_n}\rightarrow\bar{\tau}'_n}$, $\rho_0, \rho_1, \ldots, \rho_n$ a valuation sequence for (C) and $p_0\bar{t}$ a goal such that $\rho_0 = mgu(\bar{t_0}, \bar{t})$, $\rho_i = \rho_{i-1}\sigma_i$, where σ_i is the answer substitution of $p_i(\rho_i\bar{t_i})$, $1 \leq i \leq n$.*
If $\rho_{i-1}\bar{t_i}$ is a safe term of $\bar{\tau_i}$ and $\rho_i\bar{t_i}$ is a safe term of $\bar{\tau}'_i$, $1 \leq i \leq k$, then:

- *$\forall x \in vars_k(C)$, $\rho_k x$ is safe term of $A_k(x)$,*

- *$\cup_{x \in vars_k(C)} d(A_k(x), \rho_k x)$ is functional,*

where $vars_k(C) = vars(\bar{t_0}) \cup \ldots \cup vars(\bar{t_k})$.

From this lemma, it follows that in all execution using a well-typed goal $p_0\bar{t}$ with profile $p_0^{\bar{\tau}_0\rightarrow\bar{\tau}'_0}$, a clause $p_0\bar{t_0}^{\bar{\tau_0}\rightarrow\bar{\tau}'_0} :- p_1\bar{t_1}^{\bar{\tau_1}\rightarrow\bar{\tau}'_1}, \ldots, p_n\bar{t_n}^{\bar{\tau_n}\rightarrow\bar{\tau}'_n}$ and a valuation sequence $\rho_0, \rho_1, \ldots, \rho_n$:

- $\rho_0\bar{t_1}$ is a safe term of $\bar{\tau_1}$,

- If $\rho_{i-1}\bar{t_i}$ is a safe term of $\bar{\tau_i}$ and $\rho_i\bar{t_i}$ is a safe term of $\bar{\tau}'_i$, $1 \leq i \leq k$, then $\rho_k\bar{t}_{k+1}$ is a safe term of $\bar{\tau}_{k+1}$,

- If $\rho_{i-1}\bar{t_i}$ is a safe term of $\bar{\tau_i}$ and $\rho_i\bar{t_i}$ is a safe term of $\bar{\tau}'_i$, $1 \leq i \leq n$, then $\rho_n\bar{t_0}$ is a safe term of $\bar{\tau}'_0$.

So by applying assertion method, we obtain the following theorem.

Theorem 1 *For all calls $p\bar{t}$ during the execution of a Π-well-typed program, there is a profile $p^{\bar{\tau}\rightarrow\bar{\tau}'} \in \Pi$ such that $\bar{t}$ is a safe term in $\bar{\tau}$, and, if execution succeds, all answers $\sigma\bar{t}$ are safe terms in $\bar{\tau}'$.*

8 Further work

We have developed a sound type system with modes and subtypes for Prolog. Type checking works locally on each clause, hence it is fast. A prototype has been written in C-Prolog: preliminary results are satisfactory, but further experimentation is necessary to check already written programs. We think that further development could be based on two points : higher order features, and more appropriate processing of aliasing.

Higher order predicates are outside our framework. We can handle explicit calls only. Consider for instance $map/3$. The following program is well typed, and goals like $:-\ map(incr, [2], L)$ and $:-\ map(f, [a|L], [f(X), f(Y), f(Z)])$ are accepted:

   $type\ tau1 = incr,\ tau2 = f.$
   $profile$
      $apply(+tau1, +integer, \rightarrow +integer),$
      $apply(+tau2, T, +f(T)),$
      $map(+tau1, inlist(+integer), \rightarrow inlist(+integer)),$
      $map(+tau2, \rightarrow inlist(T), inlist(+f(T)).$
   $apply(incr, X1, X2) :-\ X2\ is\ X1 + 1.$
   $apply(f, X, f(X)).$
   $map(\_, [], []).$
   $map(P, [X1|L1], [X2|L2]) :-\ apply(P, X1, X2),\ map(P, L1, L2).$

We would like to extend our type language with higher order notations like [5], allowing for instance the following declaration:

   $profile$
      $map(pred(T1 \rightarrow T2),\ inlist(T1), \rightarrow inlist(T2)).$
      $map(pred(T2 \rightarrow T1), \rightarrow inlist(T1),\ inlist(T2)).$

Another problem is negation: negation as failure rule could be used to safely accept "negative profiles" of predicates, like:

   $profile$
      $islist(list(T)|U \rightarrow +list(T)),$
      $not\ islist(list(T)|U \rightarrow +U).$
   $islist([]).$
   $islist([\_|L]) :\ -\ islist(L).$

This extension would require global analysis on all clauses of a predicate. In our implementation, only primitive predicates have a predeclared negative profile, like:

   $profile\ not\ atom(+\ atom|T \rightarrow +T).$

Finally, we would like to handle variable aliasing more appropriately. The following example is rejected by our system:

   $profile\ p(a|b \rightarrow +a), q(a|b \rightarrow +a).$
   $p(X) :-\ X = Y,\ q(Y).$
   $q(a).$

A better processing of variable aliasing would require global analysis ([2]), except in simple cases, like in the example above.

References

[1] Cardelli, L. and Wegner, P. *On understanding Types, Data Abstraction, and Polymorphism*. ACM Computing Survey, Vol. 17(4), Dec. 1985, p. 471-522.

[2] Debray, S. K. and Warren, D. A. *Automatic Mode Inference for Logic Programs*. Journal of Logic Programming, N.5, 1988, p. 207-229.

[3] Dietrich, R. and Hagl., F. *A polymorphic type system with subtypes for Prolog*. Proc. 2nd European Symp. on Programming, LNCS 300, 1988, p. 79-93. See avlso Dietrich., R. *Modes and Types for Prolog*. Arbeitspapiere der GMD Nr. 285, Jan. 1988.

[4] Drabent, W. and Maluszynski, J. *Inductive Assertion Method for Logic Programs*. Proc. TAPSOFT 1987, LNCS 250, 1987, p. 167-181.

[5] Hanus, M. *Horn Clause Programs with Polymorphic Types: Semantics and Resolution*. Proc. TAPSOFT 89, LNCS 352, 1989, p. 225-240.

[6] Jacobs, D. *A pragmatic view of Types in Logic Programs* In Types in Logic Programming, F. Pfenning, editor, MIT Press, 1992, ch. 7, p. 217-228.

[7] Lakshman, T.K. and Reddy, U.S. *Typed Prolog: A Semantic Reconstruction of the Mycroft-O'Keefe Type System*. Proc. International Symposium on Logic Programming, 1991, p. 202-217.

[8] Lloyd, J. W. *Foundations of Logic Programming*. Springer Verlag, Second, Extended Edition, 1987.

[9] Milner, R. *A theory of type polymorphism in programming*. Journal of Computer and System Science, 1978, p. 348-375.

[10] Mishra, P. *Towards a Theory of Types in Prolog*. Proc. Symposium on Logic Programming, 1984, p. 289-298.

[11] Mycroft, A. and O'Keefe, R. A. *A Polymorphic Type System for Prolog*. Artificial Intelligence Vol. 23(3), Aug. 1984, p. 295-307.

[12] Naish, L. *Specification = Program + Types*. Proc. 7th Conference on Foundations of Software Technology and Theoretical Computer Science, 1987, p. 326-339.

[13] Nguyen-Phuong, L. *Un système déclaratif de types pour Prolog*. Doctoral Thesis, to appear, Grenoble, Sept. 1992.

[14] Somogyi, Z. *A system of precise modes for Logic Programs*. Proc. 4th International Conference on Logic Programming, 1987, p. 769-787.

[15] Yardeni, E. and Shapiro, E. *A type system for logic programs*. In Concurrent Prolog Vol. 2, E. Shapiro, editor, MIT Press, 1987, ch. 28, p. 211-244.

Communicating Clauses: towards Synchronous Communication in Contextual Logic Programming

Jean-Marie Jacquet
Department of Computer Science,
University of Namur, Belgium

Luís Monteiro
Departamento de Informática,
Universidade Nova de Lisboa, Portugal

Abstract

Communicating clauses are proposed as an extension to contextual logic programming aiming at specifying the synchronous communication between agents, described here as units. The expressiveness of the extended framework is argued through the coding of producer/consumer schemes and several applications combining the logic and object-oriented styles of programming. Operational and declarative semantics are designed for the new framework. The operational semantics rests on a derivation relation stating how agents can be evaluated under contextual and synchronization constraints. The declarative semantics extend the classical model and fixed point theory to take these constraints into account.

1 Introduction

Recently, contexts have been introduced in logic programming as a means to structure programs and coordinate logical derivations ([14]). To that end, a language has been proposed which supports local definitions of predicates of the kind provided by systems of units, and which supports context-dependency in the form of predicate definitions implicitly supplied by the context. Following the idea that units can also be viewed as a means to describe the behavior of objects, the concept of isa hierarchies has been developed and studied in [15]. We turn in this paper to a further extension of that work concerned with the communication of objects.

Two kinds of communication can essentially be proposed: asynchronous and synchronous. Asynchronous communication has been extensively studied for the design of concurrent logic programming languages: Concurrent Prolog ([17]), Parlog ([8]), GHC ([18]), the cc languages ([16]), ... In those languages, the communication between concurrent reductions is achieved by means of the sharing of variables between several conjoined atoms. Asynchronicity in the communication arises from the introduction of several suspension mechanisms that force the reduction of some subgoals to wait until the reduction of other subgoals has sufficiently instantiated the shared variables. Examples of such mechanisms are Concurrent Prolog read-only annotations, Parlog mode declarations, GHC suspension rules and cc ask primitives. As expected from its essence, asynchronous communication in concurrent logic programming is thus achieved by restricting one partner of the communication. Therefore, the above mechanisms can also be employed in the contextual framework and we will not add to the plethora of already existing features.

In contrast, it is worth noting that synchronous communication has received little attention in the development of concurrent logic languages. In fact, in these languages, there is no other means to tackle synchronous communication than that of coding it by means of auxiliary manager procedures and of asynchronous communication. However, the concept of synchronous communication is certainly interesting enough to provide means to code it directly. Given the object perception of units, this paper builts upon our previous work ([10, 11]) to present a new way of expressing synchronous communication directly and in a modular and distributed fashion. For that purpose, clauses of units are extended to so-called communicating clauses and the resolution principle used in contextual logic programming is extended accordingly. The aim of the paper is to sketch the resulting framework as well as to present and relate operational and declarative semantics for it.

As a snapshot, the communicating clauses allowed in units take the form

$$H \leftarrow G \quad \{H_1 : u_1, \cdots, H_m : u_m\} \tag{1}$$

where H, H_1, ..., H_m are atoms, u_1, ..., u_m are unit names, G is a conjunction of atoms and extension formulae combined with the operators " ; " and " $\|$ " and the { and } brackets denote a multi-set. All atoms may share variables. Compared with classical Horn clauses, the main innovations are thus

   i) the presence of atoms associated with unit names in the head of a clause,
   ii) the possibility of combining atoms and extension formulae with two operators
       to form goals.

These extensions induce an extension of the resolution rules developed in [14]. Basically, the operators " ; " and " $\|$ " are used for sequential and parallel compositions, respectively. The operator " $\diamond$ " is used to specify synchronization in the reductions, possibly involving communication thanks to shared variables. Reducing an atom A by the clause (1), say declared in unit named u, requires

   i) the existence of m clauses (previously renamed to avoid variable clashes)

$$H_1' \leftarrow G_1 \quad \{H' : u, H_2' : u_2, \cdots, H_m' : u_m\} \tag{2}$$

$$\cdots$$

$$H_m'' \leftarrow G_m \quad \{H'' : u, H_1'' : u_1, \cdots, H_{m-1}'' : u_{m-1}\} \tag{3}$$

   in units u_1, ..., u_m, respectively,
   ii) the existence of conjoined atoms A_1, ..., A_m to be reduced with clauses (2),
       ..., (3), respectively,

such that the (m+1)-tuples $< A, A_1, \cdots, A_m >$, $< H, H_1, \cdots, H_m >$, $< H', H_1', \cdots, H_m' >$, $\cdots$, $< H'', H_1'', \cdots, H_m'' >$ unify. In that case, assuming θ is the mgu, the atoms are simultaneously reduced to the goals $G\theta$, $G_1\theta$, ..., $G_m\theta$, respectively.

Though simple, this extension is quite suited for handling synchronous communication in a modular and distributed way. This fact is advocated in section 2. The combination of the contexts and of the extension just introduced is also shown there to be very powerful and well-suited for describing the communication between objects and, therefore, for integrating logic programming and object-oriented programming.

This paper also describes operational and declarative semantics of the extended contextual logic programming framework, precisely of the concurrent language CCL induced by the and-parallelism, the or-parallelism, the contexts and the above operators.

The operational semantics O_d rests on a derivation relation. It describes the derivations in a top-down manner and associates a computed answer substitution with each of them. It thus corresponds to the classical success set and failure set characterizations of programs. It models and-parallelism in a quite close way to real concurrent executions: to allow a goal to progress from one step, it is sufficient that one of its subgoals performs one step, although all of them are allowed to do so. Restated in other terms, in contrast with work such as [4], our modelling of and-parallelism includes the interleaving perception of parallel computations as well as the true concurrent one. For simplicity of the exposition, or-parallelism is not treated in the same way but more implicitly as a choice. Some parallelism is however still captured in the sense that no order is imposed on the way clauses should be selected for reduction.

The two declarative semantics $Decl_m$ and $Decl_f$ are based on model and fixed-point theory, respectively. They generalize the notions of Herbrand interpretation and consequence operator for classical Horn clause logic in order to account for the contextual and conjoined dependency of the truth of formulae. As suggested, an effort has been made to keep these semantics as simple as possible as well as in the main streams of logic programming semantics. However, communicating clauses and synchronized executions raise new problems, for which fresh solutions are proposed.

Communicating clauses have already been presented in similar forms in [1], [2], [3], [5], [6], [10], [11], [12], [13] and [16] in the classical logic programming framework.

As already said, this paper is a continuation of our previous work [10, 11]. In those papers, synchronous communication is expressed in a global and centralized way by extending classical Horn clauses. In contrast, this paper provides a modular and distributed counterpart based on an extension of contextual logic programming. This modularity concern introduces new problems for which fresh solutions are presented in the following sections. Besides the expected syntactic modification of the programs, the resolution principle of [10] and [11] has been extended to account for context handling and for the distribution of synchronous communication requirements. Among others, the notions of eg-goals and aggregation are peculiar to this work. At the declarative level, semantics have faced the compositionality problem caused by synchronization but also the context dependency of truth. It follows non trivial modifications of the notions of Herbrand base and truth and of the immediate consequence operator.

Compared with other related work, the work reported here differs from them both from the language point of view and from the semantic point of view.

From the language point of view, our language differs in three main respects. Firstly, it tackles the distributed context of units. Secondly, it allows *arbitrary* sequential and parallel compositions inside goals as well as an unrestricted form of variable sharing. In contrast with [1], we do not allow a forking primitive to take place in the body of clauses. However, this can be achieved easily in our model through or-parallelism. Thirdly, if the clauses (1), (2), ..., (3) can be viewed as the distributed versions of the common clause

$$H \diamond H_1 \diamond \cdots \diamond H_m \leftarrow G \diamond G_1 \diamond \cdots \diamond G_m$$

our proposal has exactly the same number of heads and bodies. This is fully justified by the fact that the reduction of a head by the corresponding body corresponds to one step of the execution of the process corresponding to the head. It should also be noted that, besides allowing to deal with unrestricted sequential composition and giving distributed expressions of synchronous communication, this requirement does not represent a real limitation as compared to the aforementioned languages. For example, the clauses $A_1 + A_2 \leftarrow A_3$ and $A_1 + A_2 \leftarrow A_3 + A_4 + A_5$ of Rose ([2]) may be rewritten respectively as

$$
\begin{array}{ll}
u_1: & A_1 \leftarrow A_3 \quad \{A_2 : u_2\} \\
u_2: & A_2 \leftarrow \triangle \quad \{A_1 : u_1\}
\end{array}
\quad \text{and} \quad
\begin{array}{ll}
u_1: & A_1 \leftarrow A_3 \quad \{A_2 : u_2\} \\
u_2: & A_2 \leftarrow A_4 \parallel A_5 \quad \{A_1 : u_1\},
\end{array}
$$

with $\triangle$ denoting the empty conjunction of atoms.

Our work also differs from related work at the semantic standpoint. To our best knowledge, semantics for communicating Horn clauses have only been proposed in [1], [2], [6] and [12]. A first difference with them is that contextual logic programming is tackled here. This requires novel extensions, as exposed in [9]. These extensions discarded, our semantics still presents several differences.

The semantics presented in [1] essentially refers to a new logic, called linear logic ([7]). In [2] and [6], the study of the declarative semantics is also conducted in terms of an extension of the Herbrand base containing parallel goals. Those goals, in the absence of a sequential composition operator, are parallel compositions of atomic formulae. By contrast, the extended Herbrand base appropriate to our language must consider parallel compositions of *arbitrary* goals. Another technical difference with our approach is our systematic use of h-structures as an auxiliary tool in the definitions of both the operational and the declarative semantics. The main reason for introducing h-structures was the need to find a concise way to specify the selection of atomic formulae in goals and their replacement by other goals. As can be appreciated from our semantic study, the use of h-structures greatly simplifies the presentation of the semantic concepts of derivability and satisfiability.

The operational semantics O_d differs from that of [2] and [6] by the use of the notion of h-structure. It differs from [12] by the use of a semantical variant of the considered system of units that allows several independent reductions to occur at the same time.

The semantics presented hereafter have been intentionally built non modular for the ease of understanding of the newly introduced concepts. Nevertheless, future research will concentrate on more modular and reactive versions. Also, it will try to generalize this work to tackle constraints as proposed in [16].

The remainder of this paper is organized into 6 sections. Section 2 suggests the interest of communicating clauses through the coding of a (classical) producer/consumer scheme and of several examples integrating the logic and object-oriented styles of programming. Section 3 describes the basic constructs of the language and explains our terminology. Section 4 defines the auxiliary concepts of extended g-goal, t-context and unit completion. Section 5 presents the operational semantics O_d. Section 6 discusses the declarative models Decl_m and Decl_f and connects them with the operational semantics O_d. Finally, section 7 sums up the relationships established in the paper and gives our conclusions.

2 Examples

2.1 Producer-consumer schemes

As a first example of the expressiveness power of communicating clauses, let us simulate, by using them, the following producer prod and consumer cons, behaving successively as follows:

i) execute some internal actions, say int_prod(M,X) and int_cons(Y), respectively; the former producing some message M;

ii) communicate synchronously the message M and treat it;

iii) apply some (undefined) resumption actions, say prod_res(M,U) and cons_res(M,V), respectively.

As suggested in section 1, prod and cons are coded in two separate units, say of name u_prod and u_cons, and the synchronization requirement is specified in a distributed way in two communicating clauses. Precisely, the program is as follows:[1]

u_prod :   prod ← int_prod(M,X) ; pexch(M)

            pexch(M) ← prod_res(M,U)   {cexch(M):u_cons}

u_cons :   cons ← int_cons(Y) ; cexch(M)

            cexch(M) ← cons_res(M,V)   {pexch(M):u_prod}

Activated by the query u_prod ≫ prod ‖ u_cons ≫ cons, it indeed reflects the behavior of the prod and cons agents [2] .

The reader will appreciate the ease of coding in this example, as opposed to that obtained by using the asynchronous communication of usual concurrent logic programming languages. It is also worth noting that it is, of course, possible to refine the above basic scheme in several ways. For instance, one could add extra arguments to the predicates and complicate the definition of the predicates prod_res and cons_res at will.

2.2 Describing objects

The previous subsection has focussed on the communication between agents. We now turn to the description of the agents or more generally objects by means of communicating clauses. In doing so, it is, in fact, shown that such clauses can also be used as a means towards the integration of logic and object-oriented programming.

The behavior of objects is classically represented in logic programming by the evaluation of a call to a procedure defined recursively, the successive values of the arguments representing the successive states of the object. Following this line, the treatment of a message mess(M) by an object obj(S) by means of a method method(M) can be schematized by the following clause: [3]

      obj(S) ← method(M,S,NewS) ; obj(NewS)   {mess(M):_}.

---

[1] Although any Horn clause $H ← B$ can be rewritten in an equivalent form $H ← B\ \emptyset$, we will stick, for the time being, to the classical Horn clause notation and reserve the communicating form for clauses involving a non-empty multi-set of communicating atoms in their head.

[2] See [14] for more information about the contextual reduction.

[3] The notation _ is used as syntactic sugar to denote any unit of the program. Hence, the clause is actually a shorthand notation of the set of clauses obtained by replacing _ by each unit name of the program.

In that framework, the object conceptually moves from the state S to the new state NewS.

As a counterpart, the units describing the producers of the message mess(M) have, for each object obj(S), declared in the unit u_obj, to which the message mess(M) is adressed, a clause of the kind

mess(M) {obj(S):u_obj}   or   mess(M) ← mess(M)   {obj(S):u_obj}

according as the message is consumed or not.

An instance of this scheme is given by the following description[4] of the class of stacks:

stack(Id,S) ← stack(Id,[X|S])   {push(Id,X):_}
stack(Id,[X|S]) ← stack(Id,S)   {pop(Id,X):_}
stack(Id,[X|S]) ← stack(Id,[X|S])   {top(Id,X):_}

Stacks are identified there by the Id argument of the stack predicate and their state, implemented as a list, moves respectively from S, [X|S], [X|S] to [X|S], S, [X|S] according as a push, pop or top message is received.

The classical airline reservation system provides another interesting instance of the above scheme. The task consists here of simulating an airline reservation system composed of n agencies communicating with a global database about m flights. Using communicating clauses, this can be achieved by evaluating the query

u_ag ≫ agency(Id1) || ⋯ || u_ag ≫ agency(Idn) || u_db ≫ air_syst(DB_init)

where agency(Idj) represents the jth agency, identified by Idj, where DB_init represents the initial information about the m flights and where u_ag and u_db are the names of the units describing the agencies and the database, respectively. The complete description of the agencies by the unit u_ag is out of the scope of this paper. For our illustrative purposes, it is sufficient to assume that some internal actions successively generate queries for the database and behave correctly according to the answers. We will consider two kinds of messages: reserve(Flight_id,Nb_seats,Ans) and ask_seats(Flight_id,Free_seats). Their goals are respectively

  i) to ask for the reservation of Nb_seats in the flight Flight_id, which yields the answer Ans;
  ii) to ask the number of free seats in the flight Flight_id.

According   to   the   above   scheme   and   using   the auxiliary predicates make_reservation and free_seats, with obvious meanings, the treatment of these messages can be coded in u_db as follows.

air_syst(DB) ←
    make_reservation(Flight_id,Nb_seats,DB,New_DB) ; air_syst(New_DB)
        {reserve(Flight_id,Nb_seats,Ans):_}
air_syst(DB) ←
    free_seats(Flight_id,Free_seats) ; air_syst(DB)
        {ask_seats(Flight_id,Free_seats):_}

The following points are worth noting. First, accessing the database is achieved without handling lists of messages explicitly and without using merge processes, as

---

[4]This description has actually been inspired by that of [3].

usual in concurrent logic programming languages. Second, mutual exclusive access to the database is ensured by the synchronous mechanism. In that, our solution also contrasts with the classical concurrent logic one which involves commitment and merge processes.

3 The language

As usual in logic programming, the language CCL comprises denumerably infinite sets of *variables*, *functions* and *predicates*, subsequently referred to as *Svar*, *Sfunct* and *Spred*, respectively. It also includes a set *Sunit* of so-called *unit names*, characterized by the property that every element u has attached a finite subset of predicates, called the *sort* of u and denoted by *sort(u)*. The sets Svar, Sfunct, Spred and Sunit are assumed to be pairwise disjoint.

The notions of term, atom, substitution, ... are defined as usual. Their sets are subsequently referred to as *Sterm*, *Satom*, *Ssubst*, ..., respectively. We do not recall these notions here but rather specify some contextual related notions as well as some useful notations.

An *extension formula* is a formula of the form $u \gg G$ where u is a unit name and G is a finite conjunction of atomic or extension formulae, combined with the operators " ; " and " || ". A *general atom* (*g-atom*) is an atomic or an extension formula. It is typically denoted by the letters A, B, C, ... A *general goal* (*g-goal*) is a finite conjunction of g-atoms, combined with the operators " ; " and " || ". It is typically denoted by the letter G possibly subsecripted. The empty g-goal is denoted by the $\triangle$ letter. The set of general goals is referred to as Sggoal. Clauses take, from now on, the communicating form $H \leftarrow G$ $\{H_1 : u_1, \cdots, H_m : u_m\}$, where the u_i's are unit names and where the $\{$ and $\}$ brackets define a (possibly empty) multi-set. Given an atom $A = p(t_1, \ldots, t_m)$, we denote by *name(A)* the predicate name of A, namely p. A set of clauses is said to *define* a predicate p if it contains a clause whose head's name is p.

A *unit* is a formula of the form $u : U$, where $u \in Sunit$ and U is a finite set of clauses such that the set of predicates defined in U is sort(u). We call u the *name* or *head* of the unit and U its *body*. A *system of units* is a set $\mathcal{U}$ of units such that no two distinct units in $\mathcal{U}$ have the same name. For a unit in $\mathcal{U}$ with name u, we denote its body by $|u|_{\mathcal{U}}$, or simply $|u|$ if $\mathcal{U}$ is understood. In the sequel, we will often abuse language and refer to u as a unit in $\mathcal{U}$ when in fact we mean the unit $u : |u|$. The set of systems of units is subsequently referred to as *Ssyst*.

A *context* is a stack of unit names. It is referred to by its name, consisting of an arbitrary sequence of unit names. The set of context names, *Scontext*, is thus the free monoid $Sunit^{<\omega}$. Context names are represented by juxtaposition, as in uv. The empty sequence λ is employed as the name of the *empty* context. The context resulting from *extending* the context c with unit u (i.e. by putting u on top of the stack) is denoted by u.c.

4 Auxiliary concepts

4.1 Extended g-goals

As sketched in sections 1 and 2, the reduction of parallel compound goals involves the parallel reductions of the subcomponents, each of which in the scope of a possibly different context. The concepts of extended g-atoms and g-goals are introduced to grasp this association of goals and contexts.

Definition 1 *Extended g-atoms (or eg-atoms, for short) are constructs of the form $A \lhd c$ where A is a g-atom and c is a context. Extended g-goals (or eg-goal, for short) are conjunctions of eg-atoms composed with the operators " ; " and " $\|$ ". They are typically denoted by the letter $\widetilde{G}$ possibly subscripted and their set is subsequently referred to by Segoal. The empty eg-goal is denoted by the $\triangle_e$ symbol. Finally, we will abuse language and write, for any g-goals G_1, G_2 and context c,*

$$G_1 \; ; \; G_2 \lhd c \text{ and } G_1 \parallel G_2 \lhd c$$

to actually denote the constructs obtained by associating c with each g-atom of G_1 and G_2. ∎

4.2 The h-structures

Forcing atoms to synchronize introduces a need for a means to express which atoms in a general goal are allowed to synchronize and for a means to create the goals resulting from the synchronized reductions. These means are provided by the notion of h-structure. Basically, a h-structure consists of a partially ordered structure where the place holder $\square$ has been inserted in some top-level places i.e. places not constrained by the previous execution of other atoms. Atoms that can synchronize are then those that can be substituted by a place holder $\square$ in a h-structure. Furthermore, the general goals resulting from the synchronized reductions are obtained by substituting the place holder by the corresponding bodies of the communicating clauses under use. As suggested by the previous subsection, atoms have to be associated with some context during the reductions. We will consequently define h-structures with respect to eg-goals rather than g-goals.

The precise definition of the h-structures is as follows.

Definition 2 *The h-structures are the functions inductively defined on the eg-goals by the following rules.*

i) *Every eg-goal is a nullary h-structure and defines the constant mapping from $Segoal^0$ to Segoal with the eg-goal as value.*

ii) *$\square$ is a unary h-structure that maps any eg-goal to itself. For any eg-goal $\widetilde{G}$, this application is subsequently denoted by $\square[\widetilde{G}]$.*

iii) *If hs is an n-ary h-structure and if $\widetilde{G}$ is an eg-goal, then $(hs \; ; \; \widetilde{G})$ is an n-ary h-structure. Its application is defined as follows : for any eg-goals $\widetilde{G}_1$, $\ldots$, $\widetilde{G}_n$, $(hs \; ; \; \widetilde{G})[\widetilde{G}_1, \cdots, \widetilde{G}_n] = (hs[\widetilde{G}_1, \cdots, \widetilde{G}_n]) \; ; \; \widetilde{G}$*

iv) *If hs_1 and hs_2 are m-ary and n-ary h-structures and if $n + m > 0$, then $hs_1 \parallel hs_2$ is an (m+n)-ary h-structure. Its application is defined as follows : for any eg-goals $\widetilde{G}_1$, $\ldots$, $\widetilde{G}_{m+n}$,*

$$(hs_1 \parallel hs_2)[\widetilde{G}_1, \cdots, \widetilde{G}_{m+n}] = (hs_1[\widetilde{G}_1, \cdots, \widetilde{G}_m]) \parallel (hs_2[\widetilde{G}_{m+1}, \cdots, \widetilde{G}_{m+n}])$$

In the above rules, we further state that the structure $(Segoal, ; , \parallel , \triangle)$ is a bimonoid. Moreover, in the following, we will simplify the eg-goals resulting from the application of h-structures accordingly. ∎

4.3 Unit aggregation

Reducing g-atoms synchronously involves combining communicating clauses in some way. To avoid repeating this task explicitly each time a reduction is performed, we now associate with any m-tuple of units u_1, ..., u_m, a new construct called the *aggregation* of u_1, ..., u_m, that performs this task once for all. It essentially consists of constructing centralized versions of the information distributed in the communicating clauses. On the way, we take profit of this centralized structure to group several independent clauses into one expressing the simultaneous reduction of independent conjoined atoms.

Definition 3 *For any unit names u_1, ..., u_m, the* aggregation *of u_1, ..., u_m, noted $agg(u_1, \cdots, u_m)$, is defined as the following program:*

i) *if $\{\nu_1, \cdots, \nu_p\} \subseteq \{1, \cdots, m\}$ and if*

$$H^i_{\nu_i} \leftarrow G_{\nu_i} \quad \{H^i_{\nu_1} : u_{\nu_1}, \cdots, H^i_{\nu_{i-1}} : u_{\nu_{i-1}}, H^i_{\nu_{i+1}} : u_{\nu_{i+1}}, H^i_{\nu_p} : u_{\nu_p}\},$$

$i = 1, \cdots, p$, *are clauses of the units u_{ν_1}, ..., u_{ν_p}, renamed to avoid variable clashes, and such that the m-tuples $< H^1_{\nu_1}, \cdots, H^1_{\nu_p} >$, $\cdots$, $< H^p_{\nu_1}, \cdots, H^p_{\nu_p} >$ unify, say with mgu θ, then*

$$H^1_{\nu_1}\theta : u_{\nu_1} \diamond \cdots \diamond H^p_{\nu_p}\theta : u_{\nu_p} \leftarrow G_{\nu_1} \diamond \cdots \diamond G_{\nu_p}$$

is a clause of $agg(u_1, \cdots, u_m)$;

ii) *if $\{\mu_1, \cdots, \mu_r, \nu_1, \cdots, \nu_s\} \subseteq \{1, \cdots, m\}$, if $(L_{\mu_1} : u_{\mu_1} \diamond \cdots \diamond L_{\mu_r} : u_{\mu_r} \leftarrow A_{\mu_1} \diamond \cdots \diamond A_{\mu_r})$ and $(M_{\nu_1} : u_{\nu_1} \diamond \cdots \diamond M_{\nu_r} : u_{\nu_s} \leftarrow B_{\nu_1} \diamond \cdots \diamond B_{\nu_s})$ are clauses of $agg(u_1, \cdots, u_m)$, previously renamed to avoid variable clashes, then*

$$L_{\mu_1} : u_{\mu_1} \diamond \cdots \diamond L_{\mu_r} : u_{\mu_r} \diamond M_{\nu_1} : u_{\nu_1} \diamond \cdots \diamond M_{\nu_r} : u_{\nu_s}$$
$$\leftarrow A_{\mu_1} \diamond \cdots \diamond A_{\mu_r} \diamond B_{\nu_1} \diamond \cdots \diamond B_{\nu_s}$$

is a clause of $agg(u_1, \cdots, u_m)$;

iii) *if $\{\nu_1, \cdots, \nu_q\} \subseteq \{1, \cdots, m\}$, if $\{\mu_1, \ldots, \mu_q\}$ is a permutation of $\{\nu_1, \ldots, \nu_q\}$, and if $(H_{\nu_1} : u_{\nu_1} \diamond \cdots \diamond H_{\nu_q} : u_{\nu_q} \leftarrow G_{\nu_1} \diamond \cdots \diamond G_{\nu_q})$ is a clause of $agg(u_1, \cdots, u_m)$, then $(H_{\mu_1} : u_{\mu_1} \diamond \cdots \diamond H_{\mu_q} : u_{\nu_q} \leftarrow G_{\mu_1} \diamond \cdots \diamond G_{\mu_q})$ is a clause of $agg(u_1, \cdots, u_m)$.*

If u_1, ..., u_m are the units of the system $\mathcal{U}$, then $agg(u_1, \cdots, u_m)$ is also rewritten as $agg(\mathcal{U})$. Furthermore, for any unit u, the general aggregation $gagg(u)$ of u is the union of all the aggregations $agg(u_1, \cdots, u_m)$ formed from all tuples of units $u_1, \cdots, u_m$. ∎

5 Operational semantics

A first semantics of CCL may be expressed operationally in terms of a derivation relation, written as $P \vdash \widetilde{G}$ *with* θ that, basically, expresses the property that, given the system of units S, the eg-goal $\widetilde{G}$ has a successful derivation producing the substitution θ. It is defined by means of rules of the form

$$\frac{Assumptions}{Conclusion} \quad if \ Conditions,$$

asserting the Conclusion whenever the Assumptions and Conditions hold. Note that Assumptions and Conditions may be absent from some rules. Precisely, the derivation relation is defined as the smallest relation of $Ssyst \times Segoal \times Ssubst$ satisfying the following rules (N-O) to (E-O). As usual, the above notation is used instead of the relational one with the aim of suggestivity.

Definition 4 (The derivation relation)

$$(N\text{-}O) \qquad \overline{S \vdash \triangle_e \; with \; \epsilon}$$

$$(E\text{-}O) \qquad \frac{S \; \vdash \; hs[G \triangleleft u.c] \; with \; \sigma}{S \; \vdash \; hs[u \gg G \triangleleft c] \; with \; \sigma}$$

$$(X\text{-}0) \qquad \frac{S \; \vdash \; hs[A \triangleleft c] \; with \; \sigma}{S \; \vdash \; hs[A \triangleleft u.c] \; with \; \sigma} \qquad if \quad name(A) \notin sort(u)$$

$$(S\text{-}0) \qquad \frac{S \; \vdash \; hs[G_1 \triangleleft u_1.c_1, \ldots, G_m \triangleleft u_m.c_m] \; with \; \sigma}{S \; \vdash \; hs[A_1 \triangleleft u_1.c_1, \ldots, A_m \triangleleft u_m.c_m] \; with \; \theta\sigma}$$

$$if \quad \left\{ \begin{array}{l} (H_1 : u_1 \diamond \cdots \diamond H_m : u_m \; \leftarrow \; G_1 \diamond \cdots \diamond G_m) \in agg(u_1, \cdots, u_m)^5 \\ < A_1, \cdots, A_m > \; and \; < H_1, \cdots, H_m > \; unify \; with \; mgu \; \theta \end{array} \right.$$

∎

The first three rules essentially rephrase the contextual rules. Rule (N-O) states that the empty conjunction is derivable with the empty substitution in any context. Rule (E-O) explains the context extension: an extension formula is derivable in a context if the 'inner' conjunction is derivable in the context extended with the unit mentioned in the extension formula. Rule (X-O) characterizes the meaning of the contextual definition: an atom is derivable in the context whose top unit does not define the atom's predicate name if the atom is derivable in the context with the top unit removed.

The last rule (S-O) specifies the synchronous reductions. Note that, thanks to the definition of $agg(u_1, \cdots, u_m)$, this rule covers both

  i) the usual reduction of an atom by means of a Horn clause,
 ii) the simultaneous reduction of independent atoms by means of independent clauses,
iii) the real synchronous reductions by means of communicating clauses.

In all these four rules, the conciseness and the expressiveness of the h-structures are also worth noting. Thanks to them, it is not necessary to specify rules for the sequential and parallel composition of goals. Rather, those cases are treated together with the synchronous reduction case in the only rule (S-O). Moreover, atoms and extension formulae are selected for reduction in a uniform manner.

An operational semantics can be derived therefrom as follows.

Definition 5 (Operational semantics) *Define the operational semantics* O_d : $Ssyst \to Scontext \to Sggoal \to \mathcal{P}(Ssubst)$ *as the following function: for any* $S \in Ssyst$, $c \in Scontext$ *and* $G \in Sggoal$, $O_d(S)(c)(G) = \{\theta : S \vdash G \triangleleft c \; with \; \theta\}$.

∎

---

[5] As usual, a suitable renaming of the clauses is assumed.

6 Declarative semantics

6.1 Model theory

One of the distinctive features of a logic programming language is that its semantics can be understood in two complementary ways, inherited from logic. The operational semantics, based on proof theory, describes the method for executing programs. The declarative semantics, based on model theory, explains the meaning of programs in terms of the set of their logical consequences. Any claim to the effect that a given language is a logic programming language must be substantiated by providing suitable logic-based semantic characterizations. The operational semantics of the language CCL under consideration in this paper has been studied in the previous section. The present section is devoted to the discussion of the declarative semantics. We assume given a system of units $\mathcal{U}$ and describe its semantics in terms of the aggregation $\mathrm{agg}(\mathcal{U})$.

Two problems must in fact be faced in order to provide suitable declarative semantics: the impact of the synchronous character of some reductions and the impact of the contextual nature of the reductions.

On the one hand, one might at first think that the usual notion of (Herbrand) interpretation for Horn clause logic carries through the synchronous communication extension. Thus an interpretation would be a set of ground atomic formulae, with the intended meaning that the formulae in the set are true under the interpretation. The truth of compound formulae would then be derived in a compositional manner. The problem with this is that the parallel composition is not a propositional operation in that its truth or falsity can not be derived from that of its arguments. More precisely, if both arguments are true then their parallel composition is also true, but if one or both are false then the parallel composition may be true or false. For example, A and B are false both for the empty program and for the program consisting of the two units

$$u: \quad A \leftarrow \triangle \quad \{B:v\} \qquad\qquad v: \quad B \leftarrow \triangle \quad \{A:u\} \quad .$$

However, $u \gg A \parallel v \gg B$ is false for the first program and true for the second one.

Note that the sequential composition is not affected by a similar problem. Indeed, a sequential composition of goals is true if and only if the component goals are true, so that declaratively the sequential composition is just the logical conjunction. In any case we can not hope to be able to specify which formulae are true by giving only the true atomic formulae. We are thus led to consider an extended Herbrand base containing parallel compositions of ground goals as our interpretations.

On the other hand, because of the context extension, the truth depends on the considered contexts. Furthermore, different parts of a goal may refer to distinct contexts, so the extended Herbrand base will in fact be described in terms of ground extended goals.

The following notions sum up the required extensions and combine them in a suitable way.

Definition 6 *The extended Herbrand base EB is the set of all ground extended atoms $A \triangleleft c$ together with all parallel compositions $\widetilde{G}_1 \parallel \widetilde{G}_2$ of nonempty ground extended goals $\widetilde{G}_1$ and $\widetilde{G}_2$. (Note that extension formulae do not enter into the composition of such extended goals because they are not required to be general.) An interpretation is a subset I of EB.* ∎

Definition 7 *Given a ground eg-goal $\widetilde{G}$, its truth in I, written $\models_I \widetilde{G}$, is defined inductively by the following rules:*

   i) $\models_I \triangle \triangleleft c$, *for every context c.*

   ii) If $\widetilde{G}$ and $\widetilde{H}$ are ground eg-goals, $\models_I (\widetilde{G} \, ; \widetilde{H})$ if $\models_I \widetilde{G}$ and $\models_I \widetilde{H}$.

   iii) If $\widetilde{G}$ and $\widetilde{H}$ are ground eg-goals, $\models_I (\widetilde{G} \parallel \widetilde{H})$ if either $(\widetilde{G} \parallel \widetilde{H}) \in I$ or $\models_I \widetilde{G}$ and $\models_I \widetilde{H}$

   iv) $\models_I u \gg G \triangleleft c$ *if* $\models_I G \triangleleft u.c$

   v) If $\widetilde{A}$ is a ground extended atom, $\models_I \widetilde{A}$ if $\widetilde{A} \in I$. ■

We may now define the truth of an arbitrary formula in an interpretation.

Definition 8 *Given a formula F, its truth in I, written $\models_I F$, is defined inductively by the following rules.*

   i) If F is a clause or a general goal, $\models_I F$ if $\models_I F_0$ for every ground instance F_0 of F.

   ii) For a ground clause, $\models_I (A_1 : u_1 \diamond \cdots \diamond A_m : u_m \leftarrow B_1 \diamond \cdots \diamond B_m)$ if, for any ground h-structure hs and any contexts $c_1, \ldots, c_m$, $\models_I hs[A_1 \triangleleft u_1.c_1, \cdots, A_m \triangleleft u_m.c_m]$ whenever $\models_I hs[B_1 \triangleleft u_1.c_1, \cdots, B_m \triangleleft u_m.c_m]$.

   iii) For a ground general goal, $\models_I G$ if $\models_I G \triangleleft \lambda$ ■

The notion of model, central for the declarative semantics, can now be defined.

Definition 9 *An interpretation I is a* model *of a system of units $\mathcal{U}$ if $\models_I C$ for every clause C of agg($\mathcal{U}$). A formula f is a* consequence *of $\mathcal{U}$, denoted $\mathcal{U} \models f$, if f is true in every model of $\mathcal{U}$.* ■

We are now in a position to define the model declarative semantics. For the ease of notation, for a context name $c = u_1 \ldots u_n$, $c \gg G$ will be used as a shorthand for the extension formula $u_n \gg \ldots \gg u_1 \gg G$. Furthermore, for any g-goal G, we will use ground(G) to denote the set of ground instances of G.

Definition 10 (Model declarative semantics) *Define the model declarative semantics as the following function $Decl_m : Ssyst \rightarrow Scontext \rightarrow Sggoal \rightarrow \mathcal{P}(Ssubst)$: for any $\mathcal{U} \in Ssyst$, $c \in Scontext$ and $G \in Sggoal$,*

$$Decl_m(\mathcal{U})(c)(G) = \{\theta : \forall G_0 \in ground(G\theta), \mathcal{U} \models c \gg G_0\}$$ ■

6.2 Fixed-point theory

The models of a system of units $\mathcal{U}$ can be characterized as the prefixed points of a continuous operator $T_\mathcal{U} : Sint \rightarrow Sint$ associated with $\mathcal{U}$, where Sint is the complete lattice of all interpretations (partially ordered by $I \leq J$ if and only if $I_u(S) \subseteq J_u(S)$ for every $u \in Sunit$ and $S \subseteq HB$). The suitable operator $T_\mathcal{U}$ to consider is as follows.

Definition 11 *Define $T_\mathcal{U} : Sint \rightarrow Sint$ as follows: for every interpretation I, $T_\mathcal{U}(I)$ is the set of all ground extended goals of the form $hs[A_1 \triangleleft u_1.c_1, \cdots, A_m \triangleleft u_m.c_m]$ such that $\models_I hs[B_1 \triangleleft u_1.c_1, \cdots, B_m \triangleleft u_m.c_m]$ for a ground h-structure hs, contexts $c_1, \ldots, c_m$ and a ground instance $(A_1 : u_1 \diamond \cdots \diamond A_m : u_m \leftarrow B_1 \diamond \cdots \diamond B_m)$ of a clause in agg($\mathcal{U}$).* ■

As expected, this mapping enjoys the usual properties of the immediate consequence operator.

Proposition 12 *For every system of unit $\mathcal{U}$, the operator $T_{\mathcal{U}}$ is well-defined and continous. Furthermore, it has a least fixed-point $M_{\mathcal{U}}$ which is also the minimal model of $\mathcal{U}$.* ∎

We are now in a position to define the fixed-point semantics.

Definition 13 (Fixed-point semantics) *Define the fixed-point semantics $Decl_f$: $Ssyst \rightarrow Scontext \rightarrow Sggoal \rightarrow \mathcal{P}(Ssubst)$ as follows: for any $\mathcal{U} \in Ssyst$, $c \in Scontext$, and $G \in Sggoal$:*

$$Decl_f(\mathcal{U})(c)(G) = \{\theta : \forall G_0 \in ground(G\theta), \emptyset \models_{M_{\mathcal{U}}} c \gg G_0\}$$ ∎

The equivalence between the model semantics and the fixed-point semantics is given by the following proposition. As usual, it essentially consists of stating that the quantification involved in the consequence relation $\mathcal{U} \models G$, namely the one over all models of $\mathcal{U}$, can be eliminated by considering only the minimal model of $\mathcal{U}$.

Proposition 14 *For every system of units $\mathcal{U}$ and g-goal G, $\mathcal{U} \models G$ if and only if $\emptyset \models_{M_{\mathcal{U}}} G$. In particular, the declarative and the fixed-point semantics coincide, that is $Decl_m = Decl_f$.* ∎

Finally, the equivalence between the operational and the declarative semantics can be stated as follows.

Proposition 15 *For every general goal G and substitution θ,*

   i) if $P \vdash G$ with θ then $P \models G_0$ for every ground instance G_0 of $G\theta$;
   ii) if $P \models G\tau$ for some substitution τ, then $P \vdash G$ with θ, for some substitution θ such that $G\tau \geq G\theta$.

In particular, if $\alpha : \mathcal{P}(Ssubst) \rightarrow \mathcal{P}(Ssubst)$ is defined by $\alpha(\Theta) = \{\theta\gamma_{|S} : \theta \in \Theta, \gamma \in Ssubst, dom(\theta) \subseteq S\}$, for any $\Theta \in \mathcal{P}(Ssubst)$, the equalities

$$Decl_m(\mathcal{U})(c)(G) = Decl_f(\mathcal{U})(c)(G) = \alpha(O_d(\mathcal{U})(c)(G))$$

hold for any $\mathcal{U} \in Ssyst$, $c \in Scontext$ and $G \in Sggoal$. ∎

7 Conclusion

The paper has presented an extension of contextual logic programming as well as operational and declarative semantics for the resulting framework. From the language point of view, the extension mainly consists in adding multisets of atoms associated with unit names to Horn clauses. Roughly speaking, those atoms are the atoms whose impending reduction by a clause of the corresponding units is required to allow the clause to be used for reduction. The extended framework has been shown to be well-suited for expressing synchronous communications between agents as well as to code several applications involving the logic and object-oriented styles of programming.

The operational and declarative semantics have extended the classical notions of success set, model and immediate consequence operator to the new framework. An effort has been made to design these semantics as simple as possible as well as in the main streams of logic programming semantics. However, the synchronization and contextual restrictions have raised new problems, for which fresh solutions have been proposed. Among the main innovations is the notion of h-structure, which constitutes a concise way of specifying the selection of atoms in goals and their replacement by other goals. All the semantics have been related in the paper, as established by propositions 14 and 15.

We regard communicating clauses - and, therefore, the work reported here – as a step in the integration of logic programming and object-oriented programming. Our future research, under development, will be concerned with more elaborated versions involving other notions such as inheritance and constraints. At a semantical level, we are developing and comparing other more modular operational semantics and denotational semantics in the style of [9]. We are also investigating the relationship of these models with semantics of the partial order type such as pomsets or event structures. Finally, the introduction of synchronous communication in concurrent logic programming (classically ruled by asynchronous communication) introduces new problems of embedding of languages, that are also under study.

Acknowledgments

The research reported herein has been partially supported by Esprit BRA 3020 (Integration). The first author likes to thank the members of the C.W.I. concurrency group, headed by J.W. de Bakker, for their weekly intensive discussions, as well as B. Le Charlier for his interest in his work. The second author wish to thank the Instituto Nacional de Investigação Científica and the Junta Nacional de Investigação Científica e Tecnológica for partial support.

References

[1] J.-M. Andreoli and R. Pareschi. Linear Objects: Logical Processes with Built-in Inheritance. In D.H.D. Warren and P. Szeredi, editors, *Proc. 7th Int. Conf. on Logic Programming*, pages 495–510, Jerusalem, Israel, 1990. The MIT Press.

[2] A. Brogi. And-Parallelism without Shared Variables. In D.H.D. Warren and P. Szeredi, editors, *Proc. 7th Int. Conf. on Logic Programming*, pages 306–321, Jerusalem, Israel, 1990. The MIT Press.

[3] J.S. Conery. Logical Objects. In R.A. Kowalski and K.A. Bowen, editors, *Proc. 5th Int. Conf. and Symp. on Logic Programming*, pages 420–434, Seattle, USA, 1988. The MIT Press.

[4] F.S. de Boer, J.N. Kok, C. Palamidessi, and J.J.M.M. Rutten. Semantic Models for a Version of PARLOG. In G. Levi and M. Martelli, editors, *Proc. 6th Int. Conf. on Logic Programming*, Series in Logic Programming, pages 621–636, Lisboa, 1989. The MIT Press.

[5] P. Degano and S. Diomedi. A First Order Semantics of a Connective Suitable to Express Concurrency. In *Proc. 2nd Workshop on Logic Programming*, pages 506–517, Albufeira, Portugal, 1983.

[6] M. Falaschi, G. Levi, and C. Palamidessi. A Synchronization Logic: Axiomatics and Formal Semantics of Generalized Horn Clauses. *Information and Control*, 60:36–69, 1984.

[7] J.Y. Girard. Linear Logic. *Theoretical Computer Science*, 50:1–102, 1987.

[8] S. Gregory. *Design, Application and Implementation of a Parallel Logic Programming Language*. PhD thesis, Department of Computing, Imperial College, London, Great-Britain, 1985.

[9] J.-M. Jacquet and L. Monteiro. Comparative Semantics for a Parallel Contextual Logic Programming Language. In S. Debray and M. Hermenegildo, editors, *Proc. of the North American Conference on Logic Programming*, pages 195–214, Austin, USA, 1990. The MIT Press.

[10] J.-M. Jacquet and L. Monteiro. Comparative Semantics of Generalized Horn Clauses. In *Proceedings of the Logic Programming Conference '91*, pages 181–191, Tokyo, Japan, 1991. to appear as Lecture Notes in Computer Science, Springer-Verlag.

[11] J.-M. Jacquet and L. Monteiro. Extended Horn Clauses: the Framework and its Semantics. In J.C.M. Baeten and J.F. Groote, editors, *Proc. 2nd Int. Conf. on Concurrency Theory (Concur'91)*, volume 527 of *Lecture Notes in Computer Science*, pages 281–297, Amsterdam, The Netherlands, 1991. Springer-Verlag.

[12] L. Monteiro. An Extension to Horn Clause Logic allowing the Definition of Concurrent Processes. In *Proc. Formalization of Programming Concepts*, volume 107 of *Lecture Notes in Computer Science*, pages 401–407. Springer-Verlag, 1981.

[13] L. Monteiro. A Horn Clause-like Logic for Specifying Concurrency. In *Proc. 1st Int. Conf. on Logic Programming*, pages 1–8, 1982.

[14] L. Monteiro and A. Porto. Contextual Logic Programming. In G. Levi and M. Martelli, editors, *Proc. 6th Int. Conf. on Logic Programming*, pages 284–302, Lisboa, 1989. The MIT Press.

[15] L. Monteiro and A. Porto. A Transformational View of Inheritance in Logic Programming. In D.H.D. Warren and P. Szeredi, editors, *Proc. 7th Int. Conf. on Logic Programming*, pages 481–494, Jerusalem, Israel, 1990. The MIT Press.

[16] V.A. Saraswat. *Concurrent Constraint Programming Languages*. PhD thesis, Carnegie-Mellon University, 1989. To be published by The MIT Press.

[17] E.Y. Shapiro. A Subset of Concurrent Prolog and its Interpreter. Technical Report TR-003, Institute for New Generation Computer Technology (ICOT), Tokyo, 1983.

[18] K. Ueda. *Guarded Horn Clauses*. PhD thesis, Faculty of Engineering, University of Tokyo, Tokyo, Japan, 1986.

A Declarative View of Inheritance in Logic Programming

M. Bugliesi

Dipartimento di Matematica Pura ed Applicata
Via Belzoni 7, Padova – ITALY
michele@blues.unipd.it

Abstract

We discuss a declarative characterization of inheritance in logic programming. Our approach is inspired both by existing literature on denotational models for inheritance and by earlier work on a compositional definition of the semantics of logic Programming. We consider a general form of inheritance which is defined with an overriding semantics between inherited definitions and incorporates two different mechanisms known in the literature as static and dynamic inheritance. The result of our semantic reconstruction is an elegant framework which enables us to capture the compositional properties of inheritance and offers a uniform basis for the analysis of the different mechanisms we consider.

1   Introduction

The interest in modular logic programming has given rise in the recent literature to several proposals for capturing, at the semantic level, the compositional properties inherent in an modular approach to software development.

Inheritance provides one of various composition tools program development whose effectiveness has become widely accepted after the experience gained by the Object-Oriented community. Although the study of inheritance is not new in the logic programming field [11,15,4], the existing solutions seem still to provide only partial answers to the semantic problem. Some of them fail to capture the whole power of the notion of inheritance as defined within the O-O community ([2]) whereas others ([15]) achieve a transformational view whereby inheritance is logically understood only from a strictly operational point of view.

In this paper we present a new approach which is motivated and inspired by both existing literature on denotational models for Object-Oriented languages [17,7] and by earlier work on a compositional definition of the semantics of Logic Programming [10,3,1].

We first consider an extended horn clause language, ObjectLog, which has an embedded form of modularity whereby a set of clauses can be collected into a named theory – a *unit* – and different units can communicate by requesting one another the evaluation of a goal. The mechanism for inter-unit communication is captured by allowing *message-goals* of the form $u : g$ to occur in the body of a clause. The intended meaning of $u : g$ is the obvious one, namely to enforce the evaluation of the goal g by using the set of clauses provided by the unit u. As in [11], units are viewed in this context as the logical re-interpretation of the Object-Oriented notion of *object*. Correspondingly, the mechanism for inter-unit goal invocation provides a primitive operation for program composition which captures the idea of *message-passing* found in Object Orientation. The semantics of ObjectLog is derived by using a composite structure for interpretations in which all the units of a program are interpreted simultaneously in much the same spirit as in [12]. In contrast to that case, this approach allows us to capture also a model-theoretic semantics for our language.

We then introduce inheritance as an orthogonal compositional mechanism for building standard logic programs out of a set of program fragments. Following the style of [17] we consider two different mechanisms. Both defined with an overriding semantics, they embed the two forms of inheritance known as static inheritance – a la' Simula67 – and dynamic inheritance– a la' Smalltalk. Our semantic characterization of inheritance relies on the assumption that the semantics of a logic program should be regarded as a function over Herbrand sets rather than as a simple Herbrand set. This idea, which we originally borrowed from Reddy's denotational model [17], has also motivated various other proposals for a compositional semantics of logic programming ([16,10,3,1]).

As the next and final step we then show how to incorporate the notion of inheritance within the linguistic framework provided by ObjectLog. The resulting language – Selflog – exhibits the typical Object-Oriented behaviour whereby the meaning of the $u : g$ is now to enforce the evaluation of the goal g not simply in the unit u but rather in the composition of u with all its ancestors. At the semantic level, the integration is obtained by combining the semantic models developed for inheritance and inter-unit goal invocation. The result is an elegant framework which enables us to capture the compositional properties of inheritance and provides a uniform basis for the analysis of the different mechanisms we consider.

The rest of the paper is organized as follows. In section 2 we show how to declaratively model the mechanism for inter-unit goal invocation. In section 3 we introduce inheritance and discuss the semantics of the dynamic and static interpretations. In section 4 we show how to combine inheritance and the idea of inter-unit goal invocation into a single framework. Finally, in section 5, we discuss the relations of our approach with the existing literature on the subject.

2　ObjectLog

ObjectLog is a logic language instrumented with two basic mechanisms to support a primitive form of modularity. ObjectLog allows one to declare a unit as a collection of clauses and it extends the syntax of horn clauses by allowing message-goals to occur in the body of a clause. The syntax for unit declaration is simply: $\langle unit\ def \rangle ::= \textbf{unit}\ \langle unit\ name \rangle \texttt{[}\langle clauses \rangle \texttt{]}$.

The bodies of the clauses of a unit may contain message-goals of the form $u : G$ where u is a unit name and G is a goal. Following the style introduced in [14], in the declaration $\textbf{unit}\ u\ \texttt{[}\cdots\texttt{]}$ we will denote with $|u|$ the set of the ground instances of the clauses defined by u. ObjectLog's operational semantics is defined in terms of the proof predicate $\vdash$ which can be viewed as a special case of the more general relation used to define the semantics of Contextual Logic Programming in [14]. In the following definition, which we give in a Natural Deduction style, we use the notation $\square$ to stand for the empty goal formula and ϵ for the identity substitution.

$$(O_1) \quad \frac{}{u \vdash_\epsilon \square} \qquad\qquad (O_2) \quad \frac{u \vdash_\sigma G\theta}{u \vdash_{\theta\sigma} g} \quad \left(\begin{array}{c} h\,\text{:-}G \in u \\ \theta = mgu(g, h) \end{array} \right)$$

$$(O_3) \quad \frac{u \vdash_\theta G_1 \quad u \vdash_\sigma G_2\theta}{u \vdash_{\theta\sigma} G_1, G_2} \qquad (O_4) \quad \frac{\hat{u} \vdash_\theta G}{u \vdash_\theta \hat{u}:G}$$

The notation $u \vdash_\theta G$ has been used here to stand for $u \vdash G\theta$. As in [12] an O-proof for $u \vdash G\theta$ is a tree rooted at $u \vdash_\theta G$, whose internal nodes are instances of one of the above inference figures and whose leaf nodes are labeled with the *initial* figure (O_1).

The interpretation of the above rules is straightforward. (O_1), (O_2) and (O_3) model the standard operational semantics of logic programming with the only difference that our programs are now units. As for (O_4), it states that evaluating a message-goal $u : G$ in any unit corresponds to evaluating the goal G in the unit u, regardless of the unit in which the message-goal occurred. This behaviour is referred to as *context freeing* in [14].

2.1 Interpretations and Models

An ObjectLog program $P(U)$ is constructed as a set of units U. Its semantics is given in terms of a composite set-theoretic structure which provides a *model* for each of the component units. This structure is defined in much the same way as standard interpretations and models are used for characterizing the semantics of a logic program. The difference is that in this latter case we interpret a single program whereas in ObjectLog we would like to interpret several programs – our units – simultaneously. An elegant solution to this problem was first given in [12] in terms of a Kripke-like structure used to interpret the possibly infinite set of programs arising in that case. The approach we follow here is similar, but simpler, being the set of units of a program always finite. This enables us to introduce a standard notion of truth as the basis for a model-theoretic characterization for the semantics of the language.

A program $P(U)$ is defined over a set Σ of function symbols and a set Π of predicate symbols. The Herbrand Universe HU for $P(U)$ is built over Σ; the Herbrand Base $\mathcal{B}$ for each $u \in U$ is built from HU over Π. An interpretation I for a program $P(U)$ is defined as the tuple of sets $\langle I(u) : u \in U \rangle$, where each $I(u)$ is the subset of $\mathcal{B}$ that interprets the associated unit. To distinguish between tuples of sets and sets we will henceforth use the term T-interpretation to refer to a tuple of interpretations. The class of T-interpretations will be denoted by $\mathfrak{I}$.

We begin by introducing a notion of satisfiability. The following definition is based on the classical notion of truth as set-membership. For any interpretation s and any T-interpretation I, we defined the *truth of a ground formula F with respect to s and I* ($s \models_I F$) as follows:

$$
\begin{array}{lll}
(1) & s \models_I G & \Longleftrightarrow \quad G \in s \\
(2) & s \models_I G_1, G_2 & \Longleftrightarrow \quad (s \models_I G_1 \text{ and } s \models_I G_2) \\
(3) & s \models_I h\text{:-}G & \Longleftrightarrow \quad (s \models_I G \Rightarrow s \models_I h) \\
(4) & s \models_I u : G & \Longleftrightarrow \quad I(u) \models_I G
\end{array}
$$

The T-interpretation I is meant to convey all the necessary information to establish the truth of a message-goal on the account of the truth of the corresponding goal in the specified unit. With this understanding, the meaning of the above definition is rather intuitive. A ground goal G is true *wrt s* and I if so are all the conjuncts of G. A clause is true if the head is true whenever the body is true. A message goal $u : G$ is true *wrt s* and I if the goal G is true *wrt* $I(u)$, the interpretation that I associates with u, and I (independently of the interpretation s).

Based on this definition of satisfiability, we have a corresponding notion of T-model.

Definition 2.1 A T-interpretation I is a T-model for a program $P(U)$ iff for every $u \in U$ and each clause C of $|u|$, $I(u) \models_I C$. □

Notice that if U is a singleton set, the notions of truth, T-interpretation and T-model coincide with the classical ones.

2.2 Model-Theoretic Semantics

The standard meaning of a logic program P is defined as the least Herbrand model M_P of P. The model-theoretic semantics for ObjectLog, based on T-models, is defined along the guidelines of the classical approach.

Partial Ordering on T-Interpretations. We first introduce the ordering relation $\sqsubseteq_{\mathfrak{I}}$ over T-interpretations. The definition of $\sqsubseteq_{\mathfrak{I}}$ is derived from the partial order $\subseteq$ (set inclusion) on interpretations in the usual way. For any program $P(U)$, if I_1 and I_2 are two T-interpretations, $I_1 \sqsubseteq_{\mathfrak{I}} I_2$ *iff* $\forall u \in U$ $I_1(u) \subseteq I_2(u)$. The set of T-interpretations associated with $P(U)$ is a complete lattice with join and meet operators defined respectively as:

$$
\begin{array}{llll}
\text{(join)} & (I_1 \sqcup I_2) & = & \forall u \in U \ I_1(u) \cup I_2(u) \\
\text{(meet)} & (I_1 \sqcap I_2) & = & \forall u \in U \ I_1(u) \cap I_2(u)
\end{array}
$$

$I_\perp = \langle \varnothing, \ldots, \varnothing \rangle$ and $I_\top = \langle \mathcal{B}, \ldots, \mathcal{B} \rangle$ denote respectively the bottom and top element of this lattice. It's easy to see that $I_\top$ is a T-model for the associated program and that the standard model intersection property holds on T-models (given two T-models M_1 and M_2, $M_1 \sqcap M2$ is also a T-model). Hence, a minimal T-model exists for any program – the intersection (meet) of all the T-models –.

2.3 Fixpoint Semantics

A constructive characterization of the minimal T-model can be given following the same idea as [12]. Given a program $P(U)$, we define a transformation $T_{P(U)}$ for whose fixpoint is the minimal T-model for $P(U)$. In contrast to [12], $T_{P(U)}$ is defined here in terms of the immediate-consequence transformation of each of the units of $P(U)$. For u in U and $I \in \mathfrak{I}$, let $T_{u,I} : \mathcal{P}(\mathcal{B}) \mapsto \mathcal{P}(\mathcal{B})$ be defined as follows:

$$T_{u,I}(s) \;=\; \{A \mid A\!:\!-G \in |u| \text{ and } s \models_I G\}$$

We then define the immediate consequence operator $T_{P(U)}$ for the program as a transformation from T-interpretations to T-interpretations as

$$T_{P(U)}(I) = \langle T_{u,I}(I(u)) \mid u \in U \rangle$$

$T_{P(U)}$ is monotonic and continuous on $\mathfrak{I}$. The proof, (see [6]), follows by showing that for any $I \in \mathfrak{I}$, $T_{u,I}$ is continuous on $\mathcal{P}(\mathcal{B})$ and that for any increasing sequence of T-interpretations $I_1 \sqsubseteq_{\mathfrak{I}} \ldots \sqsubseteq_{\mathfrak{I}} I_n \ldots$, $T_{u,\sqcup_{j=1}^\infty I_j} = \sqcup_{j=1}^\infty T_{u,I_j}$.

The continuity of $T_{P(U)}$ guarantees the existence of a least fixpoint. The fixpoint is built by simultaneously carrying on the computation of the transformations associated with each unit thus capturing the interdependency among the interpretations for the units in $P(U)$ implicit in the idea of message-goal. The fixpoint of $T_{P(U)}$ gives precisely the minimal T-model $M_{P(U)}$ for $P(U)$.

Theorem 2.1 [6] $M_{P(U)} = \mathit{lfp}(T_{P(U)}) = \sqcup_{k=1}^\infty T_{P(U)}^k(I_\perp)$. $\square$

As in the classical approach, we can now use the fixpoint construction to show that the minimal T-model for a program coincides with the set of atomic and ground logical consequences of the program.

Theorem 2.2 [6] Let $M = \langle M(u) \mid u \in U \rangle$ be the minimal model for a program $P(U)$. Then for any $u \in U$ and any ground goal G, there exists an O-proof for $u \vdash_\epsilon G$ if and only if $M(u) \models_M G$. $\square$

Example 2.1 Consider a program $P(U)$ with $U = \{u_1, u_2\}$ where:

u_1 [$p\!:\!-u_2 : q.$ $r.$] u_2 [$q\!:\!-u_1 : r.$]

The minimal T-model for $P(U)$ is the T-interpretation $M_{P(U)} = \langle\{r,p\},\{q\}\rangle$. $M_{P(U)}$ is obtained at the third step of the iteration $T_{P(U)}^{(n)}(I_\perp)$. The T-interpretation computed at the first step is $\langle\{r\},\oslash\rangle$. At the next step we are to compute $T_{P(U)}^{(2)}(I_\perp) = \langle T_{u_1,I}(\{r\}),\ T_{u_2,I}(\oslash)\rangle$, where $I = \langle\{r\},\oslash\rangle$ and $T_{u_2,I}(\oslash) = \{A \mid A\texttt{:-}G \in |u_2| \text{ and } \oslash \models_I G\}$. Now, $\oslash \models_I u_1 : r$ iff $\{r\} \models_I r$ and thus $T_{u_2,I}(\oslash) = \{q\}$ and $T_{P(U)}^{(2)}(I_\perp) = \langle\{r\},\{q\}\rangle$. Following the same argument, it's easy to see that $M_{P(U)}$ is indeed the T-interpretation obtained at the next iteration and that it is the fixpoint. $\qquad\square$

3 Inheritance

In this section we introduce inheritance as an independent composition mechanism for logic programs Throughout this section we will use the terms logic program, program fragment and unit interchangeably, with the understanding that we are now restricting ourselves to consider (the composition of) programs built over the language of horn clauses. We begin by informally introducing the interpretation of inheritance we use throughout.

A first abstract model for inheritance was developed using a denotational framework in two independent papers ([7] and [17]). In [17], Reddy carries out a systematic analysis of two different interpretations of inheritance and investigates their respective semantic characterizations. We illustrate the point here in terms of two possible ways of interpreting the hierarchical composition of logic programs (units). Let's first introduce a little notation. Given two units, u and su, we denote with u ◁ su the composition of u and su into a hierarchy where su is u's immediate ancestor (its *super* unit). We also assume an overriding semantics for ◁ whereby if both u and su in u ◁ su contain a definition for same predicate, then the definition in u overrides the one found in su.

Example 3.1 Consider a program built as the composition of su and u, where u inherits from su and redefines one of its super-unit's predicates.

$$
\text{su}\ \left[\begin{array}{l} iAm(\texttt{'su'}).\\ whoAreYou(x)\texttt{:-}iAm(x). \end{array}\right] \qquad \text{u}\ [\ iAm(\texttt{'u'}).\ ]
$$

We want to look at the evaluation of the query $whoAreYou(x)$ in u ◁ su. Clearly, the result depends on the binding for the predicate iAm in su. In fact, we can either bind it to su's local definition, or consider u ◁ su as a modified version of su where iAm is bound to the definition provided in u. Put a little differently, we can think of the invocation $iAm(x)$ as a shorthand for the typical Object-Oriented notation $\texttt{self}:iAm(x)$, and rephrase the above statement in terms of the two corresponding bindings for $\texttt{self}$. The two choices reflect the behaviour of the two different mechanisms that Reddy identifies respectively as static and dynamic inheritance. If $iAm(x)$ is evaluated in su ($\texttt{self}$ is *statically* bound to su) then the answer will be the substitution $\{x \mapsto' su'\}$. Conversely, if $iAm(x)$ is evaluated in the composition of su with u, (self is *dynamically* bound to u $\triangleleft$ su), then the resulting substitution will be $\{x \mapsto' u'\}$. □

The semantics of the composition u $\triangleleft$ su can be formally specified at different levels. At the operational level, by defining the rules for evaluating a goal into the composed program u $\triangleleft$ su. Alternatively, we can take a transformational view and define a way for constructing a new logic program which behaves as the composition of u and su. Finally, at the declarative level we can try and interpret u and su to derive the interpretation of u $\triangleleft$ su in terms of the interpretation of the components

In the next section we will consider these three approaches, the goal being to achieve a declarative characterization and to establish its relationship with the operational semantics. The transformational view provides the necessary link between these two end-points. The discussion will be carried on by assuming a dynamic connotation for the composition operator $\triangleleft$ and simply addressing analogies and differences with respect to the static case.

3.1 Hierarchies of logic programs

The operational semantics of the composition $\triangleleft$ has been already studied in the literature [2,14]. We include here a brief survey to make the discussion self-contained. We will denote with $\pi(u)$ the set predicate symbols *defined* by the unit u. The same notation will be used also for arbitrary hierarchies according to the definition: $\pi(u \triangleleft su) = \pi(u) \cup \pi(su)$. $\mathcal{H}$ will denote a generic hierarchy $u_1 \triangleleft u_2 \triangleleft \ldots \triangleleft u_n$ and for any atom A, $pred(A)$ will stand for the predicate symbol of A. Finally, for any goal G and any hierarchy $\mathcal{H}$, $u_{\mathcal{H},G}$ will stand for the first unit found in a left-to right scan of $\mathcal{H}$ such that $\pi(u)$ contains $pred(G)$.

The operational semantics of the composition $\triangleleft$ can be defined in terms of the following inference figures which we borrow from [2].

(I_1) $\qquad \dfrac{}{\mathcal{H} \vdash_\epsilon \square}$

(I_2) $\qquad \dfrac{\mathcal{H} \vdash_\sigma G\theta}{\mathcal{H} \vdash_{\theta\sigma} A}$ $\qquad (\theta = mgu(A, \bar{A})$ and $\bar{A} : -G \in u_{\mathcal{H},A})$

(I_3) $\qquad \dfrac{\mathcal{H} \vdash_\theta G_1 \quad \mathcal{H} \vdash_\sigma G_2\theta}{\mathcal{H} \vdash_{\sigma\theta} G_1, G_2}$

We say that $\mathcal{H} \vdash G\theta$ has an I-proof if there is a tree rooted at $\mathcal{H} \vdash_\theta G$ whose internal nodes are instances of one of the above figures and whose leaf nodes are labeled with figure (I_1). The meaning of (I_1) and (I_3) is straightforward. As for (I_2), it formalizes the overriding semantics of $\triangleleft$. The search for a matching clause for A stops at $u_{\mathcal{H},A}$ – the first unit in the hierarchy which defines $pred(A)$ – thus hiding any other definition for $pred(A)$ found in any of u_A's ancestors. Notice also that the evaluation of the body of the clause takes place in the whole hierarchy $\mathcal{H}$, regardless of the unit in $\mathcal{H}$ where the clause occurs. This reflects the dynamic connotation for $\triangleleft$ which we have addressed earlier in this section. If $\mathcal{H} = u_1 \triangleleft \ldots \triangleleft u_{\mathcal{H},A} \triangleleft \ldots \triangleleft u_n$, the corresponding rule for the static case would be drawn as follows ([14]):

$$(I_{2'}) \quad \frac{u_{\mathcal{H},A} \triangleleft \ldots \triangleleft u_n \vdash_\sigma G\theta}{\mathcal{H} \vdash_{\theta_\sigma} A} \quad (\theta = mgu(A, \bar{A}) \text{ and } \bar{A}\text{:-}G \in u_{\mathcal{H},A})$$

The body G of $\bar{A}$:-G is now evaluated in the sub-hierarchy whose tip node is $u_{\mathcal{H},A}$, using therefore only $u_{\mathcal{H},A}$'s local and inherited definitions. This suggests that static inheritance should indeed be understood as a scope mechanism for the clauses of a hierarchy. Later in this section we will see how its semantics can be given in essentially the same style as the semantics of the *static scope rules for local definitions* defined in [9]. This analogy was first pointed out in [2].

From figures $(I_1) - (I_3)$ it's easy to see how to construct a logic program equivalent to the composition of two programs through $\triangleleft$.

Definition 3.1 Let u_P and u_Q be two logic programs. $u_P \oplus u_Q$ denotes the logic program obtained as the union of the clauses of u_P with the clauses of u_Q which do not define any of the predicates in $\pi(u_P)$.
Formally: $u_P \oplus u_Q = \{A\text{:-}G \in u_P\} \cup \{A\text{:-}G \in u_Q : pred(A) \notin \pi(u_P)\}$. $\square$

The relation between $u_P \oplus u_Q$ and $u_P \triangleleft u_Q$ is formalized on the basis of their respective operational semantics by the following result.

Proposition 1 For any goal G, there exists an I-proof for $u_P \triangleleft u_Q \vdash G\theta$ *iff* there exists an SLD refutation for G in $u_P \oplus u_Q$ with final substitution θ.
Proof. By induction on the height of the I-proof for $u_P \triangleleft u_Q \vdash_\theta G$. The I-proof has height n if and only if G is refutable in n SLD steps from $u_P \oplus u_Q$ and θ is the computed substitution.

3.2 Declarative semantics

At the declarative level, the semantics of $\triangleleft$ is given relying on the assumption that the semantics of a logic program should be regarded as a function over Herbrand sets rather than as a simple Herbrand set. As noted in [10], this choice is crucial to achieve a compositional semantics for modular logic programming. The idea of "moving from an *object level* semantics to a *function level* semantics ([10])" has been largely investigated in the recent literature. First introduced in [16], it has been similarly exploited in [10] to define a set of algebraic operators on logic programs and, more recently, it has also inspired the study of the semantics of *open* logic programs in [1] and [3]. Here we take the same view as [10] and we base our construction on the assumption that the meaning of a program be its associated transformation T_P. This characterization has an immediate counterpart in the use of *functionals* for defining the semantics of (sub-)classes in [17] and provides a uniform basis for the analysis of the static and dynamic models for inheritance we are considering.

We first introduce a new operator on $\mathcal{P}(\mathcal{B})$ which provides the formal device for modeling, in a set-theoretic sense, the overriding semantics of $\lhd$.

Definition 3.2 Let π denote an arbitrary set of predicate symbols and let S_1 and S_2 be two sets in $\mathcal{P}(\mathcal{B})$. Then we define a function $\Diamond_\pi : \mathcal{P}(\mathcal{B}) \times \mathcal{P}(\mathcal{B}) \mapsto \mathcal{P}(\mathcal{B})$ as follows: $S_1 \Diamond_\pi S_2 = S_1 \cup \{t \in S_2 \mid pred(t) \notin \pi\}$ □

The use of $\Diamond_\pi$ for modeling the overriding semantics of inheritance can be intuitively motivated in terms of the classical minimal-model semantics as follows. For two programs u_P and u_Q, if M_P and M_Q are two models of u_P and u_Q, a model for $u_P \oplus u_Q$ is obtained as a superset of $M_P \Diamond_{\pi(u_P)} M_Q$. A more precise result holds if we assume a function-level semantics.

Now let Φ denote the set of continuous mappings from $\mathcal{P}(\mathcal{B})$ to $\mathcal{P}(\mathcal{B})$. Φ is a complete lattice under the order relation $\leq$ obtained from $\subseteq$ in the standard way (for $T_1, T_2 \in \Phi$, $T_1 \leq T2$ *iff* $\forall I \in \mathcal{P}(\mathcal{B})$ $T_1(I) \subseteq T_2(I)$). We can then lift the definition of $\Diamond_\pi$ at the function level.

Definition 3.3 Let T_1, T_2 be two continuous functions in Φ, and π be a set of predicate symbols. Then $T_1 \Diamond_\pi T_2 = \lambda I . T_1(I) \Diamond_\pi T_2(I)$ □

We have abused the notation here and let $\Diamond_\pi$ denote two different operators defined respectively over Φ and $\mathcal{P}(\mathcal{B})$. For any choice of π, $\Diamond_\pi$ can be shown to be co-continuous on $\mathcal{P}(\mathcal{B})$, and on Φ ([6]). Hence $\Diamond_\pi$ is well defined on Φ. Its use as the semantic counterpart of the syntactic operator $\oplus$ is formalized by the following result.

Theorem 3.1 For any two programs u_P and u_Q, $T_{(u_P \oplus u_Q)} = T_{u_P} \Diamond_{\pi(u_P)} T_{u_Q}$.
Proof. For any $I \subseteq \mathcal{B}$,

$$
\begin{aligned}
T_{(u_P \oplus u_Q)}(I) &= \{A \mid A\text{:-}G \in |u_P \oplus u_Q| : G \subseteq I\} \\
&= \{A \mid A\text{:-}G \in |u_P| : G \subseteq I\} \cup \\
&\quad \cup\{A \mid A\text{:-}G \in |u_Q| : pred(A) \notin \pi(u_P) \ \& \ G \subseteq I\} \\
&= T_{u_P}(I) \cup \{A \in T_{u_Q}(I) : pred(A) \notin \pi(u_P)\} \\
&= T_{u_P}(I) \Diamond_{\pi(u_P)} T_{u_Q}(I)
\end{aligned}
$$
□

As a corollary, under the assumption $[\![u_P]\!] = T_{u_P}$, we have a proof for the identity: $[\![u_P \oplus u_Q]\!] = [\![u_P]\!] \Diamond_{\pi(u_P)} [\![u_Q]\!]$. Notice that the above equality wouldn't hold if we interpreted $[\![\cdot]\!]$ as the classical minimal-model semantics. Simply take $u_P = \{p(a)\text{:-}q(b)\}$ and $u_Q = \{q(b)\}$. Then $M_{u_P} = \oslash$ and $M_{u_Q} = \{q(b)\}$ whereas $M_{u_P \oplus u_Q} = \{p(a), q(b)\} \neq M_{u_P} \Diamond_{\pi(u_P)} M_{u_Q}$. This is an instance of the well known problem due to the non OR-compositionality of the minimal-model approach to the semantics of logic programming.

Now, on the account of the relation between $u_P \oplus u_Q$ and $u_P \lhd u_Q$ established in proposition 1, we have the following *compositional* [8] definition for the declarative semantics of $\lhd$.

Definition 3.4 For any two programs u_P and u_Q,

$$[u_P \lhd u_Q] \overset{\text{def}}{=} [u_P \oplus u_Q] = [u_P] \Diamond_{\pi(u_P)} [u_Q] \qquad (1)$$

In [5] a similar construction is used to characterize the semantics of the algebraic operator *is_a* which has essentially the same connotation as $\lhd$. The key difference is that our definition is compositional whereas in [5] the semantics of u_P *is_a* u_Q is given in terms of the semantics of u_P and of a *new* program $\overline{u_Q}$ obtained by filtering out of u_Q the definitions for all the predicates in $\pi(u_P)$. As such, the overriding semantics of *is_a* is captured at the syntactic level in [5] whereas the meaning of $\lhd$ is defined entirely at the semantic level. This also makes (1) independent of the choice of the partition u_P, u_Q.

Proposition 2 For u_P, u_Q and u_R programs,

$$[u_P \lhd u_Q \lhd u_R] = [u_P \lhd u_Q] \Diamond_{\pi(u_P \oplus u_Q)} [u_R] = [u_P] \Diamond_{\pi(u_P)} [u_Q \lhd u_R]$$

Proof. Immediate by observing that, for any $S, S_1, S_2 \in \mathcal{P}(\mathcal{B})$ and any $\pi_1, \pi_2 \in \Pi$, $S \Diamond_{\pi_1} (S_1 \Diamond_{\pi_2} S_2) = (S \Diamond_{\pi_1} S_1) \Diamond_{\pi_1 \cup \pi_2} S_2$ $\qquad \square$

3.3 A note on static inheritance

Using the above characterization, we can furtherly investigate the semantic implications of the two different interpretations of $\lhd$. We will use the notation $\lhd_s$ to identify the static composition, whereas $\lhd$ will denote the dynamic one.

First notice that, according to (1), the meaning of $u_P \lhd u_Q$ is the result of the mutual dependency between u_P and u_Q. This becomes clear by observing that $[u_P \lhd u_Q] = \lambda I \,.\, T(I) = \lambda I \,.\, T_{u_P}(I) \Diamond_{\pi(u_P)} T_{u_Q}(I)$, and thus that T_{u_P} and T_{u_Q} both depend on the same interpretation I. If we took the fixpoint of T, the set computed at each step of the iterative computation $T^{(1)}(\varnothing), \ldots, T^{(n)}(\varnothing)$ would be a subset of the set obtained by performing one deduction step for u_P and u_Q based on the same set of hypothesis I. Operationally, this corresponds to the fact that the evaluation of a goal G in u_P might use a clause of u_Q (if G is not defined in u_P), and vice-versa, evaluating G in u_Q might involve a clause of u_P.

The case for $\lhd_s$ is substantially different since the behaviour of each unit in a hierarchy becomes determinate by only looking at the local and the inherited definitions. As such, in $u_P \lhd_s u_Q$, u_P depends on u_Q but not vice-versa. At the semantic level, this results into a different relation which shows how the meaning of u_Q is indeed determined independently of u_P. Namely: $[u_P \lhd_s u_Q] = \lambda I \,.\, T_{u_P}(I) \Diamond_{\pi(u_P)} T_{u_Q}^{\infty}(\varnothing)$. Notice how we are now taking the fixpoint of T_{u_Q} (instead of T_{u_Q} itself) thus *closing* the interpretation of u_Q. The resulting set, filtered by $\Diamond_{\pi(u_P)}$ is then used as the set of hypotheses for the deduction steps of T_{u_P}. A similar characterization is used in [9] to define the fixpoint semantics for the scope rules considered there. This relation between the different semantic properties of $\lhd$ and $\lhd_s$ was first similarly explained by Reddy in his denotational model.

4   SelfLog

In this section we show how to integrate the notion of (dynamic) inheritance introduced before within the linguistic framework of section 2. The integration is studied in terms of the semantics of a concrete language, SelfLog, which extends ObjectLog by allowing the hierarchical relation between two units to be declared explicitly. Syntactically, the extension amounts to adding a new production for unit declaration. The declaration unit $u \prec su$ [⟨clauses⟩] associates ⟨clauses⟩ with u and declares su as the immediate ancestor of u. The corresponding hierarchy is denoted by $u \prec su$. A SelfLog program $P(U)$ is a set of units configured as a tree-like hierarchy where for each $u \in U$ there is at most one other unit $\bar{u}$ such that $u \prec \bar{u}$. In the following $\mathcal{H}(u)$ will denote the hierarchy obtained by taking the transitive closure of $\prec$ starting from u and the term *base*-unit will be used to refer to a unit without any ancestor ($u = \mathcal{H}(u)$ if u is a base-unit).

Operationally, SelfLog can be described by simply integrating the inference figures for $\lhd$ within the operational characterization of ObjectLog.

(S_1)
$$\frac{}{\mathcal{H} \vdash_\epsilon \square}$$

(S_2)
$$\frac{\mathcal{H} \vdash_\sigma G\theta}{\mathcal{H} \vdash_{\theta\sigma} A} \qquad (\theta = mgu(A, \bar{A}) \text{ and } \bar{A} \colon\! -G \in u_{\mathcal{H},A})$$

(S_3)
$$\frac{\mathcal{H} \vdash_\theta G_1 \qquad \mathcal{H} \vdash_\sigma G_2\theta}{\mathcal{H} \vdash_{\sigma\theta} G_1, G_2}$$

(S_4)
$$\frac{u \lhd \ldots \lhd u_n \vdash_\theta G}{\mathcal{H} \vdash_\theta u : G} \qquad (\mathcal{H}(u) = u \prec u_1 \prec \ldots \prec u_n)$$

The notation $u_{\mathcal{H},A}$ has been used with the same meaning as in $(I_1) - (I_3)$. An S-proof for $\mathcal{H} \vdash G\theta$ is defined, as before, as a proof for $\mathcal{H} \vdash_\theta G$ which uses the inference figures $(S_1) - (S_4)$. Notice that we have also implicitly extended the definition of $\lhd$ to apply to arbitrary SelfLog units rather than to simple logic programs. With the same understanding, we extend the notation $u_P \oplus u_Q$ to refer to the *syntactic* composition introduced in definition 3.1 applied now to two units. We can, correspondingly, establish the relation between $u_P \lhd u_Q$ and $u_P \oplus u_Q$ in the context of SelfLog.

Proposition 3 Let u_P and u_Q be two units and G be a goal. An S-proof for $u_P \lhd u_Q \vdash G\theta$ exists if and only if there exists an O-proof for $u_P \oplus u_Q \vdash G\theta$.
Proof. By induction on the height of the proofs. For the inductive step, by considering the cases where the last inference if the S-proof is an instance of $(S_1) - (S_4)$ (and correspondingly for the O-proof and $(O_1) - (O_4)$). $\square$

4.1 Declarative Semantics

The operational characterization given in the previous section also suggests a declarative interpretation for a SelfLog program. The fact that the evaluation of $u : G$ is carried out by evaluating G in $\mathcal{H}(u)$ can be declaratively interpreted by taking as the meaning of each unit u in $P(U)$ the meaning of the associated hierarchy $\mathcal{H}(u)$. Under this assumption, a declarative characterization of a SelfLog program can be still given in terms of the notions of T-interpretation and of truth defined for ObjectLog. What changes is the definition of T-model which generalizes the definition given for ObjectLog. A T-model will again be a tuple of interpretations where now each component provides a model for the hierarchy associated with the corresponding unit.

Definition 4.1 Let $P(U)$ be a SelfLog program and let M be a T-interpretation for $P(U)$. M is a T-model for $P(U)$ iff for every u such that $\mathcal{H}(u) = u \prec u_1 \prec \ldots, \prec u_n$, $M(u) \models_M C$ for every clause C of $|u \oplus \ldots \oplus u_n|$.

Again, the top element $I_\top$ of $\Im$ is a T-model for any program and the intersection of all the T-models is the minimal T-model for the program itself.

4.2 Fixpoint Semantics

Following the same idea used for the declarative characterization, we can also give a constructive definition of the minimal T-model in terms of a fixpoint computation. Under the assumption $[\![u_P]\!] = T_{u_P}$, equating the meaning of a hierarchy with the meaning of its top unit amounts to taking as $[\![u_P]\!]$ not just T_{u_P} but rather the immediate-consequence operator for the hierarchy. For any unit u and $I \in \Im$, let then again $T_{u,I} : \mathcal{P}(\mathcal{B}) \mapsto \mathcal{P}(\mathcal{B})$ be defined as in section 2.3 by: $T_{u,I}(s) = \{A \mid A\text{:-}G \in |u| \text{ and } s \models_I G\}$. Now, if $\mathcal{H}(u) = u \prec u_1 \prec \ldots, \prec u_n$, we would like to associate with u not $T_{u,I}$ but a new transformation $\mathcal{T}_{u.I}$ which incorporates the semantics of the composition $u \lhd u_1 \lhd \ldots, \lhd u_n$. Definition 3.4 suggests how $\mathcal{T}_{u,I}$ should be defined.

Definition 4.2 For any unit u and T-interpretation I, the transformation $\mathcal{T}_{u,I} : \mathcal{P}(\mathcal{B}) \mapsto \mathcal{P}(\mathcal{B})$ is given inductively by:

$$\mathcal{T}_{u,I}(s) = T_{u,I}(s) \qquad \text{if } u \text{ is a base unit}$$
$$\mathcal{T}_{u,I}(s) = T_{u,I}(s) \Diamond_{\pi(u)} \mathcal{T}_{su,I}(s) \quad \text{if } u \prec su \qquad \qquad \Box$$

The definition of the base case is a consequence that any base units coincides with its associated hierarchy. As for the inductive case, if $\mathcal{H}(u) = u \prec u_1 \prec \ldots, \prec u_n$, the equation above can be expanded as follows:

$$\mathcal{T}_{u,I}(s) = T_{u,I}(s) \Diamond_{\pi(u)} (T_{u_1,I}(s) \Diamond_{\pi(u_1)} (\cdots (\Diamond_{\pi(u_n)} T_{u_n,I}(s))))$$
$$\text{(by prop. 2)} = T_{u,I}(s) \Diamond_{\pi(u)} T_{u_1,I}(s) \Diamond_{\pi(u \oplus u_1)} \cdots \Diamond_{\pi(u \oplus \ldots \oplus u_n)} T_{u_n,I}(s)$$

Accordingly, for any $u_j \in \mathcal{H}(u)$ we obtain the expected effect of filtering out of the interpretation for u_j all the elements which are produced by local definitions and whose predicate symbol is defined also in any of u_j's heirs.

The transformation $T_{P(U)} : \Im \mapsto \Im$ can be finally defined as for ObjectLog as: $T_{P(U)}(I) = \langle T_{u,I}(I(u)) : u \in U \rangle$. $T_{P(U)}$ can be taken as the semantics of a SelfLog program by imposing $[\![P(U)]\!] = T_{P(U)}$. This is justified by the following results which generalize the corresponding ones introduced for ObjectLog.

Theorem 4.1 [6] $\quad M_{P(U)} = lfp(T_{P(U)}) = \sqcup_{k=1}^{\infty} T_{P(U)}^k(I_\perp)$. $\qquad\square$

Theorem 4.2 [6] Let M be the minimal model for a program $P(U)$. For any u in $P(U)$ and any ground goal G, there exists an S-proof for $u \vdash_\epsilon G$ if and only if $M(u) \models_M G$. $\qquad\square$

Notice that in the computation of the fixpoint, many instances of $T_{u,I}$ for the same u may be active at the same time. As a matter of fact, there are as many active instances of $T_{u,I}$ as the number of the hierarchies which u is part of. In each of these hierarchies u assumes a different semantic connotation depending on its heirs.

Example 4.1 Let $P(U)$ be the following modified version of the program reported in example 3.1.

$$u \prec su [\, i(u). \,] \qquad su \left[\begin{array}{l} i(su). \\ w(x) :- i(x). \end{array} \right] \qquad u_1 [\, t(x) :- u : w(x). \,]$$

We have used w and i respectively as shorthands for *whoAreYou* and *iAm* and t as a shorthand for *test*. Any T-interpretation for $P(U)$ is a 3-tuple of the form $\langle I(u), I(su), I(u_1) \rangle$. The expected minimal T-model is $M_{P(U)} = \langle \{i(u), w(u)\}, \{i(su), w(su)\}, \{t(u)\} \rangle$. The fixpoint is obtained by iterating the computation of $T_{P(U)}^{(n)}(I_\perp)$ where:

$$
\begin{aligned}
T_{P(U)}(I) &= \langle T_{u,I}(I(u)), \; T_{su,I}(I(u)), \; T_{u_1,I}(I(u)) \rangle \\
&= \langle T_{u,I}(I(u)) \Diamond_{\pi(u)} T_{su,I}(I(u)), \; T_{su,I}(I(su)), \; T_{u_1,I}(I(u_1)) \rangle
\end{aligned}
$$

The fixpoint is reached in three steps: $T_{P(U)}^1(I_\perp) = \langle \{i(u)\}, \{i(su)\}, \oslash \rangle$, $T_{P(U)}^2(I_\perp) = \langle \{i(u), w(u)\}, \{i(su), w(su)\}, \{\oslash\} \rangle$ and finally $T_{P(U)}^3(I_\perp) = M_{P(U)}$. $\qquad\square$

5 Related Work

We have already pointed out analogies and differences for the approach described here with respect to various related solutions found in the literature.

An extensive study on the semantics of various forms of composition mechanisms for logic programming has also been developed in [2]. In that paper, inheritance systems are viewed as a special case of more general forms of composition mechanisms which are derived as extensions or variations of Contextual Logic Programming. The approach is rather different than the one presented in this paper, in two respects. The first is our use of functions to capture the meaning of dynamic inheritance as opposed to the use of standard set-based interpretations in [2]. The second but not less important one is that the definition of inheritance assumed in that paper is based on the notion of *extension*, rather than overriding, between inherited definitions. This assumption is crucial for the framework presented in [2] to prove the existence of a fixpoint for the immediate consequence operator they define. The same assumption constitutes the basis also for the compositional approach developed in a more recent paper ([4]) by the same authors.

A notion of inheritance which is essentially the same as the dynamic interpretation we have assumed here is also considered in [15]. The semantic problem is instead approached from a different and strictly transformational perspective. The methodology to capture the meaning of an inheritance system is to transform it into a logic program to then show the equivalence between the respective operational semantics. A declarative interpretation for inheritance is then derived indirectly on the account of the well-known equivalence between the operational and declarative semantics in logic programming.

Recently, an approach similar to the one we haved presented in this paper has been independently studied by Monteiro and Porto in a paper which is to appear in the forthcoming proceedings of the *PHOENIX Seminar on Declarative Programming* [13].

Aknowledgements. I'd like to thank Annalisa Bossi and Gilberto File' for many fruitful discussions. I'm also grateful to Cristina Ruggieri at DS Logics s.r.l for her comments on earlier versions of this paper. This work has been partially supported by "Progetto Finalizzato Sistemi Informatici e Calcolo Parallelo" of CNR under grant 89.00026.69.

References

[1] A. Bossi, M. Gabbrielli, G. Levi, and M. Meo. Contributions to the Semantics of Open Logic Programs. In *in Proceedings of FGCS'92 Int. Conf*, 1992.

[2] A. Brogi, E. Lamma, and P. Mello. Structuring Logic Programs: A Unifying Framework and its Declarative and Operational Semantics. Technical Report 4/1, Progetto Finalizzato C.N.R. Sistemi Informatic e Calcolo Parallelo, 1990.

[3] A. Brogi, E. Lamma, and P. Mello. Compositional Model-theoretic Semantics for Logic Programs. Technical Report 8-91, Comp. Sci. Dept. University of Pisa, 1991.

[4] A. Brogi, E. Lamma, and P. Mello. Objects in a Logic Programming Framework. In *Proceedings of the 2nd Russian Conf. on Logic Programming*, Leningrad, 1991.

[5] A. Brogi, P. Mancarella, D. Pedreschi, and F. Turini. Composition Operators for Logic Theories. In *Proc. Symposium on Computational Logic*. Springer-Verlag, Basic Research Series, 1990.

[6] M. Bugliesi. *Inheritance Systems in Logic Programming: Semantics and Implementation*. Ms thesis, Dept. of Computer Sciences, Purdue University West-Lafayette IN – USA, May 1992.

[7] W. Cook and J. Palsberg. A Denotational Semantics of Inheritance and its Correctness. In *Proceedings of the ACM OOPSLA'89 Int. Conf.*, pages 433–443. 1989.

[8] H. Gaifman and E. Shapiro. Fully Abstract Compositional Semantics for Logic Programs. In *Proceedings of the ACM Conf. on Principle of Programming Languages*, 1989.

[9] L. Giordano, A. Martelli, and F. Rossi. Local definitions with static scope rules in Logic Languages. In *Proceedings of the FGCS'88 Int. Conf.*, 1988.

[10] P. Mancarella and D. Pedreschi. An Algebra of Logic Programs. In *Proc. of the 5th ALP Int. Conf. on Logic Programming*, Seattle, 1988.

[11] F. G. McCabe. *Logic and Objects. Language, application and implementation*. PhD thesis, Dept. of Computing, Imperial College of Science and Technology, Univ. of London, 1988.

[12] D. Miller. A Logical Analysis of Modules in Logic Programming. *Journal of Logic Programming*, 6(2):79–108, 1989.

[13] L. Monteiro. *Personal communication*. March 1992.

[14] L. Monteiro and A. Porto. Contextual Logic Programming. In *Proceeding of the 6th ALP Int. Conf. on Logic Programming*, Lisbon, 1989.

[15] L. Monteiro and A. Porto. A Transformational View of Inheritance in Logic Programming. In *Proc. of the 7th ALP Int. Conf. on Logic Programming*, 1990.

[16] R. A. O'Keef. Towards an Algebra for Constructing Logic Programs. In *Proceeding of the IEEE Symposium on Logic Programming*, 1985.

[17] U. Reddy. Objects as Closures: Abstarct Semantics of Object Oriented Languages. In *Proceedings of the ACM Int. Conf. on Lisp and Functional Programming*, pages 289–297, 1988.

Verification I

Observational Equivalences for Logic Programs

Maurizio Gabbrielli, Giorgio Levi, Maria Chiara Meo
Dipartimento di Informatica
Università di Pisa
Corso Italia 40, 56125 Pisa, Italia
{gabbri,levi,meo}@di.unipi.it

Abstract

We first introduce a general semantic scheme for logic programs which provides a uniform framework for defining different compositional semantics parametrically wrt a given notion of observable. The equivalence of the operational (top-down) and fixpoint (bottom-up) costruction of the semantics is ensured by the scheme (provided a congruence property is verified). We then define several observational equivalences on logic programs and investigate how they are related. The equivalences are based on various observables (successful derivations, computed answers, partial computed answers and call patterns) and on a notion of program composition. For each observational equivalence we study the relation with a suitable formal semantics, by investigating correctness and full abstraction properties. All the semantics we consider are obtained as instances of the general scheme.

1   Introduction

The first application of any semantics is to help understanding the meaning of programs, and program understanding is based on our ability to detect when two programs cannot be distinguished by looking at their behaviors. Defining an equivalence on (logic) programs $\approx$ and a formal semantics $\mathcal{S}(P)$ are then two strongly related tasks.   A semantics $\mathcal{S}(P)$ is *correct* wrt $\approx$, if $\mathcal{S}(P_1) = \mathcal{S}(P_2)$ implies $P_1 \approx P_2$. $\mathcal{S}(P)$ is *fully abstract* wrt $\approx$, if the converse holds, i.e. if $P_1 \approx P_2$ implies $\mathcal{S}(P_1) = \mathcal{S}(P_2)$. While full abstraction is known to be a desirable property for any semantics, correctness is a must.

Equivalences can be defined by using logical arguments only, both considering model-theoretic and proof-theoretic properties. However the equivalences we are concerned with *must* be based on what we can observe from a computation. Indeed, when trying to understand the meaning of programs, when analyzing and transforming programs, we need equivalences (and semantics) which capture the "observational" behaviour of programs. The pure logical reading of programs fails capturing interesting properties of computations. For example, logically equivalent programs can compute different answer substitutions for the same goal (example 3.3). Once we have a formalization of program execution (given by the inference rules which specify how derivations are made), we have a choice for the equivalence by defining an *observable*, i.e. a property we want observe in the computation. We can be interested in different observable properties such as successful derivations, computed answers, partial computed answers, variables sharing, variables groundness etc. A given choice of the observable X induces an *observational equivalence* $\approx_X$ on programs. Namely $P_1 \approx_X P_2$ iff P_1 and P_2 are observationally indistinguishable according to X. For example, if the observable s denotes a *success*, $P_1 \approx_s P_2$ iff for any goal G, G is refutable in P_1 iff it is refutable in P_2. It is worth noting that abstract interpretation can simply be understood and formalized, from an abstract point of view, in terms of the choice of a suitable observable (for example groundness of goal variables in the derivation).

The most natural observable in the case of logic programs is *computed answer substitution*, which is usually considered the result of a program execution. Hence any "reference semantics" for logic programs should be correct wrt the observational equivalence based on computed answers. However, as first shown in [10], this is not the case of the classical van Emden and Kowalski's semantics [27]. The need for a different semantics (correct wrt computed answers) gave rise to several new definitions and was particularly recognized in the case of abstract interpretation [25, 2, 6] and program transformation [20, 3], where also less abstract observables (e.g. partial computed answers) have sometimes to be modeled [6].

In addition to the problem of modeling observational equivalences, there exists an important property which does not hold in the least Herbrand model semantics, i.e. *OR-compositionality*. A semantics is compositional wrt a (syntactic) program composition operator $\circ$ when the semantics of the compound construct $C_1 \circ C_2$ can be defined by (semantically) composing the semantics of the constituents C_1 and C_2. When composition of programs is considered, given an observable property we obtain different equivalences depending on which kind of program composition we consider. Given an observable X and a program composition operator $\circ$, the induced equivalence $\approx_{(\circ, X)}$ is defined as follows. $P_1 \approx_{(\circ, X)} P_2$ iff for any program Q, $P_1 \circ Q \approx_X P_2 \circ Q$, (i.e. iff P_1 and P_2 are observationally indistinguishable under any possible context allowed by the composition). Note that if semantics $\mathcal{S}(P)$ is *correct* wrt $\approx_X$ and compositional wrt $\circ$ then $\mathcal{S}(P)$ is also *correct* wrt $\approx_{(\circ, X)}$. In the case of logic programs, the least Herbrand model semantics is not compositional wrt the *union* of programs (i.e. is not OR-compositional). If the observable is successful derivation, OR-compositionality can be understood in logical terms since the set of all the (Herbrand) models is OR-compositional [24] (and correct wrt successful derivations). The only OR-compositional semantics correct wrt computed answers are described in [19, 5, 4]. Clearly, OR-compositionality is a desirable property both for theoretical (compositional semantics of modules) and for practical (modular program analysis and transformation) purposes.

Over the last few years we have developed a general approach to the semantics [13], whose aim was modeling the observable behaviors (possibly in a compositional way) for a variety of logic languages, ranging from positive logic programs [10, 11, 5, 4], to general logic programs [26, 16], constraint logic programs [12] and concurrent constraint programs [14]. Our approach is based on the idea of choosing (equivalence classes of) sets of clauses as semantic domains. Denotations (that we call π-interpretations) are not interpretations in the conventional mathematical logic sense and can be computed both by a top-down construction (a success set) and by a bottom-up construction (the least fixpoint of suitable continuous immediate consequence operators on π-interpretations). The s-semantics [10, 11] was the first (non-compositional) semantics correct wrt computed answers and which used sets of unit clauses as domain. Gaifman and Shapiro, using a proof-theoretic approach, introduced the idea of using as domain sets of non-unit clauses to achieve OR-compositionality [18] when considering successful derivations. They then defined (using a different semantic domain) a fully abstract OR-compositional semantics modeling computed answers [19]. The Ω-semantics [5, 4] is the real compositional generalization of the s-semantics and uses non-unit clauses as domain.

In this paper, following the approach of [13], we first define a semantic scheme which generalize Ω-semantics and provides a uniform framework for defining different compositional semantics for logic programs parametrically wrt a given notion of observable. The scheme allows both top-down (operational) and bottom-up (fixpoint) definitions of the semantics and ensures the equivalence of the two characterizations, provided a congruence property is verified. Moreover the scheme allows to treat in an uniform way both "concrete" and "abstract" semantics such as those arising in semantic based program analysis. Indeed, an abstract semantics is simply obtained by considering an "abstract" notion of observable (e.g. groundness, terms rigidity, variables sharing etc.). The correctness of an abstract semantics wrt a concrete one is usually stated by using a Galois connection which relates the two semantics [7]. It is worth noting that in our framework, since all the semantics are instances of the same scheme, their relations can be uniformly understood in terms of abstractions. Therefore, the relation between different semantics (not necessarily a concrete and an abstract one) can be formally expressed by using Galois connections.

We then consider various program equivalence notions and investigate how they are related to study their discriminating power. A systematic comparison of various program equivalences has already been given in [24], which, however, considers only equivalences based on logical properties or on the semantics in [27]. We have already argued that all these equivalences are too weak to correctly characterize computed answers. For example, programs $P_1 = \{p(X), p(a), q(a), q(b)\}$ and $P_2 = \{p(X), q(a), q(b)\}$ are identified by all the equivalences considered in [24] and the same is true for programs $Q_1 = \{q(X) : -q(X), q(X)\}$ and $Q_2 = \{q(X) : -q(X)\}$. However, programs P_1 and P_2 have different computed answers (see example 3.3) and, if we consider the OR-composition of programs, Q_1 and Q_2 are different too (see example 3.7). Some equivalences which consider OR-composition have already been studied in [18, 19]. However programs $R_1 = \{p(a), q(b), r(X, Y) : -p(X), q(Y)\}$ and $R_2 = \{p(a), q(b), r(X, Y) : -q(Y), p(X)\}$ are identified by all the equivalences considered in [18, 19], while, if we consider "partial computed answers" with a given selection rule, they can be distinguished (see example 5.1).

We extend the study of [24] and [18, 19] by introducing new equivalences, which are able to capture differences such as those of the previous programs, and by analyzing their relationships. The new equivalences are obtained both considering new observables such as *partial computed answers* and by considering non-standard T_P operators. For each observational equivalence we study how it is related to a suitable formal semantics (obtained as a specific instance of the general scheme) by investigating correctness and full abstraction properties. For partial answers and call patterns, we rephrase in our semantic framework some results given in [17] and we show a semantics [17] which models partial answers when considering also the selection rule (and hence allows to distinguish programs R_1 and R_2). Having related each observational equivalence to a suitable fixpoint semantics and therefore to an immediate consequence operator, we then study the equivalences induced by these operators and their relations to the observational ones.

The notion of program composition we consider is $\cup_\Omega$, which is a generalization of program union where the set of predicates $\Omega \subseteq \Pi$ specifies which predicates can be shared by different programs (Π is the set of all predicates). If $\Omega = \Pi$, $\cup_\Omega$ is the standard union $\cup$, while if $\Omega = \emptyset$ the composition is allowed only on programs which do not share predicate symbols. A program P can be composed, by means of $\cup_\Omega$, with other programs which may further specify the predicates in Ω. Formally, if $Pred(P) \cap Pred(Q) \subseteq \Omega$ then $P \cup_\Omega Q = P \cup Q$, otherwise $P \cup_\Omega Q$ is not defined

[5, 4]. The observables we analyze are successful derivations (denoted by s), computed answers (ca), partial computed answers (p), correct partial answers (cp), call patterns (pt) and correct call patterns (cpt). Successful derivations and computed answers are independent from the selection rule, while this is not the case for partial computed answers and call patterns. We then denote the various equivalences by $\approx_{(\Omega, X, R)}$, where Ω denotes the composition ($\cup_{\Omega}$), $X \in \{s, ca, p, cp, pt, cpt\}$ denotes the observable, and R is the selection rule. When R is not specified we will omit the third parameter.

The reader is assumed to be familiar with the terminology and the basic results on the semantics of logic programs [22, 1]. We assume a given signature S which contains a denumerable set F of function symbols and a set Π of predicate symbols. If t and t' are terms, $t \leq t'$ iff there exists a substitution ϑ such that $t\vartheta = t'$. $\leq$ is a preorder and the associated equivalence is called *variance*. These definitions can be extended in the obvious way to clauses. If $c_1 = A : -B_1, \ldots, B_n$ and $c_2 = C : -D_1, \ldots, D_n$, c_1 *subsumes* c_2 iff there exists ϑ such that $A\vartheta = C$ and $\{B_1\vartheta, \ldots, B_n\vartheta\} \subseteq \{D_1, \ldots, D_n\}$. By $Pred(E)$ we denote the set of predicates occurring in the expression E. The ordinal powers $f^{\alpha}(X)$ of a monotonic function f on a complete lattice are defined as usual, namely $f^0(X) = X$, $f^{\alpha+1}(X) = f(f^{\alpha}(X))$ for any ordinal α and $f^{\gamma}(X) = \bigsqcup_{\alpha < \gamma} f^{\alpha}(X)$ for γ limit ordinal. When considering the T_P operators, we use the standard notation $T_P \uparrow \alpha = (T_P)^{\alpha}(\emptyset)$. We define $(f + g)(X) = f(X) \cup g(X)$ for f, g generic functions, and $[\![P]\!](X) = (T_P + id)^{\omega}(X)$ where id denotes the identity function. The closure operator $[\![P]\!](X)$ introduced in [21] denotes the function corresponding to deductions in any number of step. When considering a function f_P obtained by a program P (such as T_P or $[\![P]\!]$) we define $f_{P_1} = f_{P_2}$ iff $\forall X$, $f_{P_1}(X) = f_{P_2}(X)$. The equality of the f_P's induces an equivalence on programs in the obvious way, namely P_1 and P_2 are equivalent wrt a given f_P iff $f_{P_1} = f_{P_2}$. If G is a goal, $G \overset{\vartheta}{\leadsto}_{P,R} B_1, \ldots, B_n$ denotes an SLD derivation of the resolvent $B_1, \ldots, B_n$ in the program P which uses the selection rule R. ϑ is the substitution γ, composition of the mgu's, restricted to the variables of G (denoted by $\gamma_{|G}$). If R is omitted, no specific selection rule is assumed (and the definition is independent from the selection rule). $G \overset{\vartheta}{\leadsto}_P \square$ denotes the refutation of G in P with computed answer substitution ϑ. $\tilde{t}$, $\tilde{X}$ denote tuples of terms and variables respectively, while $\tilde{B}$ denotes a (possibly empty) conjunction of atoms. The proofs of the results given in this paper are in [15].

2 A general semantic scheme

The scheme is a generalization of the Ω-open semantics introduced in [5, 4] to get compositionality wrt program union. The standard semantics based on atoms are not compositional wrt union of programs since the information necessary to achieve compositionality can (syntactically) only be expressed by clauses.

Let $P_1 = \{p(X) : -r(X)\}$ and $P_2 = \{r(a)\}$. The least Herbrand model semantics of $P_1 \cup P_2$ cannot be obtained from the semantics of P_1 and P_2 since P_1 has an empty model. The semantics of P_1 should contain also the clause $p(X) : -r(X)$. The open semantics is then defined on domains consisting of (equivalence classes) of sets of clauses (π-interpretations).

If we abstract from the specific equivalences in [5, 4], the open semantics can be viewed as a semantic framework for correctly modeling $\approx_{(\circ, X)}$ equivalences. Depending on the observable X and the composition operator $\circ$, the semantics for $\approx_{(\circ, X)}$ can be obtained from the general scheme by defining a specific equivalence relation $\sim$ on sets of clauses and therefore a semantic domain. We denote by $\mathcal{C}$ the set of all the clauses (on the given signature). A π-interpretation is an equivalence class $I_{/\sim}$ where $I \subseteq \mathcal{C}$. We can then define the top-down semantics $\mathcal{O}_\sim(P)$, parametrically wrt $\sim$. We use the notation $Id_\Pi = \{p(\tilde{X}) : -p(\tilde{X}) \mid p \in \Pi$ and $\tilde{X}$ are distinct variables$\}$.

Definition 2.1 *Let P be a program, R be a fair selection rule and $\sim$ be an equivalence relation on $\wp(\mathcal{C})$. Assume $P^* = P \cup Id_\Pi$. Then*
$$\mathcal{O}_\sim(P) = \{A : -B_1, \ldots, B_m \in \mathcal{C} \mid$$
$$\exists\ \vartheta\ s.t.\ p(\tilde{X}) \overset{\vartheta}{\leadsto}_{P,R} D_1, \ldots, D_k \overset{\gamma}{\leadsto}_{P^*,R} B_1, \ldots, B_m,\ m \geq 0,$$
$$A = p(\tilde{X})\vartheta\gamma\ and\ \tilde{X}\ distinct\ variables \qquad \}_{/\sim}$$

Note that $\mathcal{O}_\sim(P)$ is a π-interpretation and that definition 2.1 is independent from the fair selection rule R considered. Moreover $\mathcal{O}_\sim(P)$ is the set of all the *resultants* [23], obtained from goals of the form $p(\tilde{X})$ in P^*.

$\mathcal{O}_\sim(P)$ can equivalently be defined as the least fixpoint of an operator $T_P^{\sim}(I)$ (parametric wrt $\sim$). We require $\sim$ to be a congruence wrt $\cup$, i.e. for $i = 1, 2\ldots$, if $I_1 \sim J_i$, $I_i, J_i \subseteq \mathcal{C}$, then $\bigcup_{i=1,2,\ldots} I_i \sim \bigcup_{i=1,2,\ldots} J_i$ (all our definitions of $\sim$ satisfy such a requirement). Since $\sim$ is a congruence, the set of π-interpretations $\Im_\sim$ is a complete lattice. Let us define $\iota(I) = \{a\}$ where a is the renamed apart version of any element in $I \in \Im_\sim$. Then for any $X \subseteq \Im_\sim$ we can define $\sqcup X = [\bigcup_{I \in X} \iota(I)]_{/\sim}$ and for $I, J \in \Im_\sim$, $I \sqsubseteq J$ iff $I \sqcup J = J$. The relation $\sqsubseteq$ is an ordering on $\Im_\sim$ and $(\Im_\sim, \sqsubseteq)$ is a complete lattice (with $\sqcup$ as glb).

Definition 2.2 *Let P be a program and let $I \in (\Im_\sim, \sqsubseteq)$. Then $T_P^{\sim}(I) = [\Gamma(\iota(I))]_{/\sim}$ where, for $Q \subset \mathcal{C}$, $\Gamma_P(Q)$ is defined as follows*
$$\Gamma_P(Q) = \{(A : -B_{1,1}, \ldots, B_{1,m_1}, \ldots, B_{n,1}, \ldots, B_{n,m_n})\vartheta \in \mathcal{C} \mid$$
$$\exists A : -B_1, \ldots, B_n \in P$$
$$for\ i = 1, \ldots, n\ \exists\ B_i' : -B_{i,1}, \ldots, B_{i,m_i} \in Q \cup Id_\Pi,$$
$$m_i \geq 0,\ such\ that\ \vartheta = mgu\ ((B_1, \ldots, B_n), (B_1', \ldots, B_n'))\quad \}$$
Moreover we define $[\![P]\!]^{\sim} = (T_P^{\sim} + id)^\omega$.

In general, we require the definition of $T_P^{\sim}(I)$ to be independent from the element chosen in the equivalence class I, i.e. we require that for $Y \sim J$, $\Gamma_P(Y) \sim \Gamma_P(J)$. Also in this case all our definitions of $\sim$ satisfy this property. The following theorem shows a general property of our scheme stating the equivalence of the top-down and the bottom-up constructions of the semantics. This simplifies the treatment in specific cases since usually it is easier to prove the requirements of the theorem than the stated equivalence.

Theorem 2.3 *Let P be a program and $\sim$ be an equivalence on $\wp(\mathcal{C})$ such that if $I \sim J$ then $\Gamma_P(I) \sim \Gamma_P(J)$. Moreover assume $\sim$ being a congruence wrt infinite unions. Then $T_P^{\sim} \uparrow \omega$ is the least fixpoint of $T_P^{\sim}$ on the complete lattice $(\Im_\sim, \sqsubseteq)$ and $T_P^{\sim} \uparrow \omega = \mathcal{O}_\sim(P)$.*

By instantiating $T_P^{\sim}$ with a suitable $\sim$ equivalence, we can define various fixpoint semantics, as in the case of the operator in [8]. As previously argued, semantics arising in abstract interpretation can be obtained as well by considering suitable observables. Moreover note that our framework can be extended to constraint logic programs in a straightforward way. In the following, for each observable X and composition operator $\circ$ considered we introduce a suitable $\sim_{(X,\circ)}$ equivalence to obtain a correct (in some cases fully abstract) semantics for $\approx_{(X,\circ)}$. For example (weak) subsumption equivalence [24] can be used for the observable $X = s$ and program union ($\circ = \cup$), but is too coarse and hence not correct when considering $X = ca$ (see example 3.7). Variance is correct wrt $X = ca$, but is too fine an equivalence, since it would distinguish clauses such as $H : -A, B$ and $H : -B, A$. Such a distinction is necessary when considering as observables partial answers with a given selection rule. In general, we assume that no equivalence finer than variance is used as $\sim$ (this is consistent with the fact that clauses are renamed apart during derivations). The equivalences on sets of clauses $\sim$ are subscripted by a pair $(\circ, X)$ denoting the composition and the observable. When no subscript is specified $\sim$ denotes variance.

3   No compositions

In this section we consider $\cup_\emptyset$ as composition operator, i.e union of programs which do not share predicate symbols, with successful derivations (s) and computed answers (ca) as observables. We first consider $\approx_{(\emptyset,s)}$ and $\approx_{(\emptyset,ca)}$ showing their relations to the s-semantics and the Herbrand semantics. For the sake of brevity, we give below the formal definition of the two equivalences for the general case.

Definition 3.1 *Let P_1, P_2 be programs. Let G be a goal and Q be a program such that $P_i \cup_\Omega Q$ is defined, for $i = 1, 2$. Then*

- $P_1 \approx_{(\Omega,s)} P_2$ *if* $\forall\ G,\ \forall\ Q,\ G \stackrel{\vartheta}{\leadsto}_{P_1 \cup_\Omega Q} \square$ *iff* $G \stackrel{\gamma}{\leadsto}_{P_2 \cup_\Omega Q} \square$,
- $P_1 \approx_{(\Omega,ca)} P_2$ *if* $\forall\ G,\ \forall\ Q,\ G \stackrel{\vartheta}{\leadsto}_{P_1 \cup_\Omega Q} \square$ *iff* $G \stackrel{\vartheta}{\leadsto}_{P_2 \cup_\Omega Q} \square$.

Note that the case $\Omega = \emptyset$ is equivalent to considering no composition at all. Hence in this case the only information we need in an interpretation I is given by the unit clauses contained in I. Formally, for $I, J \subseteq \mathcal{C}$, we can then define $I \sim_{(\emptyset,ca)} J$ iff I and J contain the same unit clauses modulo variance and $I \sim_{(\emptyset,s)} J$ iff I and J have the same ground instances of unit clauses. Equivalences coarser than $\sim_{(\emptyset,ca)}$ and finer than $\sim_{(\emptyset,s)}$ arise when considering abstract semantics.

Note that for $\sim_{(\emptyset,ca)}$ all the previous definitions boil down to the case of the s-semantics. For any $I \in \Im_{\sim_{(\emptyset,ca)}}$, the set of unit clauses (modulo variance) of any element in I can be considered the canonical representative of the equivalence class of I. $T_P^{\sim(\emptyset,ca)}$ is then exactly the immediate consequence operator of [10] and its least fixpoint is the s-semantics [10, 11]. In the case of $\sim_{(\emptyset,s)}$ the canonical representative of an equivalence class J is obtained by taking the set of the ground instances of the unit clauses of an element in J. Then $T_P^{\sim(\emptyset,s)}$ (on canonical representatives) is the standard immediate consequence operator T_P [27] and its least fixpoint is the usual least Herbrand model semantics. In the following we consider $T_P^{\sim(\emptyset,ca)}$ and $T_P^{\sim(\emptyset,s)}$ defined on canonical representatives.

According to definition 3.1, $\approx_{(\emptyset,s)}$ is the equivalence induced by successful derivations, while $\approx_{(\emptyset,ca)}$ is induced by computed answers. By standard results [1, 22] $M(P)$ (the canonical representative of $\mathcal{O}_{\sim_{(\emptyset,s)}}(P)$) is correct and fully abstract wrt $\approx_{(\emptyset,s)}$. Moreover, by the strong completeness theorem in [10, 11], the s-semantics $\mathcal{O}_{\sim_{(\emptyset,ca)}}(P)$ is correct and fully abstract wrt $\approx_{(\emptyset,ca)}$.

We extend now to $T_P^{\sim(\emptyset,ca)}$ some results for the ground operator T_P [24], about the discrimination power of the various equivalences. Proposition 3.2 shows that the "non-ground" equivalences are in general strictly finer than their ground versions. Strictness can be shown by counterexamples similar to the one of example 3.3. The relations between the equivalences for the non-ground case are in proposition 3.4.

Proposition 3.2 *Let P be a program. Then $\approx_{(\emptyset,ca)}$ is strictly finer than $\approx_{(\emptyset,s)}$. Moreover the equivalence wrt $T_P^{\sim(\emptyset,ca)}$ and $[\![P]\!]^{\sim(\emptyset,ca)}$ are strictly finer than the equivalence wrt $T_P^{\sim(\emptyset,s)}$ and $[\![P]\!]^{\sim(\emptyset,s)}$ respectively.*

Example 3.3 *Let us consider the programs $P_1 = \{p(x), q(a), q(b)\}$ and $P_2 = \{p(x), p(a), q(a), q(b)\}$. Since $M(P_1) = M(P_2)$, $P_1 \approx_{(\emptyset,s)} P_2$ while $P_1 \not\approx_{(\emptyset,ca)} P_2$ since for the goal $p(Y)$ only the program P_2 computes the answer Y/a.*

Proposition 3.4 *Let P_1, P_2 be programs. Then*

1. *if $T_{P_1}^{\sim(\emptyset,ca)} + id = T_{P_2}^{\sim(\emptyset,ca)} + id$ then $[\![P_1]\!]^{\sim(\emptyset,ca)} = [\![P_2]\!]^{\sim(\emptyset,ca)}$ and the converse does not hold,*

2. *$[\![P_1]\!]^{\sim(\emptyset,ca)} = [\![P_2]\!]^{\sim(\emptyset,ca)}$ iff $P_1 \approx_{(\Pi,ca)} P_2$ (Π is the set of all the predicates, see corollary 4.11)*

3. *if $[\![P_1]\!]^{\sim(\emptyset,ca)} = [\![P_2]\!]^{\sim(\emptyset,ca)}$ then $P_1 \approx_{(\emptyset,ca)} P_2$ and the converse does not hold,*

4. *the equivalence $\approx_{(\emptyset,ca)}$ is different from (neither coarser nor finer than) the equivalences induced by $T_P^{\sim(\emptyset,s)}$, $T_P^{\sim(\emptyset,s)} + id$ and $[\![P]\!]^{\sim(\emptyset,s)}$.*

A result in [24] states that if clause c_1 subsumes clause c_2 then $T_{c_2} \subseteq T_{c_1}$ and hence $T_{P_1} = T_{P_2}$ iff P_1 and P_2 are subsumption equivalent. Therefore, by proposition 3.2 the equivalence wrt the $T_P^{\sim(\emptyset,ca)}$ operator is strictly finer than subsumption equivalence. Indeed, as shown by proposition 3.6 and by example 3.7, if clause c_1 subsumes clause c_2 we can only prove that for every atom A in $T_{c_2}^{\sim(\emptyset,ca)}(Q)$ there exists a more general atom B in $T_{c_1}^{\sim(\emptyset,ca)}(Q)$ and we cannot prove $T_{c_1}^{\sim(\emptyset,ca)} \supseteq T_{c_2}^{\sim(\emptyset,ca)}$.

Definition 3.5 *Let A, B be sets of atoms. $A \preceq B$ iff $\forall\, X \in A, \exists \theta, \exists\, Y \in B$ s.t. $Y\vartheta = X$. If f, g are functions defined on sets of atoms, $f \preceq g$ iff $\forall A, f(A) \preceq g(A)$.*

Proposition 3.6 *If c_1 subsumes c_2, then $T_{c_2}^{\sim(\emptyset,ca)} \preceq T_{c_1}^{\sim(\emptyset,ca)}$. Moreover, programs P_1 and P_2 are subsumption equivalent iff $T_{P_1}^{\sim(\emptyset,ca)} \preceq T_{P_2}^{\sim(\emptyset,ca)}$ and $T_{P_2}^{\sim(\emptyset,ca)} \preceq T_{P_1}^{\sim(\emptyset,ca)}$.*

Example 3.7 *Consider programs $Q_1 = \{c_1\}$ and $Q_2 = \{c_2\}$ where $c_1 = q(X) : -q(X)$ and $c_2 = q(X) : -q(X), q(X)$. c_1 subsumes c_2 (and vice versa). However $T_{Q_1}^{\sim(\emptyset,ca)} \not\supseteq T_{Q_2}^{\sim(\emptyset,ca)}$ since if $Z = \{q(f(a, X)), q(f(X, b))\}$ then $q(f(a, b)) \in T_{Q_2}^{\sim(\emptyset,ca)}(Z) \setminus T_{Q_1}^{\sim(\emptyset,ca)}(Z)$. Note that $Q_1 \approx_{(\emptyset,ca)} Q_2$ and $Q_1 \cup Z$ and $Q_2 \cup Z$ are subsumption equivalent. However, $Q_1 \cup Z \not\approx_{(\emptyset,ca)} Q_2 \cup Z$ since the goal $q(X)$ can compute the answer $X/f(a, b)$ in $Q_2 \cup Z$ only (and therefore $Q_1 \not\approx_{(\Omega,ca)} Q_2$ for $\Omega = \{q\}$).*

From previous example we have also that (weak) subsumption equivalence does not imply $\approx_{(\emptyset,ca)}$. Therefore, when considering computed answers, (weak) subsumption equivalent clauses cannot be considered equivalent because the logical meaning of subsumption is not adequate to replace the operational meaning of SLD (clause c_2, which is a tautology, cannot be deleted nor replaced by c_1 in $Q_2 \cup Z$). This discrepancy is of the same nature of the weakness of the completeness theorem for SLD resolution (only answers more general than correct answers can be computed [22]). (Weak) subsumption equivalence is perfectly adequate to model successful derivations. Indeed if P_1 and P_2 are (weak) subsumption equivalent, $(id+)T_{P_1} = (id+)T_{P_2}$ [24] and therefore the programs have the same least Herbrand model and the same successful derivations.

4 Compositional equivalences

We consider the general case with $\cup_\Omega$ as composition operator. We first define a syntactic equivalence $\simeq$ on clauses which is correct wrt $\approx_{(\Omega,ca)}$ (for any Ω) and hence can be used to define π-interpretations for the compositional case when considering computed answers. Two semantics correct wrt $\approx_{(\Omega,ca)}$ and $\approx_{(\Omega,s)}$ are then obtained from the general scheme by defining the equivalences $\sim_{(\Omega,ca)}$ and $\sim_{(\Omega,s)}$ on sets of clauses. Moreover we show the relation of $\simeq$ and $\approx_{(\Omega,ca)}$ to previous equivalences.

Definition 4.1 *Let* $c = H : -B_1, \ldots, B_n$ *be a clause. An atom* B_i *is relevant in* c *iff either it shares variables with* H *or, inductively, it shares variables with an atom* B_j *relevant in* c. *The multiset of relevant atoms in* c *is denoted by* $Rel(c)$.

Definition 4.2 *Let* $c_1 = A_1 : -B_1, \ldots, B_n$, $c_2 = A_2 : -D_1, \ldots, D_m$ *be two clauses which do not share variables. Let us denote by* $\subseteq^+$ *multiset inclusion and by* $Set(M)$ *the set of the elements in the multiset* M. *Then* $c_1 \leq_c c_2$ *iff* c_1 *subsumes* c_2 *and there exists a renaming* ρ *such that* $A_1 = A_2\rho$, $Rel(c_2\rho) \subseteq^+ Rel(c_1)$ *and* $Set(Rel(c_2)\rho) = Set(Rel(c_1))$. $\simeq$ *denotes the equivalence induced by* $\leq_c$.

Definition 4.3 *Let* P_1, P_2 *be programs. Then* $P_1 \trianglelefteq P_2$ *iff* $\forall c_2 \in P_2, \exists c_1 \in P_1$ *such that* $c_1 \leq_c c_2$. *We denote by* $\simeq_p$ *the equivalence induced by* $\trianglelefteq$.

It is worth noting that relevant atoms in clause bodies are considered as multisets and that clauses equivalent up to $\simeq$ are subsumption equivalent and have the same multiset of relevant atoms (up to renaming). Indeed, as shown by example 3.7, a relevant atom cannot be deleted (even if subsumed by another atom in the clause) without changing the computed answers semantics of the clause (therefore $c_2 \leq_c c_1$ while $c_1 \not\leq_c c_2$). The example can be generalized to show that also relevant atoms which contain local variables only cannot be deleted. By corollary 4.6, if $P_1 \leq_c P_2$ then P_1 behaves as P_2 under any composition, while if $P_1 \simeq_p P_2$ then the two sets of clauses are indistinguishable (up to $\approx_{(\Omega,ca)}$). As a consequence, $\simeq$ can be used to correctly define the equivalence $\sim_{(\Omega,ca)}$. Note that while $\simeq$ (on clauses) gives the same equivalence as the $T_P^{\sim(\emptyset,ca)}$'s equality (proposition 4.4), this is not the case for $\simeq_p$ (proposition 4.5).

Proposition 4.4 *Let* $P_1 = \{c_1\}$ *and* $P_2 = \{c_2\}$ *be programs. Then* $T_{P_1}^{\sim(\emptyset,ca)} = T_{P_2}^{\sim(\emptyset,ca)}$ *iff* $c_1 \simeq c_2$.

Proposition 4.5 *Let* P_1, P_2 *be programs. If* $P_1 \trianglelefteq P_2$ *then for any set of atoms* X, $T_{P_1}^{\sim(\emptyset,ca)}(X) \supseteq T_{P_2}^{\sim(\emptyset,ca)}(X)$ *and the converse does not hold.*

Corollary 4.6 *Let* P_1, P_2, Q *be programs such that* $P_1 \trianglelefteq P_2$. *If* $G \overset{\vartheta}{\leadsto}_{P_2 \cup Q} \square$ *then* $G \overset{\vartheta}{\leadsto}_{P_1 \cup Q} \square$. *Moreover if* $P_1 \simeq_p P_2$ *then* $P_1 \approx_{(\Omega,ca)} P_2$ *for any* Ω.

Let $\mathcal{C}_\Omega = \{H : -\tilde{B} \in \mathcal{C} \mid Pred(\tilde{B}) \subseteq \Omega\}$. In order to get compositionality wrt $\cup_\Omega$ we need only the information given by clauses in $\mathcal{C}_\Omega$. Then we define for $I, J \subseteq \mathcal{C}$, $I \sim_{(\Omega,ca)} J$ iff $I \cap \mathcal{C}_\Omega \simeq_p J \cap \mathcal{C}_\Omega$. Note that for $\Omega = \emptyset$, $\sim_{(\Omega,ca)}$ is the same of $\sim_{(\emptyset,ca)}$ of section 3. Theorem 4.7 shows that $\mathcal{O}_{\sim_{(\Omega,ca)}}(P)$ is compositional wrt program union and correctly models computed answers. Therefore (corollary 4.8) it is correct wrt $\approx_{(\Omega,ca)}$. Similar results (using a different semantic domain based on clauses) have already been given in [5, 4].

Theorem 4.7 *Let P_1, P_2 be programs. If $P_1 \cup_\Omega P_2$ is defined then*
$$\mathcal{O}_{\sim_{(\Omega,ca)}}(\iota(\mathcal{O}_{\sim_{(\Omega,ca)}}(P_1) \sqcup \mathcal{O}_{\sim_{(\Omega,ca)}}(P_2))) = \mathcal{O}_{\sim_{(\Omega,ca)}}(P_1 \cup_\Omega P_2). \text{ Moreover}$$
$P_1 \approx_{(\Omega,ca)} \iota(\mathcal{O}_{\sim_{(\Omega,ca)}}(P_1))$.

Corollary 4.8 *Let P_1, P_2 be programs. If $\mathcal{O}_{\sim_{(\Omega,ca)}}(P_1) = \mathcal{O}_{\sim_{(\Omega,ca)}}(P_2)$ then*
$P_1 \approx_{(\Omega,ca)} P_2$.

It is easy to show that the converse of the corollary does not hold, i.e. the semantics $\mathcal{O}_{\sim_{(\Omega,ca)}}(P)$ is not fully abstract wrt $\approx_{(\Omega,ca)}$. The difficulty here is related to the use of clauses in the semantic domain (note that the full abstractness result in [19] was obtained using a domain not containing clauses).

We now show the relation of $\approx_{(\Omega,ca)}$ to other equivalences. It is easy to prove that if $\Psi \subseteq \Omega$ then $\approx_{(\Omega,ca)}$ is strictly finer than $\approx_{(\Psi,ca)}$. Theorem 4.9 and corollary 4.11 show one interesting result which relate the $[\![P]\!]^{\sim(\emptyset,ca)}$ semantics to the $\approx_{(\Omega,ca)}$ equivalence. When we consider the semantics of a program P as the function $[\![P]\!]^{\sim(\emptyset,ca)}$ restricted to sets of atoms Q such that $Pred(Q) \subseteq \Omega$, such a semantics is correct and fully abstract wrt to $\approx_{(\Omega,ca)}$. Therefore the semantics $[\![P]\!]^{\sim(\emptyset,ca)}$ is correct and fully abstract wrt $\approx_{(\Pi,ca)}$ where Π is the set of all the predicates. Example 4.10 shows that the hypothesis $Pred(Q) \subseteq \Omega$ in theorem 4.9 is necessary.

Theorem 4.9 *If P_1 and P_2 are programs then for any Ω, $P_1 \approx_{(\Omega,ca)} P_2$ iff for any set of atoms Q, such that $Pred(Q) \subseteq \Omega$, $[\![P_1]\!]^{\sim(\emptyset,ca)}(Q) = [\![P_2]\!]^{\sim(\emptyset,ca)}(Q)$.*

Example 4.10 *Let $P_1 = \{p : -q\}$ and $P_2 = \{\}$. Then $P_1 \approx_{(\emptyset,ca)} P_2$, but*
$[\![P_1]\!]^{\sim(\emptyset,ca)}(\{q\}) \neq [\![P_2]\!]^{\sim(\emptyset,ca)}(\{q\})$

Corollary 4.11 *If P_1 and P_2 are programs then $P_1 \approx_{(\Pi,ca)} P_2$ iff $[\![P_1]\!]^{\sim(\emptyset,ca)} = [\![P_2]\!]^{\sim(\emptyset,ca)}$.*

Results similar to those of proposition 3.4 can be shown to hold for the operator $T_P^{\sim(\Omega,ca)}$, and the equivalences induced by $T_P^{\sim(\Omega,ca)}(+id)$ and by $[\![P]\!]^{\sim(\Omega,ca)}$ are strictly finer when considering a larger set Ω.

Finally let us consider the equivalence $\approx_{(\Omega,s)}$. As previously discussed, weak subsumption equivalence can be used to define π−interpretations, since we are concerned with successful derivations only. Then we can define for $I, J \subseteq \mathcal{C}$, $I \sim_{(\Omega,s)} J$ iff $I \cap \mathcal{C}_\Omega$ is weakly subsumption equivalent to $J \cap \mathcal{C}_\Omega$. Theorem 4.12 states correctness and full abstraction of the resulting semantics. A different fully abstract invariant wrt $\approx_{(\Omega,s)}$ was already given in [18].

Theorem 4.12 *Let P_1, P_2 be programs. Then $\mathcal{O}_{\sim_{(\Omega,s)}}(P_1) = \mathcal{O}_{\sim_{(\Omega,s)}}(P_2)$ iff*
$P_1 \approx_{(\Omega,s)} P_2$.

5   Partial answers and call patterns

A fixpoint semantics for partial answers has been already defined in [9] and then extended in [17] to consider also correct partial answers, call patterns and selection rules. In subsection 5.1 we show how the results of [17] can be obtained in our framework by considering suitable instances of the semantic scheme. In particular we show a fully abstract semantics for partial answers. Observables and equivalences depending on the selection rule are considered in subsection 5.2.

A *partial answer* is the substitution computed by a derivation which is not yet terminated. A distinction can be made between a partial answer and a *correct* partial answer for a goal G. The first is the restriction to the variables in G of the composition of the mgu's computed in any partial derivation for G, while the second requires also that the derivation be part of a successful derivation. For example, programs $P_1 = \{r(a) : -q\}$ and $P_2 = \{q, r(a) : -q\}$ have the same partial answers for the goal $r(x)$, but not the same correct partial answers. Note that if ϑ is a correct partial answer for the goal G in program P, then $\exists X.G\vartheta$, for $X = Var(G\vartheta)$, is a logical consequence of P. This is not the case for partial answers. As shown by example 5.1 (correct) partial answers depend on the selection rule. We then give the following definition.

Example 5.1 *The program $P = \{p(a),\ q(b),\ r(X,Y) : -p(X), q(Y)\}$ has correct partial answers X/a or Y/b for the goal $r(X,Y)$ depending on the (leftmost or rightmost) selection rule.*

Definition 5.2 *Let P be a program, R be a selection rule and G be a goal. The substitution ϑ is an R-partial answer for G in P iff $G \overset{\vartheta}{\leadsto}_{P,R} B_1, \ldots, B_n$, $n \geq 0$. ϑ is a correct R-partial answer for the goal G iff $G \overset{\vartheta}{\leadsto}_{P,R} B_1, \ldots, B_n \overset{\gamma}{\leadsto}_P \Box$, $n \geq 0$. Moreover, ϑ is a (correct) partial answer for G in P iff there exists a rule R such that ϑ is a (correct) R-partial answer for G in P.*

It is interesting to study equivalences based on partial answers, since these notions are useful in abstract interpretation [6]. Another observable which arises in the framework of program analysis is "call patterns". According to the procedural interpretation of logic programs, a selected atom $p(\tilde{t})$ in a derivation can be considered a "call" of the procedure p with parameter $\tilde{t}$. A "call pattern" is therefore any selected atom in a derivation. Also in this case we can be concerned with the selection rule and the correct call patterns. The formal definition of (correct)(R-) call pattern can then be obtained from definition 5.2 by replacing "the substitution ϑ" by "the atom $B_i\vartheta$, $1 \leq i \leq n$".

5.1   Without selection rules

We first consider the case where the selection rule is not specified. Let us formally introduce the four equivalences induced by these observables.

Definition 5.3 *Let P_1, P_2 and Q be programs such that $P_i \cup_\Omega Q$ is defined, for $i = 1, 2$. Then we define $P_1 \approx_{(\Omega,p)} P_2$, $P_1 \approx_{(\Omega,cp)} P_2$, $P_1 \approx_{(\Omega,pt)} P_2$ and $P_1 \approx_{(\Omega,cpt)} P_2$ iff $\forall\ G$, $\forall\ Q$, G has the same set of (respectively) partial answers, correct partial answers, call patterns and correct call patterns in $P_1 \cup_\Omega Q$ and in $P_2 \cup_\Omega Q$.*

For the sake of simplicity, we consider only the case $\Omega = \emptyset$. The compositional case can be obtained by techniques similar to those used in the above sections. Suitable instances of the semantic scheme can be used to model (correct) partial answers and call patterns. The key issue is that we can extract from the clauses in $\mathcal{O}_\sim(P)$ all the information needed to obtain these observables for any goal G. For example, ϑ is a partial answer for the goal $p(\tilde{t})$ iff there exists a clause $H : -B_1, \ldots, B_n$ in $\iota(\mathcal{O}_\sim(P))$ such that $\vartheta = \gamma_{|p(\tilde{t})}$ for $\gamma = mgu(p(\tilde{t}), H)$. ϑ is a correct partial answer if there exists such a clause and there exist n atoms $C_1, \ldots, C_n$ in $\iota(\mathcal{O}_\sim(P))$ such that $(B_1, \ldots, B_n)\gamma$ unifies with $(C_1, \ldots, C_n)$. Note that, when considering partial answers, we need only the information in the heads of the clauses in $\mathcal{O}_\sim(P)$. For correct partial answers instead we have to consider also the bodies. For example, if $P = \{q(X),\ p(X) : -q(X),\ q(a) : -r(a)\}$ then $\mathcal{O}_\sim(P) = [P \cup$

$\{p(X),\ p(a)\ :\ -r(a)\}]_{/\sim}$. Therefore X/a is the mgu of $p(X)$ and the head of a clause in $\mathcal{O}_\sim(P)$. However X/a is not a correct partial answer. We can then define the equivalences $\sim_{(\emptyset,p)}$, $\sim_{(\emptyset,cp)}$ and the semantics for partial answers as follows.

Definition 5.4 *Let P be a program. For $I,J \subseteq \mathcal{C}$ we define $I \sim_{(\emptyset,p)} J$ iff $\forall H :$ $-\tilde{B} \in I\ \exists K : -\tilde{C} \in J$ such that $H = K\rho$ for a renaming ρ. The partial answer semantics $\mathcal{S}_{(\emptyset,p)}(P)$ and the correct partial answer semantics $\mathcal{S}_{(\emptyset,cp)}(P)$ of P are then defined as $\mathcal{S}_{(\emptyset,p)}(P) = \mathcal{O}_{\sim_{(\emptyset,p)}}(P)$ and $\mathcal{S}_{(\emptyset,cp)}(P) = \mathcal{O}_{\sim_{(\Pi,ca)}}(P)$.*

It is possible to prove that ϑ is a partial answer for the goal $G = A_1,\ldots,A_k$ in the program P iff for $j = 1,\ldots,k\ \exists H_j \in \iota(\mathcal{S}_{(\emptyset,p)}(P))$ such that $\vartheta = \gamma_{|G}$ and $\gamma = mgu((A_1,\ldots,A_k),(H_1,\ldots,H_k))$. A similar characterization can be given for correct partial answer, considering heads of clauses in $\iota(\mathcal{P}_{(\emptyset,cp)}(P))$ and requiring also that the conjunction of the bodies of such clauses unify with a conjunction of unit clauses taken from $\iota(\mathcal{S}_{(\emptyset,cp)}(P))$.

The information needed to model call patterns can be obtained from the clauses in $\mathcal{O}_\sim(P)$ as well. For example C is a call pattern for the atomic goal A in the program P, iff $\exists H : -B_1,\ldots,B_n \in \mathcal{O}_\sim(P)$ such that $C = B_i\vartheta$, $1 \leq i \leq n$, where $\vartheta = mgu(A,H)$. Note that we only need the information on the relation between the head and the various atoms in the body (i.e. the clause $H : -B_1,\ldots,B_n$ is equivalent to the set of clauses $\{H : -B_1,\ldots,H : -B_n\}$). When considering correct call patterns we need to keep all the information on the clause bodies (viewed as multisets). The equivalence $\sim_{(\emptyset,p)}$ and the semantics for call patterns are then defined as follows.

Definition 5.5 *Let P be a program. Let us define, for $I,J \subseteq \mathcal{C}$, $I \sim_{(\emptyset,pt)} J$ iff $\forall H : -B_1,\ldots,B_n \in I$ for $i = 1,\ldots,n$, $\exists K : -C_1,\ldots,C_m \in J$ such that $H : -B_i = (K : -C_j)\rho_i$ for $1 \leq j \leq m$, ρ_i renaming and vice versa. Moreover, $\sim_{(\emptyset,cpt)}$ is variance on clauses considering bodies as multisets. The call patterns semantics $\mathcal{C}_\emptyset(P)$ and the correct call pattern semantics $\mathcal{C}_{(\emptyset,cpt)}(P)$ are defined as $\mathcal{C}_\emptyset(P) = \mathcal{O}_{\sim_{(\emptyset,pt)}}(P)$ and $\mathcal{C}_{(\emptyset,cpt)}(P) = \mathcal{O}_{\sim_{(\emptyset,cpt)}}(P)$.*

The following theorem shows the correctness of all the semantics considered and the full abstraction of $\mathcal{S}_{(\emptyset,p)}(P)$ (wrt the appropriate $\approx_x$ equivalences). The same theorem was already obtained in [17] by using a slightly different definition of the semantic domain. Note that the equivalences considered in this section are all different and no one is contained in any other. The relations to the equivalence $\approx_{(\Pi,ca)}$ are shown by proposition 5.7

Theorem 5.6 *Let P_1,P_2 be programs. For $x \in \{(\emptyset,p),(\emptyset,cp),(\emptyset,pt),(\emptyset,cpt)\}$ the following facts hold. 1) For any $I \in \mathcal{S}_x(P_1)$, $I \approx_x P_1$. 2) If $\mathcal{S}_x(P_1) = \mathcal{S}_x(P_2)$ then $P_1 \approx_x P_2$. 3) $\mathcal{S}_{(\emptyset,p)}(P_1) = \mathcal{S}_{(\emptyset,p)}(P_2)$ iff $P_1 \approx_{(\emptyset,p)} P_2$.*

Proposition 5.7 *Let P_1,P_2 be programs. If $P_1 \approx_{(\Pi,ca)} P_2$ then $P_1 \approx_{(\emptyset,p)} P_2$ and $P_1 \approx_{(\emptyset,cp)} P_2$.*

5.2 Introducing a selection rule

We will consider in this section equivalences based on partial answers with a given selection rule R, showing a correct and fully abstract semantics for them originally defined in [17]. Such a semantic is defined both top-down and bottom up, and the equivalence of the two constructions holds only when considering *local* selection rules. A local selection rule was defined in [28] as a rule which selects in a resolvent $\tilde{N}$ always one of the most recently introduced atoms in the derivation from the goal to $\tilde{N}$ (the atom A is introduced in the resolvent $\tilde{M}$ if A is in the body of the clause used to obtain $\tilde{M}$ from its parent in the derivation). This definition is modified in [17] by requiring also that a fixed ordering is given (by means of a bijection ϕ on the set of integer numbers) for the selection of atoms in the bodies, and hence for the selection of one the most recently introduced atoms. Note that PROLOG leftmost rule is local and in general local rules produce SLD trees with a simple structure, suitable for efficient searching techniques [28].

When considering the selection rule, the ordering of atoms in the body of a clause is relevant. We will therefore consider π−interpretations as sets of clauses modulo variance (denoted by $\sim$). In order to take into account the selection rule, definition 2.1 can easily be changed by deleting Id_Ω (which was used exactly to get the independence from the selection rule). Adapting definition 2.2 is more complicate and the formal definition of the $T_{(P,R_\phi)}$ operator for the rule R_ϕ is given in [17]. The intuition is that since R_ϕ is local, the ordering ϕ can also be used "locally" on the body of any clause used in the bottom-up "computation" defined by $T_{(P,R_\phi)}$. For example, considering as R_ϕ the leftmost rule, if $H : -B_1, \ldots, B_n \in P$ and for any k, $1 \leq k \leq n$, $\exists\, k-1$ unit clauses $A_1, \ldots, A_{k-1} \in X$ and $\exists\, A_k : -\tilde{B} \in X \cup Id_\Pi$, then $(H : -\tilde{B}, B_{k+1}, \ldots, B_n)\vartheta \in T_{(P,R_\phi)}(X)$ where $\vartheta = mgu((B_1, \ldots, B_k)(A_1, \ldots, A_k))$. In [17] is proved that the operator $T_{(P,R_\phi)}$ is continuous on the lattice of π-interpretations and that its least fixpoint $T_{(P,R_\phi)} \uparrow \omega$ is equal to the top-down semantics $\mathcal{O}_{(\sim,R_\phi)}(P)$.

Definition 5.8 *[17] Let P be a positive program and R be a local selection rule. Then we define*

$$\mathcal{O}_{(\sim,R)}(P) = \{A : -B_1, \ldots, B_m \in \mathcal{C} \mid \quad \exists\vartheta \text{ s.t. } p(\tilde{X}) \stackrel{\vartheta}{\rightsquigarrow}_{P,R} B_1, \ldots, B_m, \ m \geq 0,$$
$$A = p(\tilde{X})\vartheta, \text{ for } \tilde{X} \text{ distinct variables} \quad \}$$

When considering R-partial answers, we only need the information from the heads of clauses in $\mathcal{O}_{(\sim,R)}(P)$. However, we need to distinguish between partial answers (obtained by heads of clauses with non-empty bodies in $\mathcal{O}_{(\sim,R)}(P)$) and computed answers (obtained by unit clauses in $\mathcal{O}_{(\sim,R)}(P)$). Consider for example the clause $p(X, Y) : -q(X), r(Y)$ with the leftmost selection rule. Clearly if Y/b is a partial answer for $r(Y)$ and X/a is an answer for $q(X)$, then $\{X/a, Y/b\}$ is a partial answer for $p(X, Y)$, while this is not the case if X/a is a partial answer (and not an answer) for $q(X)$. A correct and fully abstract semantics (theorem 5.10) $\mathcal{S}_{(\emptyset,p,R)}(P)$ for R-partial answers and computed answers is obtained from $\mathcal{O}_{(\sim,R_\phi)}(P)$ as follows. Results based on $\mathcal{O}_{(\sim,R)}(P)$, similar to those of the previous subsections, can be shown to hold for R-correct partial answers and R-call patterns.

Definition 5.9 *[17] Let P be a positive program and R be a local selection rule. The R-partial answer semantics $\mathcal{S}_{(\emptyset,p,R)}(P)$ of P is ($\uplus$ denotes the disjoint union) $\mathcal{S}_{(\emptyset,p,R)}(P) = S \uplus T$ where*
$$T = \{A \mid A \in I \text{ for } I \in \mathcal{O}_{(\sim,R)}(P)\}_{/\sim}$$
$$S = \{A \mid \exists A : -B_1, \ldots, B_n \in I \cup Id_\Pi \text{ for } I \in \mathcal{O}_{(\sim,R)}(P)\}_{/\sim}$$

Theorem 5.10 *[17] Let P_1, P_2 be programs and R be a local selection rule. Then $\mathcal{S}_{(\emptyset,p,R)}(P_1) = \mathcal{S}_{(\emptyset,p,R)}(P_2)$ iff for any goal G, G has the same computed answers and the same R-partial answers in P_1 and in P_2.*

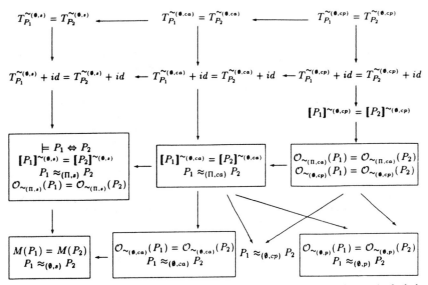

Figure 1. $A \longrightarrow B$ means that A is strictly finer than B. Equivalences included in a box coincide. The leftmost column is from [24] (apart from $\mathcal{O}_{\sim_{(\Pi,s)}}(P)$).

6   Conclusions

Some of the relations among the various equivalences we have studied are illustrated by figure 1. Equivalences in columns from the right to the left correspond to increasingly more abstract observables (partial answers, computed answers and successful derivations respectively). Fully abstract semantics wrt $\approx_{(\circ,X)}$ are those for which the equivalence $\mathcal{S}(P_1) = \mathcal{S}(P_2)$ is in the same box as $P_1 \approx_{(\circ,X)} P_2$. Moving from the top to the bottom in each column abstraction grows. In the first two columns, below compositional observational equivalence, compositionality is lost at the expense of abstraction. In the third column note that since $\mathcal{O}_{\sim_{(\bullet,cp)}}(P) = \mathcal{O}_{\sim_{(\Pi,ca)}}(P)$, $\mathcal{O}_{\sim_{(\bullet,cp)}}(P)$ is also compositional. $\mathcal{O}_{\sim_{(\bullet,p)}}(P)$ is an abstraction of $\mathcal{O}_{\sim_{(\bullet,cp)}}(P)$.

The general scheme $\mathcal{O}_{\sim}(P)$ captures several observational equivalences. For example, its instance $\mathcal{O}_{\sim_{(\bullet,ca)}}(P)$ (the s-semantics) is correct and fully abstract wrt computed answers. $\mathcal{O}_{\sim_{(\Pi,ca)}}(P)$ is correct wrt computed answers with the composition $\cup_{\Pi}$. $\mathcal{O}_{\sim_{(\bullet,p)}}(P)$ is correct and fully abstract wrt partial answers. $\mathcal{O}_{\sim_{(\bullet,pt)}}(P)$ is correct wrt call patterns. Hence $\mathcal{O}_{\sim}(P)$ can be taken as the basic semantic framework for program transformation and program analysis (where different observables correspond to different "collecting" semantics). Since $\mathcal{O}_{\sim}(P)$ has both a procedural and a fixpoint definition, equivalent top-down and bottom-up techniques are available. Finally note that most of the equivalences considered are undecidable. However some of them are decidable for specific classes of programs. For example, for Datalog programs the equivalence $\approx_{(\Omega,ca)}$ is decidable.

Acknowledgments

Part of this work was carried out while the first author was visiting IIAS, FUJITSU Ltd. Tokyo. He would like to thank all the people at IIAS and in particular Jiro Tanaka and Hiroyasu Sugano.

References

[1] K. R. Apt. Introduction to Logic Programming. In J. van Leeuwen, editor, *Handbook of Theoretical Computer Science*, volume B: Formal Models and Semantics. Elsevier, Amsterdam and The MIT Press, Cambridge, 1990.

[2] R. Barbuti, R. Giacobazzi, and G. Levi. A General Framework for Semantics-based Bottom-up Abstract Interpretation of Logic Programs. Technical Report TR 12/91, Dipartimento di Informatica, Università di Pisa, 1991. To appear in *ACM Transactions on Programming Languages and Systems*.

[3] A. Bossi and N. Cocco. Basic transformation operations for logic programs which preserve computed answer substitutions. To appear in *Journal of Logic Programming*, 1991.

[4] A. Bossi, M. Gabbrielli, G. Levi, and M. C. Meo. Contributions to the Semantics of Open Logic Programs. In *Proceedings of the Int'l Conf. on Fifth Generation Computer Systems 1992*, pages 570–580. ICOT, Tokyo 1992.

[5] A. Bossi and M. Menegus. Una Semantica Composizionale per Programmi Logici Aperti. In P. Asirelli, editor, *Proc. Sixth Italian Conf. on Logic Programming*, pages 95–109, 1991.

[6] M. Codish, D. Dams, and E. Yardeni. Bottom-up Abstract Interpretation of Logic Programs. Technical report, Dept. of Computer Science, The Weizmann Institute, Rehovot, 1990. To appear in *Theoretical Computer Science*.

[7] P. Cousot and R. Cousot. Abstract Interpretation: A Unified Lattice Model for Static Analysis of Programs by Construction or Approximation of Fixpoints. In *Proc. Fourth ACM Symp. POPL*, pages 238–252, 1977.

[8] S. Debray and R. Ramakrishnan. Generalized Horn Clause Programs. Technical report, Dept. of Computer Science, The University of Arizona, 1991.

[9] M. Falaschi and G. Levi. Finite failures and partial computations in concurrent logic languages. *Theoretical Computer Science*, 75:45–66, 1990.

[10] M. Falaschi, G. Levi, M. Martelli, and C. Palamidessi. A new Declarative Semantics for Logic Languages. In R. A. Kowalski and K. A. Bowen, editors, *Proc. Fifth Int'l Conf. on Logic Programming*, pages 993–1005. The MIT Press, Cambridge, Mass., 1988.

[11] M. Falaschi, G. Levi, M. Martelli, and C. Palamidessi. Declarative Modeling of the Operational Behavior of Logic Languages. *Theoretical Computer Science*, 69(3):289–318, 1989.

[12] M. Gabbrielli and G. Levi. Modeling Answer Constraints in Constraint Logic Programs. In K. Furukawa, editor, *Proc. Eighth Int'l Conf. on Logic Programming*, pages 238– 252. The MIT Press, Cambridge, Mass., 1991.

[13] M. Gabbrielli and G. Levi. On the Semantics of Logic Programs. In J. Leach Albert, B. Monien, and M. Rodriguez-Artalejo, editors, *18th Int'l Colloquium on Automata, Languages an Programming*, volume 510 of *Lecture Notes in Computer Science*, pages 1–19. Springer-Verlag, Berlin, 1991.

[14] M. Gabbrielli and G. Levi. Unfolding and Fixpoint Semantics of Concurrent Constraint Programs. Technical Report TR 2/91, Dipartimento di Informatica, Università di Pisa, 1991. To appear in *Theoretical Computer Science*.

[15] M. Gabbrielli, G. Levi, and M. C. Meo. Observational Equivalences for Logic Programs. Technical Report, Dipartimento di Informatica, Università di Pisa, 1992.

[16] M. Gabbrielli, G. Levi, and D. Turi. A Two Steps Semantics for Logic Programs with Negation. In *Proceedings of the Int'l Conf. on Logic Programming and Automated Reasoning*, Lecture Notes in Artificial Intelligence. Springer-Verlag, Berlin, 1992.

[17] M. Gabbrielli and M. C. Meo. Fixpoint Semantics for Partial Computed Answer Substitutions and Call Patterns. In H. Kirchner and G. Levi, editors, *Proceedings of Third Int'l Conf. on Algebraic and Logic Programming*, Lecture Notes in Computer Science. Springer-Verlag, Berlin, 1992.

[18] H. Gaifman and E. Shapiro. Fully abstract compositional semantics for logic programs. In *Proc. Sixteenth Annual ACM Symp. on Principles of Programming Languages*, pages 134–142. ACM, 1989.

[19] H. Gaifman and E. Shapiro. Proof theory and semantics of logic programs. In *Proc. Fourth IEEE Symp. on Logic In Computer Science*, pages 50–62. IEEE Computer Society Press, 1989.

[20] T. Kawamura and T. Kanamori. Preservation of Stronger Equivalence in Unfold/Fold Logic Programming Transformation. In *Proc. Int'l Conf. on Fifth Generation Computer Systems*, pages 413–422. ICOT, Tokyo, 1988.

[21] J.-L. Lassez and M. J. Maher. Closures and Fairness in the Semantics of Programming Logic. *Theoretical Computer Science*, 29:167–184, 1984.

[22] J. W. Lloyd. *Foundations of Logic Programming*. Springer-Verlag, Berlin, 1987. Second edition.

[23] J. W. Lloyd and J. C. Shepherdson. Partial Evaluation in Logic Programming. *Journal of Logic Programming*, 11:217–242, 1991.

[24] M. J. Maher. Equivalences of Logic Programs. In J. Minker, editor, *Foundations of Deductive Databases and Logic Programming*, pages 627–658. Morgan Kaufmann, Los Altos, Ca., 1988.

[25] K. Marriott and H. Søndergaard. Semantics-based Dataflow Analysis of Logic Programs. In G. Ritter, editor, *Information Processing 89*. North-Holland, 1989.

[26] D. Turi. Extending S-Models to Logic Programs with Negation. In K. Furukawa, editor, *Proc. Eighth Int'l Conf. on Logic Programming*, pages 397–411. The MIT Press, Cambridge, Mass., 1991.

[27] M. H. van Emden and R. A. Kowalski. The semantics of predicate logic as a programming language. *Journal of the ACM*, 23(4):733–742, 1976.

[28] L. Vieille. Recursive query processing: the power of logic. *Theoretical Computer Science*, 69:1–53, 1989.

On Normal Forms and Equivalence for Logic Programs

James Harland
Department of Computer Science
University of Melbourne
Parkville, 3052, Australia
jah@cs.mu.oz.au

Abstract

It is known that larger classes of formulae than Horn clauses may be used as logic programming languages. One such class of formulae is *hereditary Harrop formulae*, for which an operational notion of provability has been studied, and it is known that operational provability corresponds to provability in intuitionistic logic. In this paper we discuss the notion of a normal form for this class of formulae, and show how this may be given by removing disjunctions and existential quantifications from programs. Whilst the normal form of the program preserves operational provability, there are operationally equivalent programs which are not intuitionistically equivalent. As it is known that classical logic is too strong to precisely capture operational provability for larger classes of programs than Horn clauses, the appropriate logic in which to study questions of equivalence is an intermediate logic. We explore the nature of the required logic, and show that this may be obtained by the addition of the *Independence of Premise* axioms to intuitionistic logic. We show how equivalence in this logic captures the notion of operational provability, in that logically equivalent programs are operationally equivalent. This result suggests that the natural logic in which to study logic programming is a slightly stronger constructive logic than intuitionistic logic.

1 Introduction

It is well known that variables which appear in Horn clauses may be considered to be universally quantified at the front of the clause, so that the Prolog clause `p(X) :- q(X,Y)` may be considered a shorthand for the formula $\forall x \forall y\, p(x) \subset q(x,y)$. However, we may also consider variables which do not appear in the head of the clause as being existentially quantified at the front of the *body*, so that the above clause is equivalent to $\forall x\, p(x) \subset \exists y\, q(x,y)$. Thus we may consider Horn clauses to have the expressive power of the latter style (i.e. in which existential quantifiers are allowed in the bodies of clauses), but we need only implement the former style. In this way we may think of the more restrictive definition as a normal form for programs corresponding to the second definition.

A more general class of programs and goals was given in [11], the definition of which is given below.

$$D := A \mid \forall x D \mid D_1 \wedge D_2 \mid G \supset A$$
$$G := A \mid \exists x G \mid G_1 \wedge G_2 \mid G_1 \vee G_2 \mid D \supset G$$

where A denotes an atom. A program is a set of closed D formulae and a goal is a closed G formula.

In [11], it was shown how disjunctions may be removed from programs in the above class, in that for any program which contains a disjunction, there is a program with the same operational behaviour, which, although usually much larger, contains no disjunctions. We may think of this as removing redundancies from the program, and so programs may be given a simpler definition, in that there is a smaller class of formulae with the same expressive power. In this paper we extend this result by showing that existential quantifiers may be similarly removed from programs. Thus, the normal form will be a program which contains no disjunctions and no existential quantifications.

Another interesting property of Horn clauses [7, 8] when used as a programming language is that the class of goals used, i.e. (existentially quantified) conjunctions of atoms, sometimes seems to be somewhat restrictive, as it does not allow goals to inspect the structure of the program. For example, the success or failure of any Horn clause goal is the same no matter which of the following two programs is used.

$$\begin{array}{cc} p & p \\ r \supset q & q \supset r \end{array}$$

The problem is that conjunctions of atoms only "look" at the head of the clause, rather than the body. Were we able to ask a query such as "add q to the program and then ask r", we would indeed observe different behaviour from each of these two logically inequivalent programs.

Hence it seems that a larger class of goals (and/or a larger class of programs), such as those mentioned above, may lead to notions of operational equivalence which are more in tune with logical equivalence. It is also not at all clear what the appropriate notion of logical equivalence will be, as it is known that classical logic, intuitionistic logic and minimal logic all coincide on the Horn clause fragment [12].

The larger class of programs and goals mentioned above indeed allows additions to the program to be made during computation, and hence will be useful for determining an appropriate notion of operational equivalence for logic programs. An operational notion of provability, denoted $\vdash_o$, may be given for this class of formulae [12, 11], and $\vdash_o$ may be thought of as a generalisation of the notion of SLD-resolution [8]. The nature of proofs in this system, known as uniform proofs, was also discussed in [12].

It is known that the relation $\vdash_o$ corresponds to intuitionistic provability, in that if P is a program and G is a goal, then $P \vdash_o G$ iff $P \vdash_I G$. Hence intuitionistically equivalent formulae have the same operational behaviour. However, the converse is not true. For example the nature of $\vdash_o$ is such that $P \vdash_o D \supset (G_1 \vee G_2)$ iff $P \vdash_o (D \supset G_1) \vee (D \supset G_2)$, and these two goals are not intuitionistically equivalent. Similarly there are programs P and P' for which $P \vdash_o G$ iff $P' \vdash_o G$ but P and P' are not intuitionistically equivalent [4]. Moreover, the transformation to the normal form does not preserve intuitionistic equivalence, in that the original program and its normal form are not necessarily intuitionistically equivalent. Thus the natural logic for this class of programs needs to be stronger than intuitionistic logic. As it is known that classical logic is too strong for this purpose [11, 12], this leads us to intermediate logics. In this paper we also show how an appropriate logic may be obtained by adding the *Independence of Premise* (IP) rules to intuitionistic logic. We may think of this logic as being "fully abstract" with respect to $\vdash_o$, in that logical equivalence implies operational equivalence and vice-versa. In particular, a program and its normal form are equivalent in this logic.

This paper is organized as follows. In Section 2 we provide the technical preliminaries, and in Section 3 we show how a normal form, in which disjunctions and existential quantifiers may be eliminated from programs, may be given, and in Section 4 we discuss the relevance of the normal form for computation. Section 5 presents a useful "minimality" result for operational equivalence, and in Section 6 we discuss the intermediate logic and show the full abstraction theorem. Finally in section 7 we discuss some further work and remaining issues.

Due to space limitations, it is not possible to include proofs of all the results in this paper. Complete proofs of all results stated here and further discussion may be found in [2, 4, 5].

2   Preliminaries

Definition 2.1 D_{iH} and G_{iH} formulae are given by the grammar

$$D := A \mid \forall x D \mid D_1 \wedge D_2 \mid G \supset A$$
$$G := A \mid \exists x G \mid G_1 \wedge G_2 \mid G_1 \vee G_2 \mid D \supset G$$

We refer to this class of formulae as implicative Horn formulae.[1]
D_{hhf} and G_{hhf} formulae are given by the grammar

$$D := A \mid \forall x D \mid D_1 \wedge D_2 \mid G \supset A$$
$$G := A \mid \exists x G \mid \forall x G \mid G_1 \wedge G_2 \mid G_1 \vee G_2 \mid D \supset G$$

---

[1]In earlier work we have used the term D_{mod} and G_{mod} formulae; however, implicative Horn formulae seems to be more descriptive name.

We refer to this class of formulae as hereditary Harrop formulae.

In either case, we refer to the D formulae as definite formulae *and the G formulae as* goal formulae.

A program is a set of closed definite formulae, and a goal is a closed goal formula.

In this paper we will be mainly concerned with implicative Horn formulae, although we will refer to hereditary Harrop formulae at times.

In [12] it is shown how an operational notion of proof may be given for both of the above classes of programs and goals. Such proofs are known as *uniform* proofs, and a corresponding operational notion of provability $\vdash_o$ may be defined as follows.

We assume the existence of a finite set of constant and function symbols, and a countable set of variables.

Definition 2.2 *We refer to the set of all ground terms as the* Herbrand universe, *denoted by* $\mathcal{U}$.

We refer to the set of all terms (not necessarily ground) as the general Herbrand universe, *denoted by* $\mathcal{U}'$.

As noted in [12], we may think of a definite formula in much the same way that we think of a Horn clause. We denote the substitution of the term t for the variable x via $[t/x]$.

Definition 2.3 *We define a mapping* $| - |$ *from sets of definite formulae to sets of definite formulae by cases as follows:*

$$| \{D_1, \ldots, D_n\} | = \bigcup_{i=1}^{n} | D_i |$$

$$
\begin{aligned}
| A | &= \{A\} \\
| G \supset A | &= \{G \supset A\} \\
| \forall x D | &= \bigcup_{t \in \mathcal{U}'} | D[t/x] | \\
| D_1 \wedge D_2 | &= | D_1 | \cup | D_2 |
\end{aligned}
$$

Definition 2.4 *Let P be a D_{hhf} program. Then we define $\vdash_o$ as the least relation satisfying*

- *$P \vdash_o A$ iff $A \in | P |$ or $\exists G \supset A \in | P |$ such that $P \vdash_o G$*

- *$P \vdash_o G_1 \vee G_2$ iff $P \vdash_o G_1$ or $P \vdash_o G_2$*

- *$P \vdash_o G_1 \wedge G_2$ iff $P \vdash_o G_1$ and $P \vdash_o G_2$*

- *$P \vdash_o \exists x G$ iff $P \vdash_o G[t/x]$ for some $t \in \mathcal{U}'$*

- *$P \vdash_o \forall x G$ iff $P \vdash_o G[y/x]$ where y is not free in P or G*

- $P \vdash_o D \supset G$ *iff* $P \cup \{D\} \vdash_o G$

In [12] it is shown how the above relation corresponds to the notion of *uniform proof*, i.e. a proof in which the outermost connective of the goal is introduced in the previous step. Further discussion on this point is beyond our scope; for now we note that it is known that the above relation corresponds to a well-understood notion of proof. It was also shown in [12] that $P \vdash_o G$ iff $P \vdash_I G$ where $\vdash_I$ denotes intuitionistic provability.

3 A Normal Form for Programs

In this section we show how any D_{iH} program P is operationally equivalent to a program P' containing no disjunctions or existential quantifiers, i.e. that $P \vdash_o G$ iff $P' \vdash_o G$. This process is inspired by the intuitionistic equivalences

$$(G_1 \lor G_2) \supset A \equiv_I (G_1 \supset A) \land (G_2 \supset A)$$
$$(\exists x G) \supset A \equiv_I \forall x (G \supset A)$$

where x does not appear in A.

As in [11], dnf(G) and dfnf(P) denote respectively the *disjunctive normal form* of a goal G and the *disjunction-free normal form* of a program P. The definitions in [11] are given in a slightly modified form here, so that we may consider dnf(G) as a formula, rather than a set. We introduce along similar lines the *existential normal form* of a goal and the *existential-free normal form* of a program, here denoted by enf and efnf respectively. We will assume that each existentially quantified variable is unique, so that a goal such as $\exists x\, p(x) \land \exists x\, q(x)$ is written as $\exists x\, p(x) \land \exists y\, q(y)$. Note that goals must be closed formulae, and so cannot contain free variables.

Definition 3.1 *Let D be a D_{iH} definite formula and let G be a G_{iH} goal formula. Then we define* dfnf(D), efnf(D), dnf(G) *and* enf(G) *as follows:*

$\text{enf}(G) = \exists \tilde{x}\, \text{enf}'(G)$ $\qquad\qquad$ $\text{dnf}(G) = \bigvee \text{dnf}'(G)$

$\text{enf}'(A) = A$ $\qquad\qquad\qquad\quad$ $\text{dnf}'(A) = \{A\}$

$\text{enf}'(G_1 \lor G_2) = \text{enf}'(G_1) \lor \text{enf}'(G_2)$ $\qquad$ $\text{dnf}'(G_1 \lor G_2) = \text{dnf}'(G_1) \cup \text{dnf}'(G_2)$

$\text{enf}'(G_1 \land G_2) = \text{enf}'(G_1) \land \text{enf}'(G_2)$ $\qquad$ $\text{dnf}'(G_1 \land G_2) = \{G' \land G'' \mid G' \in \text{dnf}'(G_1),$
$$G'' \in \text{dnf}'(G_2)\}$$

$\text{enf}'(\exists x G) = \text{enf}'(G)$ $\qquad\qquad\qquad$ $\text{dnf}'(\exists x G) = \{\exists x G' \mid G' \in \text{dnf}'(G)\}$

$\text{enf}'(D \supset G) = \text{efnf}(D) \supset \text{enf}'(G)$ $\qquad$ $\text{dnf}'(D \supset G) = \{\text{dfnf}(D) \supset G' \mid$
$$G' \in \text{dnf}'(G)\}$$

$\text{efnf}(A) = A$ $\qquad\qquad\qquad\qquad$ $\text{dfnf}(A) = A$

$\text{efnf}(G \supset A) = \forall \tilde{x}\, (\text{enf}'(G) \supset A)$ $\qquad$ $\text{dfnf}(G \supset A) = \bigwedge \{G' \supset A \mid G' \in \text{dnf}'(G)\}$

$\text{efnf}(D_1 \land D_2) = \text{efnf}(D_1) \land \text{efnf}(D_2)$ $\qquad$ $\text{dfnf}(D_1 \land D_2) = \text{dfnf}(D_1) \land \text{dfnf}(D_2)$

$\text{efnf}(\forall x D) = \forall x\, \text{efnf}(D)$ $\qquad\qquad$ $\text{dfnf}(\forall x D) = \forall x\, \text{dfnf}(D)$

where $\tilde{x}$ are all the existentially quantified variables of G.

Let P be a D_{iH} program. Then we define $\mathrm{dfnf}(P) = \{\mathrm{dfnf}(D) \mid D \in P\}$, and $\mathrm{efnf}(P) = \{\mathrm{efnf}(D) \mid D \in P\}$.

An example of each of these transformations is given below.

P	$\mathrm{dfnf}(P)$	$\mathrm{efnf}(P)$
$s \subset (\exists x p(x) \vee q(x)) \wedge r$	$s \subset \exists x p(x) \wedge r$	$\forall x\ s \subset (p(x) \vee q(x)) \wedge r$
	$s \subset \exists x q(x) \wedge r$	

We may think of the process described by $\mathrm{dnf}(G)$ as pushing all disjunctions to the top level of the goal, so that $\mathrm{dnf}(G)$ is a disjunction of disjunction-free formulae. We may then apply the identity above to obtain the disjunction-free program. A similar remark applies to $\mathrm{enf}(G)$; all existential quantifiers are pushed to the top of the formula, and so we may apply the corresponding identity to obtain a program free of existential quantifications. Thus the above equivalences imply that

$$\mathrm{dfnf}(G \supset A) = \bigwedge\{G' \supset A \mid G' \in \mathrm{dnf}'(G)\} \equiv_I \mathrm{dnf}(G) \supset A$$
$$\mathrm{efnf}(G \supset A) = \forall(\mathrm{enf}'(G \supset A)) \equiv_I \mathrm{enf}(G) \supset A$$

In this way we may specify the program equivalent to D which contains no occurrences of $\exists$ or $\vee$ as $\mathrm{efnf}(\mathrm{dfnf}(D))$. We will refer to this program as $\mathrm{normal}(D)$. Similarly we will refer to $\mathrm{enf}(\mathrm{dnf}(G))$ as $\mathrm{normal}(G)$. The formal results which establish the desired operational equivalence of D and $\mathrm{normal}(D)$ are given below.

Proposition 3.1 *Let P be a D_{iH} program, and let G be a G_{iH} goal. Then*

1. $P \vdash_o G \Leftrightarrow \mathrm{dfnf}(P) \vdash_o G \Leftrightarrow P \vdash_o \mathrm{dnf}(G) \Leftrightarrow \mathrm{dfnf}(P) \vdash_o \mathrm{dnf}(G)$

2. $P \vdash_o G \Leftrightarrow \mathrm{efnf}(P) \vdash_o G \Leftrightarrow P \vdash_o \mathrm{enf}(G) \Leftrightarrow \mathrm{efnf}(P) \vdash_o \mathrm{enf}(G)$

The equivalence of the first and the fourth cases of 1 was shown in [11].

Corollary 3.2 *Let P be a D_{iH} program, and G be a G_{iH} goal. Then*

$P \vdash_o G \Leftrightarrow \mathrm{normal}(P) \vdash_o G \Leftrightarrow P \vdash_o \mathrm{normal}(G) \Leftrightarrow \mathrm{normal}(P) \vdash_o \mathrm{normal}(G)$

Thus the corollary above not only ensures that for any program there exists an operationally equivalent program which contains no disjunctions or existential quantifiers, but also shows how such a program may be derived from the original one.

4 Normal Forms and Computation

Whilst the normalisation results above are not particularly deep, they provide an insight into the way that computation is performed in this setting. In particular, we may think of the process of converting a program into its normal form as a transformation on programs which takes place at compile time, and so we may think of the above processes as statically converting the program into a more specific form.

We may also apply the above results to the goal, in that given program P and a goal G we have that $P \vdash_o G$ iff $P \vdash_o \text{normal}(G)$. Moreover, we may write $\text{normal}(G)$ as $\exists(G_1 \vee \ldots \vee G_n)$ where each of the G_i are goal formulae which do not contain disjunctions or existential quantifiers, and $\exists(G)$ is the existential closure of all free variables in G. Now as the relation $\vdash_o$ has the disjunctive and existential properties, we have that $P \vdash_o \exists(G_1 \vee \ldots \vee G_n)$ iff $P \vdash_o G_i\theta$, for some $1 \leq i \leq n$ and some substitution θ such that $G_i\theta$ is ground. In fact, we may be more precise than this. It is well known in the logic programming literature that a Prolog interpreter returns not only an answer substitution for the (existentially quantified) variables of the goal, but also a *most general* answer substitution, which essentially means that, without changing the clauses used in the derivation, we cannot find a more general way of representing the successful instances of the goal [2].

A similar property holds in our more general framework, in that we can find a most general substitution θ such that the success of $\exists(G_1 \vee \ldots \vee G_n)$ implies the success of $G_i\theta$, and moreover the success of every instance G' of $G_i\theta$, including those instances in which the variables of $G_i\theta$ are renamed. Hence we have that $P \vdash_o \exists(G_1 \vee \ldots \vee G_n)$ iff $P \vdash_o \forall(G_i\theta)$. [3] Now as G_i may any one of the formulae $G_1, \ldots, G_n$, in our framework we need not only the notion of an answer substitution, but a more general notion of an *answer formula*, in that if $P \vdash_o \forall(G_i\theta)$, then $\forall(G_i\theta)$ is an answer formula for $\exists(G_1 \vee \ldots \vee G_n)$. For example, consider the program $P = \{p(a), q(b)\}$. It is easy to see that the goal $G = \exists x\, p(x) \vee \exists y\, q(y)$ succeeds, with the answer formulae being $p(a)$ and $q(b)$. In this way an answer formula may be thought of as a *realizer* of the original goal in the sense of Kleene [6], in that the answer formula supplies information, missing from the statement that $P \vdash_o G$, which is sufficient to establish the truth of the statement. Thus the computation process determines a formula $\forall(G_i\theta)$ of sufficient precision that it satisfies the relatively weak constraint $\exists(G_1 \vee \ldots \vee G_n)$ represented by the original goal. Naturally there may be many realizers for a given goal, and the less "definite" the goal (i.e. the looser the constraint), the

---

[2] Of course, other such maximally general answers may be found by unifying the goal with different clauses in the program.

[3] Note that the universal quantification of the goal gives a particular neat characterisation of the property that if a goal G succeeds with most general answer substitution θ, then every instance of $G\theta$ succeeds. In this way we may capture an important property of a most general answer substitution simply by enlarging the class of formulae that may be used as goals.

larger is the number of answer formulae which satisfy the constraint. In this way indefinite formulae may be used to extract related pieces of definite information from the program.

An interesting footnote to this "conversion" of an existential quantifier into a more specific universal quantifier is to note that Horn clauses may be used as hereditary Harrop formulae goals, and hence a Horn clause (or in fact any closed definite formula) is its own answer formula. For example, consider the clause $\{\forall x\ p(f(x))\}$. The goal $\exists y\ p(y)$ succeeds with the answer substitution being $y \leftarrow f(x)$, and so the answer form of the goal is $\forall x\ p(f(x))$. Thus the process of converting the normal form of a goal into an answer formula makes it clear that computation in this setting is a matter of converting an indefinite constraint into a definite answer.

The answer formula is a particularly definite piece of information; in fact, it is not hard to rewrite $\forall(G_i\theta)$ as a definite formula (see [2, 3, 4]). Hence we may add answer formulae to the program, and hence *memoise* [10] successful goals. Memoisation is a well known technique, and may considerably improve performance, as we do not need to re-compute previously computed results. Whilst we cannot in general store successful goals themselves, this analysis shows that we can in fact store something more useful — the answer formulae — and the normal form of a goal partially shows how the answer formulae are related to the original goal. In this sense the normalisation process may be thought of as a pre-computation, in that by converting a program and a goal into normal form before computation we can save ourselves work which would be performed later anyway.

Hence the normalisation results, whilst simple, provide a useful insight into the computation process. It is possible to derive some stronger results than those above, in that it is possible to show that the above transformations not only preserve success, but also preserve (finite) failure. In other words, if we use $\vdash_f$ to denote (finite) failure, $P \vdash_f G$ iff dfnf$(P) \vdash_f G$ iff $P \vdash_f$ dnf(G) iff dfnf$(P) \vdash_f$ dnf(G), and similarly for the existential case. This means that the above results will still hold in the presence of Negation as Failure. More detail (including proofs) may be found in [2].

5 "Minimal" Operational Equivalence

As mentioned above, we may think of normal(P) as a transformation of P which produces an "equivalent" program P', in that every goal derivable from one is derivable from the other. Maher [9] has shown that there are several meaningful conceptions of equivalence between logic programs; one obvious such notion is to consider two programs P_1 and P_2 to be *operationally equivalent* if for every goal G, $P_1 \vdash_o G \Leftrightarrow P_2 \vdash_o G$. This may be thought of as treating the programs as two black boxes, so that the only way that we may distinguish between them is by how they react to queries from the outside world. We will denote the operational equivalence of two programs

P_1 and P_2 as $P_1 \equiv_o P_2$.

At this point, it is instructive to consider the question of "minimal testing" for observational equivalence. More formally, the question is what is the smallest class of goals for which operational equivalence needs to be established in order to show operational equivalence for all goals. It is easy to see that this smallest class must properly include all atomic goals. However as noted above, atomic goals alone are not enough, and suggests that implications are needed in goals in such a minimal class. In fact, implications are all that is necessary, as is shown in the proposition below.

Proposition 5.1 *Let Q formulae be defined by*

$$Q := A \mid D \supset Q$$

where D is any D_{iH} definite formula.

Let D_1 and D_2 be D_{iH} programs, and let G range over all G_{hhf} goals. Then

$$(\forall Q \ D_1 \vdash_o Q \Rightarrow D_2 \vdash_o Q) \Rightarrow (\forall G \ D_1 \vdash_o G \Rightarrow D_2 \vdash_o G)$$

This proposition turns out to be remarkably useful in proving subsequent results. Note that as $P \vdash_o Q$ iff $P \vdash_o \text{normal}(Q)$, we in fact need only consider formulae which contain no existential quantifiers or disjunctions.

We may think of the above result as establishing that operational equivalence for atoms and implications is sufficient to establish operational equivalence for all goals.

Alternatively, the above result may be interpreted as stating that if we can establish that all *extensions* of two programs enable the same atoms to be derived, then we have established operational equivalence. Thus if we cannot distinguish between two programs by arbitrary mutual extensions of them, even when the only goals which may be asked are atomic, then the two programs are operationally equivalent. There may be weaker conditions under which operational equivalence holds, but it would seem that any weakening of this condition would come from restricting the extensions that may be made to the programs.

6 Logical Equivalence

We saw above that intuitionistic logic is clearly important in the study of operational equivalence for hereditary Harrop formulae. In fact, it is easy to see that intuitionistic equivalence implies operational equivalence, as if $P_1 \vdash_I P_2$ and $P_2 \vdash_o G$, then as $P_2 \vdash_o G$ implies that $P_2 \vdash_I G$, we have that $P_1 \vdash_I G$, i.e. $P_1 \vdash_o G$. The corresponding case for $P_2 \vdash_I P_1$ is similar.

A natural question to ask at this point is whether programs which are operationally equivalent are logically equivalent, i.e. if $\forall G \ D_1 \vdash_o G$ iff $D_2 \vdash_o G$, does it follow that $D_1 \equiv_I D_2$? The answer is negative, as whilst the transformations above preserve operational equivalence, they do not preserve intuitionistic equivalence. A counterexample, due to Dale Miller, is given as follows:

$$D_1 \qquad\qquad\qquad \text{dfnf}(D_1)$$
$$(r \supset (p \vee q)) \supset s \qquad\qquad ((r \supset p) \supset s) \wedge ((r \supset q) \supset s)$$

A Kripke model in which $\text{dfnf}(D_1)$ is true but D_1 is not is given by a model with three worlds w_1, w_2 and w_3 where $w_1 \leq w_2$ and $w_1 \leq w_3$, and the true atomic formulae at w_1, w_2 and w_3 are $\emptyset$, $\{r, p, s\}$ and $\{r, q, s\}$ respectively. D_1 is not true as it is not true at w_1.

A similar counterexample may be given for the program $(p \supset \exists x q(x)) \supset r$.

Thus operational equivalence is not strong enough to establish (intuitionistic) logical equivalence. One way to interpret this result is that the natural choice of logic for programming in this context needs to have a stronger consequence relation than $\vdash_I$, so that operationally equivalent programs are logically equivalent. Hence, any natural logic of equivalence for logic programs will need to be stronger than intuitionistic logic. [4] Note that classical logic is too strong for this purpose; for example, the two programs below are equivalent in classical logic, but they are not operationally equivalent.

$$(q \vee (p \supset p)) \supset r \qquad\qquad ((p \supset q) \vee p) \supset r$$

The problem is that whilst $q \vee (p \supset p)$ and $(p \supset q) \vee p$ are classically equivalent, $q \vee (p \supset p)$ succeeds (i.e. $\vdash_o q \vee (p \supset p)$) whereas $(p \supset q) \vee p$ fails.

Thus any intermediate logic, say I', appropriate for this application will need to satisfy the following equivalences:

$$D \supset (G_1 \vee G_2) \equiv_{I'} (D \supset G_1) \vee (D \supset G_2)$$
$$D \supset \exists x \, G \equiv_{I'} \exists x \, D \supset G$$

where x is not free in D. Note that the $\Leftarrow$ direction of both equivalences hold in intuitionistic logic. These equivalences are natural ones to choose given that we expect that goals which are operationally equivalent are logically equivalent. The $\Rightarrow$ directions of these rules are known as the *Independence of Premise* axioms [13], and although there are some results regarding the addition of these and similar axioms to Heyting arithmetic [13], not much seems to be known about the logic obtained by adding these rules to intuitionistic logic.

We may think of such a logic as a logic of "present choice", in that the choice of witness for the existentially quantified variable cannot be postponed; if we can ever choose such a witness, then we can do so immediately,

---

[4] This may be thought of as a full abstraction problem for the relation $\vdash_o$, in that we are trying to determine a notion of consequence for which equivalence is precisely operational equivalence.

without investigating future worlds. Similar remarks apply to the disjunctive case, in that if we can ever choose between the two alternatives we can do so immediately, without waiting to see what will happen in the future (and hence the choice is "independent" of the assumption used to prove its truth). This immediacy is reflected in the computation process by the fact that in order to establish the truth of r from either P_3 or P_4 we do so by trying to prove the body of the clause, rather than considering possible future choices. In this way the knowledge which we may use to make the relevant choice is already present in the program, and so it is merely a matter of seeing if such a choice can be made. If it cannot, then we have no other way to proceed. Hence, the logic of present choice will reflect the fact that we can only use information encoded in the program.

We have seen how it is necessary for the logic I' to satisfy the IP axioms so that operational equivalence implies logical equivalence. Now for the converse to hold as well, we need to ensure that I' is not too strong. One way to analyse this requirement on the nature of I' is to explore the relation $\vdash_o \subseteq \mathcal{D} \times \mathcal{G}$ in terms of a relation on $\mathcal{D} \times \mathcal{D}$ and a relation on $\mathcal{G} \times \mathcal{G}$. The main obstacle to viewing $\vdash_o$ directly as a consequence relation in the traditional sense is that such relations are usually defined on $\mathcal{F} \times \mathcal{F}$ where $\mathcal{F}$ is the set of all well-formed (first-order) formulae. Hence, as is done in [11], we may view $\vdash_o$ as the restriction of $\vdash_I$ to $\mathcal{D} \times \mathcal{G}$. However, we cannot use $\vdash_o$ directly for questions of equivalence between programs or between goals, and so for such equivalences we need to use $\vdash_{I'}$.

It should be noted that there are some reasonably well-known intermediate logics. Perhaps the best known one is known as the *logic of constant domains*, and for various reasons, this seems an appropriate notion for the desired logic. However, this is not particularly suitable for our purposes. The standard proof-theoretic characterisation of the logic of constant domains (CD) is to add the following rule to intuitionistic logic (in a Hilbert-type proof system):

$$\forall x \ (\phi \vee \psi(x)) \supset (\phi \vee \forall x \ \psi(x))$$

We may incorporate this rule into the sequent system by adding the following inference rule:

$$\frac{\Gamma \longrightarrow \forall x \ (\phi \vee \psi(x))}{\Gamma \longrightarrow \phi \vee \forall x \ \psi(x)} \ \text{CD}$$

We refer to the extended proof system as I_{CD}. However, if we restrict our attention to D_{iH} and G_{iH} formulae, then this rule can never be used, as neither of the above two consequents are D_{iH} formulae, and as we do not allow universal quantification in G_{iH} goals, they are not G_{iH} formulae either. Hence, this rule will not affect the provability relations between D_{iH} formulae or between G_{iH} formulae. We give a formal statement of this result below.

Definition 6.1 *A sequent* $\Gamma \longrightarrow F$ *is an* **I'**-*sequent iff every element of* Γ *is either a* D_{iH} *or* G_{iH} *formula, and* F *is either a* D_{iH} *formula or a* G_{iH} *formula.*

Proposition 6.1 *Let* $\Gamma \longrightarrow F$ *be an* **I'**-*sequent. Then* $\Gamma \vdash_{I_{CD}} F$ *iff* $\Gamma \vdash_I F$.

Hence the logic of constant domains is not much help in this context. Another intermediate logic of interest is the extension of intuitionistic propositional calculus (IPC) called *lc* by Gabbay [1]. This may be characterised by adding to IPC the rule (in a Hilbert-style proof system)

$$(p \supset (q \vee r)) \supset ((p \supset q) \vee (p \supset r))$$

This is clearly an instance of the IP rule for disjunction. However, *lc* appears to be too strong, as it loses the disjunctive property, i.e. it is not true that if $A \vee B$ is provable then either A is provable or B is provable. Also, some of the alternative characterisations of *lc* do not fit in well with computational intuition. For example, another way to characterise this logic is to add the following rule to IPC:

$$(p \supset q) \vee (q \supset p)$$

This does not seem to be a rule which can be justified in terms of computation, especially due to the restrictions which first-order hereditary Harrop formulae place on implications, and so *lc* does not seem particularly helpful in this context either.

As mentioned above, we want $\vdash_{I'}$ to include all intuitionistic consequences (i.e. $\vdash_I \subseteq \vdash_{I'}$), but also for the following rules to hold:

$$D \supset \exists x G \vdash_{I'} \exists x D \supset G$$
$$D \supset (G_1 \vee G_2) \vdash_{I'} (D \supset G_1) \vee (D \supset G_2)$$

where x is not free in D.

The simplest way to define $\vdash_{I'}$ is to add the two rules above to the deduction rules of first-order intuitionistic logic. This will also ensure that I' is not too strong. In a sequent-style proof system, this means adding the following two rules to the standard system for intuitionistic logic:

$$\frac{\Gamma \longrightarrow F_1 \supset \exists x F_2}{\Gamma \longrightarrow \exists x F_1 \supset F_2} \qquad \frac{\Gamma \longrightarrow F \supset (F_1 \vee F_2)}{\Gamma \longrightarrow (F \supset F_1) \vee (F \supset F_2)}$$

We refer to proofs in the above system as **I'**-proofs. Note that the two extra rules are only applicable when the consequents are a particular kind of formulae, but that the extra rules ensure that there are programs D_1 and D_2 for which $D_1 \not\vdash_I D_2$ but $D_1 \vdash_{I'} D_2$. For example, $p \supset \exists x\, q(x) \equiv_{I'} \exists x\, p \supset q(x)$, and so $(p \supset \exists x\, q(x)) \supset r \equiv_{I'} (\exists x\, p \supset q(x)) \supset r$.

One important feature of the above proof rules is that the restriction of $\vdash_{I'}$ to $\mathcal{D} \times \mathcal{G}$ is precisely $\vdash_I$. In this way we have not altered the way that goals are derived from programs, but strengthened the provability relation between programs and between goals. In fact, this result also holds for hereditary Harrop formulae.

Proposition 6.2 *Let P be a D_{hhf} program and G be a G_{hhf} goal. Then $P \vdash_{I'} G \Leftrightarrow P \vdash_I G$.*

In this way I' proves the desired equivalences between programs and between goals, but does not affect computations, i.e. the consequence relation between programs and goals. It follows immediately from this proposition that the same goals may be derived from programs which are provably equivalent in I', and goals which are provably equivalent in I' behave identically.

Corollary 6.3 *Let P_1 and P_2 be D_{hhf} programs and let G be a G_{hhf} goal. If $P_1 \vdash_o G$ and $P_2 \vdash_{I'} P_1$ then $P_2 \vdash_o G$.*

Corollary 6.4 *Let P be a D_{hhf} program and let G_1 and G_2 be G_{hhf} goals. If $P \vdash_o G_1$ and $G_1 \vdash_{I'} G_2$ then $P \vdash_o G_2$.*

It is also not hard to show that a program is equivalent to its normal form in I', and similarly for a goal.

Proposition 6.5 *Let P be a D_{iH} program and G be a G_{iH} goal. Then $P \equiv_{I'} \text{normal}(P)$ and $G \equiv_{I'} \text{normal}(G)$.*

Naturally we expect operational equivalence to imply logical equivalence for an intermediate logic I' in which the equivalences mentioned above hold. We may think of this requirement on I' as demanding that all connectives be treated similarly, since the corresponding equivalences for the other connectives, given below, are intuitionistically valid.

$$D \supset (G_1 \wedge G_2) \equiv_I (D \supset G_1) \wedge (D \supset G_2)$$
$$D \supset (D' \supset G) \equiv_I (D \wedge D') \supset G$$
$$D \supset \forall x\, G \equiv_I \forall x\, (D \supset G)$$

where x is not free in D.

It is possible to show that operational equivalence implies logical equivalence in I'. A formal statement is given below.

Theorem 6.6 *Let P_1 and P_2 be D_{iH} programs, and let G range over G_{iH} goals. Then*

$$(\forall G\ D_1 \vdash_o G \Leftrightarrow D_2 \vdash_o G) \Rightarrow D_2 \equiv_{I'} D_1.$$

Proof: Assume that $\forall G\ D_1 \vdash_o G \Rightarrow D_2 \vdash_o G$. From lemma 5.1, we know that this implies that $\forall G'\ D_1 \vdash_o G' \Rightarrow D_2 \vdash_o G'$, where G' ranges over G_{hhf} goals. Now by Proposition 6.5, $D_1 \equiv_{I'} \text{normal}(D_1)$, and as $\text{normal}(D_1)$ may be re-written as a G_{hhf} formula G'', we have that $D_1 \equiv_{I'} G''$ and so $D_1 \vdash_o G''$, and hence $D_2 \vdash_o G''$, i.e. $D_2 \vdash_{I'} D_1$.

A similar argument shows that $D_1 \vdash_{I'} D_2$. $\qquad\qquad \square$

Thus in I', operational equivalence implies logical equivalence. In fact it is not hard to see that this result will hold in any logic for which $D \equiv$ normal(D), and so this property also holds in classical logic.

An interesting interpretation of this result is that if two programs D_1 and D_2 differ, i.e. $D_1 \not\equiv_{I'} D_2$, then there is a goal which distinguishes the two. More precisely, from the contrapositive of theorem 6.6 we have that if $D_2 \not\vdash_{I'} D_1$, then there is a goal G such that $D_1 \vdash_o G$ but it is not the case that $D_2 \vdash_o G$. As noted in the preceding remark, a similar property will also hold for classical logic.

7 Conclusions and Discussion

We have seen how a normal form for programs and goals may be given, and have shown that a slightly stronger logic than intuitionistic logic is needed in order to obtain a full abstraction property, i.e. that operationally equivalent programs are logically equivalent.

A point of further work on this matter is to obtain a normal form for full hereditary Harrop formulae, i.e. the class of formulae below.

$$D := A \mid \forall x D \mid D_1 \wedge D_2 \mid G \supset A$$
$$G := A \mid \exists x G \mid \forall x G \mid G_1 \wedge G_2 \mid G_1 \vee G_2 \mid D \supset G$$

The main difficulty is how to push the existential quantifiers and disjunctions outside universal quantifiers. One technique which may be of use is Skolemisation; another possibility is to use some form of infinitary logic. For example, Skolem functions will be useful for a goal such as $\forall x \exists y \, p(x, y)$, and some infinitary construction would presumably be necessary for a goal such as $\forall x \, p(x) \vee q(x)$.

Another point of further interest is the precise nature of the logic I'. Whilst the proof rules given above are sufficient, they are not very natural rules, and hence there may be a simpler and more informative proof system for I'. More natural inference rules would presumably shed more light on the nature of I'.

Another possibility is to show the analogous result to Theorem 6.6 for goal formulae, i.e. that

$$(\forall P \; P \vdash_o G_1 \Rightarrow P \vdash_o G_2) \Rightarrow G_1 \vdash_{I'} G_2$$

The main technical difficulty is to find a program "equivalent" to the goal G_1, which will then allow the proof to proceed as before. The techniques of infinitary logic may be useful here too.

8 Acknowledgements

The author would like to thank Dale Miller and David Pym for stimulating discussions of this material.

The support of the Australian Research Council and the Centre for Intelligent Decision Systems is gratefully acknowledged. Some of this work was performed whilst the author was a student in the Department of Computer Science, University of Edinburgh.

References

[1] D. Gabbay, *Semantical Investigations in Heyting's Intuitionistic Logic*, Reidel, 1981.

[2] J. Harland, *On Hereditary Harrop Formulae as a Basis for Logic Programming*, Ph.D. thesis, University of Edinburgh, July, 1991.

[3] J. Harland, Structural Properties of Logic Programs, *Proceedings of the Fourteenth Australian Computer Science Conference*, Sydney, February, 1991. Published as *Australian Computer Science Communications*:13:1, February, 1991.

[4] J. Harland, *Structural Properties of Logic Programs*, Technical Report 90/20, Department of Computer Science, University of Melbourne.

[5] J. Harland, *An Intermediate Logic for Logic Programs*, Technical Report 90/29, Department of Computer Science, University of Melbourne.

[6] S.C. Kleene, *Introduction to Metamathematics*, North-Holland, 1952.

[7] R.A. Kowalski, Predicate Logic as a Programming Language, *Information Processing 74*, North-Holland, Amsterdam, 1974.

[8] J.W. Lloyd, *Foundations of Logic Programming*, Springer-Verlag, Berlin, 1984.

[9] M.J. Maher, Equivalences of Logic Programs, in *Foundations of Deductive Databases and Logic Programming* 627-658, J. Minker (ed.), Morgan Kaufmann, 1988.

[10] D. Michie, Memo functions and machine learning, *Nature* 218:19-22, April, 1968.

[11] D.A. Miller, A Logical Analysis of Modules in Logic Programming, *Journal of Logic Programming* 6:79-108, 1989.

[12] D.A. Miller, G. Nadathur, F. Pfenning and A. Scedrov, Uniform Proofs as a Foundation for Logic Programming, *Annals of Pure and Applied Logic* 51:125-157, 1991.

[13] A.S. Troelstra, *Metamathematical Investigations of Intuitionistic Arithmetic and Analysis*, Lecture Notes in Mathematics 344, Springer-Verlag, Berlin, 1973.

Proof method of partial correctness and weak completeness for normal logic programs

Gérard Ferrand
University of Orléans and INRIA
LIFO, Faculté des Sciences, BP 6759, F-45067 Orléans cedex 2, France
ferrand@univ-orleans.fr

Pierre Deransart
INRIA
BP 105, Rocquencourt, F-78153 Le Chesnay cedex, France
deransar@minos.inria.fr

Abstract

We present a proof method for *partial correctness* and *weak completeness* for any normal programs, which coincides with the already known proof methods for partial correctness and completeness for definite programs. The purpose of such a validation method is to compare the actual semantics of a program with some expected properties, sometimes called specifications. We consider that the actual semantics of a normal program is the three-valued *well-founded semantics*. Thus the actual semantics of a program is defined by two sets of ground atoms: the set of the *true* atoms and the set of the *false* atoms.

The expected properties may be formulated also by two sets of ground atoms, partial correctness and weak completeness are formulated by set inclusions.

We obtain two basic results: one concerns the characterization of the well-founded model in terms of (generalized) proof trees and as the least fixed point of some operator acting on proof tree roots.

The second basic result concerns an application : a sound and complete proof method of partial correctness and weak completeness.

The method may be used also to prove that some given set of atoms characterizes exactly the set of true atoms, if the semantics is in fact bivalued and the specification is total.

1 Introduction

We present a proof method for *partial correctness* and *weak completeness* for
normal programs which coincides with the already known proof methods for
partial correctness and completeness for definite programs.

We consider that the semantics of a normal program is the *well-founded
semantics* in the sense of [21] (See [16, 18] for a procedural mechanism). It
is a three-valued semantics. Thus, given a program P, its semantics M_P is
defined by two sets of ground atoms : the set of the *true* atoms, denoted by
M_P^+ and the set of the *false* atoms, denoted by M_P^-, the set of the *undefined*
atoms being the complement in the set of all ground atoms.

The purpose of a validation method is to compare the *actual* semantics
M_P of a program with some *expected* properties, sometimes called specifications. These properties may be formulated also by two sets of ground atoms.
Let us say that S is a property which must be satisfied by all true atoms.
Then we want to have the inclusion $M_P^+ \subseteq S$. A program P is *partially
correct* w.r.t. a property S iff $M_P^+ \subseteq S$.

Conversely, the usual idea of *completeness* with a two valued approach
consists in a given set of atoms whose elements are expected to be true i.e.
$C \subseteq M_P^+$. In the three valued approach the corresponding concept is called
here the *weak* completeness. A program P is *weakly complete* w.r.t the property C (a set of atoms) iff $C \subseteq \overline{M_P^-}$, where the bar denotes complementation.
In other words a property of weak completeness specifies a subset of atoms
which must not be false.

Notice that in the case of a bivalued semantics i.e. if the three-valued
semantics is total, in particular in the case of definite programs or stratified
normal programs, a program P is partially correct w.r.t. S and weakly
complete w.r.t. C iff the double inclusion holds: $C \subseteq M_P^+ \subseteq S$.

This paper introduces a proof method of such inclusions in the general
case of the three-valued well-founded semantics for any normal programs.
The result is obtained in two steps.

First we give a new characterization of the well-founded semantics in
terms of (generalized) proof trees. Then it is defined as the least fixed point
of a new operator which is monotone thanks to the idea that it can be applied
even if the subsets of true and false atoms are not disjoint (they are disjoint
in the least fixed point). This opens for many applications. This paper
explores one of them: the validation method.

Second we develop the validation method which is a straightforward application of the fixed point theorem. This gives the results of soundness and
completeness of the method. We give the conditions which must be verified,
leading to a method of proof using a finite set of assertions. We do not
enter into the details of the formulation of the method by assertions, which
is illustrated by an example only (there are two formulas to be verified for
each clause plus some decreasing criterion). Notice that the method may be
used also to prove that some given set of atoms characterizes exactly the set

of true atoms, if the semantics is in fact bivalued and the used assertions correspond to $S = C$. In this case the proof method is a way to prove that $S = M_P^+$.

2 Characterization of 3-valued stable models in terms of proof trees

Let $\mathcal{L}$ be a first order language and P a *normal program* on $\mathcal{L}$ ([14]) i.e. a set of program clauses $A \leftarrow L_1, \cdots, L_n$ where A is an atom of $\mathcal{L}$, and L_i are literals (positive i.e. atom or negative i.e. $\neg A$, A atom) of $\mathcal{L}$.

Definition 2.1 *(Semi Proof Tree, spt)*
A Semi Proof Tree (spt) for P is a finite tree where each node is (occurrence of) a literal and such that :
- the root is an atom.
- for each non leaf node A, if its children are $L_1, \cdots, L_n$ then
$A \leftarrow L_1, \cdots, L_n$ *is an instance of a clause of P (hence only leaves can be negative literals).*
- for each leaf which is an atom A, the clause $A \leftarrow$ is an instance of a clause (fact) of P.
(There is an obvious equivalent inductive definition of spt).
A spt is ground if all its literals are ground.

In the *particular case* where P is *definite* ([14], no negation) the *spt* are exactly the classical *proof trees* (*pt*) of [5]. In such a case we denote by $ptr(P)$ the set of ground atoms which are *root of a proof tree*. So $ptr(P)$ coincides with the classical (Van Emden-Kowalski) minimum Herbrand model of P ([20]), which is also the set of (ground) atomic consequences of P.

Now as [17] we consider three new atoms t, u, f (true, undefined, false). They are not in $\mathcal{L}$. From a formal point of view t, u, f can be viewed as 0-ary predicate symbols. Let $\mathcal{L}_{t,u,f}$ be the first order language obtained by adding t, u, f to $\mathcal{L}$.

Definition 2.2 *(positive program)*
A positive program on $\mathcal{L}$ is a set of clauses $A \leftarrow A_1, \cdots, A_n$ where A is an atom of $\mathcal{L}$ and $A_1, \cdots, A_n$ are atoms of $\mathcal{L}$, or t or u or f.

So each *positive program* on $\mathcal{L}$ is a *definite program* on $\mathcal{L}_{t,u,f}$.

Let $H(\mathcal{L})$ be the Herbrand base of $\mathcal{L}$ i.e. the set of all ground atoms on $\mathcal{L}$.

For $J \subseteq H(\mathcal{L})$ let $\neg J = \{\neg A | A \in J\}$.

So $H(\mathcal{L}) \cup \neg H(\mathcal{L})$ is the set of all ground literals on $\mathcal{L}$.

For $I \subseteq H(\mathcal{L}) \cup \neg H(\mathcal{L})$ let $I^+ \subseteq H(\mathcal{L})$ and $I^- \subseteq H(\mathcal{L})$ defined by

$$I = I^+ \cup \neg I^-$$

i.e. $I^+ = I \cap H(\mathcal{L})$ and $I^- = \{A \in H(\mathcal{L}) | \neg A \in I\}$.

I is a *3-valued Herbrand interpretation* (in short : *3-interpretation*) of $\mathcal{L}$ if it is *"consistent"* i.e. $I^+ \cap I^- = \emptyset$. Moreover it is *2-valued* or *total* if $I^+ \cup I^- = H(\mathcal{L})$ ([17]).

If I and I' are 3-interpretations there are two natural orderings ([17], [4]) :

$I \subseteq I'$ i.e. I is a subset of I' (i.e. $I^+ \subseteq I'^+$ and $I^- \subseteq I'^-$)
(Fitting ordering or information ordering, [12, 19])

$I \leq I'$ iff $I^+ \subseteq I'^+$ and $I^- \supseteq I'^-$
(standard ordering or truth ordering).

A 3-interpretation can be equivalently viewed as a function

$$I : H(\mathcal{L}) \to \{0, 1/2, 1\}$$

defined by
$I(A) = 1$ if $A \in I^+$
$I(A) = 0$ if $A \in I^-$
$I(A) = 1/2$ if $A \in H(\mathcal{L}) - (I^+ \cup I^-)$

So $I \leq I'$ iff $I(A) \leq I'(A)$ for all $A \in H(\mathcal{L})$.

Each 3-interpretation is canonically extended to $H(\mathcal{L}_{t,u,f})$

$$I : H(\mathcal{L}_{t,u,f}) \to \{0, 1/2, 1\}$$

by $I(t) = 1, I(f) = 0, I(u) = 1/2$.

We need a particular case of a definition of [17] :
I is a *model* of a *positive program* P if for every ground instance

$$A \leftarrow A_1, \cdots, A_n$$

of a clause of P we have

$$I(A) \geq min\{I(A_i) | i \leq n\}$$

[17] gives a generalization of the Van Emden-Kowalski theorem ([20]) : every *positive program* has a $\leq$-*minimum 3-model*, denoted by $Min(P)$.

Now thanks to the notion of proof tree we can give a simple description of $Min(P)$:
We define two *definite* programs on $\mathcal{L}_{t,u,f}$, P_t and $P_{t,u}$, by :
$P_t = P \cup \{t \leftarrow\}$ and $P_{t,u} = P \cup \{t \leftarrow, u \leftarrow\}$.
The idea is to use for positive programs the classical notion of proof tree. So we add the fact $t \leftarrow$ in order to have t as a leaf in a proof tree. The idea with $P_{t,u}$ is to exclude some proof trees by preventing f from being a leaf but accepting t and u.

Our description is given by the following theorem (proved in appendix)

Theorem 2.1 *For each* positive P,
$$Min(P)^+ = H(\mathcal{L}) \cap ptr(P_t)$$
$$Min(P)^- = \{A \in H(\mathcal{L}) | A \notin ptr(P_{t,u})\}$$

Note that if u does not occur in the positive program P we have $Min(P)^- = H(\mathcal{L}) - Min(P)^+$ and in particular if P is *definite* on $\mathcal{L}$ (i.e. without t, u, f), $Min(P)^+ = ptr(P)$ (the classical Van Emden Kowalski minimum model) and $Min(P)^- = H(\mathcal{L}) - ptr(P)$.

Now let P be a *normal program* on $\mathcal{L}$ and $inst(P)$ the set of all ground instances (on $\mathcal{L}$) of clauses of P. Let I be a 3-interpretation of $\mathcal{L}$. As in [17] let P/I be the *positive program* on $\mathcal{L}$ obtained from $inst(P)$ by replacing in every clause all negative $\neg A$ by t if $A \in I^-$, by f if $A \in I^+$, by u if $A \in H(\mathcal{L}) - (I^+ \cup I^-)$.

P/I being positive, $Min(P/I)$ is a well defined model (but there is such a model for each P and each I).

[17] gives an extension of the notion of *stable model* of [13] : A 3-interpretation is a *stable* set of P if $I = Min(P/I)$, and then it is necessarily a ($\leq$-minimal) *model* of P, so it is called a *stable model* of P.

Now thanks to the notion of *semi proof tree* we can give a simple description of $Min(P/I)$:

For $J \subseteq H(\mathcal{L})$ we denote by $spt(P, J)$ the set of spt in which, for each negative leaf $\neg A$, we have $A \in J$, and we denote by $sptr(P, J)$ the set of ground atoms which are root of a spt in $spt(P, J)$.

Note that $sptr(P, J)$ is the least fixed point of the monotone operator $T_{P,J}$ defined by, for $J' \subseteq H(\mathcal{L})$,

$$T_{P,J}(J') = \{A | \text{ there exists } A \leftarrow L_1, \ldots, L_n \text{ in } inst(P)$$
$$\text{such that, for all positive } L_i, L_i \in J'$$
$$\text{and, for all negative } L_i = \neg A_i, A_i \in J\}$$

For $J \subseteq H(\mathcal{L})$ let $\overline{J} = H(\mathcal{L}) - J$.

Our description of $Min(P/I)$ is given by the

Theorem 2.2
$$Min(P/I) = sptr(P, I^-) \cup \neg\overline{sptr(P, \overline{I^+})}$$

Proof : we apply the previous theorem to P/I and we see that

$$H(\mathcal{L}) \cap ptr(P/I)_t = sptr(P, I^-)$$
$$H(\mathcal{L}) \cap ptr(P/I)_{t,u} = sptr(P, \overline{I^+})$$

q.e.d.

Corollary 2.1
I is a stable model of P iff $I^+ = sptr(P, I^-)$ *and* $\overline{I^-} = sptr(P, \overline{I^+})$.

If moreover I is *total*, the previous definition of stable ($I = Min(P/I)$) is equivalent to the definition of stable given (only for I total) by [13] (this equivalence is checked in [17]). But in this particular case (I total) we have $\overline{I^+} = I^-$, so I is *stable* iff $I^+ = sptr(P, I^-)$.

3 Characterization of the well-founded model

Now in [21] is defined the *well-founded model* M_P of any normal program P and in [17] it is proved that M_P is the $\subseteq$-minimum stable model of P ([4, 9] give a simple fixed point characterization of M_P).

From now on we don't use t, u, f so we can write H for $H(\mathcal{L})$ without any confusion.

P being a normal program we define the operator Ψ_P on the *power set* of $H \cup \neg H$ by :

$$\Psi_P(I) = sptr(P, I^-) \cup \neg \overline{sptr(P, \overline{I^+})}$$

for *all* $I \subseteq H \cup \neg H$.

Note that, if I is consistent i.e. a 3-interpretation, $\Psi_P(I) = Min(P/I)$.

Because of the definition of $sptr(P, J)$ and because of the double complementation in its definition it is easy to see that Ψ_P is monotone, i.e. that

$$I \subseteq I' \Rightarrow \Psi_P(I) \subseteq \Psi_P(I')$$

By the Knaster-Tarski theorem, Ψ_P has a ($\subseteq$-)least fixed point.

Theorem 3.1 *M_P is the ($\subseteq$-)least fixed point of Ψ_P*

Proof :

Let I_0 be the ($\subseteq$-)least fixed point of Ψ_P. We want to show that $I_0 = M_P$. For the time being we know only ([17]) that M_P is the ($\subseteq$-)least I consistent such that $\Psi_P(I) = Min(P/I) = I$.

Let Ψ_P' be the other monotone operator defined by $\Psi_P'(I) = Min(P/I)$ if I is consistent and $\Psi_P'(I) = H \cup \neg H$ otherwise (Ψ_P' is a natural adaptation of the operator used by [4]).

We see that M_P is the least fixed point of Ψ_P' because $\Psi_P'(I) = \Psi_P(I)$ for consistent I and $\Psi_P'(I) = H \cup \neg H$ otherwise.

But M_P is also a fixed point of Ψ_P hence $I_0 \subseteq M_P$. And I_0 is consistent hence $\Psi_P'(I_0) = \Psi_P(I_0) = I_0$ so I_0 is a fixed point of Ψ_P' hence $M_P \subseteq I_0$.

Compared with other approaches (in particular for an analogous characterization see [4, 9]) the novelty is not only using spt to describe least fixed points but it is that here I may be *any* $I \subseteq H \cup \neg H$, so it is only if I is consistent i.e. a 3-interpretation that $\Psi_P(I) = Min(P/I)$. (For the application to proof method "inconsistent" I are needed).

Now let us consider the case where M_P is *total*. Then, if M_P is a subset of an 3-interpretation I, $M_P = I$. Since M_P is a subset of every stable model of P, it is necessarily the *unique stable model* of P ([21],[17]).

Locally stratified programs ([1, 15, 2]) are examples satisfying this important condition (the well-founded model is total). For more details about this condition (dynamic or effective stratification) see [16, 3].

4   Proof method

4.1   Principle

From now on "least" means ($\subseteq$-)least. Now let us recall that the least fixed point of Ψ_P is also the least I such that $\Psi_P(I) \subseteq I$ (Knaster-Tarski). So in order to prove that $M_P \subseteq I$ it is *sufficient* to prove that $\Psi_P(I) \subseteq I$.

In order to get the completeness of the proof method, we state that, to prove that $M_P \subseteq I$ it is sufficient to find I' such that $I' \subseteq I$ and $\Psi_P(I') \subseteq I'$.

This method is *sound* because $M_P \subseteq I' \subseteq I$.

And this method is *complete* because, if $M_P \subseteq I$ is true, there is always such an I' to apply the method : at least $I' = M_P$.

Remark that in the particular case where M_P is *total*, if I is a *3-interpretation* and $M_P \subseteq I$ then I is total and $M_P = I$. So in this case if we apply the method we prove always $M_P = I$ and not only $M_P \subseteq I$.

But we can apply the method to *any* $I \subseteq H \cup \neg H$. From a practical point of view it is useful to adopt another notation :

Let $S \subseteq H$ and $C \subseteq H$ (the idea is to have $S = I^+$ and $C = H - I^-$).

Definition 4.1 *We call* validation condition *of P w.r.t. S, C the following conjunction :*

$$sptr(P, \overline{C}) \subseteq S \text{ and } C \subseteq sptr(P, \overline{S})$$

Let $I = S \cup \neg \overline{C}$, so $I^+ = S$ and $I^- = \overline{C}$.

Remark that I is a *3-interpretation* iff $S \subseteq C$, which is *total* iff $S = C$.

So in general the *validation condition* of P w.r.t. S, C is equivalent to :

$$sptr(P, I^-) \subseteq I^+ \text{ and } \overline{sptr(P, \overline{I^+})} \subseteq I^-$$

i.e. $\Psi_P(I) \subseteq I$.

So the *validation condition* of P w.r.t. S, C is *sufficient* to have $M_P \subseteq I$ i.e. :

$$M_P^+ \subseteq S \text{ and } C \subseteq \overline{M_P^-}.$$

In the important particular case where M_P is *total*, this gives

$$C \subseteq M_P^+ \subseteq S$$

and moreover, if $S = C$, this gives $M_P^+ = S$.

To sum up, we have the following theorem :

Theorem 4.1 *A normal program P is*
partially correct *w.r.t. S and* weakly complete *w.r.t. C,*
i.e. $M_P^+ \subseteq S$ *and* $C \subseteq \overline{M_P^-}$
iff
there exists S', C' such that $S' \subseteq S$ and $C \subseteq C'$ and the validation condition
of P w.r.t S', C' is satisfied.

So we have a proof method of *partial correctness* and *weak completeness*
which is *sound* and *complete*.

4.2 In practice

The *validation condition* of P w.r.t. S, C has two parts :
$sptr(P, \overline{C}) \subseteq S$, called *correctness part*
$C \subseteq sptr(P, \overline{S})$, called *completeness part.*
An interesting point is that the two parts of the validation condition can
be proved separately and there exists also sound and complete proof methods
to establish them, as stated by the following definitions and theorems :

Definition 4.2 *(bottom-up closure)*
A normal program P *is bottom-up closed w.r.t. S, C if for every ground*
instance $A \leftarrow L_1, \cdots, L_n$ of a clause of P the following holds :
if, for all positive L_i, $L_i \in S$
and, for all negative $L_i = \neg A_i$, $A_i \in \overline{C}$
then $A \in S$.
(In particular if $n = 0$ this amounts to $A \in S$).

Definition 4.3 *(top down closure)*
A normal program P *is top-down closed w.r.t. C, S if there exists a*
function f defined on C into a well ordered set (order denoted $\prec$, for which
there is no infinite decreasing sequence) such that, for every atom B of C,
there is a ground instance $A \leftarrow L_1, \cdots, L_n$ of a clause of P such that $B = A$
and
(i) for all positive L_i, $L_i \in C$
and, for all negative $L_i = \neg A_i$, $A_i \in \overline{S}$
(ii) for all positive L_i, $f(L_i) \prec f(A)$.
The condition (ii) is called decreasing criterion.

Both conditions are *local* : there is exactly one assertion to prove in
every clause for each property.

Let us recall that, for $J \subseteq H$, $sptr(P, J)$, which is the least fixed point
of the operator $T_{P,J}$ (section 2), is also the least J' such that $T_{P,J}(J') \subseteq J'$.

Theorem 4.2 *(Proof method for the correctness part)*

A normal program *P satisfies the* correctness part *for S and C if and only if there exists S' stronger than S (S' ⊆ S) such that P is bottom-up closed for S', C.*

To see that this condition is sufficient to have the correctness part, use that $sptr(P,\overline{C})$ is the least fixed point of $T_{P,\overline{C}}$ and that the condition *bottom-up closed* corresponds to $T_{P,\overline{C}}(S) \subseteq S$.

To see that it is a necessary condition, take $S' = sptr(P,\overline{C})$.

Theorem 4.3 *(Proof method for the completeness part)*

A normal program *P satisfies the* completeness part *for S and C if and only if there exists C' weaker than C (C ⊆ C') such that P is top-down closed for C', S.*

To prove this theorem, use again that $sptr(P,\overline{S})$ is the least fixed point of the operator $T_{P,\overline{S}}$. Hence the condition (i) of top down closure corresponds to show that $C \subseteq T_{P,\overline{S}}(C)$ and (ii) guarantees that each element of C is the root of a finite tree which is a semi proof tree. The only if part results from the fact that P is top down closed for $C' = sptr(P,\overline{S}), S$: C' satifies (i) because it is the least fixed point of $T_{P,\overline{S}}$ and (ii) is satisfied with the function which associates to every atom B of C' the least size of a semi proof tree of root B.

To sum up, in order to prove : $M_P^+ \subseteq S$ and $C \subseteq \overline{M_P^-}$ it is sufficient to prove the properties bottom up and top down closure, and this method can always be used.

In practice the sets C and S are defined by describing their atoms for each predicate symbol. The atoms are described by giving a property of their arguments (which are ground terms).

Example (from [8])

Let P be the following stratified program :

$$
\begin{array}{lll}
includ(L_1, L_2) & \leftarrow & \neg ninclud(L_1, L_2) \\
ninclud(L_1, L_2) & \leftarrow & elem(E, L_1), \qquad \neg elem(E, L_2) \\
elem(E, [E|L]) & \leftarrow & \\
elem(E, [H|L]) & \leftarrow & elem(E, L)
\end{array}
$$

Expected properties :

	S	C
$includ(L_1, L_2)$	L_1, L_2 *lists* $\Rightarrow L_1 \subseteq L_2$	L_1, L_2 *lists and* $L_1 \subseteq L_2$
$ninclud(L_1, L_2)$	L_1, L_2 *lists* $\Rightarrow L_1 \not\subseteq L_2$	L_1, L_2 *lists and* $L_1 \not\subseteq L_2$
$elem(E, L)$	L *list* $\Rightarrow E \in L$	L *list and* $E \in L$

Example of a verification for bottom up closed on the (ground) instance
    $ninclud(L_1, L_2) \leftarrow elem(E, L_1), \neg elem(E, L_2)$:
Suppose $elem(E, L_1) \in S$ and $elem(E, L_2) \notin C$
We have to verify that $ninclud(L_1, L_2) \in S$ i.e. L_1, L_2 *lists* $\Rightarrow L_1 \nsubseteq L_2$
Suppose L_1, L_2 *lists*
Since $elem(E, L_1) \in S$ we have $E \in L_1$
Since $elem(E, L_2) \notin C$ we have $E \notin L_2$
So $L_1 \nsubseteq L_2$ q.e.d.

Example of a verification for top down closed (i) on the (ground) atom
$ninclud(L_1, L_2) \in C$:
We have to check that there is a (ground) clause instance
$ninclud(L_1, L_2) \leftarrow elem(E, L_1), \neg elem(E, L_2)$
with $elem(E, L_1) \in C$ and $elem(E, L_2) \notin S$.
Since $ninclud(L_1, L_2) \in C$, L_1, L_2 are *lists* so it remains to find a ground
term E such that $E \in L_1$ and $E \notin L_2$.
    Such a term exists because $L_1 \nsubseteq L_2$ since $ninclud(L_1, L_2) \in C$. q.e.d.

Example of a verification for top down closed (ii) :
    Only the clauses of the predicate *elem* are concerned. There is an easy
decreasing criterion: the length of the second argument, which is a ground
list.

5   Conclusion

We have obtained two basic results: one concerns the characterization of
the well-founded model in terms of semi proof trees and as the least fixed
point of some operator acting on semi proof tree roots. Broadly we use the
characterization of the well-founded model by [17] as the least stable model
and our description of stable models in terms of semi proof trees. A difference
with the fixed point characterization of [4] is the use of "inconsistent" sets
of literals : Such an "inconsistency" is not absurd because it comes merely
(by complementation) from the fact that a specification may be partial. The
second basic result concerns an application : a sound and complete proof
method of partial correctness and weak completeness.
    The first result leads to many potential applications. It is known now
how the proof tree characterization of the semantics of definite programs
may help to design different semantics, and simplify known results ([10, 11]).
.With this characterization we may expect that the same phenomenon may
happen : simple definition of the SLS resolution and properties, extension
to non ground models.
    The second result is a remarkable generalization of already known re-
sults obtained with definite programs, or programs with a unique stable
model [7, 8]. It has different applications. Let us consider the theorem 4.1

and observe that partial correctness and weak completeness are not exactly symetric. This is due to the fact that the validation conditions are necessary and sufficient conditions to prove that the well founded model (M_P^+, M_P^-) is included into some expected partial model. But there is no simple method for proving the opposite inclusion. It follows that the validation conditions are sufficient conditions to prove partial correctness ($M_P^+ \subseteq S$). The method is complete and it uses auxiliary lemmas which are weak properties specifying certainly non false atoms.

The second application concerns the proof of completeness ($C \subseteq M_P^+$). However, due to the dissymetry between partial correctness and weak completeness, we do not obtain directly a proof method. There are two ways to overcome this default. The first one consists in modifying the notion of completeness by considering that, in the three valued approach, one is weakly complete w.r.t. C if the expected atoms of C are not false. The second one, which is a limit case of the previous one consists in limiting the method to the programs with a bivalued i.e. total well founded model. In this case theorem 4.1 provides a sound and complete method to prove completeness. It uses also auxiliary lemmas which are weak properties satisfied by any true atom. In this case it is important to have methods to prove that the well-founded model is total ([7] studies such a method for a condition more general than locally stratifiable).

There are also other applications related to the problem of the documentation of programs. Documentation must give relevant informations which facilitate the reading of the clauses. Valid assertions of partial correctness and weak completeness provide such information.

It must be noticed that the results obtained here do not give a practical proof method out of some scholastic examples. As for the inductive proof method in definite programs, whose theoretical formulation using the fixed point approach is extremely simple, some work needs to be achieved to make it a practical proof method based on assertions ([6]).

Finally the results obtained here may be considered as a new justification of the interest of the well-founded semantics for normal programs.

6 Appendix

Proof of the theorem 2.1 :
Let $I_0 \subseteq H(\mathcal{L}) \cup \neg H(\mathcal{L})$ defined by
$I_0^+ = H(\mathcal{L}) \cap ptr(P_t)$
$I_0^- = \{A \in H(\mathcal{L}) | A \notin ptr(P_{t,u})\}$

We have to prove that $I_0 = Min(P)$, i.e. that
1. I_0 is a 3-interpretation
2. I_0 is a model of P
3. If I is a model of P then $I_0 \leq I$.

Proof of 1. : $I_0^+ \cap I_0^- = \emptyset$ because $P_t \subseteq P_{t,u}$.

Proof of 2. : Let $A \leftarrow A_1, \cdots, A_n$ be a ground instance of a clause of P. We have to prove that

$$I_0(A) \geq min\{I_0(A_i)|i \leq n\}$$

If this min is 0 there is nothing to prove. If it is $\frac{1}{2}$ then $I_0(A_i) > 0$ so $A_i = u$ or t or is an atom $\notin I_0^-$ and in any case $A_i \in ptr(P_{tu})$, hence $A \in ptr(P_{tu})$ so $A \notin I_0^-$ i.e. $I_0(A) \geq \frac{1}{2}$.

If this min is 1 then $I_0(A_i) = 1$ so $A_i = t$ or is an atom $\in I_0^+$ and in any case $A_i \in ptr(P_t)$, hence $A \in ptr(P_t)$ so $A \in I_0^+$ and $I_0(A) = 1$.

Proof of 3. : from the following lemma :

Lemma 6.1 *If I is a model of P (positive)*

$$
\begin{array}{lll}
(i) & ptr(P_t) & \subseteq \quad \{t\} \cup I^+ \\
(ii) & ptr(P_{t,u}) & \subseteq \quad \{t, u\} \cup (H(\mathcal{L}) - I^-)
\end{array}
$$

Proof :
(i) $ptr(P_t)$ is a set of atoms ($\subseteq H(\mathcal{L}_{t,u,f})$) which is the classical (Van Emden-Kowalski) minimum Herbrand model of P_t so it is sufficient to prove that the set $\{t\} \cup I^+$ is a classical Herbrand model of P_t i.e. that, for every ground instance $A \leftarrow A_1, \cdots, A_n$ of a clause, if $A_1, \cdots, A_n \in \{t\} \cup I^+$ then $A \in \{t\} \cup I^+$. This comes from

$$I(A) \geq min\{I(A_i)|i \leq n\} = 1$$

(ii) same method :
if $A_1, \cdots, A_n \in \{t, u\} \cup (H(\mathcal{L}) - I^-)$ then $A \in \{t, u\} \cup (H(\mathcal{L}) - I^-)$ because now the min is > 0.
q.e.d.

Acknowledgements

This research was supported in part by the METHEOL project of the GRECO Programmation, CNRS.

Thanks are due to the anonymous referees for their comments and suggestions.

References

[1] K.R. Apt, H. Blair, A. Walker. *Toward a Theory of Declarative Knowledge*. In J. Minker, editor, Foundations of Deductive Databases and Logic Programming, 89-142, Morgan Kaufmann, 1988.

[2] N. Bidoit, C. Froidevaux. *General logical databases and programs : default logic semantics and stratification.* J. Inf. Comput. 1988.

[3] N. Bidoit, C. Froidevaux. *Negation by default and unstratifiable logic programs.* Theoretical Computer Science, 78, 1991.

[4] S. Bonnier, U. Nilsson, T. Näslund. *A simple fixed point characterization of three-valued stable model semantics.* Information Processing Letters 40 (1991) 73-78

[5] K. L. Clark. *Predicate Logic as a Computational Formalism.* Res. Mon. 79/59 TOC. Imperial College. 1979.

[6] P. Deransart. *Proof Methods of Declarative Properties of Definite Programs.* INRIA RR 1248, 1991 (to appear in Theoretical Computer Science).

[7] P. Deransart, G. Ferrand. *A Methodological view of Logic Programming with Negation.* INRIA RR 1011, 1989.

[8] P. Deransart, G. Ferrand. *An operational Formal Definition of PROLOG : a specification method and its application.* New Generation Computing 10 (1992) 121-171.

[9] W. Drabent. *Constructive negation by fail answers.* LiTH-IDA-R-91-23, Linköping University, 1991, to appear in Acta Informatica.

[10] M. Falaschi, G. Levi, M. Martelli, C. Palamidessi. *Declarative Modeling of the Operational Behaviour of logic languages.* Theoretical Computer Science 69(3): 289-318, 1989.

[11] G. Ferrand. *Tutorial : Basic Concepts of Logic Programming and PROLOG.* 8 th International Conference on Logic Programming, 1991.

[12] M. Fitting. *A Kripke-Kleene semantics for logic programs.* Journal of Logic programming, 2(4):295-312, 1985.

[13] M. Gelfond, V. Lifschitz. *The stable model semantics for logic programming.* Proc. 5 th Logic Programming Symposium, 1070-1080, MIT Press, 1988.

[14] J. W. Lloyd. *Foundations of Logic Programming.* Springer Verlag, 1987.

[15] T. Przymusinski. *On the declarative semantics of logic programs* In J. Minker, editor, Foundations of Deductive Databases and Logic Programming, 193-216, Morgan Kaufmann, 1988.

[16] T. Przymusinski. *Every logic program has a natural stratification and an iterated fixed point model.* Symp. on Principles of Database Systems, p 11-21, ACM SIGACT SIGMOD SIGART, 1989.

[17] T. Przymusinski. *Well-founded semantics coincides with three-valued stable semantics.* Fundamenta Informaticae XIII (1990) 445-463.

[18] K. A. Ross. *A procedural semantics for well founded negation in logic programs.* Symp. on Principles of Database Systems, p 11-21, ACM SIGACT SIGMOD SIGART, 1989.

[19] V. Thibau, J.P. Delahaye. *Programming in three-valued logic.* Theoretical Computer Science, vol 78: 189-216, 1991.

[20] M. Van Emden, R. Kowalski. *The semantics of predicate logic as a programming language.* Journal of the ACM, 23(4): 733-742, 1976.

[21] A. Van Gelder, K. A. Ross, J. S. Schlipf. *The well-founded Semantics for General Logic Programs.* Journal of the ACM, Vol. 38, No. 3, July 1991, 620-650.

Functions and Equations

Equational Logic Programming, Actions, and Change

G.Große, S.Hölldobler, J.Schneeberger, U.Sigmund, M.Thielscher
Intellektik, Informatik, TH Darmstadt, Germany

Abstract

Recently three approaches for solving planning problems deductively were proposed, each of which does not require to state frame axioms explicitly. These approaches are based on the linear connection method, an equational logic programming language, and on linear logic. In this paper we briefly review these approaches and show that they are equivalent. Moreover, we illustrate that these approaches are not only restricted to deductive planning, but can be applied whenever actions are to be modelled in logic. The approaches essentially amount on building predicates over the data structure multiset. Such multisets are interpreted as resources which are consumed and produced by actions. We give a minimal and complete unification algorithm for the equational theory which defines the multisets. Finally, we discuss possible extensions of the equational logic programming approach.

1 Introduction

Logical approaches to computer science and artificial intelligence offer – among others – the advantage of a declarative representation of knowledge. Originally, classical logic was designed and used for the representation of static knowledge. More recently logic has also been applied to model actions, states, and changing situations (eg. [22, 21, 18, 27, 10, 19]). The very first approaches in this direction revealed some fundamental problems such as the *frame problem* [22], ie. the problem of how to represent the invariants of a situation with respect to a given action. To handle this problem J. McCarthy, P. Hayes [22], and C. Green [12] introduced *frame axioms*. However, they needed $n \times m$ frame axioms, where n is the number of actions and m is the number of fluents,[1] in a planning problem. This number was reduced to n by Kowalski [17], who introduced a different representation of fluents using a *Holds* predicate. However, these frame axioms still pose a considerable problem to automated theorem provers as they may lead to many redundant derivations. W. Bibel [3] used a modified version of his connection method to solve the frame problem without the need of any frame axioms. He considered only *linear* proofs, ie. proofs in which each literal is used at most once. Unfortunately, Bibel was unable to give a semantics for the linear connection method and as R. Kowalski states *if Bibel's system really works, then it deserves an explanation and it deserves a semantics* (see Discussion in [4]). Recently, M. Masseron etal. [20] applied the multiplicative fragment of linear logic [11] to planning and showed that in this framework planning problems can also be solved without frame axioms.

---

[1] Ie. essential properties describing situations.

A different approach to deductive planning, which also avoids the frame axioms, was given in [15]. There, situations – viz. collections of fluents – are represented using a binary AC1-function symbol $\circ$, ie. a function which is associative, commutative, and admits a unit element $\emptyset$. For example, the situation in which two blocks a and b are on a table t and are clear can be described by the term $on(a, t) \circ on(b, t) \circ cl(a) \circ cl(b)$.[2] The planning process itself is specified using a predicate $plan(s, p, t)$ which is interpreted declaratively as *the execution of plan p transforms situation s into situation t.* Actions are defined by rules of the form

$$plan(preconditions \circ V, action(P), W) \ :- plan(postconditions \circ V, P, W),$$

where the pre- as well as the postconditions are collections of fluents connected by $\circ$. Such rules are applicable if the preconditions are part of the current situation and all remaining fluents are bound – via an AC1-unification procedure – to a variable V. For example, the mv-operator moves a block from one location to another one.

$$plan(cl(X) \circ cl(Y) \circ on(X, Z) \circ V, mv(X, Y, P), W)$$
$$:- plan(cl(X) \circ cl(Z) \circ on(X, Y) \circ V, P, W).$$

Derivations are terminated with the help of a fact, which states that there is nothing to do if the goal situation is already contained in the current situation.

$$plan(V \circ W, \Lambda, V).$$

Queries to such a program can be answered using SLDE-resolution, where the equational theory AC1 is built into the unification procedure. Moreover, the approach admits a standard semantics by applying the results from [16] or [14].

One should observe that the pre- as well as the postcondition of an action are just collections of fluents which can intuitively be understood as conjunctions of fluents. A more precise interpretation will be given in Section 4. This restriction holds also for [20]. W. Bibel allows a more general form, but all examples given in [3, 5] are restricted in precisely the same way.

The purpose of this paper is as follows.

1. We proved that the equational logic programming approach to deductive planning is equivalent to a the linear connection method and the linear logic approach to deductive planning. This result is obtained by transforming SLDE-refutations into linear connection proofs and linear logic proofs, respectively, and vice versa. With the help of these transformations, we do now obtain a semantics for the linear connection method as the standard semantics for logic programming modulo the equational theory AC1.

2. We show that the equational logic programming approach is not restricted to deductive planning, but can always be applied if situations are specified by conjunctions of fluents and if actions are defined over such situations. We illustrate this generality by specifying objects and database updates in this framework in analogy to [2] and [23].

3. We show that specifying conjunctions of fluents using an AC1-operator essentially amounts to defining predicates over the data structure multiset and

---

[2]Throughout the paper we use PROLOG-syntax.

that fluents represent resources which are consumed and produced by the actions.

4. We give an efficient AC1-unification algorithm for computing a complete and minimal set of unifiers modulo AC1.

5. We extend our approach by admitting a form of idempotent disjunction among fluents such that we can solve the 3-socks problem quite naturally. Moreover, we demonstrate that Mendel must have used some sort of non-idempotent disjunction (or linear logic) when he discovered his famous laws in genetics.

The paper concludes with a discussion and various ideas on future work.

2 Deductive Planning

In this section we briefly repeat W. Bibel's [3], S. Hölldobler and J. Schnee-berger's [15] as well as M. Masseron etal. approach [20] to deductive planning and show that these approaches are equivalent.

We illustrate the three approaches with the help of a little example. Suppose a thirsty person named Bert wants to get some lemonade from a vending machine. The lemonade costs 75 cents, which should be no problem as Bert has a one-dollar note as well as a quarter in his jacket. Unfortunately, the vending machine accepts only quarters. But there is also a cashier, which changes a dollar into four quarters. The problem of getting the lemonade can be described as a planning problem with the initial situation of Bert having a dollar note (d) and a quarter (q), the operators *get-change* (g_c) and *get-lemonade* (g_l), which allow him to change a dollar and to get a lemonade, respectively, and the goal where Bert has a lemonade (l) in his hand. Clearly, a solution to this problem is the plan with the two consecutive actions get-change and get-lemonade. One should observe that the pre- as well as the postconditions of both operators are conjunctions of fluents.

Linear Connection Method. W. Bibel's [3] approach to deductive planning is based on the connection method. Therein the initial situation is represented by the axiom $\exists Z\ [s(Z) \wedge d \wedge q]$, the operators get-change and get-lemonade by the axioms

$$\forall S\ [s(g_c(S)) \wedge d\ \rightarrow\ q \wedge q \wedge q \wedge q \wedge s(S)]$$
$$\forall S\ [s(g_l(S)) \wedge q \wedge q \wedge q\ \rightarrow\ l \wedge s(S)]$$

respectively, and the goal by $s(\Lambda) \wedge l$, where Λ is a constant denoting the empty plan. The predicate s is a so-called state literal, whose only role is to record the actions taken in order to achieve the goal. Figure 1 shows a valid connection proof for our example yielding the desired answer substitution $\{Z \mapsto g_c(g_l(\Lambda))\}$, ie. get-change first and, then get-lemonade.

The remarkable feature of the proof shown in Figure 1 is its *linearity*, ie. every literal is engaged in at most one connection. Without this linearity we might be able to connect the literal $\neg q$ occurring in the initial situation three

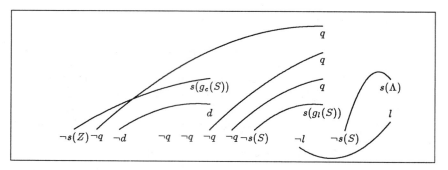

Figure 1: A linear connection proof for the get lemonade example.

times such that the conditions of the get-lemonade operator are satisfied initially. In other words, one quarter would be enough to get a lemonade.

Equational Logic Programming. In the equational logic programming approach of S. Hölldobler and J. Schneeberger [15] already sketched in the introduction the lemonade example can be expressed by the following program.

$$plan(d \circ V, g_c(P), W) :- plan(q \circ q \circ q \circ q \circ V, P, W).$$
$$plan(q \circ q \circ q \circ V, g_l(P), W) :- plan(l \circ V, P, W).$$
$$plan(V \circ W, \Lambda, V).$$

The first two clauses specify the actions get-lemonade and get-change, and the final clause states that the current situation already establishes the goal situation. The question of whether there exists a plan such that Bert can get a lemonade for a dollar and a quarter can now be answered as shown in Figure 2.

It is important to note that $\circ$ is not idempotent. Otherwise, $?- plan(d \circ q \circ q \circ q \circ q \circ q, P_1, l)$ would be an SLDE-resolvent of $?- plan(d \circ q, P, l)$ and the first program clause. But this would be like growing money on trees. Furthermore, the frame axioms are not needed as the variable V in the program clauses together with the unification computation built into SLDE-resolution take each fluent which is invariant under the action[3] to the next goal clause.

In [15] the semantics of the linear logic programming approach to deductive planning is defined as the standard semantics of a logic program with equality. It is shown that the approach is sound and complete.

---

[3] A fluent is *invariant* if it is not among the preconditions of an action.

$$?- plan(d \circ q, P, l).$$
$$?- plan(q \circ q \circ q \circ q \circ q, P_1, l).$$
$$?- plan(q \circ q \circ l, P_2, l).$$
$$\square$$

Figure 2: The SLDE-resolution of $?- plan(d \circ q, P, l)$ obtained by applying – in this order – the first, second, and third program clause yields the answer substitution $\{P \mapsto g_c(g_l(\Lambda))\}$.

$$\cfrac{\cfrac{\cfrac{q \vdash q \quad q \vdash q}{q, q \vdash q \otimes q}\small{\otimes_r} \quad q, q, q \vdash l}{\cfrac{\cfrac{\cfrac{\cfrac{q, q, q, q, q \vdash q \otimes q \otimes l}{q, q, q, q \otimes q \vdash q \otimes q \otimes l}\small{\otimes_l}}{q, q, q \otimes q \otimes q \vdash q \otimes q \otimes l}\small{\otimes_l}}{q, q \otimes q \otimes q \otimes q \vdash q \otimes q \otimes l}\small{\otimes_l}}{q \otimes q \otimes q \otimes q \otimes q \vdash q \otimes q \otimes l}\small{\otimes_l}}}{q, d \vdash q \otimes q \otimes l}\small{cut}$$

$$\cfrac{q \vdash q \quad d \vdash q \otimes q \otimes q \otimes q}{q, d \vdash q \otimes q \otimes q \otimes q}\small{\otimes_r}$$

Figure 3: A linear logic proof for the get lemonade example. For the definition of the rules $\otimes l$, $\otimes_r$, and cut see [20].

Linear Logic. The use of linear logic for planning problems was proposed by M. Massaron etal. [20]. In this approach our running example is specified by the *current state axioms* $\vdash d$ and $\vdash q$ and by the following *transition axioms*.

$$d \vdash q \otimes q \otimes q \otimes q.$$

$$q, q, q \vdash l.$$

A proof in this approach looks similar to Gentzen-like proofs. In Figure 3 a linear logic proof for our example is depicted. The plan which solves the given planning problem can be extracted from the proof by recording the used transition axioms together with their order in the proof.

One should observe that it is impossible to derive the sequent $q, d \vdash l$ instead of $q, d \vdash l \otimes q \otimes q$ in this framework. The linear logic approach as stated in [20] does not provide a mechanism for deleting essentials on the right side of a sequent.

The Equivalence Result. As the example depicted in Figures 1 and 2 already indicates, SLDE-refutations with respect to a linear logic program can be transformed into a linear connection proof and vice versa. The proof is by induction on the length of the SLDE-refutation. Similarly, as the example depicted in Figures 2 and 3 indicates, SLDE-refutations with respect to a linear logic program can be transformed into a linear logic proof. The proof is again by an induction on the length of SLDE-refutations. Conversely, it can be shown that a linear logic proof can be transformed into an SLDE-refutation by induction on the length of the linear proof. Due to lack of space, we have to omit the formal proofs. They can be found in [13] or [25].

Theorem 1 *Let $\mathcal{P}$ be a planning problem, where the pre- and postconditions of actions are conjunctions of fluents. Plan P is a solution for $\mathcal{P}$ iff P is generated by a conjunctive equational logic program iff P is generated by a conjunctive linear connection proof iff P is generated by a conjunctive linear logic proof.*

3 Objects and Database Updates

Although the approach in [15] was developed for deductive planning, it is not restricted to the planning domain. The basic ideas were to represent fluents on the object level with the help of an AC1-operator $\circ$, to specify rules for actions of the form

$$plan(preconditions \circ V, action(P), W) :- plan(postconditions \circ V, P, W)$$

and apply SLDE-resolution. The very same idea can be used to represent and manipulate objects and database items.

Objects. The combination of logic programming and object-oriented programming offers the advantage of both paradigms. From logic programming it inherits the declarative representation of data. From object-oriented programming it receives the structured representation of data in classes of objects, data structuring by inheritance among classes, and dynamic modification of data. In our approach the properties of an object are represented as fluents and connected by the AC1-operator $\circ$. For example, an object *point* which is at location $(7, 3)$ and receives the input $proj_x$ is represented by the term $point \circ input(proj_x(I)) \circ x(7) \circ y(3)$. Communication between objects is realized by shared variables as proposed in [26]. In our example, I is such a variable. Transitions are specified by rules. For example, a transition for projecting two-dimensional points on the x-axis can be specified by the rule.

$$obj(point \circ input(proj_x(I')) \circ y(Y) \circ V) :- obj(point \circ input(I') \circ y(0) \circ V). \quad (1)$$

Now the query

$$?- obj(point \circ input(proj_x(I)) \circ x(7) \circ y(3))$$

can be resolved with the transition rule (1) to

$$?- obj(point \circ input(I) \circ x(7) \circ y(0))$$

using the AC1-unifier $\{Y \mapsto 3, V \mapsto x(7), I' \mapsto I\}$. One should observe that the transition rule (1) is applicable to all objects which belong to the class of points and possess a y-coordinate or which belong to a subclass thereof. For example, a point which belongs to the subclass of coloured two-dimensional points and receives a $proj_x$–message, ie. the query

$$?- obj(point \circ input(proj_x(I)) \circ x(7) \circ y(3) \circ colour(blue))$$

is transformed to

$$?- obj(point \circ input(I) \circ x(7) \circ y(0) \circ colour(blue))$$

via SLDE-resolution with transition rule (1) using the AC1-unifier $\{Y \mapsto 3, V \mapsto x(7) \circ colour(blue), I' \mapsto I\}$. The only difference to the previous derivation is the binding of the variable V, which now contains also all additional (inherited) properties of the object.

There is no essential difference between the *plan* predicate and the *obj* predicate. One could easily rephrase objects and their transitions using a ternary predicate *object* such that $object(o, t, o')$ represents the fact that *object o is transformed into object o' after receiving messages t*. Since Theorem 1 tells us that we can transform SLDE-derivations into linear logic proofs and linear connection proofs and vice versa, we essentially incorporate objects into linear logic and the linear connection method as well.

There already exists a framework for representing objects in logic programs, which is very similar to our approach [2]. In fact, our example is taken from [2]. There, J.M. Andreoli and R. Pareschi represent the properties of objects as predicates which are connected via the binary connective @ . @ plays the same role as our ∘ except that @ is interpreted as *multiplicative disjunction* whereas we interpret ∘ as *multiplicative conjunction*. To think of @ as a disjunction is kind of counterintuitive as, then, an object like a point has an x-coordinate *or* has a y-coordinate. Formally, however, J.M. Andreoli and R. Pareschi treat @ as an AC1-operator and, thus, it corresponds precisely to ∘ . There is also a technical difference between [2] and the work reported herein. In their approach proof rules are only defined for ground goals and rules rigorously, and it is stated that these rules can be lifted via unification. In our approach, the operational semantics is rigorously defined for general goals and rules.

Database Updates. In analogy to actions in planning scenario, database transactions are specified using a predicate $db(d, t, d')$, which is read declaratively as *the execution of the transaction sequence t transforms the database d into d'*. As an example consider a toy education database specifying relations about students, courses, and grades. $enr(St, C)$ tells us that the student St is enrolled in course C, $grd(St, C, G)$ that her grade in course C is G, and $pre(P, C)$ that P is a prerequisite course for course C. A transaction for a student St to be registered for a course C is only possible if she has obtained a grade G of at least 50 in all prerequisite courses.

$$db(V, regis(St, C, S), W) : - db(enr(St, C) \circ V, S, W), \neg low\_pre(St, C, V).$$

$$low\_pre(St, C, V) : - AC1\text{-}unify(V, Y \circ pre(P, C) \circ grd(St, P, G)), G \leq 50.$$

The predicate $AC1\text{-}unify$ unifies its arguments modulo AC1 and negation is handled by negation as failure. Now, if we want to know whether *sue* can register for course $m6$ in the situation $t = enr(sue, c1) \circ pre(m4, m6) \circ grd(bill, m1, 70) \circ grd(sue, m3, 85) \circ grd(sue, m4, 55)$ we ask the following query.

$$? - db(t, regis(sue, m6, \Lambda), W).$$

Resolving this query with the clauses above and with the terminating fact $db(V, \Lambda, V)$ yields the empty clause and substitution $\{W \mapsto enr(sue, m6) \circ t\}$. This result is obtained because the proof of $low\_pre(sue, m6, t)$ fails.

This example demonstrates how complex queries – including universally quantified variables here – can be handled using general concepts from logic programming. Similarly, we can state integrity constraints employing a modified termination clause together with the necessary predicates (see [15] for a more detailed discussion).

$$db(V, \Lambda, V) \ : - consistent(V).$$

$$consistent(V) \ : - \neg inconsistent(V).$$

$$inconsistent(V \circ grd(St, C, G) \circ grd(St, C, G')), G' \neq G.$$

$$\ldots$$

The examples in this section were taken from [23]. However, it should be noted that R. Reiter's approach is more fundamental since it deals with standard situation calculus. Nevertheless, we observe that most of the examples he is able to solve are also feasible in our approach.

4   Predicates over Multisets

In our equational logic programming approach to actions and change we use terms of the form $\emptyset$ or $s_1 \circ \ldots \circ s_n$, $n \geq 1$, to represent situations, where the s_i are fluents, ie. non-variable terms which do not contain the $\circ$ function symbol. If such terms are ground, then they can be mapped to multisets with the help of an interpretation $\mathcal{I}$ as follows.[4]

$$\begin{aligned}
\mathcal{I}(\emptyset) &= \{\!\}. \\
\mathcal{I}(a) &= \{\!a\!\} \text{ if } a \text{ is a fluent.} \\
\mathcal{I}(s \circ t) &= \mathcal{I}(s) \dot{\cup} \mathcal{I}(t).
\end{aligned}$$

In other words, our predicates like *plan*, *obj*, or *db* are essentially predicates over the datastructure multiset. By the use of multisets changing situations is now like dealing with resources. By multiset operations we delete or add certain amounts of fluents to the current situation in order to yield a new situation. This update procedure is similar to the procedure used in STRIPS [8] but uses multisets instead of sets.

It is interesting to see that in all the three approaches to reasoning about change depicted in Section 2, the multiset representation for situations did not only solve the frame problem, but also led to a considerable gain of efficiency. This shall be illustrated in the following example. Suppose we had an arbitrary set of terms representing our domain in question. Certain subsets might represent certain situations. For instance, in a domain consisting of four quarters there are $16 = 2^4$ different situations. On the other hand, as common in practice, we are not really concerned with the question which quarter we got but more in how many quarters we got. The number of situations important for this knowledge is much less: just 5. Either we got none, or 1, or ... or 4 quarters. In fact what we have to do is just taking the identity of these quarters and forming the multiset of quarters. This reduction of the number of situations is not to underestimate as the following example shall demonstrate. Suppose we had two lemonades, four dollars and four quarters in our domain. Then the number of situations reduces from $1024 = 2^{10}$ to 75. This in turn affects the principle number of situation changes, which is the square of the number of situations. Instead of around 10^6 we can work with around 5×10^3; quite a difference. But as always there is no free dinner. If we use such a multiset representation we do not know with which object of the multiset we are left after some change. We cannot, for instance, say which of the 4 quarters remains in our pocket after spending three.

---

[4]Multisets are depicted using the modified curly brackets $\{\!$ and $\!\}$. Furthermore, $\dot{\subseteq}$, $\dot{\cup}$, $\dot{\setminus}$, etc. denote the multiset extensions of the usual set operations $\subseteq$, $\cup$, $\setminus$, etc.

5   AC1-Unification

So far we have given an equational logic programming approach to reasoning about action and change, but have said nothing about computational aspects. We have only mentioned that the equational theory shall be built into the unification computation. In practice, however, an efficient implementation of a special E-unification procedure is indispensable and we will give such unification procedures in this section.

AC1-unification – as required in our approach – is finitary,[5] ie. there is always a finite and minimal set of unifiers for two terms. Therefore, the aim of building in an AC1-unification algorithm is to generate a complete and minimal set of unifiers.

There are a variety of AC1-unification algorithms (cf. [7]). However, the AC1-unification problems encountered in this paper are of a special kind. The general AC1-unification algorithms perform a lot of unnecessary and redundant computations if applied to these problems. More formally, the AC1-unification problems considered herein are defined as follows. Let a *fluent* be a non-variable term, which does neither contain the $\circ$ function symbol nor the $\emptyset$ constant. For example, $colour(blue)$ and $input(I)$ are fluents. In the remainder of this paragraph let s and t (possibly indexed) denote fluents. We will consider three different unification problems with increasing complexity.

- An *AC1-matching problem* consists of two terms of the form $s_1 \circ \ldots \circ s_n$ and $t_1 \circ \ldots \circ t_m \circ W$, where the s_i, $1 \leq i \leq n$, are ground and W does not occur in t_j.
- A *restricted AC1-unification problem* consists of two terms of the form $s_1 \circ \ldots \circ s_n$ and $t_1 \circ \ldots \circ t_m \circ W$, where W does neither occur in s_i nor in t_j.[6]
- An *AC1-unification problem* consists of two terms of the form $s_1 \circ \ldots \circ s_n \circ V$ and $t_1 \circ \ldots \circ t_m \circ W$, where V and W are different variables and do neither occur in s_i nor in t_j.

The variables V and W which occur in the previous definitions are called *AC1-variables*.

In the sequel we describe three algorithms which generate complete and minimal sets of unifiers for these problem classes.

AC1-matching. It turned out that in many applications of our equational logic programming approach to planning, one of the two terms to be unified modulo AC1 was ground. Thus, we have the chance to use an AC1-matching instead of an AC1-unification algorithm quite often. A substitution σ is a matcher for an AC1-matching problem iff $\sigma(W \circ t_1 \circ \ldots \circ t_m) =_{AC1} s_1 \circ \ldots \circ s_n$, where s_i, $1 \leq i \leq n$, are ground. It is easy to prove that if σ is a solution for the AC1-matching problem then $\{\sigma t_1, \ldots, \sigma t_m\} \dot{\subseteq} \{s_1, \ldots, s_n\}$. Conversely, if we find a substitution θ such that $\{\theta t_1, \ldots, \theta t_m\} \dot{\subseteq} \{s_1, \ldots, s_n\}$, then the AC1-matching problem consisting of the terms $s_1 \circ \ldots \circ s_n$ and $t_1 \circ \ldots \circ t_m \circ W$ is

---

[5] The notions and notations concerning unification under an equational theory are taken from [28].

[6] Note that the fluents s_i may now contain variables.

solvable and the matching substitution σ can be constructed from θ as follows. Let $\{u_1, \ldots, u_k\} = \{s_1, \ldots, s_n\} \smallsetminus \{\theta t_1, \ldots, \theta t_m\}$. Then, $\sigma = \theta|_{\mathcal{V}ar(t_1, \ldots, t_m) \cup \{W \mapsto u_1 \circ \ldots \circ u_k\}}$ [7].

Let $\mathcal{S}$ and $\mathcal{T}$ be two multisets of fluents. With the previous discussion, we are now interested in computing a complete and minimal set Σ of substitutions such that for each $\sigma \in \Sigma$ we find that $\sigma \mathcal{T} \dot\subseteq \mathcal{S}$. [8] The following algorithm recursively generates this set.

1. If $\mathcal{T} = \{\}$ then $\Sigma = \{\varepsilon\}$. [9]
2. If $\mathcal{T} = \{t\} \,\dot\cup\, \mathcal{T}'$ then $\Sigma = \{\theta \sigma' \mid \sigma' \in \Sigma' \wedge \exists s \in \mathcal{S} \smallsetminus \sigma' \mathcal{T}' : \theta = mgu(\sigma' t, s)\}$ [10], where Σ' is a complete and minimal set of substitutions such that for each $\sigma' \in \Sigma'$ we find $\sigma' \mathcal{T}' \dot\subseteq \mathcal{S}$.

One should observe that for each σ' and each s the substitution $\theta \sigma' \in \Sigma$ is unique. Hence, the algorithm does no redundant computation.

Restricted AC1-Unification. Restricted AC1-unification is reduced to a subset problem over multisets, where substitutions are applied to both multisets. Let θ be a substitution such that $\{\theta t_1, \ldots, \theta t_m\} \dot\subseteq \{\theta s_1, \ldots, \theta s_n\}$, then a unifier σ of $s_1 \circ \ldots \circ s_n$ and $t_1 \circ \ldots \circ t_m \circ W$ can be constructed from θ as shown within the AC1-matching. To generate a complete set of substitutions σ such that $\sigma \mathcal{T} \dot\subseteq \sigma \mathcal{S}$ holds, we modify the algorithm shown above as follows.

1. If $\mathcal{T} = \{\}$ then $\Sigma = \{\varepsilon\}$.
2. If $\mathcal{T} = \{t\} \,\dot\cup\, \mathcal{T}'$ then $\Sigma = \{\theta \sigma' \mid \sigma' \in \Sigma' \wedge \exists s \in \sigma' \mathcal{S} \smallsetminus \sigma' \mathcal{T}' : \theta = mgu(\sigma' t, s)\}$, where Σ' is a complete and minimal set of substitutions such that for each $\sigma' \in \Sigma'$ we find $\sigma' \mathcal{T}' \dot\subseteq \sigma' \mathcal{S}$.

The resulting set Σ is complete but, unfortunately, it may contain non-minimal substitutions. Therefore, we have to test and, if necessary, to remove some substitutions.

AC1-Unification. The problem of unifying two terms that both include an AC1-variable cannot be reduced to a subset problem over multisets. However, each solution σ of the AC1-unification problem defined by the terms $s_1 \circ \ldots \circ s_n \circ V$ and $t_1 \circ \ldots \circ t_m \circ W$ can be interpreted as dividing the representing multisets $\mathcal{S} = \{s_1, \ldots, s_n\}$ and $\mathcal{T} = \{t_1, \ldots, t_m\}$ into two disjunctive parts $\mathcal{S}_1, \mathcal{S}_2$ and $\mathcal{T}_1, \mathcal{T}_2$, respectively, such that we find a most general substitution θ which unifies $\mathcal{S}_1$ and $\mathcal{T}_1$. Let $\theta \mathcal{S}_2 = \{u_1, \ldots, u_l\}$ and $\theta \mathcal{T}_2 = \{v_1, \ldots, v_k\}$. Then, $\sigma = \theta \cup \{V \mapsto v_1 \circ \ldots \circ v_k \circ Z, \ W \mapsto u_1 \circ \ldots \circ u_l \circ Z\}$, where Z is a new AC1-variable.

The algorithms for AC1-matching, restricted AC1-unification, and AC1-unification are implemented and used successfully within a PROLOG program

---

[7] $\mathcal{V}ar(X)$ denotes the set of variables occurring in the syntactic object X and $\sigma|_V$ denotes the restriction of the substitution σ to the variables in V.

[8] The notion of a minimal and complete set of substitutions is extended in the obvious way.

[9] ε denotes the empty substitution.

[10] $mgu(s, t)$ denotes the most general unifier of s and t.

of our equational logic programming approach. They turned out to be very efficient as they consider the characteristics of the AC1-terms occurring in all applications of our equational logic programming approach to actions and change. The details of the algorithms as well as a proof of their correctness, completeness, and minimality can be found in [30].

6   On Disjunction

So far we dealt only with conjunctions of fluents and we have shown how such conjunctions can be used for modelling planning problems, objects, and database updates. In certain domains, however, disjunctions arise naturally. Thus, we are faced with the problem of extending our approach to handle disjunction. In this section we will give two examples, the 3-socks problem and Mendel's law in genetics, which illustrate the need for two different forms of disjunction, and sketch how these disjunctions can be modelled in an equational logic programming language.

The 3-socks problem.   Imagine that we are standing in a dark room in front of a drawer which contains black and white socks. The 3-socks problem is now the question of how often we have to fetch a sock out of the drawer before we can be sure to have a pair of matching socks. As the name already says, the solution is 3. But how can we formalize the problem such that the solution is deduced? [3] as well as [15] give a solution within the framework of conjunctive planning, where the problem is mapped onto a pair of natural numbers. One of these numbers is incremented at each *fetch* operation until eventually one of them is 2. These solution are formally correct, but they are quite unnatural and unintuitive.

If we fetch a sock, then we know that we do have a sock, but we do not know whether this sock has the colour black or white. Hence, the result of the *fetch* operation should be formalized as a term $b \mid w$. What are the properties of $\mid$? As we intend to think of $\mid$ as an additive disjunction, $\mid$ should be associative and commutative. But $\mid$ should also be idempotent, ie. $X \mid X = X$ should hold, because if in our example all socks are white we do hold a single white sock after a *fetch* operation. These ACI-properties in mind we can now specify the *fetch* operation.

$$plan(V, fetch(P), W). \ :- \ plan((b \mid w) \circ V, P, W). \tag{2}$$

The 3-socks problem can now be specified by the following query.

$$?- \ plan(\emptyset, P, (b \circ b) \mid (w \circ w)).$$

In other words, we are looking for a plan P such that its execution transforms the empty multiset into a multiset, where we find either two black or two white socks. Resolving this goal clause three times with (new variants of) rule (2) leads to

$$?- \ plan((b \mid w) \circ (b \mid w) \circ (b \mid w), P_3, (b \circ b) \mid (w \circ w)) \tag{3}$$

and to the binding $\{P \mapsto fetch(fetch(fetch(P_3)))\}$. In order to terminate the derivation we have to resolve (3) and the terminating fact $plan(V \circ W, \Lambda, V)$. But this requires to specify the interaction between $\circ$ and $|$. If we regard fluents as resources and a term of the form $X \mid Y$ as having either resource X or resource Y but not both, then it is natural to require that $\circ$ distributes over $|$, ie.

$$X \circ (Y \mid Z) = (X \circ Y) \mid (X \circ Z).\text{[11]}$$

With the help of this axiom, the AC1 axioms for $\circ$, and the ACI axioms for $|$ we can now resolve (3) and the terminating fact leading to the binding $\{P \mapsto fetch(fetch(fetch(\Lambda)))\}$.

Mendel's law of genetics. Mendel wanted to understand how the colour of peas is determined. He crossed peas, counted the number of yellow and green peas in the following generations, and by a kind of backward reasoning discovered that the colour of peas is determined by two genes, each of which carries the hereditary factor for either yellow or green. Green is dominant and yellow is recessive, ie. peas are green if they have at least one green gene and peas are yellow if they have two yellow genes. During crossing the genes determining the colour are split and combined with a gene from another pea.

We will show how the crossing process can be modelled in an equational logic programming environment and how the ratio of yellow and green peas can be determined. We model peas with the help of a binary function symbol p, where $p(g_1, g_2)$ is interpreted as a pea with genes g_1 and g_2. The genes itself may be either yellow (y) or green (g). The colour of a pea, ie. whether the pea is *green* or *yellow*, can now be specified by the following equations.

$$\begin{aligned}
p(G_1, G_2) &= p(G_2, G_1). \\
green &= p(g, G). \\
yellow &= p(y, y).
\end{aligned} \tag{4}$$

The effect of crossing two peas is specified via a ternary predicate symbol cp, where $cp(p_1, p_2, p_3)$ is read declaratively as *crossing peas p_1 and p_2 yields p_3*. Of course, we do not know precisely how p_3 looks like; all we know is that its genes are a combination of the genes found in p_1 and p_2.

$$cp(p(X, Y), p(V, W), p(X, V) \# p(X, W) \# p(Y, V) \# p(Y, W)). \tag{5}$$

$\#$ is a binary, associative and commutative function symbol, whose intended meaning is disjunction. Because we are interested in determining the possibility of getting green and yellow peas, $\#$ must be *non*-idempotent and. thus, differs from the operator $|$ introduced in the previous section. The following example may illustrate this point.

In order to determine the outcome of crossing two green peas we ask the following query.

$$?- cp(green, green, Z). \tag{6}$$

---

[11] One should observe, that the law of distributivity of $|$ over $\circ$ does not meet our intuition. The term $X \mid (Y \circ Z)$ specifies that we have either X or $Y \circ Z$ but not both, whereas the term $(X \mid Y) \circ (X \mid Z)$ specifies that we have $X \mid Y$ and $X \mid Z$. In the latter case, we might have two resources of type X, whereas in the former case this is impossible.

(6) and (5) are unifiable modulo the equational theory (4) yielding the computed answer substitution

$$\{Z \mapsto green \,\#\, green \,\#\, green \,\#\, p(G_1, \ G_2)\}.$$

In other words, as we do not know whether the green peas were pure, we can only assume that one gene of the green peas has hereditary factor green and the other is undetermined which is indicated by the variables G_1 and G_2. It is straightforward to write a logic program to determine the probability of receiving green and yellow peas in a crossing experiment. One simply has to count the number of occurrences of *green* and *yellow* in the binding for Z. In the example these numbers will be either 4 and 0 or 3 and 1, respectively, depending on the choices made for G_1 and G_2. If $\#$ were also idempotent – viz. an ACI-operator – then

$$green \,\#\, green \,\#\, green \,\#\, p(G_1, \ G_2) =_{ACI} green \,\#\, p(G_1, \ G_2)$$

and we would never be able to compute the correct probabilities for obtaining green and yellow peas. We may speculate that Mendel must have used a non-idempotent (or multiplicative in the sense of [11]) disjunction, when he discovered his laws of genetics.

The two examples in this section illustrate that the equational logic programming approach to action and change can naturally be extended to cope with disjunction. This includes the semantics as given in [15].

7   Discussion

In this paper we have shown that three recent approaches to logic and change – viz. the linear connection method, linear logic, and equational logic programming – are equivalent if pre- and postconditions of actions are multiplicative conjunctions of fluents. This result does not only provide a standard semantics for (a fragment of) the linear connection method and linear logic, but also brings together three approaches, which were previously considered to be different. Moreover, this result allows to carry over insigths and results obtained in one approach to the other ones. However, there are still a variety of competing approaches to logic and change and their relation to the three approaches remains to be clarified. The situation calculus as used for example in [23] or labelled deductive systems [9] are just two of these approaches.

We have also shown that reasoning about action and change amounts in defining relations over the datastructure multiset and we have given complete and minimal unification algorithms for the equational theory which defines multisets. These algorithms are used in a PROLOG-implementation of the equational logic programming approach.

We believe that the equational logic programming approach to action and change has certain advantages over the linear connection method and linear logic. Equational logic admits a straightforward and well-understood standard semantics. The equational theory AC1 – used herein – can easily be added to a PROLOG system, which gives us a powerful and flexible implementation. As already demonstrated in the database example of Section 3 we can now combine reasoning over multisets with all other programming techniques in PROLOG, whereas for example in the linear logic approach Gentzen-style proofs have to be constructed.

Finally, we have outlined how the equational logic programming approach in [15] can be extended to handle two forms of disjunction – viz. idempotent and non-idempotent disjunction. Although not mentioned so far, besides the non-idempotent conjunction $\circ$, we may also have an idempotent conjunction & on the object level. On the proof theoretic level incorporating these operators in the framework of [15] amounts in building in the equational theories for these operators into the unification computation. As unification algorithms for $|$, #, and & are essentially variations of the AC1-unification algorithm for $\circ$ given in Section 5, the hard problem is to combine these algorithms (cf. [24]). On the model theoretic level, we have to understand the denotation of the operators $|$, #, and &. As disjunctions represent alternatives and $|$ as well as # shall denote disjunctions, one way to solve this problem might be by extending the interpretation $\mathcal{I}$ given in Section 4 to multisets of multisets. In this extension, a term $q \circ q$ might be interpreted as $\{\{q, q\}\}$, whereas the terms $b \mid b \mid w$ and $green \# green \# yellow$ used in Section 6 might be interpreted as $\{\{b\}, \{w\}\}$ and $\{\{green\}, \{green\}, \{yellow\}\}$, respectively. An interpretation like $\{\{b\}, \{w\}\}$ would tell us that the term $b \mid w$ denotes either a situation where we have a black sock or a situation where we have a white sock, whereas $\{\{green\}, \{green\}, \{yellow\}\}$ would tell us that the term $green \# green \# yellow$ denotes a situation where we have a green or a yellow pea, but also that it is more likely for the pea to be green. As on the proof theoretic level, the hard problem is to combine the various interpretations for the four operators. This problem is tackled in [29].

Acknowledgements. We like to thank Wolfgang Bibel for setting up such a stimulating environment which made this work possible. The reseach presented was funded by the ESPRIT BRA project 3125 MEDLAR by the (German) Ministry for Research and Technology within the project TASSO under grant no. ITW 8900 C2.

References

[1] J. Allen, J. Hendler, and A. Tate. *Readings in Planning*. Morgan Kaufmann, San Mateo, 1990.

[2] J-M. Andreoli and R. Pareschi. Linear objects: Logical processes with built-in inheritance. *New Generation Computing*, 9(3+4), 1991.

[3] W. Bibel. A deductive solution for plan generation. *New Generation Computing*, 4:115–132, 1986.

[4] W. Bibel. A deductive solution for plan generation. In J. Schmidt, C. Thanos, *Foundations of Knowledge Base Management*, pp.453–473. Springer, 1989. XII.

[5] W. Bibel, L. F. del Cerro, B. Fronhöfer, and A. Herzig. Plan generation by linear proofs: on semantics. In *Proc. of GWAI*. Springer, 1989.

[6] R. S. Boyer, editor. *Automated Reasoning. Essays in Honor of Woody Bledsoe*. Automated Reasoning Series. Kluwer Academic Publishers, Dordrecht, 1991.

[7] H.-J.Bürckert, A.Herold, D.Kapur, J.H.Siekmann, M.E.Stickel, M.Tepp, H.Zhang. Opening the AC-Unification race. *J. of Automated Reasonsing*, 4:465–474, 1988.

[8] R. E. Fikes and N. J. Nilsson. STRIPS: A new approach to the application of theorem proving to problem solving. *Artificial Intelligence*, 5(2):189–208, 1971. also published in: [1].

[9] D. M. Gabbay. LDS — labeled deductive systems. Draft, July 1990.

[10] M. Gelfond, V. Lifschitz, and A. Rabinov. What are the limitations of the situation calculus? In [6], Chapter 8, pp.167–179. Kluwer Academic Publ., 1991.

[11] J. Y. Girard. Linear logic. *Theoretical Computer Science*, 50(1):1–102, 1987.

[12] C. Green. Application of theorem proving to problem solving. In *Proc. of the IJCAI*, pp.219–239. Morgan Kaufmann, 1969.

[13] G. Grosse, S. Hölldobler, and J. Schneeberger. On linear deductive planning. Internal Report, TH Darmstadt, Informatik, 1992.

[14] S. Hölldobler. *Foundations of Equational Logic Programming*, volume 353 of *Lecture Notes in Artificial Intelligence*. Springer, 1989.

[15] S. Hölldobler and J. Schneeberger. A new deductive approach to planning. *New Generation Computing*, 8:225–244, 1990. A short version appeared in the Proceedings of GWAI'89, Springer, Informatik Fachberichte *216*, pages 63-73, 1989

[16] J. Jaffar, J-L. Lassez, and M. J. Maher. A theory of complete logic programs with equality. In *Proc. of the International Conference on Fifth Generation Computer Systems*, pp.175–184. ICOT, 1984.

[17] R. Kowalski. *Logic for Problem Solving*. North Holland, New York/Oxford, 1979.

[18] Robert Kowalski and Marek Sergot. A logic-based calculus of events. *New Generation Computing*, 4:67–95, 1986.

[19] V. Lifschitz. Toward a metatheory of action. In *Proc. of KR*, pp.376–386. Morgan Kaufmann, 1991.

[20] M. Masseron, C. Tollu, and J. Vauzielles. Generating plans in linear logic. Technical Report 90-11, Université Paris Nord C.S.P., France, 1990.

[21] J. McCarthy. Epistemological problems of artificial intelligence. In *Proc. of IJCAI*, pp.1038–1044. Morgan Kaufmann, 1977.

[22] J. McCarthy and P. J. Hayes. Some philosophical problems from the standpoint of Artificial Intelligence. In B. Meltzer and D. Michie, (eds.), *Machine Intelligence 4*, pp.463–502. Edinburgh University Press, 1969.

[23] R. Reiter. On formalizing database updates: Preliminary report. In *Proc. of the 3rd International Conference on Extending Database Technology*, 1992.

[24] M. Schmidt-Schauß. Unification in a combination of arbitary disjoint equational theories. In *Proc. of CADE*, pp.378–396. Springer, 1988.

[25] J. Schneeberger. *Plan Generation by Linear Deduction*. PhD thesis, TH Darmstadt, Informatik, 1992.

[26] E. Shapiro and A. Takeuchi. Object oriented programming in Concurrent Prolog. *New Generation Computing*, 1:25–48, 1983.

[27] Y. Shoham. *Reasoning About Change*. MIT Press, 1988.

[28] J. H. Siekmann. Unification theory. *J. of Symbolic Computation*, 7:207–274, 1989.

[29] Ute Sigmund. LLP - Lineare Logische Programmierung. Diplomarbeit, TH Darmstadt, Informatik, 1992. (in preparation).

[30] M. Thielscher. AC1-Unifikation in der linearen logischen Programmierung. Diplomarbeit, TH Darmstadt, Informatik, 1992. (in preparation).

On the Completeness of Residuation

Michael Hanus

Max-Planck-Institut für Informatik
Im Stadtwald, W-6600 Saarbrücken, Germany
michael@mpi-sb.mpg.de

Abstract

Residuation is an operational mechanism for the integration of functions into logic programming languages. The residuation principle delays the evaluation of functions during the unification process until the arguments are sufficiently instantiated. This has the advantage that the deterministic nature of functions is preserved but the disadvantage of incompleteness: if the variables in a delayed function call are not instantiated by the logic program, this function can never be evaluated and some answers which are logical consequences of the program are lost. In this paper we present a method for detecting such situations. The method is based on a compile-time analysis of the program and approximates the possible residuations and instantiation states of variables during program execution.

1 Introduction

Many proposals for the integration of functional and logic programming languages have been made during recent years (see [8] for a collection). From an operational point of view these proposals can be partitioned into two classes: approaches with a complete operational semantics and a nondeterministic search (*narrowing*) for solving equations with functional expressions (EQLOG [10], SLOG [9], K-LEAF [5], BABEL [16], ALF [11], among others), and approaches which try to avoid nondeterministic computations for functional expressions by reducing functional expressions only if the arguments are sufficiently instantiated (Funlog [20], Le Fun [3], LIFE [2], NUE-Prolog [17], among others). The former approaches are complete under some well-defined conditions (e.g., canonicity of the axioms), i.e., they compute all answers which can be logically inferred from the given program. The price for this completeness is an increased search space since there may be several incomparable unifiers of two terms if these terms contain unevaluated functional expressions. The latter approaches try to avoid this nondeterminism in the unification process. In these approaches a term is reduced to normal form before it is unified with another term, i.e., functional expressions are evaluated (if possible) before unification. If a function cannot be evaluated because the arguments are not sufficiently instantiated, the unification cannot proceed. Instead of causing a failure, the evaluation of the function is delayed until the arguments will be instantiated. This mechanism is called *residuation* in Le Fun [3]. For instance, consider the following program (we write residuating logic programs in the usual Prolog syntax but it is allowed to use arbitrary evaluable functions in terms):

```
q :- p(X,Y,5), pick(X,Y).
p(A,B,A+B).
pick(2,3).
```

together with the goal "?- q". After applying the first clause to the goal, the literals p(X,Y,5) and p(A,B,A+B) are unified. This binds A to X and B to Y, but the unification of X+Y and 5 is not successful since the arguments of the function call X+Y are not instantiated to numbers. Hence this unification causes the generation of the *residuation* X+Y=5 which will be proved (or disproved) if X and Y will be bound to ground terms. We proceed by proving the literal pick(X,Y) which binds X and Y to 2 and 3, respectively. As a consequence, the instantiated residuation 2+3=5 can be verified and therefore the entire goal has been proved.

The residuation principle seems to be preferable to the narrowing approaches since it preserves the deterministic nature of functions. However, it fails to compute all answers if functions are used in a logic programming manner. For instance, consider the function append for concatenating two lists. In a functional language with pattern-matching it can be defined by the following equations (we use the Prolog notation for lists):

```
append([],  L) = L
append([E|R],L) = [E|append(R,L)]
```

From a logic programming point of view we can compute the last element E of a given list L by solving the equation append(_,[E])=L. Since the first argument of the left-hand side of this equation will never be instantiated, residuation fails to compute the last element with this equation whereas narrowing computes the unique value for E [12]. Similarly, we can specify by the equation append(LE,[_])=L a list LE which is the result of deleting the last element in the list L. Combining the specification of the last element and the rest of a list, we define the reversing of a list by the following clauses:

```
rev([],[]).
rev(L, [E|LR]) :- append(LE,[E]) = L, rev(LE,LR).
```

Now consider the goal "?- rev([a,b,c],R)". Since the arguments of the calls to the function append are never instantiated to ground terms, the residuation principle cannot verify the corresponding residuation. Hence the answer R=[c,b,a] is not computed and there is an infinite derivation path using the residuation principle and applying the second clause infinitely many times. On the other hand a functional-logic language based on the narrowing principle can solve this goal and has a finite search space [12]. Therefore we should use narrowing instead of residuation in this example.

The last example raises the important question whether it is possible to detect the cases where the (more efficient) residuation principle is able to compute all answers. If this would be possible we can avoid the nondeterministic and hence expensive narrowing principle in many cases and replace it by computations based on the residuation principle without loosing any answers. A simple criterion to the completeness of residuation is the *groundness of all residuating variables*: if at the end of a computation all variables occurring in residual function calls are bound to ground terms, then all residuations can be evaluated and hence the answer substitution does not depend on an unsolved residuation. Since the satisfaction of this criterion depends on the data flow during program execution, an exact answer is recursively undecidable. Therefore we present an approximation to this answer by applying abstract interpretation techniques to this kind of programs. Previous approaches for abstract interpretation of logic programs (see, for instance, [1, 7, 18]) depend on SLD-resolution as the operational semantics. Hence we cannot directly apply these frameworks to our case. However it is possible to develop a similar technique by considering unsolved residuations as part of the current substitution.

In the next section we give a short description of the operational semantics considered in this paper. The abstract domain and the abstract interpretation algorithm for reasoning about residuating programs are presented in Section 3. Finally, the correctness of our method is outlined in Section 4.

2   The residuation principle

In residuating logic programs terms are built from variables, constructors and (defined) functions. *Constructors* (denoted by a, b, c, d) are used to compose data structures, while defined *functions* (denoted by f, g, h) are operations on these data structures. We do not require any formalism for the specification of functions, i.e., they may be defined by equations or in a completely different language (external or predefined functions). However, the following conditions must be satisfied in order to reason about residuating logic programs:

1. A function call can be evaluated if all arguments are ground terms.
2. The result of the evaluation is a ground constructor term (containing only constructors) or an error message (i.e., the computation cannot proceed because of type errors, division by zero etc.).

The difference between residuating logic programs and ordinary logic programs shows up in the unification procedure: if a call to a defined function $f(t_1, \ldots, t_n)$ should be unified with a term t, the function call is evaluated if all arguments $t_1, \ldots, t_n$ are bound to ground terms and the unification proceeds with the evaluated term, otherwise the unification immediately succeeds and the *residuation* $f(t_1, \ldots, t_n) = t$ is added. If all variables in $t_1, \ldots, t_n$ will be bound to ground terms in the further computation process, the residuation $f(t_1, \ldots, t_n) = t$ will be immediately verified by evaluating the left-hand side and comparing the result with the right-hand side. Precise descriptions of this algorithm can be found in [3, 13] ([4] contains a more sophisticated version) and therefore we omit the details here. The result of the residuating unification algorithm is `fail` or a substitution/residuation pair $\langle \sigma, \rho \rangle$ with

$$\sigma = \{x_1 \mapsto t_1, \ldots, x_k \mapsto t_k\} \qquad \text{and} \qquad \rho = \{s_1 = s_1', \ldots, s_m = s_m'\}$$

where each variable x_i does not occur in t_j or ρ and s_i or s_i' are unevaluable (non-ground) function calls. In the entire computation σ is part of the answer substitution and ρ will be added to the unification problem in the next resolution step. The operational semantics of *residuating logic programs* considered in this paper is similar to Prolog's operational semantics (SLD-resolution with leftmost selection rule) but with the difference that the standard unification is replaced by a residuating unification algorithm. Thus the *concrete domain of computation* $\mathcal{C}$ is not simply the set of all substitutions but a set of substitution/residuation pairs, i.e.,

$$\mathcal{C} = \{\langle \sigma, \rho \rangle \mid \sigma \text{ is a substition}, \rho \text{ is a set of residuations}\}$$

where a residuation is an equation $r = r'$ and r (or r') is a function call. Since ground function calls are evaluated during unification, we assume in the following that all elements $\langle \sigma, \rho \rangle$ of the concrete domain $\mathcal{C}$ do not contain function calls with ground terms in the residuation part ρ.

As an example consider the following residuating logic program:

```
q :- p(X,Y,5), 1 = W-V, X = V*W, Y = V+W, pick(V,W).
p(A,B,A+B).
pick(1,2).
```

If the initial goal is q, the following elements of the concrete domain are computed during the processing of the first clause:

Before "p(X,Y,5)": $\langle \emptyset, \emptyset \rangle$
After "p(X,Y,5)": $\langle \emptyset, \{5=X+Y\} \rangle$
After "1 = W-V": $\langle \emptyset, \{5=X+Y, 1=W-V\} \rangle$
After "X = V*W": $\langle \{X \mapsto V*W\}, \{5=(V*W)+Y, 1=W-V\} \rangle$
After "Y = V+W": $\langle \{X \mapsto V*W, Y \mapsto V+W\}, \{5=(V*W)+(V+W), 1=W-V\} \rangle$
After "pick(V,W)": $\langle \{X \mapsto 1*2, Y \mapsto 1+2, V \mapsto 1, W \mapsto 2\}, \emptyset \rangle$

At the clause end the residuation set is empty since all functions could be evaluated. Hence the initial goal is proved to be true.

From a semantic point of view residuations can be considered as *constraints* on substitutions and therefore the residuation framework could be viewed as a special case of the CLP framework [14]. However, this is not the case from an operational point of view. Since functions are user-defined, there need not exist a constraint solver which checks the satisfiablity of the accumulated residuations. E.g., the unsatisfiability of {append(L1,L2)=[1], append(L2,L1)=[2]} is not detected by the unification algorithms in [3, 4]. This would require a constraint solver for the defined list operations. In fact, it is reasonable to integrate the residuation principle into the CLP paradigm [19].

3 Abstract interpretation of residuating programs

In this section we present a method for checking whether the residuation part of the answer to a goal is empty, i.e., whether the residuation principle is complete w.r.t. a given program and goal. Since this problem is recursively undecidable in general, we present an approximation to it based on a compile-time analysis of the program. If this approximation yields a positive answer, then it is ensured that all residuations can be solved at run time. In the following we present the abstract domain and the motivation for it. The relation to the concrete domain and the correctness of the abstract interpretation algorithm are discussed in Section 4 in more detail. We assume familiarity with basic ideas of abstract interpretation techniques [1].

3.1 Abstract domain

There has been done a lot of work concerning the compile-time derivation of run-time properties of logic programs (see, for instance, the collection [1]). Since we have abstracted the different operational behaviour of residuating logic programs into an additional component of the concrete domain, we can use the well-known frameworks (e.g., [7, 18]) in a similar way. The heart of an abstract interpretation procedure is an abstract domain which approximates subsets of the concrete domain by finite representations. An element of the abstract domain describes common properties of a subset of the concrete domain. The properties must be chosen so that they contain relevant propositions about the interesting run-time properties. So what are the abstract properties in our case?

We are interested in unevaluated residuations at run time (second component of the concrete domain). A residuation can be verified if the function call in it can be evaluated. Since a function call can be evaluated if all arguments are ground, we need some information about the variables in it and the instantiation state of these variables in order to decide the emptiness of the residuation set. Hence our abstract domain contains information about the following properties:

Potential residuations: Residuations are generated by the unification of terms. For instance, if variable X is bound to A+B and variable Y is bound to 2 at run time, the unification of X and Y generates the residuation A+B=2. Hence, in order to state properties of all residuations which may occur at run time, we must know all potential function calls in the bindings of a program variable. Moreover, we must also know the variables in this function call in order to decide whether or not this function call can be evaluated. Therefore our abstract domain contains elements of the form "X with $+|_{\{A,B\}}$" meaning: variable X may be bound to a term containing a call to function + which can be evaluated if A and B are ground.

Dependencies between variables: Function calls can be evaluated if all variables in it are bound to ground terms. Hence we must have some information about the dependencies between variables. E.g., consider the goal

    ?- A+B = C,   C*2 = 6,   A = 1,   B = 2.

During unification of C*2 and 6 the first term cannot be evaluated since C is not ground. But the groundness of C depends on the groundness of A and B.

Thus we can deduce that the function call `C*2` can be evaluated if `A` and `B` are bound to ground terms. Hence our abstract domain contains the element "`C if {A,B}`". In general, "`X if V`" means that variable `X` is bound to a ground term if all variables in V are bound to ground terms.

Sharing between variables: The potential residuations can be copied between different variables in the unification process. E.g., consider the goal

```
?- Z = c(X),   Y = f(A),   X = Y, ...
```

After the unification of `X` and `Y` the variable `Z` contains the function call `f(A)`. In order to manage correctly the potential residuations, we must store the information that `Z` and `X` share a term. Hence our abstract domain contains the element `{X,Z}` representing the sharing between `X` and `Z`.

Summarizing the previous discussion, our *abstract domain* $\mathcal{A}$ contains the element $\perp$ (representing the empty subset of the concrete domain) and sets containing the following elements (such sets are called *abstractions* and denoted by A, A_1 etc):

Element:	Meaning:
X if V	X is ground if all variables in the variable set V are ground
X with $f\|_V$	X may be bound to a term containing a call to f which can be evaluated if all variables in V are ground
f	there may be an unevaluated function call to f depending on arbitrary variables
{X,Y}	X and Y may share a term

Obviously, $\mathcal{A}$ is finite if the set of variables and function symbols is finite. Since we use only program variables and functions occurring in the program in the abstract domain, $\mathcal{A}$ is finite in case of a finite program. For convenience we simply write "X" instead of "X if $\emptyset$". Hence an element "X" in an abstraction means that variable `X` is bound to a ground term if it does not contain any function call.

Given an abstraction A, a variable X is called *function-free* in A if A does not contain elements of the form "X with $f\|_V$" and "f". In the subset of the concrete domain corresponding to A a function-free variable can only be interpreted as a term without unevaluable function calls (compare Section 4).

To present a simple description of the abstract interpretation algorithm, we will sometimes generate abstractions containing redundant information. The following *normalization rules* eliminate some redundancies in abstractions:

Normalization rules for abstractions:		
$A \cup \{Z, X \text{ if } V \cup \{Z\}\}$	$\rightarrow A \cup \{Z, X \text{ if } V\}$	if Z is function-free in A
$A \cup \{Z, X \text{ with } f\|_{V \cup \{Z\}}\}$	$\rightarrow A \cup \{Z, X \text{ with } f\|_V\}$	if Z is function-free in A
$A \cup \{X \text{ with } f\|_\emptyset\}$	$\rightarrow A$	
$A \cup \{X \text{ if } V_1, X \text{ if } V_2\}$	$\rightarrow A \cup \{X \text{ if } V_1\}$	if $V_1 \subseteq V_2$
$A \cup \{X, \{X,Y\}\}$	$\rightarrow A \cup \{X\}$	

The additional condition in the first two rules ensures that Z is bound to a ground term containing no unevaluable function calls. We call an abstraction A *normalized* if none of these normalization rules is applicable to A. Later we will see that the normalization rules are invariant w.r.t. the concrete substitutions/residuations corresponding to abstractions. Therefore we can assume that we *compute only with normalized abstractions* in the abstract interpretation algorithm.

In order to keep the abstract interpretation algorithm simple, we assume that predicate calls and clause heads have the form $p(X_1, \ldots, X_n)$ where all X_i are distinct (similarly to the example in [7]). All other literals in the clause bodies and goals have the form $X = Y$, $X = c(Y_1, \ldots, Y_n)$ or $X = f(Y_1, \ldots, Y_n)$. It is easy to see that every residuating logic program can be transformed into a *flat residuating logic program* satisfying the above restrictions without changing the answer behaviour. For instance, the residuating logic program in Section 2 can be transformed into the following equivalent flat program:

```
q :- Z=5,  p(X,Y,Z), T=1, T=W-V, X=V*W, Y=V+W, pick(V,W).
p(A,B,C) :- C=A+B.
pick(A,B) :- A=1, B=2.
```

In the following we assume that all programs are in the required form.

3.2   The abstract interpretation algorithm

The abstract interpretation algorithm is based on several operations on the abstract domain. The first operation restricts an abstraction A to a set of variables W. It will be used in a predicate call to omit the information about variables not passed from the predicate call to the applied clause:

$$call\_restrict(\bot, W) = \bot$$
$$call\_restrict(A, W) = \{X \in A \mid X \in W\}$$
$$\cup \{X \text{ with } f|_V \in A \mid \{X\} \cup V \subseteq W\}$$
$$\cup \{f \mid f \in A \text{ or } X \text{ with } f|_V \in A \text{ with } X \in W, V \not\subseteq W\}$$
$$\cup \{\{X, Y\} \in A \mid X, Y \in W\}$$

The restriction operation for predicate calls transforms an abstraction element $X \text{ with } f|_V$ into the element f if the dependent variables are not contained in W, i.e., it is noted that there may be an unevaluated function call to f but the possible dependencies are too complex for the abstract analysis. Similarly, an abstraction element of the form $X \text{ if } V$ is passed to the clause only if $V = \emptyset$.

A similar operation is needed at the clause end to forget the abstract information about local clause variables. Hence we define:

$$exit\_restrict(\bot, W) = \bot$$
$$exit\_restrict(A, W) = \{X \text{ if } V \in A \mid \{X\} \cup V \subseteq W\}$$
$$\cup \{X \text{ with } f|_V \in A \mid \{X\} \cup V \subseteq W\}$$
$$\cup \{f \mid f \in A \text{ or } X \text{ with } f|_V \in A \text{ with } \{X\} \cup V \not\subseteq W\}$$
$$\cup \{\{X, Y\} \in A \mid X, Y \in W\}$$

The restriction operation for clause exits transforms an abstraction element $X \text{ with } f|_V$ into the element f if one of the involved variables is not contained in W, i.e., it is noted that there may be an unevaluated function call to f which depends on local variables at the end of the clause.

The following operation computes the remaining abstract information of a predicate call restriction $call\_restrict(A, W)$ in order to combine it after a predicate call:

$$
\begin{aligned}
rest(\bot, W) &= \bot \\
rest(A, W) &= \{X \text{ if } V \in A \mid X \notin W \text{ or } V \neq \emptyset\} \\
&\quad \cup \{X \text{ with } f|_V \in A \mid X \notin W\} \\
&\quad \cup \{\{X, Y\} \in A \mid X \notin W \text{ or } Y \notin W\}
\end{aligned}
$$

The *least upper bound* operation is used to combine the results of different clauses for a predicate call:

$$
\begin{aligned}
\bot \sqcup A &= A \\
A \sqcup \bot &= A \\
A_1 \sqcup A_2 &= \{X \text{ if } V_1 \cup V_2 \mid X \text{ if } V_1 \in A_1, \ X \text{ if } V_2 \in A_2\} \\
&\quad \cup \{X \text{ with } f|_V \mid X \text{ with } f|_V \in A_1 \text{ or } X \text{ with } f|_V \in A_2\} \\
&\quad \cup \{f \mid f \in A_1 \text{ or } f \in A_2\} \\
&\quad \cup \{\{X, Y\} \mid \{X, Y\} \in A_1 \text{ or } \{X, Y\} \in A_2\}
\end{aligned}
$$

Now we are able to define the abstract unification algorithm for the abstract interpretation of equations occurring in clause bodies or goals. Abstract unification is a function $au(\alpha, t_1, t_2)$ which takes an element of the abstract domain $\alpha \in \mathcal{A}$ and two terms t_1, t_2 as input and produces another abstract domain element as the result. Because of our restrictions on goal equations, the following definition is sufficient:[1]

$$au(\bot, t_1, t_2) = \bot$$

$$au(A, X, X) = A$$

$$au(A, X, Y) = closure(A \cup \{X \text{ if } \{Y\}, \ Y \text{ if } \{X\}, \ \{X, Y\}\}) \quad \text{if } X \neq Y$$

$$
\begin{aligned}
au(A, X, c(Y_1, \ldots, Y_n)) = closure(A \cup \{X \text{ if } \{Y_1, \ldots, Y_n\}, \ Y_1 \text{ if } \{X\}, \ldots, \\
Y_n \text{ if } \{X\}, \ \{X, Y_1\}, \ldots, \ \{X, Y_n\}\})
\end{aligned}
$$

$$au(A, X, f(Y_1, \ldots, Y_n)) = closure(A \cup \{X \text{ if } \{Y_1, \ldots, Y_n\}, X \text{ with } f|_{\{Y_1, \ldots, Y_n\}}\})$$

In this definition and in the rest of this paper $closure(A)$ denotes the least set A' containing A which is closed under the following rules for transitivity and distribution of sharing information:

$$
\begin{aligned}
\{X, Y\} \in A', \ \{Y, Z\} \in A' &\implies \{X, Z\} \in A' \\
\{X, Y\} \in A', \ X \text{ with } f|_V \in A' &\implies Y \text{ with } f|_V \in A'
\end{aligned}
$$

Now we can present the algorithm for the abstract interpretation of a residuating logic program in flat form. It is specified as a function $ai(\alpha, L)$ which takes an abstract domain element α and a goal literal L and yields a new abstract domain element as result. Clearly, $ai(\bot, L) = \bot$ and $ai(A, t = t') = au(A, t, t')$. The interesting case is the abstract interpretation of a predicate call $ai(A, p(X_1, \ldots, X_n))$ which is computed by the following steps:

---

[1] For simplicity we omit the occur check in the abstract unification.

1. Let $p(Z_1, \ldots, Z_n) :- L_1, \ldots, L_k$ be a clause for predicate p (if necessary, rename the clause variables such that they are disjoint from $X_1, \ldots, X_n$).
   Compute $A_{call} = call\_restrict(A, \{X_1, \ldots, X_n\})$
   $$A_0 = \langle \text{replace all } X_i \text{ by } Z_i \text{ in } A_{call} \rangle$$
   $$A_1 = ai(A_0, L_1); \ A_2 = ai(A_1, L_2); \ \ldots; \ A_k = ai(A_{k-1}, L_k)$$
   $$A_{out} = exit\_restrict(A_k, \{Z_1, \ldots, Z_n\})$$
   $$A_{exit} = \langle \text{replace all } Z_i \text{ by } X_i \text{ in } A_{out} \rangle$$

2. Let $A_{exit}^1, \ldots, A_{exit}^m$ be the exit substitutions of all clauses for p as computed in step 1. Then define $A_{success} = A_{exit}^1 \sqcup \ldots \sqcup A_{exit}^m$

3. $ai(A, p(X_1, \ldots, X_n)) = closure(A_{success} \cup rest(A, \{X_1, \ldots, X_n\}))$
   $$\text{if } A_{success} \neq \bot, \text{ else } \bot$$

Hence a clause is interpreted in the following way. Firstly, the *call abstraction* is computed, i.e., the information contained in the predicate call abstraction is restricted to the argument variables (A_{call}). The variables in this call abstraction are mapped to the corresponding variables in the applied clause (A_0). Then each literal in the clause body is interpreted. The resulting abstraction (A_k) is restricted to the variables in the clause head, i.e., we forget the information about the local variables in the clause. Potential residuations which are unsolved at the clause end are passed to the abstraction A_{out} by the *exit_restrict* operation. In the last step the clause variables are renamed into the variables of the predicate call (A_{exit}). If all clauses defining the called predicate p are interpreted in this way, all possible interpretations are combined by the least upper bound of all abstractions ($A_{success}$). The combination of this abstraction with the information which was forgotten by the restriction at the beginning of the predicate call yields the abstraction after the predicate call (step 3).

The abstract interpretation algorithm described above is useless in case of recursive programs due to the nontermination of the algorithm. This classical problem is solved in all frameworks for abstract interpretation and therefore we do not want to develop a new solution to this problem but use one of the well-known solutions. Following Bruynooghe's framework [7] we can construct a rational abstract AND-OR-tree representing the computation of the abstract interpretation algorithm. During the construction of the tree we check before the interpretation of a predicate call P whether there is an ancestor node P' with a call to the same predicate and the same call abstraction (up to renaming of variables). If this is the case we take the success abstraction of P' (or $\bot$ if it is not available) as the success abstraction of P instead of interpreting P. If the further abstract interpretation computes a success abstraction A' for P' which differs from the success abstraction used for P, we start a recomputation beginning at P with A' as new success abstraction. This iteration terminates because all operations used in the abstract interpretation are monotone (w.r.t. the order on $\mathcal{A}$ defined in Section 4) and the abstract domain is finite.

3.3 An example

The following example is the flat form of a Le Fun program presented in [3]:

```
q(Z) :- p(X,Y,Z), X=V-W, Y=V+W, pick(V,W).
p(A,B,C) :- C=A*B.
pick(A,B) :- A=9, B=3.
```

The abstract interpretation algorithm computes the following abstractions w.r.t. the initial goal $q(T)$ and the initial abstraction $\emptyset$ (specifying the set of all substitutions without unevaluated function calls):

$ai(\emptyset, q(T))$:

$ai(\emptyset, p(X,Y,Z))$: $ai(\emptyset, C=A*B) = \{C \text{ if } \{A,B\}, \ C \text{ with } *|_{\{A,B\}}\}$

$ai(\emptyset, p(X,Y,Z)) = \{Z \text{ if } \{X,Y\}, \ Z \text{ with } *|_{\{X,Y\}}\} =: A_1$

$ai(A_1, X=V-W) = \{Z \text{ if } \{X,Y\}, X \text{ if } \{V,W\}, Z \text{ with } *|_{\{X,Y\}}, X \text{ with } -|_{\{V,W\}}\} =: A_2$

$ai(A_2, Y=V+W) = \{Z \text{ if } \{X,Y\}, \ X \text{ if } \{V,W\}, \ Y \text{ if } \{V,W\},$
$\qquad\qquad Z \text{ with } *|_{\{X,Y\}}, \ X \text{ with } -|_{\{V,W\}}, \ Y \text{ with } +|_{\{V,W\}}\} =: A_3$

$ai(A_3, pick(V,W))$: $ai(\emptyset, A=9) = \{A\}$
$\qquad\qquad\qquad ai(\{A\}, B=3) = \{A, B\}$

$ai(A_3, pick(V,W)) = \{V, W, Z \text{ if } \{X,Y\}, \ X \text{ if } \{V,W\}, \ Y \text{ if } \{V,W\},$
$\qquad\qquad Z \text{ with } *|_{\{X,Y\}}, \ X \text{ with } -|_{\{V,W\}}, \ Y \text{ with } +|_{\{V,W\}}\}$
$\qquad\qquad \overset{normalize}{\longrightarrow} \{V, W, Z, X, Y\}$

$ai(\emptyset, q(T)) = \{T\}$

Hence the computed success abstraction is $\{T\}$ meaning that after a successful computation of the goal $q(T)$ the variable T is bound to a ground term and the residuation set is empty, i.e., the residuation principle allows to compute a fully evaluated answer. Similarly, the completeness of the residuation principle can be proved by our algorithm for all other residuating logic programs presented in [3]. A more complex example involving recursion can be found in [13].

4 Correctness of the abstract interpretation algorithm

In this section we will discuss the correctness of the presented abstract interpretation algorithm by relating the abstract domain to the concrete domain. Due to lack of space we omit the proofs of the theorems. The interested reader will find the proofs in [13].

To relate the computed abstract properties of the program to the concrete run-time behaviour, we have to define a *concretisation function* $\gamma: \mathcal{A} \to 2^{\mathcal{C}}$ which maps an abstraction into a subset of the concrete domain. The most difficult point in the definition of γ is the correct interpretation of an abstraction "$X \text{ if } V$". The intuitive meaning is "the interpretation of X is ground if all interpretations of V are ground". To be more precise, "$X \text{ if } V$" describes a dependency between the instantiation of X and the instantiation of the variables in V, i.e., we could define:

(*) If X if $V \in A$ and $\langle \sigma, \rho \rangle \in \gamma(A)$, then $var(\sigma(\text{X})) \subseteq var(\sigma(V))$

($var(\xi)$ denotes the set of all variables occurring in the syntactic construction ξ). Such a definition seems to justify the generation of the abstractions "X if $\{$Y$\}$" and "Y if $\{$X$\}$" in the abstract unification algorithm if X is unified with Y. But this interpretation is not true if X or Y are bound to terms containing unevaluated residuations. E.g., if X is bound to f(B) and Y is bound to c(A) during program execution, then the computation of the literal X=Y yields the substitution/residuation pair $\langle \emptyset, \{\text{f(B)=c(A)}\} \rangle$. Thus the variables contained in the bindings of X and Y are not identical after the unification step. Therefore we must weaken (*) to the condition that only the variables of $\sigma(\text{X})$ occurring outside function calls are contained in the variables of $\sigma(V)$ *w.r.t. to the residuation ρ.*

To give a precise description of the condition, we need the following definitions. By $lvar(t)$ we denote the set of all variables occurring outside function calls in the term t:

$$\begin{aligned}
lvar(X) &= \{X\} \\
lvar(c(t_1,\ldots,t_n)) &= lvar(t_1) \cup \cdots \cup lvar(t_n) \\
lvar(f(t_1,\ldots,t_n)) &= \emptyset
\end{aligned}$$

The *extension* of a set of variables V *w.r.t. to the residuation ρ* is defined by

$$var_\rho(V) = V \cup \{lvar(e) \mid f(\bar{t}) = e \in \rho \text{ or } e = f(\bar{t}) \in \rho \text{ with } var(\bar{t}) \subseteq V\}$$

(where $\bar{t}$ denotes the argument sequence $t_1,\ldots,t_n$). Note that $var_\rho(\emptyset) = \emptyset$ if ρ does not contain unevaluated ground residual function calls (which do not occur in our concrete domain) and for an empty residuation we have $var_\emptyset(V) = V$. The intuition of this definition is that we add to a set of variables V all these variables which will be ground during the computation process if all variables in V are ground. For instance, if $\rho = \{\text{f(X)=c(Y)}, \text{f(X)=c(Z)}\}$, then $var_\rho(\{\text{X}\}) = \{\text{X}, \text{Y}, \text{Z}\}$. We extend the function var_ρ to finite sets of terms by

$$var_\rho(\{t_1,\ldots,t_k\}) = var_\rho(var(\{t_1,\ldots,t_k\}))$$

Since we are interested in the property whether a function call occurring in a term can be completely evaluated, it is sufficient to look at the main function calls and not at function calls which occur inside other function calls (this is due to the fact that a unification between a function call and another term does not bind any variables in this call). Therefore we say a term t occurs *directly* in a term t' if t occurs in t' outside a function call. For instance, the term $X + (Y * 2)$ occurs directly in the term $c(X + (Y * 2))$ but the subterm $(Y * 2)$ is not a direct occurrence.

Now we are able to define the semantics of abstractions by the concretisation function $\gamma{:}\mathcal{A} \to 2^{\mathcal{C}}$ (where $\bar{t}$ denotes the argument sequence $t_1,\ldots,t_n$):

$$\gamma(\bot) = \emptyset$$

$\gamma(A) = \{\langle\sigma,\rho\rangle \in \mathcal{C} \mid 1.\ X \text{ if } V \in A \Rightarrow lvar(\sigma(X)) \subseteq var_\rho(\sigma(V))$

$\qquad\qquad 2.\ f(\overline{t})$ occurs directly in $\sigma(X)$ or ρ with $var(\overline{t}) \neq \emptyset$

$\qquad\qquad\qquad \Rightarrow f \in A$ or $var(\overline{t}) \subseteq var(\sigma(V))$ for some $X \text{ with } f|_V \in A$

$\qquad\qquad 3.\ lvar(\sigma(X)) \cap lvar(\sigma(Y)) \neq \emptyset$ for $X \neq Y \Rightarrow \{X,Y\} \in A \quad \}$

Condition 1 implies for $X \text{ if } V \in A$ that all variables occurring outside function calls in the current instantiation of X are ground if all variables in V are instantiated to ground terms. Condition 2 ensures that all unevaluated function calls in variable bindings and in residuations are contained in A. Since we are interested in potential residuations, it is sufficient to look at function calls which occur *directly* in some variable binding (and not at function calls nested in other function calls). Hence the sharing information is also restricted to *lvar* instead of *var* (condition 3). Note that for an unevaluated function call in the residuation part it is sufficient that there is an arbitrary variable X which cover this function call whereas for an unevaluated function call in the binding of a variable X there must be an abstraction element $X \text{ with } f|_V$ with the *same* variable. This is necessary for passing the correct information about potential residuations in case of a predicate call (compare call restriction operation).

From this interpretation it is clear that an abstraction without elements of the form "$X \text{ with } f|_V$" or "f" can only be interpreted as a fully evaluated pair $\langle\sigma,\rho\rangle$ if $\rho = \emptyset$ and σ does not contain unevaluable function calls. This argument has been used to state the completeness of the example in Section 3.3.

Due to this semantics of abstractions it can be proved that the normalization rules defined on abstractions in Section 3.1 are invariant w.r.t. the concrete interpretation. The following lemma justifies the application of the normalization rules.

Lemma 4.1 *If A and A' are abstractions with $A \to A'$, then $\gamma(A) = \gamma(A')$.*

For the termination of the abstract interpretation algorithm it is important that all operations on the abstract domain are monotone. Therefore we define the following order relation on normalized abstractions:

(a) $\quad \bot \sqsubseteq \alpha$ for all $\alpha \in \mathcal{A}$

(b) $\quad A \sqsubseteq A' \iff$ 1. $X \text{ if } V' \in A' \Rightarrow \exists V \subseteq V'$ with $X \text{ if } V \in A$

$\qquad\qquad\qquad\qquad$ 2. $X \text{ with } f|_V \in A \Rightarrow X \text{ with } f|_V \in A'$

$\qquad\qquad\qquad\qquad$ 3. $f \in A \Rightarrow f \in A'$

$\qquad\qquad\qquad\qquad$ 4. $\{X,Y\} \in A \Rightarrow \{X,Y\} \in A'$

It is easy to prove that $\sqsubseteq$ is a reflexive, transitive and anti-symmetric relation on normalized abstractions, the operation $\sqcup$ defined in Section 3.2 computes the least upper bound of two abstractions, and γ is monotone.

The correctness of the abstract interpretation algorithm is based on the correctness of each component of the algorithm. The entire proof can be constructed following the ideas in [7]. Due to the complex abstract domain the detailed proofs require some effort and cannot be shown in this paper. In the following we only state an important theorem which is the basis for the correctness of the abstract interpretation algorithm:

Theorem 4.2 (Correctness of abstract unification) *Let X be a variable, t be a term of the form $t = Y$, $t = c(Y_1, \ldots, Y_n)$ or $t = f(Y_1, \ldots, Y_n)$ and A be an abstraction. Then for all $\langle \sigma, \rho \rangle \in \gamma(A)$ and all unifiers $\langle \sigma', \rho' \rangle$ for $\sigma(X)$ and $\sigma(t)$, $\langle \sigma' \circ \sigma, \rho' \cup \sigma'(\rho) \rangle \in \gamma(au(A, X, t))$.*

5 Conclusions and related work

In this paper we have considered an operational mechanism for the integration of functions into logic programs. This mechanism, called residuation, extends the standard unification algorithm used in SLD-resolutions by delaying unifications between unevaluable function calls and other terms. If all variables of a delayed function call are bound to ground terms, then this function call is evaluated in order to verify the delayed unification. This residuation principle yields a nice operational behaviour for many functional logic programs but has two disadvantages. One problem is that the answer to a query may contain unsolved and complex residuations for which the user cannot easily decide their solvability. A further problem is that the search space of a residuating logic program can be infinite in contrast to the equivalent logic program. This case can occur if the residuation principle generates more and more residuations which are simultaneously not solvable. Hence it is important to check at compile time whether or not this case can occur at run time. Since this is undecidable in general, we have presented an approximation to this problem based on the abstract interpretation of residuating logic programs. Our algorithm manages information about all possible residuations together with their argument variables and the dependencies between different variables in order to compute groundness information. Hence the algorithm is able to infer which residuations can be completely solved at run time.

We can also interpret our algorithm as an attempt to compile functional logic programs from languages with a complete but often complex operational semantics (e.g., EQLOG [10], SLOG [9], BABEL [16], or ALF [11]) into a more efficient execution mechanism without loosing completeness. For this purpose we check a given functional logic program by our algorithm. If the algorithm computes an abstraction containing no potential residuations, we can safely execute the program with the residuation principle. Otherwise we must apply the nondeterministic narrowing principle to compute all answers. This method can also be applied to individual parts of the program so that some parts are executed by residuation and other parts by narrowing.

The operational semantics considered in this paper originates from Le Fun [3]. The unification procedure is very similar to S-unification [4]. However, S-unification immediately reports an error if some residuations cannot be evaluated after the unification of a literal with a clause head. E.g., the example programs in section 2 and 3.3 cannot be evaluated using S-unification. Therefore Boye has extended this framework to computation with delayed residuations [6]. He has also characterized a class of operationally complete programs based on notions from attribute grammars. Compared to our abstract interpretation procedure, Boye's characterization is mainly based on the syntactic structure of the program while we have tried to approximate the operational behaviour. Hence we obtain positive results for programs where Boye's check fails. E.g., our method yields a positive answer to the completeness question of the program

```
p(A,A+A).
p(A+A,A).
```

w.r.t. the initial goal p(2+2,1+1) while Boye's check fails (since there are external functors in input positions).

Marriott, Søndergaard and Dart [15] have also presented an abstract interpretation algorithm for analysing logic programs with delayed evaluation. The purpose of their work was to check logic programs with negation for floundering, i.e., whether a delayed evaluation of negated subgoals is complete. This has some similarities to our framework but it is a simpler problem because a delayed evaluation of a negated literal cannot bind any goal variables since this literal is evaluated only if all arguments are ground. In our context it is important that a delayed evaluation of a residuation can bind variables in order to enable the evaluation of other residuations (see the example in Section 3.3). Therefore we have to manage the dependencies between residuations and their variables in order to analyse the data flow in this case.

Since we must restrict all abstract information to a finite domain, our algorithm cannot manage all dependencies between residuations and their variables. If a residuation depends only on variables of one clause and these variables are bound to ground terms at the end of the clause, the algorithm detects the solvability of the residuation. But if a residuation depends on local variables from different clauses, then the algorithm cannot manage it and therefore it simply infers the unsolvability of this residuation. It seems to be possible to improve the algorithm at this point by refining the abstract domain (which makes the definition of the concretisation function and the correctness proofs more complex).

Another interesting topic for further research is the question whether it is possible to adapt our proposed method to the abstract interpretation of other logic languages which are not based on SLD-resolution with the leftmost selection rule. Such a method could be applied to analyse logic programs with delay primitives.

References

[1] S. Abramsky and C. Hankin, editors. *Abstract Interpretation of Declarative Languages*. Ellis Horwood, 1987.

[2] H. Aït-Kaci. An Overview of LIFE. In J.W. Schmidt and A.A. Stogny, editors, *Proc. Workshop on Next Generation Information System Technology*, pp. 42–58. Springer LNCS 504, 1990.

[3] H. Aït-Kaci, P. Lincoln, and R. Nasr. Le Fun: Logic, equations, and Functions. In *Proc. 4th IEEE Int. Symposium on Logic Programming*, pp. 17–23, 1987.

[4] S. Bonnier. Unification in Incompletely Specified Theories: A Case Study. In *Mathematical Foundations of Computer Science*, pp. 84–92. Springer LNCS 520, 1991.

[5] P.G. Bosco, E. Giovannetti, G. Levi, C. Moiso, and C. Palamidessi. A complete semantic characterization of K-LEAF, a logic language with partial functions. In *Proc. 4th IEEE Int. Symposium on Logic Programming*, pp. 318–327, 1987.

[6] J. Boye. S-SLD-resolution – An Operational Semantics for Logic Programs with External Procedures. In *Proc. of the 3rd Int. Symposium on Programming Language Implementation and Logic Programming*, pp. 383–393. Springer LNCS 528, 1991.

[7] M. Bruynooghe. A Practical Framework for the Abstract Interpretation of Logic Programs. *Journal of Logic Programming (10)*, pp. 91–124, 1991.

[8] D. DeGroot and G. Lindstrom, editors. *Logic Programming, Functions, Relations, and Equations*. Prentice Hall, 1986.

[9] L. Fribourg. SLOG: A Logic Programming Language Interpreter Based on Clausal Superposition and Rewriting. In *Proc. IEEE Int. Symposium on Logic Programming*, pp. 172–184, 1985.

[10] J.A. Goguen and J. Meseguer. Eqlog: Equality, Types, and Generic Modules for Logic Programming. In [8], pp. 295–363.

[11] M. Hanus. Compiling Logic Programs with Equality. In *Proc. of the 2nd Int. Workshop on Programming Language Implementation and Logic Programming*, pp. 387–401. Springer LNCS 456, 1990.

[12] M. Hanus. Efficient Implementation of Narrowing and Rewriting. In *Proc. Int. Workshop on Processing Declarative Knowledge*, pp. 344–365. Springer LNAI 567, 1991.

[13] M. Hanus. An Abstract Interpretation Algorithm for Residuating Logic Programs. Report MPI-I-92-217, Max-Planck-Institut für Informatik, 1992.

[14] J. Jaffar and J.-L. Lassez. Constraint Logic Programming. In *Proc. of the 14th ACM POPL*, pp. 111–119, Munich, 1987.

[15] K. Marriott, H. Søndergaard, and P. Dart. A Characterization of Non-Floundering Logic Programs. In *Proc. of the 1990 North American Conference on Logic Programming*, pp. 661–680. MIT Press, 1990.

[16] J.J. Moreno-Navarro and M. Rodríguez-Artalejo. Logic Programming with Functions and Predicates: The Language BABEL. *Journal of Logic Programming*, Vol. 12, pp. 191–223, 1992.

[17] L. Naish. Adding equations to NU-Prolog. In *Proc. of the 3rd Int. Symposium on Programming Language Implementation and Logic Programming*, pp. 15–26. Springer LNCS 528, 1991.

[18] U. Nilsson. Systematic Semantic Approximations of Logic Programs. In *Proc. of the 2nd Int. Workshop on Programming Language Implementation and Logic Programming*, pp. 293–306. Springer LNCS 456, 1990.

[19] G. Smolka. Residuation and Guarded Rules for Constraint Logic Programming. Research Report 12, DEC Paris Research Laboratory, 1991.

[20] P.A. Subrahmanyam and J.-H. You. FUNLOG: a Computational Model Integrating Logic Programming and Functional Programming. In [8], pp. 157–198.

Implementing a Lazy Functional Logic Language with Disequality Constraints

Herbert Kuchen
RWTH Aachen, Lehrstuhl für Informatik II, Ahornstraße 55
D-5100 Aachen, Germany, herbert@zeus.informatik.rwth-aachen.de

Francisco Javier López-Fraguas
UCM Madrid, Dep. Informática y Automática, Av. Complutense s/n
28040 Madrid, Spain, fraguas@emducm11.bitnet

Juan José Moreno-Navarro
UPM Madrid, Departamento LSIIS, Facultad de Informática
Boadilla del Monte, 28660 Madrid, Spain, jjmoreno@fi.upm.es

Mario Rodríguez-Artalejo
UCM Madrid, Dep. Informática y Automática, Av. Complutense s/n
28040 Madrid, Spain, mario@emducm11.bitnet

Abstract

In this paper, we investigate an implementation of a lazy functional logic language (in particular the language BABEL [MR88,MR92]) which uses disequality constraints for solving equations and building answers. We specify a new operational semantics which combines lazy narrowing with disequality constraints and we define an abstract machine tailored to the execution of BABEL programs according to this semantics. The machine is designed as a quite natural extension of a lazy graph narrowing machine [MKLR90]. Disjunctions of disequalities are handled using the backtracking mechanism.

1 Introduction

During the last years, many proposals for combining the functional and logic programming paradigms have been made [BL86,DL86]. In particular, so called *functional logic languages* [Re85] retain functional syntax but use *narrowing* – a unification based parameter passing mechanism which subsumes rewriting and SLD resolution – as operational semantics.

There are also several works aiming at the efficient implementation of logic + functional languages by means of abstract machines supporting combinations of functional and logic programming capabilities [BBCMMS89,BCGMP89,Ha90] [Mu90,KLMR90,MKLR90,Lo91]. In [KLMR90,MKLR90], we have investigated implementations of the lazy functional logic language BABEL [MR88,MR92] on the basis of *graph narrowing machines*, i.e. graph reduction machines extended by additional mechanisms for supporting logic variables, unification and backtracking.

Here, we study techniques for handling disequality constraints in BABEL. In particular, disequations of the form $X \neq t$ will be used when expressing answers.

It is well known that answer substitutions can be regarded as sets of equality constraints $X = t$. Allowing for disequalities increases the *expressivity* substantially.

For instance, the disequation $X \neq Y$ cannot be replaced by any equivalent, finite set of equations. Disequations of this kind are not well supported by non-constraint-based languages, as in the case of previous versions of BABEL (where a disequality is in general a source of infinitely many computations all giving substitutions as answers) or in PROLOG (where $\neq$ is a built-in predicate which simply checks for non-unifiability, but can neither produce variable bindings nor occur in answers).

There is a deep theoretical work on solving *equational problems*, which include both equations and disequations over a Herbrand universe as particular cases [Co90,CL89]. On the other hand, constraint solving has been integrated into many PROLOG-like logic programming languages [Co82,Co84,HS88,JL87,DVSAGB88]. In particular, the use of disequality constraints is a quite common feature in these languages as a useful programming tool. We are currently working out a general scheme for *Constraint Functional Logic Programming* [LR91,Lo92] which should help to understand the work in this paper from a broader perspective. This theoretical framework will be suitable for obtaining soundness and completeness results for the language presented here.

The rest of the paper is organized as follows. In Section 2 we define *uniform BABEL programs*, which were introduced in [MKLR90]. Section 3 discusses the motivations that led us to the representation of constraints used in our implementation. In Section 4, we give a formal specification of BABEL's operational semantics. In particular, we develop a generalization of lazy narrowing taking into account disequality constraints. Section 5 presents the design of an abstract machine which extends the lazy graph-narrowing from [MKLR90] and implements the new operational semantics. This implementation uses the existing backtracking mechanism to handle backtracking due to constraint solving. In Section 6, we summarize and point out future work.

2 Uniform BABEL Programs

In this section, we present the functional logic language which is used in the rest of the paper and we specify its syntax. It is the *uniform, first order* fragment of the language BABEL [KLMR90]. In this paper, we restrict ourselves to first order programs for simplicity. An extension to higher order programs could follow the ideas outlined in [MKLR90]. Constraints would affect only first order variables.

Uniformity [MKLR90] is a syntactic restriction, which allows a more efficient implementation of lazy narrowing. More precisely, backtracking due to different redexes can be replaced by the usual backtracking due to different rules.

2.1 Overview

Uniform First Order BABEL programs (UFO-BABEL programs, for short) consist of declarations for *data types* (together with the corresponding *data constructors*) and definitions for *functions*. *Predicates* are viewed as *boolean functions*. *Horn Clause Logic Programs* can be translated into BABEL programs as explained in [MR92,KLMR90].

In this paper, we deal with a *computation mechanism* which can be roughly described as follows: A *goal* for a program may be any expression. Goals are intended to be reduced to a *result* – a data term – by computations which also compute some *answer constraints* – both *equational* and *disequational* – for the initial variables. This differs from the operational semantics in our previous works

[KLMR90,MKLR90], where BABEL programs could compute only equality constraints (represented by substitutions) as answers. The following program computes the *size* of a list, understood as the number of different elements:

fun *member*: $\alpha \times (list\ \alpha) \rightarrow$ bool.   **fun** *size*: $(list\ \alpha) \rightarrow$ *nat*.
    member Y nil := *false*.   *size* nil := 0.
    member Y (cons X Xs) :=   *size* (cons X Xs) :=
       $X = Y \rightarrow true\ \square$ *member* X Xs $\rightarrow$ *size* Xs $\square$
          member Y Xs.   *suc* (*size* Xs).

        solve *size* (*cons* (*mkpair* X 0) (*cons* (*mkpair* Y Z) nil)).
        > 1. result: *suc* 0   answer: $X = Y$, $Z = 0$;
        > 2. result: *suc* (*suc* 0)   answer: $X \neq Y$;
        > 3. result: *suc* (*suc* 0)   answer: $Z \neq 0$;
        > no more solutions

Note that the conditional expression in the second rule for *member* implicitly introduces the disequality constraint $X \neq Y$, if the else-branch is selected. Also note that the answer constraint "$X \neq Y$" cannot be replaced by equality constraints (i.e. by a single substitution). Previous versions of BABEL would compute infinitely many solutions for this goal. As far as we know, the same holds for other existing logic + functional languages.

In the following, we explain the syntax of UFO-BABEL programs more formally.

2.2   Data Types and Data Constructors

We assume a ranked set $TC = \cup_{n \in \mathbb{N}} TC^n$ of *type constructors* δ/n (e.g. nat/0, list/1) and a countably infinite set *TVar* of *type variables* α, β etc. Any algebraic term τ built from type constructors and type variables – e.g. (list nat), (list α) – is a *data type*. A data type is *polymorphic* if it includes type variables, and *monomorphic* otherwise. We also assume a set *DC* of *data constructors* with declared principal types: $c : \tau_1 \times \ldots \times \tau_n \rightarrow \tau$, e.g. *cons*: $\alpha \times (list\ \alpha) \rightarrow list\ \alpha$. In practice, type constructors and data constructors can be introduced through **datatype** declarations; e.g. the following data types, which are predefined in BABEL:

    datatype *bool* := *true* | *false*.   **datatype** *list* α := nil | *cons* α (*list* α).
    datatype *nat*   := 0 | *suc nat*.   **datatype** *pair* α β := *mkpair* α β.

2.3   Terms and Expressions

Next, we assume a countably infinite set *Var* of (data) variables and a set *FS* of *function symbols* with declared principal types: $f : \tau_1 \times \ldots \times \tau_n \rightarrow \tau$, for example *size* : *list* α $\rightarrow$ *nat*. We can then build well typed *terms* t and *expressions* e. We understand *well typedness* in the sense of Milner's type system [Mi78].

t	::=	X	%	$X \in Var$	e	::=	X	%	$X \in Var$
	|	$(c\ t_1 \ldots t_n)$	%	$c \in DC$		|	$(c\ e_1 \ldots e_n)$	%	$c \in DC$.
						|	$(f\ e_1 \ldots e_n)$	%	$f \in FS$.

where $c : \tau_1 \times \ldots \times \tau_n \rightarrow \tau$, $f : \tau_1 \times \ldots \times \tau_n \rightarrow \tau$, and $n \geq 0$. We assume that application associates to the left and omit parentheses accordingly. The syntax allows to build expressions involving some *primitive function symbols*, assumed to be present in *FS* and used as prefix, infix and mixfix operators (we assume b, b_i : *bool*):

$\neg b$ (negation), $(b_1 \wedge b_2)$ (conjunction), $(b_1 \vee b_2)$ (disjunction), $(b \rightarrow e)$ (guarded expression, meaning: **if** b **then** e **else** undefined), $(b \rightarrow e_1 \square e_2)$ (conditional, meaning: **if** b **then** e_1 **else** e_2), and $(e_1 = e_2)$ (weak equality). A *weak equation* $(e_1 = e_2)$ is intended to be *true*, if e_1 and e_2 have the same finite and totally defined value (infinite and/or partially defined objects are possible, since our intended semantics for data constructors is not strict). $(e_1 = e_2)$ is intended to be *false*, if the values for e_1 and e_2 differ in some constructor (even if e_1, e_2 represent infinite or partially defined objects). For the *declarative semantics* of weak equality, we refer the reader to [MR88,MR92]. An *operational semantics*, based on equality and disequality constraints, will be formally specified in Section 4.

2.4   Uniform Programs

UFO-BABEL programs consist of declarations of datatypes and *shallow defining rules* for function symbols. For a function symbol $f : \tau_1 \times \ldots \times \tau_n \rightarrow \tau$, each defining rule must have the following shape:

$$\underbrace{f\ t_1 \ldots t_n}_{\text{left hand side}} := \underbrace{\underbrace{\{b \rightarrow\}}_{\text{optional guard}}\ \ \overbrace{e}^{\text{body}}}_{\text{right hand side}}$$

The following restrictions must be satisfied:

1. *Shallow Data Patterns*: Each t_i is either a variable X or a shallow pattern $(c\ X_1 \ldots X_n)$ with $X_i \in Var$ for $i = 1, \ldots, n$ $(n \geq 0)$. In the latter case, we say that f *demands* its i-th argument, and we call c the *demanded constructor*.

2. *Left Linearity*: $f\ t_1 \ldots t_n$ does not contain multiple variable occurrences.

3. *Well Typedness*: Under appropriate type assumptions for the variables, it must be possible to check the types τ_i for each t_i $(1 \leq i \leq n)$, the type *bool* for b, and the type τ for e.

4. *Restrictions on Free Variables*: Any variable that occurs only in the right hand side is called *free*. Free variables are allowed to occur in the guard, but not in the body.

Moreover, the set of defining rules for each function symbol f must satisfy two additional requirements. Given two different defining rules for the same symbol f:

$$f\ t_1 \ldots t_n := \{b_1 \rightarrow\}e_1 \qquad\qquad f\ s_1 \ldots s_n := \{b_2 \rightarrow\}e_2$$

(with variables renamed apart), we require

5. *Uniformity*: for $1 \leq i \leq n$, t_i is a variable iff s_i is a variable.

6. *Nonambiguity*: if $(f\ t_1 \ldots t_n)$ and $(f\ s_1 \ldots s_n)$ are unifiable with most general unifier σ, then either $e_1\sigma$ and $e_2\sigma$ are identical, or $b_1\sigma$ and $b_2\sigma$ are *incompatible*. For a definition of incompatibility, we refer to [KLMR92]. The conjunction of two incompatible boolean expressions is always unsatisfiable.

The restrictions 1 and 5 ensure that all the rules for a given function demand the same extent of evaluation for a considered argument. An efficient transformation of a general BABEL program (i.e. a program possibly violating restrictions 1 and 5) to a uniform one is described in [MKLR90]. This transformation may syntactically destroy nonambiguity, but we also allow programs produced in this way, even if they do not literally satisfy restriction 6. The restrictions 4 and 6 ensure that BABEL functions are functions in the mathematical sense.

We assume some *predefined rules* for the boolean operations, guarded, and conditional expressions to be present in any program:

$$X \vee Y := or1 \ X \ Y. \qquad or1 \ true \ Y \qquad := true. \qquad (true \rightarrow X) \qquad := X.$$
$$X \vee Y := or2 \ X \ Y. \qquad or2 \ X \ true \qquad := true. \qquad (true \rightarrow X \Box Y) \qquad := X.$$
$$X \vee Y := or3 \ X \ Y. \qquad or3 \ false \ false \qquad := false. \qquad (false \rightarrow X \Box Y) \qquad := Y.$$

The rules given above for "$\vee$" specify parallel disjunction in uniform format ("parallel" as far as finite failure but no infinite computation is involved). Conjunction and negation are defined correspondingly. In contrast to previous versions of BABEL [KLMR90,MKLR90], we do not assume any predefined rules for weak equality. Instead, weak equations will be reduced by constraint solving, as shown by the specification of the operational semantics in the next section.

3 Representation of Constraints: a Discussion

In a functional logic language without disequality, the only constraint-like operation is unification, which can be seen as a problem of solving sets of equations, the result being a set of bindings (equations) for variables. If one of these variables appears in a later step of the computation, its value is used instead. We claim that this nice property of having the "current constraint" as a set of pieces of information about each variable, independent of the rest, is a crucial point for an efficient implementation also in the case of disequalities.

The introduction of disequalities will require to attach more complex information to variables and to complicate the way of using it in further steps of the computation. If the language were strict, we would evaluate both sides of an equality or disequality to terms, and then we could use some of the constraint solving mechanisms proposed for the case of logic programming with disequalities [Co90,Co84,Sm91]. All of them are based on reducing a set of equalities and disequalities to some kind of *solved form*. In [Co90], solved forms are disjunctions of *basic formulas* of the form $X_1 = t_1 \wedge \ldots \wedge X_n = t_n \wedge Y_1 \neq s_1 \wedge \ldots \wedge Y_m \neq s_m$, where t_i and s_j are terms, s_j is not Y_j and each X_i occurs only once. Disjunctions appear because of disequalities between constructor applications, e.g. $(c \ t_1 \ldots t_n) \neq (c \ s_1 \ldots s_n)$ is equivalent to $t_1 \neq s_1 \vee \ldots \vee t_n \neq s_n$. These solved forms are satisfiable, if all the involved variables range over infinite domains. The case of finite domains is briefly discussed later. The finiteness of a domain can be derived from the datatype definitions, even in the case of polymorphic types (see also Section 4).

Due to the laziness of our language, a disequality may hold even between infinite objects, and therefore we lose completeness, if we force the evaluation to a (finite) term. At a first sight, it seems to be enough to allow head normal forms h_j instead of terms s_j in the disequalities $Y_j \neq s_j$. An expression is in *head normal form* (HNF), if it is a variable or a constructor application $(c \ e_1 \ldots e_n)$.

Unfortunately, a conjunction $Y_1 \neq h_1 \wedge \ldots \wedge Y_m \neq h_m$ is not guaranteed to be satisfiable, as the following example shows. Let the function f be defined by the rule $f \ (suc \ X) := X$. Then, $Y \neq 0 \wedge Y \neq (suc \ (f \ Y))$ is not satisfiable, since $Y \neq (suc \ (f \ Y))$ is only satisfied by $Y = 0$, which contradicts $Y \neq 0$. As a conclusion, we must still require terms s_j for the disequalities $Y_j \neq s_j$. This does not mean that a head normal form h in a disequality $Y \neq h$ must be reduced to a term, which would violate the lazy nature of the language. Instead, we consider two alternatives for $Y \neq (c \; e_1 \ldots e_n)$: either $Y = (c' \; X_1 \ldots X_m)$ for some $c' \neq c$ and new variables $X_1, \ldots, X_m$ $(m \geq 0)$, or $Y = (c \; X_1 \ldots X_n)$, but for some i holds $X_i \neq e_i$. Observe that the first alternative is "lazy", that is, it does not require further evaluation of the e_i's. Furthermore, the second alternative only requires the evaluation of one selected argument.

Another question is to decide whether disjunctions within constraints in solved form will be represented explicitly or handled implicitly by the backtracking mechanism. We find two reasons against the explicit representation: Firstly, it would be difficult to maintain the representation in a "variable oriented" format (for each variable, we would have to identify and link information coming from equalities and disequalities in different disjuncts). Secondly, it would be hard to maintain incrementally the structure of solved forms (if in some disjunct D we have $X \neq s$ and an equality $X = t$ is added later on, it produces $t \neq s$ which could split into a disjunction of disequalities, and we must distribute it over the conjunction constituting D). Moreover, it is difficult, to get back the old constraint, when backtracking is needed. If we do not distribute, we get an arbitrary boolean expression, which is hard to check for satisfiability. For these reasons, we have decided to avoid explicit disjunctions. Instead, a basic formula is maintained as the current constraint within any computation state, and backtracking is used for managing disjunctions introduced by disequations between constructor applications.

Finite domains introduce a new difficulty, because a basic formula needs not be satisfiable. If, e.g., the nullary constructors a, b, c enumerate all the elements in the domain ranged over by X, then the basic formula $X \neq a \wedge X \neq b \wedge X \neq c$ is not satisfiable. The solution, we have adopted, is to generate explicit alternatives for these disequalities. In the previous example $X \neq a$ would generate (by backtracking) the alternatives $X = b$ and $X = c$. In fact, this is exactly the first alternative of the above solution. In special situations (e.g. flat finite domains), some set based representation techniques as in CHIP [DVSAGB88] could also be used.

4 Operational Semantics

We present in this section an operational semantics which is rather close to the implementation proposed in Section 5, with the exception of "sharing", which is not captured here. We give a set of rules expressing how to perform computations for evaluating a given expression. These rules constitute a modification of lazy narrowing for taking into account disequality constraints. An alternative formulation of the operational semantics could replace the explicit use of unification by means of equality constraints. This is the usual approach within the CLP scheme [JL87,HS88]. Our semantics reflects more closely the behaviour of the abstract machine, which uses (efficiently implementable (compilable)) unification instead of (interpretative) constraint solving. Our aim was to develop an implementation which behaves (as efficiently) as narrowing as long as no disequalities are involved.

The basic formulas of Section 3 are represented by two components: equalities are treated as *substitutions*, while disequalities are collected in *environments*.

A computation state, called *configuration*, is a triple $\langle e, \theta, \rho \rangle$ where

- e is the *expression* to be reduced.

- θ is a *tag*, that is, a constructor symbol c or the symbol *any*. Tags are introduced for expressing that e must be reduced to a result with top-level constructor

c, or to any result in the case of *any*. Tags are interesting for avoiding in advance many useless computations by achieving a kind of "indexing by the result" mechanism and hence reducing the search space.

- ρ is an *environment*, defined as a mapping of variables to finite sets. An element of such a set can be a term or the special value *fin*.

The domain $dom(\rho)$ of an environment ρ is the set of variables X such that $\rho(X)$ is not empty. The restriction $\rho \mid_V$ of an environment ρ to a set of variables V is an environment which coincides with ρ over V and is empty for variables not in V. $fin \in \rho(X)$ indicates that X must have a finite and total value. The intended meaning of ρ is the conjunction $\bigwedge_{X \in dom(\rho)} \bigwedge_{t \in \rho(X) - \{fin\}} X \neq t$. With this reading any environment ρ is satisfiable, if no finite domain is involved. We use the notation $\rho \cup \rho'$ for the environment ρ'' with $\rho''(X) = \rho(X) \cup \rho'(X)$. For an environment ρ and a substitution σ with $dom(\rho) \cap dom(\sigma) = \emptyset$, $\rho\sigma$ denotes the result of applying σ to the elements of $\rho(X)$, for all $X \in dom(\rho)$.

Configurations are changed by the *one-step narrowing relation* $\Rightarrow_\sigma$, whose rules are given below. $\langle e, \theta, \rho \rangle \Rightarrow_\sigma \langle e', \theta, \rho' \rangle$ indicates that the configuration $\langle e, \theta, \rho \rangle$ can evolve to $\langle e', \theta, \rho' \rangle$ in one step by narrowing some variables in e as specified by the idempotent substitution σ. The rules for $\Rightarrow_\sigma$ rely on the following auxiliary construction, used to propagate bindings through the environment.

a) Given an idempotent substitution $\sigma \equiv \{X \leftarrow t\}$ and an environment ρ, we define $propagation(\sigma, \rho) := (b, \rho')$, where b is the boolean expression
$$b := \begin{cases} t \neq t_1\sigma \wedge \ldots \wedge t \neq t_k\sigma, & \text{if } \{t_1, \ldots, t_k\} = \rho(X) - \{fin\} \\ true, & \text{if } \rho(X) - \{fin\} = \emptyset \end{cases}$$
and $\rho' := ((\rho \mid_{dom(\rho) - \{X\}})\sigma) \cup \rho''$,
where $\rho''(V) := \begin{cases} \{fin\}, & \text{if } V \in var(t) \text{ and } fin \in \rho(X) \\ \emptyset, & \text{otherwise} \end{cases}$

b) Given an idempotent substitution $\sigma \equiv \{X_1 \leftarrow t_1, \ldots, X_n \leftarrow t_n\}$ and environment ρ, $propagation\,(\sigma, \rho) := (b \wedge b', \rho')$
where $(b, \rho'') := propagation(\{X_1 \leftarrow t_1\}, \rho)$
and $(b', \rho') := propagation(\{X_2 \leftarrow t_2, \ldots, X_n \leftarrow t_n\}, \rho'')$

A *computation* starting with e_0 is a sequence $\langle e_0, any, \emptyset \rangle \Rightarrow_{\sigma_1} \langle e_1, any, \rho_1 \rangle \Rightarrow_{\sigma_2} \ldots \Rightarrow_{\sigma_n} \langle e_n, any, \rho_n \rangle$. A computation *succeeds* if e_n is a term and either $\theta_n = any$ or e_n is a variable or e_n is an application of the constructor θ_n. e_n is called the *result* and $\langle \sigma, \rho \rangle$ is called the *answer* of the computation, where σ is the composition $\sigma := \sigma_1 \ldots \sigma_n \mid_{var(e_0)}$, $\rho := \rho_n \mid_{descendants(var(e_0\sigma), \rho_n)}$, and $descendants(S, \rho) := S \cup descendants(var(\rho(S)), \rho)$. If a computation has not yet succeeded, but no further narrowing steps are applicable, the computation *fails*.

Rules for $\Rightarrow_\sigma$

For reasons of space, we only include the rules which are more representative for expressing how lazy narrowing is combined with constraint solving. The full list of rules can be found in [KLMR92].

1. Goal expression $e \equiv (f\ e_1 \ldots e_n)$:

(R1.1) $$\frac{\langle e_i, \theta_i, \rho \rangle \Rightarrow_\sigma \langle e_i', \theta_i, \rho' \rangle}{\langle (f\ e_1 \ldots e_i \ldots e_n), \theta, \rho \rangle \Rightarrow_\sigma \langle (f\ e_1 \ldots e_i' \ldots e_n)\sigma, \theta, \rho' \rangle}$$
if f *demands* HNF for the i-th argument, e_i is not in HNF, e_j is in HNF for

every demanded $1 \leq j < i$ and θ_i is chosen as follows: if all the rules for f which do not contradict θ demand the same top level constructor c_i for the i-th argument, then θ_i is c_i; otherwise θ_i is *any*. A rule *contradicts* a constructor c, if its right hand side cannot yield a value with top-level constructor c. An (approximating) program analysis is needed to detect this.

Similar rules are used to reduce the arguments of "=", "$\neq$", and constructors.

(R1.2) $\langle (f\ e_1 \ldots e_n), \theta, \rho \rangle \Rightarrow_\sigma \langle b \to r\lambda, \theta, \rho' \rangle$

if e_i is in HNF for every demanded $1 \leq i \leq n$, and there is a variant $(f\ t_1 \ldots t_n) := r$ (with new variables) of a rule for f, which does not contradict θ, such that

(i) $\sigma \cup \lambda$ is a most general unifier of $(f\ e_1 \ldots e_n)$ and $(f\ t_1 \ldots t_n)$, with $dom(\sigma) \subset var((f\ e_1 \ldots e_n))$ and $dom(\lambda) \subset var((f\ t_1 \ldots t_n))$. We assume that $t_i \in dom(\lambda)$ and $e_i \notin dom(\sigma)$ if both, t_i and e_i, are variables.

(ii) $(b, \rho') := propagation(\sigma, \rho)$

2. Goal expression $e \equiv (e_1 = e_2)$ with tag *true*:

(R2.1) $\dfrac{\langle e_2, c, \rho \rangle \Rightarrow_\sigma \langle e'_2, c, \rho' \rangle}{\langle e_1 = e_2, true, \rho \rangle \Rightarrow_\sigma \langle e_1\sigma = e'_2, true, \rho' \rangle}$

if e_1 is in HNF with top-level constructor c, e_2 is not in HNF. (R2.1) is essentially an optimized version of (R1.1) for "=".

(R2.2) $\langle (c\ e_1 \ldots e_n) = (c\ e'_1 \ldots e'_n), true, \rho \rangle \Rightarrow_\epsilon \langle (e_1 = e'_1 \wedge \ldots \wedge e_n = e'_n), true, \rho \rangle$
where $(n \geq 0)$. ϵ denotes the identity function.

(R2.3) $\langle X = (c\ e_1 \ldots e_n), true, \rho \rangle \Rightarrow_\sigma \langle (b \to (X_1 = e_1\sigma \wedge \ldots \wedge X_n = e_n\sigma), true, \rho' \rangle$

if $(c\ e_1 \ldots e_n)$ is not a term, $X_1, \ldots, X_n$ are new variables,
$\sigma := \{X \leftarrow (c\ X_1 \ldots X_n)\}$ and $(b, \rho') := propagation(\sigma, \rho \cup \{X \leftarrow \{fin\}\})$.
Note that $(c\ e_1 \ldots e_n)$ needs to be evaluated because only for finite terms, "=" can yield *true*.

(R2.4) $\langle X = X, true, \rho \rangle \Rightarrow_\epsilon \langle true, true, \rho \cup \{X \leftarrow \{fin\}\} \rangle$

(R2.5) $\langle X = t, true, \rho \rangle \Rightarrow_\sigma \langle b, true, \rho' \rangle$

if t is a term, $X \notin var(t)$, $\sigma := \{X \leftarrow t\}$ and
$(b, \rho') := propagation(\sigma, \rho \cup \{X \leftarrow \{fin\}\})$.

3. Goal expression $e \equiv (e_1 = e_2)$ with tag *false*:

(R3.1) $\langle (c\ e_1 \ldots e_n) = (c'\ e'_1 \ldots e'_m), false, \rho \rangle \Rightarrow_\epsilon \langle false, false, \rho \rangle$ $\qquad$ if $c \neq c'$.

(R3.2) $\langle (c\ e_1 \ldots e_n) = (c\ e'_1 \ldots e'_n), false, \rho \rangle \Rightarrow_\epsilon \langle (e_1 = e'_1 \wedge \ldots \wedge e_n = e'_n), false, \rho \rangle$

(R3.3) $\langle X = (c\ e_1 \ldots e_n), false, \rho \rangle \Rightarrow_\sigma \langle b \to false, false, \rho' \rangle$

if $(c\ e_1 \ldots e_n)$ is not a term, $X_1, \ldots, X_m$ are new variables,
$\sigma := \{X \leftarrow (c'\ X_1 \ldots X_m)\}$ where c' is a constructor symbol of arity $m \geq 0$ different from c but with the same target type, and $(b, \rho') := propagation(\sigma, \rho)$.

(R3.4) $\langle X = (c\ e_1 \ldots e_n), false, \rho \rangle \Rightarrow_\sigma \langle b \to (X_1 = e_1 \wedge \ldots \wedge X_n = e_n)\sigma, false, \rho' \rangle$

if $(c\ e_1 \ldots e_n)$ is not a term, $X_1, \ldots, X_n$ are new variables,
$\sigma := \{X \leftarrow (c\ X_1 \ldots X_n)\}$, and $(b, \rho') := propagation(\sigma, \rho)$. Note that (R3.3) and (R3.4) are alternatives for the same situation, and that (R3.3) includes by itself several alternatives.

(R3.5) $\langle X = Y, false, \rho \rangle \Rightarrow_\epsilon \langle false, false, \rho \cup \{X \leftarrow \{Y\}, Y \leftarrow \{X\}\}\rangle$

   if X, Y are different variables with a recursive or polymorphic type.

(R3.6) $\langle X = t, false, \rho \rangle \Rightarrow_\epsilon \langle false, false, \rho \cup \{X \leftarrow \{t\}\}\rangle$

   if t is a non-variable term with a recursive or polymorphic type.

(R3.7) **(R3.8)**Like (R3.3) and (R3.4), but $(c\ e_1 \ldots e_n)$ is a term with a monomorphic non-recursive type.

(R3.9) $\langle X = Y, false, \rho \rangle \Rightarrow_\sigma \langle b \rightarrow ((c\ X_1 \ldots X_n) = Y), false, \rho' \rangle$

   if X, Y are different variables with a monomorphic non-recursive type τ, c is a constructor with target type τ, $X_1, \ldots, X_n$ are new variables, $\sigma := \{X \leftarrow (c\ X_1 \ldots X_n)\}$, and $(b, \rho') := propagation(\sigma, \rho)$.

The symmetric cases are defined analogously. The rules for disequality are similar to those for equality with the opposite tag. The rules (R3.5) and (R3.6) handle non-recursive polymorphic types (e.g. *pair α β*) like recursive types. This is only valid, if they cannot be instantiated to a type with a finite domain (e.g. *pair bool bool*). For this reason, we assume a previous program transformation, which replaces every BABEL function by the set of its used instances (depending on the considered goal). In the *size* example, the function *size* is replaced by another function with the same rules, but type *list (pair α nat) $\rightarrow$ nat*. Note that such an instance need not be monomorphic, but it is sure that occurring type variables will not be instantiated further, especially not to a type with a finite domain. We are only interested in programs, where such a transformation is possible. We use this approach in order to avoid runtime type information, which would lead to a less efficient implementation. Note that without the mentioned program transformation non-recursive polymorphic types have to be handled like non-recursive monomorphic types, since they may be instantiated to such types.

The following example computation shows how the above rules work. Consider f defined by the BABEL rule $f\ (suc\ X) := X$ and the configuration

(1) $\qquad \langle X = (suc\ (f\ X)), \quad false, \quad \{X \leftarrow \{(suc\ 0), Y, (suc\ Y)\}\rangle$.

By applying rule (R3.3) with $\sigma \equiv \{X \leftarrow 0\}$, we get

$\qquad \langle 0 \neq (suc\ 0) \wedge 0 \neq Y \wedge 0 \neq (suc\ Y) \rightarrow false, \quad false, \quad \emptyset \rangle$.

Using the rules for disequality corresponding to (R3.1) and (R3.6), the rules for conjunction and guarded expressions, we get $\langle false, false, \{Y \leftarrow \{0\}\}\rangle$.

Alternatively, we can apply (R3.4) with $\sigma \equiv \{X \leftarrow (suc\ Z)\}$ to (1), leading to $\langle (suc\ Z) \neq (suc\ 0) \wedge (suc\ Z) \neq Y \wedge (suc\ Z) \neq (suc\ Y) \rightarrow Z = (f\ (suc\ Z)), false, \emptyset \rangle$. Using the rules for disequality corresponding to (R3.2), (R3.6), and (R3.5), the rules for conjunction and guarded expressions, we get

$\qquad \langle Z = (f\ (suc\ Z)), \quad false, \quad \{Y \leftarrow \{(suc\ Z), Z\}, Z \leftarrow \{0, Y\}\}\rangle$.

Applying (R1.1) (for the 2nd argument of "=") and (R1.2) leads to

$\qquad \langle Z = Z, \quad false, \quad \{Y \leftarrow \{(suc\ Z), Z\}, Z \leftarrow \{0, Y\}\}\rangle$.

This computation fails since $Z = Z$ is not a term, but no rule can be applied.

5   The Abstract Machine

In order to implement BABEL with constraints lazily, we will use an extension of the lazy BABEL machine LBAM, presented in [MKLR90]. Before we describe this extension, let us briefly recall the LBAM.

5.1 The LBAM

The LBAM implements lazy narrowing for uniform BABEL programs, but it cannot represent and maintain constraints. In order to apply a function f to some arguments, the demanded arguments are evaluated to head normal form. Then, the rules for f are tried one after the other until an applicable rule is found.

Evaluating the demanded arguments before trying to apply a rule has the advantage that the arguments are only reevaluated (backtracking), if no rule is applicable. If, alternatively, the arguments are reevaluated, until the considered rule is applicable, non-termination can occur. Note that the number of rules is always finite, while the number of narrowings of an expression may be infinite (see also [JMM92]). Let for example the function *one* be defined by the two rules *one* $0 := suc\ 0$ and *one* $(suc\ X) := one\ X$ and consider the goal *one* $(one\ Y)$. If the first rule for *one* shall be used, $(one\ Y)$ has to be narrowed to 0. Unfortunately, there are infinitely many narrowings of $(one\ Y)$, since Y can be bound to every natural number. All these narrowings deliver the (undesired) result $suc\ 0$.

The LBAM consists of:

- a *program store* containing the abstract machine code, which the BABEL program has been translated to,

- the *graph*, which contains constructor, variable, and task nodes,

- the *active task pointer* which points at the task node representing the currently executed function application.

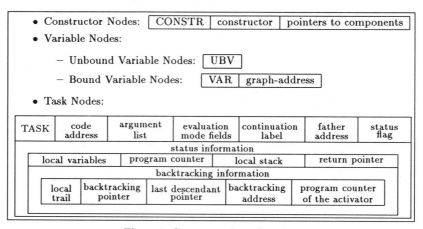

Figure 1: Structure of graph nodes.

The different kinds of nodes (see Fig. 1) are distinguished by a *tag* (first component). A *constructor node* represents a constructor application, while a *bound* or *unbound variable node* stands for a logical variable. A *task node* represents a function application. Among others, it contains the address of the code for the function, pointers to the arguments, a stack for auxiliary computations, a *status flag* (dormant, active, or evaluated), a return pointer (used to return to the activator task on successful termination), a backtracking pointer (indicating the task which must be forced to produce another solution, if the current task fails), the last descendant pointer (which points to the last (possibly indirect) descendant task, which has already finished and may produce alternative computations). This pointer is used to initialize the backtracking pointer of the next descendant task generated.

5.2 Compiling Uniform BABEL to LBAM-Code

Each BABEL rule is translated into a sequence of small graph manipulation commands. For the compilation, the rules of a uniform BABEL program are grouped according to the function symbol they define.

a) Code for a BABEL program:

```
    0:   GOALNODE (goal, k_0)
    1:   BODY_EVAL
    2:   PRINT_RESULT
    3:   MORE
    4:   JUMP_FALSE end
    5:   FORCE
         fcttrans ((⟨f_1 t^1_{i1} ... t^1_{im_1} := e^1_i⟩^{r^1}_{i=1}, k_1)
         ...
         fcttrans ((⟨f_n t^n_{i1} ... t^n_{im_n} := e^n_i⟩^{r^n}_{i=1}, k_n)
goal:    EXECUTE
         TRY_ME_ELSE fail
         exptrans (Goal)
fail:    PRINT_FAILURE
end:     STOP.
```

b) fcttrans ((⟨f t_{i1} ... t_{im} := e_i⟩^r_{i=1}, k) :=

```
    f:     LOADS j_1
           JUMP_HNF l_1
           ARG_EVAL
    l_1:   POP
           ...
           LOADS j_k
           JUMP_HNF l_k
           ARG_EVAL
    l_k:   POP
           EXECUTE
           TRY_ME_ELSE rule_2
           ruletrans (f t_{11} ... t_{1m} := e_1)
    rule_2: UNDO
           TRY_ME_ELSE rule_3
           ruletrans (f t_{21} ... t_{2m} := e_2)
    rule_3: UNDO
           ...
    rule_r: UNDO
           TRY_ME_ELSE l_{fail}
           ruletrans (f t_{r1} ... t_{rm} := e_r)
    l_{fail}: UNDO
           FAIL_RETURN
```

c) ruletrans (f t_1 ... t_m := e) :=

```
           LOAD 1
           unifytrans (t_1)
           ...
           LOAD m
           unifytrans (t_m)
    explb: exptrans (e)
           RETURN
```

d) unifytrans (X) := ε (empty code)

```
    unifytrans(c X_i ... X_{n+i-1}) :=
           UNIFY (c,n,i)
```

e) exptrans (e) :=

```
           graphtrans (e)
           JUMP_EMODE l_{hnf}        (*)
           NODE (nfe, 1, 1)          (*)
           BODY_EVAL                 (*)
           JUMP l_{end}              (*)
    l_{hnf}: JUMP_HNF l_{end}
           BODY_EVAL
    l_{end}: ...
```

f) graphtrans (X_i) := LOADX i

```
    graphtrans (X) := LOAD i
           if X is a synonym for argument i
    graphtrans ((c e_1 ... e_n)) :=
           graphtrans (e_1)
           ...
           graphtrans (e_n)
           CNODE (c, n)
    graphtrans ((f e_1 ... e_n)) :=
           graphtrans (e_1)
           ...
           graphtrans (e_n)
           NODE (f, n, k)
```

Figure 2: Code Generation Schemes

The code, which is produced for a BABEL program (see Fig. 2), works as follows. First, it generates a special dormant task node for the goal (GOALNODE(goal,k_0)) (where k_0 is the number of variables in the goal), starts its evaluation (BODY_EVAL) and prints the result (PRINT_RESULT) after a successful computation. If more solutions are desired (MORE), the machine is forced to backtrack (FORCE), otherwise the program stops (JUMP_FALSE end ...STOP). After this preliminary code, the translation of the functions (using *fcttrans*) and the code for the goal follow.

The code for a BABEL function f (with k local variables) (Fig. 2 b) first evaluates (if necessary) the demanded arguments $(j_1, \ldots, j_m)$ to HNF (LOADS j_i; JUMP_HNF l_i; ARG_EVAL; l_i: POP $(i = 1, \ldots, m)$). This code is executed, while the father of the task for f is active, in order to place the task nodes corresponding to the demanded arguments in the backtracking chain before the task node for f.

EXECUTE activates the task for f. The rules for f are tried in their textual order. The code for a rule first sets the backtracking address l (TRY_ME_ELSE l). If the rule fails, a jump to l is performed, the bindings produced by the rule are removed (UNDO) and the next rule (if existing) is tried. If all rules fail, the predecessor of the task (usually the task for the last argument, if existing) is forced to backtrack (FAIL_RETURN).

The translation of a rule (Fig. 2 c) consists of code for the unification of the arguments of the function application with the terms on the left hand side and code for the evaluation of the expression on the right hand side.

If a term t on the left hand side is just a variable X, no code for the unification is needed, but X is used as a synonym for the corresponding argument (see Fig. 2 d). If t is a constructed term, it is unified with the corresponding argument (UNIFY).

The scheme *exptrans* (Fig. 2 e) produces code, which evaluates an expression according to the evaluation mode (HNF or NF) of the current task. First, a graphical representation G of the expression is build. If a full evaluation is needed (e.g. when the result shall be shown to the user), G is given as an argument to a special function *nfe*, predefined by the rule *nfe* $X := X = X \rightarrow X$, and evaluated. Otherwise G is evaluated to head normal form, if still necessary.

If e has a type with a flat domain, the instructions marked with (*) in Fig. 2 can be omitted, because HNF and NF are then the same. For some expressions, e.g. the conditional and the equality, a more efficient translation is used. Due to the lack of space, we must omit this here.

The *graphtrans* (Fig. 2 f) scheme generates code which produces the graphical representation of an expression. In the case of an application, first the arguments are handled. Then, the pointers to their representations are taken from the local stack and included in a new constructor or task node respectively.

5.3   Extensions of the LBAM to Cope with Constraints

BABEL allows equality and disequality constraints. In Section 3, we have seen that it is sufficient to deal with basic formulas, i.e. constraints, which are the conjunction of *elementary constraints*, where the left hand side is always a variable.

If there is an equality constraint for a variable X, it will be the only constraint concerning this variable. Hence, this constraint can be handled by binding X to the corresponding right hand side. But in contrast to a binding during unification, we now have to store that the variable has to be finite, since equality is only defined for finite values. Hence, we need an additional tag in each bound variable node, indicating whether the variable may only be bound to finite values. This information will not be used during computation, since it is undecidable, whether some computation is going to be finite, but it will be given to the user at the end.

If there is no equality constraint for some variable X, there may be a conjunction of elementary disequality constraints for X. To handle this, we introduce a new kind of node called *constraint node*. The variable node for X will point to such a node. A constraint node contains the tag CONSTRAINT and a list of pointers, each pointing to the graphical representation of a term t (representing the constraint $X \neq t$).

Note that a variable node is not directly overwritten by a constraint node, but a (bound) variable node will point to it. The reason for this is that a constraint is usually changed several times during computation. While backtracking, the old constraint has to be reestablished. This is much easier, if the pointers to all the constraint nodes, representing "old" constraints, are trailed.

In addition to a new kind of node, we need a new notion of *head normal form*. Now, an expression is in HNF, if it is an unbound variable, a constructor application or a *constrained variable* (represented by a variable node pointing to a constraint node).

Furthermore, it is more complicated to decide whether a rule is applicable (see Section 4). More constraints may have to be added in order to apply a rule. It may be the case, that an actual argument is a constrained variable X which has to be unequal to a list of terms *tlist*, while the corresponding formal argument is a term $t := (c\ X_1 \ldots X_n)$. Suppose that *tlist* contains a term $t' := (c\ t_1 \ldots t_n)$. In order to apply the rule, we have to bind X to t. From the old constraint $X \neq t'$, we now get the new constraint $t \neq t'$. In order to fulfill $t \neq t'$, we have to select an argument position i $(1 \leq i \leq n)$ and to add the constraint $X_i \neq t_i$. If the selected i leads to a failure later on, we have to be able to modify this selection. One possible approach is to use a second backtracking mechanism for this (besides trying the next rule, if the considered rule leads to a failure).

In order to avoid a very complicated and probably inefficient backtracking scheme, we will use the current backtracking mechanism to handle this second source of backtracking. This constitutes a valuable simplification of the implementation. The idea is that the new constraint, which is generated while "unifying" a formal argument with a constrained variable (as the actual argument), is handled as if it would be part of the guard of the corresponding rule (see rule (R1.2) in Section 4).

Technically, this is accomplished by extending each task node by a pointer to a graphical representation of the boolean expression representing the constraint *cstr* accumulated up to now, that means while unifying the previous arguments with the corresponding formal arguments of the rule (*cstr* initially points to a node for "true"). This pointer will be redirected to the graphical representation of $t \neq t'_1 \wedge \ldots \wedge t \neq t'_k \wedge cstr$ (where $t'_1, \ldots, t'_k$ are all the terms in *tlist*) by the UNIFY command, which is responsible for the unification with t. After the unification phase and before the evaluation of the right hand side this boolean

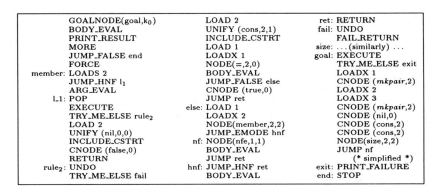

Figure 3: CBAM code for the size example

expression is pushed onto the stack and evaluated. This is done by a new command INCLUDE_CSTRT, which is inserted before label *explb* in the *ruletrans* scheme. Using this idea, constraint propagation is transformed into the evaluation of boolean expressions. The code for the example of Subsection 2.1 is shown in Figure 3.

The attentive reader may have observed that the destination oriented computing ("tag" mechanism) proposed in Section 4 has not been implemented in our abstract machine. In fact, this is not needed, since an equivalent effect can be obtained through a simple program transformation. This transformation is described in detail in [Ku92]. Due to lack of space, we only sketch it here. A rule $f\ t_1\ \dots\ t_n :=$ e is replaced by the sequence of rules $f\ t_1\ \dots\ t_n\ d_{c_i} := e_i'$ $(1 \le i \le m)$ if e may produce $c \in \{c_1, \dots, c_m\}$ as the outermost constructor, and where $d_{c_1}, \dots, d_{c_m}$ are new nullary constructors. Moreover, each application $(f\ e_1\ \dots\ e_n)$ is replaced by $(f\ e_1\ \dots\ e_n\ d)$, where d is the outermost constructor of the desired result. e_i' is the result of transforming e to receive the desired outermost constructor c_i $(1 \le i \le n)$. If arbitrary solutions are allowed, d is a new unbound variable.

6   Conclusions and Future Work

We have presented a variant of the lazy functional logic language BABEL [MR88] [MR92] which incorporates disequality constraints for solving equations and building answers. This enhances the computational power of the language, since disequalities as answers may replace infinitely many answer substitutions. We have developed an operational semantics which combines lazy narrowing with disequality constraint solving. Also a useful optimization, "result oriented computation", has been integrated in a clean way into the operational semantics.

For the implementation of the language, we have shown how the narrowing machine LBAM [MKLR90] can be extended to cope with disequality constraints. The mechanisms are rather independent of the LBAM and can be inserted into other narrowing machines, e.g. the stack based narrowing machine from [Lo91], as well. If there are no disequalities in the program, the machine behaves exactly like the LBAM, and no additional overhead is needed.

We are currently working on the implementation of the presented machine and hope to have a running prototype soon. In the future, we want to extend BABEL also by other kinds of constraints.

References

[BBCMMS89] G.P. Balboni, P.G. Bosco, C. Cecchi, R. Melen, C. Moiso, G. Sofi: Implementation of a Parallel Logic Plus Functional Language, in: P. Treleaven (ed.), *Parallel Computers: Object Oriented, Functional and Logic*, Wiley'89.

[BCGMP89] P.G. Bosco, C. Cecchi, E. Giovannetti, C. Moiso, C. Palamidessi: Using Resolution for a Sound and Efficient Integration of Logic and Functional Programming, in: J. de Bakker (ed.), *Languages for parallel architectures: Design, Semantics, Implementation Models*, Wiley, 1989.

[BL86] M. Bellia, G. Levi: The Relation between Logic and Functional Languages, Journal of Logic Programming, Vol.3, 1986, 217-236.

[CL89] H. Comon, P. Lescanne: Equational problems and disunification. J. of Symbolic Computation, 7, 1989, 371-425.

[Co82] A. Colmerauer: Prolog and infinite trees, in K.L. Clark, S.A. Tarnlund (eds.) Logic Programming, Academic Press, 1982, 231-251.

[Co84] A. Colmerauer: Equations and inequations on finite and infinite trees, Procs. FGCS'84, 1984, 85-99.

[Co90] H. Comon: Unification: A Survey, Tech. Rep. 540, LRI, Orsay, 1990.

[DL86] D. DeGroot, G. Lindstrom (eds.): *Logic Programming: Functions, Relations, Equations*, Prentice Hall, 1986.

[DVSAGB88] M. Dincbas, P. Van Hentenryck, H. Simonis, A. Aggoun, T. Graft, F. Bertheir: The constraint logic programming CHIP, Procs. Int. Conf. 5th Generation Computer Systems, FGCS'88, 1988, 693-702.

[Ha90] M. Hanus: Compiling Logic Programs with Equality, Workshop on Progr. Language Impl. and Logic Progr. (PLILP), LNCS 456, 1990, 387-401.

[HS88] M. Höhfeld, G. Smolka: Definite Relations over Constraint Languages, LI-LOG Report 53, IBM Germany, 1988 (to appear in J. of Logic Progr.).

[JL87] J. Jaffar, J.L. Lassez: Constraint Logic Programming, Procs. 14th ACM Symp. on Princ. of Prog. Lang., 1987, 114-119.

[JMM92] J.A. Jiménez-Martín, J. Mariño-Carballo, J.J. Moreno-Navarro: Efficient Compilation of Lazy Narrowing into Prolog, Procs. LOPSTR'92, to appear in: Springer Verlag, 1992.

[KLMR90] H. Kuchen, R. Loogen, J. J. Moreno-Navarro, M. Rodríguez-Artalejo: Graph-based Implementation of a Functional Logic Language, Procs. ESOP, LNCS 432, 1990, 271-290.

[KLMR92] H. Kuchen, F.J. López-Fraguas, J.J. Moreno-Navarro, M. Rodríguez-Artalejo: Implementing Disequality in a Lazy Functional Logic Language, Tech. Rep. (in preparation).

[Ku92] H. Kuchen: A Program Transformation for Destination Oriented Narrowing, Tech. Report, RWTH Aachen, 1992 (to appear).

[Lo91] R. Loogen: From Reduction Machines to Narrowing Machines, TAPSOFT'91, LNCS 494, 438-457.

[Lo92] F.J. López-Fraguas: A General Scheme for Constraint Functional Logic Programming, to appear in Procs. ALP'92, LNCS.

[LR91] F.J. López-Fraguas, M. Rodríguez-Artalejo: An Approach to Constraint Functional Logic Programming, Tech. Rep. DIA 91/4, 1991.

[Mi78] R. Milner: A Theory of Type Polymorphism in Programming, JCSS 17(3), 1978, 348-375.

[MKLR90] J. J. Moreno-Navarro, H. Kuchen, R. Loogen, M. Rodríguez-Artalejo: Lazy Narrowing in a Graph Machine, ALP, LNCS 463, 1990, 298-317; detailed version appeared as: Aachener Informatik-Bericht Nr. 90-11.

[MR88] J.J. Moreno-Navarro, M. Rodríguez-Artalejo: BABEL: A functional and logic language based and constructor discipline and narrowing, Procs. 1st Int. Conf. on Algebraic and Logic Progr. (ALP), LNCS 343, 1989, 223-232.

[MR92] J.J. Moreno-Navarro, M. Rodríguez-Artalejo: Logic Programming with Functions and Predicates: The Language BABEL, J. Logic Programming, 12, 1992, 189-223.

[Mu90] A. Mück: Compilation of Narrowing, PLILP'90, LNCS 456, 16-39 (1990).

[Re85] U.S. Reddy: Narrowing as the Operational Semantics of Functional Languages, Procs. Int. Symp. on Logic Programming, 1985, 138-151.

[Sm91] D.A. Smith: Constraint Operations for CLP(FT), Procs. 8th Int. Conf. on Logic Programming, MIT Press, 1991, 760-774.

Constraints

A constraint solver in finite algebras and its combination with unification algorithms

Hélène Kirchner & Christophe Ringeissen
CRIN-CNRS & INRIA-Lorraine
BP 239, 54506 Vandœuvre-lès-Nancy Cedex, France
{hkirchner,ringeiss}@loria.fr

Abstract

In the context of constraint logic programming and theorem proving, the development of constraint solvers on algebraic domains and their combination is of prime interest. A constraint solver in finite algebras is presented for a constraint language including equations, disequations and inequations on finite domains. The method takes advantage of the embedding of a finite algebra in a primal algebra that can be presented, up to an isomorphism, by an equational presentation. We also show how to combine this constraint solver in finite algebras with other unification algorithms, by extending the techniques used for the combination of unification.

1 Introduction

Finite algebras provide valuable domains for constraint logic programming. Unification in this context has attracted considerable interest for its applications: it is of practical relevance for manipulating hardware descriptions and solving formulas of propositional calculus; its implementation in constraint logic programming languages allowed the handling of Boolean constraints (CHIP, Prolog III), sets constraints (CAL) and constraints on finite domains (Prolog-XT). A finite algebra can be given a richer structure of primal algebra, in which every finitary function on the carrier can be composed from the basic operations. The 2-elements Boolean algebra is the simplest example of primal algebra, since every truth-function can be expressed in terms of the basic connectives, for instance $\wedge$ (and) and $^-$ (not). Other examples are finite fields, in particular modular arithmetic, Post algebras, matrix rings over finite fields and finite simple nonabelian groups. The interesting feature of these algebras is that matching, unification and disunification are equivalent and unitary. A survey on Boolean unification can be found in [11] and the unification problem in the class of primal algebras and in their varieties is extensively studied in [12]. Implementations are described in [14, 13] for Boolean unification, and in [4, 15] for unification in finite algebras.

The need for combining constraint solving in specific theories (as Booleans) with other function symbols appears in the context of programming and deduction with constraints. For instance, in theorem proving with built-in theories, free constants and function symbols are generated during skolemization. But combination problems also appear in the context of a constraint logic programming language allowing different built-in theories. The approach developed here consists in extending the techniques used to combine unification algorithms.

The combination problem for unification can be stated as follows: given two unification algorithms in two (consistent) equational theories E_1 on $\mathcal{T}(\mathcal{F}_1, \mathcal{X})$ and E_2 on $\mathcal{T}(\mathcal{F}_2, \mathcal{X})$, how to find a unification procedure for $E_1 \cup E_2$ on $\mathcal{T}(\mathcal{F}_1 \cup \mathcal{F}_2, \mathcal{X})$? Combining unification algorithms was initiated in [6, 8, 19, 20] where syntactic conditions on the axioms of the theories to be combined were assumed. Combination of arbitrary theories with disjoint sets of symbols is considered in [2, 17] and the case of theories sharing constants is studied in [16]. The general idea of unification in a combination of theories consists in breaking an equational problem into sub-problems that are pure in the sense that they can be solved in one component of the combination. In order to find solutions for the combined unification problem, the following assumptions should be satisfied, for $i = 1, 2$:

• E_i has a complete unification algorithm with free constants, i.e. a unification algorithm for terms in $\mathcal{T}(\mathcal{F}_i \cup \mathcal{C}, \mathcal{X})$ where $\mathcal{C}$ is an arbitrary set of free constants.

• A complete constant elimination algorithm for E_i is available. This is used for breaking cycles between equations, that appear during the occur-check process.

The problem considered in this paper is the combination of a constraint solver in a finite algebra with another unification algorithm that may be a unification algorithm in any equational theory, including the empty theory. In this context, we are faced to several problems:

• The finite algebras we want to consider are not in general quotient term algebras: they are defined by their carrier and some functions, but do not have an equational presentation. The method we propose here is to embed a finite algebra into a primal algebra and to take advantage of the fact that any primal algebra can be presented, up to an isomorphism, by an equational presentation.

• A unification algorithm for primal algebras was proposed in [4]. We extend it and generalize its proof to a large class of constraints. Using this constraint solver, a constraint is transformed into an equational problem with the same set of solutions.

• In order to combine this constraint solver with another unification algorithm, we need to solve constraints with free constants and to deal with the constant elimination problem in primal algebras. Using the notion of frozen variable, we derive from the constraint solver in primal algebras, a solver for constraints with frozen variables and a complete frozen variable elimination algorithm.

The paper is organized as follows: Section 2 is devoted to the definition and properties of finite and primal algebras and presents the embedding of a finite algebra into a primal algebra. In Section 3, the constraints we want to solve in primal algebras are defined together with their solutions. In Section 4, a constraint solver in primal algebras is presented. Section 5 shows how to combine it with another unification algorithm. The constraint solver for the combination is illustrated on an example. For lack of space, all proofs are omitted but can be found in [10].

2 Finite and primal algebras

In this section, we define the algebraic framework and consider the relationship between finite algebras, primal algebras and Boolean algebras. The main result is Theorem 2 that states an isomorphism between a primal algebra and an adequate term algebra.

Let $\mathcal{F}$ be a set of function symbols, $\mathcal{X}$ a set of variables, and $\mathcal{A}$ an $\mathcal{F}$-algebra, whose carrier is denoted by A. An algebra is finite when its carrier and its set of functions are both finite. $T(\mathcal{F}, \mathcal{X})$ is the free $\mathcal{F}$-algebra over $\mathcal{X}$, whose carrier is the set of terms $T(\mathcal{F}, \mathcal{X})$. Given a set of equational axioms E and the generated congruence $=_E$, the quotient $\mathcal{F}$-algebra is denoted $T(\mathcal{F}, \mathcal{X})/=_E$.

An assignment α is a mapping from $\mathcal{X}$ to A; it uniquely extends to an homomorphism $\underline{\alpha}$ from $T(\mathcal{F}, \mathcal{X})$ to $\mathcal{A}$. The restriction of an assignment α to a set of variables $V \subseteq \mathcal{X}$ is denoted by $\alpha_{|V}$. This notation is extended to sets of assignments. The set of all assignments is denoted by $ASS_A^{\mathcal{X}}$ or ASS_A, when $\mathcal{X}$ is clear from the context.

A term t built on a set of function symbols $\mathcal{F}$ and m variable symbols in an ordered set of variables $\mathcal{X}$, defines a function $t^{\mathcal{A}} : A^m \rightarrow A$ as follows:

$$\forall (a_1, \ldots, a_m) \in A^m, \ t^{\mathcal{A}}(a_1, \ldots, a_m) = \underline{\alpha}(t),$$

where α is an assignment such that $\forall i \in [1 \ldots m]$, $\alpha(x_i) = a_i$ (also denoted by $(x_i \mapsto a_i)$). Conversely,

Definition 1 *[12] An $\mathcal{F}$-algebra $\mathcal{A}$ is* primal *if any finitary function on its carrier A with an arity greater than 0 is equal to $t^{\mathcal{A}}$ for some t in $T(\mathcal{F}, \mathcal{X})$.*

Given a primal $\mathcal{F}$-algebra $\mathcal{A}$ such that $\mathcal{F}$ is a finite set of finitary function symbols, its carrier A is necessarily finite. In the sequel, only finite primal algebras are considered. To any finite algebra, we can associate a primal algebra with the same carrier and an extended set of function symbols.

Definition 2 *Given the $\mathcal{F}$-algebra $\mathcal{A}$ with the carrier $A = \{0, \ldots, n-1\}$, the* enriched finite algebra $\overline{\mathcal{A}}$ *is defined by the carrier A, and the set of function symbols*

$$\overline{\mathcal{F}} = \mathcal{F} \cup \{\bot, [1], \ldots, [n-2], \top, C_0, \ldots, C_{n-1}, +, \cdot\}$$

interpreted as follows:

$\perp_A = 0$

$\top_A = n - 1$

$\forall i \in A \setminus \{0, n-1\}, [i]_A = i$

$\forall i \in A, \forall x \in A, C_{iA}(x) =$ if $x = i$ then $n - 1$ else 0

$\forall (x, y) \in A^2, x +_A y = \max(x, y)$

$\forall (x, y) \in A^2, x \cdot_A y = \min(x, y)$.

Example 1 *The algebra defined by the carrier $A = \{0, 1\}$ together with the set of additional operators of Definition 2 is the 2-elements Boolean algebra where $+$ corresponds to $\vee$ (or), $\cdot$ to $\wedge$ (and), C_0 to $^-$ (not). The operator C_1 is the identity.*

The algebra $\overline{\mathcal{A}}$ is primal [12], since any function $f : A^m \to A$ is equal to the functional interpretation of the term

$$\sum_{(a_1, \ldots, a_m) \in A^m} C_{a_1}(x_1) \cdots C_{a_m}(x_m) \cdot [f(a_1, \ldots, a_m)] \qquad (POST)$$

where $[f(a_1, \ldots, a_m)]$ denotes the operator corresponding to the value taken by the function f on $(a_1, \ldots, a_m)$. Intuitively, this term represents the truth table of the function f.

We now exhibit a finite set AF of equational axioms such that each term $t \in T(\overline{\mathcal{F}}, \mathcal{X})$, is equal modulo AF to a specific canonical form, which is the $(POST)$ decomposition of $t^{\overline{A}}$.

Definition 3 *Let AF be the* finite set of axioms *on $T(\overline{\mathcal{F}}, \mathcal{X})$:*

$$
\begin{aligned}
x + (y + z) &= (x + y) + z & x + \perp &= x \\
x + y &= y + x & x + \top &= \top \\
x \cdot (y \cdot z) &= (x \cdot y) \cdot z & x \cdot \perp &= \perp \\
x \cdot y &= y \cdot x & x \cdot \top &= x \\
x \cdot (y + z) &= x \cdot y + x \cdot z & x + x &= x \\
x + (y \cdot z) &= (x + y) \cdot (x + z) & x \cdot x &= x
\end{aligned}
$$

$$\forall f \in \overline{\mathcal{F}}_p, \forall i \in A, \ C_i(f(x_1, \ldots, x_p)) = \sum_{f_A(i_1, \ldots, i_p) = i} C_{i_1}(x_1) \cdots C_{i_p}(x_p)$$

$$\forall i \in A, \ C_i([i]) = \top$$

$$\forall (i, j) \in A^2, i \neq j, \ C_i(x) \cdot C_j(x) = \perp$$

$$\sum_{i=0}^{n-1} C_i(x) = \top$$

$$\sum_{i=0}^{n-1} C_i(x) \cdot [i] = x$$

Example 2 *If we consider the domain size $n = 2$ and $\mathcal{F} = \emptyset$, the set of axioms given above generates the Boolean theory.*

Theorem 1 *Any term t in $T(\overline{\mathcal{F}}, \mathcal{X})$ is equal modulo AF to its* canonical form:

$$\sum_{\{\alpha: \mathcal{V}(t) \to A\}} \prod_{x \in \mathcal{V}(t)} C_{\alpha(x)}(x) \cdot [\underline{\alpha}(t)].$$

Proof: see [10]. □

The canonical form of t must be compared to the previous decomposition $(POST)$ where f corresponds to $t^{\overline{A}}$ and $f(a_1, \dots, a_m)$ to $\underline{\alpha}(t)$. In order to simplify notation, the product $\prod_{x \in V} C_{\alpha(x)}(x)$ will be denoted by $\prod \alpha(V)$ and called atom.[1]

Theorem 1 leads to the next result, useful in the context of constraint solving in primal algebras, since it justifies to work at the level of terms instead of functions and values.

Theorem 2 *The $\overline{\mathcal{F}}$-algebras $\overline{A}$ and $T(\overline{\mathcal{F}}, \mathcal{X})/{=}_{AF}$ have the same equational theorems: for any universally quantified equality $(t = t')$, $\overline{A} \models (t = t')$ iff $t =_{AF} t'$. Moreover, $\overline{A}$ and $T(\overline{\mathcal{F}})/{=}_{AF}$ are isomorphic.*

Corollary 1 *The presentation $(\overline{\mathcal{F}}, AF)$ is ω-complete, i.e. the algebras $T(\overline{\mathcal{F}}, \mathcal{X})/{=}_{AF}$ and $T(\overline{\mathcal{F}})/{=}_{AF}$ have the same equational theorems: for any universally quantified equality $(t = t')$, $T(\overline{\mathcal{F}})/{=}_{AF} \models (t = t')$ iff $t =_{AF} t'$.*

A direct proof of these results can be found in [10], but they could also be obtained as consequences of more general results on the variety of primal algebras given in [5].

3 Constraint languages

We now define a constraint language for the class of constraints we want to solve in finite algebras. We also make precise the notions of solutions and complete sets of symbolic solutions for a given constraint.

A *substitution* is an endomorphism of $T(\mathcal{F}, \mathcal{X})$. We call *domain* of the substitution σ the set of variables $\mathcal{D}om(\sigma) = \{x | x \in \mathcal{X}$ *and* $\sigma(x) \neq x\}$ that are not mapped to themselves, *range* of σ the set of terms $\mathcal{R}an(\sigma) = \cup_{x \in \mathcal{D}om(\sigma)} \sigma(x)$ and *variable range* of σ the set of variables $\mathcal{V}\mathcal{R}an(\sigma) = \cup_{x \in \mathcal{D}om(\sigma)} \mathcal{V}(\sigma(x))$. We use letters $\sigma, \mu, \gamma, \phi, \dots$ to denote substitutions. Substitutions are partially ordered by subsumption ordering, as follows: Given a (possibly empty) set of equational axioms E and the generated congruence $=_E$, a substitution ϕ is an *E-instance* on $V \subseteq \mathcal{X}$ of a substitution σ, written $\sigma \leq^V_E \phi$ (and read as σ is more general modulo E than ϕ on V), if there exists some substitution μ such that $\forall x \in V$, $\phi(x) =_E \mu(\sigma(x))$.

Definition 4 *[18, 9] Let $\mathcal{F}$ be a set of function symbols and $\mathcal{P}$ a set of predicates, a constraint language $CL_\kappa[\mathcal{F}, \mathcal{P}]$ is given by:*

---

[1]The atom terminology comes from Boolean algebras.

- *a set of* constraints *which are first-order existentially quantified formulae built over* $\mathcal{T}(\mathcal{F}, \mathcal{X})$ *and predicates* $\mathcal{P}$.

- $\mathcal{V}(c)$ *the set of free variables of the constraint* c.

- *a non-empty set* κ *of interpretations* $\mathcal{K}$. *Each interpretation* $\mathcal{K}$ *is given by a domain* K *and a solution mapping that associates to each constraint the set of assignments* $Sol_\mathcal{K}(c)$ *defined as follows:*

  - $Sol_\mathcal{K}(p(t_1, \ldots, t_j)) = \{\alpha \in ASS_K^\mathcal{X} \mid (\underline{\alpha}(t_1), \ldots, \underline{\alpha}(t_j)) \in p_\mathcal{K}\}$.
  - $Sol_\mathcal{K}(c \wedge c') = Sol_\mathcal{K}(c) \cap Sol_\mathcal{K}(c')$.
  - $Sol_\mathcal{K}(\neg c) = ASS_K^\mathcal{X} \backslash Sol_\mathcal{K}(c)$.
  - $Sol_\mathcal{K}(\exists x : c) = \{\alpha \in ASS_K^\mathcal{X} \mid$ *there exists* $\alpha' \in Sol_\mathcal{K}(c)$ *such that* $\alpha_{|\mathcal{V}(c)\backslash\{x\}} = \alpha'_{|\mathcal{V}(c)\backslash\{x\}}\}$

An assignment in $Sol_\mathcal{K}(c)$ *is* a *solution of* c *in* $\mathcal{K}$. *A constraint* c *is valid in* $\mathcal{K}$, *written* $\mathcal{K} \models c$, *if any assignment is a solution of* c *in* $\mathcal{K}$. *A constraint* c *is valid in* $CL_\kappa[\mathcal{F}, \mathcal{P}]$, *written* $CL_\kappa[\mathcal{F}, \mathcal{P}] \models c$, *if* c *is valid in any interpretation* $\mathcal{K}$ *of* κ.

As usual, we can also define abbreviations $\vee, \Rightarrow, \Leftrightarrow$ to write more complex constraints.

Two constraints c and c' are *equivalent* if they have the same set of solutions in any interpretation. This is equivalent to write that $CL_\kappa[\mathcal{F}, \mathcal{P}] \models (c \Leftrightarrow c')$.

A *symbolic solution* of a $CL_\kappa[\mathcal{F}, \mathcal{P}]$-constraint c is a substitution σ such that $CL_\kappa[\mathcal{F}, \mathcal{P}] \models \sigma(c)$. A substitution ϕ is an $CL_\kappa[\mathcal{F}, \mathcal{P}]$-*instance* on $V \subseteq \mathcal{X}$ of a substitution σ, written $\sigma \leq_\kappa^V \phi$, if there exists some substitution μ such that $\forall x \in V, CL_\kappa[\mathcal{F}, \mathcal{P}] \models \phi(x) = \mu(\sigma(x))$.

Definition 5 *A set of substitutions is* a *complete set of solutions of the* $CL_\kappa[\mathcal{F}, \mathcal{P}]$-*constraint* c, *denoted by* $CSS(c)$, *if*
(1) $\forall \sigma \in CSS(c), \mathcal{D}om(\sigma) \cap \mathcal{V}Ran(\sigma) = \emptyset$ *and* $\mathcal{D}om(\sigma) \subseteq \mathcal{V}(c)$.
(2) Each substitution in $CSS(c)$ *is a symbolic solution of* c.
(3) For any symbolic solution ϕ *of* c, *there exists* $\sigma \in CSS(c)$ *such that* $\sigma \leq_\kappa^{\mathcal{V}(c)} \phi$.
When two substitutions of $CSS(c)$ *cannot be compared with* $\leq_\kappa^{\mathcal{V}(c)}$, *the complete set of solutions* $CSS(c)$ *is minimal. If such a set is reduced to one element, this element is denoted* $mgs(c)$.

In this paper, we focus our interest on some particular constraint languages:
• An equational presentation $(\mathcal{F}, E)$ defines an *equational* constraint language $CL_E[\mathcal{F}, \{=^?\}]$ where constraints are *equational* constraints that is first-order equational formulae built over $\mathcal{T}(\mathcal{F}, \mathcal{X})$. The standard interpretation is the quotient algebra $\mathcal{T}(\mathcal{F}, \mathcal{X})/ =_E$. A symbolic solution is a

E-unifier. A complete set of solutions of a $CL_E[\mathcal{F}, \{=^?\}]$-constraint c is denoted $CSS_E(c)$ or $CSU_E(c)$ since it is also a *complete set of E-unifiers*. For instance, if $\mathcal{F} = \{a, f\}$, $\mathcal{X} = \{v, x, y\}$ and E consists of the associativity and commutativity axioms for f, then $(f(v, x) =^? f(a, f(x, y)))$ is an equational constraint.

• The $\overline{\mathcal{F}}$-algebra $\overline{A}$ (isomorphic to $T(\overline{\mathcal{F}})/ =_{AF}$), together with a set of relations $\mathcal{P}_A$ on A, is the standard interpretation of the *primal constraint language* $CL_{AF}[\overline{\mathcal{F}}, \mathcal{P}]$. $CSS_{AF}(c)$ denotes a complete set of solutions of the $CL_{AF}[\overline{\mathcal{F}}, \mathcal{P}]$-constraint c. In this constraint language, we show in the next section that a minimal complete set of solutions contains at most one element. Several predicates are interesting in practice for expressing constraints on finite domains: these are equality, disequality and ordering predicates. For instance, if $\mathcal{F} = \{0, 1, C_0, +, \cdot\}$, $\mathcal{P} = \{=^?, \neq^?, >^?\}$, $\mathcal{X} = \{v, w, x, y, z\}$, $(x =^? z \cdot (z + 1))$, $(x + y =^? v \cdot w)$, $(x \cdot y >^? z + 1)$, are elementary constraints of this primal constraint language.

4   Constraint solving in primal algebras

Unification in primal algebras has been studied in [12] by generalizing algorithms for solving equations in finite Boolean algebras. We address here the more general problem of solving any constraint expressed in the previously defined primal constraint language. Our proof technique is derived from [4], where a method is proposed for computing a most general unifier in a primal algebra whose domain is of cardinality n.

In the context of a finite algebra, the set $Sol(c)$ of solutions of a constraint c is usually easy to compute since the domain A is finite: just consider all assignments of variables to their possible values and check for each of them whether the constraint is satisfied. But we are rather interested in a more compact representation of the set of solutions, provided by a complete set of solutions, or even better by a most general solution. To analyze the problem, let us first characterize a most general solution σ of c thanks to a surjective mapping between assignments from $ASS_A^{\mathcal{V}(\sigma(c))}$ to $Sol(c)$.

For a given c, a substitution σ defines a mapping $\sigma_c : ASS_A^{\mathcal{V}(\sigma(c))} \mapsto ASS_A^{\mathcal{V}(c)}$, which maps any $\alpha \in ASS_A^{\mathcal{V}(\sigma(c))}$ to the assignment defined by $\forall x \in \mathcal{V}(c)$, $\sigma_c(\alpha)(x) = \underline{\alpha}(\sigma(x))$. This relation extends by straightforward induction, to terms built on $\mathcal{V}(c)$. Let $\mathcal{I}(\sigma_c)$ denote the range of σ_c: $\mathcal{I}(\sigma_c) = \{\sigma_c(\alpha) | \alpha \in ASS_A^{\mathcal{V}(\sigma(c))}\}$.

Example 3 *In the 2-elements Boolean algebra, consider the equation* $c = (x =^? x + y)$ *and the substitution* $\sigma = \{y \mapsto x\}$. σ_c *maps the assignment* $(x \mapsto 0)$ *onto* $(x \mapsto 0)(y \mapsto 0)$ *and* $(x \mapsto 1)$ *onto* $(x \mapsto 1)(y \mapsto 1)$.

The next result reduces the symbolic solving problem to a necessary and sufficient condition on σ_c.

Proposition 1 *A substitution σ is a symbolic solution of the constraint c if and only if $\mathcal{I}(\sigma_c) \subseteq Sol(c)_{|\mathcal{V}(c)}$. If there exists a substitution σ such that $\mathcal{I}(\sigma_c) = Sol(c)_{|\mathcal{V}(c)}$, σ is a most general solution of c.*

Proof: The proof (cf. [10]) uses an intermediate result: let σ and σ' be two substitutions and c a constraint; $\mathcal{I}(\sigma'_c) \subseteq \mathcal{I}(\sigma_c)$ if and only if $\sigma \leq_{AF}^{\mathcal{V}(c)} \sigma'$. □

Now the problem is to prove the existence of such a substitution σ. This is done by giving explicitly the construction of a mapping σ_c from assignments of new variables Y (introduced to express all assignments $\alpha : \mathcal{V}(\sigma(c)) \mapsto A$) to assignments of variables $\mathcal{V}(c)$. The number of new variables in Y must be chosen as small as possible but satisfying the condition $n^{|Y|} \geq |Sol(c)_{|\mathcal{V}(c)}|$. Indeed since σ_c is a mapping, we necessarily have

$$|ASS_A^Y| \geq |\mathcal{I}(\sigma_c)| = |Sol(c)_{|\mathcal{V}(c)}|.$$

Moreover $|ASS_A^Y|$ is equal to $|A|^{|Y|}$ where $|A| = n$. In the worst case, $|Y|$ is equal to $|\mathcal{V}(c)|$. Then any surjective mapping of ASS_A^Y onto $Sol(c)_{|\mathcal{V}(c)}$ can be used as the mapping σ_c.

Example 4 *In the 2-elements Boolean algebra, consider the equation $c = (x + yz =^? xyz)$, where the $\cdot$ symbol is omitted. An assignment (for instance $\beta = (x \mapsto 0)(y \mapsto 0)(z \mapsto 0)$) is next abusively denoted by its atom ($\bar{x}\bar{y}\bar{z}$ for β)). The reader can check that $Sol(c) = \{\bar{x}\bar{y}\bar{z}, \bar{x}\bar{y}z, \bar{x}y\bar{z}, xyz\}$. We need two new variables y_1 and y_2, since $2^{|Y|} \geq 4$ implies $|Y| = 2$ as the smallest possibility. Then the mapping σ_c can be chosen as follows:*

$$\sigma_c(\bar{y}_1\bar{y}_2) = \bar{x}\bar{y}\bar{z} \quad \sigma_c(\bar{y}_1 y_2) = \bar{x}\bar{y}z \quad \sigma_c(y_1\bar{y}_2) = \bar{x}y\bar{z} \quad \sigma_c(y_1 y_2) = xyz$$

We are now able to explicit a most general solution, thanks to the canonical form of $\sigma(x)$ in the theory AF, for each $x \in \mathcal{V}(c)$.

Theorem 3 *Let c be a constraint, Y a finite set of variables disjoint of $\mathcal{V}(c)$ and σ_c a mapping from ASS_A^Y to $ASS_A^{\mathcal{V}(c)}$ such that $\mathcal{I}(\sigma_c) = Sol(c)_{|\mathcal{V}(c)}$. The substitution*

$$\sigma = \{x \mapsto \sum_{\{\alpha:Y \to A\}} \prod \alpha(Y) \cdot [\sigma_c(\alpha)(x)]\}_{x \in \mathcal{V}(c)}$$

is a most general solution of c.

Proof: According to Theorem 1, for any $x \in \mathcal{V}(c)$,

$$\sigma(x) =_{AF} \sum_{\{\alpha:Y \to A\}} \prod \alpha(Y) \cdot [\underline{\alpha}(\sigma(x))]$$

and $\underline{\alpha}(\sigma(x)) = \sigma_c(\alpha)(x)$ by construction. □

Example 5 *(Example 4 continued: $c = (x + yz =^? xyz)$). $\sigma_c(\alpha)(x) = 1$ if α corresponds to the atom $y_1 y_2$, $\sigma_c(\alpha)(y) = 1$ if α is $y_1\bar{y}_2$ or $y_1 y_2$, $\sigma_c(\alpha)(z) = 1$ if α is $\bar{y}_1 y_2$ or $y_1 y_2$. After simplication, we get $mgs(c) = \{x \mapsto y_1 y_2, y \mapsto y_1, z \mapsto y_2\}$.*

5 Combination problem

We now consider the problem of combining two constraint languages on disjoint signatures, by extending the definition of the union of equational theories.

Definition 6 *Let $\mathcal{F}_1$ and $\mathcal{F}_2$ be disjoint signatures: $\mathcal{F}_1 \cap \mathcal{F}_2 = \emptyset$. The combined constraint language CC of two constraint languages $CL_{\kappa_1}[\mathcal{F}_1, \mathcal{P}_1]$ and $CL_{\kappa_2}[\mathcal{F}_2, \mathcal{P}_2]$ is the constraint language $CL_\kappa[\mathcal{F}_1 \cup \mathcal{F}_2, \mathcal{P}_1 \cup \mathcal{P}_2]$ such that κ is the set of interpretations preserving the validity of $CL_{\kappa_1}[\mathcal{F}_1, \mathcal{P}_1]$-constraints and $CL_{\kappa_2}[\mathcal{F}_2, \mathcal{P}_2]$-constraints.*

In the more specific case of combining the primal constraint language $CL_{AF}[\overline{\mathcal{F}}, \mathcal{P}]$ with another equational constraint language $CL_E[\mathcal{F}_2, \{=^?\}]$, $(\mathcal{F}_1, E_1) = (\overline{\mathcal{F}}, AF)$, $\mathcal{P}_1 = \mathcal{P}$ and $\mathcal{P}_2 = \{=^?\}$. The key idea is that solving any constraint in a primal algebra will result in a unique solved form, its most general solution, that can be considered as a conjunction of equational constraints. This enables us to extend the tools for combining unification problems.

The combination of the two constraint solvers relies on three operations: *abstraction* that produces pure constraints in one language by replacing subterms by new variables existentially quantified; *solving pure constraints with frozen variables* in each language, to take into account that shared variables cannot be instantiated independently; *frozen variable elimination* for breaking cycles of the form $x_1 =^? t_1[x_2] \wedge \ldots \wedge x_q =^? t_q[x_1]$ where $t_1, \ldots, t_q$ are non-variable terms pure alternately in each constraint language.

The solving process applied on a pure primal constraint c returns a most general solution of c. Let $\widehat{mgs}(c)$ denote the most general solution of the $CL_{AF}[\overline{\mathcal{F}}, \mathcal{P}]$-constraint c written as an equational constraint. Indeed, since $CL_{AF}[\overline{\mathcal{F}}, \mathcal{P}] \models c \Leftrightarrow \widehat{mgs}(c)$, $CC \models c \Leftrightarrow \widehat{mgs}(c)$. In other words, c and $\widehat{mgs}(c)$ have the same set of solutions in both the primal constraint language and the combined constrained language CC.

Variable abstraction transforms an heterogeneous atomic constraint $p(t_1, \ldots, t_j)$ where at some position ω in the term t_i, the function symbol $t_i(\omega) \notin \overline{\mathcal{F}}$, into the constraint $\exists x : p(t_1, \ldots, t_i[x]_\omega, \ldots, t_j) \wedge x = t_{i|\omega}$ where x is a new variable. By repeatedly applying this transformation, an heterogeneous atomic constraint is transformed into the conjunction of a pure atomic primal constraint with equational constraints. To summarize, for any CC-constraint c, there exists an equational constraint c' such that $CSS_{CC}(c) = CSU_{AF \cup E}(c')$. This property justifies to reuse the same techniques for breaking cycles as in the equational theories combination [1, 17], once pure constraints have been solved.

5.1 Constraint solving w.r.t. frozen variables

The $CL_{AF}[\mathcal{F}, \mathcal{P}]$-constraint solver is easily modified to avoid instantiation of frozen variables.

A *complete set of solutions* $CSS(c, \mathcal{M})$ of the constraint c w.r.t. frozen variables $\mathcal{M} \subseteq \mathcal{V}(c)$ is defined from Definition 5 by modifying the point (1): $\forall \sigma \in CSS(c, \mathcal{M})$, $\mathcal{D}om(\sigma) \subseteq \mathcal{V}(c) \backslash \mathcal{M}$. When a minimal $CSS(c, \mathcal{M})$ is at most a singleton, $mgs(c, \mathcal{M})$ denotes this unique element.

From now on, an assignment $\delta \in ASS_A^{\mathcal{M}}$ corresponds to a substitution δ, obtained by replacing the value $\delta(x) \in A$ by the corresponding constant $[\delta(x)] \in \mathcal{F}$. The substitution $mgs(c, \mathcal{M})$ is computed from the most general solutions of each constraint $\delta(c)$, thanks to the following remark that $\sigma \in CSS(c, \mathcal{M})$ if and only if for any instantiation δ of frozen variables, $\delta \circ \sigma \in CSS(\delta(c), \emptyset)$.

Theorem 4 *Let c be a constraint and $\mathcal{M}$ a set of variables included in $\mathcal{V}(c)$. The substitution*

$$\{x \mapsto \sum_\delta \prod \delta(\mathcal{M}) \cdot mgs(\delta(c))(x)\}_{x \in \mathcal{V}(c) \backslash \mathcal{M}}$$

is a most general solution of c with frozen variables $\mathcal{M}$.

Example 6 *(Example 4 continued: $c = (x + yz =^? xyz)$). Assume $\mathcal{M} = \{x\}$. We need to consider $c0 = \mathbf{0} + yz =^? \mathbf{0}yz$ where $Sol(c0) = \{\bar{y}\bar{z}, \bar{y}z, y\bar{z}\}$ and $c1 = \mathbf{1} + yz =^? \mathbf{1}yz$ where $Sol(c1) = \{yz\}$. Hence $mgs(c1) = \{y \mapsto 1, z \mapsto 1\}$ and the mapping*

$$\sigma_{c0}(\bar{y}_1 \bar{y}_2) = \bar{y}\bar{z} \quad \sigma_{c0}(\bar{y}_1 y_2) = \bar{y}z \quad \sigma_{c0}(y_1 \bar{y}_2) = y\bar{z} \quad \sigma_{c0}(y_1 y_2) = y\bar{z}$$

yields $mgs(c0) = \{y \mapsto y_1, z \mapsto \bar{y}_1 y_2\}$.
The terms $\bar{x} \cdot mgs(c0)(y) + x \cdot mgs(c1)(y)$ and $\bar{x} \cdot mgs(c0)(z) + x \cdot mgs(c1)(z)$ are respectively associated to y and z:
$mgs(c, \mathcal{M}) = \{y \mapsto \bar{x}y_1 + x, z \mapsto \bar{x}\bar{y}_1 y_2 + x\}$.

5.2 Frozen variable elimination

Let us now consider the problem of cycles of the form $x_1 =^? t_1[x_2] \wedge \ldots \wedge x_q =^? t_q[x_1]$ where $t_1, \ldots, t_q$ are non-variable terms pure alternately in each constraint language. Such cycles may have solutions in the combined constraint language. In order to find them, we need to discover instantiations that transform this cycle into another system from which solutions can be computed. This is the purpose of variable elimination.

Definition 7 *A term u is eliminating x in t w.r.t. frozen variables $\mathcal{M}$ if $x \notin u, x \notin \mathcal{M}$ and $t \leq_{AF}^{\overline{\mathcal{M} \cup \{x\}}} u$ i.e. $\exists \sigma$ s.t. $\sigma(t) =_{AF} u$ and $\mathcal{D}om(\sigma) \cap (\mathcal{M} \cup \{x\}) = \emptyset$. The set of all such terms is denoted by $STE(x, t, \mathcal{M})$. The substitution σ is an eliminator of x in t. The set of eliminators of x in t is denoted by $SE(x, t, \mathcal{M})$.*

Example 7 *Let us consider the Boolean term* $t = x + y$. *The substitution* $\phi = \{y \mapsto \bar{x}\}$ *is an eliminator of* x *in* t. *The term* $\top$ *is eliminating* x *in* t. *The substitution* $\sigma = \{y \mapsto \bar{x} + z\}$ *is also an eliminator but is more general than* ϕ.

Definition 8 *A set of terms is a* complete set of terms eliminating x *in* t *w.r.t frozen variables* $\mathcal{M}$, *denoted by* $CSTE(x, t, \mathcal{M})$, *if*
(1) $CSTE(x, t, \mathcal{M}) \subseteq STE(x, t, \mathcal{M})$.
(2) $\forall u \in STE(x, t, \mathcal{M}) \; \exists s \in CSTE(x, t, \mathcal{M}), \; s \leq_{AF}^{\overline{\mathcal{M} \cup \{x\}}} u$.
A $CSTE(x, t, \mathcal{M})$ *is* minimal *if two terms of* $CSTE(x, t, \mathcal{M})$ *cannot be compared with* $\leq_{AF}^{\overline{\mathcal{M} \cup \{x\}}}$. *When such a set is at most a singleton,* $mgte(x, t, \mathcal{M})$ *denotes this unique element.*

A complete set of eliminators of x in t, denoted by $CSE(x, t, \mathcal{M})$, is defined just like for CSS.

A term u eliminating x in t is built as follows: let $Common(x, t)$ be the set of values of t independent of the value taken by x. Formally, $Common(x, t) = \cap_{i \in A} Val(\{x \mapsto [i]\}(t))$ where $Val(t) = \{\underline{\alpha}(t) \mid \alpha \in ASS_A\}$. There is a strong connection between the inclusion $\subseteq$ on value sets and the subsumption quasi-ordering $\leq_{AF}$ on terms: $Val(u) \subseteq Val(t)$ if and only if $t \leq_{AF} u$. If u does not contain x and $t \leq_{AF} u$ then values of u are independent of those taken by x and are values of t. So $Val(u) \subseteq Common(x, t)$. Moreover, as shown next, there exists a term u satisfying $Val(u) = Common(x, t)$: it is the most general term eliminating x in t.

Theorem 5 *The problem of finding a complete set of most general terms eliminating* x *in* t *is unitary in (enriched) finite algebras.*
• *If* $\mathcal{M} = \emptyset$ *then* $mgte(x, t, \emptyset) = \sum_{i \in A} C_i(v) \cdot [S(i)]$, *where* v *is a new variable* $(v \notin V(t))$ *and* $S : A \mapsto Common(x, t)$ *is a surjective mapping.*
• *If* $\mathcal{M} \neq \emptyset$ *then* $mgte(x, t, \mathcal{M}) = \sum_\delta \prod \delta(\mathcal{M}) \cdot mgte(x, \delta(t), \emptyset)$.

Again the computation of the most general eliminator with frozen variables is based on the remark that $u \in CSTE(x, t, \mathcal{M})$ if and only if for any instantiation δ of frozen variables, $\delta(u) \in CSTE(x, \delta(t), \emptyset)$.

Example 8 *If* t *is a Boolean term without frozen variable* $(\mathcal{M} = \emptyset)$ *non equivalent to* x, *then we can choose* $mgte(x, t, \emptyset) = v$ *when* $Common(x, t) = \{0, 1\}$, *or* $mgte(x, t, \emptyset) = \mathbf{0}$ *(resp.* $\mathbf{1}$*) when* $Common(x, t) = \{0\}$ *(resp.* $\{1\}$*).*

Constraint solving w.r.t. frozen variables provides the most general eliminator: this is the most general solution of $(t =^? u)$ that does not instantiate x and v.

Theorem 6 *The frozen variable elimination problem is unitary in (enriched) finite algebras. A unique most general eliminator of* x *in* t *is* $mgs(t =^? mgte(x, t, \mathcal{M}), \mathcal{M} \cup \{x, v\})$ *where* $\mathcal{M} \cup \{v\}$ *are variables in* $mgte(x, t, \mathcal{M})$.

Example 9 *Let t be the Boolean term $\bar{x}(\bar{y}+y\bar{z})+xyz$. Since $Common(x,t)$*
$= \{0,1\}$, we consider $c = (t =^? v)$ where x and v are frozen, that is:
$c00 = \{x \mapsto \mathbf{0}, v \mapsto \mathbf{0}\}(c)$ with $Sol(c00) = \{yz\}$.
$c01 = \{x \mapsto \mathbf{0}, v \mapsto \mathbf{1}\}(c)$ with $Sol(c01) = \{\bar{y}\bar{z}, \bar{y}z, y\bar{z}\}$.
$c10 = \{x \mapsto \mathbf{1}, v \mapsto \mathbf{0}\}(c)$ with $Sol(c10) = \{\bar{y}\bar{z}, \bar{y}z, y\bar{z}\}$.
$c11 = \{x \mapsto \mathbf{1}, v \mapsto \mathbf{1}\}(c)$ with $Sol(c11) = \{yz\}$.
Hence $mgs(c00) = mgs(c11) = \{y \mapsto \mathbf{1}, z \mapsto \mathbf{1}\}$ and $mgs(c01) = mgs(c10) =$
$\{y \mapsto y_1, z \mapsto \bar{y}_1 y_2\}$ thanks to the mapping

$$\sigma_{c01}(\bar{y}_1\bar{y}_2) = \bar{y}\bar{z} \quad \sigma_{c01}(\bar{y}_1 y_2) = \bar{y}z \quad \sigma_{c01}(y_1\bar{y}_2) = y\bar{z} \quad \sigma_{c01}(y_1 y_2) = y\bar{z}$$

Finally, $mgs(c, \{x, v\}) = \{y \mapsto \bar{x}\bar{v} + \bar{x}vy_1 + x\bar{v}y_1 + xv, z \mapsto \bar{x}\bar{v} + \bar{x}v\bar{y}_1 y_2 +$
$x\bar{v}\bar{y}_1 y_2 + xv\}$.

5.3   Rules for combination

We adopt the methodology used in [7] to describe unification algorithms by
sets of rules transforming conjunctions of equations. Rules for constraint
solving in CC are given below. The parameters of these combination rules
are:

• a constraint c: it is a conjunction of atomic constraints and equations. The
constraint c_i denotes the $CL_{E_i}[\mathcal{F}_i, \mathcal{P}_i]$-constraint included in c, for $i = 1, 2$.
• two sets U_1 and U_2 of variables (initially empty) to "freeze", one for each
equational theory E_i. U denotes the union $U_1 \cup U_2$.
• two sets CV_1 and CV_2 of pairs of variables (initially empty) to record cycles, one for each equational theory E_i. CV denotes the union $CV_1 \cup CV_2$.

The combination rules for constraint solving in CC

1. Solve
$$\frac{c \wedge c_i, U, CV}{c \wedge \bigwedge_{l \in L} x_l =^? s_l, U, CV} \quad \text{if } \{x_l \mapsto s_l\}_{l \in L} \in Solve(c_i, U_i, CV_i).$$

2. Variable Abstraction(Constraint)
$$\frac{c \wedge p(t_1, \ldots, t_j), U, CV}{c \wedge p(t_1, \ldots, t_l[x]_\omega, \ldots, t_j) \wedge x =^? t_{l|\omega}, U, CV} \quad \text{if } \begin{cases} t_l(\omega) \notin \overline{\mathcal{F}} \\ x \text{ is a new variable.} \end{cases}$$

3. Variable Abstraction(Equation)
$$\frac{c \wedge s =^? t, U, CV}{c \wedge s =^? t[x]_\omega \wedge x =^? t_{l|\omega}, U, CV} \quad \text{if } \begin{cases} t(\omega) \in \mathcal{F}_i, t(\epsilon) \in \mathcal{F}_j, i \neq j \\ x \text{ is a new variable.} \end{cases}$$

4. Impure Equation
$$\frac{c \wedge s =^? t, U, CV}{c \wedge x =^? s \wedge x =^? t, U, CV} \quad \text{if } \begin{cases} s \in T(\mathcal{F}_1, \mathcal{X}) \backslash \mathcal{X}, t \in T(\mathcal{F}_2, \mathcal{X}) \backslash \mathcal{X} \\ x \text{ is a new variable.} \end{cases}$$

5. Variable Replacement
$$\frac{c \wedge x =^? y, U, CV}{\{x \mapsto y\}(c) \wedge x =^? y, \{x \mapsto y\}(U), \{x \mapsto y\}(CV)} \quad \text{if } x, y \in \mathcal{V}(c).$$

6. **Freeze**

$$\frac{c, U_i, CV}{c, U_i \cup \{x\}, CV} \quad \text{if} \begin{cases} x =^? s, \ x =^? t \text{ are equations in } c \\ s \in T(\mathcal{F}_1, \mathcal{X}) \backslash \mathcal{X}, \ t \in T(\mathcal{F}_2, \mathcal{X}) \backslash \mathcal{X}, \ x \notin U \end{cases}$$

7. **Elim_1** $\dfrac{c, U_i, CV_i}{c, U_i \cup \{y\}, CV_i \cup \{(y,x)\}}$ **Elim_2** $\dfrac{c, U_i, CV}{c, U_i \cup \{x\}, CV}$

if $x =^? t[y]$, where $t \in T(\mathcal{F}_i, \mathcal{X}) \backslash \mathcal{X}$, is in a compound cycle in c.

Rules Solve, Freeze and Elim introduce nondeterminism: one must try all branches to preserve a complete set of solutions. If E is a simple theory, that is a theory such that $x =^? t[x]$ has no solution, then rules Freeze and Elim may be deleted for this theory.

The rule **Solve** assumes the existence for each component of a "black-box" which transforms a pure constraint c_i to its solved form. It performs the successive application of variable identification, solving with frozen variables and frozen variable elimination.

Definition 9 *Given c_i a $CL_{E_i}[\mathcal{F}_i, \mathcal{P}_i]$-constraint, U_i a set of variables and CV_i a set of pairs of variables, the set of restricted solutions of c_i, denoted by $Solve(c_i, U_i, CV_i)$, is the set of all substitutions $\sigma_3 \circ \sigma_2 \circ \sigma_1$ such that*
(1) $\sigma_1 \in ID(U_i) = \{\sigma | \mathcal{D}om(\sigma) \subseteq U_i \text{ and } \mathcal{R}an(\sigma) \subseteq \mathcal{X}\}$.
(2) $\sigma_2 \in CSS(\sigma_1(c_i), \mathcal{VR}an(\sigma_1))$.
(3) $\sigma_3 \in CSE(\sigma_1(x), \sigma_2(y), \mathcal{VR}an(\sigma_1) \backslash \{\sigma_1(x)\})$ for all $(x,y) \in CV_i$.

The next completeness result can be derived from [1, 2].

Theorem 7 *The process of applying the combination rules as long as possible starting from $(c, \emptyset, \emptyset)$ terminates with any control and returns a complete set of solutions of c.*

Example 10 *Let us consider the combination of the Commutative theory defined by two function symbols $\{a, f\}$ and the axiom $C = \{f(x,y) = f(y,x)\}$, with the theory of the primal algebra 3 with function symbols $\{0, 1, 2, C_0, C_1, C_2, +, \cdot\}$. The following equational constraint $f(v, x) =^? f(a, f(x, y)) \wedge y =^? v \cdot w \wedge x =^? z \cdot (z+1)$ where a is a free constant may be solved as follows: First, we solve the first equation in the theory C. Then we obtain $x =^? a \wedge v =^? f(x, y) \wedge y =^? v \cdot w \wedge x =^? z \cdot (z+1)$. The variable x is instantiated in both theories. So x must be frozen in 3 and the related equation solved. We obtain $x =^? a \wedge v =^? f(x, y) \wedge y =^? v \cdot w \wedge z =^? x$. There still exists a compound cycle $v =^? f(x, y) \wedge y =^? v \cdot w$ which can be broken:*
At first the variable v is frozen and two cases must be considered:
(1) x and v are identified: it yields $a =^? f(x, y)$ which has no solution.
(2) v is eliminated in $v \cdot w$: it yields $w =^? C_0(v) \cdot z'$ and $y =^? 0$. The new variable z' appears during the frozen variable elimination process.
Finally we get the dag solved form $x =^? a \wedge v =^? f(x, y) \wedge y =^? 0 \wedge z =^? x \wedge w =^? C_0(v) \cdot z'$ and the corresponding solution $\{x \mapsto a, v \mapsto f(a, 0), y \mapsto 0, z \mapsto a, w \mapsto C_0(f(a, 0)) \cdot z'\}$.

6 Conclusion

A constraint solver for the combination of constraints on finite domains with AC-unification problems is being implemented in the software UNIF, developed at CRIN and INRIA-Lorraine. A feature to emphasize is that the implementation of the constraint solver on finite domains uses, as data structures, n-ary dags, a natural extension of binary decision graphs introduced by Bryant [3]. This data structure exactly reflects the set of assignments for a constraint and operations on these dags correspond to the constructions expressed by the unification algorithm in primal algebras.

To conclude, let us mention some further ideas. The techniques used in this paper extend to pseudo-boolean constraints (equations and inequations between integer-valued functions $f : \{0,1\}^n \mapsto Z$). Such constraint solvers can thus be combined with other unification algorithms with similar techniques. The combination of constraint solvers in two primal algebras is another application of the same techniques. It has interesting applications to hardware validation, for instance to mix specifications of componenets using different primal algebras. As a more general goal, embedding in a constraint logic programming language a solver for combined theories is expected to lead to interesting applications when constraints must be solved in complex algebraic domains.

Acknowledgements: We sincerely thank the UNIF group in Nancy for fruitful discussions.

References

[1] A. Boudet. *Unification dans les mélanges de théories équationelles. Application aux axiomes d'associativité, commutativité, identité et idempotence, aux anneaux Booléens, et aux groupes Abéliens*. Thèse de Doctorat d'Université, Université de Paris-Sud, Orsay (France), February 1990.

[2] A. Boudet. Unification in a combination of equational theories: An efficient algorithm. In M. E. Stickel, editor, *Proceedings 10th International Conference on Automated Deduction, Kaiserslautern (Germany)*, volume 449 of *Lecture Notes in Computer Science*. Springer-Verlag, July 1990.

[3] R. E. Bryant. Graph-based algorithms for boolean function manipulation. *IEEE Transactions on computers*, C-35(8):677–691, August 1986.

[4] W. Büttner, K. Estenfeld, R. Schmid, H.-A. Schneider, and E. Tiden. Symbolic constraint handling through unification in finite algebras. *Applicable Algebra in Engineering, Communication and Computation*, 1(2):97–118, 1990.

[5] A. L. Foster. Generalized "boolean" theory of universal algebras. *Math. Zeitschr.*, Bd. 59:191–199, 1953.

[6] A. Herold. Combination of unification algorithms. In J. Siekmann, editor, *Proceedings 8th International Conference on Automated Deduction, Oxford (UK)*, volume 230 of *Lecture Notes in Computer Science*, pages 450–469. Springer-Verlag, 1986.

[7] J.-P. Jouannaud and C. Kirchner. Solving equations in abstract algebras: a rule-based survey of unification. In J.-L. Lassez and G. Plotkin, editors, *Computational Logic. Essays in honor of Alan Robinson*, chapter 8, pages 257–321. MIT Press, Cambridge (MA, USA), 1991.

[8] C. Kirchner. *Méthodes et outils de conception systématique d'algorithmes d'unification dans les théories équationnelles*. Thèse de Doctorat d'Etat, Université de Nancy I, 1985.

[9] C. Kirchner, H. Kirchner, and M. Rusinowitch. Deduction with symbolic constraints. *Revue d'Intelligence Artificielle*, 4(3):9–52, 1990. Special issue on Automatic Deduction.

[10] H. Kirchner and C. Ringeissen. Combining unification problems with constraint solving in finite algebras. Research Report 91-R-106, Centre de Recherche en Informatique de Nancy, 1991.

[11] U. Martin and T. Nipkow. Boolean unification — the story so far. *Journal of Symbolic Computation*, 7(3 & 4):275–294, 1989. Special issue on unification. Part one.

[12] T. Nipkow. Unification in primal algebras, their powers and their varieties. *Journal of the Association for Computing Machinery*, 37(1):742–776, October 1990.

[13] A. Rauzy. Boolean unification: an efficient algorithm. Technical report, LABRI, University of Bordeaux 1, 1990.

[14] O. Ridoux and H. Tonneau. Une mise en œuvre de l'unification d'expressions booléennes. In *Actes de SPLT'90, Trégastel*. CNET, 1990.

[15] C. Ringeissen. Etude et implantation d'un algorithme d'unification dans les algèbres finies. Rapport de DEA, Université de Nancy I, 1990.

[16] C. Ringeissen. Unification in a combination of equational theories with shared constants and its application to primal algebras. In *Proceedings of LPAR'92*, Lecture Notes in Artificial Intelligence. Springer-Verlag, 1992.

[17] M. Schmidt-Schauß. Combination of unification algorithms. *Journal of Symbolic Computation*, 8(1 & 2):51–100, 1989. Special issue on unification. Part two.

[18] G. Smolka. *Logic Programming over Polymorphically Order-Sorted Types*. PhD thesis, FB Informatik, Universität Kaiserslautern, Germany, 1989.

[19] E. Tidén. Unification in combinations of collapse-free theories with disjoint sets of functions symbols. In J. Siekmann, editor, *Proceedings 8th International Conference on Automated Deduction, Oxford (UK)*, volume 230 of *Lecture Notes in Computer Science*, pages 431–449. Springer-Verlag, 1986.

[20] K. Yelick. Unification in combinations of collapse-free regular theories. *Journal of Symbolic Computation*, 3(1 & 2):153–182, April 1987.

Records for Logic Programming

Gert Smolka
Ralf Treinen
Deutsches Forschungszentrum für Künstliche Intelligenz (DFKI)
Stuhlsatzenhausweg 3
D-W6600 Saarbrücken
Germany
{smolka,treinen}@dfki.uni-sb.de

Abstract

CFT is a new constraint system providing records as logical data structure for constraint (logic) programming. It can be seen as a generalization of the rational tree system employed in Prolog II, where finer-grained constraints are used, and where subtrees are identified by keywords rather than by position.

CFT is defined by a first-order structure consisting of so-called feature trees. Feature trees generalize the ordinary trees corresponding to first-order terms by having their edges labeled with field names called features. The mathematical semantics given by the feature tree structure is complemented with a logical semantics given by five axiom schemes, which we conjecture to comprise a complete axiomatization of the feature tree structure.

We present a decision method for CFT, which decides entailment / disentailment between possibly existentially quantified constraints. Since CFT satisfies the independence property, our decision method can also be employed for checking the satisfiability of conjunctions of positive and negative constraints. This includes quantified negative constraints such as "$\forall y \forall z (x \neq f(y,z))$".

1 Introduction

Records are an important data structure in programming languages. They appeared first with imperative languages such as ALGOL 68 and Pascal, but are now also present in modern functional languages such as SML. A major reason for providing records is the fact that they serve as the canonical data structure for expressing object-oriented programming techniques.

In this paper we will show that records can be incorporated into logic programming in a straightforward and natural manner. We will model records with a constraint system CFT, which can serve as the basis of future constraint (logic) programming languages. Since CFT is a conservative extension of Prolog II's rational tree system [9, 10], the familiar term notation can still be used. We haven chosen to admit infinite trees so that cyclic data structures can be represented directly. However, a set-up admitting only

241

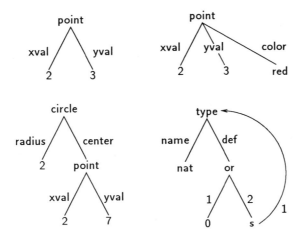

Figure 1: Examples of Feature Trees.

finite trees as in the original Horn clause model is also possible.

1.1 Records are Feature Trees

We model records as feature trees [6, 7]. A feature tree (examples are shown in Figure 1) is a tree whose edges are labeled with symbols called features, and whose nodes are labeled with symbols called sorts. The features labeling the edges correspond to the field names of records. As one would expect, the labeling with features must be deterministic, that is, every direct subtree of a feature tree is uniquely identified by the feature of the edge leading to it. Feature trees without subtrees model atomic values (e.g., numbers). Feature trees may be finite or infinite. Infinite feature trees provide for the convenient representation of cyclic data structures. The last example in Figure 1 gives a finite graph representation of an infinite feature tree, which may arise as the representation of the recursive type equation $\mathsf{nat} = 0 + \mathsf{s}(\mathsf{nat})$.

A ground term, say $\mathsf{f}(\mathsf{g}(\mathsf{a},\mathsf{b}),\mathsf{h}(\mathsf{c}))$, can be seen as a feature tree whose nodes are labeled with function symbols and whose arcs are labeled with numbers:

Thus the trees corresponding to first-order terms are in fact feature trees observing certain restrictions (e.g., the features departing from a node must be consecutive positive integers).

1.2 Record Descriptions

In CFT, records (i.e., feature trees) are described by first-order formulae. To this purpose, we set up a first-order structure $\mathcal{T}$ (CFT's standard model) whose universe is the set of all feature trees (over given alphabets of features and sorts), and whose descriptive primitives are defined as follows:

- Every sort symbol A is taken as a unary predicate, where a *sort constraint* $x\!:\!A$ holds if and only if the root of the tree x is labeled with A.

- Every feature symbol f is taken as a binary predicate, where a *feature constraint* $x[f]y$ holds if and only if the tree x has the direct subtree y at feature f.

- Every finite set F of features is taken as a unary predicate, where an *arity constraint* xF holds if and only if the tree x has direct subtrees exactly at the features appearing in F.

The descriptions or constraints of CFT are now exactly the first-order formulae obtained from the primitive forms specified above, where we include equations "$x = y$" between variables.

A feature constraint $x[f]y$ corresponds to field selection for records. A more familiar notation for $x[f]y$ might be $y = x.f$. Note that the field selection function "$x.f$" is partial since not every record has a field f.

Next we note that the familiar term notation can still be used in CFT if a little syntactic sugar is provided. For instance, the equational constraint

$$X \;=\; \mathsf{point}(Y,Z)$$

employing the binary constructor **point** translates into the conjunction

$$X\!:\!\mathsf{point} \;\wedge\; X\{1,2\} \;\wedge\; X[1]Y \;\wedge\; X[2]Z.$$

Note that constructors and features are dual in the sense that features are argument selectors for constructors.

CFT can also express constructors that identify their arguments by keywords rather than by position. For instance, the equation

$$P \;=\; \mathsf{point}(\mathsf{xval}\!:\!X,\ \mathsf{yval}\!:\!Y,\ \mathsf{color}\!:\!Z)$$

can be taken as an abbreviation for

$$P\!:\!\mathsf{point} \;\wedge\; P\{\mathsf{xval},\mathsf{yval},\mathsf{color}\} \;\wedge\; P[\mathsf{xval}]X \;\wedge\; P[\mathsf{yval}]Y \;\wedge\; P[\mathsf{color}]Z.$$

Using nesting, which can be expressed in CFT with existentially quantified auxiliary variables, we can give the following description of the infinite feature tree shown in Figure 1:

$$X \;=\; \mathsf{type}(\mathsf{name}\!:\!\mathsf{nat},\ \mathsf{def}\!:\!\mathsf{or}(0,\mathsf{s}(X))).$$

Compared to the standard tree constraint systems, the major expressive flexibility provided by CFT is the possibility to access a feature without saying anything about the existence of other features. The constraint

$$X[\text{color}]Y$$

says that X must have a color field whose value is Y, but nothing else. Hence we can express properties of the color of X without knowing whether X is a circle, triangle, car or something else. Using constructor constraints, we would have to write a disjunction

$$X = \text{circle}(\ldots, Y, \ldots) \;\vee\; X = \text{triangle}(\ldots, Y, \ldots) \;\vee\; \ldots$$

which means that we have to know statically which alternatives are possible dynamically. Moreover, disjunctions are expensive computationally. In contrast, feature constraints like X[color]Y allow for efficient constraint simplification, as we will see in this paper.

Descriptions leaving the arity of a record open are also essential for knowledge representation, where a description like

$$X: \text{person}[\text{father}: Y, \text{ employer}: Y]$$

should not disallow other features. In CFT this description can be expressed by simply *not* imposing an arity constraint:

$$X: \text{person} \;\wedge\; X[\text{father}]Y \;\wedge\; X[\text{employer}]Y.$$

1.3 Constraint Simplification

The major technical contribution of this paper is the presentation and verification of a constraint simplification method for CFT. This method provides for incremental entailment / disentailment checking as it is needed for more advanced constraint programming frameworks [17, 19].

To state our technical results precisely, let a simple constraint be a formula in the fragment

$$[x:A, \; x[f]y, \; xF, \; x = y, \; \bot, \; \top]_{\wedge,\exists}$$

obtained by closing the atomic formulae under conjunction and existential quantification. Let γ and ϕ be simple constraints. We give a method that decides simultaneously entailment $\gamma \models_{\text{CFT}} \phi$ and disentailment $\gamma \models_{\text{CFT}} \neg\phi$. This method can be implemented by an incremental algorithm having quasi-linear complexity, provided the features possibly occurring in γ and ϕ are restricted a priori to some finite set. We also prove that CFT satisfies the independence property, that is,

$$\gamma \models_{\text{CFT}} \phi_1 \vee \ldots \vee \phi_n \quad \Longleftrightarrow \quad \exists i: \; \gamma \models_{\text{CFT}} \phi_i.$$

Hence, our decision method can decide the satisfiability of conjunctions of positive and negative simple constraints since

$$\gamma \wedge \neg\phi_1 \wedge \ldots \wedge \neg\phi_n \models_{\mathrm{CFT}} \bot$$

is equivalent to

$$\gamma \models_{\mathrm{CFT}} \phi_1 \vee \ldots \vee \phi_n.$$

All results are obtained under the assumption that the alphabets of sorts and features are infinite.

1.4 Related Work

CFT can be viewed as the minimal combination of Colmerauer's rational tree system [9, 10] with the feature constraint system FT [6]. In fact, CFT is obtained from FT by simply adding arity constraints as new descriptive primitive. However, the addition of arity constraints requires a nontrivial extension of FT's relative simplification method [6], which can be seen from the fact that the entailment

$$x = f(x,y) \wedge y = f(y,y) \models_{\mathrm{CFT}} x = y$$

holds in CFT. (It of course also holds in Colmerauer's rational tree system.)

Our operational investigations are based on congruences and normalizers of constraints, two new notions providing for an elegant presentation of our results. Huet [11] uses the related notion of "équivalence simplifiable" in his study of rational tree unification. We improve on Colmerauer's [10] results for rational trees since our constraints are closed under existential quantification. For instance, our algorithm is complete for quantified negative constraints such as $\neg\exists y\exists z(z = f(y,z))$.

Feature descriptions have a long and winded history. One root are the unification grammar formalisms FUG [14] and LFG [13] developed for applications in computational linguistics (see [8] for a more recent paper in this area). Another, independent root is Aït-Kaci's ψ-term calculus [1, 2], which is the basis of several constraint programming languages [3, 4, 5]. Smolka [20] gives a unified logical view of most earlier feature formalisms and studies an expressive feature constraint logic.

Feature trees appeared only recently with the work on FT [7, 6]. To our knowledge the notion of an arity constraint is new. Carpenter's [8] extensional types are somewhat related in that they fix an arity for all elements of a type.

1.5 Organization of the Paper

Section 2 gives a formal definition of the feature tree structure, thus fixing syntax and semantics of CFT. Section 3 defines a first-order theory by means of five axiom schemes, which we conjecture to be a complete axiomatization of the feature tree structure. Section 4 presents the decision method and states its properties.

Due to space limitations the paper does not contain the proofs of the claimed results. We also cannot give an algorithmic formulation of our decision method, which would exhibit its incrementality and worst-case complexity. Both proofs and algorithmic formulation are given in the full paper [21].

2 The Feature Tree Structure

This section gives a formal definition of CFT's standard model $\mathcal{T}$. $\mathcal{T}$ is a first-order structure whose universe consists of all feature trees obtainable from given alphabets of sorts and features.

From now on we assume that an infinite alphabet SOR of symbols called **sorts** and an infinite alphabet FEA of symbols called **features** are given. For several results of this paper (e.g., independence) it is essential that both alphabets are infinite. The letters A, B will always denote sorts, the letters f, g will always denote features, and the letters F, G will always denote *finite* sets of features.

We also assume an infinite alphabet of variables, ranged over by the letters x, y, z. From the alphabets of sorts, features and variables we define the following first-order language with equality: Every sort symbol A is a unary predicate; every feature symbol f is a binary predicate; every finite set F of features is a unary predicate, called an *arity predicate*; the equality symbol $\doteq$ is a binary predicate that is always interpreted as identity; there are no function symbols, and there are no predicate symbols other than the ones mentioned. Every formula and every structure in this paper will be taken with respect to this signature. Note that under this signature every term is a variable.

For convenience, we will write Ax, xfy and xF for $A(x)$, $f(x,y)$ and $F(x)$, respectively. (In Section 1 we have used yet another, Prolog compatible syntax: $X:a$ for sort and $X[f]Y$ for feature constraints.) We assume the usual connectives and quantifiers. We write $\perp$ for "false" and $\top$ for "true". We use $\tilde{\exists}\phi$ [$\tilde{\forall}\phi$] to denote the existential [universal] closure of a formula ϕ. Moreover, $\mathcal{V}(\phi)$ is taken to denote the set of all variables occurring free in a formula ϕ.

A **path** is a word (i.e., a finite, possibly empty sequence) over the set of all features. The symbol ε denotes the empty path, which satisfies $\varepsilon p = p = p\varepsilon$ for every path p. A path p is called a **prefix** of a path q, if there exists a path p' such that $pp' = q$. We use FEA* to denote the set of all paths.

A **tree domain** is a nonempty set $D \subseteq$ FEA* that is **prefix-closed**, that is, if $pq \in D$, then $p \in D$. Note that every tree domain contains the empty path.

A **feature tree** is a partial function $\sigma\colon$ FEA$^\star \rightsquigarrow$ SOR whose domain is a tree domain. The paths in the domain of a feature tree represent the nodes of the tree; the empty path represents its root. We use D_σ to denote the domain of a feature tree σ. A feature tree is called **finite [infinite]** if its domain is finite [infinite]. The letters σ and τ will always denote feature trees.

The **subtree** $p\sigma$ of a feature tree σ at a path $p \in D_\sigma$ is the feature tree defined (in relational notation) by:

$$p\sigma := \{(q, A) \mid (pq, A) \in \sigma\}.$$

We now define the **feature tree structure** $\mathcal{T}$ as follows:

- The universe of $\mathcal{T}$ is the set of all feature trees;
- $\sigma \in A^{\mathcal{T}}$ iff $\sigma(\varepsilon) = A$;
- $(\sigma, \tau) \in f^{\mathcal{T}}$ iff $f \in D_\sigma$ and $\tau = f\sigma$;
- $\sigma \in F^{\mathcal{T}}$ iff $D_\sigma \cap \text{FEA} = F$.

Note that $\mathcal{T}$ contains all infinite feature trees. Another option is to admit only those infinite feature trees that are rational (i.e., have only finitely many subtrees). For the results of this paper this would not make a difference. We also conjecture that the rational feature tree structure and $\mathcal{T}$ are elementarily equivalent, analogous to the situation with constructor trees [18].

3 The Theory CFT

We will now define a first-order theory CFT having the feature tree structure $\mathcal{T}$ as one of its models. All results of this paper actually hold for every model of CFT. We conjecture that CFT is a complete axiomatization of the feature tree structure $\mathcal{T}$ and expect that this can be shown with a quantifier elimination technique similar to the one used in [7].

We briefly review the notion of a theory. A **theory** is a set of closed formulae. We say that a structure $\mathcal{A}$ is a **model** of a theory T ($\mathcal{A} \models T$) if $\mathcal{A}$ satisfies each formula of T. A formula ϕ is a **consequence** of a theory T ($T \models \phi$) if $\tilde{\forall}\phi$ is valid in every model of T. A formula ϕ is **unsatisfiable** in a theory T if $\neg\phi$ is a consequence of T. Two formulae ϕ, ψ are **equivalent** in a theory T ($\phi \models\!\!\models_T \psi$) if they are equivalent in every model $\mathcal{A}$ of T, that is, if $\phi \leftrightarrow \psi$ is a consequence of T. A formula ϕ **entails** a formula ψ in a theory T ($\phi \models_T \psi$) if ϕ entails ψ in every model of T, that is, if $\phi \rightarrow \psi$ is a consequence of T. A formula ϕ **disentails** a formula ψ in a theory T if ϕ entails $\neg\psi$ in T. For convenience, we will omit the index $\emptyset$ for the empty theory, that is, write $\models$ for $\models_\emptyset$.

CFT is defined by five axiom schemes. The first four schemes are straightforward:

(S)	$\tilde{\forall}(Ax \wedge Bx \rightarrow \bot)$	if $A \neq B$
(F)	$\tilde{\forall}(xfy \wedge xfz \rightarrow y \doteq z)$	
(A1)	$\tilde{\forall}(xF \wedge xfy \rightarrow \bot)$	if $f \notin F$
(A2)	$\tilde{\forall}(xF \rightarrow \exists y(xfy))$	if $x \neq y$ and $f \in F$.

The first two axiom schemes say that sorts are pairwise disjoint, and that features are functional. The last two schemes say that, if x has arity F, exactly the features $f \in F$ are defined on x.

To formulate the remaining axiom scheme, we need the notion of a determinant. A **determinant for** x is a formula

$$Ax \wedge x\{f_1, \ldots, f_n\} \wedge x f_1 y_1 \wedge \ldots \wedge x f_n y_n$$

which we will write more conveniently as

$$x \doteq A(f_1 : y_1, \ldots, f_n : y_n).$$

As we have pointed out before, a determinant as the one above is similar to a constructor equation $x \doteq f(y_1, \ldots, y_n)$. A **determinant for** pairwise distinct variables $x_1, \ldots, x_n$ is a conjunction

$$x_1 \doteq D_1 \wedge \ldots \wedge x_n \doteq D_n$$

of determinants for $x_1, \ldots, x_n$. If δ is a determinant, we use $\mathcal{D}(\delta)$ to denote the set of variables determined by δ.

The remaining axiom scheme will say that every determinant determines a unique solution for its determined variables. To this purpose we define the quantifier $\exists! x \phi$ ("there exists a unique x such that") as an abbreviation for

$$\exists x \phi \wedge \forall x, y (\phi \wedge \phi[x \leftarrow y] \rightarrow x \doteq y).$$

($\phi[x \leftarrow y]$ denotes the formula obtained from ϕ by replacing every occurrence of x with y.) The more general form $\exists! X \phi$, where X is a finite set of variables, is defined accordingly. The quantifier $\exists!$ has the important property that

$$\exists! X \phi \wedge \exists X (\phi \wedge \psi) \quad \models_{\mathcal{A}} \quad \phi \rightarrow \psi$$

holds for every two formulae ϕ, ψ and every structure $\mathcal{A}$.

Now we can state the fifth axiom scheme:

$$(D) \quad \tilde{\forall} \, (\exists! \mathcal{D}(\delta) \, \delta) \qquad \text{if } \delta \text{ is a determinant.}$$

An example of an instance of scheme (D) is:

$$\forall u, v, w \; \exists! \; x, y, z \left(\begin{array}{l} x \doteq A(f : v, \, g : y) \wedge \\ y \doteq B(f : x, \, g : z, \, h : u) \wedge \\ z \doteq A(f : w, \, g : y, \, h : z) \end{array} \right).$$

The theory CFT is the set of all sentences that can be obtained as instances of the axiom schemes (S), (F), (A1), (A2) and (D).

Proposition 3.1 *The feature tree structure $\mathcal{T}$ is a model of CFT. Moreover, the substructure of $\mathcal{T}$ containing only the rational feature trees is also a model of CFT.*

4   The Decision Method

In this section we develop in several steps a method for deciding simultaneously entailment and disentailment in CFT.

A **basic constraint** is a possibly empty conjunction of atomic constraints (i.e., Ax, xfy, xF, $x \doteq y$). The empty conjunction is the formula $\top$. We assume that the conjunction of formulae is associative and commutative, and that it satisfies $\phi \wedge \top = \phi$. We can thus see a basic constraint equivalently as a finite multiset of atomic constraints, where $\wedge$ corresponds to multiset union and $\top$ to the empty multiset. For basic constraints ϕ, ψ, we will write $\psi \subseteq \phi$ (or $\psi \in \phi$, if ψ is an atomic constraint) if there exists a basic constraint ψ' such that $\psi \wedge \psi' = \phi$.

Let γ, ϕ be basic constraints and X, Y be finite sets of variables. We will eventually arrive at an incremental method for deciding

$$\exists Y \gamma \ \models_{\text{CFT}} \ \exists X \phi$$
$$\exists Y \gamma \ \models_{\text{CFT}} \ \neg \exists X \phi$$

simultaneously. We will also see that the equivalences

$$\exists Y \gamma \models_{\text{CFT}} \exists X \phi \iff \exists Y \gamma \models_{\mathcal{A}} \exists X \phi$$
$$\exists Y \gamma \models_{\text{CFT}} \neg \exists X \phi \iff \exists Y \gamma \models_{\mathcal{A}} \neg \exists X \phi$$

hold for every model $\mathcal{A}$ of the theory CFT.

We say that a basic constraint **clashes** if it simplifies to $\bot$ with one of the following rules:

(SCl) $\dfrac{Ax \wedge Bx \wedge \phi}{\bot}$ $A \neq B$

(ACl) $\dfrac{xF \wedge xG \wedge \phi}{\bot}$ $F \neq G$

(FCl) $\dfrac{xF \wedge xfy \wedge \phi}{\bot}$ $f \notin F$

We call a basic constraint **clash-free** if it does not clash. Obviously, every basic constraint that clashes is unsatisfiable in CFT.

Consider the basic constraint

$$x \doteq y \wedge x \, f \, x' \wedge y \, f \, y' \wedge A \, x' \wedge B \, y', \tag{1}$$

where A, B are distinct sorts. Clearly, this constraint is unsatisfiable in CFT: If there was a solution, it would have to identify x' and y' (since features are functional), which is impossible since A and B are disjoint. This suggests that a constraint simplification method must infer all equalities between variables that are induced by the functionality of features (axiom scheme (F)). This observation leads us to the central notions of congruences and normalizers of constraints.

4.1 Congruences and Normalizers

We call an equivalence relation $\approx$ between variables a **congruence** of a basic constraint ϕ if:

- if $x \doteq y \in \phi$, then $x \approx y$;
- if xfy, $x'fy' \in \phi$ and $x \approx x'$, then $y \approx y'$.

It is easy to see that the set of congruences of a basic constraint is closed under intersection. Since the equivalence relation identifying all variables is a congruence of every basic constraint, every basic constraint has a least congruence.

The least congruence of the basic constraint (1) has two nontrivial equivalence classes: $\{x, y\}$ and $\{x', y'\}$.

Technically, it will be very convenient to represent congruences as idempotent substitutions mapping variables to variables. We call a substitution θ a **normalizer** of an equivalence relation on the set of all variables if

1. θ maps variables to variables;

2. θ is idempotent (that is, $\theta\theta = \theta$);

3. $\theta x = \theta y$ if and only if $x \approx y$ (for all variables x, y).

Given $\approx$, we can obtain a normalizer of $\approx$ by choosing a canonical member for every equivalence class and mapping every variable to the canonical member of its class.

Let θ be a substitution. We use $\mathcal{Dom}(\theta)$ (the **domain of** θ) to denote the set of all variables x such that $\theta x \neq x$. A substitution is called **finite** if its domain is finite. A finite substitution θ with the domain $\mathcal{Dom}(\theta) = \{x_1, \ldots, x_n\}$ can be represented as an equation system

$$x_1 \doteq \theta x_1 \wedge \ldots \wedge x_n \doteq \theta x_n.$$

For convenience, we will simply use θ to denote this formula. Now, if θ is a substitution and ϕ is a quantifier-free formula, we have

$$\theta \wedge \phi \ \Vdash\dashv\ \theta \wedge \theta\phi,$$

where the application of θ to ϕ is defined as one would expect.

We call a substitution θ a **normalizer** of a basic constraint ϕ if θ is a normalizer of the least congruence of ϕ. Every basic constraint ϕ has a finite normalizer since its least congruence can only identify variables occurring in ϕ.

The least congruence of the basic constraint (1) has two nonsingleton equivalence classes: $\{x, y\}$ and $\{x', y'\}$. Hence the constraint (1) has 4 normalizers, each representing a different choice for the normal forms of identified variables. One possible normalizer is the substitution $\{x \mapsto y, x' \mapsto y'\}$.

For a basic constraint ϕ we will write $\overline{\phi}$ for the formula obtained from ϕ by deleting all equations "$x \doteq y$".

Theorem 4.1 *Let $\mathcal{A}$ be a model of* CFT *, ϕ be a basic constraint, and θ be a normalizer of ϕ. Then:*

1. *ϕ is unsatisfiable in $\mathcal{A}$ if and only if $\theta\overline{\phi}$ clashes;*

2. *$\phi \models_{\mathrm{CFT}} \theta \wedge \theta\overline{\phi}$.*

The first statement of the theorem gives us a method for deciding the satisfiability of basic constraints, provided we have a method for computing normalizers. The second statement gives us a solved form for satisfiable basic constraints. Since the first statement implies that a basic constraint is satisfiable in one model of CFT if and only if it is satisfiable in every model of CFT, we know that the theory CFT is satisfaction complete [12].

Let ϕ be the basic constraint (1) and θ be the normalizer $\{x \mapsto y, x' \mapsto y'\}$. Then $\theta\overline{\phi}$ is the clashing constraint

$$y\,f\,y' \wedge y\,f\,y' \wedge A\,y' \wedge B\,y'.$$

The following simplification rules for basic constraints provide a method for computing normalizers:

(Triv) $\quad \dfrac{x \doteq x \wedge \phi}{\phi}$

(Cong) $\quad \dfrac{x\,f\,y \wedge x\,f\,z \wedge \phi}{y \doteq z \wedge x\,f\,z \wedge \phi}$

(Elim) $\quad \dfrac{x \doteq y \wedge \phi}{x \doteq y \wedge \phi[x \leftarrow y]} \quad x \neq y, \ x \in \mathcal{V}(\phi)$

($\phi[x \leftarrow y]$ denotes the formula obtained from ϕ by replacing every occurrence of x with y.) Each of these rules is an equivalence transformation for CFT (rule (Cong) corresponds to axiom scheme (F)). It is also easy to see that the rules preserve the congruences of a constraint, and hence its least congruence. Furthermore, the rules are terminating. Hence we can compute for every basic constraint ϕ a normal form that has exactly the same normalizers as ϕ. The next proposition says that normal constraints exhibit a normalizer (a constraint is normal with respect to a set of rules if none of the rules applies to it):

Proposition 4.2 *Let ϕ be a basic constraint that is normal with respect to the rules (Triv), (Cong) and (Elim). Then the unique substitution θ such that $\phi = \theta \wedge \overline{\phi}$ is a normalizer of ϕ satisfying $\overline{\phi} = \theta\overline{\phi}$.*

4.2   Entailment without $\exists$

Next we will give a method for deciding entailment $\gamma \models_{\mathrm{CFT}} \phi$ between basic constraints. The constraint γ will be required to have a special form called saturated graph.

A basic constraint γ is called a **graph** if it is clash-free, contains no equation, and satisfies $x\,f\,y \in \gamma \wedge x\,f\,z \in \gamma \Rightarrow y = z$. Hence a clash-free basic constraint γ not containing equations is a graph if and only if the identity substitution is the only normalizer of γ.

A basic constraint ϕ is called **saturated** if for every arity constraint $xF \in \phi$ and every feature $f \in F$ there exists a feature constraint $xfy \in \phi$.

We call a variable x **determined** in a basic constraint ϕ if ϕ contains a determinant for x (see Section 3). We use $\mathcal{D}(\phi)$ to denote the set of all variables determined in ϕ. Moreover, if θ is a substitution, $\mathcal{V}(\theta)$ denotes the set of all variables occurring in the equational representation of θ.

Theorem 4.3 *Let $\mathcal{A}$ be a model of* CFT*, γ be a saturated graph, ϕ be a basic constraint, and θ be a normalizer of $\gamma \wedge \phi$. Then:*

1. *$\gamma \models_{\mathcal{A}} \neg\phi$ if and only if $\theta(\gamma \wedge \overline{\phi})$ clashes;*

2. *$\gamma \models_{\mathcal{A}} \phi$ if and only if $\theta(\gamma \wedge \overline{\phi})$ is clash-free, $\theta\overline{\phi} \subseteq \theta\gamma$, and $\mathcal{V}(\theta) \subseteq \mathcal{D}(\gamma)$.*

The first statement follows immediately from Theorem 4.1 (since for every structure $\mathcal{A}$, $\gamma \models_{\mathcal{A}} \neg\phi$ iff $\gamma \wedge \phi$ is unsatisfiable in $\mathcal{A}$). The second statement is nontrivial. Note that deciding entailment and disentailment is straightforward once a normalizer is computed.

To see an example, let us verify

$$x \doteq A(f{:}x, g{:}y) \wedge y \doteq A(f{:}y, g{:}y) \quad \models_{\text{CFT}} \quad x \doteq y \qquad (2)$$

with the method provided by Theorem 4.3. Without syntactic sugar we have

$$Ax \wedge x\{f,g\} \wedge xfx \wedge xgy \wedge Ay \wedge y\{f,g\} \wedge yfy \wedge ygy \models_{\text{CFT}} x \doteq y.$$

The left-hand side γ is in fact a saturated graph. If we apply the simplification rule (Elim) to $\gamma \wedge \phi$ (ϕ is the right-hand side $x \doteq y$), we obtain (up to duplicates) the normal and clash-free constraint

$$x \doteq y \wedge Ay \wedge y\{f,g\} \wedge yfy \wedge ygy.$$

Hence $\theta := \{x \mapsto y\}$ is a normalizer of $\gamma \wedge \phi$. Since $\overline{\phi} = \top$ and $\mathcal{V}(\theta) = \mathcal{D}(\gamma) = \{x, y\}$, we know by Theorem 4.3 that γ entails ϕ in every model of CFT.

4.3 Entailment with $\exists$

We now extend Theorem 4.3 to the general case $\exists Y\gamma \models_{\text{CFT}} \exists X\phi$.

First we note that, after possibly renaming quantified variables, we have

$$\exists Y\gamma \models_{\text{CFT}} \exists X\phi \quad \Longleftrightarrow \quad \gamma \models_{\text{CFT}} \exists X\phi.$$

Hence it suffices to consider the case where only the right-hand side has existential quantifiers.

Next we will see that we can assume without loss of generality that γ is a saturated graph. Given a basic constraint γ, we can first apply the simplification rules (Triv), (Cong) and (Elim) and obtain an equivalent normal form $\theta \wedge \gamma'$, where θ is a normalizer and γ' either clashes or is a graph. If γ' clashes, then $\gamma \models_{\mathrm{CFT}} \exists X \phi$ trivially holds. Otherwise, we can assume without loss of generality that $\theta \wedge \gamma'$ and X have no variable in common. Thus we have

$$\gamma \models_{\mathrm{CFT}} \exists X \phi \iff \theta \wedge \gamma' \models_{\mathrm{CFT}} \exists X \phi \iff \gamma' \models_{\mathrm{CFT}} \exists X(\theta \phi)$$

since θ is idempotent and $\theta \gamma' = \gamma'$. Now we know by axiom scheme (A2) that there exists a saturated graph γ'' such that $\gamma' \dashv\vdash_{\mathrm{CFT}} \exists Y \gamma''$ for some set Y of new variables. Thus we have

$$\gamma \models_{\mathrm{CFT}} \exists X \phi \iff \exists Y \gamma'' \models_{\mathrm{CFT}} \exists X(\theta \phi) \iff \gamma'' \models_{\mathrm{CFT}} \exists X(\theta \phi).$$

Hence, it suffices to exhibit a decision method for the case $\gamma \models_{\mathrm{CFT}} \exists X \phi$, where γ is a saturated graph and X is disjoint from $\mathcal{V}(\gamma)$.

We say that a variable x is **constrained** in a basic constraint ϕ if ϕ contains an atomic constraint of the form Ax, xF or xfy. We write $\mathcal{C}(\phi)$ for the set of all variables that are constrained in a basic constraint ϕ. The basic constraint (1), for instance, constrains the variables x, y, x' and y'.

In the following X will be a finite set of variables. We write $-X$ for the complement of X. We call a normalizer θ X-**oriented** if $\theta(-X) \subseteq -X$. Given an equivalence relation between variables, we can obtain an X-oriented normalizer by choosing the canonical member of a class from $-X$ whenever the class contains an element that is not in X. To compute X-oriented normalizers, it suffices to add the rule

$$(\text{Orient}) \quad \frac{y \doteq x \wedge \phi}{x \doteq y \wedge \phi} \quad \text{if } x \in X \text{ and } y \notin X$$

to the simplification rules (Triv), (Cong) and (Elim). With this additional rule normal forms will always exhibit an X-oriented normalizer.

The **restriction** $\theta|_X$ of a normalizer θ to a set X of variables is the substitution that agrees with θ on X and is the identity on $-X$.

For basic constraints ϕ and ψ, we write $\phi - \psi$ for the constraint that is obtained from ϕ by deleting all constraints occurring in ψ.

Theorem 4.4 (Entailment) *Let $\mathcal{A}$ be a model of CFT, γ be a saturated graph, ϕ be a basic constraint, X be a finite set of variables not occurring in γ, and θ be an X-oriented normalizer of $\gamma \wedge \phi$. Then:*

1. *$\gamma \models_{\mathcal{A}} \neg \exists X \phi$ if and only if $\theta(\gamma \wedge \overline{\phi})$ clashes;*

2. *$\gamma \models_{\mathcal{A}} \exists X \phi$ if and only if $\theta(\gamma \wedge \overline{\phi})$ is clash-free, $\mathcal{C}(\theta\overline{\phi} - \theta\gamma) \subseteq X$, and $\mathcal{V}(\theta|_{-X}) \subseteq \mathcal{D}(\gamma)$.*

Theorem 4.3 is obtained from the Entailment Theorem as the special case where $X = \emptyset$.

4.4 Complexity

The decision method suggested by the Entailment Theorem can be implemented with an algorithm having quasi-linear complexity in the size of γ and ϕ, provided the features that can actually occur in γ and ϕ are restricted a priori to some finite set. The algorithm must represent a graph and a normalizer. The normalizer is maintained with an efficient union-find algorithm. Since the number of union-find steps is linear in the size of γ and ϕ and dominates the other actions of the algorithm, which are constant-time, we have quasi-linear complexity [22].

If the features that can occur in γ and ϕ are not fixed a priori, the time for obtaining y given x and f such that xfy occurs in a graph is no longer constant. In this case the method can certainly be implemented with a complexity not worse than quadratic in the size of γ and ϕ.

4.5 Independence

Theorem 4.5 (Independence) *Let* $\phi, \phi_1, \ldots, \phi_n$ *be basic constraints and* $X_1, \ldots, X_n$ *be finite sets of variables disjoint from* $\mathcal{V}(\phi)$. *Then*

$$\phi \models_{\mathcal{A}} \exists X_1\phi_1 \vee \ldots \vee \exists X_n\phi_n \quad \Longleftrightarrow \quad \exists i: \quad \phi \models_{\mathcal{A}} \exists X_i\phi_i$$

for every model $\mathcal{A}$ *of* CFT .

The Independence Theorem does not hold for finite alphabets of sorts and features. For finitely many sorts $A_1, \ldots, A_n$ we have $\top \models_{\mathcal{T}} A_1x \vee \ldots \vee A_nx$, and for finitely many features $f_1, \ldots, f_n$ we have $\top \models_{\mathcal{T}} x\{\} \vee \exists y(xf_1y) \vee \ldots \vee \exists y(xf_ny)$.

Since we allow for existential quantification, our Independence Theorem is stronger than what is usually stated in the literature [10, 15, 16]. In fact, independence for existentially quantified constraints over finite or rational constructor trees does not hold if the alphabet of constructors is finite. To see this, note that the disjunction $\exists \overline{y}_1(x = f_1(\overline{y}_1)) \vee \ldots \vee \exists \overline{y}_n(x = f_n(\overline{y}_n))$ is valid if there are no other constructors but $f_1, \ldots, f_n$.

Acknowledgements

The research reported in this paper has been supported by the Bundesminister für Forschung und Technologie, contract ITW 9105.

References

[1] H. Aït-Kaci. *A Lattice-Theoretic Approach to Computation Based on a Calculus of Partially Ordered Type Structures*. PhD thesis, University of Pennsylvenia, Philadelphia, PA, 1984.

[2] H. Aït-Kaci. An algebraic semantics approach to the effective resolution of type equations. *Theoretical Computer Science*, 45:293–351, 1986.

[3] H. Aït-Kaci and R. Nasr. LOGIN: A logic programming language with built-in inheritance. *The Journal of Logic Programming*, 3:185–215, 1986.

[4] H. Aït-Kaci and R. Nasr. Integrating logic and functional programming. *Lisp and Symbolic Computation*, 2:51–89, 1989.

[5] H. Aït-Kaci and A. Podelski. Towards a meaning of LIFE. In J. Maluszyński and M. Wirsing, editors, *Proceedings of the 3rd International Symposium on Programming Language Implementation and Logic Programming*, Springer LNCS vol. 528, pages 255–274. Springer-Verlag, 1991.

[6] H. Aït-Kaci, A. Podelski, and G. Smolka. A feature-based constraint system for logic programming with entailment. In *Fifth Generation Computer Systems 1992*, pages 1012–1021, Tokyo, Japan, June 1992. Institute for New Generation Computer Technology.

[7] R. Backofen and G. Smolka. A complete and recursive feature theory. Research Report RR-92-30, German Research Center for Artificial Intelligence (DFKI), Stuhlsatzenhausweg 3, 6600 Saarbrücken 11, Germany, July 1992.

[8] B. Carpenter. Typed feature structures: A generalization of first-order terms. In V. Saraswat and K. Ueda, editors, *Logic Programming, Proceedings of the 1991 International Symposium*, pages 187–201, San Diego, USA, 1991. The MIT Press.

[9] A. Colmerauer. Prolog and infinite trees. In K. Clark and S.-A. Tärnlund, editors, *Logic Programming*, pages 153–172. Academic Press, 1982.

[10] A. Colmerauer. Equations and inequations on finite and infinite trees. In *Proceedings of the 2nd International Conference on Fifth Generation Computer Systems*, pages 85–99, 1984.

[11] G. Huet. Résolution d'equations dans des langages d'ordre $1, 2, \cdots, \omega$. Thèse de Doctorat d'Etat, l'Université Paris VII, Sept. 1976.

[12] J. Jaffar and J.-L. Lassez. Constraint logic programming. In *Proceedings of the 14th ACM Symposium on Principles of Programming Languages*, pages 111–119, Munich, Germany, Jan. 1987.

[13] R. M. Kaplan and J. Bresnan. Lexical-Functional Grammar: A formal system for grammatical representation. In J. Bresnan, editor, *The Mental Representation of Grammatical Relations*, pages 173–381. The MIT Press, Cambridge, MA, 1982.

[14] M. Kay. Functional grammar. In *Proceedings of the Fifth Annual Meeting of the Berkeley Linguistics Society*, Berkeley, CA, 1979. Berkeley Linguistics Society.

[15] J.-L. Lassez, M. Maher, and K. Marriot. Unification revisited. In J. Minker, editor, *Foundations of Deductive Databases and Logic Programming*. Morgan Kaufmann, Los Altos, CA, 1988.

[16] J. L. Lassez and K. McAloon. A constraint sequent calculus. In *Fifth Annual IEEE Symposium on Logic in Computer Science*, pages 52–61, June 1990.

[17] M. J. Maher. Logic semantics for a class of committed-choice programs. In J.-L. Lassez, editor, *Logic Programming, Proceedings of the Fourth International Conference*, pages 858–876, Cambridge, MA, 1987. The MIT Press.

[18] M. J. Maher. Complete axiomatisations of the algebra of finite, rational and infinite trees. In *Proceedings of the Third Annual Symposium on Logic in Computer Science*, pages 348–357. IEEE Computer Society, 1988.

[19] V. Saraswat and M. Rinard. Concurrent constraint programming. In *Proceedings of the 7th Annual ACM Symposium on Principles of Programming Languages*, pages 232–245, San Francisco, CA, January 1990.

[20] G. Smolka. Feature constraint logics for unification grammars. *Journal of Logic Programming*, 12:51–87, 1992.

[21] G. Smolka and R. Treinen. Records for logic programming. Research Report RR-92-23, German Research Center for Artificial Intelligence (DFKI), Stuhlsatzenhausweg 3, 6600 Saarbrücken 11, Germany, 1992.

[22] R. E. Tarjan. Efficiency of a good but not linear set union algorithm. *Journal of the Association for Computing Machinery*, 22:215–225, 1975.

A Constraint Logic Programming Scheme for Taxonomic Reasoning

Margarida Mamede
Luís Monteiro
Departamento de Informática
Universidade Nova de Lisboa
2825 Monte da Caparica, Portugal
{mm,lm}@fct.unl.pt

Abstract

This paper presents a novel scheme for constraint logic programming, based on an abstract model of constraints that takes as primitive the notions of atomic constraint and substitution. It is shown that the constraint model generalizes the constraint languages of Höhfeld and Smolka [8], and fits well in the general framework proposed by Saraswat [17]. The semantics of the proposed logic programming scheme is an immediate generalization of the semantics of Horn clause logic, and we show that it possesses simple characterizations of the operational, declarative and fixed-point semantics. The main motivation for this work was to formalize the notion of useful and concise answers to queries to hierarchic type systems. The paper ends with a simple example illustrating this application.

1 Introduction

The usefulness of organizing information in a hierarchical fashion in computer science has been amply demonstrated in connection with the notions of subtyping and inheritance in both the programming [1, 2, 3, 6, 14, 20] and the knowledge representation fields [19]. Our work is a contribution to the subject from the point of view of querying a hierarchical type system, also called a taxonomy, in a logic programming framework. The main problem we wish to address is that of formalizing the idea of obtaining "useful" and "informative" answers to the queries.

This problem has been investigated before by Porto, mainly in connection with the semantics of natural language systems [15, 16], and our work builds on his ideas. To put the whole subject on a firm logical basis, we rely on the ideas of constraint logic programming [9, 7]. In this view, queries and answers are both seen as type constraints, the latter in some "canonical" or "solved" form intended to capture the idea of a useful answer (see Section 4.2). The knowledge base comprises both a type hierarchy in terms of which the constraints are characterized, and a constraint logic program that defines relations among the types also in terms of type constraints. The query language is richer than the language in which the knowledge can be expressed (as in [10]), and is essentially a variant of first-order logic with terms denoting types instead of individuals.

Since we deemphasize individuals in our taxonomic reasoning, we would like to base our language on a constraint system where individuals have a secondary role (if at all) when compared to the constraints themselves. None of the existing approaches to constraint languages satisfies this requirement. In the $CLP(D)$ scheme of Jaffar and Lassez [9], the emphasis on the domain D and the requirement that it be solution compact, makes this scheme not too amenable to the kind of taxonomic reasoning we have in mind. The constraint languages of Höhfeld and Smolka [8] are more abstract than the ones resulting from the previous scheme, but again individual variables and interpretations based on domains of individuals are among their main concepts.

This state of affairs led us to propose a model of constraint system with (atomic) constraints and substitutions as the primitive concepts. Thus, we start with an abstract set of atomic constraints, an abstract monoid of substitutions, and a right action of the monoid on the set formalizing the application of substitutions to constraints. A subset of atomic constraints is singled out as the set of valid constraints, and the application of a substitution to a valid constraint is required to produce a valid constraint. From these data, a notion of satisfiable constraint can be defined, as well as an entailment relation between constraints. Thus, our model fits well in the general framework proposed by Saraswat [17], which is based on a set of atomic constraints and an entailment relation.

This model was inspired by the semantics of Horn clause logic, which it seeks to generalize. Given an ordinary logic program, the set of all atoms that are logical consequences of the program is closed for instantiation. We therefore have a constraint system according to our model if we take all atoms as the atomic constraints, the substitutions as the ordinary substitutions, and the valid constraints as the atoms which are logical consequences of the given program. This fact makes it very easy to extend our model to a logic programming framework, and the main contribution of this paper is to study the resulting constraint logic programming scheme.

This paper builds on previous work, reported in [11, 12], where we characterized the notion of "useful" answer for a type hierarchy, defined the query language, and first presented our model of constraints. We still had to show how to define general relations among types and how to implement the taxonomy and the constraint solver. Here we show how to extend logic programming with our model of constraints in order to describe the knowledge-base module that handles relation definitions. We postpone to a later paper the implementation of the taxonomy and of the constraint solver, and the description of the complete system that results from the integration of these three components, namely, the (constraint) query language, the (constraint) logic program and the taxonomy.

The rest of the paper is organized as follows. Section 2.1 presents our notion of constraint system. In Section 2.2 we show how the Höhfeld-Smolka constraint system [8] can be described in our formalism.

The third Section describes the constraint logic programming scheme. We characterize a constraint logic programming system and give four equivalent semantics. In Section 3.1 we present the proof theory of the system in terms of a reduction relation and a derivation relation, while Section 3.2 is devoted to the model theory, where we show the existence of a least model, which is also the least fixed point of the immediate consequence operator.

The fourth Section presents a detailed example illustrating the main points of the theory. In Section 4.1 we characterize a constraint logic programming system that deals with taxonomic information, in Section 4.2 a canonical form of constraints is introduced in order to cater for "concise" type constraints, and in Section 4.3 we show a concrete computation done by a constraint logic program that defines relations over a wild life taxonomy.

Finally, Section 5 includes some comments on the research done in the paper.

2 Abstract constraint systems

This section presents our notion of constraint system, which relies on two primitive concepts: a set of atomic constraints and a monoid of substitutions. The application of a substitution to a constraint is formalized by a monoid action, similar to those used by Williams in his instantiation theory [21].

2.1 Constraint systems

A *right action* of a monoid Σ on a set A is a function from $A \times \Sigma$ to A, written $(p, \theta) \mapsto p\theta$, such that the following two conditions hold:

1) $p\epsilon = p$, for every $p \in A$; and
2) $p(\theta\sigma) = (p\theta)\sigma$ for all $p \in A$ and $\theta, \sigma \in \Sigma$.

Here, ϵ is the identity on Σ and $\theta\sigma$ denotes the result of applying the monoid operation to the pair (θ, σ). We call the elements of Σ *substitutions*.

A *constraint system* is a set A of *atomic constraints*, a set $V \subseteq A$ of *valid* atomic constraints, a monoid Σ of *substitutions*, and a right action of Σ on A. The set V is required to be stable under the action, that is $a\theta \in V$ for any $a \in V$ and $\theta \in \Sigma$.

A *constraint* is a finite subset of A. The intended meaning of a constraint is the conjunction of the atomic constraints comprising it. In particular, the empty constraint $\emptyset$ is interpreted as "true", and $\{a\}$ will be identified with a for $a \in A$. A constraint C is *satisfiable* if there is $\theta \in \Sigma$ such that $a\theta \in V$ for every $a \in C$. We then say that θ *satisfies* C. The set of all satisfiable constraints will be denoted by Sat.

Saraswat [17] proposed treating a constraint system as a system of partial information in the sense of Scott [18], characterized basically by a set of objects together with an entailment relation. In our model, we can specify that a constraint C "entails" another constraint C' if any substitution satisfying C satisfies C'. With this definition, it is easy to see that a constraint system in our sense is also a constraint system in the sense of Saraswat, but for lack of space we omit the details.

To illustrate these concepts, let us look at a simple and well-known example, concerning systems of equations over first-order terms. The set of atomic constraints A is formed by all equations $t \doteq u$, the subset V of valid atomic constraints has all equations of the form $t \doteq t$, and Σ is the set of usual first-order substitutions. Σ is a monoid with the standard composition, and the application of a substitution to an equation defines a right action. An atomic constraint $t \doteq u$ is satisfiable if there is $\theta \in \Sigma$ such that $t\theta \doteq u\theta$ is valid, i.e., $t\theta = u\theta$.

As noted in the introduction, the example that motivated the present formulation of a constraint system is ordinary logic programming itself. A logic program defines a constraint system as follows: The atomic constraints are the atomic formulae, the substitutions are the first-order substitutions, and the valid atomic constraints are the atoms that are logical consequences of the program.

Two more complex applications will be presented later. The first one, in Section 2.2, shows that a constraint language in the sense of Höfeld and Smolka [8] can be seen as a constraint system. The second one, in Section 4, shows a very simple constraint system built on type hierarchical knowledge.

2.2   The Höfeld-Smolka constraint scheme

As another (more complex) example of constraint system, we show how the Höfeld-Smolka constraint scheme [8] can be described in our formalism. The contents of this section will not be used in the rest of the paper.

For sets X, Y, let $p(X)$ and $\mathcal{P}(X)$ denote the sets of all finite subsets and all subsets of X, respectively, and $[X \to Y]$ the set of all functions from X to Y. A *(Höfeld-Smolka) constraint language* is a tuple

$$L = (\text{Var}, \text{Con}, \nu, \text{Int}),$$

where Var is a set of *variables*, Con is a set of *constraints*, ν is a function $\nu : \text{Con} \to p(\text{Var})$ assigning to every constraint ϕ the finite set $\nu(\phi)$ of *variables constrained by* ϕ, and Int is a nonempty set of *interpretations*. An interpretation is a pair $I = (D^I, \llbracket \cdot \rrbracket^I)$, where D^I is a nonempty set called the *domain of the interpretation* and $\llbracket \cdot \rrbracket^I : \text{Con} \to \mathcal{P}([\text{Var} \to D^I])$ is the *solution mapping*. If we call an *assignment over I* any mapping from Var to D^I, we see that the solution mapping associates a set of assignments with every constraint ϕ, called the *solutions* of ϕ in I. An interpretation must satisfy the condition that if $\alpha \in [\![\phi]\!]^I$ and β is an assignment that agrees with α on $\nu(\phi)$ then $\beta \in [\![\phi]\!]^I$.

A constraint ϕ is *satisfiable* if there exists an interpretation I in which ϕ has a solution, that is, such that $[\![\phi]\!]^I \neq \emptyset$. If this is the case, it is also said that I *satisfies* ϕ. The constraint is *valid* in I if $[\![\phi]\!]^I = [\text{Var} \rightarrow D^I]$. Finally, a *valid* constraint is one that is valid in every interpretation.

A *renaming* is a bijection $\rho : \text{Var} \rightarrow \text{Var}$ such that $\rho(x) = x$ for all but a finite set of variables. We then say that a constraint ϕ' is a *ρ-variant* of a constraint ϕ if

$$\rho(\nu(\phi)) = \nu(\phi') \quad \text{and} \quad [\![\phi]\!]^I = [\![\phi']\!]^I \rho = \{\alpha \circ \rho \,|\, \alpha \in [\![\phi']\!]^I\}$$

for every interpretation I. Note that in this case ϕ is a ρ^{-1}-variant of ϕ'. Note also that variants need not be unique. We say that ϕ' is a *variant* of ϕ if it is a ρ-variant for some ρ. Clearly, a constraint is satisfiable if and only if each of its variants is satisfiable. A similar statement applies to validity (in an interpretation I). A constraint language is *closed under renaming* if every constraint has a variant for every renaming.

We are now going to show how we can define a constraint system $S = (A, V, \Sigma)$ such that $\text{Con} \subseteq A$, leading to the same notions of satisfiability and validity when restricted to the constraints in Con.

Basically, A contains all constraints $\phi \in \text{Con}$ together with all "instances" of ϕ obtained by substituting elements of the domains D^I for the variables constrained by ϕ. More formally, any such instance is a pair $(\phi, \alpha\lceil\nu(\phi))$, where $\alpha\lceil\nu(\phi)$ is the restriction to $\nu(\phi)$ of some assignment α over an interpretation I. We denote these instances by ϕ_α, with the understanding that $\phi_\alpha = \phi_\beta$ if α and β agree on $\nu(\phi)$. The set V is formed by all valid $\phi \in \text{Con}$ (in the Höfeld-Smolka sense) and all ϕ_α such that $\alpha \in [\![\phi]\!]^I$ for some I.

The set Σ is formed by all assignments over any domain and all renamings (or just the identity of Var if the constraint language L is not closed under renaming). The composition $\theta\sigma$ is defined to be θ if θ is an assignment, otherwise is the ordinary function composition of the renaming θ with (the assignment or renaming) σ. Clearly, this operation is associative and has the identity renaming as the identity element ϵ.

To define the action $A \times \Sigma \rightarrow A$, suppose a variant ϕ_ρ has been selected for every $\phi \in \text{Con}$ and every renaming ρ. Then, for all $a \in A$ and $\theta \in \Sigma$:

$$a\theta = \begin{cases} \phi_\theta & \text{if } a = \phi \in \text{Con}, \theta \text{ a renaming or assignment,} \\ \phi_\alpha & \text{if } a = \phi_\alpha, \alpha \text{ an assignment.} \end{cases}$$

Clearly, such an application defines an action. It is immediate to verify that V is stable under Σ, so that we have indeed a constraint system.

Proposition 2.1 *Let $\phi \in \text{Con}$. Then ϕ is satisfiable (resp., valid) with respect to L if and only ϕ is satisfiable (resp., valid) with respect to S.*

Proof If ϕ is satisfiable with respect to L, there is an interpretation I such that $[\![\phi]\!]^I \neq \emptyset$. Let $\alpha \in [\![\phi]\!]^I$. By definition of S we have $\phi_\alpha \in V$, and so ϕ is satisfiable in S. The converse is also immediate. The statement on the validity of a constraint follows from the fact that $\phi \in \text{Con}$ is valid with respect to L if and only if $\phi \in V$. ∎

3   Constraint logic programming scheme

We now extend our abstract framework by showing how to embed a constraint system in a logic programming scheme.

A *constraint logic programming system* is a set A_C of *atomic constraints*, a set $V \subseteq A_C$ of *valid* atomic constraints, a set A_P of *program* atoms disjoint from A_C, a monoid Σ of *substitutions*, and a right action of Σ on $A_C \cup A_P$. The three sets A_C, V and A_P must be stable under Σ.

We employ the notational conventions used previously and constraints are defined as before. A *goal* is a finite subset G of A_P, and $\leftarrow G$ is called a *goal clause*. A *program clause*, or just *clause*, has the form $p \leftarrow C, G$, where C is a constraint, G a goal and p a program atom. By a *formula* we mean a goal, a goal clause or a program clause. An *instance* of a formula f is a formula $f\theta$ for some $\theta \in \Sigma$. A *constraint logic program* is a finite set of clauses.

3.1   Operational semantics

The operational semantics differs from the familiar treatment for Horn clause logic in two respects. In our abstract setting, it does not make sense to speak of variants of clauses with no variables in common with the goal to be reduced because there are no variables in the first place. Thus, instead of a single substitution unifying the atom selected in the goal with the head of a candidate clause, we use two substitutions, one for the goal and another for the clause. The idea of using two substitutions was borrowed from [4]. Furthermore, most general unifiers may not exist, so the substitutions are arbitrary, provided that they unify the selected atom with the clause head.

A goal G *reduces in one step* to a goal G' with constraint C and substitution θ in a program P, denoted $G \xrightarrow{C,\theta}_P G'$, if

1) $G = q, H$ for some atom q and goal H,
2) there exist $p \leftarrow C', Q \in P$ and $\rho \in \Sigma$ such that $q\theta = p\rho$ and $C = C'\rho \in$ Sat, and
3) $G' = Q\rho, H\theta$.

The *reduction* of a goal G to the goal G' with constraint C and substitution θ in a program P, written $G \xRightarrow{C,\theta}_P G'$, is now defined recursively as follows:

1) $G \xRightarrow{\emptyset,\epsilon}_P G$.
2) If $G \xRightarrow{C,\theta}_P G' \xrightarrow{C',\theta'}_P G''$ and $D = C\theta' \cup C' \in$ Sat then $G \xRightarrow{D,\theta\theta'}_P G''$.

We then say that G *reduces* to G' with C and θ in P. To simplify our notation we often omit the reference to the program P, writing $G \xrightarrow{C,\theta} G'$ and $G \xRightarrow{C,\theta} G'$.

For some purposes, viz. the equivalence between the operational and the declarative semantics (see theorems 3.4 and 3.7), it is more convenient to work with a derivation relation rather than with the reduction relation. The *derivation relation* has the form

$$P \vdash G[C; \theta],$$

where P is a program, G a goal, C a satisfiable constraint and θ a substitution. The intuitive meaning of this relation, to be clarified by the soundness theorem, is that every substitution satisfying the constraint C satisfies $G\theta$. The derivation relation is characterized by the following derivation rules.

Null goal

$$\frac{}{P \vdash \emptyset[C; \theta]} \quad \text{if} \quad C \in \text{Sat}, \theta \in \Sigma. \qquad (N)$$

Reduction

$$\frac{P \vdash Q\rho, G\theta[D; \sigma]}{P \vdash q, G[C\rho\sigma \cup D; \theta\sigma]} \quad \text{if} \quad \begin{cases} p \leftarrow C, Q \in P, \\ q\theta = p\rho, \\ C\rho\sigma \cup D \in \text{Sat.} \end{cases} \qquad (R)$$

As expected, the derivation and the reduction relations are equivalent in some sense. The precise statement of the equivalence is as follows, proved in [13].

Proposition 3.1 $P \vdash G[C; \theta]$ *if and only if there exist* $D \in \text{Sat}$ *and* $\alpha, \beta \in \Sigma$ *such that* $G \xRightarrow{D,\alpha}_P \emptyset$, $D\beta \subseteq C \in \text{Sat}$ *and* $\theta = \alpha\beta$.

3.2 Declarative semantics

The declarative semantics of our language scheme is similar to the declarative semantics of Horn clause logic, which it generalizes in two ways. Firstly, instead of being a set of atoms, an interpretation is a set of "constrained atoms" (C, p). Intuitively, the constrained atoms represent implications $C \Rightarrow p$, stating that the truth of p is conditional upon the validity of C. Secondly, in our general framework we cannot restrict ourselves to "ground" constrained atoms (a formula f can be defined to be *ground* if $f\theta = f$ for every substitution θ), but then we must require that an interpretation be closed under "specialization". This means that with every constrained atom an interpretation must contain all its instances, as well as all constrained atoms obtained by strenghtening the constraint. The precise definition of interpretation is the following.

An *interpretation* is a subset I of $\text{Sat} \times A_P$ satisfying the following conditions:

1) If $(C, p) \in I$ and $C\theta \in \text{Sat}$ then $(C\theta, p\theta) \in I$, where θ is a substitution.
2) If $(C, p) \in I$ and $C \cup D \in \text{Sat}$ then $(C \cup D, p) \in I$, where D is a constraint.

Note that $\emptyset$ and $\text{Sat} \times A_P$ are interpretations. If C is a satisfiable constraint and G a goal, we denote by (C, G) the set of all (C, p) for $p \in G$.

An interpretation I *satisfies* a goal G under constraint D if $(D, G) \subseteq I$. I *satisfies* a clause $p \leftarrow C, Q$ under constraint D if, whenever $(D, Q) \subseteq I$ and $C \cup D \in \text{Sat}$, we have $(C \cup D, p) \in I$. A *model* of a program P is an interpretation M such that, for every instance $p \leftarrow C, Q$ of a clause in P and every $D \in \text{Sat}$, M satisfies $p \leftarrow C, Q$ under D.

The next proposition collects some important properties of models of programs.

Proposition 3.2 *The following properties hold, for every program P:*
1) $\text{Sat} \times A_P$ *is a model of P.*
2) *If $(M_i)_{i \in I}$ is a nonempty family of models of P, their intersection $\bigcap_{i \in I} M_i$ is also a model of P.*
3) *P has a least model, denoted by M_P.*

We write $P \models G[C]$ if every model of P satisfies G under C. Note that this is equivalent to $(C, G) \subseteq M_P$.

We next characterize M_P as the least fixed point of the *immediate consequence operator* associated with P. This is the function $T_P : \mathcal{P}(\text{Sat} \times A_P) \rightarrow \mathcal{P}(\text{Sat} \times A_P)$ given by

$$T_P(X) = \{(C \cup D, p) | \exists p \leftarrow C, Q \in \text{inst}(P), (D, Q) \subseteq X, C \cup D \in \text{Sat}\},$$

where $\text{inst}(P)$ is the set of all instances of all clauses of P.

Now we can state the equivalence between least models and least fixed points. The proof of the next proposition is again in [13].

Proposition 3.3 *The following properties hold:*
1) *The function T_P is continuous and maps interpretations to interpretations.*
2) *An interpretation M is a model of a program P if and only if M is a pre-fixed point of T_P, that is $T_P(M) \subseteq M$.*
3) *$M_P = \text{lfp}(T_P)$, for every program P.*

The soundness theorem is easy to state and prove.

Theorem 3.4 (Soundness) *If $P \vdash H[E; \tau]$ then $P \models H\tau[E]$.*

Proof If M is a model of P, we must show that $(E, H\tau) \subseteq M$. The proof is by induction on the length of the derivation of $P \vdash H[E; \tau]$. If the length is zero then $H = \emptyset$ and the conclusion is immediate. Otherwise H has the form q, G and the last step in the derivation was obtained by an application of rule

(R). There exist $p \leftarrow C, Q \in P$, $\theta, \rho, \sigma \in \Sigma$ and $D \in \text{Sat}$ such that $q\theta = p\rho$, $P \vdash Q\rho, G\theta[D;\sigma]$, $E = C\rho\sigma \cup D \in \text{Sat}$ and $\tau = \theta\sigma$. We must show that $(C\rho\sigma \cup D, q\theta\sigma) \in M$ and $(C\rho\sigma \cup D, G\theta\sigma) \subseteq M$. By induction hypothesis, $(D, Q\rho\sigma \cup G\theta\sigma) \subseteq M$. This already shows that $(C\rho\sigma \cup D, G\theta\sigma) \subseteq M$. On the other hand, from $(D, Q\rho\sigma) \subseteq M$ it follows that $(C\rho\sigma \cup D, p\rho\sigma) \in M$, because M is a model. The conclusion follows from the equality $q\theta = p\rho$. ∎

Before we prove the completeness theorem, we need two lemmas, whose easy proof we omit.

Lemma 3.5 *If* $P \vdash H[E;\tau]$ *then* $P \vdash H\tau[E;\epsilon]$.

Lemma 3.6 *If* $P \vdash H[E;\epsilon]$ *and* $P \vdash K[F;\epsilon]$, *with* $E \subseteq F$, *then* $P \vdash H, K[F;\epsilon]$.

Theorem 3.7 (Completeness) *If* $P \models H\tau[E]$ *then* $P \vdash H[E;\tau]$.

Proof If $P \models H\tau[E]$, we have $(E, H\tau) \subseteq M_P = T_P{\uparrow}\omega$, therefore $(E, H\tau) \subseteq T_P{\uparrow}n$ for some $n \geq 0$. The result is proved by induction on n. If $n = 0$, we immediately have $P \vdash \emptyset[E;\tau]$. For $n = k+1$, the inductive step will be proved by induction on the cardinality of H. If $H = \emptyset$, again there is nothing to prove. If H has the form q, G, we have $(E, q\tau) \in T_P{\uparrow}(k+1)$ and $(E, G\tau) \subseteq T_P{\uparrow}(k+1)$. By definition of T_P, there exist $p \leftarrow C, Q \in P$, $\rho \in \Sigma$ and $D \subseteq_f A_C$ such that $q\tau = p\rho$, $E = C\rho \cup D \in \text{Sat}$ and $(D, Q\rho) \subseteq T_P{\uparrow}k$. By the induction hypothesis on n, $P \vdash Q[D;\rho]$ and, by lemma 3.5, $P \vdash Q\rho[D;\epsilon]$. On the other hand, by the induction hypothesis on the cardinality of H, $P \vdash G[E;\tau]$ and, again by lemma 3.5, $P \vdash G\tau[E;\epsilon]$. As $D \subseteq E$, we conclude by lemma 3.6 that $P \vdash Q\rho, G\tau[E;\epsilon]$. Finally, an application of derivation rule (R) gives $P \vdash q, G[E;\tau]$, as desired. ∎

4 Example

We will now look at an example of constraint logic programming involving hierarchical type systems, also called taxonomic systems, which are here formalized by a finite partially ordered set with greatest element. In [11, 12] we gave a more complex definition of taxonomy that allows infinite sets of types.

4.1 Constraint logic programming system

Let $(T, \leq, \top)$ be a finite partially ordered set of *types*, with greatest element $\top$, W a set of (type) *variables* and R a set of *relation names* each one with its arity, denoted by *relation/arity*. The set A_C of atomic constraints is defined as

$$A_C = \{x : D \mid x \in T \cup W, D \subseteq T\}.$$

In an atomic constraint $x : D$, the set D is intended to represent the union of all its types. Intuitively, $x : D$ constrains the type of x to be a subtype of a type in D. This justifies the following definition of valid atomic constraint.

A constraint $x : D$ is *valid* if $x \in W$ and $\top \in D$, or $x \in T$ and $x \leq d$ for some $d \in D$. The set of valid atomic constraints is denoted by V as before. Thus, a valid constraint $x : D$ has $D \neq \emptyset$. The set A_P of program atoms is

$$A_P = \{r(x_1, \ldots, x_n) \mid r/n \in R, x_1, \ldots, x_n \in T \cup W\}.$$

A substitution $\sigma \in \Sigma$ is a finite set of pairs $\{v_1 \backslash x_1, \ldots, v_n \backslash x_n\}$ where $v_i \in W$ and $x_i \in T \cup W$, for every $1 \leq i \leq n$, and such that the variables on the left, called the *domain* of the substitution, are all distinct. Note that we do not require that $x_i \neq v_i$. The composition of two substitutions σ and θ is a substitution whose domain is the set of all variables in the domain of σ and θ. The element $v \backslash x$ belongs to $\sigma\theta$ if and only if one of the following conditions holds:

1) $v \backslash x \in \sigma$ and x is not in the domain of θ;
2) there exist $v \backslash w \in \sigma$ and $w \backslash x \in \theta$;
3) $v \backslash x \in \theta$ and v is not in the domain of σ.

For example, if $\sigma = \{u \backslash x, v \backslash y\}$ and $\theta = \{v \backslash x, y \backslash z\}$, $\sigma\theta = \{u \backslash x, v \backslash z, y \backslash z\}$. Note that Σ is a monoid since composition is an associative operation whose identity is the empty set.

We apply a substitution σ to every $x \in T \cup W$ by

$$x\sigma = \begin{cases} y & \text{if } x \backslash y \in \sigma, \\ x & \text{otherwise.} \end{cases}$$

The right action from $(A_C \cup A_P) \times \Sigma$ to $A_C \cup A_P$ is now defined as follows:

1) $(x : D)\sigma = (x\sigma) : D$,
2) $r(x_1, \ldots, x_n)\sigma = r(x_1\sigma, \ldots, x_n\sigma)$.

It is easy to verify that this is a right action under which the sets A_C, V and A_P are stable.

4.2 Canonical form of constraints

Two constraints C and C' are said to be *equivalent* when any substitution satisfies C if and only if it satisfies C'. In this case, we write $C \equiv C'$. As we have seen, a reduction of a goal G to $\emptyset$ returns a satisfiable constraint C and a substitution σ, meaning that every substitution satisfying C satisfies $G\sigma$. In general, there are several constraints C' equivalent to C but some are more "concise" and "useful" than the others. For instance, if $d_1 \leq d_2$ in T and $v \in W$, the constraints $v : \{d_1, d_2\}$ and $v : \{d_2\}$ contain the same "information", in the sense that they are equivalent, but we prefer to give the last one as an answer since it is the most concise representation of that information. In order to formalize this concept, we need some definitions.

The *maximal part* of $D \subseteq T$ is the set of its maximal elements:

$$maximal(D) = \{d \in D \mid (\forall t \in D)d \leq t \Rightarrow d = t\}.$$

The simpler form of an atomic constraint $v : D$, with $v \in W$ and $\top \notin D$, is then $v : maximal(D)$. However, other problems arise when we deal with a generic constraint C. First of all, valid atomic constraints are uninformative and can be removed from C. Secondly, when a variable is constrained by several atomic constraints, the constraints can be combined to form a single atomic constraint. To tackle those cases we proceed as follows. The *conjunction* of two sets of types, D_1 and D_2, is defined by

$$D_1 \wedge D_2 = \downarrow D_1 \cap \downarrow D_2$$

where $\downarrow D$ is the *down-closure* of D, i.e., $\downarrow D = \{t \in T \mid (\exists d \in D)t \leq d\}$. If $C_v = \{D \mid v : D \in C\}$ is the set of all sets of types constraining a given variable v, the *canonical form* of a constraint C is the constraint

$$canonical(C) = \{v : maximal(\bigwedge C_v) \mid C_v \neq \emptyset\} \setminus V.$$

This canonical form verifies those nice properties of equivalence and uniqueness one expects, when restricted to the satisfiable constraints, as stated in the next proposition (see [13] for a proof).

Proposition 4.1 *Let C and C' be satisfiable constraints. Then:*
1) C and canonical(C) are equivalent constraints.
2) $C \equiv C'$ if and only if canonical(C) = canonical(C').

Note that there exist many canonical unsatisfiable constraints, all representing false or the contradiction, but there is no need to choose from any of them because only satisfiable constraints may occur in reductions.

4.3 Wild life

Let us see an example based on the taxonomy illustrated in Figure 1. $\top$ (top), `animal`, `habitat`, ... are the types to be considered and the partial order relation is `animal` $\leq \top$, `habitat` $\leq \top$, ... For the purposes of this paper, we are not concerned with the way this taxonomy is represented or how the constraint solver is implemented. We will assume in this example that the constraints will be automatically converted to canonical form.

To simplify the notation, an atomic constraint $x : \{t_1, \ldots, t_n\}$ will be written in the form $x : t_1 + \cdots + t_n$.

Consider the following program P:

```
carnivorous(X) ← X:feline+aquaticMammal+penguin+birdOfPrey

herbivorous(X) ← X:elephant+ruminant

habitat(X,Y) ← X:lion+elephant+ruminant, Y:savana
habitat(X,Y) ← X:tiger+antelope, Y:jungle
habitat(X,Y) ← X:cetaceous, Y:sea
```

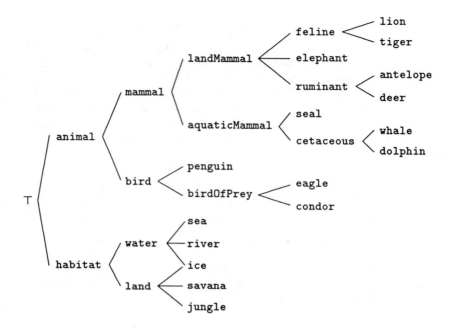

Figure 1: Wild Life Taxonomy.

```
habitat(X,Y) ← X:seal+penguin, Y:ice
fly(X) ← X:birdOfPrey
aquatic(X) ← Y:water, habitat(X,Y)
terrestrial(X) ← X:bird, fly(X)
terrestrial(X) ← Y:land, habitat(X,Y)
eat(X,Z) ← X:feline, Z:ruminant, habitat(X,Y), habitat(Z,Y)
```

We will reduce $G = \texttt{carnivorous(X)},\texttt{aquatic(X)},\texttt{terrestrial(X)}$ to the empty goal, trying all the possible clauses in each reduction step. In this particular case, all substitutions are empty. Therefore, if $G \overset{C,\epsilon}{\Longrightarrow} G' \overset{D,\epsilon}{\Longrightarrow} G''$ and $C' = C \cup D \in \text{Sat}$, we conclude $G \overset{C',\epsilon}{\Longrightarrow} G''$.

(1) $G \overset{\emptyset,\epsilon}{\Longrightarrow} \texttt{carnivorous(X)},\texttt{aquatic(X)},\texttt{terrestrial(X)}$
   We can apply the only clause that exists for *carnivorous/1*.

(2) $G \overset{C_1,\epsilon}{\Longrightarrow} \texttt{aquatic(X)},\texttt{terrestrial(X)}$
   where $C_1 = \texttt{X:feline+aquaticMammal+penguin+birdOfPrey}$.
   There is also just one clause for *aquatic/1* which will be used next.

(3) $G \overset{C_2,\epsilon}{\Longrightarrow} \texttt{habitat(X,Y)},\texttt{terrestrial(X)}$
   and $C_2 = \texttt{X:feline+aquaticMammal+penguin+birdOfPrey,Y:water}$.

Now there are four clauses for *habitat/2* but only the last two have compatible constraints with C_2 and the reduction forks in steps (4) and (5).

(4) $G \overset{C_3,\epsilon}{\Longrightarrow} \text{terrestrial(X)}, C_3 \equiv \text{X:cetaceous,Y:sea}.$

In spite of the fact that there are two clauses for *terrestrial/1*, none can be applied. The first constrains X to a **bird** and the second restricts Y to **land**. So, the computation cannot proceed.

(5) $G \overset{C_3',\epsilon}{\Longrightarrow} \text{terrestrial(X)}, C_3' \equiv \text{X:seal+penguin,Y:ice}.$

In this case both clauses for *terrestrial/1* are tried (steps (6) and (7)).

(6) $G \overset{C_4,\epsilon}{\Longrightarrow} \text{fly(X)}, C_4 \equiv \text{X:penguin,Y:ice}.$

Once again, the reduction does not succeed because the constraint associated with the clause for *fly/1*, X:birdOfPrey, joint to C_4 is insatisfiable.

(7) $G \overset{C_4',\epsilon}{\Longrightarrow} \text{habitat(X,Y)}, C_4' \equiv \text{X:seal+penguin,Y:ice}.$

Applying the last clause for *habitat/2*, the only compatible with the constraint of the reduction, we finally reach the end.

(8) $G \overset{C_5,\epsilon}{\Longrightarrow} \emptyset, C_5 \equiv \text{X:seal+penguin,Y:ice}.$

We conclude that $P \vdash G[D; \theta]$ for every satisfiable constraint D and every substitution θ such that $C_5\theta \subseteq D$ and we know that every substitution satisfying D satisfies $G\theta$. But, as usual, only the atomic constraints in the goal variables provide "useful" information and in this case "the most general answer" is the constraint X:seal+penguin.

5 Conclusions

The main purpose of the work described in this paper was to develop a constraint logic programming scheme based on an abstract notion of constraint system which, by itself, relies on two primitive concepts: constraints and substitutions. It could be argued that, since constraints are a more general concept, substitutions should not be part of the basic model. The fact is that substitutions cannot be entirely avoided. For example, when substitutions are replaced by equality constraints in the usual logic programming model, to reduce the resulting system of equations to canonical form one has to resort to the substitution concept itself. The study of the interplay between substitutions and equality constraints in our abstract setting is a topic for future research.

We tried to keep our framework as simple as possible and that led us to a very abstract scheme—perhaps too abstract to have any useful properties. As a consequence, some usual notions are not supported by the model, like the notion of most general unifier. Nevertheless, this scheme allows definitions of the declarative, fixed-point and refutation semantics, which are straightforward generalizations of the corresponding definitions in the familiar logic programming framework. Further properties should be obtained by refining the basic model, but the equivalence of the semantics remains true however complex the refinings may be. In particular, we intend to investigate conditions that guarantee the existence of most general unifiers for all pairs of unifiable atomic constraints.

There exist several works in the literature dealing with constraints and types. For example, [5] shows how concept languages can be conceived as constraint theories, and [3] presents a constraint system for logic programming with feature terms. Compared with these works our types are relatively simple, but our main aim was to formalize the notion of useful and concise answers to queries and we deliberately avoided the consideration of types with more structure that just type inclusion. We are currently investigating the extension of our techniques to concept languages, inspired by the work of Lenzerini and Schaerf [10]. The next "natural" extension will be to consider types structured as feature terms, but this is a topic for future research.

Acknowledgements

This work was partially supported by INIC and JNICT. Margarida Mamede owns a scholarship from INIC. The referees are thanked for their comments.

References

[1] H. Aït-Kaci, R. Nasr. LOGIN: A Logic Programming Language with Built-in Inheritance. *Journal of Logic Programming*, 3:185-215, 1986.

[2] H. Aït-Kaci, A. Podelski. *Towards a Meaning of LIFE*. PRL Research Report 11, DEC Paris Research Laboratory, June, 1991.

[3] H. Aït-Kaci, A. Podelski, G. Smolka. A Feature-Based Constraint System for Logic Programming with Entailment. In *Proc. FGCS'92*, ICOT, 1992.

[4] K. Akama. *Generalized Logic Programs on Specialization Systems and SLDA Resolution*. Dept. of Information Engineering, Hokkaido University, Japan, 1991.

[5] F. Baader, H.-J. Bürckert, B. Hollunder, W. Nutt, J. Siekmann. Concept Logics. In *Proc. Symposium on Computational Logic*, J. W. Lloyd (ed.) ESPRIT Basic Research Series, DG XIII, Springer-Verlag, 1990.

[6] L. Cardelli. A Semantics of Multiple Inheritance. *Information and Control*, 76:138-164, 1988.

[7] P. Van Hentenryck. *Constraint Satisfaction in Logic Programming*. Logic Programming Series, MIT Press, 1989.

[8] M. Höfeld, G. Smolka. *Definite Relations over Constraint Languages.* LILOG Report 53, IWBS, IBM Deutschland, October, 1988.

[9] J. Jaffar, J.-L. Lassez. Constraint Logic Programming. In *Proc. 14th ACM POPL Conference*, Munich, 1987.

[10] M. Lenzerini, A. Schaerf. Querying Concept-based Knowledge Bases. In *Proc. International Workshop PDK'91*, Kaiserslautern, H. Boley and M. M. Richter (eds.), LNAI 567, Springer-Verlag, 1991.

[11] M. Mamede, L. Monteiro. Answers as Type Constraints. Presented at the *International Workshop on Non-standard Queries and Non-standard Answers*, Toulouse, July 1-3, 1991.

[12] M. Mamede, L. Monteiro. A Constraint-Based Language for Querying Taxonomic Systems. In *Proc. 5th Portuguese Conference on Artificial Intelligence*, P. Barahona, L. Moniz Pereira and A. Porto (eds.), LNAI 541, Springer-Verlag, 1991.

[13] M. Mamede, L. Monteiro. *A Constraint Logic Programming Approach to Taxonomic Reasoning.* Technical Report RT 8/92-DI/UNL, Universidade Nova de Lisboa, 1992.

[14] L. Monteiro, A. Porto. A Transformational View of Inheritance in Logic Programming. In *Logic Programming: Proceedings of the Seventh International Conference*, D. H. D. Warren and P. Szeredi (eds.), MIT Press, Cambridge MA, 1990.

[15] A. Porto. A Framework for Deducing Useful Answers to Queries. In *Proc. IFIP WG 10.1 Workshop on Concepts and Characteristics of Knowledge-Based Systems*, M. Tokoro (ed.), North-Holland, 1988.

[16] A. Porto, M. Filgueiras. A Logic Programming Approach to Natural Language Semantics. In *Proc. International Symposium on Logic Programming*, IEEE Press, 1984.

[17] V. Saraswat. *Concurrent Constraint Programming Languages.* PhD thesis, Carnegie-Mellon University, January, 1989.

[18] D. Scott. Domains for Denotational Semantics. In *ICALP 82*, Springer Verlag, New York, 1982.

[19] D. S. Touretzki. *The Mathematics of Inheritance Systems.* Pitman, London, 1986.

[20] P. Wegner. Classification in Object-Oriented Systems. In *Proc. Object-Oriented Programming Workshop*, ACM Sigplan Notices 21 (10), 173-182, 1986.

[21] J. G. Williams. *Instantiation Theory.* LNAI 518, Springer-Verlag, 1991.

Deductive Databases

Controlling the Search in Bottom-Up Evaluation

Raghu Ramakrishnan
Divesh Srivastava
S. Sudarshan
Computer Sciences Department
University of Wisconsin–Madison
Madison, WI 53706, U.S.A.
{raghu,divesh,sudarshan}@cs.wisc.edu

Abstract

Bottom-up evaluation of queries on deductive databases has many advantages over an evaluation scheme such as Prolog. It is sound and complete with respect to the declarative semantics of least Herbrand models for positive Horn clause programs. In particular, it is able to avoid infinite loops by detecting repeated (possibly cyclic) subgoals. Further, in many database applications, it is more efficient than Prolog due to its set-orientedness. However, the completely set-oriented, breadth-first search strategy of bottom-up evaluation has certain disadvantages. For example, to evaluate several classes of programs with negation (or aggregation), it is necessary to order the inferences; in essence, we must evaluate all answers to a negative subgoal before making an inference that depends upon the negative subgoal. A completely breadth-first search strategy ([14]) would have to maintain a lot of redundant subgoal dependency information to achieve this.

We present a technique to order the use of generated subgoals, that is a hybrid between pure breadth-first and pure depth-first search. The technique, called Ordered_Search, is able to maintain subgoal dependency information efficiently, while being able to detect repeated subgoals, and avoid infinite loops. Also, the technique avoids repeated computation and is complete for DATALOG. We demonstrate the power of Ordered_Search through two applications. First, we show that it can be used to evaluate programs with left-to-right modularly stratified negation and aggregation more efficiently than with any previously known bottom-up technique. Second, we illustrate its use for optimizing single-answer queries for linear programs.

1 Introduction

Several studies ([11, 18, 3]) have shown similarities between different top-down evaluation methods and Magic Templates (or, Alexander Templates) based bottom-up evaluation methods for positive programs when all answers to a query are desired. In essence, the same subgoals and answers are generated by these methods when they use the same orderings of body literals in evaluating rules. However, there are important differences as well. In particular, the order in which subgoals and answers are generated and used in top-down evaluation strategies is different from the order in which they are generated and used in bottom-up evaluations. Top-down evaluations typically synchronize the generation of subgoals and answers to those subgoals, whereas bottom-up evaluations generate them asynchronously. This difference is not relevant for positive programs when all answers to a query are desired. However, when the program contains negation (or aggregation), the order in which inferences are performed becomes crucial to the correctness of the method, even when all answers to the query are desired. Again, when only a single answer to the query is desired, the order in which facts are generated and used becomes important, and the depth-first search strategy of a top-down evaluation scheme such as Prolog can perform much better than the breadth-first search strategy of bottom-up evaluation methods.

We describe a memoing technique called Ordered_Search that works on the transformed program obtained using Magic Templates rewriting, and is a hybrid between tuple-oriented top-down evaluation and set-oriented bottom-up evaluation. This technique generates subgoals and answers to subgoals asynchronously, as in bottom-up evaluation, while ordering the use of generated subgoals in a manner reminiscent of top-down evaluation. As a consequence, Ordered_Search is able to efficiently evaluate left-to-right modularly stratified programs [14] (see Sections 4.1 and 4.2), and restrict the search space in many cases when we want a single answer to the query (see Section 4.3).

1.1 Motivating Examples

Example 1.1 (Modular negation)
The class of programs with modular negation [14] naturally extends the class of programs with stratified and locally stratified negation while retaining a two-valued model. Consider the following left-to-right modularly stratified program-query pair $\langle P_{even}, Q_{even} \rangle$:

$$r1 : even(X) :- succ(X, Y1), succ(Y1, Y), even(Y).$$
$$r2 : even(X) :- succ(X, Y), \neg even(Y).$$
$$r3 : even(0).$$
$$succ(1, 0). \quad succ(2, 1). \quad \dots \quad succ(n, n-1).$$
$$\text{Query: } ?\text{-}\neg even(m).$$

Ross [14] proposed a supplementary magic sets rewriting of $\langle P_{even}, Q_{even} \rangle$ in conjunction with a bottom-up method for evaluating the rewritten program. This method explicitly stores all the subgoal dependency information for negative subgoals. Ross' approach on this example would take $O(m^2)$ space and make $O(m^2)$ derivations since it would compute and store all the dependencies between subgoals transitively.

The technique presented in this paper, Ordered_Search, would compute and store only information about direct dependencies; hence, it would use $O(m)$ space and make $O(m)$ derivations in computing the query answer. (For more details, see Example 3.2.)

We describe other top-down and bottom-up techniques that can evaluate left-to-right modularly stratified programs in Section 5. As an example, the doubled program technique of Kemp et al. [7] would also use $O(m)$ space and make $O(m)$ derivations on this example. However, if rule $r1$ were removed from P_{even}, the doubled program approach would make $O(m^2)$ derivations, though it would still use only $O(m)$ space. Even on this modified program, Ordered_Search would compute the answer to the query using $O(m)$ space and making $O(m)$ derivations. □

Example 1.2 (Obtaining a single answer)
There are many cases where the user may want a single answer to a query. Consider, for example, the following program-query pair $\langle P_{path}, Q_{path} \rangle$.

$r1 : path(X, Y, [X, Y]) : - edge(X, Y).$
$r2 : path(X, Y, [X|P]) : - edge(X, Z), path(Z, Y, P).$
$edge(1, 2). \ edge(1, 3). \ edge(2, 1). \ edge(2, 4). \ edge(3, 4).$
Query: ?-$path(1, 4, X)$.

A top-down, tuple-oriented evaluation strategy, like Prolog, would set up a query on *path*, and solve the subgoals in a depth-first fashion. However, since there is a cycle in the *edge* relation, Prolog would not terminate on the given query.

One way of obtaining a single answer to the query is to evaluate the (magic transformed) program bottom-up until we get an answer to the query, and then terminate the evaluation. With this approach, subgoals are solved in parallel as they are generated.

The technique presented in this paper, Ordered_Search, solves subgoals in a depth-first fashion for this program, but since it performs memoing, it does not repeat computation and terminates on this program. In general, it provides an alternative evaluation strategy to the breadth-first strategy of bottom-up evaluation. For many programs (the above program with the given data is one such) a depth-first search for one answer is much more efficient than a breadth-first search for one answer. (For more details, see Example 3.1.) □

The rest of this paper is organized as follows. Preliminaries are covered in Section 2. The data structures and algorithms needed to evaluate a program using Ordered_Search are described in Section 3. We present results about the soundness, completeness, and efficiency of our procedure in Section 4. In Section 4.3, we characterize the order in which generated subgoals are selected to be used in terms of a depth-first traversal of the "subgoal-dependency" graph of the original program. Related work is described in Section 5, and directions for future research are indicated in Section 6.

2   Preliminaries

We assume familiarity with logic programming terminology (see [10]) and the issues involved in the bottom-up evaluation of logic programs. In particular, we assume the reader is familiar with Magic Templates rewriting ([11]), and with semi-naive bottom-up evaluation ([1]). For the purposes of this paper, a *program* is a set of *normal rules*. The techniques described in this paper are applicable to programs with uninterpreted function symbols, though for simplicity we restrict the programs to compute only ground facts.

We use the notion of a *subgoal-dependency graph* to characterize some of the results in this paper. Intuitively, the subgoal-dependency graph of a program-query pair is an AND/OR directed graph that characterizes the dependencies between subgoals set up in a top-down evaluation of the original program. Given a subgoal on the head of a rule, there are directed arcs in the subgoal-dependency graph to each subgoal set up during the evaluation of the body of that rule. We formalize this using SLP-trees and negation trees (see [14]) in the full version of the paper.

We assume the reader is familiar with the definition of (left-to-right) modularly stratified programs and the meaning of such programs (see [14]). Intuitively, a program is modularly stratified iff its mutually recursive components are locally stratified once all instantiated rules with a false subgoal that is defined in a "lower" component are removed. In the subgoal-dependency graph for left-to-right modularly stratified programs there is no cyclic dependency involving a negated subgoal. Ross' [14] technique as well as our technique makes essential use of this property in evaluating programs with left-to-right modularly stratified negation.

2.1   Modified Magic Templates Rewriting

Intuitively, the Magic Templates rewriting of a program defines a new predicate m_p (the magic predicate) for each predicate p in the original program P. The predicate m_p contains subgoals on p that need to be solved. Additional rules (derived from rules in P) that generate these subgoals are introduced in the rewritten program. Also, original program rules defining p are guarded by an m_p literal that ensures that only p facts matching the desired m_p subgoals are generated. The supplementary variant of Magic Templates avoids some recomputation by identifying common subexpressions, but at the cost of storing additional relations.

For the purpose of this paper, we modify the Magic Templates rewriting as follows: (1) For each (magic) predicate m_p in the Magic Templates transformed program P^{mg}, we create a new predicate $done\_m\_p$, which contains those subgoals on p all of whose answers have been computed. (2) For each rule R in P^{mg}, and for each negated literal, say $\neg q_i(\overline{t_i})$ in the body of R, we add the literal $done\_m\_q_i(\overline{t_i})$ to the body of R just before the occurrence of $\neg q_i(\overline{t_i})$.

Intuitively, the literal $done\_m\_q_i(\overline{t_i})$ will be satisfied only when the complete set of q_i answers matching $\overline{t_i}$ have been computed. Hence, this literal acts as a *guard* on the use of the subsequent negated q_i literal. In a similar fashion, we can also define the modified Supplementary Magic Templates rewriting. In the rest of this paper, we use $\mathrm{SMT}(P, Q)$ to refer to the program obtained by this modified Supplementary Magic Templates rewriting of program-query pair $\langle P, Q \rangle$, using left-to-right sips.

Further, when we talk about the dependencies between magic (or supplementary) facts in the rewritten program, we refer to the dependencies between subgoals in the original program, before the (Supplementary) Magic Templates rewriting has been performed.

3 Ordered Search

We now describe our evaluation technique, which we call Ordered_Search, that works on the transformed program obtained using Magic Templates or Supplementary Magic Templates rewriting. This technique generates subgoals and answers to subgoals asynchronously, as in bottom-up evaluation, but orders the use of generated subgoals in a manner reminiscent of top-down evaluation, and is in a sense a hybrid between pure (tuple-oriented) top-down evaluation and pure (set-oriented) bottom-up evaluation. We informally describe how Ordered_Search works on a transformed program-query pair $\langle P^{mg}, Q^{mg} \rangle$ and provide a detailed algorithmic description in the full version of the paper.

3.1 An Overview

The central data structure used by Ordered_Search, the *Context*, is used to preserve "dependency information" between subgoals. Ordered_Search can be understood as modifying semi-naive bottom-up evaluation as follows:

1. Newly generated magic and supplementary facts (if any) are inserted in the *Context* instead of being directly inserted in the differential relations. Consequently, these facts are hidden from the evaluation. (Other newly generated facts are inserted in the differential relations, and made available to the evaluation, as usual.)

2. Magic and supplementary facts from *Context* are *selectively* inserted into the differential relations (i.e., made available for further use by the evaluation) when no new facts can be derived using the current set of facts available to the evaluation, i.e., a fixpoint has been reached. (When a fact in *Context* is made available to the evaluation, it is said to be "marked" on the *Context*.)

3.2 Data Structures: *Context*

The *Context* is a sequence of *ContextNodes*. Each *ContextNode* has an associated set of magic facts and supplementary facts, and each magic or supplementary fact is associated with a unique *ContextNode*. A *ContextNode* is said to be "marked" if any magic or supplementary fact associated with the *ContextNode* is marked. The sequence of marked *ContextNodes* is a subsequence of the sequence of *ContextNodes*.

In the rest of this paper, when we use adjectives like "earlier", "later", etc. to refer to *ContextNodes* in *Context*, we mean their position in the sequence and not the time (which might be different) at which these nodes were inserted in the sequence.

We now intuitively describe the various operations performed on *Context*: (1) When a new magic or supplementary fact is inserted in *Context*, it is associated with a new *ContextNode*. Facts on *Context* are stored in an ordered fashion, such that if magic fact Q_1 generates (i.e., depends on) the magic fact Q_2, then Q_2 is stored after or along with Q_1 in the *Context*. (2) On detecting a cyclic dependency between subgoals on the *Context*, the associated *ContextNodes* are collapsed into one *ContextNode*, and all the facts associated with these *ContextNodes* are now kept together. Thus, unlike the stack of subgoals in Prolog evaluation, cyclic dependencies are handled gracefully. (3) When all the answers to a subgoal have been computed, the subgoal is removed from the *Context*.

3.3 Algorithms

We give an intuitive description of the **Ordered_Search** technique and in the process make several claims informally. These are formally stated and proved in the full version of the paper.

3.3.1 Inserting Facts into *Context*

Newly generated magic and supplementary facts (obtained by applying the semi-naive rules of the Magic transformed program) are inserted in the *Context* before they are selectively made available to the evaluation. When applying these rules, **Ordered_Search** records which magic or supplementary fact was used to make each derivation. (From the form of rules in the (Supplementary) Magic Templates transformation, there is exactly one such fact.) Let Q_1 be a newly computed magic/supplementary fact derived from magic/supplementary fact Q_2.

- If Q_1 is a magic fact $m\_p(\overline{t_1})$ that has been completely evaluated, it will be present in the *done_m_p* relation.

  In this case, **Ordered_Search** does not insert Q_1 in *Context*.

- Else, since magic/supplementary facts that have been made available for use but have not been completely evaluated are marked in the

Context (see Section 3.3.2), we know that Q_2 occurs as a marked fact in a marked *ContextNode*.

The fact Q_1 is now inserted in a new unmarked *ContextNode* immediately before the next marked *ContextNode* following the marked *ContextNode* associated with Q_2 in the sequence of *ContextNodes*. (If there is no such marked *ContextNode*, Q_1 is inserted as the last *ContextNode* in the *Context*.) Thus, Q_1 is inserted after Q_2.

Since Q_2 depends on Q_1, "answers" to Q_1 could be used in computing "answers" to Q_2. Insertion, as above, is used to maintain dependency information between subgoals within the *Context* as a linear sequence. The order in which facts from *Context* are made available to the evaluation (see Section 3.3.2) will ensure that Q_1 is made available to the evaluation before Q_2 is said to be completely evaluated.

Duplicate elimination is now performed in the *Context* to ensure that there is at most one copy of Q_1 in *Context*. If there is more than one unmarked copy of Q_1 in *Context* at this stage, only the "last" copy of Q_1 is retained. If there is a marked copy of Q_1 in *Context*, i.e., if Q_1 has already been made available to the evaluation, there are two possibilities:

- If the marked copy of Q_1 occurs after the unmarked copy, only the marked copy of Q_1 is retained in *Context*.

- If the unmarked copy of Q_1 occurs after the marked copy, Q_1 depends on itself. We have thus detected a cyclic dependency between the set of all marked facts in *Context* in between the two occurrences of Q_1. Ordered_Search recognizes this and collapses this set of marked facts into the node of the marked copy of Q_1 in *Context*.

Collapsing marked facts into a single node when a cyclic dependency is detected is essential to the correctness of the technique in the presence of cycles in the subgoal-dependency graph of the original program. (Note that in left-to-right modularly stratified programs there can be positive cyclic dependencies, but no negative ones.) Since all these facts (cyclically) depend on each other, we cannot guarantee that any of these facts is completely evaluated until we know that all of them have been completely evaluated.

3.3.2 Making Facts Selectively Available

Facts from *Context* are made available to the evaluation only when no new facts can be computed using the set of available facts. If the last *ContextNode* contains at least one unmarked (magic or supplementary) fact, Ordered_Search chooses one such unmarked fact, marks it and makes it available to the evaluation by inserting it in the corresponding differential relation. (Note that this fact still remains in the *Context*.)

If all facts in the last *ContextNode* are marked, all the facts in the last *ContextNode* can be considered to be completely evaluated. Intuitively,

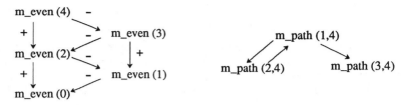

Figure 1: Subgoal Dependency Graphs for Motivating Examples

the reason for this is that a set of facts on *Context* (that have been made available to the evaluation) can be considered to be *completely evaluated* if:

1. no new facts can be generated using the currently available set of facts (i.e., the iterative application has reached a fixpoint), and

2. every magic or supplementary fact generated from these facts has been completely evaluated.

All these facts are removed from *Context* and all magic facts among these are inserted in the corresponding *done_m_p* relations. The last *ContextNode* is now removed from *Context*. Thus, when a magic fact $m\_p(\overline{t_1})$ on *Context* has been completely evaluated, it is moved to *done_m_p*.

3.4 Motivating Examples Revisited

We briefly describe how Ordered_Search can be used to evaluate the examples presented in Section 1.1.

Example 3.1 (Obtaining a single answer)

Consider the program-query pair $\langle P_{path}, Q_{path} \rangle$ from Example 1.2, where the user wants a single answer to the query. For this program-query pair, the subgoal-dependency graph is shown in Figure 1. Note that the subgoal-dependency graph has a cycle; consequently, Prolog would not terminate on this example program-query pair.

The Magic Templates transformed program $\langle P_{path}^{mg}, Q_{path}^{mg} \rangle$ is straightforward and we do not describe it further. We describe the evaluation of $\langle P_{path}^{mg}, Q_{path}^{mg} \rangle$ using Ordered_Search briefly in Table 1. Facts in *Context* marked with an * indicate facts made available to the evaluation, and facts in *Context* within { } indicate facts associated with a single *ContextNode*. Note that an answer is produced in iteration 3, as in the semi-naive bottom-up evaluation of $\langle P_{path}^{mg}, Q_{path}^{mg} \rangle$. However, the evaluation using Ordered_Search has computed fewer facts than would be computed by pure bottom-up evaluation. Also note that a cycle was detected since $m\_path(1, 4)$ was derived from $m\_path(2, 4)$, and this magic fact occurs with an * earlier in *Context*. As a result, in iteration 2, several nodes in *Context* have been collapsed together. □

Iter	Facts in	Ordered_Search
0	$path$	$\{\}$
	$Context$	$m\_path(1,4)$
1	$path$	$\{\}$
	$Context$	$m\_path(1,4)^*, m\_path(3,4), m\_path(2,4)$
2	$path$	$\{path(2,4,[2,4])\}$
	$Context$	$\{m\_path(1,4)^*, m\_path(2,4)^*\}, m\_path(3,4)$
3	$path$	$\{path(2,4,[2,4]), path(1,4,[1,2,4])\}$
	$Context$	$\{m\_path(1,4)^*, m\_path(2,4)^*\}m\_path(3,4)$

Table 1: Ordered_Search evaluation of $\langle P_{path}^{mg}, Q_{path}^{mg} \rangle$

Example 3.2 (Modular negation)
Consider the left-to-right modularly stratified program P_{even} from Example 1.1, and the query ?$\neg even(4)$. For this program-query pair, the subgoal-dependency graph is shown in Figure 1.

We omit the details of the Supplementary Magic Templates transformed program $\langle P_{even}^{mg}, Q_{even}^{mg} \rangle$. The evaluation of the supplementary magic program using Ordered_Search computes and stores only information about direct dependencies as a linear ordering of the magic and supplementary facts on $Context$; hence, the evaluation uses linear space and makes a linear number of derivations.

The technique described in [14] computes and stores the transitive dependencies in addition to the direct dependencies on this example; consequently, it would use quadratic space and make a quadratic number of derivations (of facts and dependencies). We omit details because of space limitations and describe this example in detail in the full version of the paper. $\square$

4 Results about Ordered Search

All results in this section are applicable to programs with function symbols, except where stated otherwise. We also assume for simplicity that only ground facts are generated.

4.1 Results on Soundness, Completeness and Non-repetition

The key "lemma" to establish that Ordered_Search computes the well-founded model of a left-to-right modularly stratified program states that magic facts are moved from $Context$ to the corresponding $done\_m\_p$ relations only when these facts have been completely evaluated. The soundness result below then follows from the exhaustive nature of the evaluation and the correctness of the Supplementary Magic Templates rewriting with the $done\_m\_p$ literals as guards for negative body literals (referred to as SMT rewriting).

Theorem 4.1 *Suppose* $\langle P, Q \rangle$ *is a left-to-right modularly stratified program-query pair. An evaluation of* Ordered_Search(SMT(P, Q)) *is* sound *wrt the well-founded semantics of* $\langle P, Q \rangle$. $\square$

Duplicate elimination of newly generated magic and supplementary facts in *Context* ensures that the evaluation does not repeat derivations.

Theorem 4.2 *Suppose* $\langle P, Q \rangle$ *is a left-to-right modularly stratified program-query pair. An evaluation of* Ordered_Search(SMT(P, Q)) *does not repeat derivations.* $\square$

For programs with function symbols and negation, there is no effective procedure that can guarantee completeness in general. If there is an infinite sequence of subgoals, each depending on the next one in the sequence, and Ordered_Search chooses to explore such an infinite path, it may not compute an answer to the original query, even if one exists. Such paths cannot exist for DATALOG programs. Hence, we have:

Theorem 4.3 *Suppose* $\langle P, Q \rangle$ *is a left-to-right modularly stratified DATALOG program-query pair. An evaluation of* Ordered_Search(SMT(P, Q)) *terminates and is* complete *wrt the well-founded semantics of* $\langle P, Q \rangle$. $\square$

In general, even if there are function symbols, Ordered_Search is complete wrt the well-founded semantics whenever it terminates.

4.2 Results about Space and Time Complexity

In maintaining an auxiliary data structure, the *Context*, Ordered_Search uses more space than ordinary semi-naive bottom-up evaluation (which only needs to maintain differential relations). However, there is no increase in asymptotic space complexity compared to other bottom-up evaluation strategies. Intuitively, this is because duplicate elimination on the *Context* guarantees that the same set of magic, supplementary and answer facts are computed by the various evaluation strategies, and the space used by *Context* is proportional to the space used by the magic and supplementary facts computed.

Note that Ross' technique may use asymptotically more space than Ordered_Search, since it stores transitive dependencies explicitly. For instance, in Example 1.1, Ross' algorithm uses $O(m^2)$ space, whereas Ordered_Search uses $O(m)$ space. Our technique for evaluating left-to-right modularly stratified programs is *strictly better* than the algorithm in [14], in terms of the asymptotic space complexity.

We now compare the asymptotic time complexity of Ordered_Search with other bottom-up evaluation strategies. For positive programs, it is easy to see that semi-naive bottom-up evaluation and Ordered_Search make the same set of inferences, although the order in which the inferences are performed may be different. Further, for left-to-right modularly stratified programs, it can be shown that Ordered_Search makes no more inferences than Ross' method. Note, however, that Ross' algorithm may make asymptotically more inferences than Ordered_Search since it computes transitive dependencies. For instance, in Example 1.1, Ross' algorithm to makes $O(m^2)$ inferences, whereas Ordered_Search makes $O(m)$ inferences.

In order to obtain the total time taken by the Ordered_Search evaluation in terms of the asymptotic cost of derivations, we need to obtain the cost of each derivation in the Ordered_Search evaluation. Unification of ground facts can be done in constant time using hash-consing for ground terms; indexing and insertion of ground facts in relations can also be done in constant time using hash based indexing (see [13]).

Hence, the cost of each derivation depends on the operations on *Context*, and several of these operations are operations on sets: finding the node corresponding to a fact, taking the union of facts associated with nodes on *Context*, and deleting entire sets of facts associated with a *ContextNode*. These operations can be efficiently implemented using the union-find technique [17], with an amortized cost of $O(\alpha(N))$ per operation, where N is the total number of these operations on *Context*, and $\alpha(N)$ is the inverse Ackermann function. Consequently, we have:

Theorem 4.4 *Let* $\langle P, Q \rangle$ *be a program-query pair.*

1. *If* $\langle P, Q \rangle$ *is positive, let the time taken (in terms of asymptotic derivation cost) to evaluate* $SMT(P, Q)$ *in a bottom-up semi-naive evaluation be* T*. Then, an evaluation of* Ordered_Search($SMT(P, Q)$) *takes time* $O(T\alpha(T))$*.*

2. *If* $\langle P, Q \rangle$ *is left-to-right modularly stratified, let the time to evaluate* $\langle P, Q \rangle$ *using Ross' algorithm be* T*. Then, an evaluation of* Ordered_Search($SMT(P, Q)$) *takes time* $O(T\alpha(T))$*.* □

Since $\alpha(T)$ is very small even for very large values of T, Ordered_Search compares favorably in asymptotic (space and time) complexity both to semi-naive bottom-up evaluation for positive programs, and to Ross' evaluation of left-to-right modularly stratified programs. Note that Ross' method can be asymptotically worse than Ordered_Search, as Example 1.1 showed.

As a corollary to the above result, we can show that Ordered_Search takes no more time (asymptotically) than either semi-naive bottom-up evaluation or Ross' method, when the subgoal dependency graph is acyclic.

4.3   Results on Ordering Selection of Subgoals

Recall that bottom-up evaluation of a Magic Templates transformed program generates subgoals and answers to the subgoals as in a top-down evaluation, although the order in which these are generated in the bottom-up evaluation may be quite different from a top-down evaluation. By ordering the newly generated facts in *Context*, Ordered_Search makes facts selectively available to the evaluation in a manner considerably different from pure bottom-up evaluation. We now show that the order in which generated subgoals (magic facts) are selected to be used by Ordered_Search is related to a top-down evaluation.

Theorem 4.5 *Suppose* $\langle P, Q \rangle$ *is a left-to-right modularly stratified program-query pair. In an evaluation of* Ordered_Search(SMT(P, Q)), *the order in which magic facts are marked corresponds to a* depth-first traversal *(with marking) of the subgoal-dependency graph of* $\langle P, Q \rangle$ *starting from Q.* □

The order in which Prolog explores the subgoal-dependency graph also corresponds to a depth-first traversal, although Prolog does not "mark" nodes, and hence may repeat computation. After generating an answer for a subgoal generated from a rule literal, Prolog continues with the next rule body literal, before attempting to generate more answers for the first subgoal. Ordered_Search, on the other hand, generates all answers for the first subgoal before trying to solve subgoals generated from the next rule body literal. Consequently, Prolog may perform a lot less computation than Ordered_Search in obtaining a single answer to the query. For linear programs, however, delaying the availability of subgoals to the Ordered_Search evaluation does not delay the computation of the first answer to the query (because of the asynchronous way in which answers are generated).

We conjecture that Ordered_Search is most useful for computing single answers to a query for the class of linear programs that may have cyclic subgoals (and hence Prolog is not suitable).

5   Related Work

Ordered_Search compares favorably with other top-down and bottom-up methods for evaluating logic programs in the literature. In earlier sections, we have presented a detailed comparison with semi-naive bottom-up evaluation and with Ross' technique to evaluate left-to-right modularly stratified programs. We present a brief comparison with other techniques below.

Prolog: Ordered_Search is sound, complete for DATALOG and does not repeat derivations. Prolog is not complete even for DATALOG, and may repeat derivations. Also, Prolog does not evaluate the class of left-to-right modularly stratified programs correctly.[1] Although Ordered_Search does give a measure of control for single answer queries, the Prolog search strategy is still likely to be superior in this respect (except for the class of linear programs with a large number of repeated subgoals, or cyclic subgoals).

QSQR/QoSaQ and Extension Tables: Extension Tables [5] is similar to Prolog, except that it memos facts and subgoals and can detect loops.

---

[1]Of course, a meta-interpreter can be written using Prolog to evaluate such programs.

QSQR/QoSaQ [19, 20] is a top-down, memoing, set-oriented strategy that is closely related to bottom-up evaluation with Supplementary Magic rewriting. Like Prolog, these techniques cannot deal with left-to-right modularly stratified negation/aggregation. The tuple-oriented search strategy of the Extension Tables variant ET* is closer to Prolog, and may be more useful than Ordered_Search in some settings when single answers are desired, but it repeats computation.

Ross also describes how his approach can be used to adapt QSQR to deal with left-to-right modularly stratified negation. In this case as well, dependencies between subgoals are maintained transitively, and our previous comparisons also apply to this case.

Subquery Completion: A variant of QSQR, *subquery completion*, was described in [8] to deal with recursively defined aggregates. It uses the dependencies between subgoals maintained by QSQR to handle a class of acyclic programs with aggregation. However, this technique does not deal with programs that have cycles in the subgoal-dependency graph of a strongly connected component with aggregates (even if the cyclic dependency is only between positive subgoals). Ordered_Search allows positive cycles in the subgoal dependency graph, and deals with them by collapsing nodes in the *Context*, and declaring all the facts in a collapsed node to be completely evaluated once a fixpoint is reached. There is no analogue to this step in the technique of [8].

Techniques for computing the well-founded model: There are several query evaluation techniques in the literature that compute answers under the well-founded model. For example, WELL! [2] is based on global SLS-resolution; XOLDTNF [4] is an extension of OLDT resolution; GUUS [9] is based on the alternating fixpoint semantics; and the technique of Kemp et al. [7] is based on alternating fixpoint semantics and magic sets. The class of programs handled by these techniques is larger than that handled by Ordered_Search, but each of these techniques can repeat computation even for left-to-right modularly stratified programs. This can result in a loss of efficiency of evaluation.

There are other proposed techniques that control the order of inferences in a bottom-up evaluation in some way. Sloppy Delta Iteration [15] provides a way to "hide" facts until they are to be used. Techniques for hiding facts are used in [6, 16] to evaluate programs with aggregate operations efficiently. These results are only tangentially related to Ordered_Search since the (motivation as well as the nature of the) orderings considered are quite different.

6 Conclusions and Future Work

We presented a memoing technique, Ordered_Search, that is a hybrid between breadth-first and depth-first search. This technique can be used to efficiently evaluate left-to-right modularly stratified programs, and it is also useful in computing single answers to queries. Fully set-oriented computation causes problems for the evaluation of left-to-right modularly stratified programs, as illustrated by our comparisons with Ross [14]—it can result in an order of magnitude slow-down. Hence, it is important to provide some of the benefits of tuple-at-a-time computation with bottom-up evaluation, and Ordered_Search does just this.

Ordered_Search can also be used for programs that compute non-ground facts; details are presented in the full version of the paper. Also, while our claims about correctness of Ordered_Search have been made for the class of left-to-right modularly stratified programs, we conjecture that the method is correct whenever there is no cyclic negative dependency in the subgoal dependency graph. We believe that Ordered_Search is a versatile and very useful tool in the evaluation of queries on deductive databases. Ordered_Search has been implemented in the CORAL system [12], and performance numbers will be presented in the full version of the paper.

An important direction of future research is to explore the possibility of increasing the set-orientedness of Ordered_Search, thereby increasing efficiency of evaluation, while retaining its desirable properties for evaluating left-to-right modularly stratified programs. Another direction of research is to provide a finer grain of control in making subgoals available to the evaluation such that the technique can mimic Prolog more closely, providing further benefits for queries requiring a single answer.

Acknowledgements

We would like to thank Alexandre Lefebvre for valuable discussions regarding QSQR and EKS-V1, and pointing out some related work. We would also like to thank the referees for several valuable suggestions. This research was supported by a David and Lucile Packard Foundation Fellowship in Science and Engineering, a Presidential Young Investigator Award, with matching grants from Digital Equipment Corporation, Tandem and Xerox, and NSF grant IRI-9011563.

References

[1] I. Balbin and K. Ramamohanarao. A generalization of the differential approach to recursive query evaluation. *Journal of Logic Programming*, 4(3), September 1987.

[2] N. Bidoit and P. Legay. WELL! An evaluation procedure for all logic programs. In *Proceedings of the International Conference on Database Theory*, pages 335–348, Paris, France, December 1990.

[3] F. Bry. Query evaluation in recursive databases: Bottom-up and top-down reconciled. *IEEE Transactions on Knowledge and Data Engineering*, 5:289–312, 1990.

[4] W. Chen and D. S. Warren. A practical approach to computing the well founded semantics. In *Proceedings of the Joint International Conference and Symposium on Logic Programming*, 1992.

[5] S. W. Dietrich. Extension tables: Memo relations in logic programming. In *Proceedings of the Symposium on Logic Programming*, pages 264–272, 1987.

[6] S. Ganguly, S. Greco, and C. Zaniolo. Minimum and maximum predicates in logic programming. In *Proceedings of the ACM Symposium on Principles of Database Systems*, 1991.

[7] D. Kemp, D. Srivastava, and P. Stuckey. Magic sets and bottom-up evaluation of well-founded models. In *Proceedings of the International Logic Programming Symposium*, pages 337–351, San Diego, CA, U.S.A., Oct. 1991.

[8] A. Lefebvre. Towards an efficient evaluation of recursive aggregates in deductive databases. In *Proceedings of the International Conference on Fifth Generation Computer Systems*, June 1992.

[9] N. Leone and P. Rullo. Safe computation of the well-founded semantics of Datalog queries. *Information Systems*, 17(1):17–31, 1992.

[10] J. W. Lloyd. *Foundations of Logic Programming*. Springer-Verlag, 1984.

[11] R. Ramakrishnan. Magic Templates: A spellbinding approach to logic programs. In *Proceedings of the International Conference on Logic Programming*, pages 140–159, Seattle, Washington, August 1988.

[12] R. Ramakrishnan, D. Srivastava, and S. Sudarshan. CORAL: Control, Relations and Logic. In *Proceedings of the International Conference on Very Large Databases*, 1992.

[13] R. Ramakrishnan and S. Sudarshan. Top-Down vs. Bottom-Up Revisited. In *Proceedings of the International Logic Programming Symposium*, 1991.

[14] K. Ross. Modular Stratification and Magic Sets for Datalog programs with negation. (A shorter version appeared in the Proceedings of the ACM Symposium on the Principles of Database Systems, 1990), 1991.

[15] H. Schmidt, W. Kiessling, U. Güntzer, and R. Bayer. Compiling exploratory and goal-directed deduction into sloppy delta iteration. In *IEEE International Symposium on Logic Programming*, pages 234–243, 1987.

[16] S. Sudarshan and R. Ramakrishnan. Aggregation and relevance in deductive databases. In *Proceedings of the Seventeenth International Conference on Very Large Databases*, Sept. 1991.

[17] R. E. Tarjan. *Data Structures and Network Algorithms*. Society for Industrial and Applied Mathematics, 1983.

[18] J. D. Ullman. Bottom-up beats top-down for Datalog. In *Proceedings of the Eighth ACM Symposium on Principles of Database Systems*, pages 140–149, Philadelphia, Pennsylvania, March 1989.

[19] L. Vieille. Recursive axioms in deductive databases: The query-subquery approach. In *Proceedings of the First International Conference on Expert Database Systems*, pages 179–193, Charleston, South Carolina, 1986.

[20] L. Vieille. From QSQ towards QoSaQ: Global optimizations of recursive queries. In *Proc. 2nd International Conference on Expert Database Systems*, Apr. 1988.

Query Restricted Bottom-up Evaluation of Normal Logic Programs

David B. Kemp and Peter J. Stuckey
Department of Computer Science
University of Melbourne
Parkville 3052, Australia
{kemp,pjs}@cs.mu.oz.au

Divesh Srivastava
Computer Sciences Department
University of Wisconsin–Madison
Madison, WI 53706, U.S.A.
divesh@cs.wisc.edu

Abstract

Several program transformations—magic sets, envelopes, NRSU transformations and context transformations, among others—have been proposed for efficiently computing the answers to a query while taking advantage of the query constants. These transformations use sideways information passing strategies (sips) to restrict bottom-up evaluation to facts potentially relevant to the query. It is of interest to extend these transformations to all logic programs with negation, and identify classes of programs and sips for which these transformations preserve well-founded models with respect to the query.

In a previous paper we identified classes of programs and sips for which the magic sets transformation preserves well-founded models wrt the query. We continue this line of research to other transformations that use sips. We identify classes of programs and sips for which the context transformations and the envelopes transformations preserve well-founded models wrt the query. We also define a new program transformation based on magic sets that preserves well-founded models with respect to the query for *any* choice of sips. Finally, we compare and contrast the performance of envelopes with our new program transformation using the Aditi deductive database system.

1 Introduction

Much research has been done in recent years in the efficient evaluation of queries against deductive databases. A considerable part of this has centered on the efficient bottom-up computation of logic programs using rewriting techniques that take advantage of query constants in answering queries, such as magic sets and its variants, envelopes, NRSU transformations and context transformations, among others. These techniques depend on *sideways information passing strategies* (sips) to propagate the bindings present in the query to restrict evaluation to facts that are potentially relevant to the query.

Magic sets [1, 3] is an important transformation that is used to imitate top-down computations with memoing using bottom-up computations. The transformation generates the same set of queries and the same set of answers to those queries as top-down evaluation, and is attractive because of its generality and efficiency. For some important recursions, much better algorithms than magic sets are known. The NRSU transformation [8] applies to a restricted class of programs (where predicates are factorizable) and can achieve asymptotic improvements in the efficiency of evaluation, by reducing the arity of recursive predicates. The context transformation [4, 7] can achieve similar improvements by removing the same arguments as the NRSU transformation, but it overcomes a limitation in the NRSU transformation by adding some new arguments. The importance of magic sets and context transformations can be seen from the fact that deductive database systems such as Aditi [14] and CORAL [9] use these transformations. Sagiv [11] presented an evaluation method, envelopes, that is as general as the magic sets method, and showed that in many cases may be better than magic sets. As with the magic sets, envelopes creates additional program rules that are used to compute filters to restrict evaluation to facts relevant to the query. The attractiveness of envelopes lies in the simplicity of the rules used to compute these filters.

All of these strategies were, at least originally, defined only for definite programs.[1] Extending these strategies to normal logic programs would considerably improve their utility to deductive databases. For all such programs, the well-founded semantics [16] is a three-valued semantics that is widely accepted. Kemp, Srivastava and Stuckey [5] identified classes of programs and sips for which the magic sets transformation preserves well-founded models with respect to the query. In this paper, we investigate other transformations that are based on propagating binding information using sips. Our contributions are:

1. We show that the context transformation preserves well-founded models with respect to the query for the same classes of programs and sips as does the magic sets transformation (Section 3).

2. We define a new program transformation based on magic sets and the doubled program approach for computing well-founded models ([5]) that preserves well-founded models with respect to the query for arbitrary sips applied to any program (Section 4).

3. We extend the envelopes transformation to normal logic programs and

---

[1]Sagiv [11] also presented the envelopes transformation for stratified logic programs.

show that it preserves well-founded models with respect to the query for any choice of sips (Section 5).

4. Finally, we demonstrate the practicality of our algorithms and results (Section 6).

1.1 Preliminaries

We assume familiarity with logic programming terminology (see [6]). For the purposes of this paper, a *program* is a set of *normal rules*. Although there are no algorithms that are guaranteed to effectively compute the well-founded model of a program containing function symbols, none of the technical results herein depend on a restriction to DATALOG or function-free programs. In practice, whenever the evaluation method described in [5] terminates it is the well-founded model that is computed.[2]

We use the following notation. If p is a positive literal (atom) then $\neg \cdot p \stackrel{\text{def}}{=} \neg p$. If q is a negative literal $\neg p$ then $\neg \cdot q \stackrel{\text{def}}{=} p$. If A is a set of literals then let $\neg \cdot A$ be the set of literals $\{\neg \cdot a \mid a \in A\}$.

For monotonic operators G that map subsets of the Herbrand Base of P, HB_P, to subsets of the Herbrand Base of P, we define $G \uparrow \alpha$, $G \downarrow \alpha$, $lfp(G)$, and $gfp(G)$ in the usual way.

Definition: Extend the definition of the T_P operator as follows: let M be a set of atoms.

$$T_P(M)(I) \quad = \quad \{a \mid \text{where there is a ground instance of a clause in } P$$
$$a \leftarrow q_1, \ldots, q_n, \neg p_1, \ldots, \neg p_r$$
$$\text{such that } \forall 1 \leq i \leq n, \quad q_i \in I \text{ and } \forall 1 \leq j \leq r, \quad p_j \notin M\}$$

$\diamond$

We refer the reader to [16] for a definition of the well-founded semantics, and give a slightly different formulation from that of [15], closer to that of [2], of the alternating fixpoint A_P^* of a program P.

$$F_P(T) \quad \stackrel{\text{def}}{=} \quad T_P(T) \uparrow \omega$$
$$F_P^2(T) \quad \stackrel{\text{def}}{=} \quad F_P(F_P(T))$$
$$A_P^* \quad \stackrel{\text{def}}{=} \quad lfp(F_P^2) \cup \neg \cdot (HB_P - gfp(F_P^2))$$

Theorem 1 ([15]) *The well-founded model of P, W_P^*, and the alternating fixpoint model of P, A_P^* are identical.* $\square$

We assume familiarity with sideways information passing strategies ([3]), the magic sets transformation ([3]) for program P, query Q and sips S resulting in $MP = Magic(P, S, Q)$, context transformations ([4]) and envelopes ([11]). We also assume familiarity with the doubled program technique ([5]) for computing well-founded models of a program. Intuitively, this technique is an implementation of the alternating fixpoint semantics.

---

[2]Termination can be guaranteed for function-free programs.

2 Motivation

Magic sets transformations and its variants are used to imitate top-down computations with memoing using bottom-up computation. The major advantage they provide is that they allow a bottom-up computation to be specialized with respect to the query, thus improving the efficiency of answering queries. Ideally, we would like a program P that has been magic sets transformed with respect to some query Q (giving magic program MP) to have an equivalent well-founded model with respect to Q for arbitrary sideways information passing strategies (sips). But this is not always the case, since magic transformations rely on sips that can effectively change the well-founded models.

Example 1 ([5]) Consider the following program and the program resulting from a magic sets transformation using complete left-to-right sips with respect to the query $q(a)$,

$$p(a) \leftarrow magic\_p(a), q(a), \neg r(a).$$
$$q(a) \leftarrow magic\_q(a), \neg p(a).$$
$$p(a) \leftarrow q(a), \neg r(a). \qquad r(a) \leftarrow magic\_r(a).$$
$$q(a) \leftarrow \neg p(a). \qquad magic\_q(a).$$
$$r(a). \qquad magic\_q(a) \leftarrow magic\_p(a).$$
$$magic\_r(a) \leftarrow magic\_p(a), q(a).$$
$$magic\_p(a) \leftarrow magic\_q(a).$$

Original program   **Transformed program**

The (two-valued) well-founded model of the original program is clearly $\{r(a), \neg p(a), q(a)\}$. But the well-founded model of the magic transformed program is $\{magic\_p(a), magic\_q(a)\}$, which does not agree with the original program on the query $q(a)$. $\diamond$

The problem in the above example comes from the choice of sips. In the well-founded model construction, we must determine $r(a)$ before we can infer $\neg p(a)$, and $\neg p(a)$ before $q(a)$. However, because of the choice of sips, the magic program must determine $q(a)$ before it can determine $r(a)$.

Kemp et al. [5] showed that for arbitrary programs, magic sets transformations preserve well-founded models wrt the query for a class of sips called well-founded sips.

Definition: ([5]) A (non-ground) literal Q is *two-valued* in a three-valued interpretation M if each ground instance of Q is either true or false in M.

A sip for rule R is *well-founded* if for each arc in the sip of the form

$$\{Q_1, \ldots, Q_m\} \to_{\{X_1, \ldots, X_z\}} L$$

each Q_i is either the head of R or is in an SCC lower than the SCC of the head of R and Q_i is two-valued in W_P^*. A sip strategy S is well-founded if it chooses well-founded sips for each rule in a program. $\diamond$

Kemp et al. [5] also showed that the magic sets transformation of left-to-right modularly stratified programs with left-to-right sips preserves query equivalence with respect to the well-founded semantics. (Note that there are left-to-right sips that are not well-founded sips.) We refer the reader to [10] for definitions of left-to-right modularly stratified programs.

In this paper, we continue on this line of research and examine two classes of transformations for normal logic programs:

1. Transformations that preserve well-founded models wrt the query for the same class of programs and sips as the magic sets transformations.

   This would show the naturalness of the class of programs and sips described in [5].

2. Transformations that preserve well-founded models wrt the query for arbitrary programs with any choice of sips.

We show that the NRSU and context transformations fall into the first category while the envelopes transformation falls into the second category.

3   The NRSU and Context Transformations

In [8], Naughton et al. defined a transformation that can reduce the asymptotic cost of answering some queries by reducing the arity of the recursive predicates. This transformation, which we call the NRSU-transformation, is applicable to a fairly large class of procedures that occurs frequently in real programs: those defined by right-, left-, and multi-linear rules ([8] and chapter 15 of [13]).

A fundamental limitation of the NRSU-transformation is that it works only when the call to the transformed procedure has constants in its input positions. In [4], Kemp et al. define a new transformation, called the context-transformation, that removes this restriction: it works even when the input of the transformed procedure is provided by a non-singleton relation. The context-transformation of right-linear rules is also investigated by Mumick and Pirahesh in [7].

The context transformation is defined only for linear SCCs. However, this does not prevent the program from containing negation. Indeed, a linear SCC can contain negative literals whose predicates belong to lower SCCs.

First we show that, as with magic sets, arbitrary sips can result in the program having a different well-founded model (even with respect to the query).

Example 2 Consider the following program with query $a(a)$, and the result of a context transformation of the rules for the predicate p, assuming the sips for the rule for a is the arc $\{q(X)\} \rightarrow_{\{X\}} \neg p(X, Y)$:

$a(X) \leftarrow q(X), \neg p(X,Y), t(Y).$
$q(a) \leftarrow \neg q(a).$
$p(X,Y) \leftarrow b(X,Y).$
$p(X,Y) \leftarrow b(X,Z), p(Z,Y).$
$b(a,a).$
$t(a).$

Original program

$a(X) \leftarrow q(X), \neg p(X,Y), t(Y).$
$q(a) \leftarrow \neg q(a).$
$p(W,Y) \leftarrow mc\_p(W,X), b(X,Y).$
$mc\_p(X,X) \leftarrow q(X).$
$mc\_p(W,Z) \leftarrow mc\_p(W,X), b(X,Z).$
$b(a,a).$
$t(a).$

Transformed program

The well-founded (partial) model of the original program (assuming a is the only constant in the language), is $\{b(a,a), t(a), p(a,a), \neg a(a)\}$. The well-founded model of the context transformed program is $\{b(a,a), t(a)\}$ and now $a(a)$ is undefined. $\diamond$

We investigate conditions under which the context transformation can be applied to programs containing negation. Note that as the context transformation can be applied only to predicates that are left-, right-, multi-, or mixed-linear, we assume that some SCCs are selected for context transformation, while others are selected for other types of transformation such as the magic sets transformation. Although we discuss the context transformation throughout, because it generalizes the NRSU-transformation, all of our results for the context transformation also hold for the NRSU-transformation.

3.1 Soundness of the Context Transformation

Although Example 2 shows that the well-founded model of a program can be altered by performing a context transformation on it, it turns out that answers to a query on the original program will include the answers to that query on the transformed program, i.e., the transformation is *sound*. If P is the original program, let MP be the transformed program by selectively using the context transformation for some SCCs, and the magic sets transformation for others. (We call this a *combined context and magic sets transformation*.)

The soundness of the context transformation is more difficult to prove than the soundness of the magic sets transformation since a context-magic predicate not only acts as a filter (as a magic predicate does), but it also directly contributes to the generation of new tuples. The details of the proof will appear in the longer version of this paper.

Theorem 2 *Let P be a program, S be a sip strategy for P, Q be a query, and MP be a combined context and magic sets transformation of P. Then for all substitutions θ such that $Q\theta \in W^*_{MP}$, it is the case that $Q\theta \in W^*_P$.* $\square$

3.2 Modularly Stratified Programs

For left-to-right modularly stratified programs, it can be shown that the transformed program is "two-valued with respect to the atoms that are relevant to the query". The proof of this result requires three levels of induction: an induction on the SCCs of the predicate call graph; within each SCC, an induction on the local strata resulting from a reduction of the SCC; and the inner most induction is over the fixpoint computation $T_{MP}(lfp(F_{MP}^2)) \uparrow \omega$.

This result, combined with the soundness result (Theorem 2), allows us to prove the result that the context transformation can be applied to any left-to-right modularly stratified program with left-to-right sips.

Theorem 3 *Let P be a left-to-right modularly stratified program, and say the sips for each rule in P are left-to-right sips. Let Q be a query, and MP be a combined context and magic sets transformation of P. Then P and MP agree on Q.* $\square$

The following corollary is true since all stratified programs are left-to-right modularly stratified for arbitrary sips.

Corollary 1 *Let P be a stratified program with arbitrary sips, let Q be a query, and MP be a combined context and magic sets transformation of P. Then P and MP agree on Q.* $\square$

3.3 The Context Transformation and Well-Founded Sips

A combined context and magic sets transformation can be applied to arbitrary programs. Well-founded sips allow us to transform programs that have a three-valued well-founded model while maintaining equivalence with respect to the query.

The following result is proven by induction over the SCCs of the predicate call graph, and by nested inductions over the alternating fixpoints that derive the well-founded models of P and MP. The proof also uses the "lemma" that the "relevant" context-magic tuples are two valued in the well-founded model of the transformed program.

Theorem 4 *Let P be a program, S be a well-founded sip strategy for P, Q be a query of P and MP be a combined context and magic sets transformation of P. Then MP and P agree on Q.* $\square$

4 Well-Founded Magic Sets

The fundamental problem with applying the query directed transformations to non-stratified normal programs arises from the three-valued nature of the auxiliary predicates that result. In this section we present a new transformation based on magic sets and the doubled program technique for computing well-founded models ([5]) that preserves the well-founded model with respect to the query regardless of the sips used or classes of programs that are transformed. The intuition behind this transformation is to find a nontrivial two-valued magic set which is known to be large enough to cover all the facts of interest to answering the query.

Definition: Let P be any program, let S be any sip strategy, let Q be any query and $MP = Magic(P, S, Q)$. $lfp(F_{MP}^2)$ and $gfp(F_{MP}^2)$ are two two-valued models, representing the definitely true and possibly true information respectively, obtained when computing the well-founded model of the magic program MP using the doubled program approach. Let M be the magic facts appearing in $gfp(F_{MP}^2)$.

The *well-founded magic sets* rewriting, $PM = WFMagic(P, S, Q)$, is given by the program consisting of the modified original rules[3] in MP together with the magic facts M. $\diamond$

We claim that the well-founded model of PM agrees with the well-founded model of P with respect to the query. We can of course compute the well-founded model of PM using the doubled program technique.

We begin with a technical lemma that is used in the proof that the resulting program PM is sound wrt the query and the original program.

Lemma 1 *Let P be a program, S be any sip strategy for P, Q be a query of P and $MP = Magic(P, S, Q)$.*

(a) *If q is a positive literal and $q \in W_P^*$ and magic_$q \in gfp(F_{MP}^2)$ then $q \in gfp(F_{MP}^2)$.*

(b) *If q is a negative literal $\neg r$ and $\neg r \in W_P^*$ and magic_$q \in gfp(F_{MP}^2)$ then $r \notin lfp(F_{MP}^2)$.*

(c) *If q is a positive literal and $q \notin W_P^*$ and magic_$q \in gfp(F_{MP}^2)$ then $q \notin lfp(F_{MP}^2)$.*

(d) *If q is a negative literal $\neg r$ and $\neg r \notin W_P^*$ and magic_$q \in gfp(F_{MP}^2)$ then $r \in gfp(F_{MP}^2)$.* $\Box$

We show the soundness of the program PM obtained using well-founded magic sets rewriting by proving the soundness preserving properties of each computation step: from the possibly true atoms to the definitely true atoms and vice versa. In essence the result holds because we have chosen a magic set that is large enough to ensure that all required calls are set up.

Lemma 2 *Let P be a program, S be any sip strategy for P, Q be a query of P, $MP = Magic(P, S, Q)$ and $PM = WFMagic(P, S, Q)$. If F is a set of ground atoms such that the following property holds: for all normal (non-magic) atoms q, if magic_$q \in gfp(F_{MP}^2)$, and $q \notin F$ then $q \notin gfp(F_P^2)$, then for all normal (non-magic) atoms q, if magic_$q \in gfp(F_{MP}^2)$ and $q \in F_{PM}(F) \rightarrow q \in lfp(F_P^2)$.* $\Box$

---

[3] In other words, we remove all the rules defining magic predicates from MP.

Lemma 3 *Let P be a program, S be any sip strategy for P, Q be a query of P, $MP = Magic(P, S, Q)$ and $PM = WFMagic(P, S, Q)$. If T is a set of ground atoms such that the following property holds: for all normal (non-magic) atoms q, if $magic\_q \in gfp(F^2_{MP})$ and $q \in T$ then $q \in lfp(F^2_P)$, then for all normal (non-magic) atoms q, if $magic\_q \in gfp(F^2_{MP})$, and $q \notin F_{PM}(T)$ then $q \notin gfp(F^2_P)$. $\square$*

Soundness is derived by showing each of the computed sets $F^2_{PM} \uparrow \alpha, F^2_{PM} \downarrow \alpha$ satisfy the preconditions of the above two lemmas.

Theorem 5 (Soundness) *Let P be a program, S be any sip strategy for P, Q be a query of P, $MP = Magic(P, S, Q)$ and $PM = WFMagic(P, S, Q)$. If $q \in W^*_{PM}$ and $magic\_q \in gfp(F^2_{MP})$ then $q \in W^*_P$. $\square$*

The completeness proof is almost identical in form to the soundness result, a linked induction proof of the soundness of the sets $F^2_P \uparrow \alpha$ and $F^2_P \downarrow \alpha$ with respect to W^*_{PM} for facts whose magic facts are in $gfp(F^2_{MP})$. In this case, the key preliminary results follow from the above soundness result.

Theorem 6 (Completeness) *Let P be a program, S be any sip strategy for P, Q be a query of P, $MP = Magic(P, S, Q)$ and $PM = WFMagic(P, S, Q)$. If $q \in W^*_P$ and $magic\_q \in gfp(F^2_{MP})$ then $q \in W^*_{PM}$. $\square$*

Putting the soundness and completeness results together we have the desired result: the well-founded magic sets program PM and the original program P agree on the query.

Theorem 7 *Let P be a program, let S be any sip strategy, let Q be a query and $PM = WFMagic(P, S, Q)$. Then the well-founded models of PM and P agree on Q. $\square$*

Clearly, when the magic facts appearing in the well-founded model, W^*_{MP}, of MP are two-valued, the well-founded models of MP and PM are the same. This occurs because the two programs differ only with respect to the magic facts, and in this case the magic facts for W^*_{PM} are chosen to be the same as those in W^*_{MP}. This leads to the following interesting corollary that extends the results of [5] to new programs that do not fall into any of the classes discussed there.

Corollary 2 *Let P be a program, S be any sip strategy for P, Q be a query of P and $MP = Magic(P, S, Q)$. If the model M of the magic facts in W^*_{MP} is two-valued, then the well-founded models of MP and P agree on Q. $\square$*

5 Well-Founded Envelopes

In [11], Sagiv described a program transformation, which we call *magic-envelopes*, which is as general as the magic sets transformation in that it can be applied to any program. Magic-envelopes are similar to magic sets in the sense that they restrict evaluation of a query to relevant facts, though they do not restrict computation to the same set of relevant facts as magic sets. Magic-envelopes are an attractive alternative to the magic sets transformation because of the simplicity of the rules used to compute the filters.

We now intuitively describe the magic-envelopes transformation. A *factorization* of a predicate p, denoted $\mathcal{F}\langle p \rangle$, is a collection of predicates (referred to as factors), each of which corresponds to a subset of the columns of p, such that each column of p is represented in exactly one factor. Where the factorization of p is such that there is no factor containing a bound and a free column of p, $\mathcal{F}^B\langle q \rangle$ denotes the bound factors.

Let P be any program, let S be any sip strategy and let Q be any query. An *envelope* E for program P is obtained as follows. Choose a unique factorization $\mathcal{F}$ for each adorned non-magic IDB predicate p in magic program MP such that each factor has only bound columns or only free columns, according to the adornment of p. Transform the magic program MP as follows. First, all negated literals in rule bodies of MP are removed. Next, atoms of either IDB or magic predicates are replaced in bodies of rules by their factorizations. Finally, heads of rules are also replaced with their factorizations. We now replace each rule by a separate rule for each atom in the head by making copies of the body. The resultant program $E = Env(P, S, Q, \mathcal{F})$ is said to be an *envelope* for program P.

The *magic-envelopes* transformed program $EP = MagEnv(P, S, Q, \mathcal{F})$ is obtained by taking the union of the rules in $E(P, S, Q, \mathcal{F})$ and the rules in P restricted by adding the factorization of the head of the rule to its body.

We show that the well-founded model of the magic-envelopes transformed program $EP = MagEnv(P, S, Q, \mathcal{F})$ agrees with the well-founded model of P with respect to the query Q for any choice of sip strategy S and any choice of factorization $\mathcal{F}$. We can of course compute the well-founded model of EP using the doubled program technique or any other technique to compute well-founded models.

Example 3 Consider the following non-modularly stratified program, which has a three-valued well-founded model if the p relation includes cycles, and the magic program obtained using complete left-to-right sips for the bf annotation (which are not well-founded sips).

$$a(X,Y) \leftarrow p(X,Y)$$
$$a(X,Y) \leftarrow p(X,Z), a(Z,Y), \neg a(Y,Z)$$
Original program

$$a(X,Y) \leftarrow m(X), p(X,Y)$$
$$a(X,Y) \leftarrow m(X), p(X,Z), a(Z,Y), \neg a(Y,Z)$$
$$m(Z) \leftarrow m(X), p(X,Z)$$
$$m(Y) \leftarrow m(X), p(X,Z), a(Z,Y)$$
Transformed program

The envelope program E for the two factors $b1$ and $f2$ is shown below. This can be obviously simplified by removing rules that cannot produce new facts and removing atoms in the body not connected to the head. Together with the modified original rules we obtain EP

$$b1(X) \leftarrow b1(X), p(X,Y)$$
$$f2(Y) \leftarrow b1(X), p(X,Y)$$
$$b1(X) \leftarrow b1(X), p(X,Z), b1(Z), f2(Y)$$
$$f2(Y) \leftarrow b1(X), p(X,Z), b1(Z), f2(Y)$$
$$b1(Z) \leftarrow b1(X), p(X,Z)$$
$$b1(Y) \leftarrow b1(X), p(X,Z), b1(Z), f2(Y)$$
Envelope program E

$$a(X,Y) \leftarrow b1(X), f2(Y), p(X,Y)$$
$$a(X,Y) \leftarrow b1(X), f2(Y), p(X,Z), a(Z,Y), \neg a(Y,Z)$$
$$f2(Y) \leftarrow b1(X), p(X,Y)$$
$$b1(Z) \leftarrow b1(X), p(X,Z)$$
$$b1(Y) \leftarrow f2(Y)$$
Magic Envelope program EP

$\diamond$

First we examine the relationship between the envelope filters generated by the above transformation and the magic sets computed by the well-founded magic sets transformation.

Lemma 4 *Let P be any program, let S be any sip strategy, let Q be any query and let $MP = Magic(P,S,Q)$. Let $\mathcal{F}$ be a unique factorization for the adorned IDB predicates in MP. Let $E = Env(P,S,Q,\mathcal{F})$ be the envelope generated. Then, if q is a positive literal, and $q \in gfp(F^2_{MP})$ then $\mathcal{F}\langle q \rangle \subseteq W^*_E$.* $\square$

The above result shows that the magic set $gfp(F^2_{MP})$ computed by the well-founded magic sets technique is always tighter than the magic envelope. The tradeoff made in the envelope computation is that the computations are usually considerably faster. In Section 6 we show examples where the computation of envelopes is advantageous over well-founded magic sets, and others where it leads to enormous extra computation.

The soundness and completeness of the magic-envelopes transformation for arbitrary programs is proved in a similar way to that of the well-founded magic sets transformations. In this case the essential preliminary result is the following lemma that relates the bound factorizations to the complete factorizations.

Lemma 5 *Let P be any program, let S be any sip strategy, let Q be any query and let $MP = Magic(P, S, Q)$. Let $\mathcal{F}$ be a unique factorization for the adorned IDB predicates in MP. Let $E = Env(P, S, Q, \mathcal{F})$ be the envelope generated. If $\mathcal{F}^B\langle q \rangle \subseteq W_E^*$ and $q \in T_P \uparrow \omega(A)$ for any set of atoms A then $\mathcal{F}\langle q \rangle \subseteq W_E^*$* □

The final result shows that the magic envelopes transformation is guaranteed to preserve the well-founded model of the original program P with respect to the query. This generalizes Sagiv's original result which was limited to stratified programs, where the well-founded model is guaranteed to be two-valued.

Theorem 8 *Let P be a program, S be any sip strategy for P, Q be a query of P and $MP = Magic(P, S, Q)$. Let $\mathcal{F}$ be a unique factorization for the adorned IDB predicates in MP. Let $E = Env(P, S, Q, \mathcal{F})$ be the envelope generated and $EP = MagEnv(P, S, Q, \mathcal{F})$. Then the well-founded models of EP and P agree on Q.* □

6 Performance Results

We contrast the approaches of well-founded magic sets and well-founded magic envelopes on the non-modularly stratified program given in Example 3. First we compare the well-founded magic sets and envelope evaluation of the program with the bf annotation and left to right sips as described in Example 3. Note that these sips are not well-founded and the program is not modularly stratified so simple magic sets evaluation is incorrect.

The $p()$ relation consists of a complete binary tree of height 11, with an additional arc from the bottom leftmost leaf to the leftmost node at depth 4. This means that the program is just the usual ancestor program in parts of the tree not including the leftmost subtree at depth 4. The results were obtained using the Aditi deductive database system [14] under development at the University of Melbourne. We compare the time (in seconds) taken for the well-founded magic sets and well-founded magic envelopes computations at different depths down the leftmost and rightmost branches. In comparison the full evaluation of the original program took 272 seconds and required a maximum of 93038 tuples to be stored at any time in the computation.

Method	Depth	0	1	2	3	4	5	6	7	8	9	10
Magic	Time–L	545	309	201	143	135	141	138	138	129	125	121
Magic	Time–R	561	224	132	89	66	54	45	37	27	12	11
Env	Time–L	310	157	89	57	42	51	51	51	50	49	48
Env	Time–R	325	115	63	39	28	19	16	13	11	7	6

Table 1: Time comparisons for a^{bf}

Method	Depth	0	2	4	6	8	10
Magic	Time–L	334	258	178	187	188	182
Magic	Space–L	8868	4004	2730	2730	2730	2730
Magic	Time–R	162	109	75	23	17	11
Magic	Space–R	6270	1630	446	97	21	3
Env	Time–L	6443	1149	204	232	214	210
Env	Space–L	511488	120134	22247	22247	22247	22247
Env	Time–R	445	132	58	35	27	7
Env	Space–R	61766	15536	3866	836	219	1

Table 2: Time and space comparisons for a^{bb}

For the results shown in Table 1, the magic set filters and the envelope filters computed are identical and hence because of the much simpler envelopes computation, envelopes are clearly advantageous. In contrast, we examine the results using the same original program of Example 3 but with a bb annotation and left-to-right sips, and factorizing a into a single arity 2 bound factor $b12$. The queries in this case were from a node on the leftmost branch to the leftmost node at depth 7 (midway in the cyclic path), and from a node on the rightmost branch to the rightmost node at depth 7. We compare both the time and the maximum tuples required to be stored at any time in the computation.

In the results shown in Table 2 the well-founded magic sets computation clearly shows the advantages of a tighter magic set. In this case the envelope is so large as to often dominate the computation making it far more expensive than the full computation of the a relation. Notice that the size of the envelope computed is approximately 10 times the magic set. Using an envelope consisting of two arity 1 bound factors $(b1, b2)$ for a substantially degrades the performance on queries high up the tree but improves results for the lower queries.

In summary it appears that the simpler calculations of the magic envelopes transformation are often the most efficient computation technique. But the method suffers from very bad performance for queries where the envelopes do not restrict enough, in particular when ignoring negative literals that restrict computation. In contrast the well-founded magic sets approach is always more space efficient and generally performs reasonably well.

7   Conclusions & Future Directions

We described two classes of program transformations that propagate query bindings using sideways information passing strategies for normal logic programs. First, there are those transformations that do not preserve well-founded models (wrt the query) in general. The NRSU transformations and context transformations were shown to be in this class. For these transformations, we described classes of programs and sips that preserve well-founded models wrt the query, and showed that these were the same classes that preserved well-founded models wrt the query for magic sets transformations, as described in [5]. This leads us to believe that these classes of programs and sips are extremely natural to program transformations.

Second, there are those transformations that preserve well-founded models (wrt the query) for arbitrary programs and sips. The envelopes transformation was shown to be in this class. We also defined a new program transformation based on magic sets and the doubled program technique for computing well-founded models, the well-founded magic sets technique, that preserves well-founded models for arbitrary programs and sips. Note that the context transformation cannot be extended to all sips in a manner similar to well-founded magic sets because, for right- and multi-linear rules, the computation of the context predicates replaces the computation of the original predicates, and so an overestimation of the context facts leads to incorrect answers.

We gave a preliminary performance comparison between the two program transformations applicable to arbitrary normal logic programs with arbitrary sips and showed that each strategy can win in certain situations. More research, however, is needed in determining the kinds of situations in which well-founded magic sets is superior to envelopes, and vice-versa. Another direction of future research is in extending other program transformations to normal logic programs and determining the categories they fall in.

Acknowledgements

The research of David Kemp and Peter Stuckey was supported by an Australian Research Council grant. The research of Divesh Srivastava was supported by a David and Lucile Packard Foundation Fellowship in Science and Engineering, a Presidential Young Investigator Award, with matching grants from Digital Equipment Corporation, Tandem and Xerox, and NSF grant IRI-9011563.

References

[1] BANCILHON, F., MAIER, D., SAGIV, Y. AND ULLMAN, J. Magic sets and other strange ways to implement logic programs. In *Proceedings of the 5th ACM Symposium on Principles of Database Systems* (1986).

[2] BARAL, C. AND SUBRAHMANIAN, V.S. Dualities between alternate semantics for logic programming and nonmonotonic reasoning. In *Proceedings of the 1st International Workshop on Logic Programming and Non-monotonic Reasoning*, Washington D.C. (1991), MIT Press, 69–86.

[3] BEERI, C. AND RAMAKRISHNAN, R. On the power of magic. In *Proceedings of the 6th ACM Symposium on Principles of Database Systems* (1987), 269–283.

[4] KEMP, D.B., RAMAMOHANARAO, K. AND SOMOGYI, Z. Right-, left-, and multi-linear rule transformations that maintain context information. In *Proceedings of the Sixteenth Conference on Very Large Databases*, Brisbane, Australia (1990), Morgan Kaufmann, 380–391.

[5] KEMP, D.B., SRIVASTAVA, D. AND STUCKEY, P.J. Magic sets and bottom-up evaluation of well-founded models. In *Proceedings of the Int. Logic Programming Symposium*, San Diego (1991), 337–354.

[6] LLOYD, J.W. Foundations of logic programming (second, extended edition) Springer-Verlag, New York (1987).

[7] MUMICK, I. AND PIRAHESH, H. Overbound and right-linear queries. In *Proceedings of the Tenth ACM Symposium on the Principles of Database Systems* (1991), 127–141.

[8] NAUGHTON, J., RAMAKRISHNAN, R., SAGIV, Y. AND ULLMAN, J. Efficient evaluation of right-, left-, and multi-linear rules. In *Proceedings of ACM SIGMOD '89* (1989), 235–242.

[9] RAMAKRISHNAN, R., SRIVASTAVA, D., AND SUDARSHAN, S. CORAL: Control, Relations and Logic. In *Proceedings of the International Conference on Very Large Data Bases*, Vancouver, Canada (1992).

[10] ROSS, K.R. Modular Stratification and Magic Sets for DATALOG Programs with Negation. In *Proceedings of the ACM Symposium on Principles of Database Systems* (1990), 161–171.

[11] SAGIV, Y. Is there anything better than magic? In *Proceedings of the North American Conference on Logic Programming*, Austin, Texas (1990) 235–254.

[12] ULLMAN, J. Bottom-up beats top-down for Datalog. In *Proceedings of the 8th ACM Symposium on Principles of Database Systems*, 1989.

[13] ULLMAN, J. *Principles of database and knowledge-base systems, vol. II: The new technologies.* Computer Science Press, New York, 1989.

[14] VAGHANI, J., RAMAMOHANARAO, K., AND KEMP, D. B. Design overview of the Aditi deductive database system. In *Proceedings of the International Conference on Data Engineering*, Kobe, Japan (1991), 240–247.

[15] VAN GELDER, A. The Alternating Fixpoint of Logic Programs with Negation. In *Proceedings of the ACM Symposium on Principles of Database Systems* (1989), 1–10.

[16] VAN GELDER, A., ROSS, K. AND SCHLIPF, J.S. The well-founded semantics for general logic programs. *Journal of the ACM* 38(3), 1991, 620–650.

Deductive Databases with Incomplete Information

(Extended Abstract)

Fangqing Dong   and   Laks V.S. Lakshmanan

Dept. of Computer Science, Concordia University
Montreal Quebec, Canada H3G 1M8

Abstract

We consider query processing in deductive databases with incomplete information in the form of null values. We motivate the problem of extracting the maximal information from a (deductive) database in response to queries, and formalize this in the form of *conditional answers*. We give a sound and complete top-down proof procedure for generating conditional answers. We also extend the well-known magic sets method to handle null values, and show that the transformed program executed by semi-naive evaluation (with minor extensions) is correct in the sense that it will generate all and only valid conditional answers w.r.t. the original program.

1   Introduction

Most of the works on deductive databases have only considered a complete information model for the set of facts available for the EDB (or base) relations. For many applications available information is typically incomplete. One form of incomplete information that has been researched extensively in the context of relational databases is the well-known *null values* (see [AKG 91] for a survey). Of the many different types of null values, the kind most researched are the so-called "exists but unknown" type of null values. Both logical (*e.g.*, Gallaire et al [GMN 84], Reiter [Re 86], Vardi [Va 86]) and algebraic (*e.g.*, Abiteboul et al [AKG 91]) approaches have been investigated in the literature. The main concerns have been completeness and complexity of query processing. It is well known that query processing in the presence of nulls is computationally intractable and tractability is achieved either by restricting the class of queries considered [Re 86, Va 86] or by sacrificing [Re 86, Va 86] or weakening [La 89] completeness. The question of query processing in deductive databases in the presence of incomplete information (*e.g.*, in the form of nulls) has received relatively little attention. Demolombe and Cerro [DC 88], Liu [Li 90], and Abiteboul et al [AKG 91] are the representative works (see Section 6 for more details).

In this paper, we consider query processing in deductive databases in the presence of nulls. Firstly, we set out the objective of extracting the maximal amount of information from the database in answering queries. This means that even when a tuple $\bar{d}$ is not provably an answer to a query $p(\bar{X})$, we may want to know that if certain conditions held, then $\bar{d}$ would be an answer. Aside from the theoretical interest, we believe information extracted in this manner will find applications in hypothetical query answering (see Naqvi and Rossi [NR 90]) and in answering queries in the context of design databases where specifications are often incomplete and one may want to know what would be the eventual outcomes if various design alternatives were chosen. We formalize the notion of extracting maximal information from databases using *conditional answers* (Section 2). The traditional approach of basing the semantics of programs on Herbrand models will obviously fail in the presence of null values. Indeed, unlike normal constants, nulls cannot be viewed syntactically. Also, during query processing care must be taken to ensure that the constraints on nulls are respected. To this end, we formalize the idea that nulls may be mapped to either some normal constant or to a completely new element in the domain, and preprocess a given datalog query program incorporating this idea (Section 3). We then give a sound and complete proof procedure called SLD$^\perp$-refutation for query processing (Section 4). On the bottom-up side, we develop a rewriting method which is an extension of the well-known magic sets method (see [BR 86, BR 87]) to handle null values. We also propose a complementary evaluation procedure, which is a simple extension of semi-naive evaluation. Finally, we show that all valid (conditional) answers will be generated by (extended) semi-naive evaluation of the rewritten program above and only valid answers will be generated in this manner (Section 5). We compare our work with related work in Section 6 and summarize our results and discuss future work in Section 7.

We conclude this section with an example to motivate our approach of using *conditional answers* to queries. Consider a file system design situation where it is desired to make use of available file organization strategies and their strengths in terms of efficiently supporting various types of queries. Suppose that information known to the database administrator (DBA) is represented in the form of the relations *good_for(Strategy, Query-type)* and *implemented(File, Strategy)*, where *Strategy* refers to file organization strategies and the other attributes and relations have the obvious meaning. Suppose the available knowledge is represented as the following facts together with the constraint $\mathcal{C} = \{\perp_1 \neq \perp_2\}$. Here, $b = B^+\text{-}tree$, $h = hashing$, $m = multilist$, $s = simple$, $r = range$, $bl = boolean$, and f_1, f_2, f_3 denote files.

$r_1: \ good\_for(b,s).$	$r_2: \ good\_for(b,r).$	$r_3: \ good\_for(m,bl).$
$r_4: \ good\_for(h,s).$	$r_5: \ good\_for(\perp_2,r).$	$r_6: \ implemented(f_1,h).$
$r_7: \ implemented(f_2,\perp_1).$	$r_8: \ implemented(f_3,\perp_2).$	

Here, r_5 corresponds to the DBA's knowledge that there is a strategy which is good for range queries, and this strategy could be one of the known ones, or could be something he did not encounter before (perhaps a recent invention). Also, r_7, r_8, and $\mathcal{C}$ correspond to the fact that the access strategies for files f_2, f_3 have not been decided on yet, although there is a constraint to implement them with different strategies. Let *supports(F, Q)* mean that file F supports queries of type Q efficiently. This can be defined as r_9: $supports(F, Q) \leftarrow implemented(F, S), good\_for(S, Q)$. Now, consider the query $\leftarrow supports(F, r)$, which asks for the files supporting range queries. The idea behind conditional answers is to extract tuples which would be answers if certain conditions held. Mechanically resolving the given query against rule r_9, and resolving the second subgoal in the resulting goal against r_2 gives us the new goal $\leftarrow implemented(F, b)$. Under the usual least Herbrand model semantics, an attempt to unify this subgoal with r_7 fails, essentially because b and $\perp_1$ are treated as distinct entities. However, what we really need is to be able to match the null $\perp_1$ with a (normal) constant like b as long as the constraints on the null values are not violated. In our case, since constraints are not violated, we would like to be able to conclude "$supports(f_2, r)$ provided the condition $\perp_1 = b$ holds". This reasoning is formalized in the next sections and we will eventually derive this conditional answer formally (Example 4.1). For lack of space, we suppress the proofs of our results in this extended abstract. Complete details are available in [DL 92] and will appear in the full paper as well.

2 Datalog$^\perp$ Theories

In this section, we formalize the intuition developed in the previous section. We assume the reader is familiar with the general notions of deductive databases and logic programming, SLD-refutation, bottom-up evaluation and the magic sets query rewriting method [Ul 89, Ll 87]. Datalog, the language of function-free Horn clauses, is the vehicle query language for deductive databases [Ul 89]. A datalog query program consists of (i) a finite set of unit clauses representing facts for the base (EDB) predicates, (ii) a finite set of Horn clause rules defining the derived (IDB) predicates, and (iii) a goal clause, representing the query. In this paper, we restrict attention to "pure" datalog, in which only database (base/derived) predicates (and no arithmetic predicates) are allowed in the rules. We next extend datalog programs (whose EDB contains null values) to *datalog$^\perp$ theories*, using an extension of Reiter's [Re 86] formulation of extended relational theories.

Consider a first order language L, with a vocabulary consisting of finitely many constant symbols, denoted by D, finitely many predicate symbols p_i, q_j, and infinitely many variables X_i, Y_j, Z_k. The constants d_i in D are either normal constants c_j, or nulls $\perp_k$. We assume the vocabulary includes the arithmetic relations $=, \neq, <, \leq$. (The relations $>$ and $\geq$ are redundant.) Let Π be any datalog program. Then associated with Π is a logical theory P of L, called the *datalog$^\perp$ theory* of Π, consisting of: (i) Unique Name Axioms (UNA): for every pair of distinct normal constants c_i and c_j in Π, an axiom $c_i \neq c_j$; (ii) Domain Closure Axiom (DCA): the axiom $\forall X[X = d_1 \vee \cdots \vee X = d_n]$, where $d_1, \cdots, d_n$ are all the constants mentioned in the program Π; (iii) Completion Axioms ($COMP$): for any predicate symbol p in the program Π, defined by the rules $p(\bar{t}_i) \leftarrow A_{i1} \wedge \cdots \wedge A_{im_i}$, $i = 1, \cdots, k$, the axiom $\forall \bar{X}[p(\bar{X}) \leftrightarrow (\bar{X} = \bar{t}_1 \wedge A_{11} \wedge \cdots \wedge A_{1m_1}) \vee \cdots \vee (\bar{X} = \bar{t}_k \wedge A_{k1} \wedge \cdots \wedge A_{km_k})]$ (A_{ij}'s are positive literals, $\bar{t}_i = (t_{i1}, \cdots, t_{in})$ and t_{ij}'s are constants or variables, $\bar{X} = (X_1 \cdots X_n)$, and $\bar{X} = \bar{t}_i$ is shorthand for $X_1 = t_{i1} \wedge \cdots \wedge X_n = t_{in}$); ($iv$) *Constraints*: there is a set $\mathcal{C}$ of constraints of the form $d_i R d_j$, where R is one of the arithmetic relations $=, \neq, <, \leq$, and at least one of d_i and d_j is a null. UNA force the true identity of each normal constant to be fully specified. $COMP$ ensure that any canonical model of the theory is a supported one. Constraints allow the representation of partial knowledge on the nulls. We will find the following notion of fully specified constraints convenient. We say a set $\mathcal{C}$ of constraints is *fully specified* iff (i) $\mathcal{C}$ has no equality constraints; (ii) $\mathcal{C}$ is closed under the arithmetic axioms concerning $=, \neq, <, \leq$. The fully specified constraints associated with nulls $\perp_1, \cdots, \perp_k$, denoted by $\mathcal{C}[\perp_1, \cdots, \perp_k]$, are those constraints of the form $d_i R d_j$, where d_i and d_j are either one of $\perp_1, \cdots, \perp_k$, or normal constants, at least one being a null. For simplicity, we use E to represent a set of conditions as well as the conjunction of the conditions in the set.

A query Q in L is a formula of the form $p(\bar{X})$, where $\bar{X}$ is a k-tuple of free variables. The answer to this query against a theory P is a k-ary relation, defined by $\|Q\|_P = \{\bar{d} \mid P \models p(\bar{d})\}$. We next generalize this notion of answers to that of conditional answers. Let P be a datalog$^\perp$ theory and $Q \equiv p(\bar{X})$ a query. Then we define the *conditional answers* of Q against P as

$$\|Q\|_P^c = \{(\bar{d}, E) \mid P \cup E \text{ is consistent and } P \models E \rightarrow p(\bar{d})\}.$$

In general, this answer set may include redundant answers. To exclude them, we need the notion of minimality. We say that a conditional answer $(\bar{d}, E)$ to a query Q is *minimal* provided for any conditional answer $(\bar{d}, E')$ of Q, if $P \models E' \rightarrow E$, then $P \models E \rightarrow E'$. Clearly, a set of minimal conditional answers are always non-redundant. Normal answers can be seen to be a special case of conditional answers where the condition set is empty. In future, by a datalog program, we mean a datalog program with nulls.

3 Compiling Constraints on Nulls

When processing queries in the presence of nulls, it is necessary to automatically generate all bindings for nulls which respect the associated constraints. To formalize this idea, we introduce a binary predicate *map*. For a null Ω and a variable X that ranges over the domain of the structure, $map(\Omega, X)$ asserts that Ω is mapped to the instantiation of X. It is a mapping schema in the sense that by associating different instantiations of X, we get different mappings out of it. Let Π be a datalog program with constraints $\mathcal{C}$ on nulls. Then the constraints $\mathcal{C}$ can be "compiled" into the following set of axioms:

A_1 $map(c_i, c_i)$, for each normal constant c_i;
A_2 $\forall X \exists Y [map(X, Y)]$;
A_3 $\forall XYZ[map(X, Y) \wedge map(X, Z) \rightarrow Y = Z]$;
A_4 $\forall X_1 \cdots X_k (map(\perp_1, X_1) \wedge \cdots \wedge map(\perp_k, X_k) \leftrightarrow \mathcal{C}[\perp_1 /X_1, \cdots, \perp_k /X_k])$,

where $\perp_1, \cdots, \perp_k$ are all the nulls in P, and $\mathcal{C}[\perp_1 /X_1, \cdots, \perp_k /X_k]$ is obtained from $\mathcal{C}$ by uniformly replacing occurrences of $\perp_i$ by X_i. Axiom A_1 says each normal constant is mapped to itself. Axiom A_2 and A_3 assert that *map* is a function, while axiom A_4 forces *map* to respect the constraints on the nulls.

We can transform a datalog program Π and constraints $\mathcal{C}$ into another program Π' together with a set of axioms, which incorporates the constraints on nulls and puts them in the "right" places, as follows: (i) replace the constraints $\mathcal{C}$ by the axioms above; (ii) transform each datalog rule r in Π into the rule r' obtained by replacing each null $\perp_i$ in r by a new variable X_i and adding the subgoal $map(\perp_i, X_i)$ into the rule body. Let P' be the datalog$^\perp$ theory of the transformed program Π'. Then we say that P' is obtained from P by *constraint compilation*. Notice that P' consists of the $COMP$ axioms corresponding to the transformed rules, the axioms corresponding to the constraints, and the UNA, and DCA axioms. Our main result in this section shows that the compiled theory P' is equivalent to the original theory P w.r.t. conditional answers to queries involving the database predicates.

Theorem 3.1 *Let P be a datalog$^\perp$ theory, P' be the datalog$^\perp$ theory obtained from P by constraint compilation, and $Q \equiv p(\bar{X})$ be any query. Then $\|Q\|_P^c = \|Q\|_{P'}^c$.* $\square$

In the sequel, we refer to datalog$^\perp$ theories as datalog$^\perp$ programs for convenience. The constraints and axioms that are part of a datalog$^\perp$ theory will be implicitly understood. Even through the theory has the $COMP$ axioms corresponding to the rules, we sometimes make use of the rule directly.

4 A Proof Procedure

Let P be a datalog$^\perp$ program and P' be the datalog program obtained from P by constraint compilation. Since we have already seen that P and P' are equivalent (Theorem 3.1), we can use P' for processing queries against P. Even though P' is a datalog program, existing top-down or bottom-up techniques cannot be directly applied to it, since it makes use of a special predicate map which mimics a mapping from nulls to constants, that respects the constraints on nulls. In this section, we extend the well-known SLD-refutation procedure to SLD$^\perp$-refutation, and show that it is a sound and complete proof procedure for datalog$^\perp$ programs.

Let P and P' be as above and $Q \equiv p(\bar{X})$ be a query. Consider a computation rule (see Lloyd [Ll 87] for a definition) R which is fair w.r.t. all database predicates (i.e. those excluding map). We need a few definitions. A literal is a database (map) literal if it involves a database predicate (the predicate map). A goal is a clause of the form: $\leftarrow \mathcal{E}, A_1, ..., A_n$, where A_i's are positive (database or map) literals and $\mathcal{E}$ is a conjunction of consistent constraints. A goal G is a *bottom-goal* when all literals in it are map literals or constraints.

Let $G_0 \equiv\leftarrow Q$ be the initial goal. A SLD$^\perp$-*derivation* for a program P' with initial goal G_0 is a sequence $G_0, G_1, ..., G_i, ...$ defined as follows. Let G_i be the goal$\leftarrow \mathcal{E}, A_1, ..., A_k, ..., A_n$ and let A_k be a (database) literal which is selected by the computation rule R. Suppose there is a rule r of the form: $A \leftarrow B_1, ..., B_q$ in the program. It turns out not all most general unifiers are useful for our purposes, since the mgu's we want are the ones which respect the constraints on nulls. To capture such mgu's, we introduce the notion of a *constrained mgu*. Suppose $\perp_1$ $, \cdots, \perp_l$ are the nulls such that G_i has the subgoals $map(\perp_j, X_j)$ and $map(\perp_j, X_j')$ for distinct variables X_j, X_j', $j=1, \cdots, l$. Let θ be any mgu of A and A_k. Then we call the substitution $\sigma = \theta \bullet \{X_1/X_1', \cdots, X_l/X_l'\}$ the *constrained mgu* of A and A_k (associated with θ) . Let σ be a constrained mgu of A and A_k. Then G_{i+1} is obtained as the following goal:

$$G_{i+1} \equiv \leftarrow (\mathcal{E}', A_1, \cdots, A_{k-1}, B_1, \cdots, B_q, A_{k+1}, \cdots, A_n)\sigma, \; where$$
$$\mathcal{E}' \equiv \mathcal{E} \wedge \mathcal{C}[\perp_1 /X_1, \cdots, \perp_n /X_n].$$

Here, $\perp_1, \cdots, \perp_n$ are all the nulls occurring in G_{i+1}. G_{i+1} is defined only when $\mathcal{E}'$ is satisfiable, otherwise the current goal G_i is failed[1]. A SLD$^\perp$-*refutation* from P' for query Q is a finite SLD$^\perp$-derivation $G_0, G_1, ..., G_n$, where G_n is a bottom goal. The *preanswer substitution* π associated with this SLD$^\perp$-refutation is $\pi = \theta_1 \cdot ... \cdot \theta_n$, where θ_i is the constrained mgu applied at step i in the derivation.

Let P' be a datalog program (as above), $Q \equiv p(\bar{X})$ a query, and let $G_0 \equiv\leftarrow Q, \cdots, G_n$ be a SLD$^\perp$-refutation with preanswer substitution π. Then a *conditional answer* corresponding to this refutation is obtained as follows.

I. Suppose that G_n is the empty goal ($\square$). Then $\pi(\bar{X}) = \bar{c}$ and the answer is $(\bar{c}, \phi)$, where $\bar{c}$ is a tuple of normal constants and the empty set ϕ denotes the *true* condition.

II. Suppose the bottom goal is $G_n \equiv\leftarrow \mathcal{E}, map(\perp_1, X_1), \cdots, map(\perp_m, X_m)$. Then we get a conditional answer $(\bar{d}, E)$ obtained as follows:

1. Let E be the constraints obtained from G_n as follows: (i) whenever G_n has a subgoal $map(\perp_i, c_i)$, then E has a condition $\perp_i= c_i$; (ii) if G_n has subgoals $map(\perp_i, X)$ and $map(\perp_j, X)$, $i \neq j$, for any variable X, then E has a condition $\perp_i = \perp_j$.

2. Let $\bar{d}$ be a tuple of normal constants or nulls obtained from $\bar{X}$ by replacing X_i by c_i whenever $\pi(X_i) = c_i$, and by replacing X_i by $\perp_i$ whenever G_n has the subgoal $map(\perp_i, Z_i)$, and $\pi(X_i) = Z_i$ (and $\pi(Z_i) \neq c$ for any constant c).

We next prove that $SLD^{\perp}$-refutation is a sound and complete proof procedure[2].

Theorem 4.1 *Let P be a datalog$^{\perp}$ program with fully specified constraints $\mathcal{C}$, P' be the datalog program obtained by constraint compilation from P, $Q \equiv p(\bar{X})$ be a query, and R a fair computation rule w.r.t. the database predicates. Then*

(i) If $(\bar{d}, E)$ is a conditional answer of a $SLD^{\perp}$-refutation, then we have that $P \models E \rightarrow p(\bar{d})$.

(ii) For any $(\bar{d}, E) \in \|Q\|_P^c$, there is a $SLD^{\perp}$-refutation whose associated conditional answer is $(\bar{d}, E)$. □

Example 4.1 Let us revisit the example in Section 1 and consider the query $Q \equiv supports(f_3, r)$. First, we modify the program there by constraint compilation. Thus, rules r_5, r_7 and r_8 are modified as follows. $r_5' : good\_for(X_2, r) \leftarrow map(\perp_2, X_2)$. $r_7' : implemented(f_2, X_1) \leftarrow map(\perp_1, X_1)$. $r_8' : implemented(f_3, X_2) \leftarrow map(\perp_2, X_2)$. The constraint set is $\mathcal{C} = \{\perp_1 \neq \perp_2\}$. Notice that the rewritten program P' consists of $r_1, \cdots, r_4, r_5', r_6, r_7', r_8', r_9$, the constraint $\mathcal{C}$, and the axioms UNA, DCA, and $COMP$. Consider an $SLD^{\perp}$-refutation of $\leftarrow Q$ w.r.t. the transformed program P'. It can be verified that the bottom goal $\leftarrow map(\perp_2, b)$ and the pre-answer substitution $\pi = \{F/f_3, Q/r, S/b, X_2/b\}$ are obtained. Since the condition associated with the bottom goal is satisfiable (w.r.t. constraints on nulls), we get the conditional answer $(\epsilon, \{\perp_2 = b\})$, where ϵ denotes a tuple of zero length, corresponding to the answer "yes". We next consider a recursive example. □

Example 4.2 Consider a $SLD^{\perp}$-refutation for the query $Q \equiv ancestor(paul, Y)$, from the following program.

$r_1 : \quad ancestor(X, Y) \leftarrow parent(X, Z), ancestor(Z, Y)$.
$r_2 : \quad ancestor(X, Y) \leftarrow parent(X, Y)$.

$r_3 : \quad parent(\perp_1, jim)$. $\qquad r_3' : \quad parent(X_1, jim) \leftarrow map(\perp_1, X_1)$.
$r_4 : \quad parent(paul, \perp_1)$. $\qquad r_4' : \quad parent(paul, X_1) \leftarrow map(\perp_1, X_1)$.
$r_5 : \quad parent(\perp_2, george)$. $\qquad r_5' : \quad parent(X_2, george) \leftarrow map(\perp_2, X_2)$.
$r_6 : \quad parent(john, joe)$. $\qquad \mathcal{C} : \quad \{\perp_1 \neq \perp_2, \perp_1 \neq jim, \perp_1 \neq paul, \perp_2 \neq george\}$.

We first unify the query Q with rule r_1 and the first subgoal of rule r_1 with r_4', then resolve the second subgoal of rule r_1 with rule r_2, and the only subgoal of rule r_2 with r_6. Then we get the bottom-goal $\leftarrow map(\perp_1, john)$ and the associated preanswer substitution π is $\{X/paul, Z/john, X_1/john, Y/joe\}$. So, we get a conditional answer $((joe), \{\perp_1 = john\})$ to the query Q. In a similar way, we can get two more conditional answers for Q – $((jim), \phi)$ and $((\perp_1), \phi)$. □

5 Bottom-up Query Evaluation

The bottom-up paradigm of query processing in deductive databases consists in (i) rewriting a query program into a query-equivalent program which mimics top-down computation using some "filters" like magic predicates, and (ii) evaluating the resulting program bottom-up using a method like semi-naive evaluation. For more details on bottom-up query processing and comparison with top-down approaches, the reader is referred to Ullman [Ul 89a] and Naughton and Ramakrishnan [NR 91]. Since bottom-up query processing is a popular paradigm for deductive databases, it would be desirable to be able to handle nulls within this framework. The purpose of this section is to show how this can be achieved. Throughout this section, we consider datalog$^\perp$ programs obtained from given datalog programs as discussed in section 2. We apply various transformations to such programs prior to evaluating them bottom-up. A fundamental component of bottom-up query processing is that of *sideways information passing* (SIP). Intuitively, the purpose of SIP is to transmit information about the tuples computed so far to the next subgoal while processing a rule, so that the selectivity of bound arguments can be exploited. Thus, bindings are passed on sideways. The conditions arising in handling nulls themselves constitute a form of generalized bindings. These bindings must be propagated (i) from goals to subgoals, and (ii) from one subgoal to another when processing them in a rule. Clearly, existing bottom-up techniques are incapable of handling these generalized bindings. Thus, they must be extended in order to handle them. Our approach is to associate an extra argument with each derived predicate, corresponding to the conditions associated with the tuple in the data part of that predicate. We represent sets of conditions as terms (which correspond to lists of these conditions). To this end, we extend the language L with the introduction of a distinguished constant 'ϕ' and a 3-ary function symbol f which appear in no query program. The advantage of this representation is that the conditions can be easily passed sideways just as normal data.

A second issue is that existing bottom-up techniques implement SIP by syntactic match between constants. However, this does not respect the semantics associated with nulls. For this purpose, we need SIP to be implemented via semantic match. In this section, we will introduce a new predicate *sip* to implement SIP from one argument X to another argument X' when at least one of them is bound to a null. This predicate will be placed in appropriate places in all rules so that SIP can be performed correctly incorporating the semantics of nulls. The last issue is to integrate available constraints on nulls into suitable places in programs so that those constraints can be confirmed whenever the variables associated with nulls get bound. A bruteforce approach to put the constraints in the right places is to instantiate each variable shared by (at least) two subgoals in each rule, with all possible nulls, and then impose the constraints associated with the null value with each such (partly) instantiated rule. This is clearly inefficient and will generate a huge number of rules, even when the number of nulls is limited. To avoid this problem, we make use of two meta-predicates $C(X, X')$ and $C^*(X, Y, X', Y')$. The literal $C(X, X')$ verifies that the mapping $X \longmapsto X'$ is consistent with the given constraints on nulls, while $C^*(X, Y, X', Y')$ verifies that the mappings $X \longmapsto X'$ and $Y \longmapsto Y'$ are consistent with each other.

For datalog$^\perp$ programs, the issues of binding patterns and unique binding property for IDB predicates are identical to those for normal datalog programs. We shall henceforth assume without loss of generality that our adorned programs satisfy the unique binding property [Ul 89]. We extend magic sets transformation to deal with any datalog$^\perp$ query program P in three phases. Firstly, we apply adornments to the datalog$^\perp$ program P. We then transform the resulting program P^a, incorporating SIP while respecting the semantics of nulls. At last, we apply magic sets transformation to the resulting program. Recall the map literals $map(\perp, c)$ that were introduced into datalog$^\perp$ programs in section 4. In this section, we would like to handle general situations in the context of SIP from a variable X to another variable X', where either X or X' (or both!) could be nulls. To handle these cases in a simple and symmetric manner, we will make use of literals of the form $match(X, X')$ with the meaning that both X and X' are mapped to the same individual. For uniformity, we replace all occurrences of literals of the form $map(\bot, X)$ in the datalog$^\bot$ program by the literal $match(\bot, X)$. It can be seen that the semantics is preserved since map can be viewed as a special case of $match$.

5.1 Generalizing Sideways Information Passing

The principal ideas can be summarized as follows. Let P be a datalog$^\bot$ program. With each derived literal $p(\bar{t})$, we associate a set of conditions E such that $P \models E \rightarrow p(\bar{t})$, where the conditions are of the form $\bot_j = d_j$, d_j being a normal constant or null[3]. We translate each such literal into $p(\bar{t}, E)$ in the modified program. As a special case, the condition associated with an EDB literal is empty. Recall that in arguments of predicates, we represent conditions as f-terms. A f-term is a term of the form $f(<\text{null constant}>, <(\text{null or normal) constant}>, < f\text{-term}>)$. Given an ordered list E of conditions, the f-term representation E_f of E is defined recursively as follows: $E_f = \phi$, if $E = \{\}$; $E_f = f(\bot_1, d_1, E'_f)$, if $E = \{\bot_1 = d_1, \bot_2 = d_2, \cdots, \bot_n = d_n\}$, where E'_f is the f-term representing $E' = \{\bot_2 = d_2, \cdots, \bot_n = d_n\}$. However, for simplicity, we use the same symbol E to denote a set of conditions (or their conjunction) and sometimes the term corresponding to the condition set. Besides, in rewriting programs incorporating SIP, we (suggestively) use $E, E', E^i, \cdots$ as variables ranging over such condition terms. The intended meaning should be clear from the context.

For any adorned datalog rule r^a, we modify the rule r^a by adding subgoals involving the predicate sip so that the resulting rule will implement SIP, respecting the semantics of nulls. For ease of exposition, in the following algorithm, we restrict attention to the case where no variable occurs in a subgoal more than once. The algorithm can be easily extended to deal with the general case. We remark that when we later apply the magic sets transformation, auxiliary predicates including magic and supplementary predicates will be added as subgoals in the rewritten rules. Clearly, these are derived predicates and hence conditions must be associated with each of them. Anticipating this, we suppose in the following algorithm that the initial condition set (corresponding to the magic predicate) in a rule body is E^0. Algorithm SIPN transforms each adorned rule in order to implement SIP in a correct manner.

Algorithm SIPN (SIP for nulls)
Input: An adorned datalog rule r^a: $p^a(\bar{t}) \leftarrow B_1, \cdots, B_m$, where B_i's are positive
   literals. V_b will denote the set of bound variables at any given time.
Output: A modified adorned rule $r^{a'}$, which correctly incorporates SIP.

Begin
   $V_b := \{\text{bound variables in } p^a(\bar{t})\}$; $E := E^0$;
   For $i=1$ to m **do** {

   1. If B_i is a derived literal $q(\bar{t}')$, then modify this literal to $q(\bar{t}', E^*)$, and add a literal $union(E^*, E, E')$ right after this subgoal; $E := E'$; /* The function of $union$ is to check if the union of condition sets $E' = E^* \cup E$ is consistent.*/

2. If B_i is a base literal $q(t_1, \cdots, t_k)$, then
   For $j=1$ to k **do** {

   (a) If t_j is a variable $X \in V_b$, then replace any occurrence of X in B_i or subsequent subgoals by a new variable X', and add a literal $sip(X, X', E, E')$ just before B_i; $E := E'$;

   (b) If t_j is a constant d, then replace t_j by a new variable X', and add a literal $sip(d, X', E, E')$ just before B_i; $E := E'$;
   };

3. $V_b := V_b \cup \{X'_1, \cdots, X'_k\}$; /*Here X'_i's are all the newly introduced variables.*/

}; Change the head literal to $p(\bar{t}, E)$.
End □

Example 5.1 Let us apply Algorithm SIPN to the following datalog rules, after adornment w.r.t. the query $\leftarrow sg(a, Y)$.

$$sg(X, Y) \leftarrow flat(X, Y).$$
$$sg(X, Y) \leftarrow up(X, Z), sg(Z, W), down(W, Y).$$

Then we get the following modified rules:

$$sg^{bff}(X, Y, E') \leftarrow sip^{bfbf}(X, X', E^0, E'), flat^{bf}(X', Y).$$
$$sg^{bff}(X, Y, E') \leftarrow sip^{bfbf}(X, X', E^0, E^1), up^{bf}(X', Z), sg^{bf}(Z, W, E^2),$$
$$union(E^2, E^1, E^3), sip^{bfbf}(W, W', E^3, E'), down^{bf}(W', Y).$$

Notice that the adornment is extended to the arguments representing the conditions. Clearly, this argument is *free*. □

Let $r^{a'}$ be a resulting adorned rule of the form:

$$p(\bar{t}, E) \leftarrow A_1, \cdots, A_k, sip(t_l, X'_l, E_l, E'_l), \cdots, sip(t_n, X'_n, E_n, E'_n), A_{k+1}, \cdots, A_m,$$

where A_i's can be database literals or sip, or $union$ literals. Specially, A_{k+1} is a base literal with $X'_j, j = l, \cdots, n$ among its arguments. For all $j = l, \cdots, n$:

(1) If t_j is a variable X_j, then corresponding to the literal $sip(t_j, X'_j, E_j, E'_j)$, we include a pair of rules representing the mapping patterns associated with nulls[4]:

$$match(X_j, X'_j) \leftarrow A_1, \cdots, A_k, null(X_j), A_{k+1}, C(X_j, X'_j),$$
$$match(X_j, X'_j) \leftarrow A_1, \cdots, A_k, A_{k+1}, null(X'_j), C(X'_j, X_j);$$

(2) If t_j is a normal constant c_j, then corresponding to the literal $sip(c_j, X'_j, E_j, E'_j)$, we include a rule: $match(c_j, X'_j) \leftarrow A_{k+1}, null(X'_j), C(X'_j, c_j)$;
(3) If t_j is a null $\perp_j$, then we include a rule $match(\perp_j, X'_j) \leftarrow A_{k+1}, C(\perp_j, X'_j)$.

The literal $match(X, X')$ expresses the mapping patterns between nulls and (normal or null) constants, and asserts that both X and X' are mapped to the same individual. We make use of a built-in predicate $null(X)$ which distinguishes nulls from normal constants. Intuitively, $C(X, X')$ is a meta-literal whose function is to test the consistency of the mapping patterns between X and X'. A precise definition of this test as well as details of its implementation in a bottom-up framework are discussed in Section 5.3.

Now, we give the precise definition of the predicate sip. The literal $sip(X, X', E, E')$ expresses SIP from X to X' under condition set E. Given the binding for X and E (the current conditions), it first generates a binding for X' and then tests if $E \cup \{X = X'\}$ is consistent. Then (*i*) $E' = E$ if $X = X'$ is valid, or $X = X' \in E$; (*ii*) $E' = \{X = X'\} \bigcup E$ if $X = X' \notin E$ and $\{X = X'\} \cup E$ is consistent. To generate a binding for X', sip uses *match* and confirms that the generated binding is legal w.r.t. the constraints on nulls. Finally, the definition of the predicate sip is as follows:

$sip(X, X, E, E)$.
$sip(X, X', E, E') \leftarrow match(X, X'), null(X), verify(X, X', E, E')$.
$sip(X, X', E, E') \leftarrow match(X, X'), null(X'), verify(X', X, E, E')$.
$verify(X, X', E, E) \leftarrow verify_1(X, X', E, f(X, X', E'))$.
$verify(X, X', E, f(X, X', E)) \leftarrow verify_1(X, X', E, \phi)$.
$verify_1(X, X', E, E') \leftarrow verify_1(X, X', E, f(Y, Y', E')), X \neq Y, C^*(X, Y, X', Y')$.
$verify_1(X, X', E, E') \leftarrow verify_1(X, X', E, f(Y, Y', E')), X' \neq Y', C^*(X, Y, X', Y')$.
$verify_1(X, X', E, E) \leftarrow m\_sip(X, E), match(X, X'), null(X)$.
$verify_1(X', X, E, E) \leftarrow m\_sip(X, E), match(X, X'), null(X')$.
$verify_1(X, X', E, E) \leftarrow m\_union(f(X, X', E'), E)$.
$union(\phi, E, E)$.
$union(f(X, X', E'), E'', E) \leftarrow verify(X, X', E'', E_0), union(E', E_0, E)$.

The literal $verify(X, X', E, E')$ verifies if condition $X = X'$ is consistent with the current condition set E, and generates a condition set E' defined as: (*i*) $E' = E$ if the constraint $X = X' \in E$; (*ii*) $E' = \{X = X'\} \cup E$ if $X = X' \notin E$ and $\{X = X'\} \cup E$ is consistent. In fact, *verify* is defined in a bottom-up manner using $verify_1$. The literal $verify_1(X, X', E, E')$ expresses that condition $X = X'$ is consistent with the condition set $E - E'$, provided E' is a subset of E (and that $X = X'$ remains to be confirmed to be consistent with E'). The "starting point" of the predicate $verify_1$ is defined using the magic predicates m_sip (m_union) associated with sip ($union$) predicates. The literal $union(E_1, E_2, E)$ verifies if the union of E_1 and E_2 is consistent and rewrites the union (in term form) as E. Notice that we use a special constant 'ϕ' to represent the empty set of conditions. $C^*(X, Y, X', Y')$ is a meta-literal, used to test the consistency between two mapping patterns from X and Y to X' and Y' respectively. Details associated with the two meta-predicates C and C^* are discussed in the Section 5.3. We remark that some of the rules involving the auxiliary predicates (like sip) appear unsafe but because of the binding pattern (*i.e.* sip^{bfbf}) with which they will be accessed, no problem will arise. This will be clear when we discuss a complete example in Section 5.2.

5.2   Applying Magic Sets Transformation

We integrate the techniques developed in Section 5.1 into the magic sets transformation and apply it to a given datalog$^\perp$ program P in three phases.

Phase 1 Applying adornments to P to generate an adorned program P^a.

Phase 2 Modifying the rules to correctly implement SIP, respecting the semantics for nulls and their constraints. More specifically, for every adorned rule r^a of P^a:
   (2.1) Applying algorithm $SIPN$ to the adorned rule r^a;
   (2.2) For every newly introduced literal $sip(X, X', E, E')$, generating rules to

define mapping patterns.

Phase 3 Applying magic-sets transformation to the resulting program, and using supplementary predicates to eliminate redundant subexpressions. Notice that every magic predicate *should* have an argument position associated with condition sets. Even through this argument position is *free*, we should not delete it, since it plays a crucial role in answer generation. (Also, we do not apply magic-sets transformation to the predicates *verify*, *verify₁*, and *match*, because the rules for these predicates have been designed with bottom-up computation in mind. Consequently, an application of magic sets to these predicates can not make their evaluation any more efficient.) □

Example 5.2 Consider the program of Example 5.1. On applying the SIPN and magic sets transformation to the adorned program, we get the following program which consists of three groups of rules: the *answer-generator group*, *condition-checker group*, and *mapping-generator group*. (We suppress the adornments of predicates to improve readability.)

- Answer-generator Group

$sg(X, Y, E') \leftarrow m\_sg(X, E), sip(X, X', E, E'), flat(X', Y).$

$sg(X, Y, E') \leftarrow s\_sg_2(X, W, E^3), sip(W, W', E^3, E'), down(W', Y).$

$q(Y, E) \leftarrow sg(a, Y, E).$

$sip(X, X, E, E) \leftarrow m\_sip(X, E).$

$sip(X, X', E, E') \leftarrow m\_sip(X, E), match(X, X'), null(X), verify(X, X', E, E').$

$sip(X, X', E, E') \leftarrow m\_sip(X, E), match(X, X'), null(X'), verify(X', X, E, E').$

$m\_sg(a, \phi).$

$m\_sg(Z, E') \leftarrow m\_sg(X, E), sip(X, X', E, E'), up(X', Z).$

$m\_sip(X, E) \leftarrow m\_sg(X, E).$

$m\_sip(W, E^3) \leftarrow s\_sg_2(X, W, E^3).$

$s\_sg_1(X, Z, E^1) \leftarrow m\_sg(X, E), sip(X, X', E, E^1), up(X', Z).$

$s\_sg_2(X, W, E^3) \leftarrow s\_sg_1(X, Z, E^1), sg(Z, W, E^2), union(E^2, E^1, E^3).$

- Condition-checker Group

- All rules for *verify* and *verify₁* (see Section 5.1)

$union(\phi, E, E) \leftarrow m\_union(\phi, E).$

$union(f(X, X', E'), E'', E) \leftarrow m\_union(f(X, X', E'), E''),$
$\qquad\qquad\qquad\qquad\qquad verify(X, X', E'', E_0), union(E', E_0, E).$

$m\_union(E', E_0) \leftarrow m\_union(f(X, X', E'), E''), verify(X, X', E'', E_0).$

$m\_union(E^2, E^1) \leftarrow s\_sg_1(X, Z, E^1), sg(Z, W, E^2).$

- Mapping-generator Group

$match(X, X') \leftarrow m\_sg(X, E), null(X), flat(X', Y), C(X, X').$

$match(X, X') \leftarrow m\_sg(X, E), flat(X', Y), null(X'), C(X', X).$

$match(X, X') \leftarrow m\_sg(X, E), null(X), up(X', Y), C(X, X').$

$match(X, X') \leftarrow m\_sg(X, E), up(X', Y), null(X'), C(X', X).$

$match(W, W') \leftarrow s\_sg_2(X, W, E), null(W), down(W', Y), C(W, W').$

$match(W, W') \leftarrow s\_sg_2(X, W, E), down(W', Y), null(W'), C(W', W).$

Notice that s_sg_1 and s_sg_2 are supplementary predicates introduced to avoid redundant computations of common subexpressions. Also, in the rules for *match*, the magic predicate m_sg has been used in place of sg to improve the efficiency. □

A remark about the size of the transformed program is in order. Firstly, the numbers of rules defining the predicates *sip*, *verify*, *verify₁*, and *union* are a constant, regardless of the size of the query program. Secondly, the numbers of rules defining the predicates m_sip, m_union, and $match$ are each proportional to the number of times SIP is performed in the program's rules. This in turn is determined by the number of subgoals in rule bodies and their argument sharing pattern. The numbers of rules for m_sg, s_sg_1, and s_sg_2 are just as in the usual magic sets transformation. Thus, the size of the transformed program is comparable to the size of the program obtained by traditional magic sets rewriting.

5.3   Bottom-Up Query Evaluation Based on Magic Sets

In the definition of predicates sip and $match$, we introduced two special meta-predicates C^* and C. In this section, we give formal definitions for these two meta-predicates and discuss how to integrate their implementation into the semi-naive evaluation algorithm. The meta-predicates C^* and C are defined as follows.

The literal $C^*(X, Y, X', Y')$ tests the consistency between the two mapping patterns $X \longmapsto X'$ and $Y \longmapsto Y'$ by testing if the constraints $\mathcal{C}[X/X', Y/Y']$ are consistent.

The literal $C(X, X')$ tests the consistency for the mapping pattern $X \longmapsto X'$ by testing if the constraints $\mathcal{C}[X/X']$ are consistent.

The only extra implementation detail imposed by the meta-predicates C and C^* is to test the consistency of the conditions associated with their arguments. It turns out this checking can be incorporated with a minor modification of any bottom-up evaluation algorithm such as Semi-Naive (SN) evaluation. We define $SN^\perp$-evaluation as a modification to SN evaluation as follows. An efficient way of evaluating the meta-predicate $C(X, X')$ is to use it as the condition for taking the θ-join of the relations in the body of the rule in which it occurs (e.g., see the rules in the mapping generator group in Example 5.2). As regards $C^*(X, Y, X', Y')$, it should be clear from the discussion (also see Example 5.2) that C^* is always accessed with all its arguments bound. In this case, in each iteration of the SN evaluation the conditions represented by $C^*(X, Y, X', Y')$ are tested; tuples for the rule body (and head) will be generated only when the conditions being tested are satisfied. Thus, incorporating the two meta-predicates into SN evaluation can be done relatively easily while preserving the traditional advantages of bottom-up query processing. The following result establishes the correctness of the bottom-up query evaluation method based on magic sets transformation, followed by $SN^\perp$-evaluation.

Theorem 5.1 *Let P be a datalog$^\perp$ program, and $Q \equiv p(\bar{X})$ be a query, and $MS(P)$ the transformed program obtained using the (extended) magic sets method. Let $q(\bar{d}_1, E_1), \cdots, q(\bar{d}_k, E_k)$ be the answers to the query Q obtained from $MS(P)$, using $SN^\perp$-evaluation. Let $cond(E_i) = \{\perp_j = d'_j \mid E_i$ has a subterm of the form $f(\perp_j, d'_j, t)\}$. Then*

$$\|Q\|_P^c \subseteq \{(\bar{d}_1, cond(E_1)), \cdots, (\bar{d}_k, cond(E_k))\}, \; P \models cond(E_i) \rightarrow p(\bar{d}_i), i = 1, \cdots, k,$$

that is, bottom-up query evaluation based on magic sets transformation and $SN^\perp$-evaluation will generate only valid answers and all minimal answers will be generated by this method. □

Notice that the minimality of conditions associated with answers to a query based on this algorithm may not be guaranteed because in the proposed (extended) magic sets method, we do not provide a device to check redundant condition sets. Minimality can be achieved by comparing condition sets and deleting redundant ones.

6   Comparison with Related Work

Although null values in relational databases have been studied in the framework of the so-called logical databases [GMN 84, Re 86, Va 86], it was only recently that deductive databases with null values have been considered. Demolombe and Cerro [DC 88] has extended conventional relational algebra with the idea of making it available for bottom-up evaluation of queries. However, unlike here, they have not proposed any query rewriting strategies to precede evaluation. In the absence of such strategies, bottom-up evaluation (even using semi-naive) can be prohibitively expensive. Besides, their algebra is only complete for a restricted class of (first-order) queries.

In some sense, the answers generated by Liu [Li 90] (also see section 1) are similar to conditional answers. However, there are important differences between his work and ours. Firstly, Liu's framework of S-constants corresponds to assuming that null values always assume the value of one of the known individuals, unlike our approach. Secondly, unlike us, [Li 90] does not provide any optimization strategy for bottom-up query processing computation. For deductive databases, this is particularly important. Finally, in our framework conditional answers are generated without complicating the existing notions of unification and SLD-resolution while Liu's approach uses a complex form of unification which tries to incorporate consistency checking as part of it. Also, he does not explicitly handle constraints on nulls, although they are implicit in the value ranges of S-constants. Our approach in $SLD^\perp$-refutation was inspired by constraint logic programming (see Stuckey [St 90]). Since this paradigm concerns reasoning with and about constraints, an answer to a query from a constraint logic program is essentially the answer under any model of the program generated by instantiating any variables in the constraints by constants which satisfy them. Analogously, we view null values as placeholders which can be mapped to any (normal or null) constant as long as the constraints are not violated. We remark a direct approach of transforming a datalog$^\perp$ program into a constraint logic program is inappropriate for the purpose on hand. The difficulties stem from the facts: (i) due to the modularity of rules, the bindings for local variables in rule bodies which associate with nulls can not be delivered to the heads as well as to other rules; (ii) without evaluating a (sub)goal, it is difficult for a subgoal to reason about the nulls associated with other subgoals. Indeed, a straightforward approach would produce a program which is exponentially larger than the original program [DL 92].

Two well-known query rewriting strategies are *generalized magic sets* [Ra 88] and *magic conditions* [M* 90] which appear to be capable of handling "generalized" bindings corresponding to conditions. A natural question is whether these methods can be directly used to handle (conditions involving) null values. A close examination will reveal that these methods can only deal with conditions operating at the level of relations, rather than (different) conditions applying to individual tuples. Thus, there was a need for a genuine extension to a method such as magic sets to deal with null values.

Abiteboul et al [AKG 91] has shown that for their basic model of *tables*, the question of deciding whether a tuple is an answer to a datalog query in some possible world is NP-hard. Generation of conditional answers for recursive queries can solve the above problem and the lower bound above trivially applies to it. However, we believe there are good reasons for considering this problem and developing query processing techniques for it. Firstly, incompleteness in (deductive) databases is a real problem in practice and we do need the functionality to deal with it in processing queries. Secondly, when the number of null values is bounded, we can show that conditional answers can be generated in polynomial time in the database size. Thirdly, we believe a framework such as the one developed in this paper can be the first step (i) in identifying types of queries/databases on which queries can be processed efficiently, and (ii) for devising strategies for deriving approximate answers (i.e. a subset of valid answers) to queries while achieving efficiency.

7   Summary and Future Research

We motivated the problem of generating conditional answers to queries on deductive databases containing null values. We developed a sound and complete proof procedure called SLD$^\perp$-refutation. We also developed an extension to the basic magic sets rewriting method and showed that the rewritten program evaluated bottom-up using semi-naive evaluation (with minor extensions) will generate all minimal conditional answers and will only generate valid conditional answers.

We are currently working on an implementation of the extended magic sets method and SN$^\perp$-evaluation on top of the LDL deductive DBMS [C*90]. In future research, we would like to characterize query classes and databases (based on their structure) for which conditional answers can be generated efficiently. Another attractive direction is to identify weaker forms of completeness (as was done for first-order queries – see [La 89]) w.r.t. which conditional answers for recursive queries can be generated efficiently.

Acknowledgments

The authors wish to thank V.S.Alagar for stimulating discussions. The research was supported by grants from NSERC (Canada) and FCAR (Quebec).

Footnotes

[1]Since we suppose that the constraints are fully specified, $\mathcal{E}'$ is inconsistent iff it has a constraint of the form $c \neq c, c < c, x \neq X$, or $X < X$. Fully specified constraints are used only as a theoretical device to simplify consistency checking. More efficient implementation of consistency checking for constraints is possible using graph-theoretic techniques.

[2]Notice that answers obtained using SLD$^\perp$-refutation could contain redundant ones, as we do not check minimality in the refutation process.

[3]In general, minimality of the conditions E is not guaranteed.

[4]Evidently, there are many joins which are redundantly computed several times. This can be easily avoided by using the supplementary predicates, used with magic sets rewriting. The details are discussed in Section 5.2.

References

[AKG 91] Abiteboul,S., Kanellakis,P. and Grahne,G.: "On the representation and querying of sets of possible worlds," *Theoretical Computer Science* 78 (1991), 159-187.

[BR 86] Bancillion,F. and Ramakrishnan,R.: "An amateur's introduction to recursive query processing strategies," *Proc. ACM-SIGMOD Int. Conf. on Management of Data* (1986), 16-52.

[BR 87] Beeri,C. and Ramakrishnan,R.: "On the power of magic," *Proc. of 6th ACM SIGMOD Symposium on PODS* (1987), 269-283.

[C*90] Chimenti, D. et al, "The LDL system prototype" in *IEEE Trans. on Knowledge and Data Eng.*, Vol. 2. No. 1 (1990), pp. 76-90.

[DC 88] Demolombe,R. and Cerro, L.F.D.: "An algebraic evaluation method for deduction in incomplete data bases," *The Journal of Logic Programming*, No.5 (1988), 183-205.

[DL 92] Dong,F. and Lakshmanan,V.S.: "Deductive databases with incomplete information," *Tech. Report, Dept. of Computer Science, Concordia University* (March 1992).

[GMN 84] Gallaire,H., Minker, J., And Nicolas,J.-M.: "Logic and databases:a deductive approach," *Computing Surveys*, Vol.16, No.2 (June 1984), 151-185.

[La 89] Lakshmanan, V.S.: "Query evaluation with null values: how complex is completeness?," *Proc. 9th Int. Conf. Foundation of Software Technology and Theoretical Computer Science, LNCS* vol. 405, Springer-Verlag (1989), 204-222.

[Li 90] Liu,Y.: "Null values in definite programs," *Proc. North American on Logic Programming Conference* (1990), 273-288.

[Ll 87] Lloyd,J.W.: *Foundations of Logic Programming,* Springer-Verlag, New York (1987).

[M* 90] Mumick, I.S., Finkelstein, S.J., Pirahesh, H., and Ramakrishnan, R.: "Magic conditions," *Proc. of 9th ACM SIGMOD Symposium on POPS* (1990), 161-171.

[NR 90] Naqvi,S.A. and Rossi,F.: "Reasoning in inconsistent databases," *Proc. North American on Logic Programming Conference* (1990), 255-272.

[NR 91] Naughton, J.F. and Ramakrishnan,R.: "Bottom-up evaluation of logic programs," *To appear in Journal of Logic Programming.*

[Ra 88] Ramakrishnan,R.: "Magic templates: a spellbinding approach to logic programs," *Proc. Int. Conf. and Symp. on Logic Programming* (1988), 140-159.

[Re 86] Reiter,R.: "A sound and sometimes complete query evaluation algorithm for relational databases with null values," *JACM*, Vol.33 No.2 (April 1986), 349-370.

[St 90] Stuckey, P.J.: "Constructive negation for constraint logic programming," *manuscript* (1991).

[Ul 89] Ullman,J.D.: *Principles of Database and Knowledge-Base Systems,* vol. I & II, Comp. Sci. Press, MD (1989).

[Ul 89a] Ullman,J.D.: "Bottom-up beats top-down for datalog," *In Proc. ACM Symposium on PODS* (1989).

[Va 86] Vardi, M.Y.: "Querying logical databases," *Journal of Computer and System Sciences*, No.33 (1986), 142-160.

Verification II

A Framework of Directionality for Proving Termination of Logic Programs

Francois Bronsard
T.K. Lakshman
Uday S. Reddy

Department of Computer Science
University of Illinois at Urbana-Champaign
Urbana, Illinois 61801, USA

internet: ⟨bronsard,lakshman,reddy⟩@cs.uiuc.edu

Abstract

In this paper we propose a rich notion of directionality of predicates that combines modes and regular tree types. We provide a semantic soundness result for this notion and give inference systems to decide *well-modedness* of logic programs and goals. We show how this rich notion of directionality can be used to prove the *universal* termination of LD-resolution for logic programs with non-ground goals by using simple syntactic orderings of the type used in rewriting theory.

Keywords: Directionality, Modes, Regular tree types, Mode-dependence, Well-moded programs, Universal termination, Well-founded orderings.

1 Introduction

It is widely recognized that termination[1] of logic programs depends on the *directionality* of predicates, i.e., for each predicate, the designation of some arguments to the predicate as "input" and other arguments as "output". Directionality is normally specified via notions of *modes* of predicates and *well-modedness* of programs and goals.

In general, the mode information only specifies which arguments are expected to be ground (these are the input arguments) and which arguments are expected to be non-ground (these are the output arguments) ([3, 18]). This ground/non-ground distinction which is almost always used to express directionality is however, too rigid for most programs. For example, the classical program for append terminates if the first (or the third) argument is a finite list, independently of whether the elements of this list are ground or not.

In this work, we generalize the original notion of ground/non-ground modes by combining modes and a subset of the regular tree types [11, 12] to define *mode-annotations*. Mode-annotations describe sets of (possibly non-ground) terms sharing a common structure. For example, the mode-annotation describing a set of arbitrary terms (including variables) is "?"; lists of arbitrary terms have the mode-annotation "list(?)". The essential difference between our approach and [12] is that mode-annotations describe sets of (possibly nonground) terms whereas types include only ground terms. Thus the syntax of mode-annotations includes the additional symbol, "?", which represents arbitrary terms, including non-ground terms.

---

[1] "Termination" is taken to mean *universal termination*, i.e., every branch of the SLD-tree is finite.

Hence, these mode-annotations provide a formal basis for studying termination of non-ground goals. In Section 7 we discuss the possibility of using the full regular tree types of [19, 16] to give directionality to programs using partially instantiated structures such as difference lists.

We view a predicate as a *directional* procedure which when applied to a tuple of terms satisfying an *input mode*, generates a tuple of terms satisfying a more specific[2] *output mode*. In Section 3 we propose a notion of *mode-dependency* for a predicate which defines such a relationship between the structure of inputs and outputs of the predicate. An assignment of mode-dependencies to predicates is then used to syntactically define the notion of *well-moded* clauses and goals along the lines of [18]. Well-modedness is justified by a semantic soundness result which says that when a well-moded goal is resolved with a well-moded program, then after resolution the outputs satisfy the assigned mode-dependency.

Though we assume the standard Prolog computation rule, the results extend to any other choice of a computation rule. Similarly, we assume that predicates are assigned a unique mode-dependency (or equivalently that each mode-dependency defines a different version of the predicate), although, again, our results extend to multiple mode-dependencies for predicates.

The second part of this paper deals with the use of mode information together with well-founded orderings to prove termination. Typical proofs of termination of programs involve showing that each step of the computation represents a reduction according to a well-founded ordering. Formally, this is expressed for logic programs as follows:

Remark 1 A logic program P universally terminates if and only if there exists a well-founded ordering $\succ$, such that for all goals G_1, G_2,

$$G_1 \vdash_P {}^3 G_2 \text{ implies } G_1 \succ G_2$$

This remark, first of all, justifies the need for modes. For a program which contains recursive predicates it is not normally possible to show universal termination, unless there are some restrictions on goals. For example, given the usual definition of the predicate append, from the goal $\text{append}(X, Y, Z)$ we can infer the new goal $\text{append}(X', Y, Z')$. Since this new goal is equivalent to the initial goal, up to renaming of variables, there cannot exist a well-founded ordering $\succ$ on goals such that $\text{append}(X, Y, Z) \succ \text{append}(X', Y, Z')$. Hence, such a goal cannot terminate. Consequently, unless such goals are disallowed, universal termination is impossible.

Secondly, according to this remark, showing termination requires studying all possible goals that arise during execution. To be practical, a proof technique to show termination must instead rely on the static structure of the program, for instance, relationships between heads and bodies of clauses. Hence, we must insure that the relationships between heads and bodies of clauses can be *transposed* to goals. In Section 4, we show that if the head and body of clauses are compared but the comparison is restricted to the structure described by the mode, then the ordering relation holds for *any* well-moded goal.

In order to restrict orderings to the structure described by the mode-dependency, we define a transformation, τ, which, given a term and a mode-annotation, strips the term of any structure not explicitly indicated in the mode-annotation. This

---

[2] "More specific" intuitively means that mode-annotations of the form "?" are replaced by mode-annotations such as "ground" or "list(?)".

[3] "$\vdash_P$" denotes one step of SLD resolution.

transformation is extended to atoms. We can then use syntactic orderings to compare the head and the body of clauses. In Section 5 we present some simple syntactic orderings along the lines of orderings commonly used in term rewriting theory (see [5] for a survey). Our adaptation of these orderings allows the use of *inter-argument relationships* [4] which are sometimes needed in programs with local variables.

Consider the following illustrative example:

Example 1

$$\mathsf{append}(nil, Y, Y).$$
$$\mathsf{append}(A.X, Y, A.Z) \quad \leftarrow \quad \mathsf{append}(X, Y, Z).$$

Let us assume that the mode-dependency of append is

$$\mathsf{append}(list(?), list(?), ?) \rightarrow \mathsf{append}(list(?), list(?), list(?))$$

The transformation τ applied to the the head and the body of the clause gives ($\square$ denotes arbitrary terms)

$$\tau(\mathsf{append}(A.X, Y, A.Z), \mathsf{append}(list(?), list(?), ?)) \quad = \quad \mathsf{append}(\square.X, Y, \square)$$
$$\tau(\mathsf{append}(X, Y, Z), \mathsf{append}(list(?), list(?), ?)) \quad = \quad \mathsf{append}(X, Y, \square)$$

We can conclude, using some syntactic ordering $>$ (see Section 5), that $\mathsf{append}(\square.X, Y, \square) > \mathsf{append}(X, Y, \square)$. Hence, using this clause with a well-moded goal generates a smaller goal, so the program terminates for all such goals.

The two main contributions of this paper are, first, the adaptation of regular tree types to define a powerful notion of modes which can express a rich notion of directionality, and, second, the adaptation of syntactic orderings to the context of well-moded logic programs and their use to prove universal termination[5]. Our methodology highlights the distinction between directionality, orderings, and the use of inter-argument relationships. We believe that our notion of directionality can also be used for applications other than termination such as specifying control in concurrent logic languages. Lastly, for programs which use partially instantiated structures, such as difference lists, the treatment of directionality is a difficult problem. We suggest in section 7 an extension to our approach to give directionality to such programs. A promising alternative, which we are studying, is the use of linear logic in defining *directional logic programs* [20].

1.1 Related work

The problem of improving directionality information, i.e., to go beyond the simple ground/non-ground characterization, is tackled by many recent works. In [15, 2, 21, 22], a combination of modes, orderings and inter-argument relationships is used to provide a more powerful, but more abstract, notion of directionality. Informally, the "input ⇔ ground" idea is replaced by the notion "input ⇔ terms acceptable by the ordering relation". This technique is not very different from our use of the transformation τ with the mode "?". However, we believe that there are advantages in distinguishing between the issues of directionality and orderings.

An approach very similar to our notion of modes is the notion of *integrated types* of [9] which have been used in the context of proving termination of programs

---

[4] These are also called *inter-arguments constraints*.

[5] While the use of syntactic orderings can clearly be automated, we do not address the issue of the automation of our treatment of modes.

by [23]. Although, our approach is more general than [23] because of our treatment of mode-annotations and orderings, the main differences between our modes and the *integrated types* appears when we discuss the extension of our modes with implication and quantification in section 7.

We show how termination can be shown by purely syntactic orderings. By allowing the use of inter-argument relationships, our approach can profit from the many works concerned with deriving inter-argument relationships (e.g. [14, 2, 8]). More generally, one could express the notion of propagating inter-argument relationships to prove termination (as in [14, 21, 22]) by appropriate inference systems for orderings.

The approaches of [17, 7] transform logic programs into rewrite systems and then perform termination analysis using the classical tool of rewrite theory. In contrast, our approach is more straightforward in adapting the techniques from rewrite theory directly to logic programs.

We believe that the work of [1] , although it concentrates on ground goals, could provides an abstract framework characterizing our use of syntactic orderings. The use of syntactic orderings and "don't care" types is also suggested in [6]. That approach is however, geared toward the development of programs rather than an a posteriori test of termination.

2   Mode-Annotations

2.1   Syntax of Mode-annotations

Terms and mode-annotations are defined using the following syntactic categories:

$$
\begin{array}{rcll}
\text{X} & \in & \mathcal{V} & \textit{Variables} \\
f & \in & \mathcal{F} & \textit{Function symbols} \\
t & \in & \mathcal{T} & \textit{Terms} \\
\alpha & \in & \mathcal{M} & \textit{Mode\_variables} \\
a & \in & \mathcal{A} & \textit{Mode\_annotations}
\end{array}
$$

The expressions belonging to the categories $\mathcal{T}$ and $\mathcal{A}$ are defined using the following context-free syntax:

$$
\begin{array}{rcl}
t & ::= & X \mid f(t_1,\ldots,t_k) \\
a & ::= & ground \mid ? \mid \alpha \mid f(a_1,\ldots,a_k) \mid a_1 + a_2 \mid \mathbf{fix}\alpha.a
\end{array}
$$

We impose two restrictions on the syntax of mode-annotations. First, mode-annotations must be *closed* a-terms [6], i.e., they contain no free occurrences of mode variables. Second, they must be *discriminative* [7], i.e. for mode-annotations expressed as a sum $a_1 + a_2$, the outermost symbol of a_1 and a_2 must be distinct.

As a notational convenience we allow, in addition to *ground*, mode-annotations such as *int*, whose semantics is well defined as a subset of ground terms. We also use the following shorthand notation for mode-annotations that describe commonly used structures.

$$
\begin{array}{rcl}
list(a) & = & \mathbf{fix}\alpha.(nil + a.\alpha) \\
tree(a) & = & \mathbf{fix}\alpha.(nil + node(a,\alpha,\alpha))
\end{array}
$$

---

[6] In section 7 we discuss the need to drop this condition and extend mode-annotations to full regular trees [16] in order to handle partially instantiated structures.

[7] This condition (taken from [12]) is imposed for reasons of efficiency (see Appendix B).

Terms and mode-annotations are syntactically related by the notion of *well-modedness* of terms. Well-modedness is defined via the notion of *mode contexts*. A *mode context*, is a finite set of (unique) mode-annotation assertions for variables, each of the form $X : a$ [8]. Mode contexts are needed to disambiguate the role of variables in non-ground terms. For instance, variables occurring in places such as atomic goals, should be interpreted as such, i.e. as terms with the mode annotation ?; while, in other places such as the head of a clause, variables are intended as parameters to which the context binds mode-annotations.

Definition 1 A term t is *well-moded* in a mode-annotation a relative to a mode context Γ (denoted by $\Gamma \vdash t : a$) if the judgement $\Gamma \vdash t : a$ is derivable using the inference rules given in Appendix A.

2.2   Semantics of Mode-annotations

As before, let $\mathcal{T}$ denote the set of all (possibly non-ground) terms. Note that $(2^{\mathcal{T}}, \subseteq)$ is a (reflexive) partial order where $\subseteq$ is the set-inclusion relation on sets of terms. Let $\mathcal{H}$ denote the Herbrand universe of ground terms.

Definition 2 The semantic function for mode-annotations $[\![\ ]\!] \eta : \mathcal{A} \longrightarrow 2^{\mathcal{T}}$ is defined using mode valuations $\eta \in \mathcal{M} \longrightarrow 2^{\mathcal{T}}$ as follows:

- $[\![?]\!]\eta = \mathcal{T}$.

- $[\![\alpha]\!]\eta = \eta(\alpha)$.

- $[\![ground]\!]\eta = \mathcal{H}$.

- $[\![f(a_1, \ldots, a_k)]\!]\eta = \{f(t_1, \ldots, t_k) \mid t_1 \in [\![a_1]\!]\eta \ldots t_k \in [\![a_k]\!]\eta\}$

- $[\![a_1 + a_2]\!]\eta = [\![a_1]\!]\eta \cup [\![a_2]\!]\eta$.

- $[\![\mathbf{fix}\alpha.a]\!]\eta = $ the least $S \subseteq \mathcal{T}$ such that $S = [\![a]\!](\eta[S/\alpha])$.

Since we restrict mode-annotations to closed a-terms, the mode valuation η is only a notational formalism that is convenient in defining the semantics of **fix**. In what follows we generally omit η.

We can now provide a semantic interpretation for $\Gamma \vdash t : a$. First, since the variables in the domain of Γ are intended as parameters, we need the notion of *valuations*. A *valuation* ζ is a partial mapping $\zeta : V \to \mathcal{T}$ [9]. A valuation is said to *respect* a mode context Γ if ζ and Γ have the same domain and for all $X \in Dom(\Gamma), \zeta(X) \in [\![(\Gamma(X))]\!]$. A valuation is identified with its extension to terms. Therefore, the semantics counterpart of $\Gamma \vdash t : a$ is the following: for all valuations ζ which respect Γ, $\zeta(t) \in [\![a]\!]$.

3   Mode assignment to programs

An n-ary *mode* is an n-tuple over *mode-annotations*. An n-ary mode for an n-ary predicate p is syntactically specified as : "$p(a_1, \ldots, a_n)$".

Definition 3 An n-ary *mode-dependency* is a pair of n-ary modes (written $m^i \to m^o$) where m^i (m^o) is called the input (output) mode.

---

[8] A mode context can also be viewed as a partial mapping: $V \to \mathcal{A}$.

[9] A valuation can also be viewed as a substitution.

Mode-dependencies for a predicate specify the structure of the input and output arguments to the predicate (treated as a directional procedure).

A moded clause (goal) is a clause (goal) together with an assignment of mode-dependencies to every literal occurring in the clause (goal). The notion of a well-moded clause is now defined:

Definition 4 A moded clause $A \leftarrow B_1, \ldots, B_n$, with the assigned mode-dependencies $m_a^i \rightarrow m_a^o, m_{B_1}^i \rightarrow m_{B_1}^o, \cdots, m_{B_n}^i \rightarrow m_{B_n}^o$ is *well-moded* if for all mode contexts Γ, the following hold:

1. $\forall j < n . \Gamma \vdash A : m_a^i, \ \Gamma \vdash B_1 : m_{B_1}^o \quad \ldots \quad \Gamma \vdash B_j : m_{B_j}^o \quad$ implies $\quad \Gamma \vdash B_{j+1} : m_{B_{j+1}}^i$

2. $\Gamma \vdash A : m_a^i, \ \Gamma \vdash B_1 : m_{B_1}^o \quad \ldots \quad \Gamma \vdash B_n : m_{B_n}^o \quad$ implies $\quad \Gamma \vdash A : m_a^o$

A logic program P is *well-moded* if all clauses in P are well-moded.

Definition 5 A moded goal $C_1, \ldots, C_n$ is *well-moded* if the following hold:

1. $\vdash C_1 : m_{C_1}^i$

2. For all mode contexts Γ, and for all $j \in [1 \ldots n - 1]$

$\Gamma \vdash C_1 : m_{C_1}^o \quad \ldots \quad \Gamma \vdash C_j : m_{C_j}^o \quad$ implies $\quad \Gamma \vdash C_{j+1} : m_{C_{j+1}}^i$

The well-modedness of a moded clause or a moded goal can be checked as follows: For each implication condition in the definition of well-modedness, first, the elimination rules given in Appendix A are used to construct a mode context Γ in which the atom(s) in the antecedent of the implication are in their assigned modes. Next, this mode context Γ is used to check (using the introduction rules) whether the atom in the consequent is in its assigned mode.

For example, with the mode-dependency for append assumed in section 1, the goals append($[X, 1, 2], [Y], Z$) and append($[X, 1, 2], [Y], Z$), append($Z, [Y, 1], U$) are well-moded.

Throughout the rest of this paper "programs" and "goals" denote well-moded programs and well-moded goals.

We have the following theorems to express the "correctness" of the notion of mode-dependency.

Theorem 2 Mode-consistency of LD resolution One step of LD resolution transforms a well-moded goal into another well-moded goal.

Theorem 3 Correctness of Mode dependency Consider a well-moded atomic goal $p(t_1, \ldots, t_n)$ with an assigned mode-dependency $p : m_p^i \rightarrow m_p^o$. If the LD resolution of this goal with respect to a well-moded logic program succeeds with a computed answer substitution θ then $\vdash p(t_1, \ldots, t_n)\theta : m^o$

4 Characterizing orderings to prove termination

4.1 Simplifying terms with mode-annotations

In order to prove termination it is not enough to show that the head of a clause is "greater than" the body since goals that unify with the head of a clause might be more general than the head itself. Consequently, we need to compare *generalized* versions of the head and the body. These generalizations depend on the mode-dependency of the predicates in the clause, and are obtained by the transformation τ defined below.

Definition 6 Given a term t over a set of function symbols $\mathcal{F}$ a set of variables $\mathcal{V}$, and a mode-annotation a, the transformation $\tau : \mathcal{T} \times \mathcal{A} \to \mathcal{T}(\mathcal{F} \cup (\mathcal{V} \times \mathcal{A}) \cup \{\Box, \bot\})$ which generalizes t to the most general term in the mode-annotation a, is defined recursively as follows:

$$\tau(X, a) = \begin{cases} \Box & \text{if } a = ? \\ X^a & \text{otherwise} \end{cases}$$

$$\tau(f(t_1, \ldots, t_n), ?) = \Box$$

$$\tau(f(t_1, \ldots, t_n), ground) = f(\tau(t_1, ground), \ldots, \tau(t_n, ground))$$

$$\tau(f(t_1, \ldots, t_n), g(a_1, \ldots, a_n)) = \begin{cases} f(\tau(t_1, a_1), \ldots, \tau(t_n, a_n)) & \text{if } g = f \\ \bot & \text{otherwise} \end{cases}$$

$$\tau(f(t_1, \ldots, t_n), \mathbf{fix}\alpha.a) = \tau(f(t_1, \ldots, t_n), a[\mathbf{fix}\alpha.a/\alpha])$$

$$\tau(f(t_1, \ldots, t_n), a_1 + a_2) = sup(\tau(f(t_1, \ldots, t_n), a_1), \tau(f(t_1, \ldots, t_n), a_2))$$

where the binary operator sup on terms over $\mathcal{F} \cup (\mathcal{V} \times \mathcal{A}) \cup \{\Box\}$ is defined as follows:

$$sup(t_1, t_2) = \Box \text{ if } t_1 = \Box \text{ or } t_2 = \Box$$
$$sup(t, \bot) = t$$
$$sup(\bot, t) = t$$
$$sup(f(t_1, \ldots, t_n), f(u_1, \ldots, u_n)) = f(sup(t_1, u_1), \ldots, sup(t_n, u_n))$$

The value $\Box$ denotes arbitrary terms (i.e., a lack of any structure information) while the value $\bot$ denotes an erroneous application of τ, i.e., an application $\tau(t, a)$ where t and a have different outermost function symbols. Furthermore, we require τ to be strict in $\bot$.

For a term t and a mode-annotation a, the transformation τ produces the "generalization" of t compatible with the mode-annotation a. This means that subterms of t with corresponding mode-annotations ? are replaced by the symbol $\Box$, and that variables are tagged with the corresponding mode-annotation. For example, $\tau(1.X, list(?)) = \Box.X^{list(?)}$, and $\tau(f(X, X), f(g(?), g(ground))) = f(X^{g(?)}, X^{g(ground)})$.

In the following, we identify τ with its (obvious) extension to pairs of atom and mode. We also usually omit the tag on the variables after the application of the transformation τ, unless, as in the last example above, such an omission would be ambiguous.

4.2 Simple Termination Theorem

Theorem 4 A logic program P universally terminates if there exists a well-founded stable [10] ordering $\succ$, such that for each clause $A \leftarrow B_1, \ldots, B_n$ (with mode-dependencies: $A : a^i \to a^o, B_1 : b_1^i \to b_1^o, \ldots, B_n : b_n^i \to b_n^o$,)

$$\forall j.\tau(A, a^i) \succ \tau(B_j, b_j^i)$$

This theorem can be used to prove the termination of simple programs such as append or split. However, for many programs, such as quicksort, we need to use inter-argument relationships to complete the termination proof.

4.3 Inter-argument Relationships

Given a predicate p with a mode dependence $p(a_1^i, \ldots, a_n^i) \to p(a_1^o, \ldots, a_n^o)$, an inter-argument relationship on p is expressed by the syntax:

$$p(X_1, \ldots, X_n) : R(\tau(X_1, a_1^o), \ldots, \tau(X_n, a_n^o))$$

---

[10] An ordering $\succ$ is stable if $t_1 \succ t_2$ implies for all σ, $\sigma(t_1) \succ \sigma(t_2)$.

and has the interpretation:

$$\vdash p(u_1, \ldots, u_n) : p(a_1^o, \ldots, a_n^o) \text{ and } p(u_1, \ldots, u_n) \text{ succeeds, implies}$$
$$R(\tau(u_1, a_1^o), \ldots, \tau(u_n, a_n^o))$$

In defining an inter-argument relationship, the transformation τ is needed because we must allow inter-argument relationships to hold on non-ground terms.

For example, the semantic property that in the output tuple of append the length of the first argument is less than or equal to the length of the third can be expressed by:

$$\text{append}(X, Y, Z) : X \leq Z$$

Inter-argument relationships can also be defined for (conjunction of) literals with the syntax

$$L_1, \ldots, L_n : R(\tau(t_1, a_1^o), \ldots, \tau(t_k, a_k^o))$$

where $t_1, \ldots, t_k$ are terms appearing in the literals and $a_1, \ldots, a_k$ are the corresponding mode-annotations. As an example consider the following relationship:

$$\text{append}(X, [A|L], Y), \text{append}(X, L, Z) : Y > Z$$

In general a set of inter-argument relationships can be expressed as a single relationship on a conjunction of the literals. Consequently, in the following, we assume that all inter-argument relationships have been appropriately defined on conjunctions of literals.

We define an ordering relation $\succ$ via an inference system $\vdash_\succ$. Such an inference system can use an inter-argument relationship $(L_1, \ldots, L_n : R)$ as a hypothesis for inferences. Thus, derivations have the form:

$$R \vdash_\succ t_1 \succ t_2.$$

For example, we define in the next section an inference system which establishes an ordering relation $\succ$, by combining subterm ordering, inter-argument monotonicity relationships, and lexicographic ordering.

Definition 7 We say that an inference system $\vdash_\succ$ is *stable* if

$$R \vdash_\succ t_1 \succ t_2 \text{ implies } \forall \sigma. R\sigma \vdash_\succ t_1\sigma \succ t_2\sigma$$

4.4 Termination Theorem

Definition 8 Given a stable inference system defining an ordering relation, a clause $A \leftarrow B_1, \ldots, B_n$ is τ-decreasing if

$$\forall i, R_{i-1} \vdash_\succ \tau(A, a) \succ \tau(B_i, b_i) \tag{1}$$

where R_i is defined by the following inter-argument relationship $B_1, \ldots, B_i : R_i$.

Theorem 5 A logic program $\mathcal{P}$ terminates if there exists a stable inference system $\vdash_\succ$, defining a well-founded ordering relation $\succ$, such that each clause in $\mathcal{P}$ is τ-decreasing.

The following alternative definition of τ-decreasiveness (adapted from [7]) is consistent with the termination theorem above and has proven to be quite useful in practice.

Definition 9 Given a stable inference system defining a well-founded ordering relation, a clause $A \leftarrow B_1, \ldots, B_n$ is said to be τ-*decreasing* also if

1. $\tau(A, a^i) \succ \tau(B_1, b_1^i)$
2. $\forall j, R_{j-1} \vdash_{\succ} \tau(B_{j-1}, b_{j-1}^o) \succeq \tau(B_j, b_j^i)$
3. $R_n \vdash_{\succ} \tau(B_n, b_n^o) \succeq \tau(A, a^o)$ or $R_n \vdash_{\succ} \tau(A, a^i) \succ \tau(A, a^o)$

where R_j is the inter-argument relationship of $B_1, \ldots, B_j$.

The interest of this alternative definition of τ-decreasiveness is that in some cases using this definition and a carefully chosen ordering, we can avoid the need for inter-argument relationships. The example 3 illustrates this possibility.

5   Orderings for Logic Programs

It follows from Theorem 5 that in order to show termination we need inference systems that define well-founded stable orderings and allow the use of inter-argument relationships. We now present one such system inspired by [13, 2, 4] which is based on the lexicographic ordering ([5]).

Given a precedence ordering $\succ_p$ on predicate symbols and a term ordering $\succ_t$ (discussed below), we can define the following lexicographic ordering $>$ among literals:

$$\frac{P \approx_p Q \quad \{t_i\}_i (\succ_t)_{lex} \{s_i\}_i}{P(t_1, \ldots, t_n) > Q(s_1, \ldots, s_m)} \qquad \frac{P \succ_p Q}{P(t_1, \ldots, t_n) > Q(s_1, \ldots, s_m)}$$

In general, the term ordering, $\succ_t$, must be well-founded and defined by an inference system which is stable. Moreover, it is essential that the ordering induced by the inter-argument relationships be *consistent* with the term ordering. While different term orderings are possible, in practice, however, the subterm ordering is sufficient for most programs. The set of inference rules for the subterm ordering is

- Subterm relation

$$\frac{t_i \succeq_t s}{f(\ldots, t_i, \ldots) \succ_t s} \qquad \frac{t \succeq_t g(s_1, \ldots, s_m)}{t \succ_t s_i}$$

- Structural rules : transitivity, reflexivity of $\succeq_t$, irreflexivity of $\succ_t$, ...

The correctness of these rules is straightforward as is the stability of the ordering. With the appropriate structural rules, this set is complete as well. Other terms orderings, such as the lexicographic path ordering, could easily be adapted to form sets of inference rules such as the above ([4]). It is even possible to define inference rules which use mode information for simplifications, but such inference rules do not seem to help significantly in practice.

Example 2 (Quicksort)

$$
\begin{aligned}
&\mathsf{split}(\mathsf{nil}, A, \mathsf{nil}, \mathsf{nil}). \\
&\mathsf{split}(B.X, A, B.L, H) &\leftarrow\ &B \leq A, \mathsf{split}(X, A, L, H). \\
&\mathsf{split}(B.X, A, L, B.H) &\leftarrow\ &B > A, \mathsf{split}(X, A, L, H). \\
&\mathsf{quicksort}(nil, nil). \\
&\mathsf{quicksort}(A.X, Y) &\leftarrow\ &\mathsf{split}(X, A, L, H), \mathsf{quicksort}(L, L1), \\
&&&\mathsf{quicksort}(H, H1), \mathsf{append}(L1, A.H1, Y).
\end{aligned}
$$

% Mode-dependence :

$$\begin{aligned}
\text{split}(\text{list}(\text{int}), \text{int}, ?, ?) &\rightarrow \text{split}(\textit{list}(\textit{int}), \textit{int}, \textit{list}(\textit{int}), \textit{list}(\textit{int})) \\
\text{quicksort}(\textit{list}(\textit{int}), ?) &\rightarrow \text{quicksort}(\textit{list}(\textit{int}), \textit{list}(\textit{int}))
\end{aligned}$$

To show that this program terminates, we use the lexicographic ordering $>$ described earlier, with the following precedence ordering on predicate symbols:

$$\text{quicksort} \succ_p \text{split} \succ_p \text{append} \succ_p \text{``}\leq\text{''} \succ_p \text{``}>\text{''}$$

The term ordering $\succ_t$ is simply the subterm relation.

We can show the termination of split as follows:
$\{\text{split}(B.X, A, B.L, H)\} > B \leq A, > (B > A), \text{ and } > \text{split}(X, A, L, H)\}$, since

1. $\text{split} \succ_p \text{``}\leq\text{''}$, and $\text{split} \succ_p \text{``}>\text{''}$

2. $\text{split} \approx_p \text{split}$ and $(\square.X, A, \square, \square)(\succ_t)_{lex}(X, A, \square, \square)$.

To show the termination of quicksort, we need the inter-argument relationships $\text{split}(X, A, L, H) : X \geq L$ and $\text{split}(X, A, L, H) : X \geq H$, and then we must prove:

$$\begin{aligned}
& & \text{quicksort}(A.X, \square) &> & \text{split}(X, A, \square, \square) \\
X \geq L, X \geq H &\Rightarrow & \text{quicksort}(A.X, \square) &> & \text{quicksort}(L, \square) \\
X \geq L, X \geq H &\Rightarrow & \text{quicksort}(A.X, \square) &> & \text{quicksort}(H, \square) \\
X \geq L, X \geq H &\Rightarrow & \text{quicksort}(A.X, \square) &> & \text{append}(L1, H1, \square)
\end{aligned}$$

The first and fourth case are trivially true. The second and third case can be seen to follow from the inter-argument relationships. For example, in the second case, the following deduction is possible:

$$\cfrac{\text{quicksort} \approx \text{quicksort} \quad \cfrac{\cfrac{X \geq L}{A.X \succ_t L}}{\{A.X, \square\}(\succ_t)_{lex}\{L, \square\}}}{\text{quicksort}(A.X, \square) > \text{quicksort}(L, \square)}$$

$\square$

5.1 Recursive term orderings for literals

When a term ordering is defined recursively using a precedence ordering on function symbols one can, in addition to the precedence, attach a *status* to each function symbol indicating whether its arguments should be compared lexicographically or as a multiset. For predicate symbols one can even further specify that only certain arguments of the predicate should be involved in further comparisons. Such a specification, coupled with the possibility of assigning a status and a precedence to a predicate symbol based on its mode, provides a powerful class of orderings.

Consider terms $t = f(t_1, \ldots, t_n)$ and $s = g(s_1, \ldots, s_m)$ where the status of f and g are written s_f and s_g respectively. If t and s are compared by a recursively defined ordering $>$, three cases can occur

- the arguments of t are compared with s in accordance with the status of f. This is written $\{t_1, \ldots, t_n\}(>)_{\langle s_f, \emptyset \rangle}s$. For example, if s_f indicates that only the second and third arguments should be involved in further comparison, this is equivalent to $t_2 > s \wedge t_3 > s$.

- the arguments of s are compared with t. This is written $t(>)_{\langle\emptyset,s_g\rangle}\{s_1,\ldots,s_m\}$.

- the arguments of s are compared with the arguments of t. This is written $\{t_1,\ldots,t_n\}\,(>)_{\langle s_f,s_g\rangle}\,\{s_1,\ldots,s_m\}$. For example, if both s_f and s_g specify that a lexicographic order should be used and s_f specifies that only the second and third arguments should be used, then this is equivalent to $\{t_2,t_3\}\,(>)_{lex}$ $\{s_1,\ldots,s_n\}$. Note that s_f and s_g must be mutually consistent.

Definition 10 (Recursive Ordering) Assume a precedence ordering $>_p$ on function symbols and predicate symbols such that the precedence of a predicate symbol depends on its mode and assume that each function and predicate symbols has associated with it a valid status.

Besides the usual structural rules (transitivity, ...), the inference rules specific to the recursive ordering are as follows: let $A = p(t_1,\ldots,t_n)$ and $B = q(s_1,\ldots,s_n)$

$$\frac{p >_p q \quad A(>)_{\langle\emptyset,s_q\rangle}\{s_1,\ldots,s_n\}}{A > B} \qquad \frac{p \approx_p q \quad \{t_1,\ldots,t_n\}(>)_{\langle s_p,s_q\rangle}\{s_1,\ldots,s_n\}}{A > B}$$

$$\frac{p <_p q \quad \{t_1,\ldots,t_n\}(>)_{\langle s_p,\emptyset\rangle}B}{A > B}$$

Example 3 ([7]) Consider the following program computing the transitive closure of a predicate p:

$$p(a,b).$$
$$p(b,c).$$
$$tc(X,X).$$
$$tc(X,Y) \quad \leftarrow \quad p(X,Z), tc(Z,Y).$$

% Mode-dependencies :

$$p(ground,?) \quad \rightarrow \quad p(ground,ground)$$
$$tc(ground,?) \quad \rightarrow \quad tc(ground,ground)$$

This program can easily be shown to terminate (without inter-argument relationships) by using the recursive ordering defined above with the precedence ordering: $a \succ_p b \succ_p c \succ_p p : p(ground,ground) \succ_p tc : tc(ground,?) \succ_p tc : tc(ground,ground) \succ_p p : p(ground,?)$, and status information specifying that $p : p(ground,?)$ and $tc : tc(ground,?)$ consider only their first argument for further comparisons and $p : p(ground,ground)$ and $tc : tc(ground,ground)$ consider only their second argument for further comparisons.

6 Inductive Reasoning and Symbolic Evaluation

6.1 Deriving inter-argument monotonicity relationships

Inter-argument monotonicity relationships can be derived as partial correctness properties by assuming that they hold for the recursive call to predicates (or of the goal) and using inference systems for orderings, as discussed earlier, to test that they hold for the original predicates. This technique is a special case of Hoare induction or induction on the immediate consequence operator T_p. Moreover, if the relevant literals are terminating then the inter-arguments relationships become total correctness properties.

Example 4 Given the usual definition of append (and allowing the two classical modes for append), suppose we want to prove the inter-argument relationship:

$$\text{append}(L_1, A.L_2, Y), \text{append}(L_1, L_2, Z) : Y > Z$$

We have to consider two cases: $L_1 = []$ and $L_1 = [B|L']$. In the first case, after simplification, we are left to prove $A.L_2 > L_2$ which follows by the subterm property of $>$. In the second case, the result follows by the assumption that the inter-argument relationship holds for the recursive call of the goal.

Moreover, having proved that append terminates, we can conclude that this inter-argument relationship is a total correctness property. Using this, we could, for example, easily prove the termination of the permutation program of [14].

6.2 Mutually recursive predicates

For mutually recursive predicate definitions a formal inductive argument is sometimes necessary to prove termination. The technique adopted is similar to the one advocated above for deriving inter-argument relationships. It uses symbolic evaluation with the termination of the predicates as the inductive hypotheses and syntactic orderings to justify the use of the inductive hypotheses. Moreover, once the termination of some literals is established (e.g. by the inductive hypothesis), we can use the relevant inter-argument relationships to propagate ordering information henceforth, allowing more uses of the inductive hypotheses. With this technique we can, for example, prove the termination of the mutually recursive arithmetic expression parser of [14, 22]. However, this technique is not automatic since we do not have a method to control the symbolic evaluation. Nevertheless, if we add a fixed bound to the number of unfoldings realized by the symbolic evaluation, then this technique could be automated.

7 Extensions

The techniques for showing termination presented here can be adapted to more powerful notions of mode-annotations. We can indeed extend mode-annotations [11] to regular trees as described in [16]. Given this extension we could prove the termination of programs using partially instantiated structures such as difference lists or in cases such as the following (tail recursive) clause:

$$\text{flatten}(A.X, Y) \quad \leftarrow \quad \text{list}(A), \text{append}(A, Z, Y), \text{flatten}(X, Z).$$

Mode-dependency for predicates can also be used to specify control in concurrent logic programs. For instance, a consumer process may have to suspend until an argument gets sufficiently instantiated by a producer process so as to unify with the head of a clause. Mode-annotations can be used to specify the exact structure of the arguments that would allow the consumer process to resume. Furthermore, in parallel evaluation of logic programs, the granularity of subtasks (i.e., if a subtask warrants a sub-computation large enough to outweigh the cost of forking) can be specified via the richer notion of modes.

---

[11] We note in passing that the alternative prescriptive approach to types as defined in [10] is not able to handle partially instantiated arguments.

8 Conclusions

This paper presents a rich framework of directionality for logic programs and its use in a proof method for proving universal termination of logic programs. Notions of mode-annotations (defined via a combination of modes and types) and mode-dependencies are used to give a directionality to logic programs. Well-founded orderings on the atoms in a clause are then used to show the finiteness of LD-derivations. Due to the generality of mode-annotations, the termination methodology can handle programs and goals with non-ground inputs and non-ground outputs. We believe that the richness of mode-annotations can also be used in applications other than termination proofs, such as specifying control for concurrent logic languages.

References

[1] K. R. Apt and D. Pedreschi. Studies in pure Prolog: termination. Technical Report CS-R9048, Centrum voor Wiskunde en Informatica, September 1990.

[2] A. Brodsky and Y. Sagiv. Inference of inequality constraints in logic programs. In *ACM Symp. on Principles of Database Systems*, volume 10. ACM Press, 1991.

[3] M. Bruynooghe. Adding redundancy to obtain more reliable and more readable Prolog programs. In *First Intl. Logic Programming Conf.*, pages 129–133, 1982.

[4] H. Comon. Solving inequations in term algebras. In *LICS*, pages 62–69. IEEE, June 1990.

[5] N. Dershowitz. Termination of rewriting. *Journal of Symbolic Computation*, 3:69 – 116, 1987.

[6] Y. Deville. *Logic Programming: Systematic Program Development*. International Series in Logic Programming. Addison Wesley, 1990.

[7] H. Ganzinger and U. Waldmann. Termination proofs of well-moded logic programs via conditional rewrite systems. In M. Rusinowitch and J.L. Remy, editors, *CTRS*, pages 216–222, July 1992.

[8] A. Van Gelder. Deriving constraints among argument sizes in logic programs. In *ACM Symp. on Principles of Database Systems*, volume 9, pages 47 – 60. SIGACT-SIGMOD-SIGART, ACM Press, 1990.

[9] G. Janssens and M. Bruynooghe. Deriving descriptions of possible values of program variables by means of abstract interpretation. *J. Logic Programming*, 13(2):205–258, July 1992.

[10] T. K. Lakshman and Uday S. Reddy. Typed Prolog: A semantic reconstruction of the Mycroft-O'Keefe type system. In Vijay Saraswat and Kazunori Ueda, editors, *Logic Programming: Proceedings of the 1991 International Symposium*, pages 202 – 217, Cambridge, Mass., 1991. MIT Press.

[11] P. Mishra. Towards a theory of types in Prolog. In *IEEE International symposium on logic programming*, pages 289 – 298, 1984.

[12] P. Mishra and U. S. Reddy. Declaration-free type checking. In *ACM Symp. on Principles of Programming Languages*, pages 7 – 21, 1985.

[13] Gerald Peterson. Solving term inequalities. In *Proceedings of the Eighth National Conference on Artificial Intelligence*, pages 258–263, Boston, MA, July 1990.

[14] L. Plumer. Termination proofs for logic programs based on predicate inequalities. In D.H.D. Warren and P. Szeredi, editors, *Proc. Intl. Conf. on Logic Programming*, volume 7, pages 634 – 648. MIT Press, 1990.

[15] L. Plumer. Automatic termination proofs for prolog programs operating on non-ground terms. In *Proc. Intl. Logic Programming Symp.* MIT Press, 1991.

[16] C. Pyo and U. S. Reddy. Inference of polymorphic types for logic programs. In E. L. Lusk and R.A. Overbeek, editor, *Logic Programming: Proceedings of the North American Conf.*, pages 1115 – 1134. MIT Press, 1989.

[17] M.R.K. Krishna Rao, Deepak Kapur, and R.K. Shyamasundar. A transformational methodology for proving termination of logic programs. In *5th Conference on Computer Science Logic*. LNCS, 1991. (to appear).

[18] U. S. Reddy. Transformation of logic programs into functional programs. In *Proc. Intl. Symp. on Logic Programming*, pages 187 – 196, New Jersey, USA, 1984. IEEE.

[19] U. S. Reddy. Notions of polymorphism for predicate logic programs. In *Proc. Intl. Conf. on Logic Programming*, volume 5, 1988.

[20] U. S. Reddy. A typed foundation for directional logic programming. In *Proc. Workshop on Extensions to Logic Programming, University of Bologna, Italy*, pages 199 – 222, 1992.

[21] Y. Sagiv. A termination test for logic programs. In *Proc. Intl. Logic Programming Symp.* MIT Press, 1991.

[22] K. Sohn and A. Van Gelder. Termination detection in logic programs using argument sizes. In *ACM Symp. on Principles of Database Systems*, pages 216 – 226, 1991.

[23] K. Verschaetse and D. De Schreye. Deriving termination proofs for logic programs, using abstract procedures. In *Proceedings ICLP'91*, pages 301–315, Paris, June 1991. MIT Press.

Appendix A: Mode Inference Rules

Mode judgements of the form $\Gamma \vdash t : a$ are derived using the the following mode inference rules:

Introduction Rules

In an mode context Γ, mode judgements $\Gamma \vdash t : a$ are inferred using the the following introduction rules:

$$\Gamma \vdash X : a \qquad \text{if } (X : a) \in \Gamma$$

$$\Gamma \vdash X : ? \qquad \text{if } (X \notin dom(\Gamma))$$

$$\Gamma \vdash c : ground \qquad \text{if c is a constant}$$

$$\frac{\Gamma \vdash t_1 : a_1 \quad \ldots \quad \Gamma \vdash t_k : a_k}{\Gamma \vdash F(t_1, \ldots, t_k) : F(a_1, \ldots, a_k)} \qquad \text{where F is a function or predicate symbol}$$

$$\frac{\Gamma \vdash t : a_1}{\Gamma \vdash t : a_1 + a_2}$$

$$\frac{\Gamma \vdash t : a[\mathbf{fix}\alpha.a/\alpha]}{\Gamma \vdash t : \mathbf{fix}\alpha.a}$$

Derived Rules

The following rule expresses inclusion relationship between well-moded terms.

$$\frac{\Gamma \vdash t : a}{\Gamma \vdash t : b} \qquad \text{if } b \succeq a$$

Elimination Rules

The mode-context Γ generated by a sequence of well-moded literals (each in its output mode) is determined using the introduction rules backward and the following elimination rule:

$$\frac{\Gamma \vdash t: a_1 + a_2 \quad \Gamma \cup \{t: a_1\} \vdash A \quad \Gamma \cup \{t: a_2\} \vdash A}{\Gamma \vdash A}$$

Notice that because of the implicit non-determinism involved in the backward use of the inclusion rule, in practice we might fail to effectively generate a mode-context Γ.

The soundness and completeness of these rules can be shown in a straightforward manner.

Appendix B: Inclusion Checking Rules

The following inference rules (which have been adapted from [12]) are used to infer inclusion (covering) of mode-annotations: $a_1 \preceq a_2$.

$$a \preceq a \qquad \qquad reflexivity$$

$$\frac{a_1 \preceq a_2, \quad a_2 \preceq a_3}{a_1 \preceq a_3} \qquad transitivity$$

$$a \preceq ?$$

$$\frac{a_1 \preceq ground, \ldots, a_n \preceq ground}{f(a_1, \ldots, a_n) \preceq ground}$$

$$\frac{a_1 \preceq b_1, \ldots, a_n \preceq b_n}{f(a_1, \ldots, a_n) \preceq f(b_1, \ldots, b_n)}$$

$$\frac{a_1 \preceq a, \quad a_2 \preceq a}{a_1 + a_2 \preceq a}$$

$$\frac{a \preceq a_1}{a \preceq a_1 + a_2}$$

$$\frac{a[\mathbf{fix}\alpha.a/\alpha] \preceq a_2}{\mathbf{fix}\alpha.a \preceq a_2}$$

$$\frac{a_1 \preceq a[\mathbf{fix}\alpha.a/\alpha]}{a_1 \preceq \mathbf{fix}\alpha.a}$$

The above rules can be transformed into an algorithm for checking inclusion $a_1 \preceq a_2$. Further note that the inference system is deterministic but for the rule for $+$ in a_2 and the unfolding of the **fix**. The rule for $+$ can be made deterministic by requiring that a_2 be discriminative.

The soundness of these rules can be shown by induction, and the completeness follows from the results of [12].

Handling of Mutual Recursion in Automatic Termination Proofs for Logic Programs

Gerhard Gröger
Lutz Plümer
Rheinische Friedrich-Wilhelms-Universität Bonn
Institut für Informatik III, D-5300 Bonn 1, Römerstr. 164
lutz@uran.informatik.uni-bonn.de

Abstract

An automatic termination proof procedure for logic programs with mutual recursion is presented. Argument sizes are measured by semi-linear norms. To get an upper bound for local variables in recursive literals, linear predicate inequalities are applied. They are automatically derived by associating linear constraints with program clauses. In the case of direct recursion solving these constraints is straightforward. In the general case of mutual recursion we get a system of linear constraints with several variables for which a minimal integral solution is required. Thus we end up with a problem of integer linear programming which is known to be NP-complete in general. Based on theorems of Cottle, Veinott and Chandrasekaran we show that the special structure of the constraints derived by our algorithm allows to apply an algorithm of Karmarkar which is polynomial. Based on linear predicate inequalities termination proofs are derived by showing that all elementary cycles of the strongly connected components of the program's predicate dependency graph have negative weight.

1. Introduction

The termination problem for logic programs has attracted the attention of several researchers in the last few years, see [ULG88], [BEZ89], [PLU89], [APP90], [VES91] and [GEL91] as examples. Our research aims at developing a practical tool for the automatic and efficient generation of termination proofs for (sequential or concurrent) logic programs. Unsolvability of the halting problem dictates that each necessary and sufficient characterization of terminating logic programs is undecidable. Thus an effective and even efficient algorithm can only check conditions which are sufficient but not necessary. In order to be useful these conditions should be general enough to cover a large number of procedures of practical importance.

Termination of logic programs depends on several factors. Among others the computation rule which selects atoms from goals is important. There are procedures - like *append*, *merge* etc. - which terminate for all ground queries for any computation rule. There are other programs, however, like *quicksort*, *perm* etc., which may loop forever for arbitrary computation rules, but do terminate in the special case of Prolog if the top-level query is ground on its input positions. The occurrence of local variables in recursive body literals is the main reason for this phenomenon. Look for instance at the *perm* procedure given below and assume that the top-level query is ← *perm(Ls,X)* for some ground list *Ls* and an unbound variable *X*.

p_1:   perm([],[]).

p_2:   perm(L,[H|T])   ←   append(V,[H|U],L),

                                     append(V,U,W),

                                     perm(W,T).

a_1:   append([], L, L).

a_2:   append([H|L_1],L_2,[H|L_3]) ←   append(L_1,L_2,L_3).

A recursive literal in this program is *perm(W,T)*, and a local variable is *W*. If goals are evaluated from right to left the *perm* procedure will loop forever for *perm(Ls,X)*. In the case of Prolog the subgoals ← *append(V,[H/U],L)* and ← *append(V,U,W)* are completely evaluated before calling the recursive literal *perm(W,T)*. Thus *W* will be bound to a ground list which is strictly smaller than the list *Ls* originally given. Generally speaking termination of recursion is guaranteed by the fact that the original problem is reduced to a strictly smaller one. In a formal derivation one would compare the lengths of the lists to which *L* and *W* are bound and use the definition of append in order to show that the first one is strictly greater than the latter. Since the term to which *W* will be bound when *perm(W,T)* is called is a computed answer of the goal ←*append(V,[H/U],L)*, *append(V,U,W)*, the fixpoint semantics of logic programs can be applied giving a straightforward inductive proof. This way of reasoning substantially depends on the fact that subgoals, once selected, are completely evaluated.

For a termination proof of *perm* it is not necessary to understand that *append* concatenates resp. splits the list(s) originally given. It is sufficient to know that if *append(L_1,L_2,L_3)* is in the minimal Herbrand model of the given program, the length of L_1 + L_2 equals the length of L_3. Predicate equalities resp. inequalities have been identified by several authors as a key concept for automatic termination proofs based on an approximate semantic characterization of logic programs (see [ULG88], [PLU89] and [VES91]). Predicate (in)equalities can be derived automatically. The complexity of their derivation depends on several factors. Deriving equalities is easier, but inequalities are more general. The format of the required inequalities influences the complexity of their derivation. What is of interest here is the recursive structure of the given program. It is easier to analyze programs which have only direct recursion than those with mutual recursion. Analysis of the former can be done such that whenever a predicate *p* is processed, all predicates on which the definition of *p* depends have been processed before. Bottom up traversal of the program's predicate dependency graph specifies such a sequence of processing. If there is mutual recursion - i.e. the predicate dependency graph has cycles which involve more than one predicate - several predicates have to be considered at the same time.

A logic program specifying a parser for simple arithmetic expressions gives a natural example for a termination proof which involves indirect recursion. Consider the following non-left-recursive grammar for arithmetic expressions with '+', '*' and brackets such that '*' binds stronger than '+':

$$
\begin{array}{rcl}
E & \to & T \quad | \quad T + E \\
T & \to & N \quad | \quad N * T \\
N & \to & Z \quad | \quad (E) \\
Z & \to & a \quad | \quad b \quad | \quad c
\end{array}
$$

Straightforward translation into Prolog yields the following program *parse*:

e_1:	e(L,T)	←	t(L,T).
e_2:	e(L,T)	←	t(L,['+'|C]), e(C,T).
t_1:	t(L,T)	←	n(L,T).
t_2:	t(L,T)	←	n(L,['*'|C]), t(C,T).
n_1:	n([L|T],T)	←	z(L).
n_2:	n(['('|A],B)	←	e(A,[')'|B]).
z_1:	z(a).		
z_2:	z(b).		
z_3:	z(c).		

If the query ← e(L,[]) succeeds then L, given as a list of tokens, is a well-formed arithmetic expression according to the given grammar. If ← e(L,R) succeeds with answer θ, then the difference between Lθ and Rθ (i.e. the prefix of Lθ) is a well-formed arithmetic expression.

A termination proof for this program has to consider for instance e_2, where the recursive literal *e(C,T)* contains the local variable *C*. In order to compare *C* with *L* occurring in the head literal, it is necessary to consider *t(L,['+'/C])*. A predicate inequality for *t* is required. The definitions of *e, t* and *n* are mutually recursive.

This example was already discussed in [PLU89] where it has been shown that mutual recursion can be eliminated by program transformation: *e, t* and *n* are replaced by a new predicate *parse* with a new argument representing the predicate symbols of the original program. This technique can always be applied. Flattening of program's structure, which makes verification more difficult, is an obvious disadvantage of that approach.

In this paper we show that the approach outlined in [PLU89] and [PLU90] can be extended such that mutual recursion can be handled in a natural and efficient way. In the simple case of direct recursion the algorithm deriving linear constraints gives for each predicate a set of linear constraints with one variable which can be solved immediately. In the general case of indirect recursion it gives a system of linear constraints with several variables for the different predicates which belong to the same strongly connected component of the predicate dependency graph.

The next task is to derive an optimal integral solution of these constraints. This is a problem of *integer linear programming* which is known to be *NP-complete* [PAS82]. Fortunately, the special structure of our problem allows the application of a polynomial algorithm.

The rest of this paper is organized as follows: The next section introduces the notions of *semi-linear norms, well-annotated programs* and *predicate inequalities*. The third section gives an algorithm associating linear constraints with the program's clauses. The derivation of minimal solutions for these sets of constraints is discussed in section 4 which also shows that in the case of solvability minimal integral solutions exist which are unique. Section 5 gives an algorithm deriving termination proofs by showing that all elementary cycles of the strongly connected components of the program's predicate dependency graph have negative weight. The paper ends with a discussion of related work and conclusions.

2. Basic Notions

We use standard notation and terminology of Lloyd [LLO87] or Apt [APT90]. Following [APP90] we will say *LD-derivation* for SLD-derivation with the leftmost selection rule characteristic for Prolog.

For a set T of terms a *norm* is a mapping $/\ldots/: T \rightarrow N$. According to [BCF90] a term t is *rigid* w.r.t. a norm $/\ldots/$ if $/t/ = /t\theta/$ for all substitutions θ.

Let $t[v_{(i)} \leftarrow s]$ denote the term derived from t by replacing the i-th occurrence of v with s. An occurrence $v_{(i)}$ of a variable v in a term t is *relevant* w.r.t. $/\ldots/$ if $/t[v_{(i)} \leftarrow s]/ \neq /t/$ for some s. Variable occurrences which are not relevant are called *irrelevant*. A variable is relevant if it has a relevant occurrence, and *rvars(t)* will denote the set of relevant variables occurring in a term t.

Let Δ be a mapping from a set of function symbols F to N which is not zero everywhere.

A norm $/\ldots/$ for T is said to be *semi-linear* if it can be defined by the following scheme:

$$| t | = 0 \qquad\qquad \text{if t is a variable}$$
$$| t | = \Delta(f) + \sum_{i \in I} | t_i | \qquad \text{if } t = f(t_1, \ldots t_n), \text{ where } I \subseteq \{1,\ldots,n\}.$$

Note that I depends on f.

Listsize is the most prominent example for a semi-linear norm. It is defined by the following scheme:

$$| t | = 1 + | B | \qquad \text{if } t = [H|B]$$
$$| t | = 0 \qquad\qquad \text{otherwise.}$$

Proposition 2.1: Let t be a term, $t\theta$ be a rigid term and V be the set of relevant variable occurrences in t. Then for a semi-linear norm $/\ldots/$ we have
$$|t\theta| = |t| + \sum_{v \in V} |v\theta|.$$

Proof: See [BCF90] or [PLU91].

An *annotation* d_p for an n-ary predicate symbol p is a function from the set of indices $\{1,\ldots,n\}$ to the set $\{+,-\}$. An $i \in \{1,\ldots,n\}$ such that $d_p(i) = '+'$ $(d_p(i) = '-')$ is called *input (output) position* of p. An annotation d_p for an n-ary predicate p will be denoted as $p(d_p(1)\ldots d_p(n))$, for instance $append(+,+,-)$, stating that the first two arguments of append are input and the third is output.

A program (clause) with annotations for all its predicates is called *annotated*. Let L be a literal. Then $rv_{in}(L)$ resp. $rv_{out}(L)$ denote the sets of relevant variable occurrences on the input resp. output positions of L. For a goal $G = \leftarrow A_1,\ldots,A_n$ we define $rv_{out}(G) = \bigcup_{i=1}^{n} rv_{out}(A_i)$ and $rv_{in}(G) = \bigcup_{i=1}^{n} rv_{in}(A_i)$.

Let $G = \leftarrow \ldots P,\ldots Q,\ldots$ be a goal and $V = rv_{out}(P) \cap rv_{in}(Q) \neq \emptyset$. If $v \in V$ we say that v is generated by P and consumed by Q, and that P is a generator for Q.

A (partial) LD-derivation is called *data-driven* if at each derivation step all input arguments of the leftmost subgoal are rigid.

Whether a program has only data driven LD-derivations for a certain class of goals is undecidable in general. We next give a sufficient syntactical characterization.

A goal $G = \leftarrow A_1,\ldots,A_n$ is *well-annotated* if for each A_j and each variable $v \in rv_{in}(A_j)$ there is an A_i such that $i < j$ and $v \in rv_{out}(A_i)$.

A clause $C = A_0 \leftarrow A_1,\ldots,A_n$ is *well-annotated* if

- for each $0 < j \leq n$ and each variable $v \in rv_{in}(A_j)$ we have $v \in rv_{in}(A_0)$ or there is an A_i such that $i < j$ and $v \in rv_{out}(A_i)$; and
- $rv_{out}(A_0) \subseteq rv_{in}(A_0) \cup rv_{out}(\leftarrow A_1,\ldots,A_n)$.

C is *well-annotated in a strong sense* if it is well-annotated and each body output variable has no multiple output occurrence in the body and no input occurrence in the head of C.

Theorem 2.2: If all clauses of a program P and a goal G are well-annotated, then all LD-derivations are data driven.
Proof: [PLU91].

For an n-ary predicate p in a program P a *linear predicate inequality* li_p has the form $\sum_{i\in I} p_i + c \geq \sum_{j\in J} p_j$, where I and J are disjoint sets of arguments of p, and c, the *offset* of li_p, is an integer or ∞ (infinite) or a special symbol like γ (a symbolic value which will become instantiated to an integer or ∞). I and J are called *input* resp. *output positions* of p (w.r.t. li_p).

li_p is called *valid* (for a semi-linear norm $|\ldots|$) if $P \models \forall\ p(t_1,\ldots,t_n)$ implies $\sum_{i\in I} |t_i| + c \geq \sum_{j\in J} |t_j|$. If c is ∞, li_p is trivially valid.

Let $A = p(t_1,\ldots,t_n)$. With the notations from above we further define:

- $F_{in}(A,li_p)$ $\quad = \quad \sum_{i\in I} |t_i|$
- $F_{out}(A,li_p)$ $\quad = \quad \sum_{j\in J} |t_j|$
- $F(A,li_p)$ $\quad = \quad F_{in}(A,li_p) - F_{out}(A,li_p) + c$
- $V_{in}(A,li_p)$ $\quad = \quad \bigcup_{i\in I} rvars(t_i)$
- $V_{out}(A,li_p)$ $\quad = \quad \bigcup_{j\in J} rvars(t_j)$

$F(A,li_p)$ is called the *offset* of A w.r.t. li_p.

3. Linear Inequalities for mutually recursive predicates

In this section we will present an algorithm for the automatic derivation of linear inequalities for predicates which are mutually recursive. A subproblem is how to relate variables occurring in a compound goal. It is solved by the algorithm *goal_inequality* which will also be applied in the termination proof procedure to be described in section 5.

Algorithm 3.1 *goal_inequality(G,LI,U,W,Δ,b)*
Input: A goal $\bar{G} = \leftarrow B_1,\ldots,B_n$, a set LI with one inequality for each predicate occurring in G, and two multisets U and W of variables.
Output: A Boolean variable b which will be *true* if a valid inequality relating U and W could be derived, and the offset Δ of that inequality.
begin
 $M := W;\ \Delta := 0$;
 For i := n **to** 1 **do**
  If $M \cap V_{out}(B_i,li_p) \neq \emptyset$ **then**
   $M := (M \setminus V_{out}(B_i,li_p)) \cup V_{in}(B_i,li_p)$;
   $\Delta := \Delta + F(B_i,li_p)$ **fi**;
 If $M \subseteq U$ **then** b:= *true* **else** b:= *false* **fi**
end.

The next theorem shows that algorithm 3.1 is correct.

Theorem 3.2: Assume that G is well-annotated in a strong sense, the inequalities in LI are valid, b is *true* after calling *goal_inequality(G,LI,U,W,Δ,b)* and θ is a computed answer substitution for G. Then $\sum_{u \in U} |u\theta| + \Delta \geq \sum_{w \in W} |w\theta|$ holds.

Proof: see [PLU92].

The idea of algorithm 3.1 is to substitute variables occurring on the right hand side of the desired inequality repeatedly by left-hand side variables, applying the inequalities of LI to the atoms of G and accumulating their respective offsets. Since G is well-annotated in a strong sense, each output variable has exactly one generator. This allows to give a deterministic algorithm which has a runtime complexity linear in the length of G. Extension to goals which are well-annotated in the general sense is possible but gives an exponential complexity. See [PLU89] for details.

The next algorithm derives linear inequalities for the predicates of a given program P. We assume that modes are given for the predicates of P. These modes give symbolic linear predicate inequalities: input arguments correspond to the left-hand sides, output arguments correspond to the right-hand sides of the respective inequalities. The task thus is to find values for the resp. offsets which make these inequalities valid.

Algorithm 3.3 processes the predicates of P in an order which is specified by the predicate dependency graph of P and its strongly connected components. The predicate dependency graph Γ_P of P has nodes which stand for the predicates of P. There is an edge from p to q in Γ_P if q occurs in the definition of p. Note that the strongly connected components of Γ_P form an acyclic graph Γ_P^* which can be derived in linear time (see [AHU74]). Let $SCC_1,\ldots,SCC_n$ be a bottom up traversal of Γ_P^* where the SCC_i are the sets of predicates represented by the SCCs of Γ_P.

Processing the SCCs in that sequence ensures that when a predicate p of SCC_i is considered and q is a predicate on which the definition of p depends, then q is either defined in the current SCC or in some lower SCC which implies that a predicate inequality for q has already been derived. Algorithm 3.3 derives for each clause belonging to the current SCC a *linear constraint*, i.e. a linear inequality with variables which stand for the offsets of the linear inequalities of the predicates in that SCC. Each SCC is thus mapped to a system of linear constraints. A solution of this constraint system gives the desired offsets and thus a set of valid linear inequalities for the resp. SCC. How to solve the systems of linear constraints derived by this algorithm will be discussed in the next section.

Algorithm 3.3: *predicate_inequalities(P,LI)*
Input: A program P,which is well-annotated in a strong sense;
          $SCC_1,\ldots,SCC_n$.
Output: A set LI of valid inequalities for the predicates of P.
begin LI := $\emptyset$;
  for i:= 1 to n **do**   {processing of $SCC_1,\ldots,SCC_n$}
    begin
      for j := 1 **to** r **do** **begin**   {$p_1,\ldots,p_r$ are the predicates of SCC_i}
        let M_j, N_j be index sets for the input resp. output arguments of p_j;
        let $p_{\mu,j}$ denote the μ-th argument of predicate p_j;
        $li_j := \sum_{\mu \in M_j} p_{\mu,j} + \gamma_j \geq \sum_{\nu \in N_j} p_{\nu,j}$

```
            end;
         Ki := true;
         for j := 1 to r do  begin  {processing of predicates in SCCi}
            let c1,...,cm be the clauses defining pj;
            Φj := true;
            For h:= 1 to m do
            begin  {processing of clauses defining pj}
               let ch be B0 ← B1,...,Be;
               goal_inequality((←B1,...,Be),LI∪{li1,...,lir},Vin(B0,lij),Vout(B0,lij),Δh,bh);
               c:= Δh + Fout(B0,lij) - Fin(B0,lij);
               Φj := Φj ∧ bh;
               let R = Σ(ku * γu), 1 ≤ u ≤ r and u ≠ j and integers ku ≥ 0;
               {now c has the form k * γj + R + d for some integers k, d with k ≥ 0}
```
<table>
<tr><td>(i)</td><td>If c contains '∞' then Φj := Φj ∧ false</td></tr>
<tr><td>(ii)</td><td>elseif c = R + d   then Φj := Φj ∧ (γj ≥ R + d)</td></tr>
<tr><td>(iii)</td><td>elseif c = γj + d ∧ d ≤ 0   then Φj := Φj ∧ true</td></tr>
<tr><td>(iv)</td><td>elseif c = γj + d ∧ d > 0   then Φj := Φj ∧ false</td></tr>
<tr><td>(v)</td><td>elseif c = γj + R + d ∧ R≠0 then Φj := Φj ∧ (0 ≥ R + d)</td></tr>
<tr><td>(vi)</td><td>elseif c = k * γj + R + d ∧ k>1 then Φj := Φj ∧ (0 ≥ (k-1) * γj + R + d)</td></tr>
</table>

```
            end;
            Ki := Ki ∧ Φj
         end;
(*)   If Ki is satisfiable and bounded from below
         then let (α1,...αr) be a minimal solution for (γ1,...,γr) satisfying Ki
         else let (α1,...αr) be (∞,...∞);
      For j:= 1 to r do  γj := αj;
      LI := LI ∪ {li1,...,lir}
   end
end.
```

The cases (i) - (vi) reflect different patterns of recursion in the body β of the clause c_h just considered:

(i)   occurs if β contains a predicate from a lower SCC which has an inequality containing '∞'.

(ii)   occurs if β does not have a direct recursive call; it may contain indirect recursion, however;

(iii)   and (iv) apply if β has exactly one recursive literal which has to be direct;

(v)   applies if β has exactly one direct and at least one indirect recursive call;

(vi)   applies if β has at least two direct recursive calls.

Algorithm 3.3 extends an algorithm described in [PLU92]. Its complexity depends on the statement marked by (*) which checks K_i for solvability and selects an optimal solution in the successful case. The other parts of the algorithm have a runtime complexity which is linear in program size. It is not clear from the beginning how an *optimal* solution should be characterized. Obviously a solution is optimal if it is minimal in all components $(\alpha_1,...\alpha_r)$. It is not clear, however, whether satisfiability of K_i implies that such a solution exists. If it exists, it is not necessarily integral (it could be a fraction). Offsets of linear predicate inequalities, however, must be integral. Fortunately in the next section we will be able to show that K_i is unsatisfiable, unbounded from below or there is a solution which is unique, minimal and integral. The next theorem shows that algorithm 3.3 is correct.

Theorem 3.4: The inequalities derived by the algorithm are valid.

Proof: The first induction is on the number n of SCCs in the predicate dependency graph Γ_P. The case $n = 0$ is immediate. For the inductive case assume that the inequalities derived for the predicates in $SCC_1,...,SCC_{n-1}$ are valid. Let I_0 be the minimal S-model (as defined in [FLP89]) of P restricted to the predicates in $SCC_1,...,SCC_{n-1}$. We next cancel from P all clauses which do not define predicates in SCC_n, getting P'. The T_s-operator ([FLP89]) applies only clauses from P'. Let $T_s^0 = I_0$ and $T_s^m = T_s(T_s^{m-1})$. Its limes equals the minimal S-model of P restricted to the predicates in $SCC_1,...,SCC_n$. Now we have to show that the inequalities $\{li_1,...,li_r\}$ derived for the predicates $\{p_1,...,p_r\}$ in SCC_n are valid w.r.t. T_s^m.

The proof now is by induction on the number m of applications of T_s. The case $m = 0$ is implied by the induction assumption on n. Assume that the theorem holds for $m-1$. We have to show that the inequalities $\{li_1,...,li_r\}$ hold for the elements of T_s^m.

Now let $B \in T_s^m$ and $B_0 \leftarrow B_1,...,B_e$ be the clause applied to derive B. We have $B = B_0\theta$ where θ is a computed answer substitution for $\leftarrow B_1,...,B_e$, which is well-annotated in a strong sense. Let $V = V_{in}(B_0,li_j)$ and $W = V_{out}(B_0,li_j)$. Let LI be the set of inequalities derived by algorithm 3.3 so far, and Δ_j be the result of calling $goal\_inequality((\leftarrow B_1,...,B_e),LI,V,W,\Delta_j,b_j)$. Theorem 3.2 and the induction assumption imply

$$(\ddagger) \qquad \sum_{v \in V} |v\theta| + \Delta_j \geq \sum_{w \in W} |w\theta|.$$

Since $B = B_0\theta$ by proposition 2.1 we have $F_{in}(B,li) = F_{in}(B_0,li) + \sum_{v \in V} |v\theta|$ and $F_{out}(B,li) = F_{out}(B_0,li) + \sum_{w \in W} |w\theta|$. Let α_j be the offset of li_j. We have to show

$$(\ddagger\ddagger) \qquad F_{in}(B,li_j) + \alpha_j \geq F_{out}(B,li_j).$$

If b_j is false or Δ_j is ∞ we are ready since in that case α_j is ∞. This covers case (i). Five more cases remain. (ii), (iii) and (iv) immediately imply

$$(\ddagger\ddagger\ddagger) \qquad \alpha_j \geq \Delta_j + F_{out}(B_0,li) - F_{in}(B_0,li).$$

(v) and (vi) are implied by direct transformation of the conditions characterizing these cases. ∎

We next illustrate algorithm 3.3 by the parsing example given in the introduction. The predicate dependency graph of this program has two SCCs: a trivial one with the single node z and the other with the nodes e, t and n. We use listsize as norm. Derivation of the inequality $z_1 \geq 0$ for the lowest SCC is immediate. We next consider e, starting with e_1. The call

$goal\_inequality(\leftarrow t(L,T),LI,\{L\},\{T\},\Delta_e,b_e)$

yields $\Delta_e = \gamma_t$ and $b_e = true$. Here LI is the set $\{e^1+\gamma_e \geq e^2, t^1+\gamma_t \geq t^2, n^1+\gamma_n \geq n^2\}$. We have $c = R = \gamma_t$ and thus case (ii) applies. The constraint corresponding to e_1 thus is

$\gamma_e \geq \gamma_t.$

We next consider e_2. The call

$goal\_inequality((\leftarrow t(L,['+'/C]), e(C,T)),LI,\{L\},\{T\},\Delta_e,b_e)$

yields $\Delta_e = \gamma_t + \gamma_e - 1$ and $b_e = true$. Case (v) applies. The constraint corresponding to e_2

thus is

$$0 \geq \gamma_t - 1.$$

Altogether we get the following constraints. With the matrix notation given below in mind their presentation has been slightly transformed:

$$
\begin{array}{rcrclcr}
\gamma_e & - & \gamma_t & & & \geq & 0 \\
& & -\gamma_t & & & \geq & -1 \\
& & \gamma_t & - & \gamma_n & \geq & 0 \\
& & & - & \gamma_n & \geq & -1 \\
& & & & \gamma_n & \geq & -1 \\
-\gamma_e & & & + & \gamma_n & \geq & -2.
\end{array}
$$

The minimal solution of this set of constraints is $\gamma_t = \gamma_e = \gamma_n = -1$. Thus we have derived the following valid linear predicate inequalities:

$$e^1 - 1 \geq e^2$$
$$t^1 - 1 \geq t^2$$
$$n^1 - 1 \geq n^2$$

4. Deriving minimal solutions for systems of constraints

In the nontrivial case, where no constraint equals false, algorithm 3.3 generates for each SCC a system of linear constraints in several variables for which an optimal solution has to be derived. The format of the linear predicate inequalities requires an integral solution. The components of the solution vectors are offsets which occur on the left-hand sides of inequalities. A solution which is minimal in all its components is obviously optimal with regard to termination proofs. Such a minimal solution is unique. It is not clear from the beginning, however, whether solvability implies that such a minimal integral solution exists.

Finding a minimal solution for a set of linear constraints is the problem of *linear optimization*. Simplex is the most prominent algorithm for this problem which behaves well in practice. Its worst case complexity, however, is exponential. Khachiyan and Karmarkar have presented polynomial algorithms for *linear programming* (see [SCH86]). If integral solutions are required, however, these algorithms do not suffice. The feasible set for a system of inequalities in the reals is a convex polyhedron, and a minimal solution lies in one of its corners. These corners, however, are not integral vectors in general, thus we cannot find an optimal integral solution by optimizing over corners of the polytope. For integers, the problem of linear programming is *NP-complete* (see [PAS82]).

There are special cases, however, where the structure of the problem ensures that a unique minimal solution exists which is integral. This fortunately applies to our case. Before showing this we need some further notions.

The matrix Ξ representing the (nontrivial) constraints for an SCC is constructed such that the rows represent the constraints derived by alg. 3.3 and the columns represent the predicates. $\Xi(i,j) = k$ if γ_j occurs in the i-th constraint with coefficient k. In matrix notation the linear optimization problem for the parsing example is given as follows:

$$\begin{pmatrix} 1 & -1 & 0 \\ 0 & -1 & 0 \\ 0 & 1 & -1 \\ 0 & 0 & -1 \\ 0 & 0 & 1 \\ -1 & 0 & 1 \end{pmatrix} \star \begin{pmatrix} \gamma_e \\ \gamma_t \\ \gamma_n \end{pmatrix} \geq \begin{pmatrix} 0 \\ -1 \\ 0 \\ -1 \\ -1 \\ -2 \end{pmatrix}$$

A matrix is called *pre-Leontief* if each column has at most one positive component. For instance, the *transposed* matrix of our parsing example is pre-Leontief.

A vector v is the *least* element of a set U of vectors if no other element of U is smaller than v in any component. A least element, if existing, is *unique*.

Theorem 4.1 (Cottle and Veinott, [COV72])

A non-empty set $S = \{x: \Xi * x \geq b, x \geq 0\}$ has a least element, if Ξ^t is a pre-Leontief matrix.

Proof: [COV72]

Theorem 4.2 (Chandrasekaran [CHA84])

If Ξ^t is a pre-Leontief matrix with integral coefficients , b is an integral vector and each positive component of Ξ equals 1, then a non-empty set $S = \{x: \Xi * x \geq b, x \geq 0\}$ has a least element which is integral.

Proof: [CHA84], [CHH91]

Theorem 4.3

Let $\Xi * x \geq b$ be the matrix representation of the linear optimization problem of algorithm 3.3. Then the following holds:

    1) Ξ and b are integral

    2) Ξ^t is pre-Leontief

    3)   each positive component of Ξ equals 1.

Proof: We only have to consider the nontrivial case where algorithm 3.3 generates a set of constraints which does not contain *false*. 1) is immediate. The only case where algorithm 3.3 generates a positive component of Ξ is ii), where the constraint has the form $\gamma_j \geq R + d$. In this case there is exactly one positive component which equals 1. This implies 2) and 3). ∎

Corollary 4.4

If the set K_i of constraints generated by alg. 3.3 is satisfiable and bounded from below, then it has a unique minimal solution which is integral.

Proof: If the vectors of the solution set S of K_i are positive in all their components, corollary 4.4 is immediately implied by theorems 4.2 and 4.3. For the other case let a be a lower bound for S which is integral. Then we have

K_i	$=$		$\{x:$	$A * x$	$\geq b$	$\mid$	x	$\geq$	$a\}$
	$=$		$\{a + y:$	$A * (a+y)$	$\geq b$	$\mid$	$(a+y)$	$\geq$	$a\}$
	$=$	$a +$	$\{y:$	$A * y$	$\geq b - A * a$	$\mid$	y	$\geq$	$0\}$
	$=$	$a +$	K_i'						

where K_i' is a new system of inequalities satisfying the conditions of 4.1 and 4.2. Thus K_i' and therefore also K_i has the properties stated in 4.4. ■

An immediate consequence of corollary 4.4 is that Simplex or Karmarkar's algorithm can be applied to solve the integer linear optimization problem of algorithm 3.3. Since Karmarkar's algorithm is polynomial in the number of variables, alg. 3.3 has a run-time complexity which is polynomial in the length of P.

Another interesting technique which is implemented in our prototype is the *SUP-INF-procedure* (Bledsoe [BLE75] and Shostak [SHO77]). SUP-INF, which is a semi-decision procedure for the validity problem of Presburger formulas, is complete for the reals. Thus in our special case SUP-INF derives the minimal solution of the constraints generated by alg. 3.3. if such a solution exists. In contrast to Karmarkar's algorithm, however, SUP-INF has an exponential runtime complexity in the worst case.

5. Termination proofs for mutually recursive programs

We next show how, based on the linear predicate inequalities, termination proofs for mutually recursive programs are derived. In the case of direct recursion we have to consider the recursive literals in the clauses' bodies and make sure that input becomes strictly smaller. In the general case of indirect recursion, we have to take into account all those predicates which are in the same SCC as the predicate of the clause's head. In this context new problems arise which again can be illustrated by the parse-example. Consider for instance the predicate e:

e_1: $e(L,T)$ ← $t(L,T)$.
e_2: $e(L,T)$ ← $t(L,['+'|C])$, $e(C,T)$.

Applying the predicate inequality for t and considering $t(L,['+'|C])$ in e_2 it can easily be shown that C is strictly smaller than L. This handles the case of direct recursion in e_2. But there is also indirect recursion, namely $t(L,['+'|C])$, and the input argument of this call is the same as the head input argument. Is there a potential for an infinite loop? Indirect recursion is associated with cycles in the program's predicate dependency graph, and the idea now is that if we can associate a negative number with each cycle we can show that loops cannot happen.

Proof trees, introduced in [CLA79], are a good means to make this idea more precise. Let PT be the proof tree for a goal G in the context of a program P. If P has only direct recursion, a recursive branch of PT can have only atoms with the same predicate symbol. For mutual recursion a recursive branch D may have only atoms with predicates from the same SCC. If D is infinite, there must be an infinite subsequence D' which has only one predicate p. Let $D = ...,B_i,...,B_j,...$ and B_j be the successor of B_i in D'. There is a direct correspondence between the path B_i to B_j in D and a cycle of an SCC of the predicate dependency graph of P. Let the size of an atom be the accumulated norms of its input arguments. Assume that the sizes of the respective atoms never increase in D and strictly decrease in D'. Then neither D nor D' may be infinite. In order to ensure the latter, algorithm 5.1 will show that all elementary cycles of SCCs have negative weight.

Algorithm 5.1: *termination(P,LI,b):*

Input: A program P, which is well-annotated in a strong sense;
A set LI of valid linear inequalities for the predicates of P.

Output: A Boolean variable b which will be *true* if P terminates for every
well-annotated goal.

begin.
  construct the predicate dependency graph Γ_p of P;
  for all edges (p,q) of Γ_p define weight(p,q) := $-\infty$;
  let $SCC_1,\ldots,SCC_n$ be the strongly connected components of Γ_p;
  b: = *true*;
  for i:= 1 **to** n **do**   {processing of $SCC_1,\ldots,SCC_n$}
    begin
      let $c_1,\ldots,c_m$ the clauses defining the predicates of SCC_i,
      for j := 1 **to** m **do**   {processing of clauses}
      begin
      let c_j be the clause $B_0 \leftarrow B_1,\ldots,B_r$;
      let p be the predicate symbol of B_0;
        For h:= 1 **to** r **do**   {processing of body subgoals}
      begin
        let q be the predicate symbol of B_h;
        if b **and** there is an edge (p,q) in SCC_i **then**
            begin
              $goal\_inequality((\leftarrow B_1,\ldots,B_{h-1}),LI,V_{in}(B_0,li_p),V_{in}(B_h,li_q),\Delta_h,b_h);$
              $c_h := \Delta_h - F_{in}(B_0,li_p) + F_{in}(B_h,li_q);$
              if b **and** b_h **and** $c_h \leq 0$ **then** weight(p,q) := max(weight(p,q), c_h)
                              else b:= *false*
      end
      end
    end
    end;
  if b **then**
  begin
    let Γ_p' be the graph derived from Γ_p by deleting all edges with negative weight;
    if there is a cycle in Γ_p' **then** b:=*false*
  end
end.

If *b* is *true* after calling alg. 5.1, then *goal_inequality* has been successfully applied to all
body literals which correspond to edges of SCCs of Γ_p and derived an offset Δ_h such that
c_h is not positive. The weight of an edge of Γ_p is the maximal value of c_h corresponding
to that edge. *P* is well-annotated and thus its derivations are data-driven. Thus the sizes of
the successive elements of *D* cannot increase. From the last statement of 5.1 and *b* being
true follows that all cycles of all SCCs have at least one edge with negative weight. This
implies that the sizes of the elements of *D'* are strictly decreasing. Thus neither *D'* nor *D*
can be infinite. The derivation of *G* must therefore be finite. Thus algorithm 5.1 is correct.

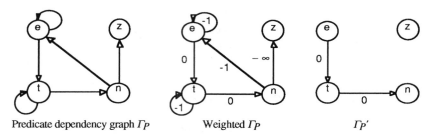

Predicate dependency graph Γ_P Weighted Γ_P $\Gamma_P{}'$

According to [AHU74] deriving the SCCs of Γ_p and testing $\Gamma_p{}'$ for cycles can both be done in linear time. The number of calls of *goal_inequality* is bound from above by the length of P, and the complexity of each call is linear in the length of the considered subgoal. Thus if n is the number of clauses of P and m the maximal number of literals of a clause of P, then the time complexity of alg. 5.1 is $O(n * m^2)$.

For illustration we come back to the parsing example. Its predicate dependency graph is given above. We consider its non-trivial SCC with predicates n,t and e. The edge (n,e) gets its weight -1 from clause n_2. Note that the head input $['('/A]$ is strictly greater than the recursive input A. Here we have no local variable. The edge (e,e) gets its weight from clause e_2. Note that the recursive literal $e(C,T)$ has the local variable C. Thus the linear inequality for the predicate t is required, giving weight -1 for that edge. Since $\Gamma_P{}'$ is cycle-free, *parse* terminates for all well-annotated queries.

6. Related Work and Conclusions

The termination problem for logic programs has been studied by several researchers. Bezem [BEZ89] has analyzed programs which terminate for all ground queries and any computation rule. By the notion of *recurrent* programs he has given a characterization which is necessary and sufficient, albeit undecidable. Apt and Pedreschi [APP90] have studied left terminating programs which terminate for ground (and bounded) queries and Prolog's computation rule. Their notion of *acceptability* is an undecidable characterization which is necessary and sufficient for left termination.

An efficient procedure for detecting terminating logic programs has been proposed Ullman and van Gelder [ULG88]. It checks for conditions which are sufficient, but not necessary. The format of their inequalities allows only one variable on either side. A more general approach has been proposed in [PLU89] which restricts attention to programs with direct recursion and shows how indirect recursion can be transformed to direct recursion. An important disadvantage of that transformation is that program structure may be flattened. Van Gelder [GEL91] and Sohn/van Gelder [SOG91] have generalized the approach of [ULG88] based on linear programming techniques. In contrast to [PLU89] their approach incorporates mutual recursion from the beginning. Their approach requires the solution of a fixpoint problem for which at present no algorithm is known. Heuristics are applied which may or may not succeed.

Verschaetse/De Schreye [VES91] have studied termination of logic programs in the context of abstract interpretation. They use equalities which are less general than inequalities. Similar to [GEL91] coefficients may be arbitrary integers.

This paper shows that the approach of [PLU89] can be extended to the general case of mutual recursion in a natural way. The algorithm of [PLU89] deriving linear inequalities is a special case of the one presented here. In the general case a system of linear constraints with several variables is generated. Although integer linear programming is NP-complete in general, it turns out that the linear constraints generated by alg. 3.3 have a simple structure. Analyzing the matrix notation of these constraints one finds that all components are integral, in each row there is at most one positive component, and this component equals one. As Cottle/Veinott and Chandrasekaran showed, these characteristics imply that there is a minimal, unique and integral solution, if any. Thus there is no problem of rounding real solutions, and Karmarkar's algorithm can be applied, which is polynomial. Note that a basic condition for applying the resp. theorems is that the matrix Ξ has at most one positive component in each row. In our algorithm this corresponds to case (ii) where all recursive literals are indirect. Roughly speaking, the component (i,j) in Ξ has value k if the number of positive occurrences minus the number of negative occurrences of predicate p_j in the i-th clause of the respective SCC equals k. Here *positive occurrence* refers to the head and *negative occurrence* refers to the body of this clause. Since we are dealing with *Horn* clauses, there cannot be more than one positive literal. Case (ii) refers to a clause which has only indirect but no direct recursion. If there is direct recursion, the head literal is counterbalanced by a recursive body literal. The point is that one reason for the relative simplicity of the linear constraints derived by alg. 3.3 stems from the fact that we are dealing with Horn clauses which is exploited in our approach to derive linear inequalities.

Based on these inequalities, termination is proved by considering all elementary cycles of the SCCs of the program's predicate dependency graph.

References

[AHU74]   Aho, A. V., Hopcroft, J. E., Ullman, J. D., *The Design and Analysis of Computer Algorithms*, Addison-Wesley, Reading, Mass., 1974.

[APP90]   Apt, K. R., Pedreschi, D., *Studies in pure Prolog: Termination*, in J. W. Lloyd (ed.), Symposium on Computational Logic, Springer Verlag Berlin 1990.

[APT90]   Apt, K. R., *Introduction to logic programming*, in Leeuwen (ed.), The Handbook of Theoretical Computer Science, North Holland 1990.

[BEZ89]   Bezem, M., *Characterizing termination of logic programs with level mappings*, in Proceedings of the North American Conference on Logic Programming, MIT Press, 1989.

[BCF90]   Bossi, A., Cocco, N., Fabris, M., *Proving Termination of Logic Programs by Exploiting Term Properties*, Technical Report Dip. di Matematica Pura e Applicata, Universita di Padova, 1990.

[BLE75]   Bledsoe, W. W., *A new method for proving certain Presburger formulas*, Advance Papers 4th Int. Joint Conf. on Artif. Intell., Tibilisi, Gerorgia, U.S.S.R, Sept. 1975, pp. 15-21.

[CHA84]   Chandrasekaran, R., *Integer Programming Problems for Which a Simple Rounding Type of Algorithm Works*, In W. R. Pulleyblank (ed.) Progress in Combinatorial Optimization, Academic Press Canada, Toronto, Ontario, Canada 1984, pp. 101-106.

[CHH91]   Chandru, V., Hooker, J. N., *Extended Horn Sets in Propositional Logic*, Journal of the ACM, Vol. 38, No. 1, January 1991, pp. 205-221.

[COV72]   Cottle, R. W., Veinott, F. Jr., *Polyhedral sets having a least element*, Mathematical Programming, Vol. 3 (1972), pp. 238-249, North-Holland Publishing Company.

[FLP89]   Falaschi, M., Levi, G., Palamidessi, C., Martelli, M., *Declarative Modeling of the Operational Behavior of Logic Languages,* Theoretical Computer Science 69, 1989.

[GEL91]   van Gelder, A., *Deriving constraints among argument sizes in logic programs*, Annals of Mathematics and Artificial Intelligence 3 (1991) 361-392.

[KAR84]   Karmarkar, N., *A new polynomial-time algorithm for linear programming*, Combinatorica 4, 1984.

[LLO87]   Lloyd, J., *Foundations of Logic Programming*, Springer Verlag, Berlin, second edition, 1987.

[PAS82]   Papadimitriou, C. H., Steglitz, K., Combinatorial Optimization, Prentice-Hall, Englewood Cliffs, NJ, 1982.

[PLU89]   Plümer, L., *Termination Proofs for Logic Programs,* Dissertation Universität Dortmund 1989, also: Springer Lecture Notes in Artificial Intelligence 446, Berlin 1990.

[PLU90]   Plümer, L., *Termination proofs for logic programs based on predicate inequalities,* in Warren, D.H.D., Szeredi, P. (eds.), Proceedings of the Seventh International Conference on Logic Programming, MIT Press 1990.

[PLU91]   Plümer, L., *Termination proofs for Prolog programs operating on nonground terms,* 1991 International Logic Programming Symposium, San Diego, California, MIT Press 1991.

[PLU92]   Plümer, L., *Automatic Verification of GHC-Programs: Termination,* Proceedings of the International Conference on Fifth Generation Computer Systems 1992, June 1-5, Tokyo 1992

[SCH86]   Schrijver, A., *Theory of Linear and Integer Programming,* Wiley, New York, 1986.

[SHO77]   Shostak, R. E., *On the SUP-INF Method for Proving Presburger Formulas,* Journal of the ACM, Vol. 24, No. 4, October 1977, pp. 529-543.

[SOG91]   Sohn, K., Van Gelder, A., *Termination Detection in Logic Programs using Argument Sizes,* Proceedings of the Tenth International Symposium on Principles of Database Systems, 1991.

[ULG88]   Ullman, J. D., van Gelder, A., *Efficient Tests for Top-Down Termination of Logical Rules,* Journal of the ACM 35, 2, 1988.

[VES91]   Verschaetse, K., De Schreye, D., *Deriving termination proofs for logic programs using abstract procedures,* KU Leuven 1991.

Synthesis and Transformation of Logic Programs in the Whelk Proof Development System

Geraint A Wiggins
Department of Artificial Intelligence
University of Edinburgh
80 South Bridge, Edinburgh EH1 1HN, Scotland
geraint@ed.ac.uk

Abstract

I present the Whelk proof development system, a tool for the synthesis and transformation of logic programs. Whelk is based on ideas used in the "Proofs-as-Programs" literature [9, 1], which enable the *extraction* of logic programs from proofs, in a similar way to that of [10]. Using Whelk, we can synthesise *pure logic programs* [4] which may be easily translated into "real" logic programming languages such as Prolog and Gödel. Delay declarations to prevent floundering and unbounded recursion may also be generated automatically. In the longer term, Whelk will form a substrate for the CLᴬM proof planner [7, 6, 8, 5], which will allow automatic generation of programs from first order specifications.

In this paper, I present a subset of the refinement rules used in Whelk. I show how a proof of correctness of both the rules and the synthesised program should be carried out. I give a detailed example of a synthesis/transformation proof.

1 Introduction

In this paper, I present and explain the Whelk proof development system. Whelk is intended for the synthesis and/or transformation of logic programs as I will explain below, though it is usable for the development of more general proofs. Whelk is designed for use with the CLᴬM proof planner [7, 6, 8, 5], which allows the automation of the proof process; currently, CLᴬM is orientated towards proofs by induction.

The rest of the paper takes the following form. Section 2 begins by outlining the notion of *proofs as programs*, summarising the problems raised and solutions proposed in [4], which arise when the idea is applied to *logic* program synthesis, rather than that of *functional* programs, which has been past practice. Section 3 summarises the operation of the Whelk system, and lists and justifies the proof rules used in the example of Section 4. Finally, Section 5 draws conclusions and outlines the next steps in the work presented here.

2 Background

2.1 Proofs as (Functional) Programs and Type Theory

Proofs-as-Programs is an existing technique for program synthesis [9]. The basic notion behind it is that mathematical proofs of certain theorems can contain the computational information required to construct a program. In particular, if we prove a conjecture of the form

$$\vdash \forall \bar{\iota}. \exists o. S(\bar{\iota}, o)$$

where $\bar{\iota}$ is a (possibly empty) vector of inputs, o is an output, and S is the specification of a program, it is sometimes possible to derive that program from the proof. I will refer to this kind of conjecture as a *synthesis conjecture*.

In order to ensure that we can derive a program from the proof, and to ensure that the program is then executable, we must place restrictions on the proof system we use. The most straightforward way to achieve the necessary restriction is to require that the logic used for the proof be *constructive*. The upshot of this is that any proof of our existential goal, above, will involve showing not merely that the output value o exists, but that it can be constructed. This is shown by constructing it in terms of any other values, functions, and relations in S, and their definitions. Since the proof shows how to construct our output for all input, we can then derive a program which will construct it for any given input value.

This construction process begs an important question: how can we know that the program we construct is correct with respect to the proof? In the literature on functional proofs-as-programs (as opposed to proofs-as-relational-programs, which I discuss below), there is a standard technique for doing this. We cast our specification conjecture and its proof in a Constructive Type Theory; once we have done so, we can derive functions, expressed in terms of the λ-calculus, as our programs, and know they are correct by virtue of the *Curry-Howard Isomorphism* [14], a one-to-one relationship between the notions of implication and function application [16, 17].

2.2 Proofs as Relational Programs

The main problem with the application of the type-theoretic proofs-as-programs technique to the synthesis of logic programs is that it synthesises functions — if we were to synthesise logic programs which were strictly functional, we would be throwing away the main advantages of logic programs: multiple outputs, partial programs, the concept of failure, and so on. So we would like to adapt the technique.

In [4], we propose an adaptation of the proofs-as-programs technique in which we view relations (*qua* logic programs called in the *all-ground mode*) as functions on to the type boole (containing just true and false). We then prove a synthesis conjecture of the approximate form

$$\vdash \forall \bar{\iota}. \exists \mathcal{B}. S(\bar{\iota}) \leftrightarrow \mathcal{B}$$

where $\mathcal{B}$ is a variable of type boole, $\bar{\iota}$ is a (possibly empty) vector of arguments and S is as before. This technique allows us to overcome the limitation of [10], which can only synthesise functional relations.

The exact form of the specification conjecture is largely a matter of taste — it can be specified as above, where the boolean variable is second-order, or in other ways which keep the logic first-order; we discuss these possibilities in [22]. The option I have chosen is to use a first order typed constructive logic with a new operator,

$$\partial : \text{formula} \mapsto \text{formula}$$

read as "it is decidable whether...". The meaning of ∂ is defined thus:

$$\vdash \forall \bar{a}. \partial S(\bar{a}) \quad iff \quad \vdash \exists P. \forall \bar{a}. S(\bar{a}) \leftrightarrow P(\bar{a}) \text{ and P, a relation, is decidable}$$

where S is a formula specifying a program. Proving decidability is equivalent to proving the existence of the boolean B in the initial approach. However, it has the advantage that the higher-order component of the specification, B, is hidden away in the definition of the logic, and we are left with a purely first order specification.

Given this operator, branches of the proof corresponding with any parts of a logic program search tree can be elaborated normally, regardless of their eventual success or failure, and then related with *true* or *false*, in a synthesised program, as appropriate. This will become clearer in the exposition of the Whelk system in Section 3, and in the worked example in Section 4.

Now, since I am not using type theory (which is for various practical reasons not ideally suited to this work), I must also motivate the construction steps associated with the proof rules — I will do this in Section 3.3.

2.3 Justification

It is necessary to justify the usefulness of this technique as opposed to the many existing techniques for program synthesis and transformation in the logic programming world. It is regrettably the case that the proofs necessary to synthesise programs are often long-winded and difficult; it seems likely that direct writing of a program will be a much quicker and less laborious approach than this. However, I suggest that the technique is very much worthwhile, for the following reasons.

1. It involves working with logical specifications with no procedural content at all. Thus, is is much closer to the original intent of Kowalski's equation [15] than working with programs which have a procedural interpretation.

2. Working with specifications in terms of equivalence means that there is only one notion of program equivalence, which simplifies matters greatly.

3. The proofs associated with a particular theorem contain much more information than a logic program usually does. This information is available for use in connection with program synthesis and/or execution, once the proof has been carried out. For example, in [21], I explain how information about applications of induction can be used to generate delay declarations.

4. In this technique, automation of the synthesis process becomes for the most part equivalent to that of the proof process. Existing work (*eg* [7, 6, 8]) can therefore be used to generate programs automatically; thus, long-windedness of the proofs no longer matters.

5. Given 3 and 4, we can expect to adapt the existing work to use the information in the proof to produce *good* programs as part of the automated process more easily than in techniques working by program transformation alone.

6. Once the proof and extraction systems are shown to be correct, we know that a complete proof will give rise to a correct program. Thus, no correctness proofs are needed for the synthesised programs.

7. We can use the technique to reproduce the behaviour of other techniques — for example, in [20], I show how a prototype of the current technique can be used to reproduce the results of [2]. Given 6 above, this means that such techniques need no longer be proven correct — if they are implemented in the synthesis logic, then they must be so, *a priori*, given that their notion of program equivalence is the same as Whelk's.

3 The *Whelk* System

3.1 Introduction

Whelk is a Gentzen Sequent Calculus proof development system, based on the *Oyster* system of [7], the Martin-Löf-based Type Theory of that earlier system having been replaced by a first order typed constructive logic with equality. *Whelk* is designed and implemented as a substrate of the CL^M proof planner, as explained in Section 5.

In this section, I will state the refinement and construction rules necessary for the example of Section 4, which constitute a good cross-section of the rules of the full *Whelk* system.

3.2 The Logic

The proof refinement system I use here is based on a sequent calculus, LJ, of [11]. LJ has been enhanced for our purposes by the addition of the ∂ operator and refinement rules for each combination of ∂ with the other operators, and with types and equality. It would take too much space here to state the rules for the whole system, so I will limit myself to those necessary for the example proof in Section 4. These rules are laid out in the following sections.

Notation is as follows: upper case Greek letters (Γ, Δ) denote sequences of formulæ and program fragments; lower case Greek letters (τ) denote types and program fragments; upper case Roman letters (A, B, C) denote formulæ; and lower case Roman letters denote variables (x, v_i) or terms (t). {} denotes contradiction. $A\langle t/x \rangle$ means "A with all free occurrences of x replaced by t". Finally, we have the usual connectives, $\forall, \exists, \wedge, \vee, \leftarrow, \rightarrow, \neg$, with the addition of $\leftrightarrow$; we have typed $=$, and we have : denoting type membership.

In all the rules, where a term substitution occurs, the type of the replacement term must be consistent with that of the term being replaced.

Note also that there must (for the moment) be no more than one occurrence of ∂ in a goal. Multiple occurrences would mean that we were synthesising meta-programs, which I defer for a future document.

3.3 Extracting Pure Logic Programs

We also need to supply a set of construction rules, in correspondence with the proof rules, to allow our program to be built. This way, the program extraction process can take place as a side effect of elaborating the proof, and then the program can simply be read off afterwards.

The language I will use for my extracted programs is that of the *pure logic program* used in [4] and [22]. It is essentially the same as the specification language used above, but functions other than constructors are not allowed, and the ∂ operator does not appear. Also, the boolean terms *true* and *false* are replaced by the predicates of the same name. There is a mapping, the *interpretation*, between the two logics, which I will now label as $\mathcal{L}_S$ and $\mathcal{L}_P$ – the *specification logic* and the *program logic*, respectively. Note that, in [22], these were called $\mathcal{L}_E$ and $\mathcal{L}_I$, the "external" and "internal" logics respectively. I no longer use this terminology, which can be misleading. The correspondent of an $\mathcal{L}_S$-formula A in $\mathcal{L}_P$ under the interpretation, is denoted by A^*; the only detail necessary here is that the connectives of $\mathcal{L}_S$ map to connectives of the same name and meaning in $\mathcal{L}_P$ under *. See [22] for more details.

The behaviour we require of our system is that, given a specification conjecture

$$\vdash \forall \overline{a}.\partial\, S(\overline{a})$$

we synthesise a pure logic program $P(\overline{a})$ such that

$$\vdash \forall \overline{a}^{*}.S(\overline{a})^{*} \leftrightarrow P(\overline{a})$$

so that P is effectively the "witness" for the decidability of the specification S – *ie* something which actually does the deciding.

For our purposes here, it is enough to say that a pure logic program, like that defining P, consists of a head and a body, connected biconditionally, and that the body is an arbitrary formula containing quantification, and maybe free occurrences of variables appearing in the head, all variables being typed. It may also contain explicit *true* and *false* predicates, so the natural expression of a pure Prolog program in these terms is its completion. For example, the Prolog `member/2` predicate

```
member( X, [X|_] ).
member( X, [_|Y] ) :- member( X, Y ).
```

could be expressed, for lists of natural numbers, as the following pure logic program:

$$
\begin{aligned}
\text{member}(x{:}nat, y{:}list(nat)) \leftrightarrow& \\
y = [] \wedge false \vee& \\
\exists v_0{:}nat.\exists v_1{:}list(nat).y = [v_0|v_1] \wedge& (x = v_0 \wedge true \vee \\
& \text{member}(x{:}nat, v_1{:}list(nat)))
\end{aligned}
$$

To generate our desired program, we need a construction rule corresponding with each proof rule. First, I introduce notions of *synthesis proof* and *verification proof*.

Synthesis proof is that part of the proof of a specification conjecture which contributes directly to the extracted program. *Verification proof* is that part which shows the synthesis part to be correct, but does not actually constitute part of the synthesised algorithm itself. This distinction is also made in the functional proofs-as-programs literature — though, in Martin-Löf type theory, both the synthesis and the verification parts of the proof contribute to the extracted program, which is undesirable for our purposes here.

It is a desirable feature of the logic $\mathcal{L}_S$ that it is possible and easy to distinguish syntactically between synthesis and verification parts of the proof: wherever there is a ∂ in one's conjecture, one is working on synthesis; elsewhere one is performing verification. This is reflected in the construction rules shown below.

The rule governing whether or not manipulation of a hypothesis contributes to the construction of a program is more subtle than that for conjectures. With a few exceptions, hypotheses in sequents are considered to be *true* and are therefore associated with the program fragment *true* by default. The only times when this is not the case are:

- when a disjunctive hypothesis is split into its disjuncts — each disjunct is then a constraint on the environments of a separate subconjecture;

- when an induction step is used — when the program fragment associated with the induction hypothesis is a recursive call to the synthesised predicate; and

- when a hypothesis is *cut* in, or a lemma is appealed to — in which case the program fragment associated with the new hypothesis is a call to the program synthesised by its proof (or just *true* if it does not contain ∂).

All of these will be demonstrated in Section 4.

Notation is as follows: each sequent or hypothesis A must now be associated with a program fragment; these fragments are written as subscripts on the expressions, each one with an explicit fragment being placed in $[\![\,]\!]$ for clarity. Where no value is given, if A is decidable by first-order unification (*eg* a function-free equality) the default is A^*; otherwise the value is a program fragment ϕ constructed by proof of the subconjecture

$$[\![\,\Gamma \vdash \partial\, A\,]\!]_{P(\mathcal{E})\mapsto\phi}$$

The body of the synthesised program fragment associated with each subconjecture is denoted by a greek letter (ϕ, ψ); the head, $P(\mathcal{E})$, is a predicate symbol, P, applied to an "environment" of variables, $\mathcal{E}$, which constitute the parameters of the predicate. $\mathcal{E}$ is written here as a list in $\langle ., \mathsf{nil}\rangle$ notation. The program fragment associated with the dominating conjecture is then expressed in terms of those of its subconjectures.

The refinement rules given in Section 3.4 are in some cases annotated with rules for program construction. Those which have no such annotation simply do not contribute to the construction; they serve only to verify its correctness. Those rules marked † do not apply to formulæ containing ∂.

Finally, note one further non-standard feature of the logic. Any formula of form

$$\partial\, A$$

where A is a formula is necessarily true — it states that A is either true or false. It is nevertheless necessary to give refinement rules for the *provability* ($\vdash$) of conjectures of this kind, because of their contribution to the synthesised program (see below).

3.4 The Refinement and Construction Rules

3.4.1 Axiom

We need two forms of axiom rule, the second deriving anything from contradiction:

$$axiom \ \frac{}{[\![\,\Gamma, [\![A]\!]_\phi, \Delta \vdash A\,]\!]_{P(\mathsf{nil})\mapsto\phi}} \qquad axiom\dagger \ \frac{}{\Gamma, \{\}, \Delta \vdash A}$$

3.4.2 ∃ Introduction

$$\exists \ intro \ \frac{\Gamma \vdash A\langle t/x\rangle}{\Gamma \vdash \exists x{:}\tau.A}$$

3.4.3 ∀ Introduction

We need two forms of ∀ introduction, distinguishing between ∀ outside and inside the scope of ∂. This is necessary because the first rule leads to the introduction of a parameter into $\mathcal{E}$ and the second does not.

$$\forall \ intro \ \frac{[\![\,\Gamma, x{:}\tau \vdash \partial\, A\,]\!]_{P(\mathcal{E})\mapsto\phi}}{[\![\,\Gamma \vdash \forall x{:}\tau.\partial\, A\,]\!]_{P(\langle(x:\tau).\mathcal{E}\rangle)\mapsto\phi}} \qquad \forall \ intro \ \frac{[\![\,\Gamma, x{:}\tau \vdash \partial\, A\,]\!]_{P(\mathcal{E})\mapsto\phi}}{[\![\,\Gamma \vdash \partial\,(\forall x{:}\tau.A)\,]\!]_{P(\mathcal{E})\mapsto\phi}}$$

3.4.4 ∧ Introduction

$$\wedge \ intro \ \frac{[\![\,\Gamma \vdash \partial\, A\,]\!]_{P(\mathcal{E})\mapsto\phi} \quad [\![\,\Gamma \vdash \partial\, B\,]\!]_{P(\mathcal{E})\mapsto\psi}}{[\![\,\Gamma \vdash \partial\,(A \wedge B)\,]\!]_{P(\mathcal{E})\mapsto\phi\wedge\psi}}$$

3.4.5 ∨ Introduction

$$\vee \ intro \ \frac{[\![\,\Gamma \vdash \partial\, A\,]\!]_{P(\mathcal{E})\mapsto\phi} \quad [\![\,\Gamma \vdash \partial\, B\,]\!]_{P(\mathcal{E})\mapsto\psi}}{[\![\,\Gamma \vdash \partial\,(A \vee B)\,]\!]_{P(\mathcal{E})\mapsto\phi\vee\psi}}$$

3.4.6 → Introduction

We need two forms of → introduction, distinguishing between → inside and outside the scope of ∂, as with $\forall$. Note that, in the construction rule, we must reject the rule of *ex falsio quod libet*, to avoid proof of anything from falsehood, which is undesirable in logic programming. Thus, that → in $\mathcal{L}_P$ is more like (local cut) in Prolog than classical implication as in Gödel, though it does not have the same (or indeed any) procedural interpretation.

$$\rightarrow intro \ \frac{\Gamma \vdash A \quad \Gamma, A \vdash B}{\Gamma \vdash A \rightarrow B} \qquad \rightarrow intro \ \frac{[\![\Gamma \vdash \partial A]\!]_{P(\mathcal{E}) \leftrightarrow \phi} \quad [\![\Gamma, A \vdash \partial B]\!]_{P(\mathcal{E}) \leftrightarrow \psi}}{[\![\Gamma \vdash \partial (A \rightarrow B)]\!]_{P(\mathcal{E}) \leftrightarrow \phi \rightarrow \psi}}$$

3.4.7 ∂ Introduction

$$\partial_{true} \ intro \ \frac{[\![\Gamma \vdash A]\!]_{P(\mathcal{E}) \leftrightarrow \phi}}{[\![\Gamma \vdash \partial A]\!]_{P(nil) \leftrightarrow true}} \qquad \partial_{false} \ intro \ \frac{[\![\Gamma \vdash \neg A]\!]_{P(\mathcal{E}) \leftrightarrow \phi}}{[\![\Gamma \vdash \partial A]\!]_{P(nil) \leftrightarrow false}}$$

3.4.8 $\forall$ Elimination

For this rule, we need all three possibilities: $\forall$ inside and outside ∂, and in expressions not containing ∂. $\mathcal{E}''$ is $\mathcal{E}'$ prepended to $(t{:}\tau).nil$.

$$\forall \ elim \ \frac{[\![\Gamma, [\![\partial \forall x{:}\tau.A]\!]_{P(\mathcal{E}')}, \Delta, [\![\partial A \langle t/x \rangle]\!]_{P(\mathcal{E}'')} \vdash A]\!]_{P(\mathcal{E}) \leftrightarrow \phi}}{[\![\Gamma, [\![\partial \forall x{:}\tau.A]\!]_{P(\mathcal{E}')}, \Delta \vdash A]\!]_{P(\mathcal{E}) \leftrightarrow \phi}}$$

$$\forall \ elim \ \frac{[\![\Gamma, [\![\forall x{:}\tau.\partial A]\!]_{P(\mathcal{E}')}, \Delta, [\![\partial A \langle t/x \rangle]\!]_{P(\mathcal{E}'')} \vdash A]\!]_{P(\mathcal{E}) \leftrightarrow \phi}}{[\![\Gamma, [\![\forall x{:}\tau.\partial A]\!]_{P(\mathcal{E}')}, \Delta \vdash A]\!]_{P(\mathcal{E}) \leftrightarrow \phi}}$$

$$\forall \ elim\dagger \ \frac{\Gamma, \forall x{:}\tau.A, A \langle t/x \rangle, \Delta \vdash B}{\Gamma, \forall x{:}\tau.A, \Delta \vdash B}$$

3.4.9 $\neg$ Elimination

$$\neg \ elim\dagger \ \frac{\Gamma, \neg A, \Delta \vdash A}{\Gamma, \neg A, \Delta \vdash \{\}}$$

3.4.10 $\vee$ Elimination

$$\vee \ elim \ \frac{[\![\Gamma, A, \Delta \vdash C]\!]_{P(\mathcal{E}) \leftrightarrow \phi} \quad [\![\Gamma, B, \Delta \vdash C]\!]_{P(\mathcal{E}) \leftrightarrow \psi}}{[\![\Gamma, A \vee B, \Delta \vdash C]\!]_{P(\mathcal{E}) \leftrightarrow (\alpha \wedge \phi) \vee (\beta \wedge \psi)}} \begin{array}{c} [\![\Gamma, \Delta \vdash \partial A]\!]_{P(\mathcal{E}) \leftrightarrow \alpha} \quad [\![\Gamma, \Delta \vdash \partial B]\!]_{P(\mathcal{E}) \leftrightarrow \beta} \end{array}$$

Here, the constructions α and β ensure that the disjuncts in the eliminated disjunction correspond with executable program fragments.

3.4.11 Induction on Lists

This is the rule which will allow us to build recursive programs. (Of course, further induction rules exist in Whelk but we do not need them for the example given here.)

$$induction \ \frac{\begin{array}{c} [\![\Gamma, x{:}list(\tau), \Delta \vdash A \langle [\,]/x \rangle]\!]_{P'(\mathcal{E}) \leftrightarrow \phi} \\ [\![\Gamma, x{:}list(\tau), \Delta, v_0{:}\tau, v_1{:}list(\tau), [\![A \langle v_1/x \rangle]\!]_{P'(\mathcal{E}')} \vdash A \langle [v_0|v_1]/x \rangle]\!]_{P'(\mathcal{E}) \leftrightarrow \psi} \end{array}}{[\![\Gamma, x{:}list(\tau), \Delta \vdash A]\!]_{P(\mathcal{E}) \leftrightarrow P'(\mathcal{E})}}$$

$\mathcal{E}'$ is the environment at the time of application of the rule, and P' is defined by

$$P'(\mathcal{E}') \leftrightarrow x =_{list(\tau)} [\,] \wedge \phi \vee \exists v_0{:}\tau.\exists v_1{:}\tau.x =_{list(\tau)} [v_0|v_1] \wedge \psi$$

Note that the program fragment associated with the induction hypothesis is a call to a procedure, as opposed to a procedure definition, such as are associated with sequents. This is always the case for hypotheses.

3.4.12 Substitution

We have two substitution rules, one under logical equivalence, which must be justified, and one for rewrites manipulating only the connectives in $\mathcal{L}_S$.

$$ sub \ \frac{\Gamma \vdash [\![B \leftrightarrow C]\!]_{P(\mathcal{E}) \mapsto \psi} \quad \Gamma \vdash [\![A\langle C/B\rangle]\!]_{P(\mathcal{E}) \mapsto \psi \wedge \phi}}{\Gamma \vdash [\![A]\!]_{P(\mathcal{E}) \mapsto \phi}} \qquad rewrite \ \frac{\Gamma \vdash [\![E]\!]_{P(\mathcal{E}) \mapsto \phi}}{\Gamma \vdash [\![D]\!]_{P(\mathcal{E}) \mapsto \phi}} $$

where $D \leftrightarrow E$, this being determined by the proof system.

In the *sub* rule, the contribution of ψ is to connect any variables instantiated in
the proof of the substituted goal with those in the original.

3.4.13 New Hypotheses

$$ lemma \ \frac{[\![\Gamma, [\![B]\!]_{P'(nil)} \vdash A]\!]_{P(\mathcal{E}) \mapsto \phi}}{[\![\Gamma \vdash A]\!]_{P(\mathcal{E}) \mapsto \phi}} $$

where P' is the program synthesised by the proof of the lemma, B.

3.5 Generating "Real" Logic Programs

Given the rules of Section 3.2, we can now perform a proof of the specification
conjecture specified in 4.1. On completion of this proof, we will have a program
which embodies the algorithm which we showed to exist during the proof process.

However, this program is a pure logic program, and not a program in a generally
accessible programming language. Fortunately, transforming pure logic programs
into Prolog and Gödel programs is easy, except for the issues of floundering and
infinite looping mentioned below. A little trivial partial evaluation quickly removes
all the failed branches of our program. Because our logic was constructive, we do
not have disjunctive heads, so we immediately generate Horn Clauses.

For the rest of this paper, I shall focus on the Gödel language [13], because it
gives us some features which are preferable, here, to those of Prolog. In particular,
Gödel allows arbitrary formulæ in the bodies of its clauses, so there is no further work
involved in unpacking the bodies of our pure logic programs. Much more importantly, Gödel admits explicit **DELAY** declarations (as found in NuProlog), which we
can use to prevent floundering and infinite looping in our synthesised programs. [21]
explains how the inductive structure of the synthesis proof encodes the information
we need to generate these declarations without further analysis.

3.6 Correctness

3.6.1 Introduction

There is not space here to give the full correctness proof for this system. I will,
however, sketch a proof for a few rules which will show how the proof is done.
Correctness of the sequent calculus is presented in terms of an existing Gentzen
Sequent Calculus, assumed correct *a priori*. Correctness of the synthesised programs
with respect to the specifications is shown in terms of the required behaviour specified
in Section 3.3. A full proof of the correctness of Whelk will be given elsewhere.

3.6.2 Correctness of the proof system

I start from $LJ_{\tau, =}$, a constructive logic based on LJ [11] with the addition of equality
and sorts in the obvious way. Connectives have their usual constructive meanings.

Theorem 3.1 (Correctness of Whelk Verification Logic) $V \vdash \phi$ *iff* $LJ_{\tau, =} \vdash \phi$
where V *is the subset of* Whelk *rules not mentioning* ∂ *and* ϕ *does not mention* ∂ .

Proof 3.1 V is identical with $LJ_{\tau, =}$ by definition. □

Theorem 3.2 (Correctness of Synthesis Logic) *The rules of* Whelk *including* ∂ *are correct with respect to the interpretation of* ∂ *given in Section 2.2.*

Proof 3.2 By definition, ⊢ ∂ A iff ⊢ A ∨ ¬A. Rewrite any Whelk rule under this equivalence. The resulting rule is necessarily derivable from the rules of LJ$_{\tau,=}$. □

Theorem 3.3 (Correctness of induction rule) *The induction rule for finite lists preserves correctness with respect to the interpretation of* ∂ *given in Section 2.2.*

Proof 3.3 In the usual way. □

Theorem 3.4 (Correctness of Whelk Logic) *The rules of* Whelk *are correct with respect to the usual constructive interpretations of the standard connectives, and to that given for* ∂ *in Section 2.2.*

Proof 3.4 From Proofs 3.1, 3.2, and 3.3. □

3.7 Correctness of the synthesis system

Theorem 3.5 (Correctness of the synthesis system) *If* $P(\overline{a})$ *is a program synthesised by* Whelk *proof of a specification conjecture*

$$\vdash \forall \overline{a}. \partial\, S(\overline{a})$$

then

$$\vdash \forall \overline{a}^*. S(\overline{a})^* \leftrightarrow P(\overline{a})$$

Proof 3.5 By induction on the structure of proofs, building on base cases of the ∂ introduction rules, each construction rule being proven correct individually.

Base Case 1:
Consider

$$\partial_{true}\ intro\ \frac{[\![\Gamma \vdash A]\!]_{P(\varepsilon) \leftrightarrow \phi}}{[\![\Gamma \vdash A]\!]_{P(nil) \leftrightarrow true}} \qquad \partial_{false}\ intro\ \frac{[\![\Gamma \vdash \neg A]\!]_{P(\varepsilon) \leftrightarrow \phi}}{[\![\Gamma \vdash \partial A]\!]_{P(nil) \leftrightarrow false}}$$

Given a specification (sub)conjecture

$$\Gamma \vdash \partial\, S$$

suppose that $\Gamma \vdash S$. Then application of ∂_{true} introduction yields subconjecture

$$\Gamma \vdash S$$

which can be shown in LJ$_{\tau,=}$. The corresponding program is defined as a proposition

$$P \leftrightarrow true$$

Therefore, ⊢ S is true and $P \leftrightarrow true$, so ⊢ $S^* \leftrightarrow P$. □

Base Case 2:
Alternatively, given a specification (sub)conjecture

$$\Gamma \vdash \partial\, S$$

such that $\Gamma \vdash \neg S$, application of ∂_{false} introduction yields subconjecture

$$\Gamma \vdash \neg S$$

which can be shown in LJ. The corresponding program is a proposition:

$$P \leftrightarrow false$$

Therefore, ⊢ S is false and $P \leftrightarrow false$, so ⊢ $S^* \leftrightarrow P$. □

Step Case

Consider $\wedge$ introduction under ∂ :

$$\wedge\ intro\ \frac{[\![\Gamma \vdash \partial A]\!]_{P(\mathcal{E}) \leftrightarrow \phi} \quad [\![\Gamma \vdash \partial B]\!]_{P(\mathcal{E}) \leftrightarrow \psi}}{[\![\Gamma \vdash \partial (A \wedge B)]\!]_{P(\mathcal{E}) \leftrightarrow \phi \wedge \psi}}$$

Suppose we have a synthesised (sub)program

$$P \leftrightarrow \phi \wedge \psi$$

from a specification conjecture

$$\Gamma \vdash \partial (A \wedge B)$$

Then the required behaviour is

$$\Gamma^* \vdash (A \wedge B)^* \leftrightarrow P$$

which is equivalent to

$$\Gamma^* \vdash (A \wedge B)^* \leftrightarrow \phi \wedge \psi$$

It is known that

$$\Gamma^* \vdash A^* \leftrightarrow \phi$$

and

$$\Gamma^* \vdash B^* \leftrightarrow \psi$$

Therefore,

$$\Gamma^* \vdash (A^* \leftrightarrow \phi) \wedge (B^* \leftrightarrow \psi)$$

Therefore (recall that the meaning of connectives is preserved under *) it is not hard to show that

$$\Gamma^* \vdash (A \wedge B)^* \leftrightarrow \phi \wedge \psi$$

The correctness of the other construction rules is proven in the same way. $\square$

4 Example: subset/2

4.1 A Simple Synthesis Conjecture

For the purposes of example here, I will use a conjecture which specifies the **subset/2** predicate using lists as a representation for sets — that is, the predicate which succeeds when all the members of the list given as its first argument are members of that given as its second. The specification in $\mathcal{W}helk$ looks like this:

$$\vdash \forall x{:}list(nat).\forall y{:}list(nat).\partial\,(\forall z{:}nat.z \in x \to z \in y)$$

where : denotes type membership, $\forall$ and $\exists$ denote the usual quantification over types, $\to$ denotes the usual implication, and $\in$ is defined by the following lemmas (which are equivalent to the completion of the familiar **member/2** predicate). Lists are denoted with the Prolog/Gödel notation.

$$\vdash \forall x{:}nat.\neg x \in [\,] \tag{1}$$

$$\vdash \forall x{:}nat.\forall h{:}nat.\forall t{:}list(nat).x \in [h|t] \leftrightarrow x = h \vee x \in t \tag{2}$$

We will also use an axiom about the decidability of equality in the natural numbers:

$$\vdash \forall x{:}nat.\forall y{:}nat.x = y \vee \neg x = y \tag{3}$$

The proof proceeds by primitive induction on lists, first on x and then on y. Note, though, that there is no reason in principle why more powerful forms of induction should not be used. For example, insertion sort and quicksort may be derived from the same specification, the former by primitive induction, the latter by course-of-values or transfinite induction [18].

Necessarily, I have skipped some steps in this proof, because the proof is far too long to present in full here. However, I have tried to focus on the points which are most relevant to the synthesis issues discussed in this paper. Note, in particular, that the proof is presented in refinement style, with the rules being applied "backwards", and that I have omitted unchanging hypotheses unless they are used in the current proof step. The finished program, after conversion to Gödel, looks like this:

```
MODULE Subset.
IMPORT Lists.
IMPORT Numbers.

PREDICATE Subset :  List( Number ) * List( Number ).
Subset(y,z) <- Subset_b(y,z).

PREDICATE Subset_b :  List( Number ) * List( Number ) * Number * Number.
Subset_b(y,z) <-
    (y = [] \/
     SOME [v1] SOME [v0] ( y=[v0|v1] &
                           SOME [x] (x=v0 -> Subset_dy(z,x)) &
                           Subset_b(v1,z)))).

PREDICATE Subset_dy :  List( Number ) * Number.
Subset_dy(z,x) <-
    SOME [v3] SOME [v2] (z=[v2|v3] &
                         (x=v2 \/ Subset_dy(v3,x))).
```

4.2 The Proof

We start with:

$$\vdash \forall x{:}\mathrm{list}(nat).\forall y{:}\mathrm{list}(nat).\partial\,(\forall z{:}nat.z \in x \to z \in y)$$

First, we introduce x, and apply primitive induction on lists. This gives us two subgoals (note the program fragment attached to the induction hypothesis in the step case — I use σ to denote the name of the synthesised predicate).

Base Case:

$$x{:}\mathrm{list}(nat)$$
$$\vdash \forall y{:}\mathrm{list}(nat).\partial\,(\forall z{:}nat.z \in [] \to z \in y)$$

Step Case:

$$x{:}\mathrm{list}(nat)$$
$$v_0{:}nat$$
$$v_1{:}\mathrm{list}(nat)$$
$$[\![\forall y{:}\mathrm{list}(nat).\partial\,(\forall z{:}nat.z \in v_1 \to z \in y)]\!]_{\sigma'((x{:}\mathrm{list}(nat)).nil)}$$
$$\vdash \forall y{:}\mathrm{list}(nat).\partial\,(\forall z{:}nat.z \in [v_0|v_1] \to z \in y)$$

At this stage, the synthesised program looks like this:

$$\sigma((x{:}list(nat)).\eta) \quad \leftrightarrow \quad \sigma'((x{:}list(nat)).\eta)$$
$$\sigma'((x{:}list(nat)).\eta]) \quad \leftrightarrow \quad (x = [] \wedge \phi) \vee$$
$$\exists v_0{:}nat.\exists v_1{:}list(nat).x = [v_0|v_1] \wedge \psi$$

where η, ϕ and ψ are uninstantiated meta-variables. Comparing this with the Gödel definitions of `Subset/2` and `Subset_b/3` in Section 4.1 will yield a clearer understanding of which parts of the proof give rise to which program fragments.

I will now follow through the base case of the proof. We proceed by introducing the remaining universal quantifiers, and then by ∂_{true} introduction:

$$y{:}list(nat)$$
$$z{:}nat$$
$$\vdash z \in [] \rightarrow z \in y$$

The synthesised program now looks like this:

$$\sigma((x{:}list(nat)).(y{:}list(nat)).nil) \quad \leftrightarrow \quad \sigma'((x{:}list(nat)).(y{:}list(nat)).nil)$$
$$\sigma'((x{:}list(nat)).(y{:}list(nat)).nil) \quad \leftrightarrow \quad (x = [] \wedge true) \vee$$
$$\exists v_0{:}nat.\exists v_1{:}list(nat).x = [v_0|v_1] \wedge \psi$$

and we are left with a verification conjecture in standard $LJ_{=,\tau}$ which is trivially proven using definition (1).

The step case is harder. First, use the *sub* $\leftrightarrow$ rule to unfold the specification according to definition (2). Then introduce the universal quantifier of y and rewrite under propositional equivalence to get:

$$y{:}list(nat)$$
$$\vdash \partial\,(\forall z{:}nat.(z = v_0 \rightarrow z \in y) \wedge \forall z{:}nat.(z \in v_1 \rightarrow z \in y))$$

The rewriting can be performed automatically, via the *rippling* paradigm of [3, 8]. The only step so far in the step case affecting the synthesised program is the $\forall$ introduction: rewrites maintain logical equivalence, and so do not change the program.

Next, we introduce $\wedge$ under ∂ to give two subconjectures:

$$\vdash \partial\,(\forall z{:}nat.z = v_0 \rightarrow z \in y) \tag{4}$$
$$\vdash \partial\,(\forall z{:}nat.z \in v_1 \rightarrow z \in y) \tag{5}$$

The proof of (4) runs as follows. After introducing $\forall$ and $\rightarrow$, we use axiom (3) to decide on the equality of z with v_0, which leaves us with the program

$$\sigma(x{:}list(nat).y{:}list(nat).nil) \leftrightarrow \sigma'(x{:}list(nat).y{:}list(nat).nil)$$
$$\sigma'(x{:}list(nat).y{:}list(nat).nil) \leftrightarrow x = [] \wedge true \vee$$
$$\exists v_0{:}nat.\exists v_1{:}list(nat).x = [v_0|v_1] \wedge$$
$$((x = v_0 \wedge true \vee \neg x = v_0 \wedge false) \rightarrow \phi) \wedge \psi$$

where ϕ and ψ correspond with the right hand branches from the $\rightarrow$ and $\wedge$ introductions, above, respectively.

The sequent corresponding with ϕ is

$$x = v_0$$
$$\vdash \partial z \in y$$

This is proven by induction, using the definition of $\in$. It yields the `member/2` predicate (`Subset_dy/2` in Section 4.1).

Finally, (5) leads to introduction of the program fragment associated with the induction hypothesis, as follows. Recall that the goal is:

$$\llbracket \forall y{:}list(nat).\partial\,(\forall z{:}nat.z \in \nu_1 \to z \in y)\rrbracket_{\sigma'((x:list(nat)).nil)}$$
$$y{:}list(nat)$$
$$\vdash \partial\,(\forall z{:}nat.z \in \nu_1 \to z \in y)$$

We eliminate y on the induction hypothesis to yield the sequent:

$$\llbracket \forall y{:}list(nat).\partial\,(\forall z{:}nat.z \in \nu_1 \to z \in y)\rrbracket_{\sigma'((x:list(nat)).nil)}$$
$$y{:}list(nat)$$
$$\llbracket \partial\,(\forall z{:}nat.z \in \nu_1 \to z \in y)\rrbracket_{\sigma'((x:list(nat)).(y:list(nat)).nil)}$$
$$\vdash \partial\,(\forall z{:}nat.z \in \nu_1 \to z \in y)$$

The proof in then completed by application of the axiom rule.

We now have the following pure logic program:

$$\sigma(x{:}list(nat).y{:}list(nat).nil) \leftrightarrow \sigma'(x{:}list(nat).y{:}list(nat).nil)$$
$$\sigma'(x{:}list(nat).y{:}list(nat).nil) \leftrightarrow$$
$$\quad x = [\,] \wedge true \vee$$
$$\quad \exists \nu_0{:}nat.\exists \nu_1{:}list(nat).x = [\nu_0|\nu_1] \wedge$$
$$\qquad\qquad ((x = \nu_0 \wedge true \vee \neg x = \nu_0 \wedge false) \to$$
$$\qquad\qquad\qquad\qquad\qquad \sigma''(y{:}list(nat).x{:}nat.nil) \wedge$$
$$\qquad\qquad\quad \sigma'(\nu_1{:}list(nat).y{:}list(nat).nil)$$
$$\sigma''(y{:}list(nat).x{:}nat.nil) \leftrightarrow$$
$$\quad y = [\,] \wedge false \vee$$
$$\quad \exists \nu_2{:}nat.\exists \nu_3{:}list(nat).y = [\nu_2|\nu_3] \wedge$$
$$\qquad\qquad ((x = \nu2 \wedge true \vee \neg x = \nu2 \wedge false) \vee$$
$$\qquad\qquad\quad \sigma''(\nu_3{:}list(nat).x{:}nat.nil)$$

This then translates, trivially, into the Gödel program of Section 4.1.

5   Conclusion and Future Work

In this paper, I have demonstrated the theory behind the Whelk program synthesis and transformation system. I have outlined a proof of correctness for the system, and I have show how it can be used to develop a simple program.

The implications of this are as follows. We now have a proof system which will allow us to synthesise programs from logic specifications. Because the proof system and associated synthesis system is known to be correct, programs synthesised by it are also correct (with respect to the specification!) *a priori*. The approach improves over similar existing approaches (*eg* [10]) because it generates true logic programs with non-determinism, rather than only functional predicates.

Because there is strong connection between the steps taken in a proof (in particular between the choice of induction scheme and the resulting algorithm), we can exercise considerable control over the program we eventually obtain. Thus, we are in a position to use proof steps which we know will lead to efficient programs. This, however, is subject to certain controls in the object-level logic to ensure that *good* programs are produced — one of which requires, for example, that negation be partially evaluated as far as possible in the synthesised program, thus reducing (or usually removing) the problem of floundering [21]. In similar vein, DELAY declarations can be generated easily and automatically, using the inductive structure of the proof.

Subject to these desirable restrictions, the close connection between the proof rules and those for construction means that we can in principle implement other techniques in our system. For example, one technique which has already been reconstructed in this framework is that of Compiling Control [2]. Another likely candidate for reconstruction is the block fold/unfolding work of [19]. A noteworthy point is that Whelk will provide a platform on which these techniques and others may not merely by developed and tested, but also combined in new and useful ways.

The next task required is to finish the implementation of the system and thence to being able to use the CℓAM proof planner to generate programs automatically. This will require the construction of new meta-level encodings of proof strategies for producing not only proofs, but proofs which correspond with *efficient* programs, as in [12]. It is known that the *rippling* paradigm [5] can usually reduce the search tree for a proof to a linear path; the search heuristics are not, however, motivated towards program synthesis, and will usually produce the shortest proof, rather than the one corresponding with the most efficient program. This, then, will be the main focus of the forthcoming work with Whelk.

6   Acknowledgements

This work was carried out as part of ESPRIT Basic Research Action #3012 ("Computational Logic"). I am grateful to my colleagues in that project (especially Danny De Schreye, Jonathan Lever, and Torbjörn Åhs) and to my colleagues in the DREAM group, in particular Alan Smaill and Alan Bundy, for their continuing interest in and support of my work. Thanks also to John Lloyd for help with Gödel.

References

[1] Joseph L. Bates and Robert L. Constable. Proofs as programs. *ACM Transactions on Programming Languages and Systems*, 7(1):113–136, January 1985.

[2] M. Bruynooghe, D. De Schreye, and B. Krekels. Compiling control. *Journal of Logic Programming*, pages 135–162, 1989.

[3] A. Bundy, A. Smaill, and J. Hesketh. Turning eureka steps into calculations in automatic program synthesis. In S.L.H. Clarke, ed., *Proceedings of UK IT 90*, pages 221–6, 1990. Also available from Edinburgh as DAI Research Paper 448.

[4] A. Bundy, A. Smaill, and G. A. Wiggins. The synthesis of logic programs from inductive proofs. In J. Lloyd, editor, *Computational Logic*, pages 135–149. Springer-Verlag, 1990. Esprit Basic Research Series. Also available from Edinburgh as DAI Research Paper 501.

[5] A. Bundy, A. Stevens, F. van Harmelen, A. Ireland, and A. Smaill. Rippling: A heuristic for guiding inductive proofs. Research Paper 567, Dept. of Artificial Intelligence, Edinburgh, 1991. To appear in Artificial Intelligence.

[6] A. Bundy, F. van Harmelen, J. Hesketh, and A. Smaill. Experiments with proof plans for induction. *Journal of Automated Reasoning*, 7:303–324, 1991. Earlier version available from Edinburgh as DAI Research Paper No 413.

[7] A. Bundy, F. van Harmelen, C. Horn, and A. Smaill. The Oyster-Clam system. In M.E. Stickel, editor, *10th International Conference on Automated Deduction*, pages 647–648. Springer-Verlag, 1990. Lecture Notes in Artificial Intelligence No. 449. Also available from Edinburgh as DAI Research Paper 507.

[8] A. Bundy, F. van Harmelen, A. Smaill, and A. Ireland. Extensions to the rippling-out tactic for guiding inductive proofs. In M.E. Stickel, editor, *10th International Conference on Automated Deduction*, pages 132–146. Springer-Verlag, 1990. Lecture Notes in Artificial Intelligence No. 449. Also available from Edinburgh as DAI Research Paper 459.

[9] R.L. Constable. Programs as proofs. Technical Report TR 82-532, Dept. of Computer Science, Cornell University, November 1982.

[10] L. Fribourg. Extracting logic programs from proofs that use extended Prolog execution and induction. In *Proceedings of Eighth International Conference on Logic Programming*, pages 685 – 699. MIT Press, June 1990.

[11] G. Gentzen. *The Collected Papers of Gerhard Gentzen*. North Holland, 1969. edited by Szabo, M.E.

[12] J.T. Hesketh. *Using Middle-Out Reasoning to Guide Inductive Theorem Proving*. PhD thesis, University of Edinburgh, 1991.

[13] P. Hill and J. Lloyd. The Gödel Report. Technical Report TR-91-02, Department of Computer Science, University of Bristol, March 1991. Revised in September 1991.

[14] W.A. Howard. The formulae-as-types notion of construction. In J.P. Seldin and J.R. Hindley, editors, *To H.B. Curry; Essays on Combinatory Logic, Lambda Calculus and Formalism*, pages 479–490. Academic Press, 1980.

[15] R. Kowalski. Algorithm = Logic +Control. *Comm. ACM*, 22:424–436, 1979.

[16] Per Martin-Löf. Constructive mathematics and computer programming. In *6th International Congress for Logic, Methodology and Philosophy of Science*, pages 153–175, Hanover, August 1979. North Holland, Amsterdam. 1982.

[17] Per Martin-Löf. *Intuitionistic Type Theory*. Bibliopolis, Naples, 1984. Notes by Giovanni Sambin of a series of lectures given in Padua, June 1980.

[18] C. Phillips. Well-founded induction and program synthesis using proof plans. Research Paper 559, Dept. of Artificial Intelligence, Edinburgh, November 1991.

[19] M. Proietti and A. Pettorossi. Construction of efficient logic programs by loop absorption and generalization. In *Proceedings of Second International Workshop on Meta-Programming in Logic*, April 1990.

[20] G. A. Wiggins. The improvement of prolog program efficiency by compiling control: A proof-theoretic view. In *Proceedings of the Second International Workshop on Meta-programming in Logic*, Leuven, Belgium, April 1990. Also available from Edinburgh as DAI Research Paper No. 455.

[21] G. A. Wiggins. Negation and control in automatically generated logic programs. In A. Pettorossi, editor, *Proceedings of META-92*, 1992.

[22] G. A. Wiggins, A. Bundy, H. C. Kraan, and J. Hesketh. Synthesis and transformation of logic programs through constructive, inductive proof. In K-K. Lau and T. Clement, editors, *Proceedings of LoPSTr-91*, pages 27–45. Springer Verlag, 1991. Workshops in Computing Series.

Implementation I

An Incremental Garbage Collector for WAM-Based Prolog

William J. Older
John A. Rummell
Computing Research Laboratory
Bell-Northern Research
P.O. Box 3511, Station C
Ottawa, Ontario, K1Y 4H7, CANADA
rummell@bnr.ca

Abstract

This paper describes the incremental compacting garbage collector developed for the WAM implementation of BNR Prolog. It exploits the specific structure of the WAM memory management architecture to localize and then simplify the garbage collection problem. It uses a fast one-pass collection algorithm, linear in the amount of recovered heap data and independent of the total heap size, which requires neither reserved bits in basic cells nor any additional reserved storage. We have observed nearly complete garbage elimination with time penalties of a few percent.

1   Introduction

Most garbage collectors for WAM-based implementations of Prolog are global (see [2], [4], and [5]). But because of their size and complexity, global garbage collections can be very expensive, and it is usual to postpone them until memory exhaustion is imminent. Thus in practice, the goal of global collection strategies is to avoid memory overflow. Conversely, the avoidance of memory overflow tends to lead to a global strategy which can collect the maximum amount of free space. Ironically, the need to do massive garbage collections when available memory is low leads to more complex algorithms, which generally increases the cost of collection, thus reinforcing the need for postponement, and so on. To break out of this circle of mutually reinforcing factors becomes difficult.

In this paper we describe a garbage collection algorithm for a WAM-based Prolog that achieves efficiency by taking advantage of detailed prior knowledge of the computing environment and the ability to alter that environment when necessary. The strategy pursued here, partly motivated by the desire to improve locality in virtual memory systems, is to significantly reduce the total memory requirements at the cost of (at most) a small, evenly distributed, time penalty. This requires that garbage collection be very fast, and hence presumably implies frequent collections over small regions, preferably using a simple algorithm. The design issues then focus on *which* regions to collect, and *when* to collect them, to best achieve the necessary performance. This leads us to exploit the relevant structural properties of the system, and even to modify them if necessary.

In section 2 we review some relevant facts about WAM memory management. Section 3 focuses on the mechanism by which garbage is created, which leads to a strategy for incremental garbage collection described in section 4. Section 5 outlines the actual collection algorithm, which is treated in more detail in the appendix. In section 6 we look at compiler modifications to aid garbage collection in some important special cases. Section 7 discusses performance evaluation.

2 WAM Memory Architecture

The memory management of the Warren Abstract Machine architecture ([1], [7]) for Prolog implementations can be described conceptually in terms of four stacks, as seen in figure 1. (Originally the C and E stacks were combined into one for implementation reasons, but they are conceptually distinct.) The environment stack E and the heap H correspond directly with the stack of procedure activation records (environments) and the heap of a conventional language such as Pascal, except the Prolog "heap" allocates as a stack. Local variables, i.e., those which do not need to survive beyond the end of the procedure call, are allocated on E; everything else is allocated on H. Variables in E can point into H, but objects in H never reference E. Pointers in E always point from newer to older, so a stack discipline can be used to manage E.

For Prolog an additional stack, the choicepoint stack C, holds choicepoints that permit backtracking. Each choicepoint holds information required to return the computation to the state just before a non-deterministic call: the current (caller's) environment, the end of E and the end of H ("critical" addresses), and the values of the arguments to the current call and other control registers. No changes are permitted in E or H above (i.e., earlier) the points remembered in the last choicepoint (LCP), unless a record of the modification is recorded on the trail stack T. The current end of the trail is also recorded in each choicepoint. This "no changes" requirement constrains the stack discipline in E significantly, since environments cannot be popped if they can be accessed directly or indirectly from a choicepoint.

Whenever a failure occurs in the current computation, i.e., an inconsistency is detected, the state is restored to that recorded in LCP by resetting E and H and using the relevant portion of the trail to undo any other modifications to the remaining part of E and H. The computation then proceeds from the restored state using an alternative choice. The cut "!" operation resets the LCP register to its state *before* the call to the currently executing procedure body, thus removing all choicepoints created since the start of this

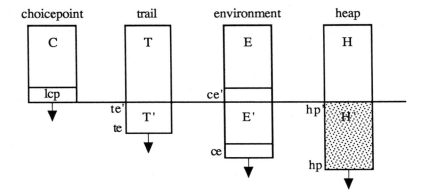

Figure 1: WAM Memory Architecture

call. Whenever choicepoints are removed by cuts, the trail is trimmed by removing any items on it which refer to locations in E or H which are now earlier than the new critical values.

The WAM architecture includes several practices designed to minimize the size of E, in addition to the basic stack discipline. One is environment trimming, which deletes variables from an environment after their last use whenever possible. Another is last call optimization (LCO), which releases an environment before the last call in the corresponding procedure body. Also, whenever environments on the E stack are made inaccessible by a cut, the next call will begin reusing the freed space. For this reason we are not concerned here with garbage collecting E, but only with H.

Several features of all Prolog implementations greatly simplify garbage collection: pointers are under complete system control, cells are already tagged, and memory is systematically organized. But garbage collectors for WAM-based Prologs require that the heap be compacted and have the additional constraint that reordering of cells is not allowed across choicepoint boundaries. These restrictions severely limit the number of feasible algorithms. Weemeeuw and Demoen [8] suggest that this is one reason why Prolog implementations (such as the ones described in [2]) favour the Morris collector, which preserves the cell order.

3 Garbage Creation

Items constructed on the heap are initially referenced by either temporary variables or local environment variables; subsequent instructions may cause these references to spread into other environment variables or heap variables. Since a variable is never unbound, garbage can only be created by the *disappearance* of a variable. For heap variables this only occurs during backtracking, and is therefore managed by the choicepoint mechanism. Temporary variables only hold values for very short periods, such as constructing temporary structures needed to make a call, and these structures often become garbage almost immediately after the call is made. Heap structures referenced by local variables in the E stack (e.g., intermediate results) may become inaccessible when those variables disappear. This happens when an environment is popped or when an environment is "trimmed", i.e., shortened by the removal of variables which are no longer needed. Finally, a cut which eliminates choicepoints, thus making some environments inaccessible, can also implicitly create garbage.

The crucial observation is that *when these operations create garbage on the heap, that garbage is always in the tip region H' past the critical point remembered in the LCP.* Temporary structures used to hold call arguments must be retained if, and only if, that call has left a choicepoint, since backtracking would need to restore those arguments. Environments need to be retained whenever they are accessible from choicepoints, so only environments created since the last choicepoint can actually be discarded. Environment trimming is also only permitted when the environment is more recent than the LCP, and this is enforced by the elegant allocation mechanism in the WAM design. Finally, whenever garbage is created by a cut, that garbage will be in the (post cut) heap tip region.

Even though garbage is only ever created at the tip of the heap, if not discarded immediately, it soon becomes buried by new data and new choicepoints. However, this indicates that if one can do a small garbage collection over the tip of the heap sufficiently often, it will eliminate garbage *before* it becomes buried. This idea is explored in the next section.

4   Incremental Garbage Collection

The principle difficulty with garbage collecting a small region in a large system is finding all the possible external references into the region. The basic idea that we will develop here is that *if the system can choose exactly when to do garbage collections, then the number of external references can be limited to a small list of known locations.* Specifically, the standard WAM choicepoint/trail mechanisms can provide all external references at no additional cost, as was noted in [2].

Let LCP be the last existing choicepoint created. Recall that LCP holds the heap register (hp'), current (caller) environment pointer (ce'), and end of trail (te') from the time of its creation. If we focus on the tip region H' of the heap (between hp' and the current hp), we notice that:

- There are no choicepoints accessing H'.

- Accessible environments possibly accessing H' are the current one (ce) and those environments accessible from ce but after ce'.

- All other permanent variables in E or heap variables outside H' (i.e., before hp' and ce') which can possibly access H' are on the trail between te' and te.

The last point is the crucial one, and very specific to Prolog. The general argument for it is:

> variables are the only things that can change and reference a heap structure,
>
> variables created before LCP could not have referenced items in H' before H' existed,
>
> hence old variables which reference into H' must have been bound since LCP was created,
>
> either they are on the trail as indicated or they are not,
>
> if they are not, then backtracking to LCP would fail to reset a variable that should be reset, which would imply an incorrect implementation,
>
> therefore, a correct implementation implies they are all on the trail.

It follows that a partial garbage collection over H' need only traverse

1. the environments from ce to ce' (via the return linkage);

2. the trail from te to te';

3. any temporary variables in current use.

This suggests an answer to the question of *where* local collections should be done. However, this conclusion has an exception: certain WAM instructions, such as `unify_variable(Yn)` (in write mode) *assign* environment variables to point into the heap, and, as an optimization, do *not* trail these bindings, even when the variable is before the critical address recorded in LCP. This causes no problems on backtracking precisely because the operation does not look at the value of the variable before overwriting it. This problem was noted in [2], where the response was to remove these optimizations. Another solution for this problem is to always include ce' in the list of environments to be scanned, since ce' is the only environment not already scanned in which this problem can occur, and then only on calls made later than the one that created LCP.

There are, however, several problems caused by the need to scan environments:

1. The worst problem is that environments may contain *uninitialized* variables, as one of the advantages of the WAM design is its ability to avoid having to initialize the variables in an environment. Usually these uninitialized cells contain leftovers from some earlier backtracking cycle, so they syntactically look like valid Prolog terms, and frequently

point into H'. Acting on them as if they were valid (and there is no conclusive way to detect all invalid terms) can cause fatal problems, e.g., if it results in the breakup of a necessarily contiguous structure. This problem was addressed in [2] by eliminating this optimization.

2. The mechanism of environment trimming operates by making environments variable length, with the current length specified only at calls. In particular, except at calls, the length of the current environment is unknown. An additional field in each environment could, of course, be used to hold the last known size between calls.

3. A one-pass algorithm (see next section) requires that every external reference is handled *exactly* once. Since a variable can only be bound at most once in any forward computation, trail entries are known *a priori* to be mutually distinct. Correctness implies that distinct environments do not overlap and therefore have distinct variables. Environments *after* ce' will not have any variables on a *trimmed* trail from te' to te, by definition of trimming, so these environments are disjoint from the trailed addresses. However, ce' may have variables which were also trailed after LCP's creation, and which will remain after trimming, so a mechanism for eliminating possible duplicates between the trail and ce' becomes necessary.

In view of these problems, we decided that it was preferable to limit the times at which garbage collection can occur - the "garbage collection opportunities" - to those in which the environment list needing scanning is empty. Note that this occurs only when returning from the call that created the last choice point. This is a partial answer to the question of *when* collections should be done.

To accomplish this, the `proceed` opcode was modified to do the garbage collection when it is returning from the specific call that created the LCP, and if other control conditions are met. (Note that while in most cases `dealloc` is followed immediately by `proceed`, it is possible, because of last call optimization, for the `proceed` to be in a different procedure entirely.) This choice implies that in the absence of "!", every computation that leaves at least one choice point will have had at least one opportunity to do garbage collection. Since this applies recursively, it suggests that there should be a sufficient number of opportunities, and that each opportunity is somewhat different, thus avoiding repeated collecting over the same data.

5 Garbage Collection Algorithm

We will now describe briefly a suitable collection strategy, and then return to the more important issue of when to execute it. A specific example, the algorithm for the WAM-based version of BNR Prolog, is given in the appendix. Since the collection algorithm may be executed many hundreds of times a second, it is important that it have very low overheads (e.g., no significant initialization costs), ideally depend linearly on the amount of *recovered* data, and be independent of the sizes of H' and H. Since the algorithm is not intended to run in conditions of critically low memory, the rest of the heap may be used for auxiliary storage.

The algorithm must of course preserve the logical structure of terms, but it need not preserve the physical structure. In particular, so far as WAM operations are concerned, the physical order of terms need not be maintained because there are no choicepoint boundaries in H'. However, reordering may cause the so-called "standard order" of variables to change without notice. The ordering of unbound variables is problematic anyway, since it has no logical foundation and is also context sensitive given that it depends on accidental and not essential properties of terms. It is also inconsistent with the WAM practice of globalizing permanent local variables on last calls. Implementations for which a *stable* standard variable order is required will need to use an order-preserving collection algorithm. Although this will make the costs linear in the size of H' rather than in the amount of recovered data, this may not make much practical difference since the average size of H' is in fact quite small.

If reordering is allowed, the most efficient algorithm appears to be of the one-pass recursive unfolding and copying variety, with a final shift of the "to-space" back over the "from-space." It requires as working store a small number of registers to hold various addresses, and a *contiguous* region of memory for a temporary stack area big enough to hold the recovered nongarbage from the collection region. The unused heap may be used for this if it is at least as big as H', since we will copy each referenced term exactly once.

This algorithm copies the accessible data out of H' to the stack area as it is encountered. At the same time references are updated to point to where the data will eventually be placed, rather than its temporary location in the stack area, so the data structure is not usable until a final phase which directly copies the stack area back over region H'. This algorithm thus assumes that each cell it examines is visited exactly once. (*What* the cells reference can, of course, be referenced many times.) During the garbage collection, region H' serves several purposes as it holds a mixture of unprocessed data structures and redirection pointers used for updating, and implicitly serves as a map for detecting areas already visited.

For each external cell (argument or trailed term) it is necessary to determine whether it is a referencing type, and if so, whether it references into the collection region H'. (Reference chains that go *through* the region can be eliminated because there are no trail items referencing into H'.) For each reference chain that terminates in H', we move the contiguous fragment being referenced (one or more cells) into the temporary stack area, and replace it with forwarding pointers into the stack area, and update the external cell to refer to the eventual destination. Note that there is no attempt here to "copy" a complete term - only individual contiguous fragments are being copied - and subterms are copied *blindly*. Hence this algorithm can be written as a pure iteration.

After all external references have been processed, the stack contains a sequence of contiguous fragments which may themselves contain references back into H'. The algorithm can then be applied (again iteratively) to each cell in the stack area, starting at the *oldest*. The stack area now becomes used as a queue that grows in front of the "read head" for the iterative algorithm as newly copied fragments are added at the end. Since every item is only ever copied once, the algorithm terminates in time proportional to the recovered data and the amount of stack needed is at most equal to the size of the collection region.

6   Refinements

We have described the mechanism of garbage collection and its preconditions, and a strategy for its use. It was found that in random samples of production code the garbage collection executed too infrequently. The principal culprit was cut "!" used at the end of a clause. For example, in

```
p :- q, r, s, !.
p :- ...
```

the return from p (i.e., the proceed opcode at the end of the first clause) would be an opportunity for garbage collection provided q, r, and s had left no choicepoints. However, the same "!" which ensures that they did not, also ensures that p does not either, so the opportunity is "lost", or, more appropriately, postponed since the caller of p now has a (bigger) opportunity. The gamble here is that some clause up the call tree will either do a more efficient garbage collection, or fail (and thus eliminate the need for one) before a new choice point gets created. Unfortunately, this gamble was lost more frequently than it was won.

A fix for this problem is fairly easy if one can alter the WAM opcode for "!" at end of clause so that if there is anything to cut, then the cut is done in two steps: the first cuts back to the choicepoint for this call if it exists, (i.e., up to, but not including, p in the above example), and the second removes the choicepoint for p. A garbage collection opportunity could then be taken between these two steps. This increases the number of opportunities significantly, but still leaves some important special cases.

Consider the typical tail-recursion optimization (TRO) of:

```
p([], ...).
p([X|Xs], ...) :- q(...), r(...), !, p(Xs, ...).
```

The use of "!" here is to ensure that q and r leave no choicepoints, so that tail-recursion optimization is in fact possible. Such procedures often run for a long time, perhaps indefinitely. However, since the second clause has no proceed there is no opportunity to garbage collect before the end, if there is an end. However, the clause logically returns to the caller's environment via the dealloc opcode just before the final call to p, so a garbage collection opportunity is possible so far as the environment restriction is concerned, but the last choicepoint is always (because of "!") one created before the call to p, and is thus unusable.

If, however, we were to write p (or transform it into)

```
p([], ...).
p([X|Xs], ...) :- q(...), r(...), !, p(Xs, ...).
p(...) :- fail.
```

then there would be an opportunity to garbage collect on each cycle of the tail recursion. Unfortunately, this is not a *cumulative* opportunity, and if we pass up one garbage collection opportunity (because the amount of heap involved is too small) the opportunity is lost forever. This example does suggest what is needed: a "virtual choicepoint" that is just at the boundary of the *first* call to p, in the sense that it is *after* the call to p with respect to the heap, but logically *before* the call to p so that "!" does not remove it, *as if* it were written:

```
p(...) :- p1(...).
p(...) :- fail.
p1([], ...).
p1([X|Xs], ...) :- q(...), r(...), !, p1(Xs, ...).
```

This would enable cumulative opportunities for garbage collection at each step of the recursion and again at the end, after which the extra choicepoint can disappear.

An efficient implementation requires modifying the WAM compiler. We chose to consider only clauses that have an environment, a final call subject to last call optimization, and a "!" immediately preceding the final call. In this case, the first modification is to change the alloc opcode in the clause head to a gc_alloc. The semantics of gc_alloc are the same as alloc, except that if the last choice point is not suitable for garbage collection of this call, then a new virtual choicepoint is created, and the cutback point (which is saved in the environment created by the gc_alloc) is set to point to it. This ensures that it will not be removed by the "!" later in the clause.

The second modification is first to transform the standard WAM sequence at the end of the clause:

```
... ecut ... <call constructors> ... dealloc exec
```

to

```
... <call constructors> ... dealloc dcut exec
```

(where `ecut` is "! from an environment" and `dcut` is "! from register"), since `ecut` commutes with the constructors and

```
ecut dealloc = dealloc dcut.
```

In the second step, to have easy access to the call arity, the `dealloc dcut exec` is combined into a new opcode, which also checks for the garbage collection opportunity.

Finally, the handling of `proceed` opcodes was altered to discard virtual choicepoints as their last action, regardless whether they chose to do a garbage collection or not. This keeps virtual choicepoints from inadvertently blocking other opportunities for garbage collection.

With these compiler changes, a tail recursion, such as p above, will result in a virtual choicepoint being created on the first call and a garbage collection opportunity will occur at the "!". Since the virtual choicepoint is not removed, the second invocation of p will not need to create one (so there is no added trailing overheads due to subsequent recursion), and the opportunity at the second invocation's "!" extends back to the time of the original call. In particular, structures created solely to make the call can be collected. Such recursions often pass some data forward for a few steps, but much past state information becomes inaccessible after a few iterations, and such structures then become collectible. Finally, at the end of the recursion there is an opportunity to collect everything not actually exported from the call.

This also applies to more complex mutual recursions, and in general to last call optimizations, provided that they are either inherently deterministic or contain a penultimate "!", as long as one of the clauses contains such a cut.

7   Evaluation

The usual trade-off between time and space appears here as a policy for deciding which garbage collection opportunities are worth taking. To explore this trade-off we initially kept the control as direct as possible by providing a single threshold parameter that can be used to adjust the frequency of garbage collection. When the value of this threshold is 0, garbage collection is inhibited; when its value is non-zero, garbage collection opportunities will be taken whenever the size (in bytes) of the heap tip is bigger than the threshold. Primitives were available to observe heap usage, the total number of garbage collections, and elapsed time.

The choice of benchmarks for evaluating garbage collection policies in Prolog is always problematic, since even small changes in coding style or cut placement can have a substantial impact on the amount of garbage and when it is created. Therefore, to serve as a realistic illustrative example we have chosen a large application program which synthesizes call processing code for a telephone switch given high level descriptions of initial and final feature states. This program is a mixture of various, but mostly deterministic, predicates rather than a single algorithm and was written before the development of the garbage collector and not modified in any way.

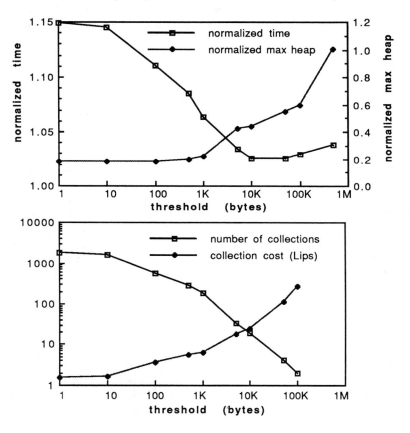

Figure 2: Incremental Garbage Collection Example

The upper graph in figure 2 shows several features that appear to be typical, based on the studies we have done to date. Normalized time and maximum space are relative to the control case with garbage collection disabled (threshold=0) but present. (We were unable to measure any performance difference between the system without garbage collection implemented and the control case.) On the left side of the graph, with garbage collection done at *every* opportunity, the maximum heap usage (i.e., the high water mark) is kept to a minimum (about 20%), but the time impact is heaviest, about 15%. On the right, as the threshold is set higher than 100Kbytes, the time impact is reduced to about 3%, but worst case heap consumption approaches the control case. In between, around a threshold of 1Kbyte, there is a narrow valley in which one gets most of the possible compression, with a time degradation of about 5%, while in the 10-100Kbytes range for the threshold one gets only about from 70% to 50% of the possible compression but a 2% penalty. Note that the optimal threshold setting for memory recovery (about 250 memory cells) is surprisingly small.

The lower graph shows the decline in the number of garbage collections as the threshold is increased, and the rise in the average cost per garbage collection. The latter is given in units of average logical inference times (for this program) and is nearly platform independent. The cost per garbage collection includes the overheads associated with virtual choicepoints, and these overhead costs are the dominant term as the number of collections becomes small.

Although this example appears typical of the code we have examined, the values of the maximum amount of compression and the time penalty for achieving it may vary for different specific algorithms. For example, highly non-deterministic predicates are usually incompressible since there is very little inaccessible data to discard; a low threshold can trigger many unprofitable garbage collections with a significant impact on time. Conversely, setting the threshold too high may result in little compaction, and the overhead caused by any virtual choicepoints is then wasted. For this reason we are currently looking at mechanisms for automatically adjusting the threshold to maintain the appropriate time and space trade-off.

8 Conclusion

This paper has described how the incremental compacting garbage collector developed for the WAM implementation of BNR Prolog exploits the WAM memory management architecture to localize garbage collection to the heap tip. It uses the existing trail mechanism to provide a convenient list of all external references, and by a careful choice of garbage collection points, minimizes the number of external references. The one-pass recovery algorithm is linear in the amount of recovered heap data and independent of the total heap size. Hundreds of garbage collections can be done per second without significant performance degradation. On realistic benchmarks we have observed nearly complete garbage elimination with little overhead.

Acknowledgements

The authors wish to thank Rick Workman and André Vellino of BNR, as well as the referees, for their suggestions and help.

Appendix: Garbage Collection Algorithm

The program given in this Appendix is a simplified version of the one developed for BNR Prolog, which requires about four pages of C. Two of the specific features of this language potentially make garbage collection more complicated: the support of cyclic terms and the use of contiguous structures (i.e., cdr coding, possibly with continuations) for representing both lists and structures. Since these continuations point to a location and refer implicitly to an indefinite number of adjacent following locations, they are interior pointers in the sense of [6]. The "end of structure" problem is handled by having all contiguous structures and lists terminated by either an end-of-seq mark or a continuation. Note that the arity of an indefinite structure is indefinite; the arity field in this case contains the physical length of the contiguous fragment and may be changed during garbage collection.

The collection region is denoted R. The description makes use of the following global variables:

bh - start of region R (hp', lowest address in R)
hp - end of region R (lowest address after R)
tsb - start of stack area (can equal hp)
tsp - top of stack (lowest unused address in stack area)
delta (= tsb - bh, used to compute final location)

A term will be considered to have two fields: tag and ptr. Generally C notation will be used: prefix * is for pointer dereferencing and postfix ++ is for incrementing. Note that a pointer p is in region R iff (p >= bh) and (p < hp).

```
void garbage_collection()
{  term  *x;
   tsp = tsb; /* empty stack at start */
   delta = tsb - bh; /* final translocation */
   foreach (arg in arglist) do
      rescue(address_of(arg));
   foreach (address on trail) do
      rescue(*addr);
   x = tsb;
   while  (x < tsp) do
      { rescue(x); x++ };
   copybytes(tsb, bh, (tsp-tsb));   /* copy  back over R */
   hp =  bh + (tsp - tsb); /* update heap pointer */
}
```

The key operation is rescue(a), where a is an address of a Prolog term. Overflow checking on the stack and the case entry for long constants have been omitted for clarity. Items salvaged from the heap are replaced by forwarding pointers into the stackarea, tagged as continuations.

```
/* uses globals: tsb, bh, hp, delta; modifies tsp */
void rescue(term *a)
{  term  t, *p, *start;
   int   count;
   while (a->tag == var) && (a->ptr in R) && (*a != *(a->ptr))
      do *a = *(a->ptr);          /* short circuit thru R */
   switch (a->tag) {
      integer, symbol: break;     /* nothing to do*/
      variable:
          if (a->ptr in region R)      /* must be self ref */
           { *tsp = *a;                 /* copy to stack */
             a->ptr->ptr = tsp;        /* make redirection */
             a ->ptr = tsp - delta; /* update ref */
             tsp++;
           }
          else if (a->ptr in stackarea)
           { a->ptr =  a->ptr - delta } /*redirect*/
          else  ;   /* nothing to do */
        break;
      list, structure, continuation: /* sequence of terms */
         if (a->tag == continuation) && (a->ptr in stackarea)
         { a->ptr = a->ptr - delta }  /*redirect*/
         else if (a->ptr->tag == continuation)
                  && (a->ptr->ptr in stackarea)
         { a->ptr = a->ptr->ptr - delta } /*redirect*/
         else if (a^.ptr in R)     /* list or structure */
          { start = tsp;            /* save for arity update */
           p = a->ptr; *tsp = *p; /*copy 1st item to stack */
           p->ptr = tsp; p->tag = continuation; /*redirect*/
           a->ptr = tsp - delta;  /*update external*/
           tsp++;                   /* advance write head */
           count = 0;
           repeat                 /* copy rest of  sequence */
              p++; t = *p;
                 p->ptr = tsp; p->tag = continuation;
                 *tsp = t;
                 tsp++; count++;
           until (t.tag == endseq) || (t.tag == continuation);
           if (a->tag == structure)
                 update_arity(start, count, t);
              };
          break;
      }   /* endcases */
}
```

383

References

[1] Ait-Kaci, Hassan. *Warren's Abstract Machine.* MIT Press, Cambridge, MA, 1991.

[2] Appleby, K., Carlsson, M., Haridi, S., Sahlin, D. Garbage Collection for Prolog Based on WAM. *Communications of the ACM*, Vol 31, No. 6, pp. 719-741, June, 1988.

[3] Barklund, J., Millroth, H. Garbage Cut for Garbage Collection of Iterative Prolog Programs. *Proceedings of the 1986 Symposium on Logic Programming*, pp. 276-283, September, 1986.

[4] Bruynooghe, M. The memory management of Prolog implementations. *Logic Programming.* eds. Tarnlund, S. A. and Clark, K. pp. 83-98, Academic Press, 1981.

[5] Bruynooghe, M. A Note on Garbage Collection in Prolog Interpreters. *Proceedings of the First International Logic Programming Conference*, September, 1982.

[6] Detlefs, David L. Concurrent, Atomic Garbage Collection. (Ph.D. Thesis) CMU-CS-90-177, Carnegie Mellon University, 1990.

[7] Warren, David H. D. An Abstract Prolog Instruction Set, *Technical Note 309*, SRI International, October, 1983.

[8] Weemeeuw, P., and Demoen, B. A la Recherche de la Memoire Perdue, or, Memory Compaction for Shared Multiprocessors. *Logic Programming:Proceedings of the 1990 North American Conference*, pp. 306-320, MIT Press, Cambridge, MA, 1990.

Improving Backward Execution in the Andorra Family of Languages

Salvador Abreu
Luís Moniz Pereira
CRIA Uninova and DCS, Universidade Nova de Lisboa
2825 Monte de Caparica, PORTUGAL
{spa,lmp}@fct.unl.pt

Philippe Codognet
INRIA-Rocquencourt
BP 105, 78153 Le Chesnay, FRANCE
Philippe.Codognet@inria.fr

Abstract

We present a new mechanism for improving the execution of non-deterministic concurrent logic languages, such as the Andorra family of languages. The basic idea is, upon failure and backtracking, to re-schedule continuation goals in order to first execute the goal that has failed. In this way, if the backtrack point is not pertinent to the failure, the original failing goal will fail again and this will immediately amount to further deeper backtracking. Such a heuristic will hence save useless deduction/backtracking work. We have implemented this scheme by modifying the Andorra Kernel Language prototype implementation developed at SICS (AKL/PS version 0.0), and evaluation results show that this backward execution strategy improves performance for a variety of benchmarks, giving speedups up to a factor two or three.

1 Introduction

Since the first research in the early 80's, the field of concurrent logic programming has raised a number of important issues about the way of executing logic programs and how to move away from the traditional, simple but rigid, search strategy of Prolog. On one hand, the depth-first left-to-right strategy of Prolog, due to its simple stack-based execution model, has led to tremendous advances in Prolog implementation technology which has been decisive for establishing logic programming as a mature declarative paradigm. But on the other hand, one sometimes prefers a more flexible control strategy, and a more adequate search strategy that reduces the overall number of inferences needed to solve the problem can make up for a slower inference speed. Moreover, a few implementations of concurrent languages now achieve raw speeds close to that of traditional Prolog systems, cf. [8, 14, 9].

Among all the concurrent logic languages, see [22] for a complete presentation and a detailed history of this programming paradigm, the Andorra family of languages is one of the most promising lines of research in this quest to tame parallelism and concurrency, as they try to encompass both Prolog and concurrent language programming styles and to take the best of both worlds. The *Andorra model* was proposed by D.H.D. Warren [25] in order to combine Or- and And-parallelism, and it has now bred a variety of idioms and extensions developed by different research groups, among which Andorra-I [6, 5] and the Andorra Kernel Language[11, 12]. The essential idea is to execute determinate goals first and concurrently, delaying the execution of non-determinate goals until no determinate goal can proceed. This was inspired by the design of the concurrent language P-Prolog[29] where synchronization between goals was based on the concept of determinacy of guard systems. However the roots of such a concept can be traced back further to the early developments of Prolog, as for instance in the *sidetracking* search procedure of [20] which favors the development of goals with the least alternatives. This is indeed but another instance of the "first-fail" heuristic often used in various fields of problem solving, that has for instance recently shown its usefulness in the area of Constraint Logic Programming [24].

An interesting aspect of the Andorra principle, is the ability to reduce the size of the computation when compared to standard Prolog, as early execution of determinate goals can amount to an *a priori* pruning of the search space. [5] shows that the reduction of the number of inferences of Andorra w.r.t. Prolog can attain one order of magnitude.

Although much work has been done to improve the forward execution in logic languages, as exemplified by the Andorra model, very little works deals with the improvement of the backward execution of programs. It is interesting, upon failure during the computation process, to take into account the information of this very failure to improve the search strategy. For instance, one can consider that the goal that has currently failed is likely to fail again after backtracking, if the backtrack point is not pertinent. This goal should thus be tried sooner after backtracking, as this could immediately amount to further deep backtracking if the backtrack point is not pertinent. In this way, the whole recomputation of the part of the proof between the backtracking point and the failing goal is avoided w.r.t. a standard (non-reordering) strategy. The point being that if this goal just failed, it is likely to be "problematic" and therefore it may fail again with the next bindings produced as a result of backtracking. In other words, *a failed goal is likely to fail again.* this can indeed be seen as yet another instance of the "first-fail" principle applied to backward execution.

Such a re-ordering of the continuation goals (goals that remain in the resolvent) upon backtracking, based only on the information of which is the current failing goal, can thus save much deduction/backtracking work. This simple idea has indeed been first proposed by Lee Naish for some years[19] as an example of heterogeneous SLD resolution. A related computation rule is presented, and it is argued that it is a form of intelligent backtracking. However, such a strategy is not well suited to the computational model of Prolog as implemented for example by stack-based architectures such as the famous Warren Abstract Machine (WAM) because a failing goal is immediately discarded, leaving no trace, and it is very hard if not impossible to relate it to its other occurrences, which will be tried anew after the last choice-point's goal has generated another solution. There is also no way to manipulate and keep part of the stacks to avoid recomputing independent parts of the proof. Also remark that Prolog's operational semantics requires a strict execution order which prevent such re-ordering. One had to wait until the development of concurrent logic languages to fully rework those ideas. Indeed at the semantic level these languages have the necessary flexibility and do not impose a strict ordering, and at the implementation level they include sufficiently versatile data-structures to make re-ordering (re-scheduling) easy, as, in one way or another, the whole computation tree has to be explicitly represented.

One important aspect of our work is that the information we use for the backward execution is very limited and the goal of this work is *not* to attempt anything like intelligent backtracking as has been proposed for Prolog [1, 3, 4] or concurrent languages [2]. Intelligent backtracking would require using data-dependency information in some way. This requires to record more information, usually during the unification process, in order to determine dependencies between failing goals and choice-points, based on data-dependencies. We preferred to experiment to what extent we could have an efficient strategy, which would behave most of the time like an intelligent backtracking scheme, without the need for data-dependency information. Also observe that in an Andorra-based model, some of the "intelligence" is already provided by the forward execution mechanism in the delaying of choices, and the eager execution of related determinate goals after the creation of a choice-point. Hence intelligent backtracking is interesting as a cure for the rigid and naive strategy of a language like Prolog, but it seems less necessary in a concurrent language as Andorra, at least when only transformational and not reactive computations are considered. We are thus only using the "fail information" as a heuristic to guide the process of pruning the search space. We shall concentrate on computationally simple strategies, guided as much as possible by information already available, this will be detailed in section 3.

We have implemented this scheme in the prototype version of the Andorra Kernel Language (AKL 0.0) developed at SICS [13]. As mentioned above, one of the main interests of the proposed scheme is its ease of implementation by simple modifications of an existing implementation of a concurrent language. One has only to integrate a re-scheduling of continuation goals upon backtracking. There is no need to modify terms or variable bindings representations as in an intelligent backtracking scheme. The overhead of our machinery w.r.t. the original AKL implementation is very small, limited to 5-10%. We have experimented with various strategies on a variety of benchmarks, and we have encouraging results: a average gain of 60% (as measured by the number of nondeterminate promotions) can be observed, with peak values up to 300%.

The rest of this article is structured as follows: section 2 summarizes the Andorra Kernel Language, and we focus on the issues most relevant for our work. Then, in section 3 we present the various methods we have experimented with. We detail some implementations issues in section 4. Section 5 illustrates this with an example. We then proceed in section 6 to present and analyze some statistics on the observed performance of the prototype implementation. Finally, in section 7 some conclusions are drawn and our projects for further developments are outlined.

2 Andorra Kernel Language

The Andorra Kernel Language (AKL) has been proposed in [12] and is a simplified instance of the framework presented in [11]. It is an attempt to fully encompass both Prolog and concurrent logic languages (aka committed-choice languages) such as Parlog, FCP or GHC [22]. It can be seen in this way as an instance of the Extended Andorra Model where the control is explicit, as opposed to [26] where the emphasis is put on an implicit control.

The main new language feature is the introduction of the guard construct borrowed from the concurrent logic programming paradigm, and its associated guard operator. However, both don't care and don't know non determinism are possible by using as guard operators either "commit" and "cut" (which prune alternatives), or "wait" (which does not prune alternatives). Guard atoms are not restricted to build-in predicates but can be program atoms, leading to non flat guards. The introduction of guards in the program's clauses is indeed a way to extend the determinacy test, which is at the core of the Andorra model, since a goal is determinate whenever a single guard check succeeds among all alternative clauses, and not only a single head unification.

AKL is a practical instance of the constraint-based framework of

[11] with three possible guard operators (cut, commit and wait) and the constraint operation tell$_\omega$ on unification constraints. A further restriction consists in allowing quiet pruning only, meaning that a pruning guard operator (cut or commit) may only be used if the head and the guard make no non-local bindings.

The semantics of the language is given by a set of rewrite rules applicable to and-or trees designated as *configurations*. Briefly the process of solving a goal G w.r.t. a given AKL program P can be formalized as finding a sequence of configurations C_i, starting with the configuration $C_0 = G$, with successive configurations obtained by application of the rewriting rules (see 2). In the simplified description that follows we omit binding environments (constraints), and consider the simplified AKL execution model, ie. without or-boxes[13].

Configurations

A configuration models the state of the computation. It can briefly be summarized by the following (very) simplified grammar:

$$
\begin{aligned}
\textit{Configuration} &\longrightarrow \textit{Goal}|\textbf{choice}(\textit{list}(\textit{And\_Box})) \\
\textit{And\_Box} &\longrightarrow \textbf{fail}|\textbf{and}(\textit{list}(\textit{Configuration})) \\
\textit{Goal} &\longrightarrow \textit{Lits}_{\text{Guard}}\%\textit{Lits}_{\text{Body}}
\end{aligned}
$$

Where *Lits* stands for a conjunction of literals, and % is a guard operator, namely wait (:), cut (!) or commit (|).

Rewriting Rules

Again these are a simplified version of the rewriting rules, making no mention of the binding environments. The rewrite rules apply to either choice-boxes or and-boxes, which may be contained in other boxes.

1. **Local Forking.** Given a subgoal A and considering that the predicate designated by A has the clauses $H_1 \leftarrow G_1\%B_1, \ldots, H_n \leftarrow G_n\%B_n$, where % is a guard operator:

$$A \Longrightarrow \textbf{choice}(\textbf{and}(G_1)\%B_1, \ldots, \textbf{and}(G_n)\%B_n)$$

2. **Failure Propagation.**

$$\textbf{and}(\ldots, \textbf{fail}, \ldots) \Longrightarrow \textbf{fail}$$

3. **Choice Elimination.**

$$\textbf{choice}(R, \textbf{fail}\%A, S) \Longrightarrow \textbf{choice}(R, S)$$

4. **Environment Synchronization.**

$$\mathbf{and}(R) \Longrightarrow \mathbf{fail}$$

iff R's constraints are incompatible with the and-box's bindings. Basically this is unification failure.

5. **Determinate Promotion.**

$$\mathbf{and}(R, \mathbf{choice}(C\%A), S) \Longrightarrow \mathbf{and}(R, C, A, S)$$

If $\%$ is a pruning guard operator (ie. cut or commit) it must also be quiet.

6. **Cut.**

$$\mathbf{choice}(R, C!A, S) \Longrightarrow \mathbf{choice}(R, C!A)$$

7. **Commit.**

$$\mathbf{choice}(R, C|A, S) \Longrightarrow \mathbf{choice}(C|A)$$

8. **Choice Splitting.**

$$\mathbf{choice}(R_1, \mathbf{and}(S_1, \mathbf{choice}(T_1, G : B, T_2), S_2), R_2) \Longrightarrow$$
$$\mathbf{choice}(R_1, \mathbf{and}(S_1, \mathbf{choice}(G : B), S_2), \mathbf{and}(S_1, \mathbf{choice}(T_1, T_2), S_2), R_2)$$

For a more extensive description, see [12] and [13].

Copying Scheme for handling Nondeterminism

The current (sequential) implementation of AKL [13] uses copying for the *choice splitting* operation (8), as described by the semantic rewrite rule. This operation is depicted in figure 1: (a) shows the configuration before applying rule (8), and (b) afterwards.

This operation leads to a very different run-time organization from that of Prolog systems where choice splitting, i.e. non-determinism is handled by choice-point creation and backtracking. In the AKL scheme, there are no choice-points, the concept being replaced by the multiple clauses of the nondeterminate goal being present in otherwise similar and-box contexts, contained in a common choice-box. This can be seen as an eager generation of alternative resolvents, as opposed to the lazy policy of using choice-points in traditional Prolog. Surprisingly enough, this scheme is related to the proof procedure of [7] where alternative resolvents are also generated eagerly.

In (b), choice-boxes S1' and S2' are *copies* of S1 and S2. This copying scheme on choice split will greatly influence the operational definition of our backward execution strategy. Indeed, our aim of re-ordering continuation goals upon failure so as to re-execute first the

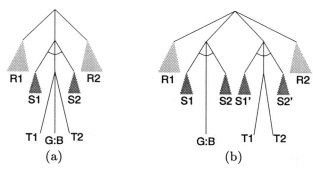

Figure 1: Configurations before and after choice split.

failing goal has to be rephrased as a transformation and reordering of the and-or tree upon failure. In particular, a goal in a given and-box has to be connected to its other occurrences in alternative ("copied") and-boxes in such a manner that that these other occurrences can be easily reordered upon failure. This leads us to define the notion of copied or re-incident node as follows:

A *re-incident node* G' is another instance of a choice-box or and-continuation for a goal G that occurs in another branch, at the same depth in the and-or tree. In other words, given configuration (1),

$$\mathbf{choice}(\cdots, \mathbf{and}(S_1, \mathbf{choice}(\cdots), S_2), \cdots) \tag{1}$$

after applying the choice-splitting rule we obtain configuration (2).

$$\mathbf{choice}(\cdots, \mathbf{and}(S_1, \mathbf{choice}(\cdots), S_2), \mathbf{and}(S'_1, \mathbf{choice}(\cdots), S'_2), \cdots) \tag{2}$$

S'_1 and S'_2 are *re-incident nodes* of respectively S_1 and S_2, as they share the same potential solutions, represented by an identical set of applicable clauses.

3   And-Or tree transformations based on failure

Intuitively, the and-or tree transformations can be viewed as a heuristic to speed up the search space scanning process by providing a means by which separate or-branches of the proof tree influence one another: one branch's early failure may be used to "draw attention" to the part of the tree that caused failure, so that it will be selected earlier than it normally would in other instances present in other parts of the tree.

In any case, reordering only takes place upon occurrence of a failure and basically consists in moving re-incident nodes of the failing goal so that they will be executed earlier that they normally would with the standard (non-reordering) strategy. This corresponds roughly to moving these nodes to the left of the tree.

Reordering strategies

We experimented with different strategies for reordering the and-or tree, that can be presented under several orthogonal aspects:

1. **Under what circumstances to reorder?**

   These are conditions that may have to be fulfilled in order for the modifications to the shape of the and-or tree to take place. Different conditions are enumerated and may have to be satisfied independently of each other.

   (a) *When the failing node is an instance of the last clause for the parent goal.* It is reasonable to impose this condition as a call to a predicate may succeed although the first clauses fail. This corresponds to reorder upon deep backtracking only.

   (b) *When the re-incident nodes have the same grandparent choice-box[1] as the failing node.* The effect of this is to further narrow the scope of the reordering operation. Nodes in a copy chain may be at different depths in a given configuration as a result of deterministic promotions, where the and-box being promoted carries with it its parent choice-box's copy information into the newly created and-continuation.

2. **What parts of the tree to reorder?**

   (a) *Reorder only the re-incident nodes.*

   (b) *Reorder all the nodes in a path from each re-incident node to the lowest common ancestor.* Using this criterion will make more extensive changes to the and-or tree, as it calls attention not only to a specific node's other instances, but also to the computation that gave rise to its failure.

3. **Where to reorder to?**

   If a a failure occurs and a given subset of the conditions specified in 1 are fulfilled, the current and-or tree (the AKL configuration) should be rewritten. The transformation will only affect the re-incident nodes of the failing literal, which will be moved. The possibilities we have considered are:

   (a) *"Bring To Front"*. This method takes all the re-incident nodes and brings them to the front of their sibling choice-boxes (or and-continuations). It can be very efficient for some rather poorly-written programs, but it easily leads to bad results because of its "randomizing" effect, as we verified experimentally. This is also the simplest method to implement efficiently.

(b) *"Incremental"*. Instead of bringing the re-incident nodes to the front it moves them to the left by one place. The intuition behind this method is that it will incrementally approximate the producer of the conflicting binding, until it *passes over* it, after which calls to the goal will suspend, waiting for the producer goal to effect its binding. This method should be more progressive than method (3a), and will hopefully provide a better approximation of a monotone gain in performance.

4   Implementation Issues

The characteristic that all of these methods have in common is their relative simplicity of implementation, and the fact that they require only small extensions to the data structures of the abstract machine emulator.

In particular, there is no modification to the representation of terms or variables. The changes consisted in modifying the structure of and-boxes, choice-boxes and and-continuations so as to make them appear as subclasses of a "copiable object", that will provide a link to other "copiable objects", as well as some information on the type of the object. Copy chains are maintained that link all the re-incident nodes of a given node. The nodes involved in the copy chains are always either choice-boxes or and-continuations.

The operations that incur an increased overhead are:

- Failure. With this scheme an and-box that is being discarded must be traversed in order to remove all the nodes below it from their copy chain. Ideally this operation should be deferred until garbage collection.

- Tree copying that occurs during choice split operations. All nodes that get copied must now be linked together.

- Tree copying that occurs during garbage collection. This operation now has to relocate a structure which is independent of the tree, the copy chains. A fix-up stack has to be maintained.

The overhead introduced by the need to maintain the structures necessary for the node-copy information results in a slowdown in the order of 5 to 10% over the un-modified AKL implementation.

5   Example Execution

We will detail the AKL execution mechanism and the effect of the reordering strategy upon failure with the simple example program:

```
p(X) :- : X=1.
p(X) :- : X=2.    q(X) :- : X=a.
                  q(X) :- : X=b.
r(X) :- : X=0.    q(X) :- : X=c.
r(X) :- : X=2.
```

An AKL configuration corresponding to the execution of goal :-
p(X), q(Y), r(X) is shown in part (a) of figure 2, before any nondeterministic step (ie. choice splitting) is made. At this stage, a choice
splitting is the only applicable rule and it is literal p that is chosen, with
its first alternative being then selected for determinate promotion. This
yields the configurations shown in parts (b) and (c) of figure 2, with p
reduced to an and-continuation.

As the nodes labeled q' and r' are copies (re-incident nodes) of those
labeled q and r, the abstract machine emulator will make this fact
explicit by establishing links from the original node to its copies, hence
the arrows that link nodes horizontally. The direction of the arrow is
not very important as the lists are circular, but an arrow $A \longmapsto B$
means that B is a (potential) re-incident node of A. The dotted lines
stand for *and-continuations* that represent the yet to be executed prefix
of the resolvent corresponding to the remainder of the body of a given
clause.

Normal AKL execution will proceed by successive application of the
rewriting rules. Whenever a goal fails, that is when rules (4) or (2) are
applied, the tree reordering mechanism will come into play, relocating
the other instances of the goal that failed (ie. the re-incident nodes),
using the strategy currently in effect, as specified by (3).

Continuing with the example, this can be seen on the tree in part
(h) of figure 2. In this case the criterion used was sbo/gp (see table 1).

6 Statistics

We have implemented the method, with various reordering strategies,
on top of the AKL 0.0 prototype implementation developed at SICS[13].
This implementation is not as efficient as state-of-the-art Prolog compilers such as SICStus Prolog, being 3 to 4 times slower. We believe
however that the results reported here can be extrapolated to a more
efficient implementation as the method is quite independent of the inference engine. For this purpose, we give as measurement of a reordering
strategy's performance the number of choice splits (ie. nondeterminate
promotions) performed, as this is probably the most expensive operation in AKL. It corresponds to choice-point creation in normal Prolog.
This numbers are thus independent of the underlying inference engine
raw speed. The results for measurements in cpu time and in overall

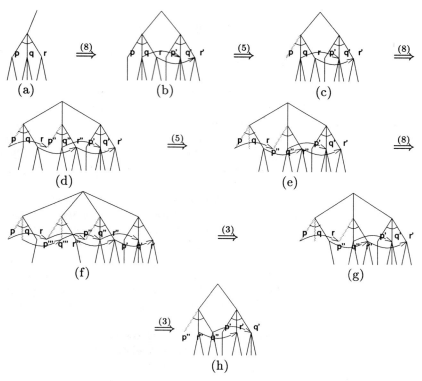

Figure 2: Configurations for `:- p(X), q(Y), r(X)`

number of inferences are similar to those in number of choice split, and are not included for this reason.

Table 2 displays the performance of these methods relative to the un-modified AKL strategy, as a ratio where numbers greater than 1 represent a speedup (ie. a lower number of choice split operations). Table 1 describes the strategies.

`bagof-circuit` generates all solutions to a digital circuit fault diagnosis problem from [18], `zebra` is a version of the "houses" problem, `crypt` is adapted from [28], `money` is the "send+more=money" cryptarithmetic puzzle, `example-g` is the example discussed in section 5, `bagof-salt-mustard` is the "salt-and-mustard" puzzle, `color-13-good` and `color-13-bad` are the traditional map-coloring puzzle from [1] with both a favorable and a bad goal ordering, `ham` and `bagof-ham` consist in finding a Hamiltonian path through a graph, and `blocks` is a simple planning problem in the blocks-world.

The overall best method seems to be the `btf` family, the fastest ones being `btf` and `btf/t`, as they obtain an average 60% gain in

Label	Strategy name	Reorder:		
		when	what	where to
btf	Bring to front	(1a)	(2a)	(3a)
btf/gp	Bring to front, same grandparent	(1a), (1b)	(2a)	(3a)
btf/t	Bring to front, tree	(1a)	(2b)	(3a)
sbo	Step by one	(1a)	(2a)	(3b)
sbo/gp	Step by one, same grandparent	(1a), (1b)	(2a)	(3b)
sbo/t	Step by one, tree	(1a)	(2b)	(3b)

Table 1: Strategy summary

Benchmark	Strategy					
	btf	btf/gp	btf/t	sbo	sbo/gp	sbo/t
circuit	1.38	1.38	1.38	1.00	1.00	1.00
bagof-circuit	2.91	2.91	2.91	1.19	1.28	1.52
color-13-good	0.56	0.68	0.56	0.26	0.91	0.27
color-13-bad	0.74	0.97	0.74	0.34	1.71	0.46
example-g	2.75	2.75	2.75	2.75	2.75	2.75
crypt	1.00	1.00	1.00	1.00	1.00	1.00
knights-5	0.97	1.00	0.97	0.97	1.00	0.97
queens-8	2.09	1.53	2.09	1.05	1.00	1.05
ham	0.90	1.00	0.95	1.00	1.00	1.00
blocks	–	1.20	–	1.97	1.00	1.97
money	1.00	1.00	1.00	1.00	1.00	1.00
bagof-salt-mustard	1.86	1.00	2.01	1.20	1.00	1.33
zebra	2.82	2.54	2.82	1.84	1.80	1.78

Table 2: ratios of Number of Choice Splits (unmodified/modified AKL)

performance on these benchmarks, with peak speedups up to a factor three. Some remarks concerning the strategies on this data:

- The methods that reorder the entire sub-tree leading to the re-incident nodes (*/t) perform almost identically to those that only reorder the re-incident nodes. This may be due to the AKL configurations being shallow.

- The "incremental" method (sbo) is more stable than the "bring to front" (btf) one. In practice this means that the gains are not as high, however, there are not as many pathological cases.

- The "same grandparent" restricting heuristic (1b, */gp) seems to restrict the gains a little, however it prevents the pathological behavior of the strategy it's being used with to appear.

- The `blocks` benchmark with the `btf` and `btf/t` heuristics took too long to complete so the figures are not in the table.

Concerning the effectiveness of the reordering strategy in general, we can make the following remarks:

- The method (all strategies taken together) is ineffective for some programs, as depicted by lines of 1.00's (or very close values) for the `crypt`, `knights`, `money`, `bagof-salt-mustard` and `ham` programs. This is because these programs are deterministic in the sense that they never require deep backtracking or are "fully" non-deterministic, in the sense that all choice points have to be explored. In such situations, where any backtracking is always pertinent, the reordering method could obviously not improve performance. However, as soon as there exist testing goals that are pending on more than one non-determinate promotion, our method can significantly improve performance.

- The Andorra Principle reduces the number of inferences needed to solve a problem when compared to Prolog, but failure information on backward execution can further improve this. *A priori* pruning should be combined with a posteriori pruning.

- Some of the non-deterministic examples were adapted[2] from similar ones used for benchmarking intelligent backtracking methods[4, 2]. They do not benefit as much from this type of manipulation as we initially expected; this is due to the fact that the Andorra principle already improves the "naive" version. A striking example of this is the `color-13` program. A good order of goals in the query gives the solution immediately and deterministically, while a bad order of goals needs 2000 times more inferences to give it in Prolog, but in AKL the two goals have roughly the same behaviour (only 1.13 times more inferences).

7 Conclusion and further work

We have shown that it is feasible to apply simple search-space pruning heuristics to improve the nondeterministic behavior in the Andorra Kernel Language. This work applies to the Extended Andorra Model as well. The experimental results are encouraging and the methods we have described are susceptible of being implemented efficiently and with few modifications to the original engine.

Hence we believe that *a priori* pruning, such as the one provided by the Andorra principle, should be combined with *a posteriori* pruning, based on failure information, to achieve the best results.

Re-scheduling based on dependency analysis is another approach, that we also intend to pursue, also assuming the Extended Andorra Model, in order to investigate what we believe is its greater appropriateness than that of the stack-based WAM model to accommodate intelligent backtracking and related notions. Such an approach combined with the Andorra Principle should be more effective in the context of reactive computations than in the purely transformational view, as independent parts of the computation need not be recalculated.

We are also interested in extending those ideas to Constraint Logic Programming, and to concurrent constraint languages in particular, and to use such heuristics to efficiently handle disjunctive constraints.

Acknowledgements

This work has been supported in part by JNICT and MRT, through the "Réseau de formation/recherche", which provided funding for Salvador Abreu's stay at INRIA during which this work was done.

Notes

[1] The grandparent choice-box is the parent choice-box of the containing and-box, ie. the closest enclosing choice-box.

[2] Many of these programs were written in Prolog and had to be hand-translated into AKL. Programs making use of the database could of course not be translated directly.

References

[1] M. Bruynooghe and L. M. Pereira. Deduction revision by intelligent backtracking. In J.A. Campbell, editor, *implementations of Prolog*. Ellis-Horwood, 1984.

[2] C. Codognet and P. Codognet. Non-deterministic stream AND-Parallelism based on intelligent backtracking. In Levi and Martelli [17], pages 63–79.

[3] Christian Codognet, Philippe Codognet, and Gilberto File. Yet another intelligent backtracking method. In Kowalski and Bowen [15], pages 447–465.

[4] Philippe Codognet and Thierry Sola. Extending the WAM for intelligent backtracking. In Furukawa [10], pages 127–141.

[5] Vítor Santos Costa, David H. D. Warren, and Rong Yang. The Andorra-I engine: A parallel implementation of the basic andorra model. In Furukawa [10], pages 825–839.

[6] Vítor Santos Costa, David H. D. Warren, and Rong Yang. The Andorra-I preprocessor: Supporting full Prolog on the basic andorra model. In Furukawa [10], pages 443–456.

[7] P. T. Cox and T. Pietrzykowski. Deduction plans : a basis for intelligent backtracking. *IEEE PAMI*, 3(1), 1981.

[8] J. Crammond. *Implementation of Committed Choice Logic Languages on Shared Memory Multiprocessors*. PhD thesis, Department of Computer Science, Herriot-Watt University, Edinburgh, May, 1988.

[9] Ian Foster and Steven Taylor. *Strand: New Concepts in Parallel Programming*. Prentice-Hall, Englewood Cliffs, New Jersey, 1989.

[10] Koichi Furukawa, editor. *Proceedings of the Eighth International Conference on Logic Programming*, Cambridge, Massachusetts London, England, 1991. MIT Press.

[11] Seif Haridi and Sverker Janson. Kernel Andorra Prolog and its Computation Model. In Warren and Szeredi [27], pages 31–46.

[12] Sverker Janson and Seif Haridi. Programming paradigms of the Andorra kernel language. In Saraswat and Ueda [21], pages 167–186.

[13] Sverker Janson and Johan Montelius. Design of a sequential prototype implementation of the andorra kernel language. Technical report, SICS, September 1991. (draft).

[14] Shmuel Klinger and Ehud Shapiro. A decision tree compilation algorithm for FCP (I , : , ?). In Kowalski and Bowen [15], pages 1315–1336.

[15] Robert A. Kowalski and Kenneth A. Bowen, editors. *Proceedings of the Fifth International Conference and Symposium on Logic Programming*, Cambridge, Massachusetts London, England, 1988. MIT Press.

[16] Jean-Louis Lassez, editor. *Proceedings of the Fourth International Conference on Logic Pro gramming*, MIT Press Series in Logic Programming, Cambridge, Massachusetts London, England, 1987. "MIT Press".

[17] Giorgio Levi and Maurizio Martelli, editors. *Proceedings of the Sixth International Conference on Logic Programming*, Cambridge, Massachusetts London, England, 1989. MIT Press.

[18] S. Morishita, M. Numao, and S. Hirose. Symbolical construction of truth value domain for logic program. In Lassez [16], pages 533–555.

[19] Lee Naish. Heterogeneous SLD resolution. *The Journal of Logic Programming*, 1(4):297–303, December 1984.

[20] L. M. Pereira and A. Porto. Intelligent backtracking and sidetracking in horn clause programs. Technical Report CIUNL 2/79, Universitade Nova de Lisboa, 1979.

[21] Vijay Saraswat and Kazunori Ueda, editors. *Logic Programming Proceedings of the 1991 International Symposium*, London, England, 1991. Massachusetts Institute of Technology.

[22] E. Shapiro. The family of concurrent logic programming languages. *ACM computing surveys*, 21(3), september 1989.

[23] Ehud Shapiro, editor. *Proceedings of the Third International Conference on Logic Programming*, Lecture Notes in Computer Science. Springer-Verlag, 1986.

[24] P. Van Hentenryck. Parallel constraint satisfaction in logic programming: Preliminary results of chip within PEPSys. In Levi and Martelli [17], pages 165–180.

[25] D. H. D. Warren. The andorra principle. Internal report, Gigalips Group, 1988.

[26] David H. D. Warren. The extended andorra model with implicit control. ICLP90 Preconference Workshop, June 1990.

[27] David H. D. Warren and Peter Szeredi, editors. *Proceedings of the Seventh International Conference on Logic Programming*, Cambridge, Massachusetts London, England, 1990. MIT Press.

[28] R. Yang. Solving simple substitution ciphers in Andorra-I. In Levi and Martelli [17], pages 113–128.

[29] Rong Yang and Hideo Aiso. P-prolog: a parallel logic language based on exclusive relation. In Shapiro [23], pages 255–269.

jc: An Efficient and Portable Sequential Implementation of Janus

David Gudeman[1], Koenraad De Bosschere[2], Saumya K. Debray[1]

1. Department of Computer Science
   The University of Arizona
   Tucson, AZ 85721, USA

2. Electronics Laboratory
   Rijksuniversiteit Gent
   B-9000 Gent, Belgium

Abstract: Janus is a language designed for distributed constraint programming [12]. This paper describes jc, an efficient and portable sequential implementation of Janus, which compiles Janus programs down to C code. Careful attention to the C code generated, together with some simple local optimizations, allows the system to have fairly good performance despite the lack (at this time) of global flow analysis and optimization.

1 Introduction

Janus [12] is an instance of a concurrent constraint programming language [11]. This report describes jc, an efficient and portable sequential implementation of Janus that compiles down to C. A Janus program is a set of *flat guarded clauses* defining its procedures. It is in many respects similar to *Strand* [6] and Flat GHC [13]. There are, however, a number of differences: the most important of these is the *two-occurrence restriction* of Janus. This restriction states, essentially, that in any clause, a variable whose value cannot be inferred to be "fixed" (i.e., ground) from the guard operations is allowed to have at most two occurrences: one of these occurrences is annotated to be the "writable" occurrence, and the other is the "readable" occurrence. Only the writable occurrence of a variable may be assigned to. Thus, variables in effect serve as point-to-point communication channels; other language constructs allow many-to-one and one-to-many communication.

The two-occurrence restriction is motivated strongly by a vision of distributed constraint programming. A fundamental concern is that syntactically correct programs should not cause the store to become inconsistent at runtime: this is enforced by the two-occurrence restriction, which ensures that any variable has exactly one producer, thereby precluding any possibility of inconsistency. This has the desirable effect that programs become efficiently implementable (at least in principle). It has been observed that while programs typically do not give rise to a great deal of aliasing, this information is not available to compilers, which have to resort to complicated and potentially expensive algorithms to recover it. The problem is addressed in Janus by specifying the default to be that there is no aliasing, and requiring the programmer to explicitly invoke certain language features when sharing between structures is necessary. Rules for syntactic well-formedness then ensure that the compile-time satisfaction of certain properties, local to a clause, regarding the number of occurrences of a variable imply the run-time satisfaction of certain global properties regarding lack of aliases.

Data objects in Janus consist of the following: askers, tellers, numbers (integers and floats), constants, arrays, lists, and bags. An *asker* for a variable X is the "read" occurrence of X: it denotes read capability on the communication channel X (if we think of a variable as a communication point-to-point channel). A *teller* for a variable X, written ^X, denotes the "write" occurrence of X, i.e., write capability on the channel X. An array of n objects $a_0, \ldots, a_{n-1}$, written $<a_0, \ldots, a_{n-1}>$, represents a sequence of values indexed by $\{0, \ldots, n-1\}$. A list is either the empty list [], or a pair [H|L]. A bag represents an unordered multiset of objects, and can be thought of as many-to-one communication channels. Ask constraints in Janus consist of various type tests and relational tests on objects (and, via selectors, to components of objects). A tell constraint is restricted to be of the form X = E, where X is a variable for which the agent has tell rights, and E can be any expression including arithmetic, array, and bag expressions.

2 The Janus Virtual Machine

2.1 Values

Janus values are represented in a single word consisting of a tag and a data portion. For integers, the data portion is the integer itself. For atoms (symbols, not atomic clauses) the data portion is a unique integer that can be looked up in a table to find the representation of the atom. For floats, the data portion is a pointer to a memory block (on the SPARC, for example, this is a 32-bit word) containing a floating point number. For lists, the data portion is a pointer to a pair of tagged values. For arrays, the data portion is a pointer to an array block. The array block contains the length of the array and a pointer to the sequence of tagged values that make up the array. For tellers, the data portion is a pointer to the corresponding asker. For askers, the data portion is a pointer to itself or to a lower value in the reference chain.

2.2 Memory Management

The Janus runtime system has two memory regions, the stack and the heap. The stack contains environments (also called stack frames), which contain a set of local variables in the form of tagged values. The heap contains tagged values as well as floating point numbers, suspension records, arrays and other sorts of data that do not fit into stack allocation. Currently, there is no garbage collection for the heap. The bottom of the stack begins at an address lower than the heap and grows toward higher memory while the heap grows toward lower memory. This makes it possible to check the allocation of stack and heap space at the same time with a single comparison of the stack and heap pointers.

Environments are allocated only at commit points: guard operations are carried out entirely in registers. When a clause commits, an environment of the appropriate size (for that clause) is allocated if necessary. The allocation and deallocation of environments is similar to the WAM, but with some important differences. First, the test to see if there is enough space for a stack frame is separate from the actual allocation of the stack frame. This allows us to combine the tests for adequate heap and stack space in a clause, so that for most procedures there is only one test that accounts for all the space that will be needed (for the stack as well as the heap) in a clause. Another difference from the WAM is that that rather than saving a "return address"—a pointer into the code of some other procedure—to which control should be transferred when the current activation has finished execution, an environment for a procedure contains a "resumption address"—a pointer into its own code—where execution should resume when control returns to it. This simplifies the management of control in the presence of arbitrary suspensions and resumptions.

Another (minor) difference from the WAM is that jc uses a stack pointer sp (to the top of the stack) rather than an environment pointer (to the base of the topmost environment). Local variables are referenced by negative offsets from sp and the resumption address is the top word on the stack. There is no pointer to the previous stack frame, instead environment allocation and deallocation uses a matched pair of instructions `NewFrame(i)`, ..., `FreeFrame(i)` where i is the number of variables in the stack frame. This scheme, like the WAM, leaves the stack with no self-defining structure. In other words, there is no way to divide the stack into frames by following pointers. This is not needed for allocating and deallocating environments, but debugging and garbage collection procedures need to know the structure of the stack so there has to be a way to re-create it. To allow this, the resumption addresses are given special tags to distinguish them from other tagged values. Since there is a resumption address at the top of each frame (except possibly the topmost frame), it is possible to divide the stack into environments by looking for tagged resumption addresses. Since currently resumption addresses are arbitrary integers, there is no run-time overhead associated with tagging and untagging them, the tagged value is just used all the time.

2.3 Registers

The virtual machine has a set of registers that are simply C variables, but many of them are declared as "register" and mapped to hardware registers. The special-purpose registers include the usual stack pointer and heap pointer. In addition, we have a register `cs` that is used to reduce the overhead of suspension (see below): this is a pointer to the current suspension record (or `NULL` if there is no such structure). There are a number of special registers that handle suspension and resumption of activations. Finally, there are several sets of general-purpose registers: *tagged value registers*, used to hold tagged values and to pass parameters to procedures (the parameter passing convention is similar to the WAM); *address registers*, used to hold machine addresses; *integer registers*, used to hold untagged integer values; and *float registers*, used to hold floating point values. There is no *a priori* bound on the number of general purpose registers: the Janus compiler generates a distinct C variable for each register needed by a program (some subset of these are given `register` declarations, based on usage counts, as discussed later).

2.4 Arithmetic

Integer values are represented as 32-bit words (30-bit value + 2-bit tag), while floating point values are represented by a tagged pointer to an untagged floating-point number, in the machine representation, allocated in the heap. The runtime system has the usual complement of arithmetic instructions. These instructions come in a number of different versions, for different types of operands and results (tagged/untagged, integer/float).

Conditional instructions in the virtual machine contain the label as one of the operands, and the jump is made immediately if the condition is met. There is a pair of conditional instructions for each type of tag, one that jumps if the tag is right, one that jumps if it is wrong.

There is also the complete set of arithmetic conditions: `EQ`, `NE`, `LT`, `LE`, `GT`, and `GE`. Like the arithmetic operations, these instructions also come in a number of different versions for comparing tagged values, tagged integers, tagged floats, untagged integers, untagged floats, and addresses. The conditions on general tagged values are all implemented as C functions to reduce code bloat.

2.5 Procedures

Parameters are all passed in tagged value registers (`t0`, `t1`, `t2`, ...). Before calling an n-ary procedure, the first n tagged value registers must be set to the n actual parameters. Then if the call is not a tail call, the stack frame must be updated to contain the resumption address of the calling procedure. When a procedure exits it just jumps to the resumption address of the top frame on the stack. The bottom frame on the stack is always initialized with a resumption address that exits the Janus portion of the program (returning to the top-level input mode).

Resumption addresses present a problem when compiling to C because in C, labels are not first-class objects. They are not values that can be assigned to variables, and it is not legal to write goto e where e is an expression other than a label name. One possible way to solve this problem is to use separate C functions for Janus procedures, since C does allow function-valued variables. But that solution is unsatisfactory for several reasons. First, the overhead of C procedure calls is much higher (for most compilers) than what is needed for Janus. Second, most C compilers do not do tail-call optimization. Third, such a strategy would preclude several other types of optimization such as call-forwarding and optimizations involving where a resumed procedure starts.

A less unsatisfactory solution, the one currently used in jc, is to use the C switch statement to give a form of "computed goto". Any address that must be stored in memory and calculated dynamically is implemented as a small integer constant (tagged as an address), and the "label" for that address is a case label with that value. However, addresses of procedures are known statically, so the jump instructions in procedure calls can have the label "hard-wired" in.

The code for the clauses of a procedure are generated contiguously, in sequence. Each guard test jumps to the next guard on failure.[1] If the last guard fails it jumps to the suspension code. After the guard code for a clause, at the "commit" point, is code to allocate an environment for that clause (if necessary). Also at the commit point is code that checks whether there is adequate space in the heap to satisfy all allocation requirements of the tell actions appearing in the body of the clause. After these allocation checks is code for in-line tell actions. Only after all possible in-line work is done are there any procedure calls.

2.6 Suspension and Resumption

In general, before a guard can test the value of a variable, it must make sure that the variable is instantiated to a value. If not, then the flag register susp_flag is set and there is a jump to the next guard or the suspension code. This action is all handled by the single instruction CheckIfAsker(lbl,var). If the flag susp_flag is set when control reaches the suspension code, then it is known that at least one guard was unable to finish due to an uninstantiated variable, so the procedure must suspend until that variable becomes known. Otherwise, all guards completed and failed, so the procedure vanishes.

As a special case, a test on a parameter does not need to be proceeded by a CheckIfAsker instruction. For parameters, the guard simply checks the type or value of the the variable and jumps to the next guard if the variable does not satisfy the test. Such tests will always fail if the variable is not instantiated. Then the suspension code must check each such parameter to see if it is instantiated as well as checking susp_flag. This strategy moves work out of the normal non-suspending code and into the suspension code, so that procedures that do not suspend do not have to pay a high performance cost for the language's suspension feature.

But this strategy does not work for variables that are not parameters, because there is no guarantee that the variable is available when the suspension code gets executed. The reason is that any non-parameter variable must get assigned some-

---

[1] We currently do not have decision tree compilation implemented: we are investigating decision tree compilation in the presence of execution weights, see [5] for details.

where in the guard, and the assignment will never be made if a preceeding test in the same guard fails. For example the guard of the clause

```
p(L) :- L = [H|T], int(H) | ...
```

(supposing it is the second guard) gets expanded into

```
G2_lbl:
JumpUnlessLcons(G3_lbl,t0)
GetCons(a0,t0)
Load(t1,a0[0])
JumpUnlessInt(t1)
...
G3_lbl:
...
```

Notice the use of t0 and t1, the tagged-value registers. The single formal parameter is initially in t0. In the code above, it is clear that if p/1 is called with an asker as its actual parameter, then the register t1 never gets assigned a value. So the suspension code cannot test t1 to check whether it is an asker.

When a procedure needs to suspend, it copies its parameters to the heap, then creates a suspension record in the heap, setting the special register cs (current suspension) to point to it. The suspension record contains a continuation address, a pointer to the parameters in the heap, a number telling how many parameters there are, and a pointer to the next suspension in a list of suspensions. Then there is a jump to suspension_label where cs is prepended to the list suspension_list of suspended activations.

When a suspension record is resumed, the register cs is set to point to the suspension record. Then the parameters are copied into the registers, and execution continues at the beginning of the procedure. If the procedure suspends again, the cs register is already pointing to the correct suspension record, so it is not necessary to create or initialize a new one. The suspension code of each procedure contains a test at the beginning that jumps directly to suspension_label if cs is non-zero, thereby avoiding the creation of a new suspension record. This greatly reduces the overhead of a program that has procedures suspending and resuming many times before they commit.

An early design decision in the jc system was that programs that did not need to suspend should not, if at all possible, incur any overhead due to the fact that the language allows suspension. One consequence of this decision was to abandon any attempt at fair scheduling: our stance is that programs written by the user should not rely on assumptions about the underlying scheduling strategy being used in an implementation for their correctness. Thus, our strategy for resumption of suspended goals makes no guarantee about when an awakened goal will actually get to execute. This allows us to optimize the implementation considerably: a tell action does not have to check whether it is awakening a suspended goal, and other common primitive operations also do not have to contend with suspensions. Indeed, there is no special tag indicating a "variable that has a procedure waiting for it to be instantiated".

When the stack is empty and there are no suspension records on rl, the suspension_list is copied to the rl and execution proceeds at the scheduler. The scheduler is simply a piece of code that checks if the register rl (the resume list) is non-empty. If so, then a suspension record is removed from the list and resumed as described above. If rl is empty, then execution continues at the resume address of the top frame on the stack. If a list of suspended procedures is resumed in this way and none of them makes any progress, it is not a good idea to repeat the process since they will continue to make no progress and an infinite loop will result. To detect this, there is another field in the suspension record, **was_resumed** that is 0 when the the record is first created and gets set to 1 when it is resumed. If any element in the **suspension_list** has a **was_resumed** field equal to 0, then that resumption is new.

Searching the entire list of suspensions to see if there is a new one can get expensive, so there are two more registers, **num_suspensions**, which counts the number of suspensions that have occurred since the last batch resumption, and **num_resumptions** which tells how many suspension records were resumed in the last batch resumption. If **num_suspensions** is different from **num_resumptions**, then some progress was made since the last batch resumption, so it is safe to resume again without traversing the list of suspensions to see if there is a new one. If **num_resumptions** is equal to **num_suspensions**, then it is necessary to traverse the list, because they may be equal either because no progress was made or because the number of new suspensions happens to be the same as the number of commits. Since these operations are carried out only on suspension and resumption, non-suspending code incurs (almost) no overhead for the possibility of suspension.

3 The Janus Compiler

The Janus compiler has been built with standard tools: the scanner is generated by lex, the parser by yacc. This is augmented by a phase that does some transformations at the syntax tree level, a code generator that generates Janus virtual machine code, and a code optimizer.

3.1 Program Transformations

The syntax tree transformations performed by the compiler can be subdivided into three groups:

Suspension-Related Transformations: These are concerned with simplifying the implementation of tell actions in the body of a clause that might suspend. To simplify the implementation, we do not want a clause to suspend once it has committed. Therefore, we create extra predicates for tell actions in the body of a clause that might have to suspend. These new predicates are generated so that they can only suspend in the guard, and not in the body: this allows all suspension to be dealt with in a uniform way, and simplifies the implementation. For example, in the factorial program

```
fact(N,^F) :- int(N), N > 0 | fact(N-1,^F1), F = F1*N.
fact(0,^1).
```

the multiplication F1*N is only allowed when F1 is known, but that depends on the condition that the recursive call to **fact/3** does not suspend. Therefore, this program is transformed to

```
fact(N,^F) :- int(N), N > 0 | fact(N-1,^F1), fact__1(F,F1,N).
fact(0,^1).
fact__1(F,F1,N) :- number(F1) | F := F1*N.
```

Note that the new program is not a legal user program: the operation :=, which is an assignment directly to an asker rather than to the associated teller, is not available to users, and the predicate **fact_1** can be seen to be assigning to a variable without checking whether it is allowed to do so (i.e., without checking for a "teller" annotation). This works because the transformation is carried out on the syntax tree of the program, after any syntax checking is carried out. The point here is that the compiler knows that the variable F has been checked for a teller annotation in the clause defining fact/2, so it is not necessary to repeat this check in fact_1/3. In general, since such auxiliary predicates are automatically generated by the compiler, they are generated in the most efficient way (maximal reuse of already available argument registers, maximal use of the information available at the call site, and omission of unneeded tests).

An alternative to this approach would be to implement virtual machine instructions operations, that can suspend if necessary—this is the approach taken in the implementation of KL1 [2]. This approach has the advantage, compared to ours, that it saves a (Janus) procedure call, but it requires a more complicated suspension scheme. Also, unless special non-suspending versions of the body goals are provided, this approach will add tests to every body goal that might suspend, which will slow down the execution.

Expression Flattening and Common Subexpression Elimination: Complex expressions are broken up into smaller pieces, which are assigned to new variables. These assignments are put immediately before the goal they are extracted from. Common expressions are merged to avoid unnecessary computations.

Goal Reordering: In order to avoid unnecessary suspension, goals are reordered, wherever possible, such that producers are generated before consumers. This transformation also has the advantage that registers can be reused more frequently because variables are only used during a short period. As part of this transformation, tell actions are moved to the beginning of the body, if possible. Having most of the tell actions at the beginning of the body goals makes register allocation somewhat more difficult, but allows better reuse of partial results, especially values in untagged registers (addresses, integer and floating point).

3.2 Code Generation

The code generator scans the syntax tree and generates code on a procedure by procedure basis. Its register allocator that is somewhat different from the ones described in literature (e.g., see [3, 8]). It uses four kinds of registers: ordinary tagged registers, untagged address registers, untagged integer registers, and untagged floating point registers. Once a variable has been untagged for any reason, its untagged version is kept in an untagged register as long as the variable is in use. These untagged registers are actually just local registers in a chunk: they are neither saved on the stack nor used as arguments.

This feature turns out to be interesting, especially for addresses of structures and the length of arrays. Since subexpressions are extracted and merged, they only have to be computed once, but can be used many times. The fact that untagged values are available for reuse contributes to the efficiency: for example, multiple references to an array element, as in the quicksort benchmark, do not cause its address to be repeatedly recomputed—instead, it is computed once into an untagged register and reused subsequently. The code generator not only tries to minimize the number of instructions, but also the number of registers. The number of hardware registers is typically limited to about 10, and the code generator reuses registers as much as possible. It keeps a static reference count of the Janus registers (tagged, as well as untagged), and the n most frequently used registers (where n depends on the target machine) are stored into hardware registers. In many Prolog implementations, by contrast, a fixed set (typically the first six or eight) "general purpose" registers are mapped to hardware registers regardless of their usage counts—an approach that may very well be suboptimal, since in our experiments we often observed more references to (untagged) address registers than to some of the first few general purpose registers.

The register allocator uses a "lazy" allocation algorithm. This essentially means that it tries to postpone the physical allocation of a register as long as possible. Therefore, assignments to a variables are not generated, but recorded internally. In case a bound expression was assigned, it can better immediately be used at the second (and last) occurrence. For example, some variables that occur only once are never generated or even assigned a register. Registers are only allocated 'on demand'.

For our current benchmark set, we end up with 90% of all the Janus register references in hardware registers by using only 8 hardware registers. The use of 10 registers covers 95% of all the register references in the benchmark set. Of course, this does not prove that 95% of the run-time register references will be covered too. Actually, however, we expect the run-time reference coverage even higher because the 5% non-covered registers occur predominantly in rarely used clauses or in the body of a clause. Most of the variables used in guards such as arguments are allocated to hardware registers. The number of hardware registers that is actually used depends on the target architecture.

3.3 Code Optimization

The code optimizer uses a special optimization called *Call Forwarding* to remove some redundant computation. The basic idea here is to generate procedures with multiple entry points: at any call site for a procedure, information specific to that call site (obtained, for example, from the guard tests preceding that call or the operations that created the actual parameters) can be used to bypass some guard tests at the callee and jump into the middle of the callee's guard tests. In order to do so, the compiler keeps track of information (mainly type information) about the contents of the Janus registers at each call site. This information is used to generate a call instruction that skips as many tests as possible at the called guard. Since many guard operations just check the type of the arguments, and since this information is often readily available at the call site, this optimization allows a call site to avoid executing many guard tests. The performance improvements resulting from this relatively simple local optimization turn out to be quite remarkable.[2] The smaller the body of the clause w.r.t. the size of the guard, the higher the savings of this optimization: the optimization is especially successful in case of small recursive predicates such as naive reverse and factorial. It is interesting to note that the optimization improves the performance of non-suspending code (in which case some tests are skipped) as well as suspending code (in which case execution is sometimes transferred directly into the suspension code).

The effects of call forwarding can be enhanced by another local optimization called *Jump Target Duplication*. This optimization replaces an unconditional jump by the target of the jump, followed by a jump to the instruction following the target. This transformation does not, of itself, improve efficiency; however, it can allow the call forwarding algorithm to skip some extra tests that could not have

---

[2] Initially, when we began the implementation, we expected that serious global dataflow analysis would be necessary to get reasonable performance—particularly in light of the fact that extensive suspension testing seemed necessary in an ask/tell language such as Janus. The improvements from our local optimizations have so surpassed our expectations that the need for global flow analysis and optimization, while not entirely eliminated, seems quite a bit less pressing at this time.

been skipped otherwise. Jump target duplication is especially useful in the special case where the jump target is a conditional jump. This situation arises due to last goal optimization, a generalization of tail recursion optimization, since the call to the last goal in a clause translates to a jump to the beginning of the code for the corresponding predicate, and this code typically consists of conditional jumps arising from guard tests. In such cases, an unconditional jump is replaced by a conditional jump that jumps directly into a particular clause: this saves one jump instruction. Repeated application can replace a procedure call by a partial decision tree.

Repeated application of jump target duplication on body goals of the called predicate will end up in an inline call of the predicate, so to prevent reduce code bloat, (not to mention infinite expansion on recursive predicates), this feature must be restricted to a limited number of instructions. In the current implementation, there is one pass of jump target duplication, where duplication is carried out only if it will allow further optimization from call forwarding.

As an important side effect, the information that is gathered about the variables is also used for other purposes. For example, specific type information (e.g., whether an operand is guaranteed to be an integer) about variables allows general arithmetic instructions to be replaced by specialized integer and floating point instructions. Other optimizations that use this information include the removal of redundant dereferencing instructions and globalizing ("put-unsafe") instructions. The net result is that the compiler consists of a small number of simple and efficient (and reliable) components, and is able to carry out significant optimizations and realize good performance, without having to deal with complicated, computationally expensive, and potentially fragile dataflow analyses.

The final optimization on intermediate code, called *Instruction-Pair Motion* involves instructions that reverse or nullify the effect of a previous instruction. The simplest case arises when there are two contiguous instructions that are complementary, e.g.:

```
..., NewFrame(6), FreeFrame(6), ...
```

Here, these instructions are analogous to the **allocate** and **deallocate** instructions, respectively, of the WAM. Clearly, the first instruction can be eliminated because the second instruction will immediately undo its effects. This optimization can be generalized to situations where the instructions under consideration are separated by a nonempty instruction sequence, in some cases containing (conditional or unconditional) jumps (see also the discussion in [4]). There are two main effects of this optimization. First, it is often the case that variables are initialized, but this action is wasted because the initialization value is subsequently overwritten without ever being used. Such useless initialization of variables can be avoided using this optimization. A similar optimization is described in [14], based on a global dataflow analysis. Our approach, which relies on local (intra-procedural) analysis instead, is simpler and more efficient, but does not work in as many cases. It is, however, quite effective for loops, where such optimizations are likely to be most effective in terms of performance improvement.

Second, in tail-recursive predicates (encoding iterative computations), most of the execution time is usually spent in the recursive clauses. In most nontrivial cases, such clauses require an environment to be allocated. Under the standard WAM model of allocation, this causes an environment to be allocated and deallocated each time around the loop, though it might be more efficient to allocate an environment once, use it through the duration of the loop, and deallocate it at the end. This can be realized using the instruction-pair motion optimization. The idea is similar to that discussed in [4]: there are some subtleties regarding the checking of stack/heap overflow, but a detailed discussion is omitted due to space constraints. A similar optimization is described in [10]. The optimizations described here can be seen as generalizing a number of optimizations for traditional imperative languages [1]:

- In the special case of a (conditional or unconditional) jump whose target is a (conditional or unconditional) jump instruction, call forwarding generalizes a flow-of-control optimization that collapses chains of jump instructions. Call forwarding is able to deal with conditional jumps to conditional jumps (this turns out to be an important source of performance improvement in practice), while traditional compilers for imperative languages such as C and Fortran deal only with the case where there is at most one conditional jump (see [1], p. 556).

- When we consider call forwarding and instruction-pair motion for the last goal in a recursive clause, what we get is essentially a generalization of code motion out of loops. The reason it is a generalization is that the code that is bypassed due to call forwarding at a particular goal need not be invariant with respect to the entire loop, as is required in traditional algorithms for invariant code motion out of loops. Moreover, our algorithm implements inter-procedural optimization and can deal with both direct and mutual recursion without having to do anything special, while traditional code motion algorithms handle only the intra-procedural case.

- When call forwarding is combined with jump target duplication, we get a generalization of subprogram inlining. The reason it is a generalization is that the extent of inlining can be controlled by limiting the number of instructions duplicated from the jump target, thus allowing "partial inlining."

- Call forwarding very often skips type tests in the guard, such as teller tests, integer tests, and floating point number tests. Usually it is possible to get integer arithmetic nearly as fast as machine arithmetic just by "declaring" the operands as integers in the guard, and depending on call forwarding to skip the tests. This goes a long way toward overcoming the performance problems of dynamic typing without requiring global type inference.

In addition, call forwarding is a useful addition to implementation techniques, such as decision tree compilation, that have been studied for committed choice languages [9], since it allows optimizations at call-sites rather than just at the callee. Thus, in the code for the predicate `fact/2` given earlier, the type of the first argument is tested in each clause, and decision tree compilation would execute this just once; however, this test would be repeated at each recursive call. Using call forwarding, the repeated tests at each recursive call would be avoided, because the code generated for the recursive call would simply bypass this test.

4 An Example of the Code Generated

Figure 1 shows the code generated for the following Janus program:

```
app([H|L1],L2,^Z) :-  Z=[H|L3], app(L1,L2,^L3).
app([],L,^Z) :- Z=L.
```

The first column is the optimized Janus virtual machine (JVM) code, while the second is the corresponding C code generated (some C macros have not been expanded due to space constraints, but their effects are described below and their implementation should be intuitively obvious). The `jc` virtual machine instructions are finer-grained than those for the WAM; in fact most of them would have simple expansions directly into assembly language. The label L3 is the beginning of the suspension code (not shown). The tag operation macros are left unexpanded to make the C code easier to read, and in any case they are quite typical of such operations. Each is_*type*() macro involves a single mask and comparison. Each get_*type*() and tag_*type*() for tellers, and integers involves a single mask *or* shift, the other types require both a mask and a shift. Askers, tellers, and integers use two-bit tags, the other types all use 5 bits. Askers have the tag 00, so they require no work to either tag or untag. All get_asker(ti) macros in the code have been expanded to ti but the tag_asker macros have been left in.

OJump(FrameResume) jumps to the resumption address in the top stack frame. What it actually does is set the value of nxt_lbl to a small integer constant then jump to the top of a switch statement

```
top: switch (nxt_lbl) {...}
```

that contains the whole janus program. Each non-tail call is followed by a case label on a unique integer. That integer is put on the top of the current frame before a call.

The Move(cs,0) at the beginning of the body sets the current suspension cs to a null value on commit. This must be done before the current procedure calls another procedure, otherwise if cs is non-null and the called procedure suspends, it will suspend on cs. The reason this instruction is at the beginning of the body instead of just before a call is so that call forwarding can skip it. another

MemCheck(i,j) tests to see whether there is room for i words of stace space plus j words of heap space plus the extra word on the stack for storing the resumption address. The reason the C code shows a check for 3 words instead of just 2 is that the extra word on the stack frame is checked for even when no stack is allocated, as in this example.

MakeTeller(t2,t2) is implemented as a special tag operation that converts an asker to a teller with one addition. TELLER and ASKER are the teller and asker tags respectively. They are static constants so the substraction is performed at C compile-time. In the unoptimized code there is a teller made and then an asker is extracted from it in the inner loop, but in the optimized code both operations are moved out of the inner loop.

MakeSafe(t1) moves t1 to the heap if it is on the stack. This is necessary in general to avoid having a lower frame in the stack point to a higher one. Because of the strict directionality of assignment in Janus it is not possible to use the WAM strategy of always just making the higher address point to the lower one. The preceeding MemCheck() is needed to make sure there is space in case t1 needs to be moved to the heap.

5 Performance

The tables below give some indication of the current level of performance of the system. The host machine in all cases is a Sun 4/60 (SPARCstation-1) with 16 MB of main memory. It should be emphasized that this is by no means a finished system: there are a number of optimizations that we have not had time to implement.

Table 1 compares the speed of the code produced by the jc compiler with the speed of the same program written in Prolog and executed on Sicstus Prolog version 2.1 (compiling to native code) and Quintus Prolog version 3.1.1. In each case, the time reported, in milliseconds, is the time taken to execute the program once. This time was obtained by iterating the program long enough to eliminate

Figure 1: Code generated for append/3 in the naive reverse benchmark

Optimized JVM code		Expanded C Code
`L0:JumpUnlessTeller(L2,t2)`	%%% CODE FOR CLAUSE 1	`L0:if (!is_teller(t2)) goto L2;`
`JumpUnlessLcons(L5,t0)`	% Is arg 3 a teller?	`if (!is_lcons(t0)) goto L5;`
`Move(cs,0)`	% Is arg 1 a cons cell?	`cs = 0;`
`GetAsker(t2)`	%	`for (t2=*get_teller(t2);t2 != *t2;t2=*t2);`
`L4:MemCheck(0,2)`	% Remove teller tag	`L4:if (sp + 3 >= hp) mem_error();`
`GetCons(a0,t0)`	% Enough space for new cons?	`a0 = get_lcons(t0);`
`Load(t3,a0[0])`	% Get address of old cons	`t3 = a0[0];`
`Load(t0,a0[1])`	% Get car of old cons	`t0 = a0[1];`
`HeapSpace(2)`	% Get cdr of old cons	`hp -= 2;`
`Assign(t2,tag_lcons(hp))`	% Allocate space for cons	`*t2 = tag_lcons(hp);`
`Store(t3,hp[0])`	% Assign new cons to arg 3	`hp[0] = t3;`
`MakeAsker(t2,hp[1])`	% Set car of new cons	`t2 = tag_asker(&hp[1]);`
`Deref(t0)`	% Make a reference to cdr	`{register tagval *v; if (is_asker(t0)`
	% Deref the cdr of old cons	`do t0=*(v=t0); while(is_asker(t0)&&v!=t0);}`
`JumpIfLcons(L4,t0)`	%	`if (is_lcons(t0)) goto L4;`
`Store(t2,hp[1])`	% Loop if old cdr is a cons	`hp[1] = t2;`
`JumpIfEqual(L6,t0,C_nil)`	% Initialize new cdr	`if (t0 == C_nil) goto L6;`
`MakeTeller(t2,t2)`	% Exit if old cdr is nil	`t2 = t2 + (TELLER - ASKER);`
`Jump(L2)`	% Make a teller for new cdr	`goto L2;`
	%	
`L1:JumpUnlessTeller(L2,t2)`	%%% CODE FOR CLAUSE 2	`L1:if (!is_teller(t2)) goto L2;`
`L5:JumpUnlessEqual(L2,t0,C_nil)`	% Teller test for clause 2	`L5:if (t0 != C_nil) goto L2;`
`GetAsker(t2)`	% Is arg 1 nil?	`for (t2=*get_teller(t2);t2 != *t2;t2=*t2);`
`L6:MemCheck(0,1)`	% Change arg 3 to an address	`L6:if (sp + 2 >= hp) mem_error();`
`MakeSafe(t1)`	% Check space for MakeSafe	`if (t1 < sp && is_varptr(t1))`
	% Make sure arg 2 is safe	`{hp-=1;*hp=*get_varptr(t1)=hp;t1=hp|(t1&3);}`
`Assign(t2,t1)`	%	`*t2 = t1;`
`OJump(FrameResume)`	% Assign arg 2 to arg 3	`nxt_lbl = ((frame)sp)->resume; goto top;`
`L2:JumpUnlessKnown(L3,t0)`	% Return from procedure	`L2:if (!is_known(t0)) goto L3;`
`JumpUnlessKnown(L3,t2)`	% Suspend if arg 1 unbound	`if (!is_known(t2)) goto L3;`
	% Suspend if arg 3 unbound	

Program	jc (J) (ms)	Sicstus (S) (ms)	S/J	Quintus (Q) (ms)	Q/J
hanoi	182	300	1.6	690	3.4
tak	267	730	2.7	2200	8.2
nrev	0.729	1.8	2.5	7.9	11
qsort	2.03	5.1	2.5	9.4	4.6
factorial	0.0494	0.44	8.9	0.27	5.5

Table 1: The Performance of jc, compared with Sicstus and Quintus Prolog

Program	unoptimized (ms)	optimized (ms)	% improvement
hanoi	283	182	36
tak	487	138	72
nrev	2.07	0.729	65
qsort	3.57	2.03	43
factorial	0.0678	0.0494	27
merge	1.19	0.623	46
susp	43.5	26.8	38
dnf	0.628	0.217	65

Table 2: Speed Improvements due to the optimizations

most effects due to multiprogramming. The experiments were repeated 20 times for each benchmark on each system and in each case, the average time was taken. The benchmarks tested were the following:

nrev – *naive reverse*: 1000 iterations on a list of length 30.
qsort– *quicksort*: 100 iterations on a list of length 50.
tak– the "Takeuchi" benchmark: we timed the call tak(18, 12, 6, _).
hanoi – The Towers of Hanoi program: hanoi(13). Adapted from [7].
factorial – A program to compute the factorial of 12.

The Janus code is typically more than twice as fast as the Sicstus Prolog, and four to eight times faster than Quintus Prolog. Table 2 gives the improvements in speed resulting from the optimizations described at the end of the previous section. Here we include three more benchmarks: susp, a program that suspends and resumes repeatedly because the consumer is always scheduled ahead of the producer. The merge benchmark is the usual nondeterministic "merge" program. The dnf benchmark is an array based implementation of the "Dutch national flag" problem (see [12]). The combined optimizations (call forwarding, jump target duplication, and instruction-pair motion), give rise to a speed improvements typically ranging from 30%–65%. For well written Janus clauses, the overhead of the guard tests that do not play a role in committing a particular clause, but are just written as a kind of sanity check for the arguments to have the proper type, is almost completely optimized away.

Finally, Table 3 compares the performance of our Janus system with C code for some small benchmarks. Again, these were run on a SPARCstation 1, with cc as the C compiler. We tested only programs where we felt C could "compete fairly" — i.e., we did not test programs such as nrev or merge, where the cost of memory

Program	Janus (ms)	C (unopt) (ms)	C (opt: -O4)
qsort[3]	1.33	1.25	0.34
tak	267	208	72
factorial	0.0494	0.049	0.036

Table 3: The performance of jc compared to C

allocation via `malloc()` would have crippled the performance of the C programs and produced misleading results. The programs were written in the style one would expect of a competent C programmer: no recursion (except in `tak`, where it is hard to avoid), destructive updates, and the use of arrays (in `qsort`).

It can be seen that even without global dataflow analysis and optimizations, we are not very far from the performance of the C code — a factor of 4 in speed from the code produced by optimizing at level -O4 by a high-quality C compiler such as `cc` on the SPARCstation is not very embarrassing, and we expect to close the gap considerably once we implement a number of optimizations that we are now investigating.

6 Conclusions

This paper describes `jc`, a portable and efficient sequential implementation of Janus [12] that compiles down to C. When we began this implementation, we expected that "heavy-duty" global flow analyses and optimizations would be necessary for credible performance, because ask/tell languages involve a great deal of testing for suspension, etc., that is absent in Prolog. Somewhat to our surprise, we discovered that with careful attention to the C code generated by the Janus compiler, and some reasonably simple "local" optimizations such as common subexpression elimination and call forwarding, we can attain reasonably good performance. We expect further performance improvements once we have implemented sophisticated compilation algorithms, such as (weighted) decision trees, heap space reuse, and global flow analysis and optimizations.

An alpha test version of this system, together with some (rudimentary) documentation, is currently available by anonymous FTP from `cs.arizona.edu` in the directory `janus/jc`.

Acknowledgements: Discussions with Mats Carlsson played a very important role in the design of the Janus virtual machine. The system also benefited from discussions with Takashi Chikayama, Ken Kahn, Jacob Levy, and Vijay Saraswat. We are also grateful to Mats Carlsson for helping with the Quintus Prolog benchmarking. The work of the first and third authors was supported in part by the National Science Foundation under grant number CCR-8901283, and that of the second author by the National Fund for Scientific Research of Belgium and by the Belgian National incentive program for fundamental research in Artificial Intelligence, initiated by the Belgian State Prime Minister's office Science Policy Programming.

---

[3] The Janus version of `qsort` used in this table is different from the one used in the previous tables: here, the predicate `split/4` has explicit `int/1` tests in its guards, to be consistent with `int` declarations in the C program and allow a fair comparison. These tests allow additional optimizations in the Janus compiler.

References

[1] A. V. Aho, R. Sethi and J. D. Ullman, *Compilers – Principles, Techniques and Tools*, Addison-Wesley, 1986.

[2] T. Chikayama, personal communication, Feb. 1992.

[3] S. K. Debray, "Register Allocation in a Prolog Machine", *Proc. 1986 IEEE Symposium on Logic Programming*, Salt Lake City, Sept. 1986, pp. 267–275.

[4] S. K. Debray, "A Simple Code Improvement Scheme for Prolog", *J. Logic Programming*, vol. 13 no. 1, May 1992, pp. 57-88.

[5] S. K. Debray, S. Kannan, and M. Paithane, "Weighted Decision Trees", *Proc. Joint International Conference and Symposium on Logic Programming*, Washington, D.C., Nov. 1992 (this volume).

[6] I. Foster and S. Taylor, "Strand: A Practical Parallel Programming Tool", *Proc. 1989 North American Conference on Logic Programming*, Cleveland, Ohio, Oct. 1989, pp. 497-512. MIT Press.

[7] A. Houri and E. Shapiro, "A Sequential Abstract Machine for Flat Concurrent Prolog", in *Concurrent Prolog: Collected Papers*, vol. 2, ed. E. Shapiro, pp. 513-574. MIT Press, 1987.

[8] G. Janssens, B. Demoen, and A. Mariën, "Improving the Register Allocation in WAM by Reordering Unification", *Proc. Fifth International Conference on Logic Programming*, Seattle, Aug. 1988, pp. 1388–1402.

[9] S. Kliger and E. Shapiro, "From Decision Trees to Decision Graphs", *Proc. 1990 North American Conference on Logic Programming*, Austin, Oct. 1990, pp. 97–116. MIT Press.

[10] M. Meier, "Recursion vs. Iteration in Prolog", *Proc. Eighth International Conference on Logic Programming*, Paris, June 1991, pp. 157–169. MIT Press.

[11] V. A. Saraswat, *Concurrent Constraint Programming Languages*, PhD thesis, Dept. of Computer Science, Carnegie-Mellon University, 1989. (To appear in the ACM Doctoral Dissertation Award series, MIT Press.)

[12] V. Saraswat, K. Kahn, and J. Levy, "Janus: A step towards distributed constraint programming", in *Proc. 1990 North American Conference on Logic Programming*, Austin, TX, Oct. 1990, pp. 431-446. MIT Press.

[13] K. Ueda, "Guarded Horn Clauses", in *Concurrent Prolog: Collected Papers*, vol. 1, ed. E. Shapiro, pp. 140-156, 1987. MIT Press.

[14] P. Van Roy and A. M. Despain, "The Benefits of Global Dataflow Analysis for an Optimizing Prolog Compiler", *Proc. 1990 North American Conference on Logic Programming*, Austin, Texas, Oct. 1990, pp. 501–515. MIT Press.

Negation I

Autoepistemic Logics as a Unifying Framework for the Semantics of Logic Programs

Piero A. Bonatti
Dipartimento di Informatica - Universita' di Pisa
Corso Italia 40, I-56125 Pisa, ITALY
bonatti@di.unipi.it

Abstract

In this paper it is shown that a 3-valued autoepistemic logic provides an elegant unifying framework for most of the major semantics of normal logic programs. The framework can immediately be extended to disjunctive logic programs, and induces the natural counterparts of the well-founded and the stable semantics. It will be shown that these semantics are inherently different from all the other semantics that have been proposed for disjunctive programs. The new semantics allow to define programs that cannot be defined through the *stationary semantics* and that seem very hard to define by means of $GWFSD$ and WF^3.

1 Introduction

It is well-known [6,7] that autoepistemic logic [11] provides an interesting semantics for negation-as-failure. In this paper we extend this result and show that a 3-valued autoepistemic logic [3,4] provides an elegant unifying framework for: the well-founded semantics [13], the stable semantics [7], the semantics introduced by Fitting [5] and Kunen [8], and ground SLDNF resolution.

It will be shown that the same autoepistemic framework can immediately be extended to *disjunctive logic programs* [9,1,2]. The resulting semantics are different from the major semantics that have been proposed so far (i.e. the *stationary semantics* [12], the *generalised well-founded semantics for disjunctive programs* (GWFSD) [1], and its extension WF^3 [2].) In fact, the formers are based on a pure notion of *negation as failure to prove*, while the latters embody different notions of *negation as assumed falsity*.

In order to motivate the new semantics, we will introduce an interesting class of programs, called *ignorance tests* that can easily be defined through the autoepistemic semantics, but can not be satisfactorily defined through the stationary semantics (it is not yet known whether ignorance-tests can be defined through GWFSD or WF^3 in a reasonable way.)

In the next section, the three-valued autoepistemic logic is defined. In section 3 we show how the three-valued autoepistemic logic captures several semantics for normal logic programs. In section 4 we introduce the autoepistemic semantics for disjunctive logic programs, and discuss the relationships with the stationary semantics, GWFSD and WF^3.

2 Three-valued Autoepistemic Logics

The language of autoepistemic logics is a propositional modal language, $\mathcal{L}$, with standard connectives ($\vee, \wedge, \leftarrow$ and $\neg$), a non-standard connective ($\Leftarrow$) and one modal operator L, to be read as "know" or "believe".

The formulae where L does not occur are called *ordinary* or *objective*. The set of ordinary formulae is denoted by $\mathcal{L}_O$. The formulae where propositional symbols occur only within the scope of L are called *purely epistemic*. The formulae of the form $L\psi$ (where ψ is an arbitrarily complex $\mathcal{L}$-formula) are called *autoepistemic atoms*.

The purpose of autoepistemic logics is to model the beliefs that an ideally rational and introspective agent should hold, given a set A of *premises* (i.e. axioms, or basic beliefs).

Definition 2.1 *A* belief-state *B is a pair $\langle B^+, B^- \rangle$, where B^+ and B^- are disjoint sets of $\mathcal{L}$-formulae.*

Intuitively, B^+ is the set of statements that the agent *believes*, while B^- is the set of statements that the agent *has no reason to believe*. The remaining statements of the language are those about which the agent is *doubtful*, that is, such statements are involved in an "epistemically inconsistent" piece of knowledge.[1]

We say that a belief state B is *complete* iff $B^+ \cup B^- = \mathcal{L}$. Belief states are partially ordered by a natural extension of set inclusion.

Definition 2.2 *Define $B_1 \subseteq B_2$ iff $B_1^+ \subseteq B_2^+$ and $B_1^- \subseteq B_2^-$.*

There is one minimal belief state $\perp = \langle \emptyset, \emptyset \rangle$, but many maximal belief states, i.e. the complete ones. Let's now introduce the models of our language:

Definition 2.3 *A* propositional interpretation *is a pair (I, B) where I is a classical (2-valued) interpretation of $\mathcal{L}_O$, and B is a belief state.*

A propositional interpretation (I, B) is also called a *B-interpretation*. A B-interpretation is *complete* iff B is complete.

---

[1] By "epistemically inconsistent knowledge" we mean any piece of conflicting information that causes the premises to have no stable expansions or many of them.

Propositional interpretations model both what is true in the "outside world" (through I) and the agent's beliefs (through B.) Ordinary atoms are given a classical truth value by I. An autoepistemic atom $L\psi$ is: *true* in (I, B) iff $\psi \in B^+$; *false* in (I, B) iff $\psi \in B^-$; and *undefined*, otherwise.

Non-atomic formulae are evaluated by extending *strong Kleene's valuation* to the non-standard connective $\Leftarrow$ as follows: formula $\psi \Leftarrow \phi$ is *true* if ψ is true or ϕ is not true, and *false* otherwise.

Note that ordinary formulae are given a thoroughly classical semantics, and that an $\mathcal{L}_O$-formula ψ is a (classical) tautology if and only if ψ is true in all propositional interpretations.

As usual, we say that a propositional interpretation (I, B) *satisfies* a formula ψ (denoted $(I, B) \models \psi$) iff ψ is true in (I, B). In this case, (I, B) is called a *B-model* (or simply a model) of ψ. We say that a set S of formulae *entails* a formula ψ (denoted $S \models \psi$) iff ψ is true in every model of S. We say that a set S of formulae *B-entails* a formula ψ (denoted $S \models_B \psi$) iff ψ is true in every B-model of S.

Definition 2.4 (I, B') *is an* **autoepistemic interpretation** *of B iff $B' = B$. (I, B') is an* **autoepistemic model** *of B if (I, B') is both an autoepistemic interpretation of B and a model of B^+. If B has an auto-epistemic model, we say that B is* **epistemically consistent**.

The basic guideline we will follow in formalising the assumptions about the agent's rationality and introspectiveness is *prudence*: we want the agent's belief state to be independent of how her doubts can be removed or, equivalently, independent of how her knowledge gaps can be filled in.

By prudence and rationality requirements, the agent's belief state should satisfy the following principle:

> **Principle 1** *The agent should believe (resp. not believe) all and only those formulae that are true (resp. not necessarily true) whenever her premises are true - no matter how she can extend her knowledge.*

By introspectiveness, the agent knows exactly what her own belief state is, and hence she knows that the actual world must be an autoepistemic interpretation of her beliefs. If no such interpretation satisfied the agent's beliefs, then the agent's rationality could be questioned, so we impose a second constraint:

> **Principle 2** *There should be a world compatible with the agent's belief state. That is, there should be an autoepistemic model of such a belief state.*

Finally, we formalise the two principles:

Definition 2.5 *Let B and B' range over belief states, and let A be a set of premises. B is a* generalised stable expansion *(GSE) of A iff*

1. $B^+ = \{\psi \mid \forall B' \supseteq B,\ A \models_{B'} \psi\}$

2. $B^- = \{\psi \mid \forall B' \supseteq B,\ A \not\models_{B'} \psi\}$

3. B *is epistemically consistent.*

For what we said before, every GSE is an admissible belief state for our agent. The next two propositions show that the three-valued autoepistemic logic generalises the autoepistemic logic introduced by Moore. More specifically, they show that stable expansions are generalised stable expansions, and that the closure properties of stable expansions are preserved. In the following, $\mathcal{L} \setminus X$ will be abbreviated by $\overline{X}$.

Proposition 2.1 X *is a* consistent *stable expansion of A iff $\langle X, \overline{X} \rangle$ is a complete GSE of A.*

Proposition 2.2 *If B is a generalised stable expansion then B is stable, that is:*

1. *If $B^+ \models \psi$ then $\psi \in B^+$*

2. $L\psi \in B^+$ *iff $\psi \in B^+$*

3. $\neg L\psi \in B^+$ *iff $\psi \in B^-$*

Finally, we prove that under fairly general conditions there exists a unique minimal GSE, that enjoys an iterative characterisation based on the operator defined below:

Definition 2.6 *Operator $\Theta_A = \langle \Theta_A(B)^+, \Theta_A(B)^- \rangle$, over belief-states, is defined by the following equations:*

$$\Theta_A(B)^+ = \{\psi \mid \forall B' \supseteq B,\ A \models_{B'} \psi\}$$
$$\Theta_A(B)^- = \{\psi \mid \forall B' \supseteq B,\ A \not\models_{B'} \psi\}$$

By definitions 2.5 and 2.6, B is a GSE of A iff B is an epistemically consistent fixpoint of Θ_A. Θ_A turns out to be monotonic:

Lemma 2.1 $B_1 \subseteq B_2$ *implies $\Theta_A(B_1) \subseteq \Theta_A(B_2)$*

It follows, by Tarski's theorem, that Θ_A has a least fixed point, $lfp(\Theta_A)$, and that $lfp(\Theta_A) = \Theta_A^\alpha(\bot)$, for some ordinal α. If $lfp(\Theta_A)$ is epistemically consistent, then it is the least stable expansion of A. From this fact a powerful result can be derived for a class of very expressive theories:

Definition 2.7 *A set of formulae A is in* **implicative form** *if and only if the members of A are either ordinary formulae, or formulae of the form: $\psi \Leftarrow \phi$, where ψ is ordinary, ϕ is purely epistemic and "$\Leftarrow$" does not occur in ϕ.*

Theorem 2.2 *If A is in implicative form then the following are equivalent:*
  1) A has a GSE
  2) $lfp(\Theta_A)^+$ has a model
  3) $lfp(\Theta_A)$ is the least GSE of A.

It can be shown that $lfp(\Theta_A)^+$ has a model iff A is coherent under Kleene's 3-valued (monotonic) logic and necessitation. Thus an implicative theory has a unique minimal GSE under fairly reasonable consistency conditions. Furthermore, the least GSE can be defined not only by means of the impredicative fixpoint conditions, but also as the limit of the ordinal sequence: $\{\Theta_A^1(\bot), \Theta_A^2(\bot), \ldots, \Theta_A^\alpha(\bot), \ldots\}$.

3 Three-valued autoepistemic logics and the semantics of normal logic programs

In this section we show how the three-valued autoepistemic logic introduced in the previous section can capture most of the major semantics of normal programs.

In this paper we restrict our attention to (possibly infinite) propositional programs. This assumption is not restrictive for the study of the declarative semantics of logic programs. In fact, all the semantics mentioned in the introduction give each program P and its ground instantiation P' the same meaning; and P' can be translated into a propositional theory by uniformly translating ground atoms into propositional symbols.

The relationships between normal logic programs and autoepistemic logics have been explored for the first time by Gelfond in [6]. The basic idea is replacing negation-as-failure ($\sim$) by "$\neg L$".

Definition 3.1 *The* **autoepistemic translation** *of a logic program P is the autoepistemic theory $\hat{P}$ obtained by translating every rule*

$$p \leftarrow q_1, \ldots, q_n, \sim q_{n+1}, \ldots, \sim q_m$$

of P into

$$p \Leftarrow q_1 \wedge \ldots \wedge q_n \wedge \neg L q_{n+1} \wedge \ldots \wedge \neg L q_m.$$

The atomic part of each stable expansion of $\hat{P}$ provides a minimal model of P. In [6] it is shown that when P is a stratified program, then $\hat{P}$ has a unique stable expansion, that corresponds exactly to what is computed by SLDNF-resolution.

In [7], the same idea has been reformulated entirely in terms of logic programming concepts, which led to the notion of *stable model*.

Stable models do not necessarily exist, and are not necessarily unique. According to the original definition [7], when P has a unique stable model M, the stable semantics of P is defined, and is equal to M. When P has no stable models, or more than one stable models, then the stable semantics is undefined. According to a more recent proposal, an atom A is *true* (resp. *false*) iff A belongs to all (resp. none) of the stable models of P.

The following proposition shows that stable models are in one-to-one correspondence with complete GSE's. $Atom(X)$, where X is a set of $\mathcal{L}$-formulae, denotes the set of ordinary atoms of X.

Proposition 3.1 *If M is a stable model of P, then there exists a complete GSE of $\hat{P}$, denoted by B, such that $Atom(B^+) = M$. Conversely, if B is a complete GSE of $\hat{P}$, then $Atom(B^+)$ is a stable model of P.*

Next we show that $\hat{P}$ has one minimal GSE, that corresponds to the well-founded semantics. For this purpose, note that the rules of $\hat{P}$ are equivalent to implicative rules of the form: $(p \Leftarrow q_1 \wedge \ldots \wedge q_n) \Leftarrow \neg Lq_{n+1} \wedge \ldots \wedge \neg Lq_m$. Moreover, for all belief states B, $\hat{P}$ is B-consistent. From these facts and Theorem 2.2, the following proposition easily follows.

Proposition 3.2 *$lfp(\Theta_{\hat{P}})$ is the least GSE of $\hat{P}$.*

The next theorem shows that the least GSE of $\hat{P}$ corresponds to the well-founded model of P

Theorem 3.1 *Let WF_P^T and WF_P^F, denote the sets of ground atoms that are true and false, respectively, in the well-founded model of P. Let B_P be the least GSE of $\hat{P}$. Then*

$$WF_P^T = Atom(B_P^+)$$
$$WF_P^F = Atom(B_P^-)$$

Summarizing, the maximal, complete GSE's of $\hat{P}$ correspond to the stable models of P, while the least GSE of $\hat{P}$ corresponds to the well-founded semantics of P.

Now we introduce a different translation, that captures the semantics introduced by Fitting [5], and its restriction, proposed by Kunen [8], which is equivalent to ground SLDNF resolution. In the new translation, every literal in the body of the rules is transformed into an autoepistemic literal.

Definition 3.2 *The autoepistemic theory $\ddot{P}$ is obtained by translating every rule*

$$p \leftarrow q_1, \ldots, q_n, \sim q_{n+1}, \ldots, \sim q_m$$

of P into

$$p \Leftarrow LLq_1 \wedge \ldots \wedge LLq_n \wedge L\neg Lq_{n+1} \wedge \ldots \wedge L\neg Lq_m.$$

Since Fitting uses sets of *annotated formulae* [5], the following conversion function is needed:

Definition 3.3 *For all belief-states B define:*

$$An(B) = \{TA \mid A \in Atom(B^+)\} \cup \{FA \mid A \in Atom(B^-)\}$$

The next theorem illustrates the correspondence between Fitting's operator Φ_P and operator $\Theta_{\ddot{P}}$.

Theorem 3.2 *For all belief-states B and all atoms A:*

- $TA \in \Phi_P(An(B))$ *iff* $A \in \Theta_{\ddot{P}}^2(B)^+$

- $FA \in \Phi_P(An(B))$ *iff* $A \in \Theta_{\ddot{P}}^2(B)^-$

The first corollary of the above theorem shows that the Kripke-Kleene semantics of P is captured by the least GSE of $\ddot{P}$.

Corollary 3.1 *Let $B = lfp(\Theta_{\ddot{P}})$ be the least GSE of $\ddot{P}$. Then*

- $TA \in lfp(\Phi_P)$ *iff* $A \in B^+$

- $FA \in lfp(\Phi_P)$ *iff* $A \in B^-$

The next corollary tells that the constructive semantics proposed by Kunen is captured by the ω power of $\Theta_{\ddot{P}}$.

Corollary 3.2 *Let $B = \Theta_{\ddot{P}}^\omega(\bot)$. Then*

- $TA \in \Phi_P^\omega(\emptyset)$ *iff* $A \in B^+$

- $FA \in \Phi_P^\omega(\emptyset)$ *iff* $A \in B^-$

Finally, we show that the ω power of $\Theta_{\ddot{P}}$ corresponds also to ground SLDNF resolution:

Theorem 3.3 *Let $B = \Theta_{\ddot{P}}^\omega(\bot)$. For all atoms A,*

- *goal $\leftarrow A$ has an SLDNF refutation in P iff $A \in B^+$*

- *goal $\leftarrow A$ has a finitely failed SLDNF tree in P iff $A \in B^-$*

Note that when P is finite or, more generally, when $\Theta_{\ddot{P}}$ is continuous, $\Theta_{\ddot{P}}^\omega(\bot)$ is the least GSE of $\ddot{P}$. In this case, by Corollary 3.2 and Theorem 3.3, both Kunen's semantics and ground SLDNF resolution are captured by the least GSE of $\ddot{P}$.

4   Disjunctive logic programs

Disjunctive logic programs [9] allow the head of the rules to be disjunctions of atoms. In order to compare the various semantics that have been proposed for disjunctive programs, the standard notions of intensional database and extensional database will be needed:

Definition 4.1 *Let the set of atoms of the language be partitioned into two sets: the set of* **extensional atoms** *and the set of* **intensional atoms.** *An* **extensional database** *is a set of disjunctive rules of the form:*

$$p_1 \vee \ldots \vee p_k \leftarrow$$

($k > 0$), where all the p_i's are extensional atoms.
An **intensional database** *is a set of disjunctive rules of the form:*

$$p_1 \vee \ldots \vee p_k \leftarrow q_1, \ldots, q_n, \sim q_{n+1}, \ldots, \sim q_m$$

($k > 0$), where all the p_i's are intensional atoms.
A **disjunctive deductive database** *is a disjunctive program*

$$P = EDB_P \cup IDB_P$$

where EDB_P is an extensional database, and IDB_P is an intensional database.

4.1   Autoepistemic semantics

The autoepistemic translations (ˆ) and (¨) can naturally be extended to disjunctive programs. In this paper, we focus our attention on (ˆ), which produces rules of the form:

$$p_1 \vee \ldots \vee p_k \Leftarrow q_1 \wedge \ldots \wedge q_n \wedge \neg L q_{n+1} \wedge \ldots \wedge \neg L q_m.$$

By analogy with the semantics of normal programs, the well-founded and the stable semantics of a disjunctive logic program P will be defined by selecting suitable formulae from the GSE's of $\hat{P}$.

Definition 4.2 ([1]) *Let $\mathbf{B}_P$ be the Herbrand base of P. The* **disjunctive Herbrand base** *of P, denoted by DHB_P is the set of all non-redundant disjunctions of atoms of $\mathbf{B}_P$.*
The **conjunctive Herbrand base** *of P, denoted by CHB_P is the set of all non-redundant conjunctions of atoms of $\mathbf{B}_P$.*

Definition 4.3 *Let P be a disjunctive program and B_{min} be the least GSE of $\hat{P}$. The* **well-founded model state** *of P is:*

$$WS_P = \langle WS_P^+, WS_P^- \rangle = \langle B_{min}^+ \cap DHB_P, \ B_{min}^- \cap CHB_P \rangle$$

A stable model state *of P is defined as:*

$$SS_P = \langle SS_P^+, SS_P^- \rangle = \langle B_{max}^+ \cap DHB_P,\ B_{max}^- \cap CHB_P \rangle$$

where B_{max} is any complete GSE of $\hat{P}$.

Proposition 3.2 holds also when P is a disjunctive program, therefore every disjunctive program has a unique well-founded model-state (while there may be none, or many, stable model-states.) The next two examples illustrate the behaviour of the new semantics.

Example 4.1 Let P be the following program:

$$a \vee b$$
$$p \leftarrow a$$
$$q \leftarrow \sim a, \sim b$$
$$r \leftarrow a$$
$$r \leftarrow b$$

The disjunctive well-founded semantics allows to derive:

- $a \vee b$ (i.e. $a \vee b \in WS_P^+$);

- $\sim a$ and $\sim b$ (i.e. $a, b \in WS_P^-$) because there is no way to derive a and no way to derive b;

- $\sim p$, because a can not be derived;

- q, because $\sim a$ and $\sim b$ can be derived;

- r, because it follows classically from P.

In this case, WS_P is also the only stable model-state of P. ∎

Note that in the above example $a \vee b$, $\sim a$ and $\sim b$ are simultaneously derived. This is not a contradiction, because "$\sim A$" means "A is not derivable" rather than "A is false". In other words, the autoepistemic formalisation of "$\sim$" captures the pure notion of negation as *failure to prove*.

Example 4.2 Let P be the following program:

$$a \leftarrow \sim b$$
$$b \leftarrow \sim a$$
$$c \vee d \leftarrow a$$
$$p \leftarrow b$$
$$p \leftarrow c$$
$$p \leftarrow d$$

According to the well-founded semantics, $\sim c$ and $\sim d$ can be derived, while $a, b, c \vee d$ and p are undefined (i.e. they do not belong to $WS_P^+ \cup WS_P^-$).

P has two stable model-states, denoted by SS_1 and SS_2, such that:

- $a, (c \lor d), p$ belong to SS_1^+ and c, d, b belong to SS_1^-;

- b, p belong to SS_2^+ and c, d, a belong to SS_2^-.

In this case there are two possible definitions for the stable semantics of P:

- the stable semantics is undefined, because there are two distinct stable model states;

- the stable semantics is given by the intersection of SS_1 and SS_2.

In the second case, it is possible to derive p and $b \lor c \lor d$, that cannot be obtained through the well-founded semantics. $\blacksquare$

The negation as failure-to-prove induced by the autoepistemic semantics is particularly helpful when specific actions have to be taken on the basis of *lack of knowledge*.

Example 4.3 Suppose that a doctor knows that some patient is affected either by disease d_1 or by disease d_2. If the doctor knows which disease is affecting the patient, then s/he can apply a specific therapy. If the doctor does not know which disease is affecting the patient, then s/he should ask for more clinical tests, because prescribing the wrong treatment may be dangerous for the patient. This example can be formalised by the following intensional database, where t_i's represent the different treatments and tests:

$$IDB_P = \{(t_1 \leftarrow d_1), (t_2 \leftarrow d_2), (t_3 \leftarrow \sim d_1, \sim d_2)\}$$

It can be shown that IDB_P correctly formalises the example, namely, for all extensional databases EDB_P:

- if $EDB_P \not\models d_1$ and $EDB_P \not\models d_2$, then $t_3 \in WS_P^+$ and $t_1, t_2 \in WS_P^-$

- if $EDB_P \models d_1$ then $t_3 \in WS_P^-$ and $t_1 \in WS_P^+$

- if $EDB_P \models d_2$ then $t_3 \in WS_P^-$ and $t_2 \in WS_P^+$

It can also be proved that, since P has a *stratified* structure, the well-founded model-state of P is also its unique stable model-state. $\blacksquare$

Example 4.4 Consider a census database DB such that, for all persons x, $male(x) \lor female(x)$ is a logical consequence of DB. At the time of the creation of DB, the data of some persons may be partially unavailable. For example, the sex of some individual x may not be known, although $male(x) \lor female(x)$ is a logical consequence of the database. In order to collect the missing information, it may be helpful to make a list of all the persons whose data is not complete. For this purpose one should define a relation r such that: $r(x)$ is inferred from DB if and only if neither $male(x)$ nor $female(x)$ can be derived from DB. With the new semantics, r can be defined simply as:

$$r(x) \leftarrow \sim male(x), \sim female(x).$$

$\blacksquare$

4.2 Stationary semantics

The stationary semantics relies on a slightly different translation of disjunctive logic programs. Every literal $\sim A$ is replaced by $\neg \mathcal{B}A$, where $\mathcal{B}A$ is a new propositional symbol.

Definition 4.4 (Generalised Closed World Assumption [10])

> $S \models_{GCWA} \psi$ *iff* ψ *is true in all the minimal Herbrand models of* S.

Definition 4.5 (Stationary semantics [12]) *The* **stationary state** *of a disjunctive program P is the limit of the monotonic ordinal-indexed sequence $S_0, S_1, \ldots, S_\alpha, \ldots$ defined below:*

$$S_0 \;=\; \emptyset$$
$$S_{\alpha+1} \;=\; \{\mathcal{B}A_1 \vee \ldots \vee \mathcal{B}A_k \mid P \cup S_\alpha \models_{GCWA} A_1 \vee \ldots \vee A_k\}$$
$$\cup \{\neg\mathcal{B}A_1 \vee \ldots \vee \neg\mathcal{B}A_k \mid P \cup S_\alpha \models_{GCWA} \neg A_1 \vee \ldots \vee \neg A_k\}$$
$$S_\lambda \;=\; \bigcup_{\alpha<\lambda} S_\alpha \;\; \textit{(where λ is a limit ordinal)}$$

Let S_β be the limit of the sequence. A disjunction of atoms $A_1 \vee \ldots \vee A_k$ is true if $\mathcal{B}A_1 \vee \ldots \vee \mathcal{B}A_k \in S_\beta$.
A conjunction of atoms $A_1 \wedge \ldots \wedge A_k$ is false if $\neg\mathcal{B}A_1 \vee \ldots \vee \neg\mathcal{B}A_k \in S_\beta$.
We say that $\sim A$ is true iff A is false.

It is easy to see that the autoepistemic semantics and the stationary semantics are different. The stationary semantics never allows $p \vee q$, $\sim p$ and $\sim q$ to be simultaneously true, while this is possible with the autoepistemic semantics (see Example 4.1.) In this sense, the stationary semantics gives non-monotonic negation some features of classical negation: a literal like $\sim p$ should be read as: "p is assumed to be false".

Example 4.5 Consider the intensional database IDB_P defined in Example 4.3. From $IDB_P \cup \{d_1 \vee d_2\}$ it is possible to derive:

- t_3, by means of the autoepistemic semantics;

- $\sim t_3$, by means of the stationary semantics; intuitively, d_1 and d_2 cannot be simultaneously assumed to be false – because this would contradict $d_1 \vee d_2$ – and hence t_3 has no justification; however, it is possible to derive $\sim d_1 \vee \sim d_2$.

This shows two facts: first, the autoepistemic and the stationary semantics are not comparable: they give completely different meanings to t_3. Secondly, it shows that IDB_P is not a correct formalisation of Example 4.3, when the stationary semantics is adopted ∎

In the following, we prove that the kind of relations captured by t_3 in Example 4.3 and by r in Example 4.4 are very difficult to capture with the stationary semantics. First we give a formal definition of such relations:

Definition 4.6 *Let* p, q *be extensional atoms, and* P *be a disjunctive program.* P *is an* **ignorance-test** *for* p, q *iff, for some intensional atom* t, *and for each extensional database* EDB, t *can be derived from* $P \cup EDB$ *iff* $EDB \not\models p$ *and* $EDB \not\models q$.

It can be easily verified that, under the autoepistemic semantics, the simple definition of t_3 in Example 4.3 is an ignorance test for d_1, d_2, and that, in Example 4.4, the definition of r is an ignorance test for all pairs of ground atoms of the form: $male(t), female(t)$. On the contrary, the next theorem shows that ignorance tests cannot be defined by means of the stationary semantics:

Theorem 4.1 *Let* p, q *be extensional atoms. No disjunctive logic program* P *can be an ignorance test for* p, q *when the stationary semantics is adopted.*

Therefore, the autoepistemic negation as failure cannot be replaced by the negation as assumed falsity induced by the stationary semantics. It seems that also the opposite should be true, i.e. there should be a class of programs that can be defined through the stationary semantics, but not by means of pure negation as failure. I leave the identification of such a class of programs as an open problem.

4.3 GWFSD and WF^3

It is not yet known whether theorem 4.1 holds for GWFSD and WF^3, too. However, there are many similarities between these semantics and the stationary semantics. For example, $p \lor q$, $\sim p$ and $\sim q$ can never be simultaneously true; as a consequence, GWFSD and WF^3 are different from the autoepistemic semantics, and the program in Example 4.3 is not an ignorance test for d_1, d_2 (actually, GWFSD and WF^3 give that program the same meaning as the stationary semantics).

5 Conclusions

The semantics based on three-valued autoepistemic logic is an elegant unifying framework for the main semantics of normal logic programs.

The autoepistemic framework can naturally be extended to disjunctive logic programs, and, in particular, it provides a well-founded and a stable semantics for these programs. The autoepistemic semantics are different from the semantics that have been proposed so far: the formers are based on a notion of pure negation as failure to prove, while the latters are based on slightly different forms of negation as assumed falsity.

In order to motivate the new semantics, we have introduced the notion of *ignorance-tests*, which formalises a class of useful programs that can easily be defined by means of the autoepistemic semantics, and that cannot be defined by means of the stationary semantics.

There are many analogies between the stationary semantics and GWFSD and WF^3. Further work is needed to see if defining an ignorance test with GWFSD and WF^3 is as difficult as with the stationary semantics.

Acknowledgements

I am grateful to V.S. Subrahmanian for his precious suggestions and encouragement.

References

[1] C. Baral, J. Lobo and J. Minker. *Generalised disjunctive well-founded semantics for logic programs.* Technical report UMIACS TR 90-39, University of Maryland at College Park, March 1989. Also in: ISMIS 90.

[2] C. Baral, J. Lobo and J. Minker. WF^3: *A semantics for negation in disjunctive logic programs.* ISMIS 91.

[3] P. Bonatti. *A more general solution to the multiple expansion problem.* In Proc. Workshop on Non-Monotonic Reasoning and Logic Programming, NACLP'90.

[4] P. A. Bonatti. *A family of three valued autoepistemic logics.* In E. Ardizzone, S.Gaglio, F.Sorbello (ed.), Trends in Artificial Intelligence: 2nd Congress of the Italian Association for Artificial Intelligence - AI*IA. Lecture Notes in Artificial Intelligence, LNAI 549. Springer-Verlag, Berlin, 1991, pp. 28-37.

[5] M. Fitting. *A Kripke-Kleene semantics for general logic programs.* The Journal of Logic Programming, Vol. 2, n. 4, Dec. 1985

[6] M. Gelfond. *On Stratified Autoepistemic Theories.* In Proceedings AAAI-87, 207-211, 1987.

[7] M. Gelfond, V. Lifschitz. *The stable model semantics for logic programming.* In Proc. of the 5th International Conference and Symposium on Logic Programming, Seattle, Washington, 1988.

[8] K. Kunen. *Negation in logic programming.* The Journal of Logic Programming, Vol. 4, n. 4, Dec. 1987

[9] J. Lobo, J. Minker, A. Rajasekar. *Extending the Semantics of Logic Programs to Disjunctive Logic Programs.* In Proc. of 6th International Conference on Logic Programming, 1989.

[10] J. Minker. *On indefinite databases and the closed world assumption.* In Lecture Notes in Computer Science 138, pp. 292-308. Springer-Verlag, 1982.

[11] R. Moore. *Semantical considerations on nonmonotonic logics.* In Artificial Intelligence 25, pp. 75-94, 1985.

[12] T. Przymusinski. *Stationary Semantics for Disjunctive Logic Programs and Deductive Databases.* In Proc. of the North American Conference on Logic Programming (1990).

[13] A. Van Gelder, K. Ross and J.S. Schlipf. *Unfounded sets and well-founded semantics for general logic programs.* In Proc. of the 7th Symposium on Principles of Database Systems, p. 221-230, 1988.

Negation as Failure in Intuitionistic Logic Programming

Laura Giordano and **Nicola Olivetti**
Dipartimento di Informatica - Università di Torino
C.so Svizzera 185 - 10149 TORINO
E-mail: (laura,olivetti)@di.unito.it

Abstract

In this paper both a top-down operational semantics and a Kripke/Kleene semantics is proposed for a logic language which combines embedded implications and negation as failure. As a difference with respect to other proposals [2,8], no restriction is put on the language; in particular, the programs we consider are not required to be stratified. Our top-down semantics is an extension of standard SLDNF [12]. The Kripke/Kleene semantics we define is a generalization of those developed by Fitting [4] and Kunen [10,11] for logic programs without embedded implications and makes use of Kleene strong three-valued logic. A three-valued interpretation provides simultaneously a meaning to all programs over a given language. The immediate consequence operator is a monotone mapping on the space of such Herbrand interpretations. In this respect our fixpoint semantics is similar to Miller's one [15].

We prove soundness and completeness of the operational semantics with respect to the fixpoint semantics both in the ground and in the non-ground case. In particular, for the non-ground case, a suitable notion of allowedness is defined for programs with embedded implications. Assuming allowedness, soundness and completeness of the operational semantics with respect to the fixpoint semantics can be proved if we cut the iteration of the T operator at a finite ordinal n. No restriction on the finiteness of the Herbrand Universe is assumed to get this result.

1 Introduction

Extensions of Horn clause logic with embedded implications have been extensively studied in these last years [5,6,15,13,14,1,16,7]. Such extensions are defined by allowing implications of the form $D \Rightarrow G$, where D is a set of clauses and G is a goal, both in goals and in clause bodies. According to the semantics chosen for implication goals, different extended languages can be obtained. In particular, when the underlying logic is the intuitionistic one, we talk of *intuitionistic logic programming*. In intuitionistic logic programming, an implication goal $D \Rightarrow G$ can be proved from a program P, if G can be proved from the extended program $P \cup D$. With this kind of operational semantics, intuitionistic logic programming is well suited to perform hypothetical reasoning [5] and it also allows module constructs to be introduced in the language [16].

In this paper we tackle the problem of defining a semantics for intuitionistic logic programming with *negation as failure*. The language obtained by adding negation as failure to intuitionistic logic programming has not a well understood operational behavior, and a general semantics for it has not yet been defined. Indeed, Gabbay in [6] pointed out several problems in dealing with negation as failure in this setting. Recently, some semantics have been proposed for logic programs with embedded implications and negation as failure. All of them, however, put some restriction on the language. In particular, Harland [8] has defined a Kripke/Kleene semantics for such programs, which works only when a distinction is made between completely and incompletely defined predicates: negation can be applied only to completely defined predicates, while only incompletely defined predicates can be extended by means of embedded implications. With the same restriction on the language, in [9] a notion of completion is defined. Bonner and McCarty in [2] have developed a generalized perfect model semantics for stratified programs with embedded implications. For the general case (without any restriction) there is a proposal by Dung [3] for a stable semantics, though a proof procedure for it is still lacking.

To motivate the interest in dealing with the unrestricted case, consider the following example, taken from [3].

Example 1. Consider the following program P:

$$\text{even} \leftarrow \neg \text{odd.}$$
$$\text{odd} \leftarrow \text{select(X)} \land (\text{ mark(X)} \Rightarrow \text{even }).$$
$$\text{select(X)} \leftarrow \text{r(X)} \land \neg \text{mark(X).}$$
$$\text{r(0). } \ldots \text{ r(n).}$$

This program is non-stratified and its behavior is the following: the goal *even* succeeds from the program P if P contains an even number of entries of r; otherwise it fails. In [2] a similar stratified program is given, but this non-stratified version seems more natural.

The purpose of this paper is, on one hand, to define a top-down proof procedure for a language which combines negation as failure and embedded implications; on the other hand, to develop a model theoretic semantics with respect to which the operational semantics of the language is sound and complete. Moreover, we do not want to put any restriction on the language. Our top-down proof procedure is an extension of standard SLDNF [12]. In our case, since different goals can be proved from different programs, a query is defined as a sequence of pairs (Program,Goal). Moreover, we define a notion of allowedness in order to prevent *floundering*, which turns out to be an harder problem than in the case of logic programs without embedded implications. Concerning the logical interpretation of this language, a modal completion has been defined in [17], where, however, the analysis mainly focused on the propositional case. Here, we define a Kripke/Kleene semantics which also works in the first order case. The Kripke/Kleene semantics we define is a generalization of those developed by Fitting [4] and Kunen [10,11] for general logic programs and makes use of Kleene strong three-valued logic. The three values *true*, *false* and *undefined* are intended to model the fact that, operationally, a query may either succeed, fail or loop.

We introduce an immediate consequence operator T, which maps interpretations to interpretations. In order to deal with embedded implications, as in [15], we regard an interpretation as a mapping from programs to valuations. Miller's proposal, however, cannot be easily adapded to the case when negation as failure is present. Since we do not want to put restriction on the language, a possible solution is to change the logical setting of the semantics. This is why we adopt a three-valued logic.

The outline of the paper is the following. In Section 2 the syntax of the language with embedded implications is given and an operational semantics is defined for the ground case. In Section 3 a Kripke/Kleene semantics is defined for the general (first order) case, by introducing the immediate consequence operator T. It is possible to prove that, when the Herbrand Universe is finite, that is when we are dealing with the ground case, the T operator is continuous and its least fixpoint can be found at iteration ω. Furthermore, the operational semantics defined in Section 2 is sound and complete with respect to the fixpoint semantics. Since the operational semantics defined in Section 2 is not effective when the Herbrand universe is infinite (i.e. in the non-ground case), in Section 4 we develop a top-down operational semantics for the full first order case. In this operational semantics the possibility of having programs with free variables makes more difficult the problem of floundering. In Section 5 the notion of *normal form* for programs and goal is introduced, together with the rules to turn an arbitrary program or goal in normal form. Moreover, a notion of *allowedness* is defined in order to cope with floundering. It may be proved that the top-down operational semantics defined in Section 4 is sound with respect to the fixpoint semantics. It is also complete if the allowedness condition is satisfied and if iteration of the operator T is cut at a finite ordinal n. This result is the analog, for the case with embedded implications, of the completeness result obtained by Kunen (see [11] Theorem 4.3, pp. 241) for logic programs without embedded implications.

2   The Operational Semantics: the ground case

In this section we define the syntax of our language, and we define an operational semantics for it, which is effective only when the Herbrand Universe is finite, that is the language only contains a finite number of constants and no function symbol. In this case, a program can be regarded as a finite set of ground clauses, obtained by groundly instantiating the clauses of the programs in all possible ways (essentially, this is a reduction to the propositional case).

Let A denote atomic propositions. The syntax of the language is the following:

$$G := A \mid G_1 \land G_2 \mid D \Rightarrow G \mid \neg G$$
$$D := A \mid G \rightarrow A \mid D_1 \land D_2 \mid \forall x D.$$

In this definition G stands for a goal and D for a clause or a conjunction of clauses. A *program* is defined as a set of clauses.

In the following, since universal quantification distributes on conjunctions, we will indifferently regard a conjunction of clauses as a set of clauses. Notice that in a clause $G \rightarrow A$ the left part G can contain embedded implications of the form $D \Rightarrow G'$. We use two different arrows $\rightarrow$ and $\Rightarrow$ for implication in clause definitions and in embedded implications (we will often call the latter *implication goals*). Moreover, the symbol $\neg$ that may occur in front of goals stands for *negation as failure*. The negation symbol can occur without restrictions in front of any goal, including conjunctions and implication goals. For the rest of this section we will make the assumption that the Herbrand Universe of the language under consideration is finite.

Notice that a program can contain free variables. Indeed, in the implication goal $D \Rightarrow G$, the conjunction of clauses D can be regarded as a program that can share some free variables with G. We will call *closed* program a set of universally closed clauses. We assume that the top-level program is always a closed program.

Let U(P) be the Herbrand Universe for the program P, that is the set of all ground terms that can be formed out of constants and functional symbols occurring in P. In order to avoid problems with variable renaming and substitution, we replace universally quantified variables in the program with terms in U(P) in all possible ways. We will denote by [P] the set of all ground instances of the clauses in P.

As in [9], to define the operational derivability of a goal from a program, we introduce two relations: $\vdash_t$ to indicate success and $\vdash_f$ to indicate finite failure. The operational semantics of the language is defined by the following proof rules, which determine when, given a closed goal G and a closed program P, G *succeeds* from P (written $P \vdash_t G$), and when G *finitely fails* from P (written $P \vdash_f G$):

1. $P \vdash_t A$ if $A \in [P]$ or there is a clause $G \rightarrow A \in [P]$ such that $P \vdash_t G$;

2. $P \vdash_t G_1 \land G_2$ if $P \vdash_t G_1$ and $P \vdash_t G_2$;

3. $P \vdash_t D \Rightarrow G$ if $P \cup \{D\} \vdash_t G$;

4. $P \vdash_t \neg G$ if $P \vdash_f G$;

5. $P \vdash_f A$ if $A \notin [P]$ and, for each clause $G \to A \in [P]$, $P \vdash_f G$;

6. $P \vdash_f (G_1 \wedge G_2)$ if $P \vdash_f G_1$ or $P \vdash_f G_2$;

7. $P \vdash_f (D \Rightarrow G)$ if $P \cup \{D\} \vdash_f G$;

8. $P \vdash_f \neg G$ if $P \vdash_t G$;

In the definition above, there are two inference rules for each principal connective in the goal: one for the relation $\vdash_t$ and the other for $\vdash_f$. Notice that an implication goal $D \Rightarrow G$ succeeds from a program P if G succeeds from the extended program $P \cup \{D\}$. Moreover, $D \Rightarrow G$ finitely fails from P if G finitely fails from $P \cup \{D\}$. The inference rules 4 and 8 define the interplay between the two relations $\vdash_t$ and $\vdash_f$.

We define a $\vdash_t$-derivation of G from P as a *finite* sequence $P_1 \vdash_{o_1} G_1, \ldots,$ $P_n \vdash_{o_n} G_n$ satisfying the following conditions: $P_1 = P$, $G_1 = G$, $o_1 = t$; for G_n, it must be that either $G_n = A$, $o_n = t$ and $A \in [P]$, or $G_n = A$, $o_n = f$ and, for each fact $B \in [P]$ and clause $G \to B \in [P]$, $B \neq A$; furthermore, for $i = 2, \ldots, n$, $o_i \in \{t, f\}$ and $G_i \vdash_{o_i} P_i$ must be obtained from some later members of this sequence by the above inference rules. A $\vdash_f$-derivation of G from P is defined in a similar way (but with $o_1 = f$).

In the next section we will define a fixpoint semantics for the language and we will state the equivalence with the above operational semantics under the assumption that the Herbrand Universe is finite.

3   Fixpoint Semantics

Given a program P, we have defined U(P) as the Herbrand Universe for P. Let B(P) be the Herbrand base for P, that is the set of all ground atoms which can be formed out by using predicates in P and terms in U(P).

We define an immediate consequence operator T for the language with negation as failure and embedded implications, by generalizing the construction by Kunen [10]. We will make use of Kleene strong three-valued logic. The three truth-values are **t, f** and **u** (true, false and undefined), where the value **u** is intended to model computations which fail to return an answer.

A *partial valuation* for P is a (total) function v from the set of all atoms of B(P) into {**t,f,u**}. The truth-values are ordered in the following way: **u**<**t** **u**<**f** and **t** and **f** are not related. From the ordering among truth-values, a partial ordering among valuations can be defined as follows: $v_1 \subseteq v_2$ iff, for all ground atoms A, $v_1(A) < v_2(A)$ or $v_1(A) = v_2(A)$.

A partial valuation v is naturally extended to all sentences, by using Kleene's truth tables for three-valued logic. We assume that the domain of interpretation is the Herbrand Universe U(P).

Let $\mathcal{W}$ be the set of all closed programs formed out of the symbols in P and let $\mathcal{V}$ be the set of all partial valuations. A *partial interpretation* is a function $I : \mathcal{W} \rightarrow \mathcal{V}$, which associates a partial valuation I(Q) to each program Q in $\mathcal{W}$.

The partial ordering among valuations can be extended to interpretations as follows:

$$I_1 \sqsubseteq I_2 \text{ iff } \forall\, Q \in \mathcal{W}\ [I_1(Q) \subseteq I_2(Q)].$$

Given two interpretations I_1 and I_2, we also define a *join* and *meet* operator as follows. Let Q be a program in $\mathcal{W}$ and A a ground atom:

$$I_1 \sqcup I_2(\text{Q})(\text{A}) := \max\{I_1(Q)(A), I_2(Q)(A)\} \text{ if the maximum exists,}$$
$$I_1 \sqcap I_2(\text{Q})(\text{A}) := \min\{I_1(Q)(A), I_2(Q)(A)\}.$$

The join of I_1 and I_2 is then defined only if, for all Q in $\mathcal{W}$, there is no ground atom A such that A is **t** in $I_1(Q)$ and **f** in $I_2(Q)$ or vice-versa. The set of all interpretations is a complete semilattice under $\sqsubseteq$, taking $\sqcup$ and $\sqcap$ respectively as the join and meet operators and the interpretation $I_\perp$ as the bottom element. The interpretation $I_\perp$ associates to each program the undefined valuation, i.e. $I_\perp(\text{Q})(\text{A}) := \mathbf{u}$, for all programs Q in $\mathcal{W}$ and all ground atoms A.

Similarly to [15], we regard an interpretation as a mapping from programs to valuations and we define the immediate consequence operator T as a function from interpretations to interpretations. The intuition is that, instead of providing a model for a single program P (as the usual T_P operator), the operator T will simultaneously provide a model for all programs. Our semantics differs from that in [15] in two respects: firstly, ourinterpretations three-valued; furthermore, we do not make the assumption that interpretations are monotonic w.r.t. programs, i.e. that

$$\text{P} \subseteq \text{Q implies } I(\text{P}) \sqsubseteq I(\text{Q}).$$

This agrees with the non-monotonic behaviour of programs with negation as failure.

In order to define the T operator, we introduce the following notion of satisfiability. Given an interpretation I, a closed program P and a closed goal G, the truth value of G in I at the world P, written $V_I(P, G)$, is defined as follows:

1. $V_I(P, A) = I(P)(A)$

2. $V_I(P, G_1 \wedge G_2) = \mathbf{t}$ if $V_I(P, G_1) = \mathbf{t}$ and $V_I(P, G_2) = \mathbf{t}$
   $\qquad\quad = \mathbf{f}$ if $V_I(P, G_1) = \mathbf{f}$ or $V_I(P, G_2) = \mathbf{f}$
   $\qquad\quad = \mathbf{u}$ otherwise;

3. $V_I(P, D \Rightarrow G) = V_I(P \cup \{D\}, G)$;

4. $V_I(P, \neg G) = \mathbf{t}$ if $V_I(P, G) = \mathbf{f}$

$\qquad = \mathbf{f}$ if $V_I(P, G) = \mathbf{t}$

$\qquad = \mathbf{u}$ otherwise;

Now we define the immediate consequence operator T. Let I be an interpretation. The interpretation J=T(I) is defined as follows:

J(P)(A):=$\mathbf{t}$, if $A \in [P]$ or there is a $G \to A \in [P]$ such that $V_I(P, G) = \mathbf{t}$
J(P)(A):=$\mathbf{f}$, if $A \notin [P]$ and, for all $G \to A \in [P]$, $V_I(P, G) = \mathbf{f}$
J(P)(A):=$\mathbf{u}$, otherwise.

It is possible to prove that the operator T is *monotone*, i.e. given two interpretations I and J, $I \sqsubseteq J$ implies $T(I) \sqsubseteq T(J)$. Therefore, T has a least fixpoint, I_∞, which can be constructed by transfinite recursion, by letting $I_0 = I_\perp$, $I_{\mu+1} = T(I_\mu)$ and taking limits at limit ordinals.

In general, since the operator T is not continuous, the least fixpoint I_∞ is reached at a larger ordinal than ω. However, when the Herbrand Universe is finite, T is *continuous*. In this case, the fixpoint I_∞ is equal to I_n, for some $n < \omega$.

It is possible to show that, when the Herbrand Universe is finite, the operational semantics introduced in Section 2 is sound and complete with respect to the fixpoint semantics presented in this section. More precisely, the following theorem holds.

Theorem 1. For all programs P and goals G,

$\qquad P \vdash_t G$ iff $V_{I_\omega}(P, G) = \mathbf{t}$.

$\qquad P \vdash_f G$ iff $V_{I_\omega}(P, G) = \mathbf{f}$. $\square$

All proofs can be found in an extended version of the paper.

In the next section, we will deal with the general case, when the Herbrand Universe is not required to be finite. Since in this case the operational semantics defined in section 2 is not effective, we will define another top-down operational semantics. We will show that such an operational semantics is equivalent (for allowed programs) to the iterative semantics defined in this section if we cut the recursion at some finite ordinal n, i.e. if we take I_n as giving the semantics of the program.

4   A top-down operational semantics

The top-down semantics we present below is intended to be an extension of standard SLDNF for programs without embedded implications. As for SLDNF procedure, our top-down semantics takes into account only searching for answer substitutions which make a goal succeed. This implies that the evaluation of a negative goal cannot create bindings, and hence the selected negative goal must be ground. If it is non-ground the evaluation process immediately halts, without returning any answer. This is the problem of *floundering*. Because of floundering, treatment of arbitrary negated goals becomes problematic. For this reason we restrict the language, by allowing negation only on atoms. From now on, we assume that there is one fixed language containing infinitely many function and predicate symbols. The syntax for goals and clauses is as follows:

$$G:= A \mid \neg A \mid G_1 \wedge G_2 \mid D \Rightarrow G$$
$$D:= A \mid G \rightarrow A \mid \forall x D.$$

A program is a set of clauses. It may contain *free* variables, to be thought of as parameters, and computed substitutions have to take into account these variables as well. Since different parts of a goal may happen to be evaluated from different programs, our operational semantics will take care of pairs (*program, goal*). For positive programs, a similar approach was followed in [5]. A *query* N is a finite sequence of pairs (P_i, G_i), where P_i is a program and G_i is a goal.

A *selection rule* R is a function that, from each query N, selects a pair $R(N) = (P_i, G_i)$. We say that R is *safe* if for no N, $R(N) = (P_i, G_i)$ is such that G_i is a negative literal and either G_i is non-ground or P_i is open. We notice that the *safeness* condition for N-programs is sharper than for ordinary general programs. Even if $\neg A$ is ground, but P_i is open, we must prevent the selection of the pair $(P_i(x), \neg A)$. Such a pair corresponds to the goal $(P_i(x) \Rightarrow \neg A)$. Intuitively, this goal succeeds if for some term t, A fails from $P_i(t)$. Thus, this case is exactly analogous to the evaluation of a non-ground literal $\neg A(x)$. An attempt to evaluate a pair $(P_i(x), \neg A)$ will immediately *flounder*.

Since we will be only concerned with safe selection rules, the safeness condition will be implicitly assumed. Given a selection rule R, and a query N, we define by simultaneous induction a *computation tree* of rank k for N via R, a *refutation* of rank k of N via R, and a *finitely failed tree* of rank k for N via R, by assuming that these notions are already defined for rank less then k. The notion of rank is the same as the one used in [12].

Definition 1 A *computation tree* T for a query N, via R, of rank k is a tree, whose nodes are labelled by queries, and whose links are labelled by substitutions. The root of T is the query N. If no stated otherwise, the substitution associated to a link is the empty substitution ε.

- Suppose that $N' = \langle (P_1, G_1), ..., (P_n, G_n) \rangle$, is a non-leaf node of T and $R(N') = (P_i, G_i)$. Then the immediate successors of N' are determined according to the following cases:

  (RA) If G_i is an atom A, then for each clause $C_j = \forall \bar{x}(G'_j \rightarrow A_j)$ in P_i, such that A and A_j are unifiable, N' has a successor N_j
  $$N_j = \langle (P_1 \sigma_j, G_1 \sigma_j), \ldots, (P_i \sigma_j, G'_j \sigma_j), \ldots, (P_n \sigma_j, G_n \sigma_j) \rangle,$$

where $\sigma_j = mgu(A, A_j)$; the substitution σ_j labels the link from N to N_j.

In applying the rule (RA), we assume that quantified variables $\bar{x}$ of a clause $C_j = \forall \bar{x}(G'_j \to A_j)$ are replaced, each time, by fresh variables. Free variables of C_j remain unaltered.

$(R\wedge)$ If $G_i = G_{i1} \wedge G_{i2}$, then N' has a unique successor N''

$$N'' = \langle (P_1, G_1), \ldots, (P_i, G_{i1}), (P_i, G_{i2}), \ldots, (P_n, G_n) \rangle.$$

$(R \Rightarrow)$ If $G_i = D \Rightarrow G'$, then N' has a unique successor N"

$$N'' = \langle (P_1, G_1), \ldots, (P_i \cup \{D\}, G'), \ldots, (P_n, G_n) \rangle.$$

$(R\neg)$ If $G_i = \neg A$, where A is ground, P_i is closed and there exists a *finitely failed tree* for $\langle (P_i, A) \rangle$, via R, of rank smaller than k, then N' has a unique successor N''

$$N'' = \langle (P_1, G_1), \ldots, (P_{i-1}, G_{i-1}), (P_{i+1}, G_{i+1}), \ldots, (P_n, G_n) \rangle.$$

$(\emptyset)$ If G_i empty, the pair (P_i, G_i) is removed from N.

- If T has some leaf, the leaves of T may be of the following kind:

  (S) the empty query $N' = \emptyset$ is a leaf; N' is called a *success* node;

  (F) let $N' = \langle (P_1, G_1), \ldots, (P_n, G_n) \rangle$, and let $R(N') = (P_i, G_i)$; then N' is a leaf, if one of the following holds: either $G_i = A$, and A does not unify with any clause of P_i, or $G_i = \neg A$, where A is ground and P_i is closed, and there is a *refutation* with rank smaller than k of $\langle (P_i, A) \rangle$; N' is called a *failure* node.

A *refutation* B of N, of rank k, via R, is a path in T, ending with a node labelled by the empty query. We say that B computes the answer θ, if θ is obtained by restricting the composition of substitutions along B to the free variables of N. We say that T is a *finitely failed tree* of rank k for N, via R, if T is a finite computation tree of rank k for N, and every leaf of T is of type (F). $\quad\square$

It is clear from Definition 1 above, that in a computation tree of rank 0, the rule $(R\neg)$ is never applied, and if N' is a failure node, the selected pair must be of the form (P_i, A_i), where A_i is a positive atom. Our definition of computation tree is essentially a generalization of the corresponding definition in [12].

We say that a query N *succeeds with answer* θ via R if for some k there is a refutation of rank k of N, via R, computing the answer θ; we say that N *fails* via R, if for some k, there is a finitely failed tree of rank k for N, via R.

Regarding the computation rule R, it may be proved, as in the case of standard SLDNF (see [18]), that *If N succeeds with answer θ, via R, then N does not fail under any other selection rule R'*. Thus we may define

- N succeeds (with answer θ) if there exists a selection rule R, such that N succeeds via R (with answer θ);

- N fails if there exists a selection rule R, such that N fails via R.

We then say that a goal G succeeds from a program P, with answer θ if the query $\langle (P, G) \rangle$ succeeds with answer θ; a similar definition may be given for failure.

The above definitions leave out the case of *floundering*. Let us call a *computation* any path (finite or infinite) in a computation tree. We say that a computation *flounders* if it is finite and its last node N is such that R cannot select any pair (P_i, G_i) in N. This implies that, for every pair (P_i, G_i), G_i is a negative literal and either G_i is non-ground, or P_i is open. The node N may be called a floundering leaf. We could have defined computation trees to include possible floundering leaves. In that case, we would have to exclude floundering leaves from the definition of finitely failed tree. Furthermore, in that case, the outcome of the evaluation of a query could be not only success, finite failure, or loop, but also floundering, the latter occurring when the computation tree is finite, there is at least a floundering leaf and every other leaf is either a failing leaf or one floundering leaf.

5 Normal forms and allowedness

Our efforts will be directed to isolate a class of programs, goals and queries, such that no computation involving them flounders. To this aim we introduce the class of programs and goals (queries) in normal form.

Definition 2 The class of programs and goals in *normal form* is defined as follows:

- A program without embedded implications is in normal form.

- A goal G is in normal form if it has the form $(Q_1 \Rightarrow L_1) \wedge \ldots \wedge (Q_n \Rightarrow L_n)$, where, for $i = 1, \ldots, n$, Q_i is a (possibly empty) program in normal form and L_i is a literal.

- A program P is in normal form if every clause C of P has the form $\forall \bar{x}(G \to A)$, where G is a goal in normal form.

- A query $N = \langle (Q_1, L_1), \ldots (Q_n, L_n) \rangle$, is in normal form if, for $i = 1, \ldots, n$, Q_i is a program in normal form and L_i is a literal. $\square$

It can be easily proved that every program, goal or query may be effectively transformed into an equivalent one in normal form. To get the normal form, one just applies the following transformations:

replace $(\ldots C \Rightarrow (D \Rightarrow G) \ldots)$ by $(\ldots \{C, D\} \Rightarrow G \ldots)$
replace $(\ldots P \Rightarrow (G_1 \wedge G_2) \ldots)$ by $(\ldots (P \Rightarrow G_1) \wedge (P \Rightarrow G_2) \ldots)$

These two transformations closely correspond to the rules $(R \Rightarrow)$ and $(R\wedge)$ in the query evaluation procedure described above. Moreover, if we do not care about the order of (logically conjuncted) subexpressions, the normal form is uniquely determined.

Proposition 1 Let N be a query and let N' be the normal form of N, then we have:

> N succeeds with answer θ if and only if N' succeeds with answer θ
> N fails if and only if N' fails.   □

A similar statement holds with respect to the fixpoint semantics, defined in Section 3.

Proposition 2 Let P be a closed program and G be a closed goal; suppose that P' and G' be the normal forms of P and G, respectively; then for every ordinal α we have:

$$V_{I_\alpha}(P,G) = V_{I_\alpha}(P',G').   \square$$

Restricting attention to normal queries —and there is no loss of generality in doing so— the top-down evaluation procedure may be considerably simplified. The rules for conjunction $(R\wedge)$ and implication $(R \Rightarrow)$ are no longer necessary. More precisely, we can replace the three rules $(R\wedge)$, $(R \Rightarrow)$ and (RA), by a single rule for atoms:

$(R'A)$:
  If $N = \langle (P_1, L_1), \ldots, (P_i, A), \ldots, (P_n, L_n) \rangle$, then for each clause $C_j \in P_i$,

$$C_j = \forall \bar{x}[(Q_1 \Rightarrow M_1) \wedge \ldots \wedge (Q_t \Rightarrow M_t) \to A_j]$$

(the M_h's are literals) such that A and A_j are unifiable via an mgu σ_j, N has a successor N_j:

$$\langle (P_1\sigma_j, L_1\sigma_j), \ldots, ((P_i \cup Q_1)\sigma_j, M_1\sigma_j), \ldots$$
$$\ldots, ((P_i \cup Q_t)\sigma_j, M_t\sigma_j), \ldots, (P_n\sigma_j, G_n\sigma_j) \rangle.$$

We introduce below the notion of allowedness, whose role is the same as the corresponding notion for general programs and goals. Because of possible occurrences of free variables in a program, the definition of allowedness is more complex than in the case of general programs. First we introduce the auxiliary notion of *degree* of a query (goal).

Definition 3 Let $N = \langle (Q_1, L_1), \ldots, (Q_n, L_n) \rangle$ be a normal query. We say that a tuple of natural numbers $\langle d_1, \ldots, d_n \rangle$ is an admissible degree for N (assigning a degree d_i to each corresponding pair (Q_i, L_i) in N) if, for each pair (Q_i, L_i), the following holds:

- if Q_i is closed and either L_i is positive or L_i is ground, then (Q_i, L_i) has degree $d_i = 0$; *otherwise*

- for every variable x, if x occurs free in Q_i, or x occurs in L_i and L_i is negative, there is a $j = 1,\ldots,n$ $(j \neq i)$ such that L_j is *positive*, x occurs in L_j and the pair (Q_j, L_j) has degree $d_j < d_i$. □

As a goal $G = (Q_1 \Rightarrow L_1) \wedge \ldots \wedge (Q_n \Rightarrow L_n)$ is the same as the query $\langle (Q_1, L_1), \ldots, (Q_n, L_n) \rangle$, an admissible degree of G is an admissible degree of the corresponding query. In particular, if all programs Q_i, are empty, that is to say $G = L_1 \wedge \ldots \wedge L_n$, we have that G has an admissible degree (namely, a tuple of 0 and 1) if and only if every variable of G occurs in a positive L_i. Notice that a normal query N (a normal goal G) may have no admissible degree.

Example 2 The goal $G_1 = (A(x) \Rightarrow B(x))$ has no admissible degree. Let G_2 be the following normal goal:
$$G_2 = (A_1(y) \Rightarrow \neg B_1(y)) \wedge (A_2(x) \Rightarrow B_2(y)) \wedge (A_3 \Rightarrow B_3(x)),$$
where, the A_i's and B_i's are atoms, and the only occurrences of variables are as shown (so that A_3 is closed). Then the tuple $(d_1, d_2, d_3) = (2, 1, 0)$ is an admissible degree for G_2.

We now define the class of normal allowed programs and goals (queries). As expected, the definition will be by mutual induction.

Definition 4 (Allowedness)

- A normal goal $G = (Q_1 \Rightarrow L_1) \wedge \ldots \wedge (Q_n \Rightarrow L_n)$, is *allowed* if, for $i = 1 \ldots n$, Q_i is *allowed* and G has an admissible degree.

- Let $C = \forall \bar{x}(G[\bar{z}] \rightarrow A[\bar{z}])$ be a clause, with free variables $\bar{z}$; replace variables $\bar{z}$ in C, by a tuple of closed terms $\bar{t}$, and hence obtain a clause $C' = \forall \bar{x}(G' \rightarrow A')$. We say that C is *allowed* if every variable of C' occurs in G' and G' is *allowed*.

- A program P is *allowed* if every clause in P is *allowed*.

- A query N is *allowed* if N has an admissible degree, and for every pair (P_i, L_i) in N, program P_i is *allowed*. □

Goal G_2 in the previous example is allowed, while goal G_1 is not. Moreover, the program for testing the parity given in the introduction is allowed.

For programs and goals without embedded implications, the above definition of allowedness reduces to the usual definition in [11]. Since every expression (program, goal, query) has a normal counterpart, we will say that an arbitrary expression is allowed if its normal counterpart is.

Proposition 3 Let N be an allowed query. No computation starting from N flounders. Moreover, if N succeeds with answer θ, then θ is ground. □

Allowedness restriction has heavy consequences also on the semantical side. The following proposition expresses the crucial fact for completeness proof with respect to finitely iterated fixpoint semantics.

Proposition 4 Let P be a closed allowed program. For every atom A, let us define the set $S_k(P, A)$:

$S_k(P, A) = \{\theta : \theta$ is ground and $dom(\theta) = Var(A)$ and $V_{I_k}(P, A\theta) = \mathbf{t}\}$.

For every k, the set $S_k(P, A)$ is finite. $\square$

If a program P is not allowed the above property generally fails. Take for instance the non-allowed program P:

$$P = \left\{ \begin{array}{l} C(f(a)) \\ \forall x[(B(x) \Rightarrow B(x)) \rightarrow A(x)] \end{array} \right.$$

It is easy to see that, for every $k > 0$, the set $S_k(P, A(x))$ is infinite.

We now come to our main results, namely soundness and completeness of our top-down query evaluation with respect to finitely iterated fixpoint semantics. For the sake of brevity, let us introduce the following notation: given a query $N = \langle (Q_1, G_1), \ldots, (Q_n, G_n) \rangle$, and a ground substitution θ, we define

- $V_I \models_\omega N\theta$ iff for some $k < \omega$, $V_{I_k}(P_j\theta, G_j\theta) = \mathbf{t}$, for each $j = 1 \ldots n$
- $V_I \models_\omega \neg N$ iff, for some $k < \omega$ and for all ground σ, $V_{I_k}(P_j\sigma, G_j\sigma) = \mathbf{f}$, for some $j = 1 \ldots n$.

Theorem 2 (Soundness) Let N be a query.

- If N succeeds with answer θ then, for every ground σ, $V_I \models_\omega N\theta\sigma$.
- If N fails, then $V_I \models_\omega \neg N$.

In particular if P is a closed program and G is a goal, we have:

- If G succeeds from P with answer θ, then for some k, and all ground σ, $V_{I_k}(P, G\theta\sigma) = \mathbf{t}$.
- If G fails from P, then for some k and all ground σ, $V_{I_k}(P, G\sigma) = \mathbf{f}$. $\square$

Before stating the completeness result, let us consider the following example.

Example 3 Let P be the following program:

$P = \{\forall x[A(x) \rightarrow A(f(x))], B(a)\}$,

and let N be the following allowed query:

$N = \langle (\{B(y)\}, \neg B(y)), (P, A(y)) \rangle$.

According to the *safeness restriction*, the only pair which may be selected is $(P, A(y))$, and by the rule $(R'A)$, one derives:

$N' = \langle (\{B(x')\}, \neg B(x')), (P, A(x')) \rangle$,

with mgu= $\{y/f(x')\}$, (a variant of the relevant clause in P has been made). This query is equivalent to N up to renaming, so that we get a looping computation. Consequently, query N does not fail as expected.

On the other hand, we have that for every ground substitution θ,

$V_{I_1}(\{B(y)\}\theta, B(y)\theta) = \mathbf{t}$, and hence
$V_{I_1}(\{B(y)\}\theta, \neg B(y)\theta) = \mathbf{f}$,

so that we get $V_I \models_\omega \neg N$. The source of this kind of incompleteness is the *safeness restriction*. If pair $(\{B(y)\}, \neg B(y))$ might be selected, we would get that $\langle (\{B(y)\}, B(y)) \rangle$ succeeds with answer ϵ, and we might regard this outcome as *failure* of $(\{B(y)\}, \neg B(y))$. Thus, relaxing the *safeness restriction*, query N would fail.

Unlike the case of programs without embedded implications, non floundering (ensured by allowedness) is not a sufficent condition for having completeness with respect to finitely-iterated three-valued semantics. This observation may lead to elaborate a stronger operational semantics in which the *safeness restriction* is left out.

In the following, however, we keep the safeness restriction and, in order to get completeness, we strengthen the notion of allowedness. We say that a goal $G = (Q_i \Rightarrow L_i) \wedge \ldots \wedge (Q_n \Rightarrow L_n)$ in normal form is *strongly allowed* if it is allowed and for every $i = 1, \ldots, n$, Q_i is closed when L_i is negative. The notion of strongly allowedness is extended to clauses, programs and queries in normal form in the obvious way. Moreover, an arbitrary query is strongly allowed if its normal form is strongly allowed.

Theorem 3 (Completeness) Let N be a strongly allowed query and let θ be a ground substitution.

- If $V_I \models_\omega N\theta$, then N succeeds with answer θ.
- If $V_I \models_\omega \neg N$, then N fails.

In particular, if P is a closed strongly allowed program, G is a strongly allowed goal and θ is a ground substitution, we have:

- If for some k, $V_{I_k}(P, G\theta) = \mathbf{t}$, then G succeeds from P with answer θ.
- If for some k, and for all ground σ, $V_{I_k}(P, G\sigma) = \mathbf{f}$, then G fails from P.

$\square$

6 Conclusions

In this work we have proposed both a top-down proof procedure and a fixpoint semantics for a language which combines embedded implications and negation as failure. We have proved that, under a suitable allowedness condition, our query evaluation procedure is complete with respect to the Herbrand interpretation obtained by iterating operator T up to stage ω. In general, such an interpretation is smaller than any fixpoint of T. For a language without embedded implications, Kunen showed (see [10]) that a stronger completeness result may be obtained, by lifting the restriction to Herbrand Universe. One can reasonably expect that the same holds for our language: i.e., that assuming allowedness our top-down query evaluation procedure is complete with respect to every fixpoint of T on *any* space of interpretations, whose domains *include* Herbrand universe. A natural development of our work will be to prove this conjecture.

Acknowledgement

This work has been partially supported by CNR - Progetto Finalizzato "Sistemi Informatici e Calcolo Parallelo" under grant n. 90.00668.PF69.

References

[1] A.J. BONNER, Hypothetical Datalog: Complexity and Expressibility, *in* Lecture Notes in Computer Science, Vol.326, pp.144-160.

[2] A.J. BONNER, L.T. MCCARTY, Adding Negation-as-Failure to Intuitionistic Logic Programming, *in* Proc. North American Conference on Logic Programming, Austin, 1990, pp.681-703.

[3] P. M. DUNG, Hypothetical Logic Programming with Negation as Failure, *in* Proc. 3rd Int. Workshop on Extensions of Logic Programming, Bologna, Febr.1992, pp.61-73. pp.144-160.

[4] M. FITTING, A Kripke/Kleene Semantics for Logic Programs, *in* J. Logic Programming 2:295-312 (1985).

[5] D.M. GABBAY, U. REYLE, N-Prolog: an Extension of Prolog with Hypothetical Implications.I, *in* J. Logic Programming 4:319-355 (1984).

[6] D.M. GABBAY, N-Prolog: an Extension of Prolog with Hypothetical Implications.II. Logical Foundations and Negation as Failure, *in* J. Logic Programming 4:251-283 (1985).

[7] L. GIORDANO, A. MARTELLI, G.F.ROSSI, Extending Horn Clause Logic with Implication Goals, *in* Theoretical Computer Science 95 (1992) 43-74.

[8] J. HARLAND, A Kripke-like Model for Negation as Failure, *in* Proc. North American Conference on Logic Programming, 1989, pp.626-642.

[9] J. HARLAND, A Clausal Form for the Completion of Logic Programs, *in* Proc. 8th Int. Conference on Logic Programming, 1991, pp.711-725.

[10] K. KUNEN, Negation in Logic Programming, *in* J. Logic Programming 4:289-308 (1987).

[11] K. KUNEN, Signed Data Dependencies in Logic Programs, *in* J. Logic Programming 7:231-245 (1989).

[12] J.W. LLOYD, *Foundations of Logic Programming*, Springer, Berlin, 1984.

[13] L.T. MCCARTY, Clausal Intuitionistic Logic. I. Fixed-Point Semantics, *in* J. Logic Programming 5(1):1-31 (1988).

[14] L.T. MCCARTY, Clausal Intuitionistic Logic. II. Tableau Proof Procedures, *in* J. Logic Programming 5(2):93-132 (1988).

[15] D. MILLER, A Theory of Modules for Logic Programming, *in* IEEE Symposium on Logic Programming, Sept. 1986, pp.106-114.

[16] D. MILLER, Lexical Scoping as Universal Quantification, *in* Proc. Sixth Int. Conf. on Logic Programming, Lisbon 1989, pp.268-283.

[17] N. OLIVETTI, L. TERRACINI, N-Prolog and Equivalence of Logic Programs, 1992, *to appear* in Journal of Logic, Language and Information.

[18] J.C. SHEPHERDSON, Negation as Failure: a Comparison of Clark's Completed Data Base and Reiter's Closed World Assumption, *in* J. Logic Programming 1:51-79 (1984).

The Stable Models of a Predicate Logic Program

V. Wiktor Marek
Department of Computer Science
University of Kentucky
Lexington, KY 40506–0027, USA

Anil Nerode
Mathematical Sciences Institute
Cornell University
Ithaca, NY 14853

Jeffrey B. Remmel
Department of Mathematics
University of California at San Diego
La Jolla, CA 92903

1 Statement of problems and results

In this paper we investigate and solve the problem classifying the Turing complexity of stable models of finite and recursive predicate logic programs.

Gelfond-Lifschitz [7] introduced the concept of a stable model M of a Predicate Logic Program P. Here we show that, up to a recursive 1-1 coding, the sets of all stable models of a finite Predicate Logic Program and the Π_1^0 classes (equivalently, the sets of all infinite branches of a recursive tree) coincide (Theorems 4.1 and 5.1). Typical consequences: 1) there are finite Predicate Logic Programs which have stable models, but which have no hyperarithmetic stable models; 2) for every recursive ordinal α there is a finite Predicate Logic Program with a unique stable model of the same Turing degree as 0^α (Corollary 5.7). Another consequence of this result is that the problem of determining whether a finite Predicate Logic Program has a stable model is Σ_1^1-complete, i.e. the set of Gödel numbers of finite Predicate Logic Programs which have stable models is a Σ_1^1-complete set.

A *support* of a ground atom p is, roughly) a subset A of the Herbrand base such that whenever M is a stable model of the program P and $A \cap M = \emptyset$ then $p \in M$ (see below for a precise definition). Among supports of a ground atom p, there are always inclusion-minimal ones. Such minimal supports are finite. We call a program P **locally finite** if every atom has only finitely many minimal supports. Under our codings, locally finite Logic Programs correspond exactly to finitely splitting trees and locally finite Logic Programs for which there is an effective algorithm which given an atom p, produces a explicit list of all the minimal supports of p correspond to recursively splitting recursive trees. We also show that local finiteness is a continuity property by associating with every Logic Program an operator on the Herbrand Base such that the program is locally finite iff the operator is continuous. It turns out that the classification of programs according to the number of supports of atoms provides additional information on the complexity of their stable models.

2   Introduction

Why are we interested in how hard it is to construct stable models M of Predicate Logic Programs P, and more generally in what the set of all stable models is like? This is because stable models are good theoretical and computational candidates for knowledge representation of the set of beliefs, or point of view, of an agent holding to a theory in one of a variety of nonmonotone reasoning systems. These systems include:

- Reiter's extensions in Default Logic [23],

- Doyle's extensions in truth maintenance systems [6],

- Marek-Nerode-Remmel's theory of extensions in non-monotone rule systems [15, 16, 17, 18],

- Reinfrank et al. theory of nonmonotonic formal systems [22],

- Gelfond-Lifschitz stable models of logic programs [7].

McCarthy ([20]) suggested that non-monotonic reasoning could be formulated as a mathematical discipline. He introduced two notions of circumscription as a first try. The other systems above followed in his wake. The Marek-Nerode-Remmel formulation ([15]) was specifically designed to abstract all important common features in a logic-free formulation. It is a convenient half-way point for reformulation of non-monotonic theories as Logic Programs. Generally, the idea behind non-monotonic reasoning is that we should be allowed to deduce conclusions using a theory consisting of premises and rules of inference which can be a combination of

- knowledge, never later revised

and

-belief, held in the absence of contrary knowledge.

If we deduce using only knowledge, we are in the traditional domain of classical logic since Aristotle. If we deduce using beliefs as well, we can then deduce due to absence of knowledge as well as from its presence. We are then in the domain of non-monotonic reasoning. A warning to the untutored is that the notion of a unique least deductively closed set containing a theory, stemming from monotonic logics, is not appropriate for any of the non-monotone reasoning systems listed above. Rather, there are many minimal deductively closed sets for the theory, no one including another. If we pick one of these minimal deductively closed sets for the theory as our current "point of view" for decision making, and later new knowledge is obtained contradicting a belief of the theory, then we are impelled, for consistency's sake, to revise our theory by abandoning the offending belief. Also, we must abandon all conclusions inferred from beliefs contradicting facts, and we then must adopt a new theory and as a new "point of view", another minimal deductively closed set for that new theory. In contrast, in traditional monotone reasoning, once a premise is established, it and its consequences are never retracted or revised later. Characteristic of non-monotonic reasoning is retraction. Beliefs may be falsified by later facts and have to be abandoned, or at least replaced by new beliefs. What we are carrying out in other papers [18] is

- representing non-monotonic theories (premises and rules of inference) of current knowledge and belief as a Logic Program P,

- representing our current choice of a model, or deductively closed "point of view", as the choice of a stable model M of that Logic Program,

thus letting a pair (P, M) represent our current "state of mind". That is, when new facts contradict old beliefs, or newly preferred beliefs replace less preferred beliefs, we have a new Logic Program P' and need a new stable model M' of that theory to move to a new revised "state of mind" (P', M'). How to do this is our proposed calculus of belief revision using stable models ([17]).

To repeat, the Logic Programming machinery is a vehicle for natural representation of the syntax, deductive structure, and intended semantics of all the non-monotonic reasoning systems alluded to above. Implementations of Logic Programming can, in principle, be used as interpreters or compilers for these non-monotone reasoning systems. These implementations now vary widely, from those based on traditional Robinson's resolution to methods based on Jeroslow's "logic as mixed integer programming" paradigm ([3]). Equally important, informal and formal semantic reasoning about extensions of a default theory or a truth maintenance system can be carried out entirely using semantic reasoning about corresponding stable models of a corresponding Logic Program.

Where do the Logic Programs corresponding to nonmonotone theories come from? When stripped of logical and syntactic finery, many different non-monotonic logic systems have the same mathematical and computational structure, including their natural semantics. This is why algorithms for Logic Programs can also be used for default logic [23], truth maintenance systems [6, 5], circumscription [12, 13]. This can be dimly seen through the ad hoc translations of such systems into one another [8, 11, 19, 22]. But the diverse symbolisms are complicated and to a large extent irrelevant. The authors [15, 16] developed a common conceptual logic-free framework of non-monotone rule systems. The computational and mathematical equivalence of most of the subjects listed above is outlined there. Non-monotonic rule systems can be used as an easy intermediate stepping stone to reformulate theories and extensions of default logic and truth maintenance systems as Logic Programs and stable models.

To summarize, Logic Programming not only is an example of a non-monotonic reasoning system, but any interpreter or compiler for Logic Programs which computes stable models can also serve to compute extensions in the other non-monotonic reasoning systems listed above. We remark that the non-monotonic rule system approach also revealed that finding stable models of logic programs and finding marriages for marriage problems and finding chain covers for partially ordered sets and many other combinatorial questions are essentially equivalent [15], allowing us to think about extensions using standard mathematics and algorithms for that standard mathematics.

STABLE MODELS. For an introductory treatment of Logic Programs, see [14]. Here is a brief self-contained account of their stable models [7]. Assume as given a fixed first order language based on predicate letters, constants, and function symbols. The Herbrand base of the language is defined as the set $B_{\mathcal{L}}$ of all ground atoms (atomic statements) of the language. A literal is an atomic formula or its negation, a ground literal is an atomic statement or its negation. A Logic Program P is a set of "program clauses", that is, an expression of the form:

$$p \leftarrow l_1, \ldots, l_k \tag{1}$$

where p is an atomic formula, and $l_1, \ldots, l_k$ is a list of literals.

Then p is called the conclusion of the clause, the list $l_1, \ldots, l_k$ is called the body of the clause. Ground clauses are clauses without variables. Horn clauses are clauses with no negated literals, that is, with atomic formulas only in the body. Horn clause programs are programs P consisting of Horn clauses. Each such program has a least model in the Herbrand base determined as the least fixed point of a continuous operator T_P representing 1-step Horn clause logic deduction ([14]).

Informally, the knowledge of a Logic Program is the set of clauses with no negated literals in the bodies, that is, the Horn clauses. The set of beliefs of a Logic Program is the set of clauses with negated literals occurring in the bodies. This use of language is sufficiently suggestive to guide the reader to translations of many nonmonotone theories in other reasoning systems into equivalent Logic Programs so that extensions as models for the non-monotonic theory correspond to stable models as models for the Logic Program.

A ground instance of a clause is a clause obtained by substituting ground terms (terms without variables) for all variables of the clause. The set of all ground instances of the program P is called $ground(P)$.

Let M be any subset of the Herbrand base. A ground clause is said to be M-applicable if the atoms whose negations are literals in the body are not members of M. Such clause is then *reduced* by eliminating remaining negative literals. This monotonization $GL(P, M)$ of P with respect to M is the propositional Horn clause program consisting of reducts of M-applicable clauses of $ground(P)$ (see Gelfond-Lifschitz [7]). Then M is called a *stable model* for P if M is the least model of the Horn clause program $GL(M, P)$. We denote this least model as $N_{M,P}$. It is easy to see that a stable model for P is a minimal model of P ([7]). We denote by $Stab(P)$ the set of all stable models of P. There may be no, one, or many stable models of P.

We should note that the syntactical condition of stratification of Apt, Blair, and Walker [2] singles out programs with a well-behaved, unique stable model, but there is no reason to think that in belief revision one could move from stratified program to stratified program; but how one might do this is an interesting and challenging question.

PROOF SCHEMES. What kind of proof theory is appropriate for Logic Programs? The key idea for our proofs is that of a proof scheme with conclusion an atom p.

Proof schemes are intended to reflect exactly how p is a finitary non-monotonic consequence of P.

Of course, a proof scheme must use, as in Horn Logic, the positive information present in the positive literals of bodies of clauses of P, but proof schemes also have to respect the negative information present in the negative literals of bodies of clauses. With this motivation, here is the definition. A *proof scheme* for p with respect to P is a sequence of triples $< \langle p_l, C_l, S_l \rangle >_{1 \le l \le n}$, with n a natural number, such that the following conditions all hold.

1. Each p_l is in $B_{\mathcal{L}}$. Each C_l is in $ground(P)$. Each S_l is a finite subset of $B_{\mathcal{L}}$.

2. p_n is p.

3. The S_l, C_l satisfy the following conditions. For all $1 \le l \le n$, one of **(a)**, **(b)**, **(c)** below holds.

    (a) C_l is $p_l \leftarrow$, and S_l is S_{l-1},

    (b) C_l is $p_l \leftarrow \neg s_1, \ldots, \neg s_r$ and S_l is $S_{l-1} \cup \{s_1, \ldots, s_r\}$, or

    (c) C_l is $p_l \leftarrow p_{m_1}, \ldots, p_{m_k}, \neg s_1, \ldots, \neg s_r$, $m_1 < l, \ldots, m_k < l$, and S_l is $S_{l-1} \cup \{s_1, \ldots, s_r\}$.

4. $\{p_1, \ldots p_n\} \cap S_n = \emptyset$.

(We put $S_0 = \emptyset$).

Suppose that $\varphi = < \langle p_l, C_l, S_l \rangle >_{1 \le l \le n}$ is a proof scheme. Then $conc(\varphi)$ denotes atom p_n and is called the conclusion of φ. Also, $supp(\varphi)$ is the set S_n and is called the support of φ.

Condition (3) tells us how to construct the S_l inductively, from the p_l and the C_l. The set S_n consists of the negative information of the proof scheme. Condition (4) eliminates consideration of the (semantically inconsistent) case when the proof scheme proves an atom which is in its own support.

A proof scheme may not need all its lines to prove its conclusion. It may be possible to omit some clauses and still have a proof scheme with the same conclusion. If we omit as many clauses as possible, retaining the conclusion but still maintaining a proof scheme, this is a *minimal proof scheme* with that conclusion. It may be possible to do this with many distinct results, but obviously there are only a finite number of ways altogether to trim a proof scheme to a minimal proof scheme with the same conclusion, since no new clauses are ever introduced. Of course, a given atom may be the conclusion of no, one, finitely many, or infinitely many different minimal proof schemes. These differences are clearly computationally significant if one is searching for a justification of a conclusion. The apparatus needed to discuss this was introduced in [15].

Formally, preorder proof schemes φ, ψ by $\varphi \prec \psi$ if

1. φ, ψ have same conclusion,

2. Every clause in φ is also a clause of ψ.

The relation $\prec$ is reflexive, transitive, and well-founded. Minimal elements of $\prec$ are minimal proof schemes.

Here are some propositions from [15, 16].

Proposition 2.1 *Let P be a program and $M \subseteq B_{\mathcal{L}}$. Let p be an atom. Then p is in $N_{P,M}$ if and only if there exists a proof scheme with conclusion p whose support is disjoint from M.*

If Z is a set of atoms we let $\neg Z$ be the conjunction of all the negations of atoms of Z. Now fix program P and atom p for the discussion. Associate with the atom p a (possibly infinitary) Boolean equation E_p

$$p \leftrightarrow (\neg Z_1 \vee \neg Z_2 \vee \ldots), \tag{2}$$

where the $Z_1, Z_2 \ldots$ is a (possibly infinite) list of supports of all minimal proof schemes with conclusion p with respect to P. In fact, for our purposes it is enough to list only the inclusion-minimal supports. This is called a defining equation for p with respect to P. If there are infinitely many distinct minimal supports for proof schemes with conclusion p, this will be an infinitary equation. We make two other conventions about the defining equation of p. Namely 1) If p is not the conclusion of any proof scheme with respect to P, then the defining equation for p is $p \leftrightarrow \perp$, equivalent to $\neg p$, so $\neg p$ must hold in every stable model of P. 2) If p has a proof scheme with empty support, that is, a proof scheme which uses only Horn clauses, then the defining equation for p is equivalent to $\top$. In this case, p belongs to all stable models of P. The set Eq_P of all equations E_p obtained as p ranges over the Herbrand base is called a defining system of equations for program P.

Example 2.1 *Let P be a program:*
$p(0) \leftarrow \neg q(X)$
$nat(0) \leftarrow$
$nat(s(X)) \leftarrow nat(X).$

Then for each n, $< \langle p(0), p(0) \leftarrow \neg q(s^n(0)), \{q(s^n(0))\} \rangle >$ is a minimal proof scheme with conclusion $p(0)$. Thus atom $p(0)$ has an infinite number of minimal proof schemes with respect to program P.

Proposition 2.2 *Let P be a logic program with defining system of equations Eq_P. Let M be a subset of the Herbrand universe $B_{\mathcal{L}}$. Then M is a stable model for P if and only if $M \cup \{\neg q : q \in B_{\mathcal{L}} \setminus M\}$ is a solution of the system Eq_P.*

Here is a second characterization of stable models via proof schemes.

Proposition 2.3 *Let P be a program. Also, suppose that M is a subset of the Herbrand universe $B_{\mathcal{L}}$. Then M is a stable model of P if, and only if, for every $p \in B_{\mathcal{L}}$, it is true that p is in M if and only if there exists a proof scheme φ with conclusion p such that the support of φ is disjoint from M.*

FSP LOGIC PROGRAMS. We now examine Logic Programs P such that every defining equation for every atom p is finite. This is equivalent to requiring that every atom has only a finite number of inclusion-minimal supports of minimal proof schemes. Such a program may have the property that there is an atom which is the conclusion of infinitely many different minimal proof schemes, but these schemes have only finitely many supports altogether among them.

Example 2.2 *Let P be the program:*
$p(0) \leftarrow q(X)$
$q(X) \leftarrow \neg r(0)$
$nat(0) \leftarrow$
$nat(s(X)) \leftarrow nat(X).$

Then the atom $p(0)$ is the conclusion of infinitely many proof schemes:

$$< \langle q(s^n(0)), q(s^n(0)) \leftarrow \neg r(0), \{r(0)\}\rangle, \langle p(0), p(0) \leftarrow q(s^n(0)), \{r(0)\}\rangle >$$

as n ranges over ω.
The single minimal support of all these proof schemes is $\{r(0)\}$.
That is, whenever $r(0)$ is not in M, then $p(0)$ will be in $N_{P,M}$.

A *finitary support* program (*FSP* program) is a Logic Program such that for every atom p, there is a finite set of finite sets S, which are exactly the inclusion-minimal supports of all those minimal proof schemes with conclusion p.

3   FSP and Continuity

In this section we study the FSP property. It turns out that this property is equivalent to the continuity property for a suitably defined operator. This is precisely the same operator whose square (that is two-fold application) determines the *monotonic* operator whose least and largest fixpoints determine the well-founded model of the program ([26]).

Associate an operator with each Logic Program as follows.

Definition 3.1 *Let P be a program. The operator $F_P : \mathcal{P}(B_{\mathcal{L}}) \rightarrow \mathcal{P}(B_{\mathcal{L}})$ is defined as follows: If $S \subseteq B_{\mathcal{L}}$ then $F_P(S)$ is the set of all atoms in $B_{\mathcal{L}}$ for which there exists a proof scheme p such that $supp(p) \cap S = \emptyset$. Thus F_P assigns to S the set $N_{S,P}$.*

Proposition 3.2 *The operator F_P is anti-monotonic, that is, if $S_1 \subseteq S_2$, then $F_P(S_2) \subseteq F_P(S_1)$.*

Proposition 3.3 *The operator F_P is lower half-continuous; that is, if $\langle S_n \rangle_{n \in \omega}$ is a monotone decreasing sequence of subsets of $B_{\mathcal{L}}$ then $\bigcup_{n \in \omega} F_P(S_n) = F_P(\bigcap_{n \in \omega} S_n)$.*

Proposition 3.4 *Let P be a Logic Program. Then following conditions are equivalent:*
(a) P is an FSP Logic Program.

(b) F_P is an upper half-continuous operator; that is, whenever $\langle S_n \rangle_{n \in \omega}$ is a monotone increasing sequence of subsets of $B_{\mathcal{L}}$, we have

$$\bigcap_{n \in \omega} F_P(S_n) = F_P(\bigcup_{n \in \omega} S_n)$$

4 Coding Stable Models into Trees

In this section, we shall give a precise statement of our claim that given any recursive Logic Program P, there is a recursive tree T such that there is an effective 1-1 degree-preserving map between the set of stable models of P and the set of paths through T.

RECURSIVE PROGRAMS. When we discuss finite programs then we can easily read off a recursive representation of the Herbrand base. The reason is that the alphabet of such a program, that is the set of predicate symbols and function symbols that appear in the program, is finite. The situation changes when P is an infinite predicate logic program representable with a recursive set of Gödel numbers. When we read off the enumeration of the alphabet of the program from an enumeration of the program itself, there is no guarantee that the alphabet of P is recursive. In particular the Herbrand base of the program is recursively enumerable but may not necessarily be recursive.

For the purposes of this paper, we define a program P to be recursive if not only the set of its Gödel numbers is recursive, but also the resulting representation of the Herbrand base is recursive.

RECURSIVELY FSP PROGRAMS. A *recursively* FSP program is an FSP recursive program such that we can uniformly compute the finite family of supports of proof schemes with conclusion p from p. The meaning of this is obvious, but we need a technical notation for the proofs. Start by listing the whole Herbrand base of the program, $B_{\mathcal{L}}$ as a countable sequence in one of the usual effective ways. This assigns an integer (Gödel number) to each element of the base, its place in this sequence. This encodes finite subsets of the base as finite sets of natural numbers, all that is left is to code each finite set of natural numbers as a single natural number, its *canonical index*. To the finite set $\{x_1, \ldots, x_k\}$ we assign as its canonical index $can(\{x_1, \ldots, x_k\}) = 2^{x_1} + \ldots + 2^{x_k}$. If program P is FSP, and the list, in order of magnitude, of Gödel numbers of all minimal support of schemes with conclusion p is

$$Z_1^p, \ldots, Z_{l_r}^p,$$

then define a function $su^P : B_{\mathcal{L}} \to \omega$ as below.

$$p \mapsto can(\{can(Z_1^p), \ldots, can(Z_{l_r}^p)\})$$

We call a Logic Program P a *recursively* FSP program if it is FSP and the function su^P is recursive.

ADDITIONAL NOTATION. Let $\omega = \{0, 1, 2, \ldots\}$ denote the set of natural numbers and let $<, > : \omega \times \omega \to \omega$ be some fixed one-to-one and onto recursive pairing function such that the projection functions π_1 and π_2 defined by $\pi_1(< x, y >) = x$ and $\pi_2(< x, y >) = y$ are also recursive. We extend our pairing function to code

n-tuples for $n > 2$ by the usual inductive definition, that is $< x_1, \ldots, x_n > = < x_1, < x_2, \ldots, x_n >>$ for $n \geq 3$. We let $\omega^{<\omega}$ denote the set of all finite sequences from ω and $2^{<\omega}$ denote the set of all finite sequences of 0's and 1's. Given $\alpha = < \alpha_1, \ldots, \alpha_n >$ and $\beta = < \beta_1, \ldots, \beta_k >$ in $\omega^{<\omega}$, we write $\alpha \sqsubseteq \beta$ if α is initial segment of β, that is, if $n \leq k$ and $\alpha_i = \beta_i$ for $i \leq n$. For the rest of this paper, we identify a finite sequence $\alpha = < \alpha_1, \ldots, \alpha_n >$ with its code $c(\alpha) = < n, < \alpha_1, \ldots, \alpha_n >>$ in ω. We let 0 be the code of the empty sequence $\emptyset$. Thus, when we say a set $S \subseteq \omega^{<\omega}$ is recursive, recursively enumerable, etc., we mean the set $\{c(\alpha): \alpha \in S\}$ is recursive, recursively enumerable, etc. A *tree* T is a nonempty subset of $\omega^{<\omega}$ such that T is closed under initial segments. A function $f: \omega \to \omega$ is an infinite *path* through T if for all n, $< f(0), \ldots, f(n) > \in T$. We let $[T]$ denote the set of all infinite paths through T. A set A of functions is a Π_1^0-class if there is a recursive predicate R such that $A = \{f: \omega \to \omega : \forall_n (R(< f(0), \ldots, f(n) >))\}$. A Π_1^0-class A is *recursively bounded* if there is a recursive function $g: \omega \to \omega$ such that $\forall_{f \in A} \forall_n (f(n) \leq g(n))$. It is not difficult to see that if A is a Π_1^0-class, then $A = [T]$ for some recursive tree $T \subseteq \omega^{<\omega}$. We say that a tree $T \subseteq \omega^{<\omega}$ is *highly recursive* if T is a recursive, finitely branching tree such that there is a recursive procedure which given $\alpha = < \alpha_1, \ldots, \alpha_n >$ in T produces a canonical index of the set of immediate successors of α in T, that is, produces a canonical index of $\{\beta = < \alpha_1, \ldots, \alpha_n, k >: \beta \in T\}$. If A is a recursively bounded Π_1^0-class, then $A = [T]$ for some highly recursive tree $T \subseteq \omega^{<\omega}$, see [10]. We let A' denote the jump of the set A and $\mathbf{0}'$ denote the jump of the empty set. Thus $\mathbf{0}'$ is the degree of any complete r.e. set. We say that a tree $T \subseteq \omega^{<\omega}$ is *highly recursive in* $\mathbf{0}'$ if T is a finitely branching tree such that T is recursive in $\mathbf{0}'$ and there is an effective procedure which given an $\mathbf{0}'$-oracle and an $\alpha = < \alpha_1, \ldots, \alpha_n >$ in T produces a canonical index of the set of immediate successors of α in T, that is, produces a canonical index of $\{\beta = < \alpha_1, \ldots, \alpha_n, k >: \beta \in T\}$.

We say that there is an effective one-to-one degree preserving correspondence between the set of stable models of a recursive program P, $Stab(P)$, and the set of infinite paths $[T]$ through a recursive tree T if there are indices e_1 and e_2 of oracle Turing machines such that
(i) $\forall_{f \in [T]} \{e_1\}^{gr(f)} = M_f \in Stab(P)$,
(ii) $\forall_{M \in Stab(P)} \{e_2\}^M = f_M \in [T]$, and
(iii) $\forall_{f \in [T]} \forall_{M \in Stab(P)} (\{e_1\}^{gr(f)} = M$ if and only if $\{e_2\}^M = f)$.
Here $\{e\}^B$ denotes the function computed by the eth oracle machine with oracle B. We write $\{e\}^B = A$ for a set A if $\{e\}^B$ is a characteristic function of A. If f is a function $f: \omega \to \omega$, then $gr(f) = \{< x, f(x) >: x \in \omega\}$. Condition (i) says that the infinite paths of the tree T, uniformly produce stable models via an algorithm with index e_1. Condition (ii) says that stable models of P uniformly produce branches of the tree T via an algorithm with index e_2. A is *Turing reducible* to B, written $A \leq_T B$, if $\{e\}^A = B$ for some e. A is *Turing equivalent* to B, written $A \equiv_T B$, if both $A \leq_T B$ and $B \leq_T A$. Thus condition (iii) asserts that our correspondence is one-to-one and if $\{e_1\}^{gr(f)} = M_f$, then f is Turing equivalent to M_f. Finally, given sets A and B, we let $A \oplus B = \{2x : x \in A\} \bigcup \{2x + 1 : x \in B\}$.

Theorem 4.1 *We suppose that the first order language $\mathcal{L}$ has infinitely many ground atoms.*

1. *Then for any recursive program P in $\mathcal{L}$, there exists a recursive tree $T \subseteq \omega^{<\omega}$ and an effective one-to-one degree preserving correspondence between the set of all stable models of P, $Stab(P)$ and $[T]$, the set of all infinite paths through*

T.

2. *If, in addition to the hypothesis of (1), program P is FSP, then the tree T is finite splitting.*

3. *If, in addition to the hypothesis of (2), program P is recursively FSP, then the tree T is a highly recursive tree.*

5   Coding Trees into Stable Models of Finite Logic Programs

In this section, we shall give the converse of the Theorem 4.1, namely that given any recursive tree T, there exists a finite Predicate Logic Program P such that there is an effective 1:1 degree preserving correspondence between $[T]$ and $Stab(P)$. We also give two refinements.

Theorem 5.1 *Let C be any Π_1^0-class. Then*

1. *There is a finite program, P, and an effective one-to-one degree preserving correspondence between the elements of C and the set of all stable models of P, $Stab(P)$.*

2. *If in addition C is of the form $[T]$ for a finitely splitting T, then P can be chosen FSP.*

3. *If in addition T is a highly recursive tree, then P can be chosen recursively FSP.*

A classical result, first explicit in [25] and [1] but known a long time earlier in equational form, is that every r.e. relation can be computed by a suitably chosen predicate over the least model of a finite Horn program. An elegant method of proof due to Shepherdson (see [24] for references) uses the representation of recursive functions by means of finite register machines. When such machines are represented by Horn programs in the natural way, we get programs in which every atom can be proved in only finitely many ways (See also [21]). Thus we can conclude:

Proposition 5.2 *Let $r(\cdot, \cdot)$ be a recursive relation. Then there is a finite program P_r computing $r(\cdot, \cdot)$ such that every atom in the least model M_r of P_r has only finitely many minimal proof schemes.*

We can combine Proposition 5.2 with the proof of Theorem 5.1, to strengthen parts (2) and (3) of that theorem. In part (2), we can require that P has only finitely many proof schemes for every atom. In part (3), we can require that there is a recursive bound on such proof schemes.

Let us think of the expressive power of a Logic Program as being crudely characterized by the kind of associated Π_1^0-class or the kind of tree which corresponds to its set of stable models in our constructions. Then, comparing the two versions of Theorem 5.1, we see that the more stringent requirement (beyond having only finitely many supports) of having only finitely many proof schemes, does not change the expressive power of Logic Programs. That is, if we can write a Logic Program P such that its stable models are "nicely" represented by the paths through a finitely splitting T, then we can write another Logic Program P' with that property plus the additional property that P' has only finitely many proof schemes for every atom.

When we compare Theorems 4.1 and 5.1, we see for Theorem 4.1 that not only for finite, but also for recursive Logic Programs P, the class of all stable models $Stab(P)$ can be encoded by a Π_1^0 class. In turn, in Theorem 5.1 we encode Π_1^0 classes as the set of all stable models of a *finite* Logic Program. This implies that from the point of view of Turing reducibility it makes no difference if we write finite or infinite (but recursive) Logic Programs. Thus we have:

Corollary 5.3 *The expressive power of the stable semantics for finite Logic Programs and for recursive Logic Programs is the same, in the sense of 1-1 Turing degree preserving transformations. That is, for every recursive program predicate P there exists a finite predicate program P' such that there is an effective 1-1 Turing degree-preserving transformation from $Stab(P')$ onto $Stab(P)$*

The degrees of elements of Π_0^1-classes have been extensively studied in recursion theory. The combined results of the theorems 4.1 and 5.1 is that we can immediately transfer results about degrees of elements of Π_0^1-classes to results about the degrees of stable models of finite Predicate Logic Programs. Below we shall state a sample of such results.

Corollary 5.4 *(Positive results for recursive Logic Programs) Suppose P is a recursive Logic Program with a stable model. Then*

1. *P has a stable model which is recursive in a complete Σ_1^1 set.*

2. *If P has denumerably many stable models, then each stable model of P is hyperarithmetic. Otherwise P has $2^{\aleph_0}$ stable models.*

If a program P is recursively FPS, then the tree T constructed in the proof of Theorem 4.1 is recursively bounded and so the class $[T]$ is highly recursive. Recursion theory again provides us with information on the Turing degrees of elements of such classes.

Corollary 5.5 *(Positive results for recursively FPS Logic Programs) Suppose that P is a recursively FPS Logic Program with a stable model. Then*

1. *P has a stable model whose Turing jump is recursive in $0'$.*

2. *If P has only finitely many stable models, then each of these stable models is recursive.*

3. *There is a stable model M in an r.e. degree.*

4. *There exist stable models M_1 and M_2 such that any function, recursive in both M_1 and M_2, is recursive.*

5. *If P has no recursive stable model, then there is a nonzero r.e. degree a such that P has no stable model recursive in a.*

The next set of corollaries follow because a recursive finitely branching tree is automatically highly recursive in $\mathbf{0}'$.

Corollary 5.6 *(Positive results for FPS Logic Programs.) For any recursively FPS Logic Program P that possesses a stable model:*

1. *There is a stable model whose Turing jump is recursive in $\mathbf{0}''$, the Turing jump of $\mathbf{0}'$.*

2. *If P has only finitely many stable models, then each of these stable models is recursive in $\mathbf{0}'$.*

3. *There is a stable model M which is in some r.e. degree in $\mathbf{0}'$.*

4. *There are stable models M_1 and M_2 such that any function, recursive in both M_1 and M_2, is recursive in $\mathbf{0}'$.*

Every finite Logic Program is certainly recursive, so positive results such as those stated above in Corollaries 5.4, 5.5 and 5.6 for recursive Logic Programs certainly also hold for finite Logic Programs. In contrast, we get stronger negative results by constructing *finite* Logic Programs which do the same tasks we previously proved could be done with *recursive* Logic Programs, see [18]. Moreover our reduction of the Π_1^0 classes to classes $Stab(P)$ for a suitably constructed finite program P not only allows us to estimate the Turing complexity of stable models, but also provides us with finite programs with "pathological" behavior. This is interesting because it means that trying to prove that all finite programs have better behavior than this is fruitless, and to get better behavior we have to look for additional hypotheses.

Corollary 5.7 *(Negative results for finite Logic Programs)*

1. *There exists a finite Logic Program P such that P has a stable model but P has no stable model which is hyperarithmetic.*

2. *For any recursive ordinal α, there is a finite Logic Program P such that P has a unique stable model M and $M \equiv_T 0^{(\alpha)}$.*

Using well-known recursion-theoretic facts about recursively bounded Π_1^0 classes we get:

Corollary 5.8 *(Negative results for Logic Programs which are recursively FSP.*

1. *There exists a finite Logic Program P_1 which is recursively FSP such that P_1 has no recursive stable model (although P_1 possesses $2^{\aleph_0}$ stable models).*

2. *There exists a finite recursively FSP Logic Program P_2 such that P_2 possesses $2^{\aleph_0}$ stable models and any two stable models $M_1 \neq M_2$ of P_2 are Turing incomparable.*

3. *If* **a** *is a Turing degree and* $0 <_T$ **a** $<_T$ **0**$'$, *then there exists a finite rfps Logic Program* P_3 *such that* P_3 *has* $2^{\aleph_0}$ *stable models, a stable model of degree* **a** *but* P_3 *has no recursive stable model.*

We can relativize all the results in Corollary 5.5 to an **0**$'$ oracle for FSP finite Logic Programs. This is due to the following result of Jockusch, Lewis, and Remmel.

Theorem 5.9 *[9] For any tree* T *which is highly recursive in* **0**$'$, *there is a recursive finitely branching tree* $S \subseteq \omega^{<\omega}$ *with an effective one-to-one degree preserving correspondence between* $[T]$ *and* $[S]$.

Encoding highly recursive in **0**$'$ trees by binary trees gives us now results on FSP finite Logic Programs.

Corollary 5.10 *(Negative results for finite FSP Logic Programs)*

1. *There exists a finite FSP Logic Program* P_1 *such that* P_1 *has no stable model which is recursive in* **0**$'$, *although* P *possesses* $2^{\aleph_0}$ *stable models.*

2. *There exists a finite FSP Logic Program* P_2 *such that* P_2 *possesses* $2^{\aleph_0}$ *stable models and any two stable models* $M_1 \neq M_2$ *of* P_2 *have the property that* $M_1 \bigoplus \mathbf{0}' \not\equiv_T M_2 \bigoplus \mathbf{0}'$.

3. *If* **a** *is a Turing degree and* **0**$'$ $<_T$ **a** $<_T$ **0**$''$, *then there exists a finite FPS Logic Program* P_3 *such that* P_3 *has* $2^{\aleph_0}$ *stable models, a stable model of degree* **a** *but* P_3 *has no stable model which is recursive in* **0**$'$.

4. *There exists a finite FPS Logic Program* P_4 *such that* P *has* $2^{\aleph_0}$ *stable models, and if* **a** *is the degree of any stable model of* P_4 *and* **b** *is a degree which is r.e. in* **0**$'$ *with* **a** $<_T$ **b**, *then* **b** $\equiv_T$ **0**$''$.

Corollary 5.6, combined with the fact that the perfect model of a program, if it exists, is the unique stable model of the Logic Program ([7]), gives the following:

Corollary 5.11 *If* P *is a recursively FSP Logic Program, and* P *has a unique stable model then that unique stable model of* P *is recursive. Consequently, if* P *is a locally stratified, recursively FSP Logic Program, then its perfect model is recursive.*

This result is in contrast to the recent result of [4]. They show that arbitrarily complex hyperarithmetic sets can be encoded by perfect models of a locally stratified finite program, so that every hyperarithmetic set is the projection of perfect model of such a program. Here, in contrast, the additional assumption of being recursively FSP reduces the complexity of such program to a recursive set!.

We end this paper with one more result which is a direct consequence of Theorems 4.1 and 5.1

Corollary 5.12 *The problem of testing if a finite Predicate Logic Program possesses a stable model is* Σ_1^1-*complete, i.e., the set of Gödel numbers of finite Logic Programs which have a stable model is a* Σ_1^1-*complete set.*

Acknowledgements

This research was partially supported by NSF grants IRI 9012902, DMS-8902797, DMS-8702473 and ARO contract DAAG629-85-C-0018.

References

[1] H. Andreka and I. Nemeti I. The Generalized Completeness of Horn Predicate Logic as a Programming Language. *Acta Cybernetica*, 4:3–10, 1978.

[2] K. Apt, H. Blair, and A. Walker. Towards a Theory of Declarative Knowledge. In J. Minker, editor, *Foundations of Deductive Databases and Logic Programming*, pages 89–142, Los Altos, CA, 1987. Morgan Kaufmann.

[3] C. Bell, A. Nerode, R. T. Ng, V.S. Subrahmanian. Implementing Deductive Databases by Linear Programming, Cornell Mathematical Sciences Institute Technical Report 91-48, August, 1991.

[4] H. Blair, W. Marek, and J. Schlipf. Expressiveness of Locally Stratified Programs. Technical report, University of Syracuse, 1991.

[5] J. de Kleer. An Assumption-based TMS. *Artificial Intelligence* 28:127–162, 1986.

[6] J. Doyle. A Truth Maintenance System. *Artificial Intelligence*, 12:231–272, 1979.

[7] M. Gelfond and V. Lifschitz. The Stable Semantics for Logic Programs. In *Proceedings of the 5th International Symposium on Logic Programming*, pages 1070–1080, Cambridge, MA., 1988. MIT Press.

[8] M. Gelfond and H. Przymusinska. On the Relationship Between Circumscription and Autoepistemic Logic. In *Proceedings of the ISMIS Symposium*, 1986.

[9] C.G. Jockusch, A. Lewis, and J. B. Remmel. π_1^0 Classes and Rado's Selection Principle. *Journal of Symbolic Logic*, 56:684–693, 1991.

[10] C.G. Jockusch and R.I. Soare. π_1^0 Classes and Degrees of Theories. *Transactions of American Mathematical Society*, 173:33–56, 1972.

[11] K. Konolige. On the Relation Between Default and Autoepistemic Logic. *Artificial Intelligence*, 35:343–382, 1988.

[12] V. Lifschitz. Computing Circumscription, *Proceedings IJCAI-1985*, Morgan Kaufmann.

[13] V. Lifschitz Pointwise Circumscription, *Proceedings AIII-1986*, pp. 406-410, Morgan Kaufmann.

[14] J. Lloyd, *Foundations of Logic Programming*, Springer-Verlag, 1989.

[15] W. Marek, A. Nerode, and J.B. Remmel. Nonmonotonic Rule Systems I. *Annals of Mathematics and Artificial Intelligence*, pages 241–273, 1990.

[16] W. Marek, A. Nerode, and J.B. Remmel. Nonmonotonic Rule Systems II. To appear in *Annals of Mathematics and Artificial Intelligence*, 1991.

[17] W. Marek, A. Nerode, and J.B. Remmel. A Context for Belief Revision: Normal Logic Programs (Extended Abstract) *Proceedings, Workshop on Defeasible Reasoning and Constraint Solving*, International Logic Programming Symposium, San Diego, CA., 1991. Also available as Cornell Mathematical Sciences Institute Technical Report 91-63.

[18] W. Marek, A. Nerode, and J.B. Remmel. How Complicated is the Set of Stable Models of a Logic Program? *Annals of Pure and Applied Logic*, pages 119-136, 1992.

[19] W. Marek and V.S. Subrahmanian. The Relationship Between Logic Program Semantics and Non-monotonic Reasoning. In *Proceedings of the 6th International Conference on Logic Programming*, 1989.

[20] J. McCarthy. Circumscription - A Form of Non-Monotonic Reasoning. *Artificial Intelligence* 13:295–323, 1980.

[21] A. Nerode and R. Shore. *Logic for Applications*. Springer-Verlag, 1993.

[22] M. Reinfrank, O. Dressler, and G. Brewka. On the Relation Between Truth Maintenance and Non-monotonic Logics. In *Proceedings of IJCAI-89*, pages 1206–1212, San Mateo, CA., 1989. Morgan Kaufmann.

[23] R. Reiter. A Logic for Default Reasoning. *Artificial Intelligence*, 13:81–132, 1980.

[24] J.C. Shepherdson. Unsolvable Problems for SLDNF-resolution. *Journal of Logic Programming*, 10:19 – 22, 1991.

[25] R.M. Smullyan. *First-order Logic*. Springer-Verlag, 1968.

[26] A. Van Gelder K.A. Ross J.S. Schlipf. Unfounded sets and well-founded semantics for general logic programs. *Journal of the ACM*, 38:587, 1991.

Concurrent Logic Programming

A Process Algebra of Concurrent Constraint Programming

Frank S. de Boer
Department of Computing Science, Technical University Eindhoven
P.O. Box 513, 5600 MB Eindhoven, The Netherlands
wsinfdb@tuewsd.win.tue.nl

Catuscia Palamidessi
Department of Computer Science, University of Pisa,
Corso Italia 40, 56100 Pisa, Italy
katuscia@apollo.di.unipi.it

Abstract

We develop an algebraic theory for the observational equivalence of concurrent constraint programs which identifies processes which have the same final results for all possible executions.

1 Introduction

In the last years there have been given several proposals to extend logic programming with constructs for concurrency, aiming at the development of a concurrent language which would maintain the typical advantages of logic programming: declarative reading, computations as proofs, amenability to meta-programming etc. Examples of concurrent logic languages include PARLOG [6], Concurrent Prolog [12, 13], Guarded Horn Clauses [16, 17] and their so-called *flat* versions. Concurrent constraint programming ([10, 14, 15]) represents one of the most successful proposals in this area.

Constraint programming is based on the notion of computing with systems of partial information. The *store* is seen as a constraint on the values that variables can assume, rather than a correspondence between variables and values. All processes of the system share a common store, which, at any stage of the computation, is given by the constraint established until that moment. The execution of a tell action modifies the current store by adding a constraint. An ask action is a test on the store: it can be executed only if the current store is *strong enough* to entail a specified constraint. If this is not the case, then the process suspends (waiting for the store to accumulate more information by the contributions of the other processes). The execution of an ask itself leaves the store unchanged. Hence both the tell and ask actions are monotonic, in the sense that after their execution the store contains the same or more information. Therefore the store evolves monotonically during the computation, i.e. the set of possible values for the variables shrinks.

This paper addresses the problem of an algebraic axiomatization for concurrent constraint programming. The algebraic approach is one of the most diffused methods in concurrency theory both for specification (i.e. definition of new operators) and for program verification (i.e. check that a certain implementation satisfies a given specification). During the last decade there have been a number of proposals for process algebras: beside the Calculus of Communicating Systems of Milner ([9]), several related formalisms have been proposed, such as the Theory of Communicating Processes of Hoare ([1]) and the Algebra of Communicating Systems of Bergstra and Klop ([2, 3, 5]).

For a given language there are, in general, various observability criteria which are of interest. Since in concurrent constraint programming processes communicate via a common store the relevant aspects of the behaviour of a process, from the point of view of the environment, are described in terms of its interaction with the common store. In this paper we consider the most abstract description: only the final results are observable. This choice is motivated by the fact that, due to the monotonic evolution of the store, the intermediate states of the computation are just approximations of the final result.

However, the equivalence induced by this notion of observables introduces too many identifications to be characterized algebraically. For an algebraic theory only those processes can be identified which not only have the same observables, but which additionally show no observable difference when immerged in any kind of context. An equivalence which satisfies this property is called a *congruence*. The coarsest of such congruences is particularly of interest since it exactly identifies those processes which cannot be distinguished by any context; it corresponds to a fully abstract semantics. In this paper we will develop a complete axiomatization of the coarsest congruence contained in the equivalence induced by observing final results only.

To prove correctness and completeness of the axiomatization, it will be convenient to define a fully abstract semantics. A compositional model is more suitable for reasoning about the axioms because it characterizes classes of processes which are observable equivalent in every context in terms of canonical representatives.

Due to space limitations in this version we have omitted the proofs which can be found in the full paper.

1.1 Plan of the paper

In the next section we define the notion of constraint system underlying the language. In particular, we discuss distributive and complemented constraint systems. In Section 3 we define the language, the operational model, and the notion of observables. In Section 4 we present the axiomatization, and in Section 5 we discuss its correctness and completeness. In section 5 we also develop a fully abstract semantics which will be useful to prove those results. In the last section we point out some directions for future research.

2 Constraint systems

The notion of constraint system we consider here is a simplification[1] of the one developed in [14].

Definition 2.1 A constraint system $\mathcal{C}$ is a complete (algebraic) lattice $\langle C, \leq, \wedge, true, false\rangle$ where $\wedge$ is the lub operation, and $true$, $false$ are the least and the greatest elements of C, respectively.

Following the standard terminology and notation, instead of $\leq$ we will refer to its inverse relation, denoted by $\vdash$ and called *entailment*. Formally

$$\forall c, d \in C. \quad c \vdash d \;\Leftrightarrow\; d \leq c.$$

In order to treat the hiding operator of the language it will be helpful to introduce a general notion of existential quantification. In this framework it is convenient to formalize this notion by means of the theory of cylindric algebras ([8]). This leads to the concept of *cylindric constraint system*.

Definition 2.2 Let *Var* be a (denumerable) set of variables $x, y, z, \ldots$. Assume that for each $x \in Var$ a function $\exists_x : C \to C$ is defined such that for any $c, d \in C$:

(i) $c \vdash \exists_x(c)$,

(ii) if $c \vdash d$ then $\exists_x(c) \vdash \exists_x(d)$,

(iii) $\exists_x(c \wedge \exists_x(d)) \sim \exists_x(c) \wedge \exists_x(d)$,

(iv) $\exists_x(\exists_y(c)) \sim \exists_y(\exists_x(c))$.

Then $\langle C, \vdash, \wedge, true, false, Var\rangle$ is a *cylindric constraint system*.

In the following $\exists_x(c)$ will be denoted by $\exists_x c$ with the convention that, in case of ambiguity, the scope of $\exists_x$ is limited to the first constraint subexpression. (So, for instance $\exists_x c \wedge d$ stands for $\exists_x(c) \wedge d$.)

We introduce now two notions taken from lattice theory: the complement and the distributivity. The complement of an element c, denoted by c^-, represents, in a sense, the negation of c. Distributivity is the usual property about combinations of lubs and glbs (in the sequel the glb of a lattice will be

---

[1]The approach of [14] follows Scott's treatment of information system ([11]): the starting point is a set of simple constraints on which a compact entailment relation is defined. Then a constraint system is constructed by considering sets of simple constraints and by extending the entailment relation on it. This construction is made in such a way that the resulting structure is a complete *algebraic* lattice, which ensures the effectiveness of the extended entailment relation. In this paper we abstract from this construction, and we just consider the resulting structure.

denoted by ∨). Constraint systems satisfying distributivity and existence of the complement are very rich structures (actually they are boolean algebras), and for this reason they are particularly suitable to reason about equalities. Furthermore, they have a very interesting feature, which will be useful for developing our axiomatization: they are able to *represent the entailment relation* as a constraint of the system itself:

Proposition 2.3 *Let* $\langle C, \vdash, \wedge, true, false \rangle$ *be a distributive and complemented constraint system. Then*

$$\forall c, d, e \in C. \ (e \wedge c \vdash d) \ \Leftrightarrow \ (e \vdash c^- \vee d).$$

We will denote $c^- \vee d$ by $c \to d$ and $(\exists_x c^-)^-$ by $\forall_x c$.

The only-if part of previous proposition is a sort of 'deduction theorem' for constraint systems.

In general, the existence of the complement and distributivity is a rather strong assumption, and it would be very restrictive to require it to be satisfied by the constraint system on which the language operates. Actually we do not need to do so. For our purpose it is sufficient to embed the constraint system of the language into a complemented and distributive one. We use this larger system only to represent terms in intermediate steps possibly needed to derive certain equalities among processes. (This is in analogy for instance with the idea of immerging the real numbers into the field of the complex numbers, in order to solve equations between real numbers.) Given a constraint system $\mathcal{C}$ we will indicate by $dc(\mathcal{C})$ the distributive and complemented closure of $\mathcal{C}$, namely the smallest distributive and complemented constraint system which contains $\mathcal{C}$ as subsystem.

Example 2.4 Consider a Herbrand domain consisting only of the constants a, b and c and let $\mathcal{C}$ be the constraint system whose elements are the equalities over this domain involving a variable x, and the entailment relation is the 'standard one', represented in Figure 1(a). This constraint system is neither distributive, nor the unicity of the complement is satisfied.

Consider now the constraint system $\mathcal{C}'$ which contains also the disequalities involving x, with the 'standard' entailment relation represented in Figure 1(b). We have that $\mathcal{C}'$ is distributive, complemented and $\mathcal{C}' = dc(\mathcal{C})$.

3 The language

In this section we present the language of concurrent constraint programming, its computational model and the intended observation criterium. The definitions we give are equivalent to the ones in [15].

We assume given a cylindric constraint system $\langle C, \vdash, \wedge, true, false, Var \rangle$. We use $A, B, \ldots$ to range over the set of processes, $p, q, r, \ldots$ to range over

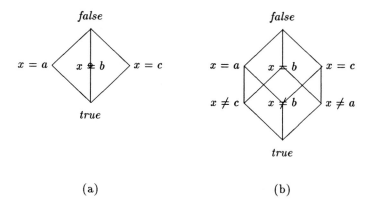

Figure 1: Herbrand constraint systems for x, a, b, c

process names, $x, y, z, \ldots$ to range over *Var* and α over the set of ask and tell actions. In addition, the notation $\vec{\chi}$ indicates a list of the form $(\chi_1, \ldots, \chi_n)$.
The processes are described by the following grammar

$$A ::= \delta \mid \alpha \cdot A \mid A + A \mid A \parallel A \mid \exists x.A \mid p(\vec{x})$$

The symbol δ denotes inaction. The process $\mathbf{ask}(c) \cdot A$ waits until the store entails c and then it behaves like A. The process $\mathbf{tell}(c) \cdot A$ adds c to the store and then it behaves like A. Sometimes we omit $\cdot$ and write, for example, $\alpha(A + B)$ instead of $\alpha \cdot (A + B)$. The operators $\parallel$ and $+$ are the parallel composition (or *merge*) and the nondeterministic choice (or *plus*), respectively. $\exists x$ is the hiding operator: $\exists x.A$ is like the process A, with the variable x seen as *local*. We will see that there is a strong relation with the existential quantifier over the constraint system, for this reason we have used the same symbol. Finally, $p(\vec{x})$ is a procedure call, p is the name of the procedure, and $\vec{x}$ is the list of the actual parameters. The meaning of a process is given with respect to a set W of declarations of the form $p(\vec{y}) :- A$. We denote by $Vrt(W)$ the set of the variants of the declarations in W, obtained by renaming their variables. In the sequel we assume W to be fixed, so we omit reference to it.

Syntactical identity between processes we denote by $\equiv$. We assume the following binding order between the operators (corresponding to decreasing priority): $\cdot$, $+$, $\parallel$, $\exists x$.

3.1 The operational model and the observables $\mathcal{O}$

The operational model is described in terms of a transition system $T = (Conf, \longrightarrow)$. The configurations *Conf* consist of a process and a constraint representing the store. The rules of T are described in Table 1. (We assume the commutativity of the parallel and the choice operator.)

Table 1: The Transition System T

R1 $\quad \langle \mathbf{ask}(d) \cdot A, c \rangle \longrightarrow \langle A, c \rangle \qquad\qquad$ **if** $c \vdash d$

R2 $\quad \langle \mathbf{tell}(d) \cdot A, c \rangle \longrightarrow \langle A, c \wedge d \rangle$

R3 $\quad \langle p(\vec{x}), c \rangle \longrightarrow \langle A, c \rangle \qquad\qquad$ **if** $p(\vec{x}) :\text{-} A \in Vrt(W)$

R4 $\quad \dfrac{\langle A, \exists_x c \rangle \longrightarrow \langle B, d \rangle}{\langle \exists x.A, c \rangle \longrightarrow \langle \exists_x^d.B, c \wedge \exists_x d \rangle}$

R5 $\quad \dfrac{\langle A, d \wedge \exists_x c \rangle \longrightarrow \langle B, e \rangle}{\langle \exists_x^d.A, c \rangle \longrightarrow \langle \exists_x^e.B, c \wedge \exists_x e \rangle}$

R6 $\quad \dfrac{\langle A, c \rangle \longrightarrow \langle A', d \rangle}{\substack{\langle A \parallel B, c \rangle \longrightarrow \langle A' \parallel B, d \rangle \\ \langle A + B, c \rangle \longrightarrow \langle A', d \rangle}}$

The way in which the store is queried and updated is described by the rules **R1** and **R2**. Note that the execution of a tell action is not constrained by consistency requirements. As a consequence a tell action can always proceed; it is an autonomous action. Also with respect to an ask action we do not require the current store to be consistent with the asked constraint, we require only that it is implied by the current store. Rule **R3** describes the replacement of a procedure call by the body of the procedure definition (in W). The hiding of variables is described by the rules **R4** and **R5**. To keep track of the local store which contains information about the local variable, we introduced an auxiliary operator $\exists_x^c$, where c represents the local store. A local computation step then proceeds from a store which consists of the local store and the global information about all the variables but the local one. The resulting store of a local computation step represents the new local store, and the new global store is obtained by adding to the old one the new information about all the variables but the local one. Finally, **R6** is the usual rule for the parallel and the choice operator, where the behaviour of a compound process is described in terms of the behaviour of the components. Notice that parallelism is described as interleaving. Furthermore, the choice operator models global non-determinism in the sense that the choices of a process which are guarded by an ask action, depend on the current store which is subject to modifications by the external environment.

The result of a terminating computation consists of the final store. This is formally represented by the notion of *observables*.

Definition 3.1 The observables are given by the function

$$\mathcal{O}[\![A]\!] = \{c \mid \langle A, true \rangle \longrightarrow^* \langle B, c \rangle \not\longrightarrow \}$$

where $\longrightarrow^*$ denotes the transitive closure of $\longrightarrow$, and $\not\longrightarrow$ indicates that there is no transition possible.

We want to identify those processes that have the same obervables in every context:

Definition 3.2 By $\doteq$ we denote the congruence $A \doteq B$ iff for all contexts $C[\,]$, $\mathcal{O}[\![C[A]]\!] = \mathcal{O}[\![C[B]]\!]$. Here a context $C[\,]$ is a process expression with occurrences of a process variable, and $C[A]$ denotes the process obtained by substituting A for this variable in $C[\,]$.

Note that the relation which identifies processes that have the same observables is not a congruence.

4 Process Algebra

In this section we investigate an axiomatization of the congruence $\doteq$. For technical convenience we restrict ourselves to finite processes, for a treatment of recursion we refer to [5]. The kernel of the algebra consists of the axiom system **aprPA** (the system in [4] restricted to action prefixing), plus the failure axioms and the axioms for τ-abstraction ([3]) .

The system **aprPA** (Table 2) axiomatizes the plus-operator (commutativity, associativity, idempotency), δ, and the merge in terms of interleaving. For the axiomatization of the merge an auxiliary operator, the left-merge ($\lfloor\!\lfloor$), is introduced. The system **aprPA** axiomatizes a notion of equivalence which is known as bisimulation [5]. The system **aprPA** plus the failure axioms (Table 3) axiomatizes the congruence induced by the equivalence which identifies processes which have the same maximal traces. Finally, the τ-abstraction rules (Table 4) allow one to abstract from 'silent steps'. In the context of concurrent constraint programming a silent-step corresponds to a **tell**(*true*) or **ask**(*true*) action.

On top of this we have first the axioms for quantification (Table 5). Quantification is axiomatized in terms of the auxiliary operator $\exists_x^c$, which acts like a kind of state-operator [5, 4]. The local store which includes information about the local variable x is represented by c. This auxiliary operator distributes over the plus, and when it passes a tell action or an ask action it quantifies the local variable (in case of an ask it also changes the constraint), and updates the local store, which is then passed on. The transformation of the constraint in the ask can be justified as follows: d is

Table 2: **aprPA**

$$\delta \cdot A \;\; = \;\; \delta$$

$A + A$	$=$	A	$A \parallel B$	$=$	$A \parallel\!\!\!\perp B + B \parallel\!\!\!\perp A$
$A + B$	$=$	$B + A$	$\delta \parallel\!\!\!\perp A$	$=$	δ
$A + (B + C)$	$=$	$(A + B) + C$	$(\alpha \cdot A) \parallel\!\!\!\perp B$	$=$	$\alpha(A \parallel B)$
$A + \delta$	$=$	A	$(A + B) \parallel\!\!\!\perp C$	$=$	$A \parallel\!\!\!\perp C + B \parallel\!\!\!\perp C$

Table 3: The Failure Axioms.

$$\alpha(\beta \cdot A_1 + B_1) + \alpha(\beta \cdot A_2 + B_2) \;\; = \;\; \begin{array}{c} \alpha(\beta \cdot A_1 + \beta \cdot A_2 + B_1) \\ + \\ \alpha(\beta \cdot A_1 + \beta \cdot A_2 + B_2) \end{array}$$

$$\alpha \cdot A + \alpha(B + C) \;\; = \;\; \alpha \cdot A + \alpha(A + B) + \alpha(B + C)$$

entailed by the local store c and an arbitrary global store $\exists_x e$ iff (by the deduction theorem) $c \rightarrow d$ is entailed by $\exists_x e$, or equivalently $\forall_x(c \rightarrow d)$ is entailed by e. Note that $\forall_x(c \rightarrow d)$ is an element of $dc(\mathcal{C})$, and remember that the deduction theorem holds in $dc(\mathcal{C})$ (this is the main reason why we have intoduced the notion of $dc(\mathcal{C})$).

Next we introduce a system of axioms which characterize the specific nature of the ask and tell actions. In the following $\alpha(c)$ and $\beta(c)$ represent ask or tell actions on the constraint c. The axiom

$$\boxed{\alpha(c)(\beta(d) \cdot A + B) = \alpha(c)(\beta(c \wedge d) \cdot A + B)} \tag{1}$$

expresses that once a constraint has been established, either by telling or asking it, it remains in the store. As a consequence, once a constraint is established, asking or telling it will have the effect of a silent transition. This is expressed by the following axiom

$$\boxed{\alpha(c)(\beta(c) \cdot A + B) = \alpha(c)(\tau \cdot A + B)} \tag{2}$$

Table 4: τ-abstraction laws

$$
\begin{aligned}
\alpha \cdot \tau \cdot A &= \alpha \cdot A \\
\tau \cdot A + B &= \tau \cdot A + \tau(A + B)
\end{aligned}
$$

Table 5: Quantification

$$
\begin{aligned}
\exists x.A &= \exists_x^{true}.A \\
\exists_x^c.\delta &= \delta \\
\exists_x^c.(A + B) &= \exists_x^c.A + \exists_x^c.B \\
\exists_x^c.\textbf{tell}(d) \cdot A &= \textbf{tell}(\exists_x(c \wedge d)) \cdot \exists_x^{c \wedge d}.A \\
\exists_x^c.\textbf{ask}(d) \cdot A &= \textbf{ask}(\forall_x(c \rightarrow d)) \cdot \exists_x^c.A
\end{aligned}
$$

The axioms

$$\boxed{\alpha(\textbf{tell}(c) \cdot A + B) = \alpha(\textbf{tell}(c) \cdot A + B) + \alpha \cdot \textbf{tell}(c) \cdot A} \tag{3}$$

and

$$\boxed{\textbf{tell}(c) \cdot A = \textbf{tell}(c) \cdot A + \textbf{ask}(d) \cdot \textbf{tell}(c) \cdot A} \tag{4}$$

together characterize the autonomous character of a tell action, namely the fact that it can always proceed irrespective of the current store. It is worthwhile noticing the similarity of axiom 3 with the I-axiom for asynchronous communication ([7]). Axiom 4 can be informally justified as follows: suppose that the current store implies the asked constraint d, in this case the process represented by the right-hand side of the axiom can select the ask-branch, execute the tell action and proceed with A. But this behaviour can be simulated with the same observable effect by the other branch. In case the current store does not imply d, the only choice left is to execute the tell-branch. It is instructive to see why axiom 4 does not hold for ask actions: let c and d be such that neither $c \vdash d$ nor $d \vdash c$. Then the processes $A \equiv \textbf{ask}(c) \cdot \delta$ and $B \equiv A + \textbf{ask}(d) \cdot \textbf{ask}(c) \cdot \delta$ can be distinguished by the context $C[\,] \equiv ([\,] + \textbf{ask}(d) \cdot \textbf{tell}(c) \cdot \delta) \parallel \textbf{tell}(d) \cdot \delta$, namely after the execution of $\textbf{tell}(d)$ the process B in $C[B]$ can select the $\textbf{ask}(d) \cdot \textbf{ask}(c) \cdot \delta$ branch after which the process terminates, whereas after the execution of **tell**(d) by the process $C[A]$ the process A is suspended, and thus the enabled branch **ask**$(d) \cdot$ **tell**$(c) \cdot \delta$ is selected, so formally we have $d \in \mathcal{O}[\![C[B]]\!] \setminus \mathcal{O}[\![C[A]]\!]$. However, the following axiom which allows the strengthening of an ask-guard can be shown to be valid:

$$\boxed{\mathbf{ask}(c) \cdot A = \mathbf{ask}(c) \cdot A + \mathbf{ask}(d) \cdot A} \tag{5}$$

provided $d \vdash c$. The axiom,

$$\boxed{\mathbf{tell}(c) \cdot A = \mathbf{tell}(d) \cdot \mathbf{tell}(e) \cdot A} \tag{6}$$

where $c \sim d \wedge e$, allows for the composition/decomposition of tell actions. Again, in a similar way as described above, it can be shown that a corresponding axiom for ask actions is not valid. The following restricted version of composition/decomposition,

$$\boxed{\mathbf{ask}(c) \cdot A + \mathbf{ask}(c \wedge d) \cdot B = \mathbf{ask}(c) \cdot A + \mathbf{ask}(c)(A + \mathbf{ask}(d) \cdot B)} \tag{7}$$

however, can be shown to be valid. We conclude with the following axiom

$$\boxed{\Sigma_i \alpha \Sigma_j \mathbf{ask}(c_{i_j}) \cdot A_{i_j} = \Sigma_i \alpha \Sigma_j \mathbf{ask}(c_{i_j}) \cdot A_{i_j} + \alpha \Sigma_k \mathbf{ask}(c_k) \cdot A_k} \tag{8}$$

provided for every $f \in I \to J$ if for every $k \in K \subseteq \{i_j \mid i \in I, j \in J\}$ we have $\bigwedge_i c_{i_{f(i)}} \nvdash c_k$ then there exist i and j such that $\mathbf{ask}(\bigwedge_i c_{i_{f(i)}}) \cdot \delta \equiv \mathbf{ask}(c_{i_j}) \cdot A_{i_j}$ (Σ denotes generalized sum, and i is to be understood to range over I, j over J). This axiom can be informally justified as follows: let c be such that for no c_k we have $c \vdash c_k$. So after the execution of α the branch $\alpha \cdot \Sigma_k \mathbf{ask}(c_k) \cdot A_k$ will terminate. Now suppose that for every i there exists j such that $c \vdash c_{i_j}$. Define $f \in I \to J$ such that $c \vdash c_{i_{f(i)}}$. It follows that there exists no k such that $\bigwedge_i c_{i_{f(i)}} \vdash c_k$ (otherwise we would have $c \vdash c_k$). So there exist i and j such that $\mathbf{ask}(c_{i_j}) \cdot A_{i_j} \equiv \mathbf{ask}(\bigwedge_i c_{i_{f(i)}}) \cdot \delta$. Thus the process represented by the left-hand side of the axiom will also terminate in the current store c after the execution of α, selecting the ith branch.

Example 4.1 Consider the following equation:

$$\alpha(\mathbf{ask}(c) \cdot \delta + A) = \alpha(\mathbf{ask}(c) \cdot \delta + A) + \alpha \cdot A$$

If $A \equiv \Sigma_i \alpha_i \cdot A_i$ contains only initial ask actions, then the equation can be obtained as an instance of the axiom 8.

5 Formal justification

In this section we discuss the formal justification (i.e., soundness and completeness) of the process algebra we have presented. We indicate with the symbol $\vdash$ (not to be confused with the entailment relation $\vdash$!) the derivation of an equality in the algebraic theory consisting of all the axioms of previous section. First we define a compositional semantics which is fully abstract with respect to $\mathcal{O}$.

In the following, $\mathcal{A}$ denotes the set of ask and tell actions. For a set S, $\mathcal{P}(S)$ is the set of all subsets of S. The domain of our semantics consists of sets of ask-tell sequences together with a constraint: formally it is given by the set $\mathcal{P}(\mathcal{A}^* \times C)$, where $C = \langle C, \leq, \wedge, true, false \rangle$ is the constraint system underlying the language. Each element of this set represents a possible run of the process within an environment (context). The constraint represents the final store (as determined by the contributions of both the process and the context), final in the sense that the process cannot proceed anymore given that store. The ask-tell sequence represents the sequence of all actions performed by the process in this run.

Before describing formally the semantics we need to introduce some technical definitions. In the following, F, F_1, F_2 will indicate elements of $\mathcal{P}(\mathcal{A}^* \times C)$.

The notation $\alpha(c) \circ F$ indicates the set obtained by prefixing $\alpha(c)$ to those sequences for which c doesn't change the final result. Formally:

$$\mathbf{ask}(c) \circ F = \begin{array}{c} \{\langle \alpha(c) \cdot f, d \rangle \mid \langle f, d \rangle \in F \text{ and } d \vdash c\} \\ \cup \\ \{\langle \tau, d \rangle \mid \langle \epsilon, d \rangle, \langle \tau, d \rangle \in F \text{ and } d \vdash c\} \\ \cup \\ \{\langle \epsilon, d \rangle \mid d \nvdash c\} \end{array}$$

and

$$\mathbf{tell}(c) \circ F = \{\langle \alpha(c) \cdot f, d \rangle \mid \langle f, d \rangle \in F \text{ and } d \vdash c\}$$

where ϵ denotes the empty sequence. The semantics of prefixing an ask action consists in adding the action to those sequences the final result of which entails the asked constraint. Moreover, we select the sequences $\langle \epsilon, d \rangle$ and $\langle \tau, d \rangle$, where d entails the asked constraint. With respect to these sequences, which model the situation that the process either terminates immediately or after some silent moves in the final store d, the action $\mathbf{ask}(c)$ behaves like a silent step. (Note that we additionally perform some τ-abstraction by contracting a number of silent steps into one.) Finally, we have to add those (empty) sequences consisting of a final result which does not imply the asked constraint, since in these cases the resulting process terminates immediately. Note that the main difference between the semantics of an ask and tell action is that for an ask action we need additionally to record those final stores which block the action. Since a tell action can always proceed this additional recording does not apply.

$F_1 \parallel F_2$ denotes the set of all possible interleavings of those sequences of F_1 and F_2 which result in the same final store:

$$F_1 \parallel F_2 = \{\langle f, c \rangle \mid \langle f_1, c \rangle \in F_1, \langle f_2, c \rangle \in F_2 \text{ and } f \in (f_1 \parallel f_2)\}$$

($f_1 \parallel f_2$ denotes the set of arbitrary interleavings of f_1 and f_2).

Finally, the local state operator is defined by

$$\exists_x^c(F) = \{\exists_x^c(\langle f, d\rangle) \mid \langle f, d\rangle \in F\},$$

where:

$$
\begin{aligned}
\exists_x^c(\langle \mathbf{tell}(d) \cdot f, d\rangle) &= \mathbf{tell}(\exists_x d) \circ \exists_x^{c \wedge d}(\langle f, d\rangle) \\
\exists_x^c(\langle \mathbf{ask}(d) \cdot f, d\rangle) &= \mathbf{ask}(\forall_x(c \to d)) \circ \exists_x^c(\langle f, d\rangle) \\
\exists_x^c(\langle \epsilon, d\rangle) &= \{\langle \epsilon, e \wedge \exists_x c\rangle \mid c \wedge \exists_x e \sim d\}
\end{aligned}
$$

Definition 5.1 The mapping $\mathcal{F}$ from processes to the set $\mathcal{P}(\mathcal{A}^* \times C)$ is defined as follows.

$$\mathcal{F}[\![\delta]\!] = \{\langle \epsilon, c\rangle \mid c \in C\}$$

$$\mathcal{F}[\![\mathbf{ask}(c) \cdot A]\!] = \mathbf{ask}(c) \circ \mathcal{F}[\![A]\!]$$

$$\mathcal{F}[\![\mathbf{tell}(c) \cdot A]\!] = \mathbf{tell}(c) \circ \mathcal{F}[\![A]\!]$$

$$\mathcal{F}[\![A + B]\!] = (\mathcal{F}[\![A]\!] \cup \mathcal{F}[\![B]\!]) \setminus C \cup (\mathcal{F}[\![A]\!] \cap \mathcal{F}[\![B]\!] \cap C)$$

$$\mathcal{F}[\![A \parallel B]\!] = \mathcal{F}[\![A]\!] \parallel \mathcal{F}[\![B]\!]$$

$$\mathcal{F}[\![\exists x.A]\!] = \exists_x^{true}(\mathcal{F}[\![A]\!]) \ .$$

The set of all possible final results of the process δ is the set C itself, since δ does not impose any constraints and all constraints are final for it.

The semantics of a process $A + B$ consists of the non-empty (with respect to the actions) sequences of A and B, plus those empty sequences the final result of which belongs both to A and B. These latter sequences represent those stores from which neither A nor B can proceed. Here C is used as an abbreviaton for $\{\epsilon\} \times C$.

Quantification is described in terms of the state operator $\exists_x^c$ where c represents the local store which contains information about the local x.

The correctness of $\mathcal{F}$ with respect to $\mathcal{O}$ is stated in the following theorem:

Theorem 5.2 *For every process A we have*

$$
\begin{aligned}
\mathcal{O}[\![A]\!] = \{c \mid \ &\exists f. \langle f, c\rangle \in \mathcal{F}[\![A]\!], con(f) \sim c, \\
&\forall f'(\ f' \cdot \mathbf{ask}(d) \preceq f \Rightarrow con(f') \vdash d)\}
\end{aligned}
$$

Here $con(f)$ denotes the conjunction of all the constraints occurring of the ask and tell actions of f, and $\preceq$ denotes the prefix relation.

However $\mathcal{F}$ is not fully abstract with respect to $\mathcal{O}$. We need the following closure conditions which characterize the monotonic nature of the computational model:

Definition 5.3 For $F \in \mathcal{P}(\mathcal{A}^* \times C)$ let $Sat(F)$ denote the smallest set containing F which is closed under the following conditions:

C1 $f \cdot \alpha(c) \cdot \beta(d) \cdot f' \in F \Rightarrow f \cdot \alpha(c) \cdot \beta(c \wedge d) \cdot f'$

C2 $f \cdot \alpha(c) \cdot \beta(c) \cdot f' \in F \Leftrightarrow f \cdot \alpha(c) \cdot \tau \cdot f'$

C3 $f \cdot \mathbf{tell}(c) \cdot \mathbf{tell}(d) \cdot f' \in F \Leftrightarrow f \cdot \mathbf{tell}(c \wedge d) \cdot f' \in F$

C4 $f \cdot \mathbf{ask}(c) \cdot \mathbf{ask}(d) \cdot f' \in F \Rightarrow f \cdot \mathbf{ask}(c \wedge d) \cdot f' \in F$

C5 $f \cdot \mathbf{ask}(c) \cdot f' \in F \Rightarrow f \cdot \mathbf{ask}(d) \cdot f' \in F \; (d \vdash c)$

C6 $f \cdot \mathbf{ask}(c \wedge d) \cdot f' \in F, \; f \cdot \mathbf{ask}(c) \cdot f'' \in F \Rightarrow f \cdot \mathbf{ask}(c) \cdot \mathbf{ask}(d) \cdot f' \in F$

C7 $f \cdot \alpha \cdot \tau \cdot f' \in F \Leftrightarrow f \cdot \alpha \cdot f' \in F$

(Note that we both use f to denote an element of $\mathcal{A}^*$ and $\mathcal{P}(\mathcal{A}^* \times C)$.) In C5 it is assumed that the constraint d is entailed by the final result.

In the full paper we show how these conditions can be expressed by the axioms.

Next we introduce the semantics $\mathcal{F}'$:

Definition 5.4 For every process A we define $\mathcal{F}'\llbracket A \rrbracket = Sat(\mathcal{F}\llbracket A \rrbracket)$.

In the full paper we show that $\mathcal{F}'$ is compositional and fully abstract with respect to $\mathcal{O}$, which together with the correctness, gives the following theorem:

Theorem 5.5 *For any processes A and B we have*

$$A \doteq B \Leftrightarrow \mathcal{F}'\llbracket A \rrbracket = \mathcal{F}'\llbracket B \rrbracket.$$

Given this characterization of the congruence we can prove the soundness and completeness of the axiom system:

Theorem 5.6 *For any processes A and B*

$$\vdash A = B \Leftrightarrow A \doteq B$$

Proof-sketch By Theorem 5.5 to prove soundness it suffices to show for any axiom $A = B$ that $\mathcal{F}'\llbracket A \rrbracket = \mathcal{F}'\llbracket B \rrbracket$. For a detailed proof of the completeness we refer to the full paper. The structure of the proof consists of a completeness result for basic processes, i.e., processes which are built up from the ask/tell primitives and δ using prefixing and choice only, and an elemination theorem which states that every process is provable equal to a basic process. In the completeness result for basic processes the following expressiveness of the closure conditions plays a crucial role: let $\mathcal{F}^0\llbracket A \rrbracket = \mathcal{F}\llbracket A \rrbracket$ and $\mathcal{F}^{n+1}\llbracket A \rrbracket = Sat(\mathcal{F}^n\llbracket A \rrbracket)$, then for every n and for every basic process A there exists a basic process A_n such that $\vdash A = A_n$ and $\mathcal{F}\llbracket A_n \rrbracket = \mathcal{F}^n\llbracket A \rrbracket$.

$\square$

6   Future Research

We investigated an algebraic axiomatization of concurrent constraint programming. An essential feature of our computational model is that the execution of a tell action is not constrained by consistency requirements; it is modelled as an autonomous action. Also with respect to an ask action we do not require the asked constraint to be consistent with the current store, we only require the asked constraint to be entailed by it. It would be interesting to study algebraically other models which do impose consistency requirements on the execution of a ask/tell action. These other models then would require additionally an algebraic theory for inconsistency or failure.

References

[1]   S.D. Brookes, C.A.R. Hoare, and W. Roscoe. *A theory of communicating sequential processes.* Journal of ACM, 31:499–560, 1984.

[2]   J.A. Bergstra and J.W. Klop. *Process algebra: specification and verification in bisimulation semantics.* Mathematics and Computer Science II, CWI Monographs, pages 61 – 94. North-Holland, 1986.

[3]   J.A. Bergstra, J.W. Klop, and E.-R. Olderog. *Readies and failures in the algebra of communicating processes.* SIAM J. on Computing, 17(6):1134 – 1177, 1988.

[4]   J.A. Bergstra, J.W. Klop, and J.V. Tucker. *Process algebra with asynchronous communication mechanisms.* S.D. Brookes, A.W. Roscoe, and G. Winskel, editors, Proc. Seminar on Concurrency, volume 197 of Lecture Notes in Computer Science, pages 76 – 95. Springer-Verlag, 1985.

[5]   J.C.M. Baeten and P. Weijland. *Process Algebra*, volume 18 of Cambridge Tracts in Theoretical Computer Science. Cambridge University Press, 1990.

[6]   K.L. Clark and S. Gregory. *PARLOG: parallel programming in logic.* ACM Trans. on Programming Languages and Systems, (8):1–49, 1986.

[7]   F.S. de Boer, J.W. Klop, and C. Palamidessi. *Asynchronous communication in process algebra.* Proc. of LICS 92, IEEE Computer Society Press, 1992. To appear.

[8]   L. Henkin, J.D. Monk, and A. Tarski. *Cylindric Algebras (Part I).* North-Holland, 1971.

[9]   R. Milner. *A Calculus of Communicating Systems*, volume 92 of Lecture Notes in Computer Science. Springer-Verlag, New York, 1980.

[10] V.A. Saraswat. *Concurrent Constraint Programming Languages.* PhD thesis, Carnegie-Mellon University, January 1989. Published by The MIT Press, U.S.A., 1990.

[11] D. Scott. *Domains for denotational semantics.* Proc. of ICALP, 1982.

[12] E.Y. Shapiro. *A subset of Concurrent Prolog and its interpreter.* Technical Report TR-003, Institute for New Generation Computer Technology (ICOT), Tokyo, 1983.

[13] E. Y. Shapiro. *Concurrent Prolog: A progress report.* Computer, 19(8):44–58, 1986.

[14] V.A. Saraswat and M. Rinard. *Concurrent constraint programming.* Proc. of the seventeenth ACM Symposium on Principles of Programming Languages, pages 232–245. ACM, New York, 1990.

[15] V.A. Saraswat, M. Rinard, and P. Panangaden. *Semantics foundations of Concurrent Constraint Programming.* Proc. of the eighteenth ACM Symposium on Principles of Programming Languages. ACM, New York, 1991.

[16] K. Ueda. *Guarded Horn Clauses.* E. Y. Shapiro, editor, Concurrent Prolog: Collected Papers. The MIT Press, 1987.

[17] K. Ueda. *Guarded Horn Clauses, a parallel logic programming language with the concept of a guard.* M. Nivat and K. Fuchi, editors, Programming of Future Generation Computers, pages 441–456. North Holland, Amsterdam, 1988.

Schedule Analysis of Concurrent Logic Programs

Andy King and Paul Soper
Department of Electronics and Computer Science,
University of Southampton, Southampton, S09 5NH, UK
amk@ecs.soton.ac.uk, pjs@ecs.soton.ac.uk

Abstract

A compilation technique is proposed for concurrent logic programs called schedule analysis. Schedule analysis deduces at compile-time a partial schedule for the processes of a program by partitioning the atoms of each clause into threads. Threads are totally ordered sets of atoms whose relative ordering is determined by a scheduler. Threads reduce scheduler activity and permit a wealth of traditional Prolog optimisations to be applied to the program. A framework for schedule analysis is proposed and this defines a procedure for creating threads. A safety result is presented stating the conditions under which the work of the scheduler can be reduced from ordering processes to ordering threads. Schedule analysis has been integrated into a compiler and implementation has suggested that it can play a central rôle in compilation. Optimisations which follow from schedule analysis include a reduction in scheduling, the removal of synchronisation checks, the simplification of unification, decreased garbage collection and a reduction in argument copying.

1   Introduction

Concurrent logic programming brings a new dimension of expressiveness to logic programming enabling a host of useful protocols and paradigms to be modeled. This flexibility has a cost, however, because it is the control strategy of Prolog which has bought efficient implementation. The depth-first search of Prolog, for instance, brings with it a stack to support local variables and continuations. On the other hand, concurrent logic programs require scheduling which introduces the extra overheads of enqueuing and dequeuing processes. Furthermore, without continuations argument copying is increased and without local variables garbage collection becomes more frequent. This is the penalty of substituting data-flow for control-flow. Schedule analysis shows how to selectively replace data-flow with control-flow and thereby reduce these overheads.

Schedule analysis is concerned with deducing at compile-time a partial schedule of processes, or equivalently the body atoms of a clause, which is consistent with the program behaviour. Program termination characteristics are affected if an atom which binds a shared variable is ordered after an atom that matches on that variable. In order to avoid this, an ordering of the atoms is determined which does not contradict any data-dependence of the program. In general the processes cannot be totally ordered and thus the analysis leads to a division into threads of totally ordered processes. In this way the work required of the run-time scheduler is reduced to ordering threads.

Scheduling threads instead of processes avoids the creation of unnecessary suspensions during evaluation. This is useful because the overhead incurred by each suspension is significant. The overhead is not merely in the extra enqueuing and dequeuing of the process, since upon resumption of the process, the guards of the associated predicate usually have to be retried. In addition to avoiding the creation of unnecessary suspensions, schedule analysis permits several useful optimisations to be applied within a thread. The optimisations all depend on the existence of a total ordering of atoms within a thread and follow from applying mode analysis, type analysis and reference analysis to the threads [8]. Mode analysis and type analysis can be used to identify: instances of unification which can be simplified; repeated synchronisation instructions which can be removed; and redundant checks which can be removed when producers are ordered before consumers in the same thread. Reference analysis can be used to identify: variables which can be accessed without dereferencing; variables for which initialisation and unification can be simplified; and local variables which can be allocated to a stack.

Schedule analysis exchanges parallelism for reduced overheads by inferring orderings for atoms. In this sense schedule analysis addresses some of the fundamental issues involved in implementing a concurrent logic program on a uniprocessor. For a multi-processor, however, there is a danger of introducing too much control-flow and therefore limiting parallelism; a balance between control-flow and data-flow needs to be struck. One way to get an efficient and balanced untilisation of a multi-processor is to partition a program into grains [4]. A grain is a set of processes, to be executed on a single processor, when it is less efficient to evaluate them in parallel. For a concurrent logic program, a consequence of data-flow is that there is no explicit ordering between the processes within a grain. Thus the processes within a grain have to be scheduled. Thus, by introducing control-flow within the scope of a grain, the benefits of reduced overheads can be obtained without compromising the parallelism. The principle is therefore to turn excess or fine-grained parallelism to good use by exchanging the parallelism for reduced overheads. King and Soper [7] describe in detail how to systematically identify fine-grained parallelism and appropriately introduce control-flow to remove the ineffective parallelism.

Section 2 describes the notation and preliminary definitions which will be used throughout. Section 3 develops a framework for schedule analysis in which the data-dependencies between the atoms of a clause are characterised in a way which is independent of the query. This enables pairs of atoms to be identified which must be allocated to different threads. Theorem 3.1, a safety result, states the conditions under which atoms can be partitioned into threads and ordered within a thread whilst preserving the behaviour of the program. This framework, however, is not tractable and section 4 outlines a practical procedure for constructing threads and gives some preliminary results. Sections 5 and 6 present related work and the concluding discussion.

2   Notation and preliminaries

To introduce schedule analysis some notation and preliminary definitions are required. Let *Atom* denote the set of atoms for a program *Prog*, with typical member $a \in Atom$. Additionally let *Goal* represent the set of goals, that is $Goal = \wp(Atom)$, with typical member $g \in Goal$. For generality, let *Clause* denote the set of clauses of the form a <- $a_{ask,1}, \ldots, a_{ask,i} : a_{tell,1}, \ldots, a_{tell,j} \mid a_{body,1}, \ldots, a_{body,k}$. The ask, tell and body atoms of a clause c are represented by the ordered sets $ask_c = \{a_{ask,1}, \ldots, a_{ask,i}\}$, $tell_c = \{a_{tell,1}, \ldots, a_{tell,j}\}$ and $body_c = \{a_{body,1}, \ldots, a_{body,k}\}$. If there are no tell atoms the $\mid$ connective is omitted from a clause, whereas if there are neither any ask atoms nor any tell atoms both the : and $\mid$ connectives are omitted from a clause. A concurrent logic program *Prog* is a finite set of clauses. Let *Subs* denote the set of substitutions for *Prog* with typical member θ. Additionally let the set of states of a transition relation for *Prog* be denoted by *State*, where $State = Goal \times Subs$, and *State* has typical member s.

Definition 1 (match, try and the transition relation) *The mappings* $match : Atom \times Atom \rightarrow \{fail, susp\} \cup Subs$, $try : Atom \times Clause \rightarrow \{fail, susp\} \cup Subs$ *and the transition relation* $\vdash$ *on State are defined by:*

$$
match(a', c) = \begin{cases}
\theta' & \theta \in mgu(a', a), \\
 & \langle ask_c, \theta \rangle \vdash^* \langle \emptyset, \theta' \rangle, \\
 & \theta' \upharpoonright vars(a') = \epsilon. \\
susp & \theta \in mgu(a', a), \\
 & \langle ask_c, \theta \rangle \vdash^* \langle \emptyset, \theta' \rangle, \\
 & \theta' \upharpoonright vars(a') \neq \epsilon. \\
fail & otherwise.
\end{cases}
$$

$$
try(a', c) = \begin{cases}
\theta' & \theta \in match(a', c), \\
 & \langle tell_c, \theta \rangle \vdash^* \langle \emptyset, \theta' \rangle. \\
susp & susp = match(a', c). \\
fail & otherwise.
\end{cases}
$$

where $\vdash^*$ *is the reflexive and transitive closure of* $\vdash$, $\vdash$ *is written infix,* $\theta \upharpoonright V$ *denotes the restriction of a substitution* θ *to a set of variables* V, $vars(a)$ *denote the variables of* a, *and* $mgu(a, b)$ *is the set of most general unifiers for* a *and* b.

   The transition relation for Prog is described piece-wise in terms of transition relations for the clauses of Prog. The transition relation for a clause

c *is described by: if* $try(a_m\theta, c') = \theta'$, c' *is renamed apart from* c *and* $body_{c'} = \{a'_1, \ldots, a'_k\}$ *then* $\langle\{a_1, \ldots, a_n\}, \theta\rangle \vdash^{c,c'} \langle\{a_1, \ldots, a_{m-1}, a'_1, \ldots, a'_k, a_{m+1}, \ldots, a_n\}, \theta \circ \theta'\rangle$.

The transition relation for Prog is described by: $\langle g, \theta\rangle \vdash \langle g', \theta'\rangle$ *if there exists a clause* c *of Prog such that* $\langle g, \theta\rangle \vdash^{c,c'} \langle g', \theta'\rangle$.

The transition relation for *Prog* engenders the notion of a proof. Thus let *Proof* denote the set of proofs for *Prog* with typical member p. A proof is a sequence $p = s_i, s_{i+1}, s_{i+2}, \ldots$ such that $s_i \vdash s_{i+1}, s_{i+1} \vdash s_{i+2}, \ldots$ and can be either finite or infinite. (The term proof has been extended to include infinite sequences for notational convenience.) Operationally a proof corresponds to a computation. A computation $p = s_i, s_{i+1}, \ldots, s_j$ is suspended if there does not exist $s \in State$ such that $s_j \vdash s$. Additionally p is resumed by ϑ if p is suspended with $s_j = \langle g, \theta\rangle$ and there exists $s \in State$ such that $\langle g, \theta \circ \vartheta\rangle \vdash s$. Alternatively if $g = \emptyset$ then p is terminated.

3   A framework for schedule analysis

The abstract framework formalises the notion of a data-dependence between two atoms of a goal and explains how to translate data-dependencies into threads.

3.1   Data-dependencies among the atoms of a goal

The existence of a data-dependency between two atoms is inferred by studying the order in which the atoms are resolved within a computation. A partial mapping resolve is used to indicate which resolution steps of a computation are responsible for solving a particular atom of the goal. The mapping resolve is defined in terms of the partial mapping solve.

Definition 2 (solve) *The partial mapping solve* : $Proof \times Atom \times \mathbb{N} \rightarrow Goal$ *is defined by:*

$$solve(p, a, j) =$$
$$\begin{cases} \{a\} & i = j, a \in g_i. \\ \{a' \mid a' \in solve(p, a, j-1), a' \neq a_m\} \cup & \\ \{a'_1, \ldots, a'_k\} & i < j, a_m \in solve(p, a, j-1). \\ solve(p, a, j-1) & i < j, a_m \notin solve(p, a, j-1). \end{cases}$$

where $p = s_i, s_{i+1}, \ldots, s_{j-1}, s_j, \ldots$, $s_j = \langle g_j, \theta_j\rangle$, $g_{j-1} = \{a_1, \ldots, a_m, \ldots, a_n\}$ *and* $g_j = \{a_1, \ldots, a_{m-1}, a'_1, \ldots, a'_k, a_{m+1}, \ldots, a_n\}$.

Definition 3 (resolve) *The partial mapping resolve* : $Proof \times Atom \rightarrow \wp(\mathbb{N})$ *is defined by:*

$$resolve(p, a) = \{j \mid a' \in solve(p, a, j), a' \notin solve(p, a, j+1)\}.$$

```
canDepend(Y) <- X = 1, canConsume(X, Y).

canConsume(X, Y) <- X = Y.
canConsume(X, Y) <- Y is X + 1.
```

Figure 1: The canDepend/1 and canConsume/2 predicates.

Intuitively a data-dependency exists from one atom to another, if the computation for the second atom can never entirely precede the computation for the first atom. The resolve mapping is useful because it indicates how atoms are scheduled thus enabling a data-dependence to be identified. Definition 5 formalises the idea of a data-dependence between two atoms which, in turn, is defined in terms of whether an atom finishes or persists.

Definition 4 (finish and persist) *If $s_i = \langle g_i, \theta_i \rangle$, $p = s_i, s_{i+1}, \ldots$ and $a \in g_i$ then*

- *a finishes in p at l if there exists $l \geq i$ such that $solve(p, a, l) \neq \emptyset$ and $solve(p, a, l + 1) = \emptyset$,*

- *a persists in p if $solve(p, a, l) \neq \emptyset$ for all $l \geq i$.*

Definition 5 (data-dependence) *Suppose $s_i = \langle g_i, \theta_i \rangle$ and $a_1, \ldots, a_j, a' \in g_i$ with $a_1 \neq a'$, $\ldots$, $a_j \neq a'$. There exists a data-dependence from a_1 or $\ldots$ or a_j to a' for $p = s_i, \ldots, s_k$ if j is the least j such that*

- *for all $p' = s_i, \ldots, s_k, s_{k+1}, \ldots$ if a' finishes in p' at l then there exists a_m with $1 \leq m \leq j$ such that $n \in resolve(p', a_m)$ and $k < n < l$.*

- *for all $p' = s_i, \ldots, s_k, s_{k+1}, \ldots$ if a' persists in p' then there exists a_m with $1 \leq m \leq j$ such that $n \in resolve(p', a_m)$ and $k < n$.*

- *there exists $p' = s_i, \ldots, s_k, s_{k+1}, \ldots$ such that either a' finishes in p' at l or a' persists in p'.*

Note that definition 5 considers all p such that $p' = s_i, \ldots, s_k, s_{k+1}, \ldots$ possibly including p which are infinite, suspended and terminated. The rôle of $p = s_i, \ldots, s_k$ in definition 5 is technical and chiefly deals with non-determinism. Its inclusion in definition 5 is necessary because, in general, the presence of a data-dependence can be decided by a non-deterministic choice. Example 1 uses the contrived but illuminating **canDepend/1** and **canConsume/2** predicates listed in figure 1 to demonstrate how non-determinism can determine the existence of a data-dependence. The example illustrates the significance of $p = s_i, \ldots, s_k$ in definition 5.

Example 1 *The non-determinism in the* **canConsume/2** *predicate of figure 1 decides whether or not a data-dependence exists from the* **X = 1** *atom to the* **canConsume(X, Y)** *atom of the* **canDepend/1** *clause. The data-dependence does not exist for* p_1 *but does exist for* p_2 *where* $p_1 = s_1, s_2, s_3, s_4, s_5$ *and* $p_2 = s_1, s_2, s_3', s_4', s_5'$ *are given below. The initial states of* p_1 *and* p_2, s_1 *and* s_2, *coincide. Different clauses of* **canConsume/2**, *however, derive* s_3 *and* s_3' *so that* s_3 *and* s_3' *and the proceeding states differ.*

$$s_1 = \langle \{canDepend(Y)\}, \epsilon \rangle \vdash$$
$$s_2 = \langle \{X = 1, canConsume(X, Y_1)\}, \{Y_1 \mapsto Y\} \rangle \vdash$$
$$s_3 = \langle \{X = 1, X = Y_1\}.\{Y_1 \mapsto Y\} \rangle \vdash$$
$$s_4 = \langle \{X = 1\}, \{Y_1 \mapsto Y, X \mapsto Y_1\} \rangle \vdash$$
$$s_5 = \langle \emptyset, \{Y \mapsto 1, X \mapsto 1, Y_1 \mapsto 1\} \rangle.$$

$$s_3' = \langle \{X = 1, Y_1 \text{ is } X + 1\}, \{Y_1 \mapsto Y\} \rangle \vdash$$
$$s_4' = \langle \{Y_1 \text{ is } X + 1\}, \{Y_1 \mapsto Y, X \mapsto 1\} \rangle \vdash$$
$$s_5' = \langle \emptyset, \{Y \mapsto 2, X \mapsto 1, Y_1 \mapsto 2\} \rangle.$$

For p_1, *no data-dependencies can exist from* **X = 1** *to* **canConsume(X, Y)** *since resolve*(s_2, s_3, s_4, s_5, **canConsume(X, Y)**) = $\{2, 3\}$ *and resolve*(s_2, s_3, s_4, s_5, **X = 1**) = $\{4\}$. *For* p_2, *however,* $3 \in$ *resolve*(s_2, s_3', s_4', s_5', **X = 1**) *and* $4 \in$ *resolve*(s_2, s_3', s_4', s_5', **canConsume(X, Y)**). *Putting* $p = s_2, s_3'$ *illustrates the rationale behind* $p = s_i, \ldots, s_k$ *in definition 5.* p *and hence* s_3' *are fixed therefore the choice of clause for* **canConsume(X, Y)** *is predefined. Therefore, a data-dependence always occurs in* $s_{k+1}, s_{k+2}, \ldots$ *allowing the data-dependence from* **X = 1** *to* **canConsume(X, Y)** *to be identified and captured.*

3.2   Data-dependencies among the atoms of a clause

Schedule analysis focuses on organising the body atoms of a clause c, $body_c$, into threads. Therefore the notion of a data-dependence between the body atoms of a clause is introduced.

Definition 6 (data-dependence relation) *The data-dependence relation* $\delta_{c,p}$ *for a clause* c *and a computation* $p = s_i, \ldots, s_k$ *is a relation on* $body_c$ *is defined by: if there exists* $s_{i-1} \in State$ *such that* $s_{i-1} \vdash^{c,c'} s_i$, *and* $body_c = \{a_1, \ldots, a_k\}$, $body_{c'} = \{a_1', \ldots, a_k'\}$, *and there exists a data-dependence from* a_{l_1}' *or* ...*or* a_{l_j}' *to* $a_{l_{j+1}}'$ *for* p *then* $\langle a_{l_1}, a_{l_{j+1}} \rangle, \ldots, \langle a_{l_j}, a_{l_{j+1}} \rangle \in \delta_{c,p}$.

Example 2 *Let fib denote the recursive clause of the the* **fib/2** *predicate presented in figure 2. Additionally let* $a_1 = $ **N1 is N - 1**, $a_2 = $ **N2 is N - 2**, $a_3 = $ **fib(N1, F1)**, $a_4 = $ **fib(N2, F2)** *and* $a_5 = $ **F is F1 + F2** *so that* $body_{fib} = \{a_1, \ldots, a_5\}$. *Since fib is deterministic consider* $p = s_1$ *where* $s_1 = \langle \{a_1, \ldots, a_5\}, \{N \mapsto 1\} \rangle$. *The data-dependence relation* $\delta_{fib,p}$ *is presented as a directed graph in figure 3.*

fib(N, F) <- N =< 1 : F = 1.
fib(N, F) <- N > 1 : N1 is N - 1, N2 is N - 2,
  fib(N1, F1), fib(N2, F2), F is F1 + F2.

Figure 2: The fib/2 predicate.

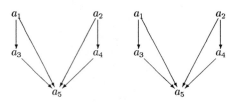

Figure 3: $\delta_{fib,p}$ and δ_{fib}.

Although the data-dependence relation $\delta_{fib,p}$ is acyclic, a data-dependence relation can contain cycles due to the possibility of coroutining, each cycle corresponding to a set of coroutining atoms. It is important that schedule analysis identifies coroutining since coroutining atoms need to be allocated to different threads. Once placed in separate threads the data-dependencies can be resolved at run-time with a scheduler.

Usually compilers do not have the benefit of a knowledge of the computation p and hence it is necessary to derive a data-dependence relation which is independent of p. In the terminology of abstract interpretation, $\delta_{c,p}$ is collected for each possible p, to construct a relation δ_c on $body_c$ which summarises the data-dependencies of $body_c$ in a way which independent of p.

Definition 7 (collecting data-dependence relation) *A relation δ_c on $body_c$ is a collecting data-dependence relation for a clause c if: $\delta_{c,p} \subseteq \delta_c$ for all p.*

If each data-dependence relation is acyclic, coroutining cannot occur. Nevertheless, cycles can still appear in a collecting data-dependence relation. This is symptomatic of atoms whose scheduling order depends on the initial computation, for instance, the query. In addition to the coroutining atoms, these atoms need to be placed in different threads so that they can be ordered at run-time by the scheduler. Example 3 illustrates how cyclic data-dependencies can be introduced into the least collecting data-dependence relation by atoms whose relative scheduling ordering depends on the query.

Example 3 *Figure 4 details the pathological abc/2, a/3 and b/3 predicates. These predicates are contrived so that for some queries AA is A + 5*

```
abc(X, C) <- C is A + B, AA is A + 5, BB is B + 6,
   a(X, BB, A), b(X, AA, B).

a(X, BB, A) <- 0 < X : A = BB.
a(X, _, A) <- 0 >= X : A = 3.

b(X, _, B) <- 0 < X : B = 4.
b(X, AA, B) <- 0 >= X : B = AA.
```

Figure 4: The **abc/2**, **a/3** and **b/3** predicates.

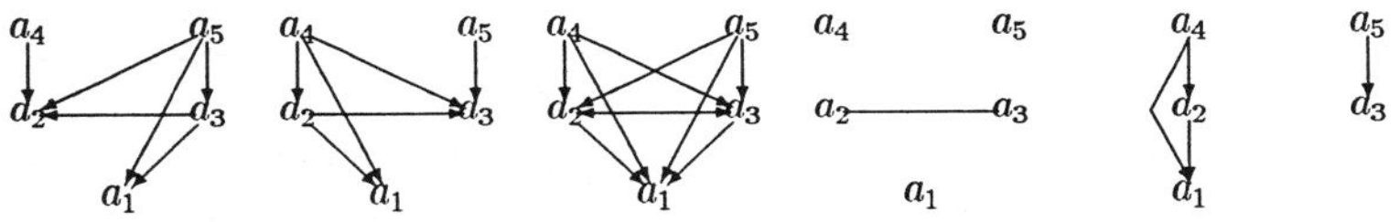

Figure 5: δ_{abc,c^+}, δ_{abc,c^-}, δ_{abc}, σ_{abc} and τ_{abc}.

is scheduled before BB is B + 6 *whereas, for others, the ordering is reversed. Specifically, the order of scheduling is predicated on* X > 0. *Let abc denote the clause the* abc/3 *predicate and* $a_1 =$ C is A + B, $a_2 =$ AA is A + 5, $a_3 =$ BB is B + 6, $a_4 =$ a(X, BB, A), $a_5 =$ b(X, AA, B) *so that* $body_{abc} = \{a_1, \ldots, a_5\}$. *Further let* c^+, c^- *and* $c^\perp$ *respectively denote* $c = s_i, \ldots, s_j$ *for which* s_i *satisfies* X > 0, s_i *satisfies* 0 >= X, *and for which* s_i *neither satisfies* X > 0 *nor* 0 >= X *because* X *is unbound. Thus* $\delta_{abc} = \delta_{abc,c^+} \cup \delta_{abc,c^-} \cup \delta_{abc,c^\perp}$. *Since* $c^\perp$ *immediately leads to a suspension,* $\delta_{abc,c^\perp} = \emptyset$, *so that* $\delta_{abc} = \delta_{abc,c^+} \cup \delta_{abc,c^-}$. *Figure 5 presents the relations* δ_{abc,c^+}, δ_{abc,c^-} *and* δ_{abc} *as directed graphs. Note that* δ_{abc} *is cyclic even though* δ_{abc,c^+} *and* δ_{abc,c^-} *are both acyclic.*

3.3 Data-dependencies among the threads of a clause

A collecting data-dependence relation is used to partition the atoms of a clause into threads. Specifically threads are formed by identifying pairs of atoms which must be allocated to different threads. There are just four ways in which data-dependencies can occur between a pair of atoms. These four ways are listed and categorised in figure 6. The data-dependencies in each category have different implications for the scheduling. By identifying which category requires run-time scheduling, a prescription for generating threads is derived.

For category one, either a data-dependence always exists from a to a' or sometimes exists from a to a'. Thus a can be ordered before a' within

Bottom of text page: no text below this line.

Category	Characteristic	Order
1	$\langle a, a' \rangle \in \delta_c$ and $\langle a', a \rangle \notin \delta_c$	a precedes a'.
2	$\langle a', a \rangle \in \delta_c$ and $\langle a, a' \rangle \notin \delta_c$	a' precedes a.
3	$\langle a, a' \rangle \notin \delta_c$ and $\langle a', a \rangle \notin \delta_c$	neither a precedes a' nor a' precedes a.
4	$\langle a, a' \rangle \in \delta_c$ and $\langle a', a \rangle \in \delta_c$	either a precedes a' or a' precedes a, or a and a' coroutine.

Figure 6: Categorising atom pairs.

the same thread at compile-time. Category two is the symmetric variant of category one. For category three, a data-dependence neither exists from a to a' nor from a' to a. Thus a and a' can be ordered at compile-time in any manner! Category four either locates coroutining activity in which data-dependencies exist both from a to a' and from a' to a; or identifies computations for which a data-dependence exists from a to a' in one computation and from a' to a in another. In either case, the atoms a and a' must be assigned to different threads and the ordering of a and a' resolved at run-time. Of these four categories only category four corresponds to pairs of atoms which require run-time scheduling. A relation σ_c on $body_c$ is introduced, called the separation relation, which is used to isolate pairs of atoms which have to be allocated to different threads.

Definition 8 (separation relation) *A relation σ_c on $body_c$ is a separation relation for a clause c if: $\langle a, a' \rangle \in \sigma_c$ if $\langle a, a' \rangle \in \delta_c$ and $\langle a', a \rangle \in \delta_c$.*

A separation relation σ_c is symmetric, that is, if $\langle a, a' \rangle \in \sigma_c$ then $\langle a', a \rangle \in \sigma_c$, and therefore can be represented pictorially as an undirected graph. σ_c is used to partition $body_c$ into sets of atoms which, when ordered, become threads.

Definition 9 (partition) *A set $part_c$ is a partition of a clause c if:*

- $part_c = \{part_{c,1}, \ldots, part_{c,t}\}$,

- $part_{c,1} \cup \ldots \cup part_{c,t} = body_c$,

- $part_{c,i} \cap part_{c,j} = \emptyset$ for all $i \neq j$,

- *if $\langle a, a' \rangle \in \sigma_c$ then $a \in part_{c,i}$, $a' \in part_{c,j}$ with $i \neq j$.*

To turn a partition $part_c$ into threads, each $part_{c,i}$ is ordered so as not to contradict a data-dependence in δ_c.

incr(X, Y) <- Y is X + 1.

incrs(Y1, Y2) <- X1 = 1, X2 = 2, incr(X1, Y1), incr(X2, Y2).

Figure 7: The incr/2 and incrs/2 predicates.

Definition 10 (thread orderings) *A set o_c is a set of thread orderings for a clause c if:*

- $o_c = \{o_{c,1}, \ldots, o_{c,t}\}$,

- $o_{c,i}$ *is a relation on* $part_{c,i}$,

- $o_{c,i} = \{\langle a_{i_k}, a_{i_l} \rangle \mid 1 \leq k < l \leq m\}$ *if* $part_{c,i} = \{a_{i_1}, \ldots, a_{i_m}\}$,

- *if* $\langle a, a' \rangle \in o_{c,i}$ *then* $\langle a', a \rangle \notin \delta_c^+$.

The transitive closure of a relation δ_c is denoted by δ_c^+.

Example 4 *Figure 3 diagrams δ_{fib}. Since δ_{fib} is acyclic, $\sigma_{fib} = \emptyset$, and therefore $part_{fib} = \{body_{fib}\}$ is a partition of c. In the notation of example 2, take $o_{fib,1} = \{\langle a_i, a_j \rangle \mid 1 \leq i < j \leq 5\}$. The clause abc is more illuminating since δ_{abc} is cyclic and therefore $\sigma_{abc} \neq \emptyset$. Adopting the atom labeling used in example 3, $\sigma_{abc} = \{\langle a_2, a_3 \rangle, \langle a_3, a_2 \rangle\}$. σ_{abc} is represented pictorially as an undirected graph in figure 5. Therefore $part_{abc} = \{part_{abc,1}, part_{abc,2}\}$ is a partition of abc where $part_{abc,1} = \{a_4, a_2, a_1\}$ and $part_{abc,2} = \{a_5, a_3\}$. In turn, the partition leads of the threads $o_{abc,1} = \{\langle a_4, a_2 \rangle, \langle a_2, a_1 \rangle, \langle a_4, a_1 \rangle\}$ and $o_{abc,2} = \{\langle a_5, a_3 \rangle\}$.*

Although threads are constructed so as to avoid contradicting any data-dependencies of the program, threads can be formed which compromise termination. Example 5 uses the incr/2 and incrs/2 predicates listed in figure 7 to illustrate circumstances in which the threads produced by schedule analysis inadvertently introduce deadlocking behaviour.

Example 5 *The incr/2 and incrs/2 predicates are presented in figure 7. Let incrs denote the clause of the incrs/2 predicate and let $a_1 = $ X1 = 1, $a_2 = $ X2 = 2, $a_3 = $ incr(X1, Y1), $a_4 = $ incr(X2, Y2) so that $body_{incrs} = \{a_1, a_2, a_3, a_4\}$ δ_{incrs} is acyclic and is diagrammed in figure 8. Since δ_{incrs} is acyclic a single thread can be constructed but, for the sake of a counterexample, divide $body_{incrs}$ according to $part_{incrs} = \{part_{incrs,1}, part_{incrs,2}\}$ where $part_{incrs,1} = \{a_1, a_4\}$ and $part_{incrs,2} = \{a_2, a_3\}$. In addition, choose the threads $o_{incrs,1} = \{\langle a_4, a_1 \rangle\}$ and $o_{incrs,2} = \{\langle a_3, a_2 \rangle\}$. $o_{incrs,1}$ and $o_{incrs,2}$ are also presented in figure 8. Note, however, that $\delta_{incrs} \cup o_{incrs,1} \cup o_{incrs,2}$ is cyclic. In operational terms, deadlock occurs, since a_4 of $o_{incrs,1}$ suspends waiting for a_2 to bind X2 and a_3 of $o_{incrs,2}$ suspends waiting for a_1 to bind X1.*

Figure 8: δ_{incrs}, $o_{incrs,1}$, $o_{incrs,2}$ and $\delta_{incrs} \cup o_{incrs,1} \cup o_{incrs,2}$.

Deadlock can occur because the constraints on the scheduling of the threads can extend beyond the constraints on the scheduling of the clause. The scheduling constraints for the threads, however, augment δ_c with the orderings imposed by the threads themselves. The cumulative ordering effect of the threads is given by $o_{c,1} \cup \ldots \cup o_{c,t}$ which is dubbed τ_c.

Definition 11 τ_c *is a relation on* $body_c$ *defined by:* $\tau_c = o_{c,1} \cup \ldots \cup o_{c,t}$.

The scheduling constraints on the threads therefore extend from δ_c to $\tau_c \cup \delta_c$. Example 5 illustrates the disastrous effect that extra cycles in $\tau_c \cup \delta_c$ can have on termination. Note, however, that if all the cycles which occur in $\tau_c \cup \delta_c$ also occur in δ_c, then termination is not compromised. This follows because the atoms which form the cycles of $\tau_c \cup \delta_c$ would occur in the cycles of δ_c and would therefore be split across different threads by schedule analysis. Theorem 3.1 confirms this observation stating the precise conditions under which the work of a scheduler can be safely reduced from scheduling processes to scheduling threads. The theorem thus provides a way for checking the integrity of the threads generated by schedule analysis. A reliable procedure for forming threads thus follows, since erroneous threads can be identified and be removed.

To introduce the safety theorem, however, the notion of an interleave is required to express a scheduling order of the threads. A scheduler can transfer control from one thread to another by suspending and resuming the evaluation of a thread. The scheduler therefore induces an ordering on $body_c$ which extends beyond τ_c. The concept of an interleave is introduced in definition 12 to capture this ordering and clarify the way in which the evaluation of the threads can be interleaved.

Definition 12 *An interleave of* τ_c *is a relation* ι_c *on* $body_c$ *defined by:*

- *if* $\langle a, a' \rangle \in \iota_c$ *then* $\langle a', a \rangle \notin \tau_c$,

- *if* $a, a' \in body_c$ *and* $a \neq a'$ *then either* $\langle a, a' \rangle \in \iota_c$ *or* $\langle a', a \rangle \in \iota_c$.

Theorem 3.1 (safety theorem [9]) *If* $\tau_c \cup \delta_c^+$ *has no more cycles than* δ_c^+ *then there exists an interleave* ι_c *of* τ_c *for arbitrary c.*

4   A procedure for schedule analysis

The framework can be regarded a compilation scheme in which the input is a collecting data-dependence relation and the output is the threads of a clause. Thus, once a collecting data-dependence relation is found, schedule analysis can be integrated into a compiler. King and Soper [9] explain how data-dependencies can be inferred with existing forms of analysis, specifically producer and consumer analysis [6, 1] or the mode algorithm of Ueda and Morita [13]; detail how a collecting data-dependence relation can be constructed; and show how the framework defines a constructive procedure, an algorithm, for generating threads.

Schedule analysis has been integrated into a compiler for a dialect of Flat Parlog. The final version of the schedule analysis module, which excludes the producer and consumer analysis, equates to about 350 lines of code. The bulk of the module equates to code for calculating the transitive closure of a relation, counting the number of cycles in a relation, and computing a partition. The transitive closure and cycle count is computed by variants of the backtracking algorithm proposed by Tiernan [12]. The partitioning is accomplished by an approximation algorithm, specifically the largest-first sequential colouring algorithm [11]. Although computing an optimal partition is equivalent to calculating $\chi(\sigma_c)$ which, in turn, is NP-complete [3], the approximation algorithm was found to frequently minimise the number of threads.

Some of the optimisations which follow from schedule analysis are best illustrated at the level of the intermediate code. The intermediate code used in the compiler is similar to Kernel Parlog [2]. Kernel Parlog is a useful basis for the intermediate language because it includes control primitives like Data/1[1] and supports the sequential and the parallel conjunction. The primitive Data(X) induces suspension if X is unbound. The parallel and the sequential conjunction, respectively denoted , and &, provide a way to order the evaluation of atoms within a clause and thereby express threads. The usefulness of Kernel Parlog extends beyond that of a representation language since Gregory (1987) proposed a suite of optimisations that can be used in connection with sequential conjunction and therefore apply to threads. The optimisations are significant because they can be used as a measure of the effectiveness of schedule analysis.

Figure 9 lists two versions of the intermediate code for fib/2, generated without and with schedule analysis. To put the optimisations into perspective, the instruction count for the Data/1 and Unify/2 primitives drops from 529 and 353 to just 1 and 177 when the tenth Fibonacci number is computed. The other primitives Less/2, Less_Equal/2, Minus/3 and Plus/3 are

---

[1]To be faithful to the intermediate code used in the compiler, primitives are denoted by Data/1, Less/2, Less_Equal/2, Plus/3 and Unify/2 rather than using the notation DATA/1, LESS/2, LESSEQ/2, PLUS/3 and =/2 introduced by Gregory (1987). The extra primitive Minus/3 required for fib/2 has the obvious interpretation.

```
fib(_1, _2) <- Data(_1) & Less_Equal(_1, 1) : Unify(_2, 1).
fib(_1, _2) <-
    Data(_1) & Less(1, _1) :
    Data(_1) & Minus(_1, 1, _4) & Unify(_4, N1),
    Data(_1) & Minus(_1, 2, _5) & Unify(_5, N2),
    fib(N1, F1), fib(N2, F2),
    Data(F1) & Data(F2) & Plus(F1, F2, _6) & Unify(_6, _2).

fib(_1, _2) <- true : Data(_1) & $fib(_1, _2).

$fib(_1, _2) <- Less_Equal(_1, 1) : Unify(_2, 1).
$fib(_1, _2) <-
    Less(1, _1) :
    Minus(_1, 1, _4) &
    Minus(_1, 2, _5) &
    $fib(_4, F1) & $fib(_5, F2) &
    Plus(F1, F2, _6) & Unify(_6, _2).
```

Figure 9: Intermediate compilation of the fib/2 predicate.

invoked 88, 89, 176 and 88 times on both occasions. Note also that the recursive clause of fib/2 requires nine variables whereas the recursive clause of $fib/2 uses seven variables. Furthermore, the $fib/2 clause has more scope for introducing local variables since five of its variables can be allocated to a stack. For the fib/2 clause, only three of its nine variables are local.

It is important to realise that although schedule analysis guarantees that a minimum number of suspensions are created for fib/2, it does not ensure that the suspension count is actually reduced. Schedulers often employ the heuristic that data-dependencies tend to flow left-to-right among the atoms of a clause to avoid creating unnecessary suspensions. In particular, for the fib/2 predicate, all the data-dependencies flow left-to-right, and therefore the scheduling heuristic minimises the number of suspensions. This does not deny the usefulness of schedule analysis since the use of threads enables other scheduling optimisations to be applied. For instance, threads permit the run-queue to be accessed less frequently and also enable a reduction in the number of arguments which are copied to and from a stack [5].

Nevertheless, schedule analysis cannot significantly improve performance when all threads it produces are small. This tends to occur with programs which use coroutining throughout. The application of schedule analysis to a prime sieve program, for example, only gave a marginal improvement in performance due to the instruction count for Unify/2 reducing from 275 to 247.

5 Related work

Korsloot and Tick [10] have presented some initial ideas on how to introduce sequentiality into concurrent logic programs. Like schedule analysis the aim is to recover "traditional procedural language optimisations that have previously been discarded by those implementing committed-choice languages". Korsloot and Tick derive data-dependencies by the mode algorithm described by Ueda and Morita [13] and give several examples of how the data-dependencies can be used to order the atoms of a clause. The procedure for sequentialisation is *ad hoc*, has no supporting theory, and consequently there is no guarantee that deadlock is avoided.

6 Conclusions

Schedule analysis is concerned with deducing at compile-time a partial schedule of the processes, or equivalently the body atoms of a clause, which is consistent with the behaviour of the program. It partitions the atoms of each clause into threads of totally ordered atoms which do not contradict any data-dependence of the program. Threads substitute data-flow with control-flow thereby reducing the load on a scheduler and also enabling a wealth of traditional control-flow optimisations to be applied to the program.

A framework for schedule analysis has been proposed, formulated in terms of the operational semantics for a program, which builds from the notion of a data-dependence to define a procedure for creating threads. All data-dependencies which can possibly occur between the atoms of a clause for any query, are collected together and compared, to identify those atoms of a clause which must be allocated to different threads. This gives a straightforward prescription for partitioning the atoms of a clause into threads. The threads generated by this procedure, however, in exceptional circumstances, can compromise the behaviour of the program. Thus, a safety result has been presented which states the conditions under which the work of a scheduler can be safely reduced from scheduling processes to scheduling threads. The theorem provides a way for checked the integrity of the threads so that erroneous threads can be identified and filtered out.

Deriving the data-dependencies for schedule analysis is non-trivial and will be a focus of future work. Nevertheless, a preliminary implementation suggests that schedule analysis is likely to be a useful compilation technique.

Acknowledgments

This research was supported in part by the UK Science and Engineering Research Council, Research Grant GR/H15042.

References

[1] FOSTER, I. & W. WINSBOROUGH (1991). "Copy Avoidance through Compile-Time Analysis and Local Reuse", *in Proceedings of the 1991 International Logic Programming Symposium*. MIT Press.

[2] GREGORY, S. (1987). *Parallel Logic Programming in Parlog, The Language and its Implementation*. Addison-Wesley.

[3] KARP, R. M. (1972). *Complexity of Computer Computations*, pp. 85–103. Plenum Press.

[4] KING, A. & P. SOPER (1990). "Granularity Analysis of Concurrent Logic Programs", *in The Fifth International Symposium on Computer and Information Sciences*, Nevsehir, Cappadocia, Turkey.

[5] KING, A. & P. SOPER (1991)a. "Implementing and Optimising Threads", Technical Report CSTR 91-13, University of Southampton.

[6] KING, A. & P. SOPER (1991)b. "A Semantic Approach to Producer and Consumer Analysis", *in International Conference on Logic Programming Workshop on Concurrent Logic Programming*, Paris, France.

[7] KING, A. & P. SOPER (1992)a. "Heuristics, Thresholding and a New Technique for Controlling the Granularity of Concurrent Logic Programs", Technical Report 92-08, University of Southampton.

[8] KING, A. & P. SOPER (1992)b. "Ordering Optimisations for Concurrent Logic Programs", *in Proceedings of the Logical Foundations of Computer Science Symposium*, Tver, Russia. Springer-Verlag.

[9] KING, A. & P. SOPER (1992)c. "Schedule Analysis: a full theory, a pilot implementation and a preliminary assessment", Technical Report 92-06, University of Southampton.

[10] KORSLOOT, M. & E. TICK (1991). "Sequentializing Parallel Programs", *in Proceedings of the Phoenix Seminar and Workshop on Declarative Programming*, Hohritt, Sasbachwalden, Germany. Springer-Verlag.

[11] MATULA, D. W., G. MARBLE, & J. D. ISAACSON (1972). *Graph Theory and Computing*, pp. 109–122. Prentice Hall.

[12] TIERNAN, J. C. (1970). "An efficient search algorithm to find the elementary circuits of a graph", *Communications of the ACM*, 13: 722–726.

[13] UEDA, K. & M. MORITA (1990). "A New Implementation Technique for flat GHC", *in International Conference on Logic Programming*, pp. 3–17, Jerusalem. MIT Press.

Variable Threadedness Analysis for Concurrent Logic Programs

R. Sundararajan, A. V. S. Sastry, E. Tick
Dept. of Computer Science
University of Oregon
Eugene, OR 97403, USA

Abstract

The single-assignment property of concurrent logic programs results in a large memory bandwidth requirement and low spatial locality in heap-based implementations. Static-analysis techniques can be used to identify data objects whose storage may be reused, and are additionally advantageous because of low runtime overheads. We present a new analysis method for local resue detection based on abstract interpretation. The analysis categorizes all variables as either single or multiple threaded, and avoids overly-conservative propagation of this information. The analysis has been demonstrated to improve the runtime performance of the PDSS KL1 system.

1 Introduction

Logic and functional programming languages are examples of languages utilizing the *single-assignment property* of variables. In logic programs, a logical variable starts its life as an undefined cell and may later hold a constant, a pointer to a structure, or a pointer to another variable. These languages do not allow in-place update of data structures. Abstractly, the effect of an update can be achieved by creating a new copy of the structure, with some new portion inserted into the copy. The single-assignment property is elegant because it is possible to use the availability of data as a means of process synchronization. However, this property has the undesirable effect of resulting in large memory turnover, due to excessive copying. The lack of economy in memory usage results in the prodigious memory requirements by programs that update aggregate data structures. Garbage collection needs to be invoked frequently as the heap space is limited.

If it is known that no references to a data object exist (other than the process inspecting the object!), then the structure can be reclaimed and used in building other structures if necessary. The detection and reuse of such data objects can be done with static analysis, known as *compile-time garbage collection* (e.g., [16, 3, 22]), at runtime (e.g., [8, 10, 12, 5]) with additional data structures and instructions, or by a combination of both. In this paper, we present a new analysis technique based on abstract interpretation for compile-time garbage collection of committed-choice logic programs. We describe the details of the algorithm and explain why it is accurate.

2 Literature Review

The application of static program analysis to infer properties of programs, and the use of this information to generate specialized and efficient code, have proved to be quite successful in logic languages. Several static analyses of logic programs to infer groundness, and sharing information (among others) have been proposed for sequential Prolog (e.g., [21, 3, 22, 9]). But these techniques do *not* extend easily to concurrent logic languages, where no assumptions can be made about the order of execution of the goals or about the interleaving of their reduction. To our knowledge, the only work in applying static analysis techniques to detect possibility of reuse in concurrent logic languages is by Foster and Winsborough [14]. They sketch a collecting semantics for Strand programs in which a program state is associated with a record of the program components that operated on it. The collecting semantics is then converted into an abstract interpretation framework by supplying an abstract domain in order to identify single consumers. The analysis details are in an unpublished draft [13], hence it is premature to compare their scheme with ours.

In other language families, research includes detecting single-threadedness of the store argument of the standard semantics of imperative languages [23], Hudak's work on abstraction of reference count for a call-by-value language with a fixed order of evaluation [15], and update analysis for a first-order lazy functional language with flat aggregates using a non-standard semantics called path semantics [1]. All the above analyses are for sequential implementations. Another important related area is shape analysis, the static derivation of data structure composition. Recent work by Chase *et al.* [4] describes an accurate and efficient method of shape analysis, which can be followed by reference-count analysis [15].

The analysis of single-threadedness or storage reusability in logic programming languages is significantly different from that of functional languages because of the power of unification and logical variables available in the former. We do not address the issue of shape analysis in this paper, only reference counting. One important use of our analysis is the reuse of "local" structures that do not require shape analysis to uncover.

3 Overview of Proposed Static Analysis

There are four distinct ways in which a logical variable can be used for sharing information in concurrent logic programs, namely, Single producer-Single consumer (*SS*), Single producer-Multiple consumer (*SM*), Multiple producers-Single consumer (*MS*), and Multiple producers-Multiple consumer (*MM*). Since a variable may be bound at most once, the notion of multiple producers implies that there are several potential producers but only one succeeds in *write-mode* unification. In a successful committed-choice program, all other potential producers perform *read-mode* unification. The purpose of our abstract interpretation is to determine which type of communication, SS or SM,[1] applies to each of the program variables. This information is used by the compiler to generate reuse instructions.

Structures appearing in the head and ask part of a clause imply *incoming* data, by the semantics of concurrent logic languages.[2] Thus if such an incoming structure is determined to be reusable, an attempt could be made to use its storage when constructing a structure in the body. Consider:

$$p(X, S, Y) :- S = t(L, C, R), \ X < C \ : \ Y = t(N, C, R) \mid p(X, L, N).$$

If the second argument in the head, S (which must be a structure $t(L, C, R)$), may be reused, it would be best to reuse it when constructing the structure $t(N, C, R)$. This is known as *instant* or *local* reuse. However, if no immediate use existed in the clause, the reclaimed storage could be stored away for future use (say, added to a free list). This is known as *deferred reuse*.

Data objects that have a single producer and single consumer are referred to as *single-threaded* and all other data objects are referred to as *multiple-threaded*. We assume structure-copying implementations. Our analysis detects single-threaded structures at compile-time. These structures can be reused at runtime if the top-level components are nonvariables. The presence of uninstantiated variable(s) in the top-level of a structure renders the structure unsuitable for reuse, even if the structure is single-threaded. The reason is that a producer of the unbound variable may bind its value *after* the enclosing structure has been reused!

We also assume that *structure sharing analysis* has been done, and that the results of the analysis are available. We envision sharing analysis similar to [26, 17], with two modifications. First, the analysis must work for concurrent languages. Second, if it is determined that two variables may share, no subsequent grounding can undo this sharing. If sharing information is not available, then we can make worst case assumptions about sharing and perform the analysis. This may produce fewer useful results.

3.1 Multiple Threadedness of Structures and Components

Compile-detection of single-threaded data structures necessarily involves some representation issues and we now discuss these issues relevant to propagating threadedness information safely and precisely. Representation of compound structures has a direct bearing on how the threadedness of a structure affects the threadedness of its components and vice versa and raises the following three questions.

- Is a substructure of a multiple threaded structure multiple threaded?

- Does a structure always become multiple threaded if one of its substructures is multiple threaded?

---

[1] We collapse MS and MM into SM in the analysis.

[2] Computation will suspend until the input arguments are sufficiently instantiated.

- How does the threadedness of a sub-term of a structure affect another sub-term of the same structure?

If a structure is multiple threaded, it means that there are (potentially) several consumers accessing the structure. Each consumer may access any substructure, implying that each substructure may also have multiple consumers. Thus multiple threadedness of a structure implies the multiple threadedness of its components.

Multiple threadedness of a component of a structure, however, does *not always* mean that the structure becomes multiple threaded. Suppose a structure is built in the body of a clause and it contains a head variable which is multiple threaded. A head variable is simply a reference to an incoming argument which has already been created. Only a *pointer* to that actual parameter resides in the structure built in the body. Because the variable is not created inside the current structure, the reuse of the structure does not affect the contents of the multiple-threaded component. Therefore the structure does not become multiple threaded.

Now suppose a structure is built in the the tell part of the guard and it contains at least one variable local to the clause (i.e., the variable does not appear in the head or the ask part) and that variable is multiple threaded. If the implementation allocates variables *inside* structures (as is usually the case), then a reuse of the structure will reclaim the space allocated for the multiple-threaded variable and is therefore unsafe. In this case, we have to make the structure multiple threaded. If the implementation creates variables *outside* structures (the structure arguments are linked to the variables by pointers), then multiple threadedness of a component would *never* make the structure multiple threaded. For the analysis presented here, we conservatively assume that variables may be created within a structure. Relaxing this assumption, whenever appropriate, leads to more precise analysis.

The answer to the third question depends on the sharing of the components of the structures. If two subterms of a structure share, then multiple threadedness of one may make the other multiple threaded. In the rest of the paper, we will discuss mainly the threadedness of variables. The threadedness of structures can be derived, with the principles discussed above, from the threadedness of its components.

4 Abstract Interpretation

In an abstract interpretation framework for a language, it is customary to define a core semantics for the language leaving certain domains and functions unspecified. These domains and functions are instantiated by an interpretation. A standard interpretation defines the standard semantics of the languages and an abstract interpretation abstracts some property of interest. The abstract and the standard interpretations are related by a pair of adjoint functions, known as the abstraction and concretization functions.

We first provide an operational semantics for the language Flat Concurrent Prolog, FCP(:), and then define our abstract interpretation method for reuse analysis. The proposed technique is also applicable to Flat Guarded Horn Clauses (FGHC), Strand, and similar languages [24].

4.1 Operational Semantics for FCP(:)

The following operational semantics is a minor variation of the standard transition system semantics for concurrent logic programs and is derived from [24]. The knowledgeable reader may wish to skip this.

A computation state is a triple $\langle G, \theta, i \rangle$ consisting of a goal G (a sequence of atoms), a current substitution θ, and a renaming index i. The index is used in renaming the variables of a clause ($PVar$ for program variables) apart from the variables of the goal. Function $rename : PVar \times \mathcal{N} \to Var$ subscripts the program variables with a renaming index and $rename^{-1} : Var \to PVar$ removes the subscript. Function $rename$ can be homomorphically extended to $rename : Clause \times \mathcal{N} \to Clause$. The initial state $\langle G, \varepsilon, 0 \rangle$ consists of the initial goal G, the empty substitution ε, and the renaming index 0.

> *Definition*: Computation
> A computation of a goal G with respect to a program P is a finite or infinite sequence of states $S_0, \ldots S_i, \ldots$ such that S_0 is the initial state and each $S_{i+1} \in t(S_i)$ where t is a transition function from S to $\mathcal{P}(S)$.

A state S is a terminal state when no transition rule is applicable to it. The state $\langle true, \theta, i \rangle$ is a terminal state that denotes successful computation and $\langle fail, \theta, i \rangle$ denotes finitely failed computation. If no transition is applicable to a state $S = \langle A_1, \ldots, A_n, \theta, i \rangle$ ($n \geq 1$) where $A_j \neq fail$, $1 \leq j \leq n$, then the state is dead-locked. We define the meaning of a program P as the set of all computations of a goal G with respect to P.

> *Definition*: Transition Rules
>
> - $\langle A_1, \ldots, A_j, \ldots, A_n, \theta, i \rangle \xrightarrow{reduce}$
> $$\langle (A_1, \ldots, A_{j-1}, A_{j+1}, B_1, \ldots, B_k)\theta', \theta \circ \theta', i+1 \rangle$$
>   if $\exists$ a clause C s.t. $rename(C,i) = H :- Ask : Tell \mid B_1, \ldots, B_k$
>   and $try(A_j, H, Ask, Tell) = \theta'$.
>
> - $\langle A_1, \ldots, A_j, \ldots, A_n, \theta, i \rangle \xrightarrow{reduce} \langle fail, \theta, i \rangle$
>   if for some j, and for all (renamed) clauses $H :- Ask : Tell \mid B_1, \ldots, B_k$,
> $try(A_j, H, Ask, Tell) = fail$.

For the standard definition of *try*, see Shapiro [24]. This sufficiently summarizes the operational semantics of flat concurrent logic languages to define our abstract interpretation scheme.

4.2 Syntactic Assumptions

Without loss of generality, the following syntactic constraints are used to simplify the analysis. These constraints can be satisfied by simple transformations at compile-time. The rationale behind the constraints (especially 2 and 3) is to ensure that the sets *Ask* and *Tell* of unification equations are in a solved form [20]. These conditions facilitate reasoning about structures that are definitely created at commit time (see Section 4.6).

1. Head arguments are distinct variables. This restriction simply moves the matching of head arguments with those of goal to the ask part of the guard.

2. Equations of the ask part may be of two forms:

   - $X = Y$, where the variables X and Y must appear in the head.
   - $X = f(...)$ where variable X must appear in the head.

   The left hand side variables must occur exactly once in the ask part. Other builtin goals, e.g., *arg/3*, can be handled similarly.

3. Equations of the tell part may be of two forms:

   - $X = Y$, where the variables X and Y must appear in the head or the ask part of the guard.
   - $X = f(...)$

   The left hand side variables must occur exactly once in the tell part.

4. All program variables have been renamed such that no variable occurs in more than one clause. This is because, when we define the abstraction function, we will merge information about various incarnations (renamed versions) of the same variable.

5. Those variables of a clause that do not appear in the head and the ask part of the guard will be referred to as local variables of the clause and are given a superscript *local*.

6. Arguments of procedure calls are variables. A goal such as $p(X, f(Z))$ can be replaced by a pair of goals $p(X, Y)$ and $Y = f(Z)$ where Y is a new variable not occurring in the clause and the unification goal $Y = f(Z)$ can be moved into the tell part of the guard. Y would be a local variable by our definition. Unification equations of the form $Y = f(...)$ may appear in the tell part but not in the body. The reason for this transformation is to make explicit the structure creation operation and to simplify the abstraction of head–goal matching.

For a state $S = \langle Goal, \theta, i \rangle$, we use $local_S$ to denote the set of variables in *Goal* that are subscripted by i and superscripted by *local*. These are the local variables of the clause used in the ith reduction step.

4.3 Abstract Domain

In the standard semantics, computation is defined as a (finite or infinite) sequence of states where two successive states are related by the transition function. Hence, the standard domain of interpretation is $\mathcal{P}(\textit{Computation})$. We are interested in determining the set of program variables that will be bound only to single-threaded data structures in *any* computation. In our abstract domain a variable can take values from the two-point complete lattice L whose least element is SS (Single Producer/Single Consumer) and the top is SM (Single Producer/Multiple Consumers). Our abstract domain *AbEnv* is *PVar* $\rightarrow \{SS, SM\}$ and the partial ordering on *AbEnv* is the usual point-wise ordering.

Our abstraction function α maps a set of computations to *AbEnv*. Function α is defined in terms of two other functions, α' and α''. Function α' maps a state to *AbEnv* and α'' maps a computation (which is a sequence of states) to *AbEnv*. We need an auxiliary predicate *multi_occurs*(*Term, State*) which is true whenever the term T occurs *more than twice* in state *State* (counting each occurrence of a term T in each atom in the state).

$$
\begin{aligned}
&\textit{Definition:}\quad \alpha' : State \rightarrow AbEnv \\
&\overline{\alpha'(S)} \quad = \quad \{Z \mapsto SM \quad \textit{if } Z \in \{rename^{-1}(X) \mid multi\_occurs(X, S) \vee \\
&\hspace{9em} (S = \langle G, \theta, i \rangle \wedge T \in sub\text{-}terms(X\theta) \wedge \\
&\hspace{9em} multi\_occurs(T, S))\} \\
&\hspace{5em} Z \mapsto SS \quad \textit{otherwise } \}
\end{aligned}
$$

A variable X (representing some data structure) can be multiple-threaded in one of two ways.

- X is multiple-threaded if it appears more than twice in the current state.

- Suppose X is bound to a term $f(...T...)$ in the current substitution θ and a sub-term, say T, occurs more than twice in the current state. Then X may or may not be multiple-threaded. Consider:

$$:\text{-}\ p(X).$$

$$p(X_1) :\text{-} \ true \ : \ X_1 = f(a) \mid q(X_1), r(X_1), s(X_1).$$

Let the initial state be $\langle p(X_1), \{\}, 0 \rangle$. The state $S1$ resulting from reducing the goal $p(X)$ with respect to the above clause is $\langle q(f(a)), r(f(a)), s(f(a)), \theta = \{X \mapsto f(a), X_1 \mapsto f(a)\}, 1 \rangle$. The sub-terms $f(a)$ of the literals q, r, and s represent the current binding of the variable X_1 (and X) shared by the literals q, r and s. Hence, in this case, both X and X_1 are multiple-threaded. On the other hand, if the goal $p(X)$ is reduced with respect to the following clause, we will obtain a similar state $S2$ but in which variables X, X_1 and X_2 will not be multiple-threaded.

$$p(X_1) :\!- true \,:\, X_1 = f(a), X_2 = f(a) \mid q(X_1), r(X_2), s(X_2).$$

There is not enough information in the states $S1$ and $S2$ to distinguish between them and hence we safely approximate X, X_1 (and X_2) to be multiple-threaded in both states.

Note that our abstract domain does not keep track of the threadedness of the top level of a structure and its sub-structures separately. This can be done by a more expressive abstract domain and corresponding abstract domain operations. We have developed such an expressive domain and are experimenting with its usefulness, the results of which will be reported elsewhere.

Different (renamed) versions of the same variable may occur in a state but we merge their threadedness. We consider a variable multiple-threaded in a state if any one of its renamed versions is multiple-threaded. It is straightforward to extend the definition of α' from $State \rightarrow AbEnv$ to $Computation \rightarrow AbEnv$, since a computation is just a sequence of states. In the following definition, $S \in Comp$ denotes each state S in the computation sequence $Comp$ (by a slight abuse of notation).

<u>Definition</u>: $\alpha'' : Computation \rightarrow AbEnv$
$$\alpha''(Comp) = \bigsqcup_{S \in Comp} \alpha'(S)$$

The abstraction function α and the concretization function γ can now be defined as follows.

<u>Definition</u>: $\alpha : \mathcal{P}(Computation) \rightarrow AbEnv$
$$\alpha(CompSet) = \bigsqcup_{C \in CompSet} \alpha''(C)$$

<u>Definition</u>: $\gamma : AbEnv \rightarrow \mathcal{P}(Computation)$
$$\gamma(X) = \{ C \in Computation \mid \alpha''(C) \sqsubseteq X \}$$

In the following subsections, we describe the abstract interpretation algorithm in detail. The algorithm consists of initialization of the abstract environment of a clause (Section 4.4), head–goal matching and guard execution (Section 4.6), local fixpoint computation and abstract entry and success environment computation (Section 4.5). Global fixpoint computation is done in the standard fashion (e.g., [9, 2]).

4.4 Initialization

The initial abstraction of the threadedness of variables is based on the number of occurrences of a variable (and the variables it shares with) in the head and the body. All occurrences of the same variable in the head and the guards are counted as a single occurrence and each occurrence of a variable in the body is counted individually.

If a variable occurs two or fewer times, it is initialized to SS. If it occurs more than twice, it is initialized to SM, implying that variables that occur only in the guard (Ask or $Tell$ part) are initialized to SS. The variables that occur only in the guard will inherit their threadedness from other terms with which they are matched/unified. The following example illustrates the computation of an initial approximation for the body occurrences.

$$f(X_1, X_2) :- X_1 < X_2 \; : \; X_3 = t(X_1) \mid p(X_1, X_4), \; q(X_1, X_2, X_3, X_4).$$

Variable X_1 is initialized to SM since it occurs three times — once in the head and twice in the body of the clause. Variable X_2 starts as single-threaded because it occurs once in the head and once in the body. Similarly, $X_3 = X_4 = SS$. We refer to the initial environment of the clause, obtained with the above rules, as $AbEnv_{init} = \{X_1 \mapsto SM, X_2 \mapsto SS, X_3 \mapsto SS, X_4 \mapsto SS\}$ and use $AbEnv^i_{init}$ to mean the initial environment of clause i.

As an example of sharing, consider the following:

$$p(X_1, X_2, X_3) :- true \; : \; X_2 = X_3 \mid q(X_1, X_2), \; r(X_3).$$

Assume the tell goal may cause X_2 and X_3 to share. Not considering sharing, the number of occurrences of X_2 and X_3 are each two. However, considering sharing, we count four occurrences of each, thus we initialize X_2 and X_3 to SM.

4.5 Threadedness Propagation

Propagation of information across procedure calls involves modeling the reduction of a goal into a set of goals by head matching, including the successful execution of the guards and the interleaved execution of body goals. The overall mechanism is summarized in Figure 1, which is described in the following sub-sections. Given a goal $Goal$, a caller's environment $AbEnv_{call}$, and a clause C we abstract the reduction process by first computing the initial environment $AbEnv_{init}$ of C, and then by safely approximating the effects of head-goal matching, Ask testing, and $Tell$ unifications. This is accomplished by safely approximating the effects of head-goal matching, Ask testing, $Tell$ unifications, and guard execution.

$Definition$: $AbsRed$: $Atom \times Clause \times AbEnv \rightarrow AbEnv$

$\overline{AbsRed(Goal, C, AbEnv_{call})} =$

let	$H :- A : T \mid B$	$=$	$rename(C)$ (1)
	$AbEnv_{init}$	$=$	$init(H :- A : T \mid B)$ (2)
	E'	$=$	$Match(Goal, H, AbEnv_{call} \cup AbEnv_{init})$ (3)
	E''	$=$	$Punify(A, E')$ (4)
	E'''	$=$	$Aunify(T, E'')$ (5)
in			

$$rename^{-1}(restrict(E''', Vars(H, A, T, B))) \tag{6}$$

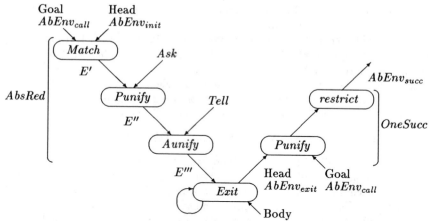

Figure 1: Abstract Interpretation Mechanism

The variables of the clause C are consistently renamed (1) to avoid capturing the goal variables. The initial environment $AbEnv_{init}$ of the renamed clause is computed using function *init* discussed in section 4.4. *Match* approximates head–goal matching in the environment of the goal and the initial environment of the renamed clause (3). *Punify* abstracts the effect of *Ask* goals of the guard (4) and *Aunify* abstracts the effect of *Tell* unification goals (5). We restrict the resulting environment E''' to the variables of the renamed clause, and then apply the inverse of the renaming function (6). This gives us the abstract environment $AbEnv_{entry}$ for the variables of clause C on reducing goal G with respect to clause C.

The success environment of a user-defined goal G is obtained, in function *Succ*, by taking the lub (least upper bound) of success environments of all the matching clauses (3 below). Although the nondeterminism in committed choice languages is the *don't-care* type, at compile time we do not know which clause will commit, and hence take the lub. The program P (an implicit parameter to *Succ*) is analyzed by calculating $AbEnv_{succ} = Succ(Query, AbEnv_{init}^{query})$, where *Query* is the top-level procedure invocation and $AbEnv_{init}^{query}$ is the initial environment for the query variables.

Definition: $Succ\colon Atom \times AbEnv \to AbEnv$
$\overline{Succ(Goal, AbEnv_{call})} =$
let $\{p_1, p_2, \ldots, p_k\}$ be the clauses whose heads match *Goal* and
$\{b_1, b_2, \ldots, b_k\}$ be their respective bodies

$$AbEnv_{entry}^i = AbsRed(Goal, p_i, AbEnv_{call}) \qquad (1)$$
$$AbEnv_{exit}^i = Exit(b_i, AbEnv_{entry}^i) \qquad (2)$$

in

$$\bigsqcup_{i=1}^{k} \{OneSucc(Goal, p_i, AbEnv_{call}, AbEnv_{exit}^i)\} \qquad (3)$$

The function *OneSucc* is similar to *AbsRed*, with two exceptions. First, we use the exit environment of a clause instead of its initial environment. Second, after simulating the head unifications, the result is restricted to the variables of the calling environment and *not* to the variables of clause C whose head matched G.

Definition: *OneSucc*: $Atom \times Clause \times AbEnv \times AbEnv \rightarrow AbEnv$

$OneSucc(Goal, C, AbEnv_{call}, AbEnv_{exit}) =$

$$\textbf{let} \quad \begin{aligned} (C', AbEnv_{exit'}) &= rename((C, AbEnv_{exit})) \\ H :- A : T \mid B &= C' \\ E &= Aunify(\{Goal = H\}, AbEnv_{call} \cup AbEnv_{exit'}) \end{aligned}$$

$\textbf{in}$

$$restrict(E, Vars(AbEnv_{call}))$$

In concurrent logic programs, body goals may execute in any order and their execution may also be interleaved. We safely approximate this by iterating the computation of abstract exit environment (given the abstract entry environment) until the exit and the entry environments are the same. This function is performed in *Exit*, as follows.

Definition: *Exit*: $Body \times AbEnv \rightarrow AbEnv$

$Exit(Body, AbEnv_{entry}) =$

$$\textbf{let} \quad AbEnv_{exit} = ExitIter(Body, AbEnv_{entry})$$
$$\textbf{in} \quad \textbf{if} \quad (AbEnv_{entry} = AbEnv_{exit}) \quad \textbf{then}$$
$$\qquad AbEnv_{entry}$$
$$\textbf{else} \quad Exit(Body, AbEnv_{exit})$$

Definition: *ExitIter*: $Body \times AbEnv \rightarrow AbEnv$

$ExitIter(Body, AbEnv_0) =$

$$\textbf{if} \quad empty(Body) \quad \textbf{then}$$
$$\qquad AbEnv_0$$
$$\textbf{else} \quad \textbf{let} \quad Body = \{l_1, l_2, \dots, l_n\}$$
$$\textbf{in} \quad \bigsqcup_{i=1}^{n} Succ(l_i, AbEnv_0)$$

A different local fixed-point calculation was first used by Codognet *et al.* [7]. Since the functions *AbsRed*, *Exit*, *Succ*, *Match*, *Punify*, and *Aunify* are monotonic and the domain L is finite, the least fixed point exists by Kleene's fixed-point theorem [25].

4.6 Abstracting Procedure Invocation

Head–Goal Matching

Function *Match*(*Goal*, *Head*, *AbEnv*), is now informally defined. Since we are dealing with canonical-form programs, head matching involves variable–variable unification only. We first unify the head H and the goal G obtaining an idempotent substitution $\theta = \{X_1 \mapsto Y_1, \dots, X_n \mapsto Y_n\}$ such that $\theta H = G$. Next the threadedness is propagated by repeating the following rules until there is no change in the abstract environment. For each $X_i \mapsto Y_i \in \theta$,

- if $\{X_i \mapsto SM, Y_i \mapsto SS\} \subseteq AbEnv$, then update $AbEnv$ with $Y_i \mapsto SM$. If Y_i is updated, for each Z that may share with Y_i, update $AbEnv$ with $Z \mapsto SM$.

- or, if $\{X_i \mapsto SS, Y_i \mapsto SM\} \subseteq AbEnv$, then update $AbEnv$ with $X_i \mapsto SM$. If X_i is updated, for each Z that may share with X_i, update $AbEnv$ with $Z \mapsto SM$.

Ask Goals

The testing of *Ask* goals is simulated by function *Punify*. Recall that ask equations do not bind goal variables; they can at most bind the variables of the clause being matched with the current goal. Function *Punify*(*Ask*, *AbEnv*), not formally defined, is discussed below. A unification equation in the ask part takes one of two forms (recall the constraints of Section 4.2):

- $X = Y$ in which both X and Y must also appear in the head. This goal simply tests for equality without creating any bindings and hence *Punify* ignores such ask goals.

- $X = f(...Y...)$ where X is a head variable. This goal does not create a binding for X in the actual execution. However, Y may be bound to a component of X, if Y doesn't appear in the head. If Y is multiple-threaded but X is not, then X (and all variables that may share with X) will become multiple-threaded. If Y is not multiple-threaded but X is, then Y (and all variables that may share with Y) will become multiple-threaded. If Y is a head variable, then Y cannot be bound to a sub-component of X but can merely be checked for equality and hence the threadedness of X and Y are not affected. Other builtin goals, e.g., *arg/3*, can be handled similarly.

Tell Unifications

We assume that tell unification equations are in solved form, i.e., the LHS variables occur exactly once in the tell part (Section 4.2). Furthermore, in each equation of the form $X = Y$ (where X and Y are variables) both X and Y must appear in the head or the ask part of the guard. The set of tell equations $X_1 = t_1, \ldots, X_n = t_n$ in solved form represents an idempotent substitution [20] $\{X_1 \mapsto t_1, \ldots, X_n \mapsto t_n\}$. An idempotent substitution can be viewed as a bipartite graph [18]. The variables X_i form a vertex set S and the variables that occur in t_i form another vertex set T and these two are disjoint. There is an edge from a vertex $X \in S$ to a vertex $Y \in T$ whenever $X \mapsto f(...Y...)$ or $X \mapsto Y$ is in θ. We propagate the threadedness by repeating the following rules until there is no change in the abstract environment.

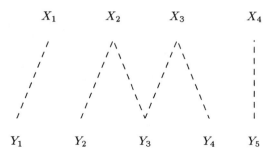

$$X_1 \qquad X_2 \qquad X_3 \qquad X_4$$

$$Y_1 \qquad Y_2 \qquad Y_3 \qquad Y_4 \qquad Y_5$$

Figure 2: Approximating Tell Unifications

1. For each $X \in S$ such that there is an edge between X and Y, and $\{X \mapsto SM, Y \mapsto SS\} \subseteq AbEnv$, update $AbEnv$ with $Y \mapsto SM$. Whenever Y is updated, for each Z that may share with Y, update $AbEnv$ with $Z \mapsto SM$. We are simply propagating the multiple-threadedness of X to its components and their aliases.

2. The symmetric case of $\{X \mapsto SS, Y \mapsto SM\}$ is treated similarly. Abstraction of a tell unification equation thus involves propagating the lub of the abstractions of the two arguments.

A more general, and therefore more precise, formulation of abstract tell unification involves keeping track of local and non-local variables and output variables,[3] in conjunction with extending the abstract domain to express information about the threadedness of sub-structures. The current formulation is imprecise in the following sense. Consider the structure created by the tell unification equation $X = f(Y_1, \ldots, Y_n)$ where X is a local variable, none of the Y_i is local and some Y_i is multiple-threaded. The structure X is reuseable if there are no more than two occurrences of X in the body of the clause, and those occurrences do not become multiple-threaded due to other reasons such as aliasing. However, our abstract domain cannot express that the top level of X is definitely single-threaded but other levels are not. This is a source of imprecision in our analysis.

As an example of the propagation steps, consider the set of tell unification equations $\{X_1 = f(Y_1, Y_2), X_2 = g(Y_2, Y_3), X_3 = h(Y_3, Y_4), X_4 = Y_5\}$ represented by the bipartite graph in Figure 2.

Assume that initially only X_3 is multiple-threaded and let $\{(X_2, X_4), (Y_3, Y_5)\}$ be the set of pairs of variables that may share. Since X_3 is SM, Y_3, Y_4 also become SM and so does Y_5 since it shares with Y_3. X_4 becomes SM because of the equation $X_4 = Y_5$ and so does X_2 since it shares with X_4. We can now apply rule one again and this time

---

[3] For languages that restrict unification to assignment, such as Strand, this condition is known precisely.

Program	Heap Usage (Words)		
	Naive	Dynamic	Static
insert	1,500,000	6,314	6,314
append	5,000,000	6,202	6,202
prime	323,786	12,128	12,158
qsort	8,000,000	61,725	61,725
pascal	167,070	127,072	147,270
triangle	543,809	539,523	—

Table 1: Heap Usage: Comparison of No Optimization, Dynamic, and Static

Y_2 becomes *SM*. Since we cannot further apply the rules, the final result is $\{X_2, X_3, X_4, Y_2, Y_3, Y_4, Y_5\}$ are *SM* and the rest $\{X_1, Y_1\}$ are *SS*.

5   Application of the Analysis

We now briefly summarize one application of the analysis involving the optimization of KL1 PDSS code [19, 6] to avoid runtime threadedness ("collect") checks within the MRB framework [5]. For each of six benchmarks, three compiled versions were generated: naive — a version with no collect or reuse instructions, used as a basis for comparison; dynamic — a version with collect instructions as generated by the existing PDSS compiler; and static — a version exploiting our static analysis, with instant reuse instructions appropriately generated and no collect operations used.

The measurements in Table 1 illustrate classes of full, partial, and no-reuse programs. The first four programs extensively use stream-based single producer/single consumer communication. Our algorithm predicted potential for full instant reuse, as confirmed in the table. Here the heap memory requirements of the static and dynamic versions are nearly identical. This demonstrates that it is possible to achieve as much efficiency as collect in programs where a large number of single-threaded structures are constructed. In pascal, only 50% of actual single-threaded structures could be detected with the static analysis. In triangle, the board structure is multiple-threaded and thus collect operations, which almost never succeed in reclaiming memory, are a waste of time. Since reuse is not possible, we did not generate a reuse version of the program. As further evidence of the utility of the analysis, the programs experienced a reduction in execution time of 4.7–7.0% attributable to the optimization. A detailed account of these experiments is give in Duvvuru *et al.* [11].

6   Conclusions and Future Work

We have introduced a new compile-time analysis method for determining single-threadedness of data structures in concurrent logic programs. The analysis is formulated in the framework of an abstract interpreter for FCP(:). The information produced is the "threadedness" of each logical variable: either single or multiple threaded, referring to the number of producer/consumer processes associated with the variable. To avoid an overly conservative approximation, the analysis imposes simple syntactic constraints that can easily be achieved at compile time without loss of generality. Structure sharing information is required to ensure correctness of the analysis, and its use is integrated into the threadedness algorithm.

Future plans include integrating both sharing and reuse analysis within the Monaco system, a native-code, shared-memory multiprocessor compiler for flat committed-choice languages.

Acknowledgements

E. Tick was supported by an NSF Presidential Young Investigator award, with funding from Sequent Computer Systems Inc.

References

[1] A. Bloss. *Path Analysis and Optimization of Non-Strict Functional Languages.* PhD thesis, Yale University, New Haven, May 1989.

[2] M. Bruynooghe. A Practical Framework for the Abstract Interpretation of Logic Programs. *Journal of Logic Programming*, 10(2):91–124, February 1991.

[3] M. Bruynooghe *et al.* Abstract Interpretation: Towards the Global Optimization of Prolog Programs. In *Int. Symp. on Logic Prog.*, pages 192–204. IEEE Computer Society, August 1987.

[4] D. R. Chase, M. Wegman, and F. K. Zadeck. Analysis of Pointers and Structures. In *SIGPLAN Conf. on Prog. Lang. Design and Implementation*, pages 296–309, June 1990. ACM Press.

[5] T. Chikayama and Y. Kimura. Multiple Reference Management in Flat GHC. In *ICLP*, pp. 276–293. MIT Press, May 1987.

[6] T. Chikayama *et al.* Overview of the Parallel Inference Machine Operating System PIMOS. In *International Conference on Fifth Generation Computer Systems*, pages 230–251, Tokyo, November 1988. ICOT.

[7] C. Codognet *et al.* Abstract Interpretation of Concurrent Logic Languages. In *NACLP*, pp. 215–232. MIT Press, October 1990.

[8] J. Cohen. Garbage Collection of Linked Data Structures. *ACM Computing Surveys*, 13:341–367, September 1981.

[9] S. K. Debray. Static Inference of Modes and Data Dependencies in Logic Programs. *ACM TOPLAS*, 11(3):418–450, July 1989.

[10] L. P. Deutsch and D. G. Bobrow. An Efficient Incremental, Automatic Garbage Collector. *CACM*, 19:522–526, September 1976.

[11] S. Duvvuru *et al.* A Compile-Time Memory-Reuse Scheme for Concurrent Logic Programs. In *International Workshop on Memory Management*, St. Malo, September 1992. ACM Press.

[12] L. H. Eriksson and M. Rayner. Incorporating Mutable Arrays into Logic Programming. In *Int. Logic Prog. Conf.*, pp. 76–82, Uppsala, 1984.

[13] I. Foster and W. Winsborough. A Computational Collecting Semantics for Strand. Research report, Argonne National Laboratory, 1990. unpublished.

[14] I. Foster and W. Winsborough. Copy Avoidance through Compile-Time Analysis and Local Reuse. In *International Symposium on Logic Programming*, pages 455–469. San Diego, MIT Press, November 1991.

[15] P. Hudak. A Semantic Model of Reference Counting and Its Abstraction. In *Conf. on Lisp and Functional Prog.*, pp. 351–363, 1986. ACM Press.

[16] P. Hudak and A. Bloss. The Aggregate Update Problem in Functional Programming Languages. In *SIGPLAN Symposium on Principles of Programming Languages*, pages 300–314, January 1985. ACM Press.

[17] D. Jacobs and A. Langen. Accurate and Efficient Approximation of Variable Aliasing in Logic Programs. In *North American Conf. on Logic Prog.*, pages 154–165. Cleveland, MIT Press, October 1989.

[18] S. B. Jones and D. L. Metayer. Compile-time Garbage Collection by Sharing Analysis. In *Conference on Functional Programming Languages and Computer Architecture*, pages 54–74. London, ACM Press, 1989.

[19] Y. Kimura and T. Chikayama. An Abstract KL1 Machine and its Instruction Set. In *International Symposium on Logic Programming*, pages 468–477. IEEE Computer Society, August 1987.

[20] J-L. Lassez, M.J. Maher, and K. Marriott. Unification Revisited. In J. Minker, editor, *Foundations of Deductive Databases and Logic Programming*, pages 587–626. Morgan Kaufmann Publishers Inc., 1988.

[21] C. S. Mellish. Some Global Optimizations for a Prolog Compiler. *Journal of Logic Programming*, 2(1):43–66, April 1985.

[22] A. Mulkers *et al.* Analysis of Shared Data Structures for Compile-Time Garbage Collection in Logic Programs. In *International Conference on Logic Programming*, pages 747–762. MIT Press, June 1990.

[23] D. Schmidt. Detecting Global Variables in Denotational Specifications. *ACM Transactions on Programming Languages and Systems*, 7(2):299–310, 1985.

[24] E. Y. Shapiro. The Family of Concurrent Logic Programming Languages. *ACM Computing Surveys*, 21(3):413–510, September 1989.

[25] J. E. Stoy. *Denotational Semantics: The Scott-Strachey Approach to Programming Language Theory.* MIT Press, first edition, 1977.

[26] R. Sundararajan. An Abstract Interpretation Scheme for Groundness, Freeness, and Sharing Analysis of Logic Programs. Tech. Report CIS-TR-91-06, University of Oregon, October 1991.

Meta and Higher-Order Programming

A Perfect Herbrand Semantics for Untyped Vanilla Meta-Programming

Bern Martens   **Danny De Schreye**
Department of Computer Science, Katholieke Universiteit Leuven
Celestijnenlaan 200A, B-3001 Heverlee, Belgium
e-mail: {bern,dannyd}@cs.kuleuven.ac.be

Abstract

We study a semantics for untyped, vanilla meta-programs, using the non-ground representation for object level variables. We introduce the notion of language independence, which generalises range restriction. We show that the vanilla meta-program associated to a stratified normal object program, is weakly stratified. For language independent, stratified normal object programs, we prove that there is a natural one-to-one correspondence between atoms $p(t_1, \ldots, t_r)$ in the perfect Herbrand model of the object program and $solve(p(t_1, \ldots, t_r))$-atoms in the weakly perfect Herbrand model of the associated vanilla meta-program. Thus, for this class of programs, the weakly perfect Herbrand model provides a sensible semantics for the meta-program. One of the main attractions of our approach is that the results can be further extended —in a straightforward way— to provide a sensible semantics for a limited form of amalgamation.

1   Introduction

Meta-programming has become increasingly important in logic programming and deductive databases. Applications in knowledge representation and reasoning, program transformation, synthesis and analysis, debugging and expert systems, the modeling of evaluation strategies, the specification and implementation of sophisticated optimisation techniques, the description of integrity constraint checking, etc. are constituting a significantly large part of the recent work in the field. In the last few years, theoretical foundations for meta-programming in logic programming have been developed in [13] and [27]. As a result, the programming language Gödel ([14]) now provides —not merely in the context of meta-programming— a fully declarative successor of Prolog, supporting the sound development of further meta-programming applications.

It should be clear however, that it can not have been the sound semantics for meta-programming, nor the existence of Gödel, that attracted so much interest into meta-programming in logic programming to start with.

(Although they have clearly accelerated the activity in the area). One attraction certainly is the desire to extend the expressiveness of Horn clause logic augmented with negation as failure. Meta-programming adds extra knowledge representation and reasoning facilities ([16]). A second attraction is related to practicality. In applicative languages —both pure functional and pure logical—, data and programs are syntactically indistinguishable. This is an open invitation to writing programs that take other programs as input. We believe that the practical success of —in particular— untyped vanilla-type meta-programming has resulted from this. However, in spite of this success, little or no effort was made to provide it with a sensible semantics. Doing just this, is the main motivation for the work reported on in this paper.

In [13], the possibility of providing a declarative semantics for untyped vanilla meta-programming is rejected immediately, on the basis that —under the usual semantics for untyped logic programs— the intended interpretations of vanilla meta-programs can never be models. Now, this statement is somewhat inaccurate. The intended *meaning* of a vanilla-type meta-theory (in which different variables range over different domains) can simply not be captured within the formal notion of an interpretation, as it is defined for untyped, first order logic. So, a more precise statement would be that *the intended meaning can not be formalised as an untyped interpretation.* However, we argue that this problem is not typical for untyped vanilla programs, but that, in general, it is a problem for the semantics of most untyped logic programs. Any untyped logic program in which a functor is used to represent a partial function suffers from the same semantical problem and, in practice, total functions seldom occur in real applications. (See [7] for a thorough discussion of this issue.)

Whether this (and other) argument(s) in favour of typed logic programs should convince us to abandon the notational simplicity of untyped logic programs all together, is an issue we do not want to address in this paper. From here on, we will assume that the semantics of an (untyped) program is captured by the alternative notion of its (least/minimal/perfect) Herbrand model(s), avoiding the problems with intended interpretations. Even in this more restricted context, there remain problems with the semantics of untyped vanilla meta-programs. In [5], we addressed these problems in the restricted context of *definite* logic programs. The present paper tackles the more general case of *normal* programs (i.e. programs with negation).

We first illustrate the difficulties on an example.

Consider the object program P:

$$p(x) \leftarrow not \ q(x)$$
$$q(a) \leftarrow$$

Let M denote the standard *solve* interpreter:

$$solve(empty) \leftarrow$$

$$solve(x \& y) \leftarrow solve(x), solve(y)$$
$$solve(\neg x) \leftarrow not \; solve(x) \qquad \text{(i)}$$
$$solve(x) \leftarrow clause(x, y), solve(y) \qquad \text{(ii)}$$

In addition, let M_P denote the program M augmented with the following facts:

$$clause(p(x), \neg q(x)) \leftarrow$$
$$clause(q(a), empty) \leftarrow$$

Now, the first problem we face is that M_P is *not* locally stratified. Consider clause (ii) of M_P. For any two ground atoms, $solve(t_1)$ and $solve(t_2)$ in the Herbrand base of the underlying language for M_P, we have that both

$$solve(t_1) \leftarrow clause(t_1, t_2), solve(t_2)$$

and

$$solve(t_2) \leftarrow clause(t_2, t_1), solve(t_1)$$

are ground instances of (ii). Therefore, in any local stratification of M_P, all the ground atoms of the form $solve(t)$ must be in the same stratum. On the other hand, by clause (i), any ground atom $solve(\neg t)$ must be placed in a higher stratum than the corresponding atom $solve(t)$. So no local stratification can be possible.

However, there is a simple way to overcome this problem. Consider the new theory, M_P', obtained from M_P by performing one unfolding step of the atom $clause(x, y)$ in clause (ii), using every available *clause*-fact of M_P. Clause (ii) is replaced by the resultants. This new theory M_P' is completely equivalent with M_P in the sense that they have identical models. But one can easily verify that M_P' *is* locally stratified. It can be shown that for any stratified object program P, the program obtained from its associated vanilla meta-program through a similar unfolding transformation, is locally stratified. In [22] and [23], Przymusinska and Przymusinski introduced *weakly* stratified logic programs and showed that they have a unique *weakly* perfect Herbrand model. Now, from their definitions, it follows that programs which can be unfolded into a locally stratified one, are weakly stratified. It can therefore be shown that a stratified object program gives rise to a weakly stratified vanilla meta-program and the weakly perfect Herbrand model of the latter can be considered as the description of its semantics.

Then the actual problem with a Herbrand model approach to the semantics of M_P can be addressed: Although the perfect Herbrand model of the object program P in the above example is $\{q(a)\}$, the weakly perfect Herbrand model of the meta-program M_P contains completely unrelated atoms, such as $solve(p(empty))$, $solve(p(q(a)))$, etc.. This is certainly undesirable, since we, in general, would like at least that the atoms of the form $solve(p(t))$ in the weakly perfect Herbrand model of M_P correspond in a one-to-one way with the atoms of the form $p(t)$ in the perfect Herbrand model of P.

In this paper, we therefore introduce the notion of *language independence* and show that it generalises range restriction. As our main result, we state that for stratified, language independent programs, the perfect Herbrand model of the program corresponds in a one-to-one way with a natural subset of the weakly perfect Herbrand model of the corresponding vanilla theory. In addition, we show how this approach can be extended to provide a semantics for various related meta-programs, including a limited form of amalgamation. The latter extension is rather interesting, since it reflects one of the main advantages the untyped approach may have over the typed one.

The paper is organised as follows. In the next section, after introducing and discussing the notions of language independence and weak stratification, we present our basic results for stratified object programs and their straightforward untyped vanilla meta-version. We consider some related (more "useful") meta-programs in section 3 and address various (limited) forms of amalgamation in section 4. We conclude with a discussion.

2 A Meta-Programming Semantics

In this section, we first briefly introduce the concepts of *language independence* and *weak stratification*. Next, we present the main results of this paper in subsection 2.3.

Throughout the rest of the paper, we assume the reader to be familiar with the basic concepts of predicate logic (see e.g. [10]) and logic programming (see e.g. [17]). We also suppose familiarity with the notions of *(local) stratification* and *perfect* model (see e.g. [1], [24]).

Finally, due to space restrictions, no proofs could be included in this text. They can be found in [20].

2.1 Language Independence

We start by extending the concept of *language independence*, introduced in [5] for definite programs, to stratified (normal) programs.

Definition 2.1 Let $\mathcal{L}$ be a (first order) language and $\mathcal{R}$, $\mathcal{F}$ and $\mathcal{C}$ its sets of predicate, function and constant symbols respectively. We call a language $\mathcal{L}'$, determined by $\mathcal{R}'$, $\mathcal{F}'$ and $\mathcal{C}'$ an *extension* of $\mathcal{L}$ iff $\mathcal{R} \subseteq \mathcal{R}'$, $\mathcal{F} \subseteq \mathcal{F}'$ and $\mathcal{C} \subseteq \mathcal{C}'$.

When considering a logic program P, it is customary to speak about the *language underlying the program*. We will use the notation $\mathcal{L}_P$. In this language, we take $\mathcal{R}_P$, $\mathcal{F}_P$ and $\mathcal{C}_P$ to be the sets of predicate, function and constant symbols occurring *in the program*.

Definition 2.2 Let P be a normal program with underlying language $\mathcal{L}_P$. A Herbrand interpretation of P in a language $\mathcal{L}'$, extension of $\mathcal{L}_P$, is called an *$\mathcal{L}'$-Herbrand interpretation* of P.

In the sequel, we will often refer to *Herbrand* interpretations and models of a program P with underlying language $\mathcal{L}_P$, when in fact, we mean $\mathcal{L}_P$-*Herbrand* interpretations or models.

Definition 2.3 A stratified program P with underlying language $\mathcal{L}_P$ is called *language independent* iff for any extension $\mathcal{L}'$ of $\mathcal{L}_P$, its perfect $\mathcal{L}'$-Herbrand model is equal to its perfect $\mathcal{L}_P$-Herbrand model.

Before concluding this subsection, we point out that the notion of language independence generalises the well-known concept of *range restriction*. We first repeat the definition of the latter.

Definition 2.4 A clause in a program P is called *range restricted* iff every variable in the clause appears in a positive body-literal.
A program P is called *range restricted* iff all its clauses are range restricted.

Range restriction has been defined for more general formulas and/or programs and was used in other contexts. See e.g. [21] and [3] for its use in the context of integrity checking in relational and deductive databases. Two equivalent notions are *safety*, used by Ullman in [29] and *allowedness* (at the clause level), defined in [17] and important for avoiding floundering of negative goals. The limitation to range restricted programs is natural in many contexts. Moreover, [19] includes a procedure to transform a non range restricted program P into a range restricted program P' that has the following property: There is a one-to-one correspondence between Herbrand models of P and P' such that they coincide for all predicates in P.

The following proposition states that this important class of logic programs is a subclass of the language independent ones.

Proposition 2.5 Let P be a stratified program. If P is range restricted then P is language independent.

A simple program that is language independent, but *not* range restricted can be found in example 3.7.

2.2 Weak Stratification

In the next subsection, we present the main result of this paper. It states that the semantics of a language independent, stratified normal object logic program and the semantics of its vanilla meta-program are related in a sensible way. We consider the semantics of a (locally) stratified program to be described by its perfect Herbrand model. However, as was pointed out in section 1, the vanilla meta-program of a stratified object program is not (locally) stratified. We need the concept of *weak stratification*, introduced in [22] and [23]. Due to space restrictions, we cannot present the rather complex formal definitions here. We refer to [22] (which is limited to function-free programs) and [23], or to [20]. Below, we introduce the concept in an informal way, hoping that the reader will acquire an understanding of the issues involved, sufficient for following through the rest of the paper.

To decide whether a normal logic program P is *weakly stratified* and if so to determine its *weakly perfect* Herbrand model, one basically proceeds as follows. Consider all ground instances of clauses in P. Choose a set A of (ground) atoms such that the clause instances whose head is in this set constitute a definite logic program only containing atoms in the chosen set. If this is not possible, then the program is *not* weakly stratified and the construction fails. Otherwise, compute the least Herbrand model H of this (definite) partial program. Consider now the clause instances left. Eliminate clause instances with a body literal the atom of which belongs to A, not satisfied according to H. Simplify the remaining clause instances by deleting condition literals with atoms in A, satisfied according to H. Repeat the above construction on this new set of ground clauses. If this construction can be carried out until no clause instances are left, take the union on the computed least Herbrand models. This is the *weakly perfect* Herbrand model of P.

The following propositions can be proved:

Proposition 2.6 If P is a weakly stratified program, it has a unique weakly perfect Herbrand model.

Proposition 2.7 If P is a stratified program, it is weakly stratified and its perfect and weakly perfect Herbrand model coincide.

2.3   Vanilla Meta-Programs

We are now finally in a position where we can address the proper topic of this paper: the semantics of meta-programs. We set out with the following definitions:

Definition 2.8 The following normal program M is called *vanilla meta-interpreter:*
   $solve(empty) \leftarrow$
   $solve(x \& y) \leftarrow solve(x), solve(y)$
   $solve(\neg x) \leftarrow not\ solve(x)$
   $solve(x) \leftarrow clause(x, y), solve(y)$

Notice M is neither language independent, nor stratified (nor locally stratified). And these properties carry over to M_P-programs, defined as follows:

Definition 2.9 Let P be a normal program. Then M_P, the *vanilla meta-program associated to P* will be the normal program consisting of M together with a fact of the form
   $clause(A, \ldots \& B \& \ldots \& \neg C \& \ldots) \leftarrow$
for every clause $A \leftarrow \ldots, B, \ldots, not C, \ldots$ in P and a fact of the form
   $clause(A, empty) \leftarrow$
for every fact $A \leftarrow$ in P.

The following theorem shows that the concept of weak stratification has a very natural application in the realm of meta-programming.

Theorem 2.10 Let P be a stratified normal program. Then M_P, the vanilla meta-program associated to P, is weakly stratified.

We can now state our basic theorem.

Theorem 2.11 Let P be a stratified, language independent normal program and M_P its vanilla meta-program. Let H_P denote the perfect Herbrand model of P and H_{M_P} the weakly perfect Herbrand model of M_P. Then the following holds for every $p/r \in \mathcal{R}_P$:
$$\forall \bar{t} \in U_{M_P}{}^r : \; solve(p(\bar{t})) \in H_{M_P} \Longleftrightarrow \bar{t} \in U_P{}^r \; \& \; p(\bar{t}) \in H_P$$

3 Extensions

Theorem 2.11 is interesting because, for a large class of programs, it provides us with a reasonable semantics for non-ground vanilla meta-programming. However, it also shows that we do not seem to *gain* much by this kind of programming. Indeed, (the relevant part of) the meta-semantics can be *identified* with the object semantics. So, why going through the trouble of writing a meta-program in the first place? The answer lies of course in useful *extensions* of the vanilla interpreter (see e.g. [26] and further references given there). The following definitions capture the essential characteristics of many such extensions.

Definition 3.1 A normal program of the following form will be called *extended meta-interpreter*:
$$solve(empty, t_{11}, \ldots, t_{1n}) \leftarrow C_{11}, \ldots, C_{1m_1}$$
$$solve(x\&y, t_{21}, \ldots, t_{2n}) \leftarrow solve(x, t_{31}, \ldots, t_{3n}), solve(y, t_{41}, \ldots, t_{4n}),$$
$$C_{21}, \ldots, C_{2m_2}$$
$$solve(\neg x, t_{51}, \ldots, t_{5n}) \leftarrow not \; solve(x, t_{61}, \ldots, t_{6n}), C_{31}, \ldots, C_{3m_3}$$
$$solve(x, t_{71}, \ldots, t_{7n}) \leftarrow clause(x, y), solve(y, t_{81}, \ldots, t_{8n}), C_{41}, \ldots, C_{4m_4}$$
where the t_{ij}-terms are extra arguments of the *solve*-predicate and the C_{kl}-literals extra conditions, defined through a stratified program included in the extended meta-interpreter (but not containing *solve* or *clause*).

Definition 3.2 Let P be a normal program and E an extended meta-interpreter. Then E_P, the *E-extended meta-program associated to* P, will be the normal program consisting of E together with a fact of the form
$$clause(A, \ldots \& B \& \ldots \& \neg C \& \ldots) \leftarrow$$
for every clause $A \leftarrow \ldots, B, \ldots, not C, \ldots$ in P and a fact of the form
$$clause(A, empty) \leftarrow$$
for every fact $A \leftarrow$ in P.

As an example of this kind of meta-programming, we include the following program E, adapted from [26]. It builds proof trees for definite object level programs and queries.

Example 3.3

$$solve(empty, empty) \leftarrow$$
$$solve(x\&y, proofx\&proofy) \leftarrow solve(x, proofx), solve(y, proofy)$$
$$solve(x, x\ if\ proof) \leftarrow clause(x, y), solve(y, proof)$$

As is illustrated in [26], the proof trees thus constructed can be used as a basis for explanation facilities in expert systems. This example can be extended to deal with normal programs by adding a clause like

$$solve(\neg x, NAF) \leftarrow not\ solve(x)$$

but this would require more complex meta-interpreters where a vanilla *solve* is also included. This presents no fundamental difficulties, but we will not explicitly address this case in what follows.

We have the following proposition:

Proposition 3.4 Let P be a stratified normal program. Let E be an extended meta-interpreter. Then E_P, the E-extended meta-program associated to P, is weakly stratified.

We include the following result from [5]:

Proposition 3.5 Let P be a definite, language independent program. Let M_P be the vanilla and E_P be an E-extended meta-program associated to P. Then the following holds for every $p/r \in \mathcal{R}_P$:
$$\forall \bar{t} \in U_{E_P}{}^r : (\exists \bar{s} \in U_{E_P}{}^n : solve(p(\bar{t}), \bar{s}) \in H_{E_P})$$
$$\Downarrow$$
$$\bar{t} \in U_{M_P}{}^r\ \&\ solve(p(\bar{t})) \in H_{M_P}\quad (\Leftrightarrow \bar{t} \in U_P{}^r\ \&\ p(\bar{t}) \in H_P)$$

The question now is: Can this result be generalised to the class of language independent, stratified normal object programs and their extended meta-programs? It is not difficult to present examples showing that this is *not* the case.

Example 3.6

P: $p \leftarrow not\ q$
$\quad q$

Notice P is language independent and (trivially) range restricted.
E: First 3 clauses as in M (definition 2.8)
$\quad solve(x) \leftarrow clause(x, y), solve(y), good(y)$
$\quad good(\neg q)$

We have $p \notin H_P$ and yet $solve(p) \in H_{E_P}$.

Example 3.7

P: $p(x, y) \leftarrow r(x), not\ q(x)$
$\quad q(a) \leftarrow h(a)$
$\quad r(a)$
$\quad h(a)$

Notice P is language independent, but *not* range restricted.

E: First 3 clauses as in M (definition 2.8)

$$solve(x) \leftarrow clause(x, y), solve(y), not\ bad(y)$$
$$bad(h(a))$$

We have $solve(p(a, empty)) \in H_{E_P}$ (and, of course, $(a, empty) \notin U_P{}^2$).

However, we *do* have the following result:

Proposition 3.8 Let P be a *range restricted*, stratified normal program and let E_P be an extended meta-program associated to P. Let H_{E_P} be its weakly perfect Herbrand model. Then the following holds for every $p/r \in \mathcal{R}_P$:

$$\forall \bar{t} \in U_{E_P}{}^r : (\exists \bar{s} \in U_{E_P}{}^n : solve(p(\bar{t}), \bar{s}) \in H_{E_P}) \implies \bar{t} \in U_P{}^r$$

4 Amalgamation

In this section, we present a semantics for different kinds of amalgamated programs. Such programs contain symbols which denote predicates as well as functions. We give a justification for this practice in subsection 4.1. It leads to an increased flexibility in considering meta-programs with several layers. In fact, as shown in subsection 4.3 below, we can now deal with an unlimited amount of meta-layers.

4.1 A Justification for Overloading

Although this was not made explicit in e.g. [17], an underlying assumption of first order logic is that the class of functors and the class of predicate symbols of a first order language $\mathcal{L}$, are disjoint (see e.g. [8]). So, if we aim to extend our results to amalgamated programs —without introducing any kind of naming to avoid the overloading— we need to verify whether the constructions, definitions and results on the foundations of logic programming are still valid if the function and predicate symbols of the language overlap.

We have checked the formalisation and proofs in [17] in detail, starting from the assumption that the set of functors and the set of predicate symbols may overlap. We found that none of the results become invalid. Of course, under this assumption, there is in general no way to distinguish well-formed formulas from terms. They as well have a non-empty intersection. But, this causes no problem in the definition of pre-interpretations, variable- and term-assignments and interpretations (see [17], p.12). It is clear however, that a same syntactical object can be both term and formula and can therefore be given two different meanings, one under the pre-interpretation and variable-assignment, the other under the corresponding interpretation and variable-assignment. But this causes no confusion on the level of truth-assignment to well-formed formulas under an interpretation and a variable-assignment ([17], p.12–13). This definition performs a complete parsing of the well-formed formulas, making sure that the appropriate assignments are applied for each syntactic substructure. In particular, it should be noted that no paradoxes can be formulated in these languages, since each formula obtains a unique truth-value under every interpretation and variable-assignment.

On the level of declarative semantics, the main results both for definite programs —the existence of a least Herbrand model and its characterisation as the least fixpoint of T_P ([17], Prop.6.1, Th.6.2, Th.6.5)— and for (weakly) stratified normal programs —the existence of a (weakly) perfect Herbrand model for P ([17], Cor.14.8; [1], [24], [22])— remain valid in the extended languages. Thus, the amalgamated programs we aim to study can be given a unique semantics.

4.2   Amalgamated Vanilla Meta-Programs

The first extension we consider is completely straightforward: We include the object-program in the resulting meta-program.

Definition 4.1 Let P be a normal program and M_P its associated vanilla meta-program (see definition 2.9). Then we call the textual combination $P + M_P$ of P and M_P the *amalgamated vanilla meta-program associated to* P.

Proposition 4.2 Let P be a stratified normal program, then $P + M_P$, its associated amalgamated vanilla meta-program, is weakly stratified.

The next theorem follows immediately:

Theorem 4.3 Let P be a stratified, language independent normal program, M_P its vanilla and $P + M_P$ its amalgamated vanilla meta-program. Let H_P, H_{M_P} and H_{P+M_P} denote their (weakly) perfect Herbrand models. Then the following holds for every $p/r \in \mathcal{R}_P$:

$$\forall \bar{t} \in U_{P+M_P}{}^r : solve(p(\bar{t})) \in H_{P+M_P} \iff p(\bar{t}) \in H_{P+M_P}$$
$$\forall \bar{t} \in U_{P+M_P}{}^r : solve(p(\bar{t})) \in H_{P+M_P} \iff \bar{t} \in U_P{}^r \,\&\, p(\bar{t}) \in H_P$$
$$\forall \bar{t} \in U_{P+M_P}{}^r : solve(p(\bar{t})) \in H_{P+M_P} \iff \bar{t} \in U_{M_P}{}^r \,\&\, solve(p(\bar{t})) \in H_{M_P}$$

Considering *extended amalgamated meta-programs* is straightforward. We will not do this explicitly and only illustrate by an example the extra programming power one can gain in this way.

Example 4.4 In applications based on the proof tree recording program from example 3.3, it may be the case that users are not interested in branches for particular predicates. To reflect this, clauses of the form:

$$solve(p(x), some\_info) \leftarrow p(x)$$

can be added (combined with extra measures to avoid also using the standard clause for these cases).

4.3   Meta2-Programs

In this subsection, we consider meta-programs that include *clause*-facts for the *solve*-clauses themselves, thus allowing the use of an unlimited amount of meta-layers. Programming of this kind is relevant in e.g. the contexts of reasoning about reasoning (see e.g. [15]) and proof-plan construction and manipulation (see e.g. [11]).

Definition 4.5 Let P be a normal program. Then $M^2{}_P$, the *vanilla meta2-program associated to P*, will be the program M (see definition 2.8) together with the following clause:

$clause(clause(x, y), empty) \leftarrow clause(x, y)$

and a fact of the form

$clause(A, \dots \& B \& \dots \& \neg C \& \dots) \leftarrow$

for every clause $A \leftarrow \dots, B, \dots, notC, \dots$ in P or M and a fact of the form

$clause(A, empty) \leftarrow$

for every fact $A \leftarrow$ in P or M.

We have the following theorems:

Theorem 4.6 Let P be a stratified normal program. Then $M^2{}_P$, the vanilla meta2-program associated to P, is weakly stratified.

Theorem 4.7 Let P be a stratified, language independent normal program and $M^2{}_P$ its vanilla meta2-program. Let H_P denote the perfect Herbrand model of P and $H_{M^2{}_P}$ the weakly perfect Herbrand model of $M^2{}_P$. Then the following holds:

$\forall t \in U_{M^2{}_P} : \ solve(solve(t)) \in H_{M^2{}_P} \iff solve(t) \in H_{M^2{}_P}$

Moreover, the following holds for every $p/r \in \mathcal{R}_P$:

$\forall \bar{t} \in U_{M^2{}_P}{}^r : \ solve(p(\bar{t})) \in H_{M^2{}_P} \iff \bar{t} \in U_P{}^r \ \& \ p(\bar{t}) \in H_P$

Various amalgamated and/or extended meta2-programs can be considered. We will not do this explicitly and conclude this section with the following proposition and example:

Proposition 4.8 Let P be a stratified, language independent normal program and let $P + M^2{}_P$ be its *amalgamated vanilla meta2-program*. Let PM be a program textually identical to $P + M^2{}_P$, except that an arbitrary number of atoms A in the bodies of clauses in the P-part of it have been replaced by $solve(A)$. Then the following holds:

$H_{P+M^2{}_P} = H_{PM}$

Example 4.9 In this framework, we can address interesting examples from [2]. Consider e.g. the following clause, telling us that a person is innocent when he is not found guilty:

$innocent(x) \leftarrow person(x), not \ solve(guilty(x))$

Of course, such possibilities only become really interesting when using extended meta-interpreters — involving e.g. an extra *solve*-argument limiting the resources available for proving a person's guilt.

5   Discussion and Conclusion

We have presented a sensible semantics for untyped vanilla meta-programs, also catering for a limited form of amalgamation. We showed that such meta-programs associated to stratified object programs are weakly stratified. In this way, we have drawn attention to a class of programs for which the notions of weak stratification and weakly perfect Herbrand model seem to provide a very natural specification of their semantics. Moreover, we conjecture that most or all results presented in this paper can be extended to meta-programs associated to *weakly* stratified *object* programs.

It should be noted that Prolog meta-predicates, such as *var*/1, *assert*/1, *retract*/1 and *call*/2 are not included in our language. A thorough discussion of the problems related to these predicates is given in [13], [12] and [18].

Not having these predicates in our language certainly puts some limitation on the obtained expressiveness. Observe, however, that in the typed non-ground representation proposed in [13], no alternative for *var*/1 was introduced either and that the declarative *var*/1 predicate introduced in the ground representation approach of [13] provides no direct support for the sort of functionalities (e.g. control and coroutining facilities) that the *var*/1 predicate in Prolog is typically used for. For the *assert*/1 and *retract*/1 predicates, the solution of [12], to represent dynamic theories as terms in the meta-program, can as well be applied in our approach.

Next, observe that the condition of range restriction —which is the practical, verifiable, sufficient condition for language independence our approach was mostly designed for— is strongly related to typing. Conversely, typing can often be expressed by means of additional atoms that are added in the bodies of clauses, expressing the range of each variable. (See e.g. [8] and [17].) In this perspective, our approach is not so different from the typed non-ground representation in [13], except that we stick to the untyped logic programming syntax.

With respect to the extension to amalgamated programs, we should point out that our use of overloading is very strongly related to the approach proposed in [25]. The main difference we can see at this time is that Richards adds each sentence as a new constant to the language, where we represent it as a new term. Here as well, more work is needed to clarify the relative merits of both approaches. The relation to the framework in [27] is much harder to investigate, since here a totally different approach based on a — much more powerful, but also more complex— explicit naming mechanism for formulas is proposed. The work described in [4] is also relevant here. It enables more powerful forms of amalgamation than we can handle (e.g. $solve(X) \leftarrow X$). However, the semantics required to support this, is a less immediate extension of the common first-order logic semantics.

Finally, it can be noted that from an operational point of view, untyped vanilla-type meta-interpreters are unproblematic in most circumstances even for object programs which are not language independent. It seems very likely that, for definite programs, this can be shown at a semantical level by a straightforward formalisation in an extended Herbrand framework as the one presented in [9]. Moreover, [28] recently extended [9], drawing from work on constructive negation, and in this way provided a setting for addressing normal object and meta-programs.

Other topics for further research include:

- possible extensions and/or alternative characterisations of the concept *language independence* and its relationship to *domain independence* and related notions ([6])

- an extension of our approach to arbitrary normal object programs in the context of well-founded semantics ([30])

- an investigation of other extensions, variants and/or applications of the meta-interpreter, as they can be found in the literature

Acknowledgements

We thank Michael Codish for interesting discussions on extended Herbrand model semantics. We also appreciate several helpful remarks made by anonymous referees.

This work was partially supported by ESPRIT BRA COMPULOG. Both authors are supported by the Belgian National Fund for Scientific Research.

References

[1] K. R. Apt, H. Blair, and A. Walker. Towards a theory of declarative knowledge. In J. Minker, editor, *Foundations of Deductive Databases and Logic Programming*, pages 89–148. Morgan-Kaufmann, 1988.

[2] K. A. Bowen and R. A. Kowalski. Amalgamating language and metalanguage in logic programming. In K. L. Clark and S.-A. Tärnlund, editors, *Logic Programming*, pages 153–172. Academic Press, 1982.

[3] F. Bry, R. Manthey, and B. Martens. Integrity verification in knowledge bases. In A. Voronkov, editor, *Proceedings 1st and 2nd Russian Conference on Logic Programming*, pages 114–139. Springer-Verlag, LNAI 592, 1992.

[4] W. Chen, M. Kifer, and D. S. Warren. HiLog: A first-order semantics for higher-order logic programming constructs. In L. Lusk and R. A. Overbeek, editors, *Proceedings NACLP'89*, pages 1090–1114, Cleveland, Ohio, October 1989. The MIT Press.

[5] D. De Schreye and B. Martens. A sensible least Herbrand semantics for untyped vanilla meta-programming and its extension to a limited

form of amalgamation. In *Proceedings Meta'92*, Uppsala, June 1992. Springer-Verlag, LNCS.

[6] R Demolombe. Syntactical characterization of a subset of domain independent formulas. *Journal of the ACM*, 39(1):71–94, 1992.

[7] M. Denecker, D. De Schreye, and Y. D. Willems. Terms in logic programs : a problem with their semantics and its effect on the programming methodology. *CCAI, Journal for the Integrated Study of Artificial Intelligence, Cognitive Science and Applied Epistemology*, 7(3 & 4):363–383, 1990.

[8] H. B. Enderton. *A Mathematical Introduction to Logic*. Academic Press, 1972.

[9] M. Falaschi, G. Levi, M. Martelli, and C. Palamidessi. Declarative modeling of the operational behaviour of logic programs. *Theoretical Computer Science*, 69:289–318, 1989.

[10] M. Fitting. *First-Order Logic and Automated Theorem Proving*. Springer-Verlag, 1990.

[11] F. Giunchiglia and P. Traverso. Plan formation and execution in a uniform architecture of declarative metatheories. In M. Bruynooghe, editor, *Proceedings Meta'90*, pages 306–322, Leuven, April 1990.

[12] P. M. Hill and J. W. Lloyd. Meta-programming for dynamic knowledge bases. Technical Report CS-88-18, Computer Science Department, University of Bristol, Great-Britain, 1988.

[13] P. M. Hill and J. W. Lloyd. Analysis of meta-programs. In H. D. Abramson and M. H. Rogers, editors, *Proceedings Meta'88*, pages 23–51. MIT Press, 1989.

[14] P. M. Hill and J. W. Lloyd. The Gödel report. Technical Report TR-91-02, Computer Science Department, University of Bristol, Great-Britain, March 1991. (Revised September 1991).

[15] J. S. Kim and R. A. Kowalski. An application of amalgamated logic to multi-agent belief. In M. Bruynooghe, editor, *Proceedings Meta'90*, pages 272–283, Leuven, April 1990.

[16] R. A. Kowalski. Problems and promises of computational logic. In J. W. Lloyd, editor, *Proceedings of the Esprit Symposium on Computational Logic*, pages 1–36. Springer-Verlag, November 1990.

[17] J. W. Lloyd. *Foundations of Logic Programming*. Springer-Verlag, 1987.

[18] J. W. Lloyd. Directions for meta-programming. In *Proceedings FGCS'88*, pages 609–617. ICOT, 1988.

[19] R. Manthey and F. Bry. SATCHMO: a theorem prover implemented in Prolog. In E. Lusk and R. Overbeek, editors, *Proceedings CADE'88, LNCS 310*, pages 415–434. Springer-Verlag, May 1988.

[20] B. Martens and D. De Schreye. A perfect Herbrand semantics for untyped vanilla meta-programming. Technical Report CW149, Departement Computerwetenschappen, K.U.Leuven, Belgium, July 1992.

[21] J.-M. Nicolas. Logic for improving integrity checking in relational databases. *Acta Informatica*, 18(3):227–253, 1982.

[22] H. Przymusinska and T. C. Przymusinski. Weakly perfect model semantics for logic programs. In R. A. Kowalski and K. A. Bowen, editors, *Proceedings ICSLP'88*, pages 1106–1120, 1988.

[23] H. Przymusinska and T. C. Przymusinski. Weakly stratified logic programs. *Fundamenta Informaticae*, XIII:51–65, 1990.

[24] T. C. Przymusinski. On the declarative semantics of deductive databases and logic programs. In J. Minker, editor, *Foundations of Deductive Databases and Logic Programming*, pages 193–216. Morgan-Kaufmann, 1988.

[25] B. Richards. A point of reference. *Synthesis*, 28:431–445, 1974.

[26] L. Sterling and E. Shapiro. *The Art of Prolog*. MIT Press, 1986.

[27] V. S. Subrahmanian. A simple formulation of the theory of metalogic programming. In H. D. Abramson and M. H. Rogers, editors, *Proceedings Meta'88*, pages 65–101. MIT Press, 1989.

[28] D. Turi. Extending S-models to logic programs with negation. In K. Furukawa, editor, *Proceedings ICLP'91*, pages 397–411, Paris, June 1991. The MIT Press.

[29] J. D. Ullman. *Database and Knowledge-Base Systems, Volume 1*. Computer Science Press, 1988.

[30] A. Van Gelder, K. A. Ross, and J. S. Schlipf. The well-founded semantics for general logic programs. *Journal of the ACM*, 38(3):620–650, 1991.

Meta-programming through A Truth Predicate

Taisuke SATO

Electrotechnical Laboratory
1-1-4 Umezono Tsukuba Ibaraki Japan 305
email: sato@etl.go.jp

Abstract

We investigate a self-referential truth predicate and its extension to a meta-interpreter for first order programs which is complete w.r.t. three-valued logical consequence semantics. First we define, in three-valued logic, a truth predicate $t_r(\ulcorner \varphi \urcorner, \theta^*)$ where $\ulcorner \varphi \urcorner$ is the code representing the structure of a formula φ and θ^* an environment assigning values to the free variables in φ. t_r will be (i) executable (ii) able to treat arbitrary formulae with arbitrary quantifications and (iii) self-referential. It turns out that this self-referential property combined with negation gives rise to paradoxes such as (a variant of) Russell's paradox, and causes the inconsistency of t_r in two-valued logic. We then extend t_r to a meta-interpreter for first order programs. It is proved, based on an equivalence preserving transformation system, that the extended one becomes a complete interpreter, i.e., it can compute every three-valued logical consequence of a first order program **P** by making use of the code of **P**.

1. Introduction

Interpreters, compilers and debuggers, in any programming language, manipulate programs as data. Programs of this type are often called metaprograms [Bo82, Hi88, Ma88, Ni90]. In logic programming, the most basic metaprogram is the "vanilla interpreter" [Bo82, Hi88].

> solve(true)← true
> solve(A&B)← solve(A)∧solve(B)
> solve(A)← clause(A←B)∧solve(B)

A *truth predicate*, t_r, is the logical counterpart of a metaprogram. A truth predicate satisfies

$$t_r(\ulcorner \varphi \urcorner) \leftrightarrow \varphi$$

where $\ulcorner \varphi \urcorner$ is the code representing the structure of a sentence (a formula without free variables) φ. A truth predicate talks about the truth value of sentences in terms of their codes [Fe84, Tu90].

Although metaprograms and a truth predicate are distinct notions, in the context of logic programming, they appear rather similar. In this paper, we present a self-referential truth predicate and its extension to a complete interpreter for first order programs[1]. We show that a logic program interpreter can be derived from a truth predicate, a fact that seems to have gone unnoticed so far.

In Section 2, after preliminaries, we define a three-valued truth predicate t_r. The departure from two-valued logic is forced upon us by Tarski's No-Truth Definition Theorem[2] denying the existence of a two-valued truth predicate. There are already many "logical" truth predicates that are semantically defined by transfinite induction, or syntactically defined by axioms or axiom schemata [Fe84, Kr75, Pe85, Tu90]. What makes t_r different from most of them is that it is a computer program.

As a program, on the other hand, t_r can, unlike the predicates "solve" and "demo" [Bo82, Hi88], explicitly manipulate quantified formulae as data. t_r is also self-referential (takes its own code as data). We will observe, however, that this self-referential property incurs paradoxes, which leads to the inconsistency of t_r in two-valued logic.

In Section 3, we extend the truth predicate with clauses for user defined predicates, and prove that the extension yields a meta-interpreter for first order programs which is sound and complete w.r.t. three-valued logical consequence semantics. It thus provides us with a way of logical meta-programming. Section 4 contains summary and related work. The reader is assumed to be familiar with logic programming and the rudiments of symbolic logic [Ll84, Sh73].

2. A truth predicate with an environment

2.1 Preliminaries[3]

We define a truth predicate with an environment (see **2.3** for its definition). Although it might be better termed as "satisfiability predicate", we opt for the name "truth predicate" for the sake of familiarity. Before proceeding, we introduce some terminology (as for syntactic conventions, see footnote 3 at the end of this paper).

Our logic is Kleene's (strong) three-valued logic [Fi85] whose vocabulary comprises denumerably many variables, finitely many function symbols, and finitely many predicate symbols. We henceforth use Σ to refer to the set of function symbols in our language. There is nothing special about three-valued logic except that formulae may take **u** (undefined) as a third truth values as well as **t** (truth) and **f** (falsehood). For example, negation obeys ~**t**=**f**, ~**f**=**t** and ~**u**=**u**. We define A∨B=**u** iff (if and only if) neither A nor B is **t**, and either A or B is **u**. A∧B is defined as ~(~A∨~B), A→B as ~A∨B. ∃xA and ∀xA are treated as an infinite disjunction and an infinite conjunction. "Strong biconditional" A⇔B is defined as A⇔B = **t** iff A=B, and = **f** otherwise. We say that a formula φ is *regular* if it does not contain "⇔". We place an ordering on truth values by **t**≥**u** and **f**≥**u**. Regular formulae are monotonic under this ordering [Sa91].

An interpretation **M** is defined as usual except that predicates may take the value **u**. We stipulate that the equality predicate = is always interpreted as the two-valued identity. For a set Γ of first order sentences, we say **M** is a model of Γ if every sentence in Γ is true in **M**. For a formula φ, three-valued logical consequence[4] "$\models_3$" is defined by

$$\Gamma \models_3 \varphi \qquad \text{iff} \qquad \forall \varphi \text{ is true in } \mathbf{M} \text{ for every model } \mathbf{M} \text{ of } \Gamma$$

where $\forall \varphi$ is the universal closure of φ.

A *first order program* is a set of predicate definitions. A *predicate definition* is a first order formula of the form $p(x) \Leftrightarrow F[x]$ such that $p(x)$ is an atomic formula and F an arbitrary regular formula with $x \supseteq Fvar(F)$. Every predicate definition, even $p(X) \Leftrightarrow \sim p(X)$, is consistent in three-valued logic [Fi85].

A predicate definition is nothing more than the iff form [Cl78] considered in three-valued logic. To write a predicate definition for p, write definite clauses $\{C_1,...,C_n\}$ for p, with their bodies being arbitrary formulae. Then construct the iff form $p(x) \leftrightarrow F[x]$ and replace the top level "$\leftrightarrow$" with "$\Leftrightarrow$" to get the predicate definition for p. We use a notation **iff**($\{C_1,...,C_n\}$) to denote the resulting $p(x) \Leftrightarrow F[x]$. For notational convenience, we present first order programs in clausal form whenever the context is clear.

We assume throughout this paper that the meaning of = is specified by $E(\Sigma)$, Clark's equational theory [Cl78, Ku89]. It is defined as

$$E(\Sigma) = \{ \ f(x)=f(y) \rightarrow x=y, \ f(x) \neq g(y) \ (f \neq g),$$
$$x \neq t[x] \ (x \text{ is a variable, } t \text{ properly contains } x \ ) \mid f,g \in \Sigma \ \}.$$

$E(\Sigma)$ deductively simulates the unification algorithm.

2.2 A coding function

To judge the truth value of a sentence φ, we have to apply some coding function to φ to obtain the code $\ulcorner \varphi \urcorner$ of φ and then apply the truth predicate to it. Needless to say, there is more than one way of coding. Assuming that two function symbols for list, nil/0 and [•|•]/2, exist in Σ (the notation follows Prolog's convention), we adopt the following coding scheme. First we assign a unique flat ground list $\ulcorner E \urcorner$ to each basic symbol (variables, function symbols, predicate symbols and logical symbols) in such a way that for no two $\ulcorner E \urcorner$s, one is part of the other. We then inductively define $\ulcorner E \urcorner$ for terms and formulae by

$$\ulcorner f(t_1,...,t_n) \urcorner = [\ulcorner f \urcorner, \ulcorner t_1 \urcorner,...,\ulcorner t_n \urcorner]$$
$$\ulcorner \varphi_1 \wedge \varphi_2 \urcorner = [\ulcorner \wedge \urcorner, \ulcorner \varphi_1 \urcorner, \ulcorner \varphi_2 \urcorner]$$
$$\ulcorner \exists V \varphi \urcorner = [\ulcorner \exists \urcorner, \ulcorner V \urcorner, \ulcorner \varphi \urcorner]$$

and so on, similar to the Go"del numbering. Since the depth of $\ulcorner E \urcorner$ is larger than that of E, we will never have $\ulcorner E \urcorner = E$.

2.3   Substitution and evaluation

By a *substitution* we mean a list $\theta = [[X_1|s_1],...,[X_n|s_n]]$ $(n{\geq}0)$ where the X_i's are variables and the s_i's terms. $E\theta$, the result of θ applied to an expression E, is obtained from E by replacing each free variable X in E such that $X{\in}\{X_1,...,X_n\}$ with a term s_i if $X_i{=}X$ and for no X_j $(j{>}i)$, $X_j{\neq}X$. Note that our definition is non-standard and allows substitutions like $[[X|Y],[X|Z]]$ and $[[X|X],[Y|Y]]$ (the former is equivalent to $[[X|Y]]$ whereas the latter is the identity mapping).

For a substitution $\theta{=}[[X_1|s_1],...,[X_n|s_n]]$, define $\theta*$ by

$$\theta* = [[\ulcorner X_1 \urcorner |s_1],...,[\ulcorner X_n \urcorner |s_n]]$$

and call it an *environment*. An environment is a list holding the value of indentifiers $\ulcorner X_1 \urcorner ,...,\ulcorner X_n \urcorner$.

Getting back to our truth predicate, it uses an evaluation predicate eval/3 as an auxiliary predicate to decode a coded term such as $[\ulcorner f \urcorner, \ulcorner X \urcorner]$ back to the original form f(X) (modulo renaming). We require that for any term t and substitution $\theta{=}[[X_1|s_1],...,[X_n|s_n]]$ such that $\{X_1,...,X_n\}{\supseteq}\mathsf{Fvar}(t)$,

$$E(\Sigma){\cup}E_{val} \models_3 eval(\ulcorner t \urcorner,\theta*,Y){\Leftrightarrow}Y{=}t\theta$$

where E_{val} denotes a program defining eval/3. E_{val} is constructed as follows. First write a program A_{ssoc} to define an auxiliary predicate assoc/3 such that for a substitution $\theta{=}[[X_1|s_1],...,[X_n|s_n]]$ and $X{\in}\{X_1,...,X_n\}$,

$$E(\Sigma){\cup}A_{ssoc} \models_3 assoc(\ulcorner X \urcorner,\theta*,Y){\Leftrightarrow}Y{=}X\theta$$

Then define eval/3 using assoc/3. If, for example, the only function symbols are nil/0 and $[\bullet|\bullet]$/2 (generalization is easy), the defining clauses for eval/3 are

$$eval(\ulcorner nil \urcorner, \theta*,Y){\leftarrow} Y{=}[]$$
$$eval([\ulcorner cons \urcorner,A,B], \theta*,Y){\leftarrow} eval(A,\theta*,C){\wedge}eval(B,\theta*,D){\wedge}Y{=}[C|D]$$
$$eval(X, \theta*,Y){\leftarrow} X{\neq}[]{\wedge}{\sim}\exists A,B(X{=}[\ulcorner cons \urcorner,A,B]){\wedge}assoc(X,\theta*,Y)$$

Put these clauses together with A_{ssoc}, and take its iff form to obtain E_{val}.

We introduce the substitution program S_{ub} for later use. It is the iff form of a definite clause program for a substitution predicate sub/4 such that, for an expression E,

$$E(\Sigma){\cup}S_{ub} \models_3 sub(\ulcorner t \urcorner,\ulcorner X \urcorner,\ulcorner E[...,X,...] \urcorner,Y){\Leftrightarrow}Y{=}\ulcorner E[...,\ulcorner t \urcorner,...] \urcorner$$

2.4 The truth predicate t_r

We are now in a position to define t_r, a truth predicate for regular formulae built up from function symbols in Σ and predicate symbols from $\{=, t_r\}$. It is self-referential and hence can talk about itself. We present t_r in clausal form.

eq: $t_r([\ulcorner = \urcorner, X_1, X_2], E_{nv}) \leftarrow eval(X_1, E_{nv}, Y_1) \wedge eval(X_2, E_{nv}, Y_2) \wedge Y_1 = Y_2$

self: $t_r([\ulcorner t_r \urcorner, X_1, X_2], E_{nv}) \leftarrow eval(X_1, E_{nv}, Y_1) \wedge eval(X_2, E_{nv}, Y_2) \wedge t_r(Y_1, Y_2)$

neg: $t_r([\ulcorner \sim \urcorner, F], E_{nv}) \leftarrow \sim t_r(F, E_{nv})$

and: $t_r([\ulcorner \wedge \urcorner, F_1, F_2], E_{nv}) \leftarrow t_r(F_1, E_{nv}) \wedge t_r(F_2, E_{nv})$

exq: $t_r([\ulcorner \exists \urcorner, X, F], E_{nv}) \leftarrow t_r(F, [[X|Y]| E_{nv}])$

Put $T_{ruth} = \mathbf{iff}(\{eq, self, neg, and, exq\})$, i.e. the iff form of a clausal program comprising above five clauses ("$\vee$" and "$\forall$" are taken care of by $\varphi_1 \vee \varphi_2 \Leftrightarrow \sim(\sim\varphi_1 \wedge \sim\varphi_2)$ and $\forall V \varphi \Leftrightarrow \sim\exists V \sim \varphi$ respectively).

[Theorem 2.1]
Let $\theta = [[X_1|s_1],...,[X_n|s_n]]$ ($n \geq 0$) be a substitution and φ a regular formula containing no predicates other than = and t_r. Suppose $\{X_1,...,X_n\} \supseteq Fvar(\varphi)$ and every s_i ($1 \leq i \leq n$) is free for X_i in φ (this is true if $s_i = X_i$). Then we have

$$E(\Sigma) \cup E_{val} \cup T_{ruth} \models_3 t_r(\ulcorner \varphi \urcorner, \theta^*) \Leftrightarrow \varphi\theta$$

[Proof] By induction on the complexity of φ. Note that all the heads of eq, self, neg, and, exq are mutually ununifiable. We show two cases (other cases are similar). Put $\theta = [[X_1|s_1],...,[X_n|s_n]]$. When φ is an atom, say $s=t$, we have $\ulcorner \varphi \urcorner = \ulcorner s=t \urcorner = [\ulcorner = \urcorner, \ulcorner s \urcorner, \ulcorner t \urcorner]$ and from $\{X_1,...,X_n\} \supseteq Fvar(s=t)$,

$E(\Sigma) \cup E_{val} \cup T_{ruth} \models_3 t_r([\ulcorner = \urcorner, \ulcorner s \urcorner, \ulcorner t \urcorner], \theta^*)$
       $\Leftrightarrow \exists Y_1, Y_2\{eval(\ulcorner s \urcorner, \theta^*, Y_1) \wedge eval(\ulcorner t \urcorner, \theta^*, Y_2) \wedge Y_1 = Y_2\}$
       $\Leftrightarrow \exists Y_1, Y_2\{Y_1 = s\theta \wedge Y_2 = t\theta \wedge Y_1 = Y_2\}$
       $\Leftrightarrow s\theta = t\theta$
       $\Leftrightarrow (s=t)\theta$

In the case of $\exists V \varphi$, suppose $\{X_1,...,X_n\} \supseteq Fvar(\exists V \varphi)$ and every s_i ($1 \leq i \leq n$) is free for X_i in $\exists V \varphi$. We see

$E(\Sigma) \cup E_{val} \cup T_{ruth} \models_3 t_r(\ulcorner \exists V \varphi \urcorner, \theta^*)$
       $\Leftrightarrow \exists Y t_r(\ulcorner \varphi \urcorner, [[\ulcorner V \urcorner|Y]|\theta^*]) \Leftrightarrow \exists Y t_r(\ulcorner \varphi \urcorner, \theta'^*)$

where $\theta'=[[V/Y] \mid \theta]$. Without losing generality, we assume that Y is a fresh variable and does not appear in θ. On the other hand, it is evident that $\{V,X_1,...,X_n\}\supseteq Fvar(\varphi)$ and Y is free for V in φ. So by applying induction hypothesis to θ' and φ, we conclude $E(\Sigma)\cup E_{val}\cup T_{ruth} \models_3 t_r(\ulcorner\varphi\urcorner,\theta'^*) \Leftrightarrow \varphi\theta'$. Now

$$\Leftrightarrow \exists Y(\varphi\theta') \qquad \text{/* } \theta' \text{ replaces every free occurrence of V in } \varphi \text{ with Y. */}$$
$$= (\exists Y\varphi[Y/V])\theta \qquad \text{/* } Fvar(\exists Y\varphi[Y/V]) = Fvar(\exists V\varphi) \text{ and every } s_i \ (1\leq i\leq n)$$
$$\text{is free for } X_i \text{ in } \exists Y\varphi[Y/V]. \text{ */}$$
$$\Leftrightarrow (\exists V\varphi)\theta \qquad \text{Q.E.D.}$$

[Corollary 2.1] (three-valued truth predicate)
Let φ be a regular sentence. Suppose that no predicates other than = and t_r appear in φ.

$$E(\Sigma)\cup E_{val}\cup T_{ruth} \models_3 t_r(\ulcorner\varphi\urcorner,[]) \Leftrightarrow \varphi$$

[Proof] Set n=0 in Theorem 2.1   Q.E.D.

2.5 Paradoxes

Due to the "self" clause and "neg" clause in its definition, t_r is potentially paradoxical. We demonstrate that paradoxes actually do emerge from the definition of t_r. Consider a program T'= **iff**({self, neg}). Define **R** by

$$\mathbf{R} = \sim t_r(X, [[\ulcorner X\urcorner \mid X]])$$

[Proposition 2.1]
Put $\varphi = t_r(\ulcorner\mathbf{R}\urcorner, [[\ulcorner X\urcorner \mid \ulcorner\mathbf{R}\urcorner]])$. φ satisfies $E(\Sigma)\cup E_{val}\cup T' \models_3 \varphi\Leftrightarrow\sim\varphi$

[Proof] $E(\Sigma)\cup E_{val}\cup T' \models_3 t_r(\ulcorner\mathbf{R}\urcorner,[[\ulcorner X\urcorner\mid X]])\Leftrightarrow\mathbf{R}$ is immediate from Theorem 2.1. Substitute $\ulcorner\mathbf{R}\urcorner$ for X on both sides. We have $E(\Sigma)\cup E_{val}\cup T' \models_3 t_r(\ulcorner\mathbf{R}\urcorner,[[\ulcorner X\urcorner \mid \ulcorner\mathbf{R}\urcorner]])$ $\Leftrightarrow \sim t_r(\ulcorner\mathbf{R}\urcorner,[[\ulcorner X\urcorner \mid \ulcorner\mathbf{R}\urcorner]])$.   Q.E.D.

[Corollary 2.2]
$E(\Sigma)\cup E_{val}\cup T'$ and $E(\Sigma)\cup E_{val}\cup T_{ruth}$ are inconsistent in two-valued logic.

[Proof] There's no two-valued model satisfying $E(\Sigma)\cup E_{val}\cup T'$.   Q.E.D.

Proposition 2.1 expresses (a variant of) Russell's paradox. Since $\mathbf{R} = \sim t_r(X,[[\ulcorner X\urcorner \mid X]])$ is a formula whose free variable is X, it is thought to define a set $\{X \mid \mathbf{R}\}$ through the equivalences

$$Y\in\{X\mid\mathbf{R}\} \quad \text{iff} \quad \mathbf{R}[Y/X] \quad \text{iff} \quad t_r(\ulcorner\mathbf{R}\urcorner,[[\ulcorner X\urcorner \mid Y]])$$

It then follows from $t_r(\ulcorner\mathbf{R}\urcorner,[[\ulcorner X\urcorner \mid \ulcorner\mathbf{R}\urcorner]])\Leftrightarrow\sim t_r(\ulcorner\mathbf{R}\urcorner,[[\ulcorner X\urcorner \mid \ulcorner\mathbf{R}\urcorner]])$ that

$$\ulcorner\mathbf{R}\urcorner \in \{X|\mathbf{R}\} \quad \text{iff} \quad t_r(\ulcorner\mathbf{R}\urcorner, [[\ulcorner X\urcorner | \ulcorner\mathbf{R}\urcorner]])$$
$$\text{iff} \quad \sim t_r(\ulcorner\mathbf{R}\urcorner, [[\ulcorner X\urcorner | \ulcorner\mathbf{R}\urcorner]])$$
$$\text{iff} \quad \ulcorner\mathbf{R}\urcorner \notin \{X|\mathbf{R}\}$$

We can identify $\{X|\mathbf{R}\}$ with $\ulcorner\mathbf{R}\urcorner$ because the set $\{X|\mathbf{R}\}$ and the code $\ulcorner\mathbf{R}\urcorner$ have a one-to-one correspondence (modulo renaming). This will lead to Russell's paradox: $\ulcorner\mathbf{R}\urcorner \in \ulcorner\mathbf{R}\urcorner$ iff $\ulcorner\mathbf{R}\urcorner \notin \ulcorner\mathbf{R}\urcorner$. For the Liar paradox, recall $\mathsf{S_{ub}}$ introduced in Subsection 2.3. Put

$$\mathbf{L_0} = \exists X(\sim t_r(X,[]) \wedge sub(V,\ulcorner V\urcorner,V,X)$$
$$\mathbf{L} = \exists X(\sim t_r(X,[]) \wedge sub(\ulcorner\mathbf{L_0}\urcorner,\ulcorner V\urcorner,\ulcorner\mathbf{L_0}\urcorner,X)$$

Since $\mathbf{L}$ satisfies $E(\Sigma) \cup \mathsf{S_{ub}} \models_3 \mathbf{L} \Leftrightarrow \sim t_r(\ulcorner\mathbf{L}\urcorner,[])$, it is interpreted as saying that "I am false", hence the Liar sentence. One easily sees that $\mathbf{L}$ leads to the two-valued inconsistency:

$$E(\Sigma) \cup \mathsf{S_{ub}} \cup \mathsf{E_{val}} \cup \mathsf{T_{ruth}} \models_3 t_r(\ulcorner\mathbf{L}\urcorner,[]) \Leftrightarrow \sim t_r(\ulcorner\mathbf{L}\urcorner,[])$$

2.6 Two valued truth predicates

Let us take $\mathsf{T_{ruth}} = \mathbf{iff}(\{eq, self, neg, and, exq\})$ and consider how to convert it into a two-valued, consistent truth predicate. In light of Corollary 2.2, we have to give up the "self" clause or the "neg" clause to recover two-valued consistency.

If we drop the "neg" clause, the resulting program, $\mathbf{iff}(\{eq, self, and, exq\})$, is a straightforward definite clause program. Therefore it is consistent with $E(\Sigma) \cup \mathsf{E_{val}}$ in two-valued logic and gives a truth predicate for the formulae constructed from $=$, t_r, conjunctions and existential quantifications.

If, on the other hand, we drop the "self" clause, the remaining program, $\mathbf{iff}(\{eq, neg, and, exq\})$, becomes an *order-consistent* program [Sa90], and hence is again two-valued consistent with $E(\Sigma) \cup \mathsf{E_{val}}$, despite the existence of "neg" clause. In this case, we have a non self-referential truth predicate for the formulae whose predicate is only $=$.

3. Extension to a complete meta-interpreter

Suppose one writes a first order program $\mathbf{P}$ to define some predicates. Let us assume, for notational simplicity, that $\mathbf{P}$ defines a unary predicate p.

$$\mathbf{P}: \quad p(Z) \Leftrightarrow F_p$$

Corresponding to this definition, we add to $\mathsf{T_{ruth}}$ the following clause.

$$\text{usr:} \quad t_r([\ulcorner p\urcorner,X],E_{nv}) \leftarrow eval(X,E_{nv},Y) \wedge t_r(\ulcorner F_p\urcorner,[[\ulcorner Z\urcorner | Y]])$$

Put T_P = **iff**({eq, self, neg, and, exq, usr}). T_P defines a truth predicate that allows us to tell about the truth of p as well as t_r and =. We claim that the new truth predicate correctly captures the meaning of the original program **P**. To prove it, we use an equivalence preserving transformation system for first order programs [Sa**].

3.1 An equivalence preserving transformation system

We briefly explain the program transformation system described in [Sa**] simplified to our case. It allows unfolding of negative goals and folding of any formulae.

Let $\Gamma_0 = \{q_i(x_i) \Leftrightarrow F_{i,0}[x_i] | 1 \leq i \leq N\}$ be an initial first order program for transformation. The q_i's are called *user predicate*s. $F_{i,0}$ ($1 \leq i \leq N$) might contain user predicates and =, a system predicate whose meaning is specified by Clark's equational theory $E(\Sigma)$. No user predicate symbol is labeled **u** in the beginning. Suppose Γ_0 has been transformed to Γ_k. To obtain the next program Γ_{k+1}, select a definition, say $q_i(x_i) \Leftrightarrow F_{i,k}$ from Γ_k, transform $F_{i,k}$ to $F_{i,k+1}$, and replace $q_i(x_i) \Leftrightarrow F_{i,k}$ with $q_i(x_i) \Leftrightarrow F_{i,k+1}$. $F_{i,k+1}$ is obtainable by applying one of the three rules: *unfolding, folding* and *replacement*. The folding and replacement rules must be applied in such a way that the new definition $q_i(x_i) \Leftrightarrow F_{i,k+1}$ satisfies $x_i \supseteq \mathsf{Fvar}(F_{i,k+1})$.

To unfold $F_{i,k}$, choose an atomic occurrence $q_j(t)$ from $F_{i,k}$, and replace it with $F_{j,0}[t]$. Label every user predicate symbol that is introduced by this unfolding by **u**. Take the result as $F_{i,k+1}$. Unfolding is the simulation of a procedure call to the initial program. Folding is the reverse operation of unfolding. To fold $F_{i,k}$, choose a subformula of the form $F_{j,0}[t]$ from $F_{i,k}$, and if it satisfies *folding conditions*: (**1**) all the user predicate symbols in $F_{j,0}[t]$ are labeled **u** and (**2**) $F_{j,0}[t]$ contains no system predicates, replace $F_{j,0}[t]$ with $q_j(t)$ without labeling **u**. The resulting formula is $F_{i,k+1}$.

Replacement allows us to replace $F_{i,k}$ with a formula $F_{i,k+1}$ such that $E(\Sigma) \models_3$ $F_{i,k+1}[q_1,...,q_N;q_1{}^{\mathbf{u}},...,q_N{}^{\mathbf{u}}] \Leftrightarrow F_{i,k}[q_1,...,q_N; q_1{}^{\mathbf{u}},...,q_N{}^{\mathbf{u}}]$. Here we have to treat the q_i's and the $q_j{}^{\mathbf{u}}$'s as independent predicates. This replacement rule covers most of the logical operations such as the renaming of bound variables, $A \wedge (B \vee C) \Rightarrow (A \wedge B) \vee (A \wedge C)$, $\exists X(X=t \wedge \varphi[X]) \Rightarrow \varphi[t]$ (provided t is free for X in φ) and $s=t \Rightarrow \mathbf{f}$ if s and t are not unifiable, and so on. We cannot, however, replace $\sim p(X) \vee p(X)$ with $\mathbf{t}$ nor $p^{\mathbf{u}}(X) \vee p(X)$ with p(X).

We show a small example. Let the initial program be $\{gtr(Y,Z) \Leftrightarrow \forall X \sim add(X,Y,Z),$ $add(X,Y,Z) \Leftrightarrow (X=0 \wedge Y=Z) \vee \exists U,V\{X=s(U) \wedge Z=s(V) \wedge add(U,Y,V)\}\}$. $gtr(Y,Z)$ reads that Y is greater than Z. The unfolding of $add(X,Y,Z)$ in $\forall X \sim add(X,Y,Z)$ and the subsequent simplifications by replacement give

$$gtr(Y,Z) \Leftrightarrow Y \neq Z \wedge \{\forall V(Z \neq s(V)) \vee \exists U,V(Z=s(V) \wedge \forall U \sim add^{\mathbf{u}}(U,Y,V))\}$$

By folding $\forall U \sim add^{\mathbf{u}}(U,Y,V)$ into $gtr(Y,V)$ (the folding conditions are met), we get

$$gtr(Y,Z) \Leftrightarrow Y \neq Z \wedge \{\forall V(Z \neq s(V)) \vee \exists V(Z=s(V) \wedge gtr(Y,V))\}$$

We have thus obtained a recursive definite clause program for gtr runnable on Prolog. Our rules preserve three-valued logical consequence.

[Proposition 3.1] (See [Sa**])

Suppose $\Gamma_0 = \{q_i(x_i) \Leftrightarrow F_{i,0} | 1 \leq i \leq N\}$ has been transformed to $\Gamma_k = \{q_i(x_i) \Leftrightarrow F_{i,k} | 1 \leq i \leq N\}$. For a sentence φ whose predicates are among $\{=, q_1, ..., q_N\}$, we have

$$E(\Sigma) \cup \Gamma_0 \models_3 \varphi \quad \text{iff} \quad E(\Sigma) \cup \Gamma_k \models_3 \varphi$$

Our transformation system is applicable to two-valued logic as well. When both Γ_0 and Γ_k are *call-consistent* (no predicate depends on itself negatively) and *strict* w.r.t. φ (φ does not depend on a predicate both positively and negatively) [Sa90,Ku89], we can replace $\models_3$ in Proposition 3.1 with $\models$ (and hence with $\vdash$). Consequently, if Γ_0 is (the completion of) a definite clause program, Γ_0 and Γ_k (Γ_k becomes a definite clause program) have the same set of provable literals. Therefore, our system preserves finite success and finite failure sets of definite clause programs.

3.2 A complete meta-interpreter

For a program $\mathbf{P} = \{p(Z) \Leftrightarrow F_p\}$ and $\mathbf{T_P} = \mathbf{iff}(\{eq, self, neg, and, exq, usr\})$, we prove, using the above transformation system, that $E(\Sigma) \cup \mathbf{P}$ and $E(\Sigma) \cup E_{val} \cup \mathbf{T_P}$ have the same three-valued logical consequence.

We will call a predicate a *user predicate* if it is defined by a user written program (other predicates such as =, eval and t_r are system predicates). Likewise, if an atom contains a user predicate, we call it a *user atom*.

[Theorem 3.1]

Suppose that F_p contains neither t_r nor eval. Then for an atom $p(t)$,

$$E(\Sigma) \cup \mathbf{P} \models_3 p(t) \quad \text{iff} \quad E(\Sigma) \cup E_{val} \cup \mathbf{T_P} \models_3 t_r(\ulcorner p(Z) \urcorner, [[\ulcorner Z \urcorner | t]])$$

$$E(\Sigma) \cup \mathbf{P} \models_3 {\sim}p(t) \quad \text{iff} \quad E(\Sigma) \cup E_{val} \cup \mathbf{T_P} \models_3 t_r(\ulcorner {\sim}p(Z) \urcorner, [[\ulcorner Z \urcorner | t]])$$

[Proof] We treat only $p(t)$ (the case of $\sim p(t)$ is similar). Consider a program $\Gamma_0 = E_{val} \cup \mathbf{T_P} \cup \{p(Z) \Leftrightarrow t_r(\ulcorner F_p \urcorner, [[\ulcorner Z \urcorner | Z]])\}$. First we transform Γ_0. Recall that due to our coding scheme, F_p and its code $\ulcorner F_p \urcorner$ are syntactically isomorphic, meaning that if F_p has an occurrence of an atom $p(t)$ at a certain position in F_p, $\ulcorner F_p \urcorner$ contains $[\ulcorner p \urcorner, \ulcorner t \urcorner]$ at the corresponding position. We transform the body of $p(Z) \Leftrightarrow t_r(\ulcorner F_p \urcorner, [[\ulcorner Z \urcorner | Z]])$ as follows.

$p(Z) \Leftrightarrow t_r(\ulcorner F_p \urcorner, [[\ulcorner Z \urcorner | Z]])$

/* Unfold $t_r(\ulcorner F_p \urcorner, [[\ulcorner Z \urcorner | Z]])$ successively as $t_r(\ulcorner \exists V(\varphi_1 \land \varphi_2) \urcorner, \lambda*) \Rightarrow$

$\exists Y t_r{}^{\mathbf{u}}(\ulcorner \varphi_1 \land \varphi_2 \urcorner, \theta*) \Rightarrow \exists Y(t_r{}^{\mathbf{u}}(\ulcorner \varphi_1 \urcorner, \theta*) \land t_r{}^{\mathbf{u}}(\ulcorner \varphi_2 \urcorner, \theta*)) \Rightarrow \cdots$ until

(the code of) an atom $\mathbf{A}$ is reached.

When unfolding an existentially quantified goal $t_r(\ulcorner \exists V\varphi \urcorner, \lambda*)$

by the "exq" clause, use an instance of the following form:

$$t_r([\ulcorner\exists\urcorner,\ulcorner V\urcorner,\ulcorner\varphi\urcorner],\lambda*)\leftarrow \exists V t_r(\ulcorner\varphi\urcorner,[[\ulcorner V\urcorner|V]|\lambda*]).$$

Now we treat the case where **A** is a user atom $p(t)$. */

$\Rightarrow F_p[...,t_r{}^{\mathbf{u}}(\ulcorner p(t)\urcorner,\theta*),...]$

/* We can assume that each component in the environment $\theta*$ is of the
form $[X|X]$. Continue unfolding $t_r{}^{\mathbf{u}}(\ulcorner p(t)\urcorner,\theta*)$ by the "usr" clause in T**p**. */

$\Rightarrow F_p[...,\exists Y\{eval^{\mathbf{u}}(\ulcorner t\urcorner,\theta*,Y)\wedge t_r{}^{\mathbf{u}}(\ulcorner F_p\urcorner,[[\ulcorner Z\urcorner|Y]])\},...]$

/* Simulate the execution of $eval^{\mathbf{u}}(\ulcorner t\urcorner,\theta*,Y)$ by unfolding and replacement.*/

$\Rightarrow F_p[...,\exists Y\{Y=t\theta\wedge t_r{}^{\mathbf{u}}(\ulcorner F_p\urcorner,[[\ulcorner Z\urcorner|Y]])\},...]$

/* Use replacement. Note that $t\theta=t$. */

$\Rightarrow F_p[...,t_r{}^{\mathbf{u}}(\ulcorner F_p\urcorner,[[\ulcorner Z\urcorner|t]]),...]$

/* Fold $t_r{}^{\mathbf{u}}(\ulcorner F_p\urcorner,[[\ulcorner Z\urcorner|t]])$ into $p(t)$ using $p(Z)\Leftrightarrow t_r(\ulcorner F_p\urcorner,[[\ulcorner Z\urcorner|Z]])$.
This folding is legal. */

$\Rightarrow F_p[...,p(t),...]$

$= F_p$

We have thus succeeded in transforming Γ_0 to $E_{val}\cup T\mathbf{p}\cup \mathbf{P}$ (the transformation for the case where **A** contains a system predicate is similar). By Proposition 3.1, we have

$$E(\Sigma)\cup E_{val}\cup T\mathbf{p}\cup\{p(Z)\Leftrightarrow t_r(\ulcorner F_p\urcorner,[[\ulcorner Z\urcorner|Z]])\}\models_3 p(t)\ \text{iff}\ E(\Sigma)\cup E_{val}\cup T\mathbf{p}\cup\mathbf{P}\models_3 p(t).$$

$E(\Sigma)\cup\mathbf{P}\models_3 p(t)$

iff $E(\Sigma)\cup E_{val}\cup T\mathbf{p}\cup\mathbf{P}\models_3 p(t)$ /* p refers neither to eval nor to t_r. */

iff $E(\Sigma)\cup E_{val}\cup T\mathbf{p}\cup\{\ p(Z)\Leftrightarrow t_r(\ulcorner F_p\urcorner,[[\ulcorner Z\urcorner \mid Z]])\ \}\models_3 p(t)$ /* see above */

iff $E(\Sigma)\cup E_{val}\cup T\mathbf{p}\cup\{\ p(Z)\Leftrightarrow t_r(\ulcorner F_p\urcorner,[[\ulcorner Z\urcorner \mid Z]])\ \}\models_3 t_r(\ulcorner F_p\urcorner,[[\ulcorner Z\urcorner|t]])$

/* t_r does not refer to p. */

iff $E(\Sigma)\cup E_{val}\cup T\mathbf{p}\models_3 t_r(\ulcorner F_p\urcorner,[[\ulcorner Z\urcorner|t]])$

iff $E(\Sigma)\cup E_{val}\cup T\mathbf{p}\models_3 t_r(\ulcorner p(Z)\urcorner,[[\ulcorner Z\urcorner|t]])$ Q.E.D.

A couple of comments follow. First of all, it is immediate to extend this result to the general case; Suppose **P** contains $p(Z_1,..,Z_n)\Leftrightarrow F_p[Z_1,...,Z_n]$. We then add to T_{ruth} the clause

usr: $t_r([\ulcorner p\urcorner,X_1,...,X_n],E_{nv})\leftarrow eval(X_1,E_{nv},Y_1)\wedge...\wedge$
$eval(X_n,E_{nv},Y_n)\wedge t_r(\ulcorner F_p\urcorner,[[\ulcorner Z_1\urcorner|Y_1],...,[\ulcorner Z_n\urcorner|Y_n]])$

If **P** uses primitives other than $=$ (for example $<$), we need to add

less: $t_r([\ulcorner <\urcorner,X_1,X_2],E_{nv})\leftarrow eval(X_1,E_{nv},Y_1)\wedge eval(X_2,E_{nv},Y_2)\wedge Y_1<Y_2$

together with an appropriate axiom (or a program) for $<$. Theorem 3.1 still remains valid with these augmentations and ensures that t_r works as a meta-interpreter for first order programs which is sound and complete w.r.t. its three-valued logical consequence semantics.

Secondly, when we stated Theorem 3.1, we require that F_p contains neither t_r nor eval. Suppose we allow F_p to contain t_r. This only means that we are now able to call an interpreter in the clause body (a call to t_r corresponds to an invocation of call/1 in Prolog). We will still have

$$E(\Sigma) \cup E_{val} \cup T_{\mathbf{P}} \cup \mathbf{P} \models_3 p(t) \quad \text{iff} \quad E(\Sigma) \cup E_{val} \cup T_{\mathbf{P}} \models_3 t_r(\ulcorner p(Z) \urcorner, [[\ulcorner Z \urcorner | t]])$$

Theorem 3.1 is stated in terms of three-valued logic. The extent to which we can carry it over to the two-valued case depends on the structure of **P**. For example, if **P** is the iff form of a definite clause program, we may replace $\models_3$ with $\vdash$ in the theorem. For other cases, see [Sa90].

3.3 Programming with t_r

3.3.1 Interpreting goals

We list some examples to show potential applications of our truth predicate. We assume that appropriate user predicates are already defined in the form of "usr" clauses. The first example is to use t_r as a usual interpreter to instantiate individual variables.

$$?- t_r(\ulcorner append([a],[b],Z) \urcorner, [[\ulcorner Z \urcorner | Z]])$$
$$Z = [a,b]$$

Moreover, using this interpreter, we can ask for (the code of) a predicate name (and other syntactic objects).

$$?- t_r([P, \ulcorner [a] \urcorner, \ulcorner [b] \urcorner, \ulcorner Z \urcorner], [[\ulcorner Z \urcorner | Z]])$$
$$P = \ulcorner append \urcorner$$
$$Z = [a,b]$$

3.3.2 Formula evaluation

With the help of t_r, not only can we declaratively compose and decompose arbitrary first order formulae (and hence goals), but we can evaluate them during execution and get variable bindings, even though they include *arbitrarily nested bound variables* like the example below.

$$?- t_r(\ulcorner \exists z \{ \exists x \{ (y=f(x,z) \wedge x=0 \wedge \exists x(z=g(x) \wedge x=1)) \} \} \urcorner, [[\ulcorner y \urcorner | Y]])$$
$$Y = f(0,g(1))$$

Look at the double occurrences of $\exists x$ in the goal. Their scopes are nested, but variable bindings are treated properly.

3.3.3 Generic procedures

Programs can be parameterized with procedures. Suppose we want to write a program that takes the transitive closure of a binary relation R defined by an arbitrary formula φ whose code is given as a parameter. All we need is to write

$$cl([R,A,B],X,Y) \leftarrow t_r(R,[[A|X],[B|Y]])$$
$$cl([R,A,B],X,Y) \leftarrow cl([R,A,B],X,Z) \land t_r(R,[[A|Z],[B|Y]])$$

and run this program with R instantiated to the code $\ulcorner \varphi \urcorner$ of φ, A and B to the codes of free variables in φ respectively. For example, let friend(A,B) be a primitive relation (A is a friend of B). To calculate a chain of people who have a common friend, and to ask if X and Y are in the chain, the query

$$?\text{-} cl([\ulcorner \exists c\{friend(a,c) \land friend(b,c)\} \urcorner, \ulcorner a \urcorner, \ulcorner b \urcorner],X,Y)$$

will do the job and give us an answer. Here $[\ulcorner \exists c\{friend(a,c) \land friend(b,c)\} \urcorner, \ulcorner a \urcorner, \ulcorner b \urcorner]$ represents the lambda abstraction $\lambda a \lambda b. \exists c\{friend(a,c) \land friend(b,c)\}$. It is applied at run time by t_r to X and Y using the environment $[[\ulcorner a \urcorner | X],[\ulcorner b \urcorner |Y]]$. Although Hilog [Ch89] and Reflective Prolog [Co90] already provide a way for such generic programming, R is restricted to atoms in their formalisms. Note that if we interpret the above goal using t_r, a self-referential goal of the form $t_r(\ulcorner t_r(R,[[A|X],[B|Y]]) \urcorner, \theta^*)$ will appear during execution and this invokes the "self" clause in T_{ruth}.

3.3.4 A complete demo predicate

If, instead of asserting the "usr" clause, we modify the T_{ruth} program so that the truth predicate carries around the code $\ulcorner DB \urcorner$ of the whole database DB as an extra argument, the resulting program, D_{emo}, will give us a three-valued complete demo predicate such that

$$E(\Sigma) \cup E_{val} \cup D_{emo} \models_3 demo(\ulcorner DB \urcorner, \ulcorner \varphi \urcorner, \theta^*) \quad \text{iff} \quad E(\Sigma) \cup DB \models_3 \varphi\theta$$

We remark that $\models_3$ can be replaced with $\vdash$ if D_{emo} does not include the neg clause, DB is (the code of) a definite clause program and φ is an atom. In this case, the demo predicate preserves the finite failure set of DB (details omitted). The demo predicate was first introduced in [Bo82], but the completeness was assumed there rather than proved.

4. Discussion

In Section 2 we have presented a three-valued truth predicate $t_r(\ulcorner \varphi \urcorner, \theta^*)$ defined by a first order program T_{ruth} (Theorem 2.1), which takes two arguments, the code $\ulcorner \varphi \urcorner$ of a formula φ and an environment θ^* of the form $[[\ulcorner X_1 \urcorner |s_1],...,[\ulcorner X_n \urcorner |s_n]]$ $(n \geq 0)$. It is (i) executable, (ii) able to refer to the truth values of arbitrary formulae and (iii) self-referential. Paradoxical sentences (Russell's paradox and the Liar paradox) were constructed based on t_r, implying the two-valued inconsistency of T_{ruth}. We have pointed to some conditions under which t_r becomes a two-valued truth predicate.

In Section 3, we have extended t_r to a meta-interpreter by adding clauses for user defined predicates, and have proven its soundness and completeness w.r.t. three-valued logical consequence semantics (Theorem 3.1). It is clear however that this completeness does not make much sense unless we have a complete interpreter for first order programs. We already have presented such an interpreter in [Sa91].

As mentioned before, we cannot expect to obtain a truth predicate which is two-valued and satisfies $t_r(\ulcorner \varphi \urcorner) \leftrightarrow \varphi$ for all sentence φ. Kripke [Kr75] proved that it is possible to define a truth predicate $T(x)$, if only we accept "truth value gaps", i.e. if we move to three-valued logic. He constructed, by transfinite induction on a given domain, a three-valued interpretation of $T(x)$ as a least fixed point (hence non-computable).

Perlis [Pe85] later showed that we can have a two-valued truth predicate $True(x)$ if we change the meaning of negation in a quoted context. He proved that for a consistent first order theory T, $T \cup \{True(\ulcorner \varphi \urcorner) \leftrightarrow \varphi *$[5] $\mid \varphi$ is a prenex sentence$\} \cup \{\sim(True(\ulcorner \varphi \urcorner) \wedge True(\ulcorner \sim\varphi \urcorner)\mid$ φ is a prenex sentence$\}$ is a conservative extension of T. Although this looks fine, the meaning of negation is not clear and $True(\ulcorner \varphi \urcorner) \leftrightarrow \varphi *$ is a schema, i.e. there exist an infinite number of formulae of this pattern. Therefore it cannot be a program, let alone an interpreter. For more on "logical approaches" to truth predicates, see [Fe84, Tu90].

In logic programming however, it seems that truth predicates have not received much attention and have not been investigated as such. The closest one is the "solve predicate". For example in [Hi88], Hill and Lloyd augmented the vanilla interpreter with a new clause $solve(not(X)) \leftarrow \sim solve(X)$ for negative goals and proved that the augmented solve predicate correctly captures the logical consequences of the original program. However it still is neither self-referential nor capable of handling arbitrary quantifications.

Our truth predicate and its extension to a complete meta-interpreter offer a way to meta-programming dealing with self-reference and quantifications all at once. A further extension to set construction is an interesting future research direction [Fe84] .

Acknowledgments:

The author would like to thank anonymous referees for helpful comments.

---

[1] First order programs are definite clause programs extended by negation, implication and universal quantification. They can be executed by an interpreter which is complete w.r.t. three-valued logical consequence semantics [Sa91]. A precise definition is given later.

[2] The theorem states that there is no consistent truth predicate in arithmetic [Sh73]. This will remain true no matter what truth predicate we define as long as it is reasonably expressive and defined in two-valued logic.

[3]Object variables are strings starting with an upper case letter. x,y,z,... are metavariables for tuples of distinct variables and s,t for terms. x also stands for a set of variables. Fvar(E) (resp., Bvar(E)) denotes the set of free variables (resp., bound variables) in an expression E. A notation like E[x] indicates that $x \supseteq$ Fvar(E). By E[F/G], we mean the result of a substitution of F for G in E.

[4] We designate the two-valued logical consequence relationship by $\models$. Note that $\models_3$ implies $\models$ and $\models$ is equivalent to $\vdash$ (provability relationship).

[5] φ^* is defined for a prenex formula φ by $\varphi^*[...,\sim True(x),...] = \varphi[...,True(\ulcorner \sim x \urcorner),...]$.

References:

[Bo82] Bowen,K.A. and Kowalski,R.A., "Amalgamating Language and Metalanguage Logic Programming", in Logic programming (Clark,K.L. and Tarnlund,S-A eds.), ACADEMIC PRESS (1982) 152-172.

[Ch89] Chen,W., Kifer,M. and Warren,D.S., "HiLog: A First-Order Semantics for Higher Order Logic Programming Constructs", in Proc. of NACLP'89 (1989) 1090-1114.

[Cl78] Clark,K., "Negation as Failure", in Logic and Databases, Gallaire,H. and Minker,J. (eds.), Plenum Press (1978) 293-322.

[Co90] Costatini,S. and Lanzarone,G.A., "A Metalogic Programming Language", in the Proc. of META'90, Leuven (1990) 218-233.

[Fe84] Feferman,S. "Toward Useful Type-Free Theories. I", J. of Symbolic Logic 49 (1984) 75-111.

[Fi85] Fitting,M., "A Kripke-Kleene Semantics for Logic Programs", J. of Logic Programming 2 (1985) 295-312.

[Hi88] Hill, P.M. and Lloyd,J.W.,"Analysis of Meta-Programs", in the Proc. of Meta'88, Bristol (1988) 23-51.

[Kr75] Kripke,S. "Outline of a Theory of Truth", J. of Philosophy 72 (1975) 691-716.

[Ku89] Kunen,K., "Signed Data Dependencies in Logic Programs", J. Logic Programming, 7 (1989) 231-245.

[Ll84] Lloyd,J.W., "Foundation of Logic Programming", Springer-Verlag (1984).

[Ni90] Nilsson,F.N., "Combinatory Logic Programming", in the Proc. of META90 Leuven (1990) 187-202.

[Ma88] Maes,P and Nardi,D. (eds.), "Meta-Level Architectures and Reflection", Elsevier Science Publishers B.V. (1988)

[Pe85] Perlis,D., "Languages with Self-Reference I: Foundations", J. of Artificial Intelligence 25 (1985) 301-322.

[Sa90] Sato,T, "Completed Logic Programs and Their Consistency", J. Logic Programming 9 (1990) 33-44.

[Sa91] Sato,T., "A Complete Top-down Interpreter for First Order Programs", in the Proc. of 1991 Int'l Logic Programming Symposium" San Diego (1991) 35-53.

[Sa**] Sato,T., "Equivalence-Preserving First Order Unfold/fold Transformation Systems", to appear in Theoretical Computer Science.

[Sh73] Shoenfield,J.R., Mathematical Logic (2nd ed.) Addison-Wesley (1973).

[Tu90] Turner,R., Truth and Modality for Knowledge Representation, Pitman (1990).

Interactive Synthesis of Definite-Clause Grammars

Juergen Haas
Bharat Jayaraman

Department of Computer Science
State University of New York at Buffalo
226 Bell Hall
Buffalo, NY 14260

E-Mail: {bharat,haas}@cs.buffalo.edu

Abstract

We discuss the mechanical transformation of an unambiguous context-free grammar (CFG) into a definite-clause grammar (DCG) using a finite set of examples, each of which is a pair $\langle s, m \rangle$, where s is a sentence belonging to the language defined by the CFG and m is the semantic representation (meaning) of s. The resulting DCG would be such that it could be executed to compute the semantics for every sentence of the original DCG. Our proposed approach is based upon two key assumptions: (a) the semantic representation language is the *simply typed λ-calculus*; and (b) the semantic representation of a sentence is a function (expressed in the typed λ-calculus) of the semantic representations of its parts (*compositionality*). With these assumptions we show that a higher-order DCG can be systematically constructed using a unification procedure for typed λ-terms. The needed procedure differs from the one in (Huet 75) in that the types for variables are not completely known in advance. As a result, there might in general be an additional source of nondeterminism in enumerating *projection* substitutions. We believe that such a system would simplify the task of building DCGs when the semantic representation involved quantified terms, and could be a useful tool for generating natural query language front-ends for various applications. We illustrate the approach with examples, including a small fragment of natural language grammar where *type raising* must be performed.

1 From Context-Free to Definite-Clause Grammars

Our goal is to develop a system that will take as input an unambiguous *context-free grammar* (CFG) and a finite set of pairs $\langle s, m \rangle$, where s is a sentence belonging to the language defined by the CFG and m is the semantic representation (meaning) of s, and will produce as output a *definite clause grammar* (DCG) (Pereira and Warren 1980) capable of computing the semantic representations for all sentences of the CFG. We envisage that the system would actually work interactively, by querying the user for the semantic representations for a series of key sentences (which it determines according to some scheme) and reporting back to the user the synthesized DCG periodically until the user accepts the DCG. In order to narrow the search space of possible solutions, we adopt the following two constraints: (1) the semantic representation language is the *simply typed* λ-*calculus*; (2) the semantic representation of a sentence is some function (expressed in the typed λ-calculus) of the semantic representations of the phrases that constitute the sentence (*compositionality*). Under these assumptions we believe that, if there is a DCG satisfying the input pairs, it is possible to systematically search for it; if there is no solution, the search may sometimes be nonterminating. The primary goal of this paper is to describe how this solution can be found, whenever it exists.

The motivation for our work stems from the fact that, although the semantic representations for typical sentences is easy to give, it is not easy to manually modify a CFG to obtain a DCG when the semantic representations involve quantified terms (as in natural languages). However, by the compositionality principle, the semantic representation of a sentence can be systematically obtained from those of its constituent phrases. Hence, it seems feasible, in principle, to have the computer assist a human in the transition from a CFG to a DCG. A potential use of our proposed system is that it might facilitate rapid prototyping of natural-language interfaces to databases, since the interface could be obtained by defining the syntax along with typical input sentences and their semantic representations. Our proposed use of the λ-calculus not only has precedent for natural language semantics (Dowty et al 81, Miller and Nadathur 86, Pereira 90), the availability of a unification procedure for simply-typed terms (Huet 75) allows us to reduce the problem of generalization from examples to a unification problem. However, as we shall see later, certain important changes to Huet's procedure are needed in our context, since the types for variables are not completely known in advance.

There are several interesting theoretical and practical issues that pertain to our stated problem: developing a methodology for writing grammars and semantic representations so that solutions can be found; exploring the constraints from different types of grammars and semantic representations; exploring the effect of different examples on the efficiency of synthesis; showing the effectiveness of the system for the intended applications; and converting when possible the higher-order DCG into a first-order DCG (through *partial execution*) for greater efficiency. We address only some of these issues in this paper; a more thorough treatment can be found in (Haas 92). Section 2 describes in detail our approach to the synthesis of a higher-order DCG from examples. Section 3 illustrates the various facets of our approach with two examples, including the synthesis of a DCG for a small fragment of a natural language grammar to illustrate how quantified terms are handled and type raising automatically performed. Section 4 presents the current status of the work and related work.

Finally, we note that natural languages are of interest in our work since they are good examples of languages whose semantics require the use of quantified terms, and hence the full use of the typed λ-calculus. However, our work is not directly concerned with devising suitable semantics for the full range of natural language sentences. Our work is concerned with that subset of natural languages that can be adequately described with CFGs and the typed λ-calculus. For applications such as natural query languages, it seems feasible to describe the language with a context-free grammar and also to insist on sentences whose meanings have no ambiguity. However, our proposed techniques appear to work even for certain forms of context-sensitive grammars as well as certain forms of ambiguous grammars.

In the remainder of this paper, we assume the reader has some familiarity with DCGs, typed λ-calculus, and higher-order unification.

2   Synthesis of a Higher-Order DCG from Examples

In the pseudo-code below, we assume, for simplicity of presentation, that a CFG rule has either a single terminal on its rhs or a sequence of one or more nonterminals (in practice, we permit both terminals and nonterminals on the rhs). As in Prolog DCGs, nonterminals are identifiers beginning with a lowercase letter, and terminals are such identifiers surrounded by [and]. A higher-order DCG is similar in structure to a first-order DCG except that typed λ-terms take the place of first-order terms. As in λProlog (Nadathur and Miller 88), (F X) stands for function application and X\E stands for λX.E (λ-abstraction). We assume that application is left-associative, i.e., (F X Y) is short-hand for ((F X) Y). The basic scheme for synthesis is given below in terms of four procedures—**SYNTH**, **SOLVE**, **SUBST**, and **DECOMP**—and is followed by a brief discussion of the salient issues.

Procedure SYNTH(G)

The procedure **SYNTH** takes as input a CFG **G** and returns a higher-order DCG after obtaining the semantic representations for sample sentences interactively.

1. Let **G** be an unambiguous CFG having n rules, with start symbol s.

2. Construct the higher-order DCG as follows:

    a. If the i-th CFG rule is $a_i \dashrightarrow b_{i1} \ldots b_{ik_i}$, the i-th DCG rule will be

    $(\forall V_1 \ldots V_{k_i}) \, a_i((F_i \, V_1 \ldots V_{k_i}), \alpha_{k_i+1}) \dashrightarrow b_{i1}(V_1, \alpha_{i1}) \ldots b_{ik_i}(V_{k_i}, \alpha_{ik_i})$

    b. If the i-th CFG rule is $a_i \dashrightarrow [t]$, the i-th DCG rule will be

    $a_i(F_i, \alpha_{i1}) \dashrightarrow [t]$.

    For the sake of clarity, we maintain the types for the function variables $F_1, \ldots, F_n$ explicitly: In 2a, the type of V_i is α_i and the type of F_i is

$\alpha_{i1} \to \ldots \to \alpha_{ik_i} \to \alpha_{i(k_i+1)}$. It is important to note that the function variables $F_1, \ldots, F_n$, as well as the type variables α_{ij}, $1 \leq i \leq n$, $1 \leq j \leq k_i$ are *free* variables of the DCG, i.e., they are not universally quantified like the variables V_i.

3. Solve for the variables F_i in the above DCG as follows.

$E \leftarrow \phi; \quad done \leftarrow false; \quad i \leftarrow 1;$

WHILE *not done* **DO**

a. Generate a set of new sentences se_{ij}, $1 \leq j \leq l_i$, for some finite l_i (selection strategy for these sentences is omitted here). For each se_{ij}, let n_{ij} be the user-supplied semantic representation, assumed to be a simply-typed term of type t_{ij}.

b. Execute the goal $s(M, t_{ij}, se_{ij}, [\,])$, $1 \leq j \leq l_i$, using the constructed DCG of step 2. For each se_{ij}, let m_{ij}, $1 \leq j \leq l_i$, be the computed semantic representation for variable M.

c. $E \leftarrow E \cup \{m_{ij} = n_{ij} \; : \; 1 \leq j \leq l_i\}$.

d. Call **SOLVE**(E). If successful, **SOLVE** nondeterministically returns one of the multiple maximally general unifiers which are possible. Assign $done \leftarrow true$ if either unification fails, *or* unification succeeds and all sentences of the CFG have been enumerated, *or* unification succeeds and the user accepts the resulting DCG after replacing all variables F_i in the DCG of step 2 according to one of the unifiers of E and reducing all λ-terms to their normal forms.

e. $i \leftarrow i + 1$

END WHILE

4. If unification failed in step **3d**, return "no solution", else return the DCG found.

Procedure SOLVE(E)

Procedure **SOLVE** tries to solve the set of higher-order equations **E** by attempting to find substitutions for the free function variables occurring in **E**.

1. $E \leftarrow \mathbf{E}; \qquad F \leftarrow \{F_i \; : \; 1 \leq j \leq n\}; \qquad \sigma \leftarrow \phi.$

2. WHILE $E \neq \phi$ **DO**

a. Select equation $e = \langle e_1, e_2 \rangle$ from E, and call **SUBST**(e)—note that e_1 is flexible and e_2 is rigid. If **SUBST** succeeds, it returns a substitution term t for the variable V at the head position of e_1.

b. $\sigma \leftarrow \sigma\{\langle V, t \rangle\}$ (composition of substitutions); $E \leftarrow E\sigma$. Reduce all terms in E and σ to their normal form.

c. $E \leftarrow \textbf{DECOMP}(E)$.

END WHILE

3. Return $\sigma \downarrow F$ (the *restriction* of σ to the variables F).

Procedure SUBST(e)

The procedure **SUBST** is similar to MATCH in (Huet 75), except for the way *projection* substitutions are enumerated. Let $\mathbf{e} = \langle e_1, e_2 \rangle^1$, where

$$e_1 = \lambda u_1 \ldots \lambda u_n.(f \; s_1 \; s_2 \; \ldots \; s_p),$$
$$e_2 = \lambda v_1 \ldots \lambda v_n.(@ \; t_1 \; t_2 \; \ldots \; t_q),$$

and the (simple) type of @ is completely known, say $\delta_1 \rightarrow \ldots \rightarrow \delta_q \rightarrow \beta$, but the type of f may not be completely known—only the number of arguments of f would in general be known. Procedure **SUBST** nondeterministically selects and returns an *imitation* or a *projection* substitution for the head of e_1, provided that the appropriate type constraints are met:

Imitation substitution: applicable only if @ is a constant
$f \leftarrow \lambda w_1 \ldots \lambda w_p.(@ \; (h_1 \; w_1 \; \ldots \; w_p) \; \ldots \; (h_q \; w_1 \; \ldots \; w_p))$, where the type of w_i is γ_i, provided the type of f can be unified with $\gamma_1 \rightarrow \ldots \rightarrow \gamma_p \rightarrow \beta$. Each new function variable h_i is assigned a type $\gamma_1 \rightarrow \ldots \rightarrow \gamma_p \rightarrow \delta_i$, for $1 \le i \le q$.

Projection substitutions:
$f \leftarrow \lambda w_1 \ldots \lambda w_p.(w_i \; (h_1 \; w_1 \; \ldots \; w_p) \; \ldots \; (h_l \; w_1 \; \ldots \; w_p))$, for each $1 \le i \le p$, provided the type (γ_i) of w_i can be unified with $\epsilon_1 \rightarrow \ldots \rightarrow \epsilon_l \rightarrow \beta$, and the type of f can be unified with $\gamma_1 \rightarrow \ldots \rightarrow \gamma_p \rightarrow \beta$. Each new function variable h_i is assigned a type $\gamma_1 \rightarrow \ldots \rightarrow \gamma_p \rightarrow \epsilon_i$, for $1 \le i \le l$.

While only one imitation substitution is possible, for projection substitutions, in general there is nondeterminism in the choice of w_i as well as the choice of number of arguments, l. The latter possibility arises because the type γ_i of w_i may not always be completely known.

---

[1]If e_1 has fewer prefix variables than e_2, we assume e_1 is η-expanded so that they have the same number of prefix variables. If it has more prefix variables than of e_2, then there is no unifying substitution.

Procedure DECOMP(E)

This procedure is similar to Huet's SIMPL (Huet 1975), except that the types of function variables are determined as the structure of the terms is recursively traversed. It is essentially the same as the procedure used in λProlog (Nadathur and Miller 88), but we reproduce it below for the sake of completeness. Note that the right-hand sides of all equations will often be closed terms, with known (simple) types, hence this procedure plays a crucial role in propagating type information.

If $\mathbf{E} = \phi$ then return ϕ.

Else if $\mathbf{E} = \{\langle e_1, e_2 \rangle\}$, then unify the type of e_1 and the type of e_2, and if e_1 is flexible then return $\mathbf{E}$, else—e_1 and e_2 are both rigid—let $e_1 = \lambda \vec{x}.(@_1\ e_{11}\ \ldots\ e_{1m})$ and $e_2 = \lambda \vec{x}.(@_2\ e_{21}\ \ldots\ e_{2m})$ be the $\beta\eta$ long forms. If $@_1 \neq @_2$ then fail, else unify the type of e_{1i} and the type of e_{2i} for $1 \leq i \leq m$, and return $\mathbf{DECOMP}(\{\langle \lambda \vec{x}.e_{1i}, \lambda \vec{x}.e_{2i} \rangle : 1 \leq i \leq m\})$.

Else $\mathbf{E}$ has greater than one equation. Let $\mathbf{E} = \{\langle e_{1i}, e_{2i} \rangle : 1 \leq i \leq n\}$. Return $\bigcup_{i=1}^{n} \mathbf{DECOMP}(\{\langle e_{1i}, e_{2i} \rangle\})$, if $\mathbf{DECOMP}(\{\langle e_{1i}, e_{2i} \rangle\})$ does not fail for any i.

Discussion of the Synthesis Technique

We clarify the salient features of the synthesis procedure just described:

1. *Compositionality:* The compositionality principle is expressed in step 2 of procedure **SYNTH** by assuming that, in a CFG rule $a \dashrightarrow b_1 \ldots b_k$, the meaning of the nonterminal a is some function F of the meanings of the nonterminals $b_1 \ldots b_k$, where F is expressible in the typed λ-calculus. As noted by van Benthem (1986) and Zadrozny (1992), compositionality is a meaningful restriction only when the semantic function is strictly weaker than a general partial recursive function. Since the typed λ-calculus has the **strong normalization** property, it does indeed restrict the kinds of semantic functions that can be synthesized. When terminal symbols are present along with one or more nonterminals on the rhs of a rule, our methodology assumes that the meaning is independent of these terminal symbols; if the semantics of any such terminal $[t]$ is to be taken into account, it should be replaced by a new nonterminal n, and a new rule $n \dashrightarrow [t]$ added to the CFG.

2. *Types*: One of the crucial issues in this synthesis is the determination of types for the free function variables. The lack of complete knowledge of these types in advance marks an important point of departure from Huet's procedure. While the unification procedure of λProlog must also work with polymorphic types, a crucial difference in our work is that there is an additional source of nondeterminism in procedure **SUBST** in enumerating *projection* substitutions. In practice, the

needed types tend not to be very complex, and therefore the additional nondeterminism may not be a practical problem. Furthermore, since large DCGs would be synthesized in a modular fashion, the number of unknown variables processed could be kept reasonably small. It seems very reasonable to restrict the user-supplied semantic representations to closed λ-terms, in which case we only need a *matching* procedure, rather than a unification procedure. When it is known that terms are of second-order type, there is a finite matching algorithm (Huet and Lang 78). Recently, even third-order matching was also shown to be decidable (Dowek 92).

3. *Termination and Multiple Solutions*: In step 3 of **SYNTH**, we incrementally generate a set of equations, where each equation relates the user's chosen semantic representation for a sentence and the semantic representation that would be derived from the higher-order DCG for this sentence. There are three possible outcomes in solving these equations: failure, success, and nontermination. In case of failure, there is no higher-order DCG satisfying the given semantic representations. In case of successful unification and if the CFG generates a finite language, then successful termination is achieved when all sentences have been enumerated. Since the unification procedure is only recursively enumerable, the search may sometimes proceed indefinitely when there is no solution. If we restricted attention to matching, our problem would reduce to general higher-order matching (beyond order 3), whose decidability is still unknown. Since the unification of typed λ-terms could result in multiple maximally general unifiers (i.e., most general unifiers do not always exist), multiple DCG solutions are possible at any stage. However, from experimentation, we have found that typed λ-terms provide strong constraints on possible generalizations, and often there is a single DCG that generalizes a given a set of examples. We are currently examining criteria that the sample sentences must satisfy so that a single solution is produced, in the sense that the DCGs corresponding to all other solutions exhibit the same input/output behavior.

3   Illustration of the Synthesis Technique

3.1   Successor function

We use a very simple example in order to illustrate the synthesis procedures, starting with the steps of the procedure **SYNTH**:

(Step **1**.) Assume the following CFG is input:

```
s --> [a].
s --> [a], s.
```

(Step **2.**) The DCG at the end of step 2 would be:

```
s(F1) --> [a].
s(F2 A) --> [a],s(A).
```

(Step **3a.**) Suppose we wanted the following semantics: [a] means 0; [a,a] means 1; [a,a,a] means 2; and so on, the meaning of a sequence of length n is the number $n-1$. Suppose further that we use *Church numerals* to encode these numbers: `0 = F\X\X`, `1 = F\X\(F X)`, `2 = F\X\(F (F X))`, etc. We will see that the desired DCG can be obtained with just three examples:

```
[a], [a,a], [a,a,a].
```

The user is asked for the corresponding semantic representations, which, in this example, would be respectively:

```
F\X\X, F\X\(F X), F\X\(F (F X)),
```

where $\tau(\texttt{F\textbackslash X\textbackslash X}) = \tau(\texttt{F\textbackslash X\textbackslash(F X)}) = \tau(\texttt{F\textbackslash X\textbackslash(F (F X))}) = (i \to i) \to i \to i$ ($\tau(t)$ denotes the type of term t).

(Step **3b.**) Executing the above DCG on the sentence [a], the computed semantic representation will be **F1**. Similarly the computed terms for [a,a] and [a,a,a] are (F2 F1) and (F2 (F2 F1)), respectively. The type of **F1** is inferred to be $(i \to i) \to i \to i$, and the type of **F2** is inferred to be $((i \to i) \to i \to i) \to (i \to i) \to i \to i$.

(Step **3c.**) The equation-set E is:

```
{F1 = F\X\X,
 (F2 F1) = F\X\(F X),
 (F2 (F2 F1)) = F\X\(F (F X))}
```

(Step **3d.**) **SOLVE** is called on the above equation-set. **SOLVE** in turn calls **SUBST** to determine the following substitution for **F1**:

```
F1 <- K\L\L
```

After reducing all terms to their normal form, **SOLVE** calls **DECOMP** to obtain the following equation-set:

```
{(F2 K\L\L) = F\X\(F X),
 (F2 (F2 K\L\L)) = F\X\(F (F X))}
```

In its next iteration, **SOLVE** obtains the following projection substitution from **SUBST**:

```
F2 <- K\L\M\(K (H2 K L M) (H1 K L M))
```

The following reduced equation-set is next passed on to **DECOMP**:

```
{A\B\(H1 K\L\L A B) = F\X\(F X),
 A\B\(H1 K\L\L (H2 K\L\(H1 M\N\N K L) A B)
                  (H1 K\L\(H1 M\N\N K L) A B)) = F\X\(F (F X))}
```

Since the left-hand-side terms are all flexible, **DECOMP** has no effect in this case. In the next iteration, **SOLVE** obtains the following projection substitution from **SUBST** for H1:

```
H1 <- K\L\L,
```

and this substitution allows **DECOMP** to eliminate one more equation, so that the only remaining equation is

```
A\B\(H2 K\L\(K L) A B (A B)) = F\X\(F (F X)).
```

The derivation continues in this manner. The correct substitution for H2 now is

```
H2 <- K\L\M\N\(L (H3 K L M N)),
```

leading to the equation

```
A\B\(H3 K\L\(K L) A B (A B)) = F\X\(F X).
```

The substitution `H3 <- K\L\M\N\N` solves this last equation, and the final substitutions are:

```
F1 <- K\L\L
F2 <- K\L\M\(K L (L M))
H1 <- K\L\L
H2 <- K\L\M\N\(L N)
H3 <- K\L\M\N\N
```

SOLVE returns the substitutions for F1 and F2 to procedure **SYNTH**.

(Step **4**.) Therefore the constructed higher-order DCG is:

```
s(A\B\B) --> [a].
s(A\B\C\(A B (B C)) D) --> [a], s(D).
```

where the term `A\B\C\(A B (B C))` in the second rule essentially encodes the successor function.

3.2 Simple Natural Language DCG

We now turn to the synthesis of DCGs for a small fragment of a natural language grammar. While the example of section 3.1 showed that the types of all function variables in the DCG can be inferred completely prior to invoking **SOLVE**, the example we now consider illustrates that this is not always the case. This example also illustrates how the constraints from multiple examples help prune the search space, by eliminating unproductive substitutions quickly. Below on the left is the input CFG and, on the right, the DCG generated after step 2.

```
s --> np, iv.           s((F1 V W)) --> np(V),iv(W).
np --> det, n.          np((F2 V W)) --> det(V),n(W).
det --> [a].            det(F3) --> [a].
det --> [every].        det(F4) --> [every].
n --> [program].        n(F5) --> [program].
n --> [computer].       n(F6) --> [computer].
iv --> [runs].          iv(F7) --> [runs].
iv --> [halts].         iv(F8) --> [halts].
```

Suppose that the sentences and their user-supplied semantic representations in step 3a of **SYNTH** are as follows: (constants `exists`, `all`, `and`, `implies`, `prog`, `comp`, `run`, `halt` are assumed to be given suitable types):

```
[a,program,runs]        (exists X\(and (prog X) (run X))))
[every,program,runs]    (all X\(implies (prog X) (run X))))
[a,computer,runs]       (exists X\(and (comp X) (run X))))
[a,program,halts]       (exists X\(and (prog X) (halt X))))
```

The equation-set E after step 3c of **SYNTH** would be:

```
{(F1 (F2 F3 F5) F7) = (exists X\(and (prog X) (run X)))
 (F1 (F2 F4 F5) F7) = (all X\(and (prog X) (run X)))
 (F1 (F2 F3 F6) F7) = (exists X\(and (comp X) (run X)))
 (F1 (F2 F3 F5) F8) = (exists X\(and (prog X) (halt X)))}
```

SOLVE obtains first an imitation substitution from **SUBST** for the function variable `F1`, as follows: `F1 <- X\Y\(exists (G X Y)`. However, this choice is immediately eliminated by **DECOMP** when `F1` is substituted for in the second equation. Hence **SOLVE** obtains the following projection substitution:

```
F1 <- K\L\(K (H1 K L)).
```

Since `F1` takes two arguments, its substitution term has two prefix variables. The first argument `K` is selected nondeterministically as the head of the substitution term. Since the type of `K` is still unknown at this point, the number of arguments of K is also selected nondeterministically. That is, the type of K is expressed as $\alpha \to \beta$, where α and β are type variables that will be instantiated later through unification by **DECOMP**. Under this substitution for F1, the above equations reduce to the following set:

```
{(F2 F3 F5 (H1 (F2 F3 F5) F7)) = (exists K\(and (prog K)
                                                (run K))),
 (F2 F4 F5 (H1 (F2 F4 F5) F7)) = (all K\(implies (prog K)
                                                 (run K))),
 (F2 F3 F6 (H1 (F2 F3 F6) F7)) = (exists K\(and (comp K)
                                                (run K))),
 (F2 F3 F5 (H1 (F2 F3 F5) F8)) = (exists K\(and (prog K)
                                                (halt K)))}
```

Since F2 has three arguments, its type is of the form $\alpha_1 \to \alpha_2 \to \alpha_3 \to \gamma$, where α_1, α_2, α_3, and γ will be instantiated later. Once again an imitation substitution can be seen to fail, and a projection substitution must be used. Due to lack of space, we do not pursue this example in detail here; the complete set of variable bindings, including those for the auxiliary function variables introduced during the derivation, is as follows:

```
F2  <- K\L\M\(K (H2 K L M) (H3 K L M))
F3  <- K\L\(exists (H4 K L))
H4  <- K\L\M\(and (H6 K L M) (H5 K L M))
H5  <- K\L\M\(K (H7 K L M))
H2  <- K\L\M\M
H1  <- K\L\L
F7  <- K\(run (H8 K))
H8  <- K\K
H7  <- K\L\M\M
H6  <- K\L\M\(L (H9 K L M))
H3  <- K\L\M\L
F5  <- K\(prog (H10 K))
H10 <- K\K
H9  <- K\L\M\M
F4  <- K\L\(all (H11 K L))
H11 <- K\L\M\(implies (H13 K L M) (H12 K L M))
H12 <- K\L\M\(K (H14 K L M))
H14 <- K\L\M\M
H13 <- K\L\M\(L (H15 K L M))
H15 <- K\L\M\M
F6  <- K\(comp (H16 K))
H16 <- K\K
F8  <- K\(halt (H17 K))
H17 <- K\K
```

Thus the constructed higher-order DCG would be:

```
s((A B)) --> np(A),iv(B).
np(A\(B A C)) --> det(B),n(C).
det(A\B\(exists C\(and (B C) (A C)))) --> [a].
det(A\B\(all C\(implies (B C) (A C)))) --> [every].
n(A\(prog A)) --> [program].
n(A\(comp A)) --> [computer].
iv(A\(run A)) --> [runs].
iv(A\(halt A)) --> [halts].
```

This example also illustrates our point that it can be easy to give the CFG and the semantic representations of typical sentences, but it is not so easy to construct the resulting DCG manually.

3.3 Type Raising

Suppose that the CFG of section 3.2 is extended to include proper nouns. Shown below on the left are three new CFG rules for this purpose, and, on the right, their corresponding DCG rules, from step 2.

```
np --> pn.              np((F9 V)) --> pn(V).
pn --> [shrdlu].        pn(F10) --> [shrdlu].
pn --> [eliza].         pn(F11) --> [eliza].
```

Note that the DCG rule obtained earlier for s,

```
s((A B)) --> np(A),iv(B)
```

computes the semantic representation of a sentence by applying the representation of np (noun phrase) to the representation of iv (intransitive verb). However, if the noun phrase is a proper noun, its semantic representation can be applied to that of the verb only after converting the constant corresponding to the proper noun into a function. This operation is known as the *type raising*—the extent to which a constant must be "raised" depends upon the context in which it is used—and represents yet another difficulty in the manual construction of a DCG. It is noteworthy that the structure of the DCG constructed from step 2 is general enough that it automatically provides for such type-raising, without any special consideration. In the rule np((F9 V)) --> pn(V), the function F9 will perform the necessary raising. We illustrate how this is achieved, assuming the following sample sentences and their user-supplied semantic representations.

```
[shrdlu,runs]        (run shrdlu)
[eliza,runs]         (run eliza)
[shrdlu,halts]       (halt shrdlu)
```

The new equations added are as follows.

```
{(F1 (F9 F10) F7) = (run shrdlu)
 (F1 (F9 F11) F7) = (run eliza)
 (F1 (F9 F10) F8) = (halt shrdlu)}
```

As before **F1** gets the substitution **F1 <- A\B\(A B)**, and the above equations reduce to:

```
{(F9 F10 F7) = (run shrdlu)
 (F9 F11 F7) = (run eliza)
 (F9 F10 F8) = (halt shrdlu)}
```

Now, an imitation substitution is not possible for **F9**, and it can be easily derived that the following substitution is the only viable choice (derivation details omitted):

```
F9 <- A\B\(B A)
```

Thus the necessary type-raising follows directly from the desired semantic representations. The substitutions for **F10** and **F11** are now easily determined to be: **F10 <- shrdlu, F11 <- eliza**.

4   Related Work and Current Status

We are not aware of any research that solves our stated problem, but research in machine learning and program synthesis by examples is closely related. Our DCG synthesis work can be considered as an example of inductive learning, since the semantics of all sentences of a grammar is induced from a finite number of examples. In this connection, it would be interesting to characterize the class of DCGs that can be learned from finite number of examples using our synthesis technique. Perhaps the most closely related area of research is program synthesis from schemas and examples. The analogy between DCG synthesis and program synthesis is the following: the context-free grammar can be viewed as a schema; the sample sentence-meaning pairs can be viewed as the sample input-output pairs of the desired program; and the unknown function variables of the DCG of step 2 of **SYNTH** correspond to the unknown function variables of the program schema. However, program synthesis seems to be the harder of the two problems, since DCG synthesis starts with the knowledge of the context-free grammar, whereas program synthesis also involves the determination of the right schema. Recently, Hagiya showed the use of the simply-typed λ-calculus and higher-order unification for program synthesis from schemas and examples (Hagiya 90, Hagiya 91). A noteworthy technical difference from Hagiya's work is that he encodes schemas using a special kind of term and provides an extended higher-order unification procedure for an extended simply-typed λ-calculus, whereas we maintain a sharp difference between the grammar (or schema) and the typed λ-terms.

In order to increase the execution efficiency of the synthesized DCGs for forward execution (i.e., for generating the semantic representations of sentences), we have developed a procedure for partially executing the higher-order terms occurring in the DCGs. Space constraints preclude a full discussion of this issue in this paper—see (Haas 92) for details—but basically the idea is to perform β-reductions at "compile time" where possible, so that first-order unification suffices to compute the correct semantic representation. For efficient reverse execution, a meta-interpretive technique can be used to ensure that subgoals with more instantiated argument terms are executed before others, so as to minimize nondeterminism. With this scheme, reverse execution appears to be as efficient as forward execution.

An implementation of our synthesis procedure has been completed, and all examples shown in sections 2 and 3 were tested out on this implementation. This implementation also supports partial execution, but presently does not automatically generate sentences; the user must instead supply sample sentences and their logical forms. Using this implementation, we have successfully synthesized larger DCGs than the ones shown in this paper, and we are in the process of synthesizing a DCG for a small natural query language. In considering the synthesis of DCGs for larger fragments of natural language than natural query languages, it becomes necessary to work with ambiguous grammars. Certain forms of ambiguous grammars can be accomodated in our scheme with only minor extensions: essentially, the user provides one semantic representation for each different parse of an ambiguous sentence; and **SYNTH** sets up multiple equations for such a sentence—the pairing-up of each user-supplied semantic representation with the computed semantic representation contributes an additional source of nondeterminism.

As noted in the discussion of section 2, there are several areas of further work, and there are reasonable constraints that we might impose on the problem to make it more tractable. With more experience in writing semantic representations in the typed λ-calculus semantics, we would be in a better position to formulate a methodology for writing CFGs and their representations so that DCGs can be synthesized more efficiently. Overall, despite the semi-decidability of the higher-order unification procedure, we feel that this approach to DCG synthesis is quite feasible.

Acknowledgments

We thank Dale Miller, Fernando Pereira, and the anonymous referees for their helpful comments and suggestions. This research was supported in part by NSF grant CCR 9004357.

References

Dowek, G. (1992) "Third Order Matching is Decidable," *Seventh Annual LICS*, pp. 2-10, Santa Cruz, CA, June 1992.

Dowty, D. R., Wall, R. E. and Peters, S. (1981) "Introduction to Montague Semantics," Dordrecht, Holland; Boston: D. Reidel Pub. Co.

Haas, J. (1992) "Automatic Generalization of Semantics: From Context-Free to Definite-Clause Grammars," Ph.D. dissertation, Department of Computer Science, SUNY at Buffalo, expected 1992.

Hagiya, M. (1990) "Programming by Example and Proving by Example using Higher-order Unification," In M. E. Stickel (ed.) *Proc. 10th CADE*, pp. 588–602, Kaiserslautern, July 1990. Springer-Verlag LNAI 449.

Hagiya, M. (1991) "From Programming by Example to Proving by Example," In T. Ito and A. R. Meyer (eds.), *Proc. Intl. Conf. on Theoret. Aspects of Comp. Software*, pp. 387–419, Springer-Verlag LNCS 526.

Huet, G. P. (1975) "A Unification Algorithm for Typed λ-Calculus," *Theoretical Computer Science*, 1 27-57.

Huet, G. P. and Lang, B. (1978) "Proving and Applying Program Transformations Expressed with Second-Order Patterns," *Acta Informatica*, vol. 11, pp. 31-55.

Miller, D. and Nadathur, G. (1986) "Some Uses of Higher-Order Logic in Computational Linguistics," *Proc. 24th Annual Meeting of the Assoc. for Computational Linguistics*, pp. 247-255.

Nadathur, G. and Miller, D. (1988) "An Overview of λProlog," *Proc. 5th ICLP*, pp. 810-827.

Pereira, F. C. N. (1990) "Semantic Interpretation as Higher-Order Deduction," *Proc. Second European Workshop on Logics and AI*, Amsterdam.

Pereira, F. C. N., and Warren, D. H. D. (1980) "Definite Clause Grammars for Language Analysis - A Survey of the Formalism and a Comparison with Transition Networks," *Artificial Intelligence*, vol. 13, pp. 231-278.

van Benthem, J. F. A. K. (1986) *Essays in Logical Semantics*, chapter 10, Reidel Pub. Co., Hingham, MA, USA, Kluwer Academic Pub.

Zadrozny, W. (1992) "On Compositional Semantics," IBM Research Report, submitted for publication.

Negation II

Representing Actions
in Extended Logic Programming

Michael Gelfond
Department of Computer Science
University of Texas at El Paso
El Paso, TX 79968

Vladimir Lifschitz
Department of Computer Sciences
and Department of Philosophy
University of Texas at Austin
Austin, TX 78712

Abstract

We represent properties of actions in a logic programming language that uses both classical negation and negation as failure. The method is applicable to temporal projection problems with incomplete information, as well as to reasoning about the past. It is proved to be sound relative to a semantics of action based on states and transition functions.

1 Introduction

This paper extends the work of Eshghi and Kowalski [4], Evans [5] and Apt and Bezem [1] on representing properties of actions in logic programming languages with negation as failure.

Our goal is to overcome some of the limitations of the earlier work. The existing formalizations of action in logic programming are adequate for only the simplest kind of temporal reasoning—"temporal projection." In a temporal projection problem, we are given a description of the initial state of the world, and use properties of actions to determine what the world will look like after a series of actions is performed. Moreover, the existing formalizations can be used for temporal projection only in the cases when the given description of the initial state is complete. The reason for that is that traditional logic programming languages automatically apply the "closed world assumption" to each predicate.

We are interested here in temporal reasoning of a more general kind, when the values of some fluents[1] in one or more situations are given, and the goal is to derive other facts about the values of fluents. Besides temporal projection, this class of reasoning problems includes, for instance, the cases when we want to use information about the current state of the world for answering questions about the past[2]. The view of logic programming accepted in this paper is strictly declarative. The adequacy of a representation of a body of knowledge in a logic programming language means, to us, adequacy with respect to the declarative semantics of that language. It is interesting to find out, of course, whether any of the currently available query evaluation procedures will actually terminate if used for answering questions on the basis of our representation, and how fast, but those are secondary issues. In fact, the language of "extended logic programs" used in this paper is a subset of the system of default logic from [16], and our work can be viewed as a development of the approach to temporal reasoning based on nonnormal defaults [15].

Two parts of this paper may be of more general interest.

First, we introduce here a simple declarative language for describing actions, called $\mathcal{A}$. Traditionally, ideas on representing properties of actions in classical logic or nonmonotonic formalisms are explained on specific examples, such as the "Yale shooting problem" from [9]. Competing approaches are evaluated and compared in terms of their ability to handle such examples. Sandewall [17] provides a systematic comparison of the most important approaches by applying them to a rather long series of problems of this kind. We propose to supplement the use of examples by a different method. A particular methodology for representing action can be formally described as a translation from $\mathcal{A}$, or from a subset or a superset of $\mathcal{A}$, into a "target language"—for instance, into a language based on classical logic or on circumscription. The soundness and completeness of each particular translation become precise mathematical questions; the possibilities and limitations of each methodology can be described in terms of the "dialects" of $\mathcal{A}$ to which it is applicable. Our method for describing properties of actions in logic programming is presented here as a translation from $\mathcal{A}$ into the language of extended logic programs, and the soundness of this translation is the main technical result of the paper.

Second, the proof of the main theorem depends on a relationship between stable models [7] and signings [11], that may be interesting as a part of the general theory of logic programming.

The language $\mathcal{A}$ is introduced in Section 2, and Section 3 is a brief review of extended logic programs. Our translation from $\mathcal{A}$ into logic programming is defined in Section 4, and the soundness theorem is stated in Section 5. Section 6 contains the lemmas that relate stable models to signings. The proof of the soundness theorem can be found in the complete version of this paper.

2   A Language for Describing Actions

A description of an action domain in the language $\mathcal{A}$ consists of "propositions" of two kinds. A "v-proposition" specifies the value of a fluent in a particular situation—either in the initial situation, or after performing a sequence of actions. An "e-proposition" describes the effect of an action on a fluent.

We begin with two disjoint nonempty sets of symbols, called *fluent names* and *action names*. A *fluent expression* is a fluent name possibly preceded by ¬. A *v-proposition* is an expression of the form

$$F \textbf{ after } A_1; \ldots; A_m, \tag{1}$$

where F is a fluent expression, and $A_1, \ldots, A_m$ ($m \geq 0$) are action names. If $m = 0$, we will write (1) as

initially F.

An *e-proposition* is an expression of the form

$$A \textbf{ causes } F \textbf{ if } P_1, \ldots, P_n, \tag{2}$$

where A is an action name, and each of $F, P_1, \ldots, P_n$ ($n \geq 0$) is a fluent expression. About this proposition we say that it *describes the effect of A on F*, and that $P_1, \ldots, P_n$ are its *preconditions*. If $n = 0$, we will drop **if** and write simply

A **causes** F.

A *proposition* is a v-proposition or an e-proposition. A *domain description*, or simply *domain*, is a set of propositions (not necessarily finite).

Example 1. The Fragile Object domain, motivated by an example from [18], has the fluent names *Holding*, *Fragile* and *Broken*, and the action *Drop*. It consists of two e-propositions:

> *Drop* **causes** ¬*Holding* **if** *Holding*,
> *Drop* **causes** *Broken* **if** *Holding*, *Fragile*.

Example 2. The Yale Shooting domain, motivated by the example from [9] mentioned above, is defined as follows. The fluent names are *Loaded* and *Alive*; the action names are *Load*, *Shoot* and *Wait*. The domain is characterized by the propositions

> **initially** ¬*Loaded*,
> **initially** *Alive*,
> *Load* **causes** *Loaded*,
> *Shoot* **causes** ¬*Alive* **if** *Loaded*,
> *Shoot* **causes** ¬*Loaded*.

Example 3. The Murder Mystery domain, motivated by an example from [2], is obtained from the Yale Shooting domain by substituting

$$\neg Alive \textbf{ after } Shoot;\ Wait \qquad\qquad (3)$$

for the proposition **initially** $\neg Loaded$.

Example 4. The Stolen Car domain, motivated by an example from [10], has one fluent name *Stolen* and one action name *Wait*, and is characterized by two propositions:

$$\textbf{initially } \neg Stolen,$$
$$Stolen \textbf{ after } Wait;\ Wait;\ Wait.$$

To describe the semantics of $\mathcal{A}$, we will define what the "models" of a domain description are, and when a v-proposition is "entailed" by a domain description.

A *state* is a set of fluent names. Given a fluent name F and a state σ, we say that F *holds in* σ if $F \in \sigma$; $\neg F$ holds in σ if $F \notin \sigma$. A *transition function* is a mapping Φ of the set of pairs (A, σ), where A is an action name and σ is a state, into the set of states. A *structure* is a pair (σ_0, Φ), where σ_0 is a state (the *initial state* of the structure), and Φ is a transition function.

For any structure M and any action names $A_1, \ldots, A_m$, by $M^{A_1; \ldots; A_m}$ we denote the state

$$\Phi(A_m, \Phi(A_{m-1}, \ldots, \Phi(A_1, \sigma_0) \ldots)),$$

where Φ is the transition function of M, and σ_0 is the initial state of M. We say that a v-proposition (1) is *true* in a structure M if F holds in the state $M^{A_1; \ldots; A_m}$, and that it is *false* otherwise. In particular, a proposition of the form **initially** F is true in M iff F holds in the initial state of M.

A structure (σ_0, Φ) is a *model* of a domain description D if every v-proposition from D is true in (σ_0, Φ), and, for every action name A, every fluent name F, and every state σ, the following conditions are satisfied:

(i) if D includes an e-proposition describing the effect of A on F whose preconditions hold in σ, then $F \in \Phi(A, \sigma)$;

(ii) if D includes an e-proposition describing the effect of A on $\neg F$ whose preconditions hold in σ, then $F \notin \Phi(A, \sigma)$;

(iii) if D does not include such e-propositions, then $F \in \Phi(A, \sigma)$ iff $F \in \sigma$.

It is clear that there can be at most one transition function Φ satisfying conditions (i)–(iii). Consequently, different models of the same domain description can differ only by their initial states. For instance, the Fragile Object domain (Example 1) has 8 models, whose initial states are the subsets of

$$\{Holding,\ Fragile,\ Broken\};$$

in each model, the transition function is defined by the equation

$$\Phi(Drop, \sigma) = \begin{cases} \sigma \setminus \{Holding\} \cup \{Broken\}, & \text{if } Fragile \in \sigma, \\ \sigma \setminus \{Holding\}, & \text{otherwise.} \end{cases}$$

A domain description is *consistent* if it has a model, and *complete* if it has exactly one model. The Fragile Object domain is consistent, but incomplete. The Yale Shooting domain (Example 2) is complete; its only model is defined by the equations

$$\sigma_0 = \{Alive\},$$
$$\Phi(Load, \sigma) = \sigma \cup \{Loaded\},$$
$$\Phi(Shoot, \sigma) = \begin{cases} \sigma \setminus \{Loaded, Alive\}, & \text{if } Loaded \in \sigma, \\ \sigma, & \text{otherwise,} \end{cases}$$
$$\Phi(Wait, \sigma) = \sigma.$$

The Murder Mystery domain (Example 3) is complete also; it has the same transition function as Yale Shooting, and the initial state $\{Loaded, Alive\}$. The Stolen Car domain (Example 4) is inconsistent.

A v-proposition is *entailed* by a domain description D if it is true in every model of D. For instance, Yale Shooting entails

$$\neg Alive \textbf{ after } Load; Wait; Shoot.$$

Murder Mystery entails, among others, the propositions

$$\textbf{initially } Loaded$$

and

$$\neg Alive \textbf{ after } Wait; Shoot.$$

Note that the last proposition differs from (3) by the order in which the two actions are executed. This example illustrates the possibility of reasoning about alternative "possible futures" of the initial situation.

Although the language $\mathcal{A}$ is adequate for formalizing several interesting domains, its expressive possibilities are rather limited. The only fluents available in $\mathcal{A}$ are propositional ones. It is impossible to say in $\mathcal{A}$ that certain fluents are related in some way (for instance, that $F1$ and $F2$ cannot be simultaneously true); for this reason, actions described in $\mathcal{A}$ have no indirect effects ("ramifications"). Every action is assumed to be executable in any situation. We cannot talk about the duration of actions, or describe actions that are nondeterministic, or are performed concurrently. The inconsistency of the Stolen Car domain illustrates the fact that $\mathcal{A}$ cannot be used for representing "causal anomalies," or "miracles" [12][3]. Defining and studying extensions of $\mathcal{A}$ is a topic for future work.

The entailment relation of $\mathcal{A}$ is nonmonotonic, in the sense that adding an e-proposition to a domain description D may nonmonotonically change the set of propositions entailed by D. (This cannot happen when a v-proposition is added.) For this reason, a modular translation from $\mathcal{A}$ into another declarative language (that is, a translation that processes propositions one by one) can be reasonably adequate only if this other language is nonmonotonic also.

3 Extended Logic Programs

Representing incomplete information in traditional logic programming languages is difficult, because their semantics is based on the automatic application of the closed world assumption to all predicates. Given a ground query, a traditional logic programming system can produce only one of two answers, *yes* or *no*; it will never tell us that the truth value of the query cannot be determined on the basis of the information included in the program.

Extended logic programs, introduced in [8], are, in this sense, different. The language of extended programs distinguishes between negation as failure *not* and classical negation $\neg$. The general form of an extended rule is

$$L_0 \leftarrow L_1, \ldots, L_m, not\, L_{m+1}, \ldots, not\, L_n, \tag{4}$$

where each L_i is a literal, that is, an atom possibly preceded by $\neg$. An extended program is a set of such rules. Here is an example:

$$\begin{aligned} &p, \\ &\neg q \leftarrow p, \\ &r \leftarrow \neg p, \\ &t \leftarrow \neg q, not\, s, \\ &u \leftarrow not\, \neg u. \end{aligned} \tag{5}$$

Intuitively, these rules say:

p is true;
q is false if p is true;
r is true if p is false;
t is true if q is false and there is no evidence that s is true;
u is true if there is no evidence that it is false.

The answers that an implementation of this language is supposed to give to the ground queries are:

$$\begin{aligned} p: &\quad yes, \\ q: &\quad no, \\ r: &\quad unknown, \\ s: &\quad unknown, \\ t: &\quad yes, \\ u: &\quad yes. \end{aligned}$$

The semantics of extended logic programs defines when a set of ground literals is an *answer set* of a program [8]. For instance, the program (5) has one answer set, $\{p, \neg q, t, u\}$.

The answer sets of a program can be easily characterized in terms of default logic. We will identify the rule (4) with the default

$$L_1 \wedge \ldots \wedge L_m \; : \; \overline{L_{m+1}}, \ldots, \overline{L_n} \; / \; L_0 \qquad (6)$$

($\overline{L}$ stands for the literal complementary to L). Thus every extended program can be viewed as a default theory. The answer sets of a program are simply its extensions in the sense of default logic, intersected with the set of ground literals ([8], Proposition 3).

4 Describing Actions by Logic Programs

Now we are ready to define the translation π from $\mathcal{A}$ into the language of extended programs.

About two different e-propositions we say that they are *similar* if they differ only by their preconditions. Our translation method is defined for any domain description that does not contain similar e-propositions. This condition prohibits, for instance, combining in the same domain such propositions as

Shoot **causes** ¬*Alive* **if** *Loaded*,
Shoot **causes** ¬*Alive* **if** *VeryNervous*.

(*VeryNervous* refers to the victim, of course—not to the gun.)

Let D be a domain description without similar e-propositions. The corresponding logic program πD uses variables of three sorts: *situation* variables $s, s', \ldots$, *fluent* variables $f, f', \ldots$, and *action* variables $a, a', \ldots$[4]. Its only situation constant is $S0$; its fluent constants and action constants are, respectively, the fluent names and action names of D. There are also some predicate and function symbols; the sorts of their arguments and values will be clear from their use in the rules below.

The program πD will consist of the translations of the individual propositions from D and the four standard rules:

$$Holds(f, Result(a, s)) \leftarrow Holds(f, s), \; not \; Noninertial(f, a, s), \\ \neg Holds(f, Result(a, s)) \leftarrow \neg Holds(f, s), \; not \; Noninertial(f, a, s), \qquad (7)$$

$$Holds(f, s) \leftarrow Holds(f, Result(a, s)), \; not \; Noninertial(f, a, s), \\ \neg Holds(f, s) \leftarrow \neg Holds(f, Result(a, s)), \; not \; Noninertial(f, a, s). \qquad (8)$$

These rules are motivated by the "commonsense law of inertia," according to which the value of a fluent after performing an action is normally the same as before. The rules (7) allow us to apply the law of inertia in reasoning "from the past to the future": the first—when a fluent is known to be true in the past, and the second—when it is known to be false. The rules (8) play the same role for reasoning "from the future to the past." The auxiliary predicate *Noninertial* is essentially an "abnormality predicate" [13].

Now we will define how π translates v-propositions and e-propositions. The following notation will be useful: For any fluent name F,

$$|F| \text{ is } F, \quad |\neg F| \text{ is } F,$$

and, if t is a situation term, $Holds(\neg F, t)$ stands for $\neg Holds(F, t)$. The last convention allows us to write $Holds(F, t)$ even when F is a fluent name preceded by $\neg$. Furthermore, if $A_1, \ldots, A_m$ are action names, $[A_1; \ldots; A_m]$ stands for the term

$$Result(A_m, Result(A_{m-1}, \ldots, Result(A_1, S0) \ldots)).$$

It is clear that every situation term without variables can be represented in this form.

The translation of a v-proposition (1) is

$$Holds(F, [A_1; \ldots; A_m]). \tag{9}$$

For instance, $\pi(\textbf{initially } Alive)$ is

$$Holds(Alive, S0),$$

and $\pi(\neg Alive \textbf{ after } Shoot)$ is

$$\neg Holds(Alive, Result(Shoot, S0)).$$

The translation of an e-proposition (2) consists of $2n + 2$ rules. The first of them is

$$Holds(F, Result(A, s)) \leftarrow Holds(P_1, s), \ldots, Holds(P_n, s). \tag{10}$$

It allows us to prove that F will hold after A, if the preconditions are satisfied. The second rule is

$$Noninertial(|F|, A, s) \leftarrow not \ \overline{Holds(P_1, s)}, \ldots, not \ \overline{Holds(P_n, s)} \tag{11}$$

($\overline{Holds(P_i, s)}$ is the literal complementary to $Holds(P_i, s)$.) It disables the inertia rules (7), (8) in the cases when f can be affected by a. Without this rule, the program would be contradictory: We would prove, using a rule of the form (10), that an unloaded gun becomes loaded after the action *Load*, and also, using the second of the rules (7), that it remains unloaded!

Note the use of *not* in (11). We want to disable the inertia rules not only when the preconditions for the change in the value of F are known to hold, but whenever *there is no evidence that they do not hold*. If, for instance, we do not know whether *Loaded* currently holds, then we do not want to conclude by inertia that the value of *Alive* will remain the same after *Shoot*. We cannot draw any conclusions about the new value of *Alive*. If we replaced the body of (11) by $Holds(P_1, s), \ldots, Holds(P_n, s)$, the translation would become unsound.

Besides (10) and (11), the translation of (2) contains, for each i ($1 \leq i \leq n$), the rules

$$Holds(P_i, s) \leftarrow \overline{Holds(F, s)}, Holds(F, Result(A, s)) \tag{12}$$

and

$$\overline{Holds(P_i, s)} \leftarrow \overline{Holds(F, Result(A, s))}, \\ Holds(P_1, s), \ldots, Holds(P_{i-1}, s), \\ Holds(P_{i+1}, s), \ldots, Holds(P_n, s). \tag{13}$$

The rules (12) justify the following form of reasoning: If the value of F has changed after performing A, then we can conclude that the preconditions were satisfied when A was performed. These rules would be unsound in the presence of similar propositions. The rules (13) allow us to conclude that a precondition was false from the fact that performing an action did not lead to the result described by an effect axiom, while all other preconditions were true.

We will illustrate the translation process by applying it to Yale Shooting (Example 2). The translation of that domain includes, in addition to (7) and (8), the following rules:

$Y1.$ $\neg Holds(Loaded, S0)$.

$Y2.$ $Holds(Alive, S0)$.

$Y3.$ $Holds(Loaded, Result(Load, s))$.

$Y4.$ $Noninertial(Loaded, Load, s)$.

$Y5.$ $\neg Holds(Alive, Result(Shoot, s)) \leftarrow Holds(Loaded, s)$.

$Y6.$ $Noninertial(Alive, Shoot, s) \leftarrow not \neg Holds(Loaded, s)$.

$Y7.$ $Holds(Loaded, s) \leftarrow Holds(Alive, s), \neg Holds(Alive, Result(Shoot, s))$.

$Y8.$ $\neg Holds(Loaded, s) \leftarrow Holds(Alive, Result(Shoot, s))$.

$Y9.$ $\neg Holds(Loaded, Result(Shoot, s))$.

$Y10.$ $Noninertial(Loaded, Shoot, s)$.

It is instructive to compare this set of rules with the formalization of Yale Shooting given by Apt and Bezem [1], who were only interested in temporal projection problems, and did not use classical negation. Instead of our four inertia rules, they have one, corresponding to the first of the rules (7). In addition, their program includes counterparts of $Y2$, $Y3$, $Y5$ and $Y6$. It does not tell us whether *Loaded* holds in the initial situation, but the negative answer to this question follows by the closed world assumption. Their rule corresponding to $Y5$ does not have $\neg$ in the head, of course; instead, the new fluent *Dead* is used. In their counterpart of $Y6$, the combination *not* $\neg$ is missing; this does not lead to any difficulties, because the closed world assumption is implicitly postulated.

5 Soundness Theorem

We say that a ground literal L is *entailed* by an extended logic program, if it belongs to all its answer sets (or, equivalently, to all its extensions in the sense of default logic). Using this notion of entailment and the entailment relation for the language $\mathcal{A}$ introduced in Section 2, we can state a result expressing the soundness of the translation π.

Soundness Theorem. *Let D be a domain description without similar e-propositions. For any v-proposition P, if πD entails πP, then D entails P.*

For an inconsistent D, the statement of the soundness theorem is trivial, because such D entails every v-proposition. For consistent domain descriptions, the statement of the theorem is an immediate consequence of the following lemma which will be proved elsewhere:

Soundness Lemma. *Let D be a consistent domain description without similar e-propositions. There exists an answer set Z of πD such that, for any v-proposition P, if $\pi P \in Z$ then D entails P.*

Note that the lemma asserts the possibility of selecting Z uniformly for all P; this is more than is required for the soundness theorem.

The set Z from the statement of the lemma is obviously consistent, because a consistent domain description cannot entail two complementary v-propositions. Consequently, if D is consistent and does not include similar v-propositions, then πD has a consistent answer set.

The converse of the soundness theorem does not hold, so that the translation π is incomplete. This following simple counterexample belongs to Thomas Woo (personal communication). Let D be the domain with one fluent name F and one action name A, characterized by two propositions:

$$A \textbf{ after } F,$$
$$A \textbf{ causes } F \textbf{ if } F.$$

It is clear that D entails **initially** F. But the translation of this proposition, $Holds(F, S0)$, is not entailed by πD. Indeed, it is easy to verify that the set of all positive ground literals other than $Holds(F, S0)$ is an answer set of πD.

6   Answer Sets and Signings

To prove the soundness lemma, we need the following definition. Let Π be a general logic program (that is, an extended program that does not contain classical negation). A *signing* for Π is any set S of ground atoms such that, for any ground instance

$$B_0 \leftarrow B_1, \ldots, B_m, not\ B_{m+1}, \ldots, not\ B_n$$

of any rule from Π, either

$$B_0, B_1, \ldots, B_m \in S,\ B_{m+1}, \ldots, B_n \notin S$$

or

$$B_0, B_1, \ldots, B_m \notin S,\ B_{m+1}, \ldots, B_n \in S.^5$$

For example, $\{p\}$ is a signing for the program

$$p \leftarrow not\ q, \quad q \leftarrow not\ p, \quad r \leftarrow q.$$

In this section we show that the answer sets of a general program Π which has a signing S can be characterized in terms of the fixpoints of a monotone operator. Specifically, for any set X of ground atoms, let θX be the symmetric difference of X and S:

$$\theta X = (X \setminus S) \cup (S \setminus X).$$

Obviously, θ is one to one. Moreover, it is clear that θ is an involution:

$$\begin{aligned}
\theta^2 X &= \{[(X \setminus S) \cup (S \setminus X)] \setminus S\} \cup \{S \setminus [(X \setminus S) \cup (S \setminus X)]\} \\
&= (X \setminus S) \cup (S \cap X) \\
&= X.
\end{aligned}$$

We will define a monotone operator ϕ such that any X is an answer set of Π if and only if θX is a fixpoint of ϕ.

Recall that, for general logic programs, the notion of an answer set (or "stable model") can be defined by means of the following construction [7]. Let Π be a general logic program, with every rule replaced by all its ground instances. The *reduct* Π^X of Π relative to a set X of ground atoms is obtained from Π by deleting

(i) each rule that has an expression of the form $not\ B$ in its body with $B \in X$, and

(ii) all expressions of the form $not\ B$ in the bodies of the remaining rules.

Clearly, Π^X is a positive program, and we can consider its "minimal model"—the smallest set of ground atoms closed under its rules. If this set coincides with X, then X is an *answer set* of Π.

This condition can be expressed by the equation $X = \alpha \Pi^X$, where α is the operator that maps any positive program to its minimal model.

Let S be a signing for Π. The operator ϕ is defined by the equation

$$\phi X = \theta \alpha \Pi^{\theta X}.$$

Lemma 1. *A set X of ground atoms is an answer set of Π iff θX is a fixpoint of ϕ.*

Proof. By the definition of ϕ, θX is a fixpoint of ϕ iff

$$\theta \alpha \Pi^{\theta^2 X} = \theta X.$$

Since θ is one-to-one and an involution, this is equivalent to

$$\alpha \Pi^X = X.$$

Note that, since θ is an involution, Lemma 1 can be also stated as follows: X is an answer set of Π iff $X = \theta Y$ for some fixpoint Y of ϕ.

Lemma 2. *The operator ϕ is monotone.*

Proof. Let Π_1 be the set of all rules from Π whose heads belong to S, and let Π_2 be the set of all remaining rules. Clearly, for any X,

$$\Pi^X = \Pi_1^X \cup \Pi_2^X.$$

Since S is a signing for Π, all atoms occurring in Π_1^X belong to S, and all atoms occurring in Π_2^X belong to the complement of S. Consequently, Π_1^X and Π_2^X are disjoint, and

$$\alpha \Pi^X = \alpha \Pi_1^X \cup \alpha \Pi_2^X.$$

Furthermore, for any expression of the form *not B* occurring in Π_1, B does not belong to S; consequently,

$$\Pi_1^X = \Pi_1^{X \setminus S}.$$

Similarly, for any expression of the form *not B* occurring in Π_2, B belongs to S, so that

$$\Pi_2^X = \Pi_2^{X \cap S}.$$

Consequently, for every X,

$$\alpha \Pi^X = \alpha \Pi_1^{X \setminus S} \cup \alpha \Pi_2^{X \cap S}.$$

In particular,

$$\alpha \Pi^{\theta X} = \alpha \Pi_1^{\theta X \setminus S} \cup \alpha \Pi_2^{\theta X \cap S}.$$

It is clear from the definition of θ that

$$\theta X \setminus S = X \setminus S,$$

$$\theta X \cap S = S \setminus X.$$

We conclude that

$$\alpha \Pi^{\theta X} = \alpha \Pi_1^{X \setminus S} \cup \alpha \Pi_2^{S \setminus X}.$$

By the choice of Π_1 and Π_2, $\alpha \Pi_1^{X \setminus S}$ is contained in S, and $\alpha \Pi_2^{S \setminus X}$ is disjoint with S. Consequently,

$$\alpha \Pi^{\theta X} \setminus S = \alpha \Pi_2^{S \setminus X},$$

$$S \setminus \alpha \Pi^{\theta X} = S \setminus \alpha \Pi_1^{X \setminus S}.$$

Hence

$$\phi X = \theta \alpha \Pi^{\theta X} = (\alpha \Pi^{\theta X} \setminus S) \cup (S \setminus \alpha \Pi^{\theta X}) = \alpha \Pi_2^{S \setminus X} \cup (S \setminus \alpha \Pi_1^{X \setminus S}).$$

Since α is monotone, and the reduct operators $X \mapsto \Pi_i^X$ are antimonotone, it follows that ϕ is monotone.

Having proved Lemmas 1 and 2, we can use properties of the fixpoints of monotone operators given by the Knaster-Tarski theorem [20] to study the answer sets of a program with a signing. The Knaster-Tarski theorem asserts, for instance, that every monotone operator has a fixpoint; this gives a new, and more direct, proof of the fact that every general program with a signing has at least one answer set.[6] Moreover, it asserts that a monotone operator has a least fixpoint, which is also its least pre-fixpoint. (A *pre-fixpoint* of ϕ is any set X such that $\phi X \subset X$.) This characterization of the least fixpoint of ϕ is used in the proof of the soundness lemma.

Footnotes

1. A *fluent* is something that may depend on the situation, as, for instance, the location of a moveable object [14]. In particular, *propositional* fluents are assertions that can be true or false depending on the situation.

2. One possible way to represent reasoning about the past in the framework of logic programming is to interpret it as "explanation" and "abduction" [19]. Our approach is more symmetric; we treat both reasoning about the future and reasoning about the past as "deductive." The precise relationship between the two approaches is a subject of further investigation

3. Our preferred approach to causal anomalies is to view them as evidence of unknown events that occur concurrently with the given actions and contribute to the properties of the new situation.

4. Using a sorted language implies, first of all, that all atoms in the rules of the program are formed in accordance with the syntax of sorted predicate

logic. Moreover, when we speak of an *instance* of a rule, it will be always assumed that the terms substituted for variables are of appropriate sorts.

5. This is slightly different from the original definition [11].

6. The existence of answer sets for such programs, and for programs of some more general types, was established by Phan Minh Dung [3] and François Fages [6].

Acknowledgements

We would like to thank G. N. Kartha and Norman McCain for comments on a draft of this paper, Kenneth Kunen for directing us to his paper on signings, and Thomas Woo for the counterexample reproduced in Section 5. This research was supported in part by NSF grants IRI-9101078 and IRI-9103112.

References

[1] Krzysztof Apt and Marc Bezem. Acyclic programs. In David Warren and Peter Szeredi, editors, *Logic Programming: Proc. of the Seventh Int'l Conf.*, pages 617–633, 1990.

[2] Andrew Baker. Nonmonotonic reasoning in the framework of situation calculus. *Artificial Intelligence*, 49:5–23, 1991.

[3] Phan Minh Dung. On the relations between stable and well-founded semantics of logic programs. *Theoretical Computer Science*, 1992. To appear.

[4] Kave Eshghi and Robert Kowalski. Abduction compared with negation as failure. In Giorgio Levi and Maurizio Martelli, editors, *Logic Programming: Proc. of the Sixth Int'l Conf.*, pages 234–255, 1989.

[5] Chris Evans. Negation-as-failure as an approach to the Hanks and McDermott problem. In *Proc. of the Second Int'l Symp. on Artificial Intelligence*, 1989.

[6] François Fages. Consistency of Clark's completion and existence of stable models. *Journal of Methods of logic in computer science*, 1992. To appear.

[7] Michael Gelfond and Vladimir Lifschitz. The stable model semantics for logic programming. In Robert Kowalski and Kenneth Bowen, editors, *Logic Programming: Proc. of the Fifth Int'l Conf. and Symp.*, pages 1070–1080, 1988.

[8] Michael Gelfond and Vladimir Lifschitz. Classical negation in logic programs and disjunctive databases. *New Generation Computing*, 9:365–385, 1991.

[9] Steve Hanks and Drew McDermott. Nonmonotonic logic and temporal projection. *Artificial Intelligence*, 33(3):379–412, 1987.

[10] Henry Kautz. The logic of persistence. In *Proc. of AAAI-86*, pages 401–405, 1986.

[11] Kenneth Kunen. Signed data dependencies in logic programs. *Journal of Logic Programming*, 7(3):231–245, 1989.

[12] Vladimir Lifschitz and Arkady Rabinov. Miracles in formal theories of actions. *Artificial Intelligence*, 38(2):225–237, 1989.

[13] John McCarthy. Applications of circumscription to formalizing common sense knowledge. *Artificial Intelligence*, 26(3):89–116, 1986.

[14] John McCarthy and Patrick Hayes. Some philosophical problems from the standpoint of artificial intelligence. In B. Meltzer and D. Michie, editors, *Machine Intelligence*, volume 4, pages 463–502. Edinburgh University Press, Edinburgh, 1969.

[15] Paul Morris. The anomalous extension problem in default reasoning. *Artificial Intelligence*, 35(3):383–399, 1988.

[16] Raymond Reiter. A logic for default reasoning. *Artificial Intelligence*, 13(1,2):81–132, 1980.

[17] Erik Sandewall. Features and fluents. Technical Report LiTH-IDA-R-91-29, Linköping University, 1992.

[18] Lenhart Schubert. Monotonic solution of the frame problem in the situation calculus: an efficient method for worlds with fully specified actions. In H.E. Kyburg, R. Loui, and G. Carlson, editors, *Knowledge Representation and Defeasible Reasoning*, pages 23–67. Kluwer, 1990.

[19] Murray Shanahan. Prediction is deduction but explanation is abduction. In *Proc. of IJCAI-89*, pages 1055–1060, 1989.

[20] Alfred Tarski. A lattice-theoretical fixpoint theorem and its applications. *Pacific Journal of Mathematics*, 5:285–309, 1955.

On Logic Program Semantics with Two Kinds of Negation

José Júlio Alferes
Luís Moniz Pereira
CRIA Uninova and DCS, U.Nova de Lisboa
2825 Monte da Caparica, Portugal
{jja|lmp}@fct.unl.pt

Abstract

Recently several authors have stressed and showed the importance of having a second kind of negation in logic programs for use in deductive databases, knowledge representation, and nonmonotonic reasoning [6, 7, 8, 9, 13, 14, 15, 24].

Different semantics for logic programs extended with $\neg$-negation (extended logic programs) have appeared [1, 4, 6, 9, 11, 12, 17, 19, 24] but, contrary to what happens with semantics for normal logic programs, there is no general comparison among them, specially in what concerns the use and meaning of the newly introduced $\neg$-negation.

The goal of this paper is to contrast a variety of these semantics in what concerns their use and meaning of $\neg$-negation, and its relation to classical negation and to the default negation of normal programs, here denoted by *not* .

To this purpose we define a parametrizeable schema to encompass and characterize a diversity of proposed semantics for extended logic programs, where the parameters are two: one the axioms $AX_\neg$ defining $\neg$-negation; another the minimality conditions not_{cond} defining *not*-negation.

By adjusting these parameters in the schema we can then specify several semantics involving two kinds of negation [6, 11, 17, 19, 24]. Other semantics, dealing with contradiction removal [1, 4, 12, 22], are not addressed yet by the schema. The issue will be briefly touched upon in section 5, as well as that of incorporating disjunction.

The structure of the paper is as follows: we begin with preliminary definitions; in section 2 we present the parametrizeable schema; next we present properties important for the study of extended logic program semantics, and show for various $AX_\neg$ whether or not the resulting semantics complies with such properties; afterwards, in section 4, we reconstruct the plurality of semantics for extended logic programs in our schema by specifying for each their set $AX_\neg$ and their condition not_{cond}; finally we address further developments.

1 Language

An *extended logic program* (or x–program) P is a set of rules of the form:
$H \leftarrow B_1, \ldots, B_n, \, not \, C_1, \ldots, not \, C_m$ where $n, m \geq 0$ and H, B_i, C_i are
objective literals. An *objective literal* is either an atom A or its negation
$\neg A$ where $\neg$ is one kind of negation introduced. The symbol *not* stands for
negation by default, an additional kind of negation. *not L* is termed a *default
literal*. *Literals* are either objective or default ones.

By the *language* of P, $\mathcal{L}(P)$ we mean the set of all ground literals built
from the symbols occuring in P.

Whenever unambigous we refer to extended logic programs simply as
programs. Without loss of generality [18], a set of rules stands for all its
ground instances wrt $\mathcal{L}(P)$. By *normal program* we mean any extended logic
program where all objective literals are atoms, so that only default negation
is present.

In the sequel, we translate every x–program P into a set of general clauses
$\bar{P}$, which we dub a *clausal logic program*. The models and interpretations of
clausal logic programs are the classical models and interpretations of sets of
general clauses. Propositions of the form *not_A* (translation in $\bar{P}$ for *not A*
in P) are called *default* ones, all other propositions being the *objective* ones.

2 Generic semantics for programs with two kinds of negation

Within this section we present the above mentioned parametrizeable schema.

First we begin by defining two generic semantics for normal logic programs extended with an extra kind of negation: one extending the stationary
semantics [18, 19] for normal programs (itself equivalent to well founded semantics [23]); another extending the stable model semantics [5]. We dub
these semantics generic because they assume little about the extra kind of
negation introduced. The meaning of the negation by default is however
completely determined in each of the two semantics (both stationary and
stable models) that we present.

Subsequently we generalize the schema in order to parametrize it as well
w.r.t. negation by default.

2.1 Stationary semantics for programs with two kinds of negation

Here we redefine the stationary semantics of [19] in order to parametrize it
with a generic second type of negation in addition to negation by default.

We start by defining stationary expansion of normal programs as in [19].

Definition 2.1 (Minimal Models) [19] *By minimal model of a theory T
we mean a model M of T with the property that there is no smaller model*

N of T which coincides with M on default propositions. If a formula F is true in all minimal models of T then we write: $T \models_{CIRC} F$ and say that F is minimally entailed by T.

This amounts to the predicate circumscription $CIRC(T; \mathcal{O}; \mathcal{D})$ of theory T in which objective propositions $\mathcal{O}$ are minimized and default propositions $\mathcal{D}$ are fixed.

Definition 2.2 (Stationary Expansion of Normal Programs) [19] *A stationary expansion of a normal program P is any consistent theory P^* which satisfies the fixed point condition $P^* = \bar{P} \cup \{not\_L \mid P^* \models_{CIRC} \neg L\}$ where L is any arbitrary objective literal, $\bar{P}$ is the program obtained from P by replacing every literal of the form not L by not_L, and where the distributive axiom $not(\neg L) \equiv \neg not\ L$ is assumed.*

Note that $\bar{P}$ is always a Horn set of clauses.

Example 1 Let $P = \{a \leftarrow not\ a; \quad b \leftarrow not\ a, c; \quad d \leftarrow not\ b\}$ whose clausal program is $\bar{P} = \{a \vee \neg not\_a; \quad b \vee \neg not\_a \vee \neg c; \quad d \vee \neg not\_b\}$. The only expansion of P is $P^* = \bar{P} \cup \{not\_b, not\_c, \neg not\_d\}$. In fact the minimal models of P^* are (throughout the examples we exhibit for clarity all literals):

$$\{ \quad not\_a, \quad not\_b, \quad not\_c, \quad \neg not\_d, \quad a, \quad \neg b, \quad \neg c, \quad d \quad \}$$
$$\{ \quad \neg not\_a, \quad not\_b, \quad not\_c, \quad \neg not\_d, \quad \neg a, \quad \neg b, \quad \neg c, \quad d \quad \}$$

As P^* entails $\neg b$, $\neg c$, and d, it must contain $\{not\_b, not\_c, not\_\neg d\}$, and no more default literals. Note that by the distributive axiom $not\_\neg d \equiv \neg not\_d$.

In order to extend this definition to logic programs with a generic second kind of negation, we additionally transform the literals it negates into new atoms:

Definition 2.3 (Clausal Program of P $\bar{P}$) *The clausal program $\bar{P}$ of an x–program P is the clausal Horn program obtained by first denoting every literal in $\mathcal{L}(P)$ of the form: $\neg A$ by a new atom $\bar{A}$; not A by a new atom not_A; not $\neg A$ by a new atom not_$\bar{A}$, and then replacing in P those literals by their new denotation and, finally, reinterpreting the rule connective $\leftarrow$ as material implication $\Leftarrow$.*

Example 2 Let $P = \{a \leftarrow \neg b\}$. The clausal program $\bar{P}$ is $\{a \vee \neg \bar{b}\}$. Note that operations must be performed in the above order. If we would begin by first reinterpreting $\leftarrow$ as material implication we would get $\{a \vee b\}$.

Remark 2.1 *The symbol $\neg$ in $\bar{P}$ stands always for classical negation; the symbol $\neg$ in P stands for a negation whose meaning will be determined by the way it relates to the $\neg$ of $\bar{P}$, through axioms added to $\bar{P}$ (cf. definition 2.6). The context always determines the correct reading; be sure not to confuse the two uses.*

The resulting models of an x–program are determined by the models of its clausal program through an inverse transformation:

Definition 2.4 (Meaning of a clausal program P^*) *The meaning of a clausal program P^* is the union of the sets of all atoms:*

A	*such that*	$P^* \models A$		*not A*	*such that*	$P^* \models not\_A$
$\neg A$	*such that*	$P^* \models \bar{A}$		*not $\neg A$*	*such that*	$P^* \models not\_\bar{A}$

In order to specify the second kind of negation we introduce in $\bar{P}$ axioms defining it. For example, if we want the second negation to be classical negation we must add to $\bar{P}$ the set of clauses $\{\bar{A} \leftrightarrow \neg A \mid A \in \mathcal{L}(P)\}$, where $\leftrightarrow$ denotes material equivalence. In this case we would expect the semantics of P to be the same whether or not the first part of the transformation to $\bar{P}$ takes place.

Since we want this generic semantics to be an extension to the stationary semantics, we must guarantee that the semantics of a program without any occurence of $\neg$-negation is the same as for stationary semantics, whatever kind of $\neg$-negation is used and defined in the generic schema. To that end we must first minimize the atoms in the language of P, and only afterwards do we minimize the bar-ed atoms.

Definition 2.5 ($M \tilde{\leq} N$) *Let M and N be two models of a program $\bar{P}$ and M_{pos} (resp. N_{pos}) be the subset of M (resp. N) obtained by deleting from it all literals of the form $\bar{L}$.*
We say that $M \tilde{\leq} N$ iff: $M_{pos} \subseteq N_{pos} \vee (M_{pos} = N_{pos} \wedge M \subseteq N)$.

This definition is similar to the classical one plus a condition to the effect that, say, model $M_1 = \{\bar{a}\}$ is smaller than model $M_2 = \{a\}$.

Minimal models are defined as in definition 2.1 but with this new $\tilde{\leq}$ relation. The equivalence between minimality and circumscription is made through the ordered predicate circumscription $CIRC(T; \mathcal{O}; \mathcal{D})$ of the theory T, in which objective propositions $\mathcal{O}$ are minimized, but minimizing first propositions not of the form $\bar{A}$ and only afterwards the latter, and where default propositions $\mathcal{D}$ are fixed parameters.

The definition of stationary expansion of x–programs is then a generalization of definition 2.2, parametrized by the set of axioms $AX_\neg$ defining $\bar{A}$, plus this new notion of ordered minimality.

Definition 2.6 (Stationary $AX_\neg$ Expansions of x–programs)
A stationary expansion of an $AX_\neg$ x–program P is any consistent theory P^* which satisfies the following fixed point condition:

$$P^* = \bar{P} \cup AX_\neg \cup \{not\_L \mid P^* \models_{CIRC} \neg L\}$$

where L is any arbitrary objective literal, and $AX_\neg$ is the set of axioms for $\neg$-negation in P.

A stationary expansion P^* of a program P is obtained by adding to the corresponding clausal program $\bar{P}$ the axioms defining $\neg$–negation, and the negations by default not_L of those and only those literals L which are false in all minimal models of P^*. The meaning of negation by default is that, in any stationary expansion P^*, not_L holds if and only if P^* minimally entails $\neg L$. Note that the definition of $AX_\neg$ can influence, by reducing the number of models, whether or not $\neg L$ is in all minimal models of P^*.

From the distributive axiom above we obtain directly (as in [19]):

Proposition 2.1 *A consistent theory P^* is a stationary expansion of an $AX_\neg$ x–program P iff:*

- *P^* is obtained by augmenting $\bar{P} \cup AX_\neg$ with some default propositions not_A and $\neg not\_A$ where A is an objective proposition;*

- *P^* satisfies the conditions: $P^* \models not\_A \equiv P^* \models_{CIRC} \neg A$ and $P^* \models \neg not\_A \equiv P^* \models_{CIRC} A$ for any objective proposition A.*

Example 3 Consider program $P = \{p \leftarrow a; \quad p \leftarrow \neg a; \quad q \leftarrow not\, p\}$, where $\neg$ in P is classical negation, i.e. $AX_\neg = \{\bar{a} \Leftrightarrow \neg a, \bar{p} \Leftrightarrow \neg p, \bar{q} \Leftrightarrow \neg q\}$. The only stationary expansion of P is:

$$P_1^* = \bar{P} \cup AX_\neg \cup \{\neg not\_p, not\_\bar{p}, not\_q, \neg not\_\bar{q}, not\_a, \neg not\_\bar{a}\}$$

In fact, the only minimal model of P_1^* is: $\{\neg not\_p, not\_\bar{p}, not\_q, \neg not\_\bar{q}, not\_a, \neg not\_\bar{a}, p, \neg\bar{p}, \neg q, \bar{q}, \neg a, \bar{a}\}$ and the conditions of proposition 2.1 hold. Note how the $\leq$ relation prefers this model to other models that would be minimal if the classical $\leq$ were to be enforced. For example, the classically minimal model:

$$\{\neg not\_p, not\_\bar{p}, not\_q, \neg not\_\bar{q}, not\_a, \neg not\_\bar{a}, p, \neg\bar{p}, q, \neg\bar{q}, \neg a, \bar{a}\}$$

is not minimal when the $\leq$ relation is considered.

If $\neg$ in P is defined by $AX_\neg = \{\bar{a} \Rightarrow \neg a, \bar{p} \Rightarrow \neg p, \bar{q} \Rightarrow \neg q\}$, i.e. $\neg$ in P is a *strong* negation in the sense that it just implies classical negation in $\bar{P}$, the only stationary expansion of P is:

$$P_2^* = \bar{P} \cup AX_\neg \cup \{not\_p, not\_\bar{p}, \neg not\_q, not\_\bar{q}, not\_a, not\_\bar{a}\}$$

In fact, the only minimal model of P_2^* is: $\{not\_p, not\_\bar{p}, \neg not\_q, not\_\bar{q}, not\_a, not\_\bar{a}, \neg p, \neg\bar{p}, q, \neg\bar{q}, \neg a, \neg\bar{a}\}$ and the conditions of proposition 2.1 hold.

We now define the semantics of a program based on its stationary expansions.

Definition 2.7 (Stationary $AX_\neg$ Semantics of x–programs)
A stationary $AX_\neg$ model of a program P is the meaning of P^*, where P^* is a stationary $AX_\neg$ expansion of P.

The stationary $AX_\neg$ semantics of an x–program P is the set of all stationary $AX_\neg$ models of P.

If $S = \{M_k \mid k \in K\}$ is the semantics of P, then the intended meaning of P is $M = \bigcap_{k \in K} M_k$.

Example 4 The meaning of the program of example 3 is $\{p, \neg q, \neg a, not\ q, not\ a, not\ \neg p\}$ if we use classical negation, and $\{q, not\ p, not\ \neg p, not\ \neg q, not\ a, not\ \neg a\}$ if we use strong negation.

Example 5 Consider $P = \{a \leftarrow not\ b;\quad \neg a\}$, where $\neg$ is a weak form of negation determined by $AX_\neg = \{\neg A \Rightarrow \bar{A} \mid A \in \mathcal{L}(P)\}$.

The only stationary expansion of P is $P^* = \bar{P} \cup AX_\neg \cup \{\neg not\_a, \neg not\_\bar{a}, not\_b, \neg not\_\bar{b}\}$, determining thus the meaning of P as $M = \{a, \neg a, not\ b, \neg b\}$. The fact that both a and $\neg a$ belong to M is not a problem since the weak form of negation allows that. Note that $\neg A \Rightarrow \bar{A}$ is equivalent to $A \vee \bar{A}$, and allows models with both A and $\bar{A}$. Literal $\neg b$ also appears in M forced by the weak negation.

Now we state in what sense this semantics is a generalization of stationary semantics.

Theorem 2.1 (Generalization of Stationary Semantics)
Let P be a (nonextended) normal logic program, and let $AX_\neg$ be such that no clause of the form $A_1 \vee \ldots \vee A_n$ where $\{A_1, \ldots, A_n\} \subseteq \mathcal{L}(P)$ is a logical consequence of it.

M is a stationary $AX_\neg$ model of P iff M (modulo the $\neg$-literals) is a stationary model of P.

The restriction on the form of $AX_\neg$ is meant to avoid unusual definitions of $\neg$-negation as, for instance:

Example 6 Let $P = \{a \leftarrow b\}$, and $AX_\neg = \{a \vee \neg\bar{b}, \bar{b}\}$. P has a stationary $AX_\neg$ model $\{a, not\ \neg a, not\ b, \neg b\}$ which is not a stationary model of P. Note however that a is in the model because it is a logical consequence of $AX_\neg$ irrespective of the program.

2.2 The parametrizeable schema

Stable Models Semantics [5] has a one-to-one correspondence with stable expansions [10], and the latter can be obtained simply by replacing $\models_{CIRC}$ by $\models_{CWA}$ in the definition of stationary expansion of normal programs.

As with the stationary semantics of extended programs, a generic definition of stable semantics for extended programs can also be obtained, with $P^* \models_{CWA} \neg L$ as the condition for adding negation by default.

So, in general a new parameter in the schema is desireable in order to specify how default negation is to be added to an expansion.

Definition 2.8 ($\langle AX_\neg, not_{cond}\rangle$ **Expansion of x–programs)**
A $\langle AX_\neg, not_{cond}\rangle$ expansion of an x–program P is any consistent theory P^* which satisfies the following fixed point condition:

$$P^* = \bar{P} \cup AX_\neg \cup \{not\_L \mid not_{cond}(L)\}$$

where L is any arbitrary objective literal.

The definition of a generic semantics is similar to that of stationary semantics.

Definition 2.9 ($\langle AX_\neg, not_{cond}\rangle$ **Semantics of x–programs)**
A $\langle AX_\neg, not_{cond}\rangle$ model of a program P is the meaning of P^*, where P^* is a $\langle AX_\neg, not_{cond}\rangle$ expansion of P.
The semantics of a program P is the set of all $\langle AX_\neg, not_{cond}\rangle$ models of P. The intended meaning of P is the intersection of all models of P.

We define Stable $AX_\neg$ Semantics as the generic semantics where:

$$not_{cond}(L) = P^* \models_{CWA} \neg L.$$

With this definition proposition 2.1 and theorem 2.1 are also valid for stable models.

3 Properties required of extended logic programs

In this section we present properties important for the study of extended logic program semantics, and show for some $AX_\neg$ whether or not the resulting semantics complies with such properties. Here we examine the cases of:

- *classical negation*   i.e. $AX_\neg = \{\bar{A} \Leftrightarrow \neg A \mid A \in \mathcal{L}(P)\}$
- *strong negation*   i.e. $AX_\neg = \{\bar{A} \Rightarrow \neg A \mid A \in \mathcal{L}(P)\}$
- *weak negation*   i.e. $AX_\neg = \{\neg A \Rightarrow \bar{A} \mid A \in \mathcal{L}(P)\}$
- *pseudo negation*   i.e. $AX_\neg = \{\}$.

for stationary and stable semantics. In section 4.1 we study our semantics $WFSX$, which relates more directly both kinds of negation, and where $not_{cond}(L) = (P^* \models_{CIRC} \neg L \vee P^* \models_{CIRC} \bar{L})$, by introducing *explicit* negation. We concentrate next only on properties determined by the $\neg$-negation. For comparative studies of semantics concerning negation by default see [2, 3].

Property 1 (Consistency) *A semantics is consistent iff, for any program P, if M is a stationary (resp. stable) model of P then for no atom $A \in \mathcal{L}(P)$ $\{A, \neg A\} \subseteq M$.*

In other words, a semantics is consistent if there is no need for testing for consistency within the final (stationary or stable) models of a program.

Example 7 Let $P = \{a \leftarrow not\,b; \quad \neg a \leftarrow not\,b\}$, where $\neg$ is weak negation. The only stationary expansion of P is $P^* = \bar{P} \cup \{\neg A \Rightarrow \bar{A} \mid A \in \mathcal{L}(P)\} \cup \{not\_b, not\_\bar{b}\}$. The only minimal model of $P^* = \{a, \neg not\_a, \bar{a}, \neg not\_\bar{a}, \neg b, \neg \bar{b}, not\_b, not\_\bar{b}\}$ is consistent. Although the meaning of $P^* = \{a, \neg a, not\_b, not\_\bar{b}\}$ is inconsistent.

As shown with the previous example, semantics with weak negation might not be consistent. The same happens for semantics with pseudo negation.

Semantics with classical or strong negation are consistent because, by the very definition of $AX_\neg$, for every atom $A \in \mathcal{L}(P)$, $\neg A \vee \neg \bar{A} \in P^*$, for every expansion P^* of any program P, and thus no model of P^* has A and $\bar{A}$. Thus the meaning of P^* can never have both A and $\neg A$.

Property 2 (Coherence) *A semantics is coherent iff, for any program P, whenever M is a stationary (resp. stable) model of P, if $\neg A \in M$ then $not\,A \in M$, and if $A \in M$ then $not\,\neg A \in M$.*

This property plays an important rôle if we consider the second kind of negation instrumental for specifying the falsity of literals. In that case coherence can be read as: *if A is declared false then it can be assumed false by default.* It turns out that, for both stationary and stable semantics, coherence is equivalent to consistency; hence the importance of coherence.

Theorem 3.1 *A stationary (or stable) semantics is coherent iff it is consistent.*

Proof: We prove this theorem here only for the case of a stationary semantics. The proof for stable semantics is quite similar and is omitted for brevity.

($\rightarrow$) If a stationary semantics is coherent then for any P^* every model M of P^* having $\bar{A}$ also has not_A. By proposition 2.1 $not\_A \in M \Leftrightarrow \neg A \in M$. Similarly we conclude that for every M if $A \in M$ the $\neg \bar{A} \in M$. Thus, given that models of clausal programs are always total, every model containing A does not contains $\bar{A}$, and every model containing $\bar{A}$ does not contain A, which is the consistency property.

($\leftarrow$) This part of the proof is similar and also omitted for brevity. $\Diamond$

Property 3 (Supportedness) *A semantics is necessarily supportive iff, for any program P, whenever M is a stationary (resp. stable) model of P then, for every objective literal L, if $L \in M$ there exists in P at least one rule of the form: $L \leftarrow B_1, \ldots, B_n, not\,C_1, \ldots, not\,C_m$ such that:*

$$\{B_1, \ldots, B_n, not\,C_1, \ldots, not\,C_m\} \subseteq M.$$

Since that for any program P, $\bar{P} \cup \{not\_L \mid P^* \models_{\overline{CIRC}} \neg L\}$ is a Horn clausal program, a stationary (or a stable) semantics such that $AX_\neg$ does not contain any clause with positive propositions is necessarily supportive. Thus, semantics with pseudo or strong negation are necessarily supportive.

Semantics that introduce in $AX_\neg$ such clauses might not be necessarily supportive. For example, if $\neg$ is classical negation necessary supportedness does not hold:

Example 8 Let $P = \{a \leftarrow b; \quad \neg a\}$. The only stationary $\{\bar{A} \Leftrightarrow \neg A\}$ model is $M = \{not\, a, \neg a, not\, b, \neg b\}$. As $\neg b \in M$, and there is no rule for $\neg b$, the semantics is not necessarily supportive.

This property closely relates to the use of logic as a programming language. One does not expect objective literals to be true unless rules stating their truth condition are introduced; in other words, except for default propositions, no implicit information should be expected. We argue that if one wants the result of the previous program one should write $P = \{\neg b \leftarrow \neg a; \quad \neg a\}$ or, if disjunction is introduced, $P = \{a \leftarrow b; \neg a; \, b \vee \neg b\}$.

4 Fixing the set $AX_\neg$ and the condition $not_{cond}(L)$

In this section we reconstruct some semantics for x–programs simply by specifying the set $AX_\neg$ and the condition $not_{cond}(L)$ w.r.t. the generic semantics defined above. We contribute this way for a better understanding of what type of second negation each of those semantics uses, and what are the main differences among them. Moreover, we show a definition for the semantics of [11] in terms of a two-valued logic, and clarifiy the meaning of its explicit negation.

We begin by reconstructing answer-sets semantics [6] for programs with consistent answer-sets (equivalent to the semantics of [24]).

Theorem 4.1 (Answer-Sets Semantics) *An interpretation M is an answer-set of a program P iff M is a stable $\{\bar{A} \Rightarrow \neg A \mid A \in \mathcal{L}(P)\}$ model of P (modulo the syntactic representation of models).*

This theorem leads us to the conclusion that answer-sets semantics extends stable models semantics with strong negation. Thus, from the results of section 3, we conclude that answer-sets semantics is consistent, coherent and supportive.

Note that if instead of strong negation one uses pseudo negation and a test for consistency in the final models, the result would be the same. However, we think that the formalization as in theorem 4.1 is more accurate because the consistency there is dealt within the fixpoint condition, with no need for meta–level constraints, and the properties exhibited are those of strong negation and not of pseudo negation. For example, coherence (a property of strong negation but not of pseudo negation) is obeyed by answer-sets semantics.

One semantics extending well founded semantics with ¬-negation is presented in [17]. There it is claimed that the method used in [6] can be applied to semantics other than stable models, and that method is used to define the proposed semantics. It happens however that the meaning of ¬ is not the same as for answer-sets, in the sense that different $AX_\neg$s are used:

Theorem 4.2 (WFS plus ¬ as in [17]) *An interpretation M is an extended stable model of a program P iff M is a consistent stationary $\{\}$ model of P.*

Note the need for testing consistency in stationary models of the semantics. As seen in section 3, this semantics does not comply with coherence, which in our opinion is an important property of ¬, satisfied by answer-sets semantics.

Next we reconstruct the semantics presented in [19]. There the semantics is defined similarly to our generic definition, but where $AX_\neg$ is absent, and no transformation on literals of the form $\neg A$ and $not\,\neg A$ occurs. With this similarity the reconstruction follows easily:

Theorem 4.3 (Stationary Semantics with classical negation) *An interpretation M is a stationary model (in the sense of [19]) of a program P iff M is a stationary $\{\bar{A} \Leftrightarrow \neg A \mid A \in \mathcal{L}(P)\}$ model of P.*

Due to lack of space we do not present here the proofs of these theorems. Nevertheless we would like to note the importance of the new minimality relation $\lesssim$ in the proof of the last one. We must ensure that the equivalences introduce via $AX_\neg$ do not affect minimal models of the program where $\bar{A}$ is replaced by $\neg A$ for every atom A. If the $\leq$ relation were used, this would not be the case since $\bar{A} \Leftrightarrow \neg A$ has two minimal $\leq$ models, $\{A, \neg\bar{A}\}$ and $\{\neg A, \bar{A}\}$. As the relation used is $\lesssim$, the only minimal model of the equivalence is the latter, which is the same model of the program after the above transformation.

From the results of section 3 we conclude that this semantics does not comply with supportedness. Nevertheless, this semantics is the only one reconstructed here that introduces *real* classical negation into normal logic programs. We argue that, comparing it with semantics with strong negation, this is not a big advantage since, once disjunction is added to logic programs with strong negation, a programmer can state in the language that the negation is classical rather than strong. This can be done simply by adding rules of the form $A \vee \neg A$. Moreover, the programmer has the opportunity of stating which negation, strong or classical, is used for each of the atoms in the language, by adding or not for each of them such disjunctive rules. This issue will be further discussed in section 5.2.

4.1 Well Founded Semantics with Explicit Negation

Recently [11] we presented the semantics $WFSX$, which extends WFS to programs with a second type of negation that we dub *explicit*.

$WFSX$ follows naturaly from the single coherence requirement: $\neg L$ implies $not\, L$ (if L is explicitly false, L must be false) for any literal L.

Example 9 [11] Consider program $P = \{a \leftarrow not\, b, \quad b \leftarrow not\, a, \quad \neg a \leftarrow\}$.

If $\neg a$ were to be simply considered as a new atom symbol, say a', and WFS used to define the semantics of P (as suggested in [17]), the result would be $\{\neg a, not\, \neg b\}$, so that $\neg a$ is true and a is undefined. We insist that $not\, a$ should hold because $\neg a$ does. Accordingly, the WFSX of P is $\{\neg a, b, not\, a, not\, \neg b\}$, since b follows from $not\, a$.

The formal definition of this semantics is made by embedding that requirement into the very definition of (3-valued) interpretation, and then by straightforwardly adapting to it the formal techniques used for WFS in [16].

Since this semantics exhibits all the above mentioned properties of strong negation and is defined as an extension of WFS, it seems that it should be closely related to stationary semantics with strong negation. In fact:

Theorem 4.4 (WFSX Semantics and Strong Negation) *If an interpretation M is a stationary $\{\bar{A} \Rightarrow \neg A \mid A \in \mathcal{L}(P)\}$ model of P then M is an (WFSX) extended stable model of a program P.*

Thus $WFSX$ gives semantics to more programs and, whenever both semantics give a meaning to a program, the WF model of $WFSX$ is a (possibly proper) subset of that of stationary semantics with strong negation. The differences between $WFSX$ and stationary semantics with strong negation are best shown with the help of an example.

Example 10 Consider the program $P = \{a \leftarrow not\, a, \quad b \leftarrow a, \quad \neg b \leftarrow\}$, which has no strong stationary models. According to $WFSX$ its well founded model (and only extended stable model) is $M = \{\neg b, not\, b, not\, \neg a\}$. Note that M is not even a model in the (usual) sense of [16], because for the second rule the truth value of the head (false) is smaller than the truth value of the body (undefined).

In [11] a new truth valuation function is defined that agrees with the required definition of extended stable models. The main difference between this and the truth valuation function of [16] is that it allows models where a rule has an undefined body and a false head, just in case the explicit negation of the head is true. In other words in $WFSX$ $\neg$–negation overrides undefinedness. The truth of $\neg L$ is an *explicit* declaration that L is false.

Any semantics complying with proposition 2.1 cannot have M as a model of the program: not_b is in an expansion iff $\neg b$ is in all minimal models of that expansion, but if this is the case then (by the second rule clause) $\neg a$ should also be in all minimal models, which would necessarily entail $not\, a$ in the expansion.

In order to reconstruct $WFSX$ in our schema, a new condition for adding default negation is required, forcing a default literal not_L to assuredly belong to an expansion also in the case where the explicit negation $\bar{L}$ is in all minimal models.

Theorem 4.5 (WFSX Semantics) *An interpretation M is an extended stable model of a program P iff M is the meaning of a P^* such that:*

$$P^* = \bar{P} \cup \{not\_L \mid P^* \models_{CIRC} \neg L \text{ or } P^* \models_{CIRC} \bar{L}\}$$

Example 11 The program P of example 10 has now an expansion $P^* = \bar{P} \cup \{not\_b, \neg not\_\bar{b}, not\_\bar{a}\}$. In fact the minimal models are:

$$\{not\_a, not\_\bar{a}, not\_b, \neg not\_\bar{b}, a, \neg\bar{a}, b, \bar{b}\}$$
$$\{\neg not\_a, not\_\bar{a}, not\_b, \neg not\_\bar{b}, \neg a, \neg\bar{a}, \neg b, \bar{b}\}$$

In all those models we have: $\neg\bar{a}$ so we must introduce $not\_\bar{a}$; have $\bar{b}$ so we must introduce $\neg not\_\bar{b}$ and, by the second disjunct, not_b. Thus P^* is an expansion.

5 Further Developments

5.1 Contradiction Removal

In [1, 4, 12] semantics are presented that avoid some contradictions by making certain *not* literals undefined.

Example 12 Let $P = \{a \leftarrow not\,b; \quad \neg a\}$. None of the semantics discussed in section 4 gives a meaning to this program. Since there are no clauses for b in $\bar{P}$, $\neg b$ is in all minimal models. Thus $not\,b$ must be in the semantics. As $not\,b$ leads to a contradiction in a no meaning is defined for P. All the semantics referred above assign a meaning to P by undefining $not\,b$. For example with the semantics of [1] the meaning of P is $\{not\,a, \neg a, not\,\neg b\}$.

The idea underlying these semantics is: *if an assumption supports a contradiction then take back that assumption.*

In order to capture this idea within the schema described above in this paper one has to allow a *not* literal possibly not to be added to $\bar{P} \cup AX_\neg$ by the fixpoint condition, thus weaking that condition. For instance, for stationary expansions one could have instead: $P^* = \bar{P} \cup AX_\neg \cup S$ where $S \subseteq \{not\_L \mid P^* \models_{CIRC} \neg L\}$.

Example 13 In the previous example, P has several such fixpoints. For instance: $P_1^* = \bar{P} \cup AX_\neg$, $P_2^* = P_1^* \cup \{not\_\bar{b}\}$, $P_3^* = P_1^* \cup \{not\_a, \neg not\_\bar{a}, not\_\bar{b}\}$. The meaning of P_3^* is the meaning ascribed to P by [1].

As shown in this example there is a choice of subsets to consider. To choose a definite subset we need a new parameter in the schema. If we choose the definite rule that elects the intersection of the maximal sets S satisfying the fixpoit condition, P_3^* is the only expansion.

The study of criteria leading to the designation of preferred subsets deserves further attention; [1] examines in detail a preference based on CWA assumptions.

5.2 Logic Programs with ¬-Negation and Disjunction

Given the similarities between this generic definition of semantics for x–programs and that of stationary semantics for normal logic programs, it is easy to extend the former for extended disjunctive logic programs (or disjunctive x–programs) based on the extension of the latter for disjunctive normal programs [19].

First we have to extend the definition of $\bar{P}$ for the case of disjunctive programs. This extension is obtained simply by adjoining to definition 2.3: "[...] *reinterpreting the connective* ∨ *in logic programs as classical disjunction*". With this new context we define:

Definition 5.1 (Stationary $AX_\neg$ Expansion of disj. x–programs)
A Stationary $AX_\neg$ expansion of a disjunctive x–program P is any consistent theory P^* which satisfies the following fixed point condition (where the distributive axiom not $(A \wedge B) \equiv$ not $A \vee$ not B is assumed):

$$P^* = \bar{P} \cup AX_\neg \cup \{not\, F \mid P^* \models_{CIRC} \neg F\}$$

where F is an arbitrary conjunction of positive (resp. negative) objective literals.

Given this definition the semantics follows similarly to section 2.

Example 14 Let $P = \{p \leftarrow not\, a; \quad p \leftarrow not\, \neg b; \quad a \vee \neg b\}$ and $AX_\neg$ be the axioms for explicit negation. The only stationary $AX_\neg$ expansion of P is

$$P^* = \bar{P} \cup AX_\neg \cup \{not\_\bar{a}, not\_b, \neg not\_p, not\_\bar{p}, not\_a \vee not\_\bar{b}, \neg not\_a \vee \neg not\_\bar{b}\}.$$

Thus the only stationary $AX_\neg$ model is $\{p, not\, \neg p, not\, \neg a, not\, b\}$.

Henceforth, the way is open for the study of the interaction between ¬ and disjunction in each of the semantics for x–programs, and comparisons between those semantics via disjunction. One result concerning the latter is the formalization of the comparison between the use of classical or explicit negation stated at the end of the previous section:

Theorem 5.1 *Let P be an x–program. M is a stationary $\{\bar{A} \Leftrightarrow \neg A\}$ model of P iff it is a stationary $\{\bar{A} \Rightarrow \neg A\}$ model of $P \cup \{A \vee \neg A \mid A \in \mathcal{L}(P)\}$.*

It is known [19] that a definition such as 5.1 makes program disjunctions exclusive. This is seen in example 14. In order to treat disjunctions as inclusive rather than exclusive, in nonextended disjunctive programs, it suffices to replace $\models_{CIRC}$ by $\models_{WECWA}$ in the definition of expansions [19], where $WECWA$ stands for Weak Extended Closed World Assumption [21] or Weak Generalized Closed World Assumption [20]. This is not the case for extended disjunctive programs.

Acknowledgements

We thank ESPRIT BRA COMPULOG (no. 3012), Instituto Nacional de Investigação Científica, Junta Nacional de Investigação Científica e Tecnológica, and Gabinete de Filosofia do Conhecimento for their support. Thanks to Joaquim Aparício, Gabriel David, and Luís Monteiro for their comments.

References

[1] J. N. Aparício, L. M. Pereira, and J. J. Alferes. Contradiction removal semantics with explicit negation. Technical report, AI Centre, Uninova, March 1992.

[2] J. Dix. Classifying semantics of logic programs. In A. Nerode, W. Marek, and V. S. Subrahmanian, editors, *Logic Programming and NonMonotonic Reasoning'91*, pages 166–180. MIT Press, 1991.

[3] P. M. Dung. On the relations between stable and well-founded semantics of logic programs. *Theoretical Computer Science*, 1992. To appear.

[4] P. M. Dung and P. Ruamviboonsuk. Well founded reasoning with classical negation. In A. Nerode, W. Marek, and V. S. Subrahmanian, editors, *Logic Programming and NonMonotonic Reasoning'91*, pages 120–132. MIT Press, 1991.

[5] M. Gelfond and V. Lifschitz. The stable model semantics for logic programming. In R. A. Kowalski and K. A. Bowen, editors, *5th Int. Conf. on Logic Programming*, pages 1070–1080. MIT Press, 1988.

[6] M. Gelfond and V. Lifschitz. Logic programs with classical negation. In Warren and Szeredi, editors, *7th Int.Conf. on Logic Programming*, pages 579–597. MIT Press, 1990.

[7] Katsumi Inoue. Extended logic programs with default assumptions. In Koichi Furukawa, editor, *8th Int. Conf. on Logic Programming'91*, pages 490–504. MIT Press, 1991.

[8] R. Kowalski. Problems and promises of computational logic. In John Lloyd, editor, *Computational Logic Symposium*, pages 1–36. Springer-Verlag, November 1990.

[9] R. Kowalski and F. Sadri. Logic programs with exceptions. In Warren and Szeredi, editors, *7th Int. Conf. on Logic Programming*. MIT Press, 1990.

[10] R. C. Moore. Semantics considerations on nonmonotonic logic. *Artificial Intelligence*, 25:75–94, 1985.

[11] L. M. Pereira and J. J. Alferes. Well founded semantics for logic programs with explicit negation. In B. Neumann, editor, *European Conf. on AI'92*. John Wiley & Sons, Ltd, 1992.

[12] L. M. Pereira, J. J. Alferes, and J. N. Aparício. Contradiction Removal within Well Founded Semantics. In A. Nerode, W. Marek, and V. S. Subrahmanian, editors, *Logic Programming and NonMonotonic Reasoning'91*, pages 105–119. MIT Press, 1991.

[13] L. M. Pereira, J. N. Aparício, and J. J. Alferes. Counterfactual reasoning based on revising assumptions. In Ueda and Saraswat, editors, *Int. Logic Programming Symp.'91*. MIT Press, 1991.

[14] L. M. Pereira, J. N. Aparício, and J. J. Alferes. Hypothetical reasoning with well founded semantics. In B. Mayoh, editor, *Scandinavian Conf. on AI'91*. IOS Press, 1991.

[15] L. M. Pereira, J. N. Aparício, and J. J. Alferes. Nonmonotonic reasoning with well founded semantics. In Koichi Furukawa, editor, *8th Int. Conf. on Logic Programming'91*, pages 475–489. MIT Press, 1991.

[16] H. Przymusinska and T. Przymusinski. Semantic issues in deductive databases and logic programs. In R. Banerji, editor, *Formal Techniques in Artificial Intelligence*. North Holland, 1990.

[17] T. Przymusinski. Extended stable semantics for normal and disjunctive programs. In Warren and Szeredi, editors, *7th Int. Conf. on Logic Programming*, pages 459–477. MIT Press, 1990.

[18] T. Przymusinski. Stationary semantics for disjunctive logic programs and deductive databases. In Debray and Hermenegildo, editors, *North American Conf. on Logic Programming'90*, pages 40–57. MIT Press, 1990.

[19] T. Przymusinski. A semantics for disjunctive logic programs. In Loveland, Lobo, and Rajasekar, editors, *ILPS'91 Workshop in Disjunctive Logic Programs*, 1991.

[20] A. Rajasekar, J. Lobo, and J. Minker. Weak generalized closed world assumptions. *Automated Reasoning*, 5:293–307, 1989.

[21] K. Ross and R. Topor. Inferring negative information from disjunctive databases. *Automated Reasoning*, 4:397–424, 1988.

[22] Chiaki Sakama. Extended well–founded semantics for paraconsistent logic programs. In *Fifth Generation Computer Systems*, pages 592–599. ICOT, 1992.

[23] A. Van Gelder, K. A. Ross, and J. S. Schlipf. The well-founded semantics for general logic programs. *Journal of ACM*, pages 221–230, 1990.

[24] G. Wagner. A database needs two kinds of negation. In B. Thalheim, J. Demetrovics, and H-D. Gerhardt, editors, *MFDBS'91*, pages 357–371. Springer-Verlag, 1991.

A Goal-Oriented Approach to Computing Well Founded Semantics

Weidong Chen
Computer Science and Engineering
Southern Methodist University
Dallas, TX 75275-0122

David S. Warren*
Department of Computer Science
SUNY at Stony Brook
Stony Brook, NY 11794-4400

Abstract

This paper presents a goal-oriented method, called *XOLDTNF resolution*, of computing the well founded semantics of general logic programs. It has the practical advantages of top-down computation, smooth integration with Prolog, and the handling of variables. Yet it avoids both positive and negative loops, and termination is guaranteed for all programs without function symbols. We establish the soundness and completeness of XOLDTNF resolution for all logic programs. An implementation of XOLDTNF resolution in Prolog is available via FTP.

1 Introduction

The well founded semantics [20] provides a natural and robust declarative semantics for *all* logic programs. It coincides with previously proposed semantics on more restricted classes of programs, including "stratified" and "locally stratified" programs [10, 12]. Several alternative formulations of the well founded semantics have also been developed [11, 18].

This paper focuses on effective and efficient query evaluation with respect to the well founded semantics. The most commonly used procedural semantics of logic programs, although less popular in deductive databases, is SLDNF resolution [5, 8]. SLDNF resolution is known to have three major problems, namely positive loops, negative loops, and floundering on non-ground negative literals.

Consider the following program [17] of graph reachability and query:

> *edge(a, b). edge(a, c). edge(b, a). edge(b, d).*
> *reach(X, Y) ← reach(X, Z), edge(Z, Y).*
> *reach(X, X).*

* Work supported in part by NSF Grant CCR 9102159 and New York State Science and Technology Foundation Grant RDG 90173.

$\leftarrow reach(a, Y).$

The SLD-tree for the query is infinite due to positive loops, leading to non-terminating computation. The following [7, 19] is an example of negative loops of SLDNF:

$move(a, b).\ move(a, c).\ move(b, a).\ move(b, d).$
$win(X) \leftarrow move(X, Y),\ \sim win(Y).$
$\leftarrow win(X).$

Notice that the programs above do not contain any function symbols and termination is normally expected by users for these programs.

Various mechanisms have been proposed to improve the termination property of SLDNF resolution by detecting and handling positive loops, such as OLDT resolution [17], extension tables [6], and QSQR [21]. The basic idea is to save intermediate results in tables, check for identical or simpler subgoals, and reuse the saved results when identical or simpler subgoals are encountered. It has been shown [3, 16] that this top-down approach with memo-ing is essentially equivalent to bottom-up computation, such as [1, 13, 16].

In order to compute the well founded semantics, we concentrate on the problem of negative loops. It should be mentioned that several top-down procedural semantics have been proposed for the well founded semantics [11, 14], but they inherit the three major problems of SLDNF resolution and thus are not effective even for function-free programs. Recently an effective top-down procedural semantics, called WELL! [2], was developed for function-free programs. WELL! is defined in terms of two sequences of trees, one for lemmas that are definitely true or false and the other for potential lemmas that are possibly true or false. As a result, the algorithm in [2] does double tree traversal.

We extend OLDT resolution with the negation as failure rule and negative contexts. OLDT resolution [17] is a variant of SLD resolution augmented with *call* and *solution* tables for avoiding positive loops. Our mechanism of negative contexts further avoids negative loops and applies tabling techniques to general logic programs. The procedural semantics, which we call *XOLDTNF resolution*, is characterized as computing a fixpoint of calls and answers. XOLDTNF resolution differs from WELL! by treating lemmas and potential lemmas in a uniform manner, thus avoiding the double traversal of trees and leading to more efficient computation. We show that XOLDTNF is sound and complete for *finitely negative* and *non-floundering* queries of general logic programs. The class of finitely negative programs properly includes all function-free programs and all stratified programs. Termination is guaranteed for all function-free programs.

The rest of the paper is organized as follows. Section 2 reviews the basic terminology and the well founded semantics of logic programs. Section 3 discusses negative loop checking and introduces a well founded semantics under negative contexts. Section 4 presents XOLDTNF resolution for general logic programs. Section 5 establishes its soundness and completeness. We conclude with a discussion of some pragmatic issues. All proofs have been omitted due to space limitations, and can be found in [4].

2 Well Founded Semantics

We assume the basic terminology of logic programs, most of which can be found in [8], and present the well founded semantics of general logic programs [15, 20].

An *atom* is of the form $p(t_1, ..., t_n)$, where p is an n-ary predicate symbol and $t_1, ..., t_n$ are terms. We consider equivalence classes of atoms equal under variable renaming. Atoms that are renaming variants of each other are viewed as syntactically identical.

If A is an atom, then A is a *positive literal* and $\sim A$ is a *negative literal*. A *literal* is either a positive or negative literal. A *clause* is of the form $A \leftarrow L_1, ..., L_n$, where A, the *head* of the clause, is an atom, and $L_1, ..., L_n (n \geq 0)$, the *body* of the clause, are literals. Each L_i is a *subgoal* of the clause. A *general logic program* (or simply *program*) is a finite set of clauses. A *query* Q is a conjunction of literals. The negation of a query Q, denoted by $\leftarrow Q$, is called a *goal*.

For any atom A, A and $\sim A$ are said to be *complements* to each other. Let I be a set of literals. We denote by $\sim I$ the set obtained by taking the complement of each literal in I. A set of literals is *inconsistent* if it contains two literals that are complements of each other; otherwise it is *consistent*. The set of positive literals in I is denoted by $Pos(I)$, and the set of negative literals by $Neg(I)$.

Given a program P, a *partial interpretation* I for P is a consistent set of literals whose atoms are in the Herbrand base of P. A ground literal l is *true* in I if $l \in I$ and is *false* in I if the complement of l is in I. There is a natural partial ordering over partial interpretations: $I \subseteq J$, where $\subseteq$ is the subset relationship.

The well founded semantics depends upon the notion of *unfounded sets* to draw negative conclusions.

Definition 2.1 (Unfounded Set[20]) Let P be a program, H be the Herbrand base of P, and I be a partial interpretation. A subset $S \subseteq H$ is an *unfounded set of P with respect to I* if for every atom $A \in S$ and every ground instance r of a clause of P whose head is A, (at least) one of the following holds:

1. some positive subgoal L in the body of r is false in I or is in S;

2. some negative subgoal L in the body of r is false in I.

A literal L that makes (1) or (2) above true is called a *witness of unusability* for clause r with respect to I.

The *greatest unfounded set of P with respect to I*, denoted by $\mathcal{U}_P(I)$, is the union of all unfounded sets of P with respect to I. ◇

The condition that some subgoal in the body of r is false in I means that rule r cannot be used to derive the head A from I. The other condition that some positive subgoal is also in S is the unfoundedness condition: of all the rules that may still be usable to derive some atom in S, each requires an atom in S to be true. That is, atoms in S depend upon each other positively in such a way that no one atom in S can be *first* established from I using rules in P.

The well founded semantics can be defined using the following *monotonic* transformations over sets of literals [15]:

- $A \in \mathcal{T}_P(I)$ if and only if there is some ground instance r of a clause in P with head A such that every subgoal in the body of r is true in I;

- $\mathcal{U}_P(I)$ is the greatest unfounded set of P with respect to I;

- $\overline{\mathcal{T}}_P(I) = \mathcal{T}_P(I) \cup I$;

- $\mathcal{V}_P(I) = (\cup_{k=1}^{\omega} \overline{\mathcal{T}}_P^k(I)) \cup \sim\mathcal{U}_P(I)$.

Let α and β be countable ordinals. The partial interpretations I_α and I^∞ are defined recursively by

- $I_0 = \emptyset$

- $I_{\alpha+1} = \mathcal{V}_P(I_\alpha)$

- $I_\alpha = \cup_{\beta<\alpha} I_\beta$ for limit ordinal α

- $I^\infty = \cup_\alpha I_\alpha$

Theorem 2.1 ([15]) *The sequence of partial interpretations I_α is monotonically increasing. I^∞ is the least fixpoint of $\mathcal{V}_P$ and is equal to the well founded partial model of P defined in [20].*

3   Avoiding Negative Loops

OLDT resolution [17] avoids positive loops by saving intermediate results and solving looping positive subgoals using only previously computed answers. Effective computation of the well founded semantics requires that negative loops be avoided. Unlike positive loops that are treated as failed, a negative loop has to be treated *undefined* according to the well founded semantics, as the following example shows.

$$p \leftarrow \sim p.$$
$$q \leftarrow p.$$

The undefinedness of the looping negative subgoal should be propagated to other subgoals appropriately.

We extend OLDT resolution with *negative contexts*, each of which is a set of ground negative literals. The initial query is evaluated under the empty negative context. When a ground negative subgoal $\sim B$ is encountered, we check to see if $\sim B$ is in the current negative context. If not, a tree for B is started by the negation as failure rule. However, B will be evaluated in a new negative context, namely the current negative context augmented with $\sim B$. If $\sim B$ is already in the current negative context, it means that a negative loop occurs, in which case $\sim B$ is treated as undefined and is resolved using the negative context. In this way some negative loops can be handled finitely.

We maintain a set of calls and a table of answers for each negative context. All calls with the same negative context will share the same table for detecting identical calls and reusing answers computed previously. As will be shown, answer sharing among tables of different negative contexts is also possible under certain conditions.

To better understand the effect of negative contexts in query evaluation, we present a different formalization of the well founded semantics that takes negative contexts into account. Let P be a program and H be the Herbrand base of P. A *negative context* is a set of ground negative literals of the form $\sim B$ where $B \in H$. Let $\mathcal{I}$ be a set of partial interpretations indexed by the set of all possible negative contexts. We denote by $\mathcal{I}_N$ the corresponding partial interpretation for a negative context N.

There is a natural partial ordering such that $\mathcal{I} \subseteq \mathcal{J}$ if for every negative context N, $\mathcal{I}_N \subseteq \mathcal{J}_N$. The least element with respect to $\subseteq$, denoted by $\{\}$, is such that $\{\}_N = \emptyset$ for every N.

We extend the notion of *unfounded set* in the well founded semantics to calls under negative contexts.

Definition 3.1 (Unfounded Set under Negative Context) A subset $\mathcal{A} \subseteq H$ is an *unfounded set of P under N with respect to $\mathcal{I}$* if for every atom $A \in \mathcal{A}$ and every ground instance r of a clause of P whose head is A, at least one of the following holds:

1. some positive subgoal L in the body of r is false in $\mathcal{I}_N$ or is in $\mathcal{A}$;

2. some negative subgoal L in the body of r is not in N and is false in $\mathcal{I}_{N \cup \{L\}}$.

Any literal that makes (1) or (2) true is called a *witness of unusability* of r in P under N with respect to $\mathcal{I}$. The union of arbitrary unfounded sets of P under N is also an unfounded set. We denote by $\mathcal{U}_{P_N}(\mathcal{I})$ the greatest unfounded set of P under N with respect to $\mathcal{I}$.

We extend transformations over sets of literals to programs with negative contexts:

- $A \in \mathcal{T}_{P_N}(\mathcal{I})$ if and only if there is some ground instance r of a clause in P with head A such that
  - every positive subgoal in the body of r is true in $\mathcal{I}_N$; and
  - every negative subgoal L in the body of r is not in N and is true in $\mathcal{I}_{N \cup \{L\}}$.

- $\mathcal{U}_{P_N}(\mathcal{I})$ is the greatest unfounded set of P under N with respect to $\mathcal{I}$;

- $\overline{\mathcal{T}}_{P_N}(\mathcal{I}) = \mathcal{T}_{P_N}(\mathcal{I}) \cup \mathcal{I}_N$;

- $\mathcal{V}_{P_N}(\mathcal{I}) = (\cup_{k=1}^{\omega} \overline{\mathcal{T}}^k_{P_N}(\mathcal{I})) \cup {\sim}\mathcal{U}_{P_N}(\mathcal{I})$;

- $(\mathcal{V}_P(\mathcal{I}))_N = \mathcal{V}_{P_N}(\mathcal{I})$.

Compared with the notion of unfounded sets and transformations in the ordinary well founded semantics, the major difference is that in both $\mathcal{T}_{P_N}(\mathcal{I})$ and $\mathcal{U}_{P_N}(\mathcal{I})$, a negative subgoal ${\sim}B$ is first checked to see if it belongs to N. Only if ${\sim}B$ is not in N will B be evaluated in context $N \cup \{{\sim}B\}$. This effectively blocks negative loops.

We define a sequence $\mathcal{I}_\alpha$ of sets of partial interpretations indexed with negative contexts. For every negative context N,

- $(\mathcal{I}_0)_N = \emptyset$

- $(\mathcal{I}_{\alpha+1})_N = \mathcal{V}_{P_N}(\mathcal{I}_\alpha)$

- $(\mathcal{I}_\alpha)_N = \cup_{\beta < \alpha}(\mathcal{I}_\beta)_N$ for limit ordinal α

- $(\mathcal{I}^\infty)_N = \cup_\alpha (\mathcal{I}_\alpha)_N$

In [4], we show that true or false answers obtained from a negative context can be shared across all negative contexts. Such sharing could have a significant impact on the efficiency of query evaluation. Our implementation supports sharing of answers of a call after it is completely evaluated.

As to the relationship between the ordinary well founded semantics (without negative contexts) I^∞ and our well founded semantics $\mathcal{I}^\infty$ under negative contexts, the ordinary well founded semantics can be viewed as computation with respect to a changing negative context. More precisely, let I be a partial interpretation, and $Und(I)$ be the set of all ground atoms that are undefined in I.

Lemma 3.1 *Let P be a program. Then $I_{\alpha+1} \subseteq (\mathcal{I}^\infty)_{N_\alpha}$, where $N_\alpha = {\sim}Und(I_\alpha)$.*

Finally, the well founded partial model coincides with the partial model under the empty negative context.

Theorem 3.2 *Let P be a program. Then $I^\infty = (\mathcal{I}^\infty)_\emptyset$.*

4 XOLDTNF Resolution

XOLDTNF resolution extends OLDT resolution in two aspects. One is that
the truth value of an answer may be *undefined*, due to the three-valued
nature of the well founded semantics in general. The other extension is that
negative loops are avoided by negative contexts. Intermediate results are
maintained in tables that are indexed by negative contexts.

4.1 XOLD Resolutions and XOLDTNF Structures

For general logic programs, their meaning is defined by the well founded
semantics, which is a partial interpretation in general. A partial interpre-
tation is essentially a three-valued model with truth values $\mathbf{t}$, $\mathbf{f}$, and $\mathbf{u}$ for
undefined. The truth ordering is $\mathbf{f} < \mathbf{u} < \mathbf{t}$. An answer of a query consists of
both an instance of the query atom and a corresponding truth value which
can be either $\mathbf{t}$ or $\mathbf{u}$.

Definition 4.1 (XOLDT Answer Table) A *truth pair* is a pair of the
form (B, v), where B is an atom, and v is either $\mathbf{t}$ or $\mathbf{u}$. An *XOLDT answer
table* T is a set of pairs $(B, (B', v))$ where B is an atom, B' is a substitution instance of B, and v is either $\mathbf{t}$ or $\mathbf{u}$. An XOLDT answer table is
reduced if whenever $(B, (B', \mathbf{t})) \in T$, $(B, (B', \mathbf{u})) \notin T$. The *reduction* of an
XOLDT answer table T, $reduce(T)$, is obtained by deleting from T elements
$(B, (B', \mathbf{u}))$ when $(B, (B', \mathbf{t})) \in T$.

Let T_1 and T_2 be reduced XOLDT answer tables. $T_1 \preceq T_2$ if for every
$(B, (B', v_1)) \in T_1$, there exists $(B, (B', v_2)) \in T_2$ such that $v_1 \leq v_2$. The
union, $T_1 \cup T_2$, is the reduction of the set union of T_1 and T_2. $\Diamond$

Henceforth we always assume that XOLDT answer tables are reduced.

Recall that in SLD-tree, each node is labeled with a query. In XOLDTNF
forests to be defined later, each node is labeled with an *X-clause*, of the form

$$(A, v) \leftarrow L_1, ..., L_n$$

where (A, v) is a truth pair, and $L_1, ..., L_n$ are literals. When $n = 0$, the
head of an X-clause represents an answer. Let R be any fixed, but arbitrary
computation rule that selects from the body of an X-clause exactly one literal
if there exists one. The atom (literal) selected by R is called the *selected
atom (literal)* of the X-clause.

Definition 4.2 (XOLD Resolution) Let G be an X-clause
$(A, v) \leftarrow L_1, ..., L_n$, where $n > 0$ and L_i be the selected atom. Let D
be a clause, and D', of the form $A' \leftarrow L'_1, ..., L'_m$, be a variant of D with
variables renamed so that G and D' have no variables in common. G is
XOLD resolvable with D if L_i and A' are unifiable. The clause

$$((A, v) \leftarrow L_1, ..., L_{i-1}, L'_1, ..., L'_m, L_{i+1}, ..., L_n)\theta$$

is the *XOLD resolvent* of G with D where θ is the most general unifier of L_i and A'. $\diamond$

Definition 4.3 (XOLD Answer-Resolution) Let G be an X-clause $(A, v) \leftarrow L_1, ..., L_n$, where $n > 0$ and L_i be the selected atom of G. Let B' be a variant of an atom B with variables renamed so that G and B' have no variables in common. G is *XOLD answer-resolvable* with a truth pair (B, v') if L_i and B' are unifiable. The clause

$$((A, v^*) \leftarrow L_1, ..., L_{i-1}, L_{i+1}, ..., L_n)\theta$$

is the *XOLD answer-resolvent* of G with (B, v'), where θ is the most general unifier of L_i and B', and v^* is **t** if both v and v' are **t** and is **u** otherwise. $\diamond$

XOLD resolution is used for a call when it is first encountered. All later occurrences of the call will be solved using XOLD answer-resolution.

In computing with general logic programs, we maintain XOLDT tables that are indexed with negative contexts.

Definition 4.4 Let P be a program. An *XOLDTNF structure* $\mathcal{S}$ is a quadruple $(\mathcal{C}, \mathcal{T}, \mathcal{D})$, where $\mathcal{C}$ and $\mathcal{D}$ are sets of atoms indexed by negative contexts; and $\mathcal{T}$ is a set of (reduced) XOLDT answer tables indexed by negative contexts. $\diamond$

In an XOLDTNF structure, $\mathcal{D}$ is the set of calls that have been completely evaluated, which provides an implicit representation of negative answers together with $\mathcal{T}$. For convenience, we write $(N, A) \in \mathcal{C}$ when $A \in \mathcal{C}_N$, and $((N, A), (A', v)) \in \mathcal{T}$ when $(A, (A', v)) \in \mathcal{T}_N$. Similarly for $\mathcal{D}$.

For every set $\mathcal{A}$ of atoms indexed by negative contexts, the set of answers for $\mathcal{A}$ in $\mathcal{S}$, denoted by $\mathcal{S}|_{\mathcal{A}}$, is the set of all elements $((N, A), (A', v)) \in \mathcal{T}$ such that $(N, A) \in \mathcal{A}$. Let $\mathcal{S}_1$ and $\mathcal{S}_2$ be XOLDTNF structures. We define $\mathcal{S}_1 \preceq \mathcal{S}_2$ if for every negative context N, $(\mathcal{C}_1)_N \subseteq (\mathcal{C}_2)_N$, $(\mathcal{D}_1)_N \subseteq (\mathcal{D}_2)_N$, $(\mathcal{T}_1)_N \preceq (\mathcal{T}_2)_N$, and $\mathcal{S}_1|_{\mathcal{D}_1} = \mathcal{S}_2|_{\mathcal{D}_1}$.

4.2 Positive XOLDTNF Forests

In the well founded semantics (with negative contexts), three transformations are involved. Positive answers are computed at each stage by iterating $\mathcal{T}_P$ ($\mathcal{T}_{P_N}$) up to ω; negative answers are computed at each stage using the largest unfounded sets $\mathcal{U}_P$ ($\mathcal{U}_{P_N}$); both transformations, which are merged into $\mathcal{V}_P$, are iterated until a fixpoint is reached.

Our definition of XOLDTNF resolution follows a similar structure. Given a program P, an XOLDTNF structure $\mathcal{S}$, and a negative context N, the notion of *XOLDTNF forest* for N under $\mathcal{S}$ corresponds to $\mathcal{T}_{P_N}$. A *positive XOLDTNF forest* corresponds to the iteration of $\mathcal{T}_{P_N}$ to ω. From the positive XOLDTNF forest, we define the set of calls that have been completely evaluated. Some of the completely evaluated calls are failed, i.e., without any answers, and they correspond to the portion of $\mathcal{U}_{P_N}$ relevant to the orginal query. The notion of *global XOLDTNF forest* corresponds to the iteration of $\mathcal{V}_P$ up to a fixpoint.

Definition 4.5 Let P be a program, R be an arbitrary but fixed computation rule, S be an XOLDTNF structure $(\mathcal{C}, \mathcal{T}, \mathcal{D})$ and, N be a negative context. The *XOLDTNF forest* for N under S is a forest constructed as follows.

For each $(N, A) \in \mathcal{C}$, there is a tree whose root node is labeled by $(A, \mathbf{t}) \leftarrow A$. Let $D_1, ..., D_n$ be all the clauses in P with which $(A, \mathbf{t}) \leftarrow A$ is XOLD resolvable, and $G_1, ..., G_n$ be the respective XOLD resolvents. The root node has n child nodes labeled with $G_1, ..., G_n$. If $n = 0$, the root node is a *dead leaf*.

Let V be a non-root node with label G of the form $(A, v) \leftarrow L_1, ..., L_n$ and, L_i be selected by R, where $1 \le i \le n$.

- If L_i is an atom B, for every $((N, B), (B', v)) \in \mathcal{T}$, V has a child node labeled with the XOLD answer-resolvent of G with (B', v);

- If L_i is a non-ground negative literal, V is a *floundered* leaf node;

- If L_i is a ground negative literal $\sim B$ and $\sim B \in N$, V has a single child node labeled with

$$(A, \mathbf{u}) \leftarrow L_1, ..., L_{i-1}, L_{i+1}, ..., L_n$$

- If L_i is a ground negative literal $\sim B$ and $\sim B \notin N$ and $(N \cup \{\sim B\}, B) \in \mathcal{D}$, there are three cases:

  - If $((N \cup \{\sim B\}, B), (B, \mathbf{t})) \in \mathcal{T}$, V is a *dead* leaf;
  - If $((N \cup \{\sim B\}, B), (B, \mathbf{u})) \in \mathcal{T}$, V has a single child node labeled with

    $$(A, \mathbf{u}) \leftarrow L_1, ..., L_{i-1}, L_{i+1}, ..., L_n$$

    (Recall that $\mathcal{T}$ is reduced.)
  - Otherwise, V has a single child node labeled with

    $$(A, v) \leftarrow L_1, ..., L_{i-1}, L_{i+1}, ..., L_n$$

If V is labeled with $(B, v) \leftarrow$, V is an *answer* leaf. If the root node is labeled with $(A, \mathbf{t}) \leftarrow A$, then $(A, (B, v))$ is an *answer pair*.

An XOLDTNF forest is *non-floundering* if there is no floundered leaf node in any tree of the forest. By *ground XOLDTNF forest* we mean XOLDTNF forests that are constructed from a ground XOLDTNF structure and the Herbrand instantiation of P. ◇

Let P be a program, and S be an XOLDTNF structure $(\mathcal{C}, \mathcal{T}, \mathcal{D})$, and F_N be the XOLDTNF forest for N under S.

- $calls_{P_N}(S)$ is the set of all selected atoms of nodes in F_N;

- $table_{P_N}(S)$ is the reduction of the set of answer pairs of F_N;

- $\overline{table}_{P_N}(S)$ is the reduction of the union of $table_{P_N}(S)$ and $\mathcal{T}_N$;

- $\mathcal{X}_{P_N}(S) = (\mathcal{C}', \mathcal{T}', \mathcal{D})$, where $\mathcal{C}'$ is identical to $\mathcal{C}$ except that $\mathcal{C}'_N = calls_{P_N}(S)$; and $\mathcal{T}'$ is identical to $\mathcal{T}$ except that $\mathcal{T}'_N = \overline{table}_{P_N}(S)$. $\Diamond$

Let $\mathcal{X}^k_{P_N}(S)$ denote the finite power of $\mathcal{X}_{P_N}$ and,

$$\mathcal{X}^\omega_{P_N}(S) = (calls^\omega_{P_N}(S), \overline{table}^\omega_{P_N}(S), \mathcal{D}) = \cup_k \mathcal{X}^k_{P_N}(S)$$

The iteration of $\mathcal{X}_{P_N}$ up to ω computes all positive and undefined answers given an XOLDTNF structure S. The XOLDTNF forest F_N for N under $\mathcal{X}^\omega_{P_N}(S)$ is called the *positive XOLDTNF forest* for N under S.

For negation-as-failure, we also need to detect when a subgoal is failed. This is accomplished implicitly by detecting all subgoals that have been completely evaluated, the subset of which that have no answers are failed.

More precisely, a subset C of $calls^\omega_{P_N}(S)$ is *completely evaluated* with respect to S if for every atom $A \in$ C, either

a. A is ground and $(A, (A, \mathbf{t})) \in \overline{table}^\omega_{P_N}(S)$; or

b. for every node V in the tree for A in the positive XOLDTNF forest F_N under S, the following holds:

  i. if the selected literal of V is an atom B, then $B \in$ C; and

  ii. if the selected literal of V is $\sim B$, then B is ground and either $\sim B \in N$ or $(N \cup \{\sim B\}, B) \in \mathcal{D}$.

In case (a), no further computation can add any more knowledge to the answer of A. In case (b), at every choice point, if the selected literal is an atom, the atom must be completely evaluated; and if the selected literal is a negative subgoal, it must be ground and its truth value must have been already determined.

The union of arbitrary completely evaluated sets of calls is also completely evaluated. For each N, the greatest completely evaluated set is denoted by $done^\omega_{P_N}(S)$. In the implementation, when a negative subgoal is solved by the negation-as-failure rule, an exhaustive search is done for answers of the corresponding the positive subgoal. Completely evaluated calls are obtained after the exhaustive search is finished.

4.3 Global XOLDTNF Forest

We are now ready to define the *Global XOLDTNF Forest* for general programs. In a global XOLDTNF forest, negative subgoals that are selected are simultaneously expanded by starting new trees for the corresponding positive subgoals if they have not been encountered before.

Definition 4.6 Let P be a program, and $\mathcal{S}$ be an XOLDTNF structure. The *global XOLDTNF forest* F is a forest of forests consisting of positive XOLDTNF forests F_N for every N under $\mathcal{S}$. We define

- $\overline{calls}^{\omega}_{P_N}(\mathcal{S})$ as the union of $calls^{\omega}_{P_N}(\mathcal{S})$ and the set of all ground atoms B such that $\sim B$ is selected in F_M for some negative context M and $\sim B \notin M$ and $N = M \cup \{\sim B\}$;

- $\mathcal{X}_P(\mathcal{S}) = (\mathcal{C}, \mathcal{T}, \mathcal{D})$ such that $\mathcal{C}_N = \overline{calls}^{\omega}_{P_N}(\mathcal{S})$; $\mathcal{T}_N = \overline{table}^{\omega}_{P_N}(\mathcal{S})$; $\mathcal{D}_N = done^{\omega}_{P_N}(\mathcal{S})$.

By *ground global XOLDTNF forest* we mean a global XOLDTNF forest that is constructed from a ground XOLDTNF structure and the Herbrand instantiation of P. ◇

Let P be a general program and, C be a set of atoms. Let $\mathcal{S}_0$ be the XOLDTNF structure $(\mathcal{C}_0, \{\}, \{\}, \{\})$, where $(\mathcal{C}_0)_\emptyset = C$ and $(\mathcal{C}_0)_N = \emptyset$ for every other negative context N. We define

$$
\begin{aligned}
\mathcal{X}_0 &= \mathcal{S}_0 \\
\mathcal{X}_{\alpha+1} &= \mathcal{X}_P(\mathcal{X}_\alpha) \\
\mathcal{X}_\alpha &= \bigcup_{\beta < \alpha} \mathcal{X}_\beta \text{ if } \alpha \text{ is a limit ordinal other than } 0
\end{aligned}
$$

Lemma 4.1 *The sequence $\mathcal{X}_\alpha$ is a monotonically increasing sequence of XOLDTNF structures.*

Let C be a set of atoms, and $\mathcal{X}^\infty = (\mathcal{C}^\infty, \mathcal{T}^\infty, \mathcal{D}^\infty) = \cup_\alpha \mathcal{X}_\alpha$. It follows by classical results of Tarski that $\mathcal{X}^\infty$ is the least fixpoint of $\mathcal{X}_P$. The Herbrand base is countable, and so for some countable ordinal α, $\mathcal{X}^\infty = \mathcal{X}_\alpha$. We call the global XOLDTNF forest for $\mathcal{X}^\infty$ the *final XOLDTNF forest* for C under P. C is *non-floundering* if the final XOLDTNF forest does not contain any floundered leaf node.

For function-free programs and queries, every $\mathcal{X}_\alpha$ must be finite. By Lemma 4.1, the sequence $\mathcal{X}_\alpha$ is monotonically increasing. Thus the fixpoint of $\mathcal{X}^\infty$ can be reached in a finite number of steps. Termination for function-free programs is therefore guaranteed.

5 Soundness and Completeness

This section states the soundness and completeness results of XOLDTNF resolution. Proofs can be found in [4].

Theorem 5.1 (Soundness of XOLDTNF Resolution) *Let P be a program, and C be a set of atoms. Then for every $A \in C$,*

1. If $((\emptyset, A), (A', \mathbf{t})) \in \mathcal{T}^\infty$, then $I^\infty \models \forall (A')$;

2. If $(\emptyset, A) \in \mathcal{F}^\infty$, then $I^\infty \models \forall (\neg A)$.

where $\mathcal{F}^\infty$ is the set of all calls $(M, B) \in \mathcal{D}^\infty$ that have no answers in $\mathcal{T}^\infty$.

The proof uses an induction over the construction of $\mathcal{X}^\infty$ and the well founded semantics under negative contexts as a link between the computation and the ordinary well founded semantics.

It turns out that XOLDTNF resolution is in general not complete. Consider the following program and query:

$$p(X) \leftarrow \sim p(f(X)).$$
$$q \leftarrow p(a), r.$$
$$\leftarrow q.$$

XOLDTNF resolution will create a tree for $(\emptyset, q)$:

$$1 : (q, \mathbf{t}) \leftarrow q.$$
$$2 : (q, \mathbf{t}) \leftarrow p(a), r.$$

At this point, a new tree for $(\emptyset, p(a))$ is started:

$$3 : (p(a), \mathbf{t}) \leftarrow p(a).$$
$$4 : (p(a), \mathbf{t}) \leftarrow \sim p(f(a)).$$

And it will start a new tree for $(\{\sim p(f(a))\}, p(f(a)))$, and continue. The computation will not return to $(\emptyset, q)$ until some answer is obtained for $(\emptyset, p(a))$, which does not exist in this case.

In Ross's global SLS resolution[15], a single list of subgoals is maintained and a *positivistic computation rule* is used that always selects positive subgoals before negative ones. For the above example, global SLS resolution will be able to fail q, by choosing and failing r before trying to expand $\sim p(f(a))$.

To support memo-ing, XOLDTNF resolution does not keep a single list of subgoals. The computation rule can select positive subgoals before negative ones, but only within a clause. In other words, the computation rule is local. This seems to be a common assumption in all procedural semantics that involve memo-ing. Nevertheless, completeness can still be achieved for quite a large class of programs and queries.

Definition 5.1 Let P be a program, C be a set of atoms. C is *finitely negative* if there exists an integer n such that such that whenever $(C^\infty)_N$ is nonempty in (possibly non-ground) $\mathcal{X}^\infty$, $|N| \leq n$.

Notice that all function-free programs and queries are finitely negative, so are stratified programs and their queries.

Lemma 5.2 *Let P be a program, and C be a finitely negative and non-floundering set of atoms. Let $\mathcal{X}^\infty = (C^\infty, \mathcal{T}^\infty, \mathcal{D}^\infty)$ be the (non-ground) final XOLDTNF forest for C under P. Then $C^\infty = \mathcal{D}^\infty$.*

Theorem 5.3 *Let P be a program, and C be a finitely negative and non-floundering set of atoms that contain only symbols from P. Let P' be the augmented program, I^∞ and $(I')^\infty$ denote the well founded partial model of P and P', respectively. Then for every atom $A \in C$,*

1. *if $I^\infty \models \exists A$, then there exists some A' such that $((\emptyset, A), (A', \mathbf{t})) \in \mathcal{T}^\infty$ of $\mathcal{X}^\infty$;*

2. *if $I^\infty \models \forall(\neg A)$, then $(\emptyset, A) \in \mathcal{F}^\infty$;*

3. *if $(I')^\infty \models \forall(B)$, where B is an instance of A, then $((\emptyset, A), (A', \mathbf{t})) \in \mathcal{T}^\infty$ of $\mathcal{X}^\infty$ such that B is an instance of A'*

where $\mathcal{F}^\infty$ is the set of all calls $(M, B) \in \mathcal{D}^\infty$ that have no answers in $\mathcal{T}^\infty$.

The notion of augmented programs is the standard one [14].

6 Discussion

We have presented a goal-oriented method of computing the well founded semantics of general logic programs. It avoids both positive and negative loops and terminates for all function-free programs. It is sound and complete for all finitely negative and non-floundering queries, which properly include non-floundering queries with respect to all function-free programs and all stratified programs.

Compared with WELL! [2], the detection of positive and negative loops in XOLDTNF resolution is similar. However, there seem to be two major differences. One is that we treat looping negative subgoals as undefined and use an explicit three-valued representation of intermediate results. This provides a uniform treatment of lemmas, i.e., true or false answers, and potential lemmas, which *also* include undefined answers. Since all lemmas are also potential lemmas, our uniform treatment avoids the double traversal of trees. The other major difference is that we consider answer sharing across different negative contexts. Our experience shows that such sharing could improve efficiency significantly. It should also be mentioned that a derivation procedure for well founded models is described in [9], but only for *ground* programs.

Pragmatically, XOLDTNF resolution can be integrated with Prolog computation in a smooth manner. In fact, it is useful to distinguish between Prolog predicates solved using SLDNF and tabled predicates solved using XOLDTNF. The former may include base predicates containing only facts or built-in predicates. During query evaluation, Prolog predicates can be easily called during XOLDTNF evaluation of other predicates, and vice versa.

An implementation of XOLDTNF resolution has been carried out using Prolog meta interpreters [22]. It is available by anonymous FTP from cs.sunysb.edu.

References

[1] F. Bancilhon, D. Maier, Y. Sagiv, and J. Ullman. Magic sets and other strange ways to implement logic programs. In *Proceedings of the Fifth Symposium on Principles of Database Systems*, pages 1–15, March 1986.

[2] N. Bidoit and P. Legay. Well!: An evaluation procedure for all logic programs. In *Proceedings of the International Conference on Database Technology*, pages 335–348, 1990.

[3] F. Bry. Query evaluation in recursive databases: Bottom-up and top-down reconciled. In *Proceedings of the First International Conference on Deductive and Object-Oriented Databases*, December 1989.

[4] W. Chen and D.S. Warren. A practical approach to computing the well founded semantics. Technical Report 92-CSE-9, Department of Computer Science and Engineering, Southern Methodist University, March 1992.

[5] K.L. Clark. Negation as failure. In H. Gallaire and J. Minker, editors, *Logic and Databases*, pages 293–322. Plenum, New York, 1978.

[6] S.W. Dietrich and D.S. Warren. Extension tables: Memo relations in logic programming. Technical Report 86/18, Department of Computer Science, SUNY at Stony Brook, 1986.

[7] M. Gelfond and V. Lifschitz. The stable model semantics for logic programming. In R.A. Kowalski and K.A. Bowen, editors, *Proc. 5th Int. Conf. and Symp. on Logic Programming*, pages 1070–1080, 1988.

[8] J.W. Lloyd. *Foundations of Logic Programming*. Springer-Verlag, New York, second edition, 1987.

[9] L.M. Pereira, J.N. Aparicio, and J.J. Alferes. Derivation procedures for extended stable models. In *Proceedings of 12th International Conference on Artificial Intelligence*, pages 863–868, 1991.

[10] H. Przymusinska and T.C. Przymusinski. Weakly perfect model semantics for logic programs. In R.A. Kowalski and K.A. Bowen, editors, *Proc. 5th Int. Conf. and Symp. on Logic Programming*, pages 1106–1120, 1988.

[11] T.C. Przymusinski. Every logic program has a natural stratification and an iterated least fixed point model. In *Proc. 8th ACM Symp. on PODS*, pages 11–21, 1989.

[12] T.C. Przymusinski. On the declarative and procedural semantics of logic programs. *Journal of Automated Reasoning*, 5:167–205, 1989.

[13] R. Ramakrishnan. Magic templates: A spellbinding approach to logic programs. *Journal of Logic Programming*, 11:189–216, 1991.

[14] K.A. Ross. A procedural semantics for well founded negation in logic programs. In *Proc. 8th ACM Symp. on PODS*, pages 22–33, 1989.

[15] K.A. Ross. *The Semantics of Deductive Databases*. PhD thesis, Department of Computer Science, Stanford University, August 1991.

[16] H. Seki. On the power of alexander templates. In *Proceedings of the Eighth ACM Symposium on Principles of Database Systems*, pages 150–159, March 1989.

[17] H. Tamaki and T. Sato. Old resolution with tabulation. In *Proceedings of the Third International Conference on Logic Programming*, pages 84–98, 1986.

[18] A. van Gelder. The alternating fixpoint of logic programs with negation (extended abstract). In *Proc. 8th ACM Symp. on PODS*, pages 1–10, 1989.

[19] A. van Gelder, K.A. Ross, and J.S. Schlipf. Unfounded sets and well-founded semantics for general logic programs. In *Proc. 7th ACM Symp. on PODS*, 1988.

[20] A. van Gelder, K.A. Ross, and J.S. Schlipf. The well-founded semantics for general logic programs. *Journal of the Association for Computing Machinery*, 38(3), July 1991.

[21] L. Vieille. A database-complete proof procedure based upon sld-resolution. In *Proceedings of the Fourth International Conference on Logic Programming*, 1987.

[22] D.S. Warren. Computing the well founded semantics of logic programs. Technical report, Computer Science Department, SUNY at Stony Brook, June 1991.

Linear Logic

Herbrand Methods in Sequent Calculi : unification in LL

Serenella Cerrito
L.R.I.,Université Paris XI
Bât.490, Centre d'Orsay
91405 Orsay Cedex, France.
serena@lri.lri.fr.

Abstract

We propose a reformulation of quantifiers rules in sequent calculi which allows to replace blind existential instantiation with unification, thereby reducing non-determinism and complexity in proof-search. Our method, based on some ideas underlying the proof of Herbrand theorem for classical logic, may be applied to any "reasonable" non-classical sequent calculus, but here we focus on sequent calculus for linear logic, in view of an application to linear logic programming. We prove that the new linear proof-system which we propose, the so called system LLH, is equivalent to standard linear sequent calculus LL.

1 Introduction

A result in classical logic which has been widely exploited in logic programming is *Herbrand theorem*. Several versions of this result are present in the literature; we recall here one of them (see [13]).

Herbrand Theorem
Let F be a prenex formula of the form $\exists w \forall x \exists y \forall z A[w, x, y, z]$ with A quantifier-free.
F is provable in predicate calculus if and only if a disjunction of the form

$$A[t_{11}, f(t_{11}), t_{12}, g(t_{11}, t_{12})] \lor \cdots \lor A[t_{n1}, f(t_{n1}), t_{n2}, g(t_{n1}, t_{n2})]$$

(called Herbrand disjunction) is provable in propositional calculus.
The terms $t_{11}, \cdots, t_{n2}$ are constructed out of variables and function symbols of F together with the new function symbols f (unary) and g (binary).

Such a result allows the use of unification rather than of blind instantiation when proofs are built up, thereby reducing non-determinism and complexity in proof-search. It would be nice to dispose of similar tools when searching for linear proofs; unfortunately not every linear formula can be put in prenex form, so that it does not make much sense trying to get exactly this kind of theorem in linear logic. Indeed, the same kind of phenomenon occurs also in other non classical logics, for instance intuitionistic logic.

However, the idea underlying the proof of the classical theorem [13] may be exploited also in the linear context : *the universally quantified variables can be expressed as functions of the existential ones*. Let us call this technique *Herbrandization*. Notice that when formulae are *Skolemized* the existential variables are expressed as functions of the universal ones. Skolemization preserves satisfiability while Herbrandization preseves provability (validity). In this paper we propose a new linear sequent calculus LLH which uses *Herbrand functions* in the very formulation of the quantifier rules, thereby achieving an effect somewhat similar to Herbrand theorem.

Our method could also be applied to *any* other "reasonable" sequent calculus, since what really matters is just the handling of quantifiers rules and of of identity axioms. Hence the results presented in this paper hold for a whole class of calculi : all the sequent calculi with "standard" quantification rules and identity axioms enjoying cut-elimination.[1] Indeed in [18] Shankar has independently developed an approach rather similar to ours to deal with the intuitionistic calculus LJ. The distinguishing features of our approach are :

- the focus on the application to linear logic programming, more precisely on possible extensions of the logic programming language LinLog [1];

- the embedding of unification *into* the sequent calculus, so to get a *new proof-system*, rather than just a search procedure over ordinary sequent proofs (as in [18]);

- the treatment of unifiers via *sets of equations*; such sets may be seen as solutions to *constraints* w.r.t. the Herbrand universe.

2 Linear Sequent Calculi

2.1 Preliminaries

Linear logic [8] is essentially obtained by removing the structural rules *contraction* and *weakening* from Gentzen sequent calculus LK. As a result of such omission one gets two conjunctions ($\otimes$, the multiplicative conjunction, and &, the additive conjunction) and two disjunctions ($\uparrow$, the multiplicative disjunction, and $\oplus$, the additive disjunction). Contraction and weakening are absent as *structural* rules, but are reintroduced as *logical rules* via the modalities ! and ?.

Let $\mathcal{F}$ be a set of function symbols. Let

$$\mathcal{P}^{pos} = \{P_1, ..., P_i, ...\} \text{ and } \mathcal{P}^{neg} = \{P_1^{\perp}, .., P_i^{\perp}, ...\}$$

be ordered sets of predicates. Linear formulae in the language $\mathcal{L} = (\mathcal{F}, \mathcal{P}^{pos} \cup \mathcal{P}^{neg})$ are built out of literals via the linear connectives, modalities and quantifiers in the usual way (see [8]).

A (right-handed) linear sequent is an expression of the form $\vdash \Gamma$, where Γ is a finite sequence of linear formulae $G_1, .., G_n$; the implicitly defined meaning of the linear sequent $\vdash \Gamma$ is

$$G_1 \uparrow G_2 \uparrow ... \uparrow G_{n-1} \uparrow G_n$$

We list the inference rules of the (right-handed) linear sequent calculus LL in the appendix; we recall that LL enjoys cut-elimination.

We will assume that formulae and proofs in LL are such that :

- no variable in a formula is simultaneously free and bound,

- in a formula, distinct quantifiers bound distinct variables and in a sequent, quantifiers occurring in distinct formulae bound different variables,

- in a LL proof D, if y is the *eigenvariable* of an universal rule, y does not occur in the fragment of branch which goes from the root to the conclusion of this rule.

---

[1]Of course, some minor technical modifications are needed, according to the specific logic considered.

These assumptions are without loss of generality because of the possibility of renaming variables.

2.2 The linear sequent calculus LLH

We modify the notion of linear formula as follows. We assume to have special variables, called *witness* variables, which have the role of instantiating existential statements and which are noted $W_1, W_2, \dots$. We suppose to have denumerably many of them. Let us call $\mathcal{L}_H$ the language obtained from $\mathcal{L}$ by adding a set $\mathcal{F}_{\mathcal{H}}$ of new function symbols called *Herbrand functions*; for any non-negative integer n, $\mathcal{F}_{\mathcal{H}}$ contains denumerably many functions of arity n.

Definition 1 *A term of $\mathcal{L}_H$ is inductively defined by :*

- *any witness variable is a term*

- *if $t_1, \dots, t_n$ are terms and f is a n-ary function symbol (ordinary or Herbrand), then $f(t_1, \dots, t_n)$ is a term.*

Definition 2 *Formulae of $\mathcal{L}_H$ are inductively defined as follows.*

- *The logical constants 1, $\perp$, T, 0 are formulae.*

- *If P is a (positive or negative) predicate and $t_1, \dots, t_n$ are terms, then $P(t_1, \dots, t_n)$ is a formula.*

- *If F and G are formulae, a new formula may be built out of them by using a linear connective or an exponential modality in the standard way.*

- *If F is a formula, Q a quantifier, w a witness variable, x an ordinary variable, then $QxF[w/x]$ is a formula.*

Notice that, by definition, formulae of $\mathcal{L}_H$ are such that the free variables are exactly the witness variables. Moreover, as in the case of $\mathcal{L}$, we will assume that in any formula distinct quantifiers bound distinct variables and in a sequent quantifiers of distinct formulae bound different variables.

The proof-system LLH acts on $\mathcal{L}_H$ formulae and terms. The identity group of LLH differs from LL just because the identity axioms are replaced by the following identity rules :

$$\frac{W_1 = t_1, \dots, W_n = t_n}{\vdash A, A'^{\perp}}$$

where the premise is such that $W_1, \dots, W_n$ are among (perhaps all) the witness variables in A, A' and the set of equations $W_1 = t_1, \dots, W_n = t_n$ represents a substitution for these variables which is the most general unifier of A and A'. This set can be empty; in this case it denotes the identity substitution, which replaces variables by themselves. Hence, a LL-identity axiom is a particular case of LLH identity rule.

For example, the following is a correct instance of identity rule :

$$\frac{W_1 = f(a), W_2 = W_3}{\vdash p(W_1, W_2), p^{\perp}(f(a), W_3)}$$

The only other rules which change in LLH w.r.t. to LL are the quantifiers rules, which now become :

$$\frac{\vdash \Gamma, A[x/f(W_1, \cdots, W_n)]}{\vdash \Gamma, \forall x A}(\forall)$$

where $W_1, \cdots, W_n$ are exactly the witness variables occurring in the lower sequent and f is a Herbrand function symbol not appearing in the lower sequent,

$$\frac{\vdash \Gamma, A[x/W_i]}{\vdash \Gamma, \exists x A}(\exists).$$

where W_i is a witness variable not appearing in the lower sequent.

Remark 1 *The intuitive meaning of the use of Herbrand functions in the LLH quantifier rules is the following. The fact that the witness variable W is the argument of the Herbrand function f in the term $f(W)$ introduced (in a bottom-up reading) by a $\forall$ rule has the effect to prevent the unification of W and $f(W)$ (at the level of identity rules). Concretely, this means that the object represented by $f(W)$ is really "arbitrary" and does not depend on any commitment on the value of W. In other terms, the use of Herbrand functions enforces the standard eigenvariable condition in the universal rule.*

Remark 2 *It is the case to point out that if if we had formulated the LLH $\forall$ rule by just imposing the following "weak" condition :*

$$W_1, \cdots, W_n \text{ are the witness variables in } \forall x A(x)$$

(rather than the witness variables in $\forall x A(x)$ and in Γ) we would have got an unsound rule. For instance, the formula $\exists x(p(x)\&q)$ would have became a consequence of $\exists x p(x)\&q$, although this kind of inference is not correct in linear logic. (See the example 3 below).

Of course, to make the above point precise we need to properly define the notion of *LLH proof*. In order to introduce this definition, we first give an example.

Example 1 *Suppose that we want to prove the validity of the formula*

$$A(a)\&B(a) \multimap \exists x(A(x)\&B(x))$$

What we actually look for is an answer for the question : "For which value of x we get that $A(x)\&B(x)$ is linearly implied by $A(a)\&B(a)$?" The following LLH proof of the corresponding sequent

$$\vdash A^\perp(a) \oplus B^\perp(a), \exists x(A(x)\&B(x))$$

tells us that the answer to that question is $x=a$.

$$\frac{\dfrac{\dfrac{W_1 = a}{\vdash A^\perp(a), A(W_1)}}{\vdash A^\perp(a) \oplus B^\perp(a), A(W_1)} \qquad \dfrac{\dfrac{W_1 = a}{\vdash B^\perp(a), B(W_1)}}{\vdash A^\perp(a) \oplus B^\perp(a), B(W_1)}}{\dfrac{\vdash A^\perp(a) \oplus B^\perp(a), A(W_1)\&B(W_1)}{\vdash A^\perp(a) \oplus B^\perp(a), \exists x(A(x)\&B(x))}}$$

We give now the formal definition of LLH-proof.

Definition 3 *Let $\vdash \Gamma$ be a linear sequent.*

- *A candidate LLH-proof for $\vdash \Gamma$ is a tree T of sequents such that :*
  i) the root is $\vdash \Gamma$
  ii) the children of a vertex v are the vertex $a_1 \cdots a_n$, where $0 \leq n \leq 2$ such that
  $$\frac{a_1 \cdots a_n}{v}$$
  is an instance of a LLH-inference rule;
  iii) distinct applications $R_1, \cdots, R_n$ of the $\forall$ rule in T make use of distinct Herbrand function symbols $f_1, \cdots, f_n$;
  iv) distinct applications $R_1, \cdots, R_n$ of the $\exists$ rule in T make use of distinct witness variables $W_1, \cdots, W_n$;
  v) a leaf is either the (empty) premise of an axiom (for 1 or T) or the premise of an identity rule.

- *Given any branch β of a candidate LLH-proof D whose leaf is a set of equations E, E is called the partial answer given by β for $\vdash \Gamma$. When this leaf is empty, we say that the partial answer given by β is the identity substitution.*

- *A candidate LLH-proof D is a LLH-proof when the partial answers $E_1, \cdots, E_p$ given by the p branches of D have a solution (an unifier). In this case, the more general of these solutions is called the answer for $\vdash \Gamma$ given by D.*

Example 2 *The following tree is a LLH-proof for*

$$\vdash \exists x (A^\perp(x) \oplus B^\perp(x)), A(a)\&B(b)$$

whose answer is $W_1 = a, W_2 = b$. Notice that W_1 and W_2 are two distinct witness variables for the very same existentially quantified variable x. Notice that the sequent may be read "$A^\perp(a) \oplus B^\perp(b)$ linearly implies $\exists x(A^\perp(x) \oplus B^\perp(x))$", so that the answer provides an information about the two possible values for the existential variable x.

$$
\cfrac{
\cfrac{
\cfrac{
\cfrac{W_1 = a}{\vdash A^\perp(W_1), A(a)}
}{\vdash A^\perp(W_1) \oplus B^\perp(W_1), A(a)}
}{\vdash \exists x(A^\perp(x) \oplus B^\perp(x)), A(a)}
\qquad
\cfrac{
\cfrac{
\cfrac{W_2 = b}{\vdash B^\perp(W_2), B(b)}
}{\vdash A^\perp(W_2) \oplus B^\perp(W_2), B(b)}
}{\vdash \exists x(A^\perp(x) \oplus B^\perp(x)), B(b)}
}{\vdash A(a)\&B(b), \exists x(A^\perp(x) \oplus B^\perp(x))}
$$

The next tree is a candidate LLH-proof for the sequent

$$\vdash A^\perp(a) \oplus B^\perp(b), \exists x((A(x)\&B(x))$$

but it is NOT a LLH-proof because the set of partial answers $\{W_1 = a, W_1 = b\}$ has no solution. Indeed, such a sequent is not a linear theorem.

$$
\cfrac{
\cfrac{
\cfrac{W_1 = a}{\vdash A^\perp(a), A(W_1)}
}{\vdash A^\perp(a) \oplus B^\perp(b), A(W_1)}
\qquad
\cfrac{W_1 = b}{\vdash B^\perp(b), B(W_1)}
\Big/ {\vdash A^\perp(a) \oplus B^\perp(b), B(W_1)}
}{
\cfrac{\vdash A^\perp(a) \oplus B^\perp(b), A(W_1)\&B(W_1)}{\vdash A^\perp(a) \oplus B^\perp(b), \exists x(A(x)\&B(x))}
}
$$

Consider now the sequent

$$\vdash \forall x \exists y A(x,y) \multimap \exists y \forall x A(x,y)$$

This sequent may be equivalently rewritten as

$$\vdash \exists x \forall y A^{\perp}(x,y), \exists k \forall z A(z,k)$$

and it is not a linear theorem. Neiher is it LLH-provable because no associated candidate proof can be constructed. One immediately sees that the formulae in the leaf of the following tree cannot be unified because of the occur check *condition :*

$$\cfrac{\cfrac{\cfrac{\cfrac{\vdash A^{\perp}(W_1, f(W_1, W_2)), A(g(W_1, W_2), W_2)}{\vdash A^{\perp}(W_1, f(W_1, W_2)), \forall z A(z, W_2)}}{\vdash \forall y A^{\perp}(W_1, y), \forall z A(z, W_2)}}{\vdash \forall y A^{\perp}(W_1, y), \exists k \forall z A(z, k)}}{\vdash \exists x \forall y A^{\perp}(x, y), \exists k \forall z A(z, k)}$$

Example 3 *The reader can easily check that the sequent*

$$\vdash \forall x p^{\perp}(x) \oplus q^{\perp}, \exists x (p(x) \& q)$$

corresponding to the incorrect inference of remark 2 is not LLH-provable. However, if we liberalize the $\forall$ rule as we indicated, we do obtain a "proof" of such a sequent. The fact that such a linear sequent is not a theorem, while the analogous classical sequent is so, depends on the fact that in linear logic the $\oplus$ rule and the $\&$ rule do not commute. This example should provide some intuition on the reason why we can not boldly liberalize the $\forall$ rule. In intuitionistic logic we have the same kind of phenomenon and, again, we cannot restrict the arguments of the Herbrand functions to the witness variables in the main formula. [18] contains a fine analysis of the relation between the arguments of the Herbrand functions and the propositional impermutabilities of LJ.

2.3 A variant of LLH

Notice that it would also be possible to define a variant of LLH, say LLH', as follows. Rather than requiring the partial answers provided by a candidate proof-tree to be compatible, one asks a stronger condition: for any witness variable W_i, they must all assign the *same* value to it. Hence, if a sequent $\vdash \Gamma$ containing W_i is the conclusion of a &-rule (or a $\otimes$-rule) and both the sub-tres rooted at $\vdash \Gamma$ contain occurrences of W_i, then the partial answers provided by the branches of both trees must declare $W_i = t_i$ for the same term t_i. The advange of LLH' over LLH is that it looks more like a "standard" proof-system, since the criteria for being a well formed proof-tree are purely *local*, while the last condition in the definition of LLH proof-trees, involving a test of compatibility of the substitutions corresponding to the various branches, is *global*. Moreover, one could find LLH' more in the spirit of logic programming : for instance, in PROLOG the substitutions for the various branches are "threaded through" rather than compiled indepently and then checked for compatibility. However, there is a problem with this formulation : *how* to select the correct term t_i to be associated to *each* occurrence of W_i in the proof?

We could think of making the various branches communicate by giving the answer calculated by one of them as *input* to the construction of the next one, but this method will not quite work for LLH'. For instance, condider the formula :

$$\forall x A(x) \otimes B(b) \multimap \exists y (A(y) \otimes B(y))$$

It is evident that it is valid and that the answer for y is b. Now, a proof of such a formula reduces to a proof of the sequent :

$$\vdash \exists x A^\perp(x), B^\perp(b)), \exists y(A(y) \otimes B(y))$$

hence to a proof of the sequent :

$$\vdash A^\perp(W_1), B^\perp(b)), A(W_2) \otimes B(W_2)$$

The $\otimes$ rule tells us that we are left with two sequents to prove :

1. $\vdash A^\perp(W_1), A(W_2)$

2. $\vdash B^\perp(b)), B(W_2)$

hence with two branches both containing the witness variable W_2. Clearly, if we do the two branches independently we come up with two different, but compatible, answers : $W_2 = W_1$ and $W_2 = b$; this exactly corresponds to the way things are described by LLH. If we start by proving the second of the above sequents and give the calculated most general unifier as an input to the construction of the remaining branch, the solution $W_2 = b$ becomes an additional constraint which must be satisfied by the next calculated unifier : so, we get the answer $W_1 = W_2 = b$ for the second branch and the resulting tree is indeed a LLH' proof. So far, so good. But obviously if we start by doing the branch corresponding to the first sequent and we give the calculated most general unifier, namely $W_1 = W_2$, as input to the construction of the remaining branch we do not get a LLH' proof as final result.

On the other hand, if we do not imbed in the calculus any strategy to calculate substitutions and witness terms, our system LLH will not internalize a search strategy w.r.t. the quantifiers and will be as "blind" as LL. This is the kind of considerations which made us choose LLH over LLH'.

Of course a third possibility is left : to make the various branches communicate as sketched above, providing substitutions as inputs, without asking the very same value to be assigned to shared witness variables; substitutions would rather be further and further refined all along the construction of the tree. This method clearly reminds PROLOG's way of calculating unifiers. But, in our opinion, this constitutes just a possible way of "implementing" proof-search in LLH, not really an alternative logical formulation of the calculus itself.

3 Equivalence between LL and LLH

We prove that the system LLH is sound and complete by proving its equivalence with the standard system LL.

First, we remark that the proof of cut elimination for LL applies to LLH as well. Hence, we can suppose LLH-proofs to be cut-free.

The next definition will allow us to formulate a correspondence between the terms used to instantiate existentials in a LL-proof and the values associated to the witness variables by the answer provided by the corresponding LLH-proof.

Definition 4 *Let t be a term in the language $\mathcal{L}_H$. Its purification t^* is the term in $\mathcal{L}$ obtained by replacing first any maximal sub-term s of t whose root is an Herbrand function by a new ordinary variable x, then any occurrence of a witness variable by a new ordinary variable y.*

Example 4 *Let t be $h(f(g(W_1)),W_1)$, where h is a function in $\mathcal{F}$, f and g are functions in $\mathcal{F}_{\mathcal{H}}$ and W_1 is a witness variable. Its purification t^* is the term $h(x,y)$. (Notice that purifications are unique up to variable renaming).*

Theorem 1 *Let $\vdash \Delta$ be a sequent of closed formulae in $\mathcal{L}$. If $\vdash \Delta$ is LLH-provable then it is LL-provable. More precisely, if D is a cut-free LLH-proof of $\vdash \Delta$ whose answer is*

$$a = \{W_1 = t_1, \cdots, W_n = t_n\}$$

then there is a LL-proof D' of $\vdash \Delta$ such that :
i) D' uses the "same" rules as D and in the same order;
ii) if

$$\frac{\vdash \Gamma, A[x/W_i]}{\vdash \Gamma, \exists x A}(\exists).$$

is an application of the existential rule in D, then the corresponding rule in D' is

$$\frac{\vdash \Gamma, A[x/t_i^*]}{\vdash \Gamma, \exists x A}(\exists).$$

where t_i^* is the purification of t_i.

Sketch of the proof
We build out of D a LL-proof D' in two steps:

- *Step 1)* We transform D into a tree T of sequents in the language $\mathcal{L}_H$ by first replacing any occurrence of any witness variable W_i by the term t_i whenever the equation $W_i = t_i$ appears in the answer a given by D, then erasing the trivial equations $t_i = t_i$ from the top of identity rules. The tree T so obtained is "almost" a LL-proof. In fact, its leaves are LL axioms and all the inferences are instances of LL-rules, with the important exception of universal inferences. An universal inference in D :

$$\frac{\vdash \Gamma, A[x/f(W_1,\cdots,W_n)]}{\vdash \Gamma, \forall x A}$$

  in T becomes :

$$\frac{\vdash \Gamma, A[x/f(t_1,\cdots,t_n)]}{\vdash \Gamma, \forall x A}$$

  which is NOT an instance of a LL universal rule; say that is a *quasi* universal rule.

- *Step 2)* We "fix" T so to obtain a LL proof D'. The Herbrand-term $f(t_1,\cdots,t_n)$ appearing in the premise of a quasi universal rule cannot appear in its conclusion; hence the replacement of the occurrences of such terms by fresh variables tranforms quasi universal inferences into patterns of the form :

$$\frac{\vdash \Gamma, A[x/y]}{\vdash \Gamma, \forall x A}$$

  where the *eigenvariable* restriction is respected, that is into correct instances of LL universal rules.

Example 5 *Consider the sequent*

$$\vdash \exists y \forall x A(x,y) \multimap \forall x \exists y A(x,y)$$

This sequent may be equivalently rewritten as

$$\vdash \forall y \exists x A^{\perp}(x,y), \forall z \exists k A(z,k)$$

and has the following LLH proof D :

$$
\frac{
\frac{
\frac{
\frac{
\frac{W_1 = b, W_2 = a}{\vdash A^{\perp}(W_1,a), A(b,W_2)}
}{\vdash A^{\perp}(W_1,a), \exists k A(b,k)}
}{\vdash \exists x A^{\perp}(x,a), \exists k A(b,k)}
}{\vdash \exists x A^{\perp}(x,a), \forall z \exists k A(z,k)}
}{\vdash \forall y \exists x A^{\perp}(x,y), \forall z \exists k A(z,k)}
$$

where a and b are Herbrand constants corresponding to two applications of the universal LLH rule. By applying the first step of the proof of theorem 1 we get the following tree T :

$$
\frac{
\frac{
\frac{
\frac{
\vdash A^{\perp}(b,a), A(b,a)
}{\vdash A^{\perp}(b,a), \exists k A(b,k)}
}{\vdash \exists x A^{\perp}(x,a), \exists k A(b,k)}
}{\vdash \exists x A^{\perp}(x,a), \forall z \exists k A(z,k)}
}{\vdash \forall y \exists x A^{\perp}(x,y), \forall z \exists k A(z,k)}
$$

By applying the second step, we get the following LL-proof :

$$
\frac{
\frac{
\frac{
\frac{
\vdash A^{\perp}(\eta,\xi), A(\eta,\xi)
}{\vdash A^{\perp}(\eta,\xi), \exists k A(\eta,k)}
}{\vdash \exists x A^{\perp}(x,\xi), \exists k A(\eta,k)}
}{\vdash \exists x A^{\perp}(x,\xi), \forall z \exists k A(z,k)}
}{\vdash \forall y \exists x A^{\perp}(x,y), \forall z \exists k A(z,k)}
$$

Notice that η is the purification of b and ξ is the purification of a.

The theorem above shows that LLH is correct; the completeness result is given below.

Theorem 2 *Let $\vdash \Delta$ be a sequent of closed formulae in $\mathcal{L}$. If $\vdash \Delta$ is LL-provable then it is LLH-provable. More precisely, if D is a cut-free LL-proof of $\vdash \Delta$ then there is a LLH-proof D' of $\vdash \Delta$ such that :*
i) D' uses the "same" rules as D and in the same order;
ii) for each of the n applications of the LL-existential rule in D :

$$\frac{\vdash \Gamma, A[x/s_i]}{\vdash \Gamma, \exists x A}(\exists)$$

the corresponding existential rule in D' is

$$\frac{\vdash \Gamma, A[x/W_i]}{\vdash \Gamma, \exists x A}(\exists)$$

and if the equation $W_i = t_i$ belongs to the answer a provided by D', then s_i is an instance of the purification t_i^* of t_i.

Sketch of the proof

Once again, we build D' in two steps.

- *Step 1*) We transform D into a tree T of sequents in the language $\mathcal{L}_H$ by performing substitutions for terms appearing in the quantifiers inferences. That is, in the case of universal inferences :

$$\frac{\vdash \Gamma, A[x/y]}{\vdash \Gamma, \forall x A}$$

we replace y by the term $f(W_{j_1}, \cdots, W_{j_k})$ where f is a new Herbrand function and $W_{j_1}, \cdots, W_{j_k}$ are the witness variables appearing in $\vdash \Gamma, \forall x A$.

In the case of existential inferences :

$$\frac{\vdash \Gamma, A[x/s_i]}{\vdash \Gamma, \exists x A}(\exists).$$

we replace s_i by the new witness variable W_i and we add the equation $W_i = s_i$ on the top of the appropriate branch. The tree T obtained is "almost" a LLH-proof : it may fail to be a true LLH-proof only because an identity rule

$$\frac{W_1 = t_1, \cdots, W_n = t_n}{\vdash A, A'^{\perp}}$$

may be such that the set of equations $\{W_1 = t_1, \cdots, W_n = t_n\}$ is a unifier of A, A' but not the most general one.

- *Step 2*) We transform T into a genuine LLH-proof D' by replacing unifiers with most general unifiers.

Example 6 *Consider the following LL-proof D :*

$$\frac{\dfrac{\vdash A^{\perp}(a), A(a)}{\vdash A^{\perp}(a), \exists k A(k)}}{\vdash \exists x A^{\perp}(x), \exists k A(k)}$$

By applying the operations of the first step of the proof of theorem 2 we get the tree T :

$$\frac{\dfrac{\dfrac{W_1 = a, W_2 = a}{\vdash A^{\perp}(W_1), A(W_2)}}{\vdash A^{\perp}(W_1), \exists k A(k)}}{\vdash \exists x A^{\perp}(x), \exists k A(k)}$$

It is clear that the substitution $\{W_1 = a, W_2 = a\}$ is an unifier of $A(W_1)$ and $A(W_2)$, but not the most general one. By applying the second step of the proof to the tree T we get :

$$\frac{\dfrac{\dfrac{W_1 = W_2}{\vdash A^{\perp}(W_1), A(W_2)}}{\vdash A^{\perp}(W_1), \exists k A(k)}}{\vdash \exists x A^{\perp}(x), \exists k A(k)}$$

The answer provided by the above LLH-proof says that the value for W_1 and W_2 (the witness variables corresponding respectively to the quantifications $\exists x$ and $\exists k$ of the conclusion) is the same witness variable, say W_1. Indeed, any ordinary variable, say y, is the purification of W_1; the term a (the term by which both the existentials were instantiated in the LL-proof D) is an instance of y.

4 Related work

In [14] a logic programming language $\mathcal{L}$ containing both universal quantifiers and implication in goals is proposed, together with an interpreter sound and complete w.r.t. intuitionistic logic. The method there described to deal with universal quantifiers has been used in a version of λPROLOG [16]. The idea is to reduce the provability of a $\forall x G(x)$ goal from a program $\mathcal{P}$ to the provability of $G(c)$ for a *new* constant c and to carefully restrict the use of this new constant in substitutions.

> All free variables, in the goal and in the program, must be restricted so that the substitution terms that will eventually instantiate them will not contain that new constant. Free variables generated by subsequent backchaining steps, however, may be instantiated with terms containing this new constant ([14], p.272).

The restriction on the scope of substitutions for the current variables is reflected by the fact that the interpeter checks the "feasibility" of a candidate unifying substitution σ with respect to the "current set of constants" before allowing the use of σ in a "backchaining step". In order to correctly handle substitutions, the interpreter needs to keep track of informations as "current goal", "current program", "current set of constants" etc, which turns out to be a rather delicate matter.

There are interesting connections between the behaviour of such an interpreter w.r.t. quantified goals and our treatement of sequent calculus quantifier rules; we think that our approach provides a very simple and natural *logical* formulation of this way of handling quantified goals. Indeed, the fact that a variable x occurring in the goal and in the program cannot be instantiated to the new constant c corresponds in our formalism to the fact that the "universal" term corresponding to c, being expressed as an Herbrand function f of the variable x, cannot provide a value to this last variable, because of the "occur-check" condition. The variable x is nothing but a witness variable in the sequent containing the program clauses and the current universal goal. Also, the fact the new generated variables do not need to obey to the same restriction has a very simple explanation in our framework : the Herbrand function introduced by (backward) application of an universal rule depends only on the witness variables already present in the sequent to be proved.

The idea of expressing the *eigenvariable* of an universal rule by a term depending on the formulae in the conclusion, when doing automatic proof-search, is breefly discussed in [17]; it corresponds to the first version of *Isabelle* theorem prover and presents similarities with our "Herbrand functions" method. However, the main technique proposed in that paper for dealing with universal quantification is rather ∀ *lifting*, a method using λ-terms. This last approach underlies more recent versions of *Isabelle* as well as a different version of λPROLOG [16].

5 Further developments

Linear Logic Programming

What do we mean, in general, by "logic programming"? We believe that the distinguished features of logic programming are :

1. the view of computations as proofs in a logic system

2. the use of a *goal-directed* approach in proof-search.

The view of goal-directed proof-search as an intrinsic feature of logic programming has first been advocated in [15] and can be found also in [12] and [11]. According to this point of view, the SLD version of the resolution method - on which PROLOG is based - is just a specific instance of goal-directed proof search, which applies to the case of consequences of Horn clauses. However, the logic underlying a logic programming language is not necessarily classical logic and the proof-method is not necessarily resolution. For instance, λPROLOG evaluation corresponds to goal-directed (succedent-directed) construction of *uniform* proofs in an intuitionistic sequent calculus [16]. LinLog [1] is a logic programming language based on search of *focusing* sequent proofs in linear logic.

Sequent calculi seem particularly adapted to goal-directed proof-search, since proof-trees are naturally built out starting from the root (the sequent to be proved) and climbing up to axioms. However, to be reasonably efficient, the search of sequent proofs must deal appropriately with several factors of non-determinism. This problem is already present in classical and intuitionistic sequent calculi, but it becomes more important in the case of LL. In fact, when one tries to build up a LL-proof starting from the root, there are several situations where a *choice* has to be done :

1. We need to choose which formula in the sequent is going to be "processed" next.

2. When we want to apply a $\otimes$-rule, we need to choose how to "split" the context.

3. When we want to apply a $\oplus$-rule, we neeed to choose between two possible rules for this connective.

4. When we want to apply an existential rule, we must choose a specific term t as instantiation.

LinLog [1] deals quite well with the first case of non-determinism mentioned above. In some sense, the "propositional part" of the search for linear proofs is optimized; the *triadic* sequent calculus corresponding to LinLog evaluation internalizes an efficient and complete search-strategy : the resulting proofs enjoy the so called *focusing* property. Solutions for the second problem (as well as partial solutions for the first problem) have been proposed in [12] and [11]. We do not see any way to wipe out the third difficulty; by the way, a similar problem already arises in the case of classical logic programming (indeed, the specificity of Horn clauses is the absence of disjunction).

None of the above works deals with the fourth problem[2]. The language LinLog [1] does allow existential and universal quantification in the body of clauses and universal quantification in goals; so the associated "triadic" sequent calculus does contain explicit quantifier rules[3]. For instance, the following clauses constitute a legitimate LinLog program :

- $1 \multimap A(x, x)$

- $\exists y \forall x A(y, x) \multimap B(z)$

---

[2]However, the problem of how to handle quantifiers is not unknown to the community of automatic deduction in non classical logics (see section on related work).

[3]Notice that LinLog logical structure is indeed richer than the one of LO, the fragment discussed for instance in [6].

and $\forall z B(z)$ is a legitimate goal. However, the quantifiers rules of the triadic calculus are essentially the "blind" standard LL rules, so that, differently from the propositional case, the calculus does not internalize any proof-search method w.r.t. quantification. The burden of handling terms and quantifiers is left to the implementation level.

The sequent calculus LLH proposed in this paper plugs unification into *standard* linear sequent calculus, but the original motivation which lead to LLH, and its final aim, is the investigation of how to build unification into the sequent calculus corresponding to LinLog. Indeed, it is not too difficult to see how one could modify the quantifiers rules and the *propagation* rule of such a calculus so to make them fit with our approach.

Sequent Calculi as systems to reason with constraints

According to our definition, the premise of a LLH identity rule is a set of equations E which represents the most general *unifier* for the formulae $A(t_1, \cdots, t_n)$ and $A^\perp(t'_1, \cdots, t'_n)$ in the conclusion. Quite equivalently, we could have said that E is the most general solution for the equation system : $\mathcal{S} = \{t_1 = t'_1, \cdots, t_n = t'_n\}$ in the initial algebra of ground Herbrand terms. This second formulation suggests a more general reading of identity rules. Given *any* algebra $\mathcal{A}$ over the signature corresponding to L_H, the set of equations E can be seen as the most general solution for the equation system $\mathcal{S}$ w.r.t. $\mathcal{A}$; in other words, $\mathcal{S}$ may be seen as a set of constraints relative to $\mathcal{A}$ and E as a solution for these constraints. This approach fits into the *constraint logic programming* framework, according to which (ordinary) unification is but one special case of constraint solving [10].

This view of premises of identity rules as solutions for constraints w.r.t. a given algebra can be pushed further. We could associate constraints to sequents; for instance, searching for a proof for the sequent $\vdash A(W_1, W_2)) \mid \{W_1 + W_2 = 4\}$ w.r.t the structure $\mathcal{N}$ would mean searching for values n_1 and n_2 such that $n_1 + n_2 = 4$ and $A(n_1, n_2)$ hold in $\mathcal{N}$. Constraints are then "pushed" in sequent proofs up to the leaves and finally solved at that level.

Aknowledgements.

We would like to thank for their useful comments : J.Y. Girard, J. Harland and particularly R. Pareschi, whose helpful remarks have significantly contributed to the development of this work. Thanks also to the anonymous referees for their criticisms and suggestions.

References

[1]   J.M. Andreoli, 1991. Logic Programming with Focusing Proofs in Linear Logic, to appear in *Journal of Logic and Computation*.

[2]   J.M. Andreoli and R.Pareschi, 1990. LO and behold! concurrent structured processes, in *Proceedings of OOPSLA/ECOOP'90*, Ottawa, Canada.

[3]   J.M. Andreoli and R.Pareschi, 1990. Logic Programming with sequent systems : a linear logic approach, in em Proc. of the Workshop on Extensions

of Logic Programming, Lecture Notes in Artificial Intelligence, Tübingen, Germany, Springer Verlag.

[4]   J.M. Andreoli and R.Pareschi, 1991. Communication as fair distribution of knowledge, in *Proceeedings of OOPSLA'91*, Phoenix, USA.

[5]   J.M. Andreoli and R.Pareschi, 1991. Dynamic programming as multi-agent programming, *ECOOP'91 workshop on Object-based concurrent computing.*

[6]   J.M. Andreoli and R.Pareschi, 1991. Linear Objects : Logical Processes with built-in inheritance. *New Generation Computing.* (Special issue, Selected papers from ICLP'90).

[7]   S.Cerrito, 1992. Herbrand Methods in Linear Logic, *Rapport de Recherche L.R.I. n.728, january 92, Université Paris XI.*

[8]   J-Y. Girard, 1987. Linear logic, *Theoretical Computer Science*, 50, pp. 1-108.

[9]   J-Y. Girard , Y. Lafont and P. Taylor, 1989. Proofs and types, *Cambridge tracts in theoretical computer science*, Cambridge University Press, Cambridge.

[10]   J.Jaffar and J.-L.Lassez, 1987. Constraint Logic Programming, *Proceedings of the Conference on Principles of Programming Languages*, Munich.

[11]   J.Harland, D.Pym, 1991. The Uniform Proof-theoretic Foundation of Linear Logic Programming, in *Proceedings of the 1991 International Symposium on Logic Programming*, Vijay Saraswat & Kazunori Uedo eds.,

[12]   J.S.Hodas, D.Miller 1991. Logic Programming in a fragment of intuitionistic linear logic. *Proceedings of the sixth annual IEEE symposium on logic in computer science (LICS)*, IEEE Computer Society Press.

[13]   S.C.Kleene 1967. *Mathematical Logic*, J.Wiley and Sons.

[14]   D.Miller, Lexical Scoping as Universal Quantification, *Proceedings of the International Conference on Logic Programming*, pp. 268-283, Lisbon, June, 1989.

[15]   D. Miller, G. Nadathur, F. Pfenning and A. Scedrov, 1991. Uniform Proofs as a Foundation for Logic Programming, *Annals of Pure and Applied Logic 51*, pp. 125-157.

[16]   G.Nadathur D.Miller, 1988. An overview of λPROLOG, ·*Proceedings of the Fifth International Conference on Logic Programming*, R.Kowalski and K.Bowen eds., MIT press, pp.810-827.

[17]   L. Paulson, 1989. The Foundation of a Generic Theorem Prover, *Journal of Automated Reasoning*, 5, pp.363-397.

[18]   N.Shankar 1992. Proof Search in the Intuitionist Sequent Calculus, to appear in *Proceedings of the Eleventh International Conference on Automated Deduction*, D. Kapur ed, MIT Press, Springer-Verlag.

APPENDIX

LL calculus

- *Identity Group*

$$\frac{}{\vdash A, A^\perp}(identity\ axioms) \qquad \frac{\vdash \Gamma, A \quad \vdash \Delta, A^\perp}{\vdash \Gamma, \Delta}(cut)$$

- *Exchange rule*

$$\frac{\vdash \Gamma}{\vdash \Gamma'}(exch)$$

where Γ' is a permutation of Γ.

- *Logical Rules*

  - *Neutral Elements*

  $$\frac{\vdash \Gamma}{\vdash \Gamma, \perp}(\perp) \quad \frac{}{\vdash 1}(axiom\ for\ 1) \quad \frac{}{\vdash \Gamma, T}(axiom\ for\ T)$$

  - *Additive rules*

  $$\frac{\vdash \Gamma, A \quad \vdash \Gamma, B}{\vdash \Gamma, A \& B}(\&) \quad \frac{\vdash \Gamma, A}{\vdash \Gamma, A \oplus B}(\oplus 1) \quad \frac{\vdash \Gamma, B}{\vdash \Gamma, A \oplus B}(\oplus 2)$$

  - *Multiplicative rules*

  $$\frac{\vdash \Gamma, A \quad \vdash \Delta, B}{\vdash \Gamma, \Delta, A \otimes B}(\otimes) \quad \frac{\vdash \Gamma, A, B}{\vdash \Gamma, A \uparrow B}(\uparrow)$$

  - *Quantifiers rules*

  $$\frac{\vdash \Gamma, A[x/y]}{\vdash \Gamma, \forall x A}(\forall) \qquad\qquad \frac{\vdash \Gamma, A[x/t]}{\vdash \Gamma, \exists x A}(\exists)$$

  if y is not free in the lower sequent.

- *Exponential Rules*

$$\frac{\vdash \Gamma}{\vdash \Gamma, ?A}(?weakening) \quad \frac{\vdash \Gamma, ?A, ?A}{\vdash \Gamma, ?A}(?contraction) \quad \frac{\vdash \Gamma, A}{\vdash \Gamma, ?A}(?) \quad \frac{\vdash ?\Gamma, A}{\vdash ?\Gamma, !A}(!)$$

Specifying Filler-Gap Dependency Parsers in a Linear-Logic Programming Language

Joshua S. Hodas
Department of Computer and Information Science
University of Pennsylvania
Philadelphia, PA 19104-6839 USA
hodas@saul.cis.upenn.edu

Abstract

An aspect of the Generalized Phrase Structure Grammar formalism proposed by Gazdar, et al. is the introduction of the notion of "slashed categories" to handle the parsing of structures, such as relative clauses, which involve unbounded dependencies. This has been implemented in Definite Clause Grammars through the technique of *gap threading*, in which a difference list of extracted noun phrases (gaps) is maintained. However, this technique is cumbersome, and can result in subtle soundness problems in the implemented grammars. Miller and Pareschi have proposed a method of implementing gap threading at the logical level in intuitionistic logic. Unfortunately that implementation itself suffered from serious problems, which the authors recognized. This paper builds on work first presented with Miller in which we developed a filler-gap dependency parser in Girard's linear logic. This implementation suffers from none of the pitfalls of either the traditional implementation, or the intuitionistic one. It serves as further demonstration of the usefulness of sub-structural logic in natural language applications.

1   Introduction

It is now standard in linguistics and natural language processing to view a relative clause as being formed by a relative pronoun followed by a sentence that is missing a noun phrase. For example, the sentence:

> John wrote the book [that Jane read].

can be thought of as having the following parse tree, where *gap* marks the spot where the missing noun phrase would be, if the clause were a sentence:

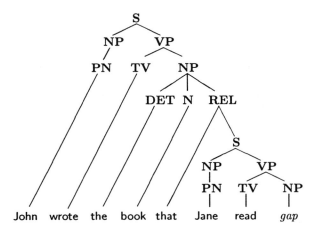

A common way to implement this idea in logic programming is the technique of *gap threading* in which a difference list of gaps is passed around as a parameter in a Definite Clause Grammar (DCG). The state of this list changes as gaps are introduced (by encountering relative pronouns, for example) and discharged (by completing a parse that uses the gap). In turn the state of the list controls whether the parse is allowed to use a gap in place of an **NP** at a given point in the parse.

Unfortunately, this technique has several drawbacks. It requires tedious modification of the entire grammar, even the parts that are not involved in parsing structures that need the gap list. Further, the difference list representation induces subtle bugs in the grammar that admit certain ungrammatical sentences which the underlying grammar being implemented rejects.

Pareschi and Miller proposed a method of handling unbounded filler-gap dependencies at the logic level, rather than in the term language. Their technique made use of the enhanced goal language of λProlog, which is based on hereditary Harrop formulas. The basic idea was to temporarily augment the grammar with a new rule for gap noun phrases only during the parse of a relative clause. Unfortunately, because the management of proof context in intuitionistic logic is too coarse, the grammars that result are unsound (though in a different way than the difference-list grammars), accepting many non-grammatical sentences.

In this paper I will begin by describing the Generalized Phrase Structure Grammar formalism which first proposed the basic ideas underlying all of these systems. I will then present the traditional gap threading technique as well as the system proposed by Pareschi and Miller and explain their shortcomings. Finally, I will present a solution to the problem inspired by Pareschi and Miller's work but implemented in Girard's linear logic. This solution, first briefly presented in joint papers with Miller [5, 7], addresses all of the failings of the previous solutions, while maintaining the naturality of Miller and Pareschi's system.

2 Generalized Phrase Structure Grammar

The Generalized Phrase Structure Grammar (GPSG) formalism developed by Gerald Gazdar [1, 2, 3] demonstrated that it is possible to parse grammatical structures involving unbounded dependencies, such as relative clauses and **wh** questions, using a phrase structure grammar. Previously it had been thought that such constructs were too complex for phrase structure grammars, which are context-free, but rather required the strength of transformational grammar.

The basic ideas in GPSG are quite simple. It posits, for instance, that the body of a relative clause is a sentence that is missing a noun phrase somewhere. So, if sentences belong to the category **S**, and noun phrases to the category **NP**, then the rule for (one particular form of) relative clause would be:

$$\textbf{REL} \longrightarrow \text{that } \textbf{S/NP}^1$$

where **S/NP** is the derived category of sentences missing a noun phrase. This requires, in turn, that rules be given for generating/parsing the derived category. These new rules are generated from the original grammar in a relatively straightforward manner. So, if the original grammar were:

$$\textbf{S} \longrightarrow \textbf{NP VP}$$
$$\textbf{NP} \longrightarrow \textbf{PN}$$
$$\textbf{NP} \longrightarrow \textbf{DET N}$$
$$\textbf{VP} \longrightarrow \textbf{TV NP}$$

then the new grammar, which allows relative clauses in noun phrases, would consist of that grammar augmented with:

$$\textbf{NP} \longrightarrow \textbf{DET N REL}$$
$$\textbf{REL} \longrightarrow \text{that } \textbf{S/NP}$$

$$\textbf{S/NP} \longrightarrow \textbf{NP VP/NP}$$
$$\textbf{VP/NP} \longrightarrow \textbf{TV NP/NP}$$
$$\textbf{NP/NP} \longrightarrow \epsilon$$

In general, for each rule in the original grammar which defines a category that could dominate an **NP** (i.e., could occur above an **NP** in a parse tree) there will be a new version of that rule for each category on the right of the

---

[1]Actually, in the years since GPSG was first proposed it has changed significantly [12]. So, while the name has remained, the formalism no longer uses this sort of phrase structure rule, but instead uses node admissibility rules. In this paper I will use the original phrase structure rule style, as it is easier to understand the connection to DCG's in that form.

rule that could dominate an **NP**. Note, however, that we have not included the derived rule:

$$\text{S/NP} \longrightarrow \text{NP/NP VP}$$

in order to block extraction from the subject noun phrase. This is an over-simplification of a standard restriction, which is intended to guard against the acceptance of such sentences as:

> * John wrote the book [that the story in *gap* is long].

3   Gap Threading in Prolog

There are many ways to approach implementing GPSG style grammars in Prolog. Obviously, the grammar could be implemented directly as a DCG with rules defining the base categories as well as each of the derived categories. This is not an attractive option, however, since, depending on the number of derived categories, the resulting grammar can be substantially (potentially quadratically) larger than the core grammar on which it is based. Gazdar points out, however, that since the rules for the derived categories are formed so uniformly from the original grammar, it is possible to use the original grammar on its own, together with some switches controlling whether the parser selects rules as is or in derived form [1, page 161].

So, for instance, the grammar above can be implemented with the following DCG:

```
s          --> s(nogap).
s(Gap)     --> np(nogap) vp(Gap).
np(gap)    --> [].
np(nogap)  --> pn.
np(nogap)  --> det n.
np(nogap)  --> det n rel.
vp(Gap)    --> tv np(Gap).
rel        --> [that] s(gap).
```

Each rule where the head is parameterized by `nogap` corresponds to a rule in the core grammar only. In contrast, those parameterized by `Gap` act as core rules when the parameter is instantiated to `nogap`, but as derived rules when it is instantiated to `gap`. It is easy to see that this DCG implements the grammar faithfully.

This system of switches is, however, too limited for grammars intended to handle multiple extractions from nested structures. Therefore gap-threading parsers (as this sort of system is called) are typically implemented with a difference list of gaps in place of the simple toggle. In such an implementation, the DCG above becomes:

```
s(S)            --> s([]-[]).
s(F0-F)         --> np([]-[]), vp(F0-F).
np([gap|F]-F)   --> [].
np(F-F)         --> pn.
np(F-F)         --> det, np([]-[]).
np(F-F)         --> det, np([]-[]), rel.
vp(F0-F)        --> tv, np(F0-F).
rel             --> [that], s([gap|F]-F).
```

Although the difference list in this grammar will never grow beyond a single element, in more complex grammars the list structure is necessary. This technique of implementing GPSG parsers has been developed extensively by Pereira and Shieber [11] and others.

There are many problems with gap-threading parsers of this sort. First, they are difficult to construct. Insuring that the gap list is properly maintained can be quite subtle. Portions of the grammar that seem unconnected with the problem at hand require significant adjustment to insure that they do not interfere with the transmission of the gap information from the gap's introduction to its discharge, since with unbounded dependencies the two may be separated by almost any structure.

More importantly, due to the lack of "occurs check" in the unification algorithm used in languages like Prolog, serious soundness problems can occur with the difference list representation [8]. For instance, it is possible for the difference list to "go negative" in advance of the relative pronoun, only to balance out due to the presence of an extra noun phrase in the relative clause. Similar problems arise in complex grammars that allow multiple extractions from nested structures.

Thus, it is difficult to design a gap threading grammar intended to accept sentences like:

> Which violins are these sonatas difficult to play *gap* on *gap*.

or:

> I told Mary [that John wondered [who Jane saw *gap*]].

without it also accepting:

> * I told *gap* [that John wondered [who Jane saw Sally]].

4 Gap Threading in Intuitionistic Logic

In 1990 Pareschi and Miller proposed using the expanded goal structure of λProlog to enhance the power of DCG's [10]. That paper focused both on parsing and the construction of semantics. Here we are concerned only with the former, so I will summarize only that aspect of the work. λProlog is based on the hereditary Harrop formula fragment of intuitionistic logic.

Its enriched formula language provides a number of control structures not available in Prolog, and hence DCG's.

In particular, intuitionistic logic has the following rule for implication introduction:

$$\frac{\Gamma, D \longrightarrow G}{\Gamma \longrightarrow D \Rightarrow G} \Rightarrow R$$

If we take the view, as λProlog does, that logic programming is the bottom up search for cut-free proofs in intuitionistic logic, then this rule can be seen as giving a notion of scoping of clauses not available in the logic of Horn clauses. The clauses in D are available only during the proof of G [9].

Pareschi and Miller used this rule to provide a clean implementation of filler-gap dependency parsers. The basic idea is relatively simple: rather than use a complex system of parameters to control when the np --> [] clause can be used – which is what all the mechanics of gap threading is really about – use the control provided by the above rule to scope the gapped-**NP** clause only over the derivation of the **S** that forms the body of the relative clause.

Using their implementation, the sample grammar would become:

```
s  L1 L2 :- np  L1 LA, vp LA L2.
np L1 L2 :- pn  L1 L2.
np L1 L2 :- det L1 LA, n  LA L2.
np L1 L2 :- det L1 LA, n  LA LB, rel LB L2.
vp L1 L2 :- tv  L1 LA, np LA L2.
rel (that::L1) L2 :- (np Z Z) => s L1 L2.
```

Here the syntax of λProlog, which uses a curried notation (i.e. no parentheses) and does not include DCG's, is used directly. As such, the difference list of words being parsed, which is implicit in DCG's, is explicit here. The key feature of this implementation is that the bulk of the grammar is unchanged from the core grammar. The only mention of a gapped noun phrase is in the final rule. When this rule is invoked the unit clause np Z Z is added to the grammar and an attempt is made to parse for an **S**. Since the input and output lists of the assumed rule are the same, the rule represents a noun phrase with no phonological content: a gap. This rule may be used to complete any rule looking for an **NP** during the parse of the subordinate **S**.

The quantifier rules of λProlog are used to insure that an introduced gap is used only once. In particular, while λProlog uses the standard Prolog quantifier assumption that variables (identifiers beginning with a capital letter) are universally quantified at the outside of the clause in which they occur, it makes no such assumption about variables in clauses loaded using implication. Therefore the Z in the last clause above is quantified at the same level as the other variables in that clause. When the clause is used, the unit clause that is temporarily loaded into the grammar contains Z as an uninstantiated logic variable. Once the rule is used to fill in for a missing noun phrase, Z is instantiated to that location in the parse. It cannot be instantiated for some other location, unless the parse fails back to some point before this. If we wanted to be able to use the gap to fill in for more than one noun phrase, then the last rule in the grammar would be written with Z explicitly universally quantified (for historical reasons, λProlog uses the operators pi and sigma for universal and existential quantification respectively):

```
rel (that::L1) L2 :- (pi Z\ (np Z Z)) => s L1 L2.
```

In order to handle restrictions on where a gap is allowable (such as the restriction on extraction from a subject noun phrase already discussed), Miller and Pareschi propose modifying the scheme to load gap locator rules rather than the gaps themselves. While this works, it is roughly equivalent to simply defining the grammar to include rules for derived categories up front; and as described earlier, that is quite cumbersome.

A serious problem with Pareschi and Miller's work, which the authors recognized, is that there is no logical method to require that an introduced gap be used. That is, if the goal s L1 L2 can succeed, then so can (np Z Z) => s L1 L2. This leads to the erroneous acceptance of:

* John wrote the book [that Jane read a magazine].

since

Jane read a magazine.

is a valid sentence, regardless of the presence of the assumed gap.

Technically, the problem is that in intuitionistic logic the freely available rule of weakening:

$$\frac{\Gamma \longrightarrow B}{\Gamma, A \longrightarrow B} \; W$$

allows unused assumptions to be simply discarded. This problem is familiar to knowledge representation and artificial intelligence researchers, and has led to the interest in relevance logic. In that system weakening is not allowed, so any assumptions must be *relevant* to the goal in order for a proof to exist.

5 Gap Threading in Linear Logic

In recognizing the limitations of their system, Pareschi and Miller suggested that a solution might be found in Girard's linear logic [4], which places strict limitations on the use of weakening and contraction. That proposal is the idea which underlies this work.

While the rules of intuitionistic linear logic are similar to those of ordinary intuitionistic logic, there is a significant difference: only formulas specifically designated (by being marked with the operator !) can be weakened or contracted. Further, because of the restrictions on the structural rules there are two forms of conjunction, disjunction, and truth, which differ based on the way they treat the proof context. To understand the need for two conjunctions, for instance, consider two ways of axiomatizing conjunction introduction in intuitionistic logic:

$$\frac{\Gamma \longrightarrow A \quad \Gamma \longrightarrow B}{\Gamma \longrightarrow A \wedge B} \wedge R \qquad \frac{\Gamma \longrightarrow A \quad \Delta \longrightarrow B}{\Gamma, \Delta \longrightarrow A \wedge B} \wedge R$$

In the presence of the contraction rule, these two formulations are equivalent, since the former rule can be replaced with the proof:

$$\frac{\dfrac{\Gamma \longrightarrow A \quad \Gamma \longrightarrow B}{\Gamma, \Gamma \longrightarrow A \wedge B} \wedge R}{\Gamma \longrightarrow A \wedge B} C^*$$

In this work we are concerned with only a fragment of intuitionistic linear logic, given by the rules in figure 1. The proof theory of this fragment, and a logic programming language based on it, have been discussed extensively in two joint papers with Dale Miller [5, 7] and is the main topic of this author's dissertation [6]. A crucial point is that there is a straightforward bottom-up, goal-directed proof procedure (conceptually similar to the one used for Prolog) that is sound and complete for this fragment of linear logic[2].

The solution, then, is simple. The rules of the grammar are represented by !'ed formulas in the proof context (the left hand side of the sequent arrow) since they are intended to be available for use as many times as needed, or not at all. In contrast, the temporary rules for gapped noun phrases are loaded without the !. Since a gap is stored as a linear resource, it must be used, and cannot simply be discarded.

The syntax of Lolli[3], the language described in [5, 7], is intended to be familiar to logic programmers. And, while the elements of the concrete syntax represent different operators than they do in Prolog, they are designed to have the same operational behavior. That is, if a pure-Prolog program is entered into Lolli, its behavior will be the same as it was in Prolog. The linear nature of the language is not evident if the program does not make use of it. This operational equivalence is explained and proved in [7]. To accomplish it, the following assumptions are made:

- ':-' represents reverse $\multimap$, ',' represents $\otimes$, '&' (which does not occur in Prolog) represents &, and '{}' around a formula represent !. Finally, as in λProlog, 'pi' and 'sigma' are used for universal and existential quantification, respectively.

- The quantifier assumptions are the same as in Prolog (or more accurately λProlog). To wit, variables not explicitly quantified within a

---

[2]This statement should be qualified. First, there are restrictions on the ways the logical operators can be combined. Second, it is the non-deterministic or breadth-first algorithm which is complete. The deterministic depth-first implementation actually used suffers from the same failings as standard Prolog interpreters.

[3]The language takes its name from the linear logic implication operator $\multimap$ which, for obvious reasons, is generally referred to as "lollipop".

$$\frac{}{B \longrightarrow B} \text{ identity} \qquad \frac{}{\Delta \longrightarrow \top} \top R$$

$$\frac{\Delta, B_i \longrightarrow C}{\Delta, B_1 \,\&\, B_2 \longrightarrow C} \,\&L \ (i = 1, 2) \qquad \frac{\Delta \longrightarrow B \qquad \Delta \longrightarrow C}{\Delta \longrightarrow B \,\&\, C} \,\&R$$

$$\frac{\Delta_1 \longrightarrow B \qquad \Delta_2, C \longrightarrow E}{\Delta_1, \Delta_2, B \multimap C \longrightarrow E} \multimap L \qquad \frac{\Delta, B \longrightarrow C}{\Delta \longrightarrow B \multimap C} \multimap R$$

$$\frac{\Delta, B_1, B_2 \longrightarrow C}{\Delta, B_1 \otimes B_2 \longrightarrow C} \otimes L \qquad \frac{\Delta_1 \longrightarrow B \qquad \Delta_2 \longrightarrow C}{\Delta_1, \Delta_2 \longrightarrow B \otimes C} \otimes R$$

$$\frac{\Delta \longrightarrow C}{\Delta, !B \longrightarrow C} \,!W \quad \frac{\Delta, !B, !B \longrightarrow C}{\Delta, !B \longrightarrow C} \,!C \quad \frac{\Delta, B \longrightarrow C}{\Delta, !B \longrightarrow C} \,!D \quad \frac{!\Delta \longrightarrow B}{!\Delta \longrightarrow !B} \,!R$$

$$\frac{\Delta, B[t/x] \longrightarrow C}{\Delta, \forall x.B \longrightarrow C} \,\forall L \qquad \frac{\Delta \longrightarrow B[y/x]}{\Delta \longrightarrow \forall x.B} \,\forall R,$$

provided that y is not free in the lower sequent.

Figure 1: A proof system for a fragment of linear logic

clause are assumed to be universally quantified at the clause's boundaries.

- Clauses are assumed to be !'ed at the clause's boundary. For proof theoretic reasons, the implicit !'s are placed outside the implicit quantifiers.

Given these assumptions, the Lolli version of this grammar is changed little from its λProlog counterpart. Only the implication in the last clause need be changed:

```
s  L1 L2 :- np  L1 LA, vp LA L2.
np L1 L2 :- pn  L1 L2.
np L1 L2 :- det L1 LA, n  LA L2.
np L1 L2 :- det L1 LA, n  LA LB, rel LB L2.
vp L1 L2 :- tv  L1 LA, np LA L2.
rel (that::L1) L2 :- (np Z Z) -o s L1 L2.
```

It is important to note that due to the linear constraint, it makes no difference if the last rule is given as:

```
rel (that::L1) L2 :- (pi Z\ (np Z Z)) -o s L1 L2.
```

The loaded rule, representing a gapped noun phrase, can still be used only once. Each time a $\otimes$ conjunction goal is encountered during the parse of the subordinate **S**, the gap is carried up into the proof of only one side of the conjunction.

In addition to yielding a solution to the problems that Pareschi and Miller encountered, the linear logic setting affords simple treatments of other parsing issues. One particularly attractive feature of this system is its ability to specify the management of gaps across coordinate structures, such as conjuncts. GPSG proposes that any category can be expanded by the conjunction of two or more structures of the same category. So, for instance:

S $\longrightarrow$ S and S.

If the language level conjunction is represented in the grammar by the second form of logical conjunction, &, then coordination constraints are handled automatically. That is, if the clause:

```
s  L1 L2 :- s L1 (and::LA) & s LA L2.
```

is added to the grammar, then the system will accept the sentences

John wrote the book and Jane read the magazine.

and

John wrote the book [that Jane read *gap* and Jill discarded *gap*].

but will reject:

* John wrote the book [that Jane read *gap* and Jill discarded the magazine].

Because & duplicates linear resources into both branches of the proof, both of the subordinate clauses must consume the same gaps. This scheme does not seem to provide any particular insight into the parsing of so-called "parasitic gaps", though it is not clear that they are beyond the capabilities of the system.

In a similar manner, it is possible to use the ! operator to specify restrictions on extraction in the grammar. For example, in order to block extraction from subject noun phrases, the first rule of the grammar is rewritten as:

```
s  L1 L2 :- {np  L1 LA}, vp LA L2.
```

Recall from Figure 1 that the proof rule for ! in a goal is:

$$\frac{!\Gamma \longrightarrow A}{!\Gamma \longrightarrow !A} \; !R$$

where $!\Gamma = \{!D | D \in \Gamma\}$. In essence this states that a !'ed goal can only be proved in the presence of exclusively !'ed assumptions. Thus, if $!\Gamma$ is the grammar above, with the first rule modified as stated, then attempting to parse the relative clause:

[who Jane saw *gap*]

leads to a proof of the form:

$$
\cfrac{
  \cfrac{
    !\Gamma \longrightarrow np((jane::saw::nil),(saw::nil))
  }{
    !\Gamma \longrightarrow !np((jane::saw::nil),(saw::nil))
  }
  \qquad
  \cfrac{
    \cfrac{
      !\Gamma \longrightarrow tv((saw::nil),nil) \qquad !\Gamma, np(Z,Z) \longrightarrow np(nil,nil)
    }{
      !\Gamma, np(Z,Z) \longrightarrow tv((saw::nil),nil) \otimes np(nil,nil)
    }
  }{
    !\Gamma, np(Z,Z) \longrightarrow vp((saw::nil),nil)
  }
}{
  \cfrac{
    \cfrac{
      !\Gamma, np(Z,Z) \longrightarrow !np((jane::saw::nil),(saw::nil)) \otimes vp((saw::nil),nil)
    }{
      !\Gamma, np(Z,Z) \longrightarrow s((jane::saw::nil),nil)
    }
  }{
    !\Gamma \longrightarrow rel((who::jane::saw::nil),nil)
  }
}
$$

The proof is somewhat abridged, in that applications of the various left hand
! rules (dereliction, weakening, and contraction), as well as implication on
the left, have been hidden. In contrast, attempting to parse the clause:

> * [that the story in *gap* is long]

will fail, because the gap *np* formula will be unavailable for use in the branch
of the proof attempting to parse the **NP** "*the story in", since the !'ed *np*
goal forces the gap *np* in the context to the other side of the tree.

Unfortunately, this technique is at once a bit too coarse-grained and too
fine-grained. For instance, it blocks the acceptance of

> [who saw Jane]

which should be allowed – the restriction on extraction from the subject noun
should not block gapping of the entire subject, only its substructures. This
problem can be circumvented by having multiple rules for relative clauses:
one, as we have already shown, which introduces a gap and attempts to
parse for an **S**, and one which simply attempts to parse for a **VP**.

A subtler problem is that the use of ! blocks all extractions from the
subject, not just the extraction of noun phrases. This will become an issue
when other types of gaps are introduced. Thus, while this technique can
be used to implement this and other similar "island constraints", there are
some complications.

While the examples in the paper thus far have dealt only with relative
clauses, GPSG proposes solutions to many other sorts of unbounded dependencies. For instance, given a category **Q** of non-**wh** questions, the category
can be expanded to cover some **wh** questions with GPSG rules of the form:

> **Q** $\longrightarrow$ **wh-PP Q/PP**

So that from questions like:

> Did Jane read the book under the table?

one gets:

> Where did Jane read the book?

It should be apparent that such extensions are easy to add in this setting.
Figure 2 shows a larger grammar than those presented up till now that parses
several forms of sentences and questions. (Only the grammar itself is shown,
the pre-terminals and lexicon are removed for the sake of brevity.) Figure 3
shows a sample interaction with the parser, with several examples like those
from the paper properly parsed or rejected.

```
parse Str Tree :- explode_words Str Lst, (s Lst nil Tree ; q Lst nil Tree).

s P1 P2 (s NP VP)  :- {np P1 PA NP}, vp PA P2 VP.
s P1 P2 (and (s NP1 VP1) (s NP2 VP2)) :-
    ({np P1 PA1 NP1},vp PA1 (and::P0) VP1) & ({np P0 PA2 NP2},vp PA2 P2 VP2).

q P1 P2 (q VFA NP VP) :- vfa P1 PA VFA, np PA PB NP, vp PB P2 VP.
q P1 P2 (q NW Q) :- NW P1 PA NW, {(pi P\ np P P (np gap)) -o q PA P2 Q}.
q P1 P2 (q PPW Q) :- ppwh P1 PA PPW,{(pi P\ pp P P (pp gap)) -o q PA P2 Q}.
q P1 P2 (q NW VP) :- NW P1 PA NW, vp PA P2 VP.

npwh P1 P2 (NW NWH) :- nwh P1 P2 NWH.
npwh (which::P1) P2 (npwh which N) :- n PA P2 N.
ppwh P1 P2 (ppwh PWH) :- pwh P1 P2 PWH.

sb (that::P1) P2 (sbar that S) :- s P1 P2 S.
qb P1 P2 (qbar NW VP) :- npwh P1 PA NW, vp PA P2 VP.
qb P1 P2 (qbar NW S) :- npwh P1 PA NW,{(pi P\np P P (np gap)) -o s PA P2 S}.

np P1 P2 (np PNposs) :- pnposs P1 P2 PNposs.
np P1 P2 (np Det Nposs OptPP OptRel) :-
    det P1 PA Det, nposs PA PB Nposs, optpp PB PC OptPP, optrel PC P2 OptRel.

pnposs P1 P2 (pnposs PN) :- pn P1 P2 PN.
pnposs P1 P2 (pnposs PN s Nposs) :- pn P1 (s::PA) PN, nposs PA P2 Nposs.

nposs P1 P2 (nposs OptAP N) :- n PA P2 N.
nposs P1 P2 (nposs OptAP N s Nposs) :- n PA (s::PB) N, nposs PB P2 Nposs.

vp P1 P2 (vp DV NP PP) :- dv P1 PA DV, np PA PB NP, pp PB P2 PP.
vp P1 P2 (vp TV NP) :- tv P1 PA TV, np PA P2 NP.
vp P1 P2 (vp IV OptPP) :- iv P1 PA IV, optpp PA P2 OptPP.
vp P1 P2 (vp Stv Sb) :- stv P1 PA Stv, sb PA P2 Sb.
vp P1 P2 (vp TV NP Sb) :- tv P1 PA TV, np PA PB NP, sb PB P2 Sb.
vp P1 P2 (vp Qv Qb) :- qv P1 PA Qv, qb PA P2 Qb.
vp P1 P2 (vp Vfa VP) :- vfa P1 PA Vfa, vp PA P2 VP.

optpp P1 P1 (optpp epsilon).    optpp P1 P2 (optpp PP) :- pp P1 P2 PP.
pp P1 P2 (pp P NP) :- p P1 PA P, np PA P2 NP.

optrel P1 P1 (optrel epsilon).  optrel P1 P2 (optrel Rel) :- rel P1 P2 Rel.
rel (that::P1) P2 (rel that VP) :- {vp P1 P2 VP}.
rel (who::P1)  P2 (rel who VP)  :- {vp P1 P2 VP}.
rel (that::P1) P2 (rel that S) :- {(pi P\ np P P (np gap)) -o s P1 P2 S}.
rel (whom::P1) P2 (rel whom S) :- {(pi P\ np P P (np gap)) -o s P1 P2 S}.
rel P1 P2 (rel P whom S) :-
p P1 (whom::PA) P, {(pi P\ pp P P (pp gap)) -o s PA P2 S}.
rel P1 P2 (rel P which S) :-
p P1 (which::PA) P, {(pi P\ pp P P (pp gap)) -o s PA P2 S}.
```

Figure 2: An expanded filler-gap dependency parser

```
%lolli
Starting Lolli version 0.6, July 10, 1992
  (built with Standard ML of New Jersey,
   Version 75, November 11, 1991)...

?- nl2 --o top.

?- parse 'the program that john wrote halted' T.

?T <- s (np (det the) (nposs (n program)) (optpp epsilon)
          (optrel (rel that (s (np (pnposs (pn john)))
                               (vp (tv wrote) (np gap))))))
          (vp (iv halted) (optpp epsilon)).


?- parse 'i told mary that john wondered who jane saw' T.

?T <- s (np (pnposs (pn i)))
        (vp (tv told) (np (pnposs (pn mary)))
            (sbar that (s (np (pnposs (pn john)))
                         (vp (qv wondered)
                             (qbar (npwh (nwh who))
                                   (s (np (pnposs (pn jane)))
                                      (vp (tv saw) (np gap)))))))) .


?- parse 'i told that john wondered who jane saw sally' T.

no


?- parse 'which computer did john write the program on' T.

?T <- q (npwh which (optap epsilon) (n computer))
        (q (vfa did) (np (pnposs (pn john)))
           (vp (dv write) (np (det the) (nposs (n program))
                              (optpp epsilon) (optrel epsilon))
           (pp (p on) (np gap)))) .


?- bye.
Closing proLLog.
```

Figure 3: A sample interaction with the expanded gap-threading parser

6 Conclusion

In this paper I have shown that the use of a linear logic programming language yields an extremely attractive and understandable implementation of many of the features of Generalized Phrase Structure Grammar. These include proper management of gaps in unbounded dependencies, as well as the handling of a simple form of island constraint and some forms of coordinate structures.

In addition, the implementations that result from using these techniques are particularly perspicuous, in that, in contrast to traditional techniques such as gap threading, they require very few changes to the core grammar. Finally, the system is immune to the soundness problems that occur in many difference-list-based gap threading systems.

7 Availability of the Lolli System

An implementation of Lolli, written in Standard ML of New Jersey, can be retrieved by anonymous ftp from `ftp.cis.upenn.edu`, in the directory `pub/lolli`. The system comes with several example programs including the full version of the parser given in Figure 2. The directory also includes DVI versions of most of the papers pertaining to Lolli. If you do retrieve the Lolli system, please send mail to `hodas@saul.cis.upenn.edu` so that you can be informed of updates to the system.

8 Acknowledgements

The author is grateful to Mark Steedman, Dale Miller, Fernando Pereira, Pat Lincoln, and Elizabeth Hodas for their helpful conversations about this work, and to Remo Pareschi for conversations about the work that led up to it. He is also thankful to Mark Johnson for his ideas relative to the problems with traditional gap threading systems. Finally he is most grateful to the paper's referees, who helped correct certain mis-statements about GPSG, and provided improved example sentences.

The author has been funded by ONR N00014-88-K-0633, NSF CCR-91-02753, and DARPA N00014-85-K-0018 through the University of Pennsylvania.

References

[1] Gerald J. M. Gazdar. Unbounded dependencies and coordinate structure. *Linguistic Inquiry*, 12(2):154–184, 1981.

[2] Gerald J. M. Gazdar. *Phrase Structure Grammar*, pages 131–186. Reidel, Dordrecht, 1982.

[3] Gerald J. M. Gazdar, Ewan Klein, Geoffrey K. Pullum, and Ivan Sag. *Generalized Phrase Structure Grammar*. Harvard University Press, Cambridge, Mass., 1985.

[4] Jean-Yves Girard. Linear logic. *Theoretical Computer Science*, 50:1–102, 1987.

[5] Joshua Hodas and Dale Miller. Logic programming in a fragment of intuitionistic linear logic: Extended abstract. In G. Kahn, editor, *Sixth Annual Symposium on Logic in Computer Science*, pages 32 – 42, Amsterdam, July 1991.

[6] Joshua S. Hodas. *Logic Programming in Intuitionistic Linear Logic: Theory, Design, and Implementation*. PhD thesis, University of Pennsylvania, Department of Computer and Information Science, expected 1993.

[7] Joshua S. Hodas and Dale Miller. Logic programming in a fragment of intuitionistic linear logic. *Journal of Information and Computation*, 1992. To appear.

[8] Mark Johnson, 1992. Private electronic mail correspondence.

[9] Gopalan Nadathur and Dale Miller. An Overview of λProlog. In *Fifth International Logic Programming Conference*, pages 810–827, Seattle, Washington, August 1988. MIT Press.

[10] Remo Pareschi and Dale Miller. Extending definite clause grammars with scoping constructs. In David H. D. Warren and Peter Szeredi, editors, *1990 International Conference in Logic Programming*, pages 373–389. MIT Press, June 1990.

[11] Fernando C. N. Pereira and Stuart M. Shieber. *Prolog and Natural-Language Analysis*, volume 10. CLSI, Stanford, CA, 1987.

[12] Peter Sells. *Lectures on Contemporary Syntactic Theories*. Number 3 in CSLI Lecture Notes. Center for the Study of Language and Information, Stanford, Ca., 1985.

Implementation II

Multistage Indexing Algorithms for Speeding Prolog Execution

Ta Chen and I.V. Ramakrishnan
Department of Computer Science
State University of New York at Stony Brook
Stony Brook, NY 11794

R. Ramesh
Department of Computer Science
University of Texas at Dallas
Richardson, TX 75083

Abstract

In [11] we had proposed a new and efficient indexing technique that utilized all the functors in the clause-heads and the goal. The salient feature of this technique was that the selected clause-head *unified (modulo nonlinearity)* with the goal. In unification (modulo nonlinearity) all the variables in the terms being unified are assumed to be unique; so the only operation performed is one of matching their constant portions. So use of our indexing technique can result in sharper discrimination, fewer choice points and reduced backtracking.

A naive and direct translation of our indexing algorithms considerably slowed down the execution speeds of a wide range of programs typically seen in practice, viz., those having small procedures and shallow clauses. The main problem with the naive implementation was that deep and shallow terms, terms with few indexable arguments, small and large procedures were all being handled *uniformly*. To beneficially extend the applicability of our algorithms required mechanisms in our implementation that are "sensitive" to term structures and size and complexity of procedures. We accomplish this in the ν-*ALS* compiler by carefully decomposing our indexing process into *multiple stages*. The operations performed by these stages can gradually increase in complexity ranging from as simple an operation as first argument indexing done in the first stage to the complex operation of unification (modulo nonlinearity) performed in the last stage. The indexing process can be terminated at any stage whenever it is not beneficial to continue further. So small procedures with simple terms can be indexed quickly using the first few stages whereas large and complex procedures may require all the stages. To handle large and small procedures we carefully interleave the indexing process with algorithms appropriate for the respective sizes.

We have now completed the design and implementation of ν-*ALS*. Using it we have enhanced the performance of a broad range of programs typically encountered in practice. In conclusion, our experience with ν-*ALS* strongly suggests that indexing based on unification (modulo nonlinearity) is a viable idea in practice and that a broad spectrum of realistic programs can realize all of its benefits.

1   Introduction

In [11] we had proposed a new and efficient indexing technique for quickly filtering clause-heads in a prolog program into a smaller set of clause-heads that are more likely to unify with the goal. The salient feature of this technique was that the selected clause-head *unified (modulo nonlinearity)* with the goal. We say that a clause head unifies (modulo nonlinearity) with the goal iff it unifies with the goal after uniquely renaming multiple occurrences of variables in both the clause-head and the goal. Therefore, a clause-head selected by such an indexing algorithm *may* fail to unify with the goal iff there are multiple instances of a variable either in the clause-head or in the goal.

Indexing based on unification (modulo nonlinearity) has the following three main advantages over methods used in existing prolog compilers (such as Quintus, *ALS* and Stony Brook Prolog) that index on the first (or some other prespecified) argument.

- It is more effective. The filtered set produced by indexing based on unification (modulo nonlinearity) will in general have considerably fewer clause-heads than that produced by indexing based on the first argument alone. This is because the former method examines many more symbols (and so discriminates more sharply) than the latter method. The number of choice points can decrease resulting in reduced backtracking.

- It is transparent to the programmer. When using indexing based on unification (modulo nonlinearity), programs need no longer be organized for effectively exploiting the indexing method. In contrast, programs indexed on the first argument are typically written in such a way so as to exploit it.

- Indexing alone sometimes suffices to compute the unifiers. When doing unification (modulo nonlinearity), if every variable gets at most one substitution, then these substitutions alone are the unifiers. The unification step that typically follows every indexing step can now be skipped.

Note that the fast unification algorithms of Paterson and Wegman [10] and Martelli and Montanari [6] can be used to perform unification (modulo nonlinearity). The main problem in doing so is that when there are several clause-heads to be selected the symbols in the goal may need to be reinspected several times. This is quite wasteful and not appropriate for fast indexing.

In our approach, each clause-head is transformed into a set of strings by doing a left-to-right preorder traversal and removing the variables. Thus $f(a, g(X, b))$ is transformed into *fag* and *b*. Observe that the *clause-head strings* so obtained contain all the nonvariable symbols in the head. These clause-head strings are then compiled into a string-matching automaton. At run time the goal is scanned and the state transitions made by the automaton are recorded. The information embodied in these states is now used to avoid reinspection of symbols in the goal and thereby improve the running time of the technique. Specifically, our running time is proportional to the number of variables in the clause-head and the goal as opposed to sum of their sizes. In addition to the above algorithm, which we will refer to as *indexing based on string-matching*, we had also briefly outlined in [11] another indexing method suitable for small procedures. However the method uses a bit-vector model; sets of clause-heads are represented by bit vectors and intersection and union operations on them are assumed to require constant time. So the above method, which we will refer to as *indexing based on bit vectors*, is suited for prolog programs in which the number of clause-heads with the same predicate name does not exceed the wordsize. In [4], Hickey and Mudambi also proposed a compilation scheme to reduce choice points. Their technique uses a decision tree whose construction is based on input parameters only. Therefore, unlike our technique, they need to perform mode inference. Note that size of the decision tree can become exponential. Palmer and Naish described a method to reduce this blow up in [8].

Our algorithms were not incorporated into any compiler and so their practical utility had not been established. We therefore began a project in June '91 in collaboration with Applied Logic Systems (in Syracuse, New York) to seamlessly incorporate our indexing algorithms in their portable *ALS* compiler.

A preliminary implementation based on a naive and direct transformation of our algorithms into code showed that its usefulness was very limited. Only large and complex procedures (not often encountered in practice) seemed to benefit from them. But typical prolog programs have small procedures with shallow terms and few indexable arguments. Such programs did not benefit at all from the naive implementation. Even worse it slowed down their execution speeds considerably.

The main problem with our preliminary implementation was that deep and shallow terms, terms with very few indexable arguments, small and large procedures were all being handled *uniformly*. A serious drawback with such a uniform use of our algorithms is that indexing small procedures with shallow clause-heads and few indexable arguments is expensive as it results in poor discrimination despite seeing many symbols. For such procedures it is advantageous to use the simple method of first argument indexing. Although the latter indexing method can result in a lot of backtracking the deterioration in overall execution speed is quite small when compared to using the former method. The problem now was how to realize the full benefits of our indexing technique (such as transparency, effectiveness and reduced backtracking) over a broad spectrum of prolog programs ranging from small procedures with a few shallow rules to complex procedures with deep structures, without unduly compromising the performance of any program in the spectrum.

Based on the above observations it was evident that our implementation required mechanisms "sensitive" to term structures and sizes of procedures in order to beneficially extend its practical applicability. One approach to build-in such mechanisms is to do indexing in *multiple stages* ; each stage further shrinks the size of the filtered set produced by the preceding stage using operations relatively more complex than the one used in earlier stages. The indexing process can be terminated at any stage whenever it is not beneficial to continue further. So small procedures with simple terms can be indexed quickly using the first few stages whereas all the stages are used for large and complex procedures.

Our indexing method lends itself quite nicely for decomposition into multiple stages. The operations performed by these stages can gradually increase in complexity ranging from as simple an operation as first argument indexing done in the first stage to the complex operation of unification (modulo nonlinearity) performed in the last stage. To handle large and small procedures we carefully interleave our string-matching based algorithm (beneficial for large procedures) with the bit-vector based algorithm (useful for small procedures) during the indexing process.

We have now completed the design and implementation of the ν-*ALS* compiler that incorporates our indexing algorithms based on the ideas described above. Using it we have improved the performance of a broad range of programs. Through a careful decomposition of our apparently complex indexing process into multiple stages and interleaving algorithms appropriate for large and small procedures we have been able to extend the range of its practical utility considerably. We have now demonstrated that indexing based on unification (modulo nonlinearity) is a viable idea in practice and that even small and simple prolog programs can realize all of its benefits. We remark that contrary to current practice, programmers can now write programs with complex heads. Such programs can be efficiently indexed by our algorithms resulting in fewer choice points and reduced backtracking.

This paper is an extended summary of the design, implementation and impact on the run time performance of prolog programs compiled using the ν-ALS compiler. The paper is organized as follows. In the next section we present an overview of the compiler and its impact on the run time performance of prolog programs. In section 3 we briefly review the ideas underlying our indexing techniques. Section 4 describes the design and implementation of ν-ALS compiler. Section 5 discusses run time performance of prolog programs compiled using ν-ALS compiler. In section 6 we discuss some of the implications of our experience with ν-ALS on the practice of prolog programming.

2   Overview of ν-ALS

In the current implementation of ν-ALS, we have decomposed our indexing method into *three* stages. The first stage discriminates among the clause-heads based on the first argument. This is essentially the same as WAM indexing. The clause-heads selected by the first stage are further filtered in the intermediate stage using "appropriate" symbols that follow the first argument in preorder. In essence the operation done by this stage can be viewed as a "generalization" of first argument indexing. The third and final stage completes unification (modulo nonlinearity) of the clause-heads with the goal. Herein we use both the string-matching based and bit-vector based algorithms. Specifically, if the number of clause-heads selected by the intermediate stage is less than the wordsize of the computer we then only use the bit-vector based algorithm. Otherwise we deploy the string-matching based algorithm to reduce the size of the filtered set and finally finish off the process using the bit-vector based algorithm.

We mention that in the entire indexing process no symbol is *ever examined more than once* and hence no stage ever repeats the work done by any other stage. Furthermore symbols in the goal subterms that occur within variable substitutions of every clause-head are never examined.

Finally we remark that it is possible to introduce additional stages in between the intermediate and final stage. For example, one such stage can be designed to do the same operation as that of the intermediate stage but using the last argument instead. Our main objective in this first prototype of ν-ALS was to validate the practical applicability of our indexing method. For ease and simplicity of implementation we chose to design only one intermediate stage.

2.1   Impact on Prolog Execution Speed

In our experiments we compiled programs using the ALS and ν-ALS compiler. We then ran them on a Sun-3/160 and measured the total time of execution. These programs (see Figures 2, 3, 4) include the *dutch national flag* problem given in [9], the *border* predicate in the CHAT-80 system [12], the *replace* program and the *8-queens* problem, both of which are ALS benchmarks, and programs to parse strings using $LL(k)$ grammars. The speedup of a program in our performance figures refers to the ratio of execution speed of the program compiled using ν-ALS over that of the same program compiled using ALS. Based on our experiments we can make the following conclusions on the impact of ν-ALS on execution speeds of prolog programs

- Prolog programmers typically tend to write programs in which all the input arguments precede the outputs. We can speedup such programs especially if some of the input arguments are nonvariables. An example is the *dutch national flag* problem where we obtain speedups ranging from 28% to 36% on our test queries. These speedups can be larger or smaller but are never lower than *ALS*.

- We can quickly selects facts; the lower the priority[1] of the selected fact the faster is the selection. An example is the *border* program where we show speedups of 97% when searching through a very small database of eight facts. Each fact is a flat structure with only two arguments.

- Extant techniques cannot index programs in which variables as arguments precede those that have nonvariables as arguments. We speedup such programs by running the indexing process through all the stages. We demonstrate this on the *replace* program wherein we obtain speedups of 322%!.

- We can reduce nondeterminism in prolog programs that have a lot of nonvariable symbols in clause-heads; the larger the number of such symbols the faster the execution. For example, by putting the lookahead symbols in the clause-head we can parse $LL(k)$ grammars deterministically, i.e. our indexing method always chooses only one clause-head. We obtain speedups of 11%, 23% and 31% for parsing $LL(1)$, $LL(2)$ and $LL(3)$ programs respectively. Note that the nonvariable symbols in clause-heads keep increasing for larger k and hence our speedups also rise accordingly.

- Finally, we do not degrade performance of programs that do not benefit from our indexing algorithms. An example of this is *8-queens*. Our running times are almost identical to that obtained using *ALS*.

3 Review of Indexing Algorithms

We briefly review the main conceptual ideas underlying string-matching based and bit-vector based algorithms. For details, the readers are referred to [11].

3.1 String-Matching Based Algorithm

Let us superpose the goal and the clause-head at their roots. We say that $< u, v >$ is a node-pair if upon superposition node u in the goal falls on node v in the clause-head. A node is either labeled with a function symbol or a variable. If u (or v) is labeled with a variable X then the subtree rooted at v (respectively u) is called a *substitution* for X. In case u is labeled with X then we delete u and the subtree rooted at v from the goal and clause-head respectively. On the other hand if v is labeled with X then we remove v from the clause-head and the subtree rooted at u from the goal. After this step all the nodes in the remaining node-pairs are labeled with function symbols only. Note that in order for the goal and the clause-head to unify, the function symbols of both the nodes in all of these remaining node-pairs must be identical. An indexing algorithm that selects a clause-head only when the labels in each of these node-pairs match, utilizes all the nonvariable symbols.

---

[1] We say that clause p has higher priority over clause q if p appears before q in the program text.

The main problem is that a naive implementation will examine every node-pair for comparing node labels.

The key idea in our approach is not to examine every node-pair. Instead we compare a sequence of node-pairs in $O(1)$ time. We are able to do this by transforming the operation of comparing node-pairs to a string-matching problem. As mentioned earlier in our approach each clause-head is transformed into a set of *clause-head strings* by doing a left-to-right preorder traversal and removing nodes labeled with variables.

Given a goal, we perform a series of complex string-matching steps that involve clause-head strings and goal strings. The outcome of these steps are then correlated to obtain the filtered set. We have shown that all the string-matching questions that can possibly arise in selection, based on the conceptual description above, are special cases of the generic question - "Does the prefix of length l (not necessarily a proper prefix) of a clause-head (or goal) string occur at the ith position in a goal (respectively, clause-head) string". By suitably compiling the clause-head strings into a string-matching automaton we are able to answer these questions in $O(1)$ time at run time.

The automaton is constructed at compile time by preprocessing all the clause-heads. Its worst-case time complexity is $O(min(k_i + k_g, l_i, l_g))$ (here k_i and l_i are the number of variables and leaf nodes, in the clause-head, respectively and k_g, l_g are the respective number of variables and leaf nodes in the goal). In contrast, using the unification algorithms in [10, 6] would result in a worst-case time complexity of $O(|\ g\ | + |\ s\ |)$ ($|\ g\ |$ and $|\ s\ |$ are the sizes of the goal and clause-head respectively.) The time needed to construct the automaton (at compile-time) and its space requirements are both quadratic in the size of the clause-heads (in the worst case).

3.2 Bit-Vector Based Algorithm

We use the notion of a *position* to refer to subterms in a term as follows. A position is either the empty string Λ that reaches the root or $p.i$ (where p is a position and i is an integer) which reaches the ith argument of the subterm reached by p. The *pathstring* up to position p in a term t is the sequence of node labels on the path from root of t to the node at p. We define a prefix tree $pre(v)$ with respect to a node v in a term t as the tree[2] obtained by replacing by new variables the subtrees rooted at the children of v and those children of the ancestors of v that appear after v in preorder.

Now suppose the goal has been traversed in preorder up to node v at position p. Let Π denote the set of all those clause-heads that have unified (modulo nonlinearity) with $pre(v)$. Let S_v denote all those clause-heads whose pathstrings up to position p are identical to the pathstring in the goal up to p. Let M_v denote all those clause-heads that have a variable at position p. Clearly $\Pi \subseteq M_v \bigcup S_v$. Now the objective is to extend the prefix tree one node at a time by visiting the subtree at v in preorder. Suppose the next node visited in the goal is v'. If v' is a variable then we simply continue the traversal. If it is a functor symbol then we delete from Π all those clause-heads that do not appear in $S_{v'}$. This is because the symbol at v' will not match the corresponding symbols in the deleted clause-heads. Thus Π is updated continuously as we visit more and more nodes in the subtree at v. Let Π' denote the updated Π on exiting from v. On exiting from v we finally add the clause-heads in $M_v \bigcap \Pi$ to Π'. These clause-heads now unify (modulo nonlinearity)

---

[2]Note that terms have an obvious labeled tree representation

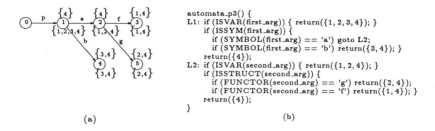

```
                                                  automata_p3() {
                                                  L1: if (ISVAR(first_arg)) { return({1, 2, 3, 4}); }
                                                      if (ISSYM(first_arg)) {
                                                          if (SYMBOL(first_arg) == 'a') goto L2;
                                                          if (SYMBOL(first_arg) == 'b') return({3, 4}); }
                                                      return({4});
                                                  L2: if (ISVAR(second_arg)) { return({1, 2, 4}); }
                                                      if (ISSTRUCT(second_arg)) {
                                                          if (FUNCTOR(second_arg) == 'g') return({2, 4});
                                                          if (FUNCTOR(second_arg) == 'f') return({1, 4}); }
                                                      return({4});
                                                  }
```

(a)   (b)

Figure 1: The Automaton and Its Translated C Code.

with $pre(v)$ augmented with the subtree at v. Observe that by maintaining S_v, M_v and Π as bit strings in a word it is possible to update Π in $O(1)$ time using logical *and* and *or* operations.

4 Design and Implementation of ν-ALS

Recall that our indexing method is decomposed into three stages. We now describe their design and methods for efficiently implementing them. We also describe the interfaces (or *hooks*) between the stages and the criterion used for continuing the indexing process beyond a particular stage.

Design of the first stage is relatively straightforward. In this stage, selection is done by examining the first argument symbol only. This is exactly the operation done by WAM indexing which is also the indexing method adopted in the ALS compiler. We therefore chose to retain WAM indexing to do the selection operation in the first stage of ν-ALS also.

4.1 Second Stage

Recall we had mentioned that this stage is a generalization of first argument indexing. Specifically, this stage will select a set of clause-heads such that the first string of every clause-head in the set is either a prefix of the goal's first string or vice versa. More importantly, clause heads not included in this set will fail to unify because of symbol mismatches. To describe the ideas underlying the design we first need the following concepts related to the Aho-Corasick automaton [2]. The automaton consists of nodes called *states* and two types of links - *goto* and *failure*. The goto links are labeled with symbols from the alphabet of the strings recognized by the automaton. These links together with the states form a trie structure known as the *goto trie* whose root is the start state. We refer to strings recognized by the automaton as its *keywords*. In Figure 1(a), *paf*, *pag*, *pb*, *p* are keywords of the automaton. We say that string λ *represents* state γ if the path in the trie from the start state (the root node) to state γ spells out λ. For example state 3 in the figure represents the string *paf*. We say that γ is the *primary accepting* state of a keyword string α if it is both an accepting state and also represents α.

Now let g_1 be the goal's first string. Let S_1 be the set of all those clause-heads whose first strings are prefixes of g_1. Let S_2 be the set of all those clause-heads such that g_1 is a prefix of their first strings. The objective of stage 2 is to compute

$S_1 \bigcup S_2$. The clauses corresponding to the above set will constitute a *try_me-retry_me-trust_me* chain at the end of the second stage.

Computation of $S_1 \bigcup S_2$ is done as follows. Suppose the first string β of a clause-head r matches a prefix α of g_1. Recall that there is a path in the automaton that spells out β. This implies that α can be entirely scanned by the automaton without making any failure transitions. Based on this observation S_1 can be constructed as follows. The automaton scans the symbols in g_1 (from left to right) and makes transitions. It continues scanning these symbols as long as it makes only *goto* transitions. During such a scan if the automaton makes a goto transition to a primary accepting state of β then r is included in S_1. On the other hand suppose g_1 is a prefix of β. Once again the automaton can scan g_1 entirely without making any failure transitions. So S_2 is constructed as follows. Let A denote the state reached on completely scanning g_1. If g_1 is a prefix of β then the primary accepting state of β must be a descendant of A in the goto tree. Therefore S_2 will consist of only those clause-heads such that the primary accepting states of their first strings are descendants of A in the goto tree.

During compilation we maintain the following information. With each state A, we keep a set C_A of all those clause-heads for which A is the primary accepting state of their first strings. We also maintain another set D_A of clause-heads such the primary accepting states of their first strings are descendants of A in the goto tree. At run time the automaton starts off by reading the symbols in g_1. It continues scanning them as long as it makes only goto transitions. During this scan if it enters an accepting state A then C_A is added to S_1. Computation is finished when either g_1 is completely scanned without making any failure transitions or a failure transition occurs before all the symbols in g_1 have been read. In the former case, if B is the state of the automaton on completely scanning g_1 then S_2 becomes D_B. In the latter case $S_2 = \emptyset$.

A preliminary implementation of the second stage based on the ideas described above resulted in poor performance. In what follows we discuss methods used to speed it up.

4.1.1 Efficient Implementation

There were two sources for improving the efficiency of the implementation. Firstly $S_1 \bigcup S_2$ was being computed at run time by doing several unions of C_A's. Secondly the automaton was being used interpretively. Consequently, to make any transition from one state to another state required one memory reference to fetch the symbol based on which the transition is made. Moreover a test for empty transition (i.e. no goto transition) is also made at every state. (Note a state with empty transition denotes a final state.)

Optimization 1: The first optimization done was to precompute $S_1 \bigcup S_2$ at compile time. With every state A we keep a set C'_A where $C'_A = \bigcup_{\forall B} C_B$ such that B is an ancestor of A in the goto tree. It can be shown that the (worst-case) blow-up in space now is at most quadratic in the sum of sizes of the clause-heads.

In addition we also have D_A as before. On scanning g_1 at run time suppose the first state at which a failure occurs is γ. Then $S_1 = C'_\gamma$ and $S_2 = \emptyset$. In the case we are able to completely scan g_1 without making failure transitions and the state reached upon scanning is β then $S_1 = C'_\beta$ and $S_2 = D_\beta$. Thus the *try_me-retry_me-trust_me* chain is computed at compile time for every state. We illustrate the above idea using the following example. For expository purposes the program consists of facts alone.

```
p(a, f(X), d).          p(a, g(X, h(1, 2, 3)), e).
p(b, Y, Z).             p(X, Y, Z).
```

The first strings for the above facts are *paf, pag, pb* and *p* respectively. Figure 1(a) shows the part of the automaton relevant for the second stage. In the figure the list above a state u is its C'_u list and the one beneath it is $C'_u \bigcup D_u$.

Given a goal, e.g. p(a, g(A, B), e), the transitions for its first string *pag* end at state 4 successfully, therefore $C'_4 \bigcup D_4$, which contains fact 2 and 4, is returned. If the goal is p(a, h(1, 2, 3), c), its first string *pah123c* fails at state 2 on symbol h, so C'_2, which includes fact 4 only, is returned.

Optimization 2: Our second optimization step was not to use the automata interpretively. Instead we compile the automata into *case statements*[3]. In our current version we translate it into case expressions in C. Consequently, the symbols on which transitions are made now become C constants, thereby saving a memory reference for each symbol comparison. Furthermore, at the final states where no transition is possible, the translated code simply returns without checking for the null list condition. Each prolog procedure's corresponding automaton is translated into a C procedure, which is called when necessary to perform the intermediate stage indexing. To illustrate the idea, consider the same program as above. The translated C procedure corresponding to the automaton in Figure 1(a) is shown in Figure 1(b). Although our current implementation translates the automata into C, it can also be directly translated into assembly codes or even machines codes, which will make it even more efficient.

4.2 Third Stage

Recall that in this stage we do unification (modulo nonlinearity) completely. Our strategy here is to use either the bit-vector algorithm or a combination of string-matching and bit-vector algorithms. We use the former when the number of clause-heads remaining after selection by the previous stages does not exceed the word-size. Otherwise we employ the latter strategy. Implementation of both the string-matching and bit-vector based algorithms is rather routine. For efficiency we again compile the trie used in the bit-vector based algorithm into case expressions in C. The interesting part is design of the combination. Note that we are able to compute the *try_me-retry_me-trust_me* chains at compile time for both the first and second stages. One such precomputed chain will serve as the input to the third stage. So at compile time we examine all such chains. Suppose the number of clauses in one such chain is more than the wordsize. Specifically, suppose the wordsize is say 32 bits and the number of clauses in the chain is n and $n > 32$. We then construct a trie for the last 32 clause-heads in the chain. At run time if this chain is selected as the input to stage 3 then we initiate our string-matching based algorithm on the first $n - 32$ clauses and then finish off the selection process on the last 32 clauses using the bit-vector based algorithm. Note that it is possible for a clause-head to appear in more than one chain and hence may appear in more than one trie. But we can again show that the (worst-case) blow-up in space is at most quadratic in the sum of sizes of all the clause-heads.

---

[3] We mention that when the the branching factor from a state is quite small as in Figure 1(b) we compile it into *if* instead of *case* statements.

4.3 Criterion for Continuation Beyond a Stage

Note that it should be possible to stop the indexing process at any stage whenever it is not beneficial to continue any further. We have a simple criterion for doing so in our current version. We stop the indexing process whenever the number of clause-heads selected is 1. From both the first and second stages we move on to the next stage whenever the *try_me-retry_me-trust_me* chain selected has more than one clause. It is possible to develop a more sophisticated criterion by doing program analysis. For instance we can analyse the clause-heads to identify nonvariable positions in them. We can continue indexing if among the clause-heads in the selected chain there are nonvariables symbols that have not been examined. Note that for any clause-head in a selected *try_me-retry_me-trust_me* chain we can identify at compile time exactly all of its symbols that would have been seen so far. Another possibility is to do mode analysis. If the remaining unscanned arguments of the goal are all outputs, then obviously there is no point continuing the indexing process any further.

4.4 Interstage Interface

We now describe how the stages are hooked together. For this purpose we create the following three new WAM instructions - *switch_on_automata, switch_on_string* and *switch_on_trie*. The *switch_on_automata* instruction is used to begin the selection process of the second stage whereas the latter two instructions are used for starting the third stage. The *switch_on_string* instruction starts off our string-matching based algorithm whereas the *switch_on_trie* instruction initiates the bit-vector based algorithm.

For describing the interface between the first and second stage we will assume familiarity with the internal organization of WAM appropriate for WAM indexing (see section 5.9 on indexing in [1] for details). Recall that in WAM indexing all clauses are partitioned into four (not necessarily distinct) chains - *variable, list, constant* and *structure*. The *variable* chain merely links together all the clauses constituting a procedure. The index block begins with the WAM instruction *switch_on_term* followed by four pointers, each one pointing to one of the four chains. Note that the *variable* chain is used whenever the goal's first argument is a variable (i.e. its first string is empty). We can therefore regard its first string as being vacuously scanned and hence bypass the second stage altogether. So the pointer to the *variable* chain in the index block is replaced by a pointer to a memory block whose first instruction is either *switch_on_string* or *switch_on_trie* that when executed will initiate the third stage. For the *list* chain the pointer is modified only when the number of clauses in it is more than one. In that case the pointer is set to point to a memory block whose first instruction is a *switch_on_automata* that starts off the second stage. Recall that for *constant* and *structure* chains their corresponding pointers in the index block points to a table beginning with *switch_on_constant* and *switch_on_structure* respectively, followed by a sequence of entries. Each entry is a pair of the form $< k, @single\text{-}clause >$ or $< k, @multiple\text{-}clauses >$. The first component in a pair is the *key*. The pair $< k, @(single\text{-}clause) >$ is entered into the table whenever there is only one clause in the procedure that matches the key in the pair whereas the other one is used when there is more than one clause. In the former case @(*single-clause*) points to the first instruction of the clause and in the latter case @(*multiple-clauses*) points to the *switch_on_automata* instruction that starts off the second stage. The *switch_on_automata* instruction is always followed

Program	Query	Loops	ALS	ν-ALS	Speedup
const	c(f(100))	50000	168.76	9.48	17.74
	c(f(50))	50000	90.37	8.83	10.23
	c(f(1))	50000	7.97	8.68	0.92
full16	f(1, 3, X, 32)	50000	62.12	21.15	2.94
border	borders(yugoslavia, mediteranean)	50000	16.03	8.15	1.97
	borders(yugoslavia, hungary)	50000	12.68	8.48	1.50
	borders(yugoslavia, albania)	50000	7.12	8.48	0.84
dnf	s1 (see Figure 2)	5000	93.17	68.48	1.36
	s2 (see Figure 2)	5000	43.98	34.65	1.27
	s3 (see Figure 2)	5000	22.95	19.48	1.18
replace	replace(neg(expr), A, B)	50000	9.92	9.82	1.01
	replace((2 < 4), A, B)	50000	10.72	10.82	0.99
	replace(mul(expr1, expr2), A, B)	50000	9.02	9.22	0.98
replace.sw	replace(1, A, B, neg(expr))	50000	69.08	21.43	3.22
	replace(1, A, B, (2 < 4))	50000	48.18	22.43	2.15
	replace(1, A, B, mul(e1, e2))	50000	15.90	22.50	0.71
replace.all	replace(1, A, B, neg(expr))	50000	68.60	21.37	3.21
	replace(1, A, B, (2 < 4))	50000	69.70	22.45	3.10
	replace(1, A, B, mul(e1, e2))	50000	73.33	21.57	3.40
ll(1)	p (see Figure 4)	10000	62.98	56.68	1.11
ll(2)	q (see Figure 4)	10000	87.32	70.80	1.23
ll(3)	r (see Figure 4)	10000	59.50	45.37	1.31
queens	get_solutions(A)	20	49.28	49.68	0.99

Table 1: Speedup Figures

by a parameter which is the state of the automaton from which the second stage will begin its transitions. We can thereby avoid rescanning the key symbol already seen in WAM indexing.

We now describe the interface to the third stage. Note that since any state of the automaton can be reached via the second stage, transition into the third stage can be done from any one of them. So we maintain a pointer *final* with each state. If the number of clauses in the *try_me-retry_me-trust_me* chain for a state is only one, then the *final* pointer of that state points to the starting address of the single clause. Otherwise, it points to a block of memory which starts off either with a *switch_on_trie* instruction when the number of clauses is less than the wordsize or with a *switch_on_string* instruction otherwise. Finally, we outline briefly how symbols seen in previous stages are not reexamined in the third stage. In the string-matching based algorithm the problem is nonexistent since the the same data structure (i.e. the aho-corasick automaton) is used uniformly in all the stages. The difficulty arises when combining the aho-corasick automaton with the trie used in the bit-vector based algorithm. But observe that each state in the aho-corasick automaton corresponds to a position reached in the trie. So we maintain a pointer $pos(s)$ in every state s to its corresponding position in the trie. Whenever the bit-vector based algorithm is initiated from a state, say α at run time, then we traverse the trie from $pos(\alpha)$ onwards thereby avoiding reexamination of symbols seen prior to reaching $pos(\alpha)$.

5 Discussion of Benchmarks

Table 1 lists timing results of the benchmark programs we have tested. Each program is tested on one or more queries. The figures under *Loops* indicate the number of times the corresponding query is run. Times are measured in seconds and speedups are computed as the ratio of the running time of programs compiled using

c(f(1)). c(f(2)). . . c(f(100)).	f(1, 2, X, 1). f(1, 2, X, 2). . . f(1, 2, X, 16). f(1, 3, X, 17). f(1, 3, X, 18). . . f(1, 3, X, 32).	borders(yugoslavia,albania). borders(yugoslavia,austria). borders(yugoslavia,bulgaria). borders(yugoslavia,greece). borders(yugoslavia,hungary). borders(yugoslavia,italy). borders(yugoslavia,romania). borders(yugoslavia,mediteranean).

```
top(In, Out) :- dnf( In, Out, Out1, Out1, Out2, Out2, []).
dnf([], R, R, W, W, B, B).
dnf([r | Item], [r | R1], R, W0, W, B0, B) :- dnf(Item, R1, R, W0, W, B0, B).
dnf([w | Item], R0, R, [w | W1], W, B0, B) :- dnf(Item, R0, R, W1, W, B0, B).
dnf([b | Item], R0, R, W0, W, [b | B1], B) :- dnf(Item, R0, R, W0, W, B1, B).
s1 :- top([b,b,b,b,b,b,b,b,b,b,b,b,b,b,b,b,b,b,b,b,b,b,b,b,b,b,b,b,b,b,b,b,b,b,b,
          b,b,b,b,b,b,b,b,b,b,b,b,b,b,b,b,b,b,b,b,b,b,b,b,b,b,r,r,r,r,r,r], A).
s2 :- top([b,b,b,b,b,b,b,b,b,b,b,b,b,b,b,b,b,b,b,b,b,b,b,b,b,b,b,r,r,r,r,r], A).
s3 :- top([b,b,b,b,b,b,w,w,w,w,w,w,r,r,r,r,r,r], A).
```

Figure 2: const (upper left), full16 (upper center), border (upper right), dnf

ALS over that using ν-*ALS*. All programs are run on a Sun-3/160. The programs include the *dutch national flag* (Figure 2) problem given in [9], the *border* (Figure 2) predicate in the CHAT-80 system [12], the *replace* (Figure 3) program and the *8-queens* (Figure 3) problem, both of which are *ALS* benchmarks, and programs to parse $LL(k)$ grammars (Figure 4). The first two programs in the table viz. *const* and *full16* (both in Figure 2) are *atypical* programs contrived to highlight key aspects of our indexing algorithm.

The *const* program illustrates the advantage of ν-*ALS* whenever it is beneficial to look beyond the first argument. On the query *c(f(100))* WAM indexing stops after inspecting the principal functor *f* of the first argument. But nothing is achieved at all since all the one hundred clauses have the same symbol there. Therefore, it has to resort to unification and backtracking through ninety-nine clauses before the right one is finally found while the intermediate stage in our method will inspect one more symbol and find the right answer without doing any unification. The response to queries *c(f(1))* and *c(f(50))* are essentially the same except that backtracking is done only once and fifty times respectively in WAM indexing.

The *border* program illustrates the performance of ν-*ALS* on facts, especially *ground* facts wherein the arguments are all constant terms. Since the arguments are all constant terms we can pick the correct fact at the end of the second stage. Note that the lower the priority of the selected fact the bigger the speedup (compare the speedups on *?-border(yugoslavia,mediterranean)* vs *?-border(yugoslavia,albania)*). This can also be seen on the *const* program (see speedups on *?-c(f(1))* vs *?-c(f(50))*).

Our method can naturally exploit the extant practice of writing programs with input arguments preceding all output arguments. We can speedup such programs especially in those cases in which input arguments that are nonvariables precede those that have variables as arguments. For eexample, consider the program for the *dutch national flag* problem. With the exception of the first clause, every other clause's first argument is a list whose first element is a constant. WAM indexing will look through the clauses one by one while our intermediate stage finds the right clause based on a single transition.

Our indexing method has the potential to reduce nondeterminism in prolog programs that have many nonvariable symbols in clause-heads; the larger the number

```
size(8).        int(1).       int(2).       int(3).
int(4).         int(5).       int(6).       int(7).       int(8).
get_solutions(Soln) :- solve([], Soln).
newsq([], sq(1, X)) :- int(X).
newsq([sq(I,J) | Rest], sq(X,Y)) :- X is I + 1, int(Y), no_threat(I, J, X, Y),
       safe(Rest, X, Y).
safe([], X, Y).
safe([sq(I,J) | L], X, Y) :- no_threat(I, J, X, Y), safe(L, X, Y).
no_threat(I, J, X, Y) :- I =\= X, J =\= Y, I−J =\= X−Y, I+J =\= X+Y.
solve([sq(Bs,Y) | L], [sq(Bs,Y) | L]) :- size(Bs).
solve(Init, Fin) :- newsq(Init, Next), solve([Next | Init], Fin).
```

```
replace(mul(A,B),   Z,   mul(A,B,Z)).      replace(1, Z, mul(A,B,Z),   mul(A,B)).
replace(abs(X),     V,   abs(X,V)).        replace(1, V, abs(X,V),     abs(X)).
replace((A+B),      Z,   (Z is A+B)).      replace(1, Z, (Z is A+B),   (A+B)).
replace((A−B),      Z,   (Z is A−B)).      replace(1, Z, (Z is A−B),   (A−B)).
replace((A*B),      Z,   (Z is A*B)).      replace(1, Z, (Z is A*B),   (A*B)).
replace((A/B),      Z,   (Z is A/B)).      replace(1, Z, (Z is A/B),   (A/B)).
replace((A<B),      Z,   lt(A,B,Z)).       replace(1, Z, lt(A,B,Z),    (A<B)).
replace((A>B),      Z,   gt(A,B,Z)).       replace(1, Z, gt(A,B,Z),    (A>B)).
replace((A>=B),     Z,   ge(A,B,Z)).       replace(1, Z, ge(A,B,Z),    (A>=B)).
replace((A=<B),     Z,   le(A,B,Z)).       replace(1, Z, le(A,B,Z),    (A=<B)).
replace(eq(A,B),    Z,   eq(A,B,Z)).       replace(1, Z, eq(A,B,Z),    eq(A,B)).
replace(neg(X),     T,   neg(X,T)).        replace(1, T, neg(X,T),     neg(X)).
```

Figure 3: 8-queens, replace (lower left) and replace.sw (lower right)

of such symbols the better is the speedup. For example, by putting the lookahead symbols in the clause-heads we can parse *LL(k)* grammars deterministically, i.e. our indexing method always selects only one clause-head. Therefore no choice points are ever created thereby resulting in deterministic execution. Observe that the speedups increase with larger *k*.

In all of the examples discussed above we only needed to use the first two stages of our indexing algorithm. We now discuss the impact of the third stage. We use program *replace* (an *ALS* benchmark) for illustration. In this program WAM indexing suffices to pick the right clause in all the queries shown in the table. Hence our speeds are comparable to that of *ALS*. So in *replace.sw* we switch the first argument of every clause in *replace* to the last and put a constant 1 at its original position in order to nullify the effect of the first two stages. Therefore all the twelve clauses appear as input to the final stage. The queries that look for the last and fourth clause in the program obtain speedups of 3.22 and 2.15 respectively. There is a slowdown when selecting the first clause. This is because the overhead in our final stage becomes a dominant factor when selecting very high priority clauses. (See discussion on improving such cases in section 6.) In our current implementation we have observed that we start gaining whenever we have to select clauses with priority greater than *three*. Program *full16* is another example that uses all the three stages.

However observe that we always gain when handling queries that need *all* answers. See the results for the program *replace.all*. This program is identical to *replace.sw*; the only difference being that iterations are now done without a cut. The iterations for all other programs are done using a cut in order to stop the search on finding the first correct answer to the query. Finally, the 8-queens problem in the *ALS* benchmarks is representative of programs that do not benefit from our indexing. Our results show that the run time performance of such programs is not affected by our technique. In other words the additional overhead due to our algorithms is almost negligible.

```
Grammar
E →TE'     E'→+TE' | ε     T →FT'     T'→*FT' | ε     F →id
Program
  e(A, B) :- t(A,C), e1(C, B).                    e1([], []).
  e1([ id | A ], [ id | A ]).                     e1([ * | A ], [ * | A ]).
  e1([ + | A ], B) :- t(A, C), e1(C, B).          t(A, B) :- f(A, C), t1(C, B).
  t1([], []).                                     t1([ id | A ], [ id | A ]).
  t1([ + | A ], [ + | A ]).                       t1([ * | A ], B) :- f(A, C), t1(C, B).
  f([ id | A ], A).
  p :- e([id,+,id,+,id,+, id, +, id, +, id, +, id, *, id, *, id,*, id, *, id, *,
         id, *, id, *, id], A).
```

```
Grammar
S →ε | abA     A →b | SA'     A'→aa
Program
s([a,a|A],[a,a|A]).
s([a,b|A],B) :- a(A,B).
a([a,a|A],B) :- a2([a,a|A],B).
a([b|A],A).              a2([a,a|A],A).
a([a,b|A],B) :- a(A,C), a2(C,B).
q:- s([a,b,a,b,a,b,a,b,a,b,a,b,a,b,a,b,a,b,
     a,b,a,b,a,b,a,b,a,b,a,b,a,b,a,b,b,a,
     a,a,a,a,a,a,a,a,a,a,a,a,a,a,a,a,a,a,a,
     a,a,a,a,a,a,a,a,a,a,a,a], A).
```

```
Grammar
S → ε | abA     A →ab | aabAA' | aA'
A'→aa
Program
s([a,a|A],[a,a|A]).
s([a,b|A],B) :- a(A,B).
a([a,a,a|A],B) :- a2([a,a,a|A],B).
a([a,b|A],A).              a2([a,a|A],A).
a([a,a,b|A],B) :- a(A,C), a2(C,B).
r :- s([a,b,a,a,b,a,a,b,a,a,b,a,a,b,a,a,b,
     a,a,b,a,a,b,a,a,b,a,a,b,a,a,b,a,a,a,
     a,a,a,a,a,a,a,a,a,a,a,a,a,a,a,a,a], A).
```

Figure 4: ll(1), ll(2) (lower left), ll(2) (lower right)

6   Implications to Practical Prolog Programming

This paper described the design and implementation of ν-ALS compiler that incorporates an indexing technique based on unification (modulo nonlinearity). The technique appeared to be beneficial to *atypical* prolog programs (e.g. deep term structures and large number of clauses constituting procedures). To extend its applicability to a broad spectrum of prolog programs we decomposed the technique to do indexing in multiple stages. Each stage further shrinks the size of its input set by employing operations relatively more complex than those used in previous stages. We validated the practical viability of our approach by showing good speedups over a range of prolog programs typically encountered in practice.

We remark that there is room for further improvement such as optimizing our code and incorporating analysis information as mentioned earlier. There is yet another important optimization step that we have not yet implemented. This has to do with doing unification following indexing. If during the indexing step we compute at most one substitution for any variable then there is no need to do unification. In case we do have to perform unification then we must avoid rescanning symbols already seen during indexing. Incorporating these optimizations into ν-ALS will further improve the performance of programs. It is quite likely that even such queries as $c(f(1))$, $borders(yugoslavia, albania)$ and $replace(1, A, B, multiple(expr1, expr2))$ may not exhibit any slowdown.

We conclude with some remarks on the implication of our experience with ν-ALS to the practice of prolog programming. Prolog programmers typically write programs whose input arguments precede all output arguments. In ν-ALS this practice continues to be well supported. However much better performance can be accrued if programmers refine this practice so that all input arguments that are nonvariables precede the others. But more importantly ν-ALS now encourages programmers to write programs with complex clause-heads. By doing so it is possible to decrease the number of choice points and thereby reduce nondeterminism.

Acknowledgements

We express our sincere thanks to David S. Warren for stimulating ideas, enthusiasm and constant encouragement that enabled the completion of this project. We also thank Dr. R.C. Sekar for valuable discussions that made us focus on tangible implementation goals. The paper was written at INRIA Lorraine and CRIN in Nancy, France where I.V. Ramakrishnan was on sabbatical during the spring and summer of 1992. His stay was supported by a grant from the French Ministère de la recherche et de la Technologie. Chen was supported in part by New York State S&T grant RDG-90173 and NSF grants CCR-8805734 and CR-9102159. Ramesh was supported by NSF grant CCR-9110055.

References

[1] H. Aït-Kaci. The WAM: A (real) tutorial. Technical Report, Paris Research Laboratory, Digital Equipment Corporation, January 1990.

[2] A.V. Aho and M. J. Corasick. Efficient string matching: An aid to bibliographic search. *Communication of the ACM*, 18(6):333–340, 1975.

[3] C.M. Hoffmann and M.J. O'Donnell. Pattern matching in trees. *JACM*, 29(1):68–95, 1982.

[4] T. Hickey and S. Mudambi. Global compilation of Prolog. *Journal of Logic Programming*, 7(3):193–230, November, 1989.

[5] J.H. Morris, D.E. Knuth and V.R. Pratt. Fast pattern matching in strings. *SIAM Journal of Computing*, 6(2):323–350, 1977.

[6] A. Martelli and U. Montanari. An efficient unification algorithm. *Transaction on Programming Languages and Systems*, 4(2):258–282, April 1982.

[7] E. M. McCreight. A space-economical suffix tree construction algorithm. *JACM*, 23(2):263–272, April 1976.

[8] D. Palmer and L. Naish. NUA-Prolog: an extension to the WAM for parallel Andorra. In *Proceedings of the Eighth International Conference on Logic Programming*, K. Furukawa, ed., pages 429–442, 1991.

[9] R. A. O'Keefe. *The Craft of Prolog*. MIT Press, 1990.

[10] M.S. Paterson and M.N.Wegman. Linear unification. *Journal of Computer and System Sciences*, 16:158–167, 1978.

[11] R. Ramesh, I.V. Ramakrishnan and D.S. Warren. Automata-driven indexing of prolog clauses. In *Seventh Annual ACM Symposium on Principles of Programming Languages*, pages 281–290, San Francisco, 1990.

[12] D.H.D. Warren and F.C.N. Pereira. An efficient easily adaptable system for interpreting natural language queries. *American Journal of Computational Linguistics*, 8(3-4):110–122, 1982.

Weighted Decision Trees

Saumya Debray   Sampath Kannan   Mukul Paithane

Department of Computer Science
University of Arizona
Tucson, AZ 85721, USA
{debray, kannan, mukul}@cs.arizona.edu

Abstract: While decision tree compilation is a promising way to carry out guard tests efficiently, the methods given in the literature do not take into account either the execution characteristics of the program or the machine-level tradeoffs between different ways to implement branches. These methods therefore offer little or no guidance for the implementor with regard to how decision trees are to be realized on a particular machine. In this paper, we describe an approach that takes execution frequencies of different program branches, as well as the costs of alternative branch realizations, to generate decision trees. Experiments indicate that the performance of our approach is uniformly better than that of plausible alternative schemes.

1 Introduction

There has been a great deal of research, in recent years, on the design and implementation of concurrent logic and constraint programming languages (see, for example, [12, 13, 14, 15, 17]). Much of the implementation effort in this context has focussed on the so-called "flat" versions of these languages: here, a procedure definition consists of alternatives, each alternative preceded by a *guard* that consists of a set of *ask actions* or *primitive tests*. An alternative can be selected at runtime only if the corresponding guard tests can be satisfied. For such languages, a compilation technique called *decision tree compilation* seems quite promising [6, 7, 8]. The idea here is to improve program efficiency by structuring the collection of all guard tests for a procedure into a "decision tree", thereby reducing the number of redundant tests executed. Algorithms for decision tree compilation have been given by Kliger and Shapiro [6, 7] and Korsloot and Tick [8].

The algorithms given by the authors cited above are concerned primarily with generating a decision tree for a set of tests by choosing an order in which the tests should be executed. They use various heuristics to accomplish this, e.g., by first considering tests that are "cared about" by the largest number of clauses (the *max-care* heuristic), then choosing from such tests one that has the fewest different results (the *min-variability* heuristic). These algorithms generate "conceptually reasonable" decision trees. However, as far as we can see, these algorithms give little or no guidance towards the actual *machine realization* of a decision tree, i.e., the actual structure and nature of branch instructions that should be generated at the machine level for a particular program in a particular implementation, assuming that certain characteristics of the program and the machine are given. There are a number of reasons why this problem is not entirely trivial:

1. Procedures are typically defined by more than one clause, and not all clauses are executed with equal frequency. For example, since programs typically spend most of their execution time in loops, the recursive clauses for a procedure are likely to be executed much more often than the non-recursive clauses that terminate recursion. If the different clauses for a procedure have differ-

ent "weights", or execution frequencies, then the decision tree should be constructed in such a way that the "heavier" a clause, i.e., the more frequently it is executed, the shorter the path from the root of the decision tree to the node corresponding to a decision on that clause. (Note that this notion of the "weight" of a clause refers only to its frequency of execution, which determines its importance in the context of decision tree compilation—it has nothing to do with its "granularity", i.e., computational cost.) Moreover, a good decision tree compilation algorithm should be robust with respect to program transformations such as *loop unrolling* or *partial evaluation*, which can change control flow characteristics and affect the relative execution frequencies of different branches.

2. It is not enough to consider the weights of different clauses in isolation when generating decision trees. For example, one could imagine a compilation scheme where a partial decision tree is generated considering the tests for the heaviest clause first, after which any remaining tests for the next heaviest clause are "grafted" onto this tree, and so on down the other clauses. Such an approach can give surprisingly poor performance, because a set of clauses may have weights that are not individually very large, but are collectively much heavier than the clause with heaviest weight (we discovered this the hard way while experimenting with decision trees for the lexical analysis phase of a compiler).

3. Conditional jumps can be implemented in a variety of ways using different addressing modes, and the alternatives have different capabilities and different costs. For example, a multi-way jump can be implemented using a tree of 2-way conditional branches, or by an indirect jump through a "jump table". The former is cheaper—typically, one or two machine instructions—but is limited to two alternatives; the latter is more expensive—typically, six to ten machine instructions—but can address many different alternatives. Unless the realization choices are made intelligently, the machine-level overheads may reduce considerably, or even nullify, the benefits of using decision trees.

This entire discussion is predicated on being able to associate execution frequencies (or, when normalized, estimated execution probabilities) with the clauses defining a procedure. For a discussion of this issue in the context of compilers for traditional languages, see [2, 9, 10, 18, 19]; techniques for estimating execution frequencies of logic programs from their call graph structure are discussed in [3, 16]. A point to note is that the techniques described in [3, 16] involve a simple and efficient linear-time traversal of the call graph of the program (i.e., a graph describing the caller-callee relationships between predicates): there is no iterative fixpoint computation of the sort encountered in global dataflow analyses. Thus, the overhead of estimating execution frequencies using such techniques is small. An alternative is to profile the program on sample inputs to estimate execution frequencies: as the results of Gorlick and Kesselman [5] indicate, the overhead for this approach is also small.

The primary technical contribution of this paper is to give an algorithm to construct "weighted" decision trees. The idea is to reduce the expected machine-level cost of executing the decision tree by taking into account estimated execution probabilities of the different clauses of a procedure, together with the execution costs of alternative machine realizations for (conditional) branches. We argue that in general, it is not enough to consider only the probabilities given, but that a related information-theoretic notion of *entropy* can be used to advantage. One interesting—and apparently novel—aspect of our algorithm is that in the process of generating a "good" decision tree for a procedure, it may generate tests that do not appear in the original source program, but which can be used to improve the execution characteristics of the decision tree. Experiments indicate that in most cases, the decision trees so generated correspond very closely to what one would desire for the particular weight distributions and machine instruction costs.

2 Preliminaries

2.1 Normalized Programs

To simplify the discussion that follows, we assume that programs are in a normalized form satisfying the following two properties:

1. the guards for any procedure are *exhaustive*, i.e., for any possible values of actual parameters to that procedure, there is at least one guard that will not fail; and

2. all ask actions are of the form '$f(v_1, \ldots, v_n)$ **op** c', where **op** is a comparison operator, $f(\cdots)$ is an n-ary "evaluable function", and c is a constant over a totally ordered domain.

These requirements may appear to be very restrictive, but it turns out that programs can be transformed to satisfy these conditions fairly easily. First, consider a procedure p whose guards are $\{G_1, \ldots, G_n\}$: such a procedure can be made exhaustive simply by adding "default" clauses that catches any input that causes each of the guards $G_1, \ldots, G_n$ to fail: the guards for these default clauses is obtained by transforming the formula $\neg G_1 \wedge \cdots \wedge \neg G_n$ to disjunctive normal form. The details are fairly obvious, and not pursued here further. An important point to note is that there is no need to determine whether the guards $G_1, \ldots, G_n$ in the original definition are already exhaustive: the "default" clause(s) can be added blindly without affecting the behavior of the program in any way. If $G_1, \ldots, G_n$ are exhaustive, then the guard of each default clause so generated is unsatisfiable, so the transformation does not affect program semantics.

Next, consider transforming ask actions to normal form: we assume that the language under consideration allows (only) the following kinds of ask actions:

Relational Tests on Values : Given a test of the form '$expr_1$ **op** $expr_2$' where **op** is a comparison operator,[1] let $expr_1 \equiv expr_1' + c_1$ and $expr_2 \equiv expr_2' + c_2$, then the normal form test is '$(expr_1' - expr_2')$ **op** $(c_2 - c_1)$.' E.g., the test '$X > Y + 5$' becomes transformed to the normal form test '$X - Y > 5$'.

Tests on Types : We assume that the language has a finite set of base types $\tau_1, \ldots, \tau_n$, with corresponding type tests $\mathbf{is\_}\tau_1, \ldots, \mathbf{is\_}\tau_n$. In the transformation to normal form, the extraction and checking of type tags is made explicit via an operation $tag(e)$ that returns the tag bits of the value of the expression e. Assume that the tag bit patterns for the types $\tau_1, \ldots, \tau_n$ are $\kappa_1, \ldots, \kappa_n$ respectively. Then, a type test '$\mathbf{is\_}\tau_i(expr)$' is transformed to a normal form test '$tag(expr) = \kappa_i$'.

---

[1] We assume that there is some reasonable set of operators can be allowed in the expressions $expr_1$ and $expr_2$, e.g., the usual arithmetic operators, selectors for extracting components of compound structures and aggregates, etc.

2.2 Definitions and Notation

The techniques in this paper for generating decision trees rely heavily on our ability to "decompose" the set of primitive tests in a procedure definition into subsets of tests where tests in any subset are "independent" of the other tests. To formalize this notion we need the following definitions. An *outcome* of a primitive test is the result of the test for a particular assignment of values to the variables in the test. The set of possible outcomes of a test t is denoted by $\mathsf{outcomes}(t)$. The idea can be extended to a set of tests S: assume an arbitrary (but fixed) ordering for the elements of S, then the set of possible outcomes for S is denoted by $\mathsf{outcomes}(S)$, where an element $\sigma \in \mathsf{outcomes}(S)$ is a tuple $\langle \sigma_1, \ldots \sigma_{|S|} \rangle$ where σ_i represents the outcome of the ith test in S.

Definition 2.1 An outcome $\sigma = \langle \sigma_1, \ldots \sigma_{|S|} \rangle \in \mathsf{outcomes}(S)$ is *consistent* if there is some substitution of values for the variables of S that makes the outcome of the ith test in S equal σ_i for every i, $1 \leq i \leq |S|$. The set of all consistent outcomes of a set S of primitive tests is denoted $\mathsf{outcomes}^*(S)$. ∎

Definition 2.2 Given a set of tests U, $S \subseteq U$ is an equivalence class if S is minimal with respect to the property that for every σ in $\mathsf{outcomes}^*(S)$ and τ in $\mathsf{outcomes}^*(U - S)$, there exists a valuation θ of the variables in U such that $\theta(S)$ has outcome σ and $\theta(U - S)$ has outcome τ. ∎

Although it is not immediately obvious, it can be shown that the classes defined above are indeed equivalence classes and induce a partition on the set of tests. A point to note is that this generalizes the intuitive notion of a pair of tests being (in)dependent: according to this notion, we can only talk of the dependence of a *set* of tests, which means that the outcome of one of them provides some information about the possible outcomes of the others (this is roughly analogous to the notion of a set of vectors being linearly (in)dependent).

Example 2.1 Consider the following clause:

```
p(X, Y) :-  X < 0, X > Y | ...
```

Previous authors have considered the notion of a clause "caring" about a test (e.g., see [7]): a clause C cares about a test g if there is a test g' in the guard of C such that exactly one of the tests $g' \wedge g$, $g' \wedge \neg g$ is satisfiable. By this definition, the clause given above does not care about the test $\mathtt{Y > 0}$. However it is clear that the guard tests '$\mathtt{X < 0}$, $\mathtt{X > Y}$' cannot be satisfied if $\mathtt{Y > 0}$ is true. In our notion, the three tests $\{\mathtt{X < 0},\ \mathtt{X > Y},\ \mathtt{Y > 0}\}$ would be in the same equivalence class, since it is the minimal set of tests in this case that satisfies the definition of an equivalence class above (no proper subset of this set satisfies the definition). □

As this example illustrates, the notion of an equivalence class differs from the notion of "cares about" in that we consider all possible outcomes of the tests in an equivalence class, not just the outcomes where the guard tests are true. The intuitive justification for this is that we get valuable information not only from finding out that certain guard tests hold, but also from finding out that certain guard tests do not hold.

The algorithmic problem of breaking up a set of primitive tests into equivalence classes is in general rather complex. A sophisticated algorithm would analyze the relations (if any) between the variables mentioned in the primitive tests and take these relations into account in deciding equivalence classes. It is not hard to prove that the general equivalence class finding problem is NP-Complete. In practice, however, a good heuristic is to put two tests in the same equivalence class if the tests both involve a common variable. Algorithms for finding equivalence classes are not the main focus of this paper, since in most examples that we have encountered, this is far easier than the other tasks involved in finding the optimal decision tree.

In the next section we describe the algorithm to find the optimal decision tree. At a very high level, the algorithm breaks up the problem of sequencing the primitive tests in a procedure definition into hierarchical problems of sequencing the various equivalence classes of queries and sequencing the queries within an equivalence class. We show that there is no loss of optimality in this hierarchical breakup and that the sequencing between equivalence classes is independent of the weights on the various possible actions. The weights only affect the sequencing of tests within each equivalence class.

In order to describe our heuristic for ordering the tests within an equivalence class we borrow the notion of *entropy* (also known as the *uncertainty function*) from information theory[1]:

Definition 2.3 Let X be a random variable that takes on a finite number of possible values $x_1, x_2, \ldots, x_m$ with probabilities $p_1, p_2, \ldots, p_m$, respectively, such that $p_i > 0, 1 \leq i \leq m$, and $\sum_{i=1}^{m} p_i = 1$. The *entropy* of X, denoted $H(X)$, is defined to be $\sum_{i=1}^{m} -p_i \log_2(p_i)$. ∎

At first glance the choice of this particular function seems somewhat arbitrary, but it can be shown that this is the *only* function that satisfies some very reasonable axioms on the behaviour of an uncertainty function (see [1] for details). The notion of entropy extends in a straightforward way to tests: if a test t has m possible outcomes, with probabilities $p_1, \ldots, p_m$ respectively, then the entropy of t is $H(t) = \sum_{i=1}^{m} -p_i \log_2(p_i)$. The underlying idea here is that execution frequencies for different clauses (i.e., guards) can be normalized to give us estimates of execution probabilities for the guard tests, whence we can use entropies to guide the generation of decision trees.

Intuitively, the way to think of entropies in our situation is that, when we enter a procedure definition, the average amount of uncertainty we have to dispel before choosing the clause to execute is represented by the entropy. Each test that we perform dispels a certain amount of uncertainty based on the probabilities of each of the outcomes of that test. The relevant property of entropy here is that, given an initial entropy e_1, if we perform a test with etropy e_2, then the average amount of uncertainty that remains given the outcome of the test is $e_1 - e_2$. Hence, tests that dispel a greater amount of uncertainty make greater progress towards our goal. Another feature that makes this approach very attractive is that the entropy function (and a normalized version of it) is especially useful for comparing tests that take differing numbers of instructions to perform (i.e., have different costs) and have different numbers of outcomes.[2] For instance we can use a normalized entropy function to compare a binary decision, as exemplified by an **if** statement,

---

[2]Initially, we looked for more elementary ways to solve what we hoped would be a simple compilation problem. However, we were unable, after considerable thought, to come up with a

with a multiway decision, as exemplified by a **case** or **switch** statement. To this end we define the normalized entropy of a test as follows:

Definition 2.4 The *normalized entropy* of a test t with entropy $H(t)$ and cost C is given by $\widehat{H}(t) = H(t)/C$. ∎

We defer a discussion of the use of this definition to the next section. In the next section we will see the application of entropy (or uncertainty) to ordering tests within an equivalence class.

3 Generating Weighted Decision Trees

3.1 The Mutually Exclusive Case

Recall that a set of guards is exhaustive if any consistent outcome of the primitive tests comprising the guards turns on *at least* one of the guards. In practice most procedure definitions satisfy a further property which we call *mutual exclusion*.

Definition 3.1 A pair of tests t_1 and t_2 is *mutually exclusive* if and only if $\exists (t_1 \wedge t_2)$ is not satisfiable.

A set of tests is mutually exclusive if the tests are pairwise mutually exclusive. ∎

In this section we will focus on procedure definitions where the set of guards are exhaustive as well as mutually exclusive — i.e. every consistent outcome of the primitive tests turns on *exactly one* of the guards.

For such procedure definitions we can rigorously establish the 'form' of the (provably) optimal decision tree. Our results in this section will apply to arbitrary procedure definitions that are mutually exclusive and exhaustive (note that that the general problem of generating an optimal decision tree where the tests may not be mutually exclusive and exhaustive is NP-Complete [4]). We can show that in any procedure definition where the guards are mutually exclusive and exhaustive, there is a single equivalence class such that each guard "cares about" this class. In other words, the outcome of the tests in the equivalence class *must* be determined before we can decide which guard is turned on.

Definition 3.2 An equivalence class is said to be *dominant* if the outcome of the tests in the equivalence class must be determined before we can decide if any of the guards is true. ∎

Theorem 3.1 *In any procedure definition where the guards are exhaustive and mutually exclusive, there is a dominant equivalence class of tests.* ∎

The proof is omitted due to space constraints. This result immediately suggests an optimal algorithm for generating a decision tree in the case where the procedure definition is mutually exclusive and exhaustive:

1. Find a dominant equivalence class.

---

reasonable approach using only execution weights that would be able to compare the relative costs of two-way branches using conditional branches and multi-way branches using a branch table.

2. Produce a decision tree for the equivalence class (along the lines of Figure 1), and recursively construct trees for the subproblems at each of the leaves of this tree.

The optimality of the algorithm follows from the fact that the outcome of tests in the dominant equivalence class must be determined by *any* scheme to evaluate the procedure definition.

The central part of the above algorithm is to produce an optimal decision tree for an equivalence class. This is the subject of our next subsection.

3.2   Generating the Decision Tree for an Equivalence Class

In this section we present a heuristic for finding a near-optimal decision tree for an equivalence class using the notion of normalized entropy defined in the previous section. This is the portion of our general algorithm for mutually exclusive and exhaustive procedure definitions that is not necessarily optimal. Recall that each test is assumed to be of the form '$f(\bar{x})$ **op** c', where f is an evaluable function and c is a constant over a totally ordered domain. Given an equivalence class of tests S for which to generate a decision tree, we first group the elements of S into partitions, called *families*, such that tests in the same family compute the same "left hand side" expression $f(\bar{x})$. For example, given the tests

    {I > 0, J > 0, I-J < 0, I-J = 0, I-J >= 1}

we get three families: $\{\texttt{I > 0}\}$, $\{\texttt{J > 0}\}$, and $\{\texttt{I-J < 0, I-J = 0, I-J >= 1}\}$. To generate the decision tree for the original equivalence class, we have to construct the decision tree for each family so generated. As discussed at the end of the previous section, at each point we construct a decision tree for a dominant equivalence class of tests. There may be semantic dependencies that impose an ordering, e.g., it may be necessary to test that a variable is bound to a cons cell before attempting to access the head of that cell: if there are such dependencies, we assume that the different families are ordered in a way that respects these dependencies and yields a legal ordering. Our choice of an order for processing these families may also be guided by low-level considerations, e.g., we may choose an order that groups together different families that test the same variables, so as to improve our use of registers and better exploit the cache. For all these reasons, we do not focus on the ordering between families in this paper, although this ordering has a bearing on the average number of instructions executed.

According to earlier treatments of decision tree compilation, the next step, namely the construction of a decision tree for a family of tests, which is of the form $\{f(\bar{x}) \ \mathbf{op}_1 \ c_1, \ldots, f(\bar{x}) \ \mathbf{op}_n \ c_n\}$, is trivial: we generate a multi-way jump based on the value of the expression $f(\bar{x})$. This does not address the crucial implementation decision of how this multi-way branch is to be realized. Depending on the addressing modes available on our target architecture, there may be a variety of options available, with different capabilities and costs: for example, we may use a tree of conditional branches (corresponding to **if-then-else** statements), or an indirect jump through a branch table (corresponding to a **case** or **switch** statement), or possibly a combination of both. In general, each option has different capabilities and different costs: for example, a conditional branch takes two or three machine instructions but is able to address only two alternatives, while an indirect jump through a branch table may take a total of six to ten machine instructions, but can address a large number of alternatives. Further, even if we decide to use a conditional test rather than jump through a branch table, we still have to make the choice of what that test should be. Typically, the best choice will be a test that tries to balance, as far as possible, the weights corresponding to each of its outcomes: this may produce a test that does not appear in the original source program. One of the novel features of our algorithm is that it (when appropriate) generates tests which do not occur in the source program, resulting in improved performance.

Our aim is to generate a decision tree that reduces, as far as possible, the expected length (in machine instructions) over all paths. To do this, we use normalized entropies (see Definition 2.4) to compare the "merit" of alternative realizations, and pick the best.[3]. The justification for using normalized entropy is as follows: What we would like to do is to minimize the average path length which is the weighted average of the number of instructions it takes to get to each leaf of the tree. On the average, we need to dispel an amount of uncertainty equal to the entropy of the probability distribution induced by the weights on the leaves before we can get to the leaves. In order to find the way that takes the fewest number of instructions to dispel this uncertainty, we use the greedy heuristic and pick the test that dispels the greatest amount of entropy per instruction. Of course, this is only a heuristic and we can construct somewhat pathological examples where it is not optimal. Our algorithm is described below and the decision trees produced by our algorithm for some examples are described in the next section. To simplify the discussion that follows, we assume that there are only two alternative realizations possible: conditional jumps, with cost C_{branch}, and indirect jumps through a branch table, with cost C_{switch}: the algorithm can be extended to deal with other realizations (e.g., where a set of tests is realized using a `switch` after "lopping off" the boundaries using two `if-then-else` statements) without much trouble. We use the following notation:

- the probability (i.e., normalized weight) of a test t is denoted by $prob(t)$;

- because not every set of tests can be realized using a branch table (for example, if there are tests of the form `x > 0`), we assume that there is a predicate $switchable(S)$ that is true if and only if the set of tests S can be implemented using a branch table; and

- given a family of tests S, we use the notation '$\langle S_1, c, S_2 \rangle = split(S)$' to indicate that

  (i) S is partitioned into two pieces S_1 and S_2 such that the total weight of the tests in S_1 is as close as possible to the total weight of tests in S_2; and

  (ii) c is the "dividing line" between the tests S_1 and S_2, i.e., tests in S_1 imply that the expression being evaluated has a value less than c, while tests in S_2 imply that this value is greater than (or equal to) c.

The algorithm, which is given in Figure 1, can be extended in a straightforward way to consider more than two alternative realizations. In the function gen_tree, it is

---

[3] If one were only interested in finding the optimal binary decision tree for the example above, techniques for generating optimal binary search trees using dynamic programming would apply, but these techniques do not permit an easy comparison of this tree with a decision tree using multiway branches.

Input : A set of tests S forming an equivalence class.

Output : A decision tree T realizing the tests S.

Method : **return** $T := gen\_tree(S)$;

> **function** $gen\_tree(S)$: **decision_tree**
> **begin**
> > normalize the weights of tests in S;
> > partition S into families;
> > arrange these families in some order $\{S_1, \ldots, S_n\}$;
> > **for** $i := 1$ **to** n **do**   /* construct decision trees for each family */
> > > **if** $switchable(S_i)$ **and** $entropy\_switch(S_i) > entropy\_cond(S_i)$ **then**
> > > > **gen_switch**(S_i);
> > > **else**
> > > > **gen_cond**(S_i);
> > > **fi**;
> > **od**
> **end**;
>
> **procedure** $gen\_switch(S)$
> **begin**
> > implement the tests in S at n as an indirect jump through a jump table;
> **end**
>
> **procedure** $gen\_cond(S)$
> **begin**
> > let S be a family of tests $\{\mathcal{E}(\bar{x}) \ \mathbf{op}_1 \ c_1, \ldots, \mathcal{E}(\bar{x}) \ \mathbf{op}_n \ c_n\}$;
> > let $\langle S_1, c, S_2 \rangle = split(S)$;
> > let $p_1 = \sum\{prob(t) \mid t \in S_1\}$ and $p_2 = \sum\{prob(t) \mid t \in S_2\}$;
> > generate the decision tree "**if** $\mathcal{E}(\bar{x}) < c$ **goto** U_1 **else goto** U_2;"
> > > **where** $U_1 = gen\_tree(S_1)$ **and** $U_2 = gen\_tree(S_2)$;
> **end**
>
> **function** $entropy\_switch(S)$: **real**
> **begin**
> > **return** $(\sum\{-prob(t) \log_2(prob(t)) \mid t \in S\})/C_{switch}$;
> **end**
>
> **function** $entropy\_cond(S)$: **real**
> **begin**
> > let $\langle S_1, c, S_2 \rangle = split(S)$;
> > let $p_1 = \sum\{prob(t) \mid t \in S_1\}$ and $p_2 = \sum\{prob(t) \mid t \in S_2\}$;
> > **return** $-(p_1 \log_2(p_1) + p_2 \log_2(p_2))/C_{branch}$;
> **end**

Figure 1: An Algorithm for Ordering Tests Within an Equivalence Class

important that the weights be normalized before proceeding with the construction: otherwise, in subsequent invocations of *gen_tree* from within *gen_cond*, the computations of weighted entropies may become distorted. Note that the procedure *gen_cond* can introduce tests into the decision tree that are not present in the original source program. Given the treatment of type tests such as `integer/1`, `atom/1`, etc., described in Section 2.1, an esthetically pleasant consequence of this is that a set of type tests on a variable may compile into decision tree tests with non-equality comparisons on type tags, e.g., something like 'if $tag(X) < $ LIST ...'

Example 3.1 The following example illustrates the working of the algorithm of Figure 1. Let the cost of an indirect branch through a jump table be 10 instructions, while that of a test/conditional-branch combination is 2 instructions (these are the assembly instruction counts for `switch` and `if` statements in C on Sparcstations). Consider the predicate `p/1` defined by 100 clauses:

```
p(X)  :- X = 1    | true.
   ...
p(X)  :- X = 100 | true.
```

Suppose that the weights of the clauses, for different values of the argument `X`, are given by the following table (the distribution is somewhat artificial, but it illustrates the algorithm in a simple way and produces a pretty decision tree):

X	weight	normalized wt.
1	520	0.5200
2–49	3	0.0030
50	236	0.2360
51–100	2	0.0020

We first consider the root node of the decision tree. The weighted entropy $\widehat{H}_{jt}$ for a jump table implementation of this node is given by

$$\widehat{H}_{jt} = \tfrac{1}{10}((-0.52\log_2 0.52) + \sum_{i=2}^{49} -0.003\log_2 0.003 + (-0.236\log_2 0.236) + \sum_{i=51}^{100} -0.002\log_2 0.002)$$
$$= 0.308.$$

For a conditional branch implementation, the "split point" that balances the normalized weights best, given the distribution given above, is 2 (i.e., the test generated will be 'X < 2'). The weighted entropy $\widehat{H}_{cb}$ for a conditional branch implementation is given by

$$\widehat{H}_{cb} = \tfrac{1}{2}((-0.52\log_2 0.52) + (-0.48\log_2 0.48)) = 0.499.$$

Since $\widehat{H}_{cb} > \widehat{H}_{jt}$, a conditional branch 'if (X < 2) ...' is used to implement this node.

One of the children of this node is the node 1, which is a leaf node that does not need a decision tree. The other child requires a decision tree for the cases 2–100. For this, the recursive call to the function *gen_tree* results in a renormalization of the relevant weights, which produces the following:

X	weight	normalized wt.
2–49	3	0.0063
50	236	0.4917
51-100	2	0.0042

Computing weighted entropies as above, with the split point for the conditional branch case being at 50, we get $\widehat{H}_{jt} = 0.437$, $\widehat{H}_{cb} = 0.442$. Since $\widehat{H}_{cb} > \widehat{H}_{jt}$, a conditional branch 'if (X < 50) ...' is used to implement this node.

One of the children of this node is for the cases 2–49. Each of these cases has a normalized weight of 0.0208. With the split point for the conditional branch at 25, the weighted entropies are computed as $\widehat{H}_{jt} = 0.558$, $\widehat{H}_{cb} = 0.500$. Since $\widehat{H}_{jt} > \widehat{H}_{cb}$, this subtree is implemented using a jump table.

The other child is for the cases 50–100. On normalization, we have

X	weight	normalized wt.
50	236	0.7024
51-100	2	0.0059

In this case, with the split point for the conditional branch at 51, the weighted entropies are computed as $\widehat{H}_{jt} = 0.254$, $\widehat{H}_{cb} = 0.439$. Since $\widehat{H}_{cb} > \widehat{H}_{jt}$, a conditional branch 'if (X < 51) ...' is used to implement this node.

One child of this node is the leaf node 50, which does not need a decision tree. The other child is for the cases 51–100, for which each test has a normalized weight of 0.02. In this case, with the split point for the conditional branch at 25, the weighted entropies are computed as $\widehat{H}_{jt} = 0.564$, $\widehat{H}_{cb} = 0.500$. Since $\widehat{H}_{jt} > \widehat{H}_{cb}$, this subtree is implemented using a jump table.

The overall decision tree that is produced for this example is shown in Figure 2. The average number of instructions executed for this tree, given the weight distribution and implementation costs assumed above, is 5.78. By comparison, the average cost is 10 instructions if the decision tree is implemented as a single `switch` statement, and between 12 and 14 instructions (depending on the exact structure of the tree) if it is implemented as a binary tree without taking weights into account. (A cursory examination of the tree in Figure 2 suggests that it may be better, given the weight of the leaf labelled 50, to test for this case earlier, e.g., using the test 'X = 50' immediately after the test 'X < 2'. However, a careful examination indicates that the average number of instructions executed for such a tree would be 5.94, which is slightly higher than that of the tree obtained using our algorithm.)

To simplify the discussion in this example, we have ignored the possibility of suspension due to underinstantiated inputs. To deal with suspension, it suffices to add a clause that specifies when suspension should occur:

```
p(X) :- tag(X) = VARIABLE | suspend(...).
```

The weight of such a "suspension clause" will depend on the execution characteristics of the program. For example, if p/1 is almost always called with a non-variable argument, and therefore rarely suspends, then the suspension clause will have a very small weight, and the corresponding node in the decision tree generated using our approach will be fairly deep, i.e., it will be considered towards the end. On the

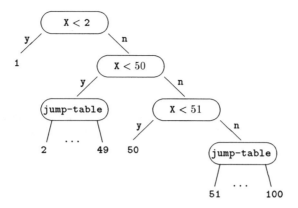

Figure 2: The decision tree produced for Example 3.1

other hand, if p/1 is usually called with a variable argument and has to suspend (as might happen in programs written in an "object-oriented" style), then the suspension clause will have a high weight and its node in the decision tree will be close to the root, i.e., it will be considered early in the execution of the predicate. As far as we can tell, earlier approaches, e.g., those of Kliger and Shapiro [6, 7], generate decision trees that consider suspension in *otherwise* branches, which appear to be considered at the end if none of the non-*otherwise* branches is taken, and therefore do not offer this flexibility. □

3.3 The Non-Mutually Exclusive Case

In this case, at any point there is a *set* of equivalence classes of tests, each of which is "cared about" by some subset of the set of clauses under consideration, rather than a single dominant equivalence class that every clause cares about. Theoretically, the notion of entropies seems less obviously applicable here, because the tests are not mutually exclusive. However, it turns out that we get intuitively reasonable results if we use weights or normalized entropies to order the different equivalence classes, then apply the previous algorithm to the equivalence classes in this order.

4 Performance

In this section, we compare the performance of the entropy based technique described earlier with those of a number of other plausible ways of implementing decision tree for an equivalence class. Our experiments considered an equivalence class consisting of a single multiway branch, which corresponds to several tests on the same group of variables. Our decision tree compiler takes a (switchable) set of tests with weights, together with machine cost parameters, and emits C code for these tests. The results reported are execution times for the code so generated, compiled using **gcc** on a Sparcstation-2: this allows us to examine the relative machine-level costs of different realizations of decision trees without obscuring the results by including time spent in non-decision-tree computations. The results are given in Table 1. The different approaches that we compare with our entropy-based approach are as follows:

If-Then-Else : Here, the n-way branch is implemented as a series of *if-then-else* statements. As a result, the last branch is executed only after $n-1$ tests have been performed. (This is not quite the same as not compiling a decision tree at all, since it is possible, in such a scheme, that tests from different guards are shared.)

Weighted If-Then-Else : Similar to the above, except that the tests are ordered in decreasing order of weight, with the branch with the highest weight tested for first.

Weighted Binary Tree : When the underlying set of values is totally ordered, it is possible to organize a set of tests so that we effectively use a binary search tree. The tests at the leaves of the tree are the tests that appeared originally in the program and the tests on the internal nodes are the ones that are inserted such that the probability of execution of either branch is as equal as can be made, depending on the probability values of the original program branches. Unlike the decision tree compilation schemes suggested in the literature, this scheme can generate (internal node) tests that do not appear in the original program.

Jump Table : The most obvious way of coding an n-way branch is using an indirect jump through a jump table. However, this approach is not suitable for non-equality tests, e.g., **x > 2**.

The benchmarks tested were the following:

1. Lexical Analyzer: In a compiler front-end, a lexical analyzer must examine each character of the input program to determine the lexical structure of the program. This requires a decision tree with an n-way branch, where n is the size of the alphabet. We restricted our alphabet to digits and lower case letters, so that the decision tree had 36 leaves. Letters were given heavier weight than digits (each letter had a weight of 10, and each digit a weight of 1). We used a 2 Mbyte text file as test input for our experiments. The decision tree produced by the entropy-based scheme in this case was a binary tree.

2. Final Code Generator: After all final code generation decisions have been made in the back end of a compiler, it is necessary to actually emit the instructions to create an object file. For this, the compiler must examine the opcode of each instruction (which is typically in some internal representation) to determine the exact bit patterns to emit. Thus, it is necessary to create a decision tree based on the relative (static) frequencies of different opcodes. We used **gcc** to compile itself on a Sparcstation and generate an assembler file, then used the static instruction counts obtained from this to estimate the relative frequency of different opcodes. The decision tree in this case had 53 leaves. The decision tree produced by our entropy-based approach was an indirect jump through a branch table. The time reported is the time taken to process the **gcc** opcodes.

Approach	Lexical Analyser	Code Generator	Byte-Code Interpreter
entropy-based	1.000	1.000	1.000
jump table	1.114	1.000	1.000
binary tree	1.114	1.347	1.470
if-then-else	2.770	1.732	> 5
weighted-if-else	1.033	1.732	2.625

Table 1: Normalized Performance Figures

3. Byte-Code Interpreter: Many programming language implementations use byte code interpreters, where programs are compiled to (a byte-code encoding of) a virtual machine instruction set, which is then interpreted by a machine-level program. Many well-known Prolog implementations follow this approach. Such an interpreter requires a decision tree on byte-code instruction opcodes. While the inner loop of such interpreters is typically implemented as an indirect branch through a jump table, it is not obvious that this is necessarily the best implementation, since this fails to take into account the relative (dynamic) frequencies of different opcodes. For our experiments, we instrumented SB-Prolog to obtain dynamic opcode traces for a number of medium-sized Prolog programs (e.g., **boyer**, the SB-Prolog compiler, the Berkeley PLM compiler, a dataflow analyser for Prolog, etc.), then used the opcode frequencies so obtained to measure the time taken by different decision tree realizations to process the traces so obtained. In this case, the decision tree had 91 leaves, and the particular byte-code encodings used, the dynamic opcode distribution, and the relative machine level costs assumed caused the entropy-based method to generate an indirect branch through a jump table.

5   Conclusions

While decision tree compilation is a promising way to carry out guard tests efficiently, the methods given in the literature do not take into account either the execution characteristics of the program or the machine-level tradeoffs between different ways to implement branches. These methods therefore offer little or no guidance for the implementor with regard to how decision trees are to be realized on a particular machine. In this paper, we describe an approach that takes execution frequencies of different program branches, as well as the costs of alternative branch realizations, to generate decision trees. Experiments indicate that the performance of our approach is uniformly better than that of other plausible alternatives.

Acknowledgements: Comments by Evan Tick and the anonymous referees helped improve the presentation of the paper. The work of the first and third authors was supported in part by the National Science Foundation under grant number CCR-8901283; that of the second author was supported by the National Science Foundation under grant number CCR-9108969.

References

[1] R. B. Ash, *Information Theory*, Dover Publications, NY, 1965.

[2] T. Ball and J. Larus, "Optimally Profiling and Tracing Programs", *Proc. 19th. ACM Symp. on Principles of Programming Languages*, Albuquerque, NM, Jan.

1992, pp. 59–70.

[3] S. K. Debray, "A Remark on Tick's Algorithm for Compile-Time Granularity Analysis", *Logic Programming Newsletter* vol. 3 no. 1, July 1989.

[4] M. R. Garey and D. S. Johnson, *Computers and Intractability: A Guide to the Theory of NP-Completeness*, Freeman, New York, 1979.

[5] M. M. Gorlick and C. F. Kesselman, "Timing Prolog Programs Without Clocks", *Proc. Fourth IEEE Symp. Logic Programming*, San Francisco, CA, Sept. 1987, pp. 426-432. IEEE Press.

[6] S. Kliger and E. Shapiro, "A Decision Tree Compilation Algorithm for FCP(|, : , ?)", *Proc. Fifth Int. Conf. on Logic Programming*, Seattle, Aug. 1988, pp. 1315–1336. MIT Press.

[7] S. Kliger and E. Shapiro, "From Decision Trees to Decision Graphs", *Proc. NACLP-90*, Austin, Oct. 1990, pp. 97–116. MIT Press.

[8] M. Korsloot and E. Tick, "Compilation Techniques for Nondeterminate Flat Concurrent Logic Programming Languages", *Proc. Eighth Int. Conf. on Logic Programming*, Paris, June 1991, pp. 457–471. MIT Press.

[9] S. McFarling, "Program Optimization for Instruction Caches", *Proc. Third Int. Symp. on Architectural Support for Programming Languages and Operating Systems*, pp. 183–191.

[10] K. Pettis and R. C. Hansen, "Profile Guided Code Positioning", *Proc. SIGPLAN-90 Conf. on Programming Language Design and Implementation*, White Plains, NY, June 1990, pp. 16–27.

[11] M. L. Powell, "A Portable Optimizing Compiler for Modula-2", *Proc. SIGPLAN-84 Symp. on Compiler Construction*, Montreal, June 1984, pp. 310–318. SIGPLAN Notices vol. 19 no. 6.

[12] V. Saraswat, K. Kahn, and J. Levy, "Janus: A step towards distributed constraint programming", in *Proc. 1990 North American Conf. on Logic Programming*, Austin, TX, Oct. 1990, pp. 431–446. MIT Press.

[13] E. Shapiro, "The Family of Concurrent Logic Programming Languages", *Computing Surveys*, vol. 21 no. 3, Sept. 1989, pp. 412-510.

[14] E. Shapiro (ed.), *Concurrent Prolog: Collected Papers*, MIT Press, 1987.

[15] S. Taylor, *Parallel Logic Programming Techniques*, Prentice Hall, 1989.

[16] E. Tick, "Compile-time Granularity Analysis for Parallel Logic Programming Languages", *Proc. Int. Conf. on Fifth Generation Computer Systems*, Tokyo, Japan, Nov. 1988, pp. 994-1000.

[17] K. Ueda, "Guarded Horn Clauses", in *Concurrent Prolog: Collected Papers*, vol. 1, ed. E. Shapiro, pp. 140-156, 1987. MIT Press.

[18] D. W. Wall, "Global Register Allocation at Link-time", *Proc. SIGPLAN-86 Conf. on Compiler Construction*, June 1986, pp. 264–275.

[19] D. W. Wall, "Predicting Program Behavior Using Real or Estimated Profiles", *Proc. SIGPLAN-91 Conf. on Programming Language Design and Implementation*, June 1991, pp. 59–70.

Abduction

A Query Evaluation Method for Abductive Logic Programming

Ken Satoh, Noboru Iwayama
Institute for New Generation Computer Technology
1-4-28 Mita, Minato-ku, Tokyo 108, Japan
ksatoh@icot.or.jp, iwayama@icot.or.jp

Abstract

We present a query evaluation method for abduction. In artificial intelligence, abduction has been recognized as an important human reasoning applied in various fields [2]. In logic programming, Eshghi and Kowalski [2] introduce abduction to handle negation as failure and Kakas and Mancarella [4, 5] extend the framework to include any arbitrary abducible predicate.

We have already proposed a correct bottom-up procedure to compute abduction [8]. However, this procedure is not suitable for query evaluation. Although [5] proposes a query evaluation method by extending the procedure in [2], there is a problem of incorrectness in the procedure in [2] and this problem is inherited in the procedure in [5]. Also, their procedure can handle only a limited class of integrity constraints.

The procedure we propose in this paper is correct for any consistent abductive framework. If the procedure succeeds, there is a set of hypotheses which satisfies a query, and if the procedure finitely fails, there is no such set. We guarantee correctness since we adopt a forward evaluation of rules and check consistency of "implicit deletion" [7]. Thanks to the forward evaluation of rules, we can also handle any form of integrity constraints.

1 Introduction

In this paper, we present a query evaluation method for abduction in logic programming. Researchers in artificial intelligence have recently recognized that abduction plays an important role in various applications such as diagnosis, planning and design (for example, see [2]).

Eshghi and Kowalski [2] are the first to consider abduction based on stable model semantics [3] in logic programming. They show the relationship between negation as failure and abduction. And they provide a proof procedure to compute negation as failure through abduction for a call-consistent logic program.

This work has been extended intensively by Kakas and Mancarella [4]. They show the relationship of abductive logic programming with autoepstemic logic, assumption-based truth maintenance system and updates, and also they extend Eshghi and Kowalski's procedure to manipulate arbitrary abducibles [5].

In [8], we also give a bottom-up method of computing a generalized stable model [4] which is a basis of abduction defined by Kakas and Mancarella. Although this method is correct for any general logic program with integrity constraints, it is not goal-directed; that is, even if a goal is given, we might explore some irrelevant parts to a query. Eshghi and Kowalski's top-down procedure [2] solves this problem of irrelevant computation to a query. However, their procedure has a problem of incorrectness for some non-call-consistent programs [2, p.251]. This problem is inherited in the procedure of [5].

Here, we provide a query evaluation method that is correct for every consistent abductive framework [1]. If our procedure answers "yes", then there is a set of hypotheses which satisfies a query. If our procedure answers "no", then there is no set of hypotheses which satisfies a query.

Our procedure can be regarded as an extension of Kakas and Mancarella's procedure [5] in the following two points.

Forward evaluation of rules:
It is important to use integrity constraints to exclude undesirable results from abduction. However, their procedure manipulates a class of integrity constraints in which there is at least one abducible predicate in each integrity constraint.

For example, their procedure cannot handle the following program with an abducible predicate $normal\_bird^\dagger$ [2].

$$fly(X) \leftarrow bird(X), normal\_bird^\dagger(X) \tag{1}$$
$$bird(tweety) \leftarrow \tag{2}$$
$$non\_fly(tweety) \leftarrow \tag{3}$$
$$\perp \leftarrow fly(X), non\_fly(X) \tag{4}$$

$fly(tweety)$ seems to be derived with an assumption $normal\_bird^\dagger(tweety)$ from (1). However, deriving $fly(tweety)$ leads to contradiction by an instance of (4):

$$\perp \leftarrow fly(tweety), non\_fly(tweety).$$

Therefore, $fly(tweety)$ cannot be derived.

This example shows that we need another method to detect contradiction. In our procedure, we use a forward evaluation of rules so that we can check any form of integrity constraints. In the example above, we first derive $fly(tweety)$ from (1), then check the integrity constraint

---

[1] Consistency of an abductive framework means that there is a generalized stable model for the framework.

[2] Upper-case letters, lower-case letters and $\perp$ express variables, constants and inconsistency, respectively.

$\bot \leftarrow non\_fly(tweety)$ with a forward evaluation of (4) and find contradiction.

Check for Implicit Deletions:

We check consistency for "implicit deletions" first observed by Sadri and Kowalski [7]. For example, consider the following program with an abducible predicate $normal\_barber^\dagger$ [3].

$$
\begin{align}
&man(noel) \leftarrow &(1)\\
&barber(noel) \leftarrow &(2)\\
&shaves(noel, X) \leftarrow man(X), \sim shaves(X, X) &(3)\\
&shaves(X, X) \leftarrow barber(X), normal\_barber^\dagger(X) &(4)\\
&shaves(casanova, X) \leftarrow barber(X), \sim normal\_barber^\dagger(X) &(5)
\end{align}
$$

$shaves(casanova, noel)$ seems to be derived with an assumption $\sim normal\_barber^\dagger(noel)$. However, if we assume it, an instance of (4):

$$shaves(noel, noel) \leftarrow barber(noel), normal\_barber^\dagger(noel)$$

is implicitly deleted since its body becomes false. Therefore, contradiction occurs from the instance of (3):

$$shaves(noel, noel) \leftarrow man(noel), \sim shaves(noel, noel).$$

Consequently, $shaves(casanova, noel)$ cannot be derived.

This example shows that we must consider the integrity of rules deleted by the hypothesis. However, the proposed methods [2, 4] do not check consistency of implicit deletion. We believe that this lack of check is a major culprit of incorrectness in these methods. Inversely, we check the implicit deletion in our procedure. So, we can show that if we assume $\sim normal\_barber^\dagger(noel)$, neither $shaves(noel, noel)$ nor $\sim shaves(noel, noel)$ can be consistently derived in the example above.

Also, our procedure is important in the following respects.

1. If we do not consider abducible predicates, then our method can be used for query evaluation of every consistent general logic program with integrity constraints based on stable model semantics.

2. Our procedure adopts integrity checking for addition of a rule by accumulating hypotheses. In some cases, it avoids infinite loops which occur in other methods of integrity checking such as [7].

The structure of the paper is as follows. Firstly, we review the definitions of an abductive framework. Then, we show the procedure for query evaluation of an abductive framework and give some examples. Finally, we compare our method with related researches. For proofs of the theorems, see [9].

---

[3] $\sim$ expresses negation as failure.

2 A Semantics of Abductive Framework

We mainly follow the definition of abductive framework in [4], but we modify it slightly for notational conveniences. Firstly, we define a rule and an integrity constraint.

Definition 2.1 *Let H be an atom, and $L_1, ..., L_m (m \geq 0)$ be literals each of which is an atom or a negated atom of the form $\sim B$. A rule is of the form:*

$$H \leftarrow L_1, L_2, ..., L_m.$$

We call H the *head* of the rule and $L_1, ..., L_m$ the *body* of the rule. Let R be a rule. $head(R)$, $body(R)$ and $pos(R)$ denote the head of R, the set of literals in the body of R and the set of positive literals in $body(R)$ respectively.

Definition 2.2 *Let $L_1, ..., L_m (m \geq 0)$ be literals. An integrity constraint is of the form:*

$$\perp \leftarrow L_1, L_2, ..., L_m \ ^4.$$

We write integrity constraints as the above form so that we do not have to distinguish integrity constraints and rules. So, from this point, we do not distinguish rules and integrity constraints.

Moreover, we impose that rules in a program must be *range-restricted*, that is, any variable in a rule R must occur in $pos(R)$. However, [1] pointed out that any rule can be translated into range-restricted form by inserting a new predicate "*dom*" describing Herbrand universe for every non-range-restricted variables in the rule.

For a given program (with integrity constraints), we define a stable model as follows.

Definition 2.3 *Let T be a logic program and Π_T be a set of ground rules obtained by replacing all variables in each rule in T by every element of its Herbrand universe. Let M be a set of ground atoms from Π_T and Π_T^M be the following (possibly infinite) program.*

$$\Pi_T^M = \{H \leftarrow B_1, ..., B_k | \ H \leftarrow B_1, ..., B_k, \sim A_1, ..., \sim A_m \in \Pi_T$$
$$and \ A_i \notin M \ for \ each \ i = 1, ..., m.\}$$

Let $min(\Pi_T^M)$ be the least model of Π_T^M. A stable model for a logic program T is M iff $M = min(\Pi_T^M)$ and $\perp \notin M$.

This definition gives a stable model of T which satisfies all integrity constraints. We say that T is *consistent* if there exists a stable model for T.

For a query evaluation procedure, it is better to limit ground instances which should be considered. For example, consider the following program.

---

[4] Although we only consider the above form of integrity constraints (denials) in this paper, there is a transformation from a more general form of integrity constraints to denials as shown in [7].

$$p(1,2) \leftarrow p(2,1) \tag{1}$$
$$p(2,1) \leftarrow \sim q(2) \tag{2}$$
$$q(X) \leftarrow p(X,Y), \sim q(Y) \tag{3}$$
$$r(f(1)) \leftarrow \tag{4}$$

From the above definition, we have to consider infinite ground rules for (3) because of the function symbol f in (4). However, it is clear that there is no possibility to make any instances for $p(X,Y)$ other than $p(1,2)$ and $p(2,1)$ to be true, and so, all we have to consider are actually the following two ground rules.

$$q(1) \leftarrow p(1,2), \sim q(2) \tag{3.1}$$
$$q(2) \leftarrow p(2,1), \sim q(1) \tag{3.2}$$

We formalize this phenomenon as follows.

Definition 2.4 *Let T be a logic program and T^- be a negation-removed program obtained by removing all integrity constraints in T and all the negative literals in the body of remaining rule and $min(T^-)$ be the least minimal model of T^-. We define a relevant ground program Ω_T for T as follows:*

$$\Omega_T = \{H \leftarrow B_1, ..., B_k, \sim A_1, ..., \sim A_m \in \Pi_T | B_i \in min(T^-) \text{ for each } i = 1, ..., k.\}$$

Proposition 2.5 *Let T be a logic program. A set of stable models for T is equal to a set of stable models for Ω_T.*

The above proposition actually holds for any logic program, but if we impose a program to be range-restricted, we can construct Ω_T directly from T^- without considering instantiation of variables with every elements in Herbrand Universe.

Example 2.6 *Let T be the above program (1), (2), (3) and (4).*
Then, $min(T^-)$ is $\{p(1,2), p(2,1), q(1), q(2), r(f(1))\}$ and so, Ω_T becomes (1), (2), (3.1), (3.2) and (4).
Ω_T has only one stable model which is equal to the unique stable model for T, that is, $\{p(1,2), p(2,1), q(1), r(f(1))\}$.

Now, we define an *abductive framework*.

Definition 2.7 *An abductive framework is a pair $\langle T, A \rangle$ where A is a set of predicate symbols, called abducible predicates and T is a set of rules each of whose head is not in A.*

We call a set of all ground atoms for predicates in A *abducibles*. As pointed out in [4], we can translate a program which includes a definition of abducibles to an equivalent framework that satisfies the above requirement. Moreover, we impose an abductive framework to be range-restricted, that is, any variable in a rule of a program must occur in non-abducible positive literals of the rule.

Now, we define a semantics of an abductive framework.

Definition 2.8 *Let* $\langle T, A \rangle$ *be an abductive framework and* Θ *be a set of abducibles. A generalized stable model* $M(\Theta)$ *is a stable model of* $T \cup \{H \leftarrow |H \in \Theta\}$.

We say that $\langle T, A \rangle$ is *consistent* if there exists a generalized stable model $M(\Theta)$ for some Θ. The similar proposition to Proposition 2.5 holds for an abductive framework.

Proposition 2.9 *Let* $\langle T, A \rangle$ *be a logic program and* T^- *be an abducible-and-negation-removed program obtained by removing all negative literals and abducibles in the body of each rule in a program* T. *We define a relevant ground program* Ω_T *for* $\langle T, A \rangle$ *as follows:*
$$\Omega_T = \{H \leftarrow B_1, ..., B_k, C_1, ..., C_l, \sim A_1, ..., \sim A_m \in \Pi_T|$$
$$B_i \in min(T^-) \text{ for each } i = 1, ..., k \text{ and } C_1, ..., C_l \text{ are abducibles.}\}$$
Then, a set of generalized stable models for $\langle T, A \rangle$ *is equal to a set of generalized stable models for* $\langle \Omega_T, A \rangle$.

3   Query Evaluation for Abduction

Before showing our query evaluation method, we need the following definitions. Let l be a literal. Then, $\bar{l}$ denotes the complement of l.

Definition 3.1 *Let* T *be a logic program. A set of resolvents w.r.t. a ground literal* l *and* T, $resolve(l, T)$ *is the following set of rules:*

$resolve(l, T) =$
$\quad \{(\perp \leftarrow L_1, ..., L_k)\theta| \; l \text{ is negative and}$
$\qquad\qquad H \leftarrow L_1, ..., L_k \in T \text{ and } \bar{l} = H\theta \text{ by a ground substitution } \theta\} \cup$
$\quad \{(H \leftarrow L_1, ..., L_{i-1}, L_{i+1}, ..., L_k)\theta|$
$\qquad\qquad H \leftarrow L_1, ..., L_k \in T \text{ and } l = L_i\theta \text{ by a ground substitution } \theta\}$

The first set of resolvents are for negation as failure and the second set of resolvents corresponds with "forward" evaluation of the rule introduced in [7].

Example 3.2 *Consider the following program* T.

$$p(1, 2) \leftarrow p(2, 1) \qquad\qquad\qquad\qquad\qquad\qquad\qquad\qquad (1)$$
$$p(2, 1) \leftarrow \sim q(2) \qquad\qquad\qquad\qquad\qquad\qquad\qquad\qquad (2)$$
$$q(X) \leftarrow p(X, Y), \sim q(Y) \qquad\qquad\qquad\qquad\qquad\qquad\quad (3)$$

Then, $resolve(\sim q(2), T)$ is a set of the following rules:

$p(2, 1) \leftarrow$ *with the literal in the body of (2)*
$\perp \leftarrow p(2, Y), \sim q(Y)$ *with the head of (3)*
$q(X) \leftarrow p(X, 2)$ *with the second literal in the body of (3)*

Definition 3.3 *Let T be a logic program. A set of deleted rules w.r.t. a ground literal l and T, $del(l, T)$, is the following set of rules:*

$$del(l, T) = \{(H \leftarrow L_1, ..., L_k)\theta|$$
$$H \leftarrow L_1, ..., L_k \in T \text{ and } \bar{l} = L_i\theta \text{ by a ground substitution } \theta\}$$

Example 3.4 *Consider the program T in Example 3.2. Then, $del(q(2), T)$ is a set of the following rules:*

$$p(2, 1) \leftarrow \sim q(2) \qquad \qquad \text{from (2)}$$
$$q(X) \leftarrow p(X, 2), \sim q(2) \qquad \qquad \text{from (3)}$$

Our query evaluation procedure consists of 4 subprocedures, $derive(p, \Delta)$, $literal\_con(l, \Delta)$, $rule\_con(R, \Delta)$ and $deleted\_con(R, \Delta)$ where p is a non-abducible atom and Δ is a set of ground literals already assumed and l is a ground literal and R is a rule.

$derive(p, \Delta)$ returns a ground substitution for the variables in p and a set of ground literals. This set of ground literals is a union of Δ and literals newly assumed during execution of the subprocedure. Other subprocedures return a set of ground literals.

The subprocedures have a **select** operation and a **fail** operation. The **select** operation expresses a nondeterministic choice among alternatives. The **fail** operation expresses immediate termination of an execution with failure. Therefore, a subprocedure succeeds when its inner calls of subprocedures do not encounter **fail**. We say *a subprocedure succeeds with (θ and) Δ* when the subprocedure successfully returns (θ and) Δ.

The informal specification of the 4 subprocedures is as follows.

1. $derive(p, \Delta)$ searches a rule R of p in a program T whose body can be made true with a ground substitution θ under a set of assumptions Δ. To show that every literal in the body can be made true, we call *derive* for non-abducible positive literals in the body. Then, we check the consistency of other literals in the body with T and Δ. Note that because of the range-restrictedness, other literals in R become ground after all the calls of *derive* for non-abducible positive literals.

2. $literal\_con(l, \Delta)$ checks the consistency of a ground literal l with T and Δ. To show the consistency for assuming l, we add l to Δ; then, we check the consistency of resolvents and deleted rules w.r.t. l and T.

3. $rule\_con(R, \Delta)$ checks the consistency of a rule R with T and Δ. If R is not ground, we must check the consistency for ground instances of R. But by Proposition 2.9, it is sufficient to consider every ground instance $R\theta$ in $\Omega_{T \cup \{R\}}$. We can prove the consistency by showing that either a literal in $body(R\theta)$ can be falsified or $body(R\theta)$ can be made true and $head(R\theta)$ consistent.

This procedure can also be used to check integrity for rule addition.

4. $deleted\_con(R, \Delta)$ checks if a deletion of R does not cause any contradictions with T and Δ. To show the consistency of the implicit deletion of R, it is sufficient to prove that the head of every ground instance $R\theta$ in Ω_T [5] can be made either true or false.

Thanks to the range-restrictedness, we can compute all ground instances of a rule R (if they are finite) in Ω_T (or $\Omega_{T \cup \{R\}}$). For this, we compute every SLD derivation of a query which consists of all non-abducible positive literals in $body(R)$ to the abducible-and-negation-removed program T^- (or $(T \cup \{R\})^-$).

Example 3.5 *Consider T and the second resolvent of $resolve(\sim q(2), T)$ in Example 3.2. Let R be the second resolvent and T_1 be $T \cup \{R\}$. In order to obtain possible ground instances of R in Ω_{T_1}, we compute every SLD derivation of a query $? - p(2, Y)$ to the program T_1^-. Then, since only the returned substitution from SLD derivation is $\{Y/1\}$, we have the following ground instance in Ω_{T_1} for R:*

$$\bot \leftarrow p(2, 1), \sim q(1)$$

Now, we describe in detail the subprocedures in Figure 1 and Figure 2. In Figure 1, ε denotes empty substitution and $\theta_i \sigma_i$ expresses a composition of two substitutions θ_i and σ_i. Also, we denote a set of non-abducible positive literals, non-abducible negative literals, and abducibles (either negative or positive) in a rule R as $pos(R)$, $neg(R)$ and $abd(R)$.

If we remove $deleted\_con$ and do not consider resolvents obtained with "forward" evaluation of the rule, then this procedure coincides with that of Kakas and Mancarella [4]. That is, our procedure is obtained by augmenting their procedure with an integrity constraint checking in a bottom-up manner and with an implicit deletion checking.

We can show the following theorems for correctness of successful derivation and finite failure.

Theorem 3.6 *Let $\langle T, A \rangle$ be a consistent abductive framework. Suppose $derive(p, \{\})$ succeeds with (θ, Δ). Then, there exists a generalized stable model $M(\Theta)$ for T such that Θ includes all positive abducibles in Δ and $M(\Theta) \models p\theta$.*

This theorem means that if the procedure $derive(p, \{\})$ answers "yes" with (θ, Δ), then there is a generalized stable model which satisfies $p\theta$. However, we cannot say in general that we make $p\theta$ true only with positive abducibles in Δ, because there might be some hypotheses which are irrelevant to a query but which we must assume to get consistency.

The following is a theorem related to correctness for finite failure.

---

[5] Note that $\Omega_{T \cup \{R\}} = \Omega_T$ since R is an instance of a rule in T.

$derive(p, \Delta)$ p: a non-abducible atom; Δ: a set of literals
begin
  if p is ground and $p \in \Delta$ **then return** (ε, Δ)
  elseif p is ground and $\sim p \in \Delta$ **then fail**
  else
  begin
    select $R \in T$ s.t. $head(R)$ and p are unifiable with an mgu θ
    if such a rule is not found **then fail**
    $\Delta_0 := \Delta$, $\theta_0 := \theta$, $B_0 := pos(R\theta)$, $i := 0$
    while $B_i \neq \{\}$ **do**
    begin
      take a literal l in B_i
      if $derive(l, \Delta_i)$ succeeds with (σ_i, Δ_{i+1})
        then $\theta_{i+1} := \theta_i \sigma_i$, $B_{i+1} := (B_i - \{l\})\sigma_i$, $i := i + 1$ and **continue**
    end
    $\delta := \theta_i$
    for every $l \in neg(R\delta) \cup abd(R\delta)$ **do**
    begin
      if $literal\_con(l, \Delta_i)$ succeeds with Δ_{i+1}
        then $i := i + 1$ and **continue**
    end
    if $literal\_con(p\delta, \Delta_i)$ succeeds with Δ' **then return** (δ, Δ')
  end
end $(derive)$

$literal\_con(l, \Delta)$ l: a ground literal; Δ: a set of literals
begin
  if $l \in \Delta$ **then return** Δ
  elseif $l = \bot$ or $\bar{l} \in \Delta$ **then fail**
  else
  begin
    $\Delta_0 := \{l\} \cup \Delta$, $i := 0$
    for every $R \in resolve(l, T)$ **do**
      if $rule\_con(R, \Delta_i)$ succeeds with Δ_{i+1}
        then $i := i + 1$ and **continue**
    for every $R \in del(l, T)$ **do**
      if $deleted\_con(R, \Delta_i)$ succeeds with Δ_{i+1}
        then $i := i + 1$ and **continue**
  end
  return Δ_i
end $(literal\_con)$

Figure 1: The definition of $derive$ and $literal\_con$

$rule\_con(R, \Delta)$ R: a rule; Δ: a set of literals
begin
   $\Delta_0 := \Delta$, $i := 0$
   for every ground rule $R\theta \in \Omega_{T \cup \{R\}}$ **do**
   begin
     select (a) or (b)
     (a) **select** $l \in body(R\theta)$
       if $l \in pos(R\theta) \cup abd(R\theta)$ and $literal\_con(\bar{l}, \Delta_i)$ succeeds with Δ_{i+1}
         then $i := i + 1$ and **continue**
       elseif $l \in neg(R\theta)$ and $derive(\bar{l}, \Delta)$ succeeds with $(\varepsilon, \Delta_{i+1})$
         then $i := i + 1$ and **continue**
     (b) $\Delta_i^0 := \Delta_i$, $j := 0$
       for every $l \in body(R\theta)$ **do**
       begin
         if $l \in pos(R\theta)$
           and $derive(l, \Delta_i^j)$ succeeds with $(\varepsilon, \Delta_i^{j+1})$
           then $j := j + 1$ and **continue**
         elseif $l \in neg(R\theta) \cup abd(R\theta)$
           and $literal\_con(l, \Delta_i^j)$ succeeds with Δ_i^{j+1}
           then $j := j + 1$ and **continue**
       end
       if $literal\_con(head(R\theta), \Delta_i^j)$ succeeds with Δ_{i+1}
         then $i := i + 1$ and **continue**
   end
   return Δ_i
end $(rule\_con)$

$deleted\_con(R, \Delta)$ R: a rule; Δ: a set of literals
begin
   $\Delta_0 := \Delta$, $i := 0$
   for every ground rule $R\theta \in \Omega_T$ **do**
   begin
     select (a) or (b)
     (a) **if** $derive(head(R\theta), \Delta_i)$ succeeds with $(\varepsilon, \Delta_{i+1})$
       then $i := i + 1$ and **continue**
     (b) **if** $literal\_con(\sim head(R\theta), \Delta_i)$ succeeds with Δ_{i+1}
       then $i := i + 1$ and **continue**
   end
   return Δ_i
end $(deleted\_con)$

Figure 2: The definition of $rule\_con$ and $deleted\_con$

Theorem 3.7 *Let* $\langle T, A \rangle$ *be an abductive framework. Suppose that every selection of rules terminates for* $derive(p, \{\})$ *with either success or failure. If there exists a generalized stable model* $M(\Theta)$ *for* $\langle T, A \rangle$ *and a ground substitution* θ *such that* $M(\Theta) \models p\theta$, *then there is a selection of rules such that* $derive(p, \{\})$ *succeeds with* (θ, Δ) *where* Θ *includes all positive abducibles in* Δ.

This theorem means that if we can search exhaustively in selecting the rules and there is a generalized stable model which satisfies a query, then the procedure always answers "yes".

With this theorem, we obtain the following corollary for a finite failure.

Corollary 3.8 *Let* $\langle T, A \rangle$ *be an abductive framework. If* $derive(p, \{\})$ *fails, then for every generalized stable model* $M(\Theta)$ *for* $\langle T, A \rangle$ *and for every ground substitution* θ, $M(\Theta) \not\models p\theta$.

When the procedure $derive(p, \{\})$ answers "no", there is no generalized stable model which satisfies the query. Also, this corollary means that we can use a finite failure to check if the negation of a ground literal is true in all generalized stable models since finite failure of $derive(p, \{\})$ means that every generalized stable model satisfies $\sim p$.

4 Examples

Example 4.1 *Consider the program* T *in Example 3.2 and an abductive framework* $\langle T, \emptyset \rangle$. *Then, Figure 3 shows a sequence of calling procedures obtained for* $derive(q(V), \{\})$.

In Figure 3, we firstly search a rule whose head is unifiable with $q(V)$ (Step 2) and try to make the body of the rule to be true (Step 3~20). There are two literals in the body, $p(V, Y_1)$ and $\sim q(Y_1)$. We find a ground substitution for $p(V, Y_1)$ (Step 3~19) and then show consistency of $\sim q(2)$ (Step 20).

While finding a substitution for the first literal $p(V, Y_1)$, we check consistency of $\sim q(2)$ (Step 7~17). To show its consistency, we check three resolvents for $\sim q(2)$ shown in Example 3.2 (Step 8, 16 and 17).

During the check for the first resolvent, we check implicit deletion of an instance of rule (3) deleted by $q(1)$ (Step 14) in order to show consistency of $q(1)$ (Step 13). In this case, we have a non-ground deleted rule and so, we compute every ground instance in a relevant ground program. There is only one such ground rule $(q(2) \leftarrow p(2, 1), \sim q(1))$ and since $\sim q(2)$ has been already assumed, Step 14 succeeds.

Similarly, at Step 16 and 17, we have non-ground rules and so, we compute ground instances in a relevant ground program. Such instances are $(\perp \leftarrow p(2, 1), \sim q(1))$ for Step 16 and $(q(1) \leftarrow p(1, 2))$ for Step 17. Both steps succeed since $q(1)$ and $p(1, 2)$ has been already assumed.

$$derive(q(V), \{\})$$ 1

   select $q(V) \leftarrow p(V, Y_1), \sim q(Y_1)$ 2

    $derive(p(V, Y_1), \{\})$ 3

     select $p(1, 2) \leftarrow p(2, 1)$ 4

      $derive(p(2, 1), \{\})$ 5

       select $p(2, 1) \leftarrow \sim q(2)$ 6

       $lit\_con(\sim q(2), \{\})$ 7

        $rule\_con((p(2, 1) \leftarrow), \{\sim q(2)\})$ 8

        $lit\_con(p(2, 1), \{\sim q(2)\})$ 9

         $rule\_con((p(1, 2) \leftarrow), \{p(2, 1), \sim q(2)\})$ 10

         $lit\_con(p(1, 2), \{p(2, 1), \sim q(2)\})$ 11

          $rule\_con((q(1) \leftarrow \sim q(2)), \{p(1, 2), p(2, 1), \sim q(2)\})$ 12

          $lit\_con(q(1), \{p(1, 2), p(2, 1), \sim q(2)\})$ 13

           $del\_con((q(X_2) \leftarrow p(X_2, 1), \sim q(1)),$

                $\{q(1), p(1, 2), p(2, 1), \sim q(2)\})$ 14

         $rule\_con((q(2) \leftarrow \sim q(1)), \{q(1), p(1, 2), p(2, 1), \sim q(2)\})$ 15

       $rule\_con((\bot \leftarrow p(2, Y_3), \sim q(Y_3)), \{q(1), p(1, 2), p(2, 1), \sim q(2)\})$ 16

       $rule\_con((q(X_4) \leftarrow p(X_4, 2)), \{q(1), p(1, 2), p(2, 1), \sim q(2)\})$ 17

      $lit\_con(p(2, 1), \{q(1), p(1, 2), p(2, 1), \sim q(2)\})$ 18

     $lit\_con(p(1, 2), \{q(1), p(1, 2), p(2, 1), \sim q(2)\})$ 19

   $lit\_con(\sim q(2), \{q(1), p(1, 2), p(2, 1), \sim q(2)\})$ 20

  $lit\_con(q(1), \{q(1), p(1, 2), p(2, 1), \sim q(2)\})$ 21

ANSWER

$V = 1$ under $\{q(1), p(1, 2), p(2, 1), \sim q(2)\}$

Figure 3: Calling Sequence for $derive(q(V), \{\})$

Finally, we check consistency of $q(1)$ (Step 21) and get a ground substitution of $\{V/1\}$ for $q(V)$.

Example 4.2 *Consider the following program T and an abductive framework $\langle T, \{normal\_bird^\dagger\}\rangle$.*

$fly(X) \leftarrow bird(X), normal\_bird^\dagger(X)$ (1)

$bird(tweety) \leftarrow$ (2)

$non\_fly(tweety) \leftarrow$ (3)

$\bot \leftarrow fly(X), non\_fly(X)$ (4)

Then, Figure 4 shows a sequence of calling procedures obtained for $derive(fly(tweety), \{\})$ by left-most depth-first search [6].

In Figure 4, we firstly try to search the rule for $f(t)$ and find the rule (1) (Step 2) and try to make the body true. Then, we check consistency for one of the literal $b(t)$ in the body (Step 5~15) and assume $\sim nb^\dagger(t)$ at Step

---

[6]In Figure 4, f, b, $nb^\dagger$, nf and t mean fly, $bird$, $normal\_bird^\dagger$, non_fly and $tweety$ respectively.

$derive(f(t), \{\})$ 1

   select $f(t) \leftarrow b(t), nb^\dagger(t)$ 2

    $derive(b(t), \{\})$ 3

     select $b(t) \leftarrow$ 4

     $lit\_con(b(t), \{\})$ 5

      $rule\_con((f(t) \leftarrow nb^\dagger(t)), \{b(t)\})$ 6

     $lit\_con(\sim nb^\dagger(t), \{b(t)\})$ 7

      $del\_con((f(t) \leftarrow b(t), nb^\dagger(t)), \{\sim nb^\dagger(t), b(t)\})$ 8

      $derive(f(t), \{\sim nb^\dagger(t), b(t)\})$ 9

      select $f(t) \leftarrow b(t), nb^\dagger(t)$ 10

       $derive(b(t), \{\sim nb^\dagger(t), b(t)\})$ 11

       $lit\_con(nb^\dagger(t), \{\sim nb^\dagger(t), b(t)\}) \Longrightarrow$ **fail** (back to 8)   12

      $lit\_con(\sim f(t), \{\sim nb^\dagger(t), b(t)\})$ 13

       $rule\_con((\perp \leftarrow b(t), nb^\dagger(t)), \{\sim f(t), \sim nb^\dagger(t), b(t)\})$ 14

       $del\_con((\perp \leftarrow f(t), nf(t)), \{\sim f(t), \sim nb^\dagger(t), b(t)\})$ 15

    $lit\_con(nb^\dagger(t), \{\sim f(t), \sim nb^\dagger(t), b(t)\}) \Longrightarrow$ **fail** (back to 6)   16

     $lit\_con(nb^\dagger(t), \{b(t)\})$ 17

      $rule\_con((f(t) \leftarrow b(t)), \{nb^\dagger(t), b(t)\})$ 18

     $lit\_con(f(t), \{nb^\dagger(t), b(t)\})$ 19

      $rule\_con((\perp \leftarrow nf(t)), \{f(t), nb^\dagger(t), b(t)\})$ 20

     $lit\_con(\sim nf(t), \{f(t), nb^\dagger(t), b(t)\})$ 21

      $rule\_con((\perp \leftarrow),$

       $\{\sim nf(t), f(t), nb^\dagger(t), b(t)\}) \Longrightarrow$ **fail**(back to 20)   22

     $derive(nf(t), \{f(t), nb^\dagger(t), b(t)\})$ 23

     select $nf(t) \leftarrow$ 24

     $lit\_con(nf(t), \{f(t), nb^\dagger(t), b(t)\})$ 25

      $rule\_con((\perp \leftarrow f(t)),$

       $\{nf(t), f(t), nb^\dagger(t), b(t)\}) \Longrightarrow$ **fail**   26

Figure 4: Calling Sequence for $derive(fly(tweety), \{\})$

7. After showing consistency of $\sim nb^\dagger(t)$ (Step 7~15), we try to make the other literal $nb^\dagger(t)$ in the body of the selected rule at Step 2, but we fail (Step 16). Then, we backtrack and assume $nb^\dagger(t)$ instead (Step 17). Since $nb^\dagger$ is an abducible predicate, it is sufficient to show consistency of $nb^\dagger(t)$. However, to show its consistency, we must show consistency of $f(t)$ (Step 19). Unfortunately, contradiction occurs by the integrity constraint (4) (Step 20~26) and therefore, we cannot conclude $f(t)$.

5 Related Work

5.1 The procedure of Kakas and Mancarella

As stated in Section 3, if we do not check the consistency for implicit deletion and we do not consider the "forward" evaluation of rules, our procedure is identical to that of Kakas and Mancarella [5]. Although "forward" evaluation of rules is used mainly to forward-check the integrity constraint, it is also necessary for implicit deletion check. This is because a rule might be deleted by both an assumed literal itself; and also by other literals derived from the assumed literal. Therefore, the whole procedure is necessary for consistency checking of an abductive framework; and also of a general logic program even *without* integrity constraints.

5.2 Integrity check method of Sadri and Kowalski

Sadri and Kowalski [7] propose an integrity check method by augmenting the SLDNF procedure with "forward" evaluation of rules and consistency check for implicit deletion. Although we use also the same techniques, our method differs from theirs in accumulating hypotheses during integrity check. The technique of hypothesis accumulation enables us to prove the consistency for addition of rules for a wider class of logic programs more than with their method. For example, consider the following program:

$$p \leftarrow \sim q \qquad (1)$$
$$q \leftarrow \sim p \qquad (2)$$

To check the consistency for addition of p, they invoke a query $\leftarrow p$ and see if it finitely fails. However, their procedure enters an infinite loop, whereas $rule\_con((p \leftarrow), \{\})$ of our procedure succeeds in showing the consistency for addition because of the accumulation of hypotheses.

Moreover, their method guarantees consistency for addition of a rule not for every general logic program, but for a limited class of logic programs which contain no negative literals in the body of each rule. On the other hand, if $rule\_con(R, \{\})$ succeeds, we can guarantee that R is consistent with the current program even if it contains negative literals in its body.

5.3 Poole's Theorist

Poole [6] develops a default and abductive reasoning system called *Theorist*. Our method differs from *Theorist* in the following points.

1. The basic language for *Theorist* is a first-order language whereas we use a logic program. So, in *Theorist*, a contrapositive inference must be considered, while in our setting, it is not necessary. Instead of that, however, we must consider the consistency checking of implicit deletion.

2. Assumptions in *Theorist* correspond with normal defaults without prerequisites in Default Logic, whereas in our setting, rules in a logic program can be regarded as arbitrary defaults. So, our procedure deals with a default theory with only arbitrary default rules and no proper axioms.

6   Conclusion

In this paper, we propose a query evaluation method for an abductive framework. Our procedure can be regarded as an extension of the procedure of Kakas and Mancarella by adding forward evaluation of rules and consistency check for implicit deletion.

We think that we need to investigate the following research in the future.

1. In our method, a literal l for $literal\_con(l, \Delta)$ must be ground. This restriction imposes a program to be range-restricted. However, if we can manipulate non-ground hypotheses, range-restrictedness is no longer necessary. Therefore, we would like to investigate a direct treatment of non-ground hypotheses.

2. We should investigate the computational complexity of our procedure and compare it with our bottom-up procedure for abduction [8].

Acknowledgments

We thank Katsumi Inoue from ICOT, Bob Kowalski from Imperial College, Tony Kakas from University of Cyprus, Phan Minh Dung from AIT, Chris Preist from HP Labs. and anonymous referees for instructive comments.

References

[1] Manthey, R., Bry, F., SATCHMO: A Theorem Prover Implemented in Prolog, *Proc. of CADE'88*, pp. 415 – 434 (1988).

[2] Eshghi, K., Kowalski, R. A., Abduction Compared with Negation by Failure, *Proc. of ICLP'89*, pp. 234 – 254 (1989).

[3] Gelfond, M., Lifschitz, V., The Stable Model Semantics for Logic Programming, *Proc. of LP'88*, pp. 1070 – 1080 (1988).

[4] Kakas, A. C., Mancarella, P., Generalized Stable Models: A Semantics for Abduction, *Proc. of ECAI'90*, pp. 385 – 391 (1990).

[5] Kakas, A. C., Mancarella, P., On the Relation between Truth Maintenance and Abduction, *Proc. of PRICAI'90*, pp. 438 – 443 (1990).

[6] Poole, D., Compiling a Default Reasoning System into Prolog, *New Generation Computing*, Vol. 9, No. 1, pp. 3 – 38 (1991).

[7] Sadri, F., Kowalski, R., A Theorem-Proving Approach to Database Integrity, *Foundations of Deductive Database and Logic Programming*, (J. Minker, Ed.), Morgan Kaufmann Publishers, pp. 313 – 362 (1988).

[8] Satoh, K., Iwayama, N., Computing Abduction Using the TMS, *Proc. of ICLP'91*, pp. 505 – 518 (1991).

[9] Satoh, K., Iwayama, N., A Query Evaluation Method for Abductive Logic Programming ICOT Technical Report, ICOT(1992).

SLDNFA: an abductive procedure for normal abductive programs

Marc Denecker and Danny De Schreye
Department of Computer Science, K.U.Leuven,
Celestijnenlaan 200A, B-3001 Heverlee, Belgium
e-mail : {marcd, dannyd}@cs.kuleuven.ac.be

Abstract

A family of extensions of SLDNF-resolution for normal abductive programs is presented. The main difference between our approach and existing procedures is the treatment of non-ground abductive goals. A completion semantics is given and the soundness and completeness of the procedures has been proven. The research presented here, provides a simple framework of abductive procedures, in which a number of parameters can be set, in order to fit the abduction procedure to the application under consideration.

1 Introduction

Negation as failure and abduction have been recognized as important forms of nonmonotonic reasoning ([13], [18]). We present a general procedure for logic programs which integrates both paradigms. This procedure resulted from research in the domain of temporal reasoning. Temporal reasoning is an excellent domain for testing nonmonotonic reasoning techniques because of the *frame problem*. The frame axiom has a correct representation in situation and event calculus with negation as failure, as was illustrated in [1] for the famous Yale Turkey Shooting problem. A major restriction of negation as failure is its incapacity of representing *incomplete knowledge*. The original event calculus only supports the prediction of a goal state, starting from a complete description of the initial state and the set of events. In planning, however, the set of events is the subject of the search, and thus, a priori unknown. A solution to this problem is to extend event calculus with abduction ([8], [20]). In planning problems for example, the predicates which describe the events, i.e. $happens/1, act/2$ and $<$ are abducible. An abductive solution for a goal, describing the goal state, gives a description of a set of events and their order.

A crucial property of the underlying abductive procedure is the treatment of non-ground abductive goals. To see the problem, consider the following clause:

$$p \leftarrow happens(E), act(E, initiate\_p)$$

Observe that when executing the goal $\leftarrow p$, the abductive atoms cannot become ground. A procedure for planning should be able to cope with such situations. This condition is not satisfied by the abductive procedure defined in [11]. In the past, special abductive procedures for temporal reasoning with abductive event calculus have been presented ([8], [20], [16, 17]). However, as the three authors argue, the treatment of constraints in [8] and the treatment of non-ground abductive failure goals in [20], [16, 17] can be very inefficient.

The abductive procedure SLDNFA presented in this paper, provides an improved treatment of non-ground abductive atoms. We have proven its sound- and completeness. Although the inspiration for the design of SLD-NFA stems from temporal reasoning, we formulate it in full generality and it can be applied in any domain where abduction is useful, such as fault diagnosis, natural language understanding, knowledge assimilation, and default reasoning (see [13]).

In section 2, we present the intuitions behind SLDNFA and define the basic inference operators. In section 3 we formalise SLDNFA and its soundness and completeness. In section 4, we present variants of SLDNFA, which yield other completeness results. Finally, we end with a discussion. Due to space restrictions, we refer to [5] for all proofs.

2 Basic computation steps in SLDNFA

The SLDNFA procedure is an abductive procedure for normal abductive programs. An abductive logic program is a normal logic program (with negation as failure), except that a set of abductive predicates occurs which are undefined. For a given query Q, an abductive procedure computes a set Δ of (ground) abducible facts such that $P + \Delta \models Q$.

SLDNFA is an extension of the well-known SLDNF procedure (SLD resolution with Negation as Failure) for non-abductive programs. Basically the SLDNF procedure proves an initial goal by constructing a set $\mathcal{PG}$ of goals that must succeed and a set $\mathcal{NG}$ of goals that must fail. SLDNF tries to reduce goals in $\mathcal{PG}$ to the empty goal $\square$ and tries to build a finitely failed tree for the goals in $\mathcal{NG}$. When a ground negative literal $\neg A$ is selected in a goal in $\mathcal{PG}$, $\leftarrow A$ is added to $\mathcal{NG}$ and vice versa. In the sequel, we call a goal from $\mathcal{PG}$ a *positive goal* and a goal from $\mathcal{NG}$ a *negative goal*. Keep in mind that these names refer to the mode of execution for the goal, not to the sign of the literals in the goal. For SLDNFA, this computation scheme must be extended for the case that an abductive atom is selected in a positive or negative goal. Let the goal be $\leftarrow L_1, \ldots, L_{m-1}, \underline{A}, L_{m+1}, \ldots, L_k$ with A the selected abductive atom.

The case where an abductive atom A is selected in a positive goal, can be solved by skolemising the atom, replacing all of its variables with skolem constants, and adding the resulting atom to Δ. It is this solution which has been applied in [8], [20] and [16]. The definitions below formalise this.

Definition 2.1 (abduction) *A skolemising substitution θ for a set of basic* *expression (terms or atoms) is a substitution which assigns a fresh skolem constant to each variable occurring in one of the expressions.*

Let Q be a goal $\leftarrow L_1, \ldots, L_m, \ldots, L_k$, with L_m an abducible atom. Q' is derived from Q by abducing L_m using the skolemising substitution θ iff θ is a skolemising substitution for L_m and Q' is $\theta(\leftarrow L_1, \ldots, L_{m-1}, L_{m+1}, \ldots, L_k)$.

As can easily be imagined, the introduction of skolem constants causes additional problems with the unification in positive and negative goals. An example illustrates the problem in positive goals. Take the fact $p(f(g(Z), V)) \leftarrow$ and the query $\leftarrow r(X), p(X)$ where r/1 is an abducible predicate. Consider the following partial derivation:

$$\mathcal{PG} = \{ \leftarrow \underline{r(X)}, p(X) \} \qquad \qquad Abduction$$
$$\mathcal{PG} = \{ \leftarrow \underline{p(sk)} \} , \quad \Delta = \{ r(sk) \}$$

Solving the positive goal $\leftarrow p(sk)$ is not trivial: classical unification cannot be applied since the unification of sk and $f(g(Z), V)$ fails. We extend unification as in [20] and [16]. In a first phase, extended unification performs unification, treating skolem constants as variables; in a second phase, it skolemises the terms bound to the original skolem constants. In the example, SLDNFA's positive unification procedure substitutes sk by $f(g(sk_1), sk_2)$ and returns $\Delta = \{ r(f(g(sk_1), sk_2)) \}$.

Below we extend unification and resolution in this spirit.

Definition 2.2 *An equality set in solved form is a set of atoms of the form $x = t$ where x is a variable X or a skolem constant sk, t is a term and each x occurs only once at the left and not at the right. Moreover, if x is a skolem constant then t is not a variable.*

The equality reduction is the process of transforming a set E of equalities to a set E_s of equalities in solved form by a modified version of the Martelli-Montanari algorithm ([15]). The modified algorithm consists of the same rewrite rules, except that skolems constants are treated as variables, and one additional rewrite rule, which replaces an atom of the form $sk = X$ by the symmetrical atom $X = sk$. This rule is evoked at the end of the reduction as a post-processing. E_s is called a solved form of E.

We define a substitution as an equality set in solved form. Using the definition of equality reduction, we define *positive unification* and then *positive resolution*.

Definition 2.3 (positive unification) *Given is an equality set E with a solved form E_s. Let θ_{sk} be a skolemising substitution for the terms which are assigned to skolem constants in E_s. A positive unifier of E is given by the substitution $\theta_{sk} o E_s$.*

Definition 2.4 (positive resolution) *Let Q be a goal $\leftarrow L_1, \ldots, L_k$ and let C be a normal clause $H \leftarrow B_1, \ldots, B_q$ sharing no variables with Q. Q' is derived from Q and C by positive resolution on an atom L_m and using a positive unifier θ if the following conditions hold:*

- θ is a positive unifier of L_m and H.

- Q' is the goal $\theta(\leftarrow L_1, \ldots, L_{m-1}, B_1, \ldots, B_q, L_{m+1}, \ldots, L_k)$.

So far, the procedures that we introduced, can be found elsewhere in the literature. The procedures defined below for negative goals are new. The case where an abductive atom A is selected in a negative goal (in the sequel, *a negative abductive goal*), is more complex than the positive case. We must compute the failure tree obtained by resolving the goal with all abduced atoms in Δ. The main problem is that the final Δ may not be totally known when the abductive goal is selected. The procedures of ([20], [17]), solve this problem by storing all negative literals for which a failure tree is to be computed and rebuilding their failure trees each time a new fact is abduced. As indicated by the authors, this may introduce a serious overhead. SLDNFA avoids this by interleaving the computation of this failure tree with the construction of Δ. This is implemented by storing in a set $\mathcal{NAG}$ the triplet (Q, A_Q, D_Q) where Q is a negative abductive goal, A_Q is the abductive atom selected from Q and D_Q is the set of abduced atoms which have already been resolved with Q. We illustrate this strategy with an example. Consider the program with abducible predicate r/1:

$$q \leftarrow r(X), \neg p(X)$$
$$p(X) \leftarrow r(b)$$

Below, an SLDNFA refutation for the query $\leftarrow r(a), \neg q$ is given. Only the modified sets at each step are given. Initially $\mathcal{NG}$, $\mathcal{NAG}$ and Δ are empty.

$\mathcal{PG} = \{\leftarrow \underline{r(a)}, \neg q\}$	*Abduction*
$\mathcal{PG} = \{\leftarrow \underline{\neg q}\}$, $\Delta = \{r(a)\}$	*Adding negative goal*
$\mathcal{PG} = \{\Box\}$, $\mathcal{NG} = \{\leftarrow \underline{q}\}$	*Negative resolution*
$\mathcal{NG} = \{\leftarrow \underline{r(X)}, \neg p(X)\}$	*Selection of negative abd. goal*

$r(X)$ has to be resolved with all facts already abduced or to be abduced about r/1. The only abduced fact that can be applied now is $r(a)$. The triplet $(" \leftarrow r(X), \neg p(X)", "r(X)", \{r(a)\})$ is saved in $\mathcal{NAG}$ and the resolvent $\leftarrow \neg p(a)$ is added to $\mathcal{NG}$:

$\mathcal{NG} = \{\leftarrow \underline{\neg p(a)}\}$, $\mathcal{NAG} = \{(" \leftarrow r(X), \neg p(X)", "r(X)", \{r(a)\})\}$	
$\mathcal{PG} = \{\Box , \leftarrow \underline{p(a)}\}$, $\mathcal{NG} = \{\}$	*Positive resolution*
$\mathcal{PG} = \{\Box , \leftarrow \underline{r(b)}\}$	*Abduction*
$\mathcal{PG} = \{\Box\}$, $\Delta = \{r(a), r(b)\}$	*Selection of negative abd. goal*

Due to the abduction of $r(b)$, another branch starting from the goal in $\mathcal{NAG}$ has to be explored:

$\mathcal{NG} = \{\leftarrow \underline{\neg p(b)}\}$, $\mathcal{NAG} = \{(" \leftarrow r(X), \neg p(X)", "r(X)", \{r(a), r(b)\})\}$	
$\mathcal{PG} = \{\Box , \leftarrow \underline{p(b)}\}$, $\mathcal{NG} = \{\}$	*Positive resolution*
$\mathcal{PG} = \{\Box , \leftarrow \underline{r(b)}\}$	*Abduction*
$\mathcal{PG} = \{\Box\}$	

At this point, a solution is obtained: all positive goals are reduced to □, the set of negative goals is empty and with respect to Δ, a complete failure tree has been constructed for the negative abductive goal in $\mathcal{NAG}$.

The occurrence of skolem constants in negative goals causes additional problems. The following example illustrates them. Consider the clause:

$$p(f(g(Z), V)) \leftarrow q(Z, V)$$

and the execution of the query $\leftarrow r(X), \neg p(f(X, a))$, where, again, $r/1$ is abducible:

$$\mathcal{PG} = \{\leftarrow \underline{r(X)}, \neg p(f(X, a))\} \qquad \text{\textit{Abduction}}$$
$$\mathcal{PG} = \{\leftarrow \overline{\neg p(f(sk, a))}\}\ , \quad \Delta = \{r(sk)\} \qquad \text{\textit{Adding negative goal}}$$
$$\mathcal{PG} = \{\square\}\ , \quad \mathcal{NG} = \{\leftarrow \underline{p(f(sk, a))}\} \qquad \text{\textit{Negative resolution}}$$

To solve the negative goal $\leftarrow p(f(sk, a))$, we must unify $f(sk, a))$ and $f(g(Z), V)$. Here V and a unify as in normal unification. If we make the default assumption that sk is different from $g(Z)$ for each Z, then the unification fails and therefore $\leftarrow p(f(sk, a))$ fails. However, in general sk may appear in other goals and may be unified there with other terms at a later stage. Assume that due to some unification, sk is assigned a term $g(t)$. In that case, we must retract the default assumption and investigate the new negative goal $\leftarrow q(t, a)$. Otherwise, if all other goals have been refuted, we can conclude the SLDNFA-refutation as a whole by returning $sk \neq g(Z)$ as a constraint on the generated solution. As we will show later on, adding these constraints explicitly is not even necessary.

SLDNFA's *negative unification procedure* obtains this behavior as follows. First the equality reduction is applied on $f(sk, a)) = f(g(Z), V)$, producing $\{V = a, sk = g(Z)\}$. The variable part $\{V = a\}$ is applied as in normal resolution. The skolem part $\{sk = g(Z)\}$, which contains the negation of the default assumption, is added as a residual atom to the resolvent and the resulting resolvent $\leftarrow sk = g(Z), q(Z, a)$ is added to $\mathcal{NG}$. The selection of the entire goal can be delayed as long as no value is assigned to sk. If such an assignment occurs and for example the term $g(t)$ is assigned to sk, then the goal $\leftarrow g(t) = g(Z), q(Z, a)$ reduces to the negative goal $\leftarrow q(t, a)$ which then needs further investigation. Otherwise, no further refutation is needed.

This extension of unification and resolution for negative goals is formalised in the following definitions.

Definition 2.5 (negative unification) *Given is an equality set E with a solved form E_s. Let θ be the part of E_s with a variable at the left and E_r the part of E_s with a skolem at the left. We say that E negatively unifies with substitution θ and residue E_r.*

Definition 2.6 (negative resolution) *Let Q be a goal $\leftarrow L_1, \ldots, L_k$, with an atom L_m and let C be a normal clause $A \leftarrow B_1, \ldots, B_q$ sharing no variables with Q.*

Q' is derived from Q and C by negative resolution on L_m if the following holds:

- L_m and A negatively unify with variable substitution θ and residue E_r.

- Q' is the goal $\theta(\leftarrow L_1, \ldots, L_{m-1}, E_r, B_1, \ldots, B_q, L_{m+1}, \ldots, L_k)$.

3 The SLDNFA procedure

Below we define an SLDNFA-derivation as a sequence of transitions for multisets of goals.

Definition 3.1 *Let P be a normal program based on a language $\mathcal{L}$. Let $\mathcal{L}_{sk}$ be an alphabet of skolem constants.*

An SLDNFA derivation for a query Q_0 consists of finite or infinite sequences:

- $\{Q_0\} = \mathcal{PG}_0, \mathcal{PG}_1, \ldots$ *of multisets of goals,*

- $\{\} = \mathcal{NG}_0, \mathcal{NG}_1, \ldots$ *of multisets of goals,*

- $\{\} = \mathcal{NAG}_0, \mathcal{NAG}_1, \ldots$ *of multisets of triplets (Q, A_Q, D_Q), where Q is a goal, A_Q is an abductive atom in Q and D_Q is a set of abduced atoms, negatively unifiable with A_Q,*

- *a sequence $\{\} = \Delta_0, \Delta_1, \ldots$ of sets of ground abducible facts, and*

- *a sequence $\theta_1, \theta_2, \ldots$ of substitutions.*

For each i, there is a selection (Q, L_m) or (Q, L_m, B) such that Q occurs in $\mathcal{PG}_{i-1}, \mathcal{NG}_{i-1}$ or $\mathcal{NAG}_{i-1}$ and L_m is a literal in Q. B is selected only if $(Q, L_m, D_Q) \in \mathcal{NAG}_{i-1}$. In that case, B is negatively unifiable with L_m and occurs in $\Delta_{i-1} \setminus D_Q$. $\theta_i, \mathcal{PG}_i, \mathcal{NG}_i, \mathcal{NAG}_i$ and Δ_i are obtained in one of the following ways:

a) $Q \in \mathcal{PG}_{i-1}$, L_m *is a non-abductive atom*

   Q' *is derived from Q and a variant of a program clause by positive resolution on L_m and using a positive unifier θ_i. $\mathcal{PG}_i$ is $\theta_i(\mathcal{PG}_{i-1} \setminus \{Q\} \cup \{Q'\})$; $\mathcal{NG}_i, \mathcal{NAG}_i$ and Δ_i are obtained by applying θ_i on $\mathcal{NG}_{i-1}$, $\mathcal{NAG}_{i-1}$ and Δ_{i-1}.*

a_1) $Q \in \mathcal{PG}_{i-1}$, L_m *is of the form $s = t$*

   This is a special case of a). Q' is derived from Q and a variant of the reflexivity atom $X = X \leftarrow$ by positive resolution on L_m and using a positive unifier θ_i. $\mathcal{PG}_i$ is $\theta_i(\mathcal{PG}_{i-1} \setminus \{Q\} \cup \{Q'\})$; $\mathcal{NG}_i, \mathcal{NAG}_i$ and Δ_i are obtained by applying θ_i on $\mathcal{NG}_{i-1}, \mathcal{NAG}_{i-1}$ and Δ_{i-1}.

b) $Q \in \mathcal{PG}_{i-1}$, L_m *is an abductive atom*

   Q' *is derived from Q by abducing L_m using the skolemising substitution θ_i. $\mathcal{PG}_i$ is $\mathcal{PG}_{i-1} \setminus \{Q\} \cup \{Q'\}$; Δ_i is $\Delta_{i-1} \cup \{\theta_i(L_m)\}$; $\mathcal{NG}_i$ and $\mathcal{NAG}_i$ remain unchanged.*

c) $Q \in \mathcal{PG}_{i-1}$, L_m is a negative literal $\neg A$

Q' is derived from Q by deleting $\neg A$. θ_i is ε; $\mathcal{PG}_i$ is $\mathcal{PG}_{i-1} \setminus \{Q\} \cup \{Q'\}$; $\mathcal{NG}_i$ is $\mathcal{NG}_{i-1} \cup \{\leftarrow A\}$; $\mathcal{NAG}_i$ and Δ_i remain unchanged.

d) $Q \in \mathcal{NG}_{i-1}$, L_m is a non-abductive atom

Let S be the set of all resolvents that can be derived by negative resolution on L_m from Q and at most one variant with fresh variables for each clause. θ_i is ε; $\mathcal{NG}_i$ is $\mathcal{NG}_{i-1} \setminus \{Q\} \cup S$; $\mathcal{PG}_i, \mathcal{NAG}_i$ and Δ_i remain unchanged.

Note that when S is empty, the result of the operation is to delete Q from $\mathcal{NG}_{i-1}$.

d_1) $Q \in \mathcal{NG}_{i-1}$, L_m is of the form $s = t$

Q' is derived from Q and a variant of the reflexivity atom $X = X \leftarrow$ by negative resolution on L_m. θ_i is ε; $\mathcal{NG}_i$ is $\mathcal{NG}_{i-1} \setminus \{Q\} \cup \{Q'\}$; $\mathcal{PG}_i, \mathcal{NAG}_i$ and Δ_i remain unchanged.

e) $Q \in \mathcal{NG}_{i-1}$, L_m is an abductive atom

θ_i is ε; $\mathcal{NG}_i$ is $\mathcal{NG}_{i-1} \setminus \{Q\}$; $\mathcal{NAG}_i = \mathcal{NAG}_{i-1} \cup \{(Q, L_m, \{\})\}$; $\mathcal{PG}_i$ and Δ_i remain unchanged.

f) $Q \in \mathcal{NG}_{i-1}$, L_m is a negative literal $\neg A$

θ_i is ε; $\mathcal{PG}_i$ is $\mathcal{PG}_{i-1} \cup \{\leftarrow A\}$; $\mathcal{NG}_i$ is $\mathcal{NG}_{i-1} \setminus \{Q\}$; $\mathcal{NAG}_i$ and Δ_i remain unchanged.

g) $Q \in \mathcal{NG}_{i-1}$, L_m is a negative literal $\neg A$

Let Q' be obtained from Q by deleting L_m. θ_i is ε; $\mathcal{NG}_i$ is $\mathcal{NG}_{i-1} \setminus \{Q\} \cup \{Q', \leftarrow A\}$; $\mathcal{PG}_i, \mathcal{NAG}_i$ and Δ_i remain unchanged.

h) $(Q, L_m, D_Q) \in \mathcal{NAG}_{i-1}$, $B \in \Delta_{i-1} \setminus D_Q$

Q' is the resolvent derived from Q and B by negative resolution on L_m. θ_i is ε; $\mathcal{NG}_i$ is $\mathcal{NG}_{i-1} \cup \{Q'\}$; $\mathcal{NAG}_i$ is $\mathcal{NAG}_{i-1} \setminus \{(Q, L_m, D_Q)\} \cup \{(Q, L_m, D_Q \cup \{B\})\}$; $\mathcal{PG}_i$ and Δ_i remain unchanged.

We denote the set of skolem constants occurring in Δ by $Sk(\Delta)$.

We require the selection in an SLDNFA-derivation to be safe: a negative literal may only be selected when L_m is ground. Observe that when the selection is safe, then two goals in $\mathcal{PG}_i \cup \mathcal{NG}_i \cup \mathcal{NAG}_i$ do not share variables, only skolem constants can be shared. Therefore, only the skolem part of θ_i can have an effect when applying θ_i on other goals or abduced atoms. That is why in b), θ_i, which is a variable substitution, does not need to be applied on other goals.

Another point for which some explanation is in order is the addition of the negative goal $\leftarrow A$ to $\mathcal{NG}_i$ in step g). The correctness of the approach follows from the tautology $Q \leftrightarrow A \vee (\neg A \& Q')$. Step f) tries to prove Q by building a successful derivation for $\leftarrow A$, thus proving A; step g) tries to prove Q by finitely failing $\leftarrow A$ and Q', thus proving $\neg A \& Q'$. An alternative for g) (say g') would be to add only Q'. The correctness of g') follows from the simpler equivalence $Q \leftrightarrow A \lor Q'$. This approach is followed in the procedure defined in [11]. However, this variant appears to be in general less efficient, due to the fact that redundant solutions in both branches can be explored: solutions constructed via g') may satisfy A and thus are investigated when applying f). Stated otherwise, g) implements a form of *complement splitting*.

Definition 3.2 *An SLDNFA-derivation is finitely failed if it is finite, say of length n and one of the following situations occurs at n:*

- *the selected goal Q occurs in $\mathcal{PG}_n$ and L_m is a positive atom such that no positive resolution is possible on L_m.*

- $\Box \in \mathcal{NG}_n$.

Definition 3.3 *We say that $s = t$ is irreducible when s is a skolem constant and t is a non-variable term, different from s.*

As explained in the previous section, an irreducible equality atom $sk = t$ in a negative goal can be used as the default assumption that sk and t are unequal. A smart selection rule will never select a negative goal which contains an irreducible equality goal because it will fail anyway if, eventually, the default assumption is added as a constraint on the solution.

Definition 3.4 *An SLDNFA refutation K for a goal Q is a finite SLDNFA derivation (say of length n) such that $\mathcal{PG}_n$ contains no other goals than $\Box$, each goal Q in $\mathcal{NG}_n$ comprises an irreducible equality atom and for each (Q, A_Q, D_Q) in $\mathcal{NAG}_n$: D_Q contains each $B \in \Delta_n$ which negatively unifies with A_Q.*

The answer substitution is $\theta_a = \theta_n o \ldots o \theta_1|_{var(Q)}$. The solution generated by K is (Δ_n, θ_a).

A refutation generates not only abducible facts but also constraints in $\mathcal{NG}_n$ of the form $\leftarrow L_1, \ldots, sk = t, \ldots, L_k$. These constraints are valid under the default assumption that $sk \neq t$. Clearly this assumption is satisfied in the theory $FEQ(\mathcal{L} + Sk(\Delta_n))$ (the theory of Free Equality or Clark Equality on the language $L + Sk(\Delta_n)$). Therefore $FEQ(\mathcal{L} + Sk(\Delta_n)) \models \leftarrow L_1, \ldots, sk = t, \ldots, L_k$. Thus, we do not need to add these constraints explicitly to the solution after all, as announced earlier.

Another issue is the relation to SLDNF. Although the definition of SLDNFA refutation is structured rather differently than the definition of SLDNF refutation ([14]), for non-abductive programs, we have proved that the definitions of SLDNFA and SLDNF are equivalent: for programs without abducible predicates and for every SLDNFA refutation, it is possible to construct an SLDNF refutation with the same goals, resolution steps and substitutions. Vice versa, for every SLDNF refutation an equivalent SLDNFA can be constructed.

We have proved the following soundness result for the SLDNFA procedure with respect to completion semantics (see [5]). Below, $comp(\mathcal{L} + Sk(\Delta), P +$

Δ) denotes the Clark completion ([3]) of the non-abductive program consisting of the clauses of P and Δ. $\&(Q_0)$ denotes the open conjunction of literals of Q.

Theorem 3.1 (soundness) *If (Δ,θ) is the result of an SLDNFA refutation for a goal Q_0 then $comp(\mathcal{L} + Sk(\Delta), P + \Delta) \models \forall(\theta(\&(Q_0)))$.*

The theorem does not guarantee the consistency of the generated abductive solution. However, for most programs (i.e. stratified or locally stratified programs) this problem does not occur. A more radical solution for the problem would be to consider 3-valued completion semantics ([9]). SLDNFA is still correct wrt to these semantics and for each Δ, $P + \Delta$ is consistent. Another issue to be investigated is the soundness of SLDNFA wrt other more *fine-grained* semantics such as the Generalised Stable Models ([12]).

A completeness result on SLDNFA has been proven with respect to the completion semantics defined for abductive normal programs in [4]. The definition is an extension of the definition for non-abductive programs.

Definition 3.5 *Let P be a normal abductive program based on some language $\mathcal{L}$. The completion of P wrt to $\mathcal{L}$, is the theory consisting of $FEQ(\mathcal{L})$ and the if-and-only-if definitions for all non-abducible predicates. We denote this theory by $comp_A(\mathcal{L}, P)$.*

The completion of an abductive program puts no constraints on the abductive predicates. This is totally different than the case of a non-abducible predicate p with an empty definition: according to the completion, p is always false.

The next concept needed to formulate the completeness result is the SLDNFA-tree. First we define how the computation branches, given some selection.

Definition 3.6 *Given is a finite SLDNFA derivation K, and a selection (Q, L) or (Q, L, B) at step n-1.*

The set S of computable children of K is the set of all tuples $(\mathcal{PG}_n^i, \mathcal{NG}_n^i, \mathcal{NAG}_n^i, \Delta_n^i, \theta_n^i)$, that can be obtained by applying one of the computation steps a)-h) on the selected tuple.

In practice, only in two situations more than one child can exist:

- when Q is selected from $\mathcal{PG}_n$ and L is a non-abductive atom, then there are as many children as there are program clauses with a head unifiable with L.

- when Q is selected from $\mathcal{NG}_n$ and L is a negative literal, then the computation steps f) and g) can be applied, and we obtain two children.

Definition 3.7 *An SLDNFA-tree for a query Q is a tree in which each branch is either a failed SLDNFA derivation or an SLDNFA refutation. For each nonleaf N, a selection (Q, L) or (Q, L, B) exists such that the children of N are the computable children of the derivation up to N.*

As a completeness result, we have proved that (under certain conditions expressed below), SLDNFA generates all minimal and most general solutions (see [5]). More precisely: given any abductive solution Δ, there exists a solution Δ' generated by SLDNFA, and a substitution σ for the skolem constants of Δ' such that $\sigma(\Delta') \subseteq \Delta$. This does not imply that Δ' contains less elements than Δ: indeed it is possible that σ maps two or more facts of Δ' into one fact of Δ. In the next section, we come back to this phenomenon. Below, we call an abductive solution (Δ, θ) consistent if the theory $comp(\mathcal{L} + Sk(\Delta), P + \Delta)$ is consistent.

Theorem 3.2 (completeness) *Let P be a normal abductive program based on a language $\mathcal{L}$ and a normal query Q which has a finite SLDNFA-tree W.*

a) *if all branches of W are finitely failed, then $comp_A(\mathcal{L}, P) \models Q$*

b) *if $comp_A(\mathcal{L}, P) + \exists(\&(Q))$ is satisfiable, then W contains a successful branch.*

c) *let (Δ, θ) be a consistent abductive solution for Q based on an extension $\mathcal{L}'$ of $\mathcal{L}$. There exists a successful branch in W generating a solution (Δ', θ') and a ground skolem substitution σ_{sk} such that $\sigma_{sk}(\Delta') \subseteq \Delta$ and $\sigma_{sk} \circ \theta'(Q)$ and $\theta(Q)$ unify.*

SLDNFA, like SLDNF, can only be complete under severe restrictions. The condition of having a finite computation tree is quite restrictive. It subsumes the condition that the computation does not flounder. It is needed because the proof relies on an equivalence between the goal and the leaves of the SLDNFA-tree. This equivalence can only be proven for finite trees. This proof technique is in the same spirit as Clark's proof of the completeness of SLDNF for hierarchical programs. Similarly as for SLDNF, completeness results for infinite SLDNFA-trees could be obtained by imposing conditions such as allowedness and strictness on the abductive programs (see [2]). This is subject to future research.

4   Extensions of the abductive procedure.

The current SLDNFA procedure can be extended in different ways, in order to obtain even more solutions. As a result, the computation trees become larger, the computation is less efficient but additional interesting solutions are obtained. Below an example shows the relevance of the first extension.

Consider the following simplified planning program. An action E initialises a condition p if some initial condition $r(E)$ holds when the action takes place. The same type of action initialises q if an initial condition $s(E)$ holds. The problem is to find a situation in which both p and q hold. The query is $\leftarrow p, q$. The predicates $action/1$, $r/1$ and $s/1$ are abducible.

$$P = \{p \leftarrow action(E), r(E) \qquad q \leftarrow action(E), s(E)\}$$

Intuitively, there seem to be two interesting solutions: $\{action(sk), r(sk), s(sk)\}$ and $\{action(sk_1), r(sk_1), action(sk_2), s(sk_2)\}$.

SLDNFA only generates the second solution while the first is definitely more interesting from the perspective of planning, since it contains less actions. Observe that the substitution $\{sk_1/sk, sk_2/sk\}$ maps the two *action* facts on the same fact in the first solution. Below we extend SLDNFA such that it dynamically tries to merge abduced facts. As a result the first solution will also be generated.

The extended SLDNFA has the more interesting completeness property that for any abductive solution Δ, there exists a generated solution Δ' and a skolem substitution σ_{sk} which maps Δ' into Δ, but no facts of Δ' are merged. The cost for this is that the extended procedure crosses a much larger computation tree. Our extended algorithm allows a compromise between the improved completeness and the larger computation tree. It provides the opportunity to specify exactly for what abducible predicates the improved completeness should be obtained. The other abducible predicates are dealt with like in SLDNFA. The special abducible predicates will be called *strongly abducible*.

Below $\bar{t}$ denotes a tuple $(t_1, \ldots, t_n)$. $\bar{t} = \bar{s}$ denotes $t_1 = s_1, \ldots, t_n = s_n$.

Definition 4.1 *Let P be an abductive normal program with disjunct sets of abducible predicates and strongly abducible predicates.*

An SLDNFA^o procedure is an extension of the SLDNFA procedure obtained by applying steps e) and h) for abductive and strongly abductive atoms and by adding steps b_1) and b_2):

b_1) $Q \in \mathcal{PG}_{i-1}$, L_m *is a strongly abductive atom*
Q' *is derived from Q and an abduced fact from Δ_{i-1} by positive resolution on L_m and using a positive unifier θ_i. $\mathcal{PG}_i$ is $\theta_i(\mathcal{PG}_{i-1} \setminus \{Q\} \cup \{Q'\})$; $\mathcal{NG}_i, \mathcal{NAG}_i$ and Δ_i are obtained by applying θ_i on $\mathcal{NG}_{i-1}$, $\mathcal{NAG}_{i-1}$ and Δ_{i-1}.*

b_2) $Q \in \mathcal{PG}_{i-1}$, L_m *is a strongly abductive atom $p(\bar{t})$*
Q' *is derived from Q by abducing L_m using the skolemising substitution θ_i. $\mathcal{PG}_i$ is $\mathcal{PG}_{i-1} \setminus \{Q\} \cup \{Q'\}$; $\mathcal{NG}_i$ is $\mathcal{NG}_{i-1} \cup \{\leftarrow \theta_i(\bar{t}) = \bar{s} \parallel p(\bar{s}) \in \Delta_{i-1}\}$; Δ_i is $\Delta_{i-1} \cup \{\theta_i(L_m)\}$; $\mathcal{NAG}_i$ remains unchanged.*

SLDNFA^o differs from SLDNFA in its treatment of strongly abductive atoms, by allowing that either resolution with existing abduced facts is performed, or that a new abduced fact is introduced which is different from the previous ones.

Theorem 4.1 *The SLDNFA^o procedure is sound. It satisfies the same completeness result that was proven for the SLDNFA procedure in Theorem 3.2. In addition to the assertion c), the skolem substitution σ_{sk} maps distinct strongly abduced facts of the generated solution Δ' to distinct facts in Δ.*

For other applications of abduction such as diagnosis, the above completeness result may still be insufficient. The following example clarifies this:

$$P = \{q_1(a) \leftarrow \qquad q_2(a) \leftarrow \qquad p(X) \leftarrow q_1(X), \neg q_2(X)\}$$

The query is $\leftarrow r(X), \neg p(X)$, where $r/1$ is abducible. SLDNFA generates one solution $(\{r(sk)\}, \{X = sk\})$. The set of remaining constraints $\mathcal{NG}_n$ is $\{\leftarrow sk = a, \neg q_2(sk)\}$ with $sk = a$ as the selected atom.

An alternative solution is $(\{r(a)\}, \{X = a\})$. The substitution $\{sk = a\}$ maps the generated solution to this solution. Observe that under this skolem substitution, the remaining constraint $\leftarrow sk = a, \neg q_2(sk)$ still holds, but for a different reason: $q_2(a)$ holds, thus $\neg q_2(sk)$ finitely fails. The application of the skolem substitution does not preserve the fact on which the generated solution depends (namely $sk \neq a$). The two solutions represent two different justifications for the observation given by the goal.

SLDNFA can easily be extended in order to find these solutions. The idea is the following: a constraint containing an atom $sk = t$ is satisfied when $sk \neq t$ is satisfied or when sk equals t and the remainder of the constraint finitely fails. Two new computation steps explore these two alternatives.

Definition 4.2 *The SLDNFA$_+$ procedure is an extension of the SLDNFA procedure with two additional steps:*

i) *$Q \in \mathcal{NG}_i$, L_m is an irreducible equality atom $sk = t$*
   θ_i is ε; $\mathcal{NG}_i$ is $\mathcal{NG}_{i-1} \setminus \{Q\} \cup \{\leftarrow sk = t\}$; $\mathcal{PG}_i, \mathcal{NAG}_i$ and Δ_i remain unchanged.

j) *$Q \in \mathcal{NG}_i$, L_m is an irreducible equality atom $sk = t$*
   Q' is the goal obtained by deleting L_m from Q and σ is a skolemising substitution for t. θ_i is $\sigma \circ \{sk=t\}$; $\mathcal{NG}_i = \theta_i(\mathcal{NG}_{i-1} \setminus \{Q\} \cup \{Q'\})$; $\mathcal{PG}_i$, $\mathcal{NAG}_i$ and Δ_i are obtained by applying θ_i on $\mathcal{PG}_{i-1}$, $\mathcal{NAG}_{i-1}$ and Δ_{i-1}.

Observe that it makes no sense to apply i) or j) on a negative goal if it contains no additional literals. The result of step i) is the same goal, the result of step j) is failure.

Definition 4.3 *An SLDNFA$_+$ refutation K is a finite SLDNFA$_+$ derivation (say of length n) which satisfies the same conditions as an SLDNFA refutation. In addition, we require that all constraints in $\mathcal{NG}_n$ are atomic irreducible equality goals.*

Theorem 4.2 *SLDNFA$_+$ is sound. It satisfies the same completeness result that was proven for the SLDNFA procedure. Additionally to the assertion c) in Theorem 3.2, if $\leftarrow sk = t$ belongs to $\mathcal{NG}_n$ then $\sigma_{sk}(sk)$ and $\sigma_{sk}(t)$ do not unify.*

Observe that the modifications to SLDNFA in SLDNFA^o and SLDNFA$_+$ stand orthogonal to each other. That is, they can be combined to a new procedure SLDNFA$^o_+$. This procedure is sound, and as a completeness result it can be stated that σ_{sk} preserves the disequality constraints and the disequality of strongly abduced atoms.

5   Discussion

We have implemented a prototype of the abductive procedure in Prolog. The prototype was extended to an abductive planner for abductive event calculus by adding a module with a constraint solver for temporal reasoning. Our prototype is implemented as a vanilla meta-program on top of Prolog (about 240 lines of code). In [7] the power of the system is showed by applying it to planning with context dependent events and solving well-known temporal reasoning problems involving prediction and postdiction under uncertainty (e.g. Yale Turkey Shooting, Russian Turkey Shooting, Stanford Murder Mystery, stolen car problem ([19])). Our experiences have highlighted the need for an intelligent control strategy. Our implementation uses the straightforward *depth first, left to right* control strategy. In many examples, the system enters an infinite branch of the search tree. A solution for this is to execute the planner according to an iterative deepening regime. Loop detection, intelligent control and intelligent backtracking could be of use to the system.

In [4], an abductive procedure is presented which for a given hierarchical normal abductive program P and query $\leftarrow Q$, derives an *explanation formula* E equivalent with Q under the completion of P:

$$comp_A(P) \models (Q \Leftrightarrow E)$$

This is done by repeatedly substituting atoms of defined predicates by the equivalent part in their if-and-only-if definition, until no defined atoms are left over. Thus, the explanation formula is built of abducible predicates and equality only. It characterises all abductive solutions in the sense that for any set Δ of abducible ground atoms, Δ is an abductive solution iff it satisfies E.

SLDNFA can be considered as a (more sophisticated) procedure for rewriting goals using the definition of the defined predicates. An advantage of the procedure in [4] is that it also applies for non-ground negative literals. On the other hand, observe that in the case of a recursive predicate, repeated naive rewriting of a defined atom by its definition necessarily goes into a loop. SLDNFA can avoid this (in many cases) by checking the consistency of generated equality and disequality atoms (this is done implicitly in the resolution steps) and eliminating an inconsistent branch. Even when provisions for equality would be built into the procedure in [4], there would still be the problem that if the computation tree contains an infinite branch, then the explanation formula cannot be computed. SLDNFA on the other hand investigates the tree branch per branch and, using an iterative deepening regime, will ultimately find all solutions in finite branches.

Another related procedure has been presented in [10]. This belief revision procedure tries to construct an SLDNF-refutation for a given goal by adding facts to the program (as in SLDNFA) to succeed positive goals and by deleting clauses of the program to fail negative goals. We believe that there is a big conceptual gap between this procedure and SLDNFA. They are in general not applicable in the same context. Whether in a given context the procedure in [10] or SLDNFA is applicable depends totally on the reliability of the general domain knowledge which is formulated in the clauses of the program. When reliable, as in planning, no clauses should be retracted.

A remaining restriction of SLDNFA is its incapability to deal with non-ground negative atoms (the problem of floundering negation). Here is an intriguing relationship with the view of *negation by failure as abduction* ([8], [11]). In this view, the problem with non-ground negative atoms is a subproblem of the problem with non-ground abductive literals. Strong indications exist that the techniques incorporated in SLDNFA can solve the problem of floundering negation for positive goals but not for negative goals.

In ([6]), we have formalised a procedural duality between abduction and model generation. A current limitation of the duality framework is its restriction to definite abductive programs. In future work we intend to extend the framework to describe a duality between SLDNFA and an extended notion of model generation. This extended model generation will be based on the notion of *justification*, well-known from the work on truth maintenance systems.

Acknowledgments

We thank Maurice Bruynooghe and Lode Missiaen for many helpful suggestions.

References

[1] K.R. Apt and M. Bezem. Acyclic programs. In *Proc. of the seventh International Conference on Logic Programming*, pages 579–597. MIT press, 1990.

[2] L. Cavedon and J.W. Lloyd. A completeness theorem for sldnf resolution. *Journal of logic programming*, 7:177–191, 1989.

[3] K.L. Clark. Negation as failure. In H. Gallaire and J. Minker, editors, *Logic and databases*, pages 293–322. Plenum Press, 1978.

[4] L. Console, D. Theseider Dupre, and P. Torasso. On the relationship between abduction and deduction. *journal of Logic and Computation*, 1(5):661–690, 1991.

[5] Marc Denecker and Danny De Schreye. A family of abductive procedures for normal abductive programs, their soundness and completeness. Technical Report 136, Department of Computer Science, K.U.Leuven, 1992.

[6] Marc Denecker and Danny De Schreye. On the duality of abduction and model generation. In *proceedings of FGCS, Tokyo*, 1992.

[7] Marc Denecker, Lode Missiaen, and Maurice Bruynooghe. Temporal reasoning with abductive event calculus. In *proceedings of ECAI92, Vienna*, 1992.

[8] K. Eshghi. Abductive planning with event calculus. In R.A. Kowalski and K.A. Bowen, editors, *proc.of the 5th ICLP*, 1988.

[9] M. Fitting. A kripke-kleene semantics for logic programs. *journal of Logic Programming*, 2(4):295–312, 1985.

[10] A. Guessoum and J.W. Loyd. Updating knowledge bases ii. Technical Report TR-90-13, Department of Computer Science, University of Bristol, 1990.

[11] A.C. Kakas and P. Mancarella. Database updates through abduction. In *proc. of the 16th Very large Database Conference*, pages 650–661, 1990.

[12] A.C. Kakas and P. Mancarella. Generalised stable models: a semantics for abduction. In *proc. of ECAI-90*, 1990.

[13] R.A. Kowalski. Logic programming in artificial intelligence. In *proceedings of the IJCAI*, 1991.

[14] J.W. Lloyd. *Foundations of Logic Programming*. Springer-Verlag, 1987.

[15] A. Martelli and U. Montanari. An efficient unification algorithm. *Transactions on Programming Languages and Systems*, 4(2):258–282, 1982.

[16] L. Missiaen. *Localized abductive planning with the event calculus*. PhD thesis, Department of Computer Science, K.U.Leuven, 1991.

[17] L. Missiaen, M. Bruynooghe, and M. Denecker. Abductive planning with event calculus. Internal report, Department of Computer Science, K.U.Leuven, 1992.

[18] D. Poole. A logical framework for default reasoning. *Artificial Intelligence*, 36:27–47, 1988.

[19] Erik Sandewall. Features and fluents. Technical Report LiTH-IDA-R-91-29, Institutionen for datavetenskap, Linkoping University, 1991. preliminary version of a forthcoming book.

[20] M. Shanahan. Prediction is deduction but explanation is abduction. In *IJCAI89*, page 1055, 1989.

Implementation of Parallelism

Exploiting Or-parallelism in Optimisation Problems

Péter Szeredi*

IQSOFT—SZKI Intelligent Software Ltd.,
Iskola u. 10, H-1011 Budapest, Hungary,
`szeredi@iqsoft.hu`

Abstract

Several successful multiprocessor implementations of Prolog have been developed in recent years, with the aim of exploiting various forms of parallelism within the Prolog language. Or-parallel implementations, such as Aurora or Muse were among the first to support the full Prolog language, thus being able to execute existing Prolog programs without any change. There are, however, several application areas where the simple built-in control of Prolog execution hinders efficient exploitation of or-parallelism.

In this paper we discuss the area of optimisation problems, a typical application area of this kind. The efficiency of an optimum search can be dramatically improved by replacing the exhaustive depth-first search of Prolog by more sophisticated control, e.g. the branch-and-bound algorithm or the minimax algorithm with alpha-beta pruning. We develop a generalised optimum search algorithm, covering both the branch-and-bound and the minimax approach, which can be executed efficiently on an or-parallel Prolog system. We define appropriate language extensions for Prolog—in the form of new higher order predicates—to provide a user interface for the general optimum search, describe our experimental implementation within the Aurora system, and present example application schemes.

Keywords: Logic Programming, Programming Methodology, Parallel Execution, Optimum Search.

1   Introduction

Development of parallel Prolog systems for multiprocessor architectures has been one of the new research directions of the recent years. Implementation techniques have been developed for various parallel execution models and for various types of parallelism. Or-parallel execution models were among the first to be implemented. Several such systems have been completed recently, such as PEPSys [6], Aurora [8], ROPM [9] and Muse [2].

Our present work is based on Aurora, a prototype or-parallel implementation of Prolog for shared memory multiprocessors. Aurora provides support for the full Prolog language, contains graphics tracing facilities, and gives a choice of several scheduling algorithms [4, 5, 3].

One of the major outstanding problems in the context of parallel execution of Prolog is the question of non-declarative language primitives. These primitives,

---

*Part of the work reported here has been carried out while the author was at the Department of Computer Science, University of Bristol, U.K.

e.g. the built in predicates for modification of the internal data base, are quite often used in large applications. As these predicates involve side effects, they are normally executed in strict left-to-right order. The basic reason for this is the need to preserve the sequential semantics, i.e. compatibility with the sequential Prolog. Such restrictions on the execution order, however, involve significant overheads and consequent degradation of parallel performance.

There are two main directions for the investigation of this problem. First, one can look at using the unrestricted, "cavalier" versions of the side effect predicates. This opens up a whole range of new problems: from the question of synchronisation of possibly interfering side effects, to the ultimate issue of ensuring that the parallel execution produces the required answers. Since one is using the non-logical features of Prolog here, it is natural that the problems encountered are similar to those of imperative parallel languages. We have explored some of these issues in [15].

Another approach, that can be taken, is to investigate why these non-logical features are used in the first place. One can try to identify typical subproblems which normally require dynamic data base handling in Prolog. Having done this, one can then define appropriate higher order language extensions to encapsulate the given subproblem and thus avoid the need for explicit use of such non-logical predicates. A typical example already present in the standard Prolog is the 'setof' predicate: this built-in predicate collects all solutions of a subgoal, a task which otherwise could only be done using dynamic data base handling.

In this paper we attempt to pursue the second path of action for the application area of optimum search problems. Efficient optimum search techniques, such as the branch-and-bound algorithm and the minimax algorithm with alpha-beta pruning, require sophisticated communication between branches of the search tree. Rather than to rely on dynamic data base handling to solve this problem, we propose the introduction of appropriate higher order predicates. We develop a general optimum search algorithm to be used in the implementation of these higher order predicates, which covers both the branch-and-bound and the minimax algorithm, and which can be executed efficiently on an or-parallel Prolog system such as Aurora.

The structure of the paper is the following. Section 2 introduces the *abstract domain*, i.e. the abstract search tree with appropriate annotations, suitable for describing the general optimum search technique. Section 3 presents our *parallel algorithm* for optimum search, within this abstract framework. Section 4 describes appropriate *language extensions* for Prolog, in the form of new built-in predicates, for embedding the algorithm within a parallel Prolog system. Section 5 outlines our experimental Aurora *implementation* of the language extensions using the parallel algorithm. In Section 6 we describe two *application schemes* based on the language extensions, preliminary *performance data* for which is given in Section 7. Section 8 discusses related work, while Section 9 summarises the conclusions.

2 The Abstract Domain

The abstract representation of the optimum search space is a tree with certain annotations. Leaf nodes have either a numeric value associated with them, or are marked as failure nodes. The root node and certain other non-leaf nodes are called *optimum nodes*. These nodes are annotated with either a *min* or a *max* symbol, indicating that the minimal (maximal) value of the given subtree should be calculated. Some non-leaf nodes can be annotated with constraints of form <*relational-op*> *Limit*, where *Limit* is a number, and <*relational-op*> is one of the comparison operators $<$, $\leq$, $>$ or $\geq$. Constraints express some domain related knowledge about values associated with nodes, as explained below. Figure 1 shows an example of an annotated tree.

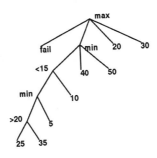

Figure 1: AN EXAMPLE ANNOTATED TREE

We will use the term *value node* for the non-failure leaf nodes and the optimum nodes together. We define a value function, which assigns a value to each value node. For a leaf node, the value is the one given as the annotation. For a max (min) node, the value is the maximum (minimum) of the values of all the value nodes directly below the given node. If there are no value nodes below an optimum node (i.e. all nodes below are failure nodes), then the value of a max node can be assumed to be $-\infty$ and that of a min node to be $+\infty$. To simplify the initial discussion we will assume that each optimum (and also each constraint node) has at least one value node below it, and so there is no need for infinite values. We will discuss the general case at the end of Section 3.

A node annotated with a constraint $<relational\text{-}op>$ *Limit* expresses the validity of the following fact:

> For each of the value nodes directly below the constraint node their value V satisfies the following relation: $V <relational\text{-}op>$ *Limit*.

The example tree in Figure 1 contains two constraints. To check that e.g. the upper one ($<$**15**) is valid, one has to examine the value nodes directly below (the min node and the leaf node with value **10**) both of which do have a value smaller than **15**.

The goal of the optimum search is to find the value of the root node. In our example the two min nodes both have a value **5**, and the value of the root node is **30**.

The notion of search tree presented here is more general than that required by the branch-and-bound and minimax algorithms. The branch-and-bound algorithm uses a search tree with only a single optimum node (the root) and several constraint nodes below. The minimax algorithm applies to trees where there are several layers of alternating optimum nodes but there are no constraint nodes.

We have to introduce a further type of annotation in the search tree to cover some aspects of scheduling: each node can have a numeric priority assigned to it. This priority value will be used to control a best-first type search, i.e. nodes with higher priorities will be searched first (see the examples in Section 6).

3 The Parallel Algorithm

In our model several processing agents (workers) explore the search tree in parallel, in a way analogous to the SRI model [16]. The workers traverse the tree according to some exhaustive search strategy (e.g. depth-first or best-first) and maintain a "best-so-far" value in each optimum node.

We introduce the notion of *neutral interval*, generalising the alpha and beta values used in the alpha-beta pruning algorithm. A neutral interval, characterised by a constraint of form <*relational-op*> *Limit* can be associated with a particular node if the following condition is satisfied:

> The value of the root node will not be affected if we replace the value of a (value) node directly below the given node, which falls into the neutral interval, by another value falling into the neutral interval.

As the workers traverse the tree they assign neutral intervals to constraint and optimum nodes. When a constraint node is processed, the complement of the constraint interval is assigned to the node as a neutral interval. This neutral interval must be valid, according to the above definition, as there can be no value nodes directly below the given constraint node, that have a value falling into the neutral interval[1]. For example, when the constraint <15 of the tree in Figure 1 is reached, the neutral interval ≥15 is assigned to the given constraint node.

In a similar way, a neutral interval $\leq B$ ($\geq B$) can be associated with each max (min) node, which has a best-so-far value B. For example, when the child of the root with the value 20 is reached in our sample tree, the root's best-so far value becomes 20, and so a neutral interval ≤20 can be associated with the root. This can be interpreted as the statement of the following fact: "values $\leq$ 20 are indifferent, i.e. need not be distinguished from each other"[2].

An important property of neutral intervals is that they are inherited by descendant nodes, i.e. if a neutral interval is associated with a node, then it can be associated with any descendant of the node as well. This can be easily proven using the continuity property of intervals, as outlined below.

The only non-trivial case of inheritance is the one when a neutral interval is associated with the parent P of an optimum node N. To prove that the same neutral interval can be associated with node N, let us consider the effect of changing the value of a node directly below N within the given neutral interval (say the value is changed from V_1 to V_2, where both V_1 and V_2 are within the neutral interval). A simple examination of cases shows that if the old value of N or the new value of N is outside the closed interval bounded by V_1 and V_2, then the value of N (and consequently the value of the root) could not have changed. This means that if the value of N changes, it changes within the closed interval bounded by V_1 and V_2, that is within the given neutral interval. Using the premise that this neutral interval is associated with node P, we can conclude that the value of the root is unchanged in this case as well. This finishes the proof that the given neutral interval is inherited by the child node N.

There are basically two types of neutral intervals, ones containing $+\infty$ and the ones containing $-\infty$. Two intervals of the same type can always be replaced by the bigger one. This, together with the inheritance property, means that the worker

---

[1]Note that because of the inheritance of neutral intervals this seemingly trivial fact can be utilised for pruning subtrees below the constraint node (see later).

[2]For value nodes directly below the root a stronger statement is valid: "values ≤20 can be discarded". For the sake of inheritance, however, the above weaker form is required.

can keep two actual neutral intervals as part of the search status, when the tree is being traversed (which is analogous to the alpha and beta values of the minimax search).

Neutral intervals can be used to prune the search tree. When a worker reaches a node the constraint of which is subsumed by a currently valid neutral interval, then the tree below the constraint node does not have to be explored, and a single solution with an arbitrary value within the neutral interval can be assumed[3]. Optimum nodes act as special constraint nodes in this respect: a max (min) node with a best-so-far value B is equivalent to a constraint $\geq B$ ($\leq B$).

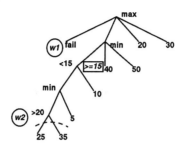

Figure 2: FIRST SNAPSHOT OF EXPLORATION OF THE SAMPLE TREE

Figure 2 shows a snapshot of the exploration of the tree in Figure 1 by two workers. Worker **w1** has reached the leftmost failure node, while worker **w2** descended on the second branch down to the second constraint. Processing of the upper constraint resulted in a neutral interval $\geq$**15** being created (shown as a rectangular box in the figure). When the lower constraint of >**20** is reached, the worker notices that the constraint is subsumed by the inherited neutral interval and so the subtree below is pruned (as shown by the dotted line).

A second snapshot is shown in Figure 3. Worker **w1** has now reached the third child of the root, with the value **20**. As outlined earlier, this results in a neutral interval $\leq$**20** being associated with the root. This neutral interval is now propagated downwards, and its interaction with the constraint <**15** results in the whole subtree rooted at that constraint being pruned, i.e a solution with an arbitrary value <**15** is assumed (say **0**). This example shows why it is necessary to assume an arbitrary solution, instead of discarding the whole subtree. The latter approach would result in an incorrect solution **40** being assigned to the min node, and consequently to the root node as well.

The propagation of neutral intervals, as exemplified by Figure 3, is one of the crucial features of our algorithm. In general, propagation is required when a worker is updating the best-so-far value (and so the neutral interval) of an optimum node, while other workers are exploring branches below this node. The new neutral interval should now be brought to the attention of all workers below the given node. There are two basic approaches for handling this situation:

---

[3] This is the point where we use our simplifying assumption (the existence of a value node below each constraint node).

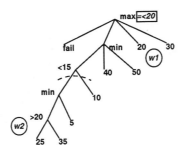

Figure 3: SECOND SNAPSHOT OF EXPLORATION OF THE SAMPLE TREE

- The workers below are notified about the new neutral interval, i.e. the information on changes is propagated downwards.

- The downwards propagation is avoided at the expense of each worker scanning the tree upwards every time it wants to make use of the neutral interval (e.g. for pruning).

Reynolds and Kefalas [10] have used the second approach in their proposed extension of the Brave system. A serious drawback of this approach is, however, that it slows down the exploration, even if only a single worker happens to be working on a subtree. Therefore the first approach seems to be preferable, i.e. the worker updating a best-so-far value in an optimum node should notify all the workers below the given node about the new neutral interval.

So far we have assumed that each optimum and constraint node has at least one value node below it. Let us now expand the domain of discussion to include trees where this condition is not enforced. If we extend the range of values that can be associated with nodes to include the infinite values $-\infty$ and $+\infty$, then each failure node can be viewed as a proper value node, with the actual value being $-\infty$ if the optimum node immediately above is a max node, and $+\infty$ if the optimum node immediately above is a min node.

The notion of constraint can have two interpretations in this extended framework. One can consider *strong* constraints, which actually guarantee the presence of a (finite) value node below; and *weak* constraints which may still hold if there is no proper value node in the subtree below. The implicit constraints generated by optimum nodes are obviously of the strong type. On the other hand, not all constraints can be assumed to be strong, as e.g. the constraints used in the branch and bound algorithm are normally of the weak type.

A weak constraint can be utilised (for pruning or for producing a neutral interval) only in one of the two kinds of optimum searches. For example, a weak constraint $< B$ occurring in a minimum search expresses the fact that the contribution of the current subtree to the minimum search will either be a value $< B$, or $+\infty$. This means that such a constraint can not be used to prune the subtree, as it can not guarantee that all values will be part of a single neutral interval. On the other hand a weak constraint of form $> B$ occurring in a minimum search will be equivalent to a strong constraint, and thus can safely be used for pruning, as the "failure" value

$+\infty$ is actually part of the constraint interval $> B$.

In our example this means that the first pruning step, shown in Figure 2, which is based on the constraint >20 in a minimum search, can be carried out even if the constraint is weak, i.e. if all value nodes below the constraint are replaced by failure nodes. On the other hand, the second pruning step (Figure 3) can not be carried out if the the constraint is weak.

4 Language Extensions

We propose new higher level predicates to be introduced to encapsulate the algorithm described in the previous section. The optimum search is generalised to allow arbitrary Prolog terms, and an arbitrary ordering relation *LessEq* instead of numbers and numerical comparison. The optimum search returns a pair of terms *Value-Info*, where the *Value* is used for ordering and *Info* can contain some additional information. To simplify the user interface, our experimental implementation assumes all (user-supplied) constraints to be weak.

The proposed new built-in predicates are the following:

maxof(*+LessEq*, *?Value-Info*, *+Goal*, *?Max*)
minof(*+LessEq*, *?Value-Info*, *+Goal*, *?Min*)

> *Max*(*Min*) is a *Value-Info* such that *Goal* is provable, and *Value* is the largest (smallest), according to the binary relation *LessEq*, among these *Value-Info* pairs. *LessEq* can be an arbitrary binary predicate, either user-defined or built-in, that defines a complete ordering relation. If *Goal* is not provable, maxof and minof fails (this failure replaces the infinite values of our abstract algorithm of the previous section). The following example is an illustration for the use of maxof:

```
        biggest_country(Continent, Country, Area) :-
            maxof(=<, A-C,
                    country(Continent, C, A),
                    Area-Country).
```

bestof(*+Dir*, *+LessEq*, *?Template*, *+Goal*, *?Best*)

> *Dir* can be either max or min. bestof(max, ...) is equivalent to maxof(...) and bestof(min, ...) is equivalent to minof(...). This predicate is just a notational tool for writing minimax-type algorithms.

constraint(*?Term1*, *+LessEq*, *?Term2*)

> *Term1* is known to be less or equal to *Term2* according to the binary relation *LessEq*. This means that all solutions of the current branch will satisfy the given condition. One of *Term1* and *Term2* is normally a *Value* of a maxof, minof or bestof, in which case the constraint can be used for pruning. An example:

```
        country(europe, Country, Area) :-
            constraint(Area, =<, 600000),
            european_country(Country, Area).
```

priority(*+Priority*)

> *Priority* should be an integer. This call declares that the current branch of

execution is of priority *Priority*. Several calls of the `priority` predicate can be issued on a branch, and the list of these priorities (earlier ones first), ordered lexicographically, will be used when comparing branches. Examples for the use of the `priority` primitive will be given in Section 6.

5 Implementation

We have designed an experimental implementation of the language primitives described in the previous section, within the current Aurora system itself. This uses a simplified version of the proposed algorithm, as it does not implement the propagation of neutral intervals. The implementation applies the best-first search strategy by default, but depth-first control is also available. This section gives a brief description of the experimental implementation.

Introduction of new control features is normally done via interpretation. We have decided to avoid the extra complexity and overheads of interpretation by introducing a meta-predicate called `task`, to be used to encapsulate the new control primitives within the application program. A call of `task` has the following form:

`task(`*Goal,* *NewContext* – *OldContext*`)`

Here *Goal* is normally a conjunction, which begins with calls of the control predicates `priority` and `constraint`. The invocation of `task` should always be the last subgoal in the surrounding `bestof`. If the *Goal* in `task` contains an embedded call to `bestof`, this should be the last subgoal in the conjunction, to make the minimax algorithm applicable.

The second argument of `task` is required for passing the control information on surrounding tasks and optimum searches. Similarly, the `bestof` (and `maxof`/`minof`) predicates acquire an additional last argument of the same structure. We use the form *NewContext* - *OldContext* to indicate that the role of this argument is similar to a difference list. The *OldContext* variable links the given call with the surrounding `bestof` or `task` invocation (i.e. it is the same variable as the *NewContext* variable in the extra argument of the surrounding control call). Similarly the *NewContext* variable is normally passed to the *Goal* argument, for use in embedded `task` or `bestof` invocations.

Let us show an example from the previous section in this modified form:

```
country(europe, Country, Area, Ctxt) :-
    task(
        (constraint(Area, =<, 600000),
         european_country(Country, Area)),
        _ - Ctxt).
```

Here we assume, that `european_country` does not contain any further invocations of `task` or `bestof`, hence *NewContext* is a void variable.

The execution of an application in this experimental implementation is carried out as follows. If there are no calls of `task` embedded in a `bestof`, then the optimum search is performed in a fairly straightforward way: a best-so-far value is maintained in the Prolog database which is updated each time a solution is reached.

When an invocation of `task` is reached within the `bestof` predicate, first the constraints are processed: if a constraint indicates that the subtree in question will not modify the best-so-far value (i.e. the constraint is subsumed by the currently applicable neutral interval), then the `task` call fails immediately. Otherwise the goal of the task, paired with information on the constraint, priority and context, is asserted into the Prolog database and the execution fails as well. When all the subtasks have been created and the exploration of the **bestof** subtree finishes, a best-first scheduling algorithm is entered: the subtask with the highest priority is selected and its goal is started. Such a subtask may give rise to further **bestof** and/or **task** calls, which are processed in a similar way.

For the sake of such nested task structure the best-first scheduling is implemented by building a copy of the search tree in the Prolog database, but with the branches ordered according to the user supplied priorities (in descending order). This tree is then used for scheduling (finding the highest priority task), as well as for pruning.

Pruning may be required when a leaf node of the optimum search is reached and the best-so-far value is updated. Following this update the internal tree is scanned and every task, which has become unnecessary according to its constraint, is deleted.

A more detailed description of the implementation can be found in [14].

6   Applications

Two larger test programs were developed to help in evaluating the implementation: a program for playing the game of kalah, using alpha-beta pruning, which is based on a version presented by Sterling and Shapiro [13]; and a program for the traveling salesman problem based on the branch-and-bound technique, as described in [1]. This section presents the general program schemes used in these programs, namely the branch-and-bound and alpha-beta pruning schemes. For the sake of readability we omit the additional context arguments in this presentation, but we do include the invocation of the **task** predicate.

6.1   The Branch-and-Bound Algorithm

We describe a general program scheme for the branch-and-bound algorithm. We assume that the nodes of the search tree are represented by (arbitrary) Prolog terms. We expect the following predicates to be supplied by the lower layer of the application:

child_of(*Parent, Child*) Node *Child* is a child of node *Parent*.

leaf_value(*Leaf, Value*) Node *Leaf* is a leaf node, with *Value* being the value associated with it.

node_bound(*Node, Bound*) All leaf nodes below the (non-leaf) node *Node* are known to have a value greater or equal to *Bound*.

Figure 4 shows the top layer of the branch-and-bound scheme based on the above predicates. The program uses a single **minof** call invoking the predicate **leaf_below(Node, Leaf, Value)**. The latter predicate simply enumerates all the **Leaf** nodes and corresponding **Values** below **Node**. The logic of this predicate is very simple: either we are at a leaf node (first clause), in which case we retrieve its value, or we pick up any child of the node and recursively enumerate all the descendants of that child (second clause). This logic is complemented with the calls providing the appropriate control (shown with a deeper indentation): calculating a lower bound for the relevant subtree (**node_bound**), calculating the **Priority** as the

```
% Leaf is the leaf below node with the minimal Value
branch_and_bound(Node, Leaf, Value):-
   minof(=<, V-L,  leaf_below(Node, L, V),  Value-Leaf).

% Node has a Leaf descendant with value Value
leaf_below(Node, Node, Value):-
   leaf_value(Node, Value).
leaf_below(Node, Leaf, Value):-
   child_of(Node, Child),
      node_bound(Child, Bound),
      Priority is -Bound,
                                          task((
      constraint(Bound, =<, Value),
      priority(Priority),
   leaf_below(Child, Leaf, Value)            ))
```

Figure 4: THE GENERAL SCHEME FOR THE BRANCH-AND-BOUND ALGORITHM

negated value of **Bound** (so that the subtrees where the bound is lower have higher priority), notifying the system about the bound (**constraint**) and the priority for the best-first search (**priority**). The last three calls in the clause are encapsulated within the auxiliary predicate **task** (shown with the deepest indentation).

This general scheme of Figure 4 can be concretised to support a specific application by designing an appropriate node data structure, and providing the definition of the lower level predicates (**child_of** etc.). This has been done for the traveling salesman problem, the preliminary performance results for which are presented in Section 7.

6.2   The Alpha-Beta Pruning Algorithm

We now proceed to describe a similar scheme for the minimax algorithm with alpha-beta pruning (Figure 5). Again we allow the nodes of the game tree to be represented by arbitrary Prolog terms. The topology of the tree and the values associated with nodes are expected to be supplied through predicates of the same form as for the branch-and-bound algorithm (**child_of**(*Parent, Child*) and **leaf_value**(*Leaf, Value*)). We require two additional auxiliary predicates:

node_priority(*Node, Prio*) *Prio* is the priority of node *Node*.

absolute_min_max(*Min, Max*) *Min* and *Max* are the absolute minimum and maximum values for the whole of the game tree[4].

This scheme can be invoked by the **alpha_beta(Node, max, Child, Value)** call. Here **Node** represents a node of the game tree, and **max** indicates that this is a maximum node. The call will return the **Child** with the maximal **Value**, from among all children of **Node**.

The **alpha_beta** predicate is defined in terms of a **bestof** search over all **Child-Value** pairs enumerated by the **child_value** predicate. This predicate, in its turn, issues appropriate constraint directives, enumerates the children (**child_of**),

---

[4]Note that the scheme is still usable if no such absolute bounds are available—one just has to delete those parts of the program, which deal with the constraints based on the absolute bounds.

```
% Node of type Type (min or max) has the value Value,
% produced by Child.
alpha_beta(Node, Type, Child, Value):-
    bestof(Type, =<, V-C,
           child_value(Node, Type, V, C),  Value-Child).

% Node of type Type has a Child with Value.
child_value(Node, Type, Value, Child):-
    opposite(Type, OppType),
        absolute_min_max(Min, Max),
                                                     task((
        constraint(Min, =<, Value),
        constraint(Value, =<, Max),
    child_of(Node, Child),
    node_value(Child, OppType, Value)            ))


% Node of type Type has Value.
node_value(Node, _, Value):-
    leaf_value(Node, Value).
node_value(Node, Type, Value):-
        node_priority(Node, Priority),
                                                     task((
        priority(Priority),
    bestof(Type, =<, V-null,
           child_value(Node, Type, V, _),  Value-null)   ))


opposite(max,min).
opposite(min,max).
```

Figure 5: THE MINIMAX ALGORITHM WITH ALPHA-BETA PRUNING

and invokes **node_value** for every child. The **node_value** predicate has two clauses, the first is applicable in the case of leaf nodes, while the second invokes the opposite **bestof** over **child_value** recursively, after having informed the system about the priority applicable to the given subtree.

Note that the algorithm presented in Figure 5 calculates the optimum with respect to the complete game tree. It is fairly easy, however, to incorporate an appropriate depth limit, as usually done in game playing algorithms, by a simple modification of this scheme.

7 Performance Results

Table 1 gives some early performance figures for the applications discussed in Section 6, using the experimental implementation described in Section 5.

The tests have been run on a Sequent^{TM} Symmetry S27 multiprocessor with 12 processors, and the Manchester scheduler [5] has been used. Time (in seconds) is given for the one-worker case, and speedups are shown for 2-10 workers.

The two traveling salesman sample runs involve complete graphs with 9 and 11

Version	1	Workers				
		2	4	6	8	10
	(Time)	(Speedup)				
Traveling salesman						
9 nodes	32.2	1.68	2.66	3.24	3.71	4.07
11 nodes	152.86	1.64	2.67	3.48	3.93	4.37
The game of kalah						
board 1	13.71	1.39	1.83	2.35	2.96	3.32
board 2	57.33	1.71	2.88	3.75	4.72	5.65
board 3	31.20	1.70	3.08	4.04	5.18	5.67
board 4	65.66	1.55	2.47	3.66	4.73	5.00

Table 1: RUN TIMES AND SPEEDUPS FOR VARIOUS OPTIMISATION PROBLEMS

nodes, and 36 and 55 edges, respectively. A variant of the game of kalah is used as the second test program. Four different board states are tested with a limited depth of search (4 steps). Because of the search tree being so shallow, the depth-first strategy is used, rather than the best-first one.

Considering the prototyping nature of our experimental implementation we view the results as quite promising. We plan to carry out a detailed performance evaluation in the near future to identify the overheads involved in various parts of the algorithm.

8   Related Work

An important issue is the relation of our work to the mainstream of research in constraint logic programming (CLP). In current CLP frameworks (as e.g. in the one described by van Hentenryck in [7]) the constraints arising in optimum search algorithms are handled by special built-in predicates. The reason behind this is that the generation of constraints is implicit in an optimum search, as the applicable constraint depends on the best-so-far value. We believe that by replacing such special predicates with the **bestof** construct, our extended algorithm can be smoothly integrated into a general CLP system.

Another aspect of comparison may be the type of parallelism. Current CLP systems address the issues of and-parallel execution of conjunctive goals as e.g. in the CLP framework described by Saraswat [12]. Our approach complements this by discussing issues of exploiting or-parallelism. Combination of the two types of parallelism can lead to much improved performance as shown by existing and-or-parallel systems, such as Andorra [11].

The problems of or-parallel execution of optimum search problems have been addressed by Reynolds and Kefalas [10] in the framework of their meta-Brave system. They introduce a special database for storing partial results or *lemmas*, with a restricted set of update operators. They describe programs implementing the minimax and branch-and-bound algorithms within this framework. They do not, however, address the problem of providing a uniform approach for both optimisation algorithms. Another serious drawback of their scheme is that pruning requires active participation of the processing agent to be pruned: e.g. in the minimax algorithm each processing agent has to check all its ancestor nodes, whether they make further processing of the given branch unnecessary.

9   Conclusions

The design and the implementation of the `bestof` predicate has several implications. First, we have developed a new higher order extension to Prolog, with an underlying algorithm general enough to encapsulate two important search control techniques: the branch-and-bound and alpha-beta pruning algorithms. The `bestof` predicate makes it possible to describe programs requiring such control techniques, in terms of special control primitives such as constraints and priority annotations. On the other hand we gained important experience by implementing the new predicates on the top of Aurora system. We believe that this experience can be utilised later, in a more efficient, lower level implementation as well.

We view the development of the `bestof` predicate as a first step towards a more general goal: identifying those application areas and special algorithms where the simple control of Prolog is hindering efficient parallel execution, and designing appropriate higher order predicates that encapsulate these algorithms. We believe that the gains of this work will be twofold: reducing the need for non-declarative language components as well as developing efficient parallel implementations of such higher order primitives.

Acknowledgements

The author would like to thank his colleagues in the Gigalips project at Argonne National Laboratory, the University of Bristol, the Swedish Institute of Computer Science and IQSOFT. Special thanks go to David H. D. Warren for continuous encouragement and help in this work. Thanks are also due to the anonymous referees, for valuable comments and suggestions for improvement.

This work was supported by the ESPRIT project 2025 "EDS", and the Hungarian-U.S. Science and Technology Joint Fund in cooperation with the Hungarian National Committee for Technical Development and the U.S. Department of Energy under project J.F. No. 031/90.

References

[1] Alfred V. Aho, John E. Hopcroft, and Jeffrey D. Ullman. *Data Structures and Algorithms*. Addison-Wesley, 1983.

[2] Khayri A. M. Ali and Roland Karlsson. The Muse or-parallel Prolog model and its performance. In *Proceedings of the North American Conference on Logic Programming*. The MIT Press, October 1990.

[3] Anthony Beaumont, S Muthu Raman, Péter Szeredi, and David H D Warren. Flexible Scheduling of Or-Parallelism in Aurora: The Bristol Scheduler. In *PARLE91: Conference on Parallel Architectures and Languages Europe*, pages 403–420. Springer Verlag, June 1991. Lecture Notes in Computer Science, Vol 506.

[4] Ralph Butler, Terry Disz, Ewing Lusk, Robert Olson, Ross Overbeek, and Rick Stevens. Scheduling OR-parallelism: an Argonne perspective. In *Logic*

Programming: Proceedings of the Fifth International Conference, pages 1590–1605. The MIT Press, August 1988.

[5] Alan Calderwood and Péter Szeredi. Scheduling or-parallelism in Aurora – the Manchester scheduler. In *Logic Programming: Proceedings of the Sixth International Conference*, pages 419–435. The MIT Press, June 1989.

[6] J. Chassin de Kergommeaux and P. Robert. An abstract machine to implement efficiently OR-AND parallel Prolog. *Journal of Logic Programming*, 7, 1990.

[7] Pascal van Hentenryck. *Constraint Satisfation in Logic programming*. The MIT Press, 1989.

[8] Ewing Lusk, David H. D. Warren, Seif Haridi, et al. The Aurora or-parallel Prolog system. *New Generation Computing*, 7(2,3):243–271, 1990.

[9] B. Ramkumar and L.V. Kalé. Compiled execution of the reduce-OR process model on multiprocessors. In *Proceedings of the North American Conference on Logic Programming*, pages 331–331. The MIT Press, October 1989.

[10] T. J. Reynold and P. Kefalas. OR-parallel Prolog and search problems in AI applications. In *Logic Programming: Proceedings of the Seventh International Conference*, pages 340–354. The MIT Press, 1990.

[11] V. Santos Costa, D. H. D. Warren, and R. Yang. The Andorra-I Engine: A parallel implementation of the Basic Andorra model. In *Logic Programming: Proceedings of the Eighth International Conference*. The MIT Press, 1991.

[12] Vijay A. Saraswat. *Concurrent Constraint Programming Languages*. PhD thesis, Carnegie-Mellon University, January 1989.

[13] Leon Sterling and Ehud Shapiro. *The Art of Prolog*. The MIT Press, 1986.

[14] Péter Szeredi. Design and implementation of Prolog language extensions for or-parallel systems. Technical Report, IQSOFT and University of Bristol, December 1990.

[15] Péter Szeredi. Using dynamic predicates in an or-parallel Prolog system. In Vijay Saraswat and Kazunori Ueda, editors, *Logic Programming: Proceedings of the 1991 International Logic Programming Symposium*, pages 355–371. The MIT Press, October 1991.

[16] David H. D. Warren. The SRI model for or-parallel execution of Prolog—abstract design and implementation issues. In *Proceedings of the 1987 Symposium on Logic Programming*, pages 92–102, 1987.

Exploiting Dependent And-parallelism in Prolog: the Dynamic Dependent And-parallel Scheme (DDAS)

Kish Shen[§]
Department of Computer Science
University of Bristol
Bristol BS8 1TR
U.K.
kish@compsci.bristol.ac.uk

Abstract

DDAS (Dynamic Dependent And-parallel Scheme) is an and-parallel execution scheme for Prolog, designed to exploit both dependent and independent and-parallelism efficiently in full Prolog programs. In particular, DDAS can exploit non-deterministic and-parallelism, a form of and-parallelism that has been under-exploited in parallel Prologs. DDAS can exploit and-parallelism without th need for annotations, but for efficiency reasons, the and-parallelism is extracted by means of an annotation scheme called the Extended Conditional Graph Expressions, an extension to the Conditional Graph Expressions as proposed by Hermenegildo. Backtracking is kept simple in DDAS in order to optimise forward execution.

This paper presents a high-level overview of DDAS. The emphasis is on describing the model rather than implementation issues, although some of the design decisions are discussed in the context of implementation considerations. A prototype pseudo-parallel WAM-based implementation of DDAS has been implemented, and the initial results suggest that an efficient implementation is feasible.

1 Introduction

Implicit exploitation of parallelism in Prolog has until recently concentrated on extracting two forms of parallelism: or-parallelism and independent and-parallelism (IAP); both individually (*e.g.* [24, 11, 1, 6, 8]) and some combination of the two (*e.g.* [5, 7]). Comparatively little attention has been given to exploiting dependent and-parallelism (DAP)[1] within Prolog, although interest has grown recently (*e.g.* [14, 20]).

In this paper, the Dynamic Dependent And-parallel Scheme (DDAS), a scheme designed to exploit DAP and IAP, will be presented. The main aim of DDAS is to run *full* Prolog programs in parallel, extracting as much and-parallelism as possible, without seeking to change the Prolog language, or impose too high a cost in exploiting the parallelism.

It is generally considered to be difficult and inefficient to exploit unrestricted DAP within Prolog, especially because of its interaction with the backtracking behaviour of Prolog. Proposals to exploit DAP either did not give much attention to efficiency, or restrict

---

[§]Most of the research reported in this paper was carried out while the author was at the Computer Laboratory, University of Cambridge, Cambridge, U.K.

[1]In this paper, "dependent and-parallelism" is defined as starting the resolution of body goals which *might* affect each other's search-space (through the unifications they perform) in parallel.

the parallelism in order to achieve efficiency. One advantage of DDAS is that in many ways it is less restrictive in its exploitation of DAP than other efficient approaches such as Andorra-I [14]; but at the same time efficiency considerations played an important rôle in the design of the scheme.

The rest of this paper is organised as follows: first the basic concepts behind DDAS will be introduced, followed by a more detailed overview of the forward and backward execution of the scheme. Efficiency issues are then briefly discussed, followed by a summary of the initial results obtained from a prototype implementation. Finally, related work in the field is briefly compared to DDAS. A reasonable familiarity with Prolog and the basic issues of parallelism in Prolog is assumed throughout this paper.

Many important issues, such as the characteristic of the parallelism within application programs, details of dealing with side-effects, and detailed implementation considerations, cannot be addressed within the limited space of this paper. The interested reader is referred to my thesis [15] for a more detailed discussion of some of these issues.

2   Basic Approach

Following Warren [23], the term **worker** will be used to refer to the entities that perform the computation, or **work**. In common with many previous approaches (*e.g.* [24, 11, 1, 8, 6]), DDAS takes the subtree-based approach to parallelism, *i.e.* parallelism is achieved by allowing more than one worker to explore the search-space of a program simultaneously. Each worker performs work in much the same way as a sequential Prolog engine, thus the search-space is divided into "chunks" or subtrees that are each executed sequentially. Each such subtree is referred to as a **task**, and represents the execution of a goal. A task finishes successfully if the goal returns a solution.

The most common way to represent the search-space is the search-tree, but for and-parallelism, it is more convenient to use a proof tree [3] to represent the search-space, as the subtrees can be more directly and simply defined. A proof tree is an and-tree, where each node represents a call to a goal. A node can be **extended** or **non-extended**. If extended, the node represents a successful unification for the goal, and its immediate descendants are the body goals of the clause that unified with the goal. A non-extended node has yet to be unified. When all nodes are extended, the proof tree represents a successful evaluation of the query, and corresponds to a branch of the search-tree that terminates in a successful evaluation. Backtracking can be viewed as replacing an extended node with an alternative extension (*i.e.* an alternative unification for the goal), which then leads to a new proof tree. Each extended node can form the root of a subtree for and-parallel execution.

In the subtree-based approach, equivalence to Prolog is achieved by ensuring that the search-space explored in parallel is the same as that explored sequentially by Prolog.[2] For or-parallelism and IAP, this equivalence is achieved because each task cannot affect the computations performed in the other tasks, and each task performs the same computation as in the equivalent part of the sequential search-space. For DAP, the tasks running in parallel may affect each other's search-space, so it is more difficult to maintain the equivalence to sequential Prolog. With DDAS, the equivalence is maintained by synchronising at a finer level than that done with an IAP system: instead of synchronising the execution at the level of a task to ensure independence, synchronisation is at the level of the unifications performed by the tasks. The synchronisation must ensure that the same computations are performed in parallel as in sequential Prolog, *i.e.*, the same search-space is explored, and that corresponding unifications in the parallel and sequential execution make the same substitutions for variables to non-variables, up to the renaming of variables. Thus,

---

[2] This is a simplified view that ignores differences due to speculative work and work avoided by intelligent backtracking.

execution of goals which are not independent of other goals executing in parallel is allowed, giving rise to DAP.

DDAS can be viewed as consisting of two main components: the mechanism for synchronisation just discussed, which ensures the equivalence to sequential Prolog during forward execution; and a backward execution component for ensuring that the equivalence is preserved when a unification fails. These components will now be presented in more detail.

3 Forward execution

3.1 Basic concepts

The main problem with DAP is that when tasks (working on different subtrees) which are not independent (*i.e.* they share variables) are executed in parallel, they may try to bind the same variable during their execution. In DDAS, such binding conflicts are resolved using a priority system to synchronise the unifications — unifications which would be executed first in sequential Prolog have a higher priority than unifications that would be executed after them in sequential Prolog. That is, *the left-to-right ordering of goals (and hence unifications) of sequential Prolog is maintained for the priority system*. Thus, for several tasks that share the same variable, the task that is executing the goal with the highest priority (the leftmost), is the task that is allowed to bind the variable. The other tasks must suspend if they try to bind the variable to a non-variable term. Abstractly, this can be regarded as allowing sequential Prolog execution at all time (the leftmost goal), with parallelism allowed for goals to the right as long as their unifications executing in parallel do not interfere with the sequential computation.

This suspension mechanism is similar to the synchronisation mechanism used by the committed choice languages in that the goal allowed to bind the variable can be regarded as the producer for the value of the variable, and the other goals as the consumers of the value. However, there are two crucial differences:

- No explicit annotations are required: the producer/consumer positions are fixed implicitly by the order of sequential Prolog execution. A producer can never appear to the right of its consumer.[3]

- The producer status applies to the whole proof of a goal, and not just a particular unification. Therefore, any subgoals of the goal inherit the producer status.

Note that the binding conflict problem does not arise for variables which are accessed by only one or none of the goals executing in and-parallel. These variables are *non-dependent* variables, in that no synchronisation on binding is needed for them. All variables which cannot be determined to be non-dependent are *assumed* to be *dependent*. Thus the DAP exploited by DDAS is a natural superset of IAP: IAP goals are simply those goals which do not contain any dependent variables.

This classification of variables has definite advantages from an implementation viewpoint: non-dependent variables can be implemented as normal Prolog variables, avoiding any overheads of the dependent variables.

All goals can *potentially* be executed in and-parallel, but executing all goals in and-parallel will almost certainly not be the most efficient way of executing the program in parallel, as will be discussed later. Therefore, annotations are used to indicate which goals are to be executed in and-parallel, allowing for a more efficient exploitation. Such

---

[3] Although GHC does not contain visible annotations, the programmer still needs to control and direct the parallelism *explicitly*.

annotations are not necessary for correct parallel execution, but are needed for effective parallel execution. Many annotation schemes are possible. The annotation scheme that is developed is an extension of the Conditional Graph Expression (CGE) notation proposed by Hermenegildo (as a refinement to the notation of DeGroot [6]) for IAP [8], and like the CGE notations, they indicate *where* parallelism should be exploited, and not *how* it should be exploited. It is simply a matter of convenience to choose such annotations over a scheme which specifies where parallelism should *not* be exploited. The annotations can be supplied by the system as part of the compilation process, or by the programmer directly.

3.2   Syntax of annotation used for DDAS

The extended CGE scheme used is called the *Extended Conditional Graph Expressions* (ECGEs). Like the CGEs, ECGEs are annotations that enclose a set of two or more consecutive body goals, which are to be run in parallel:

```
(<CGE conditions> => b1(...) & ... & bn(...))
```

The dependent status of a term is determined at run-time. The proposed extended annotations in the ECGE must therefore be able to dynamically label variables as dependent. This is done by extending DeGroot's idea of static annotations with dynamic tests as used in the CGEs by adding an additional CGE "condition": dep/1. This is an annotation that marks the variable(s) (or the unbound variables inside a structure if the annotated variable is bound to a structure) which occurs textually inside the CGE as a path to a dependent variable (or variables).[4] These dependent variables obey the producer/consumer rules already outlined. Variables that are not annotated by this annotation are assumed to be non-dependent.

Note that non-strict IAP, as described by Hermenegildo and Rossi [10] can also be exploited in DDAS: with non-strict IAP, goals which are run in and-parallel can contain some variables which are dependent variables, but which will only be bound by one of the and-goals. With DDAS, depending on the ECGE conditions, these goals can be run in and-parallel either with such variables labelled as dependent (this may cause unnecessary suspensions), or "non-strictly" with the variables not labelled as dependent.

3.3   Conditions for suspension

To more precisely define the condition for suspension, the concept of *nv-binding*, as defined by Hermenegildo and Rossi [10], is extended to deal with dependent variables:

v-binding, nv-binding, non-variable access   A binding x/t, where x is a non-dependent variable is a *v-binding* if t is a variable (dependent or non-dependent). Otherwise (that is, if x is a dependent variable, or t is a non-variable), it is a *nv-binding*.

A non-variable access to a dependent variable is any access to the variable that is not a v-binding.

A task will suspend if it tries to nv-bind a dependent variable, and there is an active task to its left that also has access to that dependent variable. The task is said to be in a *consumer* position for the variable. The leftmost active task is said to be in the *producer* position for the variable, and is allowed to bind the variable. Note that the definition

---

[4] Note that if the dependent variable is aliased to another variable before entering the ECGE, and both variables occur textually inside the ECGE, then both should be annotated with dep/1 as they represent different paths of access to the term represented by the dependent variable. If a variable is aliased to a dependent variable inside the ECGE, then this represents the same path of access, and only the dependent variable has to be marked as dependent.

of nv-binding implies that an attempt to bind a dependent variable to another dependent variable will always suspend unless both dependent variables are in a producer position.

A stronger condition for suspension is required for full Prolog, in oder to cope with the meta-logical and extra-logical predicates. To a task that is a consumer for an unbound dependent variable, the variable is an entity whose value cannot yet be determined. All non-variable accesses to the dependent variable require the value of the variable be known, so all such accesses are suspended.

3.4 Unsuspending a suspended goal

After suspending, a task can be unsuspended and execution resumed if the dependent variable it is suspended on becomes bound to a non-variable. Note that other tasks suspended on the same variable will also be unsuspended. This is similar to the unsuspension mechanism of the committed choice languages. However, in order to maintain Prolog behaviour, a further case of unsuspension has to be supported. Consider the following case:

```
foo(X) :- (dep(X) => a(X) & b(X)).

a(_).
b(1).
```

a(X), in a producer position for the dependent variable X, does not bind X; but b(X), in a consumer position for X, will try to bind the dependent variable. If it then suspends, there is the problem of how it would be unsuspended. This is achieved by introducing the concept of *dynamic producer*:

> The producer for a dependent variable is the goal which is the leftmost active (still executing) goal in the ECGE which has access to that variable.

A consequence of the above concept is that when a goal finishes execution successfully, the producer status is passed to the next leftmost still active (if any) goal that has dependent variable(s) in the ECGE. If the task executing this goal was suspended on a dependent variable for which it has now become the producer for, the task is unsuspended.[5] Thus, in the above example, initially a(X) is the producer for X, until it is resolved. At that point, the producer status is passed to b(X). If b(X) was suspended on X, it can now wake up and bind X as it has become the producer for the variable. This second route to unsuspension guarantees that a suspended goal will always be unsuspended *if* goals to its left terminate.

3.5 A simple example

If the standard naïve reverse program is executed under normal conditions (*i.e.* first argument instantiated to a list, second argument uninstantiated), it can be annotated with the following ECGE:[6]

---

[5] The reason that the leftmost status is not traced for each individual dependent variable is because of the complications of aliasing between dependent variables. The actual scheme used in the implementation of DDAS is more elaborate and allows more precision in both the leftmost status and the restricted backward execution scheme [15]. The less precise scheme is described here for simplicity.

[6] The normal conditions can be guaranteed and parallel execution allowed only if those conditions are met by providing extra ECGE condition. These are left out to simplify the presentation.

```
nrev([], []).
nrev([E|L], R) :-
    (dep([R1]) =>
        nrev(L, R1) &
        append(R1, [E], R)
    ).
```

Initially, when `nrev/2` is first executed, the two body goals (`nrev(L, R1)` and `append(R1, [E], R)`) are executed in and-parallel, with the task executing `append` suspending when it attempts to nv-bind `R1`. This is repeated at every call to `nrev/3` until the original list is traversed. The first clause of `nrev/3` is called, and a reversed list starts to be built up in `R1`. This causes the various calls to `append/2` to unsuspend, and eventually the reversed list is produced.

4   Backward execution

The important consideration for backward execution is that correct behaviour with respect to Prolog is preserved. That is, the same termination behaviour as Prolog is maintained, and the same solutions as Prolog are returned, in the same order. Within such specifications, many schemes are possible. Here, one possible scheme, which seeks to limit speculative computation, would be presented.

4.1   Unbinding a dependent binding

The execution of the naïve reverse example is very similar to the way a committed choice language would execute the program. The reason is that there is no need to deal with failures in this example. The committed choice languages are defined to not allow failures without the whole program failing, but DDAS must allow failure so as to be equivalent to Prolog. Some previous schemes that tried to unite a committed choice framework with a more Prolog-like framework have to deal with this problem also. Two such schemes [18, 4] both choose to use some form of intelligent backtracking as the means to deal with failures. The main advantage of intelligent backtracking is that much unneeded work can be avoided. The disadvantages are that firstly intelligent backtracking imposes some overhead to the normal forward execution of a program as extra information to allow intelligent backtracking has to be carried; secondly, such schemes are likely to be quite complex; and thirdly strict equivalence to Prolog is not maintained (especially with regards to side-effects).

For these reasons, and also because of the belief that it is not clear how practical the benefits of intelligent backtracking are, and that with careful programming and annotations, a much less intelligent backtracking scheme can be used without a high cost, only very limited effort has been made to make the backtracking scheme "intelligent" in DDAS. This allows the forward execution to be optimised, as it minimises the information needed for backtracking, which has to be generated and carried during forward execution. The assumption is that the and-parallelism will generally be exploited in situations where the goals are likely to succeed. The backward execution scheme is also relatively simple (and so is probably easier to implement) because of this lack of intelligence.

In the basic backward execution scheme, if a dependent binding is undone during backtracking, then all tasks executing goals to the right in the ECGE, and which have access to the dependent variable, are told to redo their computation. The reason is that such tasks are those which *might* be affected by the unbinding of the dependent variable as they might have consumed the binding. A task told to redo its goal's computation would discard all the computation the task performed, and execute the goal from the start again — this is unlike more intelligent schemes, where the system would try to undo as little work as possible.

The actual scheme used for DDAS is a slight optimisation of this basic scheme: no redo is sent by the producer if the dependent binding has not been consumed by any consumer, and a consumer does not carry out the redo unless it has consumed at least one dependent binding. The implementation cost of this scheme is low: a bit is needed for each dependent variable to record if it has been consumed or not; and a bit is needed for each task executing a goal to indicate if it has consumed any dependent bindings or not. The information is not precise: the task may have consumed a different dependent binding from the one causing the redo, and there is no record of which task consumed which binding.

Preliminary results presented in [15] do suggest that, as expected, the "optimised" scheme can reduce the amount of work that have to be discarded. However this scheme cannot be considered to be very intelligent, as it is still possible to redo much work that need not be discarded. It is not clear *in practice* how much useful work will be thrown away. However, there is one quite common case which can lead to a significant amount of wastage, but which can be quite easily detected and avoided through compile-time analysis. The problem occurs because of a premature binding of a dependent variable: the dependent variable is bound at a clause head, followed by some simple tests which fail. This causes the unbinding of the dependent variable, and the possibility of discarding a large amount of work. This problem is closely related to that of finding deterministic goal in systems that execute deterministic goals in parallel, such as PNU-Prolog [13] and Andorra-I [14]. So similar methods of determinacy analysis as Andorra-I at compile time can be used to avoid this problem. The purpose of the determinacy analysis is somewhat different, however: in DDAS it would be used to provide more efficient parallel execution, whereas in Andorra-I it is needed to extract and-parallelism. Other forms of compile time analysis can probably also be used to reduce the risk of wasting useful work in other situations (*e.g.* by avoiding and-parallel execution of goals with a high probability of failure).

For deeper failures, it should be noted that only failures in the producer which lead to unbinding of the dependent variable would cause wasted work. The possibility of wasted work can be reduced by reducing the chances of failure of the producer. One possible way is through constraints, so that the constraints prevent the binding of variables to values which would later lead to failure. This would probably be effective in reducing the amount of wasted work performed by DDAS, in addition to reducing the size of the search-space in some programs.

4.2   Backtracking to the top of a sibling and-goal

Consider the following example:

```
foo :- (dep([A]) => f(A) & g(A) & h(B) & i(A)), j.
```

The goals inside the ECGE in this example can be classified into two types: *dependent and-goals*, which have dependent variables (in this case A, so f(A), g(A) and i(A) are dependent and-goals), and *independent and-goals*, which do not have dependent variables (in this case, h(B)).

For independent and-goals, the "restricted" intelligent backtracking scheme of Hermenegildo [8] is retained (and thus break the strict equivalence to Prolog — so if side-effect exists in a sibling and-goal, restricted intelligent backtracking cannot be allowed locally). That is, if a task tries to backtrack pass the top of a independent and-goal (*e.g.* in this case, if the task executing h(B) backtracks to the top of h(B), and cannot find an alternative), then the whole ECGE fails. However, if any of the goals to the left of h(B) (f(A) and g(A)) contain side-effects, then only goals to the right (i(A)) can be killed.

For a dependent and-goal, the situation is slightly more complex: the failure of a dependent and-goal does not mean the failure of the entire ECGE, as dependent and-goals to the left of the one that failed may bind the dependent variable(s) to different values and allow the failed goal to then execute successfully. Thus, the task executing the dependent and-goal that is immediately to the left of the failed dependent and-goal is informed of the failure, in the absence of side-effects. Dependent and-goals may be separated by non-dependent and-goals, so the left dependent neighbour of i(A) is g(A) in the example, separated by h(B). Thus if i(A) fails, then if h(B) contains no side-effects, g(A) is informed of the failure; otherwise h(B) is informed.

If the informed task has already finished, it immediately backtracks. If it has not finished, it will begin backtracking once it is finished (it does not start backtracking immediately in this case to retain equivalence to Prolog). If the failing dependent and-goal is the leftmost dependent and-goal, and so has no dependent and-goal to its left (in this case, f(A)), the failure is treated like the failure of an independent and-goal — *i.e.* the whole ECGE can fail.

The co-ordination between tasks during backtracking — *i.e.* redoing a task because of the unbinding of a dependent variable to the left, informing a task to the left of failure, and the killing of tasks because an independent and-goal has failed — can be done by "signals" being sent between tasks. The signals for the three situations described are "redo", "fail" and "kill" respectively.

4.3 Dealing with cuts

The cut prunes away part of the search-space. For correct parallel execution, any work done in the pruned search-space is wasted work and has to be discarded. Thus, ideally, no work should be performed in the pruned search-space.

Like &-Prolog, and unlike the committed choice languages and Andorra, goals to the left and right of the pruning operator (cut for DDAS) can execute in parallel at the same time. However, the pruning needs to be co-ordinated across these goals, when the cut prunes away search-space in other and-goals. Consider the following clause:

```
foo :- (true => a & b & (c, !) & d).
```

This cut prunes away the choices for a, b, c, as well as foo. The main problem is that a and b are executing in parallel, and may still be executing when the cut is encountered. The effect of the cut is performed in two stages: the choices for c are pruned when the cut is encountered. The tasks executing a and b are then informed that a cut has occurred to their right. The pruning of choices on a and b then takes place when all sibling and-goals between them and the cut have returned a solution, *i.e.* b is pruned when b returns a solution, a is pruned when both a and b have returned a solution (the finishing of the task that finishes later initiates the pruning). The reason that a cannot be pruned before b is finished is because b might fail due to some dependent binding it consumed, and this would cause a to generate another solution before the cut would be encountered in sequential execution.

Note that no parallelism is lost (except for whatever overhead is needed to perform the cut) in dealing with cuts. This is in contrast to dealing with other side-effects, where the task performing the side-effect must in general suspend until it is leftmost.

4.4 An example

In the example shown in figure 1, the program fails because one of the list element is not a number. One possible execution of the program is shown in the figure. In the figure,

```
qsort([H|T], S, X) :-
        (dep([A, B, Y]) =>
            split(H, T, A, B) &
            qsort(A,S,[H|Y]) &
            qsort(B,Y,X)
        ).
qsort([], X, X).

split(H, [A|X], L, Z) :- A =< H, L = [A|Y], split(H,X,Y,Z).
split(H, [A|X], Y, L) :- A > H, L = [A|Z], split(H,X,Y,Z).
split(_,[],[],[]).

:- qsort([7,8,apples,9], S, []).
```

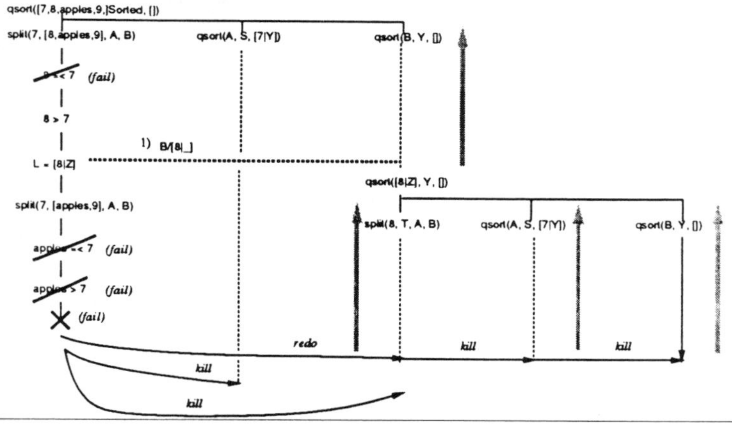

Figure 1: Execution of quick sort with failure

unifications which occur at the same time are shown at the same horizontal level. Each task is shown executing successive goals in the same column. Vertical dotted lines indicates a suspended task, and a horizontal dotted line indicates the binding of a dependent variable and the subsequent unsuspension of the task(s) suspended on that variable. The "redo" and "fail" signals sent from one task to another are indicated by thin arrows. A crossed-out goal indicates a unification failure.

The execution proceeds as follows: the task running split(7,[8,apples,9],A,B) binding B to [8|_] at point 1) in figure 1. This unsuspends qsort(B,Y,[]), which then enters a new ECGE, and starts off three descendant and-goals. All these and-goals suspend. Meanwhile, the split(7,[8,apples,9],A,B) task fails when it tries to do arithmetic comparisons with apples. This causes the task to backtrack, unbinding the binding made to B. The task sends a "redo" signal to the task running qsort(B,Y,[]), which has split into three descendant and-tasks, these descendant ECGE's tasks are killed, and the "redo" then continues to undo the computations performed before creating the descendant ECGE, as illustrated by the grey arrows in the figure. The split(7,[8,apples,9],A,B) task finally fails to the start of the goal, and sends a "kill" signal to the and-tasks running qsort(A,S,[H|Y]) and qsort(B,Y,X), as shown at the bottom of the figure (the latter task may still be in the middle of a "redo", in which case the "redo" simply continues, but forward execution is not restarted. If forward execution has already resumed, then it is killed).

5   A Simple Example

It is beyond the scope of this paper to fully demonstrate the utility of DDAS. Instead, a simple example would be given here to illustrate the exploitation of non-determinate dependent and-parallelism, a form of parallelism that has not yet been efficiently exploited in parallel Prolog systems. Consider the example in figure 2, where given a list of persons, People, and a person Person, languages_of_sgs/4 finds from People the people who are "cousins of the same generation"[7] of Person, and from these cousins, produces the list Speakers of people who speaks language L. The predicate has as many solutions as there are languages in the database, and in general a person can speak more than one language, so the program has non-deterministic and-parallelism.

```
languages_of_sgs(Person, People, L, Speakers) :-
    (dep([Sgs,L]) =>
        find_sgs(People, Person, Sgs) &
        language(L) &
        all_speak(Sgs, L, Speakers)
    ).

find_sgs([X|People], Person, Sgs) :-
    sg(Person, X), !, Sgs = [X|Sgs1],
    find_sgs(People, Person, Sgs1).
find_sgs([_|People], Person, Sgs) :-
    find_sgs(People, Person, Sgs).
find_sgs([],_,[]).

sg(X, X) :- person(X).
sg(X, Y) :-
    parent(X,Xp), sg(Xp, Yp), parent(Y, Yp).

all_speak([X|Sgs], L, [X|Speakers]) :-
    speak(X, L), !,
    all_speak(Sgs, L, Speakers).
all_speak([_|Sgs], L, Speakers) :-
    all_speak(Sgs, L, Speakers).
all_speak([],_, []).

/* followed by database of people, parent, language, speak */
```

Figure 2: Example program with non-deterministic DAP

DDAS, with the ECGE annotations shown, can execute this program in and-parallel: find_sgs/3 generates the list of cousins, Sgs, which is incrementally consumed in parallel

---
[7] The sg/2 predicate, which defines "cousins of the same generation", is taken from Ullman [21, page 797].

by `all_speak/3`, generating the list of speakers for the first language, and subsequently the lists for other languages can be generated through backtracking.

This program will also benefit from or-parallelism: the lists of speakers for the different languages could be generated in or-parallel. DDAS can be readily extended to exploit or-parallelism: a proposal to do so, based on the "or-under-and" method of combining IAP and or-parallelism [17], is called Prometheus [15], and is able to exploit and- (IAP and DAP) and or-parallelism. As each branch of the search-tree is computed independently in the "or-under-and" method, the addition of dependent and-goals add no extra complications to the conceptual model. There have been some recent proposals to implement the "or-under-and" [7], and such implementation models can be extended to cope with DDAS.

6 Efficiency of DDAS

The design of DDAS attempts to achieve efficiency at two levels:

- the execution scheme is kept as close to Prolog as possible, with parallelism exploited only if extra resources are available. This ensures that, ignoring implementation overheads, the system will never perform worse than sequential Prolog.

- Implementation costs are considered during the design. Two somewhat conflicting aims have to be balanced: minimising potential implementation overheads, and maximising the amount of exploitable parallelism.

The unbinding of a dependent variable may cause a lot of work to be redone, but it is important to note that this wasted work would only be performed if resources are available. Nevertheless, the available resources can be better utilised if they are directed to non-wasted work. I believe that with a good preprocessor, efficient allocation and usage of resources can be achieved. However, this needs to be confirmed by actual results from real programs.

In addition, the question of whether the implementation overheads are acceptable or not cannot be answered at a high-level, and can only be properly addressed with an actual implementation. To this end, a prototype pseudo-parallel DDAS implementation — DASWAM, has been implemented.

It is beyond the scope of this paper to discuss the details of DASWAM. A very brief summary will be given here. More details can be found in my thesis [15], with the more novel aspects of the system summarised in [16]. DASWAM is derived from suitably modifying a sequential WAM [22] to execute in parallel. The modifications are based on the marker scheme proposed for the RAP-WAM [8], suitably extended for DDAS. The major addition to the RAP-WAM is a new tagged data-type: the dependent cell, which is used to represent the dependent variable. In addition, the markers need to carry extra information to allow the determination of producer-consumer status.

7 Initial Results from the DASWAM

The main reasons of implementing the prototype DASWAM is to:

- verify that the abstract design of the DASWAM is valid and feasible.

- use the prototype to study the behaviour and characteristics of DDAS.

- verify that DASWAM can be implemented relatively efficiently.

The prototype implementation is under active development, and is still at an early stage. The current state of the prototype is sufficient to demonstrate the validity of the design of DASWAM, and also to at least suggest that the implementation overhead is not prohibitively high. However, the behaviour and characteristics of DDAS have not yet been studied extensively. A compiler is being developed by modifying the SICStus V0.6's compiler [2], and is currently able to compile some programs. Programs tested include naïve reverse, various versions of quick-sort (differing mainly in the ECGE used), a N-queens program, and a clustering algorithm, which is the core part of a network management application developed by British Telecom.[8]

The prototype DASWAM is not a truly parallel system. Rather, programs are executed in pseudo-parallel: parallelism is simulated by cycling through all the workers, executing one DASWAM instruction from each worker at a time. The main reason for implementing a pseudo-parallel system is that it is more flexible: it is not limited by the physical limitations (such as number of processors) of a parallel system, thus allowing a more extensive study of the high-level issues and characteristics of DDAS. In addition, it is easier to monitor a pseudo-parallel system, as such monitoring would not perturb the system. This is important in the initial stages of studying the design of a system.

The prototype was developed by first implementing a sequential SICStus WAM as specified in [2], and then adding the DASWAM extensions. The initial results suggest that sequential programs run at about half the speed on DASWAM when compared to running on a sequential SICStus WAM. Programs with annotations that exploit DAP running on one worker run at about a quarter the speed of the sequential version of the program running on the sequential SICStus WAM. Although the program is run on one worker, much of the extra work associated with DASWAM, such as allocating the markers, conversion of dependent variables, testing for producer and consumer status, is performed.

It must be noted that no attempt has been made to optimise the parallel modifications to the WAM in DASWAM. It is expected that the overheads can be substantially reduced, and that the overhead for executing sequential code can be reduced to that seen in Aurora [19], because almost none of the parallel modifications are invoked, except for using an unbound tag, and some extra tests for the dependent tag during unification. The overhead for executing parallel code should be reducible as well, as the independent parallel version of quicksort seems to account for half the parallel overhead of the dependent parallel version — the IAP version ran in 533ms on a DECSystem 5400, the DAP version in 783ms, compared to 383ms for the sequential version. Running programs with IAP only on DASWAM does not invoke any of the machinery associated with DAP (as all variables are non-dependent), except for some tag tests, so similar efficiency as &-Prolog should be achievable, which is much lower than the current overheads (see [9] for a study of &-Prolog performance). Thus there does seem to be much potential for reducing the overheads.

The initial results do suggest that DDAS is a feasible approach for exploiting DAP, and that the potential amount of parallelism is higher than that derived IAP alone. For example, figure 3 shows the potential speed-ups for three versions of quick-sort: an IAP only version (IAP), and two DAP versions — (i) DAP, wasted work: a version containing shallow failures after binding the dependent variable, leading to a large amount of work being redone (about 1.8 times the amount of useful work with 20 workers), and (ii) DAP, no wasted work: a version which do not have the wasted work problem (and can be obtained from the wasted work version by compile-time analysis). This last version of the program is able to achieve significantly greater speed-ups than the IAP version. In fact, even the DAP, wasted work version has better speed-ups than the IAP version. Note that machine dependent overheads (such as time for locking, and contention on memory) are not modelled in the prototype.

---

[8] Some of these programs were hand-modified from SICStus WAM code as the compiler was not ready when the data was gathered.

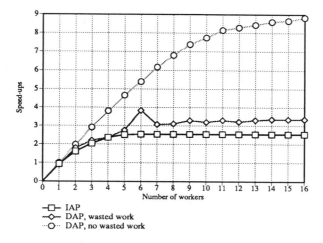

Figure 3: Comparison of speed-ups for various versions of quick-sort on DASWAM

8 Comparison with related work

DDAS can potentially exploit more parallelism than most of the other proposed systems that exploit DAP, as it is able to exploit non-deterministic DAP. Thus, for example, it is able to exploit parallelism not exploited in schemes which exploits deterministic and-parallelism such as PNu-Prolog [13] and Andorra-I [14]. In addition to "true" non-deterministic DAP such as the speakers example, simulation results for IAP [17, 15] suggest that it is quite common for a goal to only have one solution, but have many side branches which do not lead to a solution. It seems likely that this characteristic exists in dependent and-goals as well. Such goals can theoretically be executed in and-parallel by Andorra-I, but in practice it may be difficult to recognise that such goals are really deterministic, and thus the and-parallelism is not exploited. DDAS would be able to exploit such parallelism.

DDAS can also exploit more and-parallelism than schemes which exploit only IAP, such as the AND/OR process model [5] and &-Prolog [8, 9].

Some proposed systems can exploit more parallelism than DDAS. For example, Tebra's OMI [20] exploits and-parallelism in an "optimistic" way, and is similar to DDAS as the same priority system for binding of dependent variables is used. It can exploit more and-parallelism than DDAS, as a task can nv-bind a dependent variable in a consumer position. The parallelism is also more speculative than in DDAS; so for example, it will perform more work than DDAS in the speakers example. In addition, implementation of OMI is likely to be more expensive than DDAS because of the more complicated behaviour associated with the dependent variables.

DDAS is designed to be as close to Prolog as possible, and is thus not able to exploit the implicit co-routining of languages such as Andorra-I [14]. Like Prolog, co-routining can be added as an extension to the language. An advantage with being very close to Prolog is that the impact of side-effects on the parallel computation is easier to deal with. In addition, the traditional Prolog debugging methods could be used with DDAS.

9 Conclusions

In this paper, DDAS, a parallel execution model for Prolog capable of exploiting DAP (with the traditional IAP as a subset) is presented. Initial results suggest that this scheme is feasible: it can be implemented without prohibitive overheads, and can extract more parallelism than an IAP-only scheme.

Much development work, including extending the prototype to include or-parallelism, is still needed. A particularly interesting area of research is that of a compile-time analyser (similar in spirit to those of &-Prolog [12] and Andorra-I [14]), which would make the and-parallelism truly transparent. In addition, a detail study of the behaviour of DDAS with respect to realistic applications is also needed.

10 Acknowledgements

I like to thank all the people who have helped with the research presented in this paper, in particular Vítor Santos Costa, Manuel Hermenegildo, Gopal Gupta and David Warren, for the discussions on the various aspects of DDAS. This paper itself has benefited greatly from comments by Inês Dutra, Vítor Santos Costa, Rong Yang, and the anonymous referees, whom I would also like to thank.

I was partly supported by an Overseas Research Studentship from the Committee of Vice-Chancellors and Principals of the Universities of the United Kingdom when the early part of this research was carried out. I am currently supported by a BT (British Telecom) Fellowship at the University of Bristol.

References

[1] K. A. M. Ali and R. Karlsson. The Muse Approach to Or-Parallel Prolog. Technical Report SICS/R-90/R9009, Swedish Institute of Computer Science, 1990.

[2] M. Carlsson. *SICStus Prolog Internals Manual*. Swedish Institute of Computer Science, Box 1263, S-163 12 Spånga, Sweden, Jan. 1989.

[3] K. L. Clark. Predicate Logic as a Computational Formalism. Technical report, Department of Computing and Control, Imperial College, 1979.

[4] C. Codognet and P. Codognet. Non-deterministic Stream And-Parallelism Based on Intelligent Backtracking. In G. Levi and M. Martelli, editors, *Logic Programming: Proceedings of the Sixth International Conference*, pages 83–79. The MIT Press, 1989.

[5] J. S. Conery. *The AND/OR Process Model for Parallel Interpretation of Logic Programs*. PhD thesis, University of California at Irvine, 1983. Available as technical report 204.

[6] D. DeGroot. Restricted And-Parallelism. In *Proceedings of the International Conference on Fifth Generation Computer Systems 1984*, pages 471–478, 1984.

[7] G. Gupta and M. V. Hermenegildo. Recomputation based Implementation of And-Or Parallel Prolog. In *Proceedings of the International Conference on Fifth Generation Computer Systems 1992, Volume 2*, pages 770–782. Institute for New Generation Computing, June 1992.

[8] M. V. Hermenegildo. *An Abstract Machine Based Execution Model for Computer Architecture Design and Efficient Implementation of Logic Programs in Parallel*. PhD thesis, The University of Texas At Austin, 1986.

[9] M. V. Hermenegildo and K. J. Green. &-Prolog and its Performance: Exploiting Independent And-Parallelism. In D. H. D. Warren and P. Szeredi, editors, *Logic Programming: Proceedings of the Seventh International Conference*, pages 253–268. The MIT Press, 1990.

[10] M. V. Hermenegildo and F. Rossi. On the Correctness and Efficiency of Independent And-Parallelism in Logic Programs. In *1989 North American Conference on Logic Programming*. The MIT Press, Oct. 1989.

[11] E. L. Lusk, R. Butler, T. Disz, R. Olson, R. A. Overbeek, R. Stevens, D. H. D. Warren, A. Calderwood, P. Szeredi, S. Haridi, P. Brand, M. Carlsson, A. Ciepielewski, and B. Hausman. The Aurora Or-Parallel Prolog System. In *Proceedings of the International Conference on Fifth Generation Computer Systems 1988, Vol. 3*, pages 819–830. Institute for New Generation Computer Technology, 1988.

[12] K. Muthukumar and M. V. Hermenegildo. The CDG, UDG, and MEL Methods for Automatic Compile-time Parallelization of Logic Programs for Independent And-Parallelism. In D. H. D. Warren and P. Szeredi, editors, *Logic Programming: Proceedings of the Seventh International Conference*, pages 221–236. The MIT Press, 1990.

[13] L. Naish. Parallelizing NU-Prolog. Technical report 87/17, The Department of Computer Science, University of Melbourne, 1987.

[14] V. Santos Costa, D. H. D. Warren, and R. Yang. The Andorra-I Preprocessor: Supporting Full Prolog on the Basic Andorra Model. In *Proceedings of the Eighth International Conference of Logic Programming*, 1991.

[15] K. Shen. *Studies of And/Or Parallelism in Prolog*. PhD thesis, Computer Laboratory, University of Cambridge, 1991. Submitted.

[16] K. Shen. An Overview of DASWAM — An Implementation of DDAS. Technical Report CSTR-92-08, Computer Science Department, University of Bristol, 1992.

[17] K. Shen and M. V. Hermenegildo. A Simulation Study of Or- and Independent And-parallelism. In V. Saraswat and K. Ueda, editors, *Logic Programming: Proceedings of 1991 International Symposium*, pages 135–151. The MIT Press, 1991.

[18] Z. Somogyi, K. Ramamohanarao, and J. Vaghani. A Stream AND-Parallel Execution Algorithm with Backtracking. In R. A. Kowalski and K. A. Bowen, editors, *Logic Programming: Proceedings of the Fifth International Conference and Symposium, Volume 2*, pages 1142–1159. The MIT Press, 1988.

[19] P. Szeredi. Performance Analysis of the Aurora Or-Parallel System. In E. L. Lusk and R. A. Overbeck, editors, *Logic Programming: Proceedings of the North American Conference, 1989, Volume 2*, pages 713–732. The MIT Press, Oct. 1989.

[20] H. Tebra. *Optimistic And-Parallelism in Prolog*. PhD thesis, Vrije Universiteit te Amsterdam, 1989.

[21] J. D. Ullman. *Principles of Database and Knowledge-Base Systems*, volume II. Computer Science Press, 1803 Research Boulevard, Rockville, MD 20850, 1989.

[22] D. H. D. Warren. An Abstract Prolog Instruction Set. Technical Note 309, SRI International, 333 Ravenswood Ave., Menlo Park CA 94025, USA, 1983.

[23] D. H. D. Warren. The SRI Model for Or-Parallel Execution of Prolog – Abstract Design and Implementation Issues. In *Proceedings 1987 Symposium on Logic Programming*, pages 92–102. Computer Society Press of the IEEE, Sept. 1987.

[24] D. S. Warren. Efficient Prolog Management for Flexible Control Strategies. In *Proceedings of the Second Symposium on Logic Programming*, 1984.

Program Analysis

Understanding Finiteness Analysis Using Abstract Interpretation

Peter A. Bigot
Saumya Debray
Department of Computer Science
The University of Arizona
Tucson, AZ 85721
{pab, debray}@cs.arizona.edu

Kim Marriott
IBM T.J. Watson Research Center
P.O.Box 704
Yorktown Heights, NY 10598
kimbal@watson.ibm.com

Abstract

Finiteness analyses are compile-time techniques to determine (sufficient) conditions for the finiteness of relations computed during the bottom-up execution of a logic program. We examine finiteness analyses from the perspective of abstract interpretation. However, problems arise when trying to use standard abstract interpretation theory for finiteness analysis. They occur because finiteness is not an *admissible* property and so naïve application of abstract interpretation leads to incorrect analyses. Here we develop three simple techniques based on abstract interpretation theory which allow inadmissible properties to be handled. Existing approaches to finiteness analysis may be explained and compared in terms of our extension to abstract interpretation theory, and we claim that their correctness is more easily argued in it. To support our claim we use our techniques to develop and prove correct a finiteness analysis which is the most precise that we know.

1 Introduction

Recently a great deal of attention has been devoted to the study of bottom-up execution models for logic programs in which programs are executed by evaluating entire relations and then "joining" them. In implementations of such systems, it is necessary to ensure that the relations computed during any evaluation are finite. In this paper, we are concerned with compile-time analysis techniques to determine (sufficient) conditions for the finiteness of relations computed during the bottom-up execution of a logic program. We examine finiteness analyses from the perspective of abstract interpretation [3, 4]. Abstract interpretation provides a simple semantic basis for dataflow analysis of logic programs. Early work in this area focussed on top-down execution models, as exemplified by Prolog (e.g., see [12, 19]); more recently, researchers have considered abstracting from the bottom-up T_P semantics [1, 11]. However, problems arise when trying to use standard abstract interpretation theory for finiteness analysis. They occur because finiteness is not an *admissible* property (i.e., the union of a chain of finite sets may not be finite), and so naïve application of abstract interpretation leads to incorrect analyses. This is because Scott-induction, the cornerstone of proving correctness of an abstract interpretation, is not valid for inadmissible properties.

Here we develop three simple techniques based on abstract interpretation theory which allow inadmissible properties to be handled. For each technique we illustrate its use in finiteness analysis. The first technique is based on the idea of not developing an analysis for the inadmissible property itself, but rather an analysis for an admissible property which implies the inadmissible. The second technique is to approximate the greatest fixpoint, rather than the least. The third approach is to combine the first two, giving rise to an approach somewhat akin to the widening/narrowing technique of Cousot & Cousot [4, 5].

This paper has two main technical contributions. The first is the development of generic methods for developing and understanding the dataflow analysis of inadmissible program properties. These methods are interesting theoretically as an extension of abstract interpretation theory and are also important practically as some pragmatically interesting program properties, such as finiteness and fairness, are inadmissible. The second main technical contribution is a framework for the better understanding and development of finiteness analysis. Existing approaches to finiteness analysis may be explained and compared in terms of our extension to abstract interpretation theory, and we claim that their correctness is more easily argued in it. To support our claim we use our techniques to develop and prove correct a finiteness analysis which is the most precise that we have seen.

2 Preliminaries

2.1 Basic Definitions

We assume that the reader is familiar with the basic concepts of lattice theory. A subset Y of a complete partial order (cpo) X is a *lower set* iff $\forall y \in Y . \forall x \in X . x \leq y \Rightarrow x \in Y$. *Upper set* is defined dually. A lower set is a *principal ideal* iff it has a maximum element, and an upper set is a *principal filter* iff it has a minimum element. A function F is *monotonic* iff $\forall x, x' \in X . (x \leq x') \Rightarrow (F(x) \preceq F(x'))$. Dually F is *co-monotonic* iff $(x \leq x') \Rightarrow (F(x') \preceq F(x))$. Unless stated to the contrary, all functions will be assumed to be monotonic. The powers of a function $F : X \to X$ on a complete lattice X are defined by

$$F{\uparrow}_x^{\beta} = \begin{cases} x \sqcup F \left(F{\uparrow}_x^{(\beta - 1)} \right) & \text{if } \beta \text{ is a successor ordinal} \\ x \sqcup \bigsqcup \{ F {\uparrow}_x^{\beta'} \mid \beta' < \beta \} & \text{otherwise.} \end{cases}$$

$$F{\downarrow}_x^{\beta} = \begin{cases} x \sqcap F \left(F{\downarrow}_x^{(\beta - 1)} \right) & \text{if } \beta \text{ is a successor ordinal} \\ x \sqcap \bigsqcap \{ F {\downarrow}_x^{\beta'} \mid \beta' < \beta \} & \text{otherwise.} \end{cases}$$

We let $F{\uparrow}^{\beta}$ denote $F{\uparrow}_{\perp}^{\beta}$ and $F{\downarrow}^{\beta}$ denote $F{\downarrow}_{\top}^{\beta}$. Note that by definition $F{\uparrow}_x^0 = F{\downarrow}_x^0 = x$. Let X be a cpo and $F : X \to X$ be monotonic. It is well known that F has a *least fixpoint*, denoted by $lfp(F)$, such that $lfp(F) = F{\uparrow}^{\beta}$ for some ordinal β; if X is a complete lattice then F also has a *greatest fixpoint*, denoted by $gfp(F)$, such that $gfp(F) = F{\downarrow}^{\beta}$ for some ordinal β. We call the sequence $F{\uparrow}^0, F{\uparrow}^1, ..., F{\uparrow}^{\beta}$ the *Kleene sequence* of F.

2.2 Abstract Interpretation

Abstract interpretation provides the basis for a semantic approach to the development of dataflow analyzers. Abstract interpretation formalizes the idea of "approximate computation" in which computation is performed with descriptions of data rather than the data themselves. Correctness of the analysis with respect to the standard interpretation is argued by providing an "approximation relation" which holds whenever an element in a non-standard domain describes an element in the corresponding standard domain. Equivalently, an approximation relation may be defined in terms of a "concretization function" which maps elements in a non-standard domain to those elements in the standard domain which they describe, or an "abstraction function" which maps standard elements to the elements which describe them. Note that these definitions are non-standard because both the concretization and abstraction function map to sets of objects rather than a single object. This generalization is necessary because in the standard framework it is impossible to express an inadmissible approximation relation. The approximation relation can be viewed as a *logical relation* [20] and so it can be lifted from the "base" or "primitive" domains to functions.

Definition. A *description* $Desc = \langle D, \propto, C \rangle$ consists of a *description domain* (a complete lattice) D, a *data domain* (a cpo) C, and an *approximation relation* $\propto \subseteq D \times C$. The function $\gamma : D \to \wp(C)$ defined by $\gamma(d) = \{c \mid d \propto c\}$ is called the *concretization function*, and the function $\alpha : C \to \wp(D)$ defined by $\alpha(c) = \{d \mid d \propto c\}$ is called the *abstraction function*. We require γ to be monotonic and α to be co-monotonic. Let $\langle D_1, \propto_1, C_1 \rangle$ and $\langle D_2, \propto_2, C_2 \rangle$ be descriptions, and $F_D : D_1 \to D_2$ and $F_C : C_1 \to C_2$ be functions. Then the approximation relation is lifted to functions by defining $F_D \propto F_C$ iff $\forall d \in D_1 . \ \forall c \in C_1 . \ d \propto_1 c \Rightarrow F_D(d) \propto_2 F_C(c)$. By an abuse of notation we will let $Desc$ denote both the description and the description domain. ∎

In this paper our example descriptions will have the desirable property that every object and function has a best or most precise description. This occurs when the description is "singular", and is necessary later to show the existence of description domain analogs to given data domain functions.

Definition. A description $\langle D, \propto, C \rangle$ is *singular* iff the associated abstraction function $\alpha : C \to \wp(D)$ maps to principal filters. In this case we define an associated *inducement function* $\widehat{\alpha} : C \to D$ by $\widehat{\alpha}(c) = \sqcap \alpha(c)$. $\widehat{\alpha}(c)$ is monotonic, and yields the single "best" (i.e., most informative) element of the description domain that describes c.

We lift the inducement function to function spaces as follows. Let $\langle D_1, \propto_1, C_1 \rangle$ be a description, $\langle D_2, \propto_2, C_2 \rangle$ a singular description with inducement function $\widehat{\alpha}_2$, and $F : C_1 \to C_2$ a function. We define $\widehat{\alpha}(F) : D_1 \to D_2$ to be:

$$\widehat{\alpha}(F)(d) = \bigsqcup \{\widehat{\alpha}_2(F(c)) \mid d \propto_1 c\}.$$

We say that $\widehat{\alpha}(F)$ is the function *induced* from F. ∎

Just as $\widehat{\alpha}(c)$ is the description that best describes a data domain element c, the induced function $\widehat{\alpha}(F)$ best describes, over the description domain, the effect of the data domain function F. We will use this notion later to derive operators that describe the effect, in terms of finiteness, of the familiar T_P operator for logic programs.

In traditional abstract interpretation, additional requirements are placed on descriptions so as to ensure that the approximation relation is *admissible*.

Definition. A predicate Q on cpo C is *admissible* iff for all chains $L \subseteq C$,

$$(\forall l \in L . \ Q(l)) \Rightarrow Q(\sqcup L)$$

Dually, Q is *co-admissible* iff for all chains $L \subseteq C$,

$$(\forall l \in L . Q(l)) \Rightarrow Q(\sqcap L)$$

A description is (*co-*)*admissible* iff its approximation relation is (co-)admissible. ∎

Admissibility of the approximation predicate is required so that Scott induction can be used to prove Proposition 2.1, which is the basis for proving an abstract interpretation is correct.

Proposition 2.1 Let D be an admissible description for C and let $F_D : D \to D$ approximate $F_C : C \to C$. Then $lfp(F_D) \propto lfp(F_C)$. ∎

Common restrictions to ensure admissibility are that the abstraction function maps to principal filters and is continuous as in Nielson [16], or that the concretization function maps to principal ideals as in Marriott & Søndergaard [11], or the combination of these two restrictions yielding the Galois connection approach of Cousot & Cousot [3, 4]. See Marriott [10] for more details on the relationships between these restrictions. Abstract interpretation in the presence of inadmissible approximation relations is addressed by Mycroft and Jones [13], but in a limited context as they ignore recursion.

However, Proposition 2.1 does not hold if the admissibility requirement is dropped, so when the approximation relation is inadmissible there is no guarantee that an analysis developed using the traditional techniques of abstract interpretation will be correct. Such inadmissible approximation relations do occur in practice, whenever we are interested in inferring a property P of a program or database where P itself is not admissible. Any precise natural description domain for the analysis will contain an element which describes exactly those objects with property P, and the approximation relation for such descriptions will therefore be inadmissible. As we shall see, finiteness is an example of such a property.

2.3 Finiteness Analysis

The language we consider is that of Horn logic. We assume that there is some fixed set of *intensional* predicate symbols, *IP*, and some disjoint set of *extensional* predicate symbols, *EP*. Given a set of predicate symbols S, HB_S denotes the set of ground atoms that can be constructed from S. Note that we allow an infinite number of constant symbols. In the case S is the set of all predicate symbols we simply write *HB*. A *program* P is a finite set of definite clauses (or rules) in which only intensional predicates appear in the heads of the clauses. A *relation* for predicate set S is a subset of HB_S. The *projection* of relation R onto predicate Q, written R_Q and sometimes also called the (sub-)relation for Q, is the set $\{Q(\vec{t}) \mid Q(\vec{t}) \in R\}$. The *projection* of relation R onto argument i of predicate Q, written $R_{Q,i}$, is the set $\{\vec{t}_i \mid Q(\vec{t}) \in R\}$ where $\vec{t}_i$ denotes the ith element of the tuple $\vec{t}$. When R is known to contain only ground atoms for Q, we will use the simpler notation R_i.

The *input* to a program P is a relation for EP. This is called the *extensional database* (EDB). The extensional predicates may have *integrity constraints* associated with them, which restrict the possible input relations in some way (in this case, by specifying finiteness relationships between argument positions in the relations). The *output* of P is a relation for all of the predicates. The output restricted to the intensional predicates is called the *intensional database* (IDB). The output is computed as the least fixpoint of the "immediate consequence" operator T_P^E where

E is the EDB. The operator $T_P^E : \wp(HB) \to \wp(HB)$ is defined by:

$$T_P^E(R) = E \cup \left\{ A \;\middle|\; \begin{array}{l} A :- A_1, \ldots, A_n \text{ is a ground instance of a clause in } P, \text{ and} \\ \{A_1, \ldots, A_n\} \subseteq R \end{array} \right\}$$

When E is unspecified or unimportant, we make it a parameter and refer to $T_P : \wp(HB) \to \wp(HB) \to \wp(HB)$; we do the same for description domain analogues to T_P and T_P^E.

The *finiteness analysis problem* for a program P, intensional predicate Q, and integrity constraints $\mathcal{E}$ is to determine whether the relation for Q in $lfp(T_P^E)$ is guaranteed to be finite for every input relation E satisfying $\mathcal{E}$.

Finiteness analysis is clearly decidable for Datalog programs, i.e., programs where all function symbols have arity 0, if the EDB relations are always finite. The problem becomes undecidable if programs contain function symbols with nonzero arity; it can be simplified somewhat by approximating the effect of each function symbol of arity $n > 0$ by an infinite EDB relation of arity $n + 1$ with certain associated finiteness constraints. The language where programs contain no function symbol of nonzero arity, but where EDB relations may sometimes be infinite, is referred to as *extended Datalog*. As far as we know, the finiteness analysis problem for extended Datalog is not known to be either decidable or undecidable (see, for example, [18]). In this paper, we primarily consider extended Datalog programs. However the analyses are still correct in the presence of arbitrary function symbols.

Before presenting analyses for finiteness, we must define the basic domains which constitute the descriptions on which the analyses are based, and show how integrity constraints are specified. The idea is to describe each R_Q by a propositional formula describing the finiteness dependencies between the arguments of predicate Q. For instance, the description $p(x, y) : x \to y$ is read as "for any finite assignment of values to the first argument of predicate p, there are only finitely many assignments to the second argument which satisfy the relation assigned to p."

Definition. Let *Prop* denote the subset of propositional formula constructed from the constants *true* and *false* and a suitably large but finite set of propositional variables using the propositional connectives $\wedge, \vee, \leftrightarrow, \to$.

A *predicate description* for predicate Q has the form $Q(\vec{x}) : \phi$ where $\vec{x}$ represents a sequence of distinct propositional variables which serve as placeholders or names for relation attributes, $\phi \in Prop$, and $\text{vars}(\phi) \subseteq \text{vars}(\vec{x})$. Predicate descriptions for predicate Q are pre-ordered by $\leq$ defined by $(Q(\vec{x}) : \phi) \leq (Q(\vec{x}') : \phi')$ iff $\phi \Rightarrow \phi''$, where $Q(\vec{x}) : \phi''$ is a variable renaming of $Q(\vec{x}') : \phi'$, required to reconcile the relation attribute names.

A *relation description* is a set of predicate descriptions in which a predicate occurs at most once. If there is no predicate description for Q in a relation description $\mathcal{R}$ we implicitly include the description $Q(\vec{x}) : false$. We define $\mathcal{R}_Q$ to be the predicate description of Q in $\mathcal{R}$. We let *RDesc* denote the set of relation descriptions. Relation descriptions are pre-ordered by $\leq$ where $\mathcal{R} \leq \mathcal{R}'$ iff $\forall Q . \mathcal{R}_Q \leq \mathcal{R}'_Q$. $\blacksquare$

By an abuse of notation we will treat relation and predicate descriptions modulo the equivalence induced by $\leq$ and order them by the partial order induced from $\leq$. Thus *RDesc* is a finite lattice.

Relation descriptions will be used both to specify integrity constraints and as descriptions in our finiteness analyses.

Definition. Given a relation R and predicate Q, R_Q *satisfies* predicate description $Q(\vec{x}) : \phi$ iff

$$\forall R' \subseteq R_Q . R' \neq \emptyset \Rightarrow \tau_{R'} \text{ satisfies } \phi$$

where the truth assignment $\tau_{R'}$ to the variables $\vec{x}$ is given by $\tau_{R'}(\vec{x}_i)$ iff R_i' is finite. Relation R *satisfies* relation description $\mathcal{R}$, written $R \vdash \mathcal{R}$ (or $\mathcal{R} \dashv R$), iff for all predicates Q, R_Q satisfies $\mathcal{R}_Q$.

The *finiteness description FDesc* is the description $\langle RDesc, \dashv, \wp(HB) \rangle$. ∎

Other descriptions for finiteness analysis may be naturally obtained by restricting the type of propositional formulae in the predicate descriptions. Natural restrictions are to disallow disjunction, to disallow implication, or to disallow both. These restrictions will not be addressed here.

Example 2.1 Consider the infinite relation s representing the immediate successor relation. Given a finite restriction on the first argument position, the set of satisfying tuples has only finitely many values appearing in the second argument position and vice versa. Thus s satisfies $s(x, y) : x \leftrightarrow y$. As another example, the only relation for q to satisfy $q(x) :$ *false* is the empty relation. ∎

Lemma 2.2 *FDesc* is singular. ∎

Definition. Let $\alpha\widehat{_{FDesc}}$ be the inducement function from $\wp(HB)$ to $RDesc$ defined in terms of $\dashv$. $\alpha\widehat{_{FDesc}}$ exists as a consequence of Lemma 2.2.

Let P be a program. Define $U_P : RDesc \to RDesc \to RDesc$ to be the function induced from $T_P : \wp(HB) \to \wp(HB) \to \wp(HB)$ using the description *FDesc*. ∎

Using the above definitions for a given integrity constraint $\mathcal{E} \in RDesc$, we determine the description domain analog of the T_P operator by computing the induced function for T_P^E, allowing $E \in \wp(HB)$ to range over all possible EDBs described by $\mathcal{E}$. Formally,

$$U_P^{\mathcal{E}}(\mathcal{R}) = \sqcup \{\alpha\widehat{_{FDesc}}(T_P^E(R)) \mid \mathcal{R} \dashv R \wedge \mathcal{E} \dashv E\}$$

In more concrete terms, consider a clause $p(\vec{x}) :- q_1(\vec{v}_1), \ldots, q_n(\vec{v}_n)$ in a program P. Suppose we are given a relation description $\mathcal{R}$ for the predicates of P. Then, given a relation R that satisfies $\mathcal{R}$, an evaluation of the body of this clause over R will satisfy $\psi = \phi_1 \wedge \cdots \wedge \phi_n$, where (some alphabetic variant of) $q_i(\vec{v}_i) : \phi_i$ is in $\mathcal{R}$. Letting $\vec{y} = \mathrm{vars}(\psi) \setminus \mathrm{vars}(\vec{x})$ be the variables that occur only in the body of the clause, the finiteness information inferred for the head is given by $\exists \vec{y} : \psi$; the quantification removes the effect of the variables that do not appear in the head of the rule. Of course, just as the T_P operator evaluates all the clauses in a program and collects together the results, U_P should consider all the clauses and collect together the finiteness information obtained for each predicate. Thus, we have:

$$U_P^{\mathcal{E}}(\mathcal{R}) = \mathcal{E} \cup \{p(\vec{x}):\phi \mid \phi = \bigvee_{p(\vec{x}) :- q_{i,1}(\vec{v}_{i,1}), \ldots, q_{i,n_i}(\vec{v}_{i,n_i}) \in P} \exists \vec{y}_i : \psi_i\}$$

where $\psi_i = \bigwedge_{q_{i,j}(\vec{v}_{i,j}):\phi_{i,j} \in_{\alpha} \mathcal{R}} \phi_{i,j}$ and $\vec{y}_i = \mathrm{vars}(\psi_i) \setminus \mathrm{vars}(\vec{x})$. $\in_{\alpha}$ indicates that some alphabetic variant of the constraint appears in $\mathcal{R}$, and ϕ in this case is taken to be the propositional equivalent of the existentially quantified formula, so the result remains in $RDesc$.

By definition $U_P \dashv T_P$, so naïvely we would expect that $lfp(U_P^{\mathcal{E}}) \dashv lfp(T_P^E)$ whenever $\mathcal{E} \dashv E$, and a finiteness analysis might be performed by computing $lfp(U_P^{\mathcal{E}})$. However, the following example shows that $lfp(U_P^{\mathcal{E}}) \not\dashv lfp(T_P^E)$ for some programs.

Example 2.2 Consider program P:

```
p(X) :- z(X).
p(X) :- s(X,Y), p(Y).
```

in which s is a extensional predicate intended to be the successor relation, and z an extensional predicate defining a zero element. The associated integrity constraint is $\mathcal{E} = \{s(x,y) : x \leftrightarrow y, z(x) : x\}$. The computation of the least fixpoint of $U_P^\mathcal{E}$ proceeds starting from $\bot_{FDesc} = p(\bar{x}) : false$ for all predicates p. Tracing the computation using the propositional formula for $U_P^\mathcal{E}$ above we get:

$$
\begin{aligned}
U_P^\mathcal{E} \uparrow 0 = \bot_{FDesc} &= \{p(x) : false, s(x,y) : false, z(x) : false\} \\
U_P^\mathcal{E} \uparrow 1 = U_P^\mathcal{E}(\bot_{FDesc}) &= \mathcal{E} \cup \{p(x) : false \vee \exists y . (false \wedge false)\} \\
&= \{p(x) : false, s(x,y) : x \leftrightarrow y, z(x) : x\} \\
U_P^\mathcal{E} \uparrow 2 &= \mathcal{E} \cup \{p(x) : x \vee \exists y.((x \leftrightarrow y) \wedge false)\} \\
&= \{p(x) : x, s(x,y) : x \leftrightarrow y, z(x) : x\} \\
U_P^\mathcal{E} \uparrow 3 &= \mathcal{E} \cup \{p(x) : x \vee \exists y.((x \leftrightarrow y) \wedge y)\} \\
&= U_P^\mathcal{E} \uparrow 2
\end{aligned}
$$

So $(p(x) : x) \in lfp(U_P^\mathcal{E})$, which leads to the incorrect conclusion that p is finite for P and $\mathcal{E}$. ∎

The problem arises because:

Proposition 2.3 *FDesc* is inadmissible.

Proof: Let $a_1, a_2, ...$ be distinct constant symbols. Define relation S_β to be $\{p(a_i) \mid i \leq \beta\}$ where β is either finite or the first infinite ordinal ω. Let $\mathcal{S}$ be $\{p(x) : x\}$ indicating that p is a finite relation. Let L be the chain $\bigcup_{i \leq \omega}\langle \mathcal{S}, S_i \rangle$. Clearly $\sqcup L = \langle \mathcal{S}, S_\omega \rangle$. Now, for all $i < \omega$, $\mathcal{S} \dashv S_i$, but $\mathcal{S} \not\dashv S_\omega$. Therefore, $\dashv$ is inadmissible, and so is FDesc. ∎

3   Inadmissible Predicates and Abstract Interpretation

We have seen that the traditional abstract interpretation approach for developing dataflow analyses does not apply when the description is inadmissible. In this section we suggest three simple techniques to develop analyses in this case. The techniques are illustrated by using them to develop finiteness analyses.

3.1   Using a Stronger Admissible Property

The first approach is based on a simple idea: rather than finding an analysis to directly show that an inadmissible property P' holds, develop an analysis for an admissible property P which implies P'. The approach is strengthened by the observation that we do not require admissibility for all chains in the cpo, only those that will be encountered when computing the least fixpoint. That is, we need only show that the description is admissible for chains based on the Kleene sequence of the operator to be approximated.

We first clarify how the result of one analysis on some description domain can be used to infer something about the program in another description domain.

Definition. Let D, D' be descriptions for C. A function $F : D \to D'$ is *approximation preserving* if $\forall c \in C \,.\, \forall d \in D \,.\, d \propto_D c \Rightarrow F(d) \propto_{D'} c$.   ∎

Given an approximation preserving mapping from D to D' we can use it to map the results of an analysis on D to the descriptions in D'. If D' is singular, then there is a best (in the sense of most precise) approximation preserving function. We call this the *induced approximation preserving function*.

Definition. Let $\langle D, \propto, C \rangle$ be a description and $\langle D', \propto', C \rangle$ a singular description with inducement function $\hat{\alpha}'$. The *induced approximation preserving function* $\delta : D \to D'$ is simply the function induced from the identity function for C; i.e., $\delta(d) = \sqcup\{\hat{\alpha}'(c) \mid d \propto c\}$.   ∎

Intuitively, $\delta(d)$ finds the "best" element of D' that describes everything that d describes.

The following definition makes precise what it means for a description to be admissible for a particular operator.

Definition. The description $\langle D, \propto, C \rangle$ is *admissible for* $F : C \to C$ iff, for all chains $L \subseteq D \times C'$ where $C' \subseteq C$ is the Kleene sequence of F, we have $(\forall l \in L \,.\, Q(l)) \Rightarrow Q(\sqcup L)$. Co-admissibility of a description for a function is defined dually.   ∎

Correctness of this technique is captured by the following theorem:

Theorem 3.1 Let D, D' be descriptions for C and $F : D \to D'$ be approximation preserving. Let $F_D : D \to D$ approximate $F_C : C \to C$. If D is admissible for F_C, then $F(lfp(F_D)) \propto_{D'} lfp(F_C)$.   ∎

Proof: It follows from Proposition 2.1 that $lfp(F_D) \propto_D lfp(F_C)$. Thus the result follows from the definition of approximation preserving.   ∎

We can now determine the behavior of a function in data domain C by using a description D which is admissible but does not give exactly the information we want. We then use an approximation-preserving function to translate the answer from the admissible domain to the desired description domain, even if the latter is inadmissible.

One might hope that for a given inadmissible property P there is a "best" or "strongest" admissible property implying P. Unfortunately this is not necessarily true as the property of being admissible is itself an inadmissible property.

We now give two finiteness analyses which illustrate this technique. The first example relies on the simple observation that for operators with a finite Kleene sequence, all descriptions are admissible.

FINITENESS ANALYSIS 1: WEAKLY-BOUNDED PROGRAMS

If we can guarantee that a program P being analyzed is *weakly-bounded* for integrity constraint $\mathcal{E}$ on the EDB (in the sense that for all E where $\mathcal{E} \dashv E$, T_P^E has a finite Kleene sequence), then any description is admissible for T_P^E, and in particular *FDesc* is. Thus we can analyze whether Q is finite for P by computing $lfp(U_P^{\mathcal{E}})$ and checking that this implies finiteness. More formally:

Theorem 3.2 Let P be weakly-bounded for the integrity constraint $\mathcal{E}$. Then predicate Q is finite for P and $\mathcal{E}$ if $(Q(\vec{x}) : \bigwedge \vec{x}) \in lfp(U_P^{\mathcal{E}})$.   ∎

This idea is essentially the same as that behind finiteness analyses based on "weak finiteness", which was introduced by Sagiv and Vardi [18]. The hard part in this type of analysis is showing that a program is weakly-bounded. Many analyses to detect sub-cases of weak-boundedness are found in the database literature. There are various notions of boundedness (e.g., see [6, 7, 8, 14, 15]), and Naughton and Sagiv give a decision procedure for a class of bounded recursions [15].

FINITENESS ANALYSIS 2: CONTAINMENT

The second example is more complex. The underlying idea is that, given a fixed finite set B, the property of being contained in B is admissible, and clearly containment in a finite set implies finiteness. Descriptions of containment can be simply captured using propositional variables and formulas much as we used these to capture finiteness. Thus the description $p(x, y) : x \vee y$ is read as "the values in the first argument of the relation assigned to p are contained in B or the values in the second argument of the relation are contained in B." More formally,

Definition. Given a relation R and predicate Q, R_Q *C-satisfies* predicate description $Q(\vec{x}) : \phi$ for set B iff

$$\forall R' \subseteq R_Q \, . \, R' \neq \emptyset \Rightarrow \tau_{R'} \text{ satisfies } \phi$$

where the truth assignment $\tau_{R'}$ to the variables $\vec{x}$ is given by $\tau_{R'}(\vec{x}_i)$ iff $R'_i \subseteq B$. ∎

The key problem is to choose the set B so that it gives good results for all programs and EDBs. One solution is to make the choice of B dependent on the current relation assigned to the extensional predicates. We choose B to be the set of all arguments which come from an attribute in the EDB which has a finite number of values.

Definition. Relation R *C-satisfies* relation description $\mathcal{R}$, written $R \vDash_c \mathcal{R}$ (or $\mathcal{R} \dashv R$) iff for all predicate symbols Q, R_Q satisfies $\mathcal{R}_Q$ for B_R, where

$$B_R = \cup\{R_{Q,i} \mid Q \in EP \text{ and } R_{Q,i} \text{ is finite}\}.$$

The *finite containment description CDesc* is the description $\langle RDesc, \dashv, \wp(HB) \rangle$. ∎

Intuitively, a *CDesc* analysis traces the flow of terms from base relation attributes that are known to be finite through the computation, and reveals the computed attributes which depend only on the original finite set. Although the relation $\dashv$ is defined in terms of the actual input E, we can ignore this for the analysis by using an appropriately sized set of symbolic constants to represent the elements of B_R.

Example 3.1 Consider again the predicate s representing the immediate successor relation. s is described in *CDesc* only by $s(x, y) : true$, since for any finite set of ordinals B, there is some element whose successor is not an element of B. The relation $p(x) :- x \text{ is a prime less than } 1000$ satisfies $p(x) : x$. Again, only the empty relation satisfies $p(x) : false$. ∎

The descriptions *CDesc* are admissible for any T_P^E because the set B_R is finite and does not change in the Kleene sequence, since it depends only on extensional predicates, which are by assumption disjoint from the intensional predicates (i.e., those defined by the program). Other analyses can be made by using a different set for B; of course, making the choice of B dependent on the current relations assigned to the intensional predicates can lead to an inadmissible description for T_P^E.

Lemma 3.3 *CDesc* is admissible for T_P^E. ∎

Lemma 3.4 *CDesc* is singular. ∎

Definition. Let P be a program. Define $V_P : RDesc \to RDesc \to RDesc$ to be the function induced from $T_P : \wp(HB) \to \wp(HB) \to \wp(HB)$ using the description *CDesc*. ∎

While this definition specifies V_P non-constructively in terms of T_P, it is not difficult to see that it gives rise to a terminating dataflow analysis, since V_P is defined on the finite domain *RDesc*. As *CDesc* is admissible for T_P^E, we can analyze the containment properties of Q by computing $lfp(V_P^{\mathcal{E}})$. More formally:

Theorem 3.5 Predicate Q is finite for program P and containment integrity constraints $\mathcal{E}$ if $Q(\vec{x}) :\wedge \vec{x}) \in lfp(V_P^{\mathcal{E}})$. ∎

This analysis may be interesting in itself; note that it does determine "finiteness", but this sense of finiteness is limited, and we may not be explicitly given containment properties of the EDB. However, we can use it as an intermediate step for determining finiteness in the following manner:

Definition. $\delta_{FC} : RDesc \to RDesc$ is the induced approximation preserving function from *FDesc* to *CDesc*. $\delta_{CF} : RDesc \to RDesc$ is the induced approximation preserving function from *CDesc* to *FDesc*. ∎

Theorem 3.6 Predicate Q is finite for program P and finiteness integrity constraints $\mathcal{E}$ if $Q(\vec{x}) :\wedge \vec{x}) \in \delta_{CF}(lfp(V_P^{\delta_{FC}(\mathcal{E})}))$. ∎

In other words, we can approximate the inadmissible finiteness analysis by translating the information we have about finiteness conditions for the EDB into containment information, determining the containment properties of the program, and translating them back into finiteness conditions.

Example 3.2 Consider the following program taken from Example 7 in [9]:

```
p(X1,Y1) :- f(X1), i(Y1).
p(X2,Y2) :- i(X2), f(Y2).
p(X3,Y3) :- p(X3,Y3).
q(X4) :- p(X4,X4).
```

Let $\mathcal{E}$ be the finiteness integrity constraint $\{f(x) : x, i(x) : true\}$, asserting that E_f is a finite set. Since $f(x) : x$ in *FDesc* implies that f is a finite relation, the set B_R constructed from the (eventually) supplied E will contain its constants, and f satisfies $f(x) : x$ in *CDesc*. Then $\delta_{FC}(\mathcal{E}) = \mathcal{E}$. As we are still operating on the *RDesc* lattice, $V_P^{\mathcal{E}}$ is syntactically similar to the formula given earlier for $U_P^{\mathcal{E}}$; only the interpretation has changed. The fixpoint computation proceeds as follows:

$$V_P^{\mathcal{E}} \uparrow 0 = \perp_{CDesc} = \{p(x,y) : false, q(x) : false, f(x) : false, i(x) : false\}$$
$$V_P^{\mathcal{E}} \uparrow 1 = V_P^{\mathcal{E}}(\perp_{CDesc})$$
$$= \mathcal{E} \cup \{p(x,y) : x \vee y, q(x) : false\}$$
$$V_P^{\mathcal{E}} \uparrow 2 = \mathcal{E} \cup \{p(x,y) : x \vee y, q(x) : x\}$$
$$V_P^{\mathcal{E}} \uparrow 3 = V_P^{\mathcal{E}} \uparrow 2$$

An argument similar to that above shows that $\delta_{CF}(\{q(x) : x\}) = \{q(x) : x\}$, so $(q(x) : x) \in \delta_{CF}(lfp(V_P^{\delta_{FC}(\mathcal{E})}))$. Thus, the analysis concludes that q is finite. ∎

Note that this example is not handled by the methods in [9] nor any other finiteness analysis that we know of. We conjecture that the containment analysis when restricted so that only conjunctions of propositional variables are allowed in the descriptions is equivalent to the graph based analysis given in Section 9 of [9].

3.2 Approximate From Above

The second technique is also quite simple. Rather than computing an approximation to the least fixpoint we instead compute an approximation to the greatest fixpoint. Soundness of this approach does not require that the approximation be admissible, since we are already starting from above the least fixpoint. Formal correctness of the technique is captured as a corollary of the following somewhat stronger result.

Theorem 3.7 Let D be a (possibly inadmissible) description of C, and let $F_D : D \to D$ approximate $F_C : C \to C$. Let c be any fixpoint of F_C and let $d \propto c$; then:

(i) For any finite $k \geq 0$, $F_D\!\downarrow_d^k \propto c$; and

(ii) If D is co-admissible, then for any ordinal β, $F_D\!\downarrow_d^\beta \propto c$.

Proof: (Sketch) By hypothesis, $d \propto c$, so since F_D approximates F_C we have $F_D(d) \propto F_C(c) = c$. Using finite induction (i) holds. Co-admissibility of $\propto$ allows us to use transfinite induction to prove (ii). ∎

Corollary 3.8 Let D be a co-admissible description of C, and let $F_D : D \to D$ approximate $F_C : C \to C$. Then $gfp(F_D) \propto c$ where c is any fixpoint of F_C. ∎

Interesting cases of this corollary are when c is the least fixpoint or when it is the greatest fixpoint. A related technique was suggested by Codish et al. [2] for analyses in which the Kleene sequence for the approximating operator is too long. However, they did not consider inadmissible descriptions.

FINITENESS ANALYSIS 3: APPROXIMATION OF THE GFP
Thus we can analyze whether Q is finite for P by computing $gfp(U_P^{\mathcal{E}})$ and checking that this implies finiteness.

Lemma 3.9 *FDesc* is co-admissible. ∎

Theorem 3.10 Predicate Q is finite for program P and integrity constraint $\mathcal{E}$ if $(Q(\vec{x}) : \bigwedge \vec{x}) \in gfp(U_P^{\mathcal{E}})$. ∎

Example 3.3 Consider the following program P taken from [9]:

```
p(X1,X1) :- f(X1).
p(X2,Y2) :- f(Y2), g(X2,V2), h(X2,W2), p(V2,W2).
p(X3,Y3) :- f(X3), g(Y3,V3), h(Y3,W3), p(V3,W3).
```

with integrity constraints $\mathcal{E} = \{f(x) : x, h(x,y) : y \to x, g(x,y) : y \to x\}$ stating that f represents a finite set, and both h and g are finite in the first argument for subrelations with a finite set of second arguments. Leaving some intermediate steps out for space, the greatest fixpoint computation proceeds as follows:

$$
\begin{aligned}
U_P^{\mathcal{E}} \!\downarrow 0 &= \{f(x) : true, g(x,y) : true, h(x,y) : true, p(x,y) : true\} \\
U_P^{\mathcal{E}} \!\downarrow 1 &= \mathcal{E} \cup \{p(x,y) : true\} \\
U_P^{\mathcal{E}} \!\downarrow 2 &= \mathcal{E} \cup \{p(x,y) : x \vee y\} \\
U_P^{\mathcal{E}} \!\downarrow 3 &= \mathcal{E} \cup \{p(x,y) : x \wedge y\} \\
U_P^{\mathcal{E}} \!\downarrow 4 &= U_P^{\mathcal{E}} \!\downarrow 3
\end{aligned}
$$

Thus $(p(x, y) : x \wedge y) \in \mathit{gfp}(U_P^{\mathcal{E}})$, and the analysis determines that p is finite. ∎

An examination of the details of the $U_P^{\mathcal{E}}$ operator as defined in Section 2.3 leads to the conclusion that a $\mathit{gfp}(U_P^{\mathcal{E}})$ calculation is equivalent to the axiomatic superfiniteness analysis given by Kifer et al. in [9], in that each axiom set presented therein has a corresponding component in the $U_P^{\mathcal{E}}$ operator.

3.3 Combination

Our final technique is to combine the two previous techniques. First an admissible description is used to find an approximation to the least fixpoint, then we use this approximation as an upper bound in the second method and iterate downwards, while still staying above the least fixpoint. From Theorem 3.1 and Theorem 3.7, we have:

Theorem 3.11 Let D, D' be descriptions for C and $F : D \to D'$ be approximation preserving. Let $F_D : D \to D$ and $F_{D'} : D' \to D'$ approximate $F_C : C \to C$. Let D be admissible for F_C and $d = F(\mathit{lfp}(F_D))$. Then:

(i) for all finite ordinals k, $F_{D'}\!\downarrow_d^k \propto_{D'} \mathit{lfp}(F_C)$; and

(ii) if D is co-admissible, for all ordinals β, $F_{D'}\!\downarrow_d^\beta \propto_{D'} \mathit{lfp}(F_C)$.

∎

The combination approach given here is somewhat related to the widening/ narrowing approach to abstract interpretation introduced by Cousot and Cousot [3]. The widening/narrowing approach was developed to handle the case when the description domain has infinite ascending chains, and so it is not possible to compute the least fixpoint of the approximating operator using a finite Kleene sequence. An extreme use of this technique is when the description domain coincides with the data domain. The idea is to use a widening operator to "jump above" the least fixpoint and then a narrowing operator to move downwards from this point and improve the approximation.

It is implicit in the widening/narrowing approach of Cousot and Cousot that there is a Galois connection between the original domain and the domain on which the widening and narrowing operator are defined. This ensures that the approximation relation is admissible. Thus our combination approach is, in some senses, a relaxation of widening/narrowing in which the widening and narrowing operators are allowed to work on different domains and the approximation relation for the narrowing operator's domain is not required to be admissible. It is also a specialization, as when couched in these terms we are using the trivial widening operator "lub" and the trivial narrowing operator "glb". However it should be emphasized that the two techniques were developed to handle very different problems.

FINITENESS ANALYSIS 4: COMBINATION
Thus we can analyze whether Q is finite for P by combining Finiteness Analysis 2 with Finiteness Analysis 3.

Theorem 3.12 Predicate Q is finite for program P and integrity constraints $\mathcal{E}$ if $(Q(\vec{x}) : \bigwedge \vec{x}) \in \mathit{gfp}(W_P^{\mathcal{E}})$, where $W_P^{\mathcal{E}}$ is defined by $W_P^{\mathcal{E}}(\mathcal{R}) = \delta_{CF}(\mathcal{R}_V) \sqcap U_P^{\mathcal{E}}(\mathcal{R})$ and $\mathcal{R}_V = \mathit{lfp}(V_P^{\delta_{FC}(\mathcal{E})})$. ∎

Notice that, although both *lfp* and *gfp* computations are over the *RDesc* domain, the *lfp* computation uses the *CDesc* interpretation, while the *gfp* computation uses *FDesc*. $\sqcap$ on *RDesc* is essentially component-wise conjunction of the propositional formula. The use of $\sqcap$ in the definition of $W_P^{\mathcal{E}}$ ensures that, after the first step, the *gfp* computation is operating no higher than the results of the *lfp* when converted to the *FDesc* domain.

Example 3.4 Consider the following program, created by grafting together the programs in Example 3.2 and Example 3.3.

```
pl(x,y) :- f(x), i(y).
pl(x,y) :- i(x), f(y).
pl(x,y) :- pl(x,y).
pg(x,y) :- f(x).
pg(x,y) :- f(y), g(x,v), h(x,w), p(v,w).
pg(x,y) :- f(x), g(y,v), h(y,w), p(v,w).
q(x,y,z) :- pl(x,x), pg(y,z).
```

We are given EDB constraints $\mathcal{E} = \{f(x) : x, i(x) : \mathit{true}, g(x,y) : y \rightarrow x, h(x,y) : y \rightarrow x\}$, so f is a finite set, we know nothing about i, and for both g and h, if the second argument can be shown to be finite, the first is also.

Converting $\mathcal{E}$ to *CDesc* leaves f and i unchanged; however, the implication in the description for g and h is lost, since we don't know if membership in the containment set is preserved between the two arguments. Thus $\delta_{FC}(\mathcal{E}) = \mathcal{E}' = \{f(x) : x, i(x) : \mathit{true}, g(x,y) : \mathit{true}, h(x,y) : \mathit{true}\}$. The bottom-up computation is straightforward, and yields:

$$lfp(V_P^{\mathcal{E}'}) = \mathcal{E}' \cup \{pl(x,y) : (x \vee y), pg(x,y) : (x \vee y), q(x,y,z) : (x \wedge (y \vee z))\}$$

The results of the bottom-up calculation, when converted back to the *FDesc* domain, are unchanged; i.e.

$$\delta_{CF}(lfp(V_P^{\mathcal{E}'})) = \mathcal{E} \cup \{pl(x,y) : (x \vee y), pg(x,y) : (x \vee y), q(x,y,z) : (x \wedge (y \vee z))\}$$

We can then proceed with a greatest fixpoint computation on $W_P^{\mathcal{E}}$:

$$W_P^{\mathcal{E}} \downarrow 0 = \top_{FDesc} = \{pl(x,y) : \mathit{true}, pg(x,y) : \mathit{true}, q(x,y,z) : \mathit{true}, \ldots\}$$
$$U_P^{\mathcal{E}}(W_P^{\mathcal{E}} \downarrow 0) = \mathcal{E} \cup \{pl(x,y) : \mathit{true}, pg(x,y) : \mathit{true}, q(x,y,z) : \mathit{true}\}$$
$$W_P^{\mathcal{E}} \downarrow 1 = \delta_{CF}(lfp(V_P^{\mathcal{E}'})) \sqcap U_P^{\mathcal{E}}(W_P^{\mathcal{E}} \downarrow 0)$$
$$= \mathcal{E} \cup \{pl(x,y) : (x \vee y), pg(x,y) : (x \vee y), q(x,y,z) : (x \wedge (y \vee z))\}$$
$$U_P^{\mathcal{E}}(W_P^{\mathcal{E}} \downarrow 1) = \mathcal{E} \cup \{pl(x,y) : (x \vee y), pg(x,y) : (x \wedge y), q(x,y,z) : (x \wedge (y \vee z))\}$$
$$W_P^{\mathcal{E}} \downarrow 2 = \delta_{CF}(lfp(V_P^{\mathcal{E}'})) \sqcap U_P^{\mathcal{E}}(W_P^{\mathcal{E}} \downarrow 1)$$
$$= \mathcal{E} \cup \{pl(x,y) : (x \vee y), pg(x,y) : (x \wedge y), q(x,y,z) : (x \wedge (y \vee z))\}$$
$$U_P^{\mathcal{E}}(W_P^{\mathcal{E}} \downarrow 2) = \mathcal{E} \cup \{pl(x,y) : (x \vee y), pg(x,y) : (x \wedge y), q(x,y,z) : (x \wedge y \wedge z)\}$$
$$W_P^{\mathcal{E}} \downarrow 3 = \delta_{CF}(lfp(V_P^{\mathcal{E}'})) \sqcap U_P^{\mathcal{E}}(W_P^{\mathcal{E}} \downarrow 2)$$
$$= \mathcal{E} \cup \{pl(x,y) : (x \vee y), pg(x,y) : (x \wedge y), q(x,y,z) : (x \wedge y \wedge z)\}$$
$$U_P^{\mathcal{E}}(W_P^{\mathcal{E}} \downarrow 3) = U_P^{\mathcal{E}}(W_P^{\mathcal{E}} \downarrow 2)$$
$$W_P^{\mathcal{E}} \downarrow 3 = W_P^{\mathcal{E}} \downarrow 2$$

Note that, although $lfp(V_P^{\mathcal{E}'})$ was a fixpoint in the bottom up *CDesc* computation, it is not a fixpoint in the top-down *FDesc* computation, and we can get more information about the finiteness properties. This is because the *CDesc* computation was unable to use information about g and h to propagate the inference about pg through; when the implications were restored, it could be shown that R_{pg} satisfies not only $pg(x, y) : x \lor y$, but also $pg(x, y) : x \land y$. Thus, it requires both directions to determine that q is a completely finite relation. ∎

To our knowledge, no other finiteness analysis can infer the above result.

4 Conclusions

We have systematically investigated the development of dataflow analyses for inadmissible program properties. This is important as some practical program properties, such as finiteness, are inadmissible, and blindly applying traditional techniques from abstract interpretation leads to incorrect analyses. We have illustrated workable extensions to these techniques by means of four finiteness analyses, the last of which is the most precise finiteness analysis that we are aware of.

The advantage of developing finiteness analyses in the framework given here is that it simplifies their description and proof of correctness. Essentially a dataflow analysis is given by simply specifying the description domain and choosing one of the techniques given here. Another advantage is that the analyses can be lifted to the case of non-constant function symbols.

Acknowledgements Discussions with Raghu Ramakrishnan were very helpful in clarifying the relationships between the various finiteness analyses proposed in the deductive database literature. Comments by Mike Codish and the anonymous referees helped improve the presentation of the paper. The second author was supported in part by the National Science Foundation under grant number CCR-8901283.

References

[1] R. Barbuti, R. Giacobazzi and G. Levi, "A Declarative Approach to Abstract Interpretation of Logic Programs", TR-20/89, Dept. of Computer Science, University of Pisa, 1989.

[2] M. Codish, J. Gallagher and E. Shapiro, "Using Safe Approximations of Fixed Points for Analysis of Logic Programs", *Proc. META88, Workshop on Meta-programming in Logic Programming*, Bristol, June 1988.

[3] P. Cousot and R. Cousot, "Abstract Interpretation: A Unified Lattice Model for Static Analysis of Programs by Construction or Approximation of Fixpoints", *Proc. 4th ACM Symp. on Principles of Programming Languages*, 1977.

[4] P. Cousot and R. Cousot, "Systematic Design of Program Analysis Frameworks", *Proc. 6th ACM Symp. on Principles of Programming Languages*, 1979.

[5] P. Cousot and R. Cousot, "Comparing the Galois Connection and Widening/Narrowing Approaches to Abstract Interpretation", Manuscript, 1991.

[6] H. Gaifman, H. Mairson, Y. Sagiv, and M. Vardi, "Undecidable Optimization Problems for Database Logic Programs", *Proc. 2nd IEEE Symposium on Logic in Computer Science*, Ithaca, 1987.

[7] Y. Ioannidis, "Bounded Recursion in Deductive Databases", Technical Report, UCB/ERL M85.6, University of California, Berkeley, Feb. 1985.

[8] P. Kanellakis, "Logic Programming and Parallel Complexity", Technical Report CS-86-23, Dept. of Computer Science, Brown University, Oct. 1986.

[9] M. Kifer, R. Ramakrishnan, and A. Silberschatz, "An Axiomatic Approach to Deciding Finiteness of Queries in Deductive Databases", manuscript (Preliminary version appeared in *Proc. 7th ACM Symp. on Principles of Deductive Databases*, Austin, TX, March 1988).

[10] K. Marriott, "Frameworks for abstract interpretation", *Acta Informatica* (to appear).

[11] K. Marriott and H. Søndergaard, "Bottom-up dataflow analysis of normal logic programs", *J. Logic Programming* vol. 13 nos. 2-3, July 1992, pp. 181–204.

[12] C. S. Mellish, "Abstract Interpretation of Prolog Programs", *Proc. 3rd International Conference on Logic Programming*, London, July 1986. Springer-Verlag LNCS vol. 225.

[13] Mycroft, A. and Jones, N., "A Relational Framework for Abstract Interpretation", *Programs as Data Objects*, LNCS 154, Springer-Verlag, 536-547 (1986).

[14] J. Naughton, "Data Independent Recursion in Deductive Databases", *Proc. 5th ACM Symp. on Principles of Database Systems*, March 1986.

[15] J. Naughton and Y. Sagiv, "A Decidable Class of Bounded Recursions", *Proc. 6th ACM Symp. on Principles of Database Systems*, San Diego, CA, March 1987.

[16] F. Nielson, "Strictness analysis and denotational abstract interpretation", *Information and Computation* **76** (1) : 29–92, 1988.

[17] R. Ramakrishnan, F. Bancilhon, and A. Silberschatz, "Safety of Recursive Horn Clauses with Infinite Relations", *Proc. ACM Symp. on Principles of Database Systems*, 1987.

[18] Y. Sagiv and M. Y. Vardi, "Safety of Datalog Queries over Infinite Databases", *Proc. 8th ACM Symposium on Principles of Database Systems*, Philadelphia, PA, March 1989.

[19] H. Søndergaard, "An application of abstract interpretation of logic programs: Occur check reduction", In B. Robinet and R. Wilhelm, editors, *Proc. ESOP 86* (LNCS 213), pages 327–338. Springer-Verlag, 1986.

[20] R. Statman, "Logical relations and the typed lambda calculus", *Information and Control*, vol. 65, pages 85–97, 1985.

Reexecution in Abstract Interpretation of Prolog
(Extended Abstract)

Baudouin Le Charlier
University of Namur,
21 rue Grandgagnage, B-5000 Namur (Belgium)
Email: ble@info.fundp.ac.be

Pascal Van Hentenryck
Brown University,
Box 1910, Providence, RI 02912 (USA)
Email: pvh@cs.brown.edu

Abstract

Logic programming, because of referential transparency, enjoys the property that a goal may be reexecuted arbitrarily often without affecting the meaning of the program. This property, although not interesting computationally in general, can be exploited in abstract interpretation to improve the accuracy of the analysis, as noted by Bruynooghe in [1].

In this paper, we study reexecution from its theoretical foundations to its experimental evaluation. We define a new abstract semantics for Prolog, which incorporates the notion of reexecution, and we study its correctness and precision properties. A fixpoint algorithm to compute (parts of) the abstract semantics is then presented. The accuracy and efficiency of the algorithm is evaluated experimentally on two abstract domains, a simple domain and an elaborate domain, and compared with conventional approaches.

The experimental results indicate that (1) reexecution can provide significant gain in accuracy at a very reasonable computation cost and that (2) reexecution on a simple domain is a versatile alternative to the standard approach on a more sophisticated domain.

1 Introduction

Abstract interpretation of Prolog has attracted many researchers in recent years. This effort is motivated by the need of optimization in logic programming compilers to be competitive with procedural languages and the declarative nature of the languages which makes them more amenable to static analysis. Considerable progress has been realised in this area in terms of the frameworks (e.g. [1, 10, 11]), the algorithms (e.g. [1, 5, 6, 13]), the abstract domains and the implementations (e.g. [3, 4, 7, 14]). Recent results indicate that abstract interpretation can be competitive with specialized data flow algorithms and could be integrated in industrial compilers.

Traditionally, an application of abstract interpretation for Prolog requires the definition of an abstract domain which captures, through abstract substitutions, the information relevant to the application. A generic algorithm (e.g. [1, 6]) can then be instantiated to this abstract domain. If the level of precision provided by

```
append( X₁ , X₂ , X₃ ) :- X₁ = [] , X₃ = X₂.
append( X₁ , X₂ , X₃ ) :- X₁ = [ X₄ | X₅ ] , X₃ = [ X₄ | X₆ ] ,
          append( X₅ , X₂ , X₆ ).
```

Figure 1: The Normalized Version of Append

```
TRY CLAUSE 2
   EXIT EXTC (Any,Var, Ground,Var,Var,Var)
   CALL UNIF-FUN  (Any,Var,Ground,Var,Var,Var)
   EXIT UNIF-FUN   (Any,Var,Ground,Any,Any,Var) PS: [{1,4,5}]
   CALL UNIF-FUN  (Any,Var,Ground,Any,Any,Var) PS: [{1,4,5}]
   EXIT UNIF-FUN   (Any,Var,Ground,Ground,Any,Ground) PS: [{1,5}]
   CALL PRO-GOAL  append(Any,Var,Ground)
   EXIT PRO-GOAL  append(Ground,Ground,Ground) SV: [{2,3}]
   EXIT EXTG  (Any,Ground,Ground,Ground,Ground,Ground) SV: [{2,6}]
   EXIT RESTRC  (Any,Ground,Ground)
   EXIT UNION  (Any,Ground,Ground)
EXIT CLAUSE 2
```

Figure 2: The Second Iteration on the Simple Domain

the resulting algorithm is not satisfactory, another, more sophisticated, abstract domain is defined to overcome the limitations.

In this paper, we investigate another (complementary) approach. The approach exploits the referential transparency of logic programming which guarantees that a goal may be reexecuted arbitrarily often without affecting the program. Although not interesting computationally in general, this property can be used in abstract interpretation to improve the precision of the analysis as noted by Bruynooghe as early as 1987.

As a motivating example, consider abstract interpretation using a simple domain, containing modes, sharing, and same value components on the append program depicted in Figure 1. Assume also that the input substitution includes the modes (Any,Var,Ground) for X_1, X_2, X_3. The output modes (Ground,Ground,Ground) should ideally be contained in the output substitution. However, the simple domain returns an output substitution with modes (Any,Ground,Ground). Figure 2 depicts the second iteration of the algorithm on the second clause and illustrates why the analysis loses precision. On return of the recursive call, the algorithm needs to propagate the fact that variable X_5 is Ground. Since X_4 is ground as well, X_1 should now be Ground. However, the pattern information relating X_1 to X_4 and X_5 has been lost and the mode of X_1 cannot be improved upon. The traditional way of overcoming the problem amounts to preserving more information on the variables, e.g. remembering that X_1 is bound to [X_4|X_5] as done in the elaborate domain used later in the paper.[1] However, a similar effect can be achieved (for the append program) simply by reexecuting the first goal of the clause. The reexecution automatically assigns the mode Ground to X_1.

The research described in this paper originates in an attempt to study theoretically and experimentally an algorithm that would automatically reexecute goals to

---

[1] Other approaches have been explored including covering and the Prop domain.

achieve more precision. We propose a new abstract semantics which generalizes the traditional basic abstract semantics and incorporates the idea of reexecution. The reexecution semantics makes use of a new operation REFINE. The abstract semantics is safe wrt the operational semantics and improves (or at least preserves) the precision of the basic semantics. A fixpoint algorithm computing the abstract semantics is also presented and its implementation choices discussed. The algorithm is then evaluated experimentally on a simple domain and a much more elaborate one. Results comparing the standard algorithm (described in [3, 6, 7]) with the reexecution algorithm are given both in terms of accuracy and efficiency of the analysis. We also compare the reexecution algorithm on the simple domain with the standard algorithm on the elaborate domain to demonstrate that reexecution on a simple domain provide a complementary and versatile alternative to the standard algorithm on a more sophisticated domain.

The rest of the paper is organized as follows. The next section recalls some basic notions from previous papers. Section 3 presents the reexecution abstract semantics. Section 4 presents the fixpoint algorithm for the reexecution semantics while section 5 reports the experimental results. The last section contains the conclusion of the paper. Only parts of our theoretical and experimental results are presented here. See the technical report version of this paper [8] for a comprehensive coverage.

2 Preliminaries[2]

In this section, we mainly recall the basic concrete operations used in the semantics. We use $var(o)$ to represent the set of variables in the syntactical object o, $dom(\theta)$ and $codom(\theta)$ to denote the domain and codomain of a substitution and $mgu(t_1, t_2)$ to denote the set of most general unifiers of t_1 and t_2. Let θ be a substitution and $D \subseteq dom(\theta)$. The *restriction* of θ to D, denoted $\theta_{/D}$, is the substitution σ such that $dom(\sigma) = D$ and $x\theta = x\sigma$ for all $x \in D$.

The operational semantics uses five primitive operations. In the definitions, we assume that $var(c) = \{x_1, \ldots, x_m\}$, $var(head(c)) = \{x_1, \ldots, x_n\}$, and $x_{i_1}, \ldots, x_{i_n}$ is the sequence of variables occurring in g (from left to right).

$$\text{EXTC}(c, \theta) = \{ \{x_1 \leftarrow t_1, \ldots, x_n \leftarrow t_n, \ldots, x_{n+1} \leftarrow y_1, \ldots, x_m \leftarrow y_{m-n}\} :$$
$$t_i = x_i\theta \ (1 \leq i \leq n) \text{ and } y_1, \ldots, y_{m-n} \text{ are all distinct variables}$$
$$\text{and } var(t_1, \ldots, t_n) \cap \{y_1, \ldots, y_{m-n}\} = \emptyset \}.$$

$$\text{RESTRC}(c, \theta) = \{\theta_{/\{x_1, \ldots, x_n\}}\}.$$

$$\text{RESTRG}(g, \theta) = \{\{x_1 \leftarrow x_{i_1}\theta, \ldots, x_n \leftarrow x_{i_n}\theta\}\}.$$

$$\text{EXTG}(g, \theta_1, \theta_2) = \{ \theta_1\sigma : \exists\theta_3 \text{ such that } \theta_3 = \text{RESTRG}(g, \theta_1) \text{ and } \theta_2 = \theta_3\sigma \text{ where}$$
$$dom(\sigma) \subseteq codom(\theta_3) \text{ and } (codom(\theta_1) - codom(\theta_3)) \cap codom(\sigma) = \emptyset \}.$$

$$\text{RENAME}(g, \theta) = \{\{x_{i_1} \leftarrow x_1\theta, \ldots, x_{i_n} \leftarrow x_n\theta\}\}$$

In the following, we also use $\langle \theta, cons \rangle$ for a computation state, $cons$ being a procedure name, a clause, an atom (i.e. built-in or procedure call), or a sequence of atoms. We use $\langle \theta, cons \rangle \longmapsto \theta'$ to denote that θ' is an answer substitution obtained from $\langle \theta, cons \rangle$ using SLD-resolution.

---

[2]The reader is refered to [6] for a more comprehensive and rigorous presentation.

3 The Abstract Semantics

3.1 Preliminaries

The abstract semantics is based on the basic abstract semantics proposed in [12] and used subsequently in [3, 6, 7]. We recall only the main concepts here.

For each finite set D of program variables we assume the existence of a *cpo* AS_D whose elements are called abstract substitutions on domain D and denoted by β. Let CS_D be the set of program substitutions having domain D. The meaning of each abstract substitution is given through the concretization function: $Cc : AS_D \to \mathcal{P}(CS_D)$. We assume in the following that Cc is monotone.

The abstract semantics uses seven (families of) abstract primitive operations EXTC, RESTRG, EXTG, RESTRC, UNION, AI_VAR and AI_FUNC. The first four operations are safe abstractions of the corresponding "concrete" operations used by the operational semantics. The last three operations are safe in the following sense (assuming $D = \{x_1, \ldots, x_n\}$):

$$\forall \theta \in CS_D : (\theta \in Cc(\beta_1) \text{ or } \theta \in Cc(\beta_2)) \Rightarrow \theta \in Cc(\text{UNION}(\beta_1, \beta_2))$$

$$\left. \begin{array}{cc} \forall \theta \in CS_{\{x_1, x_2\}} & \sigma \in mgu(x_1\theta, x_2\theta) \\ \forall \beta \in AS_{\{x_1, x_2\}} & \theta \in Cc(\beta) \end{array} \right\} \Rightarrow \theta\sigma \in Cc(\text{AI\_VAR}(\beta))$$

$$\left. \begin{array}{cc} \forall \theta \in CS_D & \sigma \in mgu(x_1\theta, f(x_2, \ldots, x_n)\theta) \\ \forall \beta \in AS_D & \theta \in Cc(\beta) \end{array} \right\} \Rightarrow \theta\sigma \in Cc(\text{AI\_FUNC}(\beta))$$

The abstract semantics of a program P is defined as a set of abstract tuples $(\beta_{in}, p, \beta_{out})$ where p is a predicate symbol of arity n occurring in P, $D = \{x_1, \ldots, x_n\}$ and $\beta_{in}, \beta_{out} \in AS_D$. For convenience, we assume in the following an underlying program P. The *underlying domain* UD of the program is the set of all (β_{in}, p) such that $\beta_{in} \in AS_D$ and p occurs in P. We denote $SATT$ the set of all functional, total, and monotone sets of abstract tuples *sat*.

$SATT$ is endowed with the following ordering: $sat_1 \leq sat_2$ iff $\forall (\beta, p) \in UD : sat_1(\beta, p) \leq sat_2(\beta, p)$. We note $\beta_{out} = sat(\beta_{in}, p)$ iff $(\beta_{in}, p, \beta_{out}) \in sat$.

3.2 The REFINE Operation

In this section, we introduce a novel abstract operation.

Motivation The abstract interpretation of a clause c for an input abstract substitution β_{in} can be viewed as the annotation of c with abstract substitutions $\beta_{in}, \beta_0, \ldots, \beta_m$, say

$$\beta_{in} \; p(x_1, \ldots, x_n) \leftarrow \beta_0 \; g_1 \; \beta_1 \, , \, \ldots \, , \; \beta_{m-1} \; g_m \; \beta_m.$$

satisfying $\theta_i \in Cc(\beta_i)$ for all $\theta_0, \theta_1, \ldots, \theta_m$ such that $\theta_{in} \in Cc(\beta_{in})$; $\theta_0 \in \text{EXTC}(c, \theta_{in})$; $\langle \theta_{i-1}, g_i \rangle \longmapsto \theta_i$ ($1 \leq i \leq m$). θ_i is more instantiated than θ_j when ($i > j$). Hence $\langle \theta_i, g_j \rangle \longmapsto \theta_i$ due to referencial transparency of logic programs. The above property allows the reexecution of subgoal g_j on abstract substitution β_i and guarantees that the resulting abstract substitution β_i' safely approximates θ_i (i.e. $\theta_i \in Cc(\beta_i')$). Moreover, the property holds for any subgoal g_j ($1 \leq j \leq i$) and allows for multiple reexecutions. However naive reexecution is not guaranteed to improve the accuracy of β_i. In fact, it may even decrease accuracy. The purpose of the REFINE operation is to make sure that reexecution improves (or at least preserves) accuracy.

Axiomatic Characterization   For some set of variables $D = \{x_1, ..., x_n\}$, let us note $Aseq_D$ the set of finite sequences $(\beta_1, \ldots, \beta_q)$ such that $q \geq 0$ and $dom(\beta_i) \subseteq D$ $(\forall i : 1 \leq i \leq q)$.

Definition 1   A *refinement* operation on D is any operation

$$\text{REFINE} : AS_D \times Aseq_D \rightarrow AS_D$$

satisfying

1. $\forall \beta \in AS_D \; \forall (\beta_1, \ldots, \beta_q) \in Aseq_D : \text{REFINE}(\beta, \beta_1, \ldots, \beta_q) \leq \beta$.

2. For all $D_1, \ldots, D_q \subseteq D$, $\beta \in AS_D$, $(\beta_1, \ldots, \beta_q) \in AS_{D_1} \times \ldots \times AS_{D_q}$ and $\theta \in Cc(\beta)$:

   $$\theta_{/D_1} \in Cc(\beta_1) \; \& \; \ldots \; \& \; \theta_{/D_q} \in Cc(\beta_q) \; \Rightarrow \; \theta \in Cc(\text{REFINE}(\beta, \beta_1, \ldots, \beta_q)).$$

3. Let $\beta \in AS_D$ and $seq_1, \ldots, seq_i, \ldots$ be an infinite sequence of elements from $Aseq_D$. The following properties hold

   (a) the sequence $\beta_0, \ldots, \beta_i, \ldots$ has a greatest lower bound denoted $\sqcap_{i=1}^{\infty} \beta_i$,

   (b) $Cc(\sqcap_{i=1}^{\infty} \beta_i) = \cap_{i=1}^{\infty} Cc(\beta_i)$,

   for all infinite decreasing sequence $\beta_0 \geq \ldots \geq \beta_i \geq \ldots$ defined by

   $$\begin{aligned} \beta_0 &= \beta, \\ \beta_i &= \text{REFINE}(\beta_{i-1}, seq_i) \quad (i \geq 1). \; \square \end{aligned}$$

Conditions 1-3 guarantees respectively that REFINE increases accuracy, is safe and remains safe when applied infinitely often (a continuity requirement). It is a formal requirement for the abstract semantics but has few practical consequences. Existence of refinement operations for actual applications is rather obvious.

Example 2   On some domains, REFINE can be defined in terms of an *exact join* operation, say $\bowtie$. For all $\beta_1 \in AS_{D_1}$, $\beta_2 \in AS_{D_2}$, the exact join satisfies

$$Cc(\beta_1 \bowtie \beta_2) = \{\; \theta : dom(\theta) = D_1 \cup D_2 \; \& \; \theta_{/D_1} \in Cc(\beta_1) \; \& \; \theta_{/D_2} \in Cc(\beta_2) \;\}$$

Note that $dom(\beta_1 \bowtie \beta_2) = dom(\beta_1) \cup dom(\beta_2)$. With the exact join, REFINE is then defined as

$$\text{REFINE}(\beta, \beta_1, \ldots, \beta_n) = \beta \bowtie \beta_1 \bowtie \ldots \bowtie \beta_n. \; \square$$

3.3   The Reexecution Semantics

We are now in position to define the reexecution semantics which is depicted in Figure 3. The semantic functions T_p and T_c are shared with the basic abstract semantics (see [6, 7, 12]) and the main novelty is to be found in semantic function T_b. T_b makes use of two other semantic functions T_g and T_r corresponding respectively to a normal goal execution and to a goal reexecution. It also makes use of the greatest lower bound and the operation REFINE. Note also that the semantic function T_r makes use of the renaming operation RENAME which is a safe abstraction of the corresponding concrete operation.

The abstract semantics of a program is defined as the least fixpoint of $TSAT$. It is guaranteed to exist if the primitive operations are monotone. In practice, this

$TSAT(sat) = \{(\beta, p, \beta') : (\beta, p) \in UD \text{ and } \beta' = T_p(\beta, p, sat)\}.$

$T_p(\beta, p, sat) = \text{UNION}(\beta_1, \ldots, \beta_n)$
where $\beta_i = T_c(\beta, c_i, sat),$
$c_1, \ldots, c_n$ are the clauses of p.

$T_c(\beta, c, sat) = \text{RESTRC}(c, \beta')$
where $\beta' = T_b(\text{EXTC}(c, \beta), b, sat),$
b is the body of c.

$T_b(\beta, <>, sat) = \beta.$
$T_b(\beta, (g_1, \ldots, g_k), sat) = \bigsqcap_{i=1}^{\infty} \beta_i \quad (k \geq 1)$
where $\beta_0 = T_b(\beta, (g_1, \ldots, g_{k-1}), sat)$
$\beta_1 = T_g(\beta_0, g_k, sat)$
$\beta_{i+1} = \text{REFINE}(\beta_i, T_r(\beta_i, g_1, sat), \ldots, T_r(\beta_i, g_k, sat)) \quad (i \geq 1)$

$T_g(\beta, g, sat) = \text{EXTG}(g, \beta, \beta_2)$
where $\beta_2 = sat(\beta_1, p)$ if g is $p(\ldots)$
$\text{AI\_VAR}(\beta_1)$ if g is $x_i = x_j$
$\text{AI\_FUNC}(\beta_1, f)$ if g is $x_i = f(\ldots),$
$\beta_1 = \text{RESTRG}(g, \beta).$

$T_r(\beta, g, sat) = \text{RENAME}(g, \beta_2)$
where $\beta_2 = sat(\beta_1, p)$ if g is $p(\ldots)$
$\text{AI\_VAR}(\beta_1)$ if g is $x_i = x_j$
$\text{AI\_FUNC}(\beta_1, f)$ if g is $x_i = f(\ldots),$
$\beta_1 = \text{RESTRG}(g, \beta).$

Figure 3: The Reexecution Semantics

may be too strong a requirement, especially for an operation like REFINE. Fortunately, postfixpoints of $TSAT$ (i.e. the sets sat such that $sat \geq TSAT(sat)$) are always guaranteed to exist which is sufficient for the purpose of abstract interpretation [2, 12]. The reexecution algorithm is of interest provided that the computed postfixpoint is more accurate than the least fixpoint of the basic semantics.

3.4 Safeness and Accuracy of the Reexecution Semantics

To establish the safeness of the reexecution semantics, it is only necessary to establish the safeness of the function T_b. The result then follows from the safeness of the basic abstract semantics. To simplify notations, we denote by sg_k the sequence of goals $g_1, \ldots, g_k$.

Theorem 3 Let sat be any postfixpoint of $TSAT$. Let D, θ, β be such that $var(sg_k) \subseteq D = var(\theta) = var(\beta)$. Then

$$\left.\begin{array}{l} \theta \in Cc(\beta) \\ \langle \theta, sg_k \rangle \longmapsto \theta' \\ \beta' = T_b(\beta, sg_k, sat) \end{array}\right\} \Rightarrow \theta' \in Cc(\beta').$$

The reexecution semantics is at least as precise as the basic semantics.

Theorem 4 Let T_b^r and T_b^b denote the reexecution and basic versions of the T_b function. Then, for any β, sg_k and sat, $T_b^r(\beta, sg_k, sat) \leq T_b^b(\beta, sg_k, sat)$.

3.5 Notes on Operation REFINE

Practical Computation The semantic functions should not be seen as suggesting any particular practical implementation. In fact, the expression

$$\text{REFINE}(\beta_{i-1}, T_r(\beta_{i-1}, g_1, sat), \ldots, T_r(\beta_{i-1}, g_k, sat))$$

is best viewed as an operation which automatically chooses which arguments to reevaluate using, say, *call by name* instead of *call by value*.[3] The choices taken in our implementation are discussed in a subsequent section and amounts to applying REFINE on a single goal.

Exact Join In presence of an exact join, $\text{REFINE}(\beta_{i-1}, \ldots)$ may be computed as $\beta_{i-1} \bowtie T_r(\beta_{i-1}, g_j, sat)$ for a *selected goal* g_j.

The existence of an exact join is rather natural in the context of abstract interpretation and has empirical and theoretical justifications. On the empirical side, the two domains used in our experiments enjoy an exact join although they were originally designed for the basic semantics. On the theoretical side, the exact join operation is a generalization of an abstract intersection operation which is often exact in actual abstract domains. In this case, abstract intersection coincides with the *glb*, which is not a safe abstraction of intersection otherwise.

4 The Algorithm

We now present a fixpoint algorithm to compute the abstract semantics. The fixpoint algorithm is an instance of a universal top-down fixpoint algorithm [9] whose correctness has been proven. It is also a generalization of the standard algorithm designed for the basic abstract semantics [6, 7].

The algorithm makes use of all the operations and data structures of the original algorithm. In addition, it makes use of the REFINE operation on two substitutions, of operation RENAME, and of a new operation RECONSIDER.[4] The last operation is generic but should satisfy

$$\text{RECONSIDER}(set, \beta_{old}, \beta_{new}) \subseteq \{ g \in set \mid \text{RESTRG}(\beta_{old}, g) \neq \text{RESTRG}(\beta_{new}, g) \}.$$

The algorithm is depicted in Figures 4 and 5. Compared to the standard algorithm, the novelties are to be found in Procedure solve_clause. This procedure makes use of two sets: the ready set, which contains all atoms that can be executed (or reexecuted) and the queue set which contains the atoms to execute or which are thought to be interesting to reexecute. An atom to be executed needs to be present in both sets. Operation EXTG is used after the first execution while operation REFINE is used after reexecution. The ready set is updated to include the next goal which can be executed while the queue set is updated using the RECONSIDER operation.

---

[3]Strictly speaking, it would be more precise to add one more argument to the operation to provide the relevant information. This would however complicate the exposition.

[4]RECONSIDER was considered part of the REFINE operation in the reexecution semantics.

```
procedure solve(in β_in,p; out sat,dp)
begin
    sat := ∅;  dp := ∅;
    solve_call(β_in,p,∅,sat,dp)
end

procedure solve_call(in β_in,p,suspended; inout sat,dp)
begin
    if (β_in,p) ∉ (dom(dp) ∪ suspended) then
    begin
        if (β_in,p) ∉ dom(sat) then
            sat := EXTEND(β_in,p,sat);
        repeat
            β_out := ⊥;
            EXT_DP(β_in,p,dp);
            for i := 1 to m with c_1,...,c_m clauses-of p
            do begin
                solve_clause(β_in,p,c_i,suspended ∪ {(β_in,p)},β_aux,sat,dp);
                β_out := UNION(β_out,β_aux)
            end;
            (sat,modified) := ADJUST(β_in,p,β_out,sat);
            dp := dp \ REMOVE_DP(modified,dp)
        until (β_in,p) ∈ dom(dp)
    end
end
```

Figure 4: The Algorithm: Part I

Implementation Choices The basic algorithm leaves open a number of decisions such as the choice of the next goal to execute, the implementation of REFINE, and the implementation of RECONSIDER. Our implementation always gives priority to reexecution of goals. The underlying motivation is to provide the best possible substitution for the first execution of a goal, yielding the best possible input modes. It may also avoid calling a goal recursively with a greater (i.e. less precise) substitution. As a consequence, it tends to produce substitution preserving programs which is an important property for complexity reasons [6]. The experimental results indicate the effectiveness of this heuristics. The domains used in the experimental evaluation both enjoy an exact join operation. Hence it was natural to use it as a basis for REFINE. Our basic implementation always reconsiders all possible goals, i.e.

$$\text{RECONSIDER}(set, \beta_{old}, \beta_{new}) = \{ g \in set \mid \text{RESTRG}(\beta_{old}, g) \neq \text{RESTRG}(\beta_{new}, g) \}.$$

This gives maximal precision at the cost of additional complexity.

5 Experimental Evaluation

This section reports the experimental evaluation of the reexecution algorithm. Section 5.1 and 5.2 give an overview of the programs tested and of the abstract domains. Sections 5.3 and 5.4 compare the standard and reexecution algorithms on the simple and the elaborate domains respectively. Section 5.5 compares reexecution on the

```
procedure solve_clause(in β_in,p,c,suspended; out β_out;inout sat,dp)
begin
    Let g_1,...,g_m body-of c in
        β_ext := EXTC(c,β_in);
        ready := {g_1};
        queue := {g_1,...,g_m};
        while queue ≠ ∅ do
        begin
            select g_i from ready ∩ queue;
            β_aux := RESTRG(g_i,β_ext);
            switch (g_i) of
            case X_j = X_k:
                β_int := AI_VAR(β_aux)
            case X_j = f(...):
                β_int := AI_FUNC(β_aux,f)
            case q(...):
                solve_call(β_aux,q,suspended,sat,dp);
                β_int := sat(β_aux,q);
                if (β_in,p) ∈ dom(dp) then
                    ADD_DP(β_in,p,β_aux,q,dp)
            end;
            if firstExecutionOf(g_i) then
                β_next := EXTG(g_i,β_ext,β_int)
            else
                β_next := REFINE(β_ext,RENAME(g_i,β_int))
            ready := ready ∪ {g_{i+1}};
            queue := queue \ {g_i} ∪ RECONSIDER({g_1,...,g_m},β_ext,β_next);
            β_ext := β_next;
        end;
        β_out := RESTRC(c,β_ext)
end
```

Figure 5: The Algorithm: Part II

simple domain with standard execution on the elaborate domain. See [8] for the complete tables and other measures evaluating the implementation choices.

5.1 The Programs Tested

The programs tested were an alpha-beta procedure kalah, an equation-solver Press, a cutting-stock program cs, the generate and test version of a disjunctive scheduling program Disj, the tokeniser and reader Read of R. O'Keefe and D.H.D. Warren, a program PG by W. Older to solve a specific mathematical problem, the Browse program Grabriel taken from Gabriel benchmark, a planning program Plan (PL for short), an n-queens program Queens, the peephole optimizer Peep from SB-Prolog, and the traditional concatenation and quicksort programs, say Append (with input modes (var,var,ground)) and Qsort (difference lists).

5.2 Overview of the Abstract Domains

The Elaborate Domain The elaborate abstract domain contains patterns (i.e. for each subterm, the main functor and a reference to its arguments are stored), sharing, same-value, and mode components. It should be related to the *depth-k abstraction* of [5], but no bound is imposed a priori to the terms depth. Program normalization does not lose precision on this domain. However, as the domain is infinite widening operations must be used by the algorithms. The domain is fully described in [12] which contains also the proofs of monotonicity and safeness.

The Simple Abstract Domain The mode domain of [12] is a reformulation of the domain of [1]. The domain could be viewed as a simplification of the elaborate domain discussed where the pattern information has been omitted and the sharing has been simplified to an equivalence relation. Only three modes are considered: ground, var and any. Equality constraints can only hold between program variables (and not between subterms of the terms bound to them). The same restriction applies to sharing constraints. Moreover algorithms for primitive operations are significantly different. They are much simpler and the loss of accuracy is significant.

5.3 Simple Standard Versus Simple Reexecution

In this section, we compare the standard and reexecution algorithm on the simple domain. The simple domain may lose much precision since no information on types (e.g. the form of the terms bound to variables) is preserved. The reexecution algorithm recovers part of this information by repeating the execution of built-ins and procedure calls. It may thus improve the accuracy substantially. The purpose of this section is to quantify experimentally this gain in accuracy and its cost in performance on the simple domain. Experimentals results are depicted in table 1. meq_o (meq_i) gives the number of output (input) arguments for which the same mode is derived by both algorithms. mgt_o and mgt_i are the number of arguments for which reexecution is strictly better. sps, ss_s and ss_r respectively provide the total number of unifications in the programs and the number of unifications which can be specialized according to the information derived by the standard and the reexecution algorithm. t_s and t_r are the corresponding execution times.

5.3.1 Accuracy

Input and Output Modes To compare the accuracy of the standard and the reexecution algorithm, we first collect the input and output modes for each procedure in the program. Only one input and output mode is associated to each procedure (hence no program specialization is performed).

The experimental results show substantial gains on the output modes for the reexecution algorithm on most programs. On the average, the gain is over 50%. Reexecution also improves Queens, CS, PG, and Plan by more than 70% and produces more than 30% improvement on 9 programs. The results at the procedure granularity are in fact higher and factor out the fact that ground input modes give ground output modes that cannot be improved upon. The average improvement here is over 70%. Reexecution also produces an improvement of over 75% for 7 programs, 4 of which show a 100% improvement.

The improvements for the input modes are somewhat lower than for the output modes which is intrinsic to the reexecution framework because reexecution provides its maximum effect at the end of a clause (where all subgoals may be reexecuted). The average improvement at the mode granularity is over 30%. It is over 49% at the procedure granularity. Note also that 7 programs are improved by more than 30%

	meq_o	mgt_o	meq_i	mgt_i	sps	ss_s	ss_r	t_s	t_r
Append	2	1	3	0	4	2	2	0.01	0.01
Kalah	57	66	78	45	283	186	249	1.67	1.88
Queens	2	9	5	6	17	6	15	0.14	0.07
Press	130	13	137	6	432	185	203	3.74	7.73
Peep	38	25	46	17	543	393	477	2.71	2.92
CS	28	66	57	37	203	83	148	3.37	4.32
Disj	24	36	33	27	183	138	163	1.89	2.42
PG	8	23	18	13	52	28	43	0.35	0.27
Read	116	5	122	0	437	279	279	3.71	4.37
Plan	8	24	16	16	36	12	24	0.30	0.21
QSort	3	6	4	5	12	2	11	0.23	0.11

Table 1: Standard Versus Reexecution: the Simple Domain.

at the mode granularity while 8 programs exhibit a gain over 45% at the procedure granularity. Peaks of 81% and 80% are achieved on Kalah and Queens.

It is interesting to point out as well that the modes inferred are now optimal or close to optimal for many programs. This will be discussed in more detail in a subsequent section.

Unification Specializations To provide a more complete picture of the gain in accuracy, we also indicate how many unifications (i.e. executions of $x_i = x_j$ et $x_{i_1} = f(x_{i_2}, \ldots, x_{i_n})$) can be specialized using the modes inferred by both strategies. We assume that $x_i = x_j$ can be specialized when one of its arguments is either ground or variable and that $x_{i_1} = f(x_{i_2}, \ldots, x_{i_n})$ can be specialized when its first argument is either ground or a variable. For both strategies, we report the number of static specializations (which requires a unique procedure for all uses). A program uses the results of abstract interpretation to associate a substitution to each program point corresponding to a unification operation. This substitution is then used to decide whether the unification can be specialized or not.

The results indicate that reexecution produces an average improvement of over 25%. The programs with the least improvements are Press (since reexecution still loses much information) and Read (since not much information is to be gained). They are also the programs with the smallest number of specializations. The measures also show that reexecution produces over 75% of static specializations in the average, illustrating the potential for specializations in the programs.

5.3.2 Efficiency

We now investigate the computational cost of the reexecution algorithm. We measure the computation times on a SPARC-1 (Sun 4/60), the number of executions of Procedure Solve_Goal, and the number of executions of Procedure Solve_Clause.

The results indicate that reexecution is in the average 8% slower than the standard algorithm. The highest increase in computation time occurs for the Press program which is about twice as slow with reexecution (7.73 sec. instead of 3.74 sec.). Four programs are faster using reexecution thanks to the additional precision: Queens (0.07 sec. instead 0.14 sec.), Plan (0.21 sec. instead of 0.30 sec.), PG (0.27 sec. instead of 0.3), and QSort (0.11 sec. instead of 0.23). The number of executions at the goal and procedure level is always lower using reexecution but for

	meq_o	mgt_o	meq_i	mgt_i	sps	ss_s	ss_r	t_s	t_r
Append	3	0	3	0	4	4	4	0.01	0.01
Kalah	123	0	123	0	283	278	278	5.41	8.65
Queens	11	0	11	0	17	17	17	0.16	0.18
Press	43	100	61	82	431	249	416	24.64	12.12
Peep	61	2	63	0	543	526	526	6.31	9.75
CS	94	0	94	0	203	203	203	5.82	30.83
Disj	60	0	60	0	183	183	183	3.19	7.43
PG	31	0	31	0	52	47	47	0.77	0.99
Read	122	0	122	0	437	280	280	25.08	123.69
Plan	32	0	32	0	36	28	28	0.58	0.72
QSort	8	1	9	0	12	11	11	0.09	0.41

Table 2: Standard Versus Reexecution: the Elaborate Domain.

the Press program (for the abovementioned reasons) and the Read program where little information can be gained.

We also measured some results to find out about the execution profile. The results indicate that the maximum number of times an atom is reexecuted for a single clause activation is atmost 4 and in the average 2.36, indicating that few reexecutions are in fact needed. On the whole execution, an atom is atmost reexecuted 9 times and the average on all programs is close to 5. The measures also indicate that reexecution is concentrated in only about 16% of all atoms, indicating that only a small portion of the program needs reexecution.

5.4 Elaborate Standard Versus Elaborate Reexecution

We now consider the elaborate domain (see table 2). This domain produces optimal results or near-optimal results for many programs. The main exceptions are Press and Qsort where the UNION operation loses some dependencies between variables in a difference list, leading to a significant loss in accuracy. Peep has a small loss in accuracy for the same reason. Finally, Read has some imprecision due to the lack of a data type for lists in the present domain.

5.4.1 Accuracy

Improvements for the output modes are produced on 3 programs. Press exhibits improvements of 69.93% and 90.38% at the mode and procedure granularity, Peep produces improvements of 3.17% and 10.53%, and Qsort obtains 11.11% and 33.33%. Only Press exhibits an improvement for the input modes (respectively 57.34% and 92.31% at the mode and procedure granularities)and for the unification specializations where 25% improvement is obtained.

5.4.2 Efficiency

As far as efficiency is concerned, it is interesting to note that reexecution is, in the average, 2.31 times slower than the standard algorithm. Reexecution is two times faster than the standard algorithm for the Press program (12.12 sec. instead of 24.64 sec.) and, in the worst case, less than 5.3 times slower than the standard algorithm (30.83 sec. instead of 5.82). The worst case occurs for program CS which builds up large terms that requires reexecution although no information can

	meq_o	mgt_o	mlt_o	meq_i	mgt_i	sps	ss_{sr}	ss_{es}	t_{sr}	t_{es}
Append	3	0	0	2	1	4	4	4	0.01	0.01
Kalah	123	0	0	116	7	283	249	278	1.88	5.41
Queens	11	0	0	9	2	17	15	17	0.07	0.16
Press	142	1	0	133	10	431	203	249	7.73	24.64
Peep	61	0	2	57	6	543	477	526	2.92	6.31
CS	94	0	0	79	15	203	148	203	4.32	5.82
Disj	60	0	0	54	6	183	163	183	2.42	3.19
PG	31	0	0	29	2	52	43	47	0.27	0.77
Read	121	0	0	114	7	437	279	280	4.37	25.08
Plan	32	0	0	29	3	36	24	28	0.21	0.58
QSort	8	0	1	9	0	12	11	11	0.11	0.09

Table 3: Simple Reexecution versus Elaborate Standard

be gained. Except for Press, reexecution makes always more iterations than the standard algorithm which is easily explained since not much precision is gained that could compensate for reexecution.

The execution profile indicates once again that reexecution is focused on a small subpart of the program (10.58% of the possible atoms are reexecuted).

5.5 Simple Reexecution Versus Elaborate Standard

As mentioned previously reexecution on a simple domain provides an alternative to standard execution on a more sophisticated domain. In this section, we evaluate experimentally the potential of this idea, both in terms of efficiency and in terms of accuracy (see table 3).

5.5.1 Accuracy

We compare the output modes obtained by reexecution on the simple domain with standard execution on the elaborate domain. The results indicate that over 95% of the modes are the same in both strategies. Moreover, reexecution on the simple domain improves upon the standard execution on the elaborate domain in two programs: Peep (3.17% and 10.53% improvement) and qsort (11.11% and 33.33% improvement). It only loses precision on Press (0.7% and 1.92% loss). For output modes, it appears that reexecution on the simple domain compares favourably with standard execution on the elaborate domain.

As far as the input modes are concerned, it turns out that 92% of modes are the same in both approaches. Although the result is slightly below those obtained for the output modes, reexecution on the simple domain still compares well with standard execution on the elaborate domain.

Finally, the unification specializations obtained by both approaches indicate that reexecution on the mode domain loses about 8% in dynamic specializations and about 14% in static specializations. This is in fact very much in accordance with the input modes and shows that reexecution bridges most of the gap between the simple and the elaborate domains.

5.5.2 Efficiency

The comparison of execution times for both approaches indicates that reexecution on the simple domain is more than two times faster than the standard execution on the elaborate domain. The improvements are particularly high on the large programs such as Read (5.77 sec. versus 25.08 sec.), Press (7.73 sec. versus 24.64 sec.), and Kalah (1.88 sec. versus 5.41 sec.), reaching 4.35, 3.19, and 2.88. The numbers of executions of goals and procedures are also smaller but with a reduced factor (indicating that the operations on the simpler domain are less expensive).

6   Conclusion

In this paper, we have studied, in a comprehensive manner, the idea of reexecution for the abstract interpretation of Prolog. A new abstract semantics embedding the idea of reexecution has been proposed, based on a new operation REFINE whose properties have been studied and which has been related to the notion of exact join. A fixpoint algorithm to compute the reexecution semantics has been presented and the implementation choices have been discussed, including the strategy of giving priority to reexecution over first execution. The algorithm has been tested experimentally on two domains: a simple domain (simple modes, simple sharing and same value constraints) and an elaborate domain (patterns, elaborate modes, elaborate sharing and same value constraints) and measures concerning accuracy and efficiency have been reported. They indicate that reexecution produces significant gain in precision at almost no computational cost for the simple domain. On the elaborate domain (which produces optimal or near-optimal results for almost all programs), reexecution produces gains on the non-optimal programs and is about twice as slow as the standard algorithm on the average. It was also demonstrated that reexecution on the simple domain is a valuable alternative to the standard algorithm on the elaborate domain. The accuracy of reexecution on the simple domain improves upon the standard algorithm on the elaborate domain for the output modes and comes close for the input modes and the unification specializations. Reexecution on the simple domain is also twice as fast as standard execution on the elaborate domain.

Acknowledgements

This research was partly supported by the Belgian National Incentive-Program for fundamental Research in Artificial Intelligence (Baudouin Le Charlier) and by the National Science Foundation under grant number CCR-9108032 and the Office of Naval Research under grant N00014-91-J-4052 ARPA order 8225 (Pascal Van Hentenryck).

References

[1] M. Bruynooghe. A practical framework for the abstract interpretation of logic programs. *Journal of Logic Programming*, 10(2):91–124, February 1991.

[2] P. Cousot and R. Cousot. Inductive definitions, semantics and abstract interpretation. In *Conference Record of Nineteenth ACM Symposium on Programming Languages (POPL '92)*, Albuquerque, New Mexico, U.S.A., January 1992.

[3] V. Englebert, B. Le Charlier, D. Roland, and P. Van Hentenryck. Generic abstract interpretation algorithms for prolog: Two optimization techniques and their experimental evaluation (extended abstract). In M. Bruynooghe and M. Wirsing, editors, *Proceedings of the Fourth International Workshop on Programming Language Implementation and Logic Programming (PLILP'92)*, Lecture Notes in Computer Science, Leuven, August 1992. Springer-Verlag.

[4] M. Hermenegildo, R. Warren, and S. Debray. Global Flow Analysis as a Practical Compilation Tool. *Journal of Logic Programming*, 1991. To appear in the Journal of Logic Programming (also published as Technical Report Computer Science Dept, Universidad Politecnica de Madrid, Spain, 1991).

[5] T. Kanamori and T. Kawamura. Analysing success patterns of logic programs by abstract hybrid interpretation. Technical report, ICOT, 1987.

[6] B. Le Charlier, K. Musumbu, and P. Van Hentenryck. A generic abstract interpretation algorithm and its complexity analysis. In K. Furukawa, editor, *Proceedings of the Eighth International Conference on Logic Programming (ICLP'91)*, Paris, France, June 1991. MIT Press.

[7] B. Le Charlier and P. Van Hentenryck. Experimental evaluation of a generic abstract interpretation algorithm for Prolog. In J. Cordy, editor, *Proceedings of the IEEE fourth International Conference on Programming Languages (ICCL'92)*, Oakland, U.S.A., April 1992. IEEE Press.

[8] B. Le Charlier and P. Van Hentenryck. Reexecution in abstract interpretation of prolog. Technical Report 92-1, Institute of Computer Science, University of Namur, Belgium, (also Brown University: Technical Report No. CS-92-12), March 1992.

[9] B. Le Charlier and P. Van Hentenryck. A universal top-down fixpoint algorithm. Technical Report 92-22, Institute of Computer Science, University of Namur, Belgium, (also Brown University), April 1992.

[10] K. Marriott and H. Søndergaard. Semantics-based dataflow analysis of logic programs. In G. Ritter, editor, *Information Processing'89*, pages 601–606, San Fransisco, California, 1989.

[11] C.S. Mellish. Abstract interpretation of Prolog programs. In S. Abramski and C. Hankin, editors, *Abstract Interpretation of Declarative Languages*, chapter 8, pages 181–198. Ellis Horwood Limited, 1987.

[12] K. Musumbu. *Interprétation Abstraite de Programmes Prolog*. PhD thesis, Institute of Computer Science, University of Namur, Belgium, September 1990. In French.

[13] R.A. O'Keefe. Finite fixed-point problems. In J-L. Lassez, editor, *Proceedings of the Fourth International Conference on Logic Programming (ICLP'87)*, pages 729–743, Melbourne, Australia, May 1987. MIT Press.

[14] R. Warren, M. Hermenegildo, and S.K. Debray. On the practicality of global flow analysis of logic programs. In R.A. Kowalski and K.A. Bowen, editors, *Proceedings of the Fifth International Conference on Logic Programming (ICLP'88)*, pages 684–699, Seattle, Washington, August 1988. MIT Press.

Practical Aspects of Set Based Analysis

NEVIN HEINTZE *(nch@cs.cmu.edu)*
School of Computer Science
Carnegie Mellon University
Pittsburgh, PA 15213

Summary

The set based approach to compile time analysis of logic programs has numerous advantages over other approaches, including a simple, intuitive definition, and an accurate and uniform treatment of term structure. However the algorithms for set based analysis that have been presented to date have focussed on establishing decidability results, and do not provide a practical basis for program analysis. This paper demonstrates that very substantial progress can be made towards a practical system by redesigning the algorithms, employing appropriate representation techniques, and removing redundancy. An implementation is described and experimental evidence is given that suggests set based analysis of logic programs can be made practical.

1 Introduction

The set based approach to program analysis [5, 6, 7] has its origins in the use of constraints to perform type analysis of programs [10, 11, 13]. In essence, set based analysis involves first writing set constraints (a calculus for expressing relationships between sets of program values) to describe the runtime behavior of a program, and then solving these constraints to find their least model. The fundamental difference between set based analysis and other approaches in literature (which are based on abstract interpretation) is that set based analysis does not employ an iterative least fixpoint computation over a finitary domain[1]. Instead of using an abstract domain to approximate program computation, set based analysis employs a single notion of approximation: all dependencies between the values of program variables are ignored. In particular, there are no depth bounds on term size, or other *a priori* restrictions on the sets of terms that can be manipulated during the analysis.

If one takes a very broad view of abstract interpretation as a framework for defining program approximations (as opposed to the more algorithmic iterative fixpoint view), then set based analysis can be formulated as an abstract interpretation. However, the corresponding iterative fixpoint computations do not terminate, and so iterative fixpoint computation cannot be used in set based analysis. In fact one of the main issues addressed by works on set based analysis has been to show that set based analysis is decidable.

In summary, set based analysis uses a simple, intuitive and uniform approximation that avoids the inelegant and *ad hoc* nature of the abstract domains used in abstract interpretation. In particular, set based analysis yields an accurate and uniform approximation of term structure[2]. In contrast, the finitary non-uniform nature

---

[1] The domain must be "finitary" in the sense that it satisfies some property (such as no infinite ascending chains) so that the iterative fixpoint computation terminates. Note that narrowing/widening can be used to address this restriction, but at the cost of computing something other than the least fixpoint.

[2] Although set based analysis is provides an accurate approximation of term structure, it is not uniformly more accurate than abstract interpretation because abstract interpretation admits a limited form of inter-variable dependencies. However, the techniques developed for set based analysis can be extended

of abstract domains typically used in abstract interpretation leads to non-intuitive and chaotic interaction between the domain and the operations of the language. For these reasons, we believe that set based analysis has substantial advantages in terms of uniformity, predictability and stability, and that this has important consequences for scaleability.

This paper is a progress report on an ongoing effort to incorporate set based analysis in an experimental compiler. The main focus of this paper is to investigate one of the main remaining doubts about set based analysis: its computational cost. It is clear that solving set constraints can be expensive in the worst case, and this is due to the exponential behavior of the intersection operation (see [2] for a formal account of the exponential behavior of one class of set constraints). However it is not clear whether worst case behavior is a good indication of the practicality of set based analysis, since programs rarely exhibit the extremes of behavior used in worst case analysis. To address this question, we develop and evaluate an implementation of set constraints. Although straightforward implementation of the algorithms described in [5, 6] is unworkable, substantial progress has been made towards a practical system by redesigning the algorithms, employing appropriate representation techniques, and exploiting the redundancy that is typically present.

After reviewing how set constraints can be used for program analysis, we begin the main part of the paper (in Section 3) by reformulating the set constraint algorithm in a way that is more appropriate for implementation purposes. In section 4, we identify some of the central operations required by the algorithm. This motivates a number of key design decisions, which lead to a basic implementation approach. Section 5 describes a crucial modification for more effectively dealing with the intersection operation. Section 6 contains some experimental results, with particular focus on justifying the design decisions outlined in the paper.

2 Background: Set Constraints and Analysis

We briefly outline how set constraints may be used to obtain safe approximations of program execution (see [4, 5, 6] for more details). For each point in the program, we wish to obtain a safe description of the possible substitutions that are encountered at that point during program execution. First introduce set variables to capture the sets of values of each program variable at each point in the program. Then write constraints between these sets to safely approximate the local consistency conditions of the program. The following example gives a logic program, constraints to approximate the program's success set, and a model of these constraints.

$$
\begin{array}{lll}
& Ret_p = p(\mathcal{X}) & Ret_p \mapsto \{p(f(a)), p(f(f(a))), \cdots\} \\
p(X) \leftarrow q(X), r(X). & Ret_q = q(a) \cup q(f(\mathcal{Y})) & Ret_q \mapsto \{q(a), q(f(a)), \cdots\} \\
q(a). & Ret_r = r(f(\mathcal{Z})) & Ret_r \mapsto \{r(f(t)) : \text{for all terms } t\} \\
q(f(Y)) \leftarrow q(Y). & \mathcal{X} = q^{-1}(Ret_q) \cap r^{-1}(Ret_r) & \mathcal{X} \mapsto \{f(a), f(f(a)), \cdots\} \\
r(f(Z)). & \mathcal{Y} = q^{-1}(Ret_q) & \mathcal{Y} \mapsto \{a, f(a), f(f(a)), \cdots\} \\
& \mathcal{Z} = \top & \mathcal{Z} \mapsto \{\text{all terms}\}
\end{array}
$$

The variables Ret_p, Ret_q and Ret_r capture the sets of ground atoms in the success set corresponding to the predicates p, q and r respectively. The variables $\mathcal{X}$, $\mathcal{Y}$ and $\mathcal{Z}$ capture the sets of values for the program variables X, Y and Z respectively. The symbols q^{-1} and r^{-1} denote projection with respect to q and r, so that $q^{-1}(Ret_q)$ denotes the set $\{t : q(t) \in Ret_q\}$. Hence, the constraint $\mathcal{X} = q^{-1}(Ret_q) \cap r^{-1}(Ret_r)$

---

to give an analysis algorithm that is strictly more accurate than abstract interpretation (see [9]).

indicates that the set of values for the program variable X equals those values t such that $q(t)$ is in Ret_q and $r(t)$ is in Ret_r. The symbol $\top$ denotes the set of all ground terms. A model of the constraints maps each set variable into a set of ground terms in such a way that each constraint is satisfied. The model given above is in fact the least model of the constraints, and the set based analysis of the program corresponds exactly to the program's success set. This is not true in general because set constraints ignore dependencies between program variables by collecting the values of program variables into sets, as illustrated by the following example[3].

$$p(X, Y) \leftarrow q(X, Y). \qquad \begin{aligned} Ret_p &= p(\mathcal{X}, \mathcal{Y}) \\ Ret_q &= q(a, b) \cup q(c, d) \\ \mathcal{X} &= q_{(1)}^{-1}(Ret_q) \\ \mathcal{Y} &= q_{(2)}^{-1}(Ret_q) \end{aligned} \qquad \begin{aligned} Ret_p &\mapsto \{p(a, b), p(a, d), p(c, b), p(c, d)\} \\ Ret_q &\mapsto \{p(a, b), p(c, d)\} \\ \mathcal{X} &\mapsto \{a, c\} \\ \mathcal{Y} &\mapsto \{b, d\} \end{aligned}$$

$q(a, b).$
$q(c, d).$

Not only can set constraints be used to approximate the success set of a program, but rather they can be adapted in a straightforward manner to deal with other strategies such as top-down left-to-right execution or parallel execution. The following example illustrates a program and the constraints constructed to approximate a top-down left-to-right execution of the program[4].

$$\begin{aligned} ① : p(X) &\leftarrow ②q(X), ③r(X). \\ ④ : q(a). \\ ⑤ : r(Y). \end{aligned} \qquad \begin{aligned} Ret_p &= p(\mathcal{X}^①) \\ Ret_q &= q(a) \\ Ret_r &= r(\mathcal{Y}^⑤) \\ Call_q &= q(\mathcal{X}^②) \\ Call_r &= r(\mathcal{X}^③) \end{aligned} \qquad \begin{aligned} \mathcal{X}^② &= p^{-1}(Call_p) \\ \mathcal{X}^③ &= p^{-1}(Call_p) \cap q^{-1}(Ret_q) \\ \mathcal{X}^① &= p^{-1}(Call_p) \cap q^{-1}(Ret_q) \\ & \qquad \cap r^{-1}(Ret_r) \\ \mathcal{Y}^⑤ &= r^{-1}(Call_r) \end{aligned}$$

To construct these constraints, program points must be introduced to indicate the various stages of execution of the body of a rule. For example point ② indicates program execution just before $q(X)$ is called in the body of the first rule, point ③ indicates execution just before $r(X)$, and point ① indicates execution after both body atoms have succeeded. For each variable and relevant program point, a set is introduced to describe the values of the variable at that program point. For example $\mathcal{X}^①$, $\mathcal{X}^②$, and $\mathcal{X}^③$ respectively denote the values of $\mathcal{X}$ at ①, ② and ③. The main difference between these constraints and the previous constraints is that variables $Call_p$, $Call_q$ and $Call_r$ have been introduced to capture the possible calls to p, q and r. For example the constraint $\mathcal{X}^③ = p^{-1}(Call_p) \cap q^{-1}(Ret_q)$ indicates that the values of X at point ③ consists of all t such that $p(t)$ is in $Call_p$ and $q(t)$ is in Ret_q.

The construction of set constraints corresponding to a program has only been informally outlined here. Further details and correctness proofs can be found in [5, 7, 8, 4]. The key point is that, given a notion of program execution (such as topdown left-to-right, topdown parallel) we can give a schema for generating appropriate constraints from a program. We note that the constraints used in this paper are simpler and slightly less accurate than those used in [5]. However the differences are only minor, and it is easy to adapt the correctness proofs in [5] to the constraints considered here. Most importantly, the constraints used here provide a similar uniform treatment of structures, and in some sense represent the core part of the more complex constraints.

We conclude this section with a formal definition of set constraints and a statement of what is involved in constructing their least model. A *set expression* (denoted

---

[3] $q_{(1)}^{-1}(Ret_q)$ and $q_{(2)}^{-1}(Ret_q)$ denote projection on q at the first and second arguments respectively.

[4] The set of initial goals is specified by appropriately modifying the equations for $Call_p$, $Call_q$ and $Call_r$. For example, the single goal $?-p(Z)$ could be modeled by $Call_p = p(\top)$.

$sexp$, possibly subscripted) is either a set variable (denoted $\mathcal{X}, \mathcal{Y}, \cdots$), the empty set symbol $\perp$, the universal set symbol $\top$, a constant, the union of two set expressions, the intersection of two set expressions, or of one of the forms $f(sexp_1, \cdots, sexp_n)$ or $f_{(i)}^{-1}(sexp)$ where f is an n-ary function symbol, $1 \leq i \leq n$ and $sexp, sexp_1, \cdots, sexp_n$ are set expressions. The set constraints considered in this paper have the form $\mathcal{X}_1 = sexp_1, \cdots, \mathcal{X}_m = sexp_m$, where $\mathcal{X}_1, \cdots, \mathcal{X}_m$ are distinct set variables, and the $sexp_i$ are set expressions. An *interpretation* $\mathcal{I}$ of these constraints is a mapping from the set variables in the constraints into sets of ground terms. Such a mapping can be extended to map set expressions into sets of terms in an obvious way, for example $\mathcal{I}(f(sexp_1, \cdots, sexp_n)) = \{f(x_1, \cdots, x_n) : x_i \in \mathcal{I}(sexp_i)\}$, $\mathcal{I}(f_{(i)}^{-1})(sexp) = \{x_i : f(x_1, \cdots, x_n) \in \mathcal{I}(sexp)\}$, and $\mathcal{I}(sexp \cap sexp') = \mathcal{I}(sexp) \cap \mathcal{I}(sexp')$. An interpretation $\mathcal{I}$ of the constraints $\mathcal{X}_1 = sexp_1, \cdots, \mathcal{X}_m = sexp_m$ is a *model* if $\mathcal{I}(\mathcal{X}_i) = \mathcal{I}(sexp_i)$ for each $1 \leq i \leq m$. Models are ordered as follows: $\mathcal{I} \leq \mathcal{I}'$ iff $\mathcal{I}(\mathcal{X}) \subseteq \mathcal{I}(\mathcal{X})$ for all relevant set variables $\mathcal{X}$.

The constraints considered in set based analysis always have least models, and [6] shows that least models are always describable by regular term grammars in the sense that, in the least model, the set for each set variable is definable using a regular term grammar. The algorithm implemented in this paper, when input a collection $\mathcal{C}$ of set constraints, outputs a collection $\mathcal{C}'$ that has the same least model as $\mathcal{C}$, but is in *explicit form*. The importance of explicit form constraints is that they are essentially a regular tree description of their own least model. To define explicit form constraints, first define that a set expression is *atomic* if it is $\top$, a set variable, or of the form $f(aexp_1, \cdots, aexp_n)$ where each $aexp_i$ is an atomic set expression. Then, an explicit form collection of set constrains is of the form $\mathcal{X}_1 = sexp_1, \cdots, \mathcal{X}_m = sexp_m$ where each $\mathcal{X}_i$ is a distinct set variable, and each $sexp_i$ consists of a (possibly empty) union of non-variable atomic set expressions.

3 The Basic Set Constraint Algorithm

We present an algorithm for computing the least model of a collection of constraints $\mathcal{X}_1 = sexp_1, \cdots, \mathcal{X}_m = sexp_m$. This algorithm is closely related to the algorithm in [6] (also see [5]); we shall discuss the differences at the end of this section. For convenience of presentation, we shall ignore the symbol $\top$. The details of the transformations to deal with $\top$ are straightforward and can be found in [6]. The first step of the algorithm is a preprocessing stage that puts the constraints in a standard form. This standard form can be defined as follows. An *intersector* is of the form $aexp_1 \cap \cdots \cap aexp_n$ where the $aexp_i$ are atomic set expressions. A *projector* is of the form $f_{(i)}^{-1}(aexp)$ where $aexp$ is an atomic set expression. A constraint is in *standard form* if it is of the form $\mathcal{X} = sexp_1 \cup \cdots \cup sexp_n$ where <u>at most one</u> of the $sexp_i$ is either a projector or an intersector, and the remaining $sexp_i$ are atomic expressions. A collection of constraints $\mathcal{X}_1 = sexp_1, \cdots, \mathcal{X}_m = sexp_m$ is in *standard form* if each $\mathcal{X}_i$ is a distinct set variable, and each constraint is in standard form. The most important aspect of standard form constraints is that they do not have any "nested" occurrences of union, intersection and projection symbols. Constraints can be converted into normal form by repeatedly identifying an occurrence of a set expression that does not satisfy the standard form definition, replacing it by a new variable and then adding a new equation between the new variable and the replaced set expression. The details of this are straightforward and can be adapted from [6]. Importantly the resulting equations are equivalent to the original equations in the sense that the least model of the resulting equations, when restricted to the variables in the original equations, is the least model of the original equations.

The bulk of the algorithm consists of the exhaustive application of three transformations to standard form constraints. Such constraints are represented using an array, indexed by set variables. Specifically, if the equation $X = sexp_1 \cup \cdots \cup sexp_n$ appears in constraints where each $sexp_i$ is either a projector, an intersector or an atomic expression, then define that $rhs(X)$ is $\{sexp_1, \ldots, sexp_n\}$. For all other variables X appearing in the constraints, define that $rhs(X)$ is $\{\}$. We can now describe the first two of the three transformation steps.

Transformation 1 *If $Y \in rhs(X)$ and $s \in rhs(Y)$ is an atomic expression then add s to $rhs(X)$.* ☐

Transformation 2 *If $f_{(i)}^{-1}(s) \in rhs(X)$ and $f(t_1, \cdots, t_n) \in rhs(s)$ is nonempty then add t_i to $rhs(X)$.* ☐

The nonempty condition in the projector transformation is needed to deal with constraints such as $X = f_{(1)}^{-1}(f(a, U))$, $U = a \cap b$. The least model of this constraint maps both X and U into the empty set. Now, if the projector transformation is applied to this constraint, it would lead to the constraint $X = a \cup f_{(1)}^{-1}(f(a, U))$ whose least model now maps X into $\{a\}$. To determine whether an atomic expression is empty or not at some stage in the algorithm, we proceed as follows. We associate a boolean value $nonempty(X)$ with each variable X that appears in the constraints. Initially each value $nonempty(X)$ is set to *false*. These values are then repeatedly updated using the following step: if $nonempty(X)$ is *false* and t is an atomic expression appearing in $rhs(X)$ such that $nonempty(Y)$ is *true* for all variables Y appearing in t, then update $nonempty(X)$ to *true*. On termination of these updating steps, an atomic expression t is determined to be nonempty iff all variables that appear in the term are nonempty.

The last transformation simplifies intersectors, and its main complexity is that it introduces new variables. To ensure termination, these new variables must be carefully controlled using a special naming scheme. Specifically, each introduced variable is of the form $V_{\{t_1, \cdots, t_n\}}$, $n \geq 1$, where the t_i are atomic expressions appearing in the constraints at the start of the algorithm. Intuitively such a variable, call it a *composite variable*, is equivalent to the expression $t_1 \cap \cdots \cap t_n$. Thus a variable such as $V_{\{f(X), Y, f(Z)\}}$ not only represents $f(X) \cap Y \cap f(Z)$, but also expressions such as $V_{\{f(X), Y\}} \cap f(Z)$ and $V_{\{f(X), f(Z)\}} \cap V_{\{f(X), Y\}}$. To facilitate the manipulation of composite variables, introduce a mapping $\mathcal{N}$ such that $\mathcal{N}(V_T)$ is T, and $\mathcal{N}(t)$ is $\{t\}$ if t is not of the form V_T. For example, $\mathcal{N}(V_{\{f(X), f(Z)\}} \cap V_{\{f(X), Y\}})$ $= \{f(X), Y, f(Z)\}$. Similarly $\mathcal{N}(V_{\{f(X), Y\}} \cap f(Z))$ and $\mathcal{N}(f(X) \cap Y \cap f(Z))$ are also equal to $\{f(X), Y, f(Z)\}$. Also define that $atm(aexp)$ is $rhs(X)$ if $aexp$ is the variable X, and $\{aexp\}$ otherwise. Finally, we can state

Transformation 3 *If $s_1 \cap \cdots \cap s_m \in rhs(X)$ and $f(t_{i,1}, \cdots, t_{i,n}) \in atm(s_i)$, $1 \leq i \leq m$, then let S_j is $\mathcal{N}(t_{1,j}) \cup \cdots \cup \mathcal{N}(t_{m,j})$, $1 \leq j \leq n$, and add $f(V_{S_1}, \cdots, V_{S_n})$ to $rhs(X)$. For each j, if $rhs(V_{S_j}) = \{\}$ then add $t_{1,j} \cap \cdots \cap t_{m,j}$ to $rhs(V_{S_j})$.* ☐

The set constraint algorithm can now be stated as: exhaustively apply those instances of transformations $1 - 3$ that change rhs, and on termination output the explicit form constraints resulting from the deletion of all intersectors, projectors and variables from rhs. The main difference between this presentation of the set constraint algorithm and [6] is that here we have attempted to minimize the number of transformation steps that have to be performed by combining the substitution, projection simplification and intersection simplification transformations of [6]. In particular, transformations 2 and 3 combine elements of the substitution transformation with the projection and intersection transformations respectively. Transformation 1 is all that remains of the original substitution transformation. Another difference is that [6] uses an extended version of regular grammars, as opposed to directly dealing with set equations. We now briefly outline the new algorithm's correctness.

Theorem 1 *When input with constraints $\mathcal{C}_{in}$ in standard form, the algorithm terminates with output $\mathcal{C}_{out}$ in explicit form. Moreover $\mathcal{I}_{in}(\mathcal{X}) = \mathcal{I}_{out}(\mathcal{X})$ for all $\mathcal{X}$ appearing in $\mathcal{C}_{in}$, where $\mathcal{I}_{in}$ and $\mathcal{I}_{out}$ are the least models of $\mathcal{C}_{in}$ and $\mathcal{C}_{out}$ respectively.*

Proof Outline: First, it is clear that there are only a finite number of variables $\mathcal{V}_S$ added by the algorithm since, for each such variable, S must be a subset of the atomic expressions contained in the input collection $\mathcal{C}_{in}$. Now, each atomic expression considered by the algorithm must either be an atomic expression from $\mathcal{C}_{in}$, or an expression of the form $f(\mathcal{V}_{S_1}, \cdots, \mathcal{V}_{S_n})$, hence there are only a finite number of such expressions. Termination of the algorithm then follows from the fact that each productive transformation adds an atomic expression to the *rhs* of some variable, and such additions are never repeated.

We now address correctness. Let $\mathcal{C}'$ be the constraints obtained after the exhaustive application of the transformations and before the deletion step. It is clear that the transformations preserve the least model of the input constraints (although these transformation may introduce new variables), and so it follows that the least model of $\mathcal{C}'$ is equivalent to $\mathcal{I}_{in}$ when restricted to the variables in $\mathcal{C}_{in}$. It remains to show that the least model of $\mathcal{C}'$ is equal to the least model of $\mathcal{C}_{out}$. This follows from that fact that $\mathcal{I}_{out}$ is a model of $\mathcal{C}'$. To prove this, consider an equation in $\mathcal{C}' - \mathcal{C}_{out}$. Such an equation must be of the form $\mathcal{X} = s_1 \cup \cdots s_n \cup op$ where $X = s_1 \cup \cdots \cup s_n$ appears in $\mathcal{C}_{out}$ and op is either a projector or intersector. We prove the former case; the latter is similar. By definition $\mathcal{I}_{out}(\mathcal{X}) = \mathcal{I}_{out}(s_1 \cup \cdots \cup s_n)$, and so it suffices to show that $\mathcal{I}_{out}(f_{(i)}^{-1}(t)) \subseteq \mathcal{I}_{out}(s_1 \cup \cdots \cup s_n)$, where op is $f_{(i)}^{-1}(t)$. Let $x_i \in \mathcal{I}_{out}(f_{(i)}^{-1}(t))$. By definition, there must exist a term $f(x_1, \cdots, x_m) \in \mathcal{I}_{out}(t)$. Now, t is either a variable or a non-variable atomic expression. If it is a variable, say $\mathcal{X}$, then there must be an equation for $\mathcal{X}$ of the form $\mathcal{X} = s_1' \cup \cdots \cup s_k'$ in $\mathcal{C}_{out}$ such that one of the s_l' is $f(t_1, \cdots, t_m)$ and $x_j \in \mathcal{I}_{out}(t_j)$, $1 \leq j \leq m$. Hence at the end of the algorithm, $f(t_1, \cdots, t_m) \in rhs(\mathcal{X})$ and $f(t_1, \cdots, t_m)$ is nonempty. Since the projector transformation has been exhaustively applied, it must be the case that t_i appears in $rhs(\mathcal{X})$ on termination. This means that t_i is in fact one of $s_1, \cdots, s_n$. Hence $x_i \in \mathcal{I}_{out}(t_i) \subseteq \mathcal{I}_{out}(s_1 \cup \cdots \cup s_n)$. The case where t is a non-variable atomic expression is similar. []

We conclude this section with an example of the execution of the algorithm. When input with the constraints shown below on the left, the algorithm performs steps A, B, C and D, corresponding to applications of transformations $2, 3, 1$ and 3 respectively. The final output of the algorithm is $\mathcal{W} = f^2(\mathcal{W}) \cup f(\mathcal{W}) \cup f(\mathcal{V}_{\{y,a\}})$, $\mathcal{X} = f(\mathcal{V}_{\{y,a\}})$, $\mathcal{Y} = a$, $\mathcal{Z} = f(a) \cup g(a)$, and $\mathcal{V}_{\{y,a\}} = a$.

$$
\begin{aligned}
\mathcal{W} &= \mathcal{X} \cup f^2(\mathcal{W}) \cup f^{-1}(\mathcal{W}), \\
\mathcal{X} &= f(\mathcal{Y}) \cap \mathcal{Z}, \\
\mathcal{Y} &= a, \\
\mathcal{Z} &= f(a) \cup g(a),
\end{aligned}
$$

A. Add $f(\mathcal{W})$ to $rhs(\mathcal{W})$;

B. Add $f(\mathcal{V}_{\{y,a\}})$ to $rhs(\mathcal{X})$, and add the equation $\mathcal{V}_{\{y,a\}} = \mathcal{Y} \cap a$;

C. Add $f(\mathcal{V}_{\{y,a\}})$ to $rhs(\mathcal{W})$;

D. Add a to $rhs(\mathcal{V}_{\{y,a\}})$;

4 Outline of Implementation

Consider the possible expressions that can appear on the rhs of an equation. First, there are non-variable atomic expressions, and these shall be called *constructed* terms. In essence, these are the central objects that are manipulated by the algorithm. Second, there are the projectors, and these can be viewed as operators on constructors. For example, if $rhs(\mathcal{X})$ contains the constructed term $f(t_1, t_2)$, then $f_{(2)}^{-1}(\mathcal{X})$ produces the term t_2 (which must either be a constructed term or a variable). Specifically, corresponding to each projector of the form $f_{(i)}^{-1}(\cdots)$, we define a partial function $proj_{f,i}$ that maps $f(t_1, \ldots, t_n)$ into t_i and is otherwise undefined. The third class of expressions consists of the intersectors. Again these can be viewed as operators on constructors, and corresponding to each n-ary intersection expression, we define a partial function $intersect_n$ as follows: for each function symbol f, $intersect_n(f(t_{1,1}, \ldots, t_{1,n}), \cdots, f(t_{m,1}, \ldots, t_{m,n})) = f(\mathcal{V}_{S_1}, \ldots, \mathcal{V}_{S_n})$ where each S_j is $\mathcal{N}(t_{1,j}) \cup \cdots \cup \mathcal{N}(t_{m,j})$, and is otherwise undefined. Finally, there are variables, and their effect is to directly transfer constructed terms from one equation to another.

Using this classification of $rhs(\mathcal{X})$ into constructed terms, variables and operators (projectors and intersectors), we split the array rhs into three separate arrays, con, var and op, respectively denoting the constructed terms, variables and operators in $rhs(\mathcal{X})$. For example, the equation $\mathcal{X} = f^2(\mathcal{X}) \cup f(\mathcal{X}) \cup f^{-1}(\mathcal{X}) \cup \mathcal{Y}$ is represented as $con(\mathcal{X}) = \{f^2(\mathcal{X}), f(\mathcal{X})\}$, $op(\mathcal{X}) = \{f^{-1}(\mathcal{X})\}$, and $var(\mathcal{X}) = \{\mathcal{Y}\}$. Note that $op(\mathcal{X}_i)$ is either the empty set or a singleton set and remains fixed throughout the algorithm. Redefine $atm(aexp)$ to be $con(\mathcal{X})$ if $aexp$ is the variable $\mathcal{X}$, and $\{aexp\}$ otherwise. The transformation steps of the algorithm can now be rephrased as:

- If $f_i^{-1}(\mathcal{Y}) \in op(\mathcal{X})$ and $t \in atm(\mathcal{Y})$ is nonempty, then if $proj_{f,i}(t)$ is a variable, add it to $var(\mathcal{X})$, and otherwise add it to $con(\mathcal{X})$.

- If $s_1 \cap \cdots \cap s_m \in op(\mathcal{X})$ and $t_i \in atm(s_i)$, then add $intersect_n(t_1, \ldots, t_m)$ to $con(\mathcal{X})$, and construct appropriate equations for any new composite variables introduced.

- If $\mathcal{Y} \in var(\mathcal{X})$ and $t \in con(\mathcal{Y})$, then add t to $con(\mathcal{X})$.

where add means that if the operation is defined, then add the resulting atomic expression to the specified set if it does not already appear there. Note that the sets $con(\mathcal{X})$, $var(\mathcal{X})$ are monotonically increasing.

Our implementation is essentially based on the above formulation of transformations. Two key observations about this formulation motivate a number of major implementation design decisions. First, a frequent operation in the algorithm involves comparison of constructed terms, and in particular, the determination of whether a new constructed term is already an element of a set. Second, at any particular instance, there may be many possible steps, but only a few of these are likely to be productive. It is therefore important to be able to focus on those steps that are likely to be productive. We now elaborate.

Term Representation: To provide cheap comparison for constructed terms, we code each atomic term as an integer in the following simple manner. As each variable is encountered, a unique positive integer is allocated for it. Notationally we shall write $\#\mathcal{X}$ to denote the integer associated with the variable $\mathcal{X}$. Function and constant symbol are also identified by positive integers; we write $\#f$ to denote the integer for the function or constant symbol f. The coding of constructed terms is essentially performed by incrementally building a mapping ζ from sequences of integers into negative integers (ζ is initially empty). Specifically, the coding $\#t$ of a constructed term t is achieved as follows. Let t be $f(t_1, \ldots, t_n)$ and first compute the sequence $(\#f, \#t_1, \ldots, \#t_n)$. Then, return $\zeta(\#f, \#t_1, \ldots, \#t_n)$ if it is already defined, and otherwise allocate a negative integer say j, update ζ appropriately and then return j. An array is also maintained to map each coding into the sequence it represents. This is used mainly by the projection operation.

Coding constructed terms as integers provides a very compact representation of atomic terms, since there is maximal sharing between atomic terms that have common subterms. It also allows the set $con(\mathcal{X})$ to be represented efficiently. Specifically, we represent the relationship $t \in con(\mathcal{X})$ using ordered pairs $(\#t, \#\mathcal{X})$, and this in turn is implemented using a hash table. Similar comments apply to a number of other operations of the algorithm, and hashing techniques are heavily used throughout. Although fairly simple methods have proved effective for moderate sized problems, it is likely that specialized hashing techniques will be important for handling very large analysis problems.

In some sense this coding represents a tradeoff: term comparison is dramatically improved, but projection is more expensive and also there are overheads in initializing and maintaining the data structures used. However, term comparison is the most frequently used operation, and its cost in a PROLOG style term representation is very high in comparison to the overheads of integer coding. This was borne out experimentally: a very early implementation using PROLOG style term representation was substantially inferior to a later implementation using coding.

Dependency Directed Updating: Once a particular instance of a step has been applied, it never needs to be applied again. For example if $op(\mathcal{X})$ is the projector $f_{(1)}^{-1}(\mathcal{Y})$ and the constructed term $f(a, b)$ appears in $con(\mathcal{Y})$, then once a has been added to $con(\mathcal{X})$, we never again need to apply $op(\mathcal{X})$ to $f(a, b)$. We exploit this by using a dependency directed updating scheme, so that operations are only applied to new constructed terms. Specifically, define an array dep such that $dep(\mathcal{X})$ indicates where any new constructed terms for $\mathcal{X}$ have to be propagated:

$$dep(\mathcal{X}) \stackrel{\text{def}}{=} \begin{array}{l} \{vdep(\mathcal{Y}) : \mathcal{X} \in var(\mathcal{Y})\} \ \bigcup \ \{pdep(\mathcal{Y}) : f_{(i)}^{-1}(\mathcal{X}) \in op(\mathcal{Y})\} \\ \bigcup \ \{idep(\mathcal{Y}) : (s_1 \cap \cdots \cap s_n) \in op(\mathcal{Y}) \text{ where some } s_i \text{ is } \mathcal{X} \} \end{array}$$

The forms $vdep(\mathcal{Y})$, $pdep(\mathcal{Y})$ and $idep(\mathcal{Y})$ respectively denote variable, projector and intersector dependencies. As an example, consider the following constraints and their representation in terms of arrays con, var op and dep.

$$\begin{aligned}
\mathcal{X} &= b \cup f(\mathcal{X}) \cup \mathcal{Z} \\
\mathcal{Y} &= c \cup (\mathcal{X} \cap \mathcal{Z}) \\
\mathcal{Z} &= d \cup f_{(1)}^{-1}(\mathcal{X})
\end{aligned}$$

	con	var	op	dep
$\mathcal{X}$	$b, f(\mathcal{X})$	$\mathcal{Z}$		$idep(\mathcal{Y}), pdep(\mathcal{Z})$
$\mathcal{Y}$	c		$\mathcal{X} \cap \mathcal{Z}$	
$\mathcal{Z}$	d		$f_{(1)}^{-1}(\mathcal{X})$	$vdep(\mathcal{X}), idep(\mathcal{Y})$

Using this representation, the algorithm can essentially be written as

```
update(t, dep, X) {
    if dep is vdep(Y) then add(t, Y);
    if dep is pdep(Y) and f⁻¹₍ᵢ₎(X) ∈ op(Y) then add(projf,i(t), Y)⁵;
    if dep is idep(Y) and s₁ ∩ ··· ∩ sₘ ∈ op(Y) then
        let X be sⱼ;      /* note that X must appear in s₁ ... sₘ */
        foreach sequence (t₁,...,tₙ) such that tᵢ ∈ atm(sᵢ), j ≠ i, and tᵢ = t
            add(intersectₙ(t₁,...,tₙ), X);
        construct equations for any new composite variables;
}

add(t, X) {
    if t ∉ con(X) then
        con(X) := con(X) ∪ {t};
        foreach dep' ∈ dep(X)
            update(t, dep', X);
}
```

The algorithm is initiated by inspecting each variable $\mathcal{X}$ and calling $add(proj_{f,i}(t), \mathcal{X})$ for each $t \in atm(s)$ if $f_{(i)}^{-1}(s) \in op(\mathcal{X})$, and calling $add(intersect_n(t_1, \ldots, t_n))$ for each sequence $(t_1, \ldots, t_n)$ such that $t_i \in atm(s_i)$, if $s_1 \cap \cdots \cap s_n \in op(\mathcal{X})$.

Composite Variables and Nonempty: The generation and management of composite variables is essentially straightforward. Corresponding to the function $\mathcal{N}$, an array is used to record, for each new composite variable allocated, the set of terms corresponding to this variable. The mapping from a set of terms $\{s_1, \cdots, s_n\}$ into a composite variable is performed by first constructing $\mathcal{N}(s_1) \cup \cdots \cup \mathcal{N}(s_n)$. The elements of this set are then sorted and the resulting sequence is looked up in a hash table, where each entry of this table consists of a sorted list of atomic expressions and the corresponding composite variable identifier. If the sequence is found in the table, the appropriate variable identifier is returned. If the sequence is not found, then a new variable $\mathcal{V}_S$ is generated and the table is updated appropriately. Also a new equation is generated by setting $var(\mathcal{V}_S) := \emptyset$, $con(\mathcal{V}_S) := \emptyset$ and $op(\mathcal{V}_S) := \{s_1 \cap \cdots \cap s_n\}$ where S is $\{s_1, \ldots, s_n\}$, and updating the dependencies for each variable $\mathcal{X}$ in S using $dep(\mathcal{X}) := dep(\mathcal{X}) \cup \{idep(\mathcal{V}_S)\}$, and then finally, if each s_i is a non-variable atomic expression, calling $add(intersect_n(s_1, \ldots, s_n), \mathcal{V}_S)$

We now address *nonempty*. To avoid recomputing *nonempty* each time it is needed, an incremental approach is employed. Let *nonempty* be an array that maps each atomic expression t into *true* if t is currently known to be nonempty, and *false* otherwise. Initially each entry in *nonempty* is set to *false*. The value of $nonempty(f(t_1, \cdots, t_n))$ is updated to *true* if $nonempty(t_i)$ is *true* for all $1 \leq i \leq n$. The value of $nonempty(\mathcal{X})$ for a variable $\mathcal{X}$ is updated to *true* if $con(\mathcal{X})$ contains a nonempty atomic expression. Again this updating is managed using lists of depen-

---

[5] The nonempty condition has been omitted here for reasons of simplicity. See the subsection "Composite Variables and Nonempty" for the full details of the interaction of projection and nonempty.

dencies. In this case, for each atomic expression t, we maintain the list of the atomic expressions directly dependent on $nonempty(t)$. When $nonempty(t)$ changes from *false* to *true*, the terms dependent on t are recomputed.

Now, the updating of projectors depends on the nonempty function. Recall that the projector updating step is: if $f_{(i)}^{-1}(\mathcal{X}) \in op(\mathcal{Y})$, $t \in con(\mathcal{Y})$ and t is nonempty, then add $proj_{f,i}(t)$ to $con(\mathcal{X})$ or $var(\mathcal{X})$. If this step is executed and $nonempty(t)$ is *true*, then $proj_{f,i}(t)$ can be immediately add to the appropriate set and the step completed. However, if $nonempty(t)$ is *false* then the step must be suspended, and only completed when (and if) $nonempty(t)$ eventually becomes *true*. This is achieved using an extension to the dependency lists used in the implementation of nonempty.

5   Intersectors

This section focuses on improving the performance of intersectors, which are the most difficult operations to implement efficiently. Not only do they introduce new variables, but they also have a combinatorial nature. For example consider an intersector $t_1 \cap \cdots \cap t_n$, and suppose that one of the t_i is the variable $\mathcal{X}$ and that s has been freshly added to $con(\mathcal{X})$. Then, in updating this intersector using this constructed term, we must consider all possible combinations of $s_j \in atm(t_j)$, $j \neq i$.

A first step in dealing with this problem is to partition the terms in $con(\mathcal{X})$ according to their principal function symbol. For example, consider updating the intersector $\mathcal{X} \cap \mathcal{Y} \cap \mathcal{Z}$ using a newly constructed term $f(\mathcal{Y})$ for $\mathcal{Z}$. If $con(\mathcal{X}) = \{f(\mathcal{X}), f(\mathcal{W}), g(\mathcal{X})\}$ and $con(\mathcal{Y}) = \{f(\mathcal{Z}), g(\mathcal{Y})\}$, then clearly we only need to consider the intersections $f(\mathcal{X}) \cap f(\mathcal{Z}) \cap f(\mathcal{Y})$ and $f(\mathcal{W}) \cap f(\mathcal{Z}) \cap f(\mathcal{Y})$, and we can ignore intersections such as $f(\mathcal{X}) \cap g(\mathcal{Y}) \cap f(\mathcal{Y})$, since they will always be empty. Although this simple modification is extremely important, more fundamental changes are required to implement intersection efficiently. In essence we need to exploit the substantial redundancy that is typically present in set constraints.

Minimal DNF Expansion: Consider the intersector $\mathcal{X} \cap \mathcal{Y} \cap \mathcal{Z}$ where $con(\mathcal{X})$, $con(\mathcal{Y})$ and $con(\mathcal{Z})$ are respectively $\{A, B, C\}$, $\{A, C, D\}$ and $\{A, B, D\}$, and A, B, C and D are distinct constructed terms. To recompute this intersector, we essentially need to construct $(A \cup B \cup D) \cap (A \cup C \cup D) \cap (A \cup B \cup D)$. A naive expansion of this expression would lead to 27 intersections: $A \cap A \cap A$, $A \cap A \cap B$, etc. However for this example, we only need to compute the expressions A, $B \cap D$, $C \cap B$ and $C \cap D$, and so we can reduce 27 intersections to just three. The problem of minimizing the number of expressions to be computed can be viewed as a special case of computing a minimal DNF form, given an expression in CNF. A number of different approaches were tested. The essence of the current approach is to precompute information about the pattern of occurrences of constructed terms that appear in more than one "disjunction", and then to use this information to sequentially build up minimal conjunctions. For space reasons we omit the details of this algorithm.

We now outline how this approach to intersection is incorporated. It is clear that updating intersectors is very expensive, and should therefore be done as infrequently as possible. This can be achieved by giving precedence to updates involving projectors. Specifically, the updating is split into two phases. The first consists of the exhaustive updating using projectors. The second consists of updating using intersectors. The algorithm then proceeds by repeatedly alternating these two phases. As a side effect, this organization of updating steps also enhances the performance of the DNF minimization algorithm, since by delaying its application, the amount of redundancy increases. The algorithm can now be described as

```
repeat
    exhaustively apply all possible projector steps;
    recompute each intersector;
until no change;
```

Approximating Subsumption Relationships: Consider an intersector $\mathcal{X} \cap \mathcal{Y}$. If $con(\mathcal{X}) = \{A, B\}$ and $con(\mathcal{Y}) = \{C, D\}$ and in the least model of the equations, $A \subseteq B$ and $C \subseteq D$, then clearly the recomputation of the intersector can be reduced to computing $B \cap D$. However, establishing whether subsumption relationships such as $A \subseteq B$ hold in the least model can only be done, in general, once the least model is known. The approach used here involves approximating the least model using the information contained in the array con. Specifically, for each variable X, this array defines an equation $\mathcal{X} = t_1 \cup \cdots \cup t_n$, where $con(\mathcal{X}) = \{t_1, \cdots, t_n\}$. Hence con can be considered to define a collection of equations in explicit form, and this in turn defines an interpretation, call it $\mathcal{I}_{con}$. This interpretation represents the part of the least model that has been computed by the algorithm so far. If $\mathcal{I}_{lm}$ denotes the least model of the constraints input to the algorithm, then $\mathcal{I}_{con}(\mathcal{X}) \subseteq \mathcal{I}_{lm}(\mathcal{X})$ for all variables $\mathcal{X}$ appearing in the input constraints. Now, we can use $\mathcal{I}_{con}$ to approximate the subsumption relationships that hold in $\mathcal{I}_{lm}$, and hence simplify the intersector computation, as follows.

```
repeat
    exhaustively apply all possible projector steps;
    for each variable X
        max_con(X) := {t ∈ con(X) : ¬∃s ∈ con(X) s.t.   I_con(s) ⊃ I_con(t)}⁶;
    recompute each intersector using max_con instead of con;
until no change;
```

Note that there is no formal connection between the subsumption relationships that hold in $\mathcal{I}_{lm}$ and $\mathcal{I}_{con}$. Hence, in general, $max\_con(\mathcal{X})$ is just a subset of $con(\mathcal{X})$ for each $\mathcal{X}$. In practice the correlation between the subsumption relationships that hold in $\mathcal{I}_{lm}$ and $\mathcal{I}_{con}$ is close, especially after the early stages of the algorithm (this issue is discussed further in the next section). The correctness of using max_con instead of con follows from the fact that $\mathcal{I}_{con} = \mathcal{I}_{max\_con}$, where $\mathcal{I}_{max\_con}$ is the model defined by max_con. We omit the details.

6   Empirics

The implementation described in this paper has been developed over a period of three years. A very early version used an explicit representation for constructed terms. However term comparison was prohibitively expensive and only very small programs such as naive reverse could be analyzed. The next version employed the term representation described here and exploited redundancy using a dnf minimization algorithm and an early form of the subsumption approximation algorithm. Most of the basic notions described in this paper were contained in this version. A subsequent version reimplemented these notions more efficiently. Greater use was made

---

⁶If this set contains terms that are equal under $\mathcal{I}_{con}$, then we pick one of them and delete the others.

		time				space				
		total (secs)	proj (%)	sub (%)	∩ (%)	input eqns	output eqns	∩	con terms	model size
nrev	bu	0.01	0	100	10	10	10	0 + 0	11	10
	tdlr	0.21	10	76	14	20	35	8 + 5	20	26
dnf	bu	0.65	29	68	3	88	96	3 + 4	82	159
	tdlr	12.59	6	59	35	156	440	53 + 254	313	1739
lcm		13.86	0	99	1	3	145	3 + 142	171	148
hcf		27.54	1	99	0	1	34	0 + 0	148	4

Table 1: Time and space measurements for six set constraint benchmarks.

of dependency directed update, and the subsumption algorithm was completely re-designed using bit vectors. This reimplementation resulted in average speedups of at least a factor of 10, and a reduction in the number of equations generated by a factor of 4. The preceding sections contain only an outline of some of the major design decisions of this implementation. For space reasons we have omitted many details, including a large number of small modifications that, in sum, make an important contribution to the system's performance.

The current implementation is approximately 4,500 lines of Standard ML (this includes programs to construct the set constraints corresponding to a program as well as the set constraint solver and its front end). All timings are on a Sun Sparc 1+ (24MB) running Mach and using version 0.75 of Standard ML of New Jersey. Table 1 presents some execution statistics for a number of example set constraints. The nrev program is the standard naive reverse program. The dnf program is a program to convert a propositional logic formula into a formula in disjunctive normal form. It contains 10 facts and 22 rules (with an average of about 2 body atoms per rule) and contains a large number of mutually recursive calls. For both of these programs we consider the set constraints corresponding both bottom-up (bu) and top-down left-to-right (tdlr) execution. The final two example constraints, lcm and hcf, are essentially pathological cases designed for testing the intersector and projector parts of the algorithm respectively. These constraints are $\mathcal{X} = a \cup f^{11}(\mathcal{X}), \mathcal{Y} = a \cup f^{13}(\mathcal{Y}), \mathcal{Z} = \mathcal{X} \cap \mathcal{Y}$ and $\mathcal{X} = a \cup f^{-33}(\mathcal{X}) \cup f^{144}(\mathcal{X})$ respectively, where $f^{11}(\mathcal{X})$ denotes 11 applications of f to $\mathcal{X}$ and $f^{-33}(\mathcal{X})$ denotes 33 applications of the projector $f_{(1)}^{-1}$ to $\mathcal{X}$. For each example, we give timing information, equation counts and an indication of the space used. The first column of the table is total time, and the next three columns break this down into time spent on projectors, inferring subsumption relationships and intersectors, each expressed as a percentage of total time. Columns 5, 6 and 7 respectively give the number of equations input to the algorithm, the total equations generated during execution, and the number of equations that deal with intersections (entries in this column are of the form $x + y$ where x is the number of intersectors in the input equations, and y is the number of intersectors introduced during execution). Column 8 is the total number of distinct constructed terms. Column 9 provides a measure of the complexity of the least model constructed by the algorithm, and is obtained as follows. First, list all of the sets $max\_con(\mathcal{X})$, for each set variable $\mathcal{X}$. Some of these sets will be the same (in which case the corresponding variables are equal in the least model). The complexity measure is then obtained by summing the cardinalities of the distinct sets that appear in this list. These results show that bottom-up constraints are substantially easier to solve than top-down left-to-right constraints. This general relationship holds because, by their nature, top-down constraints are more complicated and more accurate than

		subsumption				no subsumption			
		time (secs)	total eqns	con terms	table size	time (secs)	total eqns	con terms	table size
nrev	bu	0.01	10	11	16	< 0.01	10	11	16
	tdlr	0.21	35	20	75	0.11	35	20	75
dnf	bu	0.65	96	82	1689	1.01	184	126	5309
	tdlr	12.59	440	313	9317	≈ 218	2669	1510	280K
lcm constraints		13.86	145	171	292	0.26	145	171	292
hcf constraints		27.54	34	148	1644	0.31	34	148	1644

Table 2: Effects of the subsumption component of the algorithm.

	Iterations								
	1	2	3	4	5	6	7	8	9
% time	2	8	18	31	47	61	81	91	100
% ∩ eqns	19	24	40	67	85	96	100	100	100
% model	23	43	58	68	78	86	93	100	100

Table 3: Cumulative consumption of resources during execution.

the bottom-up constraints. The subsumption approximation part of the algorithm accounts for the majority of execution time. The lcm and hcf examples show extreme behavior – in fact the subsumption approximation component of the algorithm is not used at all during the execution of the main body of the algorithm, although it is responsible for producing a compact representation of the output constraints. In the case of lcm, the output for $\mathcal{X}$ is $\mathcal{X} = a \cup f^{143}(\mathcal{X})$, and for hcf the output is $\mathcal{X} = a \cup f^3(\mathcal{X})$.

The driving example used during the development of this implementation was the top-down left-to-right constraints for the dnf program. These constraints are difficult to solved because they exhibit substantial mutual recursion and intersection. We believe that adequately addressing these two issues (mutual recursion and intersection) is at the core of obtaining practical implementations of set based analysis, and so solving the dnf constraints was considered to be an important test case. It was these constraints that motivated the subsumption approximation part of the implementation, whose effects are illustrate in table 2. For the analysis of nrev, and for the lcm and hcf constraints, there is little redundancy and the subsumption component is expensive and provides no direct benefit. However for the more substantial dnf program, it is clearly of benefit, and in the case of top-down analysis, it is crucial. Specifically, in this case the difference in time is nearly a factor of 20, and for one measure of memory usage (the number of entries in the central hash table of the implementation), the difference is a factor of 30. (In fact the measurements for this entry in the table had to be made on a 64MB DECstation 5000, and then converted to equivalent Sparc 1+ times).

Table 3 illustrate the dynamic behavior of the algorithm by giving cumulative measures of the consumption of resources during execution of the top-down dnf constraints. One "iteration" corresponds to an exhaustive application of the projector transformation followed by a recomputation of each intersector. The measure of the amount of the least model computed at each stage is obtained as follows. Let $max\_con(\mathcal{X})|_{final}$ denote the value of the set $max\_con(\mathcal{X})$ on termination of the algorithm. Let $\delta(\mathcal{X})$ denote the proportion of the elements in $max\_con(\mathcal{X})|_{final}$ that currently appear in $con(\mathcal{X})$, and this represents a pessimistic estimate of the proportion of $\mathcal{X}$ that has been currently computed. Finally, the measure of the amount of the least model computed is just the average of $\delta(\mathcal{X})$ over all variables $\mathcal{X}$ currently appearing in the equations. The behavior of this measure indicates that the model grows quickly in the early stages, and that most of the time is spent obtaining the last few components of the model. This supports the notion that during most of the execution of the algorithm, $max\_con(\mathcal{X})$ provides a fairly good approximation to the least model for the purposes of obtaining subsumption relationships.

To illustrate the effects of the minimal dnf expansions algorithm, we again use the top-down dnf constraints. When applied to these constraints, the implementation constructs 1270 conjunctions. In comparison, a simple expansion of these formulas would have led to 1921 disjunctions. Although this only represents a direct saving of 649 disjunction, or about a third, the indirect savings, in terms of intersectors that never need to be constructed, is much larger.

7   Concluding Discussion

The driving example of this implementation effort was a moderate sized program (dnf) exhibiting properties that are problematic for analysis, such as substantial mutual recursion and intersection. Very significant progress has been made and this example can now be analyzed within a reasonable time and space bound. We believe that this provides strong evidence that set based analysis can be made practical. However to realize this goal, much work remains. Our experience suggests that a number of components of the algorithm can be further improved. Currently the major expense is the subsumption algorithm, and one reason for this is that it is not by nature incremental. We are investigating ways to overcome this, including trading some of its effectiveness for the ability to reuse results from previous iterations. Another avenue for improvement lies in the use of specialized hashing techniques.

Thus far we have focussed extensively on efficiency aspects of the analysis. However we have now reached a stage where moderate sized programs can be analyzed. We therefore plan to use this implementation to investigate set based analysis, with particular emphasis on the quality of the information obtained[7] and its relevance to compilation. Practical program analysis must also deal with operations such as call, assert and retract. Preliminary work suggests that it may be possible to directly model these operations in a set constraint framework. One extension that is in the current implementation, but has not been described due to space reasons, is a limited form of mode analysis. For example, when run on the nrev program where the initial goal has its first argument ground, our implementation computes that both arguments will be ground lists after goal execution, and that all calls to append are such that the first argument is always a ground list. Although this extension has been incorporated into the implementation with very little additional overhead, it is somewhat restricted because interdependencies between variables are ignored, and such dependencies can be important for mode analysis. An algorithm in [9] may provide a basis for more accurately dealing with modes while retaining the important advantages of structural accuracy.

We conclude with a discussion of related work. Most of the work on implementation of analysis for logic programs is based on abstract interpretation and the algorithms used are fundamentally different in nature. Our work is more closely connected to work on types for logic programs in which types are defined by ignoring

---

[7] As an example of the output of the algorithm, the top-down analysis of the dnf program constructs the following set $\mathcal{X}$ to describe the set of terms that are the result of putting an arbitrary input formula into dnf: $\mathcal{X} = or(\mathcal{X}, \mathcal{X}) \cup and(\mathcal{X}, \mathcal{X}) \cup not(\mathcal{C})$ where $\mathcal{C}$ describes the set of propositional constants.

inter-variable or inter-argument dependencies. Implementations have been reported in [12] and [14], but the former does not focus on practical issues, and the latter is not directly comparable to our work since it deals with type checking rather than type inference. The most closely related work to ours is [1], which describes an implementation of type inference for the functional language FL. In very general terms their observations about the complexity of the intersection operation are similar to ours. However the two algorithms are completely different in structure. In particular their algorithm does not include the projection operation, and this appears to substantially alter the tradeoffs and design decisions that are made. Furthermore, our implementation has been specifically designed to deal with constraints where there is substantial mutual dependency between variables. Such constraints are typical in the constraints generated for the top-down analysis of logic programs.

8 Acknowledgments

I would like to thank Joxan Jaffar, Spiro Michaylov and Frank Pfenning for many useful comments and suggestions.

References

[1] A. Aiken and B. Murphy, "Implementing Regular Trees", *Proceedings 5th ACM Conference on Functional Programming and Computer Architecture*, Cambridge, MA, August 1991, LNCS 523, pp 427 – 447.

[2] T. Fruhwirth, E. Shapiro, M.Y. Vardi, E. Yardeni, "Logic Programs as Types for Logic Programs", *Proceedings 6th IEEE-LICS*, Amsterdam, June 1991, pp 300 – 309.

[3] F. Gècseg and M. Steinby, "Tree Automata", Akadèmiai Kiadò, Budapest, 1984.

[4] N. Heintze, "Set Based Program Analysis", forthcoming Ph.D. thesis, School of Computer Science, Carnegie Mellon University, September 1992 (expected).

[5] N. Heintze and J. Jaffar, "A Finite Presentation Theorem for Approximating Logic Programs", *Proceedings 17th ACM-POPL*, San Francisco, January 1990, pp 197 – 209.

[6] N. Heintze and J. Jaffar, "A Decision Procedure for a Class of Herbrand Set Constraints", *Proceedings 5th IEEE-LICS*, Philadelphia, June 1990, pp 42 – 51.

[7] N. Heintze and J. Jaffar, "Set Based Program Analysis", draft manuscript, January 1991.

[8] N. Heintze and J. Jaffar, "Semantic Types for Logic Programs" in *Types in Logic Programming*, F. Pfenning (Ed.), MIT Press, 1992, pp 141 – 155.

[9] N. Heintze and J. Jaffar, "An Engine for Logic Program Analysis", *Proceedings 7th IEEE-LICS*, Santa Cruz, June 1992, pp 318 – 328.

[10] N.D. Jones and S.S. Muchnick, "Flow Analysis and Optimization of LISP-like Structures", *Proceedings 6th ACM-POPL*, San Antonio, January 1979, pp 244 – 256.

[11] P. Mishra, "Toward a Theory of Types in PROLOG", *Proceedings 1st IEEE Symposium on Logic Programming*, Atlantic City, July 1984, pp 289 – 298.

[12] C. Pyo and U.S. Reddy, "Inference of Polymorphic Types for Logic Programs" *Logic Programming, Proceedings of the North American Conference, 1989*, Cleveland, MIT Press, October 1989, pp 1115 – 1134.

[13] J.C. Reynolds, "Automatic Computation of Data Set Definitions", *Information Processing 68*, North-Holland, 1969, pp 456 – 461.

[14] E. Yardeni and E.Y. Shapiro, "A Type System for Logic Programs", *Journal of Logic Programming*, Vol. 10, 1991, pp 125 – 153.

Semantics

Normal Logic Programs as Open Positive Programs

A. Brogi*, E. Lamma+, P. Mancarella* and P. Mello+

*Dipartimento di Informatica
Corso Italia, 40
I-56125 Pisa, Italy
{brogi, paolo}@di.unipi.it

+DEIS
Viale Risorgimento 2
I-40136 Bologna, Italy
{evelina, paola}@deis33.cineca.it

Abstract

There is no general agreement on what the meaning of a logic program with negation is, as shown by the number of different semantics which have been defined so far. We give an alternative characterisation of existing semantics for normal programs. We interpret normal programs as positive programs, and denote them by their Herbrand models. The approach allows easy comparisons of different existing semantics of logic programs with negation which can be drawn by reasoning on properties of Herbrand models. This way, we show that stationary expansions and complete scenaria coincide.

1 Introduction and motivations

Negation-as-failure is a powerful inference rule widely adopted in logic programming to express some forms of non-monotonic reasoning. Unfortunately, there is no common agreement on what is the intended meaning of a normal logic program, that is a program (possibly) containing negative atoms in clause bodies. In the past years, a number of different semantics have been proposed to characterise logic programs with negation. Among others, we mention: the *well-founded semantics* [12], the *stable model semantics* [5] and its extensions (e.g. *partial stable models* [10], *P-stable models* [11], and *3-valued stable models* [8]), the *preferential semantics* [3] and the *stationary semantics* [9].

These semantics approach similar problems from different perspectives. The well-founded semantics is based on the concept of unfounded set, and the well-founded model of a program is computed as the fixpoint of a suitable transformation function. Stable models are defined in terms of a syntactic program transformation. Recent extensions of the stable model semantics relate to 3-valued logic, and are also based on syntactic transformations. The preferential semantics, instead, exploits the idea of treating negation as hypothesis (following [4]) and relates to autoepistemic logic. Finally, the stationary semantics treats negation as negation by default, and is based on the principles of minimisation and predicate circumscription.

Although some relations between these semantics are intuitively clear, formal comparisons are not easy to be drawn mainly because of the different constructions which are used in their definitions. Some correspondences have already been stated. In [8] it is shown that the well-founded model of a program corresponds to the intersection of all its 3-valued stable models, as well as that P-stable models [11] are 3-valued stable models. Moreover, in [7] it is shown that preferred extensions [3] are partial stable models [10].

This paper intends to represent a contribution to the studies on the semantics of logic programs with negation from different perspectives. First of all, we compare different semantics for logic programs within a unifying framework, which takes into account only the Herbrand models of programs. This is done, according to [3, 4, 9], viewing normal programs as positive ones, by considering each negative literal $not\ A$ as a new positive literal not_A. We first associate with each program its Herbrand models following the approach presented in [2] for open positive programs. Then, we identify among them those models which characterise the intended meaning of negation, and prove that they provide an alternative characterisation of both stationary semantics and preferential semantics.

A first advantage of this approach is that different semantics for programs are defined on purely model-theoretic arguments (i.e., Herbrand models) rather than in terms of the syntax of programs. For example, the definition of (3-valued) stable models given through syntactic transformations over programs is reformulated in terms of simple properties on the Herbrand models of programs.

Secondly, this approach suggests a general methodology for comparing different semantics. For each given semantics S, a suitable function ψ_S could be defined which, given the Herbrand models of a program P, $HM(P)$, yields the models $S(P)$ corresponding to the semantics S:

$$\psi_S : HM(P) \mapsto S(P)$$

In this way, it is possible to draw comparisons between different semantics for negation in logic programming, even though they tackle the negation issue from different perspectives. In other words, equivalencies between different declarative semantics can be proved, as well as differences between them can be formally clarified. Given two different semantics S_1 and S_2, this can be achieved by simply comparing the corresponding functions ψ_{S_1} and ψ_{S_2}.

In particular, we prove that complete scenaria [3] and stationary expansions [9] coincide, and are equivalent to a suitable projection function on Herbrand models. (For the lack of space, all the proofs of the formal results are omitted in this paper and can be found in [1]).

2 Normal programs as positive programs

Recently, many authors have exploited the idea of considering normal programs as *positive* programs, by looking at negative literals *not p*(...) as positive atoms with predicate symbol *not_p* [3, 4, 9]. Following this approach, we will simply consider normal programs as (open) positive programs, and apply the same approach as in [2] to normal programs.

In [2] the semantics which associate with a positive program P the set of all its Herbrand models has been proposed and it has been shown that this semantics is *compositional*. For example, the semantics of the union $P \cup Q$ of two programs can be obtained in terms of the semantics of the components programs P and Q, which is not the case if the standard minimal Herbrand model semantics is adopted. Roughly, the non-minimal Herbrand models of a program characterise possible extensions of it, corresponding to compositions with different programs.

In [2] this is outlined by showing that each Herbrand model of a program is *supported* by a set of assumptions (atoms), and this set fully characterises the extensions corresponding to that model. In this paper we show that, by viewing normal programs as positive programs, the same semantics framework can be adopted, and we show that various existing semantics can be recovered within this framework by defining suitable projection functions on the set of all *supported* models. On the one hand, this allows one to relate and compare different semantics within a unifying framework, and on the other hand this provides scope for addressing compositionality also in the case of normal programs. In the sequel, we will mainly concentrate on the first aspect, by showing that several, well known semantics for negation in logic programming can be easily recovered also in the purely semantic framework of supported interpretations. As far as compositionality is concerned, we will mention in section 6 how the results of [2] can be exploited to provide normal programs with a compositional semantics.

We devote the rest of this section to setting up these preliminary notions and the notations we will be using throughout the paper. We will refer to the basic concepts and terminologies of standard logic programming. Then, a *normal program* P is a set of clauses of the form $A \leftarrow L_1, \ldots, L_n$, $(n \geq 0)$, where A is an atom and $L_1, \ldots, L_n$ are literals. Negative literals in clause bodies will be denoted by *not A*, to keep the distinction between negation by failure (or by default) *not* and classical negation $\neg$ clear. Without loss of generality, we consider only (possibly infinite) propositional programs, thus assuming that a program P has already been instantiated (as done, e.g., in [9]).

Let P be a program and HB the Herbrand Base associated with P. As mentioned above, negative literals $not\ A$ will be looked at as positive atoms not_A, where not_A is a new propositional symbol (as done, for instance in [9]). In other words, P is transformed into its *positive version* P' by replacing each negative literal $not\ A$ in P's clause bodies with the corresponding positive literal not_A. By the Herbrand base associated with P' we mean the set obtained extending HB with

$$not\_HB = \{not\_A | A \in HB\}$$

regardless of whether a literal $not\ A$ occurs in any clause body. This is due to the fact that we are going to define the intended meaning of P by selecting suitable Herbrand models of P', that is subsets of $HB \cup not\_HB$. Given a Herbrand model, M say, the meaning of $not\_A \in M$ is that $not\ A$ is true in M.

We will not distinguish any further between P and its positive version P', that is we will denote directly by P its positive version. Moreover, we will refer to the elements of HB (resp. not_HB) as *positive* (resp. *negative*) atoms. A Herbrand interpretation I of P is, as usual, a subset of its Herbrand Base, that is a subset of $HB \cup not\_HB$. Since we will be only interested in Herbrand interpretations and models, from now onwards we will refer to them simply as interpretations and models. Given an interpretation I, I^+ and I^- will stand for $I \cap HB$ and $I \cap not\_HB$, respectively. The next definition introduces the notion of *coherency* of an interpretation I, which is needed to avoid confusion with the classical notion of *consistency*.

Definition 2.1 *An interpretation I is* coherent *iff for no atom $A \in HB$ both $A \in I^+$ and $not\_A \in I^-$. I is* incoherent *otherwise.*

Notice that, if normal programs are viewed as positive programs, a Herbrand model of a program can possibly be incoherent. For this reason, from now onwards we will use the term interpretations for arbitrary (possibly incoherent) Herbrand models of a program, and we will call models only *coherent* ones.

As mentioned above, the Herbrand models of a (positive) program P can be given an alternative, though equivalent, characterisation in terms of a *supportedness* notion which has been used in [2]. This characterisation is given in the next definition, where we make use of the standard *immediate consequence operator* T_P associated with a positive program P.

Definition 2.2 *Let P be a program, M an interpretation of P (i.e., $M \subseteq HB \cup not\_HB$), and $H \subseteq M$ such that $M = T_{P \cup H} \uparrow \omega$. Then M is called a* supported interpretation *of P and M is said to be* supported by H, written as M^H. We will denote by $SI(P)$ the set of supported interpretations of P.

It is worth observing that the minimal Herbrand model of a program is always supported by $H = \{\}$. Moreover, for any set H there is a unique interpretation M supported by H, namely $M = T_{P \cup H} \uparrow \omega$, whereas an interpretation M can be supported by several sets.

Example 2.3 Let P be the following program:

$\quad a \leftarrow not\_b$

Recall that the underlying Herbrand Base we are referring to is $\{a, b, not\_a, not\_b\}$, so the set of supported interpretations of P contains, among others: $\{\}$, $\{a\}$, $\{a, not\_b\}$, $\{a, not\_a, not\_b\}$, $\{not\_a\}$. Notice that, for instance, the interpretation $\{a, not\_b\}$ is supported by two different sets, namely $\{a, not\_b\}$ itself and $\{not\_b\}$.

Herbrand models as supported interpretations can be characterised in several, yet equivalent, ways (see [2]).

Proposition 2.4 *Let P be a program and M an interpretation of P supported by H. Then, the following are equivalent statements:*

(i) $M = T_P \uparrow \omega(H)$

(ii) $M = \cap \ \{M' | M'$ is a Herbrand model of $P \cup H\}$

(iii) $M = \cap \ \{M' | M'$ is a Herbrand model of P and $H \subseteq M'\}$

3 Semantics of negation

Once a normal program has been denoted by the set of its supported interpretations, the question arises whether it is possible to define suitable projections on this set, which capture different, well-known declarative semantics for negation. In this section, we introduce the notion of *complete supported models* and show that it is possible to capture through them both Dung's preferential semantics and Przymusinski's stationary semantics. As a by-product, we obtain a proof of equivalence of these two semantics and a unifying view of them. This is particularly interesting in view of the fact that they tackle the problem of assigning a declarative meaning to negation from different perspectives, negation through abduction in Dung's view and circumscription in Przymusinski's view. Similar results can be achieved for other semantics of negation (e.g. well-founded semantics [12], partial stable models semantics [10], 3-valued stable semantics [8]): we will mention some in section 5.

In the case of positive programs the usual, minimal model semantics can be obviously recovered in the framework of supported interpretations, by considering only the interpretation supported by the empty set. In the case of normal programs, we define in a stepwise fashion a projection which identifies those supported interpretations assigning to negative atoms not_A the correct meaning of negation by default.

Definition 3.1 *Let P be a program. A supported interpretation M of P is a negatively supported interpretation of P iff M is supported by M^-. We will denote by $NSI(P)$ the set of negatively supported interpretations of P.*

It is worth recalling that M is supported by M^- iff $M = T_{P \cup M^-} \uparrow \omega$. Hence, if a supported interpretation M is negatively supported, then the set of positive atoms true in M (i.e., M^+) contains exactly those which are derivable by assuming the truth of the negative atoms in M^-. We avoid to denote explicitly the set H supporting a negatively supported interpretation, since $H = M^-$.

Example 3.2 Let P be the program of example 2.3. Then:
$$NSI(P) = \{\{\}, \quad \{not\_a\}, \quad \{a, not\_b\}, \quad \{a, not\_a, not\_b\}\}$$
Notice that: $\{a\} \in SI(P)$ but $\{a\} \notin NSI(P)$, since $\{a\}$ is supported only by $\{a\}$ itself.

We now introduce the notion of conservative extension of a negatively supported interpretation. Roughly, given two negatively supported interpretations N and M, N conservatively extends M if every negative atom which is true in M is also true in N, and N does not assume the truth of not_A whenever A is true in M.

Definition 3.3 *Let M, N be two negatively supported interpretations of a program P. N is a conservative extension of M iff $M^- \subseteq N^-$ and $M^+ \cup N^-$ is coherent. The set of all conservative extensions of M is denoted by $CE(M)$.*

Notice that incoherent interpretations have no conservative extensions: in fact, if M is incoherent then obviously for any $N \in NSI(P)$ such that $M^- \subseteq N^-$, also $M^+ \cup N^-$ is incoherent. Nevertheless, coherent interpretations can have incoherent conservative extensions. Up to this point, however, we are not much concerned with coherency, which will be taken into account later to identify admissible models among admissible interpretations.

Example 3.4 Let P be the program of example 2.3. Then:
$$CE(\{\}) = \{\{\}, \{not\_a\}, \{a, not\_b\}, \{a, not\_a, not\_b\}\}$$
$$CE(\{not\_a\}) = \{\{not\_a\}, \{a, not\_a, not\_b\}\}$$
$$CE(\{a, not\_b\}) = \{\{a, not\_b\}\}$$
$$CE(\{a, not\_a, not\_b\}) = \{\}$$
Notice that $\{a, not\_a, not\_b\} \in CE(\{not\_a\})$, but $\{a, not\_a, not\_b\} \notin CE(\{a, not\_b\})$.

We now introduce the notion of admissible supported interpretation. Intuitively, a negatively supported interpretation M is admissible if no conservative extension of M can contradict any negative atom in M^-.

Definition 3.5 *Let M be a negatively supported interpretation of a program P. M is an admissible supported interpretation iff:*
$$\forall N \in CE(M) : M^- \cup N^+ \text{ is coherent.}$$
The set of all admissible supported interpretations of P is denoted by $ASI(P)$.

Example 3.6 Let P be the program of example 2.3. Then:
$$ASI(P) = \{\{\}, \{a, not\_b\}, \{a, \ not\_a, \ not\_b\}\}$$
Notice that $\{not\_a\} \notin ASI(P)$ since a belongs to its conservative extension $\{a, \ not\_b, \ not\_a\}$.

According to definition 3.5, incoherent interpretations are always admissible: this is due to the fact that an incoherent interpretation admits no conservative extension. Of course, we do not want to accept incoherent interpretations as models, and this is achieved by the next definition.

Definition 3.7 *Let M be an admissible supported interpretation of a program P. If M is coherent then M is an admissible supported model of P. The set of all admissible supported models of P is denoted by $ASM(P)$.*

Example 3.8 Let P be the program of example 2.3. Then:
$$ASM(P) = \{\{\}, \{a, \ not\_b\}\}.$$
In fact, $\{a, \ not\_a, \ not\_b\} \in ASI(P)$, but it is not an admissible supported model since it is incoherent in its own.

The admissibility condition of a negatively supported interpretation M can be obviously restated as follows:
$$M^- \subseteq \{not\_A \mid \forall N \in CE(M) : \ A \notin N\}$$
Among admissible models, we can select those that make as many negative hypotheses as possible, on the grounds that all their conservative extensions do not contradict those hypotheses. These are the models for which the above condition turns into an equality. This leads us to the definition of *complete* supported models.

Definition 3.9 *Let M be a negatively supported model of a program P. M is complete iff: $M^- = \{not\_A \mid \forall N \in CE(M) : \ A \notin N\}$. The set of all complete supported models of P is denoted by $CSM(P)$.*

Example 3.10 Let P be the program of example 2.3. Then:
$$CSM(P) = \{\{a, \ not\_b\}\}.$$
The model $\{\} \in ASM(P)$ is not complete, since it does not contain not_b, even though any conservative extension of $\{\}$ does not make b true (see example 3.4).

The next proposition shows that negatively supported models which are total are indeed complete: an interpretation I is *total* if and only if for each $A \in HB$, either $A \in I^+$ or $not\_A \in I^-$.

Proposition 3.11 *Let M be a negatively supported interpretation of a program P. If M is total and coherent then M is a complete supported model of P.*

The next proposition states that complete supported models capture the intended meaning of locally stratified programs, which admit a unique complete supported model corresponding to their unique perfect (or stable) model. Notice that this also implies that positive programs have a unique complete supported model corresponding to their minimal Herbrand model.

Proposition 3.12 *Let P be a locally stratified logic program, and let M be its unique stable model. Then P', the positive version of P, admits a unique complete supported model M', such that:*

$$M'^+ = M$$
$$M'^- = \{not\_A \mid A \notin M\}.$$

Summarising, what we are proposing here is to denote a logic program P by the set of its supported interpretations, and then to select among them its complete supported models, which give the declarative semantics of P. The previous proposition states that this yields the usual declarative semantics for locally stratified programs. In the rest of the paper we will show that complete supported models allows us to capture both Dung's preferential semantics and Przymusinski's stationary semantics, and as a by-product, the (3-valued) stable semantics and the well-founded semantics.

4 Relation with preferential and stationary semantics

In this section, we state the correspondence between our semantic framework and other existing proposals for the semantics of normal logic programs. In particular, we will show that complete supported models have a direct correspondence with Dung's complete scenaria and with Przymusinski's stationary expansions, thus giving a unifying view of those semantics while proving their equivalence.

4.1 Dung's Preferential Semantics

In his recent work [3], Dung has studied the treatment of negation as hypothesis in logic programming, which was first introduced in [4] in the framework of abductive reasoning. The main idea of this approach is to look at negative literals as possible abductive hypotheses, and to give the semantics of a program P through the notion of admissible extensions of the theory represented by P. These extensions are obtained augmenting P with a set of abductive hypotheses Δ, which satisfy appropriate conditions of acceptability.

In the sequel we recall the basic definitions and results of [3]: in order to better understand the relationships with our framework, we restate Dung's definitions according to our terminology and notations. Given a logic program P and a set of hypotheses $H \subseteq not\_HB$, Dung introduces the notation $Der(P, H)$ to stand for the set $\{A \in HB | P \cup H \vdash A\}$. Since, obviously, $Der(P, H)$ is the set of positive atoms in the minimal Herbrand model of $P \cup H$, in our terminology $Der(P, H) = M^+$, where M is the negatively supported interpretation such that $M^- = H$, and this fact will be used in the sequel.

Definition 4.1 *Given a logic program P, a scenario is a first order theory $P \cup H$, such that $Der(P, H) \cup H$ is coherent.*

Among scenaria, Dung first identifies those which contain an hypothesis not_A only if it satisfies the "no evidence to the contrary" criterion. Roughly speaking, given a scenario $P \cup H$ and an hypothesis not_A, not_A has no evidence to the contrary with respect to $P \cup H$ if all possible ways of deriving A are incoherent with $Der(P, H)$. This is formally stated in the next two definitions.

Definition 4.2 *An hypothesis not_A is acceptable with respect to a scenario $P \cup H$ if for every set of hypotheses $E \subseteq not\_HB$ such that $P \cup E \vdash A$, $Der(P, H) \cup E$ is incoherent.*

Notice that any such E is "evidence" for A, that is "evidence for the contrary" of the hypothesis not_A. If any such evidence to the contrary is incoherent with the conclusions of the original set H, then not_A can be safely accepted in H.

Definition 4.3 *A scenario $P \cup H$ is admissible if every hypothesis in H is acceptable with respect to $P \cup H$. A preferred extension is a maximal (with respect to set inclusion) admissible scenario of P.*

The *preferential semantics* of a program P is then given by the set of all its preferred extensions. As shown in [3], preferred extensions can also be viewed as the maximal elements of the space of *complete scenaria*. A scenario is complete if it contains all the hypotheses acceptable with respect to it.

Definition 4.4 *An admissible scenario $P \cup H$ is complete if every hypothesis acceptable wrt $P \cup H$ is accepted in $P \cup H$, i.e., for every not_A, if not_A is acceptable wrt $P \cup H$ then $not\_A \in H$.*

In the next proposition we summarise some of the results in [3].

Proposition 4.5 *Let P be a logic program. Then:*
(i) P admits at least one preferred extension;
(ii) P admits at least one complete scenario;
(iii) The well-founded model of P corresponds
    to the least complete scenario.

We are now in the position of stating the direct correspondence between complete/admissible scenaria and complete/admissible supported models. First of all, we observe that there is an obvious direct correspondence between coherent negatively supported interpretations and scenaria.

Proposition 4.6 *Let P be a logic program, $H \subseteq not\_HB$ and $M = T_{P \cup H} \uparrow \omega$. Then, $P \cup H$ is a scenario iff M is a coherent negatively supported interpretation. Moreover, $Der(P, H) = M^+$.*

The next theorem relates admissible scenaria with admissible supported models.

Theorem 4.7 *Let P be a logic program. Then, M is an admissible supported model of P iff $P \cup M^-$ is an admissible scenario of P.*

Finally, we get a one-to-one correspondence between complete supported models and complete scenaria.

Theorem 4.8 *Let P be a logic program. Then, M is a complete supported model of P iff $P \cup M^-$ is a complete scenario of P.*

4.2 Przymusinski's Stationary Semantics

In [9], Przymusinski interprets negation in (disjunctive) normal programs as negation by default. The negation by default *not F* of a propositional formula *F* is treated as a new propositional symbol The introduction of default propositions *not_F* allows one to deal with both classical negation *¬F* and negation by default *not F*. In Przymusinski's framework, a formula *F* of the form *A* or *¬F* is called an *objective proposition*, while *not_F* is called a *default proposition*. Since *not_A* is considered as a new predicate symbol, and classical negation is also taken into account, we talk about consistency and inconsistency in the classical sense, as opposed to the notion of coherency and incoherence previously introduced.

In the sequel we recall the basic definitions and results of [9]. The idea of Przymusinski is to define the semantics of a program *P* in terms of *stationary* expansions, namely theories obtained by augmenting *P* with some default propositions of the form *not_A* or *¬not_A*, and by imposing a stationarity condition on them. Let us go into the details of Przymusinski's definitions. Given a logic program *P*, an expansion *T* is a *theory* obtained by augmenting P with some default propositions of the form not_A or $\neg not\_A$. In the sequel, we will use the classical notions of Herbrand interpretations and models of a theory T.

Recall that, given a theory T, a Herbrand interpretation I of T can be identified with a subset of the (extended) Herbrand base $HB \cup not\_HB$. Given an interpretation I, a default or objective proposition F of the kind A or not_A is true in I if $F \in I$, false otherwise. Moreover, I is a model of T if it satisfies all the statements in T.

Definition 4.9 *Given a theory T, a model M of T is* minimal *iff there is no model N of T such that $N \subset M$ and N coincides with M on default propositions.*
We denote by $\mathcal{MIN}(T)$ the class of all minimal models of a theory T.

According to [9], if a formula F is true in all minimal models of T, we write $T \models_{min} F$. As pointed out in [9], this notion of minimal model corresponds to considering predicate circumscription $CIRC(T; O; D)$ of the theory T, in which objective propositions O are minimised and default propositions D are fixed.

Among expansions of a program P, Przymusinski identifies those expansions T which are obtained by adding to the original program P some default propositions of the form not_A (resp. $\neg not\_A$), in such a way that the corresponding objective propositions A are false (resp. true) in all minimal models of T.

Definition 4.10 *A consistent theory $T = P \cup H \cup K$, with $H \subseteq not\_HB$ and $K \subseteq \{\neg not\_A | A \in HB\}$, is a* stationary expansion *of a program P iff T satisfies the conditions:*
  (S1) $T \models not\_A \Longleftrightarrow T \models_{min} \neg A$
  (S2) $T \models \neg not\_A \Longleftrightarrow T \models A$
for any objective proposition A.

Example 4.11 Consider the following program P, taken from [9]:
  $a \leftarrow not\_b$
  $b \leftarrow not\_a$
  $c \leftarrow a, b$
The program has three stationary expansions, namely:
  $T_0 = P$
  $T_1 = P \cup \{not\_a, \neg not\_b, \ not\_c\}$
  $T_2 = P \cup \{not\_b, \ \neg not\_a, not\_c\}$
Notice that T_1 and T_2 have only one minimal model, namely:
  $M_1 = \{b, \ not\_a, \ not\_c\}$ for T_1, and
  $M_2 = \{a, \ not\_b, \ not\_c\}$ for T_2.

In order to state the relationship between stationary expansions and complete supported models of a program P, we first need to relate the framework of supported interpretations to the one of theories and expansions of theories. This is achieved by the following definition.

Definition 4.12 *Let P be a program, M be a supported interpretation of P and T be a theory obtained by augmenting P with some default propositions of the form not_A and $\neg not\_A$. Then:*

(i) $T(M)$, *the* theory *associated with M, is defined as follows:*
$$T(M) = P \cup M^- \cup \{\neg not\_A | A \in M^+\}$$

(ii) $S(T)$, *the* supported interpretation *associated with T, is the supported interpretation N such that $N^- = T \cap not\_HB$.*

The next two propositions clarify the meaning of the above mapping, by showing the correspondence between minimal models of theories and conservative extensions of supported interpretations. More precisely, the first proposition states that for any *coherent* supported interpretation M, the set of conservative extensions of M coincides with the set of minimal models of $T(M)$. On the other hand, the second proposition states that, for any theory T satisfying condition $(S2)$ of definition 4.10, the set of minimal models of T coincides with the set of conservative extensions of $S(T)$.

Proposition 4.13 *Let M be a coherent supported interpretation. Then N is a conservative extension of M iff N is a minimal model of $T(M)$.*

Proposition 4.14 *Let T be a theory which satisfies condition $(S2)$ of definition 4.10. Then, N is a minimal model of T iff N is a conservative extension of $S(T)$.*

Finally, we get to the result which states that there is a one-to-one correspondence between complete supported models and stationary expansions.

Theorem 4.15 *Let P be a program. Then:*
(i) *if M is a complete supported model of P*
     then $T(M)$ is a stationary expansion of P
(ii) *if T is a stationary expansion of P*
     then $S(T)$ is a complete supported model of P.

As a corollary of theorem 4.8 and theorem 4.15, we directly obtain the equivalence of complete scenaria and stationary expansions.

Corollary 4.16 *Let P be a program. We have:*
(i) *if $P \cup H$ is a complete scenario of P then*
     $P \cup H \cup \{\neg not\_A | A \in Der(P, H)\}$ *is a stationary expansion of P.*
(ii) *if T is a stationary expansion of P then*
     $P \cup (T \cap not\_HB)$ *is a complete scenario of P.*

5 Relations with other semantics

In his paper [9], Przymusinski showed that stationary expansions give an alternative characterisation of 3-valued stable models, which has the advantage of being defined in terms of classic, two-valued logic. As a consequence of the results of Przymusinski and of theorem 4.15, we have that also complete supported models correspond directly to 3-valued stable models. However, as in the case of [9], our description lies completely on model-theoretic arguments, as opposed to the original definition of 3-valued stable models [8] which used the language of 3-valued logic and a syntactic transformation on the original program clauses.

It is also worth observing that both stationary semantics and preferential semantics extend Gelfond and Lifschitz's stable model semantics for normal programs. In fact, the stable models of a program P (if any) coincide with *total* stationary expansions and complete scenaria. Notably, the same result can be restated in our framework as follows.

Proposition 5.1 *Let P be a program and $M \subseteq HB$. Then M is a stable model of P iff $M \cup \{not\_A | A \notin M\}$ is a total negatively supported model of the positive version of P.*

This result is due to proposition 3.11 and the equivalence between complete supported models and 3-valued stable models.

Finally, both Dung and Przymusinski have related their semantics to the well-founded semantics defined in [12]. Indeed, given a program P, both the least complete scenario and the least stationary expansion correspond to the well-founded model of P. Thus, as a consequence of the results of section 4, the least complete supported model corresponds to the well-founded model.

Proposition 5.2 *Let P be a program and $W = \cap\{M \mid M \in CSM(P)\}$. Then W is still a complete supported model, and it corresponds to the well-founded model of P, that is:*
$$M_W = W^+ \cup \{\neg A | not\_A \in W^-\}$$
is the well-founded model of P.

6 Conclusions and future work

In this paper we have given an alternative characterisation of some existing semantics for negation, in terms of simple properties of the Herbrand models of a normal program, when interpreted as a positive one. This semantics is given on purely model theoretic grounds, without referring to the syntax of the program and it is shown to be equivalent to other existing semantics for negation.

Future work will be devoted to extend the results of the present paper in two main directions. On the one hand, we plan to consider other existing semantics for extended logic programs. In [9] the author extends the notion of stationary expansions to disjunctive logic programs, while in [6] the stable model semantics is extended to deal also with classical negation. We plan to further exploit the relations between our framework and these semantics, to cope with both disjunctive programs and programs with classical negation.

As mentioned in section 2, another interesting aspect of our approach is concerned with compositionality issues. Compositionality is not addressed by the existing semantics of normal programs. It is not clear how to determine the models of a normal program from the models of its components. For instance, there is no way of determining the stable models of the union of two programs from the stable models of the two separate programs. Consider the two programs: $p \leftarrow not \; q$ and $p \leftarrow$ which have the same stable model $\{p\}$. If these are composed with the program $q \leftarrow$ we obtain two programs which have different stable models ($\{q\}$ and $\{p, q\}$, respectively). The main reason why the existing semantics for normal programs do not properly cope with program union derives from the way they interpret negation. Whatever semantics for negation is adopted, a program is interpreted as a "complete" knowledge specification, and the meaning of negation basically interprets what "complete" is intended to mean. This does not reflect the implicit assumption underlying program composition, namely that a program is conceived as *open* (i.e., as an incomplete chunk of knowledge to be possibly completed with other knowledge).

Similar considerations apply to positive programs as well, where the standard minimal Herbrand model semantics is not compositional with respect to program union. Instead, the semantics given in [2], which associate with a positive program the set of all its Herbrand models, accounts for compositionality. The same idea applies then to normal programs, when they are treated as open positive ones. Once programs are denoted by their Herbrand models, the results presented in [2] apply to normal programs as well, and the Herbrand models of the union of normal programs can be obtained from those of the component programs. At this point, the intended semantics can be recovered by applying the corresponding projection function on Herbrand models, as the one introduced in the paper for complete supported models. Referring back to the example of stable models, the stable models of $P \cup Q$ can be determined from the Herbrand models of $P \cup Q$, in the same way as the stable models of P can be determined from the Herbrand models of P (i.e., by applying the projection function for stable models).

Compositionality induces also interesting insights on the equivalence of programs. A *compositional* notion of equivalence states that a part P of a program can be replaced by an equivalent, although syntactically different, part Q without affecting the semantics of the whole program. The compositionality of the Herbrand models semantics, along with the projections defined in this paper, do induce an interesting equivalence relation on normal programs, which is worth investigating further. Programs which have the same Herbrand models also have the same stable models, preferred extensions, stationary expansions and so on.

Acknowledgements: We thank Michael Gelfond and Phan Minh Dung for their useful comments and suggestions on earlier versions of this paper. Work partially supported by C.N.R. PFI "Sistemi Informatici e Calcolo Parellelo" under grants n. 91000921.PF69 and n. 9100880.PF69.

References

[1] Brogi, A., Lamma, E., Mancarella, P., and Mello, P., "Normal Logic Programs as Open Positive Programs", Technical Report, Dipartimento di Informatica, Università di Pisa, 1992.

[2] Brogi, A., Lamma, E., and Mello P., "Compositional model-theoretic Semantics for Logic Programs", In *Proc. 2nd WELP*, 1991.

[3] Dung, P.M., "Negation as Hypothesis: An Abductive Foundation for Logic Programming", In *Proc. 8th ICLP*, MIT Press, 1991.

[4] Eshghi, K., and Kowalski, R.A., "Abduction Compared with Negation by Failure", In *Proc. 6th ICLP*, MIT Press, 1989.

[5] Gelfond, M., and Lifschitz, V., "The stable model semantics for logic programming", In *Proc. 5th ICSLP*, MIT Press, 1988.

[6] Gelfond, M., and Lifschitz, V., "Logic Programs with Classical Negation", In *Proc. 7th ICLP*, MIT Press, 1990.

[7] Kakas, A.C., and Mancarella, P., "Preferred Extensions are Partial Stable Models", to appear in *Journal of Logic Programming*.

[8] Przymusinski, T.C., "Extended Stable Semantics for Normal and Disjunctive Programs", In *Proc. 7th ICLP*, MIT Press, 1990.

[9] Przymusinski, T.C., "Semantics of Disjunctive Logic Programs and Deductive Databases", In *Proc. DOOD'91*, 1991.

[10] Saccà, D., and Zaniolo, C., "Stable models and non determinism in logic programs with negation", In *Proc. PODS'90*, 1990.

[11] Saccà, D., and Zaniolo, C., "Partial Models and Three-Valued Models in Logic Programs with Negation", In *Logic Programming and Non-Monotonic Reasoning*, MIT Press, 1991.

[12] Van Gelder, A., Ross, K., and Schlipf, J., "Unfounded sets and the well- founded semantics for General Logic Programs", In *Proc. PODS'88*, 1988.

Classifying Semantics of Disjunctive Logic Programs
(Extended Abstract)

Jürgen Dix
University of Karlsruhe,
Institute of Logic, POBox 6980
D-W-7500 Karlsruhe, Germany
dix@ira.uka.de

Abstract

Our aim is to look from a structural point of view at the various semantics for disjunctive logic programs with negation that have been considered in the last years. These semantics induce nonmonotonic entailment relations " $\vdash$ "; we ask for the properties they satisfy and try to distinguish between these semantics by looking at the requirements they meet.

In previous work on programs without disjunctions, we have shown that two important properties turned out to be useful: *Cumulative* and *Rational Monotony*. We introduce some further interesting principles: *Modularity*, *Relevance*, and *PPE*. All these conditions seem to be strongly related to the complexity of computing a semantics. We argue that any reasonable semantics should satisfy them.

We also distinguish between an *inclusive* and an *exclusive* interpretation of "∨" in disjunctive programs: the condition *Or* and its converse turn out to be useful. For exclusive "∨", we discuss Przymusinski's *stationary* approach and point out a serious shortcoming, the failure of *Modularity*. For inclusive "∨", we define extensions of Minker's WGCWA for stratified and general disjunctive programs.

Finally, we show how to extend a given semantics for the class of stratified programs to the whole class of arbitrary disjunctive programs. Using this construction, we get two cumulative semantics: DWFS (extending PERFECT and WFS) and DWGCWA (extending WGCWA and WFS).

1   Introduction

This paper is a continuation of [Dix91a] and [Dix91b]. The overall aim is to get a clear picture of the various existing semantics of disjunctive logic programs and their mutual relations.

While there is only one canonical semantics for positive programs without disjunctions, the least Herbrand model, the situation changes when disjunctive heads are allowed: we can interpret "∨" *exclusive*, this leads to GCWA, or *inclusive*, this leads to WGCWA (or, equivalently, to the DDR-rule). In both cases, it is an interesting question, and a field of active research, to ask for extensions of the respective semantics to larger classes of programs, eg to the class of *stratified* disjunctive programs or, finally, to the whole class of *all* disjunctive programs. Recently, various semantics have been proposed:

- the "WGCWA" (or, equivalently the DDR-rule as introduced in [RT88]), that interprets $\vee$ *inclusive* ([RLM89]), and the "GCWA" (defined by Minker), that interprets $\vee$ *exclusive*, for *positive* disjunctive programs,

- the *perfect* "PERFECT" and "GCWAS" (see [Prz88], and [MLR91]) for *stratified* disjunctive programs,

and some semantics defined for general disjunctive programs:

- the *stationary* semantics $\mathcal{STN}$ of Przymusinski ([Prz91b]),

- an extension of " STABLE" to arbitrary disjunctive programs ([GL91, Prz91a])

- "GDWFS" and "WF^3" of Baral/Lobo/Minker ([BLM90a, BLM91]).

The starting point of most of these semantics was a particular program that was not handled correctly, according to the intuitions of the researchers, by the existing semantics. The new semantics was then designed to give the desired conclusions.

We propose another approach: we associate, uniform for all semantics, a consequence relation $\mathrel{\vrule\,}\!\!\sim_P$ between sets of atoms and sets of literals to each program P: for any semantics SEM and any program P, a relation $\mathrel{\vrule\,}\!\!\sim_P$ is canonically defined. We can now ask for the properties of this $\mathrel{\vrule\,}\!\!\sim$ relation.

For programs without disjunctions, our results in [Dix91a] and [Dix91b] have shown that the properties of *cumulativity* and *rationality* play an important role: they are valid for the supported SUPP semantics for stratified programs([ABW88]). Among the known extensions of SUPP to the class of all normal programs, only the wellfounded semantics WFS satisfies them: the competing approaches STABLE and GWFS ([BLM90b]) satisfy neither of them.

These abstract properties are also interesting in themselves. They seem to be related to the complexity of computing a semantics: note that as far as propositional programs are considered, WFS (rational and cumulative) is computable in quadratic time, while the computation of STABLE (neither cumulative nor rational) is hard as well as the computation of GWFS.

This view is also supported by our results in this paper, e.g. WGCWA is not only cumulative, but also rational, unlike GCWA, which is only cumulative. Indeed, WGCWA was originally introduced as a weaker form of

GCWA in that a certain costly operation, the *can*-operation, was deleted in the procedural definition of GCWA.

We also introduce some new interesting properties: the *principle of partial evaluation* PPE, which allows to partial evaluate a program under certain conditions, *Modularity*, a principle that enables to compute a semantics in a modular fashion, and *Relevance*, a principle that ensures that the derivation of a literal only depends on the *relevant rules*.

As already mentioned, the situation for disjunctive programs is more complicated than for normal programs: we have to ask for extensions of both semantics GCWA and WGCWA to the whole class of programs. Among the existing semantics, there is the perfect semantics "PERFECT" of Przymusinski and the weaker version GCWAS of Minker, Lobo and Rajasekar: they are both extensions of GCWA but they are only defined for the class of stratified disjunctive programs. It turns out that these semantics still are cumulative (they are not rational, since GCWA is not).

Among the existing semantics for the whole class of disjunctive programs, the stationary semantics of Przymusinski is very interesting. As pointed out by Przymusinski, $\mathcal{STN}$ not only extends PERFECT (as do GDWFS and WF^3) but it also extends WFS. We show, however, that $\mathcal{STN}$ not only fails to be cumulative, it also does not satisfy the weaker property of *Modularity*.

While Przymusinski needs a certain *disjunctive inference rule* to get an extension of PERFECT, such inference rules are not needed for an inclusive interpretation of "∨". We modify his construction to define $\mathcal{WSTN}$: an extension of WGCWA to the class of disjunctive programs. This semantics still is cumulative, but rationality is lost (a restricted version of rationality still holds). For normal logic programs $\mathcal{WSTN}$ coincides with WFS. $\mathcal{WSTN}$ is therefore a promising candidate to be a reasonable semantics for an inclusive interpretation of "∨". Unlike in the case for stratified programs under an exclusive interpretation of "∨", there seems to be no unique candidate under an inclusive meaning of "∨": we will define WPERFECT, a semantics that is stronger than $\mathcal{WSTN}|_{strat}$, the restriction of $\mathcal{WSTN}$ to stratified programs.

Given a semantics SEM_{strat} for stratified programs (disjunctive or not, interpreting "∨" exclusive or inclusive), we describe how to construct a cumulative extension SEM to the whole class of arbitrary programs. In the case of normal programs (choosing SEM_{strat} to be Apt, Blair and Walker's supported semantics) we get WFS. But the construction generalizes to the class of disjunctive programs. Choosing SEM_{strat} to be PERFECT, we get a cumulative extension DWFS, which is weaker than $\mathcal{STN}$.

We intend to use these and further principles in order to obtain representation theorems for the various different semantics: see [Dix92] where we began to do so for *normal* programs.

In section 2 we introduce some terminology which is needed later on, state some interesting properties of a nonmonotonic relation " $\vdash\!\!\!\sim$ " due to Kraus, Lehmann, Magidor and Makinson, introduce the sceptical entailment SEM_P^{scept} of a semantics SEM and present our conditions *Modularity* and *Relevance*.

In section 3 we consider positive and stratified disjunctive programs. We illustrate the behaviour and the abstract properties of GCWA, WGCWA and consider the extensions PERFECT and WPERFECT.

Section 4 recapitulates the stationary approach of Przymusinski. We discuss two different versions (based on different disjunctive inference rules), show some "clash of intuitions" and the failure of Cumulativity and Modularity. We introduce $\mathcal{WSTN}$, a semantics based on WGCWA instead on GCWA and determine its properties. Finally, we show how to extend a semantics defined on the class of stratified programs to the class of arbitrary programs in a *cautious* way.

We end in section 5 with Figure 1 which summarizes our results, and give some additional remarks and a short outlook.

2 Notation and Terminology

A general *disjunctive* logic program consists of rules, that allow arbitrary *positive* clauses to appear in their heads:

$$A_1 \vee ... \vee A_n \leftarrow B_1, ... B_m, \neg C_1, ... \neg C_l \quad \text{where } n \geq 1 .$$

If $l = 0$, the program is *positive disjunctive*; if $n = 1$ the program is *normal*; if $n = 1$ and $l = 0$ the program is *positive* (or *definite*). A program is, in addition, called *propositional* or *Datalog*, if it does not contain any function symbols, but only propositional variables or their negations. It is convenient to assume that all programs are fully instantiated, i.e. we consider only propositional programs in this paper. This is without loss of generality: all our results generalize to the class of arbitrary programs. Let MIN-MOD(T) denote the class of all *two-valued* minimal Herbrand-models of T.

We also need some notions from 3-valued logic. We use truth values t "true", f "false", u "undefined" and the Kleene connectives $\vee, \wedge, \neg$ and $\leftarrow$. $\leftarrow$ is the *weak* implication, where "$u \leftarrow u$" is considered to be *true*. Additionally, we can use two different orderings of the truth values: the lattice $\mathbf{3}_t$ defined by $f \leq_t u \leq_t t$ (truth-ordering) and the semi-lattice $\mathbf{3}_k$ defined by $u \leq_k t, u \leq_k f$ (knowledge-ordering).

We will consider in this paper sets of literals. A set $\{a, \neg b, c, \neg d\}$ will also be denoted by $< \{a, c\}; \{b, d\} >$ and thus can be seen as a three-valued structure: the first part describes the atoms that are considered true, the second part describes atoms that are considered to be false. $< T; F > \leq_k < T'; F' >$ means therefore, that $T \subseteq T'$ and $F \subseteq F'$.

2.1 Kraus, Lehmann and Magidor' s Rules

The following structural properties for an entailment relation " $\vdash$ " *between single formulae* were considered by Kraus, Lehmann and Magidor:

Cautious Mon.:	$\alpha \vdash \beta$	*and*	$\alpha \vdash \gamma$ *imply* $\alpha \wedge \beta \vdash \gamma$.
Cut:	$\alpha \vdash \beta$	*and*	$\alpha \wedge \beta \vdash \gamma$ *imply* $\alpha \vdash \gamma$.
Rationality:	*not* $\alpha \vdash \neg\beta$	*and*	$\alpha \vdash \gamma$ *imply* $\alpha \wedge \beta \vdash \gamma$.
Disjunctive Rat.:	$\alpha \vee \beta \vdash \gamma$	*implies*	$\alpha \vdash \gamma$ *or* $\beta \vdash \gamma$.
Or:	$\alpha \vdash \gamma$	*and*	$\beta \vdash \gamma$ *imply* $\alpha \vee \beta \vdash \gamma$.

The property *Cut* is uncontroversial: it is satisfied by any known nonmonotonic system. *Cautious Monotony* combined with *Cut* is the following condition, called *cumulativity*:

$$\text{If } \alpha \vdash \beta \text{ then: } \alpha \vdash \gamma \text{ iff } (\alpha \wedge \beta) \vdash \gamma.$$

It states that whenever a fomula β has been derived from α, then β can be used as a "lemma" and does not affect the set of formulae derivable from α alone. If this condition is not valid, intermediate lemmas are of no use: this indicates, that reasoning in non-cumulative systems may be more expensive.

Under some very weak conditions (that are always satisfied for the relations $\vdash$ considered in this paper) *Rationality* implies both *Cautious Monotony* and *Disjunctive Rationality*. Since *Cut* is always satisfied, we will in the sequel use the terms "cautious" and "cumulative" interchangeably.

The property *Or* will turn out useful to distinguish between an *exclusive* and an *inclusive* meaning of $\vee$. In particular its converse

$$(\alpha \vee \beta) \vdash \gamma \text{ implies } \beta \vdash \gamma \text{ and } \alpha \vdash \gamma$$

will turn out to describe semantics interpreting "$\vee$" inclusive.

The next section states the precise definitions we are using later on. The greatest difference to the formulations in this section is, that we do not have " $\vdash$ " (or C) as a relation on the *whole* set of formulae.

2.2 Sceptical Semantics $SEM_P^{scept}(U)$

Model theoretically, all of the semantics we will be presenting are defined as subsets of $\text{MOD}(P \cup U)$ (the set of all models of $P \cup U$). More precisely, $\text{SEM}_P(U) \subseteq \text{MOD}(P \cup U)$[1]. For all semantics it is possible to define a *sceptical* notion of entailment for arbitrary literals L:

$$\text{SEM}_P^{scept}(U) := \bigcap_{\mathcal{M} \in SEM_P(U)} \{L : L \text{ is a (pos. or neg.) literal with: } \mathcal{M} \models L\}$$

---

[1] We consider three-valued Herbrand-models of the underlying language $\mathcal{L}_{P \cup U}$.

We also write SEM(P) instead of $SEM_P^{scept}(\emptyset)$. Thus, $SEM_P^{scept}(U)$ can be seen as a threevalued model of $P \cup U$. With this notion, we are able to introduce two sorts of *extensions* of semantics. When we say that a semantics SEM *extends* another semantics SEM', we have to distinguish between:[2]

- SEM $\leq_k$ SEM': this means, that SEM' classifies more atoms as true or false than SEM, or

- SEM' is defined for a class of programs that strictly includes the class of programs for which SEM is defined and for all programs of this smaller class, the two semantics coincide.

Comparing with the " $\mathrel{|\!\sim}$ " framework of Kraus, Lehmann and Magidor, each of our semantics induces such a " $\mathrel{|\!\sim}$ "-relation between sets of *atoms* (positive literals) on the left hand side, and sets of arbitrary *literals* on the right hand side:

- $a_1 \wedge \ldots \wedge a_n \mathrel{|\!\sim} l_1 \wedge \ldots \wedge l_m$:iff $\{l_1, \ldots l_m\} \subseteq SEM_P^{scept}(\{a_1, \ldots a_n\})$

Note, that for the rule of *Disjunctive Rationality,Or* or *Converse of Or*, we not only allow the addition of atoms, but also the addition of disjunctions $\alpha \vee \beta$ to P. Note also, that we do not *derive* disjunctions: we only derive literals. It is possible to extend our framework and also allowing to derive positive disjunctions. In this case, however, special care has to be taken and the definition of $\mathrel{|\!\sim}$ has to be slightly modified: this point will be discussed in the full paper.

2.3 Modularity, Relevance

In the sequel, we assume the reader is familiar with the notion of the *dependency-graph* of a program. This graph induces a natural relation *depends on* between atoms of B_P. We define

- $dependencies\_of(X) := \{A : X \text{ depends on } A\}$, and

- $rel\_rul(P, X)$ is the set of *relevant rules* of P with respect to X, i.e. the set of rules that contain an $A \in dependencies\_of(X)$ in their head.

It is perfectly reasonable that the truthvalue of a literal L, with respect to a semantics SEM(P), only depends on the subprogram formed from the relevant rules of P with respect to L.[3] This idea is formally captured by:

Definition 2.1 (Relevance)
For all literals L: $SEM(P)(L) = SEM(rel\_rul(P, L))(L)$.

---

[2]The first notion also makes perfectly sense for semantics defined for the same class of programs.

[3]$rel\_rul(P, \neg X) := rel\_rul(P, X)$, $dependencies\_of(\neg X) := dependencies\_of(X)$

The principle of *Modularity* enables us to compute a semantics by modularizing it into certain "subprograms" (formed of the relevant rules). The semantics of these modules can be computed first and the semantics of the whole program can be determined by reducing this program with atoms that were already determined.

Definition 2.2 (Modularity)
Let P be instantiated, $P = P_1 \cup P_2$, $B_{P_1} \cap B_{P_2} = \{A\}$ and $P_2 = rel\_rul(P, A)$. If $A \in SEM(P_2)$, then $SEM(P) = SEM(P_1 \cup \{A\}) \cup SEM(P_2)$.

It is possible to strengthen this principle by allowing reductions with arbitrary literals L (not only atoms). For our purposes, however, this weaker version is sufficient. Even this version fails for $\mathcal{STN}$. [Dix92] contains some more principles, e.g. *Reduction* and *PPE* together with a more detailed discussion. Obviously, *Modularity* is a very special form of *Cumulativity* and therefore implied by it.

3 From Positive to Stratified Disj. Programs

All semantics defined for the whole class of general disjunctive programs, considered so far in the literature, e.g. Baral, Lobo and Minker's GDWFS ([BLM90a]), Baral, Lobo and Minker's WF^3 ([BLM91]), and the very recent STATIONARY-semantics of Przymusinski ([Prz91b]) coincide on the class of *positive* disjunctive programs: the respective semantics was first considered by Minker and is given by $SEM_P(U) = \text{MIN-MOD}(P \cup U)$. It interprets "$\vee$" exclusive and is called GCWA. In [RT88] and [RLM89] two complementary approaches, interpreting $\vee$ inclusive, were introduced and turned out to be equivalent: WGCWA. We will investigate its properties in the next section.

3.1 GCWA, WGCWA

In [Dix91a], we already pointed out that GCWA is cumulative but not rational. In [MR90] a fixpoint operator $T_P^{\mathcal{C}}$ operating on the powerset of DHB$_P$, the disjunctive Herbrand base, was introduced. DHB$_P$ consists of all positive ground clauses formed by using distinct atoms of the usual Herbrand base. For a set $S \in 2^{DHB_P}$, they defined the canonical form of S, can(S):=$\{C : C \in S$ and there is no $C' \in S$ such that C' is a subclause of $C\}$, and showed, that the set of atoms, the negations of which are derivable under GCWA, is exactly $HB_P \setminus \{$atoms in $can(T_P^{\mathcal{C}} \uparrow \omega(\emptyset)\}$.

Originally, WGCWA was defined by modifying the set of derivable negated atoms. Instead of considering $HB_P \setminus \{$atoms in $can(T_P^{\mathcal{C}} \uparrow \omega(\emptyset)\}$ Minker and Rajasekar declared $HB_P \setminus \{$atoms in $T_P^{\mathcal{C}} \uparrow \omega(\emptyset)\}$ to be the set of derivable negated atoms under WGCWA. The set of derivable atoms is for both semantics the same.

In [RLM89], they gave an equivalent and more intuitive definition of WGCWA. The idea is to restrict the inference of negative literals with respect to GCWA. For this purpose, the disjunctions are interpreted *inclusively* rather than *exclusively* (but only for the inference of *negative* literals). This idea is formalized by transforming any clause $A_1(\underline{t_1}) \vee ... \vee A_n(\underline{t_n}) \leftarrow B_1(\underline{s_1}) \wedge ... \wedge B_m(\underline{s_m})$ into n clauses "$A_1(\underline{t_1}) \leftarrow B_1(\underline{s_1}) \wedge ... \wedge B_m(\underline{s_m})$", "$A_2(\underline{t_2}) \leftarrow B_1(\underline{s_1}) \wedge ... \wedge B_m(\underline{s_m})$", ... , "$A_n(\underline{t_n}) \leftarrow B_1(\underline{s_1}) \wedge ... \wedge B_m(\underline{s_m})$". Using this transformation, any positive disjunctive program P can be transformed into a definite program P^*, which has a least Herbrand model M_{P^*}. WGCWA(P) can then be defined as the following set:

$$\{\alpha : \ \alpha \in B_P \text{ and } \text{MIN-MOD}(P) \models \alpha \ \} \cup \{\neg\beta : \ \beta \in B_P \text{ and } M_{P^*} \models \neg\beta\}$$

The difference of GCWA and WGCWA may be illustrated with the program P consisting of "$a \vee b$" and "$c \leftarrow a, b$". While GCWA(P) derives $\neg c$, WGCWA(P) does not derive it. The set of derivable atoms, however, is in both cases the same: GCWA and WGCWA only differ on negated atoms.

The difference between GCWA and WGCWA can also be illustrated with the rule *Or*: while GCWA satisfies *Or*, WGCWA does not: it satisfies its converse. Indeed, it turns out that *Or* is no specific property of GCWA: STATIONARY also satisfies *Or* as well as the other extensions of GCWA: see theorem 4.3.

The failure of the *Or*-rule can be illustrated with the program consisting of the single clause $x \leftarrow \alpha, \beta$. We obviously have $\alpha \vdash \neg x$ and $\beta \vdash \neg x$ but we have not $(\alpha \vee \beta) \vdash \neg x$, since $M_{P^*} = \{\alpha, \beta, x\}$.

3.2 Stratified Disj. Programs: PERFECT and WPERFECT

Analogously to the situation for programs without disjunction, there is also the notion of a *stratified* disjunctive database together with canonical models associated to it: the *perfect* models defined by Przymusinski. It turns out that PERFECT is cumulative, but, as an extension of GCWA, not rational nor even disjunctive rational. The definition of stratification naturally extends from normal programs to disjunctive programs (see [Prz88]).

In Figure 1, the semantics PERFECT is the counterpart of Apt, Blair and Walker's supported semantics. This is partly justified by [MLR91], where the methods of [ABW88] were successfully extended to disjunctive databases: the unique model constructed there is, however, weaker than the perfect model for stratified disjunctive programs.

A straightforward extension of WGCWA to stratified programs is the following semantics WPERFECT:

$$WPERFECT(P) = PERFECT(P) \cap M_{P^*}^{supp}$$

We can prove the following results:

Theorem 3.1 (Properties of GCWA, WGCWA)

a) *GCWA, WGCWA, PERFECT and WPERFECT are cumulative.*

b) *While GCWA and PERFECT satisfy* Or, *WGCWA and WPERFECT satisfy* Converse of Or. *In addition WGCWA is rational.*

4 General Disjunctive Programs

The motivation to define GDWFS or WF^3 are similar to the motivations underlying GWFS: finding an extension of WFS (for normal programs) in order to solve more complicated floating conclusions problems (see [Dix92], where WFS$^+$, an extension of WFS, is defined). While GDWFS, WF^3 and STATIONARY all extend the perfect semantics (in the sense that they coincide on the class of stratified disjunctive programs), only STATIONARY also extends WFS in this sense. In general, we have $WFS(P) \leq_k GDWFS(P) \leq_k WF^3$, where the first $\leq_k$ has only a meaning for programs P without disjunctions. The failure of our PPE-principle (formally introduced in [Dix92]), can be illustrated with the following program P, which also applies to GDWFS and WF^3: all these semantics coincide on this particular program.

$$
\begin{array}{llll}
P: & p & \leftarrow & \neg b \\
   & b & \leftarrow & c \\
   & c & \leftarrow & p, \neg a \\
   & a & \leftarrow & \neg b
\end{array}
\qquad\qquad
\begin{array}{llll}
P_c: & p & \leftarrow & \neg b \\
     & b & \leftarrow & p, \neg a \\
     & a & \leftarrow & \neg b
\end{array}
$$

Note that c has only been replaced by the rule defining it, but yet the semantics of P and P_c differ: P derives p and a while P_c does not.

Przymusinski's stationary approach $\mathcal{STN}$ satisfies PPE. This approach is very elegant: for normal programs, $\mathcal{STN}$ turns out to be equivalent to WFS. The advantage of this new construction is, that it also applies to *arbitrary* disjunctive programs. There is, however, a problem: the straightforward generalization does not extend PERFECT. Since there is no doubt that PERFECT is the right semantics for stratified programs (under an *exclusive* interpretation of "∨"), Przymusinski was forced to introduce a *disjunctive inference rule* to obtain an extension of PERFECT. In a preliminary draft, he used a different rule than in the final paper ([Prz91b]). The following two programs show, that neither versions are cumulative and that his final version even fails to satisfy *Modularity*.

$$
\begin{array}{llll}
P_1: & b & \leftarrow & y \\
     & y \vee x & & \\
     & z \vee y & & \\
     & m & \leftarrow & x, z, b \\
     & y & \leftarrow & \neg m
\end{array}
\qquad\qquad
\begin{array}{llll}
P_2: & a & \leftarrow & e, \neg g \\
     & a & \leftarrow & f, \neg g \\
     & a & \leftarrow & f, \neg e \\
     & a & \leftarrow & g, \neg e \\
     & e \vee f \vee g & &
\end{array}
$$

P_2 is a stratified program that derives a under PERFECT. Concerning P_1, different intuitions seem possible. One can argue, that $\neg m$ should be derivable, since the only way to derive m is by using the fourth clause, which means deriving b, which means deriving y which excludes deriving x or z. This is the way, P_1 is handled by the first version of $\mathcal{STN}$. The second (final) version $\mathcal{STN}$ does not derive $\neg m$. But if we replace the second and third line of P_1 by $y \vee x \leftarrow a$ and $z \vee y \leftarrow a$ and apply $\mathcal{STN}$ to $P_1 \cup P_2$, then $\neg m$ is derivable. This shows that *Modularity* is not satisfied: we consider this to be a serious shortcoming.

During an e-mail discussion with Teodor Przymusinski, the following simpler counterexample to Cumulativity (but not to Modularity) was found: "$a \leftarrow \neg d$", "$c \leftarrow \neg d$", "$c \vee d \leftarrow a$". While Przymusinski argues that $\neg d$ should be derivable in this example and $\neg m$ should not be derivable in P_1, we argue that both examples should be handled in the same way: either both $\neg m$ and $\neg d$ are derivable or neither of them. We feel that such a "clash of intuitions" should be solved by principles such as *Modularity*.

We now recapitulate Przymusinski's definition of $\mathcal{STN}$. We present it in a fashion that is more suited for our purposes.

Definition 4.1 ($\mathcal{STN}$)
$\mathcal{STN}$ is defined in two steps.

1. Step: *First, we have to transform a given program by replacing any negated atom $\neg a$ by a new predicate not_a. We obtain a positive disjunctive program P containing new not_a_i-atoms. Note, that these new predicates not_a_i only occur in the bodies of rules. For any assignment $I \subseteq \{not\_a_1, .. not\_a_n\}$ of the not_a_i-predicates, we will consider the set $Min_I(P)$ of all minimal models of $P \cup I$. We will also consider I as a (two-valued) model: this allows us to evaluate formulae that are boolean combinations of not_a_i-atoms.*

2. Step: *In a second step, we try to derive more and more positive or negative disjunctions consisting solely of not_a_i-atoms. These disjunctions can be seen as constraints that should be satisfied by the minimal models that we consider. Thus, in the course of the computation, more and more constraints C_i will be computed. The assignments I have to respect these constraints. More precisely, let $C_0 := \{true\}$ and*

$$\mathcal{MIN}_i(P) := \bigcup_{I \models C_i} Min_I(P)$$

together with

$$C_{i+1} = \begin{aligned} &\{ \ not\_a_1 \vee ... \vee \ not\_a_r : \ \mathcal{MIN}_i(P) \models \neg a_1 \vee ... \vee \neg a_r \} \\ &\cup \{\neg not\_a_1 \vee ... \vee \neg not\_a_s : \ \mathcal{MIN}_i(P) \models a_1 \vee ... \vee a_s \} \end{aligned}$$

This is done, until $C_\alpha = C_{\alpha+1}$.

$\mathcal{STN}$ is defined as[4]

$$\mathcal{STN}(P) := \{l : \ l \text{ a literal with } \mathcal{MIN}_\alpha(P) \models l\}.$$

As it stands, this version of $\mathcal{STN}$ does not extend PERFECT: for the program P_2, $\mathcal{STN}$ does not derive a. In addition, the rule Or is not satisfied: in P_2 we have $(e \vee f) \vdash a$ and $(f \vee g) \vdash a$ but not $(e \vee f \vee g) \vdash a$. To get an extension of PERFECT, Przymusinski added a disjunctive inference rule. We can also incorporate this rule into our framework: this amounts to replacing the sets $\mathcal{MIN}_i(P)$ by $\mathcal{MIN}_i(P_i)$ and $Min_I(P)$ by $Min_I(P_i)$, together with setting $P_0 = P$, and

$$P_{i+1} = P_i \cup \{(a_1 \wedge ... \wedge a_s) \rightarrow (not\_a_{s+1} \vee ... not\_a_k) : \ not\_a_1 \vee ... \vee not\_a_k \in C_i\}$$

We obtain various variants of STATIONARY by adding other closure conditions for P_i. For example, Przymusinski used the following rule for his final definition of STATIONARY: $P_0 = P \cup \{(not\_a_1 \wedge ... \wedge not\_a_s) \rightarrow (a_{s+1} \vee ... \vee a_k) : \ not_{a_1} \vee ... \vee not_{a_k} \in P\}$ and

$$P_{i+1} = P_i \cup \{(not\_a_1 \wedge ... \wedge not\_a_s) \rightarrow (a_{s+1} \vee ... \vee a_k) : \ not\_a_1 \vee ... \vee not\_a_k \in C_i\}.$$

We are now in a position to define $\mathcal{WSTN}$. The only difference to $\mathcal{STN}$ is that we restrict the derivation of negative disjunctions $\neg a_1 \vee ... \vee \neg a_r$ in the same way as does WGCWA. Note that we defined for any positive disjunctive program P the definite program P^*, which has a least Herbrand model M_{P^*}.

Definition 4.2 ($\mathcal{WSTN}$)
Analogously to definition 4.1. In step 2., we need some new sets $\mathcal{M}_i$:

$$\mathcal{MIN}_i(P) := \bigcup_{I \models C_i} Min_I(P) \quad and \quad \mathcal{M}_i := \{M_{(P \cup I)^*} : \ I \models C_i\}$$

to constrain the derivation of negative disjunctions in the following way:

$$
\begin{aligned}
C_{i+1} \quad = \quad & \{ \ not\_a_1 \vee ... \vee \ not\_a_r : \quad \mathcal{M}_i(P) \models \neg a_1 \vee ... \vee \neg a_r \} \\
\cup \ & \{\neg not\_a_1 \vee ... \vee \neg not\_a_s : \ \mathcal{MIN}_i(P) \models a_1 \vee ... \vee a_s \}
\end{aligned}
$$

until $C_\alpha = C_{\alpha+1}$.
 $\mathcal{WSTN}(P)$ is then defined as

$$\{a : \ a \in B_P \text{ with } \mathcal{MIN}_\alpha(P) \models a\} \cup \{\neg a : a \in B_P \text{ with } \mathcal{M}_\alpha(P) \models \neg a\}$$

---

[4]For our purposes and in contrast to Przymusinski, we only derive literals, not disjunctions.

As remarked earlier, GCWA satisfies *Or*. This rule seems to be strongly related to the *exclusive* interpretation of ∨ as the next theorem shows. While *Or* is not valid for $\mathcal{WSTN}$ (we constructed a counterexample for WGCWA in section 3.1), the converse of *Or*: If $(\alpha \vee \beta) \hspace{0.2em}\vdash\hspace{-0.5em}\sim\hspace{0.2em} \gamma$ then $\alpha \hspace{0.2em}\vdash\hspace{-0.5em}\sim\hspace{0.2em} \gamma$ and $\beta \hspace{0.2em}\vdash\hspace{-0.5em}\sim\hspace{0.2em} \gamma$ holds. This is a very strong property, that can be seen as a restricted form of rationality. Besides, $\mathcal{WSTN}$ is also cumulative:

Theorem 4.3 (Cumulativity and Or)
a) *STATIONARY, GDWFS and WF³ satisfy* Or.
b) $\mathcal{WSTN}$ *is cumulative and satisfies the converse of* Or. *Its restriction to stratified programs is weaker than WPERFECT.*

We now give a method to extend a given semantics for the class of *stratified* programs to the whole class of arbitrary (disjunctive) programs. To this end, we will define, for a fully instantiated program P, $P^{\#}$ to be the program obtained from P by *deleting all rules of P that contain in their bodies an atom x (occurring in P) depending negatively on itself*. $P^{\#}$ is therefore a stratified program. We will construct a semantics SEM which is obtained by iteratively computing $P_{\alpha}^{\#}$ and using a given semantics for stratified programs in an appropriate way.

We need the notion of *reducing a program using a set of literals M*. We define "P reduced by M" as the program $P^M := \{rule^M : rule \in P\}$, where $rule^M$ is defined by

$$(H \leftarrow B_1, ..., B_n, \neg C_1, ... \neg C_m)^M := \begin{cases} true & \text{if } \exists j : C_j \in M \text{ or } \neg B_j \in M \\ rule' & \text{otherwise} \end{cases}$$

Here, $rule'$ stands for $H \leftarrow B'_1, ..., B'_{n'}, \neg C'_1, ... \neg C'_{m'}$, where the set $\{B'_i : i \in I'\}$ (resp. $\{\neg C'_i : i \in I'\}$) is just an enumeration of the set $\{B_i : B_i \in I\} \setminus M$ (resp. $\{\neg C_i : \neg C_i \in I\} \setminus M$).

Definition 4.4 (SEM)
Let P be an instantiated program. Set $P_0 := P$ and

$$P_{\alpha+1} := P_{\alpha}^{M_{\alpha}^+ \cup M_{\alpha}^-}, \ where$$

$M_{\alpha}^- = \{\neg x : x \in B_{P_{\alpha}^{\#}} \text{ not dep. neg. on itself in } P_{\alpha} \text{ and } M_{P_{\alpha}^{\#}}^{supp} \models \neg x\}$ and $M_{\alpha}^+ = \{x : x \in B_{P_{\alpha}^{\#}} \text{ and } M_{P_{\alpha}^{\#}}^{supp} \models x\}$.[5] *Note that $\mathcal{L}_{P_{\alpha+1}} \subseteq \mathcal{L}_{P_{\alpha}}$. The construction stops, if $\mathcal{L}_{P_{\lambda+1}} = \mathcal{L}_{P_{\lambda}}$.*
We define: SEM(P)$= \bigcup_{\alpha=0}^{\lambda} M_{\alpha}^+ \ \cup \ \bigcup_{\alpha=0}^{\lambda} M_{\alpha}^-$

---

[5]It may happen, that $\mathcal{L}_{P_{\alpha+1}}$ still contains atoms x that are not contained in any head of $P_{\alpha+1}$. We therefore reduce with $\{\neg x\}$ until the condition "x occurs in $P_{\alpha+1} \implies x$ occurs in the head of a rule of $P_{\alpha+1}$" is satisfied.

It turns out, that SEM(P) coincides with WFS(P). The advantage of our construction is, however, that it generalizes to the case of disjunctive programs: for an *exclusive* interpretation, we only have to replace

$$M_{P_\alpha^{\#}}^{supp} \quad \text{by} \quad PERFECT(P_\alpha^{\#}),$$

to obtain a semantics for general disjunctive programs: DWFS. We are able to show that DWFS is a cumulative extension of WFS, satisfies *Or* and our principles *Modularity* and *PPE*.

For an *inclusive* interpretation, we may replace

$$M_{P_\alpha^{\#}}^{supp} \quad \text{by} \quad WPERFECT(P_\alpha^{\#})$$

(to obtain DWGCWA) or by $\mathcal{WSTN}\,|_{strat}\,(P_\alpha^{\#})$ to obtain still another semantics.

A more detailed discussion of these semantics will be contained in the full paper.

5 Conclusions and Outlook

Figure 1 illustrates how the semantics dicussed so far are related and summarizes their properties. Semantics on the same level (1st level (positive programs): M_P, 2nd level (positive disjunctive): WGCWA, GCWA, 3rd level (stratified): M_P^{supp}, 4th level (stratified disjunctive): PERFECT, GCWAS, WPERFECT, $\mathcal{WSTN}|_{strat}$, 5th level (normal): WFS, GWFS, STABLE, WFS$^+$, 6th level (general disjunctive): $\mathcal{WSTN}$, DWFS, $\mathcal{STN}$, GDWFS and WF^3) are defined for the same class of programs. A line between two semantics indicates that one semantics is an extension of the other (in the sense that it coincides with the semantics on the lower level). As already said in Section 2, this notion of an extension has to be distinguished from $\leq_k$.

We argue that the question "What is the *right* declarative and what the *appropriate* procedural semantics of general disjunctive logic programs?" should be answered by general principles like *Cumulativity*, *Rationality*, *Modularity*, *Relevance* and similar properties and not only by examples and counterexamples appealing more or less to one's intuition.

We have shown that there are *cumulative extensions* of WGCWA (namely WPERFECT and $\mathcal{WSTN}$) as well as a semantics DWFS for general disjunctive programs extending PERFECT and WFS and satisfying our conditions of PPE, Modularity, Relevance and Cumulativity.

These principles, although inspired by theoretical investigations, turned out to be very useful for implementing semantics for disjunctive programs (see [Mül92]). This work is still in progress and it seems that more refined versions could be defined and used to decrease the complexity of computing semantics.

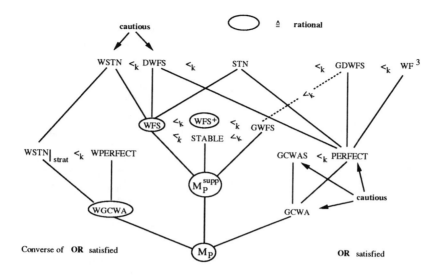

Figure 1: Semantics for disjunctive programs

Acknowledgements

Many thanks to Martin Müller for lots of useful comments and many fruitful discussions. The comments of some anonymous referees also helped to improve the paper.

References

[ABW88]   K. Apt, H. Blair, and A. Walker. Towards a theory of declarative knowledge. In Jack Minker, editor, *Foundations of Deductive Databases*, chapter 2, pages 89–148. Morgan Kaufmann, 1988.

[BLM90a] Chitta Baral, Jorge Lobo, and Jack Minker. Generalized Disjunctive Well-founded Semantics for Logic Programs. CS-TR 2436, Computer Science Dept., Univ. Maryland, University of Maryland College Park, Maryland 20742, USA, March 1990.

[BLM90b] Chitta Baral, Jorge Lobo, and Jack Minker. Generalized Well-founded Semantics for Logic Programs. In M. E. Stickel, editor, *10th International Conference on Automated Deduction, LNAI 449, subseries LNCS*, pages 102–116. Springer, J. Siekmann, July 1990.

[BLM91]   C. Baral, J. Lobo, and J. Minker. WF^3: A Semantics for Negation in Normal Disjunctive Logic Programs. In Z.W. Ras and M. Zemankova, editors, *Methodologies for Intelligent Systems*, pages 459–468. Springer, Lecture Notes in Artificial Intelligence 542, 1991.

[Dix91a] Jürgen Dix. Classifying Semantics of Logic Programs. In Anil Nerode, Wiktor Marek, and V. S. Subrahmanian, editors, *Logic Programming and Non-Monotonic Reasoning, Proceedings of the first International Workshop*, pages 166–180. Washington D.C, MIT Press, July 1991.

[Dix91b] Jürgen Dix. Cumulativity and Rationality in Semantics of Normal Logic Programs. In J. Dix, K. P. Jantke, and P. H. Schmitt, editors, *Proceedings of the first Workshop on Nonmonotonic and Inductive Logic 1990 in Karlsruhe*, pages 13–37. LNCS 543, Springer, October 1991.

[Dix92]   Jürgen Dix. A Framework for Representing and Characterizing Semantics of Logic Programs. In B. Nebel, C. Rich, and W. Swartout, editors, *Principles of Knowledge Representation and Reasoning: Proceedings of the Third International Conference (KR92)*. San Mateo, CA, Morgan Kaufmann, 1992.

[GL91]   Michael Gelfond and Vladimir Lifschitz. Classical Negation in Logic Programs and Disjunctive Databases. *New Generation Computing*, 9, 1991.

[MLR91]   Jack Minker, Jorge Lobo, and Arcot Rajasekar. Circumscription and Disjunctive Logic Programming. In V. Lifschitz, editor, *Artioficial Intelligence and Mathematical Theory of Computation. Papers in Honor of John McCarthy*, pages 281–304. Academic Press, 1991.

[MR90]   Jack Minker and Arcot Rajasekar. A fixpoint semantics for disjunctive logic programs. *Journal of Logic Programming*, 9:45–74, 1990.

[Mül92]   Martin Müller. Implementations of semantics for disjunctive logic programs. Technical report, Master Thesis, Karlsruhe University (in german), 1992.

[Prz88]   Teodor Przymusinski. On the declarative semantics of deductive databases and logic programs. In Jack Minker, editor, *Foundations of Deductive Databases*, chapter 5, pages 193–216. Morgan Kaufmann, 1988.

[Prz91a] Teodor Przymusinski. Stable Semantics for Disjunctive Programs. *New Generation Computing Journal*, 9:401–424, 1991.

[Prz91b] Teodor Przymusinski. Stationary Semantics for Normal and Disjunctive Logic Programs. In C. Delobel, M. Kifer, and Y. Masunaga, editors, *DOOD '91, Proceedings of the 2nd International Conference*. Muenchen, Springer, LNCS 566, December 1991.

[RLM89]   Arcot Rajasekar, Jorge Lobo, and Jack Minker. Weak Generalized Closed World Assumption. *Journal of Automated Reasoning*, 5:293–307, 1989.

[RT88]   Kenneth A. Ross and Rodney A. Topor. Inferring negative Information from disjunctive Databases. *Journal of Automated Reasoning*, 4:397–424, 1988.

Propositional Semantics
for Disjunctive Logic Programs

Rachel Ben-Eliyahu
Cognitive Systems Laboratory
Computer Science Department
University of California
Los Angeles, California 90024
rachel@cs.ucla.edu

Rina Dechter
Information & Computer Science
University of California
Irvine, California 92717
dechter@ics.uci.edu

Abstract

In this paper we study properties of the class of head-cycle-free extended disjunctive logic programs (HEDLPs), which includes, as a special case, all nondisjunctive extended logic programs. We show that any propositional HEDLP can be mapped in polynomial time into a propositional theory such that each model of the latter corresponds to an answer set, as defined by stable model semantics, of the former. Using this mapping, we show that many queries over HEDLPs can be determined by simply solving propositional satisfiability problems, that is, without enumerating answer sets.

This mapping suggests an alternative definition of stable model semantics, expressed in the familiar language of propositional logic, and it has several important implications: It establishes the NP-completeness of this class of disjunctive logic programs, allows existing algorithms and tractable subsets for the satisfiability problem to be used in logic programming, facilitates the evaluation of the expressive power of disjunctive logic programs, and leads to recognition of useful similarities between stable model semantics and Clark's predicate completion.

1   Introduction

Stable model semantics, proposed by Gelfond and Lifschitz [GL91], successfully bridges the gap between two lines of research, default reasoning and logic programming. Gelfond and Lifschitz pointed out the need for explicit representation of negated information in logic programs and accordingly defined *extended logic programs* as those that use classical negation in addition to the *negation-as-failure* operator.

One advantage of stable model semantics is that it is closely related to the semantics of Reiter's default logic [Rei80], in the framework of which an extended logic program may be viewed as a default theory with special features. This duality allows transference of insights, techniques, and analytical results from default logic to logic programming, and vice versa.

The work presented here puts this duality into practice. We use techniques developed for answering queries on default theories [BED91a] to compute answer sets for disjunctive logic programs (according to stable model semantics). We also show how this semantics can be given an interpretation in propositional logic.

Specifically, we show that a large class of extended disjunctive logic programs (EDLPs) can be compiled in polynomial time into a propositional theory such that each model of the latter corresponds to an answer set of the former. Consequently, query answering in such logic programs can be reduced to deduction in propositional logic. This reduction establishes the NP-completeness of various decision problems regarding query answering in such logic programs and suggests that any of a number of existing algorithms and heuristics known for solving satisfiability are now applicable for computing answer sets. Moreover, known tractable classes for satisfiability induce the identification of new tractable subsets of logic programs. As an example we introduce new tractable subsets of logic programs which correspond to tractable subsets of *constraints satisfaction problems* (CSPs).

Aside from the computational ramifications, our translation provides an alternative representation of stable model semantics, expressed in the familiar language of propositional logic. This facilitates the comparison of various semantic proposals for logic programs and also allows evaluation of their expressive power. In particular, it leads to the discovery of useful similarities between stable model semantics and Clark's predicate completion.

Our translation does not apply to the full class of EDLPs but only to a subclass (albeit a large one) of *head-cycle-free* extended disjunctive logic programs (HEDLPs). Note that this class contains any extended nondisjunctive logic program. The question of whether stable model semantics for the class of *all* disjunctive logic programs can be expressed in propositional logic in polynomial time remains open.

The rest of the paper is organized as follows: In Section 2 we review the definition of EDLPs and their stable model semantics and present some new characterizations of answer sets for such programs. Section 3 shows how an HEDLP can be mapped into a propositional theory and discusses the properties of our mapping. Section 4 illustrates four outcomes of the translation concerning the language's expressiveness, complexity, tractable classes, and relationship to Clark's predicate completion. In Section 5 we mention relevant work by others, and in Section 6 we provide concluding remarks. Omitted proofs can be found in the full paper [BED91b].

2 Extended Disjunctive Logic Programs

EDLPs are disjunctive logic programs with two types of negation: negation by default and classical negation. They were introduced by Gelfond and Lifschitz [GL91], who defined an EDLP as a set of rules of the form

$$L_1|...|L_k \longleftarrow L_{k+1}, ..., L_{k+m}, \text{not } L_{k+m+1}, ..., \text{not } L_{k+m+n} \qquad (1)$$

where each L_i is a literal and *not* is a negation-by-default operator. The symbol '|' is used to distinguish it from the '∨' used in classical logic. A literal *appears positive* in the body of a rule if it is not preceded by the *not* operator. A literal *appears negative* in the body of a rule if it *is* preceded by the *not* operator.[1]

Example 2.1 *Suppose we know that a baby called Adi was born. We also know that a baby, if there is no reason to believe that it is abnormal, is normal and that normal babies are either boys or girls. This information could be encoded in a disjunctive logic program as follows:*

> *Baby(Adi)* ⟵
> *Normal_baby(x)* ⟵ *Baby(x), not Abnormal(x)*
> *Boy(x) | Girl(x)* ⟵ *Normal_baby(x).*

The literal Abnormal(x) appears negative in the body of the second rule. The literal Normal_baby(x) appears positive in the body of the third rule.

Gelfond and Lifschitz have generalized stable model semantics so that it can handle EDLPs. We next review this semantics with a minor modification: while Gelfond and Lifschitz's definition allows inconsistent answer sets, ours does not. Given a disjunctive logic program Π, the set of answer sets of Π under this modified semantics will be identical to the set of *consistent* answer sets under Gelfond and Lifschitz's original semantics. With slight changes, all the results in this paper apply to their semantics as well.

First, an *answer set* of an EDLP Π without variables and without the *not* operator is defined. Let $\mathcal{L}$ stand for the set of grounded literals in the language of Π. A *context of* $\mathcal{L}$, or simply "context", is any subset of $\mathcal{L}$.

An *answer set* of Π is any minimal[2] context S such that

1. for each rule $L_1|...|L_k \longleftarrow L_{k+1}, ..., L_{k+m}$ in Π, if $L_{k+1}, ..., L_{k+m}$ is in S, then for some $i = 1, ..., k$ L_i is in S, and

2. S does not contain a pair of complementary literals.[3] □

---

[1] Note that *positive (negative) literal* and *a literal that appears positive (negative) in a body of a rule* denote two different things (see Example 2.1).

[2] Minimality is defined in terms of set inclusion.

[3] Under Gelfond and Lifschitz's semantics this item would say, "If S contains a pair of complementary literals, then $S = \mathcal{L}$".

Suppose Π is a variable-free EDLP. For any context S of $\mathcal{L}$, Gelfond and Lifschitz define Π^S to be the EDLP obtained from Π by deleting

1. all formulas of the form *not L* where $L \notin S$ from the body of each rule and

2. each rule that has the formula *not L* where $L \in S$.

Note that Π^S has no *not* , so its answer sets were defined in the previous step. If S happens to be one of them, then we say that S is an *answer set* of Π. To apply the above definition to an EDLP with variables, we first have to replace each rule with its grounded instances.

Consider, for example, the grounded version of the program Π above:

Baby(Adi) $\longleftarrow$
Normal_baby(Adi) $\longleftarrow$ Baby(Adi), *not* Abnormal(Adi)
Boy(Adi) | Girl(Adi) $\longleftarrow$ Normal_baby(Adi).

The reader can verify that Π has two answer sets:
$\{Baby(Adi), Normal\_baby(Adi), Girl(Adi)\}$ and
$\{Baby(Adi), Normal\_baby(Adi), Boy(Adi)\}$.

We will assume from now on that all programs are grounded and that their dependency graph has no infinitely decreasing chains. The *dependency graph* of an EDLP Π, G_Π, is a directed graph where each literal is a node and where there is an edge from L to L' iff there is a rule in which L appears positive in the body and L' appears in the head[4]. An EDLP is *acyclic* iff its dependency graph has no directed cycles. An EDLP is *head-cycle free* (that is, an HEDLP) iff its dependency graph does not contain directed cycles that go through two literals that belong to the head of the same rule. Clearly, every acyclic EDLP is an HEDLP. We will also assume, without losing expressive power, that the same literal does not appear more than once in the head of any rule in the program.

We next present new characterizations of answer sets. The declarative nature of these characterizations allows for their specification in propositional logic in a way such that queries about answer sets can be expressed in terms of propositional satisfiability.

We first define when a rule is satisfied by a context and when a literal has a proof w.r.t. a program Π and a context S.

A context S satisfies the body of a rule iff each literal that appears positive in the body is in S and each literal that appears negative in the body is not in S. *A context S satisfies a rule* iff either it does not satisfy its body or it satisfies its body and at least one literal that appears in its head belongs to S.

A *proof* of a literal is a sequence of rules that can be used to derive the literal from the program. Formally, a literal L has a *proof* w.r.t. a context S and a program Π iff there is a sequence of rules $\delta_1, ..., \delta_n$ from Π such that

---

[4] Note that our dependency graph ignores the literals that appear negative in the body of the rule.

1. for each rule δ_i, one and only one of the literals that appear in its head belongs to S (this literal will be denoted $h_S(\delta_i)$),

2. $L = h_S(\delta_n)$,

3. The body of each δ_i is satisfied by S, and,

4. δ_1 has an empty body, and for each $i > 1$, each literal that appears positive in the body of δ_i is equal to $h_S(\delta_j)$ for some $1 \leq j < i$.

The following theorem clarifies the concept of answer sets:

Theorem 2.2 *A context S is an answer set of an HEDLP Π iff*

 1. S satisfies each rule in Π,

 2. for each literal L in S, there is a proof of L w.r.t Π and S, and

 3. S does not contain a pair of complementary literals. $\square$

Note that the above theorem will not necessarily hold for programs having head cycles. Consider, for example, the program having the set of rules $\{P|Q \longleftarrow, P \longleftarrow Q, Q \longleftarrow P\}$. The set $\{P, Q\}$ is an answer set of this program but it violates condition 2 of the theorem, since neither P nor Q has a proof w.r.t. the answer set and the program.

Is there an easy way to verify that each literal has a proof? It turns out that for an acyclic EDLP the task is easier:

Theorem 2.3 *A context S is an answer set of an acyclic EDLP Π iff*

 1. S satisfies each rule in Π,

 2. for each literal L in S, there is a rule δ in Π such that

  (a) the body of δ is satisfied by S,

  (b) L appears in the head of δ, and

  (c) all the literals other than L in the head of δ are not in S,

 and

 3. S does not contain a pair of complementary literals. $\square$

To identify an answer set when Π is *cyclic*, we need to assign indexes to literals that share a cycle in the dependency graph:

Theorem 2.4 *A context S is an answer set of an HEDLP Π iff*

 1. S satisfies each rule in Π,

 2. there is a function $f : \mathcal{L} \mapsto N^+$ such that, for each literal L in S, there is a rule δ in Π such that

(a) the body of δ is satisfied by S,

(b) L appears in the head of δ,

(c) all literals in the head of δ other than L are not in S, and,

(d) for each literal L' that appears positive in the body of δ, $f(L') < f(L)$,

and

3. S does not contain a pair of complementary literals. □

The above characterizations of answer sets are very useful. In addition to giving us alternative definitions of an answer set, they facilitate a polynomial time compilation of any finite grounded HEDLP into a propositional theory, such that there is a one-to-one correspondence between answer sets of the former and models of the latter. The merits of this compilation will be illustrated in the sequel.

3 Compiling Disjunctive Logic Programs into a Propositional Theory

Each answer set of a given logic program can be viewed as representing a possible world compatible with the information expressed in the program. Hence, given an EDLP Π and a context V, the following queries might come up:

Existence: Does Π have an answer set? If so, find one or all of them.

Set-Membership: Is V contained in *some* answer set of Π?

Set-Entailment: Is V contained in *every* answer set of Π?

In this section we will present algorithms that translate a finite HEDLP Π into a propositional theory T_Π such that the above queries can be expressed as satisfiability problems on this propositional theory.

The propositional theory T_Π is built upon a new set of symbols $\mathcal{L}_\Pi$ in which there is a new symbol I_L for each literal L in $\mathcal{L}$. Formally,

$$\mathcal{L}_\Pi = \{I_L | L \in \mathcal{L}\}.$$

Intuitively, each I_L stands for the claim "The literal L is *In* the answer set", and each valuation of $\mathcal{L}_\Pi$ represents a context, which is the set of all literals L such that I_L is assigned **true** by the valuation. What we are looking for, then, is a theory over the set $\mathcal{L}_\Pi$ such that each model of the theory represents a context that is an answer set of Π.

Consider procedure *translate-1*, below, which translates an HEDLP Π into a propositional theory T_Π.

translate-1(Π)

1. For each body-free rule $L_1|...|L_k\longleftarrow$ in Π, add $I_{L_1} \vee ... \vee I_{L_k}$ into T_Π.

2. For each rule

$$L_1|...|L_k\longleftarrow L_{k+1}, ..., L_{k+m}, \textit{not } L_{k+m+1}, ..., \textit{not } L_{k+m+n} \qquad (2)$$

with no empty body add

$$I_{L_{k+1}} \wedge ... \wedge I_{L_{k+m}} \wedge \neg I_{L_{k+m+1}} \wedge ... \wedge \neg I_{L_{k+m+n}} \longrightarrow I_{L_1} \vee ... \vee I_{L_k}$$

into T_Π.

3. For a given $L \in \mathcal{L}$, let S_L be the set of formulas of the form

$$I_{L_{k+1}} \wedge ... \wedge I_{L_{k+m}} \wedge \neg I_{L_{k+m+1}} \wedge ... \wedge \neg I_{L_{k+m+n}} \wedge \neg I_{L_1} \wedge ... \wedge \neg I_{L_{j-1}} \wedge$$
$$\neg I_{L_{j+1}} \wedge ... \wedge \neg I_{L_k}$$

where there is a rule of the form (2) in Π in which L appears in the head as L_j.

For each L in $\mathcal{L}$ such that the rule "$L\longleftarrow$" is not in Π add to T_Π the formula $I_L \longrightarrow [\vee_{\alpha \in S_L} \alpha]$ (note that if $S_L = \emptyset$ we add $I_L \longrightarrow \textbf{false}$ to T_Π).

4. For each two complementary literals L, L' in $\mathcal{L}$, add $\neg I_L \vee \neg I_{L'}$ to T_Π. $\square$

The theory T_Π, produced by the above algorithm, simply states the conditions of Theorem 2.3 in propositional logic: the first and second steps of algorithm *translate-1* express condition 1 of the theorem, step 3 expresses condition 2, and step 4 describes condition 3. Hence:

Theorem 3.1 *Procedure* translate-1 *transforms an acyclic EDLP Π into a propositional theory T_Π such that θ is a model for T_Π iff $\{L|\theta(I_L) = \textbf{true}\}$ is an answer set for Π.*

What if our program is cyclic? Can we find a theory such that each of its models corresponds to an answer set? Theorem 2.4 suggests that we can do so by assigning indexes to the literals.

When we deal with finite logic programs, the fact that each literal is assigned an index and the requirement that an index of one literal will be lower than the index of another literal can be expressed in propositional logic. Let $\#L$ stand for "L is associated with one and only one integer between 1 and n", and let $[\#L_1 < \#L_2]$ stand for "The number associated with L_1 is less than the number associated with L_2". These notations are shortcuts for formulas in propositional logic that express those assertions (see [BED91b]).

The size of the formulas $\#L$ and $[\#L_1 < \#L_2]$ is polynomial in the range of the indexes we need. We can show that the index variables' range can be bounded by the maximal length of an acyclic path in any *strongly connected component* in G_Π (the dependency graph of Π).

The strongly connected components of a directed graph are a partition of its set of nodes such that, for each subset C in the partition and for each $x, y \in C$, there are directed paths from x to y and from y to x in G. The strongly connected components can be identified in linear time [Tar72]. Thus, once again we realize that if the HEDLP is acyclic, we do not need any indexing.

The above ideas are summarized in the following theorem, which is a restricted version of Theorem 2.4 for the class of *finite* HEDLPs.

Theorem 3.2 *Let Π be a finite HEDLP, and let r be the length of the longest acyclic directed path in any component of G_Π. A context S is an answer set of an HEDLP Π iff*

1. *S satisfies each rule in Π,*

2. *there is a function $f : \mathcal{L} \mapsto 1, ..., r$ such that, for each literal L in S, there is a rule δ in Π such that*

   (a) *the body of δ is satisfied by S,*

   (b) *L appears in the head of δ,*

   (c) *all literals other than L in the head of δ are not in S, and,*

   (d) *for each literal L' that appears positive in the body of δ and shares a cycle with L in the dependency graph of Π, $f(L') < f(L)$,*
   and

3. *S does not contain a pair of complementary literals.* □

Procedure *translate-2* expresses the conditions of Theorem 3.2 in propositional logic. Its input is any finite HEDLP Π, and its output is a propositional theory T_Π whose models correspond to the answer sets of Π. T_Π is built over the extended set of symbols $\mathcal{L}_\Pi' = \mathcal{L}_\Pi \bigcup \{L = i | L \in \mathcal{L}, 1 \le i \le r\}$, where r is as above. Steps 1, 2, and 4 of *translate-2* are identical to steps 1, 2, and 4 of *translate-1*, so we will show only step 3.

translate-2(Π)-step 3

3 Identify the strongly connected components of G_Π. For each literal L that appears in a component of size > 1, add $\#L$ to T_Π.

For a given $L \in \mathcal{L}$, let S_L be the set of all formulas of the form

$$I_{L_{k+1}} \wedge ... \wedge I_{L_{k+m}} \wedge \neg I_{L_{k+m+1}} \wedge ... \wedge \neg I_{L_{k+m+n}} \wedge \neg I_{L_1} \wedge ... \wedge \neg I_{L_{j-1}} \wedge$$
$$\neg I_{L_{j+1}} \wedge ... \wedge \neg I_{L_k} \wedge [\#L_{k+1} < \#L] \wedge ... \wedge [\#L_{k+t} < \#L]$$

such that there is a rule in Π

$$L_1|...|L_k \longleftarrow L_{k+1}, ..., L_{k+m}, \textit{not } L_{k+m+1}, ..., \textit{not } L_{k+m+n}$$

in which L appears in the head as L_j and $L_{k+1}, ..., L_{k+t}$ $(t \leq m)$ are in L's component.

For each L in $\mathcal{L}$ such that the rule "$L \longleftarrow$" is not in Π add to T_Π the formula $I_L \longrightarrow [\vee_{\alpha \in S_L} \alpha]$ (note that if $S_L = \emptyset$ we add $I_L \longrightarrow \textbf{false}$ to T_Π). $\square$

Note that if *translate-2* gets as an input an acyclic HEDLP it will behave exactly the same as *translate-1*, thus it is a generalization of *translate-1*.

The following proposition states that the algorithm's time complexity and the size of the resulting propositional theory are both polynomial:

Proposition 3.3 *Let Π be an HEDLP. Let $|\Pi|$ be the number of rules in Π, n the size of $\mathcal{L}$, and r the length of the longest acyclic path in any component of G_Π. Algorithm* translate-2 *runs in time $O(|\Pi|n^2r^2)$ and produces $O(n + |\Pi|)$ sentences of size $O(|\Pi|nr^2)$.*

The following theorems summarize the properties of our transformation. In all of them, T_Π is the set of sentences resulting from translating a given HEDLP Π using *translate-2* (or *translate-1* when the program is acyclic).

Theorem 3.4 *Let Π be an HEDLP. If T_Π is satisfiable and if θ is a model for T_Π, then $\{L|\theta(I_L) = \textbf{true}\}$ is an answer set for Π.*

Theorem 3.5 *If S is an answer set for an HEDLP Π, then there is a model θ for T_Π such that $\theta(I_L) = \textbf{true}$ iff $L \in S$.*

Corollary 3.6 *An HEDLP Π has an answer set iff T_Π is satisfiable.*

Corollary 3.7 *A context V is contained in some answer set of an HEDLP Π iff there is a model for T_Π that satisfies the set $\{I_L|L \in V\}$.*

Corollary 3.8 *A literal L is in every answer set of an HEDLP Π iff every model for T_Π satisfies I_L.*

The above theorems suggest that we can first translate a given HEDLP Π to T_Π and then answer queries as follows: to test whether Π has an answer set, we test satisfiability of T_Π; to see whether a set V of literals is a member in some answer set, we test satisfiability of $T_\Pi \cup \{I_L|L \in V\}$; and to find whether V is included in every answer set, we test whether $T_\Pi \models \wedge_{L \in V} I_L$.

Example 3.9 *Consider again the program Π from the previous section ("Ba" stands for "Baby(Adi)", "Bo" stands for "Boy(Adi)", and each of the other literals is represented by its initial):*

$$Ba \longleftarrow$$
$$N \longleftarrow Ba, \textit{not } A$$
$$Bo|G \longleftarrow N$$

The theory T_Π, *produced by algorithm* translate-2 *(and also by algorithm* translate-1, *since this program is acyclic), is as follows:*

{*following step 1:*

$$I_{Ba}$$

following step 2:

$$I_{Ba} \wedge \neg I_A \longrightarrow I_N, \ I_N \longrightarrow I_{Bo} \vee I_G$$

following step 3:

$$I_N \longrightarrow I_{Ba} \wedge \neg I_A, \ I_{Bo} \longrightarrow I_N \wedge \neg I_G, \ I_G \longrightarrow I_N \wedge \neg I_{Bo}, \ \neg I_A$$

(no sentences will be produced in step 4 since there are no complementary literals in $\mathcal{L}$)

}.

This theory has exactly two models (we mention only the atoms to which the model assigns **true**): $\{I_{Ba}, I_N, I_G\}$, which corresponds to the answer set { Baby(Adi), Normal_baby(Adi), Girl(Adi) }, and $\{I_{Ba}, I_N, I_{Bo}\}$, which corresponds to the answer set { Baby(Adi), Normal_baby(Adi), Boy(Adi) }.

4 Outcomes of Our Translation

4.1 NP-completeness

Gelfond and Lifschitz [GL91] have shown that there is a close relationship between default theories and logic programs interpreted by stable model semantics. Their observation allows techniques and complexity results obtained for default logic to be applied to logic programming, and vice versa. For example, the complexity results obtained for default logic [KS91, Sti90] establish the NP-hardness of the existence and membership problems and the co-NP-hardness of the entailment problem for the class of HEDLPs.

In view of these results, the polynomial transformation to satisfiability that we have presented in the last section implies the following:

Corollary 4.1 *The existence problem for the class HEDLP is NP-complete.*

Corollary 4.2 *The membership problem for the class HEDLP is NP-complete.*

Corollary 4.3 *The entailment problem for the class HEDLP is co-NP-complete.*

4.2 Tractability

The results obtained in the last subsection suggest that in general many types of queries on a disjunctive logic program are NP-hard or co-NP-hard under stable model semantics.

Our mapping of HEDLPs into propositional theories suggests a new dimension along which tractable classes can be identified. Since our transformation is tractable, any subset of HEDLPs that is mapped into a tractable subset of satisfiability is tractable too. Among other known techniques, we can apply techniques from the CSP literature that solve satisfiability and characterize tractable subsets by considering the topological structure of the problem (for a survey, see [Dec92]).

For instance, in [BED91a] we have shown how a CSP technique called *tree-clustering*, developed by Dechter and Pearl [DP89], can be used to solve satisfiability. Based on this technique, we can characterize the tractability of HEDLPs as a function of the topology of their *interaction graphs*. The *interaction graph* is an undirected graph where each literal L in $\mathcal{L}$ is associated with a node and the set of all literals that appear in rules with L in the head are connected in a clique.

The first theorem considers the *clique width* of the interaction graph.

Definition 4.4 (clique width) *A graph is chordal if every cycle of length at least 4 has a chord. The* clique width *of a graph G is the minimal size of a maximal clique in any chordal graph that embeds G.*

Theorem 4.5 *For an HEDLP whose interaction graph has a clique width q, existence, membership, and entailment can be decided in $O(\pi^4(2r)^{q+2})$ steps.*

In the above theorem and in the next, π stands for the number of rules or the number of literals used in the program, whichever is bigger, and r stands for the length of the longest acyclic path in any component of the dependency graph of the program (so if the program is acyclic, $r = 1$).

Note that an upper bound to the clique width is the number of literals used in the program and that the upper bound is always at least as large as the size of the largest rule in the program. We believe, however, that tree-clustering is especially useful for programs whose interaction graphs have a repetitive structure. Programs for temporal reasoning, where the temporal persistence principle causes the knowledge base to have a repetitive structure are a good example. In [BED91b] we demonstrate the usefulness of tree-clustering for answering queries on such programs.

The next theorem relates the complexity to the size of the cycle-cutset of the interaction graph.

Theorem 4.6 *For an HEDLP(D, W) whose interaction graph has a cycle-cutset of cardinality c, existence, membership, and entailment can be decided in $O(\pi^4(2r)^{c+4})$ steps.*

4.3 Expressiveness

Are disjunctive rules really more expressive than nondisjunctive rules? Can we find a nondisjunctive theory for each disjunctive theory such that they have the same answer sets/extensions? This question has been raised by Gelfond *et al* [GPLT91]. They consider translating a disjunctive logic program

Π into a nondisjunctive program Π' by replacing each rule of the form (1) (see Section 2 above) with k new rules

$$L_1 \longleftarrow L_{k+1}, ..., L_{k+m}, \textit{not } L_{k+m+1}, ..., \textit{not } L_{k+m+n}, \textit{not } L_2, ..., \textit{not } L_k,$$

$$\cdot$$
$$\cdot$$
$$\cdot$$

$$L_k \longleftarrow L_{k+1}, ..., L_{k+m}, \textit{not } L_{k+m+1}, ..., \textit{not } L_{k+m+n}, \textit{not } L_1, ..., \textit{not } L_{k-1}.$$

Gelfond *et al* show that each extension of Π' is also an extension of Π, but not vice versa. They gave an example where Π has an extension while Π' does not. So, in general, Π' will not be equivalent to Π. We can show, however, that equivalence does hold for HEDLPs.

Theorem 4.7 *Let* Π *be an HEDLP.* S *is an answer set for* Π *iff it is an answer set for* Π'. $\square$

The reader can verify the above theorem by observing that our translation will yield the same propositional theory for both Π and Π'. The theorem implies that under stable model semantics no expressive power is gained by introducing disjunction unless we deal with a special case of recursive disjunctive logic programs.

4.4 Relation to Clark's Predicate Completion

Clark [Cla78] made one of the first attempts to give meaning to logic programs with negation ("normal programs"). He has shown how each normal program Π may be associated with a first-order theory $COMP(\Pi)$, called its *completion*. His idea is that when a programmer writes a program Π, the programmer actually has in mind $COMP(\Pi)$, and thus a formula Q is implied by the program iff $COMP(\Pi) \models Q$ (See [BED91b] for review of these well-known results).

The translation that we provided in Section 3 leads to the discovery of a close relationship between stable model semantics[5] and Clark's predicate completion.

Theorem 4.8 *Let* Π *be a normal acyclic propositional logic program. Then* M *is a model for* $COMP(\Pi)$ *iff* $\{I_P | P \in M\}$ *is a model for* T_Π. $\square$

proof (sketch): Let Π be an acyclic normal logic program, $\mathcal{L}$ the language of Π, and T'_Π the theory obtained from T_Π by replacing each occurrence of the atom I_P, where P is an atom in $\mathcal{L}$, with the symbol P. It is easy to see that the set of models of T'_Π projected on $\mathcal{L}$ is equivalent to the set of models of $COMP(\Pi)$. $\square$

---

[5] Note that in normal logic programs we have only one negation operator, which we regard as a negation by default operator for the sake of computing answer sets.

Corollary 4.9 *Let* Π *be an acyclic normal propositional logic program.* Π *has a stable model iff* $COMP(\Pi)$ *is consistent. Furthermore, M is a model for* $COMP(\Pi)$ *iff M is an answer set for* Π. $\square$

Corollary 4.10 *Let* Π *be an acyclic normal propositional logic program. An atom P is in the intersection of the answer sets of* Π *(as defined by stable model semantics) iff* $COMP(\Pi) \models P$. $\square$

Corollary 4.11 *Let* Π *be an acyclic normal propositional logic program. An atom P does not belong to any of the answer sets of* Π *(as defined by stable model semantics) iff* $COMP(\Pi) \models \neg P$. $\square$

It is already known that each stable model for a normal logic program is a model of its completion [MS89] and that if an atom is implied by the completion of a locally stratified normal program, then it belongs to its (unique) answer set [ABW88, Prz89]. We believe that the observations in Corollaries 4.9-4.11 are new because they identify the class of *acyclic* normal propositional logic programs as a class for which stable model semantics (under "skeptical reasoning"[6]) is equivalent to Clark's predicate completion.

5 Related Work

Elkan [Elk90] has shown that stable models of *normal* logic programs can be represented as models of propositional logic, but did not provide an explicit propositional theory to characterize these models. The mapping described in Section 3 above can be regarded as one such characterization.

Marek and Truszczynski [MT91] have shown how questions of membership in expansions of an autoepistemic theory can be reduced to propositional provability and have stated that this reduction can be used for checking whether an atom is in the intersection of all stable models of a *normal* logic program. Since they do not provide an explicit algorithm for such decisions, it is hard to assess the complexity of their method, and it is not clear whether it would yield results similar to those presented here.

6 Conclusions

This paper provides several characterizations of answer sets of HEDLPs according to stable model semantics. It shows that any grounded HEDLP can be mapped in polynomial time into a propositional theory such that models of the latter and answer sets of the former coincide. This allows techniques developed for solving satisfiability problems to be applied to logic programming. It also enables evaluation of the expressive power of these programs,

---

[6] "Skeptical reasoning" means that a program entails an atom iff the atom belongs to all of the program's answer sets.

identification of their tractable subsets, and discovery of useful similarities between stable model semantics and Clark's predicate completion.

One of the possible drawbacks of stable model semantics is that it entails multiple answer sets. The approach proposed in this paper suggests that in order to compute whether a literal belongs to one or all answer sets we do not need to compute or count those sets. Thus, multiplicity of answer sets may not in itself be a severe computational obstacle to the practicality of disjunctive logic programming.

We are currently investigating extensions of our work to a class of ungrounded logic programs.

Acknowledgments

This work was partially supported by NSF grant IRI-9157636, by the Air Force Office of Scientific Research grant AFOSR 900136, by GE Corporate R&D, and by Toshiba of America.

The authors thank Michael Gelfond, Vladimir Lifschitz, Jack Minker, Stott Parker, Teodor Przymusinski, and Carlo Zaniolo for helpful conversations on the relations between logic programming and default reasoning. Michael Gelfond pointed out to us the difference between the uses of disjunction in default logic and in logic programs. Vladimir Lifschitz drew our attention to the close connection between our translation and Clark's predicate completion. We also thank Judea Pearl and Halina Przymusinska for valuable comments on earlier drafts of this paper.

References

[ABW88]   K.R. Apt, H.A. Blair, and A. Walker. Towards a theory of declarative knowledge. In Jack Minker, editor, *Foundations of Deductive Databases and Logic Programs*, pages 89–148. Morgan Kaufmann, 1988.

[BED91a]   Rachel Ben-Eliyahu and Rina Dechter. Propositional semantics for default logic. Technical Report R-172, Cognitive systems lab, UCLA, 1991. Presented at the 4th international workshop on nonmonotonic reasoning, May 1992, Plymouth, Vermont. A short version appears in the proceedings of AAAI-91 under the name "Default Logic, Propositional logic, and Constraints".

[BED91b]   Rachel Ben-Eliyahu and Rina Dechter. Propositional semantics for disjunctive logic programs. Technical Report R-170, Cognitive systems lab, UCLA, 1991. Submitted.

[Cla78]   Keith L. Clark. Negation as failure. In H. Gallaire and J. Minker, editors, *Logic and Databases*, pages 293–322. Plenum Press, New York, 1978.

[Dec92]   Rina Dechter. Constraint networks. In Stuart C. Shapiro, editor, *Encyclopedia of Artificial Intelligence*, pages 276–285. John Wiley, 2nd edition, 1992.

[DP89]   Rina Dechter and Judea Pearl. Tree clustering for constraint networks. *Artificial Intelligence*, 38:353–366, 1989.

[Elk90]   Charles Elkan. A rational reconstruction of nonmonotonic truth maintenance systems. *Artificial Intelligence*, 43:219–234, 1990.

[GL91]   Michael Gelfond and Vladimir Lifschitz. Classical negation in logic programs and disjunctive databases. *New Generation Computing*, 9:365–385, 1991.

[GPLT91]   Michael Gelfond, Halina Przymusinska, Vladimir Lifschitz, and Miroslaw Truszczynski. Disjunctive defaults. In *KR-91: Proceedings of the 2nd international conference on principles of knowledge representation and reasoning*, pages 230–237, Cambridge,MA, 1991.

[KS91]   Henry A. Kautz and Bart Selman. Hard problems for simple default logics. *Artificial Intelligence*, 49:243–279, 1991.

[MS89]   Wiktor Marek and V.S. Subrahmanian. The relationship between logic program semantics and non-monotonic reasoning. In *Logic Programming: Proceedings of the 6th International conference*, pages 600–617, Lisbon, Portugal, June 1989. MIT Press.

[MT91]   Wiktor Marek and Miroslaw Truszczynski. Computing intersection of autoepistemic expansions. In *Logic Programming and Non-monotonic Reasoning: Proceedings of the 1st International workshop*, pages 37–50, Washington, DC USA, July 1991.

[Prz89]   Teodor Przymusinski. On the declarative and procedural semantics of logic programs. *journal of Automated Reasoning*, 5:167–205, 1989.

[Rei80]   Raymond Reiter. A logic for default reasoning. *Artificial Intelligence*, 13:81–132, 1980.

[Sti90]   Jonathan Stillman. It's not my default: The complexity of membership problems in restricted propositional default logics. In *AAAI-90: Proceedings of the 8th national conference on artificial intelligence*, pages 571–578, Boston,MA, 1990.

[Tar72]   Robert Tarjan. Depth-first search and linear graph algorithms. *SIAM Journal on Computing*, 1:146–160, 1972.

Addendum

The Logic of Architecture: Programming the Invention of Physical Artifacts

William J. Mitchell
School of Architecture and Planning
Massachusetts Institute of Technology
77 Massachusetts Avenue, Room 7-231
Cambridge, MA 02139, USA
wjm@mit.edu

Abstract

Architects and other designers invent physical artifacts to serve human needs. Although serendipity and inexplicable flashes of insight can certainly play a role in the production of such inventions, the basic process of deriving them is describable and formalizable, and can be automated. This paper outlines an approach to accomplishing this formalization and automation, and relates it to some fundamental ideas of logic programming.

The basic idea is to represent by means of shape transformation rules the knowledge that is needed to solve a problem of artifact invention. Each such rule tells how to combine shapes standing for components or subsystems in such a way that the resulting subsystem accomplishes some useful end. Artifact designs are derived by recursive application of the rule system to a starting shape. Thus artifact designs are treated as expressions in languages specified by specialized types of shape grammars known as *artifact grammars*.

1 Artifact Invention

Many of the most important transformations of human society have been marked by the invention of new types of useful physical artifacts—the axe, the bow and arrow, the wheel and axle, the plough, the irrigation ditch, the city, the arch, the aqueduct, firearms, the printing press, the steam engine, the camera, the automobile, the airplane, the telephone, television, the computer, the transistor, the microchip, and many more. Some would claim (though, of course, this is hotly contested in our fretful postmodern era) that the evolutionary *development* of human society has been *driven* by the successive emergence of such inventions. In any case, the invention of physical artifacts is an undeniably important human activity.

This paper is a preliminary exploration of the logic of artifact invention. It sketches a framework for the formalization of this task, and it demonstrates how inventions can be derived automatically. The discussion is developed primarily through architectural examples, but the approach that is described can readily be generalized to other design domains.

2 Part Vocabularies

Invention is grounded in the possibilities of available materials and fabrication techniques; inventions are things that you can actually or potentially *make*. Indeed, the usual proof of an invention is production of a working prototype. A first step in formalization of a framework for invention, then, is specification of a domain of shape and material possibilities.

Let us consider a shape vocabulary V. Each shape in V is a parametric closed solid—the type of element represented and manipulated by a sophisticated solid modeling system. Let us also introduce a material vocabulary M. A *part*, then, is a pair $<v, m>$ from the

Cartesian product formed by V with M.

In a given practical context, available fabrication techniques—cutting, turning, extruding, milling, moulding, and so on—will establish the shape vocabulary V. Sometimes, as in pre-industrial societies with access only to simple hand tools and a craft tradition of limited range, or where an inventor must work with a restricted catalog of ready-made components, V will be narrowly bounded and fairly easy to establish. At other times, as when the entire range of fabrication resources of modern industrial society is to be considered, specification of V may be a very challenging task. But, as a practical matter, it should always be possible to establish some reasonable working conception of the relevant shape vocabulary.

Specification of the material vocabulary M can be approached in similar pragmatic fashion. Typically, in pre-industrial contexts, only a very few natural materials are available—stone, wood, clay, and so on. In modern industrial society the range is very much wider, and materials scientists are continually extending it. But in practice, once again, it should always be possible to list the most relevant possibilities.

Typically, fabrication techniques apply effectively to some materials and not to others, so that materials tend to take certain shapes and not others. Thus, if we examine the ways that artifacts are actually made, we find characteristic part vocabularies of sawn and turned timber, rolled and cast steel, extruded and moulded plastic, and so on. In other words, there are practical fabrication constraints, so that the part vocabulary is actually a subset—perhaps quite a small one—of the set of all possible combinations of shapes and materials. Furthermore, in a given context, *resource constraints* may apply to the part vocabulary—limitations on the number of instances of a given part in stock, limitations on the amount of material available, limitations on the total fabrication cost, and the like.

Establishment of a part vocabulary captures and formalizes some of the knowledge on which an inventor draws. Generally it is a feasible task but a nontrivial one—potentially requiring consideration of developments in materials science and fabrication technology, and the kind of practical knowhow that informs work on the shop floor and the construction site. Furthermore, it is never a definitively finished task, since technological developments can always extend the ranges of available materials and fabrication techniques, and the exigencies of economic and social conditions (the availability of skilled labor, for example) can constrain what is actually possible in practice at a particular moment in a particular context.

3 Association of Behavioral Descriptions

An inventor has knowledge not only of what parts can be *made*, but also of how these parts *behave*. In general, the behaviors of parts can be specified in terms of inputs and outputs. A beam, for example, takes input of a structural load at some point within its span and produces outputs of loads at its support points. A column takes input of a load at its top end and produces output at its bottom end. A light bulb has input and output of electric current at its connection points and produces output of light at the filament.

To be more precise, we must specify exactly *where* the inputs and outputs of a part act, and the form of the *relation* between inputs and outputs. This is a matter of everyday practical observation and of applied physics. Inputs and outputs can act at points, along lines, over areas, or throughout volumes. Their locations can be represented graphically, or by equivalent numerical information in digital geometric models; for example, a structural load acting at a point can be represented by an arrow. Relations between input and output values can be represented, in the usual way, by means of mathematical functions that express scientific laws. I will call a part with associated descriptions of behaviors an *interpreted* part.

Any part has indefinitely many behaviors—structural behaviors, thermal behaviors, electrical behaviors, and so on. An inventor cannot know all of these behaviors, and may not be concerned with many of those that are known. (A structural engineer who seeks to invent a new type of structural system, for example, is not normally concerned with the electrical behavior of a steel beam.) Some potentially interesting behaviors may not even be known to science. Thus a part can never be *fully* interpreted; an inventor always works with a vocabulary of partially interpreted parts.

A second step in capture and formalization of an inventor's knowledge, then, is to associate behavioral descriptions with the parts in the vocabulary (figure 1). This brings to bear available practical and scientific knowledge of what things *do*. As relevant experience accumulates and relevant applied science advances, the interpretations of the parts can be made correspondingly more complete and accurate. One might speculate that successful inventors—the Thomas Edisons of the world—have richer and more accurate interpretations of their part vocabularies than their less successful rivals.

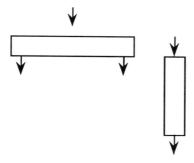

Figure 1. Simple functional descriptions associated with column and beam vocabulary elements.

4 Capacity Constraints

In general, the capacity of a part to transform given inputs into desired outputs will be subject to constraints. There are limits, for example, on the load-carrying capacity of a given steel beam spanning a given distance. If these limits are exceeded, then the beam will fail and cease to behave as a load-carrying part of a structural system. An inventor must take account of such capacity constraints.

The way to handle this is a commonplace of design practice. Capacity constraints are established by empirical observation, laboratory testing, and derivation from known scientific laws. They are expressed as functions of a part's shape and material properties. (Thus, for example, the load-carrying capacity of a rectangular beam is well-known to be a function of its length, depth, and width, and the strength of its material in tension, compression, and shear. The precise form of this function depends on the support conditions.) Failure—rather than behavior as intended—is anticipated when input values result in violation of a constraint.

An inventor's knowledge of relevant constraints may be incomplete and imprecise, but this limitation need not prohibit innovation. The great gothic cathedrals are superbly daring and inventive structures, for instance, and they sometimes push the capacities of masonry parts very close to their limits—yet their builders operated without detailed, precise, scientific knowledge of the constraints. Incomplete and imprecise knowledge of constraints simply creates areas of uncertainty about whether an invention will actually work when it is prototyped.

5 Functions and Functional Connections

A functional connection is formed between parts when the parts are put together in such a fashion that the output of one becomes the input of another, and the resulting ensemble transforms given inputs into desired outputs. Consider the functional connection of a beam and two columns to form a frame, as illustrated in figure 2. The beam takes a central load as input, distributes components of this load to its support points, and there produces two output loads. Each output load becomes an input load to a column. The columns, in turn, transmit their loads to the ground. The ensemble as a whole serves the useful purpose of carrying an elevated central load down to the ground.

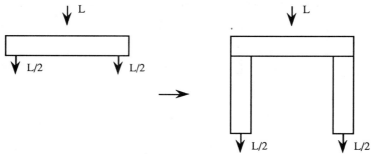

Figure 2. Rule for creation of a structural frame by forming functional connections between a beam element and two column elements.

The fact that juxtaposition of a beam and columns in this spatial relationship creates a functional connection is an important piece of practical knowhow. Indeed, the trabeated frame was one of the most important inventions in the history of architecture. Knowledge of this invention made possible the Greek temples, as well as innumerable subsequent buildings.

This piece of knowhow can be expressed in the form of a shape transformation rule, as illustrated. Programmers will recognize that the rule is a production—but one that rewrites three-dimensional arrangements of elements from a shape vocabulary rather than one-dimensional strings of symbols drawn from some symbol vocabulary. Essentially it says that, if you have two columns standing upright on the ground, you can span a beam between them to create a frame. An alternative expression is illustrated in figure 3. This says that, if you want to use a beam to support a load at an elevated point, you can put two columns under the ends to provide the support that will be needed there. The result is the same in either case.

To complete the picture, the rules should specify the internal mappings of outputs to inputs. In this case, simple equality relations describe the relationships of beam outputs to column inputs, but connections may sometimes be described by more complicated functions. The set of expressions describing the behaviors of the parts and the internal interconnections can be simplified to abstract away from the internal details and describe the outputs of the ensemble as a whole as functions of its inputs.

Notice the distinction that has now been drawn between behaviors and functions. A part may have many behaviors, just as the dictionary definition of a word may give many different senses. But, where a part is put to *use* in a particular practical context—by being functionally connected to one or more other parts in order to accomplish some practical purpose—one of these behaviors is picked out as a function. (Similarly, where a word is used in a sentence, one of its senses is picked out as the meaning in that particular context.

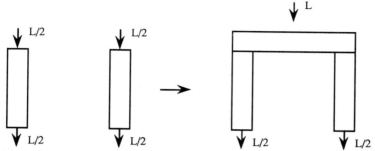

Figure 3. Alternative expression of the rule for forming a frame.

6 Abstraction and Subsystems

Just as a programmer may not want to be confronted with the internal details of a procedure, and may prefer the abstraction of a procedure call by name and argument list (once, of course, it is clear that the procedure really works), so an inventor may want to abstract away from the internal details of an assembly of functionally-connected parts.

Geometric abstraction can be accomplished by replacing the depiction or geometric model of an assembly by a depiction or model of its external envelope —much as you might literally put a complex mechanism inside a simple box, or conceal it under a cover. I will refer to these abstracted geometric descriptions as *markers*. These serve as a place-holder in a drawing or geometric model, much as a procedure name serves as a place-holder for a low-level procedure in a computer program. Conversely, a design can be detailed by replacing a marker with an assembly of lower-level markers or terminals (figure 4). (For graphic clarity, I shall distinguish markers from terminals by shading the markers and leaving the terminals unshaded.)

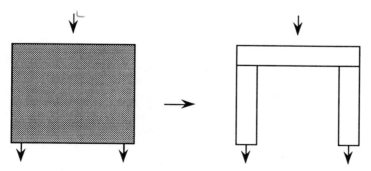

Figure 4. Rule for detailing a structural frame by replacing a marker depicting its external envelope with an appropriate assembly of terminals.

Similarly, *functional* abstraction can be accomplished by showing only the locations of the inputs and outputs of the assembly as a whole, and ignoring the internal chains of connection that relate the inputs to the outputs. In other words, a functionally abstracted representation focuses on *what* is accomplished by an assembly, while ignoring the details of *how* it is done. I have a geometrically and functionally abstracted view of my automobile, for example; I know its external shape, and I have a fairly complete picture of its inputs and outputs, but (so long as it continues to function effectively) I have little interest in lifting the hood to see how it is organized internally or to trace the chains of causality that make it work.

Usually it is convenient to refer to a useful assembly by name, such as "frame." Thus we arrive at the familiar concept of a physical subsystem—a named assembly of parts that accomplishes a practical purpose and that can be represented abstractly when the internal details do not concern us.

7 Nesting of Subsystems

In the same way that parts can be connected functionally to form low-level subsystems, so these low-level subsystems can be connected functionally to form higher-level subsystems, and so on recursively. Inventors not only discover useful ways to combine elements from a part vocabulary, but also useful ways to combine known types of subsystems. Once the carriage and the internal combustion engine had been invented, for example, it was only a matter of time before somebody put them together to produce the horseless carriage. Then, of course, the horseless carriage could be hooked to the Airstream trailer to produce the mobile dwelling.

Thus a complex physical artifact can be thought of as a hierarchy of nested subsystems. It can be described at any level of abstraction—at the highest level as an overall geometric envelope with input and output locations, at intermediate levels as assemblies of functionally interconnected subsystems, and at the lowest level as a functional assembly of actual physical parts. Programmers will immediately see an analogy; a program can also be seen as a hierarchy of procedures, and this hierarchy can be described at different levels of abstraction.

8 Substituting Parts and Subsystems

Parts and subsystems can be removed from assemblies and, provided that they fit in the space available, new ones can be substituted. In the simplest case, the new part or subsystem is identical in form and function to the old. This is the principle of standardized interchangeable parts—a cornerstone of artifact production in industrialized contexts. The usual purpose of such substitution, of course, is to replace a failed or worn-out part so that the functionality of the system is maintained.

Alternatively, the new part or subsystem might fit in the same space and have the same inputs and outputs at the same locations, but have different internal form and functional organization. For example, as all architects know, there are several practical alternatives to the trabeated frame—the triangular frame, the arch, and so on. The existence of these alternatives can be represented by rules in which the left side is a marker and the right side shows how the marker can be replaced by an assembly of lower-level vocabulary elements or subsystems (figure 5). These rules express knowledge of how to detail a subsystem. The alternatives are functional equivalents, or synonyms, just as words are synonyms when they can be substituted for each other in a sentence without altering that sentence's meaning. The choice between available functional equivalents is not, however, a matter of indifference; the alternatives may have different side effects and aesthetic qualities, consume different types and amounts of resources, and operate at different levels of efficiency. A pioneering inventor might initially be satisfied with finding *one* element or subsystem capable of doing the required job, but a sophisticated designer wants to consider the alternatives and choose the *best*.

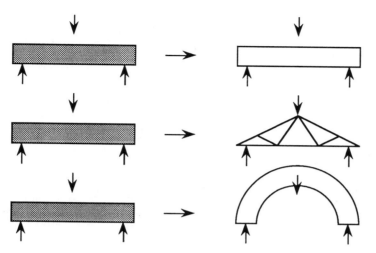

Figure 5. Rules showing alternative, functionally equivalent ways of replacing a marker. A beam, a truss, and an arch all distribute a central load to two support points.

Finally, the new element or subsystem might fit in the same space and accept the same inputs but produce different outputs. For example, an electric light and an electric shaver can be plugged into the same power outlet with strikingly different results. Parts and subsystems that can be substituted for each other in this fashion to produce different useful effects are analogous to words and phrases that can be substituted for each other to vary the meaning of a sentence—words and phrases belonging to the same parts of speech. We can substitute nouns for nouns or verbs for verbs, but it does not "fit" to substitute a noun for a verb, and an attempt to do so does not produce a meaningful sentence. Similarly, all plug-in electrical devices (lights, shavers, radios, and so on) can be grouped together as things that fit within physical systems in certain well-defined ways.

The combinatorial possibilities available to inventors depend on the existence of such alternatives, in much the same way that the sentence possibilities available to a writer depend on the existence of varieties of nouns, verbs, and so on. Long ago, this point was vividly made by Aristotle. He imagined that an animal must be a functional assembly of certain essential types of organs—perceptive organs, digestive organs, locomotive organs, *etcetera*. For each type of organ there were many alternatives—varieties of eyes, mouths, stomachs, legs, tails, and whatever. The combination of these differences, then, yielded the immense diversity of animals to be found on earth.

9 Artifact Grammars

These definitions and observations may now be brought together to yield the definition of an *artifact grammar*. Formally, an artifact grammar is a 4-tuple $<Vp, Vm, R, S>$, where Vp is a finite vocabulary of three-dimensional physical parts that can be obtained or fabricated, Vm is a finite vocabulary of three-dimensional marker shapes (as described above in the discussion of subsystems and abstraction), R is a finite set of shape transformation rules, and S is a starting shape. The starting shape S, the shapes on the left sides of rules, and the shapes on the right sides of rules are all three-dimensional assemblies of parts and markers. Application of a shape transformation rule results in replacement of the assembly on the left side by the assembly on the right side. Inventions in the language specified by the grammar are derived by recursive application of the rule system to the starting shape. A derivation terminates when no subassembly in the current configuration matches the left side of a rule, so that no rule can be applied. A realizable invention results when a derived assembly contains no markers—that is, when it consists entirely of physical parts that can be obtained or fabricated. The overall function of this invention is described by its inputs and outputs, and the chains of causality that yield this function can be traced by examining the internal connections of inputs to outputs.

Artifact grammars can be used not only to derive inventions, but also to parse existing designs to determine whether they belong to the language of artifact designs specified by the grammar. In this case, shape transformation rules are reversed, to act as reductions rather than as productions. A given assembly of components and subsystems can be shown to be in the language specified by a grammar by using the reductions to reduce the design back to that grammar's starting shape.

Figure 6 shows the starting shape for a simple example of an artifact grammar—one which derives designs for the framing of open-sided garden pavilion structures. It is a simple rectangular box, that is, a marker standing for the spatial envelope of the complete pavilion. The function is to carry roof loads down to the ground and resist lateral wind loads. The input to this marker is a uniformly distributed roof load over the top face. The outputs are point loads at the four bottom corners. (For graphic clarity, the arrows indicating these functions are omitted.)

Figure 6. The starting shape for an artifact grammar which derives designs for simple garden pavilion structures.

The marker vocabulary is illustrated in figure 7. The markers establish four types of subsystems: secondary roof subsystem, primary roof subsystem, vertical support subsystem, and lateral stability subsystems. These subsystems are represented by their bounding envelopes.

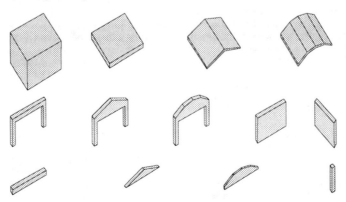

Figure 7. The marker vocabulary for the example artifact grammar.

Figure 8 shows the terminal vocabulary. It consists of wooden beams, trusses, and columns, masonry columns, and various types of bracing elements. It represents a plausible vocabulary of components for small-scale pavilion construction, but clearly there is nothing absolute about it: depending on actual availability, economic conditions, and so on, it could be expanded or contracted. Steel members could be introduced, for example. All the terminal vocabulary elements have well-defined internal constraints, given by the standard structural engineering formulae.

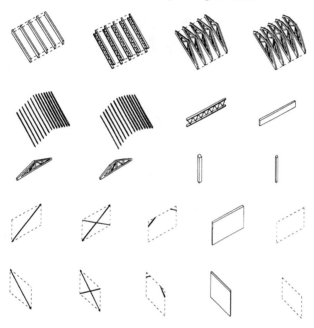

Figure 8. Terminal vocabulary of the example artifact grammar.

The rules of the grammar are illustrated in figure 9. (Input and output arrows are omitted, and the dimensional parameters associated with parts and subsystems are not listed.) Basically, this grammar treat the structure as an assembly of secondary roof subsystem, primary roof subsystem, vertical support subsystem, and lateral stability subsystems in two directions—all fitted together within the rectangular box. The secondary roof subsystem takes a roof load as input and converts it into loads acting along the edges of the box. The primary roof subsystem forms an interface with the secondary roof subsystem such that it collects those edge loads and converts them into four point loads acting at the top corners of the box. The vertical support subsystem fits under the primary roof subsystem such that it collects those four point loads and converts them into point loads acting at the bottom corners. Finally, lateral stability subsystems fit into the faces of the box and provide necessary cross-bracing. In most cases, there are alternative ways to refine a subsystem design by substituting subassemblies or terminals.

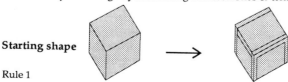

Starting shape

Rule 1

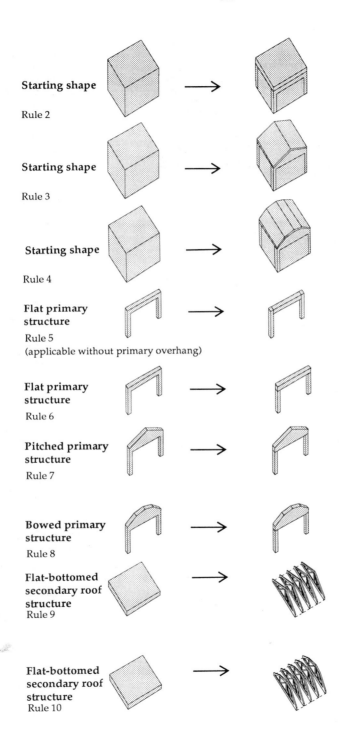

Starting shape

Rule 2

Starting shape

Rule 3

Starting shape

Rule 4

**Flat primary
structure**

Rule 5
(applicable without primary overhang)

**Flat primary
structure**

Rule 6

**Pitched primary
structure**

Rule 7

**Bowed primary
structure**

Rule 8

**Flat-bottomed
secondary roof
structure**
Rule 9

**Flat-bottomed
secondary roof
structure**
Rule 10

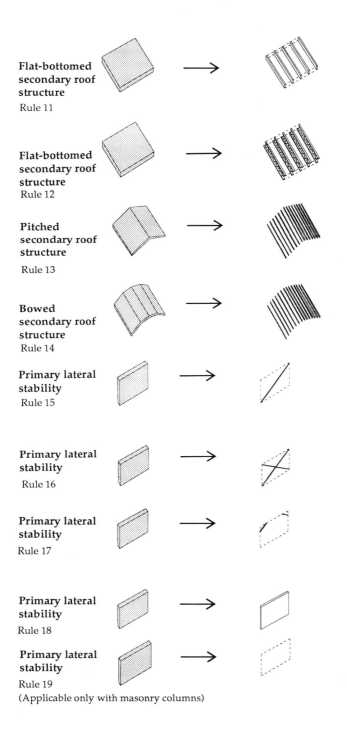

Flat-bottomed secondary roof structure
Rule 11

Flat-bottomed secondary roof structure
Rule 12

Pitched secondary roof structure
Rule 13

Bowed secondary roof structure
Rule 14

Primary lateral stability
Rule 15

Primary lateral stability
Rule 16

Primary lateral stability
Rule 17

Primary lateral stability
Rule 18

Primary lateral stability
Rule 19
(Applicable only with masonry columns)

842

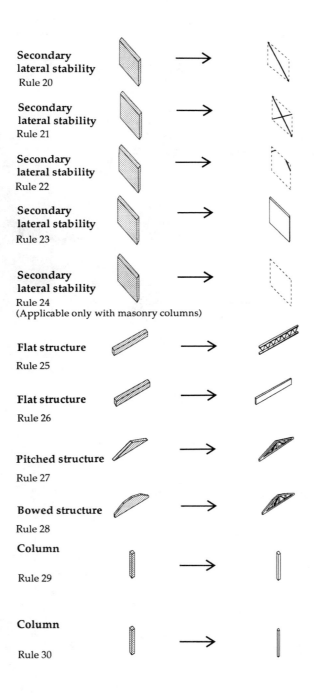

Secondary lateral stability
Rule 20

Secondary lateral stability
Rule 21

Secondary lateral stability
Rule 22

Secondary lateral stability
Rule 23

Secondary lateral stability
Rule 24
(Applicable only with masonry columns)

Flat structure
Rule 25

Flat structure
Rule 26

Pitched structure
Rule 27

Bowed structure
Rule 28

Column
Rule 29

Column
Rule 30

Figure 9. Rules of the example artifact grammar.

Artifact grammars such as this are closely related to shape grammars [1, 2], which have been employed successfully since the 1970s to specify languages of decorative designs [3, 4], villas in the style of Andrea Palladio [5, 6, 7], Mughul gardens [8, 9], traditional Japanese teahouses [10], Queen Anne houses [11], houses in the style of Frank Lloyd Wright [12], and so on. But whereas shape grammars simply derive abstract, uninterpreted designs (that is, just shapes), artifact grammars make the functions of components and subsystems explicit and derive *functionally interpreted* designs. Thus shape transformation rules appear not as arbitrary conventions of form, but as expressions of substantive knowledge about how things work, how they can be assembled, and how they can be used. The knowledge of artifact functionality that is encoded in the rules of an artifact grammar can potentially be used to support automatic evaluation of derived designs for functional adequacy, and to control the process of deriving designs that meet specified functional requirements.

10 Formulating and Solving Problems of Artifact Invention

A problem of artifact invention is formulated by specifying the artifact grammar that is to be employed to construct the domain of possibilities, the functions that are to be performed by the desired system, and any relevant constraints on space and material availability. Then the problem can be solved by a generate-and-test procedure of deriving designs in the language specified by the artifact grammar (figure 10) and testing them for feasibility and required functionality.

Sometimes the domain of alternative physical configurations specified by an artifact grammar is small, and therefore easy to search exhaustively. In general, though, it may be large or even countably infinite. Furthermore, where a configuration is assembled from parametric parts with many associated dimensional and other variables, there may be a non-trivial problem of assigning values to these variables such that the constraints are satisfied and the value of some objective function is minimized. As a practical matter, then, problems of artifact invention can turn out to be difficult to solve—even where the available computational resources are extensive.

As elsewhere, it helps to employ clever control strategies that minimize the searching needed to find solutions. For example, as recent work of Cagan and Mitchell demonstrates, simulated annealing can successfully be used to control the derivation of optimal floor plan layouts and structural designs in languages specified by artifact grammars [13, 14]. But it is better to *avoid* extensive search, wherever possible, by employing a grammar that specifies exactly the right domain of possibilities. A grammar for airplane designs, for example, should not also generate automobiles; if you want a flying machine, automobiles just will not do, and there is no point in generating designs for them. If inventive genius is some blend of inspiration and perspiration, the inspiration is in coming up with the artifact grammar that elegantly specifies the appropriate domain to search, and the perspiration is in actually doing the searching.

11 Artifact Grammars and Logic Programming

Shape grammars in general and artifact grammars in particular, like other sorts of formal grammars (phrase structure grammars, L-systems, array grammars, tree grammars, graph grammars, and so on) may be regarded as specialized examples of *production systems* [15]. But, whereas phrase structure grammars consist of rules that rewrite one-dimensional strings of symbols to derive sentences, artifact grammars consist of rules that rewrite three-dimensional arrangements of physical elements and subsystems to derive functional artifacts—buildings, mechanical devices, electronic devices, and so on. Instead of expressing the vocabulary and syntax of software (as, for example, in the BNF definition of Pascal), they express the vocabulary and syntax of hardware.

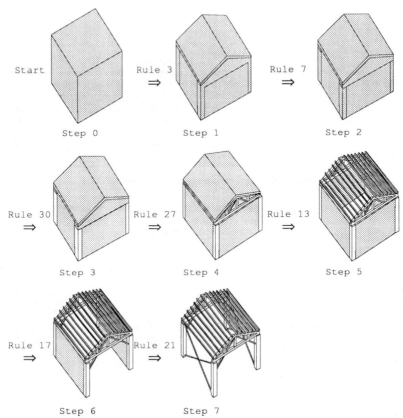

Start

Rule 3
⟹

Rule 7
⟹

Step 0

Step 1

Step 2

Rule 30
⟹

Rule 27
⟹

Rule 13
⟹

Step 3

Step 4

Step 5

Rule 17
⟹

Rule 21
⟹

Step 6

Step 7

Figure 10. Derivation of a design in the language of garden pavilions.

At a certain level of consideration, there is a very close analogy between an artifact grammar and the textbook conception of a logic program [16, 17]. A logic program deals with a set of discrete objects represented by their names, while an artifact grammar deals with a set of discrete physical parts (components and subassemblies) represented by their shapes. A logic program represents relations between objects in the notation of first-order logic, while an artifact grammar graphically represents spatial relations that establish functional connections. A logic program consists of sentences encoding knowledge about the problem that is to be solved, while an artifact grammar consists of shape rules encoding knowledge of how to put together the sort of artifact that is required.

Both logic programs and artifact grammars employ substitution as a fundamental mechanism and execute non-deterministically. Whereas the interpreter for a logic program proceeds by unification and resolution, and derives a chain of denials to solve a problem by refuting an initial denial, the interpreter for an artifact grammar proceeds by subshape recognition and substitution, and it derives a chain of solutions to design sub-problems—partial designs—in order to produce a complete design with specified functional properties. (Note that, in this process, the replacement of a marker by a more detailed subassembly with the same inputs and outputs is closely analogous to replacing a call by a procedure body in interpretation of a program.)

The major issues in development of interpreters for shape grammars and for artifact grammars are those of generalized, efficient subshape recognition, and of control strategy. Some work has been done on subshape recognition, and this has resulted in implementation of prototype shape grammar interpreters [18, 19, 20, 21, 22]. (The general problem of subshape recognition in shape grammar interpretation is harder than the specific problem of subshape recognition in artifact grammars, since shape grammar interpretation in general must contend with the emergent shapes resulting from subshape superimposition [23, 24], while artifact grammars deal only with assemblies of discrete, non-overlapping, physical parts.) Little has been done on the problem of controlling search; the interpreters that have been implemented mostly do nothing more than perform exhaustive depth-first search. This is an important topic for future research.

12 Conclusions

Artifact grammars provide a bridge between traditional CAD—with its emphasis on geometric modeling and engineering analysis—and ideas about knowledge representation and solution derivation that are fundamental to logic programming. They are motivated by the presumption that a designer's or an inventor's professional knowledge consists largely of knowledge about how to put available physical components together to form functioning systems, and they provide a way of capturing such knowledge. Thus they can provide the foundation for CAD systems which do not just represent and analyze design proposals, but which automatically derive solutions to practical invention and design problems.

References

[1]   Stiny, G. 1975. *Pictorial and Formal Aspects of Shape and Shape Grammars: On Computer Generation of Aesthetic Objects.* Birkhauser, Basel.

[2]   Stiny, G. 1980. *Introduction to Shape and Shape Grammars.* Environment and Planning B, 7. pp. 343-351.

[3]   Stiny, G. 1977. *Ice-Ray: A Note on the Generation of Chinese Lattice Designs.* Environment and Planning B, 4. pp. 89-98.

[4]   Knight, T.W. 1986. *Transformations of the Meander Motif in Greek Geometric Pottery.* Design Computing, 1. pp.29-67.

[5]   Stiny, G. and Mitchell, W.J. 1978. *The Palladian Grammar.* Environment and Planning B, 5. pp. 5-18.

[6]   Stiny, G. and Mitchell, W. J. 1978. *Counting Palladian Plans.* Environment and Planning B, 5. pp. 189-198.

[7]   Mitchell, W. J. 1990. *The Logic of Architecture.* MIT Press, Cambridge, MA.

[8]   Stiny, G. and Mitchell, W. J. *The Grammar of Paradise: On the Generation of Mughul Gardens.* Environment and Planning B, 7. pp. 209-226.

[9]   Knight, T.W. 1990. *Mughul Gardens Revisited.* Environment and Planning B, 17. pp. 73-84.

[10]   Knight, T.W. 1981. *The Forty-One Steps: The Language of Japanese Tea-Room Designs.* Environment and Planning B, 8. pp. 97-114.

[11]   Flemming, U. *More than the Sum of Parts: The Grammar of Queen Anne Houses.* Environment and Planning B, 14. pp. 323-350.

[12]   Koning, H. and Eizenberg, J. 1981. *The Language of the Prairie: Frank Lloyd Wright's Prairie Houses.* Environment and Planning B, 8. pp. 295-323.

[13]   Cagan, J. and Mitchell, W.J. 1992. *Optimally Directed Shape Generation by Shape Annealing.* Environment and Planning B, forthcoming.

[14]   Cagan, J. and Reddy, G. 1992. *An Improved Shape Annealing Algorithm for Optimally Directed Shape Generation.* In Gero, J. S. (ed.), Artificial Intelligence in Design '92. Kluwer Academic Publishers, Dordrecht. pp. 307-24.

[15]   Gips, J., and Stiny, G. 1980. *Production Systems and Grammars: A Uniform Characterization.* Environment and Planning B, 7. pp. 399-408.

[16]   Clocksin, W.F. and Mellish, C.S. 1981. *Programming in Prolog.* Springer-Verlag, Berlin.

[17]   Hogger, C.J. 1984. *Introduction to Logic Programming.* Academic Press, London.

[18]   Krishnamurti, R. 1980. *The Arithmetic of Shapes.* Environment and Planning B, 7. pp. 463-484.

[19]   Krishnamurti, R. 1981. *The Construction of Shapes.* Environment and Planning B, 8. pp. 5-40.

[20]   Chase, S. C. 1989. *Shapes and Shape Grammars: From Mathematical Model to Computer Implementation.* Environment and Planning B, 16. pp. 215-242.

[21]   Tan, M.. 1990. *Saying What It Is by What It Is Like—Describing Shapes Using Line Relationships.* In McCullough, M., Mitchell, W. J., and Purcell, P. (eds.), The Electronic Design Studio. MIT Press, Cambridge MA.

[22]   Heisserman, J. A. 1991. *Generative Geometric Design and Boundary Solid Grammars.* PhD Dissertation, Department of Architecture, Carnegie Mellon University

[23]   Stiny, G. 1990. *What Designers Do that Computers Should.* In McCullough, M., Mitchell, W. J., and Purcell, P. (eds.), The Electronic Design Studio. MIT Press, Cambridge MA.

[24]   Stiny, G. 1991. "The Algebras of Design," *Research in Engineering Design*, 2. pp. 171-81.

Author Index

The MIT Press, with Peter Denning as general consulting editor, publishes computer science books in the following series:

ACL-MIT Press Series in Natural Language Processing
Aravind K. Joshi, Karen Sparck Jones, and Mark Y. Liberman, editors

ACM Doctoral Dissertation Award and Distinguished Dissertation Series

Artificial Intelligence
Patrick Winston, founding editor
J. Michael Brady, Daniel G. Bobrow, and Randall Davis, editors

Charles Babbage Institute Reprint Series for the History of Computing
Martin Campbell-Kelly, editor

Computer Systems
Herb Schwetman, editor

Explorations with Logo
E. Paul Goldenberg, editor

Foundations of Computing
Michael Garey and Albert Meyer, editors

History of Computing
I. Bernard Cohen and William Aspray, editors

Logic Programming
Ehud Shapiro, editor; Fernando Pereira, Koichi Furukawa, Jean-Louis Lassez, and David H. D. Warren, associate editors

The MIT Press Electrical Engineering and Computer Science Series

Research Monographs in Parallel and Distributed Processing
Christopher Jesshope and David Klappholz, editors

Scientific and Engineering Computation
Janusz Kowalik, editor

Technical Communication and Information Systems
Edward Barrett, editor